KORZYBSKI
A BIOGRAPHY

BRUCE I. KODISH

Korzybski: A Biography
by Bruce I. Kodish

Copyright © 2011 by Bruce I. Kodish

All rights reserved. No part of this book may be reproduced or transmitted in any form or by any means, electronic or mechanical, including photocopying, recording or any information storage or retrieval system without prior permission from the publisher, except for brief quotations in an article or review.

Published by Extensional Publishing
          Email: ExtensionalPubl@aol.com

Publisher's Catalogue in Publication Data
Kodish, Bruce I.
Korzybski: A Biography/
by Bruce I. Kodish
Pasadena, CA: Extensional Publishing, © 2011
694 pp. includes endnotes, bibliography, index, 56 illustrations
ISBN 978-0-9700664-0-4 (softcover, perfect binding)
ISBN 978-0-9700664-2-8 (hardcover, case binding)
Library of Congress Control Number: 2010939737

1. Korzybski, Alfred, 1879–1950 2. Scientists—Poland—United States—Biography 3. Anthropology, General 4. Time-Binding 5. *Manhood of Humanity* 6. Epistemology, Applied —'General Semantics' 7. *Science and Sanity* 8. Mental Hygiene 9. Education—Critical/Creative Thinking 10. Unification of Knowledge 11. Non-Aristotelian Systems I. Title. II. Kodish, Bruce I.

Cover Design by David Presby

All illustrations and photographs used with permission of the Alfred Korzybski Literary Estate, unless otherwise indicated. "About the Author" photograph of Bruce I. Kodish, © John G. Blair.

Quotations from the Alfred Korzybski Archives and the Mira Edgerly Korzybska Archives at Columbia University and elsewhere, and from the works of Alfred Korzybski, all used with permission of the Alfred Korzybski Literary Estate.

    For articles, links, and other materials related to Korzybski and his work,
       go to www.driveyourselfsane.com and korzybskifiles.blogspot.com

          Follow Bruce I. Kodish on twitter.com/brucekodish
            and facebook.com/korzybski.biography

To
**Charlotte Schuchardt Read
and Robert P. Pula
Who Guided My Way**

Contents

Preface: Does Korzybski Matter? 8
Acknowledgements 11
Language Note and Pronunciation Guide 13
Part I   Final Day
Chapter 1   "We Only Coagulate." 16
Part II   Beginnings
Chapter 2   Young Alfred 24
Chapter 3   A Good Engineer 35
Chapter 4   To Rome 39
Chapter 5   Sick of Everything 44
Part III The Great War
Chapter 6   Germany Must Be Beaten. 52
Chapter 7   On the Eastern Front 56
Chapter 8   Battle and Retreat 61
Chapter 9   At the Disposal of the Minister of War 68
Chapter 10 Oh! Petawawa 72
Chapter 11 1917 80
Chapter 12 "Buy Liberty Bonds and Work Like Hell." 85
Chapter 13 A Veteran of the Great War 97
Chapter 14 Mira 102
Chapter 15 "Let The Dead Be Heard" 109
Part IV   Time-Binder
Chapter 16 "Binding Time" 122
Chapter 17 Dear Dear Old Men 132
Chapter 18 Alfred and the Jews 141
Chapter 19 The Time-Binding Club 148
Chapter 20 Manhood of Humanity 155
Part V   Science and Sanity
Chapter 21 Leibniz's Dreams 164
Chapter 22 "Just Work, Work, Work" 169
Chapter 23 Strange Footprints 179
Chapter 24 A Visitor from Mars 189
Chapter 25 "The Brotherhood of Doctrines" 198
Chapter 26 "Fate and Freedom" 212
Chapter 27 Measure of Man 223
Chapter 28 Advancing Human Engineering 239
Chapter 29 A Quiet Place in the Country 250
Chapter 30 Saint Elizabeths 255
Chapter 31 "The Tragedy of My Work" 274
Chapter 32 Trial-By-Headline 282

Chapter 33 First Draft 295
Chapter 34 "Don't You See the Electron?" 304
Chapter 35 Zero Hour 314
Chapter 36 A Short Trip to Poland 320
Chapter 37 Knowledge, Uncertainty, and Courage 328
Chapter 38 "General Semantics" 342
Chapter 39 A Monkey on His Lap 349
Chapter 40 Science and Sanity 356

Part VI   Words Are Not Enough!
Chapter 41 What Had Alfred Wrought? 366
Chapter 42 Reviewing Reviews 371
Chapter 43 'Scientists Don't Read' 380
Chapter 44 On the Road 395
Chapter 45 Seminars 406
Chapter 46 "Shoot All the Mothers!" 416
Chapter 47 One Weary Man 429

Part VII   The Institute
Chapter 48 The Institute of General Semantics 438
Chapter 49 Growing Pains 449
Chapter 50 The August Intensive 454
Chapter 51 Nothing To Do But Continue 461
Chapter 52 "Recognition But Very Little Money" 465
Chapter 53 Question Marks 476
Chapter 54 War Work 490
Chapter 55 Poland Fights 502
Chapter 56 Time To Try New Things 509
Chapter 57 "Release of Atomic Energy" 521
Chapter 58 "Shoot Yourself!" 532
Chapter 59 A Matter of Character 538
Chapter 60 SNAFU 545
Chapter 61 "I Don't Care A Damn About Those Yahoos..." 563
Chapter 62 "Without Publicity There Is No Prosperity." 580
Chapter 63 "What–Me Worry?" 588
Chapter 64 Hardly A Day Off 595
Chapter 65 Farewell 622

Notes 625
List of Photographs and Illustrations 656
Bibliography 657
Index 670
About the Author 693

Alfred Korzybski lecturing at the August Intensive Seminar, 1940

*Man [can live] in glory
but does not understand;
he is likened to
the silenced animals.*
—Psalm 49:20[1]

Preface
DOES KORZYBSKI MATTER?

"Let me give you [some] advice when you read a book. Read not only what you read, but study the author." —Alfred Korzybski [1]

On January 8, 2005, the *San Francisco*, a U.S. Navy nuclear submarine on a routine mission to Australia, was cruising 500 feet below the surface of the Pacific, 360 miles southeast of its home port of Guam. The sub's navigational chart indicated clear passage with no obstacles. Nonetheless, the vessel collided with an undersea mountain. One sailor was killed, 60 were wounded—some seriously. The sub, its nuclear reactor undamaged, got back to Guam two days later. Its chart, prepared by the Defense Mapping Agency (now part of the Defense Department's Geospatial-Intelligence Agency), had not been updated since 1989, although satellite data gathered in 1999 showed the mountain's presence. Hindsight didn't erase disaster.[2]

"A map is not the territory." Alfred Korzybski's often-repeated statement irritated some people in his day who considered the message trivial. Irritation may also have resulted from his insistence on the daily—indeed moment-to-moment—use of the principle. But remembering a map (or chart) is not the territory it represents (and that a map cannot cover all of the territory and remains subject to revision) obviously has continuing—sometimes life or death—relevance.

The relation of maps to territories was central to the life and work of Korzybski. And not only for navigation charts or road maps. He proposed that these kinds of literal maps and the processes by which they're produced (or not produced) serve as models for broader processes of human awareness, perception, thinking, decision-making, language use, etc. As Robert P. Pula wrote,

> By 'maps' [in the korzybskian sense] we should understand everything and anything that humans formulate…including (to take a few in alphabetical order), biology, Buddhism, Catholicism, chemistry, Evangelism, Freudianism, Hinduism, Islam, Judaism, Lutheranism, physics, Taoism, etc., etc., …![3]

Thus, anything proposed as knowedge—including whatever 'ism' one follows—has at best the usefulness but also the limitations of a map: "a map is not the territory", etc. As a form of mapping, the process of gaining knowledge (performed by human nervous systems) precludes the possibility of absolute certainty. Rather a generalized uncertainty rules: all statements only probable in various degrees.

Korzybski determined that nihilistic despair over this was not called for. Indeed, if seen properly, knowledge and uncertainty are not incompatible qualities but necessary concomitants of a new orientation. Locally precise knowledge-at-a-date, which gives a degree of predictability, is still possible for definite and intelligent action in a given time and place. But accepting generalized uncertainty *does* mean that in the absence of absolute knowledge, absolute confidence in one's decisions is not called for either. In Korzybski's view, knowledge and uncertainty belonged together. In addition, to live with both required courage—the courage to act despite imperfect knowledge and the courage to self-reflect and self-correct when needed, i.e., with frequency. The implications of this went well beyond scientific, academic interests. In particular, considering personal maladjustments in such terms revealed to him new and powerful possibilities and methods to promote sanity.

Alfred Korzybski was born into the waning Polish nobility living in the Russian-occupied sector of partitioned Poland in the latter half of the 19th century. "I was born silent",[4] he said—an observer, looking around, wondering what was going on. From a very early age, he found a natural role as a "troubleshooter".[5] His engineer father conveyed to him a deep respect for mathematics and science and their practical application. (Alfred later trained as an engineer himself.) He grew up as a Polish patriot under the hostile Tsarist dictatorship. Later in the Russian Army intelligence service, he saw first-hand the horrors of the Eastern Front of World War I. When he came to North America later in the war, he had already spent half a lifetime observing the results of human folly (including his own). "I simply was getting sick and tired of human stupidity. That's all that bothered me."[6]

Korzybski spent the remainder of his days in the nearly single-minded quest of a life-long dream: to promote human agreement by understanding and ameliorating human stupidity (preventable misevaluation) and its effects on human welfare. What was it about human beings that leads to such awesome progress in some areas (mathematics, science, and limited areas of technology) and to such awful poverty of results in others? Was there a way to prevent at least some of the individual unhappiness and societal problems he had witnessed? Was it possible to update our maps (in both the more limited and in the broader senses of the term), including our maps of ourselves, to avoid social 'collisions', i.e., unnecessary misunderstandings and conflicts with others?

His experiences convinced him that humans must learn to improve their thinking abilities (which for Korzybski did not exist entirely separate from emotional life). The lack of a focused and systematic way to help people learn how to think distressed him. ("Where do we learn how to think? No where."[7]) His knowledge of science and mathematics also convinced him he could draw out from these disciplines a method of thinking applicable to everyday language and living.

As a result Korzybski pursued an 'odd' research hypothesis : *unacknowledged factors of personal and social adjustment (sanity) exist within the professional behavior—including the language—of scientists and mathematicians.* He also realized scientists and mathematicians did not necessarily understand these factors or use them to their own best advantage either in their labs or in their daily lives. Korzybski's research led him to study not only the behavior of scientists and mathematicians but also of psychiatric patients. Relating these concerns—*science and sanity*—provided Korzybski with a unique angle of vision. For an engineer, a highly abstract theory was not sufficient. He wanted something practical as well. Without such an approach, he joked, "You can bring a horse to water, but cannot force the horse to drink. You can send a boy to college, but you cannot teach the boy how to think. It cannot be done. Why? Lack of method."[8]

He called the practical theory-method which he formulated, "general semantics", applicable to the most deeply personal problems and to the most lofty philosophical and scientific ones. Once he had formulated the theory, he devoted his life to elaborating and testing it. Did it work? He was interested first and foremost with helping individuals, whom he referred to as $Smith_1$, $Smith_2$, $Smith_3$, etc. He saw himself as another Smith—perhaps $Smith_n$—and, as he pointed out, the main "guinea pig" for his methods. His efforts to see if it worked brought him into personal contact with at least a couple thousand other 'Smiths', to whom he taught his methodology and how to apply it. (1800 people studied with Korzybski at Institute of General Semantics seminars from 1938 on. Korzybski had already been teaching for years before that.[9]) By the time of his death, he felt great confidence his system did work—*for those willing to work at it.*

More than half a century has now passed. There remains a lively, if still limited, audience for Korzybski's writings. Detractors have called his work "highly dubious". Others have viewed it as a useful public service, and some consider it a significant contribution to human civilization. In these first years of a new millennium—a time of terrorism—individual unhappiness/maladjustment and societal collisions of various sorts appear depressingly omnipresent and perhaps not unrelated. The life and work of Alfred Korzybski deserve attention.

For some readers, this book will be an introduction. Korzybskian echoes can be found in a variety of fields such as cognitive neuroscience, cognitive-behavioral psychotherapy, communication, media ecology, medicine, organizational development, philosophical counseling and philosophy, etc. In spite of this, Korzybski's cross-disciplinary work remains relatively unassimilated into standard academic fields and hard to accurately fit into familiar popular categories. Thus, Korzybski remains a relatively neglected and misunderstood figure.

There are other folks who do 'know' something about Korzybski and/or general semantics. Some of these individuals may feel eager to learn more. For others, both Korzybski and his system are "dead issues" to be consigned to the trash bin of once popular and trivial trends that have come and gone along the fringes of intellectual history. There are also some people whose interest in general semantics has come and stayed. For these individuals—I count as one—Korzybski's work is not passé and has provided a starting point for many fascinating and fruitful explorations of the world and self.

I did not know Alfred Korzybski personally (I was born two years after his death). However, as a result of my research for this book, as well as close contacts over many years with people who knew and worked with him, I have come to see him as a remarkably kind and well-balanced person, despite some hard edges and personal foibles. He did not seem to act from any hidden agenda, indeed he put off some people with his blunt directness. He was not interested in guru-worshiping followers; he sought out a remarkable set of well-grounded, independent individuals as his closest associates. He 'practiced what he preached', and indeed had many characteristics of the self-actualizing personality psychologist Abraham Maslow delineated in his work. There is little if anything in his life for a scandal-loving scribe or a salivating psycho-biographer to write about. It is quite possible some antagonistic readers may consider his work itself, despite my sympathetic portrayal, as evidence enough for Korzybski's 'nuttiness'. I can't do anything about that.

Korzybski considered his life and work inseparable. Indeed, he considered the events of his life, in themselves, "nothing much to report".[10] He thought a biographer ought to cover them in relatively few pages and focus instead on his work—what he produced, recorded in his writings. I haven't strictly taken that advice. Attention to his fascinating (to me) life enriches an understanding of his work. So in this book, I show the interplay of his life and work. I explore his lifetime mission—the amelioration of human stupidity, conflict, and misery through a scientific-philosophical reorientation of humanity, one individual at a time. What were the motivating forces which drove him to create what he did? Why did he and his work become the object of such widely and wildly different reactions by supporters and detractors? What relevance, if any, do Korzybski and his work have for us today? Does Korzybski still matter to 21st century culture and concerns? The following pages contain my affirmative answer. Here is my map of the life and work of Alfred Korzybski—a story of knowledge, uncertainty, and courage.[11]

Bruce I. Kodish
May 28, 2011

ACKNOWLEDGEMENTS

Since mid-2004, when I first decided to write Korzybski's biography, I have devoted most of my time to researching and writing this book. For much of that time, it has seemed—frankly—a grueling solitary effort. But I've had assistance too, which has eased much of the pain. Here, I want to acknowledge those individuals who helped me.

First, I feel indebted to the late Charlotte Schuchardt Read, Alfred Korzybski's confidential and editorial secretary and his literary executor, whom I knew for 23 years as my teacher/mentor and dear friend. Charlotte encouraged and empowered me as a writer, administrative troubleshooter, and teacher. Without her efforts to preserve a substantial portion of Korzybski's papers and correspondence, this book would seem much poorer and weigh somewhat less. Over the years, Charlotte shared material about Korzybski with me and—perhaps more importantly—inspired me with her warmly matter-of-fact point of view. When she died in 2002, she didn't know I would be writing this book (neither did I). I believe she would have felt pleased to see the result.

I also feel a large debt to the late Robert P. Pula, another dear friend with whom I worked at the Institute of General Semantics during its post-Korzybski but still quite korzybskian heyday in the latter part of the 20th Century. Bob, the lead lecturer at IGS seminar-workshops for over 30 years, qualified until his death as the world's foremost living general-semantics and Korzybski scholar. When he died unexpectedly at the start of 2004, he had been seriously moving ahead on a biography of Korzybski he'd begun work on several decades before. Picking up the torch from Bob seemed like the right thing to do; I had studied and worked closely with him and others at the Institute at the peak of its educational program and had developed friendships with a number of people who studied with Korzybski (like Helen Hafner, Harry Holtzman, Ann Dix Meirs, and Penelope Russianoff), including—besides Charlotte—individuals who had become some of Korzybski's closest "co-workers" (a term he liked using), for example, Robert Redpath and Charlotte's husband, Allen Walker Read. This provided me with a personal feel for Korzybski's life and work I believe few others alive have had, a personal feel which I thought might get lost if I left the biography for someone else to do years later. Although I couldn't get access to Bob's working notes or manuscript, we had many face-to-face discussions over the years about Korzybski and his work; Bob thus provided me with guidance on background reading and research that I have found as valuable as his writings. This book, written out of a deep sense of time-binding duty, completes the task Bob set out to do but couldn't complete.

Sanford I. Berman's financial grants took a significant bite out of initial expenses involved in dedicating myself to the book. Much thanks to him and his wife Sande for their ongoing friendship, interest and support.

Thanks as well to the members of the 2004 Board of Trustees of the Institute of General Semantics, who enthusiastically embraced my project when I announced it to them. I do appreciate their encouragement. Steve Stockdale, Executive Director of the IGS from 2004 through 2007, did a tremendous job consolidating and organizing the Institute archives and digitizing microfilm and other records, which made my research both easier and more extensive and demanding than I could ever have imagined. Both he and Lance Strate, Professor of Communication and Media Studies at Fordham University and IGS Executive Director from 2008–2011, have aided and encouraged me along the way. My research work would also have taken much longer without the substantial material help of Kristen Harford, Marisa Sleeter, Judy Clarke, and Zack Clarke who for varying periods administered and worked at the IGS office in Fort Worth, Texas during my numerous visits to the library and archives there from 2005 through 2009.

My thanks also go to the staff of the Columbia University Rare Book and Manuscript Division of the Butler Library in New York City. I not only received full access to all of the Alfred Korzybski and Mira Edgerly Korzybska archives located there, but they also allowed me to begin organizing some of the non-microfilmed material remaining in those collections. I greatly appreciate their professional help and careful preservation of those valuable historical materials. I also feel grateful to the Huntington Library in San Marino, California, which accepted me as a Reader (visiting scholar) and thus allowed me to take advantage of its extensive collection of materials in general history and the history of science. I've had few pleasures like the one of sitting in the Huntington's secured and pristine reading room—no pens or pencils allowed—reading Jack London's personal copy (underlined by him) of the 1912 book, *The Mechanistic Conception of Life*, by Korzybski's friend and mentor Jacques Loeb. My special thanks go to biological anthropologist and brain researcher John Allman of Caltech and mathematics professor David Linwood of the University of Tennessee, Knoxville, for their recommendations which allowed me to become a Huntington Reader. The Caltech Library, the Pasadena/Glendale Public Libraries, and the Los Angeles Public Library also served as indispensible sources of otherwise hard-to-obtain volumes.

I also got help from friends: Polymathic classicist, musician, and financial analyst Lloyd Chappell generously shared historical and other books from his personal library, which I found most helpful. Gary David, a musician as well as an epistemic counselor, shared information about his mentor, J. Samuel Bois, one of the most important continuators of Korzybski's work. Korzybskian scholar-teacher Milton Dawes read parts of the evolving manuscript and offered advice and encouragement, as did Homer J. Moore, Jr., fellow GS "student-practitioner"—his own designation even though he taught advanced classes on Korzybski's work. (Sad to say, Homer did not live long enough to see this book get into print.) Two of my friends on the IGS Board of Trustees deserve special mention for the help they've given me. Ben Hauck, working as my research assistant, spent many hours at Columbia University's Butler Library photographing several boxes of non-microfilmed documents and letters. Ben's hard work helped make this a much richer book. Corey Anton provided valuable research assistance to me during our joint one-week visit to Fort Worth in 2009 with Lance Strate, where I showed those two communication scholars what was to be found in the archives and library there. When research time got short, Corey stepped in to do some necessary 'grunt work' for me. I have since learned a great deal from him in our ongoing discussions about Korzybski, the stoic tradition, and much else.

Two men who served as personal assistants to Korzybski, David (Levine) Linwood and Ralph C. Hamilton generously gave their time for numerous interviews mainly by phone and letter. Their perspectives on living and working with Korzybski were indeed irreplaceable, and they've become my friends. Thanks as well to Billie Jane Baguley for interview insights on her time as a student in Korzybski's 1945 summer seminar. I also extend my gratitude to John McClaughry of Vermont's Ethan Allen Institute who generously allowed me to make use of his father Richard T. McClaughry's unpublished account of his experiences with Korzybski, an unforgettable depiction of the kind of work that Korzybski did with individual students.

I also extend my thanks to George Kruszewski, Teresa G. Silverstein and Zehava Sweet for their translations from Polish and Maximilian Sandor for his translations from German. My stepson, David Presby provided valuable editorial advice and designed the cover. James D. French, Editor Emeritus of the *General Semantics Bulletin*, provided additional editorial help for which I am most grateful. My friend Nikzad "Benny" Toomarian of the Jet Propulsion Laboratory helped me protect valuable computer files. Jeffrey A. Mordkowitz, IGS Executive Director from 2000–2004, provided a sympathetic ear over the years of writing and research. And over those years, my granddaughter Rebecca Adler nudzhed me with her insistent question: "Grandpa, when are you going to finish the book?" Here you have it, Rebecca.

Finally, this book would certainly not have come into existence without both the support and the careful editorial work of my wife Susan Presby Kodish, a psychologist, veteran scholar-teacher of korzybskian methodology, and experienced writer and editor. As the book's main editor, Susan shaped its form-content and deserves major credit for whatever good that readers will find within these pages. Susan has sacrificed a great deal (as have I) over the years it has taken to produce this. Obsessed with getting it done, I sometimes neglected other important things. Thanks, dear one, for putting up with me in the process.

LANGUAGE NOTE AND PRONUNCIATION GUIDE

Throughout this book, I've used "extensional devices", linguistic techniques originated by Korzybski or his students which include indexing, dating, using etc., quotes, hyphens, using non-absolutistic terms and phrases (English Minus Absolutism), using non-elementalistic terms, avoiding the 'is' of predication and identity, etc. I explain these further in various parts of the text. But since I use quotes quite often, I will explain here what I'm doing with them. As an extensional "safety device" device, I've used single quote marks at times to indicate terms and phrases which in varying degrees require caution for general methodological reasons, e.g., 'mind', 'meaning', 'space' or 'time' used alone, etc. I've also used single quotes to sometimes mark off terms used metaphorically, playfully, etc.[1] Double quote marks indicate direct quotes from a named source (more extensive direct quotes are indicated simply by text blocks with smaller font). Double quotes also indicate terms or phrases used by someone but not necessarily indicating a direct quote. Within both single and double quotes, I endeavor to include only the exact material quoted—with just the original punctuation whenever possible.

In addition, Korzybski did not typically capitalize adjectives derived from proper names, such as "aristotelian"; I have followed this convention.

Regarding the two-word but unitary term "general semantics", it refers to the applied general theory of evaluation (verbal and *non-verbal*) formulated by Korzybski. I abbreviate it with capital letters as "GS". As in the phrase "a general-semantics approach", when using the term as a modifier I use a hyphen (standard usage) to indicate its unitary nature. Somewhat apologetically, I have chosen to spell Polish names and words without the special diacritical marks of the Polish language. Polish words generally have their stress on the next to last syllable. Otherwise, I'll limit my Polish pronunciation guide to one name: *Korzybski* (KAWR – ZHIB' –SKEE). Pronounce ZH like the Z in azure.

Part I
Final Day

"All flesh is grass."
— RUDYARD KIPLING[1]

Chapter 1
"WE ONLY COAGULATE."

"In the Institute [of General Semantics], we don't die"—it was one of Korzybski's serious 'jokes'—"we only coagulate."[1]

He had persistently made a point of teaching his students to remember that their very own consciousness involved the operation of stuff—especially the three or so pounds of brain-stuff inside their skulls. Following Jacques Loeb, Jerome Alexander, and others, Korzybski liked to emphasize the colloidal nature of this stuff that not only dreams but all mentality, the best and the worst, mathematics and madness, are made on.

In a colloidal system, like a living cell or organization of cells, nanometer-sized molecules such as fats, proteins, etc., are dynamically dispersed and in flowing motion in the liquid mediums inside and outside the cells. On a sub-microscopic level, these dispersed materials and their mediums form, change and move as energetic functions of surface tensions, electrical repulsions and attractions, interactions with other materials, etc. Eventually, under the 'right' or the 'wrong' conditions, the elements—as in eggs being heated—will come out of dispersion to clump together, i.e., coagulate. No more colloidal system. Fried eggs and mortality.

Several months short of his 71st birthday, Alfred Korzybski 'coagulated' around 3:00 a.m. on Wednesday, March 1, 1950. Until he collapsed at his desk in the early evening, his previous day at the Institute of General Semantics had not seemed entirely 'untypical'. Here, in a sprawling house in the small Northwest Connecticut village of Lime Rock (so small that the postal address was in the nearby town of Lakeville), he had lived and worked for the previous four years along with a few of the Institute's small staff and Daffodil, the cat of Charlotte Schuchardt, his confidential secretary and editorial assistant.[2]

For Korzybski, his not-untypical days had their routines but, of course, they were never exactly the same. Varying details might include Institute business, correspondence, writing and editing, counseling students and staff, et cetera, et cetera, et cetera. One factor remained constant—the work never stopped.

Charlotte and the Institute's Associate (and Education) Director, Marjorie Mercer Kendig (known in official correspondence as "M. Kendig" and to her friends and associates as just "Kendig") took care of most of the Institute business along with the small office staff. Korzybski received regular status reports which brought issues to his attention related to maintenance of the building and grounds, personnel problems, bills, fund-raising efforts, publicity, etc. He understood the need for delegating work, and did so. He had learned to trust Charlotte and Kendig, and depended on them. But he also understood the need—apparently eternal and sometimes infernal—for close supervision, checking to see jobs got done and done right. In turn, they also 'supervised' him—as best they could.

At his desk he also dealt with a mountainous correspondence from students and colleagues. As the Director of the Institute, Alfred had devised an elaborate system to deal with the mail. Important letters from close friends, etc., would go directly to him. His colleagues and office staff would read, mark, and respond first to other mail. This provided some selecting and filtering function to unburden his attention from 'trivial' correspondence. Nonetheless, he ended up with a constant backlog of letters awaiting response. If no one was available to take dictation, he would type his own letters, as he had done for most of his life. Because of his two-finger typing technique, he sometimes had to tape his fingertips to protect them when they started to get raw.

He welcomed getting reports from students who had used his methods to work on their personal difficulties. But in recent years "Poor Alfred", as Kendig sometimes affectionately referred to him, had also been receiving irksome communications from colleagues, some of whom had watered down his work in ways Korzybski found objectionable. On his desk that Tuesday February 28, he had a notice from the International Society for General Semantics (ISGS) announcing the newest selection of their "Semantics Book Club", S. I. Hayakawa's *Language in Thought and Action*. Both the Society and Hayakawa had become thorns in his side, drawing the interested public and their funds away from Institute functions and at times, in his opinion, seriously misrepresenting his work in the name of popularization. Korzybski had worked at remaining cordial to Hayakawa and others at the Society while vigorously protesting their attempts to change his formulations to supposedly make his work more popularly accessible. Not only did these attempts seem unnecessary but he felt they also wore away at the foundations of the discipline he had started.

Emphasizing these foundations, he had begun to refocus on the notion of *time-binding*. On his desk were notes and the latest draft for an introduction to the Second Edition—then in preparation—of his first book, *Manhood of Humanity*. In *Manhood* he had originally defined time-binding as the human capacity to build on the experience of ones' fellow humans, including previous generations, with ever-accelerating results. (Before he decided on the title *Science and Sanity* for his second book, Korzybski had at one time planned to call it *Time-Binding: The General Theory*.)

Time-binding provided the basis of what Korzybski had envisioned as a natural science of man, a "General Anthropology" including all human activities, the best, e.g., science, mathematics, etc., and the worst, e.g., the behavior of seriously disturbed patients in "mental hospitals". In its applied aspect, Korzybski came to call this study—much to his and others' later regret—"general semantics".

Perhaps Korzybski's refocusing on time-binding and "general anthropology" might help correct some of the misinterpretations of the name "general semantics" by students and critics alike who had confused his theory with "semantics", the narrower study of linguistic meanings. Indeed, general semantics or GS, as Korzybski abbreviated it, involved much more.

By "general semantics", Korzybski had intended a general, applied theory for improving human *evaluation*—a term which for him combined 'thinking' and 'feeling', and was not necessarily limited to language. In his usage 'semantic reaction' was equivalent to *evaluation*. (The term 'semantic' as a modifier was used in this context as equivalent to *evaluational*.) Thus general semantics, a general theory of *evaluation*, studied organism-as-a-whole-in-environment, 'semantic' (*evaluational*) reactions. Although Korzybski eschewed much traditional academic philosophy, at the very least GS was related to the area of philosophy—epistemology—having to do with the question, *how do we know what we think we know?* Korzybski saw GS as a *scientifically-based, applied epistemology* applicable to all fields and to everyday life. There was resistance enough to this program, even without misinterpreting its name. Nonetheless, the name "general semantics" had a history now. Korzybski and his colleagues and students seemed 'stuck' with it and would continue having to deal with the misunderstandings surrounding the term.

Other projects had crossed Korzybski's desk in recent days. He, Kendig, and Charlotte had begun work on the first issue of the *General Semantics Bulletin,* a journal/yearbook for inter-communication among co-workers in the field of general semantics. (This has continued to be published annually up to the present.)

More pressing, he was still working on a manuscript for a paper he was scheduled to deliver in April for a Clinical Psychology Symposium on Perception at the University of Texas. Travel arrangements to Austin had been made. He had spent much of January and February writing and was presently in the stage of "delousing", his term for the 'painful' process of editing a manuscript and removing typographical, grammatical, and formulational 'vermin'. He took this analogy from his days on the Eastern Front of World War I Poland, where the actual vermin—lice—were numerous and took blood. The paper, eventually published under the title "The Role of Language in the Perceptual Processes", offered an up-to-date (1950) summary of GS with connections to recent work in linguistics (Benjamin Lee Whorf), psychology, and the new science of cybernetics. (Charlotte Schuchardt, whom Korzybski had appointed as his literary executor, would complete the editing after his death and present the paper in Texas.)

Also on the schedule for April was a trip for Korzybski to visit Adelbert Ames' Institute for Associated Research at Dartmouth College in Hanover, New Hampshire. Korzybski had recently learned of Ames' visual demonstrations, such as his now famous "distorted room", which jibed with Korzybski's teachings about the constructed aspects of human perceptual processes. On his desk sat a reprint of a three-part article Ames had sent to him "with compliments" on "Psychology and Scientific Research". Korzybski had underlined it throughout with pencil. It seemed clear that Ames and his colleagues, who were also exploring the role of assumptions in human behavior and scientific inquiry, were moving along the road Korzybski had traveled. He was eager to see what he could learn from the whole array of Ames' demos. (One of Ames' graduate assistants, Thomas E. Nelson, had only recently learned of Korzybski's work and would become an important member of the teaching staff at Institute of General Semantics seminar-workshops.)

So Korzybski had a lot of work to do. Engaging, no doubt—also incessant. The pressing demands did not stop—whatever his accumulated fatigue from years of effort. Despite his commitment to his work, Korzybski's pace was slowing. He was looking appreciably worn.

His last seminar, starting the day after Christmas and ending on January 3, his 12th annual Winter Intensive, had been held at the Sharon [Connecticut] Inn. Although his hours of lecturing had remained lively and stimulating, he mostly sat. Severe painful arthritis and sciatica—sequelae to his World War I injuries—appeared to be wearing him down at last. As Kendig observed, "He no longer tramped up and down the platform shaking his cane."[3]

He was also set to teach at the Institute Summer Seminar-Workshop running from mid-August to the beginning of September. And another Winter Holiday Seminar was planned as usual at the end of the year—a relatively light schedule given his past teaching load (in the previous 15 years, Korzybski had given approximately 80 seminars, lectures, presentations, etc.).

After work, Korzybski would sometimes spend the evening listening to his recordings of classical music. Sometimes, like Wittgenstein, he read detective stories. These relaxations might be accompanied by his favorite rum. The evening of February 28, however, was not spent relaxing.

He spent his final moments at his desk conferring with young D. David Bourland, Jr., who at the time was living in Lime Rock, near the Institute. Bourland had attended several IGS seminars. From April to September, 1949, he had done volunteer staff work at the Institute (as a minor at the time he started, he did this with his parent's permission—at Korzybski and Kendig's insistence). In September 1949 he had been awarded a fellowship to study and work with Korzybski while on a hiatus from Harvard. Bourland brought with him the perennial adolescent problems of parents, romantic interests, school, etc. His friend Alfred—in loco parentis—felt some responsibility to David and to his parents and had been doing his best to help him.

This kind of coaching or consultation by Korzybski was not exceptional. He had designed general semantics "for the sake of solving human problems."[4] He didn't expect his students to be able to adequately tackle more 'impersonal' problems before—first and foremost—applying it to themselves. So throughout his teaching career, he asked any student wishing to work with him to write a brief autobiographical statement highlighting problems, dilemmas, 'hang-ups', etc. An optional personal interview—occasionally more than one—based on this material, could be scheduled with him after he completed his series of lectures. In the interview he would as usual "troubleshoot", seeking—perhaps more than anything else—to help the student translate his or her story into a different, more fact-based form of language.[5]

The interview with Bourland turned out to be Korzybski's last labor. Since Bourland had received the fellowship, Korzybski had found him increasingly distracted and inaccessible. During this time, Bourland—just turned 21—had become involved with Virginia McMullen, a radio-television producer around 17 years his senior. McMullen, whom Kendig described as "a pleasant, chatty person of the nervous high-powered sales type",[6] had been known to Korzybski and Kendig for several years starting when the Institute had been in Chicago. In 1944, McMullen had tried to promote to Kendig a radio program on general semantics. After a number of meetings, Kendig did not feel McMullen's understanding of the discipline sufficed by Institute standards for her to do an adequate job of popularizing. (Indeed, in Kendig's opinion, "One has to know the discipline and feel it in one's 'guts' very much more securely to popularize it correctly than to write so-called scholarly articles on the subject."[7]) Miss McMullen attended the 1949-1950 Winter Intensive seminar (after a number of her phone calls to Kendig pleading for free tuition, Kendig had agreed to a reduced fee). As Kendig noted, "Bourland [who had met McMullen when she visited the Institute that summer] saw a great deal of her during the Seminar."[8]

And he continued to see her afterwards. By the end of February, he and McMullen, then living in New York City, had wedding plans. Bourland must have told one or more of his friends on the Institute staff because sometime that Tuesday morning, February 28, Korzybski found out about the wedding, set for the following weekend. Korzybski asked Werner von Kuegelgen (the Institute accountant and sales manager), Kendig, and Charlotte to come to his office for a conference. They met at 12:45 p.m. Von Kuegelgen wrote on the following day that Alfred expressed deep concern about the marriage and emphasized his sense of responsibility for David and to his parents. With the three others advising him, Korzybski decided to talk with David, hoping to convince the young man to notify his parents himself.

After the meeting, Von Kuegelgen found Bourland who, with strong encouragement, agreed to request an interview with Korzybski. Dave wrote a note and gave it to Werner in a sealed envelope to place on Korzybski's desk.[9] The note said:
> Dear AK,
> This week-end I shall be married.
> May I discuss this briefly with you?
>   Dave [10]

Around 5 o'clock in the afternoon Bourland went to Korzybski's office for the interview. At 5:15 he came out and called for help. Korzybski had collapsed at his desk while they were talking and was now unconscious. Bourland, Charlotte, Kendig, Lynn Gates (assistant and later the husband of Kendig), and von Kuegelgen carried Korzybski to his bed across the hall. In a memorandum written several weeks afterwards, Kendig recounted what happened next:

> At 5:45 [Korzybski] regained consciousness, looked at Bourland standing at the foot of his bed, and said, 'How can I convey anything to him!' Then he asked Bourland, 'Will you wait, etc.?' Bourland said, 'Yes, I will wait'. The Doctor arrived at about 6:15. I took Bourland with me to get prescriptions and to dinner. I talked with him very seriously about the recent trends I had observed in his evaluations...At the time Bourland evinced some insight and verbalized same. We returned to the Institute at 9:00 PM. A.K. was in intense pain. The Doctor was called again. Morphine did not kill the pain, and the Doctor said, 'This is very serious.' He said in sum, with A.K.'s general condition, an intense emotional strain would have produced a coronary thrombosis.
>
> At about one AM, March first, the Doctor decided that A.K. should go to the Sharon Hospital for X-Rays to determine the reason for the intense pain in lower abdomen (a mesentery thrombosis as the autopsy showed). The ambulance was summoned and arrived at about 1:45 AM. Schuchardt and the Doctor accompanied A.K. At about 2:30, Schuchardt telephoned me to come at once. I telephoned Bourland, dressed, and he drove me to the Hospital. A.K. was dead when we arrived about 3:15 AM, March first. We all remained in the Hospital until morning. ....[11]

Regarding his promise to Korzybski, Bourland did wait—for one week. On March 10, the Friday following the Memorial Service for Korzybski, he had told one of his co-workers "If anyone wants to know, I am not marrying this weekend." Kendig was informed he got married that night. Feeling some responsibility toward Bourland's parents—who had not been informed of the wedding—Kendig did not consider Bourland's operationally correct definition of 'waiting' as adequately honoring his death-bed promise to Korzybski. To her, his behavior didn't indicate the kind of mature evaluation which she expected from a Korzybski Fellow. On March 13 after further consultation with colleagues, Kendig—as Acting Director of the Institute—terminated Bourland's Korzybski Fellowship at a staff meeting which he attended. For his part, Bourland felt deep regret about Kendig's decision.[12]

Whatever bad feelings may have existed afterwards between Kendig and Bourland didn't last. Neither did Bourland's marriage to Virginia McMullun. In later years, Bourland became a professor of English and also worked in the field of operational research. He became well-known as the developer of E-Prime, his extension of general semantics which consists of English minus any form of the verb "to be". He also renewed his relationship with Kendig, maintained a friendly collegial correspondence with her, and did work for the Institute including a stint as editor of the *General Semantics Bulletin*. Bourland, who died in 2000, remained devoted to Korzybski's memory and work and later fondly recalled Korzybski's statement to him during their last interview: "Dave, you'll never have a better friend than me."[13]

Alfred's wife Mira, living in Chicago, incapacitated with arthritis, was notified at once, nigh undoubtedly by telephone. She wanted to come but later that morning, Charlotte received a telegram sent from Chicago at 8:12 a.m. from Mira's physician:

> I have heard from the Countess the death of her husband and her wish to go to Connecticut I made her aware that it would be unwise for her to attempt such a journey in her present crippled condition.[14]

Others who had been close to Alfred got telegrams like this one to David Levine, also in Chicago: "Alfred died suddenly this morning. Funeral Saturday 12:30 Institute Kendig Schuchardt".[15] Levine "felt his death as a personal loss" and scrambled to get there.[16]

Notices to the media went out. *The New York Times* printed a same-day obituary. Arrangements were made for the Saturday memorial service, etc. And phone calls, telegrams, cards, letters and flowers came pouring into the Institute from those whose lives he had touched: the 'well-known' and 'lesser known'. Bourland was not the only person on whom Korzybski had lavished his attention. Ralph C. Hamilton—his student, friend, and co-worker at the Institute—later compared his fabulous energy to that of a rodeo rider leaping from his horse to 'bulldog' a steer. With his attention to detail, it often seemed like Korzybski was leaping from his horse to 'bulldog a mouse', but for Korzybski—especially with his students—there were no small things or unimportant people.[17]

One of Alfred's friends, Clarence B. Farrar, M.D., Editor of the *American Journal of Psychiatry*, wrote to Kendig on March 2:

> Dear Miss Kendig, I can't tell you how grieved I was to get your message that Count Alfred had died, and I wish that I could be with you on Saturday to pay in that way a tribute of affection and admiration for our great friend. You will know however, although I cannot be there, that no one shares more deeply with you all the sense of loss of a teacher and leader such as he. Over the years I have had [many] courtesies and kindnesses from Count Alfred and it is my great regret that our paths have not crossed oftener; but I have been proud to feel that he was my good friend. His work has been so fundamental that it is most gratifying to see its expanding application and usefulness. To you his closest associates, who will carry on this work I send my deep sympathy and most cordial good wishes. Sincerely yours
>
> Clarence B. Farrar [18]

With little doubt, Farrar was responsible for the obituary comment in the May 1950 issue of the *American Journal of Psychiatry* which stated, "The death of this great teacher… deepens appreciation of his essential contribution to human understanding, on an individual, widely social, or international scale."[19]

Korzybski's old friends, famed botanical explorer David Fairchild and his wife Marian (daughter of Alexander Graham Bell)—whose home in Florida, "The Kampong", later became the National Tropical Botanical Garden—telegrammed to Kendig and Charlotte Schuchardt on March 2:

> How vast a void his departure leaves in the thought world of our troubled times His ideas on the uses of words will make a saner more peaceful world He has not lived in vain[20]

Cultural historian and polymath Erich Kahler—friend of Einstein and Thomas Mann—had studied Korzybski's work, and attended his April 1946 New York City Intensive Seminar (thirty hours of lecture over eight successive evenings) given at the New York Historical Society. On March 25, Kahler wrote to Kendig:

> Only a few days ago I heard the news of Count Korzybski's death, and I feel the urge to convey to you my sincere grief and sympathy. Korzybski was a great mind and his energy seemed indestructible. One would have expected him to last and grow into the ages like a grand old tree. His death is a frightful loss to our world. But I trust that you will find the courage and the strength to carry on his work which is badly needed in these times of utter confusion and peril.[21]

A lesser-known but just-as-valued friend, G. C. McKinney, a physician from Lake Charles, Louisiana, who had studied with Korzybski, got a telegram from the Institute notifying him of his mentor's death. On March 5, McKinney wrote back to Kendig and Charlotte about his profound sense of loss:

> My Dears,
> ...I have been formulating what I would say since the telegram came but that now the moment of saying has arrived it becomes very hazy. That I am concerned about both [of you] in a very personal way—to try to say that sounds rather silly since you both know it very well. That I regarded Alfred Korzybski as I have never regarded any one before, nor shall ever again, you also know. After all it is concern for whether any one is 'big' enough or whether one can be found so, to carry on, and personal concern for you that has cut so deep. Fact that I shall never see Alfred again, hear his beautiful voice, movement of his beautiful hands and (perhaps most of all) the expression of that mobile face, ranging all the way from heavy anger and sternness to almost-tears...can be laid to selfishness, ego...No use. I can go no further. Love and Love...Mac[22]

The March 3 telegram from Blanche and Harry Weinberg (Korzybski considered Harry one the most promising of his students) perhaps said best what could be said about what could not be said: "How inadequate is the verbal level now".[23]

Korzybski's desk, March 1, 1950

Part II
Beginnings

All beginnings are arduous.
— THE TALMUD (MECHILTA YITRO)[1]

Chapter 2
YOUNG ALFRED

School was done. Vacation time had come. Fourteen year old Alfred Korzybski took the train from Warsaw. He was traveling from his family's home there to spend the summer at Rudnik, their country estate located in the gubernia (government district) of Piotrkow about 100 miles to the southwest. The rail line ran south from Warsaw—the main city of the Russian Empire's Vistula land, formerly known as Poland—through Mazovia toward the homeland of the ancient Polish Kings. After a while, one line split off west to the city of Lodz which at the end of the 19th Century had become a major textile manufacturing center. Alfred's train would continue further to his stop at the village of Bedkow. A horse and cart would come to take him to Rudnik.

Looking out at the landscape from the train window, Alfred would have seen plains and rolling hills abundant with "wide expanses of heath and scrubland."[1] Alfred felt deeply connected to this poor land and to his beloved Poland, even if no one could find "Poland" on any current map. In 1894 (the year of this journey), the Republic of Poland had not existed for nearly 100 years. Alfred had studied the history thoroughly—though not at school.

In 1795, the autocratic empires surrounding Poland—Austria, Prussian Germany and Tsarist Russia—completed the partition process by which they had begun gobbling up the country twenty-two years before. These imperial powers "solemnly swore to banish the very name of 'Poland' from the record."[2] The rest of the 'civilized' world looked on but provided no rescue. For them Poland had seemed, as Edmund Burke ruefully noted, as if it was "situated on the Moon."[3] The Poles, with nearly 1000 years of national life behind them, were squeezed in a vise of political and cultural oppression. The armies of Napoleon, various shifts in jurisdiction, and a few periods of reform by the imperial powers occasionally raised the hopes of those who sought to keep their culture alive and to raise a new Polish state. To no avail. Over the years the vise had tightened. There had been uprisings—one in 1832 and one in 1863—centered in the Russian section. These had resulted in further repression. While Austria allowed a measure of freedom for its Poles to express themselves as Poles, the situation had definitely worsened in the German and Russian parts. In 1874, five years before Alfred's birth, the Tsarist Empire had fully incorporated its share of Poland—where Warsaw, Lodz, and Rudnik were located—into the Russian fatherland. As far as it was concerned, young Alfred, a descendent of the old szlachta (Polish nobility)[4], was simply a Russian citizen, a subject of the Tsar.

As part of this incorporation, "russification"—the plan to supress Polish culture—had taken off with a vengeance. Tsarist authorities designated Polish a 'foreign language' with the use of Russian obligatory in the courts and schools. Polish literature and history were banned from publication in Poland. Only some leeway was given in labeling street signs, where Polish (written in Latin script) was allowed to accompany the Russian Cyrillic names.[5] At schools such as the realschule in Warsaw that Alfred attended for something like eight years, Polish students received their lessons—even Polish language instruction—in Russian. But at home, alone with his family, or when speaking with the servants or with the peasant workers at the farm, Alfred could use his native language.

With servants and peasants working for them, the Korzybskis, if not enormously wealthy, surely qualified as well-to-do. Despite the oppressive atmosphere of the Russian regime, the family had managed to retain both the emblems of status and the means for comfortable living. Unlike many of the pre-partition Polish szlachta, the noble status of Alfred's family continued to be recognized. His ancestors were among the ancient Polish Counts (or landlords of counties) allowed to use a title in pre-partition Poland.[6] As to means, besides the perquisites of his father's position in the Russian Ministry of Communication, the family owned property in Warsaw. And with their farm estate, they retained the tradition of the Polish landed nobility.

The run-down property at Rudnik had come from Alfred's mother's family, the Rzewuskis, who had used it (one of many estates they owned) to raise hunting dogs. (Alfred's father had inherited another estate, as well as other properties in Warsaw, but had given them away to his brothers.) Without records—destroyed as the result of two World Wars—Korzybski later estimated Rudnik's size as somewhere from five to eight hundred acres, an average size estate for nobility with means. Its poorly-draining clay soil did not naturally suit Rudnik for agriculture. But lately, thanks to his father's efforts to improve the soil—a major avocation of considerable expense—Rudnik had become a model farm.

Although this was school vacation, Alfred didn't expect to idle. He would have time, no doubt, for recreation but he also had plenty of work to look forward to and also, no doubt, what he ruefully referred to as "troubles". As he later described himself, "I was a troubleshooter since [the age of] five. At home, servants, peasants, whenever we had troubles: [I heard] 'Alfred, do it.' And Alfred had to do the dirty work."[7] It started as soon as he arrived home that day:

> I came to the station and a man was with horses and cart...to take me home. The moment I arrived home here burst [in] a peasant, 'Master, master, save my wife'. What happened? She just had a child. And she had a hemorrhage. She's bleeding white. I just came, a boy of fourteen—'save her'. I knew nothing about that part of it, so I asked my mother, 'What in hell can I do?' To mama I didn't say hell. I meant it probably, but I didn't say it. What shall I do? And my mother gave me orders, put pillows under her fanny, and put cotton in her...And I remember my doing that, putting her fanny up, and filling her with cotton. Of course, not knowing what I am doing. I did the best I could successfully. It stopped the hemorrhage somehow. Helping nature, but all the time, remember, what happens, they ran to the boss and my mother didn't want to be with them that way, so I had to do it. [8]

Troubleshooter

Alfred's skill as a troubleshooter had often come in handy at Rudnik where the distances required for traveling to, from, and within the estate demanded self-sufficiency. A doctor might take six or seven hours to arrive, a veterinarian twenty. The peasants on the farm learned to depend on "the little master" who might be seen going about with a veterinary or medical textbook under his arm. In another medical emergency, a peasant girl had tried to commit suicide by swallowing iodine. He related,."I knew enough to wash my hands in dirty water and make her drink it. It saved a life. It worked. It was an actual primitive first aid, but what else to do?"[9]

Alfred had begun to take on responsibilities at a fairly young age. During the summer, his parents might need to hire anywhere from 50 to 100 people in addition to the local peasants for several months of harvesting. They hired mainly Russian soldiers from almost every part and ethnic group within the Russian empire, looking to supplement their meager salaries. Korzybski's parents provided barracks and food—and Alfred to supervise.

He already had experience supervising the peasant workers. For example, when a horse or cow died, which happened occasionally, the body would be skinned in order to obtain the hide, worth money—if it didn't get cut or otherwise damaged in the skinning process. Little Alfred would supervise the procedure as well as the digging of the hole for burying the carcass, so the dogs couldn't pull it out. Initially, he may have tried to push the workers beyond what they could reasonably do. But he listened to them and learned when they protested, "Master, we are not brutes." He would recall that phrase of protest when later trying to formulate what distinguished humans from animals.

Supervising the soldier-workers provided other things for him to learn about people. Picture eight year old Alfred, standing in a field in a military uniform and cap—which he had discovered gave him more authority with the Russian soldiers—showing them how to cut the rye and wheat, directing their work, telling them when and even how to take a break. Young Alfred could speak Russian well. Attending to the varying psychologies he observed among the soldiers, he discovered there were different ways to best handle men from different ethnic groups. He worked hard and had a commanding presence. The workers paid attention. For Alfred the job opened up what would become a life-long fascination with the issues of management and human relations. For example, he soon realized the importance of the alternating rhythm of work and rest:

> [The soldiers] worked like hell, actually like machines, for say fifteen, thirty minutes, I gave orders STOP. LAY DOWN. SMOKE. They were accustomed to orders. I didn't let them fool around, talk, chatter. No—lay down, rest, smoke, drink water. Do anything you want. Don't waste time. And I gave them say after thirty minutes, I gave them something like ten minutes rest. The result was management. That they, after that rest under orders, then they became again strong, and virile and they had rest. A great many people don't know how to rest. If you rest, don't dawdle about it. Just relax, lay down, or something like that.[10]

The Little Master

"You cannot fool a horse"

At the age of ten, Alfred had begun another job he enjoyed greatly, despite the inevitable falls and mishaps: training young horses. About fifty new ones arrived every summer and Alfred had the job of breaking them in as work horses. Although most of them would eventually work under harness, Alfred trained them by first breaking them in under saddle.

He came to generally admire horses for their loyalty and intelligence. As he later said, they taught him a great deal and influenced his future work. "I discovered something which everybody knows by now that you can fool a human being, but you cannot fool a horse. I learned that. It's really true."[11]

> Handling horses, as far as I'm concerned, has been an awfully good lesson to me. Training men is eventually easier and eventually more difficult. That with horses you have to have rapport if you want to be a good rider. From horses I also learned what I call mechanical justice. This what I call a formula, what I call mechanical justice is a most important human problem. To jump into speeches about justice in the abstract is quite… metaphysical. Now the question of mechanical justice…involves an animal level even, if so, then so. It is the beginning of logic, the beginning of mathematics [as well as science, education, and law]—if so, then so…the beginning was, if you wish, with horses.[12]

Alfred would usually pick one horse from the bunch as his "pet". He recalled a particular saddle horse he once had:

> We lived like two brothers…I took him into trouble, he took us into trouble, but ultimately we were awfully well adjusted. Now in the stable there was a corridor and there little compartments for horses. Now he of course had his own, let's call it room. I went there, I took him things, I talked to him. Oh, I don't know, we were just like two good friends. And mutual trust. The horse trusted me and I trusted the horse. Wonderful horse…When I was using him, inspecting the farm work,…I got tired of riding …so when I came to a piece of particular work done by [a] peasant, agricultural work, I dismounted, but I didn't keep the bridle in my hand. The horse was trained to work[,] he handled like a dog without being held by it.

> Now, our mutual relationship, here he got tired walking behind me and my stopping here and there telling a peasant how to do the work or showing him, physically, what to do, how to do, and he got annoyed. He was well-fed. He was not tired. He was tired simply from the drudgery of routine, but not otherwise. When he got disgusted with the routine, he nudged me with his nose in my back, I speak saying "Alfred, hurry on." Which translated means let's go. This was his way of telling me tactfully with just his nose at the middle of my back…if I didn't pay attention there. Very seldom he did it. He just ran away. Tail up and galloping away leaving me alone miles away from home. I was left without a horse. He was not supposed to do that. In addition he usually—just a few times he did it—few times, I don't know how many, [h]e went into a field where there was sand and rolled around and rolled around in the sand ruining a hundred dollar or two hundred dollar saddle. Ruined it.

> And then he went into the stable after having his fun. Now when I came back to the stable, a question of justice. When I came to the stable, oh, hours afterwards, he immediately began to tremble. Somehow he knew that he did something which he should not do. Somehow he knew. He knew that punishment is coming. And he was trembling and he got a licking like hell. Just because of that. That running away which he was not supposed to do. After the good beating, I went into his stall and did a lot of talking to him and putting my finger in the Uncle Sam manner you know—you know the Uncle Sam finger, you so and so, you know that—which I did to him. Finally he was nodding his head and going brr-r, brr-r, brr-r, and after all that lesson, then I petted him, kissed his nose. Then he again went brr-r, brr-r all over quite happy. We are good friends again. In this particular case,…I wonder if you understand that mechanical justice. He knew by himself that he did something which he shouldn't do.[13]

"We Were Sort of Strangers"

As in the case of the peasant woman bleeding to death, young Alfred at times depended on advice from his mother, Helena Rzewuska Korzybska, but he did not become a doting son. (He did remain a dutiful one, corresponding regularly with her until her death in Poland in 1937.) On the whole, family relations in the Korzybski household could not exactly be called "warm". Within Polish aristocratic families, that was probably not so unusual. Alfred, born on July 3, 1879 in Warsaw, and his sister Adrianna, two years older, were raised by servants. French and German governesses took care of the details of their daily existence.

Alfred and his sister Adrianna

The children's daily contact with their parents, at meals and other times, was limited and tended towards formality.

> ...my sister and I were at the mercy of very fine governesses and servants and had very little to do with papa, mama, very little...In a broader sense, both mother and father were interested in the future of their children...But there was not much of so-called family coordination...we were sort of strangers altogether. Friendly, nice, civilized, but well, there was no interconnection. We didn't have any particular psycho-logical problems. We were just civilized mild people going along the best we could. But the old-fashioned ties of family were absent.[14]

Helena Korzybska came from a well-known szlachta family, the Rzewuskis who had large landholdings in the Ukraine and whose reputation had become tainted by the questionable loyalty to the Polish cause of some of its members. Born around 1857 and much younger than her husband, she had grown up in the oversheltered manner common at the time for raising aristocratic girls. She ended up, in the later opinion of her son, a rather superficial and infantile woman for whom raising children seemed like playing with dolls. As Alfred recounted, Helena occupied herself in a seemingly endless round of attending and organizing parties, balls, and dinners.

As a very young child, Alfred accompanied her to various spas in Germany and other parts of Europe for one or two months a year, as she pursued a rest cure for various real or imagined illnesses. Once on a visit with her to Vienna, five or six year old Alfred threw a bouquet of flowers into the coach of Franz Josef, smacking His Apostolic Majesty, the Emperor of Austria and King of Hungary, in the nose.

Korzybski later referred to his mother as a "back seat driver" possessing a combination of apparent helplessness and underlying manipulativeness which he found irksome and sought to avoid in later relationships with women.[15] (His closest female associates in later life were women notable for their self-sufficiency and directness.) Helena's demandingness undoubtedly helped Alfred develop his troubleshooting skills. As he noted, "She drove servants usually frantic, and I was the peace-maker, alibiing, explaining."[16]

Alfred's sister definitely did not get along well with mama. To the relief of both mother and daughter, Adrianna was sent away to school at the Convent of the Sacred Heart in Vienna. When she returned to Warsaw after about five years, Alfred noted, "She was a complete stranger." She later returned to live in Vienna because of her facility in German. Her brother corresponded with her for a time but eventually lost touch with her, especially after he came to America, except for seeing her during his visit to Poland in 1929. After World War II, as with many other relatives and friends he had in Poland, he never learned what happened to her, whether she was alive or dead.

Alfred felt closer to his father Wladyslaw Korzybski, born in 1839, and one of the three sons of Wincenty Andrzej Korzybski, who had served both as attorney general of Mazovia and as a member of the Warsaw Sejm (Parliament), just prior to the 1863 insurrection. Wladyslaw had trained as an engineer and had an international outlook, having studied all over Europe, including England. Indeed, as Alfred later described it, his father "fell in love with England. Everything was British but the cook (French)."[17] This may account for Alfred's Anglo-Saxon first name. A "general" in the Russian Ministry of Ways and Communications (bureaucratic positions received military ranks), Wladyslaw Korzybki spent a great deal of time away from home traveling for his work, which encompassed the improvement of bridges and roads, including railroads, throughout Russia. However he devoted as much of his spare time and income as he could to improve the old Rzewuski dog farm. Working for the Russians while seeking to improve life at home, Wladyslaw Korzybski embodied a new spirit of conciliation and practical idealism that had captured many Poles by the 1870s—a belief that they could accomodate (or even work for) the powers-that-be while still preserving Polish culture and improving the lot of the Polish people. This attitude, exemplified by Korzybski's father and his work at Rudnik, had a lasting impact on Alfred.

A Practical Idealist

What actualities did a practical idealist like Wladyslaw Korzybski have to deal with on the farm? Rudnik had little naturally fertile land. With clay lying below the topsoil, water couldn't adequately drain through. Instead it would sit above the clay layer and evaporate, making the soil cold and acidic. At the time, the standard and very costly method of draining such soil involved inserting baked clay tubes into the clay bottom. The clay tubes would absorb the water and allow it to drain through. Wladyslaw Korzybski had no special education in agriculture, but his engineering mentality found a better, less expensive solution.

Taking advantage of the cheap labor available at Rudnik, he dug ditches into the clay layer and filled them with stones (Alfred sometimes supervised some of this stone-laying work). The elder Korzybski graded the ditches so that the underground water drained into a large, ten-feet-deep pond he had dug over an area of a city block, called "the bath", which Alfred used for swimming. (Apparently, Alfred was the only one who would swim in the year-round icy cold water whose clay residue required taking a bath after going in "the bath". He swam in it regularly every summer and became an expert swimmer.)

Eventually the spaces between the stones in the ditches would become clogged with clay. But such a ditch might drain for twenty years before needing to be redug. In the meantime, the dried-out soil turned warm and less acidic. Due to Wladyslaw Korzybski's drainage method as well as his innovative use of contour ploughing to prevent soil erosion on its hillsides, the farm became fruitful. He wrote two books, one of which had the title *Melioracje Rolne* (*Agricultural Amelioration*). Both he and his work at Rudnik became internationally known.

As a small boy, Alfred spent a great deal of time traipsing after the men at work on the ditches. The unspoken lessons were invaluable for a scientist/engineer in the making. For one thing, Alfred could experience for himself the earthliness of any kind of measurement, along with the limitations of naked eye observation. "By the eye you cannot tell [whether or not the water would go down the hill], you simply have to measure with instruments." He could see that, despite this, methods existed for getting reliable and accurate knowledge—knowledge for getting important things done. "I was witnessing…all the time a technician trying to find the measurements of the levels to get that goddamn water, that underground water away."[18] Observing his father's efforts to improve Rudnik, Alfred gained not only a life-long interest in the problems of soil conservation and farm production but more importantly he imbibed his father's deep appreciation of mathematical and scientific knowledge (Wladyslaw's hobbies were mathematics and physics) and the importance of a hands-on approach to developing and applying it.

At the tender age of five, Alfred's father gave him a "feel of [the] differential calculus".[19] It is not hard to imagine how work on the ditches may have played a part here. Given the young boy's interest in the technicians' efforts to measure the slopes of hillsides, I can imagine the elder Korzybski giving his son a simple spirit level, such as carpenters use, and showing him how to measure the grade of the slope along every few feet of a given span of hillside, then showing him how to record his measurements. Korzybski's father then might show him how to use these results to map the slope on a piece of graph paper. Shortening the intervals of measurement would result in slightly altered, more precise curves. From here it would be a short step to ask the child to imagine the intervals getting smaller and smaller, closer and closer to one point on the slope. In this way, they would have reached the governing notion of the differential calculus—a method for determining the slope at any point along a curve. Once Alfred had learned about slope-finding on the actual slopes of hillsides, he would eventually be able to grasp that other aspects of the world involving measurable relationships could also be represented on graph paper as slopes with rates of change he could determine. Integral calculus, finding the area under a curve by summing up smaller increments of it, would follow. Whatever way he first got the feel of it, Alfred remained fascinated with the underlying notions of the calculus for the rest of his life.

In later life, one of Alfred's pet phrases was, "I don't know, let's see." Wladyslaw Korzybski may or may not have said this to his son. But he surely conveyed to Alfred his curiosity, respect for facts, and engineering attitude of practicality—"how can I make this work?" As an avid follower of the latest trends in physics and mathematics, Wladyslaw Korzybski also gave his son a feel for the newest (in the latter half of the 19th Century) scientific discoveries such as the electro-magnetic field theory of Maxwell and Hertz, and a feel for developments in mathematics such as non-euclidean geometry. The father's enthusiasm caught something in the boy and Alfred often dreamt of becoming a mathematician or a physicist when he wasn't considering becoming a lawyer.

Gradually as he mastered newtonian physics and euclidean geometry in school, Alfred found that discrepancies between these disciplines and the newer theories were chipping away at his sense of certainty in the solid foundations of science and mathematics. But whatever uncertainties developed, he had trouble putting his difficulties into words and found the situation deeply unsatisfying. Something one of his high school teachers had said to him in class stuck with him:

> Here I [was] called to the blackboard. I [was] asked questions which I didn't prepare…[The teacher was] a Pole, a professor of German, [who] talked to me in Russian. How do you like that? And he was a rough-neck. I disliked him. Everybody disliked him. So here is the conversation: He asked a question. I began to answer, to bluff through as best I could. And then he asked me in his deep basso, Did you learn your lesson? He answered for me in falsetto, Yes, sir, I did. Did you know it? Yes, sir. I, I know, but [I] cannot say. Sit down, damn fool! Or Ass, or whatever. And I got the lowest mark available and I learned that lesson that if we know something, we can say. And the fellow who cannot say, does not know. And if you can say any old rot, you don't know either. So this lesson…is one of the outstanding lessons of my life.[20]

School Days

The summer vacation at Rudnik provided a lively break from Alfred's studies at the realschule (high school) which he attended in Warsaw the remainder of the year. (The family stayed in Warsaw during the winter, leaving the maintenance of Rudnik in the hands of a manager and the resident peasants.) The school routine kept him busy.

> [G]oing to school meant getting out of the house at about 8 o'clock in the morning. Having some hasty breakfast, putting on my uniform, go to school, and in school I stayed up to three, four o'clock every day. And when I came home I was supposed to do three, four hours of home study of lessons.[21]

'Supposed to' indeed. As the incident in the German class illustrates, Alfred did not do well with preparing his lessons. So he was by no means the best school student. He simply 'got by' on his examinations. Nonetheless he had become an excellent and eager learner by the time he left the realschule.

Alfred's education had begun at home. From infancy, besides Polish and Russian, he had learned French and German from nurses and governesses. As a young child, he learned to read and write in those four languages and to do simple arithmetic. (He also may have had a rudimentary reading knowlege of English.) These early experiences with multiple languages (which he came to see as including mathematics) provided literal training in the notion which his work later helped to popularize—"the word is not the thing." His ability to communicate in many tongues also made him conscious of the effects and importance of translation, i.e., finding different forms of representation and expression. His facility for learning languages also allowed him in later life to make himself at home wherever he lived.

Once Alfred knew how to read, he consumed books omnivorously. "The moment I began to read, I was reading whatever I could and then [inspired by] the training that my father had given me in physico-mathematical method. …I was personally indulging in scientific training, reading, reading, reading."[22]

One book he read quite early gave him a phrase which epitomized what seemed to him (even as a child) like an ideal attitude, that he later described in terms of delaying automatic reactions towards difficulties (not allowing them to unduly disturb him). In the book, an adventure story, the characters had gotten shipwrecked and were paddling away on some sort of flimsy raft surrounded by sharks. A shark went for the leg of one character, a British lord. To divert the shark the other passengers poked at the creature, who happily took a bite out of one of their paddles instead. Upon seeing the bitten-off paddle the lord exclaimed "Oh, how extraordinary!" Even as a young boy, Alfred found the attitude of ironic acceptance represented by this statement worth cultivating. For example, once at Rudnik a horse he was attempting to break to saddle threw him onto a pile of rocks. He felt considerable pain. Alfred recalled the phrase as he sat on the stones checking himself for broken bones (he had none)—"Oh, how extraordinary!" Korzybski applied the phrase to numerous 'bitten-off paddles' he encountered throughout his life. He recommended the phrase to his students as a salutary reminder.

After his formal schooling had begun, Alfred had spent several years at what he described as a "high-grade" private school where "we got less mathematics and physics, but we had a lot, too much, Latin and Greek" [23] (which he did not like or ever master). Then, his parents entered him in the realschule through what would roughly equal his middle school and high school years. The curriculum did not include Latin or Greek but rather focused on mathematics, physics, modern languages, and literature.

Alfred's involvement with his own program of reading left him with little time for class preparation. In the course of his personal studies, he had evolved a system for approaching any subject. This approach helped him to keep up in class and get by on examinations. (The schools in Russian Poland gave out numerical marks and Alfred maintained the numerical equivalent of a C average.) In class during lectures he would sit in the first or second row. There he would scribble notes while closely attending to the teacher. "I listened like the dickens, trying to figure out what we are doing something for."[24] Generally, his teachers seemed to like him although some of them may have felt intimidated at times as Alfred sat there watching them with his seriously furled brow and intent gaze. He was trying to find "the general principle…[the] general method" behind what they were presenting.[25] The principle of "grasping the whole", and the methods he developed to do it, served as the basis for his later ability to understand different and difficult areas of scientific and mathematical knowledge (to the satisfaction of specialists) when developing his theory. He later recommended this approach, which included a method of reading and marking books, to his seminar students.

Alfred's devotion to self-study was not an anomaly in the Poland of the 1890s (although the intensity with which he pursued it may have qualified as unusual even there). A self-education movement had sprung up among those seeking to perpetuate and peacefully advance Polish culture. For many Poles, study had become a revolutionary act as people held classes in their homes on Polish history and literature as well as in science, philosophy, etc.—in Polish. This could not be done openly at the time in the schools and universities of Russian Poland.

There was more than book-learning to Alfred's life in Warsaw, however. Although he did not have the opportunities for physical activity that he had in the summer at Rudnik, Alfred participated enthusiastically in sports—despite, or perhaps because of, a slight congenital hip displacement. At the realschule, he had physical education classes consisting of the Russian version of Swedish gymnastics exercises which included faux-military drills and marching with sticks. Alfred didn't actually dislike the drilling and later on expressed some appreciation for the attitude of discipline it encouraged. This may have been around the time Alfred started his solitary swims in the Vistula River, which flows through Warsaw. In what he called "competitions with myself" he would swim across and back the wide and wild waterway. Whenever he could he continued this kind of adventurous swimming, in the Vistula and elsewhere, into his adult life. (In his early years in the United States, he swam in both the Atlantic and Pacific Oceans when he had the opportunity.) It was also probably while still at the realschule that Alfred began fencing, taking lessons from a well-known Warsaw fencing teacher.

Alfred's parents provided him with piano lessons. He learned how to play, but not well. He confessed, "I didn't work enough to become an expert." Nonetheless, he could read music and sing, studied the great composers, and beside Chopin, found two favorites, Wagner and Tchaikovsky. He memorized much of their work, enjoying their "sad music" most of all.[26]

Alfred also received 'religious instruction'. His parents, nominal Roman Catholics, did not regularly go to church although his mother had wanted him to become a priest. As part of its program, the realschule required classes on Catholicism for at least an hour a week. Alfred appreciated one teacher, a seven-foot tall priest named Count Ledochowski. The class turned out to be only peripherally about Catholic religion. Rather, Ledochowski lectured on comparative religions and was in Korzybski's words "only slightly partial toward Catholicism." Alfred thoroughly enjoyed the class and became friendly with Ledochowski. "We saw each other privately after school for discussion of the great world movements in the field of philosophy, if you wish, dogmatism if you wish, but all of that was so extremely flexible..."[27] Later on as a teacher, Korzybski promoted the benefits of studying comparative religions. Throughout his life, he remained more or less an agnostic disdaining as he did both "rabid theism" and "active atheism".[28]

Despite his friendship with the priest, who was rumored to be a member of the Jesuit Order (banned in Tsarist Russia), Alfred had also begun to develop a distaste for the Catholic Church and in particular the Jesuit Order, which he sometimes privately referred to in later life as the "Catholic Gestapo".[29] Many of the old szlachta, including apparently Korzybski's family, considered themselves noblemen first before any religion. In addition, they may have felt that despite the efforts of some individual clerics, the Church had not done enough to promote the Polish cause. Some also resented what they perceived as the Church's hostility to science. Korzybski's negative attitude toward Catholicism as a creed and the Church as an institution reflected such views.

"The First and Greatest Frustration"

Alfred turned 18 in the summer of 1897 and may have graduated from the realschule earlier that year or in the spring of 1898 (no record exists of when he actually did so and in later years Korzybski could not recall the exact year). Alfred's great ambition had been to become a mathematician, a physicist, or lawyer. So it came as a shock to him, around this time, when he realized that his parents' choice to place him in the realschule, rather than in a classical gymnasium, would prevent him from entering a university program in any of his favored professions. The fact of the matter remained: he had not studied Latin or Greek. Facility in both languages was necessary at that time to enter a university program in mathematics, science, or law in Poland, the rest of Russia, or anywhere else in Europe. His parents had wanted him to become an engineer, like his father. They believed, in particular, that with the growing chemical industry, Alfred would be able to make good money as a chemical engineer. They had enrolled him in the realschule to put him on a track for an engineering career, not for the professions he most desired.

Alfred's discovery that he couldn't get into a university became what he later called "the first and greatest frustration I ever had."[30] Despite his middling grades, he felt that he had a decent background in mathematics and science, as well as literature and the humanities. He spoke and read French, German and Russian well and thus had linguistic access to the major languages, other than English, in which scientific research was conducted at the end of the 19th Century. As far as he was concerned, he definitely had what it took to do decent work as a mathematician, physicist, or a lawyer. Yet, as far as he knew, he would not be able find employment researching mathematics or physics anywhere in Europe with just an engineering degree and not a university PhD. And to become a lawyer, he also needed Latin, Greek, and university.

Alfred at the Realschule in Warsaw, 18 or 19 years old

Did Korzybski overestimate the problem of pursuing a mathematical/scientific research career with just a Polytechnic degree? After all, such a degree did not ultimately stop Albert Einstein (also born in 1879). On the other hand, even Einstein had initial difficulties finding what he considered suitable employment after graduating from the Swiss Federal Polytechnic in Zurich. Einstein could only get temporary jobs in a technical school and in tutoring before finding a position as a clerk in the Swiss Patent Office. Even after he had produced his epoch-making papers of 1905 (written while working at the patent office) he had to work as a Privatedozent, a poorly paid lecturer, at the University of Bern before he finally obtained his first professorial post at the University of Zurich in 1909, with pull from supporters there. Alfred was probably not exaggerating his own obstacles.

He looked into the possibility of getting tutored in Latin and Greek. Since he knew French well, he had some entry point into Latin, but Greek, was simply...well, Greek to him. He would need more time to become proficient in it. "In the meantime", as he described it later, "life was pressing. My parents were getting old. Father was getting ill; father was retired. I became more and more important in family management."[31] And though they still remained "comfortable" financially, finances were becoming more and more a concern. Alfred just couldn't see getting side-tracked to study Latin and Greek for possibly two more years to fulfill what he considered a useless formal requirement. So he decided. He simply would not waste his time studying them. He would become an engineer.

Chapter 3
A GOOD ENGINEER

Alfred had no passion for chemistry. But he would do as his parents wished. Deeply frustrated, he resigned himself to attend the Warsaw Polytechnic.

The original Polytechnic, the Preparatory School for the Institute of Technology was founded in 1826. The Tsarist government closed the Institute after the failed Polish Insurrection of 1831. It was reopened as the Emperor Nicholas II University of Technology in 1898.[1] Fifty years later, in 1948, the 68-year-old Korzybski wrote that he spent four years there, from 1898 to 1902.[2] Having lost his personal records from Poland, he did not feel definite about those dates. But other references he gave for events around this part of his life, are consistent with this time period. That four-year period would have placed him among the new students of the entering class at the just-reopened school.

The reopening, after so many years, of a Polytechnic in Warsaw would likely have felt like a day of celebration to Polish students. Whatever joy Alfred may have felt would not have come unmixed with disappointment. As a Polish patriot, he would have found grating the official Russian name for the school and the use of Russian as the language of instruction. And personally, he also felt cut adrift from the dreams he had held for so many years: "My life became aimless. I could say deal in chemical engineering... I just went ahead, [but I] lost interest, certainly lost interest in engineering..."[3]

A Chemical Education

In the late 19th Century, chemical engineering had just emerged as a separate profession from mechanical engineering. With a boom in industrial chemical technology, Wladyslaw Korzybski seems to have hoped his son would be able to leap onto a lucrative bandwagon. So in spite of Alfred's clear attraction to mechanical engineering—he enjoyed working with electrical and mechanical tools and in subsequent years invented and constructed a number of mechanical devices for his own and others' use—he majored in Chemical Engineering and minored in Organic Chemistry in order to satisfy papa.[4] His classes also covered mathematics, physics, and basic engineering subjects.

In 1898 the science of chemistry had not yet reached the level of theoretical, mathematical treatment that physics had achieved and which Alfred, the lover of mathematics, seemed to yearn for. Yet it seems hard to imagine that he did not find interest in at least some of what he was learning. For example, in chemistry, as in the rest of 1898 science, fundamental discoveries and changes in basic understandings had been coming fast and furiously. This followed a relatively stagnant 2000 or so years from Democritus until Lavoisier at the end of the 18th Century.

Only at the start of the 19th Century had John Dalton developed his atomic hypothesis and attempted to classify the elements. New elements had been discovered throughout the century. And then in 1869, only 10 years before Alfred's birth, the Russian Mendeleev had his vision of the periodic table, which revolutionized chemistry with its systemization of the qualities of elements by their atomic weights. The periodic table allowed Mendeleev to predict new elements and their characteristics, which were then subsequently discovered. Throughout the 1890s, elements forming an entirely new chemical group, the inert gases, were being found. They fit into Mendeleev's schema with remarkable ease.

In the physics of matter, the invisible atom, the basic elemental unit once thought indivisible, had begun to reveal an inner structure. In 1897, two years after Rontgen discovered x-rays emanating from cathode tubes, the British researcher J. J. Thomson found a particle discharged from such tubes which he named the "electron", thought to be a constituent of the atom. Strange energy related to certain elements had also recently been discovered—phenomena that scientists could not easily understand in terms of established chemistry or physics. In 1896 Becquerel had discovered a powerful kind of ray labeled "radioactivity" coming out of the element uranium. Recently in Paris, Alfred's compatriot Marie Curie, with her French husband Pierre, had begun to isolate another new element, radium, from pitchblende ore and to explore its radioactive properties. Matter was beginning to seem like something other than a solid brick. Alfred nigh undoubtedly followed many of these developments.

Thermodynamics had become a separately recognizable discipline within the previous 50 years. Here, Maxwell's, Bolzmann's, and Gibbs' independent but related work in statistical mechanics challenged older accepted notions of determinism. This work demonstrated probability as basic to the study of the energetic changes in the physical-chemical systems Alfred was studying. As time went on probabilistic thinking would take on ever greater importance to Alfred in his understanding of the world beyond physics and chemistry and how humans think about it.

Alfred's minor field of organic chemistry, the chemistry of carbon-based compounds, had also been born in the 19th Century. Its applications to the manufacture of dyes, synthetic materials, explosives, drugs, etc., had great importance for a chemical engineering career. One aspect of organic chemistry probably had more lasting interest for him: its emphasis on structure. Louis Pasteur had found that the characteristics and reactivity of molecules depends not just on the proportions of their constituent atoms but also on their arrangements in space. Investigating samples of racemic acid, a residue seen on the wooden barrels used to ferment grapes, he isolated two crystalline forms. He discovered that the two forms of the acid rotate polarized light in opposite directions. In other words, they exist in right-handed and left-handed versions. He went on to find that these mirror-image molecules of the 'same' substance have different chemical and biological properties as well. With his minor in organic chemistry, Alfred would have had to learn about and visualize such molecules. He would not have been able to miss the significance of structure, which, in a much more generalized form, became central to his later work.

The Machine of Alfred Korzybski

In his coursework, Alfred continued the pattern he had found so useful at the realschule for getting by with a passing grade. He attended classes consistently, following his teachers' lectures closely, taking notes, participating in labs as needed, and building for himself a comprehensive view of the various subjects. Outside of class, though, he continued to pursue his own reading and barely touched his textbooks, except to cram for examinations. Such cramming sessions often took place on the day of the exam. His lack of preparation led to some 'interesting' situations. He had already learned how to successfully take shortcuts on exams based on his understanding of the underlying principles of a subject. This had allowed him to deal with test problems whenever he had failed to learn a specific formula and other significant details, or whenever he felt he could save time and effort. He probably had perfected this method at the realschule.

The instructor of one mathematics class there had given the students a difficult problem and told them he wanted them to solve it using only algebra. At Rudnik, multi-lingual Alfred had sometimes accomplished his troubleshooting by translating between speakers of different languages. His method for solving the algebra problem followed this method of translation. Alfred first solved the problem by using differential calculus—ultimately simpler than using algebra, if one knew calculus—then translated what he had done back into algebra. He not only passed the test but, in addition, gained something even more important. Having to translate between algebra and calculus gave him greater insight into the interconnections between these two branches of mathematics. Furthermore, a sense of mathematics as language seemed to have taken shape in Alfred's awareness. His experience with algebra and calculus as forms of language provided a clear example of the fact that different modes of expression could serve a particular purpose with different degrees of usefulness.

At the Polytechnic, Alfred discovered that his failure to adequately prepare for lessons could backfire and that his subsequent need for 'short-cuts' might actually result in having to take a longer way around. During one final examination in higher mathematics, he needed some formulas he hadn't memorized. So before he could solve the test problem, he had to derive the formulas from scratch. He finished the test—thirteen hours later. The instructor, though livid, had allowed him to complete it. Alfred passed but realized the professor had justification to fail him.

In order to graduate, Alfred also had to pass an oral examination for a physics/mechanics course. As he remembered it years later:

I was told to build up a machine or instrument by X,Y, Z. Some famous stuff. Now I knew the principle of the…machine, but I didn't know the details. …I knew what the machine was supposed to do. Oh, it took me an hour or two to do that on the blackboard, but I did it. And the professor in the meantime was busy with somebody else…Then the professor [asked] "What is it?" and I say "Well, this is the machine of XY." "What! XY. I'm sorry. There was never a machine like that." My answer was "But, professor, this machine is supposed to do so and so." "Yes," answered the professor, "But this is not the machine of XY. This is the machine of Alfred Korzybski." I say, "Never mind, the machine does work." The professor say[s], "Prove it to me." And damn it, I went on to prove it to him that the machine does work…The professor told me…that it has nothing to do with the machine of XY, but he approved that the machine worked. So I passed the examination.

In the meantime somehow I was not feeling so well about the machine so at home I began to verify my machine, not XY machine, but my machine, and I came to the conclusion that the machine does not work. The professor…also felt uneasy about it. He sweated all night on that machine and discovered that the machine did not work. Several days later I met the professor after the graduation and all that successfully. And we were then no more in the relation of student and professor. So he told me "You certainly are a so and so. You kept me awake all night verifying your damn machine…But I'm not sorry that I passed you in the examination because you have shown by independent work that you are fit to solve problems." Of course, granting the mistake, the professor praised my independence. He was a very big man.[5]

Alfred had successfully graduated. Yet afterwards, he did not look for engineering work. Indeed, for the remainder of his life he never held a formal job as an engineer—chemical or otherwise. In spite of this, as he later said, he continued to operate with the attitude of an engineer: "I was always a good engineer. I had always to do with engineering of some sort. Practically I was."[6]

Like Leibniz, another scientific-philosophical synthesizer, Alfred's early desire to "grasp the whole" by finding underlying connections, included the necessity of connecting theory with practice. His time at the Warsaw Polytechnic refined his natural way of behaving by socializing him into the professional engineer's ethos of making things work by applying what we know. He had not completely wasted his time there.

At the Polytechnic, Alfred also had gotten a thorough grounding in the technical details of the physical science of 1898–1902, a period in the midst of great changes. This helped prepare him for his later assimilation of relativity, quantum theory and other innovations in 20th Century science and mathematics, which had such importance for his own formulating. His Polytechnic experiences also confirmed for him his sense that he could solve problems. In relation to this, he had gained an increasing respect for what he later called "the miracles of mathematics". His seat-of-the-pants troubleshooting experiences since childhood were now supplemented by an even greater appreciation of the 'magic' in a mathematical approach to problems, where and when one could employ exact methods. Indeed, the exactness of mathematics, which seemed to assure agreement, became an ideal for him that he would struggle to understand. What stopped it from being extended to areas that seemed beyond the reach of traditional mathematics?

Chapter 4
TO ROME

In 1902, Alfred finished school. He had had his encounter with chemistry. His family had sufficient money; he didn't need a regular job in engineering or otherwise. Now he had more time to study on his own. Besides physics and mathematics, his interests in law, philosophy, and history had gotten somewhat submerged during his time at the Polytechnic. He could also keep himself busy helping his parents manage their properties, including the farm. Still, Alfred felt somewhat at loose ends. What to do? Poles had traditionally looked West and South, especially towards Italy, to draw from the sources of Western European culture. For centuries, a European tour had been de rigueur for young noble Poles. So not surprisingly, 22-year-old Alfred looked West and South as well. The rest of Europe beckoned.

Vagabond

Between the years 1902 and 1904, Alfred traveled throughout Europe. Among other places, he visited Danzig (now Gdansk), Dresden, Berlin, Paris, Budapest, Vienna, and Rome. He may have returned to Warsaw for a brief period after one or more of these visits. But he probably spent most of his time outside of Poland, in Rome.[1]

> While traveling [by train] he rode third class, eating his dark bread and garlic together with the laborers and others by whom he was surrounded. When he came to a strange city he found an inexpensive room, secured a map and studied it. Then he took long rides through the town, roamed through the slums, ate his sandwich at the aristocratic cafes (for he had little money to spend), and studied how the different people lived.[2]

Alfred would often visit the local university, where he would sit in on lectures and read in the library. Looking up to see this stranger perusing books, a library habitué would have seen a young man "…rather thin, broad-shouldered and muscular, of medium height, [about 5'8"] with blue, alert, contemplative eyes, his hair very blond,…[with] a mustache which he habitually twirled up at its ends."[3]

Given his appearance and manner, Alfred did not lack female company when he wanted it. In a tete-a-tete with one young lady in Schoenbrunn Park in Vienna, Alfred had his second encounter with Austrian Emperor Franz Josef. The park, located next to the Imperial Palace, opened to the public during the day but closed in the evening for Franz Josef's private use, at which time the Emperor would take a solitary stroll. Alfred, sitting in the park with his lady friend, got distracted in conversation with her and didn't heed the closing-time warning bell or whistle. Soon afterwards, the Emperor surprised them on their bench. Alfred and the young lady jumped up and Alfred took off his hat. Franz Josef said, "Oh, never mind, never mind. Be comfortable, never mind." As Korzybski recalled, "we clear[ed] out like hell."[4]

"Maladetto Pollaco"

Alfred got to Rome, probably sometime in early 1902, having reached that goal via the way-stations of Budapest, Vienna, Paris, etc. In Rome, Alfred settled down to drink from what many Poles had long considered the wellspring of Western European culture. He studied Italian, learning it quickly and thoroughly, and attended law, philosophy, and other classes at the University of Rome. He also became known at the Vatican and among members of the Roman nobility in the court of Italian king Victor Emanuel III, whose reign had begun in 1900. Alfred's fencing skills and horsemanship, in particular, led to his associating with members of the king's bodyguard and members of the Cavalry School. Especially with the king's bodyguards, these associations led to his reputation among the gossiping Roman nobility as "Maladetto Pollaco" ("Accursed Pole").[5]

Alfred had studied fencing in Warsaw and began taking lessons again in Rome. His Italian fencing teacher had the improbable-sounding name of Greko, "the Greek".[6] Supplementing his lessons, he practiced fencing for hours each day with acquaintances among the officers of Victor Emanuel's bodyguard. Even with dueling on the decline in Italy and the rest of Europe, Alfred soon found himself dueling for his 'honor' with a sharp, naked saber and real danger of bloodshed.

Fortunately for him, the dueling tradition in Rome dictated sword rather than pistol. Otherwise he might have killed someone, since he was a good shot and his ingrained sense of noble honor and innate boldness at times still tended to merge with a stupid impulsiveness. Once at a drinking party at Rudnik, the estate manager had taken up Alfred's wine glass. Alfred pulled out his pistol and shot the glass out of the man's hand. Alfred had also imitated William Tell several times by shooting drinking glasses off of the heads of friends. In later years Korzybski considered it only luck he didn't wound or kill someone this way; it made him shudder to recall these youthful follies.

He also had luck in his sword fights in Rome. His skill with the saber, together with the conventions of Italian dueling—a fight would come to an end when someone drew "first blood"—prevented him from killing anyone or getting himself killed. The 'insults' to Alfred that led to his saber duels resulted, perhaps not surprisingly, from affairs of the heart.

Alfred had become close friends with one of Victor Emanuel's bodyguards. The young man had started an affair with a married noblewoman from the Bourbon family (the former French rulers of Italy). One of the most beautiful women in Rome, she had a reputation for carrying on extra-marital affairs. Meanwhile, Alfred had taken up with another young woman, a cousin of the king, and had already had some unpleasantness with the king in regard to her. (While the king's nickname among Roman nobles was "Il regazzo" or "The boy" because of his relative youth and unregal, diminutive appearance, Alfred referred to him as "Il stronzetto" or "The little shit".[7]) In an effort to confuse gossip-mongers at the royal court, Alfred and his friend came up with a plan to use when they went out with their ladies. They decided that in public, Alfred would escort his friend's girlfriend and his friend would escort Alfred's. Korzybski recalled attending evening concerts thusly with his friend and their ladies at the Pincio Garden, near the Villa Borghesa. The Garden with its terraced, statue-lined walkways and its beautiful views of the city had become one of the favorite meeting places of Roman noble society, members of the court, groups of clerics, students, etc. Alfred would stroll, sit, and chat in French with his friend's beautiful lover (whom he actually considered one of the nastiest women he'd ever met) while his friend would do likewise with Alfred's girlfriend. Their ruse worked. Soon Romans were gossiping about Alfred's supposed scandalous carrying on with a married woman. Insults from several Italian officers, regarding him and the lady he detested, fell within Alfred's earshot. This resulted in a number of saber duels. He always won these fights, which he actually seemed to enjoy. He liked to play with his opponent and would slap him numerous times with the flat part of the saber blade while easily blocking ineffective blows. When he decided the time had come to take first blood he would cut "a bit of ear, a bit of nose" and the contest would end. Alfred's reputation as the "Maladetto Pollaco" was ensured.

Alfred's association with a Roman cavalry school, where he met officers who admired his riding ability, added to the rough-and-tumble renown he was developing. However, an incident during a riding contest there deflated at least some of the bravado of the Maladetto Polacco. A friend at the school had a horse named Caesar whom Alfred considered a potentially excellent but mistrained jumper. Caesar invariably would stop at an obstacle and send his rider flying. Alfred agreed to train him and worked with him for months until he felt confident about the horse's jumping ability. Alfred and Caesar practiced their jumps over fences, steep ditches, etc., where success or failure greatly depended on the timing of the rider who would pace the horse through its moves. For Caesar's 'graduation' Alfred rode him in a steeplechase competition, where many spectators expected to see the 'old' Caesar throwing his cocky rider. On the day of the contest, they began their run through the course with Alfred dressed up in full regalia including red coat and fancy high hat. After a first-place run, they came up to their last obstacle—a high fence followed by a ditch. Alfred thought he had the jump timed perfectly when suddenly his hat started to fall off and he grabbed for it before he realized what he was doing. Caeser made the jump but, because of Alfred's loss of rhythm during their approach, landed with its rear legs in the ditch. That lost the race for them. Later Alfred watched as a gray-haired cavalry officer riding his equally elderly horse, flew across every obstacle with seeming effortlessness and won the competition. Alfred felt suitably impressed by their performance and by his own comeuppance.

"The Relationship of the Polish Youth Toward the Clergy..."

During his time in Rome, Alfred also developed acquaintances among clerics and officials at the Vatican. This came about through a chance meeting while walking down the street one day. Alfred came face to face with one Prince Radizwill, a friend of his father, whom he had also known in Poland. This particular Prince Radizwill, from a famous Polish-Lithuanian Magnate family of enormous wealth, espoused a staunch Catholicism — Korzybski considered him a "fanatic"—along with Polish patriotism. Several years before, Radizwill had approached Alfred's father requesting that he allow Alfred to join an organization of aristocratic Polish Catholic youth. As a friendly gesture, Alfred joined for the price of the nominal membership fee (equivalent perhaps to a dollar) and with no further involvement. When Radizwill saw Alfred on the Roman street he immediately invited him, as a 'dedicated Polish Catholic youth', to speak the next day at a meeting Radizwill had arranged before a group of Cardinals and the Governor of the Jesuits. Alfred demurred but Prince Radizwill insisted.

The next day Alfred found himself in a meeting room of an old convent sitting at the end of a long table next to Radizwilll with a roomful of Catholic clergy and Vatican dignitaries. Radizwill introduced him as "a representative of Polish youth" speaking on "The Relationship of the Polish Youth Toward the Clergy, and the Clergy Toward Polish Youth". Some of the priests in attendance may have felt a shock when they recognized the young man they had seen before at Pincio Garden concerts—the "Maladetto Pollaco". Alfred, who had never spoken in public before, didn't seem to have any difficulty getting up before this distinguished audience and taking the next hour or so to "give hell" to the Catholic Church since, in his opinion, the Church as a whole had betrayed the Polish national cause.[8]

The speech didn't please Radizwill who began to pinch Alfred's leg under the table, presumably to get him to shut up. Alfred, who had been "boiling against the clergy" for years, continued his speech. Under the table, in turn, he kicked Radizwill in the shins. Despite these distractions and the nature of the speech, his audience seemed to find his presentation impressive. Every Cardinal there invited Alfred for lunch or dinner. Alfred also got an audience with Pope Leo XIII, who despite his views against Polish nationalism, impressed Alfred as a "high grade" individual.[9] For the rest of his life, Alfred disdained the Catholic Church as an institution, considering it totalitarian in outlook. However, he continued to like and make friends with individual Catholics, including clerics.

In Rome, Alfred became friendly with one cleric in particular—an educated and intelligent monk named Bernardine. Korzybski would visit Bernardine, born a wealthy French marquis, in his simple monastic cell which had only a couple of hard wooden benches to sit and sleep on. They would talk for hours about philosophy, science, etc. One thing Bernardine told him made a great impression on Alfred—the monk's admission of the agnosticism or at least the non-literal, "philosophically minded" 'religion' of the "upper crust" of the Catholic hierarchy of those days. This revelation surprised him. It is not clear whether this mollified or increased Alfred's cynicism towards the Church.

"A Roma"

After perhaps a year in Rome, Alfred left to see some of the rest of Italy including Florence, Pisa, and Milan, in the north. South of Rome, he visited Naples but on his way further south towards Sicily, an earthquake occurred, his train was stopped, and he was forced to make his way back to Rome. While he'd been gone, Pope Leo had died (in July 1903) and Pius X, the new Pope had come into office (August 1903). Alfred was not impressed with Pius, whom he considered an ignorant peasant compared to Leo. But by this time, issues of the church or the romantic intrigues of the Italian court may have ceased to have much interest. Alfred was preparing to return home. It would have made sense for him to spend the winter of 1903 in the milder climate of Rome. But whether he waited until sometime in the spring of 1904 to return to Poland or left Rome somewhat earlier, he tried to enjoy the remainder of his time in the "Eternal City".

Probably in this last period in Italy, Korzybski met a Polish journalist through a friend, a cousin of the famous Polish author Henryk Sinkiewicz. The journalist took Alfred to see an Italian theatre production of Sinkiewicz's novel, *Quo Vadis*, which had been published to international acclaim in 1895. The play, about the early days of Christianity in Nero's Italy, ended with one of the characters having a vision of Christ, who though unseen could be heard to speak. The character asks, "Quo Vadis, Domine?" (Where are you going, Lord?"). In the final line of the play, the voice of Christ answers, "A Roma." ("To Rome.")[10] The beautiful, deep, rich baritone voice of the actor portraying Christ particularly impressed Alfred. For him, this final scene and that memorable last line 'made' the play. The journalist took Alfred backstage afterwards, introducing him to the actors as Sinkiewicz's cousin. Alfred found it difficult to correct this misconception and, besides, the actors seemed impressed—the man playing Nero removed the golden crown from his head when introduced to 'the cousin of the famous author'. Alfred made use of his 'in' with the actors later when he came back for another performance of the play.

Despite the pinching and kicking battle during Alfred's speech to the Cardinals, Prince Radizwill, along with his wife, had shown considerable hospitality to Alfred during his time in Rome. He decided to show his gratitude to them by treating them to a performance of *Quo Vadis* and he purchased a box in the theatre for the three of them. In the previous performance, the actors playing "St. Peter" and a female character named "Eunice", stood so close to each other during their onstage dialogue that they rubbed bellies. Alfred thought the prim Radizwills might get offended seeing this, so before the performance he talked to 'St. Peter' and 'Eunice' asking them if they could back away from each other during the show. Happily for Alfred, "St. Peter and Eunice behaved." He anticipated with relish the final scene and the last line of the play. He hoped this would impress his guests as much as it had impressed him.

Little did he know that the actor doing the voice of Christ had gotten too drunk to say even his small part. In the final scene, the question came: "Quo Vadis, Domine?" Instead of the beautiful, deep, rich voice Alfred expected, the vocal stand-in for Christ screeched "A Roma." in a grating falsetto. One can imagine the collective wincing in the audience. As Korzybski said later, "…it's a bad thing for a Christ to get drunk."[11]

Chapter 5
SICK OF EVERYTHING

Alfred had arrived home by sometime in early 1904. Russian Poland, with the rest of the Tsarist Empire, was entering a turbulent period and Alfred, a Polish patriot, got pulled into the maelstrom along with everyone else.

The Russo-Japanese War had just begun in February 1904 with a Japanese attack on the Russian fleet at Port Arthur, Manchuria, which the Russian government had leased from China. The Japanese army and navy overwhelmed the smaller Russian forces there and the war, which continued until Russian defeat in the autumn of 1905, strained the Russian economy and showed up the weaknesses of the Tsarist military administration, top-heavy with incompetent careerists and crippled by outdated, 19th-Century notions of warfare.

Meanwhile in Russian Poland, various political factions including but not limited to all sorts of Polish nationalists (reactionary, classical liberal, and socialist); non-Polish, minority nationalist groups; and internationalist socialists and communists, found in the war a demonstration of government frailty and an opportunity to become more organized. These groups sought in various ways (some violently) to push the Tsarist government to make concessions towards their various goals. The government with its secret police department, the Ochrana, either banned or had many of these organizations (violent or not) under investigation. As a result, a significant 'underground' network developed in Russian Poland (mirrored by similar groups in other parts of Russia).

Alfred never involved himself in political violence. But he did participate in the amorphous underground. Not long after his return, he very nearly got sent to prison. Alfred's 'crime' seemed to flow naturally out of the self-education movement, which he had taken part in for so long. As Norman Davies pointed out, "If terrorism and political activism were for a few, cultural activism was for the many...[T]he typical patriot at the turn of the century was a young lady of good family with a textbook under her shawl. This generation of the niepokorni, 'the unsubdued', went forth as missionaries into their own land."[1]

As a cultural 'missionary', Alfred need go no further than the estate at Rudnik:
> When he returned from Rome he was shocked with the realization that his former playmate, the gardener's son, as well as all the other peasants, could neither read nor write, yet their labor had for generations earned the money for landowners. He found release for his reactions against this injustice by building a small schoolhouse for the peasants on the country estate. It was against the [Tsarist] law, however, to educate the peasants, who were deliberately kept illiterate. He was sentenced to Siberia, but his father had the sentence suspended.[2]

This turned out to be one of the last things Wladyslaw Korzybski did for his son before dying in October 1904. His father's death left Alfred not only with the management of his family's properties but with the management of his mother as well. Alfred had already experienced Helena's style of playing at helplessness while trying to control results. He had expressed views about how to modernize methods at Rudnik which she 'shot down'. Alfred feared he would become tied to her and become subject to her "backseat driving" in a way he could barely tolerate even imagining. He was only too happy to foist off this role on a cousin who—under Helena's thumb—administered their properties. When this cousin died a few years later, Alfred again relinquished his expected role as main estate administrator to an unrelated man hired for the job.[3] Nonetheless, he still had an economic interest in family business and could not entirely break free from his mother or her influence. As a compromise, he restricted himself to those areas of management that didn't take much time, "administrative drudgery, fixing things here and there...nothing fundamental... ."[4]

One of these tasks involved managing a large apartment house his mother had bought in Warsaw several years before—probably the 66 Wilcza address that served for many years as his and his mother's residence in Warsaw. With some 25 to 30 apartments, the building had both civilian and Russian military renters. Managing the building required only about two to three hours of his attention per day but at times provided challenges. While still at the Polytechnic, he had dealt with problems resulting from some of the building's military tenants—educated peasants working as secretaries for the Russian Army in Warsaw. These men drank and partied loudly and violently during their time off. Civilian tenants, disturbed by this ruckus, threatened to leave. Alfred had to assuage the civilians, quiet the unruly soldiers, and prevent anyone from moving out in disgust—a daunting task in which he apparently succeeded.[5] After his return to Poland and with his father's death, Alfred continued with this property management and other administrative tasks for the family business.

66 Wilcza

Revolution In Poland

As if the stress of dealing with his father's death and his mother's demands was not enough, Korzybski, with other Poles, faced economic and political strains which had reached a breaking point by the end of 1904 with massive unemployment related to the war. People taking to the streets throughout Poland had increasingly violent clashes with police, who had fired into crowds of protesters. In Warsaw in November, gendarmes (Russian state-security police) attacked a group of demonstrators who were waving a red banner which said,

> "Down with the war and with Tsardom, Long live the free Polish people." [The gendarmes] were met by a hail of bullets from a squad of gunmen. Six men were killed, scores injured, and hundreds arrested. This was the first open challenge to Russian authority in Poland for forty years.[6]

Massive political violence soon followed in Poland and throughout Russia as well. In Poland, a general strike was called at the end of January 1905 and went on for at least a month. For the rest of the year, universities remained empty while work stoppages, riots, and additional general strikes, as well as "diversionary" anti-Jewish pogroms by the police, sporadically occurred.[7]

At Rudnik the peasant workers wanted to participate and decided they should strike too. As usual they consulted with master Alfred, who told them to go ahead and strike—as long as they maintained the farm and continued to feed and care for the animals. Not wanting to stay at Rudnik himself and needing money, he got a job teaching French, German, mathematics, and physics at a junior-college level girls' school or "gymnasium" in Warsaw. Although he had done private tutoring throughout his time at the Polytechnic, this was his first experience in classroom teaching. The students ranged in age from 16 to 19. Alfred took his teaching role very seriously and taught his subjects in the way he had studied them himself—as forms of human behavior. This helped him to put life into what otherwise could seem like dry, boring topics.

His students liked his classes and worked hard. They seemed fond of him too, but unlike some of the other male teachers at the school, Alfred never received 'love letters' from any of the girls during his year of teaching, a record in which he took pride. Apparently the young ladies felt a bit intimidated by him. Not because of any sternness or standoffishness on his part but rather because of his sense of humor. One time as Alfred entered his classroom, he noticed a yellow spot on the ceiling, probably the result of the roof above them leaking. When a teacher entered a classroom, the students were expected to come to standing until the teacher arrived at his desk and signaled for them to sit down. The students had risen and as he arrived at his desk, Alfred looked up at the yellow spot and in his words:

> I put my blue innocent eyes on them and I asked an innocent question...: Do you have your dormitories over this class?...The hell I got from the director...of the college. Oh, yes, I was scolded. The girls of course, giggled...and this is the kind of...humor which prevented them to write love letters because you can't imagine with that kind of sense of humor what I could not say about some silly love letter.[8]

In his later career lecturing and teaching, Korzybski's at times earthy humor remained prominent and also sometimes got him into trouble with those who considered it inappropriate.

While Alfred taught at the school, the social turmoil continued. Tsarist authorities tried to calm things down by making concessions to the protestors. In April 1905, after years of prohibition, they permitted Polish schools to once again teach classes in the Polish language. I imagine Korzybski must have relished switching from Russian to Polish in his classroom. In September 1905, the Russo-Japanese war ended in a humiliating defeat for the Russian government, which led to further unrest at home. A month later the Tsar felt impelled to call for a written constitution and to announce the formation of a Russian parliament—the Duma—elected in the spring of 1906. With economic problems easing, Russia appeared to have become a constitutional monarchy. On July 3, 1906, Alfred celebrated his 27th birthday.

"Sick of Everything"

Alfred did not continue at the girl's gymnasium after his year of teaching there. He would not go to work as a chemical engineer. He also renewed his decision not to take any major role in administering the family properties. So what now for Alfred?

He decided to continue working in peripheral aspects of the family business, things like managing the apartment in Warsaw that didn't take a lot of time and where Mama didn't involve herself much. This included working at Rudnik—training horses in the summer and working to improve the farm equipment. (He designed a mechanical potato digger that he later sought to patent during his first years in the United States.) However, while Korzybski enjoyed aspects of living in the country, he liked living in the city more, appreciating the opportunities Warsaw provided. One of the opportunities he took there was to fulfill, to some degree, his childhood dream of becoming a lawyer.

Little documentation exists about Korzybski's legal career. In the United States immediately after World War I, he described himself as a lawyer, as well as an engineer, in some letters and job applications (one for a job as an agent in the Department of Justice). Although he attended classes in Rome, there is no evidence he earned a law, or other, degree. So, in order to work as a lawyer in Poland, he would have had to apprentice himself to a lawyer there. Perhaps he did do this in the law office of a relative or friend. However, he may also have only worked for a lawyer without ever officially becoming one himself. Existing records showing his facility with legal documents and proceedings corroborate the view that he did have familiarity with legal work. A statement on an application in the U.S. would be difficult to check in chaotic, post-World War I Poland. Even if he had only worked as a legal assistant, Alfred would probably have been able to perform adequately if he had gotten hired in a law-related field, say as an investigator (once he had learned the specific, American, job-relevant laws and procedures). Alfred had a special interest in criminal behavior and law and his actual law-related work in Warsaw for an indeterminate period of time could have included working as an investigator, interviewing clients and witnesses, preparing documents, and assisting in courtroom presentations. He made little reference to this aspect of his life after the early 1920s.

A Young Man in Warsaw

In later years, discussing his life in Poland before World War I, he described himself as basically resigned and frustrated. Whatever he did didn't quite seem to suit him. A need for solitude and a passion for learning kept him from spending his time drinking and partying with friends despite his earlier 'wild' reputation as the "Maladetto Pollaco". That doesn't mean he had no pleasures. He enjoyed his pet English bulldog Taft, named after the U.S.

President of 1909–1913. He also kept fit with his athletic activities, which included daily bouts—which he kept up for years—of wrestling on his carpet with an expert professional wrestler, a butler of his, to whom he gave fencing lessons in return. Surely, he had girlfriends. Despite these diversions, Alfred did indeed feel himself "maladetto", i.e., accursed, at least in one major sense. Full of creative energy, he couldn't find a way to express it as he wished. Feeling restricted by his education and family commitments, he was looking for something he couldn't articulate but knew he hadn't found. Still, he did feel grateful for the time he had available for study. He read widely in literature, history, and philosophy[9], etc. But reading in mathematics and physics took up much of his studies. Where did he focus his interest?

Like many of the details of his pre-World War I days in Poland, it's hard to know. As a natural visualizer, he grew up loving geometry. His study of Euclid in school encouraged an early sense of reverence towards mathematics which he maintained throughout his life. As for many others before him, geometry—as an exemplar of mathematics as a whole—appeared to Korzybski as the ideal of rigorous thought. Introduced as a child by his father to four-dimensional geometry (an extension of euclidean geometry), he later said it took him three years to internalize non-euclidean geometry. When this happened is not clear, but it's possible he had already begun to explore this area of mathematics in the pre-war period.

He explained why it took him three years. Although he was ready for new ways of thinking, his thorough euclidean training gave him some difficulties—as it did for many others—in absorbing the implications and, especially in getting the feel, of non-euclidean views. Euclid had for centuries been considered the model of rationality, his postulates constituting the 'self-evident' rules for *the* geometry of the world. The consequent development of alternative geometries provided a shock because the certainty with which people had considered Euclid and his postulates as *the* geometry was no longer acceptable. It was no longer *the* geometry but only *a* geometry.[10] Acceptance of this loss of certainty would come to play a large part in Korzybski's later work.

Alfred also had an interest in symbolic or mathematical logic and the related area of mathematical foundations. After Leibniz's initial forays, the modern study of these areas can be traced back to George Boole's work in the mid-1800s. Prior to World War I, Korzybski knew about the more recent work of the Italian mathematical logician Giuseppe Peano. He probably also already had some familiarity with Georg Cantor's related theory of sets and Cantor's discussion of infinity. However, in Poland before World War I, he didn't have facility with English and didn't know about the epoch-making work being done in England by Bertrand Russell and Alfred North Whitehead (the first volume of their *Principia Mathematica* was published in 1910). Korzybski's intensive study of mathematical logic, including Russell and Whitehead's work, didn't begin until 1920, after he had met mathematician Cassius J. Keyser in New York City.[11]

Major revolutionary changes in physics were also occurring in the period just before World War I. Korzybski surely followed the general trend of this research. In 1900, Max Planck had formulated the notion of a quantum, or fundamental discrete unit of action, in the relationship between the energy and frequency of electromagnetic radiation emitted or absorbed from hot bodies. Planck's work, along with Albert Einstein's formulation of the photoelectric effect in 1905, provided the basis for further work in quantum theory, which would become one of the major areas of physics by the mid-1920s. Einstein's formulation of the electrodynamics of light, also in 1905, introduced relativity as another major area of theoretical physics. In addition to these areas, research into radioactivity and the structure of the atom was changing previous notions of 'solid' matter. According to Korzybski he did not make any significant study of Einstein's work until after World War I.[12] Nonetheless, he knew enough in the pre-war period to see major changes in the air, as profoundly challenging to the classical newtonian physics which he had mastered in school, as the non-euclidean geometries were to the classical view of mathematics. Korzybski was not alone in experiencing this time as an uncertain and puzzling one for the sciences.

Puzzlement also characterized Alfred's views on pre-war Russian and Polish politics. His puzzlement was likely a function of the expectations generated by his political ideals. His life-long affinity in politics had probably become formed by this time and could generally be characterized as 'liberal' (in the classical sense)—dedication to democratic ideals and constitutional representative government. Regarding economics, he may have had an earlier student flirtation with socialism. In the pre-World War I years of Russian Poland, his Polish nationalism may also have become connected for a time to some form of democratic socialism, which he then moved away from over the years. By the time of his early days in America, Alfred had many friends in socialist circles. He expressed sympathy for their ultimate aim for a better society, but questioned their methods. In later life, he became more 'conservative'. But even then, although he favored private enterprise, he also didn't necessarily reject government interventions in the economy, interventions the strictest "classical liberals" would have criticized.

The Tsarist government's constitutional reforms of 1905 must have fed Alfred's political hopes. These were soon brought low as the Russian government regressed towards absolutism in the years leading up to World War I. By the 1913 celebration of 300 years of Romanoff rule in Russia, it had become clear that the shifting of political power from the autocratic bureaucracy of the Tsar to a more democratic form would move only glacially at best.

In addition, by 1913 many people in Poland, including Alfred, were expecting a major war. The relatively late unification and industrialization of Germany (under Prussian leadership) in the last half of the 19th century had been accompanied by brief wars with France and Austria. These wars resulted in Germany's acquisition of French territory and in a dominating role in its alliance with the Austro-Hungarian Empire. The Germans had accomplished this with legendary Prussian efficiency. While the Russian government concerned itself with possible German expansion east, the French were equally concerned with Germany expanding westward and were eager to get back the former French areas of Alsace and Lorraine that Germany had acquired. Alliances between France, Russia and England and between Germany and Austria seemed to ensure that a conflict between any members of the two opposing sides would draw in the other members.

In Russian Poland, financier and railroad developer Jan Bloch had analyzed the consequences of technological advances upon warfare and, in a book published in 1898, predicted that a future war would involve massive firepower, defensive stalemates, and huge numbers of casualties and civilian losses. The future war's outcome would depend on which nation's socio-economic fabric broke down first. Korzybski read Bloch's book. In addition, his contacts in the anti-Tsarist underground provided him with information that made war seem almost inevitable. If predictable, why couldn't it be stopped?

Korzybski's studies had led him to the conclusion that "all sciences need[ed] a thorough revision and elimination of childlike fallacies at the bottom."[13] Why should politics, economics, etc. appear any different? Indeed, they didn't—they seemed in worse shape than the so-called exact sciences. Korzybski's dissatisfaction had become severe. "I was sick of everything, arithmetic, science, logic, politics…every goddamn thing…"[14] He had already attempted to clarify his confusions in writing but had ended up destroying his efforts. He felt he had no good "language to speak, therefore I could only express my private opinions for which I had no use."[15]

Feeling "sick of everything" indicated a healthy attitude, given that the 'civilized' world actually did seem sick. The sickness had been festering under the surface for years. Its gross eruption in World War I—a war of a scale never before seen in history—would force Korzybski to put aside his more theoretical dissatisfactions with science, etc. On June 28, 1914, less than a week before Alfred's 35th birthday, the heir to the Austro-Hungarian throne, Archduke Franz Ferdinand, and his wife were assassinated in Sarajevo. Austria-Hungary held the Serbian government responsible for the act, committed by Gavriel Princip, a Yugoslav nationalist student from Austrian-controlled Bosnia. On July 28, Alfred's 'acquaintance', the Emperor Franz Josef, declared war on Slavic Serbia, Russia's ally. Three days later, the Tsar ordered full mobilization of Russia's military, and the next day, Germany, under the Tsar's cousin Kaiser Wilhelm II, declared war on Russia. Two days later, August 3, Germany declared war on France and on August 4 invaded Belgium. Great Britain then declared war on Germany. The "Great War" had begun—the main players on each side chosen: Germany and Austria-Hungary (with the Ottoman Empire soon to enter with them) against France, Great Britain, and Russia. Alfred's beloved Poland would become the Eastern battleground.

Part III
The Great War

"Sentimentalism in questions concerning a war is a crime,..."
— ALFRED KORZYBSKI[1]

Chapter 6
GERMANY MUST BE BEATEN.

In the starting days of the war, Austria-Hungary and Germany (the Central Powers) and Russia (representing the Allies) issued declarations to the Poles under their regimes. Each declaration promised to unify Poland and sought to gain Polish help and recruits for their respective sides. Alfred felt quite sure about what he had to do. Having assessed the possibilities of a return to Polish sovereignty under each side, he decided he must help the Russians. This was not because of any patriotic feeling for the Tsarist dictatorship he had lived his life under. Rather, he had become convinced that the victory of the Central Powers would mean the death of any hopes for the recovery of Polish nationhood. Given the relative weakness of Austria-Hungary, the success of the Central Powers depended on the Germans. As Alfred saw it, if there was any future for Poland, Germany could not be allowed to win.

Korzybski had good reasons for distrusting the Central Powers' stated good intentions toward Polish nationalism. His views were based on his knowledge of history. Ethnic German expansionism led by the so-called Prussians, at the expense of Poles, had been going on for centuries.[1] More recently, vicious anti-Polish as well as anti-Jewish sentiments had found a nurturing home within German culture. In 1861, Bismarck—who ten years later as German chancellor unified Germany under Prussian dominance—had recommended genocide against the Poles: "Hit the Poles till they despair of their very lives…if we are to survive, our only course is to exterminate them."[2] Adolf Hitler's later doctrine of lebensraum, or living space, which involved the destruction and enslavement of Slavs and the colonization of their lands by Germans, was enunciated much earlier in Frankfurt in 1848 at an all-German conference. This reflected an even earlier Teutonic imperative of "Drang nach dem Slavischen Osten" ("Push east to conquer Slavic lands").[3]

German industry, perhaps the fastest growing in Europe, had been mobilized for war. Although not invincible, the relatively unified and efficient German military command had long ago prepared a detailed plan for fighting a two-front war with France and Russia. Alfred knew the success of the German efforts to Prussianize the Poles in their portion of partitioned Poland, only about fifty miles west of Lodz. Polish towns, like Poznan and Wroclaw, had been renamed as German towns (Posen and Breslau). German colonists had come in mass to settle. A large proportion of land there had been bought up by a small number of wealthy German magnates. Although the majority of the population of Prussian Poland still remained ethnically Polish, there were now some districts where Poles constituted a minority. Of all the partitioning powers, the Germans seemed to Alfred the most successful in their efforts to rub out Polish nationality in ancient Polish lands.

Korzybski felt no hesitancy; Germany must be beaten. The success of Germany's two-front war required German and Austrian troops to gain access to Russian Poland, especially to the rich agricultural land there and in the Ukraine, with the least amount of destruction to the local infrastructure. In this way, the Central Powers could avoid getting starved out by an allied economic blockade. Korzybski felt that both the Russian military and civil administrations did not by themselves have the capacity for much sustained resistance to such a German push.

Despite the size of its army (something like 1.5 million troops with another 3 million men in reserves)[4], Korzybski knew from personal experience the general poor quality of the Russian military. He had worked with Russian soldiers since childhood and had observed Russian officers and soldiers who had offices and lived in his family's apartment house in Warsaw. Despite some very competent men, the army command structure had failed to overcome many of its problems—antiquated doctrines, lack of coordination, poor intelligence, inadequate attention to supplies, etc.

By way of his father's experiences in the Ministry of Ways and Communications, he was also aware of the vast inefficiencies of Russian government bureaucracy, riddled as it was with self-aggrandizing careerists. Besides this, Korzybski had information from his contacts in the underground that the Tsarist court, civil administration, secret police, army general staff, etc., were riddled with German agents and sympathizers. Polish help, he believed, constituted a major factor to counter these negative influences, bolster Russian resistance, and prevent German victory.

Premature Evacuation

In the first days of August 1914, Korzybski saw corroborating evidence of the undermining effect of German influence on the Russians. German propaganda had insinuated that the Poles of Russian Poland would murder their Russian overseers after the declaration of war by the Tsar. Having apparently accepted this German scenario, much of the Russian general staff and civil administration (including police) fled east of the Vistula River from Warsaw when war was declared, thus effectively abandoning Russian Poland's major city. Korzybski witnessed the "flight of [the] Russian army and the whole officialdom. They left everything. They ran away, just wife, children and suitcases, to safety—means the other side of the Vistula which is a minor part of Poland."[5]

The people of Russian Poland reacted swiftly. As Korzybski noted, in a day or two citizens formed committees to take over the civil administration, some for example tying white handkerchiefs on their arms to act as policemen, e.g., directing traffic, etc. Poles, including Korzybski, also approached fleeing Russians to reassure them they would not be murdered. Grand Duke Nicholas—Commander-in-Chief of the Army General Staff, uncle of Tsar Nicholas II, and probably the only Romanoff that Korzybski respected—had already headquartered east of the Vistula at Baranovichi, 220 miles from Warsaw. According to Korzybski, Grand Duke Nicholas soon realized the Poles were not behaving as expected and reacted quickly when he realized the danger resulting from Russia's premature evacuation:

[Russian] officers were drunk in the hotels of Warsaw celebrating the departure. The [few Russian] patrols [still remaining on the fringes of Warsaw] suddenly discovered that small detachments of German cavalry were already on the outskirts of Warsaw. It was the very first days of the war. German cavalry, small detachments of no importance already penetrated the outskirts of Warsaw. Can you imagine that? And then telephoning…to the drunken officers to put up some sort of defense against those little patrols…The Grand Duke Nicholas, on the other side of the Vistula [was] immediately informed. So immediately infantry and cavalry were pouring down and those little patrols, German, were dispersed or retreated, I don't know which. And then the whole might of the Russian army came back and they marched directly to the German frontier.[6]

Indeed some of these troops, patrols from the Second Army, briefly crossed over into Germany, the furthest the Russians would ever get in the war. And on the way to the frontier, Poles welcomed the Grand Duke with flowers.[7]

With the Russians returned, the danger had passed of an immediate capitulation of Russian Poland to Germany. Korzybski remained convinced that this early failure of Germany's psychological campaign to capture Poland without a fight, sealed the outcome of World War I:

> The direct result, tragic this all was—that at this time Germany already lost the war. That one psychological issue lost the war for Germany because they did not get what they planned, undevastated Poland. They got only devastation after Poland became a battlefield...the Allies were saved.[8]

Private With a String

Whether living in Russia, Prussia or Austria, Poles generally seemed to support the side of the country in which they had citizenship. (Somewhere between 600,000 to 800,000 Polish men fought for the Russian army. 200,000 to 300,000 Poles fought on the German side, with a comparable number for the Austrians.[9]) This led to a tragically ironic result: many Poles found themselves somewhere in the Polish countryside sitting in trenches at opposite ends of gun barrels aimed at each other, despite the fact that they probably all agreed on the goal of a restored, independent Poland.

Nevertheless, Korzybski maintained throughout his life that intelligent Poles wanted the Allies to win.[10] Many Poles fighting for the Central Powers eventually came to agree with him especially after Germany and Austria had overrun Russian Poland. These included Poles who began as soldiers in the Austrian army but who finished the war by joining the "Blue Army" of General Haller who had defected from Austria and eventually fought on the Western Front for the French. Josef Pilsudski, who had started the war at the head of Austria's Polish Legion, eventually came to agree with Korzybski's view as well. Despite his initial belief that the Central Powers would support Polish independence, Pilsudski eventually realized that their 'independent' Poland meant existing under Germany's rule. He, along with many of his Legionnaires, was imprisoned by the Germans later in the war.

Having decided which side he must support, Korzybski went to Russian Army General Headquarters and volunteered soon after war was declared. He felt he had something useful to offer with his German-language skills and knowledge of Germany. His left hip displacement combined with numerous prior falls from horseback and other mishaps (he may have limped slightly when tired) made him a poor candidate for the regular army. They wouldn't take him but sent him instead to the Headquarters of the Second Army in Warsaw to see Lieutenant Colonel Terechoff who headed the Intelligence Department there. The Second Army's territory covered parts of East Prussia and Central Poland, including Warsaw and Lodz. Terechoff, who had already met Korzybski, was organizing his office; he could make use of Korzybski's enthusiasm and talents. But Korzybski, rejected by the army, would not be allowed to work there as a civilian. Terechoff, however, knowing of Alfred's abilities as a horseman, had the notion of forming a special intelligence cavalry unit to scout and gather data on enemy forces for the Second Army and for *Stavka*, Grand Duke Nicholas's General Staff Headquarters. He applied to the Grand Duke who immediately approved the plan. Although technically a volunteer, Korzybski was given a private's uniform in this newly-formed Second Army Headquarters, secret, Intelligence Department Cavalry with the official title—because of his multi-lingual talents—"Translator of the General Staff".[11]

Korzybski never did any extensive translating work, at least in the office. The unit, which had no more than fifty men, was independent of the regular army and directly under the command of Colonel Terechoff. Alfred liked the Colonel although he considered him "a lazy bones".[12] Korzybski, in turn, quickly became a favorite of the Colonel, who had learned he could depend on Alfred to get things done. In the first few weeks, Alfred helped organize the office, manage the secretarial workers, etc.; but soon Terechoff began to send him on special assignments.

Next to Alfred's private's stripes hung a string or cord indicating his special status as the Colonel's emissary. The string—along with written credentials he carried—meant that wherever he went, Alfred (for the most part) received the deference due to the Colonel. He also had certain privileges not usually accorded to privates: he could live at home (while in Warsaw) and not in the barracks, and was able to avoid having to scrub floors, do kitchen duty, and other menial jobs given to privates. He was also allowed to eat in restaurants—something ordinary Russian army privates couldn't do—although he had to request permission if an officer was present.

Once, later that year, he was sitting in a café in Lodz (soon to be captured by the Germans) drinking coffee with Zurowski, a close friend of his from the unit, and two young ladies they knew. Three drunken officers came in and, as protocol demanded, Alfred stood up and asked for permission to stay. One of the officers yelled at them to get out. Alfred, feeling reluctant to leave under the circumstances, lied and told the officer they were in the café on official business. The officers, unhappy, had to let them stay but took down their names. Later, Korzybski reported what happened to Terechoff, who chewed him out for lying to the officers. But when the officers came to Terechoff to check on Korzybski's story, the Colonel not only backed up Alfred but reprimanded the officers. Indeed, he had them arrested and court-martialed for drunkenness on duty. They each got three months in the brig.

Although Korzybski did not enter military service in the usual way, i.e., recruitment, basic training, etc., he found he fit quite easily into military life—especially in Terechoff's unit. He appreciated the esprit de corps he found there—the sense of group loyalty and responsibility under trying conditions. This, to him, represented military values at their best, which he distinguished from the militarism and regimentation the Prussians loved so much and that he hated. With his long-time experience managing soldiers and his expertise in horsemanship, shooting, and the saber, Korzybski had in effect been in training for the cavalry all his life. Soon after his enlistment, his 19th Century military skills would be severely challenged in a sobering awakening to 20th Century warfare.

Chapter 7
ON THE EASTERN FRONT

The first stages of the war had not gone well for Russia. By the end of August an invasion of East Prussia by the First and Second Russian Armies had resulted in the encirclement and destruction of much of the Second Army, in the Battle of Tannenberg, near Grunwald, the place where Polish forces had defeated the Teutonic Knights centuries before.

Korzybski did not participate in the East Prussian battles. However, while the Second Army was getting demolished, he had been sent by Terechoff to try and find the First Army under General Rennenkampf. He observed the terrible results:

> I could not find Rennenkamp[f]. [He]completely failed in attacking East Prussia. In the meantime, Grand Duke Nicholas was already bound to help the allies by attacking East Prussia and the 200,000 men of Rennenkampf were not there—especially prepared for that attack. So we put in our front some body, some sort of army, and the Second Army was sent to East Prussia, of course, complete disaster, complete. I was ordered there, but I came already after the disaster. I only saw the fleeing remnants, five men out of [every] 4,000.[1]

Initial efforts against the Austrians were more successful, with Russian armies in the south managing to capture Lwow, pushing their way into Galicia, and reaching the Carpathian mountains as autumn advanced into winter. Meanwhile, in Central Poland, where Korzybski's work was focused, initial forays towards Warsaw by the Germans got foiled. However, by October German armies were starting to advance from Prussia southeastwards into Russian Poland toward Plock (west-northwest of Warsaw) and Warsaw, and from Germany proper eastwards toward Lodz.

Greenhorns and Idiots

Around this time, on a scouting patrol, Korzybski probably had his first experience with direct artillery bombardment. Russian positions defending Lodz had begun to come under attack by German artillery using their 16.5 inch howitzer, known as "Big Bertha". The Big Bertha had a range of about seven miles. Korzybski's Colonel ordered him to go out with Zurowski to "find where the Big Berthas are." Both men were dressed in simple uniforms, but made of expensive material similar to what the Grand Duke wore. They took with them a sergeant from the Imperial Guard who wore a Cossack uniform which made him look even more impressive, though Korzybski considered him "the worst soldier I ever knew."

> We green horns saddled our beautiful horses and here we are riding, hunting for the Big Bertha. The most idiotic stuff. Now what happened. We got between the Russian army and the German army…The Russians thought we were some German officers…The Germans also thought that we were some high Dukes of the Russians…So we found ourselves, the three of us, in a concentrated cross-fire from both the German and Russians…Artillery shells were bursting all around us. Do you know what the famous imperial Cossack did? He jumped from the horse and began to run on foot. My friend and I—our horses had more sense than we, so they ran away on their own. And we let them do it. We had sense enough for that…A little girl of a peasant cottage caught the [Imperial Cossack's] horse and brought it back to him…When we ran away from that mess, the first thing I ran to my Colonel and reported what happened, and by this time all the field telephones were ringing, "Who is responsible for that monkey business?"…My Colonel, oh he gave me

hell. Of course, I gave him hell too. "How come you send a little green horn with an idiot—Imperial Bodyguard—without giving instructions?" And my Colonel said, "How could I expect that you were such a dumb idiot."

In the ensuing brouhaha with the higher authorities, the Colonel denied any knowledge of the three "Ghost riders".[2]

Korzybski subsequently learned the right way to locate the source of enemy artillery while under fire:

Don't take horses to find the Big Bertha…under fire find out where the shells are dropping. When you hear the noise of the shell coming…They make a noise like a streetcar in an empty street. So you know it's coming. The only thing to do is to lay down until the shell explodes. Of course, if the shell hits you, well, then you are sort of out of luck. But if you lay down you are pretty safe. So finally we found the craters where the shells burst and we picked fragments for the artillery man to tell the caliber and the angle—it means the source, where the battery was.[3]

Eventually, as Korzybski's work took him away from his headquarters in Warsaw to various parts of the Eastern Front, he got acclimated to the sound of artillery fire and wasn't much bothered by it. In fact, when artillery fire stopped, he would sometimes have trouble sleeping while waiting for an impending barrage. He later realized the silliness of this, since the silence often meant that an enemy battery had been hit or otherwise put out of commission and that the situation had in fact improved.

Throughout his time on the battlefields of Poland, Korzybski realized he might die. But he felt he was doing what he needed to do by helping the 'hopeless' Russians to at least slow down, if not stop, the German juggernaut. Although he did not seem blasé about death, he did come to take a rather matter-of-fact, even fatalistic, attitude about the possibility of dying. What else could he do?

Once, not far from the front line, he was sitting in a dugout drinking tea and smoking cigarettes with some intelligence scouts. He had been briefing them and was in the middle of a funny story when suddenly a Big Bertha shell came down with a whomp—hitting the earth at such an angle that it buried itself underneath the dugout:

We heard that big bomb and felt the big shake of that big fellow…We were lifted when the damn thing came under us. We were lifted…There were about six men and myself… Now the reaction of the six men…three of them, undelayed reaction, ran immediately… Three didn't move, for they realized that running away would not help. I knew also as a flash that running away would not help. So what is to do? Finish your story…I was waiting after, oh, ten seconds, fifteen seconds, perhaps twenty seconds. Of course, I didn't count the seconds. The problem was I stopped finally telling the story. It was a question of seconds and then I say, "What the hell is wrong with that shell?" It was a dud. Then as the shell still didn't explode, then I gave orders, "Run." So did I. When we ran far enough, then I [said] "Lay down." We lay down. Nothing happened. But believe me, we never went back to that dugout because you cannot trust a dud. It may explode anytime.[4]

Korzybski remembered this as one of those episodes of his life where the most appropriate thing he could say was, "How extraordinary!"

Safe-Crackers, Spies, and Secret Police

Unlike what one might gather from some histories of the time, Russian military intelligence was not completely primitive nor utterly incompetent. Indeed, Korzybski often scored successes in his work for Colonel Terechoff's unit which, among other things, involved the training and running of Russian spies and the catching of German ones.

In one of these jobs, he taught a class of thieves. Terechoff, wanting to rob the safes of the German General Staff, got a half-dozen or so safe-crackers released from Warsaw jails. Korzybski gave a series of lectures to the thieves. Not on how to crack safes—which they knew quite well how to do—but rather on details about German military organization, what the burglars could expect to find in the setup of German headquarters, what documents to look for, the best ways to escape from German areas, etc. Korzybski measured his success by the fact that most of his men returned safely from their missions.[5]

Some of the agents with whom Korzybski dealt, worked for the Russians strictly for money. Korzybski considered these people the lowest of the low and didn't even like to shake their hands after briefing them. For a time, Korzybski was put in charge of dealing with double agents. The double agents were people spying for the Russians who also spied for the Germans but represented themselves to the Russians as 'really' working for them, not the Germans. It could get confusing. Korzybski often didn't know with any confidence where the loyalty of such people lay. In such cases he would often provide a double agent with true but useless information, such as the location of a Second Army Division about to be moved somewhere else. In this way, he might at least mislead German battle planners.[6]

With other double agents, Korzybski could more definitely 'smell a rat'. One such case involved a German officer who had come over to the Russian side. He was placed in Korzybski's charge, to be put up in Korzybski's Warsaw apartment. The man claimed to have information on German positions, etc., and managed to convince Terechoff of his sincerity. But Korzybski didn't trust him. Terechoff brought the officer to the Grand Duke's headquarters, along with Korzybski. The man sat with Korzybski at one end of the room telling him in German about German positions southwest of Warsaw (so this incident must have occurred sometime early in 1915 after the Germans had already captured Lodz and the surrounding area). The man didn't realize he was telling Korzybski details about Korzybski's property at Rudnik and its adjacent territory. Since Korzybski was familiar with almost every stone for twenty miles around the estate, discepancies in the man's story indicated the man was fibbing. Korzybski kept a poker face and took notes, then excused himself as he got up to talk to Terechoff and the Grand Duke at the other side of the room. Saluting both men he reported, "That man is not an honest spy. Every word he said is just nothing but a damn lie."[7] The German officer may have heard this or may have guessed in some other way that his ruse had failed. He jumped up and ran to the window. Alfred pulled out his gun and yelled for the sentries, who grabbed the man and took him away.

Korzybski avoided involving himself in the disposal of rogue Russian agents. The Russian side would somehow let the Germans know that such-and-such a person worked for the Russians. This provided a way for the Russians to get rid of those they considered unreliable—the Germans could shoot or hang them. Korzybski considered this a dirty business and wanted nothing to do with it.

He himself soon became a target for German spying efforts. He often carried documents with him that could include information of great value to the enemy, e.g., lists of agents, where they had been sent, etc. Coming home to Warsaw from the front for several days, he met a beautiful young woman who immediately fell in love with him. This made him suspicious. He wondered if she was a spy sent—as others had been—to sleep with him and steal his papers. Colonel Terechoff had an opposite on the German side named

Colonel Mueller. Korzybski guessed Mueller would have been the one most likely to send such a spy. So Korzybski wrote a letter to him with the address of the town where German Army Intelligence Headquarters was located:

> Dear Colonel Mueller, I am deeply grateful to you for sending to me such beautiful young girl spies. In the meantime in the future when you do so, I would appreciate it but I would just advise you to brief the girls better not to be so obvious. Yours very truly,...[8]

Several days later, Korzybski was preparing to leave home and the young lady came to his apartment to say goodbye. He had gotten several soldiers to wait outside his apartment building and instructed them to arrest the woman leaving his apartment if he waved his handkerchief outside the window. Korzybski handed her the open letter and told her to read it since it was written to her friend the Colonel. At this point he hadn't yet determined if she was a spy or not. He watched her turn pale when she saw the address and become faint when she read the letter. Her reaction confirmed his suspicions, he asked her to go, and she left. Alfred signaled with his handkerchief and the soldiers arrested her. He never learned what happened to her. His attitude here may seem harsh, but he did not take his duties lightly. He knew a good spy could cost the lives of many men.

As Terechoff's unit captured German spies and people suspected of being spies, new problems arose. Even in Tsarist Russian and under severe wartime conditions, those suspected of spying could not just be shot. Rather, such prisoners were sent for confinement to an old fortress about 30 miles from Warsaw manned by the Russian state-security police, known as the "gendarmes", who later inspired the Nazi German Gestapo. As a Pole, Alfred especially loathed the gendarmes, since over the years many of his acquaintances, friends, and relatives had been harassed, imprisoned, or murdered by them. Indeed he himself had only just escaped getting sent by them to Siberia. It was already bad enough that many people in the regular army confused Korzybski's army intelligence unit with them. To have to work with them seemed especially galling. Even worse, the gendarmes had begun to release the prisoners that Terechoff's unit had already sent to them. This was not really surprising given that most of the gendarmes, Baltics of German descent, had strong pro-German sympathies. Neither Terechoff (nor Korzybski) would stand for the possibility that active spies might go free to continue their activities against Russia. Terechoff sent Korzybski to deal with the problem.

Korzybski arrived at the gendarmes' fortress in a broken-down, chauffer-driven, German-made automobile. Even with credentials from Terechoff, he had difficulty getting through the front gate. What business could this Private Korzybski have with the Colonel of the secret police? Finally, accompanied by a guard, he was allowed through and escorted into the commandant's office. Carrying his cavalry sword under his arm, Korzybski entered, clicked his spurs and saluted. After being invited to do so, he removed his hat, sat down, and handed his credentials to the Colonel, who asked, "What is the problem?"

Korzybski very politely and diplomatically explained: "The officers, your men, you harm the General Staff by releasing suspect spies which, if spies, go on being spies…I was sent by Colonel Terechoff of the Intelligence Department simply to report to you." The Colonel seemed very sympathetic, promised that no more prisoners would be released without consulting Terechoff's office, and asked Korzybski to give his report to the fortress's staff of captains.

They gathered in the assembly room, an old vault in the fortress with a floor of flat, uncemented stone. The Colonel sat at one end of a huge, long table. Korzybski stood at the other end with his sword under his arm. Along each side of the table sat the gendarme captains—ten in all. Korzybski was invited to sit and give his report. He did so. Then the various secret police captains began to question him aggressively and with increasing hostility. How is your unit organized? How does it operate? What activities is it currently involved with? Et cetera, et cetera. Korzybski was not about to reveal any information about his unit to this group of likely German sympathizers and possible traitors. The atmosphere of the room got more and more intimidating and Korzybski felt more and more enraged. Finally, he stood up, unsheathed his saber, and struck it against the floor with an enormous blow. The stone cracked. For grabbing the attention of a room full of secret police, there is nothing like breaking the floor with your sword.

Korzybski addressed the shocked and silent assembly. "Gentlemen, we are at war. For whom are you working? For the German or for the Russian?" The atmosphere immediately changed. The captains, suddenly solicitous, agreed to do everything they could to cooperate with Colonel Terechoff's intelligence unit. As they left the assembly room all smiles, Korzybski refused to shake hands with any of them. He did shake hands with the Colonel, who gave him a letter promising the gendarmes' full cooperation.[9]

Chapter 8
BATTLE AND RETREAT

As October 1914 ended, the Russian Army's Northern Command—which included the Second Army and Terechoff's irregular cavalry intelligence group—faced the Germans across the frontier of East Prussia and across central Poland towards Germany. Meanwhile, the armies of the Russian Southern Command were keeping up pressure on the Austrians and moving deeper into Galicia (Austrian Poland). Despite large numbers of Russian casualties and Russian prisoners taken, Russia still remained a threat. And despite their tactical successes in East Prussia and elsewhere, the Germans had taken tremendous losses themselves. As did the Austrians, who could not claim much tactical success against the Russians so far. Such were the circumstances on the Eastern Front as Stavka (the Russian Army General Staff) and its Northern Command, prepared for an invasion of Germany which would include the Second Army. They planned to start with the capture of Silesia, the southwestern section of partitioned Poland that Prussia had annexed more than a century before.

As part of Terechoff's unit, Korzybski worked to find out what the Germans were up to. But he had limited data. With just a few planes piloted by Frenchmen, the Russians could do only minimal aerial reconnaissance of German positions and movements. Setting up a field office in a tent, with a chair and a folding table wherever he went, Korzybski provided an up-to-date picture of the general arrangement of German troops as best he could. He would interrogate captured German prisoners and study documents brought to him (such as letters taken from German corpses or prisoners). He typically had no radio, so he would communicate his findings to Colonel Terechoff by messenger (horse or foot) or by field telephone.

Whatever successes Korzybski and his unit may have had, their activities constituted only a small part of the Russian intelligence and counter-intelligence effort, which remained on the whole quite pathetic. Via poorly-coded, intercepted Russian radio transmissions, the Germans had gotten vital information on Russian invasion plans. In the beginning of November, they began shifting by rail a quarter million men of their Ninth Army from Silesia—where they kept a remnant of defenders—to Thorn in West Prussia. From Thorn, the Ninth army looked southeast into Russian Poland toward Lodz, Plock and Warsaw. Hoping to catch the outer right flank of the advancing Russian armies, they prepared for their own invasion, which began on November 11 and took Russian forces by surprise. Within a week they had driven back Russian positions at least 100 miles, all the way to the outskirts of Lodz, though Warsaw still felt no immediate threat.

As it happened, Korzybski and Zorowski had been in Plock—located on a high cliff overlooking the Vistula, about 60 miles west-northwest of Warsaw and 70 miles north of Lodz—for at least a week before it fell to the Germans. Terechoff had sent them there to meet some of their agents and to try to get some agents across the Vistula. There were already German patrols around, and Korzybski couldn't get anyone across. The Germans had not yet appeared in the city but were expected to occupy it in a day or two. The Russian army and civil administration were making an orderly retreat.

In the meantime, Korzybski and Zurowski were organizing Poles in the town to provide help and information to their intelligence unit after the retreat. They got up to leave their nice hotel while it was still dark. Russian troops had completely cleared out and the two of them, as far as they knew, were the last remaining representatives of the Russian army. They expected the Germans to be coming in at any time. They should have gone too, but had heard that some German deserters nearby wanted to surrender. So, like fools, they rode out onto the German side, searching for the deserters whom they wanted to take as prisoners.

They ended up in a forest, stumbling around on their horses in the dark—falling into holes and getting bruised and scratched for their efforts. Finally, at daybreak they got to a small clearing and came upon a German cavalry reconnaissance patrol of a half dozen men. They stopped a few hundred yards away. Should they attack? The Germans stopped too, looking across at the two Poles. After a pause, the German lieutenant saluted them. Korzybski and Zorowski saluted back, turned their horses around (as did the Germans) and rode out of Plock and onto Russian territory as fast as they could go.[1]

10,000 German Corpses

As the last Russian army men out of Plock, Korzybski and Zorowski almost got shot by their own men as they straggled back across the Russian line. They rode to meet Captain Wolkoff, from their intelligence unit, who was staying at the home of a landowner whom Korzybski knew. Korzybski usually took orders directly from Colonel Terechoff, but in Terechoff's absence he had to take orders from Wolkoff, his superior. After the two men briefed the Captain, whose fine dinner they had disturbed by their arrival, he presented them with some news that confirmed Korzybski's judgement of him as incompetent. Wolkoff had forgotten to give important orders to some people working for the unit in Plock. Korzybski and Zorowski would have to return there to give the orders. Since the Germans probably now had control of the city, this mission seemed suicidal to Alfred. But he could only say "Yes, sir" and proceed to ride off again with Zorowski, who borrowed another horse from the landowner, since his own animal had injured a leg.

The two approached the town with trepidation, their rifles ready, but reached the center of town without finding any evidence of a German presence. After carrying out Wolkoff's orders, they found their favorite restaurant, had a nice dinner, and went back to the hotel where they had stayed before and got a good night's sleep. They got up early—still no sign of the Germans. As they started their ride out, they looked across the Vistula and saw a squadron of Death's Head Hussars, an elite Prussian bodyguard cavalry unit noted for its ruthlessness. Alfred and Zorowski couldn't resist. They hid their horses behind a house and commenced firing across the river at the Hussars. They dropped about ten of the Hussars but the whole squadron fired back, lightly wounding both of them. Alfred got struck in the knee; "nothing serious", he recalled. As they escaped, Alfred realized the stupidity of their 'heroism' since the Germans could easily have blamed the civilian inhabitants of Plock for their actions.

On the way back to their own side, Zorowski's horse took an unexpected detour and came to a stop in front of a country house. The horse would not budge and Zurowski and Korzybski had to pull the horse by the bridle and whip it from behind to get it going again. Afterwards, they again had to get through the line of Russian sentries who had bayonets raised and rifles aimed—"Are you German spies?", etc. When they finally reached Colonel Wolkoff, they reported. Then Korzybski asked the landowner, "What in the hell is wrong with your horse?" The man replied that a girlfriend of his lived at the house where the horse had stopped. The horse had gotten used to staying there for hours waiting for its owner inside.[2]

After the Russian retreat from Plock, a furious battle ensued as the Germans advanced and the Russians engaged in rearguard action. The German's paid dearly for every mile they advanced. Korzybski did his part to make them pay. Gathering information where he could, he went to a cellar where another intelligence officer had set up office with a field telephone. Alfred went to say hello to the man who—with his ear to an earphone—put his finger up to his mouth to indicate to Alfred to shut up. He motioned for Alfred to come over, gave him another earphone, and pushed a pad and pencil towards him. The officer gestured for Alfred to listen and write. As Korzybski described it:

Somehow the telephone lines on ground—a shell probably did it—the telephone lines of the Russian General Staff with the German General Staff got crossed. And what the officer was listening to was the orders of the General Staff of Germany directing the battle. Priceless stuff...So I was listening to the orders of German headquarters and writing them down on a pad, and listening, writing down, using my hand to call orderlies, send to headquarters immediate news... It was a very bloody battle, very bloody...We were in the midst of it. And because we knew...the orders of the General Staff of Germany how they directed the battle, we counteracted immediately. The result—10,000 [German] corpses.[3]

Retreat from Lodz

Possibly this crossed German phone transmission, recorded by Korzybski, finally alerted the Russian Northern Command and Stavka to the nature and extent of the German invasion. To the north, the Russian First Army under Rennenkampf, which had defended Plock, retreated and took up defensive positions in the direction of Warsaw. The capital of Russian Poland seemed safe for now but Lodz became the main target of the German Ninth Army's southwest advance. The Russians did manage to keep Lodz from falling at once. In a masterful defensive move, the Russian Second and Fifth Armies—positioned miles west and southwest of the city as the main force for a planned invasion of Germany—beat the Germans to the city. By November 17, 1914—within two days of the order to fall back—the Russian forces had formed a defensive ring around the western, northern and eastern borders of Lodz. The Germans could no longer just march in, but Lodz was now under siege.

Korzybski—his unit having set up temporary headquarters there—had arrived a few days earlier. To the west and north, the main forces of the German Ninth Army commanded by General Mackensen stood outside the Russian defensive ring. And to the east, that ring protected the city from an isolated German force under General Scheffer (including a reserve corp, a cavalry division, and a guard division) that had managed to slip through a gap in the Russian line during the retreat from the north. Scheffer's forces presented a problem. They were postioned to block the escape route towards Warsaw if the Russians decided to abandon the city. It seemed like the Russians were surrounded.

By November 21, the Germans were shelling the city. The Russians were returning the fire and hoping Rennenkampf's First Army would come down to take care of Scheffer's eastern divisions. Perhaps the Russians might have even been able to defeat the Germans if the First Army had arrived en masse to reinforce the besieged Russian armies. Instead, Rennenkampf sent down a much smaller relief force, which was only able to convince Scheffer to retreat to the northwest, where he eventually joined the rest of the German Ninth Army. Scheffer did lose half of his men in the process but he also captured 16,000 Russian soldiers and 64 artillery pieces. Nonetheless, the Russians now had a more or less unobstructed path of retreat out of Lodz.

By December 6, Russian forces had lost 100,000 men. City hospitals overflowed with casualties. Winter had set in and some Russian soldiers had no boots. They were running short of rifles, ammunition, and artillery shells as well. The Germans had already begun to enter the city. The time for retreat had come. Korzybski managed to find a rickety, straw-filled horse-cart with a flimsy harness and a worn-out rope, along with a few broken-down horses to pull it. With Zurowski, and a duty sergeant—who technically outranked Korzybski but to whom Korzybski gave orders—Korzybski loaded bundles of intelligence documents onto the cart. On the straw, along with these papers, he had placed a five-gallon glass bottle of gasoline which he planned to shatter with his sword and put a match to, if there was any threat of getting captured. The valuable information about Terechoff's intelligence operations could not be allowed to fall into German hands.

Colonel Terechoff, who had gone to say goodbye to a girlfriend, put Korzybski in charge. However, he deliberately didn't tell Alfred exactly where they were headed. This turned out to show a certain wisdom on Terechoff's part. While Alfred and Zorowski stood guard by the wagon waiting for the Colonel, a man in the uniform of a Russian Siberian infantry captain came from across the street. He walked up to Korzybski, who saluted him. The friendly Siberian captain told him not to bother with the military formalities. "I lost my regiment and as you are of the General Staff, please tell me where is your staff going?" Korzybski replied, "I'm sorry, sir, I don't know. I am waiting orders." The captain said, "I'm sorry", saluted, and returned to the other side of the street. Zorowski went up to Alfred and told him he'd been talking with a German spy. In a flash, Korzybski realized this was probably right. The captain didn't wear his uniform quite correctly. His Russian sounded somehow foreign. He hadn't stayed with the Russians but walked back in the direction from where the Germans were entering the city. Alfred immediately called for the military police, who arrested the 'Siberian captain'.[4]

When Terechoff returned, he, Korzybski, and his other men made their way along with the other Russian forces leaving Lodz. The retreating troops headed northeast, towards Warsaw, with some artillery and infantry staying behind to cover their withdrawal. Meanwhile German artillery did its best to impede their progress. Members of Korzybski's unit either rode on horseback or rode along on the horse-drawn wagon filled with intelligence documents.

Traffic soon became a major problem. Many officers seemed to have disappeared. None of the officers on the road, including his Colonel, were—in Alfred's opinion—taking command as needed to direct traffic, e.g, "Keep that traffic clear, move that wagon to the side, wait for that cavalry group to pass the intersection, etc." In fact, Korzybski's Colonel seemed to lose his head. As Alfred described it later:

> ...he was here dumb Dora, doing nothing. And the mess was going on, blocking the traffic. So I poked him in the ribs quite hard with my sword, with the handle of my sword because he wouldn't listen otherwise. I said, "Order that, so, so, etc." He looked at me with enormous surprise but he obeyed and he barked orders.[5]

After they started to move again, Terechoff rode ahead leaving Alfred in charge of getting to their new headquarters. And now traffic management became a life-threatening issue. Melting snow and the trampling of men, horses, and wagons on the dirt roads leading out of Lodz had turned the retreat into a muddy mess. German artillery provided the 'musical' accompaniment of a loud and deadly percussion. The traffic had stopped again and Korzybski went up ahead to investigate the source of the tie-up. An artillery shell had landed on the road, making a large, impassable hole. There were no officers to be found. Korzybski—sword in one hand, pistol in the other—took command and began yelling orders at the unfamiliar men around him, telling them to fill the hole with anything they could find, e.g., pieces of wood from broken wagons, sacks of food, boxes of ammunition, etc. Some of the men looked at him and asked "Who are you?" He replied, "Never mind—obey. Never mind who am I." The hole got filled and they once more began to move.[6]

Soon enough they reached another impasse. A three-inch field artillery piece had gotten stuck in the half-frozen mud in the middle of the narrow road. The line of traffic once again came to a stop. With marshes on either side, they couldn't go around. The three-inch gun, though one of the smallest and lightest of artillery pieces, was normally pulled by a team of horses. The men trying to move it somehow couldn't get the horses attached and lined up properly to dislodge it. Then a group of six men, including Korzybski, attempted to lift it out of the mud enough to shift it from the road and into the marsh. Working at odds with one other, they couldn't coordinate themselves sufficiently to budge it. With all their straining and sweating, nothing useful was happening. Out of desperation, Korzybski motioned the men aside. With an enormous effort, he dislodged the gun from the mud by himself and tipped it into the marsh. In the process, he felt his "inside[s] got busted." Indeed, he had severely herniated himself—an injury he never fully recovered from. But he had done what needed to get done at the time. The column of men, horses and wagons once more flowed. Korzybski rested by the side of the road and waited for his men and their cart of precious documents to come by.[7]

Korzybski now had to join up with Terechoff at the new General Staff headquarters. He had learned the destination and decided to switch to side roads, some even worse than the main one they had already traversed. Sometimes they passed close to German troops. Alfred decided it might be safer to go through some villages where the Germans had already passed. But these had been set afire by the Germans and he worried about sparks igniting his document-laden cart with its straw and gasoline. He and his dozen-or-so men took more side roads. They ended up in a forest with a deep, sandy path. The tired horses had more and more trouble pulling and then could pull no more.

As luck would have it, they saw ahead of them a large brewery wagon pulled by a team of big, strong-looking horses. They decided to requisition it—which they did with as much official flourish as they could muster—giving the brewery driver their broken-down wagon and tired horses in exchange. After they transferred their documents and before they drove away, Korzybski handed the driver a hastily-written note to the German General Mackensen, kindly requesting that he pay the bill for the hijacked beer-wagon. They proceeded with no further problems. Korzybski described their reception at Russian headquarters:

>...finally we arrived at the headquarters, I would say, in state, with that big, big beer wagon; big, big, heavy, well-fed horses—beautiful harnesses and what not; and my documents intact. So when I reported [to Colonel Terechoff]...that everything is safely back, he accepted my report and said, "Well, you were pretty long coming." He didn't thank me. I didn't have a chance to tell him what hell I went through before I arrived, and I just made [an] ordinary report...[Colonel Terechoff] just cocked his head, looked at me and said, "Korzybski, next time you poke me in the ribs with your sword, please don't do it so hard." I smiled and I [said], "Yes, sir."[8]

Used To Be A Horseman

Since the start of the war only four months before, Korzybski had remained pretty much in constant motion. Shifting from place to place, locations blurred. Time distorted, days passing like hours and hours like days. August 1914 already seemed like the distant past. In the field, though not for the most part directly involved in combat, he usually worked under artillery bombardment. And he had seen up-close the results of artillery, rifle, and machine gun fire. Once while walking in a forest, he had stepped through a pile of leaves and onto something soft—parts of a decaying, unburied human body that he then had to scrape off his boots. For long periods of time he had to get by with very little sleep. He often had no food since, when traveling as a representative of his special headquarters unit, he was not attached to a regular army kitchen. Once while getting chauffeured in a dilapidated car to a new location, he and his driver saw a big piece of black bread, probably dropped from a field kitchen wagon, lying on the road in a muddy hole: "We reverently stopped the car, retrieved that muddy loaf of bread, and began to eat it."[9]

Somewhere on the Eastern Front, probably early 1915

After the fall of Lodz, Alfred's nearby family estate came under German control. His mother by this time had moved to her place in Warsaw. So she was safe. But he didn't know when he would see Rudnik again. Probably not long afterwards (he later had trouble remembering the exact time or location of the incident), Alfred found himself in the middle of a pitched battle. His horse, a beloved white Arabian bred at Rudnik, got shot during a barrage of gunfire. The Arabian fell on Alfred, crushing his pelvis and severely dislocating his left hip. The horse died and Alfred somehow managed to pull himself from underneath and crawl away.[10] Instead of reporting to a hospital, he stayed at the front working, managing to walk—although doubled up in pain—by using his sword as a crutch. A couple of days later, he happened to meet a general, a physician from the medical corps. The general took one look at the hobbling, bent-over Alfred and asked him, "What is wrong with you?" Korzybski replied, "Your Excellency, there is nothing wrong with me." General: "Go to the hospital." Korzybski: "I'm sorry, your Excellency, but I cannot do that. I have work to do." General: "Go to the hospital. Those are orders." Korzybski: "Yes, sir." So Alfred got himself to the hospital.[11]

His memory of what happened there remained cloudy. He wasn't even sure where the hospital was located. He remembered getting tied down to a surgical table and then being put under with chloroform or ether. He was later told that some screws were put into his leg and pelvis. He was put into a cast from his leg to his chest. It all seemed like a daze, except for the pain:

> The only thing I [clearly] remember in the hospital [is] that once the pain was so acute—I am not a suicidal type at all—but the pain was [so] extremely acute that I decided to suicide, to kill myself. Couldn't stand it any longer. I preferred to die than to suffer so much. The point was that I didn't have the strength to get up to get at the gun. So the result was that I didn't shoot myself, but just endured the pain.[12]

After he left the hospital (perhaps a month or two later), he found that he had a more or less permanent stiffness in his joints. For the rest of his life he tended to limp and within a few years regularly used a cane as well as a shoe lift extension on the left side. (That leg became shortened after the hip injury.) In later life he preferred sitting on a high, firm chair. His sciatic nerve had also somehow gotten injured and he had a predisposition towards sciatica for the remainder of his life.

Immediately after leaving the hospital, he became most aware of one fact: he could no longer jump onto a horse. He had to be lifted. This didn't impede his military duties since by this time (the spring of 1915) his work required little time on horseback. The fact remained: Alfred could no longer get onto a horse or ride one with any ease. He had ridden and trained horses since childhood. He loved those animals. Over the course of the next year, he came to a poignant realization: his life as a horseman was over. Years later, in 1948, on a biographical form he filled out for the 8th Edition of *American Men of Science,* he wrote under Hobbies (along with "Electric, Mechanical Tools"): "Horse Training", years: "1890–1916". For "Degree of Skill" he marked an "x" under "Excellent" and wrote in the box, "Used to be".[13]

Chapter 9
AT THE DISPOSAL OF THE MINISTER OF WAR

In the winter of 1914–1915, Russian forces had some apparent success. They seemed about to capture Kracow and had reached the mountain passes of the Carpathians, which led down into the Austrian heartland. But the Austrians, with help from the Germans, pushed them back. By April, Warsaw was under threat. In addition to their losses, the shortages of shells, ammunition, rifles, clothing, and food further demoralized Russian troops.

From April to September of 1915, the Germans and Austrians relentlessly pushed forward. In the initial stages of the German-Austrian advance, Korzybski seemed to accelerate his efforts, traveling from one front to another gathering intelligence, not just for Stavka and the Second Army, but for the other Russian armies as well. But by the end of June it become clear that Russian forces would have to retreat from most, if not all, of Poland in order to just survive. The war was changing from one of mobility to one of positions and entrenchment. There would be no more need for Terechoff's highly mobile cavalry intelligence group. It was disbanded on June 20. Korzybski helped organize the breakup of the office in Warsaw, including the disposal of equipment and the dispersal of men to other units. Where would he go?

He had been thinking about an invention—a bomb. To work on it, he was sent to the Artillery Department Laboratory of the Headquarters of the Second Army. Korzybski's invention, an incendiary device, seemed extremely simple but nasty. He manufactured some samples for a demonstration at General Staff Headquarters. His bomb consisted of a 12 by 4 inch wooden box that could easily break apart when dropped from a plane. The box was stuffed with tar and kerosene-soaked rags wrapped around a center portion containing smokeless powder. The powder in turn surrounded a thin metal capsule holding some phosphorous in a liquid solution. Since phosphorous burns when exposed to air, the bomb was set off by first breaking the capsule with an icepick. The surrounding fluid would evaporate, the phosphorous would start to burn, ignite the powder and then, in 5 to 10 minutes, the rags and then the box would begin to burn as well. At this point, the box could be dropped to do its work on a field or a roof of straw or wood.

After one successful demonstration in front of the General Staff, Korzybski was asked to do another one before Grand Duke Nicholas, who had missed it. The Grand Duke wanted to see an actual aerial demonstration, with Korzybski dropping his incendiary-box bombs from a plane onto a target field. Alfred did not relish going up in an airplane. He had not enjoyed his last plane ride—to say the least.

On the front, he had become friendly with a French flyer glad to have someone to speak with in his native language. One day the flying ace invited him to come along for a flight over the German trenches. Alfred described the ride:

> I was not tied up. I had no safety belt. Not tied up and he wanted to give me the thrill which he assumed would be the thrill of my life, he began to make the loop over the German trenches and of course, the Germans did not appreciate the joke and they riddled us with machine guns. Well, I had very little to say about that because that son of a gun was doing the driving. We were in the meantime riddled with bullets on one side and on the other side, retaliating to the Germans, out of the window I was vomiting like hell on

them. It was one of my first rides. How much I got to them I don't know. Their bullets got to us all right. The rest of my reaction was probably lost in the winds. But anyway I did it. Naturally when we came back home, [so to] speak home, naturally I gave him 'a piece of my mind', so to say in quotation marks, no more airplanes for me. Well I did not calculate properly. Grand Duke Nicholas wanted to see....[1]

The Grand Duke insisted and Alfred considered it his duty not to refuse:
I took my incendiary bombs with me and then we began to fly...What I was doing was putting the ice pick into the phosphorus—oh, I don't want to make a monkey out of myself... and I don't know I dropped a half dozen of them, or a dozen, it doesn't matter because they were small things and the question was just to make fire for five, ten minutes. They were timed deliberately for a short exposure, so to say, for air. They all collapse and they start burning, and in the meantime, I nearly, somehow, I nearly burned down the airplane by mistake and the pilot got nervous and so when we were landing he nearly smashed the airplane. So, of course, we have an interchange of opinions about his capacity as a pilot and my capacity as a bombadier. Just an exchange of opinions, that's all...In the meantime in front of Grand Duke Nicholas both of us had to keep our opinions in rather polite language. And there were two of my airplane rides. And since then [Alfred was telling this story in 1947], no more airplane rides, thank you.[2]

Although in later life he realized commercial airline travel had become "not so unpleasant",[3] it seems he never did fly again. As for his incendiary-box bomb, although the demonstrations impressed the Russian and French officers watching them, his bomb was not used, since, with the diminishing front and the relatively short range of their planes, the Russians were worried about burning up parts of their own territory. The French later used their own version of an incendiary bomb using glass bottles which, in Korzybski's opinion, didn't work nearly as well.

At the Disposal of the Minister of War

Korzybski's career as a bomb-maker lasted only a short time—until July 4. He had impressed the Grand Duke and other members of the General Staff, not only for his invention (despite their inability to use it) but also because of his work with Terechoff. Korzybski was still looking to help. So by the orders of Grand Duke Nicholas, the Commander-in-Chief of the Russian Army, Korzybski was sent to Petrograd (the name of the Russian capital which had recently been changed from "St. Petersburg") to be "at the disposal of the Minister of War." Alfred arrived in Petrograd at the end of July.[4] Soon afterwards, he went to the Ministry of War office and was ushered in to see General A. A. Polivinov, recently promoted from Deputy Minister to Minister of War after a scandal involving his predecessor, Sukhomlinov, who was getting blamed for the accumulating war failures.

Polivinov was one of the few people in the Tsarist regime, along with the Grand Duke, whom Korzybski felt any respect for. Men like them, whatever their personal merits, were severely hemmed in by the ineptness and corruption of so many of their subordinates, colleagues, and superiors—along with the extreme inertia of the Tsarist administration, in general, and the dullness of the Tsar on top, more specifically. The resultant Russian inefficiency seemed inevitable and responsible for the debacle on the battlefield. Russian industry, although technically quite capable of providing adequate stocks of shells and other military supplies, had been stopped from doing so by dishonest businessmen, corrupt officials, and inadequate planning. With better leadership, the Russians could at least have held back the Germans from capturing so much of Russian Poland. Korzybski expected that the Grand Duke, unable to adequately replace equipment or men, would soon resign out of tiredness and desperation. The situation indeed looked desperate. The Germans were about to overrun Warsaw. And the Russian Army was retreating.

Having already heard about Korzybski, Polivinov embraced him and asked, "What can I do for you?"[5] Alfred could have chosen any situation he wanted. He wanted to serve at the front. He could no longer run around in a cavalry or infantry unit. But he had a friend serving as an officer in the Bodyguard Heavy Artillery Regiment. So he requested to be put there. He felt he could make a quite adequate artillery officer and asked permission to take the officer's exam at the Artillery Acadamy:

> Polivinov knew, and he knew that I knew that a complete collapse of the Russian front was in view, this request in a way was suicide, we both knew it. The so very nice old man got very excited, he jumped to his feet and exclaimed "Are you crazy?" I said, "No Excellence but I am cut away by the enemy from my home and property, so I better enlist." With reluctance he agreed.[6]

So with an order from the Minister of War, Korzybski went to the Commandant of the City of Petrograd who took care of such enlistments. Just to forgo potential trouble, Korzybski had paid 50 of his last 100 rubles to a military doctor to get a medical clearance certifying his fitness for service. The Commandant looked through Korzybski's papers and then at Korzybski and refused to take him. Korzybski returned to Polivinov who went to the Tsar himself to obtain an imperial decree for Alfred to join the Regiment.

With the imperial decree in hand, Alfred spent a good deal of time fruitlessly searching for the Bodyguard Heavy Artillery Regiment supposedly located somewhere in or around Petrograd. He couldn't find it. Meanwhile, the news from the front had not been good. On August 5, within 2 weeks of Alfred's arrival in Petrograd, the Germans had captured Warsaw and the Russians were steadily retreating east of the Vistula. The Grand Duke resigned at the end of August. Tsar Nicholas—whom Alfred considered a "half wit"[7]—took over the position of Commander-in-Chief in early September. *Hopeless.*

Korzybski also felt personally desperate. He had less than 50 rubles left in his pocket, no income, and was wondering how he was going to live. Luckily, one day on a street in Petrograd, he ran into a general whom he had known at the front. The general lent Alfred 100 rubles to tide him over and Alfred, not one to ever beg, gratefully took it. The general also suggested that Alfred, with his engineering background, might be able to get a job in the Russian armaments industry. Alfred began to consider this, and the general said he would keep a lookout for any job possibilities.

All through September and October, Korzybski remained in purgatory in Petrograd while the Russian retreat continued. By the end of September, the Germans had reached Riga, Pinsk, and Baranovichi, the former headquarters of the Russian General Staff. But the Germans had major problems too. They had reached the end of their supply lines. Along with the general destruction of battle, both the Germans and the retreating Russian forces had stripped much of the Polish infrastructure. As Korzybski had unhappily predicted, the German juggernaut could not depend on an undevastated Poland. By October, the Germans and Austrians—stuck in the White Russian and Ukrainian mud—dug into trenches facing the Russian side. Their advance had stopped.

How Many Horse-Miles to New York City?

Probably sometime late in October or in early November, Alfred happened to bump into Captain Sobanski, another friend from the front and a fellow Pole. Alfred told him about his frustrations with the war, with the ineptness of the Russian army, with the inability of Russian industry to provide adequate ammunition and supplies, and with the Tsar and his regime. He felt utterly disgusted.

Sobanski, an engineer, told him about a Russian Military Commission forming. About 200 technical experts were being sent to America to supervise the manufacture and testing of ammunition for the Russian Army. Sobanski was going as a "Senior Inspector". He suggested Korzybski visit Colonel Moisiev who was organizing the project. Korzybski went to see the Colonel as soon as he could, presented his credentials, and asked for a job. Moisiev immediately accepted Korzybski, though he apologized that the best paying jobs had already been taken. Alfred didn't care. He was appointed "Junior Inspector". Their ship was scheduled to leave shortly. (According to Korzybski's 1915 pocket calendar they sailed from Petrograd on November 17.)

Korzybski needed to get his affairs arranged, i.e., officially resign from his military appointment, obtain a passport, and get his travel stipend:

> I immediately got something like $3000 or more—dollars, not rubles—in cash. Cash in hand for the travel to the United States and back. Can you imagine traveling from Petrograd to New York $3000, and say $200 for round trip. Is that a crazy price? You know how they calculated? I was entitled to four horses and the mileage between Petrograd and New York was calculated on the price of horses. Mileage by horses and I was supposed to have four horses. Do you follow the idiocy of it? So the trip was calculated on the basis of four horses and the legal cost of four Russian horses by the mile amounted to $3200 or so. So I got the money—can you imagine what was the relief of being free of the [Tsar], hav[ing] a huge amount of money in cash, as it was in rubles...7000 rubles or so. Unheard of money. Of course, idiotic all through, granted. So finally I got the money in dollars and passport and everything. And sailing in three days, five. And what I did, I wanted to pay the 100 [rubles] back to that kind general...who lent me the 100 [rubles]. And I paid 100 [rubles] for some beautiful ivory snuff-box with diamonds and I don't know what-not. All antique or some such. And I put the 100 rubles in it, and I saw the general and thanked him so much for his trying to help me and I paid the money that way. It means a 100 [ruble] box of some sort with 100 [rubles] inside.[8]

Then, as he put it, "I resigned from my former appointments and sailed in a few days, deciding to have an educational trip, which I did."[9]

Chapter 10
OH! PETAWAWA

Korzybski and about 200 Russian technicians left Petrograd in mid-November, 1915. The boat trip to Stockholm took several days. Then after a couple days layover, they continued on to Bergen, Norway. The last week of November they sailed to New York aboard the Norwegian S/S Kristianiafjord. That spring German U-Boats had sunk the Lusitania, a British passenger ship, with a loss of nearly 1200 passengers, about 10% of them Americans. With the resulting hue and cry in America, the Germans had ceased their unrestricted attacks on shipping. They did not want to risk pushing the United States into the war. So there seemed like little danger to Alfred's journey, especially as his mission was aboard the ship of a neutral country.

Korzybski just felt glad to be out of Petrograd. As a civilian "inspector", he would be doing quality control work on ammunition manufactured somewhere in North America for the Russian army. Despite his frustrations with the Russians, he still wanted to usefully contribute to the defeat of the Central Powers. To keep his possibilities open, he brought with him a press pass he obtained in Petrograd from the North-South Press Agency, a French language news bureau. Just in case the ammunition inspection job didn't work out.[1]

Unfortunately, about half of the technicians on the ship seemed to have profiteering as their main motive. Their slogan would have been 'praise the cash and pass bad ammunition'. Alfred made friends with two other men, Colonel Kolantaiew and Colonel Sachanow, who had been at the front and disdained the petty grafters on board as much as he did. The three men stayed together and talked among themselves about the war, the shortage of shells and other essential items, and the mentality of their fellow passengers. They were not very discreet. Apparently someone listened in on their conversations and the three men came to be considered 'dangerous'.

The passage to New York took about a week. After docking in the first week of December, they reported to the Russian Military Commission in New York. They figured the grafters had transmitted news about them to friends at headquarters because they found themselves sent to what seemed like the least desirable locations in North America—places providing minimal opportunities and/or rewards for profiteering. Alfred and Colonel Kolantaiew were sent to the Remington arms factory in Bridgeport, Connecticut. Colonel Sachanow was sent to Petawawa Camp, a military proving ground located where the Petawawa River, a small tributary, empties into the Ottawa River in southern Ontario. Neither Korzybski nor Kolantiew lasted long at Remington (perhaps because the plant was run efficiently and there wasn't much for them to do there even if they weren't interested in graft). Kolantiew soon went back to Europe. After only a few days in Bridgeport, Korzybski was sent on to Petawawa "where", as he put it, "Sachanow was already exiled amongst the skunks…and bears."[2]

Where One Hears the Noise of the Water

The Canadian Army base and proving ground was adjacent to the tiny village of Petawawa. A few miles southeast on the Ottawa River was the slightly larger village of Pembroke, which contained nothing much of interest to Alfred—just a few stores, a movie house, and a church. The Canadian capital of Ottawa was a two-hour trip further east, with

Montreal only a few hours further by train. The proving ground stood on the edge of the white pine forests of the Algonquin Provincial Park. The name "Petawawa" came from the Algonquin Indian word for "where one hears the noise of the water".[3] By the time Alfred arrived there—on December 30, 1915—he more likely heard the noise of artillery fire.

Alfred had been exiled there because he didn't want to take any part in graft. He had the official title of "Junior Inspector of the Commission for the Acceptance of the Orders of the [Russian] Imperial Artillery Department in North America". He knew almost nothing about artillery, except what it felt like to be on the receiving end. Yet he was expected to be in charge of a battery of Russian Q.F. (Quick Firing) three-inch field guns used to test shells the Canada Car and Foundry Company had begun to manufacture for the Russian government. He spoke little or no English but was expected to work with British "Tommies" and Canadian soldiers on the base. In spite of these obstacles, his exile felt heavenly to him.

His nerves needed a rest. On the Eastern Front, he had begun to suspect his superiors in Second Army Headquarters Intelligence of using him as a subject for an efficiency study on how to work under the constant threat of death. He had gotten used to the continuous noise of shooting at the front and had only recently begun to sleep soundly without the sound of artillery bombardment, having realized this indicated greater—not less—safety. Over the last year and a half, he had developed the habit of sleeping with his arms folded over his chest to protect precious papers he carried. Now he still found himself waking up clutching his chest with both arms, a habit he no longer needed and worked to break.

Yes, Petawawa seemed in many ways like bliss. He had a Ford car and a comfortable furnished and heated cabin provided by the Canadian Car and Foundry Company. He had a decent salary and minimal expenses. He had only three or four hours of work per day—or at night when testing shrapnel—firing and maintaining the field guns with a crew made up of British Tommies. Otherwise, his time was his own. Any lag in getting a shipment of artillery from the manufacturer would give him a few days free, which he used to visit Ottawa or Montreal. He made such trips as often as he could.

One of Alfred's first main tasks was to learn decent English. He needed it for his work and, as a multi-lingual person, he also knew learning the language of a place provided the key to feeling at home there. He got his first few words of English from the Tommies who worked on his gun crew: "Yes", "No", and "God Damn!"[4] They soon helped him learn even more 'colorful' terms. He also studied English on his own. He had known and loved Shakespeare and Byron in translation. He now began to read the originals with an English grammar in hand. But he realized he could use still more help. For one thing, he knew he had lousy pronunciation. He needed a tutor. A Canadian customs official named Gilchrest lived at the camp. A military man, Gilchrest's health had deteriorated from overwork and he had been sent to Petawawa by kindhearted superiors in order to get a good rest. His perfunctory job of signing off on train deliveries of ammunition to the Russians took him about an hour a day—if there was a delivery. Soon enough, he began to feel lonely and bored. Both he and Korzybski found a mutual solution to their problems. Gilchrest studied French with Alfred, while Alfred worked on his English with Gilchrest. Soon Korzybski was speaking fluent Canadian-British English with the Polish accent he never lost. In later years, his U.S.-born wife helped him, and he made an effort to Americanize his English as much as he could.

Junior Inspector

Korzybski also had to get quickly up to speed in his knowledge of artillery. When he wasn't studying English, he spent much of the rest of his spare time reading artillery textbooks. The senior inspectors in the Russian Artillery Commission at Petawawa, Colonel Sachanow and Captain Goodima, were seasoned artillery men but in the main did not deal directly with the field guns. Although Korzybski had the title of junior inspector, his responsibility was not inspecting the ammunition. Rather, his civilian job consisted of test-firing and maintaining the field guns, and seemed more military than not. Basically, he functioned as an artillery lieutenant and when at work he found it most convenient to wear one of his old uniforms.

His bosses would give him samples to test. These might include shells (empty shells, loaded high explosive shells, and shrapnel shells) or shell components (primers, brass casings, timed fuses for shrapnel, etc.). Korzybski supervised the test-firing and acted as range observer. When the gunner was sick, he would take his place and operate the gun, which could hit a target several miles away. Afterwards he would report the results to Sachanow and Goodima, who had chosen the test samples and were responsible for analyzing the results, passing or rejecting lots of ammunition, corresponding with the manufacturer, etc.

In order to deal with such correspondence, Sachanow and Goodima had a small office staff of immigrant clerks who would take their dictation in Russian and write the necessary letters in English. But Sachanow and Goodima soon found they needed someone with more linguistic and technical knowledge than what the clerks could offer. So Korzybski soon had additional work acting as their liaison with the Canadian Car and Foundry Company and with Colonel Mackie, the Officer in Charge at Petawawa Camp.

If either Korzybski, Sachonow, or Goodima had wanted to do a little 'business on the side' they certainly had the opportunity even at Petawawa. The company could lose tens of thousands of dollars if dishonest inspectors rejected a carload of good ammunition. As grafters, the three men could easily have squeezed one or two thousand dollars out of the company in this way. But none of them had any inclination to do so. Canadian Car and Foundry behaved honestly as well, although Korzybski considered their prices high. For example, they might charge three times the production cost for a shrapnel fuse. Nonetheless, they had a low rejection rate for their products. They clearly were on the up and up and showed no interest in bribing the Russians to pass faulty ammunition. Indeed they seemed quite interested in cooperating with Sachanow and Goodima who would present Korzybski with advice in Russian on technical problems which Korzybski would then communicate in English or French to company representatives, engineers, etc., who seemed eager to improve their products. With Sachanow spending more and more of his time drinking and Goodima allowing Alfred a certain degree of independence, Alfred was using his abilities with language and troubleshooting once more.

As in his previous position as a "translator" in which he did intelligence work, Alfred's title at Petawawa didn't accurately represent what he did there. Though officially a civilian inspector, he inspected no ammunition. He spent his working time in a military role on the firing range supervising soldiers operating and maintaining field guns. And in the office, acting as a go-between, the 'junior' inspector was taking on responsibilities of the senior inspectors (with their permission).

Korzybski's bosses depended on him for some of their informal obligations as well. Because of his language facility and his noble bearing, they designated him the "host" when visitors such as foreign military officers came to see the Russian operation. The practice in military circles of the time involved a ritual, with the host and guests trying to drink each other under the table. Korzybski had orders to be a good host and go along. Though not a non-drinker, he cheated:

> I had a special bottle of whiskey which was just plain tea and my man, or orderly if you wish, was keeping my particular tea bottle, means whiskey bottle, filled with tea separately so I would not be caught red-handed… I had to be on my feet and personally I don't like that kind of hell drinking.[5]

There were also a number of international military meetings, during which the French, British and Russians demonstrated their artillery. Although as a civilian it was not Korzybski's role to do so, Sachanow and Goodima had him demonstrate the Russian guns wearing his old "private with a string" uniform. One day Korzybski was informed that the Duke of Connaught, one of Queen Victoria's sons and the Governor General of Canada, would be coming within a few days to tour Petawawa with his daughter Patricia. Korzybski was ordered to take care of a royal parade and demonstration for the Duke at the proving ground. "My god. What did I know about that [?] Nothing. No instructions. Just orders to do it. So I had to take care of my side which means the troops, guns, shooting , etc."[6] Alfred was certainly not overawed at the prospect of seeing the Duke. As a Count, he had been around nobility all of his life and he had encountered royalty. Besides, he had already met the Duke and his daughter on one of his visits to Ottawa and had seen and become friendly with them on subsequent visits. The royal parade came off well and they were ready for the artillery demonstration. Korzybski had been flirting with Patricia and did not notice a photographer who had placed himself directly in front of the muzzle of the field gun. Luckily, before giving the order to fire, Korzybski turned his eyes from the young woman long enough to see the man and get him out of the way. The Duke appeared impressed with Korzybski's efforts and sent him copies of the photographs and an invitation to a garden party in Ottawa.

Artillery demonstration for Duke of Connaught, 1916
(Korzybski seen toward left, behind wheel of field gun)

Gossips, Bugs, and Skunks

Alfred had become aware that some people at the Petawawa Camp considered him in an unfavorable light as an arrogant attention-seeker. He seemed so familiar with the Duke and his daughter, he had so many responsibilities not fitting his job description, he kept so much to himself, etc., etc., etc. The negative opinion about him might be summarized in the statement "Who the hell does that Korzybski think he is?" Alfred did not let it bother him. He knew that he skirted trouble and misunderstanding because of his independent attitude and direct manner. He wasn't going to change just because people might misunderstand his actions and words and then gossip about him or believe other people's gossip.

For example, he felt he had very little in common with most of the Russians, who spent their off-hours drinking. At the camp—when he wasn't working or studying on his own—he tended to socialize with the Canadian and British officers stationed there. (Goodima had his wife and children with him and spent his time at home with them.) When the Canadian officers invited him to join their mess hall, he felt glad to stop eating with the Russians. He liked the food at the Canadian officers' mess better and it didn't cost as much. And he had a chance to practice his English with people he felt he had more in common with than the Russians. He had no interest in insulting anyone. However, not eating with the Russians could easily be viewed by some Russians as an insult. He did not feel inclined to expend much energy trying to correct such impressions:

> In my country, gentlemen speak the truth, do not compromise with themselves, and are simple about it, of course this was misinterpreted, they laughed maybe, I smiled because I understood quite well their misinterpretations, which doubtless added to their irritation, but after all of what importance was it?...what through the narrow, petty and often ignorant lenses of bureaucracy was considered "pose" or "bluff" is known today, as it was before the war as simplicity, frankness, straightforwardness. I hate "diplomacy" which I refuse to emulate, I did so always, and will continue to do. To my mind simplicity and straightforwardness is the biggest luxury a gentleman can indulge in, and so I remain the same. [8]

Besides the gossips, other minor annoyances of life at Petawawa included the bugs and skunks. Korzybski had run-ins with both. Other than the multitudes of mosquitoes, the camp—at the edge of a wilderness area—had many different kinds of insects he had never seen before. Many of them bit. He found them quite bothersome, especially at night on the gun range. Alfred tried repellents that didn't work. So when shooting, he often wore gloves and used a veil under his cap to reduce the bites to his hands and face.

As for the run-ins with skunks, many of these actually consisted of run-overs at night when, once they had finished shooting, Alfred would drive to the target area five miles away with a few of his men. In the dark, his car would typically hit a few skunks along the way. He wasn't happy about hitting them. As he said "They can certainly mess up the air all right." He once came back to his cabin and found a skunk wandering around inside. He just waited until it left. "You don't argue with a skunk."

The bugs, skunks, and other disagreeable aspects of camp life became the subject of the dark humor of Alfred and his friends. One, James A. Robinson, wrote "The Popular Song of Petawawa" which they sang to commiserate among themselves. Korzybski, still learning how to spell in English, dutifully recorded the lyrics for posterity:

OH! PETAWAWA

Oh! Petawawa Oh! Petawawa Oh! Petawawa
Down where the Ottawa flowes,
We will never go there anymore anymore,
We will never go there anymore anymore,
We will never go there anymore anymore,
Down where the Ottawa flowes.

There are skunks in the gras overthere overthere,
There are skunks in the gras overthere overthere,
There are skunks in the gras they piss from their ass
Down where the Ottawa flowes
Oh! Petawawa * * * * We wont go there

There is magets in the cheese overthere overthere,
There is magets in the cheese overthere overthere,
There is magets in the cheese you can hear the beggar snees
There is magets in the cheese overthere.
Oh! Petawawa Oh! Petawawa * * * We will never go there.

There are bugs on the wall overthere overthere,
There are bugs on the wall overthere overthere,
There are bugs on the wall you can see the beggar crawl
There are bugs on the wall overthere.
Oh! Petawawa *************We will never go there.

There lots of skunks overthere overthere,
There is lots skunks overthere overthere,
If you anywhere near they'll piss in your ear
There is lots of skunks overthere.
Oh! Petawawa ********** We'll never go there.[9]

By the end of July 1916, Korzybski had been at Petawawa for more than half a year. He felt gratitude for the kindness of the Canadian officers he had met. Wanting to express his thanks, he decided to throw a grand party for the officers and their ladies aboard the river boat steamer, the "Oiseau". He arranged an elaborate multi-course banquet on board, with a variety of wines for the 40 or 50 couples whom he invited as guests (the Russians whom he had invited seemed too shy to attend). They dined while cruising up the river and back to Petawawa in the course of several evening hours. The guests seemed especially charmed by Korzybski's personal performance. In the szlachta tradition of hosting—which dictated "Gosz v dom, Bog v dom" ("Guest in the house, God in the house")—he moved among his guests, filling glasses, supervising the staff of military waiters from the base, and leading a series of toasts to the King, the Tsar, the Allies and to the health of the war injured. After the ices and fruits and before the coffee, liqueurs, and cheese, Korzybski also made a toast to his guests and to Canada. By this time they had returned to dock at Petawawa once more and danced until after midnight to the orchestra Korzybski had assembled.

Alfred may have considered the bill the most exciting part of the event. Renting the steamer cost him only $40 (he had expected to pay 3 or 4 times as much). He paid only around $100 for the food and drink, and nothing for the cooks, the waiters, or the orchestra. He didn't ask questions.[10] People talked about the evening for months afterwards. A local newspaper account of the evening noted:

Every lady carried away a beautiful Nippon dish as a souvenir of the trip. The gentlemen each received, as a remembrance, an ash tray cut from a shrapnel shell, and engraved, prophetically "World War, 1914-1917."[11]

Incident at a Train Station

By January 1917, the 'prophecy' Korzybski had engraved on the ash tray seemed as fanciful as fairy-dust. The war, in its third year, seemed to have no end in sight. Both fronts in Europe saw little overall movement of the entrenched sides.[12] Inside Russia there were lines for bread and signs of open revolt. Devastated Poland now had German overlords. The grim situation did nothing to change Alfred's conviction that he had chosen the right side to fight for. It had become clear—even to Poles who had fought on the German or Austrian side—a victory for the Central Powers would mean the end of any hope for Polish independence.

The Russian Imperial Artillery Commission completed its work at Petawawa in the first week of February. Alfred never knew exactly why. Probably, the contract with Canadian Car and Foundry had ended. At any rate, he no longer had a job at the proving ground. The Artillery Commission retained him a bit longer in order to supervise the packing and loading of the field guns and remaining ammunition onto railway cars. After he shipped them out of Petawawa, he packed up his own belongings and went to Ottawa, where he was staying with a friend. He had sent the ammunition—including high explosive shells and gun powder—to the Eddystone Ammunition Company in Pennsylvania. The Russian guns, loaded in two open cars, went to Ogdensberg, New York, where Alfred met them and arranged for the next step of their transport to Weehauken, New Jersey, for transfer to the Aberdeen Proving Ground in Maryland. By the end of the month, he had handed over the guns to the representative from Aberdeen, and returned to Ottawa.

He no longer worked for the Russian Artillery Commission. Over the previous year he had written letters trying to find the location of the Body Guard Heavy Artillery, still holding some possibility of joining them. But he heard nothing. He didn't know what he would do next.

During this period, an incident happened one night at the Ottawa train station. Korzybski, probably on his way to Ogdensberg to deal with the Russian guns, happened to meet two Canadian officers, Lieutenant Consitt and Captain Bothwell, whom he knew from Petawawa. They were in the company of a Captain Maloney, whom they introduced to Korzybski. What happened is not exactly clear but the following day, Korzybski sent a letter to Lieutenant Consitt.:

Dear Sir,
Wednesday 14th February at 11-45 pm. at the central station in Ottawa I made through you and Captain Bothwell the acquaintance of an officer whose name I do not remember. The conduct of the said officer toward me was perfectly insolent, as you are the witness. Not wishing to make trouble in a public place, I kept still for the few minutes to the train, but was decided to ask satisfaction. Therefore I invite very kindly you and Capt. Bothwell to be my seconds, this is friends, and challenge the said officer in my name to fight a duel. I accept all conditions fixed by you and Capt. B. Sword or pistol are without difference to me, for pistol I suggest 10-15 yards. Believing Sir, that my invitation you will honor me by accepting my invitation, I remain very truly yours. Formerly of the Imperial Body Guard Heavy Artillery, now officer of R. I. Art. Com. In N. Am. 15 February 1917.[13]

Over the next week a flurry of letters ensued. Bothwell and Consitt met with Maloney. They all wanted to avoid a duel and Maloney wrote a letter of apology. Alfred wrote back as soon as he received it, "Dear Friend. ...I am glad to learn that you did not intentionally hurt my feelings. Therefore I am pleased to accept your apology and also hope to meet you again under more favorable circumstances. ..."[14] Later in life, he sometimes received petty, unwarranted, even insulting criticism—which he sometimes responded to. However, after this episode, as far as I know, he never challenged anyone to a duel again.

Chapter 11
1917

Alfred spent March and most of April of 1917 in Ottawa. While he was there, important news came from Russia. Early in March (still February according to the Julian calendar then used in Russia), workers had gone on strike in Petrograd to protest a lack of bread and other essentials. With the military garrison in Petrograd deciding to support the workers, the popular uprising centered in Petrograd became a revolution that spread to Moscow and other parts of Russia. Within a little more than a week, the Tsar had abdicated. A new provisional government was formed with a core of constitutional liberals from the Duma (Russian Parliament). This weak government shared authority with the Petrograd Soviet (Workers Council), made up of various socialist factions. What would this mean for the Russian war effort, as costly and ineffective as it had become? What would it mean for Poland? Alfred didn't know. He had never considered himself a Russian but he did have Russian citizenship and a Russian passport. And for the time being, Russia still fought on the allied side. So for the sake of Poland, he still hoped to be able to somehow work for the Russians in order to defeat Germany.

In the meantime he was occupied with a number of inventions he had been working on and which he hoped might eventually provide some income. These included a rain protector for clothing (which appears never to have gotten beyond the initial drawing stage), a repair kit for broken iron wagon-wheels, and a mechanical potato digger/sorter. He had been developing the latter two for some time. Alfred made detailed mechanical drawings, technical descriptions, and promotional material. He also researched and wrote to several hundred manufacturers in Canada and the U.S., trying to get someone interested in the devices. Despite this intensive campaign, he had no takers. He also found an attorney in Ottawa who helped him to apply for U.S. patents. Later, once he had left Ottawa, his extensive travel and incessant activity over the next few years diverted him from doing much with the "wheel red cross"[1] or the potato digger. It appears he never got the patents.

On April 6, the United States entered the war against Germany. President Wilson had terrific reluctance about the U.S. becoming one of the combatants. Nonetheless, the German government had attempted to get Mexico to go to war against the U.S. (the infamous Zimmerman Telegram). It had also declared that it would begin unrestricted submarine attacks against all shipping in French and British waters. This would imperil U.S. citizens and U.S. trade with France and Great Britain. With U.S. ships already being sunk and U.S. citizens killed, Wilson could no longer resist the overwhelming American support for entering on the side of the Allies. Alfred, still in Ottawa, had already been thinking about how to protect allied ships from torpedoes.

One device consisted of a moveable-chain net, loaded with small bombs in the interstices. The net would be suspended from a mast and could be positioned by means of a rail to cover all or part of the ship anywhere along its circumference. The net could be lowered quickly whenever a submarine or torpedo was spotted. Either an electrical charge or the impact from a torpedo would set off the bombs which would in turn explode the torpedo before it reached the ship. The position of the net would be calculated to be far enough away from the ship to prevent the explosions from damaging the hull. He also suggested using protective net bags around ships, and on-board machine gun crews using high explosive shells for exploding oncoming torpedoes. Korzybski offered these suggestions, with drawings, gratis to the Canadian Naval Attaché in Ottawa and, later that summer, to the British Naval Attaché in New York. He corresponded and met with both men, who had numerous objections but still appreciated his inventiveness and desire to help.

Alfred had never held a professional job as an engineer. Yet his inventions demonstrated his orientation towards science as a "form of action"[2] to be applied to practical concerns. Since absorbing this engineering attitude from his father as a young child, he seemed naturally inclined to apply what he knew to matter-of-fact problems of living, e.g., wheels to repair, potatoes to be dug, ships to protect from torpedoes.

Alfred's engineering bent definitely leaned towards mechanical devices. Over the next few years, he made other inventions but once he started writing, his creative energies got focused there. Nonetheless, he continued to make things with his hands and fiddle with mechanical and electrical tools for the rest of his life. His hands-on experiences with designing and making things taught him that a workable solution might require much trial, effort, ingenuity, and revision. However, the science and mathematics behind it might remain relatively simple. His engineering mentality probably also contributed to his appreciation for the beauty of simple artifacts displaying an economy of form with a maximum of function—like the crafted ebony wooden boxes and other objects he liked to keep on his desk at one time or another.

On the Waterfront

It seemed clear; nothing much was going to happen with his inventions anytime soon. Korzybski left Ottawa near the beginning of May 1917 and moved to New York City, where he had friends. He also had some remaining connections with the Russian—no longer Imperial—Artillery Commission. He was asked to work as their chief inspector at the Brooklyn waterfront where they were having serious difficulties loading ammunition shipments destined for Russia. All the men previously assigned to the job had quit after one or two weeks. Alfred agreed to do it.

Some ships were getting loaded from smaller freighters. Korzybski, given a little motor boat he could use to putt-putt around the harbor, went to talk to the junior supervisors overseeing the work on one of the ships. He asked how things were going. Terrible—they told him—the longshoremen were disobeying them and, as a result, dangerously mishandling volatile ammunition. Korzybski watched the work being done for about twenty minutes and confirmed what the inspectors had said. Then he went to speak to the dockworkers' foreman, whom Korzybski described as "a New York Harbor roughneck".[3] Korzybski told him that his men would have to start listening to the Russian inspectors who wanted to make sure the ammunition got loaded in a safe manner. The foreman brushed him off. Realizing he would get nowhere with the man, Korzybski proceeded to the office of the ship's Captain.

The Captain accepted his credentials and greeted him warmly. When he heard Korzybski's concerns, he said that loading the ammunition on the ship was not his business but a matter between the Russian government and the private company the longshoremen worked for. "Then I asked the Captain just a simple question: 'Captain, do you wish to be blown up?'" Korzybski had gotten his attention:

> "What do you mean? What do you mean by 'blown up'?"
> I made a gesture of the ship being blown up going into the air and I told him, "By 'blown up' I mean blown up." Then I showed my hands going into the air, "A big puff and it's all over. That's all I mean by blowing up."
> "Oh, for pity's sake."
> I told him I was never more serious in my life.
> He got alarmed...quite alarmed. ...Then he asked me, "What to do?"[4]

Korzybski quickly devised a plan. The work depended on steam. The longshoremen used steam-powered machinery to do their loading. If the steam stopped, the workmen would not be able to earn their money. And the Captain controlled the supply of steam. The Captain would have someone wait for a signal from Alfred, who would—if necessary—wave his handkerchief to indicate he wanted the steam turned off. And the Captain would then order the steam off. Alfred returned to speak to the foreman and quietly repeated his request. The foreman told him to go to hell.

> I said nothing. I just took my hankie and waved. Suddenly, of course, the steam stopped. Means the whole loading stopped. [The foreman] and all the workers said, "What happened? What happened?" Then I [said]—I won't repeat...what I said. I used good military language then because I had him by the neck. "You so and so and so"—it was a long list. I was quite expert at it. I had learned from the Canadian and British soldiers. "Will you obey, you so and so?" Well, he was terrified by that expediency of stopping the steam. Not my so and so stuff. So immediately the whole thing changed. It means the man began to obey orders of my men...When the ships were loaded, they went... and when the ships were changed I had to flirt that way with [each] captain, [i.e.,] make that arrangement that when I wave my handkerchief the loading stops. That's all and then I [took] care of the rest. So the whole thing was organized. It went beautifully... I reported to my general[s], how I solved it. To them it was a miracle. Somehow it solved the problem. This was inherited by my successors. They were told how to solve the situation. It solved the problem completely.[5]

After a few months, Alfred was also out of a job. In the meantime, he had some money to tide him over. He had found an apartment in Manhattan on 21st Street, where he had moved after first living in Brooklyn, and then coming to the city to stay with his friend Sobanski on 15th Street. Alfred had few possessions beside some items of clothing. He had brought only a few things with him from Poland. These included some pictures from home, some uniforms, his cavalry saber and spurs, and his credentials and letters of recommendation related to his various positions on the Eastern Front. He also had a small but growing collection of books, music scores, and document files—including letters, recommendations, newspaper clippings, calendars, memos, bills, etc.—he'd gathered since he came to North America. He typed almost all his letters and made carbon-copies of nearly every one he wrote, saving them along with the letters he received. He had found it useful to have a record of what he had done and of his communications with others. In subsequent years the files and books would accumulate. Undoubtedly, storing them presented difficulties at times but he had systematic habits and was able to keep things more or less organized.

For Want of a Horseshoe

September had come. Given the uncertainties of the Russian government and its war effort, he felt relief that the U.S. had entered the war and that the U.S. Army was in the process of mobilizing men and resources to join its allies in Europe. Despite the horrors he had witnessed on the Eastern Front, despite the terrible waste of life in the bloody maw of the Great War, he was neither a pacifist nor neutral. He considered the future of Poland and Polish culture, among other things, at stake. He had already paid his dues with his war service but he wanted—needed—to do more. In July he had tried to enlist at the British Recruitment Center in New York but had not passed the physical.[6] Now, he saw a newspaper notice: "MEN wanted (50), bet. 25 and 40 yrs. for Intelligence Corps, National Army; must speak French fluently; former investigating experience desirable; good pay and allowances. Call or write, Army Recruiting Station, 280 Broadway, New York."[7] Alfred saw an opportunity to help. He immediately sent a letter to the recruiting office. After describing his background, language skills, and prior war service, he requested a job.

…I am not able to fight on account of an accident with a horse and Wounds, so I am perfectly free to accept work. Misfortunately it must be in the rear. As is shown in my documents, I am discharged from the Russian service and have the right to apply to the armies of the Allies. I can be useful as interpreter at the front, or as censor, having practice and knowing well what news can be useful to the enemy. I know that for positions that are not directly in the firing line the vacancies are always taken in advance, but I suppose that a man who has offered all he had to the war and is not able for front service and can be very useful having knowledge capacities and experience may have the right to apply for a position. …I remain Sir your obedient servant[8]

In a few days he got a reply from the Chief of the Military Intelligence section of the War Department in Washington D.C., where his letter had been forwarded. The Lieutenant Colonel respectfully turned down his offer. They already had more applicants than they needed.[9]

Alfred continued looking for employment. Finally, he landed another job with the Russian government. Horses had continued to provide one of the main forms of military transport (an estimated eight million horses died by the end of the war) and the Russians needed horseshoes in large numbers. The Russian Supply Commission in America contracted in July with The U.S. Horseshoe Company to obtain at least several thousand of them. Now, there were problems with getting the job completed and the Supply Commission needed someone to deal with the company. Korzybski was appointed as Chief Inspector and went to Erie, Pennsylvania sometime in October or the first few days of November. He knew almost nothing about manufacturing horseshoes.[10]

After meeting L. E. McElroy, the President of the company, he spent his first few days there simply walking around the factory and observing the operation. The company had lost many of its older and most qualified workers through the military draft. It had also been hit with a number of strikes. He could see significant disarray in the operation. For one thing, workers seemed to have no system for separating good horseshoes from rejects. They mixed piles of both on the shop floor, which meant good shoes could get thrown away as scrap while bad shoes got packed.

Once he started inspecting lots of completed shoes, he found more problems. The shoes were already packed in barrels before he was able to inspect them. So he had to unpack them by hand—a dirty, time-intensive job. The condition of the packing room and the inspection room he used appeared chaotic. He found a large percentage of the shoes he unpacked of sub-standard quality. He had to send them back. Completion of the order was getting further delayed. The company would not be able to finish the job by the agreed-upon deadline in November. Initially there may have been some tension between him and McElroy, who had to request a time extension from the Russian commission. However, McElroy soon realized that Alfred was simply concerned about the quality of the product and would do whatever it took to help the company get the job done properly.

Alfred had discovered some other production problems at the plant. Some parts of the shoes were too thin, which he attributed to the metal getting cut poorly. In addition, many nail holes appeared poorly placed in the smaller shoes. The holes, made with a punch machine, needed to be placed centrally, away from the edge of the metal, to keep a shoe from breaking. This was not getting done consistently. It may have seemed like a little thing, but he took the placement of the holes quite seriously, since he knew the consequences of a horse breaking its shoe and getting hobbled on the battlefront.[11] He also saw a problem with the shoes getting packed in old fertilizer bags before being put in the barrels. The acids from the unwashed bags could corrode the metal of the shoes.

Korzybski made specific suggestions to McElroy for each of the problems he uncovered. To assist with quality control, Korzybski invented an automatic horseshoe holder/counter made of a simple, round iron base and a screwed-in wire handle. The base and handle were constructed for the circumference and thickness of various sizes of shoes, so a production worker could fit, say, 100 shoes of one particular type onto an appropriately-sized counter. The counter was labeled with the name of the worker and carried into the packing area, where the shoes could be easily inspected and recounted as necessary before packing.

By early December, the Russian contract had been completed. Because of railroad delays, all of the horseshoes couldn't be sent to New York at once. Alfred stayed a little longer to arrange the shipments. When he left Erie, he had been at United States Horse Shoe for two months and had helped reorganize the entire operation of the factory. Both the Russians and McElroy were happy and wrote him glowing recommendation letters. In addition, McElroy had become intrigued with Alfred's iron-tire repair kit and agreed to build a prototype. If they could get some outside concerns interested in it, he even seemed willing to become the manufacturer. Despite his support, nobody else seemed much interested. McElroy corresponded with Korzybski into the following year but by early 1918, Korzybski had little time or energy to invest in marketing the device. He was involved in other things.

Chapter 12
"BUY LIBERTY BONDS AND WORK LIKE HELL."

While Alfred was in Erie making horseshoes, the Bolsheviks under V. I. Lenin had staged a coup against the provisional government of Russia—the "October Revolution" (which by our calendar took place on November 7, 1917). Lenin and his colleagues (Trotsky, Stalin, et al) and followers knew what they wanted— power—and acted ruthlessly to get it. They used the disenchantment with the war and the economy to get enough support among soldiers, sailors, and workers to make a relatively bloodless takeover. Lenin immediately announced his desire for an armistice with Kaiser Wilhelm's Germany, which was declared by December. Although the Bolsheviks and Germans didn't sign a peace treaty until March 1918, the war on the Eastern Front was effectively over.

The Russian Supply Commission was to be dissolved. Korzybski received orders to return to Russia. Alfred, still a Russian citizen, had no love for the Bolsheviks and no longer felt any obligation to Russia. Neither did he want to get involved in the social chaos there. He refused to go. Anyway, as a Pole he would not have been able to actually return home to Warsaw or Rudnik. Poland was still in German hands, and having fought against them, Korzybski might still have been considered an enemy. The Germans were shifting the majority of their forces to the Western front and the Americans were beginning to send troops to fortify their French and British allies there. The greatest chance for an independent Poland now was to directly help the remaining allied forces to defeat Germany.

"You Told Me to Make You Mad."

After his time in Erie, Alfred returned to New York City. It was January 1918. He had maintained contact with the Polish émigré community in New York and continued to follow the news related to Poland. The previous year had been a hopeful one for Polish revival. Concert pianist Ignacy Jan Paderewski, an associate of the right-wing Polish nationalist Roman Dmowski, had been in the United States since 1915 to raise money for war relief and to get support for Polish independence. By 1917 he had managed to get the ear of Colonel House, close advisor to President Woodrow Wilson. Wilson had sympathy for the nascent national movements forming out of the dissolving Russian and Austro-Hungarian Empires. In his "Fourteen Points" Speech to Congress on January 8, he laid out his idealistic vision for a non-vengeful peace agreement after allied victory. The 13th point announced the goal of establishing an independent Poland with access to the sea.

While this was going on, Polish nationalists in Europe had not been idle. In 1917, Dmowski's Polish National Committee had gained acceptance by the French as the main representative of Poles in the West. This group had formed a Polish army under French command, and now at the start of 1918 was looking to America for recruits. With some one million Polish immigrants in North America, mostly in the U.S., and about three million more next-generation Polish-Americans, there was a significant pool of men who might want to fight for the allied cause under a French-Polish banner. A French-Polish Military Commission, with headquarters in New York City, was formed.

Alfred had already read in the newspaper about the Polish novelist Waclaw Gasiorowski—who had become a captain in the French-Polish army—coming to the United States in late 1917 in order to encourage Poles to enlist. By February, Korzybski had managed to get a job with the French-Polish Military Commission as Gasiorowski's man Friday. The writer was making a whirlwind lecture tour through the northeast and mid-west states before returning to Europe.[1]

Since Gasiorowski didn't speak English, Alfred's main job was to serve as his translator and take care of the logistical aspects of the tour, i.e., scheduling, train tickets, dealing with local committees, etc. Alfred found him a "very fine man" although a rather "explosive prima donna". As he explained:

> I had orders that [Gasiorowski is] at his best as a lecturer when he gets mad, and I had orders to make him mad under any excuse before a lecture, so that he could deliver a good lecture. You know "orders is orders" and, of course, I didn't mind doing that. It was part of the job. How I managed to make him mad offhand I don't remember. I remember only one instance...We were supposed to move immediately after the lecture, so I was ordered to get Pullman reservations, we always traveled in a compartment together so of course I got the tickets. No doubt about that. I exhausted my repertoire of making him mad. I didn't know any more tricks to do...So before the lecture he asked me, "Korzybski, did you order the tickets?" I say "What tickets?" Oh, he was exploding,..."Pullman tickets!" I said, "Why should I?" [Gasiorowski:] "I ordered them." [Korzybski:] "What do I care." He got perfectly boiling mad and actually delivered a very good lecture. In conversation after the meeting, we had to go immediately to the station... He was already exhausted after lecturing two hours in a very strong tension. He asked me very peacefully, "Now, Korzybski, really and truthfully, do you have those tickets? Yes or not?" I said, "Why, of course, I have." [Gasiorowski:] "Why in hell did you tell me that you don't? [Korzybski:] Because, Captain, you told me to make you mad."[2]

"Poland Is Not a Piano."

His work with Gasiorowski completed, Korzybski decided to enlist in the French-Polish Army. Despite his tremendous energy, he was not considered fit for service at the front. In April, he received a blue uniform (the French colors), the title of Captain (although he was technically a civilian), and an assignment to head the recruiting office in Toronto.[3]

The North American training camp for "The Polish Army in France" was located in Niagara-on-theLake, Ontario. The pool of potential recruits consisted of Polish immigrants who were not Canadian or U.S. citizens or who had not already declared their intent to become citizens. As resident aliens, they were not subject to serve in either the Canadian or U.S. Armies and were permitted to sign up with the Polish-French force. Recruiting in Canada had been poor and it was hoped Korzybski might be able to produce some results.

In Toronto, Korzybski had a small staff and a limited budget from which he had to pay salaries, travel expenses, etc. When he wasn't in the office, he traveled throughout the city and province, speaking to church groups, union meetings, etc., where Polish immigrants gathered. Since Ontario had no Polish language newspapers, he also made contacts with the English language papers, writing press releases and generally trying to keep recruiting office activities in the public eye. It didn't take him long to realize the main recruiting obstacle among Poles in Canada.

Many of the immigrant Poles only felt willing to fight—and perhaps to die—in France if they knew the Polish Army existed there as an autonomous entity equal to its French and British allies. This was not the case. After almost a year of existence, the Polish Army in France by May 1918 still functioned as a unit of the French Army. This situation seemed as unacceptable to Korzybski as it did to the Poles he was supposed to recruit. They felt that the French and British were simply exploiting Polish national sentiments for their own purposes—so Poles could serve as cannon-fodder for them. How could Alfred recruit other Poles when he himself had little confidence that the allies had any interest in the ultimate independence of Poland? Rightly or wrongly, he believed that Paderewski, et al, in setting up the basic terms with the allies, had—for personal aggrandizement— agreed "to sell Polish Blood to the French."[4] "The Polish were pretty radical, and they simply knew that the Paderewski army was lousy in principle. They knew it and I knew it. I went into the army to make it not rotten."[5] What to do?

Korzybski felt if he could get Polish community leaders on his side he would have a better chance of getting the rank and file to enlist. In early May he met with Polish leaders in Toronto. He stood in front of the group in his blue officer's uniform and spoke about the war, the necessity of defeating the Germans, etc. Afterwards one of the men asked a question: "Officer, you look like a decent man. How [do] you happen to be in that rotten army?" Korzybski replied:

> As you understand, men, I am in uniform, so I am a little bit tied up to be too frank in statements. So I cannot admit that the army is rotten. I cannot speak about that, but for argument's sake, let's assume—I don't admit it, I just assume it—that the army is rotten. What shall you do? Enlist and make it good.[6]

On May 12, Korzybski presided over a meeting in Toronto at Massey Hall to celebrate the anniversary of the Polish Constitution of May 3, 1791, and to raise funds and get recruits for the Polish Army in France. 800 to 1000 people attended the gathering. Alfred presided over the program, which featured a band and a variety of speakers for the Polish cause. Toronto newspapers reported the event:

> Captain Korzybski opened the meeting with a vigorous speech in the Polish language. He spoke as a man who had a message to deliver and was aflame with the urgency of it. A man of soldierly bearing and intense enthusiasm; the Captain busied himself about the platform as if he was in the midst of a campaign when every minute counted.[7]
>
> He referred to the days when there was a Poland free as the [old] days when the hand of the Hohenzollern was unknown, when the elector, Frederick the Great, was an unknown quality, and the legislature of the then famous kingdom of the Sobieskis was as constitutional as any in the world.[8]

By implication, Alfred also acknowledged the negative attitude of many people in the crowd towards the Polish-French Army when he repeated to them, "[E]nlist and make the army good."[9] Afterwards, he guessed that his honesty here and in the prior meeting with Toronto's Polish community leadership had some effect on the success of the meeting, which resulted, according to one news account, in two dozen recruits and $800 in contributions for military hospital equipment. But he also didn't feel entirely surprised when, within a short time, he was recalled from his Toronto post. He later learned British and French authorities had gotten word of his speeches, felt threatened by his honesty, and had exerted some force to have him removed.[10]

He returned to New York City at the end of May. His chiefs at the Polish Military Commission actually approved of his plain speaking and warmly embraced him. They immediately reassigned him to their office in Pittsburgh, Pennsylvania, to become head of recruiting for Ohio, Pennsylvania, and West Virginia. Again, with a miniscule budget and small office staff, he began a round of traveling and speaking, as well as managing the office and dealing with the day-to-day business of recruiting.

Since there were clear stipulations that only non-U.S. citizens could apply for the Polish Army in France, Korzybski had to write letters to various Selective Service Boards for men who didn't know English. He also had to deal with the problem of enlistees who had deserted from the Polish Army training camp in Ontario. Although he preferred signing up single men with no dependents, some men who enlisted had wives and children or other dependent family. He helped those who needed it to arrange their financial affairs for loved ones in case they didn't return. He also became involved in fund-raising efforts to support the families of men who would not return. Grim business.

In hindsight, it may be difficult to remember that as the summer of 1918 arrived, the outcome of the war did not seem at all certain. The Germans had launched a major offensive in the spring, which brought them less than 100 miles from Paris. Although their troops were exhausted and their advance was petering out, they were far from defeated. Perhaps out of a sense of desperation, by mid-June the Allies finally decided to recognize the Polish Army as a separate entity. Alfred must have felt some satisfaction when he read the news about the ceremony in France, at which Polish troops under Polish command received a Polish Flag from French authorities, and gave their vow of loyalty to Poland.[11]

Still Alfred remained suspicious of Paderewski and the Polish nationalists he represented. Probably just after the war, during a talk he gave in Washington to some U.S. military officers who wanted to learn about his work with Russian Army military intelligence, conditions in Russia and Poland, etc., one of the officers asked him, "Is there a possibility that Paderewski will become a Polish king?" Korzybski bristled, "Your Excellency, please remember Poland is not a piano."[12]

Despite Korzybski's success as a recruiter, this attitude did not endear him to the top leadership of the Polish Army, even though his immediate superiors in New York City approved of his performance. At the end of July he was dismissed from his position in Pittsburgh and called back to New York City where he stayed with his friend Sobanski. He was out of the Polish-French Army. The letter of recommendation he received said, "We have found [Korzybski] to have fulfilled his duties with knowledge and zeal to our full satisfaction. He is leaving on his own accord in order to restore his health."[13] In truth, he *had* been driving himself hard and did feel the need for some rest.

Not only had he done his best as a military recruiter, but he had made some good friends during his stays in Toronto and Pittsburgh—people like the landscape painter and muralist Leon Dabo. Still in the U.S. Army, Dabo had been to France and had spoken at a rally in Pittsburgh where Alfred also spoke. Korzybski would continue corresponding with Dabo for a number of years. Alfred also became friendly with Pittsburgh civic and business leaders like Judge Joseph Buffington and Taylor Allderdice. Alfred made friends with some of the unrenowned folk of Toronto and Pittsburgh as well. Wherever he went, he could make himself at home with both 'commoners' and 'kings'.

Alfred had some time to think about what he wanted to do next and also when the war ended. The Germans' advance of the last few months was being reversed. They were retreating from Allied forces. Recently-arrived American troops had joined in the counterattack. In a letter to Allderdice dated July 28, Korzybski wrote that,

> The news from the front are truly astonishing, how your boys in such a short time are able to do such a good work, and I think I will not be very mistaken if I say that next spring will see the Allies fighting on the German soil, and finishing this war by taking Berlin.[14]

Likely thinking about job opportunities, Alfred realized he still might want to work in something related to engineering. As already noted, his interests lay more with mechanical engineering and inventions. On stationary and job applications, he took to labeling himself as "Alfred Korzybski, M.E. [Mechanical Engineer]".

Still, for some time his main focus of interest had been more on human behavior than mechanical devices. His lifelong observing of people, and wondering about what makes them tick, were now supplemented by his wartime experiences. He had pondered a great deal about the sources of the various messes he had witnessed on the Eastern Front, Petawawa, and elsewhere. As in his pre-war ruminations about the state of the sciences, he had become more and more conscious of the ineffectiveness—indeed hopelessness—of so many people's ways of thinking-reacting.

Korzybski wrote to his friend Sloane Gordon, an American journalist he had met while still in Poland. Gordon, back in the U.S., worked for the Wheeler Newspaper Syndicate. Alfred requested any advice or leads Gordon might have about jobs that could make use of his knowledge of human behavior. He felt an intelligence or propaganda job would still allow him to contribute to Allied victory.

> I feel you are the right man to put me on the right road. As you know I have two specialties, Law and Mechanical Engineering, but to say the truth I like better to utilize my knowledge of Psychology and Languages rather than Engineering, and feel sure that these capacities are most needed nowadays. ...Psychology is a very important factor to win this war in the cheapest way and this is why I think this would be the most efficient way to serve the common cause. ...[15]

"Buy Liberty Bonds and Work Like Hell."

On June 4, while still at his Pittsburgh recruiting job, Korzybski had spoken at an event sponsored by the U.S. Fuel Administration (U.S.F.A.). The following day an article headlined, "Soldiers Make Pleas To Miners for Coal" in the *Pittsburgh Gazette Times* began:

> Appealing to 2,000 miners employed at the Jamison Coal Company to do at least a part as much over here as the boys are doing "over there," and asking for steady, hard work as a matter of patriotism and national necessity, three former soldiers of the Allies [Korzybski, his colleague Klimecki from the Pittsburgh office, and Canadian Army Sergeant Major J. Armstrong Young], accompanied by Joseph T. Miller, assistant fuel administrator for the Pittsburgh district, addressed a meeting in Hannahstown, Westmorland county, last night.[16]

Alfred's speaking impressed Miller, who recommended him to the main Fuel Administration office.[17] Two months later Alfred received a telegram from the U.S.F.A. offering him a job. He accepted and began a flurry of activity that would run him ragged for the next four months.

The United States Fuel Administration was one of a number of emergency governmental agencies founded on the order of President Woodrow Wilson to bring various aspects of the U.S. economy under federal control during World War I.[18] Founded in 1917, the U.S. Fuel Administration had a mandate to regulate the "production, distribution, and consumption of coal, coke, natural gas and fuel products of petroleum."[19] Korzybski was brought into the agency's Bureau of Production as a traveling speaker, to go into coal-mining areas of the country and get audiences in general, and miners in particular, to do what they could to support the war effort. In other words, as Alfred put it, to "Buy Liberty Bonds and work like hell."[20]

One of his first items of business was to obtain a uniform. His bosses felt—and he agreed— that he needed to wear one in order to increase his clout as a Fuel Administration speaker. A request was sent to the Polish-French Army to get permission for Alfred to continue to wear the blue uniform he had worn as a recruiter. But he had become persona non grata at Polish Army headquarters in New York; the request was refused. Next stop was the Russians. Alfred realized that many people listening to him would probably not be able to distinguish a Pole from a Russian. He agreed to John Willis, head of the U.S.F.A. Speaker's Bureau, sending a request to the Russian embassy in Washington. The Military Attaché, Colonel Nikolaieff, gave immediate permission for Alfred to wear a Russian uniform. Alfred may have worn it for as long as a month. However, at this stage he felt no loyalty to the Russian Bolshevik government and didn't want any credit to go to it. So he sought another option.

Some Russian Poles, who had decided to continue fighting for the Allies after the Bolsheviks' treaty with Germany, had formed another Polish army and sought to join hands with the Polish-French forces. They had designed their own uniform. This group, the Polish Chief Military Commission in Russia (Polish Army in Russia), sent their man Lieutenant Tadeusz Yurkowski to the United States to work out some kind of arrangement with Polish Army representatives there. According to Korzybski, the Paderewski contingent initially got Yurkowski a salary and then gradually began to isolate him. He ended up in Chicago unable to do anything for his organization and in the meantime working as a clerk in the office of a Polish parish priest. However, by mid-October, Alfred got permission from him to wear the "Polish Army in Russia" uniform. Indeed Yurkowski gave his own uniform to Alfred. It fit him and he became "Lieutenant Korzybski". So Alfred carried on until the end of the war lecturing in a Polish uniform—the Polish-French Army 'be damned!'[21]

Korzybski's first assignment in August involved attending some meetings in the anthracite-coal producing region of northeastern Pennsylvania. Then he headed down to Washington, D.C. for an orientation with the man who had hired him, John Willis, the head of speakers at the U.S.F.A. Production Bureau. (Willis would be replaced by W.E.E. Koepler in the beginning of September.) A week later, Alfred got on a train bound for Bluefield, West Virginia where he arrived the following day. For the next month and a half, he toured the coal-mining towns of West Virginia and Maryland: Weyenoke, Vivian, Bear Wallow, Eckman, Kyle, Matoaka, Mayberry, Landgraff, Berwind, Cumberland, Mt. Savage, etc. He spoke at churches, Liberty Bond rallies, miners' meetings, etc. Occasionally he would speak in as many as three places in a day. His itinerary was planned by the regional representatives of the U.S.F.A., which had offices in the main towns.

He usually stayed at someone's home—for example, a mine owner, a labor inspector, or the local U.S.F.A. official. This gave him a little bit of time to relax and to make new friends, which he seemed to do easily. In Cumberland, Maryland his hosts, the Neuhoffs, had some "interesting evenings" with him. They enjoyed his singing of composer Walter Damrosch's version of Rudyard Kipling's poem "Danny Deever" following along with a phonograph record of the song (he would buy the sheet music later).[22] This may have provided his introduction to Kipling, who clearly knew something about the tough life of soldiers. Alfred became a fan of his work.

Korzybski's coal-country audiences were mixed and included native English speakers as well as immigrants, blacks and whites, poorly educated workers as well as members of the middle and upper classes. Initially he had tried to give his speeches in as many of the different languages of his audiences that he knew—Polish, Italian, Russian, etc., as well as English.[23] After doing this a few times, he found that rapidly switching between multiple languages gave him a severe headache and so he tried to limit himself, for the most part, to giving his talks in English. He prided himself on speaking plainly and simply with an attitude reminiscent of his days on the farm in Poland:

> I was a good lecturer…never appealing to passion or patriotism. This was one of the very important points of my whole work. My lecture was matter of fact, …and if you describe the facts as facts, you don't need to put any kind of bluff. So I gave them the technicalities of winning the war. If we don't supply the front with enough ammunition, which means work at home, we will not win. If we do not enrich the coffer of the United States Government then we will again not win the war.[24]

He filed reports of every meeting. The reports included comments by whomever was presiding at the meeting, as well as Korzybski's notes. Reverend John Dowling made the following remarks about a speech by Korzybski for the workers of the Union Mines and their families in Mt. Savage, Maryland, on September 28, 1918. Dowling's glowing praise was typical of the responses Korzybski received:

> The audience which was composed of [500-800] men, women and children listened most attentively to the very clear and force[ful] remarks of the gentleman — He gave us a very striking picture of all the activities of the different branches of the army. His appeal to the miners to produce more and cleaner coal was most effective. The results of the meeting cannot help but be very good. [signed] John H. Dowling

Alfred himself noted, "The audience was pleased."[25] A local newspaper report provided more details on this joint Liberty Loan and Fuel Administration meeting:

> The electric wiring was not quite finished…it looked as though the only light on the stage would come from the two illuminated box signs which flanked it on either side, but which gave only enough light for one to read the messages on them consigning the Kaiser and his kind to everlasting perdition.
>
> An S.O.S. was sent out and an obliging miner in the crowd went after his carbide lamp, which in the hands of a man in the front row made a first rate "spot." No light could have been more appropriate for the occasion. Mr. Alfred Korzybski, M.E., who was introduced to the gathering of about five hundred people by Father Dowling, talked coal, coal, coal. He said, in part: "I do not need to speak of Victory, for victory is certain. But, what sort of a victory are you going to have? That is up to you. Let me put it in this way. Supposing ten sons of these men in the front row have gone to war. How many do you wish to come back: Nine, or five? It depends on how many shells and how many guns and how many bombs and how many hand grenades those boys have to fight with. Now all these things depend on coal, first in their manufacture, and second in their transportation. Consider for a moment the case of T.N.T. As you all know it is the chief of the high explosives used in this war. As many of you may not know, it is practically the only high explosive

used today by the allies; and it is a by-product of coal. From one ton of coal you get but five pounds of T.N.T. and when you remember that all high explosive shells are filled with it, that the bombs dropped from the aeroplanes are filled with it, and that the hand grenades are filled with it, you will get some idea of the amount of coal that is needed to supply the one important item alone."

Speaking in regard to the Liberty Loan, Mr. Korzybski said: "One opportunity which you miners have, which we in the trenches do not have, is the chance to strike at the enemy twice at the same time, once when you produce the coal, when every blow with the pick is a blow at the Kaiser, and again when you take your wages, or a part of them, and invest them in Liberty Bonds. And don't forget in doing both of these things while you are responding to the call of patriotism, you are doing the best things you can do for yourselves. You are making the world a safe place for your women and children, and you are laying aside something, which you might otherwise have spent, and that is a long stride on the road of financial independence. And above all things don't get the idea that you might be doing more for your country in the army than you are doing in the mines. Uncle Sam wants you to stay on your jobs. Victory, as I said before, is certain. Give us the coal and ammunition and we will do the rest."

Preceding the meeting at Mt. Savage, which was arranged by Mr. James Aldou, Mr. Korzybski said a few words at the opening of the Liberty Loan meeting in Cumberland. On Sunday afternoon he addressed a large crowd at Westernport at a flag raising, and Sunday evening he spoke at the Centre Street M.E. Church.

Mr. Korzybski will tour the George's Creek and Upper Potomac regions under the auspices of Production Manager Howard P. Brydon.[26]

Despite these plans, Korzybski's speaking tour of the mining regions of Maryland and West Virginia was just about over. By the time he gave this speech, in late September, it was starting to become clear to the administrators at the Fuel Administration: they were going to have to drastically change, perhaps curtail, their speakers' program. The country, indeed the world, had plunged into a disastrous influenza epidemic.

"Spanish Flu"

The first flu case in the U.S. had occurred at the military base of Ft. Riley, Kansas, in March 1918. Over 1000 soldiers had fallen ill and about 50 had died, but this first wave of illness, at least in the United States, soon diminished. However, many soldiers sent to the Western Front in Europe subsequently fell ill and many died, either having caught the illness in the crowded conditions of troop transport ships or in the trenches. Although it may have started in China and was beginning to devastate large parts of Europe and Asia, war censorship conditions had blocked the news of deaths in France, England, and Germany. When uncensored news of flu cases began to be reported from Spain, a neutral country, the illness became generally known as "Spanish Influenza" or the "Spanish Lady", in spite of protests from Spaniards.

In August a second wave of influenza in the U.S. started around Boston, where many troops and sailors had returned from abroad. The illness began to spread to the civilian population. Very shortly, it was raging through the East Coast into the population centers of New York and Philadelphia, although cities like Chicago and rural areas throughout the U.S. were also affected.

From March 1918 until February 1919, the "Spanish flu" would kill over 600 thousand Americans. More U.S. soldiers died from the flu than were killed in combat. The worldwide death toll from the 1918 flu has been conservatively estimated to be at least 20 million. It was the most devastating and deadly episode of contagious disease since the Black Death, which killed 1/3 of the population of Europe in the 1300s. Although public health officials understood it as a communicable disease, they did not know its exact source—an especially virulent form of virus which would only be discovered a decade later. They had no effective medical treatments or preventive measures. The illness came on very rapidly. A healthy man might begin to have symptoms in the morning and be dead by nightfall, drowned in the fluids of his blood-drenched lungs. And the number of deaths seemed to be increasing exponentially. In Boston for example, 46 people died in the week ending September 14. 1,214 people died in the week ending October 5.[27]

On October 4, all U.S.F.A. meetings in the Georges Creek Region of Western Maryland were cancelled. It soon became clear that mass meetings anywhere in Maryland or West Virginia were probably unsafe. Alfred's speaking tour there was finished.[28] On October 7, he traveled back to Washington, D.C. and got reassigned to the Kansas City, Missouri District of the U.S.F.A. On October 11, he took a train to Chicago, where he met with Yurkowski and got the Polish Army uniform from him.[29] On October 14 he arrived in Kansas City where the next day he met Ira Clemens, the head of the U.S.F.A. regional office.

The Kansas district, which included large parts of the Great Plains and Texas, had not suffered the number of flu deaths experienced elsewhere. But a day after his arrival, after addressing one joint meeting of miners and mine operators, Alfred had no work to do. Clemens could not find suitable engagements for Alfred, since public meetings had been banned in many of the areas where he would speak. Since the Fuel Administration was having this problem in other areas where its speakers couldn't address large groups, it was decided to reclassify them as "production inspectors" who would actually visit mines and talk to individual operators, miners, and small groups. On Oct. 22, Alfred took a train from Kansas City and arrived the next day in Bridgeport, Texas as a United States Fuel Administration production inspector.

For the next few weeks, Alfred traveled around Texas visiting mines in Bridgeport, Thurber, Strawn, Lyra, New Castle, Eagle Pass, etc. Although going into the mining pits was rigorous, especially with his lame leg, Alfred enjoyed it. In his talks with individual miners, he continued the message he had developed in his speeches. He also spoke to small groups of 15 to 20 men. In his travels he visited or passed through Wichita Falls, Fort Worth, and San Antonio. Where permitted, he gave speeches to gatherings as large as 150, 200, or even 300 people. Ongoing concerns about influenza in Texas kept gatherings from becoming much larger than this, although Texas had missed the brunt of the epidemic and the nationwide death tolls had begun to abate by the first week of November.

Armistice

Soon after he got to Texas, Alfred met John Wilkinson, District 21 President of the United Mine Workers Union. They became friendly while both were visiting the mines in Thurber. Wilkinson, entranced by Alfred's lively manner and fascinated by his discussion of developments in Europe, sponsored a speech by him on "The General War Situation", at the Thurber Opera House on October 28. The end of the war seemed imminent. Allied forces had been steadily recapturing territory in German-occupied France (American forces and Polish troops were both playing their part), pushing the Germans back towards the

Belgian border. The government of the Kaiser's Germany, steadily losing ground, pressed by an economic blockade, and threatened with revolution at home, was hoping to prevent Allied armies from marching to Berlin. It had already begun to 'fish' for the possibility of an armistice with a number of the Allied powers, including the United States.

Alfred had just received a letter from Koepler, his boss at U.S.F.A. headquarters. With coal production high and a possible end of the war in sight, the bureau would be reducing its speaking personnel. Speakers were encouraged to look for other positions and Alfred began to send out feelers for jobs. As an astute networker, he made use of his contacts and friends, who were only too happy to help him. He wrote to Koepler, expressing his interest in continuing government service and asking Koepler to keep an eye out for any positions open. Wilkinson wrote a number of letters on Alfred's behalf to United Mine Workers colleagues, letting them know that Alfred would be available and able to do speaking and organizing work. Wilkinson also wrote letters of recommendation for Korzybski, which he sent to Senators Owens and Gore from Oklahoma and Senator Morris Sheppard from Texas.

From Wilkinson, Alfred learned about the upcoming Pan-American Labor Conference to be held from November 13 to 16 in Laredo. American Federation of Labor (A.F.L.) President Samuel Gompers and other A.F.L. representatives would be meeting with labor representatives from Mexico and South America. Since Alfred had been working as a production inspector in Texas, he had learned about labor issues related to Mexican miners, who constituted a large and problematic group for both Texas mine operators and union organizers. Wilkinson suggested that Alfred would be the 'perfect' person to represent the U.S.F.A. at the conference, where Inter-American labor issues were to be addressed. Korzybski, strongly anti-Bolshevik, supported the organized labor movement as represented by Gomper's group and felt enthusiastic about going.

Wilkinson wrote a letter to James Neale, head of the Fuel Administration Production Department, promoting Alfred's attendance. Already expecting to get permission, Alfred headed on to Laredo. However, because of his constant traveling he only got the letter giving him the definite go-ahead two days after the start of the conference, which he was already attending.

On November 11, on his way to Laredo, Alfred had found himself in San Antonio. It was the day Armistice was declared (although the United States didn't officially end its state of war with Germany until 1921). He was not entirely pleased. This was not the way he wanted to see the war end. The day before, he had addressed an audience of 1400 soldiers at Camp Eagle Pass.[30]

> I was in that military camp delivering, not officially, but by invitation, a long lecture on what not, in connection with this war. We were smelling already that some monkey business with the armistice was coming, I call that deliberate[ly] monkey business. The great mistake the French did, and this was strictly French, they were bled to such an extent that they simply refused to fight anymore. That was the high command, not the soldiers. Simply a question of self-preservation of the country—they were bled so white. So they agreed in a hurry to an armistice instead of marching in comparatively small doses to Berlin. That is what they should have done. In [the] long run it would have been much cheaper to have done [it] this way. It would have prevented future troubles and eventual future preparations for war and what not. And then the Versailles treaty would appear

more reasonable. The Germans for the long time advertised after the war that they lost the war, but they were not defeated in the field. It was not really true. They were defeated in strategy and with ammunition. And they bit more than they could chew, but the fact that they [the Allies] were not marching on Berlin but began to negotiate an armistice, and the officers and myself we felt very bad about it, very bad, because we knew the consequences. And I remember I was on the streets of San Antonio and talking to an officer, an American officer, when through the loud speakers, newspapers headlines, came news that the armistice was signed. We both hugged and cried.[31]

November 11 was momentous for Korzybski for more than the end of the war. He was no longer 'a man without a country'. In Warsaw, a new independent Polish government had been declared, with Pilsudski, just released from German captivity, at its head.[32]

Korzybski in San Antonio, November 1918

The Pan-American Labor Conference

While he was in San Antonio, one of the local newspapers carried a quadruple headlined story about Alfred—"Polish Officer Has Served In Three Armies. Lieutenant Karzybski [sic] Now Wishes to Help Uncle Sam Win the War. Mine Coal, His Plea. He Speaks Seven Languages and Talks to Miners in Native Tongue."[33] By now this kind of coverage had become somewhat routine for Korzybski. Reporters tended to find him, "a remarkably interesting man".[34] His background as a Polish nobleman and soldier added to his appeal and his work as a public speaker for the government added to his news value. As he developed his work in later years, he would continue to get press coverage—not all of it welcome. Whether complimentary or not, he remained interested enough in what got written about him to clip the articles and later to employ clipping services to keep tabs on pieces about him, and reviews of his work.

At the Laredo conference, he met Samuel Gompers, a man he came to admire. Korzybski characteristically came prepared, having researched Mexican miners' problems. He had wanted to speak about what he considered to be the negative influence of the Bolsheviks and the I.W.W.—a radical labor organization at odds with Gompers' group—in fomenting discontent among these workers. Alfred had some ideas about alternative ways of promoting fraternity among the nations of the world, but he couldn't get an official place on the program. He tried to have his say anyway. He considered it ironic: he, a Polish national, was "representing [the] United States government in a Pan-American Congress of labor." Referring to a picture of the attendees, he said:

> Everybody there looks like a criminal, and you will recognize me easily because I was the only one in a uniform. I also was so damn sick of the whole group, South American sort of communists, anarchists, I don't know what not, and poor old Gompers [who had just lost a daughter to influenza]…conservative, solid man and here dealing with us crackpots, you know. And I had to address that group in the name of the American government. By jove, I did my best, but I was so sorry and bitter that I don't believe I did any good. I believe…that the Laredo meeting was one of the last which I had in the government service in this war.[35]

Chapter 13
A VETERAN OF THE GREAT WAR

After the Pan-American Labor Conference, Korzybski returned to San Antonio, wrote up his report about it for the Fuel Administration, and rested a few days. He had gotten word that his job would be terminated at the end of the month. On November 25, he took a train to New Orleans and from there to Washington (riding in Pullman Sleepers, his custom on long trips). He arrived in Washington on November 27, checked into a hotel, and spent the next few weeks settling his accounts with the U.S.F.A. and exploring job possibilities.

Alfred did not yet know how his mother, other family members, and friends were doing back home in Poland. He assumed he would probably be going back sometime soon. On the other hand, he did not seem in a great hurry to return. Throughout his time in Canada and the U.S., he had maintained contact with individuals and organizations in the Polish émigré community. Of course, he felt interested in helping to relieve the immediate desperate social-political-economic situation in Poland and Europe. But he considered that by staying in the United States for a while he might be able to do something constructive, not only in regard to his own immediate welfare but also for Poland and Europe.

He had already come to some conclusions about the role of America in the world. In a speech he had given at a Chamber of Commerce meeting in Texas, Alfred compared the cramped spaces and dense population of Europe to the wide-open and less densely-peopled U.S., which seemed to him like a giant "department store" of opportunity for more people to flourish—closer to an "ideal state of democracy" than anyplace else he knew. With the end of the war, he thought the U.S. was in a position of potentially great influence and might be able to help turn Europe into "a large department store of democracy" as well.[1]

This 'store' would be based on President Wilson's vision of peace as presented in his "Fourteen Points", in particular the final one—the establishment of an association with the purpose of mediating just and peaceful settlements among disputing nations. Of course, independent Poland—the thirteenth point of Wilson's program—would play a significant part in this community of nations. But Korzybski feared that opposition to the League of Nations, as well as other factors, might prevent the League from acting effectively. Alfred had some ideas about how to improve its chances for success. He wasn't shy about writing a letter to the President to offer his help. He hoped to meet with a representative of Wilson to present his ideas before the President left for the Peace Conference in Europe. Unfortunately, Korzybski must have missed seeing the news of when the President's ship for Europe was leaving (December 4). There is no indication anyone at the White House ever responded to Alfred's offer.[2]

Along with such lofty goals, if Alfred was going to stay in the U.S.—even for a brief time—he needed to address some more immediately practical concerns. For one thing, still technically a Russian national, he needed to clarify his status as a resident alien. One of the first things he did after his arrival in Washington was to fill out a form for the Naturalization Service of the U.S. Department of Labor, declaring his intent to "renounce allegiance to The Present Government of Russia."[3] As an ethnic Pole born in Warsaw, he soon was recognized as a citizen of Poland.

And in the meantime, though he had collected salaries and spent little money since coming to North America almost three years before, he needed to find some employment. Among other possibilities, Alfred offered his services as a translator to Harry Garfield, the head of the U. S. Fuel Administration, whom—he had learned—was planning a trip to Europe. No go. An anticipated job with the Anthracite Board of Conciliation in Scranton, Pennsylvania also didn't come through. Then, since government service appealed to him, he applied to the Department of Justice – Bureau of Investigation (the immediate forerunner of the F.B.I.) for a position as a "Special Agent". With his intelligence background and experience with legal work, he probably would have made a good one. His application came armed with recommendation letters from three U.S. senators and his sterling record of wartime service. With his status as a foreign national and his war injury ("Am very healthy, and strong but a little lame.") working against him, he lied about his age. Being just about six-months short of his 40th birthday, he gave his age as "34".[4] It didn't help. He kept on looking. With connections he was making with Poles in Washington and elsewhere in the U.S., and with contacts he had made in the U.S. government, in military intelligence, and elsewhere, he hoped to find something soon.

In Flanders Fields

In the first few months after the armistice, one thing seemed abundantly clear—the war had left things in disarray. Alfred, lover of the mathematical sciences and an engineer, had already started wondering, analyzing, trying to figure out what could be done, not only for himself but for Poland and the larger world. His lifework was on the verge of being born.

Alfred had gotten a Little Leather Library edition of Kipling's *Barrack-Room Ballads* (which included "Danny Deever") and in the back of the book— small enough to fit into his breast pocket—he kept a card printed with John D. McCrae's poem "In Flanders Fields".[5] McCrae, a Canadian-army field surgeon, had composed the poem just outside his surgical tent in the rear of an ambulance after the bloody Second Battle of Ypres in war-torn Belgium in the spring of 1915. McCrae had seen many men die and by the time he himself died in early 1918, his poem was already becoming famous. Alfred had likely heard it recited and sung at many Liberty Bond rallys and memorials for the war dead:

In Flanders fields the poppies blow
Between the crosses, row on row,
That mark our place; and in the sky
The larks, still bravely singing, fly
Scarce heard amid the guns below.

We are the Dead. Short days ago
We lived, felt dawn, saw sunset glow,
Loved and were loved, and now we lie,
In Flanders fields.

Take up our quarrel with the foe:
To you from failing hands we throw
The torch; be yours to hold it high.
If ye break faith with us who die
We shall not sleep, though poppies grow
In Flanders fields.

Alfred had pasted "America's Answer" by R.W. Lillard, to the back of the card with McCrae's poem. The last verse of Lillard's poem, read:

'Fear not that ye have died for naught.
The torch ye threw to us we caught.
Ten million hands will hold it high,
and Freedom's light shall never die!
We've learned the lesson that ye taught in Flanders Fields!'[6]

Years later, in 1934 Korzybski recalled both poems while writing a letter explaining the origin of his work to the psychiatrist Helen Flanders Dunbar (Dunbar's middle name had jogged his memory).

Do you remember the answer? 'Fear not that ye have died for naught. The torch ye threw to us we caught. Ten million hands will hold it high, and Freedom's light shall never die! We've learned the lesson that ye taught in Flanders Fields!' Did we? 'that is the question'. Well Gen. Sem. [General Semantics] was born through pain and in pain. It is an illegitimate child of Mars and the World War, and like Oedipus it fulfills an ancient prophecy and kills the father. If I may quote from my 'Manhood of Humanity': 'Is this climax of the pre-war civilization to be passed unnoticed except for the poetry and the manuring of the battlefields, that the "poppies blow" stronger and better fed?...Is the great sacrifice worth analyzing? There can be only one answer—yes. But, if truth be desired, the analysis must be scientific.' This is approximately the birth certificate of Gen. Sem.[7]

Painful Legacy

The war's legacy included an exhausted and wary state of the world. The leaders of England, France, Italy, and the United States were now working things out in France at a peace conference—with representatives of what was left of the disempowered Central Powers awaiting results. President Wilson had with hope declared "The Great War" (as it had come to be called) as the "war to end all wars". Would wars end? Alfred didn't feel so sure. He wondered what it would take to actually make world peace an actuality.

More specifically, Alfred's thoughts turned to the pain of Poland, the battleground of the Eastern Front, where millions of soldiers and civilians had died or been injured and where many had been rendered homeless. The economic infrastructure had been wrecked. True, there was now an independent state, a Second Polish Republic—Alfred's lifelong dream. But uncertain borders, and problematic relations with neighboring national groups and with its own ethnic minorities, made the new state's peaceful existence tenuous.

With this general situation at the start of 1919, the war's personal legacy for Alfred included his own portion of ongoing insecurity, loss, and pain. Korzybski had not been able to establish contact with his mother and friends at home, but he was still trying to reach them by means of people he knew who were traveling to Poland. Had they survived and were they reasonably alright? They were. He would get a letter from his mother later in the year and continued a regular correspondence with her throughout her life. But he had reasonable assurance that the family properties had been ruined in the war. A lot of work would be needed to repair the damages and restore the farm's productivity.

The war had not only damaged his property. It had left its traces on Alfred himself in the form of scars clearly—and not-so-clearly—visible. Ever since his hip injury and the terrible pain he had felt afterwards, he had observed in his gait a certain more-or-less unconscious carefulness. He knew he never wanted to experience such pain again. Beyond that, he had to contend with a definite stiffness in his left leg, now shorter than the right; he needed to wear a specially-made shoe extension and lift which in turn caused other problems, a sore and callused foot. For the rest of his life, he used a cane and walking was never normal.

His hearing too had suffered. The incessant din of artillery both at the front and at the Petawawa testing range had caused damage and sensory loss. Within the next few years, he would notice difficulty with telephone conversations, which he learned to avoid. Later, as he aged, he had difficulty hearing even in personal conversations unless the room was quiet and the other person enunciated loudly and clearly enough. This led to Alfred appearing at times like a "one way conversationalist". [8]

Other war-related health problems which he considered nuisances persisted. Every so often, some extra exertion and the resulting heart palpitations or shortness of breath would remind him of the strain he had sustained from lifting that artillery piece singlehandedly during the retreat of the Russian Army from Lodz. The resulting hernia also required a truss later on. Poor hygiene and irregular diet during the war also left him with dental problems he would have to deal with later, eventually requiring dentures.

The nervous tics he had first noticed when he arrived in North America had long since vanished. Yet a residue of anxiety remained from his war experiences. For example, he would find himself looking upwards at times and realize he was unconsciously reacting to a plane flying overhead as if expecting a bomb attack. And he had vivid memories of the Eastern Front still charged with painful feelings. (The unpleasantness of these memories would diminish but never entirely vanish.) Alfred's later interest in helping those with shell shock, or battle fatigue as it was called during World War II (now termed "post-traumatic stress disorder"), was stimulated by his own experiences with the phenomenon.

In spite of these negatives, Alfred could see things after the war as not entirely dark. For one thing, at least for the next few months, he had some money to live on. He had not spent much of his stipend from the Tsarist government or his wartime salaries. Altogether he may have had about $5000 in savings. And the exigencies of his wartime service had led to another benefit—he had been forced to learn and become fluent in English. A new world of literature, scientific and otherwise, had become available to him. And now he would have some time to read. Since the start of the war he had been too busy to be able to follow much of what had been happening in the scientific world. In 1915, for example, Einstein had proposed a general theory of relativity which was turning the world of physics topsy-turvy. Alfred's work as a speaker for the French-Polish Army and the U.S. Fuel Administration also opened up another new world for him. He realized that he could move an audience with his words and that, furthermore, having an audience helped him to develop his ideas. A career as a writer and speaker now seemed like a definite possibility. And in his brief time in North America (he had arrived only a little over three years before) he had managed to develop a network of contacts throughout Canada and the United States. His file of correspondence with friends and acquaintances was growing.

The war also left him with a definite preference in clothing which he felt most grateful for: khaki. "Since the first day of war, I got into khaki and never got out of it." Although he occasionally would wear a jacket and tie or even more formal evening clothes when required, these seemed to him like so-much uncomfortable "armor". He considered anything as formal as a suit and tie, a "monkey suit". [9] In his khakis he had room to move and felt comfortable. A clean and pressed khaki 'uniform' had all the decorum he felt he needed.

In regard to his personal grooming, he seems to have started shaving his head long before the war, as he began losing his hair: "I decided to abandon what was abandoning me."[10]

Undoubtedly conditions during the war (with lice and other vermin) confirmed for him the wisdom of that decision. He continued to shave his head for the rest of his life.

Alfred's many close calls with death during the war left him with what to some people at first might *not* seem like a benefit—a significant sense of his own mortality. For Korzybski this appears to have served as a gift. He may not have dwelled on it but I believe a consciousness of his own mortality—and therefore of the preciousness of every life-moment—remained in the daily background of his awareness, more or less as a constant, for the rest of his life. On the back flyleaf of his copy of *Barrack-Room Ballads*, he had written a line from another Kipling poem, *Arithmetic on the Frontier*, that had obviously struck him:

The flying bullet down the pass
that whistles clear
"all flesh is grass." [11]

On the Eastern Front, Alfred had actually heard the flying bullet (and artillery shell) and seen the results for those to whom the bullet had *not* whistled clear. If 'all flesh was grass'—he was no exception. He was lucky to be alive. Already naturally inclined to involve himself fully in whatever he was doing, from this time on he seemed to make a concerted effort to live 'balls out' with the greatest intensity. Later, he would tell his students—with passion—to do what he worked to do in his own life—"Be conscious!" [12]

Such was the mixed legacy of the Great War for Korzybski. Though not especially happy with the state of the post-war world, he didn't seem so constituted as to become consumed with bitterness. In the way he would put it, he didn't have a 'bad liver', so for him the world didn't seem bad through and through—only 'hopeless'. Some ways forward for the world and for himself might exist—some unknown possibilities for hope. Before the war, he had attempted to write and to burst through some of the blockages he had perceived in the sciences, politics, etc. He had not succeeded. His experiences during the war had filled him with a new sense of urgency—an urgency that now seemed as if it was going to burst through him.

Chapter 14
MIRA

While attending to business in Washington, D.C., Alfred was staying at the Sterling Hotel (giving Sobanski's New York City apartment number as his permanent U.S. address and 66 Wilcza St., in Warsaw, as his home). As a genuine Polish count and a well-publicized war veteran, he had a certain cachet within the D.C. social scene and got invited to various parties, teas, and other gatherings. With some spare time now, he went—even if for the most part they bored him. Sometime at the very end of November or in early December, he attended one such event:

> Some Vasser students [were giving] a party for young "returning heroes" you know and we had, there were several American officers, a Britisher, a Frenchman, and I was the only Pole. So I entered, bored, there's another god damn tea party. Nothing exciting about that. Tired. And here on a two-seat little sofa was some very queer woman sitting. She just came from a riding party. Oh, dressed in britches, boots, and stock, tailored, with a most hideous one of those derbies you know. And she had some hideous, perfectly hideous Chinese…wide rim…glasses. She looked like hell. But I was looking around…I don't know what to do. In the meantime, my wife-to-be immediately moved aside, left space for me. She was also bored with the party. So I had nothing better to do than to sit opposite her …And we began to chat…I began to learn that she was a very famous artist.[1]

Indeed, Mira Edgerly (her first name sometimes got misspelled as Myra) was at the peak of her career as a painter specializing in portraits on ivory. Her work had become sought after by the nobility and well-to-do of Europe and England, and now by nouveau-riche patrons in the United States. Within the last year she had come to Washington, set up a studio at Stoneleigh Court, and was painting portraits of members of Washington high society like Assistant Secretary of State Breckenridge Long and his family, Captain and Mrs. Perry Belmont, and members of the Washington foreign diplomatic corps. An exhibition of her paintings was being held at the Belmont's Washington, D.C. mansion. She was charging something like $2000 to $5000 per portrait and was making $10,000 to $15,000 a year, which in 1918 amounted to a substantial sum.

Mira had struggled hard to succeed. She was born in Aurora, Illinois, the youngest of three daughters of Sam Edgerly and Rose Haskell, on January 16, 1872 or 1876. (The year remains uncertain. Though previous accounts of her life give the year of birth as 1872, affidavits provided by a family neighbor and one of her sisters give 1876 as the year.)[2] The family moved to Jackson, Michigan and later Detroit where Sam Edgerly worked as an official of the Michigan Central Railroad. The family lived a well-to-do, upper middle class existence. Mira attended a private school. But things dramatically changed when she reached her teens. Her father, well-liked in the community and generous to a fault, made a large loan to a friend who then defaulted on the payment. When Sam died soon afterwards, the family was left destitute.

After his death, the family lived in Kansas City, Missouri for a few years. Then Rose Edgerly and her two younger daughters moved to San Francisco. Rose, a wise and caring woman, gave her daughters some important advice. First, she told them she would not be able to continue to take care of them as they got older so they would have to learn to make do on their own. Second, in regard to the opposite sex, she warned each of them to ask herself one question if she became interested in a man—"Do I want this man to be the father of my child?" All three of the brilliant and beautiful sisters managed to achieve some success in later life. Minnie had been married and was a gifted artist, although she struggled financially. Amy, the oldest, had studied mathematics at the University of Michigan, married a Missouri politician, Rush C. Lake, and lived with him on a farm outside of Kansas City. Lake had died near the start of the 1918 influenza epidemic. Afterwards, Mira had stayed with Amy on the farm before coming to Washington.

At sixteen, Mira had started out by selling encyclopedias. She did that for about a week but didn't like getting pinched by her boss and quit. Possibly inspired by Minnie, she decided to try her hand at painting. She had read about miniature portraits done on ivory, got herself some old ivory poker chips and a discarded watercolor kit, and began to paint and learn. She soon realized she could carve out a niche for herself in the art market by doing something unique. Instead of painting the standard miniature portraits, she would paint portraits on larger pieces of ivory. She began to develop new techniques for doing this. In the San Francisco art world, her reputation grew. (She met art photographer Arnold Genthe there, who noted her talent and also used her as a model.)

**Mira Edgerly,
Portrait by Arnold Genthe**[3]

Charlotte Schuchardt Read, who knew Mira for many years, detailed Mira's artistic development in a short biography, from which I will quote here at length[4]:

[Mira's] first contact with great paintings of the world was through Arnold Genthe, the portrait photographer. Genthe fermented her ambition to achieve high standards of portraiture. Of this mutually inspiring friendship Genthe wrote in 1936 in his book *As I Remember*, 'Among my friends was a young miniature painter, Mira Edgerly, who besides being a gifted artist had great beauty and intelligence. Sure that I had started something new in photography, she not only posed for me but gave me many valuable suggestions on arrangement and composition.'

During these years she was invited through a client to be a guest in Guatemala, with her mother and sister, at the home of a retired president of Guatemala, halfway up a mountainside above the ocean. This was a most exciting event for her.

Although she was making rapid progress in San Francisco, she was determined to eventually get to Paris. About 1900 she came to New York, where she had a studio on 35th Street. There began a lifelong friendship with Burges Johnson, who was starting out in New York in his profession as a writer. Looking back at those days, he wrote in 1944 in *As Much as I Dare*:

> Mira Edgerly was an artist entirely self-taught, who was experimenting with miniatures in her own original fashion... She made her way on the strength of real talent plus skillful self-management plus an engaging personality...I do not remember how she broke into the magic circle in New York City, if I ever knew; but I do know that within an astonishingly short time a list of her subjects was a roll of the inner circle of the so-called Four Hundred. She was always wise in the management of herself; never granting interviews or encouraging the sort of newspaper publicity she would have found easy to secure.

When Mrs. Patrick Campbell, whom she had met at a social gathering in New York, urged her to come to London and be her guest, she made her decision to go. Now she began to establish herself as a portrait painter in London, and with her resourcefulness, pluck and tenacity, she was soon winning commissions among the pre-World War I 'privileged classes' [devastatingly portrayed in *Kind Hearts and Coronets*, the 1949 British movie satirizing Edwardian high society–BIK]. She painted in their homes in England, Scotland, Ireland and Wales, and in Germany and France.

She learned to know her clientele intimately, and many times she was deeply disturbed about the socio-economic system of that era. Often she was able to get sums of money from those to whom it meant little, for the purpose of giving it to a friend in need. In 1913 she crossed the Atlantic to New York in the steerage of the Mauretania 'to study the poor', and in September 1914 she brought seven penniless but gifted creative workers, who otherwise would have been in the breadline, with her from London to the United States, and helped them find work here.

For some years between 1905 and 1914 she also had a studio in Paris. There she enjoyed a friendship with Gertrude Stein, [And Alice B. Toklas–BIK][5]...

In 1914, as the war was breaking out in Europe, she returned to this country. Here she had to create contacts anew. But she had learned to accept it as a challenge to arrive in a strange city almost penniless, get a first commission within a few days, and go on from there. During the war years she painted in New York, Aiken, South Carolina (where her potential clientiele kept their horses for hunting), Newport, Rhode Island, Washington, D.C., Philadelphia, etc.

And now here she was at a tea party sitting next to Alfred Korzybski, whom she had just met. They were both trying to be polite and made some conversation.

A Quick Romance

Alfred had decided some time before that he would probably remain a bachelor. Not that he was a puritan. As he put it, "all my life in many ways I was spoilt by women."[6] But many of the women he had previously met, while charming, did not live up to his expectations for a mate. He didn't want to end up with some version of his mother whom, though educated in a literary sense, he considered both frivolous and manipulative.

Now here beside him sat another charming lady. He had heard about her before while visiting the Duke of Connaght and his daughter Patricia in Ottawa during his time at Petawawa. Mira had stayed with them earlier and painted their portraits. As Mira told him about her work, he realized she was far from frivolous, but indeed rather industrious and dedicated. Despite her "queer" horseback-riding getup, he found her attractive. She also had a directness he liked. She seemed to have a genuine concern for the larger circle of humanity beyond herself. As a child, she had gotten a "little 2-inch gold ruler with the golden rule engraved on it" as a gift "and she took it with her everywhere."[7] As Alfred put it years later, "her feeling and my feeling went parallel....she's not a radi≠cal, just an honest, intelligent person who knows how to face facts."[8]

He found out fairly quickly that they also had some very different ways of looking at and talking about things.:

From a linguistic point of view our temperament somehow did not agree, …she was a flowery, verbally very polite [person] in a parlor sort of way and I was a solid, scientific man who was teaching hard stuff all his life. So linguistically we did not fit."[9]

They immediately got into an argument. Alfred described it as follows:

She began to talk about nothing and blurt out opinions that were perfectly unjustified, not based on facts. And I had to say something. I couldn't get up and say go to hell. That's not done in polite society, so I was sitting and having clever conversation, and finally whatever she said somehow I cornered her that she does not know what she is talking about, of course, very polite, very polite. But I couldn't help it. I would be either silent or if I said something, I had to say what I meant. And so finally, this is already [a] funny thing, when she could not argue at all, because whatever she said, it was turned around…she began to kick, and being a horseman, when a horse misbehaves, you put your hand on the horse and quiet it down. This was not very parlor-like. I put my hand on her knee this way. You see. Pipe down. I didn't say pipe down, but I said, If you want to argue, argue, but don't kick. …She piped down immediately, stopped kicking…I just looked at her, by jove, perhaps that woman could eventually fit me. So far…I was fitting her.[10]

They left the tea party and went to a restaurant where they talked into the early morning hours. They met the next day and talked some more. "She told me about her life. I told her about my life…We became more and more acquainted."[11] Mira may have told him at this time about her brief marriage in 1914 to a fellow artist, Frederick Burt.[12] At any rate, Alfred certainly knew he was not getting involved with an inexperienced young girl. Nor did he want to. After a brief courtship, they got married in January, one day after Mira's birthday.

Alfred and Mira, Wedding Day

A wedding notice appeared in the *Washington Herald*:
Announcement is made of the marriage of Mrs. [sic] Mira Edgerly and Col. Count Alfred Skarbek de Korzybski. The wedding took place yesterday morning [Friday, January 17] in the chambers of Associate Justice Ashley M. Gould of the Supreme Court of the District of Columbia, with a little group of intimate friends of the bride and bridegroom to visit the ceremony. Mrs. Edgerly wore a traveling costume and the bridegroom was in uniform.[13]

The story of the wedding was picked up in many of the major newspapers in the U.S. and Canada. The romance of the well-known portraitist of the rich and famous with a Polish Count had definite news value. Mira Edgerly had now become Countess Mira Edgerly-Korzybska. The noble title would give her a notch up on the social scale and thus perhaps some advantage in appealing to her wealthy clientele. Conversely, Alfred was now married to a U.S. citizen and thus had an added bit of security if he wanted to stay in America. A Washington gossip columnist speculated on what seemed like a marriage of convenience:
Myra Edgerly, who has been about Washington for a year or more painting all the notables she could lure into purchasing her ivories or sitting for them, has swapped the name she has made famous for that of something less pronounceable...Myra has an excellent eye to business for she could have found few better ways of advertising her miniature exhibition now being held in the Perry Belmont house. The count is one of those romantic characters brought to the shores of this country by the war...Myra should certainly get some new commissions from her clever publicity work.[14]

Despite whatever side benefits either might have gotten from their marriage, the primary reason for it clearly seems to have been love, i.e., mutual attraction and—despite their differences in intellectual style—companionability. Mira, who had not found fulfillment among her artistic and intellectual friends, found in Alfred someone who lived up to her high ideals in a man. As she was entering middle age, she had finally found someone whom she would want to be the father of her child. Mira's friend, the writer Mildred Aldrich, who introduced her to Gertrude Stein, had described Mira as an "altruistic enthusiast in search of a great mission."[15] In their early conversations, she sensed Alfred was at the brink of starting such a mission and she could think of nothing better than to help him bring it to fruition. For Alfred's part, he could clearly feel her encouragement. This, combined with her attitude of independence (so different from his mother and other aristocratic ladies he had known), drew him to her—beyond her physical attractiveness. (Years later, Alfred told Ralph Hamilton privately, "We had a glorious sex life.")[16]

Just before meeting Mira, he had been thinking about returning to Poland. The country needed good men for the work of reconstruction. His family's properties required his attention. Mira and he had discussed going to Poland and simply living together, since as far as he knew the country had no civil marriages at the time and neither of them wanted a church wedding. However, she was in debt. Despite her significant income, money seemed to fly out of her hands. She was in the midst of a painting "campaign" where she could earn a significant amount of money. If they went to Poland immediately, she probably would not have been able to get commissions, given the bleak post-war economic circumstances of the country. So in the meantime, having married here, they could enjoy each other and the Washington social scene, while Mira could paint and have exhibits and Alfred could see about getting some income. They could go to Poland in the fall.[17]

Newlyweds

As soon as they got married, Alfred moved from the hotel where he had been staying to Mira's studio at the landmark Stoneleigh Court apartments at Connecticut and K Streets. The technical details and problems of Mira's painting methods had interested him when she first described them. With the opportunity to observe her at work, he came up with a couple of inventions to help her.

One problem she had struggled with involved the drying of the large ivories which she used as her canvases. Watercolor paint on ivory was unforgiving and did not allow for much starting and stopping or correction of mistakes after it dried. Telltale spotting and lines and streaks could appear. Thus she had little leeway for error. To get around this, Mira had devised a method of "painting backwards"—doing the entire background of the portrait quickly without a place for her subject. Then while the paint was still wet she would daub off the intended areas for the face and body with a small moistened cotton swab, leaving an unpainted outlined surface for the actual portrait which she could then spend more time with or do later. With this two-step method, the final portrait would appear seamless. Unfortunately, her ivories still had a tendency to crack as they dried.

> She was painting [a] $2,000 portrait. One nice morning after [a] night [drying] we come to the portrait—a big crack, the whole thing. Then I made immediately, invented a box with sponges with water on the bottom and some screen on the top so that when for the night she put them in the damp air…it did not crack.[18]

Another problem involved the large and expensive pieces of ivory themselves. They had to be cut or trimmed, which Mira did with a large scissors. Unfortunately, the pieces often got cracked and ruined with this process:

> I immediately bought a little electric motor, put some saws on it, and made a little table, metal, so she could saw [the ivories more precisely]. It saved an enormous amount of waste because cutting with scissors, they cracked like the dickens, so I eliminated the cracks, and this remained with her for life. The rest of her life she used those things.[19]

The newlyweds continued the marathon conversations they had had when they first met. They had a lot to talk about. The Paris Peace Conference had begun the day after their wedding. A Polish delegation was preparing to make its case before the so-called "Council of Ten" of Allies at the Conference. Alfred still hoped the Council would strongly support Polish aspirations. He also hoped that a properly constituted League of Nations proposed by President Wilson might provide some kind of stable foundation for peace among nations. Meanwhile the Russian Bolshevik regime loomed with an ominous presence. With growing labor unrest, not only in the United States but throughout Europe, the spread of Bolshevism seemed like a real threat, even to people like Alfred and Mira who both strongly supported the organized labor movement. Schemes for social reform were in the air—prohibition, woman's rights, etc. Years later, Mira recalled one early conversation she had with Alfred on how to 'fix' the world. It mirrors Alfred's account of their differences:

> In those days we drank five to ten cups of tea a day. One day at tea time I held forth how civilization should be run, repeating the conclusions that were given every night when a group of us used to talk in the Latin quarter of Paris. I had a very clear verbal pattern of an ideal civilization, and I burst into speech, repeating an artist's notion of running the world. Then he asked me to repeat what I said—in other words, "Do you know what you are saying?", and I did. Then with a very firm voice he said,

"Dearest, that's only a private opinion. I'm very glad you have it, but until human beings become aware of the natural laws of our environment as Newton and Leibnitz did in physics, there can only be a clash of private opinions." Then he analyzed my statements and I was losing out, as very shortly he had me with no logical legs to stand on. I would try to beguile him into making love to me, but he would push me away and say this has nothing to do with making love. He said, "You stay on your side of the room and I'll stay on my side, and we'll thrash this out."[20]

Their discussions did not necessarily denote serious discord. Alfred noted, "we were on the same side...except that she had no technique of expression in a harder language."[21] Mira sensed that Alfred was beginning a struggle to express something significant about the world situation and encouraged him to make a serious effort as a writer and speaker.

Chapter 15
"LET THE DEAD BE HEARD"

Alfred's first opportunity as a speaker came soon after the wedding. At the beginning of February, he gave a speech at Carroll Hall on behalf of the Polish Relief Committee, in which he pleaded for the recognition of Poland and for funds for relief work there.[1] He was also writing an article about the war and the need for a League of Nations, that he hoped to get published in a magazine or newspaper. He completed it in the first part of March and began sending out copies to potential publishers, government officials (including the Secretary of State and President Wilson), and some of his contacts in Canada and the U.S.

Near the start of "Let the Dead Be Heard" by "a Polish Soldier" he wrote, "The value of life can be only appreciated facing death."[2] The article never reached print. However, as perhaps his first publicly-offered piece of writing, it seems worth examining here for its revelation of Korzybski's raw feelings about the war and its aftermath. The article consisted of ten dense pages beginning with a depiction of the suffering of the soldier in the trenches— a "bloody game...a moral hell of despair and hope." His depiction undoubtedly reflected his own experiences:

>...Before killing an enemy he watched his agony and saw the deep bitterness, not against him, the direct slayer, but against those indirect slayers who created conditions leading to those wholesale crimes. He heard whispers of desperate love to the beloved ones, and the last worry "What will become of them?" Hour after hour he witnessed this hellish agony of hope and despair of life and death, and hour after hour, month after month, year after year, he grew more grim, more old, more nerve-broken, with a sterner and every day more pronounced determination to kill everybody who would stand in his way to kill wars. ...

The essay ended with a plea for an effective "League of Nations". To be effective it would have to involve some kind of world federation limited to "self-governing countries with European culture" (including, presumably, some form of representative government). The body would include an "international general staff, at the disposal of the League..." which would be empowered militarily by member nations to be able to severely punish any instigators of an aggressive war:

>...War is a crime—a nation, including women, voting for a crime, are criminals and they should be tried by this League of Nations, sentenced and punished according to verdict, through economic repression...or even executed through an aeroplane army with thousands of tons of bombs...

>The flying machines will be of commercial value, and a few thousand flyers in each country would be always ready to punish the criminal offender. The only country at present whom no one could trust is Germany, and Germany should be forcibly disarmed and put under definite control for many years, with a league or without.

>Sentimentalism in questions concerning a war is a crime, because it encourages war, which is nothing but a crime. Let everybody know what they may expect by starting war, and the ruthless punishment in store for them in mind and on paper, that will stop even the attempt and will be in practice the highest and truest humanitarianism...

The plausibility in 1919 of the nations of the world giving up some of their sovereignty to a world body such as the League of Nations may seem unrealistic in the hindsight of the early 21st Century. But Korzybski genuinely felt such an arrangement would be needed if a future aggressive war by Germany or any other aggressive power was to be prevented. (Clearly his proposal of the need for a viable threat of force against international aggression—not the vision of a pacifist—was subsequently borne out by the failure to prevent the rearmament of Germany or to punish the aggressions of Japan. Twenty years later, a second round of world war would begin.)

The middle sections of the essay included comments about war profiteering, the various nations involved in the war, the causes of the Russian Revolution, the spirit of Poland, the improvement of the masses, and other topics. Its final lines alluded to "In Flanders Fields":

...Justice is what the masses are crying for today. Then those things will be understood and done, those millions of dead will be honored as they deserve to be, by a living "monument of a better world." "If ye break faith with us who have died, we shall not sleep", they whisper.

Alfred received some polite letters of response to his "interesting" article, including a reply from the League to Enforce the Peace. Former President Taft, who headed the organization, read the article and had the director of its speakers' bureau write a letter inviting Alfred to apply to become a speaker for the group.[3] The League to Enforce Peace may have provided the original inspiration for Woodrow Wilson's promotion of the League of Nations. Founded in 1915, it had pushed for an international association of states as well as an international court and conflict mediation.[4] Alfred filled out their questionnaire and received a speaker's card but decided not to work for them since he was beginning to have doubts about the people and purpose behind the organization.[5] News from the Paris Peace Conference was already indicating that the other Allied powers were lining up to water down Wilson's grand vision of the League. In the U.S., opposition in Congress to the Peace Treaty—especially to U.S. membership in the League of Nations—had already begun to develop. Alfred would look for some other way to help the cause of Poland.

Meanwhile, Mira and Alfred did not spend all of their time working. In the first few months of their marriage they had time to attend a number of posh gatherings in Washington, such as the Mardi Gras costume charity ball, and a "paper chase" and "hunt supper" at the Washington Riding and Hunt Club. Mira's work also had some social requirements, appearances by her and Alfred at exhibits of her work, such as the one she had in early April at the home of Madame Zaldiver, the wife of the retiring minister of Salvador.

Probably some time in late March or early April, Alfred and Mira were able to get away to visit Colonel George Patton and his wife at the army base at Fort Meade, Maryland. Patton had spent the war in France where he had served, first as an aide to General Pershing and then as organizer of the American Tank School and commander of one of the first existing tank brigades of the U.S. Army before getting badly wounded. He spent the last days of the war in a military hospital and had just returned to the U.S. in March. Mira may have met Mrs. Patton—a formidable horsewoman—at the Washington Riding Club. Around this time she painted the Pattons' portraits. Mira and Alfred were invited out to Fort Meade, where they played among the tanks with the Pattons. As fellow cavalry men and swordsmen (Patton had written an army manual on saber fighting), Alfred and Colonel Patton undoubtedly had a lot to talk about comparing notes about their experiences on the Eastern and Western fronts. Alfred admired Patton's military prowess and later followed his World War II career with great interest.

At the end of March, something else happened that would have great importance for Alfred—an expedition led by British astronomer Arthur Stanley Eddington left for the tropics. On May 29, Eddington and his team on Principe island, off the coast of West Africa, photographed starlight passing near the sun during a total solar eclipse. They found that the light was indeed deflected by the sun's gravity, just as Einstein had predicted in his theory of General Relativity. Korzybski would have read the news when it was announced later that year in November. The implications of this for the world of physics were profound. In the next few years, Korzybski would become more and more involved in attempting to understand the einsteinian revolution and its broader human implications.

"The Profiteers and How to Fight Them"

Alfred and Mira still had hopes of getting to Poland in the fall. He planned to leave in August or September, with Mira to follow soon afterwards. Until then Mira planned to finish up her commissions in Washington and then go to Newport in late June for an exhibit at the Belmont's home there (where she would stay) and perhaps to get an additional portrait commission or two.[6] In the meantime, Alfred hoped to make some extra money.

At the end of April, he took a job at the Hanover Trust Company, a bank in Boston. Through his network, he had made contact with one of the bank's officers, a Pole, who offered him a bank teller's salary and a job selling securities to members of Boston's Polish immigrant community. However, Alfred quickly found Hanover Trust untrustworthy. The certificates he was asked to sell were phony. The bank was not honestly investing the money it received from investors. Probably, interest payments made to early investors were to get paid out of the payments made by other later investors or were not to get paid at all—what would become known as a "Ponzi scheme". Alfred refused to participate in such shenanigans and quit after only a few weeks. Within a year Hanover Trust actually did get involved with Charles Ponzi, the man for whom the "Ponzi scheme" was named. Ponzi, who first deposited his ill-gotten money at Hanover and then joined its board of directors, eventually went to jail. Hanover Trust closed down after a federal investigation.

Since Mira would be shutting her studio in Washington and going to Newport in about a month, Alfred decided to relocate to New York City. They would be close enough to visit each other on weekends. Probably because of Mira, he was able to stay at the National Arts Club on Gramercy Park where he was elected an associate member.[7] Just as he was getting settled, Alfred (an inveterate newspaper reader) saw news of anti-Jewish pogroms, which disturbed him greatly. Such pogroms had been going on in Poland, the Ukraine, and Russia for some time. But something in the May 26th edition of the *New York Herald* seemed to trigger a response in him. He clipped a pair of pictures from the paper: one photograph of the destitute survivors of a pogrom in Kishinieff and one photo showing stacks of bodies of the pogrom's murdered victims. Above the pictures, the headline read "Jews Robbed, Murdered And Driven From Homes In Polish Pogroms".[8]

As I will soon show, Alfred at this time maintained antisemitic (anti-Jewish) prejudices. He likely had grown up with such views, endemic among ethnic Poles since the latter half of the 19th Century.[9] (The Poles should not necessarily be picked upon as exceptional in this regard. Antisemitism had become quite prevalent throughout Europe, the U.S., and elsewhere.) But whatever Korzybski's prejudices as of May 1919, he could not countenance the wholesale murder of Jews. Furthermore, he probably also took offense at the fact that these pogroms in Kishinieff, in the Ukraine, were being blamed on Poles. He sent a telegram to Mira in Washington at the end of the month: "Have solution for pogroms. Telephone White [an American diplomat?] let wire to Smulski [an influential member of the Polish-American community]. Able two hours lecture English with facts, pictures. World wide importance."[10]

Mira probably contacted White immediately. Alfred received a telegram on May 31: "Appreciate the sincerity of your suggestion but I feel that we are in danger of adding fuel to flames. Will write you in detail. JCW".[11] On June 1 Mira telegramed Alfred: "White just made long call bad letters to him he made it so clear to me now not time for your idea he goes New York midnight meet minister from Warsaw going see you stay in tomorrow be sure not to miss him love [—] Monky."[12] I've found no further documention about this meeting. But it seems likely that Korzybski's knowledge about the persecution of Jews in Eastern Europe, including Poland, would continue to eat into his conscience for some time.

Newly planted in New York City, Korzybski persisted in trying to get articles published. He produced some translations of items from the Polish press and a few articles on Poland and Russia which he offered to a foreign press service. Nothing was accepted. He was out of work now and should he return to Poland, with Mira to follow, their prospects there were not clear. It isn't hard to conclude he may have been feeling somewhat 'at loose ends'. By August, Mira had relocated to Newport. Alfred was going up to see her on weekends and was planning to leave for Europe in four to five weeks.[13] At this time, he produced a new article, "The Profiteers and How To Fight Them",[14] which shows his growing attention to economic issues, his still quite sympathetic view towards socialism, and perhaps some of the economic roots of the antisemitic attitudes he held at this time.

"The Profiteers and How to Fight Them" begins with a few paragraphs in which he rails at "the rulers and war lords of both sides looking for their narrow, selfish aims". Korzybski claimed, "Legislation in the old way can not help, if legislation is chosen to do the work, then the legislation must be very radical, around the socialistic lines of nationalizing the production of the essentials of life." But he held out little hope for such legislation to happen since "parliaments of the world…are still under strong influence of the ruling classes, bankers and trusts". If change is to happen the public must get involved. A people's cooperative movement must be established. Here he pointed to the example of the Polish cooperative movement which came to prominence after the first Russian Revolution of 1905. It is here where Korzybski's misevaluation of Jews and their influence becomes apparent:

> We had in Poland several years ago a tremendously strong Jewish trust which boycotted for several centuries Polish economic life. Every wholesale dealer in the country was a Jew and every Jewish retailer had the goods cheaper and paid by long drafts, the Christian dealers had to pay dearer and cash.
>
> The situation was hope and helpless. This Jewish Trust was broken by an appeal to the people, who mobilized money and men. Polish wholesale dealers and retailers were established.
>
> This system took away from the Jews the power of exclusiveness and made them equal and not privileged in comparison to the Polish natives. And the fight was won.

From Korzybski's account one would get no sense of the extent of Jewish poverty in every part of partitioned Poland or the significant wealth of some of the members of his own class, the Polish szlachta—and their frequent exploitation of the less privileged. (The excesses of some of the szlachta have been well-documented by Davies and Zamoyski among others.) The Jews of Poland had indeed specialized for centuries as economic "middlemen" (traders, shopkeepers, money-lenders, etc.) in the feudal Polish agricultural economy. (The Polish princes had originally invited them to come to Poland for that very purpose.) But Korzybski's statement about a "Jewish trust which boycotted Polish economic life" surely seems like the kind of exaggeration criticized by economist Thomas Sowell in his studies of "middleman minorities".[15]

Middleman minorities have traditionally been misunderstood and persecuted throughout the world. The Jews, as perhaps the archetypal middleman minority, became targets for all those Poles who didn't understand the legitimate role they played in the economy. As Poland emerged from feudalism, Jewish entrepreneurs had a natural advantage in the developing capitalistic and industrializing economy. Undoubtedly there were Jewish crooks, as there were Polish ones. Korzybski may have met some. But it was too easy in Poland as in other places, for people to see that "Fagin was a Jew" and come to the incorrect conclusion, as Korzybski seems to have done, that "Every Jew was a Fagin."[16]

Korzybski analyzed this kind of misevaluation in his later work, but at this stage in his life, he was still not immune to it himself. The Polish cooperative movement's attempted boycott of Jewish businesses, which Korzybski described above, gained momentum after the 1905 revolution. Not only did it *not* make the Jews "equal" as he claimed, it marked the blossoming of an extreme and exclusionary version of Polish nationalism which became associated with severe antisemitism.

The New Machine

At the National Arts Club, Korzybski soon made contact with the writer Charles Ferguson, who had been living there. Ferguson, trained as a lawyer, and a former Episcopal and then Unitarian minister, had written a number of books and articles on social and economic reform and had traveled to Europe and Asia on study missions for President Wilson and the U.S. State Department. In New York, Ferguson had gotten involved with a circle of people centered around the industrial engineer, H. L. Gantt, whom Korzybski met just before Gantt's sudden death from food poisoning at the end of 1919. (Gantt gave Alfred a signed copy of his last book *Organizing for Work*.)[17]

Gantt, considered one of the founders of Project Management, had earlier worked with Frederick W. Taylor, who founded the discipline of "Scientific Management". Gantt had developed a method of charting found useful for large-scale industrial planning (indeed, it is still being used today). Ferguson, Gantt and others, mostly members of the American Society of Mechanical Engineers, had hopes of applying this and other methods of industrial engineering to social problems and had formed an organization in 1916 called "The New Machine", later called "The Technarchy". This group had a natural attraction for Alfred, with his engineering bent and his urgency for political-social-economic reform. Korzybski became friendly with Ferguson and began to read his work.

In Ferguson's 1915 book, *The Great News*, he had coined the term "social credit" to label his own and related notions of economic reform developed by the English writer

C. H. Douglas and others. In their view, cooperatives, under the advice of scientists and engineers, could wrest control of the credit system from bankers in order to insure a more equitable distribution of buying power. Shortly, Korzybski became enthralled with Ferguson's ideas and, for a time, seriously advocated them, recommending Ferguson's 1918 book, *The Revolution Absolute,* to friends and correspondents.

Alfred may have rejected what he saw as the extremes of capitalistic commercialism but he also viewed socialism as unrealistic though he did seem to find it appealing. As can be seen in his "Profiteers" article, he already had an interest in cooperative economics and saw in Ferguson's book a theoretical basis for the co-op movement—a kind of "social capitalism"—which he hoped could become strengthened in Poland and elsewhere.

At this time, Korzybski also had an interest in the efforts of Glenn Plumb, an attorney for the Railworker's Union, who had formed an organization dedicated to nationalizing the U.S. railway system. The railroads would be purchased by the federal government with funds from a bond issue. The government would then lease them for an extended period of time to a managing organization made up of representatives from the government, present management, and railroad workers. The "Plumb Plan" was criticized as a move toward Bolshevism and never materialized. Korzybski had hoped to get Plumb together with Ferguson and Samuel Gompers, but was unable to arrange a meeting.

By the fall, Mira and Alfred had decided to put off the trip to Poland—the first of many times they did so. He had applied to become a manufacturer's representative in Poland for International Harvester and for Ford Motor Company. They turned him down. But he was still looking for business opportunities which would enable him to inject something useful into the Polish economy while making a living there.

In the meantime, Korzybski threw his considerable energy into the cause of the "New Machine". Perhaps there was some way to use Polish community resources in the U.S. and Canada to finance and create cooperative enterprises in Poland. Promoting Ferguson's work might help inspire such activities. Alfred participated in several meetings of the New Machine which were held in New York. He was full of ideas. He contemplated editing a shortened version of *The Revolution Absolute* with added commentary by himself, and also doing a Polish translation of the work. Ferguson was grateful for Alfred's offers to promote his work and eventually gave him translation rights to the book. He inscribed the following in Alfred's copy of *The Revolution Absolute*:

> To Alfred Korzybski Soldier–Publicist, living spokesman of the dead who have been slain by the abominable politics—a man who thinks with emotion and feels with discretion, and so is fit for the greatest things. With affection and gratitude for wise counsils [sic].[18]

At the end of September, Alfred had occasion for severe disappointment. The U.S. Senate struck down the proposed Peace Treaty in a test vote. The sticking point had been U.S. membership in the League of Nations (the Treaty and the League were definitively voted down in November). A few days later, President Wilson—whom Alfred greatly admired—had to cut short his nationwide speaking tour promoting the Treaty, after suffering a stroke. (Amazingly, Wilson—bedridden and severely disabled—continued serving as President until the end of his term in March 1921, his wife and staff maintaining a kind of surrogate presidency in his name.) Notwithstanding these events, Washington was made the site of a League of Nations' International Labor Conference starting at the end of October. Alfred was selected to serve the Polish delegation as a secretary.

A Villain With A Smiling Cheek

Before heading to Washington where he was to meet Mira, Alfred attended a meeting of Ferguson's group on October 31, where he introduced an acquaintance of his—Boris Brasol—to the group. Brasol, a cultured Russian émigré, worked for the Army Military Intelligence Department (MID). Korzybski, who had contacts at MID, may have met Brasol while visiting or lecturing there:

> Mr. Brasol, who I am expecting this evening, is one of the most brilliant brains that Russia has ever produced. He is a lawyer and attorney general here for the old Russian Government. His analytical brain belongs to the international world. He may be some day a tremendous power in putting the New Machine in Russia.[19]

Herein lies a curious tale of misevaluating. The literate and sophisticated Brasol, who arrived late to the October 31 meeting, surely qualified as what Shakespeare would call "a villain with a smiling cheek".[20] Would Korzybski—hardly a lover of Tsarism—have spoken so highly of Brasol if he had known more about this "goodly apple rotten at the heart",[21] a member of the notorious "Black Hundreds" organization in Tsarist Russia? The Black Hundreds had supported the most extreme ideology of authoritarian monarchism with an associated army of thugs to terrorize those whom they considered enemies of the Tsarist state—among them Jews. As a lawyer in the Ukraine, Brasol had worked for the Tsarist Ministry of Justice assisting in the government prosecution of a Jew, Mendel Beilis, on charges of ritually murdering a boy in order to obtain his blood to make matzah. Beilis sat in jail from 1911 to 1913 before finally being released after trial; the jury accepted his innocence while agreeing that Jews sometimes *did* murder children to make matzah. (His travails were fictionalized in Bernard Malamud's 1966 novel, *The Fixer*.) Brasol's "analytic brain" now belonged to the expanding international world of proto-Nazi antisemitism that had infected Tsarist Russia and was spreading throughout Europe and the U.S. like an epidemic. Sometime during the war, Brasol—who had been working for the Russian government in London—met members of the MID. After the Russian Revolution, they helped him to come to the U.S., where he soon became an agent for the intelligence organization.

Brasol brought with him a copy of the *Protocols of the Elders of Zion*, which detailed a supposed secret meeting of Jewish leaders—the Elders of Zion—in Switzerland in 1897. (The place and date corresponded to those of the well publicized meeting of the First Zionist Congress in Basel, presided over by Theodore Herzl.) First published in 1905, the forged *Protocols* document was put together by agents of the Ochrana, the Tsar's Secret Police which, as historian Norman Davies described it, "…learned how to invent the problems which it was supposed to solve. Working on the fail-safe principle of provokatsiya (provocation), the Ochrana fomented conspiracies in order to break them,…".[22] The *Protocols*, which provided 'proof' of a 'Jewish plot' for world domination, was its pièce de résistance. (See Norman Cohn's *Warrant for Genocide* and Will Eisner's *The Plot*.)

People at the MID, as in other places, were becoming more and more concerned about the possible expansion of Bolshevism beyond Russia. For this very reason, at MID after the war there was strong support for the Polish national cause as a bulwark against a Soviet advance into Europe. This was probably one of the main reasons for Korzybski's visits to MID headquarters. As Joseph Bendersky documents in his book *The Jewish Threat*, many of the MID staff found it relatively easy to at least seriously consider the possibility that the Russian

Revolution was part of a Jewish plot to take over the world. In 1918, Brasol gave a copy of the *Protocols* to Natalie DeBogory, another Russian émigré employed as the assistant of Captain Harris Houghton, M.D, another MID intelligence officer. DeBogory translated it into English with Brasol's help. Houghton, already obsessed with Jews and Bolshevism, became interested. He and Brasol began introducing the document to select people at MID and the State Department.

By the beginning of 1919, Brasol's and Houghton's missionary work was succeeding. The notion of a Jewish-Bolshevik conspiracy seemed to spread exponentially and was becoming familiar to many people in the U.S. government, especially in the Army and the State Department. One who believed this fundamentally unwarranted rumor about the Jews would transmit it (like an infectious disease) to others who, if they accepted it, would spread it to others still. At some point along the way, such a one might hear the rumor again from someone else, which to an uncritical person would 'confirm' the rumor's correctness. A Senate Committee on Bolshevik Propaganda, headed by North Carolina Senator Lee S. Overman, began investigative hearings in February 1919. The Overman Committee heard hours of testimony concerning the supposed Jewish plot. Reverend George A. Simons of New York City, who had lived in Russia from 1907 to 1918, introduced the *Protocols* to the committee. Simons believed Jews from New York's Lower East Side had fomented the Bolshevik Revolution.[23] Representatives of the American Jewish community testified to the Overman Committee to refute these claims.

By 1920 Boston publisher Small, Maynard & Company issued *The Protocols and World Revolution*, Brasol's translation of the *Protocols* with his commentary. (Brasol seems to have decided he could insinuate his poison better if he remained anonymous as the author.) Brasol got a copy to the rabidly antisemitic automaker Henry Ford who then hired him to help promulgate the anti-Jewish creed in a series of articles based on the *Protocols*, which were published from 1920 to 1922 in Ford's newpaper, *The Dearborn Independent*. Millions of copies of *The International Jew*, a book by Ford based on these articles, were distributed internationally. Ford's book inspired Hitler and the Nazi movement. Later, in the 1930s, Brasol wrote for *Social Justice*, a magazine published by the antisemitic radio priest Father Coughlin. Brasol was suspected of working as a Nazi agent then and throughout World War II. He spoke modestly when, in 1921, he claimed in a letter to a friend: "Within the last year I have written three books, two of which have done the Jews more injury than would have been done by ten pogroms."[24]

No direct evidence exists that Brasol gave Alfred a copy of the *Protocols* or described its contents to him in 1919. (Korzybski later obtained a copy of the 1920 Small, Maynard book.) Yet it doesn't seem unlikely that Brasol may have introduced the *Protocol's* message to Korzybski and to the other people involved with the New Machine. He definitely had the opportunity at or around the time of the October 31, 1919 meeting. Although Ferguson himself seems to have remained free of antisemitism, many of his colleagues in the "Social Credit" movement did not. C. H. Douglas, the main social credit theorist, became a life-long advocate of the *Protocols*. (Korzybski probably met Douglas in New York in 1919 after Ferguson arranged a meeting between the two men.) Becoming acquainted with people like the M.I.D. conspiracy theorists, Boris Brasol, and C.H. Douglas was probably not the best way to reduce whatever stereotypes about Jews that Alfred had absorbed from his earlier days in Poland—where anti-Jewish sentiments had been festering since the last quarter of the 19th Century.[25]

Only a few days after the New Machine meeting where he had introduced Brasol, Korzybski arrived in Washington for the International Labor Conference. He seemed to 'have a bee in his bonnet' about the *Protocols* since he almost immediately began trying to find the whereabouts of Harris Houghton, Brasol's collaborator.[26] He also obtained a copy of the report of the Overman Committee—Mira had requested it from the office of California Senator James D. Phelan, who sent a copy of the document to the Korzybskis' hotel room.[27] Whether he ever found Houghton is unknown. And until August 1920, there is little if any hint of what he did with the Overman Committee material or of his developing views about Jews.

The International Labor Conference

An International Labor Organization (I.L.O.) had been established earlier that year at the Paris Peace Conference. Although a separate body, it was set up to work in cooperation with the League of Nations. Even though Congress had rejected the peace treaty and U.S. membership in the League, the U.S. had membership among the I.L.O. National delegations, which included representatives from governments, labor unions, and employers, meeting periodically in international conferences throughout the life of the organization. The first International Labor Conference was held in Washington, D.C. from Oct. 29, 1919 until Jan. 27, 1920. Korzybski attended in November and December, as a member of the Polish delegation.

Conference sessions involved discussions on proposals for reducing work hours, providing unemployment benefits, establishing child labor policies, setting up policies for working women, etc. The most memorable point of the meeting for Korzybski had less to do with these issues per se than with how they were evaluated and addressed by those attending:

>...a problem [came up.] They were talking at cross-purposes. The groups [of employers, union representatives, etc.] could not understand each other at all. They were talking English, perfectly good English, but they were speaking such a language that it was [getting] in the way of intercommunication. Finally, [Samuel] Gompers got up,..."Ladies and gentlemen, may I ask a question?" Of course when Gompers was asking a question everybody was at attention. He was a real fellow, a very reasonable man. The answer, of course, was "Go ahead, Mr. Gompers." And he asked, "Does yes mean always yes, or does yes sometimes mean no?" The conference was thrown into a panic. They adjourned. The verdict came back. Some professors of Harvard and Yale they were specialists in languages of some sort, or economists, I don't know, wrote down the verdict that yes always means yes and no means always no. The most idiotic thing any group of scholars could do because even the question may be asked in such a way, the same question, that in one way you may answer yes, the same question, the same answer, and if you put the question otherwise you might have to answer no. It is so idiotic to have that kind of stuff...[28]

>[Some time later] Gompers...rose to his feet, waited solemnly for a longer while, and when everybody was expecting a flood of words, he said very calmly one word "YES." The whole conference burst into laughter.[29]

Korzybski and everyone else who laughed with Gompers could sense the folly of the professors' approach to language. But they had no decent language themselves to talk about it. It bothered Korzybski that "the whole conference collapsed. No results whatsoever." He came away feeling disgusted: "...those international meetings, the League of Nations, they simply cannot talk sense."[30] It would take a number of years before Korzybski would be able to explain the mechanism of the professors' folly in terms of his future theory of human evaluating. His more immediate response was to run to do something practical. He was still planning to return to Poland and he wanted to get beyond the realm of empty words he had been listening to, to do something with down-to-earth value for his homeland.

The Polish Mechanics Company

The International Labor Conference had not adjourned, but Alfred—either because his official role had ended or because he had resigned in disgust—left Washington with Mira at the end of December. The new year—1920—found them in New York City with their base of operations at the National Arts Club on 15th Street. Since they were delaying their move to Poland, Mira was in search of new painting commissions. In the meantime, Alfred had gotten involved with the Polish Mechanics Company, recently formed in Toledo, Ohio with branches in Chicago, New York, Detroit, Philadelphia, Rochester, and Warsaw, Poland. The company leaders, a group of Polish-American engineers and businessmen, hoped to get Polish immigrants in America to invest in manufacturing ventures in Poland. The firm, which continued operating until 1940, became the largest and most successful of a number of such companies set up by Poles in the U.S.

In mid-January, Korzybski began a whirlwind speaking/fund-raising tour for the company. From January 17 until the end of the month he traveled and lectured in Philadelphia, Chester, Wilmington, Camden, Trenton, Perth Amboy, Elizabeth, Passaic, Paterson, Jersey City, Newark, Schenectady, Amsterdam, Utica, Syracuse, Fulton and Oswego. Then it was back to New York City for a couple of weeks—he and Mira had moved to an apartment on 8th Street—before going on another lecture tour. In mid-February he went to Toledo, then Grand Rapids, Kalamazoo, Battle Creek, Jackson, Detroit, and back to Toledo before returning to New York on February 25.[31] A poster in Polish advertised one of Korzybski's talks in Michigan:

> WHY? Every Pole and Polish Woman to whose hands this flyer will fall should participate in the great rally of the Polish Mechanics Company in America. Engineer A. Korzybski, the most gifted speaker in New York, a veteran of the last war, will speak on Saturday February 14 at 7 p.m. in the Polish Falcons' Hall on Larch Ave. 1) The government of Poland and the whole society support our work. 2) You will assure a better future for your children. 3) You will return to Poland to your own benchwork. 4) You won't give away the industry into foreign hands. 5) You will hear about the first cooperative organization in the world. 6) You will be a member of an organization numbering 6,000 intelligent Poles in the United States. 7) You will not disappoint the hope invested in you by your brothers and sisters waiting with happiness for you in the father land. 8) You will move the industry in Poland and you will pull from misery the Polish worker. 9) You will create an exemplary school. 10) You will be among your own where your heart and your understanding are calling you. All these questions will be mostly clarified at the rally. The attendance is free to everyone. No political disputes...[32]

Soon after Alfred's return to New York City in the beginning of March, Mira went to Detroit to do a portrait. Meanwhile Alfred, continuing his work for the Polish Mechanics Company, applied to the Fidelity and Deposit Company in Maryland to become the company's bonded representative, worked to set up a private banking business for the company in New York in order to help Poles forward money to their relations in Poland without the excessive exchange rates demanded from other banks, and investigated New York City real estate for the company, which wanted to buy an apartment building in the city. He was applying himself to company business with vigor. In turn, the people at the company seemed appreciative and eager for him to continue the relationship.

In April, he went to Michigan to meet Mira. Having completed the portrait in Detroit, she visited her childhood home of Jackson, where the Art Association was sponsoring an exhibition of her paintings. Alfred got there in time to attend a reception in Mira's honor. From Michigan, they made their way to Kansas City to visit Mira's sister, Amy, on her farm. From there they planned to return to New York and leave for Europe and Poland in the fall.

Before leaving New York City, at the beginning of April, Alfred had written a note to Ferguson, still expressing his admiration for *The Revolution Absolute*. He wanted to shorten the text and add more explicit chapters on cooperatives. It seems likely he was still planning to do this when he and Mira got to Amy's farm in mid-April. However, Alfred's focus was already shifting from Ferguson's work, from his business with the Polish Mechanics Company, and from Poland. He had gotten sidetracked by a vision.

Part IV
Time-Binder

"We have indeed known that the character and status of the so-called human or social sciences depend upon what man is; *but we have not reflected upon the fact that they depend also, in equal or greater measure, upon what humans* think *man is."*
— Cassius J. Keyser[1]

Chapter 16
"BINDING TIME"

By mid-April 1920, Mira and Alfred were in Missouri, visiting Mira's sister Amy before heading back east to New York City, from where they planned to go on to London and then to Poland. Amy's farm in Lees Summit, Missouri—on the outskirts of Kansas City—served as a refuge for all of the Edgerly sisters at one time or another. Mira had last spent time there with Amy in the summer of 1918 after the unexpected death of Amy's husband, Rush Lake, a well-liked Missouri politician.

Korzybski would often return to Kansas City and its environs over the next couple of decades, either to visit Amy's farm or to work with associates in the city. He found the city and region around it unusually beautiful. But among many of the inhabitants he felt a certain "sad" quality, something he couldn't quite put his finger on. Since, with whatever he observed, he was in the habit of looking for functional relationships, he wondered if there wasn't something in the soil or water.

But he didn't spend much time thinking about Kansas City's denizens. He hoped to use his time on the farm to write. He had come there with a notion to abridge, and then write a commentary upon, the specific ideas for social-economic reform in Ferguson's *The Revolution Absolute*. He had wanted to come up with a shorter and more widely accessible book in English that he could then translate into Polish and other languages. However, in conversations with Mira and others, it had become clear that the specific solutions suggested by Ferguson, Plumb, and the League of Nations advocates, among others, didn't go far enough for him. Clearer answers to more general questions that had been plaguing him for a long time could make these efforts at specific solutions more useful. Alfred continued to circle around these questions.

One of the questions had started in childhood. Alfred had spent a lifetime observing animal behavior (horses, farm animals, etc.) He didn't doubt that animals such as horses could 'think'. Indeed he had known horses whose 'sense' seemed to greatly exceed that of humans he had known. Yet he also remembered the peasants who had exclaimed to him, "Master, we are not beasts." That stuck with him. What made the difference between humans and animals?

Since the end of the war he had had more time to think, not only about the difference between a man and an animal, but along a second line of questioning. He had spent his life observing people and what they do in a variety of settings. Since childhood, he had managed and observed workers and peasants on his family's farm. As a young man, he had studied extremes of human behavior in places that others might prefer to neglect, for example visiting jails to observe criminals, prostitutes, etc. And he had read, read, read: history, philosophy, science, mathematics, etc. These, as well as his personal experiences of the 1905 revolution and especially of the tragedies and suffering of World War I, had brought him to his present perplexity: What made the differences between different kinds of human activity and enterprise?

Perhaps he had been stimulated in this line of thinking by his "thrashing out" discussions with Mira and in his discussions with Ferguson, who felt strongly about "the need for science and engineering intelligence to govern the administration of credit, etc."[1] His, by this time habitual, inclination to read a book by studying its author and to understand a subject by seeing it as a product of human behavior, led him along the following track:

Look [at] historical facts. Again I will not be exact because I would say among others that bridges do not collapse, and if they collapse we can always find the error in the calculations or blueprint. If they do collapse you always can trace. But in principle they do not collapse. And our civilization, also man-made, collapses all the time. War, revolution; war, revolution; war, revolution, through all history. Why is it, that bridges do not collapse—man-made—and human civilizations fall one after another?

The question comes, who makes bridges, and how, that they do not collapse? Engineers make bridges. How do they do it? They are talking to themselves in mathematical language. They use a language which is similar in structure to the 'facts' they are dealing with, and therefore they are successful; their bridges and what not don't collapse. They have predictability in their language, what will happen if they do that and that; and therefore they can do what is needed to make the given bridge or whatever function properly, and avoid doing something which will make it collapse.

In the meantime who is building up civilization, culture and what not? Lawyers, politicians, philosophers—you know philosophers all through history have played a tremendously important role in building a given culture, a given civilization; I will not go into a long line of who built it, because we can add indefinitely—newspaper men among others, and so on and so on and so on. And the question is, how do they do [it]? They talk to themselves and talk to others, like the engineer—except they talk the vernacular, a language unfit to talk sense, and this is why the result collapse, collapse, collapse, one after another. Now this was the beginning. This was a long stretch of time: this was not simple. It was agony to analyze and come to these conclusions.[2]

These questions and his pondering about them had been providing an ever-increasing internal background to Alfred's activities over the past year. Sometime before in New York City between his various trips, he had visited the Woolworth Building in downtown Manhattan, at the time the tallest building in the world. As he stood atop it, Alfred looked down at the streets of New York and his puzzlement seemed to crystallize:

...I was looking over New York. That enormous city, steaming, boiling with life...And I asked myself the question, how it happens, the physical side of it looking at the street, at Broadway. You saw vermin crawling, and the vermin were humans. They were so small because the height was so great, and a streetcar was a caterpillar. ...Looking at that, I was much intrigued. I was fully aware that everyone of those little bits of humans there, everyone was full of joy, sorrows, and what not. And who did that tremendous thing called New York? That vermin did it. I didn't get my answer there, but I was asking how humans, little things like that with such a wealth of personal life, how in the dickens can they do such a thing as New York, London, Paris, wars, revolutions, and what not?[3]

Epiphany

"What makes humans human?" and "Why do our social institutions collapse while bridges mostly don't?" In his quest for answers to his questions Korzybski clearly seemed in part to have been inspired by Charles Ferguson. In *The Revolution Absolute* Ferguson had announced that,

The day has come to apply the Baconian principle [of inductive science] to politics. Inductive science has ruled for three hundred years in the realm of physics, and the whole body of modern technology is an achievement of the Baconian method. But in politics we are still sitting in the grove of Socrates discussing high abstractions...[p. 205]

[Bacon had avoided discussing] the inevitable antagonism between inductive science and the Aristotelian abstractions enthralling the politics of his day...[p. 8]

> [Pursuing a Baconian sociology means dealing with] the all-inclusive social question...:
> *How can the social constitution achieve the highest possible power over the forces and materials of nature?* [p. 13]⁴

The desire to extend the reach of science into human life—even the criticism of "Aristotelian abstractions"—was already there in Ferguson's work. Yet Alfred's emphasis on the importance of mathematics was leading him further. If he could come up with a clear, definite, and scientifically sound definition of Man, he thought he would have something more exact and solid than a Baconian inductive science. He would have the basis for a deductive—a mathematics-like—science of humanity.

For their room, Amy had given Alfred and Mira the large, glass-enclosed porch of the farmhouse. They had a double bed and a table with a typewriter where Alfred began to peck in his two-fingered style. As he described it, "I spit out everything I could in big generalities about god and the devil, the world, and what not, science and mathematics." He didn't feel he was getting very far. "What makes man think? What is the special characteristic of humanity? This bothered me and bothered me and the sight from the Woolworth building..."⁵

> ...I was brooding about the role of plants in this world. What did they do? They synthesized the chemistry of the soil and air and sun (I didn't have the term chemistry-binding then). 'What is the role of a dog or a horse or a monkey? 'Well, they eat.' 'What do they eat?' Animals depend on eating [plants or other animals], drinking, and then trotting around. They begin where they began, they end where they end.' I was sitting on Amy's farm on the porch. At night one night I sat up in bed. I knew about plants, then animals. Animals – you can not deny them communication – 'talking'. They can transmit nothing. I sat up in bed – *'We can transmit from generation to generation'* [Italics mine – BIK]. I solved this in sleep. I cried. I didn't have the term 'time-binding' then. It took me a day, [maybe] about 2 or 3 – I had to have a label. Then I built up the terminology. We <u>can</u> transmit —whether we do or not — theories, religion, tabus — they cut their heads off in some tribes, [a] method [of] stopping time-binding [that] is simple and effective.⁶

"Binding Time"

The main formulation of what would become Alfred's first published book, *Manhood of Humanity* (1921), had popped up in his sleep. But it had resulted from years of reading, contemplating and internal struggle. 'Man'—a term which Korzybski used in the accepted 1920s sense as equivalent to all humankind, i.e., men, women, and children—constitutes the "binding time" class of life. (In the final published version, perhaps under the influence of native English-speaking editors, he changed the term to "time-binding").

Our symbolic/linguistic capacities allow us humans to 'bind' or organize our experiences and/or the products of our experiences so as to transmit and receive from one person and one time to another. Because we have the potential to begin where the prior individual or generation left off, we can benefit from and build upon the experiences of others at an accelerating rate. Even though animals might communicate and transmit their experiences to some extent, the facility that humans have to do this puts us in a qualitatively different dimension from other creatures.

Alfred finished the first draft of the book rather quickly, possibly within a week or two. He had little in the way of reference books. The most 'scientific' book on his sister-in-law's shelves seems to have been an old copy of Herbert Spencer's *The Principles of Biology*. Korzybski's completed manuscript entitled *The Manhood of Humanity and its Universal Language*⁷—the language being mathematics—made no direct reference to Charles Ferguson's program of social reforms, although it seemed in keeping with Ferguson's goal for a scientific sociology. More specifically, the manuscript explored what Alfred considered necessary for building an applied science of humanity, a *human engineering* as he termed it. Human engineering would make conscious use of the human capacity to "bind time" and thus apply it more usefully to all human activities. This would allow humanity as a whole to close the period of its childhood.

The Language and Logic of Nature

The definitions of the different classes of life remained somewhat muted in this first draft, indeed the definitions of plant and animal life are implied but not given explicitly. Korzybski chose to spend considerable time discussing mathematics—"the universal language" mentioned in the original title. Much of the detail of this discussion of mathematical thinking in the first draft was subsequently deleted. However, some of it seems worth noting here. It highlights, perhaps even more clearly than what eventually got published in the book, some long-standing motivational factors which persisted in influencing Korzybski's subsequent work.

For Alfred, the science of human engineering required embracing mathematics as its main helpmate. The processes and products of mathematical reasoning provided a level of security unattainable anywhere else. He indicated this with the introductory quote from Louis Brandeis that he retained in the published book:

"For a while he trampled with impunity on laws human and divine but, as he was obsessed with the delusion that two and two makes five, he fell, at last a victim to the relentless rules of humble Arithmetic. "Remember, O stranger, Arithmetic is the first of the sciences and the mother of safety." [8]

Alfred noted what continued to be one of the main articles of his scientific credo: that mathematics provides a language and logic of nature, including human nature. As he wrote, this 'logic' seems especially tied up with the study of mathematical functions (relations between variables)—the basis of the infinitesmal calculus that his father had introduced to him as a young child. The feel of the calculus had long since permeated Alfred's view of the world since he tended to look at the world in terms of indefinitely-varying functional relationships.

If human life was to be rightly understood and changed for the better, this kind of mathematical thinking had to be applied to human problems. As Alfred saw it, this didn't necessarily require great complexity or elaborate calculations. Although it became a secondary part of the published version of his first book, the notion of mathematics—or more precisely physico-mathematical method—as a guide to life began to emerge as a major theme in Alfred's subsequent writings.

Man as an Exponential Power

Alfred believed that the growth of knowledge in the sciences and technology exemplified time-binding progress. Could he represent this mathematically? If time-binding was cumulative, the result of time-binding in any generation would be proportional to the amount of knowledge already present. This would have to involve an exponential or geometrical function. By early May, he was playing with this kind of progression—$Y = 2^x$—on a piece of scrap stationary that he had already used to draft some letters. On the stationary he also doodled some branching lines whose geometric growth followed the equation. It was a diagram of what 25 years later would become widely known as a "chain reaction"—the secret of the atomic bomb.

Starting with X=1, then 2, then 3, etc., he had written the successive values of Y: 2, then 4, 8, 16, 32, 64, 128, 256, 512, 1024, etc. The series showed an accelerating rate of growth since each successive number was proportional to the quantity already present—it came from multiplying that quantity by another 2. Underneath this set of numbers, Alfred had written the arithmetical or linear sequence of Y=2X—2, 4, 6, 8, 10, 12,14,16,18, 20, etc. Relative to the geometric sequence, this sequence grew at a constant, slow rate because each number came from adding—not multiplying—2 to its predecessor.

1920 Doodle – Chain Reaction (Y= 2^x) [9]

For Alfred, it seemed that he had gotten to the core of the distinguishing characteristic of humanity: "...a man is some exponential function where the exponent or power is <u>Time</u>." [10] But what was the specific function? As an examination of both the draft and final versions of the book shows, "power" was an important term for Korzybski—not only in its limited sense as a mathematical exponent. For him, time-binding involved 'power' in both the physical science and the social-cultural senses. The accumulated achievements of past generations provided the present generation with increasing means of power for doing productive work. Starting from the notion of power in physics and extending this into the social-cultural realm led Alfred to what he considered "the natural law for the human class of life."[11]

In the physics formula for power, P=W/T. P stands for power, W stands for work (defined in term of energy—force times distance) and T stands for time. The formula defines power as the rate at which work (energy) is expended. Multiplying both sides by T gives the formula W=TP, Work equals Time x Power. It seemed to Alfred that if 'man' was a part of the natural universe, human social-cultural life could be understood by extending the framework of such physical terms.

Wealth could be viewed, for example, in terms of work, i.e., as the accumulated work or products of work of previous generations. He made P equal to progress (the accumulated time-bound work inherited from the dead at any point in time). T times P gave it the same kind of unit as W. To account for the growth from one time-binding generation to the next, he brought in a factor R which represented the ratio of progress having the exponent of time—i.e. R^T. The time exponent T could be represented most simply by an integer showing the number of generations. Voilà—he had a formula for time-binding—W=TPR^T—with Wealth equaling human progress as an exponential function of time. In the published book, Korzybski dropped T as a factor, and ended up with the basic formula, PR^T:

> ...The typical term of the progression is *PR^T* where *PR* denotes the ending progress made in the generation with which we agree to start our reckoning. *R* denotes the ratio of increase, and *T* denotes the number of generations after the chosen "start." The quantity *PR^T* of progress made in the *T*th generation contains *T* as an exponent, and so the quantity, varying as *T* passes, is called an exponential function of time.[12]

Korzybski theorized that the growth of knowledge in the physical sciences and technology approaches exemplary time-binding. Its relatively high rate of growth seemed to show a rapidly-rising exponential character—its curve growing steeper with each generation of scientists as more and more knowledge accumulated. For the most part, our social/behavioral knowledge—law, politics, economics, morals, human relationships, etc.—did not appear to represent successful time-binding. These areas of knowledge, what Korzybski called the semi-sciences, seemed to grow at a much slower rate, as if in an arithmetical straight line, in comparison with the more rapidly rising geometrical growth curve of science.

Consequences

With his behavioral definition of humanity and his exponential formula of progress in hand, Korzybski sought to draw out the social-cultural implications of time-binding. For one thing, he now had an answer to the second question that had bothered him for so long: "Why do our social institutions collapse while bridges mostly don't?" (Except for some rewriting for brevity, form, and order, most of his analysis in the first draft found its way into the published book.) Our social institutions continued to collapse because of the growing gap between our increasing knowledge of and power over the 'physical' world (exemplified by bridge-building technology) and our inadequate and/or inadequately-applied knowledge of ourselves and our social relationships. According to Korzybski, this growing gap accounted to a significant degree for the continuing cycle of wars and revolutions, as humans unsuccessfully attempted to cope with the effects of increasing technological progress. He predicted that more and greater disasters would ensue—collapsing social structures—until humans somehow managed to narrow the divide between science and the rest of human affairs.

A major step in narrowing the gap would occur, according to Korzybski, when we abandoned theological and zoological definitions of ourselves. He insisted that humans could not understand themselves adequately if they continued defining themselves as some additive combination of supernatural ('soul', 'spirit', etc.) and 'animal'. To Alfred, this view (man as an animal plus a divine spark) appeared to make a comprehensive scientific study of humanity impossible. Neither could humans understand themselves adequately if they insisted on viewing themselves simply as 'animals' destined to play out brutal competitive games for goods and territory. This view—"man is an animal"—diminished humanity and could justify the worst kind of behavior as "survival of the fittest". Rather, viewing 'Man' as a time-binder would naturally include altruism:

> ..."survival of the fittest" for human beings *as such*—that is, for *time-binders*—is survival *in time*, which means intellectual or spiritual competition, struggle for excellence, for making the *best* survive. The-fittest-in-time—those who make the best survive—are those who do the most in producing values for all mankind including *posterity*.[13]

Korzybski spent considerable effort elaborating on the economic implications of time-binding. In terms of time-binding, wealth consisted of

> ...those things—whether they be material commodities or forms of knowledge and understanding—that have been produced by the time-binding energies of humanity, and according to which *nearly all the wealth of the world at any given time* is the *accumulated fruit of the toil of past generations*—the living work of the dead.[14]

Economically, money represented but didn't constitute wealth. Korzybski warned "...against confusing the "*making*" of money by hook or crook, by trick or trade, with the *creating* of wealth, by the product of labor."[15]

Clearly, for Korzybski, knowledge constituted the basis of wealth. Later on in the 1930s, Austrian economist Friedrich Hayek—following in the free market tradition of Adam Smith, Ludwig von Mises, et al—wrote about the role of knowledge in human social-economic life. However, I've seen little indication that Hayek or his colleagues had any awareness of Korzybski's formulation of time-binding. And Korzybski didn't pursue a connection with their work. Indeed, in 1920, Korzybski seemed to tilt toward socialistic views and denounced Adam Smith as an apostle of selfishness and greed (his animus against Smith got somewhat toned down in the journey from manuscript to published book). After writing *Manhood,* Korzybski's interests shifted from the political-economic applications of time-binding and he never made any major study of economics.

From his time-binding view of wealth, Korzybski criticized both capitalists and socialists in the pages of the book:

> There are capitalists and capitalists; there are socialists and socialists. Among the capitalists there are those who want wealth—mainly the fruit of dead men's toil—for themselves. Among the socialists there are those—the orthodox socialists—who seek to disperse it. The former do not perceive that the product of the labor of the dead is itself dead if not quickened by the energies of living men. The orthodox socialists do not perceive the tremendous benefits that accrue to mankind from the accumulation of wealth, if *rightly used.*[16]
>
> ..."capitalistic" lust to *keep* for SELF and "proletarian" lust to *get* for SELF are both of them *space*-binding lust—animal lust—beneath the level of time-binding life.[17]

A different political-economic approach must result from a time-binding perspective. He did not elaborate its details, but at its base he conceived it to involve a political-economic order, neither 'socialist' nor 'capitalist' as many people understand those terms, but focused on cooperation which would benefit all humans.

In his related political-economic analysis of the causes of the Great War, Alfred placed major, but not sole, responsibility on Germany. He noted the Germans' first rate ability to maintain group cohesion and apply their time-binding energies, i.e., scientific/technical prowess, in concerted mass effort towards narrow national aims. The Allies had barely won the war with great difficulty. Apropos German and other forms of nationalism, to the extent that members of different nations could not extend their views beyond their narrow group interests, further conflicts seemed inevitable.

Forerunners

Although what he expressed in his manuscript resulted from his own process of questioning, observation, and discovery, Korzybski would have been the first to admit that his notions were not entirely original. He had forerunners.

First of all, he had been prepared for the formulation of time-binding by the very time and location of his birth. By 1879, even a Pole born in Warsaw was in a real sense born into exile. For Poland did not exist—except in the history, culture, language, and literature that ethnic Poles sought to preserve and carry on to their younger generation. Since the beginning of the 19th century, Poles had been emigrating in large numbers from the oppressive conditions of post-partition existence. To remain a Pole required conscious effort whether one remained in the former Polish lands or went abroad. The mere fact of Alfred's beginning his life as a Pole seems likely to have sensitized him to the significance of preserving and transmitting a culture under difficult circumstances. In addition,

Korzybski's emphasis in *Manhood* on the value of a scientific-mathematical attitude to human affairs—leading to a "human engineering"—also seems like a natural outgrowth of his upbringing by an engineer father in the heyday of Polish positivist philosophy and its esteem of science.

A number of decades before Alfred's birth, the Polish national poet Adam Mickiewicz had called Poland, "the Christ of the Nations." Jesus, as we know, was a Jew. Poles had lived for hundreds of years in relative harmony among, what became for a time, the largest concentration of Jews in the world. The Jews, the people of Israel, had managed for millennia to preserve an independent social-cultural life and sense of peoplehood under the most trying conditions of oppression and exile from their ancient homeland. Does it take a great leap of imagination to consider that post-partition Poles, interested in preserving their unique culture and sense of nationhood, may have learned something from the example of the Jews in their midst? It would be surprising if Korzybski, who had a major life-long interest in Jews and Jewish themes, was not affected.

From ancient days, the Jewish tradition had certainly displayed a recognition of the phenomenon of time-binding. An important part of the Jewish tradition had always been its emphasis on the importance of tradition itself. The Hebrew word for tradition, *masorah* or *masoret,* originally had referred to a "bond" or "fetter".[18] The obligation for all Jews to study and transmit this tradition *l'dor v'dor* (from generation to generation) as well as the mechanism for interpreting and applying it to new conditions (Talmudic discourse), remained accepted and important parts of the tradition. Acceptance of this tradition as the birthright of every Jew led to the high literacy rates among Jews compared to other groups.

Korzybski's study of the humanist tradition of Europe, strongly represented in Poland, probably exerted a more direct effect on Alfred's formulation of the time-binding notion. Renaissance thinkers like Leonardo da Vinci (1452-1518) showed how one could acknowledge and learn from the past to develop one's excellence in the present and in this way contribute to future generations. In his 1902 biographical novel, *The Romance of Leonardo da Vinci* (English translation 1928), Russian writer Dmitri Merejkowski described a passage from da Vinci's notebooks:

> Once, desiring to present the development of human spirit, he drew a row of cubes: the first, falling, knocks down the second; the second, a third, the third, a fourth, and so on, *ad infinitum*. Underneath he wrote: "One jolts the other." And he also added: "The cubes designate the generations of mankind and the stages of its knowledge." On another drawing he represented a plough, turning up the earth, with the inscription: "*Persistent Rigour.*" He believed that his turn, too, would come in the row of falling cubes,—that at some time or other men would respond to his summons also.[19]

Continuing the humanist theme of the human origins of human culture, Korzybski's formulation of time-binding generalized his habit of reading a book by studying its author. Time-binding implied that any aspect of culture had an author—in fact multiple authors. In his later writing and teaching, Alfred would often emphasize art, mathematics, religion, science, etc., as "...manmade and nothing but." This didn't necessarily make them dependent on arbitrary foundations but, on the contrary, seemed to provide an approach for understanding, appropriating, and using them more effectively. And revising them when needed.

By the mid-1800s, the general notion of the process of transmission basic to time-binding had become widely accepted. George Boole, creator of the first system of mathematical logic, was able to clearly describe it in this passage from his address on "The Social Aspects of Intellectual Culture" to the Cuvierian Society, a science club in Cork, Ireland:
> Each generation as it passes away bequeathes to its successor not only its material works in stone and marble, in brass and iron, but also the truths which it has won, and the ideas which it has learned to conceive; its art, literature, science, and, to some extent, its spirit and morality. This perpetual transmission of the light of knowledge and civilization has been compared to those torch races of antiquity in which a lighted brand was transmitted from one runner to another until it reached the final goal. Thus it has been said do generations succeed each other, borrowing and conveying light, receiving the principles of knowledge, testing their truth, enlarging their application, adding to their number, and then transmitting them forward to coming generations—*Et quasi cursores vitai lampada tradunt [And like runners they pass on the torch of life]*. [Boole was quoting a line from *De Rerum Natura* by the Roman poet-philosopher Lucretius who lived from 99 B.C.E.–55 B.C.E. Not surprisingly, Greek thinkers prior to Lucretius had also recognized aspects of the process of time-binding.] [20]

In his manuscript and book, Korzybski had observed that,
> ...in animal life time does not play the role it plays in human life. Animals are limited by death permanently. If animals make any progress from generation to generation, it is so small as to be negligible. A beaver, for example, is a remarkable builder of dams, but he does not progress in the way of inventions or further development. A beaver dam is always a beaver dam.[21]

At the time he wrote this, there is no indication that he was aware of Abraham Lincoln's "Lecture on Discoveries and Inventions" first delivered in 1858. In this lecture, Lincoln clearly pointed out the difference between humans and animals (also using the example of beavers)[22] and provided a brief history and discussion of the conditions of human progress as he saw it. Lincoln noted the importance that cooperation, the use of speech, and the inventions of writing and the printing press, had in the sharing and transmission of knowledge. He pointed out a given generation's dependence on the discoveries and inventions of the past, including the discovery and invention of methods of discovery and invention. He also mentioned the accelerating aspect of the growth of human knowledge especially notable after the invention of the printing press: "...discoveries, inventions, and improvements followed rapidly and have been increasing their rapidity since."[23]

Interest in the idea of "progress" had become widespread by the mid-19th Century due in part to the work of Auguste Comte, founder of the discipline of sociology and of "positive philosophy". Korzybski's distinction between the childhood and the manhood of humanity echoed Comte's discussion of the three phases in the development of human knowledge: the Theological, the Metaphysical, and the Scientific or "Positive" stages. The flavor of optimism and sense of the inevitability of human progress expressed by Comte seem present in *Manhood* as well.

By the late 19th Century, in his work *Progress and Poverty* (a volume in Korzybski's personal library), American political economist Henry George demonstrated a sense of both the transmission of culture and of progress, consistent with the notion of time-binding:
> The narrow span of human life allows the individual to go but a short distance, but though each generation may do but little, yet generations, succeeding to the gain of their predecessors, may gradually elevate the status of mankind, as coral polyps, building one generation upon the work of the other, gradually elevate themselves from the bottom of the sea.[24]

Then in the first decade of the 20th Century, writer Henry Adams—noting the breathtaking changes brought on by expanding scientific knowledge and technological advances—had suggested a historical law of acceleration to account for them. Adams did not supply an actual equation, although he did suggest its exponential nature.

Clearly, the main factors that entered into Korzybski's formulation of time-binding had been recognized by many others before him. Granted, he stood on their shoulders. Still Korzybski's formulation of time-binding did do something new: It brought together the various related factors that others had previously noted, under one unifying, functional formulation and term. Making time-binding the distinguishing feature of the human class of life gave the phenomenon a greater significance. His attempt to quantify it with the equation PR^T and his emphasis on the implications and applications of conscious time-binding for human welfare gave added value to the formulation. It seemed to him that his new definition, with these accompanying aspects, constituted a proper starting point for an applied science of humanity—a new art and science of human engineering.

For both him and Mira, the book provided a kind of 'spiritual' satisfaction as well. With the formulation of time-binding, he had found some resolution for the questions that had been plagueing him for so long. By helping people to become more conscious and better time-binders, he might be able to encourage the kind of culture that could prevent future, more devastating wars. In addition, despite some of the manuscript's stylistic clumsiness, which he realized came in part from writing in a new language, he felt happy about his writing. In places he had managed to combine a degree of rigor with a simplicity of expression that pleased him.

The significance of Alfred's book certainly struck Mira. Since they had met, she had felt that he had something to express to the world that reflected her deepest values. She had been encouraging and encouraging him to write. Sometime later in the year, she wrote him this note:

I have told you from the beginning — my dearest one — how I <u>couldn't "get through"</u> to life — always cut off — always an individual — always an observing outsider — and do you know how I feel now — as if you and I had opened our veins and my blood is flowing into you and your blood into me — and <u>you</u> have made me a <u>part of life</u>, of humanity, in giving me this manuscript by which the ache of my heart to do something for humanity is satisfied. I am completely happy in being your wife...[25]

Mira's 1921 portrait of herself and Alfred

Chapter 17
DEAR DEAR OLD MEN

As Korzybski would insist throughout his life, without Mira's encouragement and help he would not have written his first book nor developed his work afterwards. Indeed, as he often stated, he wrote primarily for her. Without her to motivate him, he said he would have likely gone back to Poland and—at most—possibly written a book in the style of "Let the Dead Be Heard". Perhaps.

But Alfred was clearly not indifferent to his own formulations. His enthusiasm comes through in his writing, his letters, and the reports of other people. It seems clear; he too was struck with the implications of what he had come up with. At a certain point, he developed his work not only because of Mira's pushing but because he had his own, not inconsiderable, internal push as well.

He wanted a science of man, more specifically a science and art of human engineering. Although his formulation of time-binding was certainly not without precedents, it seemed to him he had made a genuine advance toward such a science and art—an advance in the mathematical 'spirit'. The sharp term "time-binding" pointed to what seemed the main distinction between the separate classes of humans and animals. His exponential formula for human progress seemed to quantitatively show the entirely different dimension of life humans lived in. But he knew he needed help—not only with editing his English prose.

Perhaps he recalled his final exam back in engineering school, when he and his professor belatedly discovered his theoretical machine, devised on the blackboard, couldn't possibly work. He wanted someone competent to check what he had done. Through contacts—perhaps by way of Amy—Alfred got a letter of introduction to the University of Chicago mathematician E. H. Moore. By the beginning of July 1920, having completed his manuscript, he and Mira left Lees Summit for New York via Chicago. They checked into the Morrison Hotel there and Alfred went to see Moore.

A world-renowned mathematician, Moore had served as Vice-President and President of the American Mathematical Society. Korzybski seemed to have no difficulty getting an appointment. Moore glanced through the manuscript quickly, immediately taking note of the PR^T formula. Though Moore seemed intrigued, he honestly told Alfred he had no time to read the whole thing, so Alfred spent the next half hour explaining human engineering and time-binding to him. Moore found it interesting but protested he was not competent to judge Alfred's idea. He did refer Alfred to Professor Cassius J. Keyser at Columbia University in New York, and wrote a letter of introduction. Alfred felt encouraged.[1]

While in Chicago, Alfred and Mira also met a man named Murray Schloss who had organized something called the "Hilltop Club" where Alfred gave a talk. The club's purpose was to provide "An interchange, propaganda place, and clearing house for all manner of movements, Philosophies, Organizations and Practical Projects that AIM FUNDAMENTALLY at a Better Age."[2] As Alfred and Mira had already discovered, post-World War I America was full of educated people trying to make sense of the war and its aftermath and looking for answers to social problems. Indeed for several years, beginning in 1919, Mira had a "black book" where the two of them kept names and clippings of anyone who seemed to have 'ideas' related to Alfred's. Eventually they stopped bothering with this, since they found many of these individuals had little interest in Alfred's work. But the people at the Hilltop Club certainly seemed interested and gave him his first public forum to speak about time-binding.

At the end of July, Alfred and Mira, with their multiple trunks and suitcases, took a train to New York City. In a few days, they had found a simple apartment at 1 University Place in Greenwich Village. On August 6, within a week of settling in, Alfred sent a letter to Cassius Keyser—together with Moore's introduction and a copy of his manuscript.

Cassius J. Keyser

Cassius J. Keyser, Adrain Professor of Mathematics at Columbia University, turned out to be just the man Alfred needed. Keyser had an abiding interest in the human aspects of mathematics and its connections to every aspect of education and life. For Keyser, mathematics constituted the prototype of rigor and excellence for human thinking. He sought as a teacher and writer, "…to engage in a dignified popularization of mathematics and science, to humanize and democratize them, to make the orientation of mathematicians and scientists available to the 'educated layman.'"[3] When he got Alfred's manuscript, Keyser quickly recognized someone who shared his aims and, furthermore, someone with an urgency and ability to put them into practice.

Keyser was born in 1862 in Rawson, Ohio in a log cabin. Young Cassius appeared to have learned a great deal about the practical aspects of life from his father, a farmer. He entered academia at an early age—by 1920 he had spent most of his working life as a teacher, first in public schools, and then in universities throughout the United States, while pursuing advanced studies. In 1901, he received his PhD in Mathematics at Columbia with a dissertation entitled *The Plane Geometry of the Point in Space of Four Dimensions*. Since then he had been on the Columbia Mathematics faculty, heading the department from 1910 to 1916. His students had included distinguished mathematicians such as E.T. Bell and Edward Kasner (both of whom later became friends with Korzybski), and Emil Post, a Polish-born Jew raised in the U.S. who had just gotten his PhD in 1920 on a topic inspired by a seminar he took with Keyser on Bertrand Russell and Alfred North Whitehead's recently published, three-volume *Principia Mathematica*. Post—whose writing on incompleteness and undecidability in mathematical systems (unpublished) predated the work of both Godel and Turing—gave credit to Keyser for the truth-table methods he used in developing his work.

Keyser had already published a number of books of essays on what Korzybski would call "the human, civilizing, practical life, point of view"[4] of mathematics including: *Science and Religion: The Rational and the Superrational*, *The New Infinity and the Old Theology*, and *The Human Worth of Rigorous Thinking*. When he got Korzybski's letter, he was in the midst of preparing the manuscript of a book he had been working on for a number of years, *Mathematical Philosophy: A Study of Fate and Freedom, Lectures for Educated Laymen*.

Something about Korzybski's manuscript grabbed Keyser immediately. In a letter to George Brett of MacMillan Publishing Company written several weeks later, Keyser wrote about his first impressions:

> I began the reading of it with indifference and misgiving. But it quickly aroused my interest, which grew deeper and deeper, and when I had finished reading I felt as I feel now, that the book is a timely one of great originality, great power and great importance.

Physically it is small but spiritually—philosophically and scientifically—it is big, the biggest thing I believe in its fundamental conceptions, that our extraordinary times have evoked. As its ideas are reflected upon and developed (for they are here presented in the rough and raw) they will be found to penetrate every cardinal interest of human kind.[5]

Within two days Keyser finished his initial reading and wrote back to Korzybski to arrange a meeting. Both men quickly realized their shared aims and what they could do for each other. In the notions of "time-binding" and "human engineering" Keyser found a clarification of his own understanding of mathematics and science as human activities and a general program to apply this understanding to human concerns. He decided he would have to do some rewriting of his own work-in-progress in order to include the insights he was getting from Korzybski. Korzybski, in turn, had long felt but only recently begun to verbalize a view of the significance of a mathematical approach to thinking and living, already worked out in some detail by Keyser. Building on Keyser's formulations, Alfred was later able to extend this view as he sought to understand the foundations of time-binding. Besides this, Keyser was able to suggest books for Alfred to read and people for him to meet. Through Keyser, Alfred became aware of a world of scientific, mathematical, philosophical, historical, and other formulators who had already worked on some of the areas he had stumbled upon more or less on his own.

Cassius J. Keyser

A look at Keyser's particular and—in some people's views—peculiar take on mathematics and the psychology of mathematics reveals some of the ground from which Korzybski further developed his work. For one thing, Keyser had reached the following conviction, based on long contemplation: "Logic is not a tool of mathematics—Logic *is* mathematics. All strictly mathematical propositions are propositions in logic and conversely." (Keyser's view of mathematics and logic as equivalent or coextensive should not be confused with Frege's and Russell's program of "logicism", which sought to reduce all of mathematics to formal logic. Ultimately for him—and Korzybski—the field of mathematics was larger than, and included, formal logic.)[6]

Mathematics, Keyser also held, could not be separated from psychology without impoverishing both mathematics and the understanding of human behavior. Instead, Keyser looked at mathematics, for him the prototype of rigorous thinking, as a form of mental phenomena "unsurpassed as means in the study of mind."[7] In this, Keyser followed in the tradition of George Boole, whom Keyser considered to have started the modern revolution in mathematics with his *Investigation of the Laws of Thought*. In that book Boole had made clear, he intended his work to throw light on "the nature and constitution of the human mind."[8]

Subsequent mathematicians and logicians had focused on improving and refining Boole's symbolical calculus, which later in the 20th century served as the basis of computer science. However, as Boole's wife, Mary Everest Boole, wrote: "...nearly all the logicians and mathematicians ignored the statement that the book was meant to throw light *on the nature of the human mind...*"[9] Keyser appeared to be one of the few mathematicians in 1920 who continued to take seriously Boole's opening statement from the *Laws of Thought*.

Keyser became Alfred's mentor—if anyone could be called that—as Alfred developed his work. Both Alfred and Mira developed close friendships with Keyser and his wife Ella (and after she died in 1927, with Keyser's second wife Sara). Within a year Keyser was beginning his letters, "Dear Korzybski," which Alfred certainly preferred to "Dear Count" or "Dear Mr. Korzybski". Alfred came to normally address Keyser in letters as "My dear dear old Man", a greeting he reserved for Keyser. Until Keyser's death at the age of 85 in 1947, he remained the man whose opinion mattered most to Korzybski.

After their first meeting, Keyser wrote a note to a former student of his, Arthur Harcourt, recommending the book—still entitled *The Manhood of Humanity and Its Universal Language*—for Harcourt's publishing company, Harcourt, Brace and Howe. Korzybski sent Harcourt a copy of the manuscript along with Keyser's note, but within a few weeks got back a rejection letter. The book did not fit Harcourt's current publishing needs. Thus began the first round of queries to publishers. Alfred wrote to Open Court and MacMillan (where Keyser knew an editor), among other places. The chapter headings and Alfred's accompanying explanation of the book seemed to elicit interest. But he had no takers. It was not really surprising, given his status as an untested new author writing in a new tongue for a general readership about the 'esoteric' subject of "human engineering or mathematical sociology" (as he was labeling it at the time).[10]

When they first got to New York City, Alfred had thought he could get the publication of the book in English done quickly. He and Mira had originally planned to leave for Europe after only a couple weeks in the city. As reality began to sink in, they began to push back their departure time, first a couple of weeks, then another few weeks, then a month or two, etc. (This became a familiar pattern over the next few years.) Still, many people who heard about the book, saw the chapter headings, or who read a copy of the manuscript got excited about it. By the middle of September, Alfred and some friends met to consider starting a "Human Engineering Publishing Company" and getting out the book themselves. Keyser was encouraging but by then felt he had neither the time nor money to get involved. Nothing came out of the meeting and Alfred continued to contact people, make inquiries, and hope to find a publisher. He felt he had something good. But from his discussions and correspondence with Keyser and others, he also realized he would have to do some editing and rewriting to get the book into publishable shape.

As Keyser pointed out in a letter to Alfred at the start of October, despite the book's "energy and pungence" the English needed polishing. Keyser apologized about his inability to do more to help.[11] Two months later Keyser, who had continued seeing and corresponding with Korzybski and wanted the book to succeed, offered some candid remarks on what he thought Alfred needed to do.[12] Among other things, he thought Alfred had obscured his central theme in a mass of unnecessary details. Besides that, Alfred had offered an appendix on mathematics which, among other things, went into some detail on the concept of the continuum. Keyser told him it contained insufficient explanatory detail for mathematicians to take it seriously and too much technical jargon and detail for laypeople to understand. Keyser had latched onto a central problem Alfred would confront throughout his career: how to communicate with the diverse audiences—from educated laypeople to professional mathematicians and scientists—he felt he needed to address in order to promote the science and art of human engineering.

Keyser was also instrumental in helping Alfred update himself in the latest work in mathematics, mathematical logic, and physics. Since the start of the war, Korzybski had experienced a drought in his serious reading. He was now catching up with a vengeance. Before the war, Alfred had not had any awareness of the work on the foundations of mathematics being done by British writers such as Bertrand Russell, Alfred North Whitehead, and others. He had only been able to peripherally follow Einstein's work on general relativity. Now, as quickly as he could, Alfred began to obtain and consume a number of seminal books in mathematics and mathematical physics suggested by Keyser.

How to Read a Book

Besides the manuscript of Keyser's *Mathematical Philosophy*, which Alfred gobbled up with relish, Alfred read Keyser's other published books. He then either bought or borrowed, and then read, Russell and Whitehead's *Principia Mathematica*; Russell's *The Principles of Mathematics, The Problems of Philosophy, Our Knowledge of the External World,* and *Introduction to Mathematical Philosophy*; Whitehead's *An Introduction to Mathematics, The Organization of Thought, An Enquiry Concerning the Principles of Natural Knowledge,* and *The Concept of Nature*; and Henri Poincaré's *The Foundation of Science*, a one volume compendium of three of Poincaré's books, *Science and Hypothesis, The Value of Science,* and *Science and Method*.

Poincaré's style, even in translation, struck him as especially beautiful. In his notebook, Alfred copied a quote from Poincarés book: "To doubt everything and to believe everything are two equally convenient solutions; each saves us from thinking." (*The Foundation of Science,* p. 27).[13] In the clearest example in Korzybski's writing of anything approaching plagiarism, Alfred paraphrased this as follows without attribution in his final published text: "There are two ways to slide easily through life: Namely, to believe everything, or to doubt everything; both ways save us from thinking." (*Manhood of Humanity*, p. 4). Ironically, this remains one of the most widely-cited 'Korzybski quotes'. In his later writings, he became much more careful with quotes and attributions.

How could anyone get through the above list of books in the period of only a few months—while reading other books as well—in addition to revising a manuscript, looking for a publisher, carrying on a large and lively letter correspondence, and meeting friends and associates throughout the city on a-not-infrequent basis? Someone who did not know Korzybski's reading habits might find it unbelievable. However, during his years as an independent scholar, Korzybski had honed a consistent approach to reading, allowing him to rather quickly absorb large amounts of material in new and difficult fields. He freely shared this reading method with his friends and students.

His main habit, acquired as a schoolboy, consisted of opening himself to the presentation of the speaker/writer—at the start—with a minimum of criticism. His main aim consisted of "try[ing] to get what they wanted to say, not what they say, but what they wanted to say."[14] In a letter he wrote in 1927 to his student, psychiatrist Phillip Graven, he detailed the method itself:

> ...I found that it is extremely useful to read [a] book <u>many</u> time[s], it is better to read them as wholes so that the whole configuration works. But to do so we must have some special means or otherwise we never could go through for lack of time. I use such [a] method. In reading the first time I mark with black pencil <u>key words</u> so that one glance at one paragraph tells me all about it the most important word in the paragraph or two or three, or a name. With this ready and one quick but honest reading I never need to read the book so laboriously again unless I especially want some material. Whenever I find in my first reading something which I <u>like</u> or something I <u>dislike</u> I mark it also specially with black pencil. I never for myself make any writings in the books simply because they <u>ALWAYS</u> are confusing and formal. I usually find in my own as well as other markings that they express something premature. If on my <u>second</u> reading, which usually takes 2-3 hours for the second reading because I <u>glance</u> only through <u>my pencil marks,</u> I use next a blue pencil and again make independent marking, namely what at the second reading I like or dislike I mark again blue, on a <u>third</u> reading I rapidly turn over the pages and read only the blue marks and if interested I mark them again in red, next comes green etc.[,] each successive reading is more rapid. It [is] <u>extremely useful</u> to glance books over [,] all over rather often although use very little time on it. Then you will have boiled down a book to perhaps 20 minutes reading, but all the time turning the pages over you will deal with the whole[,] the whole configuration and context which always better explains the words of a writer.[15]

A number of the books suggested by Keyser became the objects of multiple and deep re-readings over the next few years. But Alfred's initial readings and his contact with Keyser had some more immediate results. They helped inspire him to edit much of his discussion of mathematics in his manuscript and put some of this material into what became a rewritten appendix in *Manhood of Humanity* ("Appendix I – Mathematics and Time-Binding") where he consolidated some of his ideas about the role of mathematics in time-binding. Written in an admittedly "suggestive form," this material presaged his entire life work: "As a matter of fact, scientific psychology will very much need mathematics, but a special *humanized* mathematics. Can this be produced? It seems to me that it can."[16]

Jacques Loeb

At the end of August, after having been in New York City only a few weeks, Alfred and Mira had moved from their first Greenwich Village apartment to another one nearby at 50 Washington Mews. After it became apparent that more work would have to be done on his book and that they were not going to leave immediately for Poland, they moved once again, in the beginning of October, to an apartment on 13 West 12th Street.[17] The new place became a source of ongoing troubles for them.

The previous tenant had left the place a mess and they had to wait an extra week while the manager of the building did what she could to clean it up. After they moved in they still found a mess: a filthy rug too disgusting to do anything about other than try to ignore it; ragged and dirty furniture which they dealt with by placing their own velvet covers on top; and a mattress blackened by bedbugs which they worked to clean as best they could. After they had gotten settled, they got robbed—the thief managing to gain entrance to the apartment with an extra key the owner of the building had failed to secure. The following May, after they had left and gone to California, the owner, a Mrs. Bonner, had the gall to have both her building manager and a lawyer write to them asking for extra money for cleaning, repairs, and lost items. Alfred fired back sharp letters—Mrs. Bonner actually owed them for *their* losses—and that apparently was the end of it.[18]

The bothersome apartment did not become the focus of their attention however. While Mira—looking for connections useful for her and Alfred—renewed acquaintances in the New York City art and social world, Alfred rallied his own tremendous enthusiasm and energy to promote the notion of time-binding and to try to get his book published. To some people he may have seemed like a "bull in the china shop of old theories."[19] His liveliness, sometimes coming at "two hundred words a minute",[20] could overwhelm a listener (he gradually learned how to modulate this to some degree). Undoubtedly, some people got 'turned off' while others, like Keyser, felt charmed. Not surprisingly, soon after arriving in New York City, Korzybski had developed a circle of friends and associates interested in his work.

One of the people he became friendly with was biologist Jacques Loeb (1859–1924). Indeed, Loeb became another "dear old man" who personally encouraged Alfred and whose work had a continuing influence on him. Born in Germany as Isaac Loeb, he had come to the U.S. in the 1890s, where he solidified his already growing reputation in the biological research world as a wide-ranging physiologist. By the time Korzybski met him, Loeb worked at the Rockefeller Institute in the Upper East Side of New York City, and was perhaps best-known to the general public for his successful efforts to artificially induce parthenogenesis (the development of a complete organism) from the unfertilized eggs of sea urchins, frogs, etc., some twenty years earlier. He had also done ground-breaking research on plant and animal tropisms and on the comparative physiology of the nervous system and comparative psychology. Utterly devoted to scientific research, in his earlier work Loeb had made himself a disciple of Ernst Mach and had developed an anti-metaphysical, engineering approach to his investigations. Loeb considered behavior as a legitimate part of physiological study, embraced the importance of studying the organism as a whole, and held a staunch belief in the unity of nature, which meant for him the necessity of demonstrating the physico-chemical nature of biological functions or, what he called in the title of his 1912 book of essays,

The Mechanistic Conception of Life. He became a major advocate for that conception in the "mechanist-vitalist" debates, opposing those who believed a 'vital' element in life would always evade scientific explanations. Having suffered from antisemitism most of his life, he had also become an outspoken opponent of the biologically-based rationales for racism and discrimination becoming popular by the start of World War I.

By 1920, the time Korzybski met him, Loeb was studying the colloidal behavior of proteins, which he thought promised to reveal more of the underlying mechanisms of living phenomena. In 1922, the writer Paul DeKruif, a formally-trained bacteriologist who had worked as a junior colleague of Loeb's at Rockefeller for a few years, wrote a portrait of Loeb which was published in *Harpers*, much to Loeb's embarrassment. DeKruif, who later became famous for his 1926 book, *The Microbe Hunters*, collaborated with Sinclair Lewis in the writing of Lewis's 1925 novel *Arrowsmith*, wherein the character Max Gottleib was modeled in large part upon Loeb.[21]

Alfred had first learned about Loeb from his friend Julian Grove-Korski, working at the Polish Consulate in New York, who recommended some of Loeb's writings. Loeb's approach supplied a clear, well-stated, scientifically-based rationale for some things Alfred had been groping to express in his writing, including one of Alfred's main points: the zoological and mythological conceptions of humankind had harmful effects on the time-binding process, whilst his new definition enhanced it. Loeb's work affirmed that life—including human consciousness and behavior—had to be understandable on a physiological and physico-chemical basis, and provided a plausible mechanism for how this harm or help might occur.

Loeb had written, "Since [Pavlov] and his pupils have succeeded in causing the secretion of saliva in the dog by means of optic and acoustic signals, it no longer seems strange to us that what the philosopher terms an "idea" is a process which can cause chemical changes in the body."[22] In other words, correct or wrong ideas could promote or foul up the time-binding process in a directly physiological way.

Alfred expanded on this in a new Appendix II on "Biology and Time-Binding" begun at the end of the year. As he often did when trying to formulate more clearly, he drew a diagram—a spiral seemed quite fitting.[23] The "spiral theory" of time-binding became a major theme of his subsequent work. Korzybski considered culture, i.e.,'thoughts', 'languages','symbols', 'images', etc., as the natural product of the "physico-chemical base... of the human time-binding energy" of individual nervous systems in association with one another. A 'thought' gets embodied in a language or some other symbolism. It represents a residual effect or product of time-binding. This effect provides a new incentive for action by modifying the physico-chemical base of the individual who created it or anyone else who interprets it. The physico-chemical base thus modified can produce a new 'thought' which may provide yet again some new incentive for action.

For Korzybski, this cyclical or spiral process of causality had serious implications for all aspects of human functioning:

>...Every word has its energy and produces some physico-chemical effects in the time-binding apparatus in accord with the idea which we associate with the sound of the word. If we teach ideas which are untrue, then the physico-chemical effects produced are not proper—in other words the human mind does NOT WORK PROPERLY, that is, it does not work *naturally* or *normally* or true to the human dimension. There is every reason why the standards in our civilization are so low, because we have "poisoned," in a literal sense of the word, our minds with the physico-chemical effects of wrong ideas.

This correct NATURAL APPROACH to the "Time-binding" energies will make it obvious how unmeasured is the importance of the manner in which we handle this subtle mechanism, as the poisoning with wrong ideas or with careless or incorrect words does not in any way differ in consequences from poisoning with any other stupor-producing or wrongly stimulating poison.[24]

As he noted 13 years later in *Science and Sanity*, "Neural products are stored up or preserved in extra-neural form [various observable aspects of language, symbolism, media, culture, etc., e.g., books], and they can be put back in the nervous system *as active neural processes*"—for better and worse.[25] In his first book, he emphasized how this spiral process gives vital importance to how we define ourselves both as individuals and as members of the human race. As Korzybski only later realized, his "spiral theory" of time-binding required a nonlinear, 'circular' notion of causality, not well-formulated in 1920. (See *Science and Sanity*, p. 12.) His spiral theory preceded by some years the notion of negative feedback in control theory and cybernetics. (Indeed, control theory and cybernetics did not yet exist as discrete scientific disciplines.) When the notion of feedback began to be discussed in the late 1940s, Korzybski latched onto it at once.

By the middle of December 1920, Korzybski and Loeb had begun corresponding and had met. Loeb generously offered to look at the manuscript and helped Alfred with comments and support throughout its path to publication. Loeb also provided Alfred with names of people to contact for his trip to California the following year. And later, according to Alfred, Loeb's encouragement more than anyone else's got him to stay in the United States to do his work.

Their friendship and correspondence lasted until Loeb's sudden death in Bermuda from a heart attack in early 1924. Ironically, Alfred—back in New York City by then and not knowing Loeb was away—had written to Loeb at his lab on the day of Loeb's death, February 10. Alfred wanted to meet to discuss some important issues. Loeb's secretary, still unaware of Loeb's death the night before, wrote back on February 11 suggesting Alfred write another note to Loeb after March 1 when the biologist was expected home. Alfred attended the funeral and felt Loeb's sudden death as a great blow.[26]

Chapter 18
ALFRED AND THE JEWS

Alfred had reached a view of human potential, fertile in its implications and applications, that could appeal to humanists and scientists, the religious and non-religious. He felt awe-inspired by the vista, like an urban dweller who for the first time has visited a place with a night sky not obscured by city lights. And yet, while 'looking up at the stars' he had fallen into an 'open pit'. Soon after he and Mira arrived in New York City in the fall of 1920, he was openly expressing the meanest antisemitism.

His enmeshment in what has been called "the longest hatred", as evidenced in a letter he wrote to Cassius Keyser soon after meeting him, seems never to have become known to more than a few people. If he had continued along the pathological path of Jew-hatred, it seems unlikely he would have been able to continue his work and develop it as he did over the remainder of his life. Happily, by the spring of 1921, he had left it behind and even flipped over into a kind of philosemitism, a respect for Jews and Jewish culture, which seems rather marked. His self-examination and subsequent turning away from antisemitism is documented in the records of archived notebooks from the fall and winter of 1920–21, and in later letters, published writings, and public documents.

Alfred certainly had many opportunities to pick up the prejudices against Jews common during the time he was growing up in Poland—a time of increasing conflict between ethnic Poles and Polish Jews. Once he came to the United States, his contact with antisemitic people in the U.S. Army and the State Department, who believed in a Jewish-Bolshevik conspiracy, may have reinforced such attitudes. His connection with Social Credit advocates, some of whom believed in a conspiracy of Jewish bankers against the public, could have provided a further boost to his prejudices. And his personal contact with and misevaluation of the character of Boris Brasol—proponent of the *Protocols of the Elders of Zion*—could have given even more weight to Alfred's misevaluations about Jews.

A Remarkable Letter

By the fall of 1920, having completed the first draft of *Manhood*, Korzybski seemed full of the importance of his formulation of time-binding—perhaps too full of it. He felt convinced of the detrimental nature of what he considered a wrong definition of humanity—one which posited 'Man' as having an animal aspect combined with a divine spark. To him such a view *must* be incompatible with the notion of 'Man' as a time-binder. He found it easy to pick on the Jews as the obvious culprits for this 'travesty'.

A letter he wrote to Keyser on August 16, soon after their first meeting, seems worth quoting at length since it provides the sole evidence for the extremity of Korzybski's negative attitudes toward Jews and Judaism at this time. After a quite extensive discussion of issues related to his book, he ended the letter with the following rant:

....Human = Animal X Spark of god has formed the old testament utterly capitalistic, brutally selfish, with hatred as a base. Every not Jew was not human, a beast to be cheated, killed, and so forth. They [the Jews] violated the human nature for centuries. Their theory of selfishness and hatred could not have of course creative constructive inclination, THEY BECAME PARASITES preying upon other people['s] [work]. They are today bankers and merchants, they follow their creed and their culture...It happens to be that the Christians are the biggest producers, it may happen that Christianity made productiveness, or naturally productive races, accepted the theory of love it means productiveness, no doubt any way that Christianity is strictly related to productiveness. The Jews remained parasites, and they had to be such, the productive element was lacking in them. Selfishness as a creed (in a particularly accentuated form) compelled them to their efforts to accumulate other people's work and be parasites in the newer civilization. Selfishness and greed upon other people's success, in capitalism made them more selfish and greedy, they got in their second stage of their selfish capacity to prey. To prey on the farmer and the poor was not enough. They proclaimed a new creed to prey on the accumulation of dead men's work, to prey on the wealthy and the products of work of brain workers. They do not acknowledge the highest form of binding time, the brain work, practically they prey upon it. That's socialism in the binding time light. If we analyze the lesser subdivision of the same series we will find a strange but so natural fact that modern capitalism has been the most developed on the survival of the fittest theory and selfishness by those nations who have adopted the reformation, it means BOTH BIBLES without discrimination, in those countries the church is mostly the church of the wealthy, with Adam Smith and his creed of selfishness as an economic prophet, the catholic countries have the churches for the poor, as leading spirit the new testament. Here the binding time scale of thinking explains these phenomena without mistakes. The degree of binding time element in all those theories and creeds is the crucial base which shapes life, and is the only base for understanding those apparently strange phenomena. [They're] so simple [after] all if we only start from the right base. Today we see Jewish old testament creed Bolshevism build upon hate and DESTRUCTION (it cannot be different) in Mongol lands [knocking] at the doors of white people christian, love, constructive domain. Those things are not understood completely, because of the NOT analyzing of the human class of life from the binding time base. In my book I did not want to show too much of the value of this binding of time starting base, I put it in general terms only, not wanting to antagonize people in the start, I wanted them first to digest the first dose. Then it would [be] time enough to give the next dose, when the base for understanding would be prepared. I wonder if this is wise. I simply am afraid of the bad effect of putting too much upon the people for the start. Too much of a medicine brings often a new illness. I will keep a copy of this letter to you as notes for my further books. I would love if time will permit you to have a short expression of your opinions about these few important points I have touched in this letter. Of course I have to apologize for taking too much of your time, and for the rotten language, but I had not time to correct the letter and copy it again. The time is pressing a shake up of human thoughts is imperative, or unprecedented calamities are in store. We are in the stage of confusion here, the very existence of the white race is in danger, only vigorous thinking, Mathematical thinking, binding of time standards can save the Aryan race from the semits [sic] and Mongols.

With every appreciation and gratitude [1]

Antisemitism[1920]

Whew!—a remarkable document indeed—coming as it did from a man who would soon start to formulate a system-discipline designed to promote sane evaluating. The letter characterized the Hebrew Bible as a hate-filled document which served as the basis of a centuries-old Jewish conspiracy of immorality against non-Jews. According to the letter, not only were Jews responsible for the worst of Capitalism but they were responsible for Bolshevism too. The letter also expressed a notable favoritism towards Christianity, in particular Catholicism, odd for someone who claimed to have freed himself in his youth from the restrictions of his religious background. In Korzybski's schema here, the Jews taught hatred and parasitism while Christians—especially Catholics—embodied love and productiveness. Korzybski ended with a sentence that, except for its emphasis on "Mathematical thinking", sounded as if inspired by the *Protocols of the Elders of Zion*.

In Post-War America$_{1920}$ the attitudes Korzybski expressed in the letter were not uncommon. Henry Ford had just begun the initial publication of "The International Jew" series in his newspaper, *The Dearborn Independent*. Boston publisher Small, Maynard & Company had recently published Boris Brasol's anonymous *The Protocols and World Revolution* which apparently sold well by mail-order (bookstores, for the most part, wouldn't carry it). The book was getting widely distributed in U.S. Army Military Intelligence Department circles.[2] (Korzybski had his own copy[3] and probably obtained it around this time.) The Ku Klux Klan, which defined both Jews and Blacks as threats to the 'white race', had been founded only a few years before and was now experiencing a tremendous growth in membership throughout the U.S. More genteelly expressed anti-Jewish views were also held by many 'upper crust' members of the social register—some of the people whom Mira had as clients for her portraits in ivory. Some so-called freethinkers, rejecting all religious moorings as crude superstitions, were also likely to see the Hebrew scriptures and the Jews (especially those who continued on with their traditions) as the 'deplorable' source of the 'nonsense' they were seeking so hard to reject. And not to be forgotten, there existed—then as now—the not-uncommon phenomenon of "Jewish self-hatred" (so-called) in varying degrees. 'Self-hating' Jews included an extreme antisemitic contingent with a hard-to-match disdain for their brother and sister Jews.[4] As has remained the case throughout history, 'The Jews' provided an all-purpose 'projection screen' for many of those frustrated with the perceived failings of society. With the recent influx into the U.S. of a large number of Eastern European Jews (the Jewish population approximately tripled from 1900 to 1920),[5] Yiddish-accented, tradition-oriented Jews and their children were more visible and served as convenient targets of disdain for many other Americans, both rich and poor.

So Korzybski's views circa 1920 don't seem so unusual. Perhaps this accounts for the lack of any specific response to them in Keyser's subsequent letters (which doesn't necessarily mean Keyser didn't try to correct Alfred in person.) Keyser, who gave no indication anywhere I could find of anti-Jewish prejudices, had likely heard this kind of talk before. At any rate, for various reasons Keyser seems to have decided, at least in his correspondence with Alfred, to overlook this outburst from his new friend.

Turning

What Korzybski subsequently did about his antisemitic views seems more unusual—he consciously examined and turned against them. Unlike many other antisemites, Alfred's expression of prejudice in his August 16, 1920 letter functioned for him as an impetus for serious self-evaluation and change. In the letter he had put his prejudices clearly out in the open, keeping a carbon copy for himself (as he nigh always did). They had become facts on record available for his inspection, introspection, and correction. And there is every indication he did so via conscious use of the spiral 'thought' process he was formulating about.

A number of factors probably pushed his effort to rid himself of the poison of anti-semitism. For one thing, he was beginning to associate with many individuals who—if not socialists or communists—at least had liberal sympathies towards what they perceived at the time as more 'progressive' notions for organizing society. And the year 1920 had been a difficult year for people with such views. In 1919, a small number of fringe extremists had indulged in violence and bombings against 'capitalist' targets throughout the U.S. In response, the U.S. government began to clamp down indiscriminately on people perceived as communists or communist sympathizers, whether violent or not. On New Years Day 1920, with little or no control from the infirm President Wilson, U.S. Attorney-General A. Mitchell Palmer launched raids around the country, arresting and detaining over 6,000 communists or presumed communists. Eventually many if not most of those arrested and held illegally were released. But despite considerable outcry against the unconstitutional nature of the Attorney General's actions, Palmer's raids, as part of what became known as "the Red Scare", had a chilling effect even among many peaceful and well-intentioned liberals, who did not want to be considered radical. Although there were Jews among the 'radicals' (some of them prominent), not all radicals nor even a majority of them were Jewish. (And, the majority of Jews had nothing to do with radical politics.) Alfred and Mira knew many people in the so-called progressive camp, so Alfred had direct evidence of the nonsensical nature of claims about the specifically Jewish nature of radical politics.

In his letter to Keyser, and in keeping with the message of the *Protocols*, Alfred had also proposed a conspiratorial Jewish marriage of capitalism and communism—Jews controlling both Bolshevism and the banks. The theory, advanced in the *Protocols,* would likely strike any sensible person as contradictory and absurd. At some point, it must have begun to seem so to Alfred as well. He began to investigate.

He had been familiar with the contents of the *Protocols* for some time. As noted in a previous chapter, at the end of 1919 he had obtained a copy of Senator Overman's Committee Report on Bolshevik Propaganda. In a notebook entry labeled "The Overman Committee on the Bolshevik activities", he wrote out the following, which copies part of page 135 of the Overman Report:

> Testimony of Rev. Mr. George A. Simons parson of the Washington Square Methodist Episc. Church 121 W Fortieth Str there is a gentleman Dr. Harris A. Houghton in Bayside a Captain in the Intel. Service "Jewish protocols book Redasti anti Christ". But the average person in official life here in Wash. and elsewhere is afraid to handle it Houghton says that even in his Intelligence bureau they were afraid of it.[6]

The rumor of a Jewish plot of world domination had come into the news again with the fall 1920 publication, by G.P. Putnam & Sons, of *The Cause of World Unrest*. Alfred had clipped out the book notice for his notebook:

> History of a conspiracy in which the author contends that the plans for domination outlined in the document upon which this volume is based have apparently been followed in the recent movements in Russia.[7]

This book, by an anonymous author, offered a compendium of articles on the alleged Jewish-Freemason-Bolshevik conspiracy against the Christian World that the 'reputable' *London Morning Post* had printed earlier in the year. The book also announced the forthcoming publication by Putnam of Harris Houghton's version of the *Protocols*. In October Louis Marshall, President of the American Jewish Committee, wrote to Major George

Putnam protesting the publication of both books. Letters between the two men continued through the month and in early November Putnam decided to not publish Houghton's book.[8]

Despite the vehement tone of Alfred's letter to Keyser, he clearly was not unremittingly invested in the views put forth in the *Protocols*. Once he began investigating, its claims began to unravel for him. Having had the Overman report in his possession since the end of 1919, it would be surprising—given his reading habits—if he didn't at least look through the 1,265 page document. He probably wouldn't have missed the testimonies of Louis Marshall; Simon Wolf, chairman of the board of delegates on civil rights of the Union of American Hebrew Congregations; and Herman Bernstein, a journalist with the *New York Herald* and an anti-Tsarist, anti-Bolshevik Jew who had reported in Russia in 1917 and 1918. Marshall, in a letter, and the other two men in personal testimony, provided substantial refutations of the idea of a Jewish-Bolshevik plot.

Korzybski, a kindly man at heart, had not reacted with indifference to the post-war anti-Jewish pogroms in Eastern Europe. Even earlier, during his time serving in the Russian Intelligence Service on the Eastern Front, he had saved from further prosecution a number of Jews, who had been brought to him as spies on the flimsiest of charges.[9] He could not have read Simon Wolf's introductory remarks to the Overman Committee and comfortably maintained the views expressed in his letter to Keyser. Wolf had stated:

> I am not at all surprised by the accusations against a certain portion of the human family entitled the Jewish...always made the scapegoat of every movement. It has been so from time immemorial. I am also reminded of the Irishman who beat the Jew and when asked why he did so said that he had killed Christ. When the answer came that had been done thousands of years ago, the Irishmen replied that he had never heard of it until that day.
>
> And again, when a Jew was walking along the street, a stone was thrown from the opposite side. Naturally the Jew dodged and the stone went crashing into the plate-glass window. The owner sued the Jew for damages and the judge decided that the Jew must pay, for had he not dodged the window would not have been broken. A great judge—but the misfortune is that the Jew throughout all history has been dodging those kinds of missiles and subjected to such unjust decisions.[10]

Now, Alfred had another 'bee in his bonnet' and set off on a program of serious research in Jewish history, religion, and philosophy. One page of his notebook is devoted to Jewish libraries, publishers, and communal organizations in New York City.[11] Elsewhere in the archives, several pages of notes show extensive annotated lists of various sources of Hebrew literature and history, including translations of the Talmud (Jewish Law Commentaries) and Kabbalah (Jewish mystical literature).[12] A number of the books he acquired on Jewish topics became part of the Institute of General Semantics library, including Arsene Darmesteter's *The Talmud*, and Emanuel Deutsch's *The Talmud*, Abraham Schomer's 1909 book *The Primary Cause of Antisemitism*, Gustave Karpeles' *Jews and Judaism in the Nineteenth Century*, Philip C. Friese's *Semitic Philosophy*, William F. Bode's *The Old Testament in the Light of Today*, and Rabbi Sigmund Hecht's *Post-Biblical History: A Compendium of Jewish History*. Korzybski's collection of Judaica also included the curious 1889 volume, *Anglo-Israel or The Saxon Race Proved to be the Lost Tribes of Israel in Nine Lectures* by Rev. W. H. Poole, which he probably acquired in 1919 or earlier (the book is marked with Alfred's stamp from the National Arts Club). Clearly his interest in Jews and Judaism was not entirely new.

One book he took extensive notes on was Richard J. H. Gottheil's *Zionism*, published in 1914, part of a series on "Movements in Judaism". The book documented the history to that date of Modern Political Zionism, which sought to restore a significant Jewish presence to the land of Israel. The passages Korzybski copied into his notebook indicate, among other things, the diversity of opinions among Jews regarding options towards the increasingly hostile environment of Europe. Korzybski's notes also refer to the book's accounts of public meetings of Zionists in Europe starting in 1898.[13] What Gottheil's book documented could hardly have been more different than the monolithic, hidden conspiracy depicted in the *Protocols*. Korzybski's reading of Gottheil's book may mark the beginning of his support for Zionism. (Almost a decade later, in 1929, two Jewish newspapers in Kansas City, Missouri—where he was speaking at The Young Men's and Young Women's Hebrew Association, declared him "an outspoken Zionist" in articles announcing his lecture. Korzybski never denied that 'charge'. Indeed, he seemed proud of it, clipping the articles and writing positively to friends about the "enthusiastic" newspaper coverage.[14]

Alfred's personal contact with Jews such as Jacques Loeb and Walter N. Polakov (see the following chapter) may also have influenced his changing attitude toward Jews and Judaism. For example Loeb, a German Jew, had had plenty of first-hand experience with anti-Jewish bigotry both in Germany and the U.S. He made no secret of his ethnic origins or of his opposition to racism and unfair treatment. But we will probably never know to what extent Loeb contributed to the attitude change Korzybski was in the midst of undergoing.

In the text of *Manhood*, which he was revising, Alfred wrote "...if we teach humans false ideas, we affect their time-binding capacities and energies very seriously, by affecting in a wrong way the physico-chemical base."[15] This reflected not only his new spiral theory but also the sober result of his own self-examination. Among the books Alfred read around this time was Freidlander's translation of Moshe ben Maimon's (Maimonides') *Guide for the Perplexed*. Alfred copied this quote from Chapter XI into his notebook:

> All the great evils which men cause to each other because of certain intentions, desires, opinions or religious principles, are likewise due to non-existence, because they originate in ignorance, which is absence of wisdom.[16]

Was Korzybski somehow acknowledging here his earlier mistaken opinions about Jews? (Later he would often emphasize the dual nature of ignorance—passive ignorance and, to him, the much more dangerous, active ignorance of false knowledge/half-truth.) At any rate, in later letters and published works after 1920, there is no trace of the Jew-hatred contained in the Keyser letter. Although he referred to the 'white race' in later writings, his references could not be considered 'racist' by a careful reader, except perhaps *against* the so-called white race.[17]

For the rest of Korzybski's life he maintained an interest in antisemitism and talked and wrote about Judaism and the Jewish people with sympathy. Throughout the following decade, in letters to his friend psychologist A. A. Roback, who wrote a number of books on Jewish topics, Alfred would often inquire about the Jewish ethnicity of various mathematicians and scientists. He came to feel that the Jews as a group, like the Poles and the Scots, had especially developed a "'time' or process orientation" foreshadowing the modern way of thinking he wanted to formulate more clearly—although he felt that creative individuals from all groups also tended to express this. The Jewish people constituted the only ethnic or religious group (including the Poles) about whom Korzybski ever published anything specific (see his *Foreword to "The Essence of Judaism" by Hans Kohn*, first published and distributed in 1943 by the Institute of General Semantics, along with a reprint of Kohn's 1934 article).[18] He was also an early outspoken critic of the Nazis and wrote openly and condemningly about their ideology and their persecution of Jews—quite a shift for someone who had once sounded like a proto-Nazi himself.

Korzybski's efforts at self-education regarding Jews and Judaism reflected an all too rare but much to be wished for condition, something writer Erich Kahler (a Jew) later noted:

One day when I was discussing the problem of anti-Semitism with the eminent Austro-Jewish poet, Richard Beer-Hofmann, he said to me: "I am not at all astonished at the fact that they hate us and persecute us. But what I cannot understand is, why they do not marvel at us more than they do."

Well, marveling at the strange phenomenon of the Jewish people would imply some knowledge of their history, some general perception of the Jewish destiny. And if there were such knowledge and such perception, there could not be so much hatred and persecution. ....[19]

Lifelong Misconceptions

Notwithstanding Korzybski's subsequent greater knowledge and more accurate perception (which indeed did lead him to marvel), he never quite overcame certain misconceptions about Jews. For example, reinforced by a misreading of the Hebrew Bible, he considered the notion of "the chosen people" a doctrine of racial superiority and a precursor of Nazism.[20] For someone who prided himself as a constructive and sympathetic reader, I opine that Korzybski failed by his own measure here. Without knowing the accompanying rabbinic commentary based on oral tradition, the Hebrew Bible—in terms of the normative Jewish interpretation—cannot be adequately understood. Korzybski gave no indication that he ever recognized the importance of this commentary and tradition where, as Chaim Potok later pointed out, "...The notion of chosenness...is an assumption of responsibility, not superiority."[21] Korzybski's error here may have resulted in part from a tendency towards a crude anti-clericalism that he never quite got away from—despite his stated opposition to dogmatic atheism. His truncated view of Jewish belief was one that he shared with many 'enlightened' people, including a number of assimilated Jewish intellectuals. That alone didn't make him an antisemite—only mistaken.

Chapter 19
THE TIME-BINDING CLUB

Since Alfred was describing his work as an effort in "human engineering or mathematical sociology",[1] he believed progressive-minded engineers, like the ones who had been involved with Gantt's and then Ferguson's "New Machine", would find something of value in what he had to say. Not surprisingly, just after he got back to New York in the autumn of 1920, a couple of men he knew recommended his getting in touch with Walter N. Polakov, a Russian-born engineer living in New York City who had worked with H. L. Gantt. Alfred wrote to Polakov and the two men soon began a lifelong friendship.[2]

"Poly"

If Keyser could be called Alfred's formulational father, then Polakov (whom Alfred usually addressed as "Walter" or "Poly") qualifies as Korzybski's main intellectual 'brother'. Polakov grasped more quickly than most the overall shape of Alfred's developing work. After all, for Polakov—a lover of mathematics and a practicing engineer with a strong sense of social responsibility—Alfred's work seemed more than anything like a clarification and confirmation of what he already felt and knew. Walter became close with both Alfred and Mira. He also became friends with Keyser, Loeb, and many of the other people Alfred was also meeting at this time—indeed he introduced Alfred and Mira to some of them. Soon after he met Korzybski, Polakov began to study Keyser's work and many of the other works Alfred was also discovering at this time. Polakov's studio in upper Manhattan become a place where Alfred could share his views, receive criticisms, and get suggestions. Polakov not only contributed to Alfred's formulating, he also became the earliest significant popularizer of the world view and methodology Korzybski was trying to delineate through the 1920s—although Polakov's published writings are now relatively unknown.

Walter N. Polakov

Polakov was born in Luga, Russia in the same year and month as Alfred. Apparently Jewish (his name appears in the 1922-1923 *American Jewish Year Book* in the listing of "Jews of Prominence in the United States)[3], he seems to have had a completely assimilated upbringing. (None of his later published writings or letters show a trace of Jewish background or interest, although he certainly did not seem antisemitic—just indifferent.) He got his degree in Mechanical Engineering at Dresden's Royal Institute of Technology in 1902, and did advanced graduate work in psychology and industrial hygiene at the University of Moscow. After working for the Tula Locomotive Works and as Chief Engineer and Naval Instructor in the Russian Department of Navigation and Harbors, he emigrated to the United States with his wife and a daughter in 1906, just after the first Russian Revolution. He quickly became proficient in English and became well-known in the U.S. as an expert in power plant operations and in industrial engineering and management.[4]

Before he met Alfred, Polakov had already come to a clear understanding of the power of a form of representation to affect behavior and the added importance of using a dynamic form of representation (adequately accounting for the time factor) to represent dynamic events. His work with the Gantt Chart, which focused on the element of time, no doubt enhanced this. He had worked closely with H. L. Gantt to develop this system of project management during the war and was rightly considered one of the world's leading experts in its use. (Polakov helped edit and supplied an appendix to Walter Clark's definitive book on the subject, *The Gantt Chart: A Working Tool of Management*, published in 1922.)

In his consulting work, Polakov was obsessed with reducing waste in industry—defined as restricted, reduced, interrupted, or lost productivity. Since for him the ultimate waste resulted from workers getting treated like animals or commodities, his use of the Gantt methodology required worker involvement and brain power. Indeed, as indicated in the title of a talk he gave at the December 1921 meeting of The American Society of Mechanical Engineers, he considered "making work fascinating as the first step toward reduction of waste".[5] The connection to Korzybski's emphasis in *Manhood* that "Man is not an animal", seems obvious. Polakov's career as an industrial engineering consultant to businesses and governments could be summarized in a credo he had gotten from Gantt: the purpose of technology and business was "rendering rigorous service". Both he and Gantt belonged to a larger movement in 1920s America among socially-conscious engineers and management thinkers.[6] In applying the notion of "making work fascinating" to industrial management, Polakov qualifies as a precurser to the movement for Total Quality Management.

Universal Labor and Time-Binding
In the fall of 1920, the U.S. economy was in a recession, as was Walter's consulting firm. Though Polakov was not making much money, he was at least trying not to waste his time. He was keeping himself busy writing—he had just finished the "Preface" of *Mastering Power Production*, a book analyzing the economics and technology of industrial power production in the U.S. Although now ready for publication (with a 1921 copyright date), the book did not actually come out until January 1922; Walter's publisher couldn't pay the printer's bill. In the meantime, when he met Alfred, probably sometime in late August, he had already started working on a new book, *Quo Vadis, America?* (an analysis of the 1920 U.S. economy which Walter ultimately abandoned). The two men exchanged manuscripts.

Polakov found Alfred's work compelling. Korzybski's explicit formulation of time-binding and emphasis on a mathematical and engineering approach to social problems affirmed Polakov's own views. After only a short time with the manuscript, he concluded that Korzybski's "philosophy of Human Engineering" constituted "a foundation of new philosophic thought".[7] Even Polakov's revered Marx, whom he considered "the founder of the science of political economy", had not come to the clear definition of the human class of life that he felt Korzybski had reached.⁸ Polakov spoke modestly here. While working on *Mastering Power Production* during and after the war, he had independently arrived—in passing—at a recognition of the phenomenon that Korzybski had defined, labeled, and put at the center of his book. Korzybski readily saw this and agreed about the congruence of his and Polakov's views. After reading the manuscript of *Mastering Power Production*, Korzybski accepted Polakov's notion of "Universal Labor" as "*Corresponding exactly to Time-binding*".⁹ Alfred had typed out for himself some material from Polakov's "Preface", including the following:

> …in my discussion of Universal labor, I attempted to show that the cumulative work of past generations lives through the ages and benefits posterity thus, through creative work of engineering minds, we approach the eternity.
>
> If we apply this criterion to all our work—the human energy expended for production of any result—we must apply it in relation to *time* not only because we live within a limit of time, not even because time can not be created, stopped or extended but principally because the conception of time is distinctively human, is the factor and the exponent of the entire progress of human life.¹⁰

"Ideals of Socialism"

The compatibility of Korzybski's and Polakov's views extended to socialism. Korzybski may not have wanted to call himself a socialist or to do away with private enterprise, but he certainly admired the goals of socialism. In a letter to Lincoln Steffens in 1922, Korzybski wrote,

> Old capitalism is not scientific, [it is] based on animal standards and therefore it breaks down every little while. Socialism must be built upon REALLY scientific premises or it will also have sad failures. As far as the ideals of socialism go I have nothing to say and am in accord with them. BUT THE METHOD the PREMISES must be made scientific.¹¹

That his biases in the early 1920s inclined towards socialism can definitely be seen in a 1922 letter to Luella Twining, recounting a dinner he and Mira had just attended in Milwaukee:

> …Some bankers gave us a dinner, and they asked me what I think about the bloodshed and terror in Russia, it was a trap because obviously the question was idiotic. I answered that as a soldier I have no use for killing whomever, but I said that I refuse to be blind on either sides, and explained that I do not see no [sic] difference between Lenin and Trotzki lets us say and Morgan and Rockfeller [sic] let us say, both groups have corpses behind them, the difference is that the first COUNT them at least the others HIDE them, in this respect I have more use for those who at least are not cowards.¹²

Throughout his life, Korzybski continued to disparage "commercialism" and felt strong antipathy (perhaps with some justification) towards what he considered the excesses and abuses of the banking system, unrestricted profit motive, etc. (See *Science and Sanity*, passim.) However, his general political-economic views moved further away from those of Polakov. Perhaps Keyser exerted some moderating influence here. Keyser once wrote to Alfred, "The gabble of a 'radical' tends to make me conservative and the gabble of a 'conservative' tends to make me radical."¹³ By the mid-1940s, Korzybski had became a qualified supporter of Harry Truman and later felt positive about the possibility of Eisenhower for President—hardly radical political choices.

Nonetheless, he maintained some of his old sympathies until the end of his life. For example, speaking at a luncheon given in his honor in 1948, he was strongly critical of "the anti-human character of Soviet Communism", and its leadership, but still spoke positively about socialism.¹⁴ In the 1930s, Korzybski had given general support to Roosevelt's "New

Deal", and apparently continued to have no objection to applying statist solutions to socio-economic problems. Ralph Hamilton had many conversations with him and noted, "He thought the government should take a more decisive hand in controlling and managing natural resources instead of letting them be claimed by any chance venturer. And of course it should support worthy causes like [his work]."[15]

In his 1944 book, *The Road to Serfdom* (which Mira got and Alfred may have perused) economist Friedrich Hayek expressed an alternative viewpoint that ran against the current of then popular economic opinion. Hayek, following von Mises and other economists of the Austrian school, argued that inevitable limitations on human knowledge meant that any centralized, "New Deal"-like governmental planning and control would inevitably lead to economic foul-up and point a democracy in the direction of totalitarianism. This suggested that a market economy, whatever the flaws of commercialism, might better serve a time-binding class of life. At around this time, Korzybski had begun to more fully explore the relation of democracy and dictatorship to time-binding, but he never got around to grappling with the implications of the work of Hayek, et al., for his own formulations.

The Time-Binding Club

Alfred, Mira, Polakov, and Keyser had been promoting "time-binding", "human engineering", etc., among people they met. Interest was growing. Walter decided to organize a "binding time" club which, by October, was getting together once a week at his studio apartment at the Hotel des Artistes on 1 West 67th Street.[16] (Polakov had become single again, though his teen-age daughter, Catherine, was still living with him.) Among others, the group of regulars at the meetings included Polakov and Alfred; Robert B. Wolf, an engineer, management consultant, and Vice-President of The American Society of Mechanical Engineers; Alfred's friend Julian Grove-Korski who worked at the Polish Consulate in New York; William John Fielding, an advertising copywriter for Tiffany's and Company who reviewed books and wrote articles on "free thought" and sexology; and Charles W. Wood, an editorial writer for *The World* newspaper and, for a time a couple of years later, a contributing editor to *The Liberator*, Max Eastman's monthly radical socialist newspaper. In addition, people like Mira, Keyser, Catherine Polakov, Jacques Loeb, historian James Harvey Robinson, and E. A. Ross, a sociology professor from the University of Wisconson and former President of the American Sociology Association, occasionally attended. The meetings continued at Polakov's home for several years—sometimes when Alfred was not in town—before finally petering out by the fall of 1923.[17]

Among the members of what soon became known as the "Time-binding Club", Korzybski's formulations seemed to have the effect of a "brain revolution", as Polakov called it. Keyser was rewriting *Mathematical Philosophy* to include his new conscious awareness of time-binding. Polakov now understood Gantt's method as a way of consciously implementing it in business/industrial planning.[18] In light of his ongoing reading and his discussions with Alfred and others, Polakov was also moving away from orthodox Marxism. In a few years, in the first of a series of articles on "Science and Labor" for *The American Labor Monthly*, he would write, "Marxism and the so-called radical theories springing from it are not free from this [scientific] criticism. Let us be impersonal. The theory of scientific socialism is based on gross materialism which is no longer tenable in view of the strides made by the positive sciences."[19]

Robert B. Wolf, somewhat younger than Alfred and Walter, also found time-binding an "epoch-making concept".[20] His enthusiasm was indicative of a larger fact: Korzybski's work by no means appealed only to so-called free-thinking, radical types. Wolf had written a number of pamphlets and articles such as "Individuality in Industry", "Non-Financial Incentives", and "Creative Spirit in Industry". His approach had struck a chord in industrial engineering and management audiences and he had built a successful business in industrial consulting. Wolf espoused a kind of mystical Christianity and in his management work attempted to combine Gantt's methods with the esoteric theories of Fabre d'Olivet, among others.[21] Now he was trying to fit time-binding into this framework as well. Hard-headed Poly had his suspicions. But Alfred seems to have enjoyed mentoring Wolf.

The engineers in the group had a strong influence on Korzybski. He decided to increase his emphasis on "Human Engineering". For a time he even changed the title of the book to the unwieldy *Human Engineering or The Science of The Manhood of Humanity and Its Universal Application*. In this regard he started writing a third appendix to the book entitled "Engineering and Time-Binding".

Discussions with fellow "time-binders" in the club, as well as critiques from others to whom he had sent parts of the manuscript, were definitely helping him to refine his ideas and tighten up his writing. For example, Alfred had noted in the manuscript that the three classes of life (plants, animals and humans) could be said to represent different and incommensurable dimensions (using examples from algebra). Polakov apparently gave a presentation discussing these classes of life in terms of geometrical dimensions, specifically the co-ordinates of a cube, using a simple illustration with three lines. This illustration made clearer Alfred's argument about confusing dimensions. By focusing only on its components—i.e., points, lines, or surfaces—a cube could get mistakenly characterized in terms, say, of its surfaces. Its higher-dimensionality—its 'cubeness'—could get entirely neglected. In a similar manner, viewing humans—a higher dimension of life—as animals appeared as wrong as calling a cube a "square". The geometric analogy seems obvious in hindsight but Alfred apparently had not developed it on his own. When the book was finally published, he included Polakov's illustration (see *Manhood of Humanity*, p. 61) but didn't mention Polakov as the source of it, even though Walter had requested he do so.[22] Probably an innocent oversight by Korzybski in the rush to publication, this may have contributed to some of the tension which later surfaced between the two friends.

Steinmetz

Club members were also helping Alfred to make important outside connections. Alfred never hesitated in approaching the 'biggest' people in whatever field he was writing about. Probably at the suggestion of Polakov, Alfred had read the 1916 book, *America and the New Epoch,* by Charles Steinmetz, a mathematician, engineer, and socialist born in Prussian Poland in 1865. Steinmetz—a wizened hunchback and, in Polakov's words, a "big-hearted" genius—had come to the U.S. in 1889. Since then Steinmetz had established the mathematical theory of alternating currents, made possible the expanding national power grid, and become the head of the research laboratory at General Electric Corporation. Steinmetz's book had analyzed what he saw as a necessary historical shift from an era emphasizing individualism and competition to one emphasizing cooperation. To Korzybski writing his engineering appendix, Steinmetz's book gave "a most correct engineering picture of the political situation in the world..."which fit in with the message of human engineering that Alfred wanted to convey in his own book.[23] He hoped he might be able to get Steinmetz interested in his work and perhaps get his critique and endorsement.

Polakov, who knew Steinmetz, wrote a letter of introduction for Korzybski. At the beginning of September, Alfred sent it, along with his own letter and a manuscript of his book, to Steinmetz's home and office in Schenectady, north of New York City.[24] About a week later two mysterious men—special government agents?—visited Polakov asking questions about "the Korzybski theory". Walter and Alfred wondered: Did some of Palmer's 'red hunters' intercept the manuscript sent to Steinmetz? After he had heard no word from Steinmetz for a month, Alfred sent another letter to him and also one to General Electric.[25] The letter addressed to G.E. finally got through. Within a few weeks, Steinmetz wrote back to him indicating he had not received the manuscript or the two previous letters addressed to him.[26] Alfred sent him another manuscript in mid-November via private messenger but didn't hear back from him for another month. It was certainly not lack of interest on Steinmetz's part. He had a busy laboratory at his home at "Liberty Hall" and was now in the midst of an exhaustive research project on lightning which would lead two years later to the first effective lightning arrester for the power industry. It turns out that both of Korzybski's manuscripts had gotten misplaced in Steinmetz's lab. Steinmetz finally wrote back to Korzybski on December 21; the manuscript had finally reached him: "...I started reading it [and] am getting interested; will write you soon."[27]

In early 1921, with Korzybski madly revising his manuscript, Steinmetz wrote expressing further interest in the new material on human engineering but provided no other comments.[28] He was just too busy to do much more than express his sympathy for Alfred's work. Korzybski wrote back expressing some frustration he wasn't able to personally meet and get more input from Steinmetz as the book neared publication—although he had decided to add Steinmetz to his list of people acknowledged in the "Preface".[29] Steinmetz didn't object.

Steinmetz spent his last few years extremely fruitfully. He built an artificial lightning machine, formulated a method of suppressing lightning damage to power lines, and wrote one of the earliest books explaining the theory of relativity. Korzybski apparently never met him in person. Steinmetz died unexpectedly in October 1923 of heart failure—probably related to the strain of his severe kypho-scoliosis, i.e., "hunchback", combined with his relentless activity. Polakov wrote the following in an obituary of him published in that year's November 7 issue of *The Nation*:

> ...[Steinmetz] often stated that the aim of engineering is to control the forces of nature for the well-being of mankind. What are these "forces of nature"? Are they limited to "non-human nature," or do they embrace as well the forces of "human nature"? On this point Steinmetz never wavered.
>
> In interviews that were broadcasted across two continents he sharply defined the goal of success for the engineer—"to find out how human forces work." For only then," according to Steinmetz, "can we expect any great human progress." That is why he became such a warm supporter of Korzybski's theory of man...[30]

Maggots In The Cheese

The 'Time-Binders' were not all about serious discussion. They had fun while they sat in Walter's apartment and, as Walter remembered much later, "…discussed many aspects of our problems, drank homemade brew [Prohibition had taken effect on Jan. 15, 1920 and would last until 1933], ate sardines and hoped for the best."[31] Alfred regaled his friends with stories and gave them his rendition of the Petawawa Camp Song: '...There are maggots in the cheese over there. over there,.....'. To people in the group, this seemed to describe the condition of those who operated without sufficient awareness of their time-binding debts to the past or their time-binding responsibilities to the future. As Keyser put it later, "We have been and are living in the midst of a great civilization like maggots in a cheese." Both he and Walter used the analogy in later writings.[32]

Alfred still didn't have a publisher by the end of the year. The 'Time-Binders' had briefly considered putting together their own publishing company but decided against it. Meanwhile, the Management Section of the American Society of Mechanical Engineers was planning a tribute to H. L. Gantt and Walter for the Society's Annual Meeting, scheduled for December 7–10 in New York. Walter planned to formally introduce "time-binding" in the course of summarizing Gantt's contribution to management thinking. In November, Walter was circulating a draft of his presentation to his friends and invited Alfred, Wolf, Wood and another engineer, Hugh Archibald to serve as discussants to the paper at the meeting. (Both Polakov's paper and the comments of Korzybski and the others were published in the April 21, 1921 issue of *Mechanical Engineering*.) The meeting provided Alfred with his first national audience (at least among the engineers attending the conference). "Time-Binding" had been launched.

Chapter 20
MANHOOD OF HUMANITY

By January 1921 Alfred's book, now renamed *Human Engineering* and significantly revised, had boosters and 'buzz'. The January 16 Sunday *New York Times* had an article on Alfred, with the headline "NEW THEORY AS TO MAN". The subheading read "Polish Mathematician's Conclusions That Human's Function Is to "Bind Time" Attracts Scientists' Attention".[1] Still, there was the 'little' matter of getting a publisher. Mira had been in touch with an old friend from her starving-artist days, writer Burges Johnson, an English professor and director of publications at Vassar College. Johnson, with connections in the publishing world, promised to write a letter to the Vice-President of E. P. Dutton & Company, one of the biggest publishers in New York. After already receiving a number of rejection letters, neither Alfred nor Mira had prepared for what happened next.

E. P. Dutton

Mid-morning on January 4, the phone rang in their apartment. The doorman of their building had called up to tell them, "E. P. Dutton…is here to see you." E. P. Dutton![2] Alfred and Mira got excited: "We didn't want E. P. Dutton to wait, so we told him to send him up. We tidied ourselves up the best we could in one minute and here comes, not E. P. Dutton at all [by this time a nearly 90-year-old man] but a bell-boy from E. P. Dutton [Publishing Company] to deliver a letter…[from Dutton's Vice-President, John Macrae.]"[3] Macrae's letter, dated that day and addressed to "Count Korzybski," read:

Dear Sir,

I have to-day received a letter from my friend, Burges Johnson of Vassar College, bringing to my attention a manuscript which you have lately completed on HUMAN ENGINEERING, and I can tell you at once that I am tremendously interested in this manuscript and I should like to have it for consideration at the very earliest possible. I can further say that I think there is no doubt whatever from what I hear of your manuscript, that I should like to publish the book for you. The information of the existence of your manuscript has just this moment come to my attention, and I am sending you this letter by special messenger…

I should prefer, if agreeable to you, to make an appointment to meet you here at my offices almost any time, at your convenience. If practical and agreeable to you, you could, on receipt of this note, call me over the telephone, Plaza 7400, and we could then make an appointment at once which would be agreeable to your engagements.

Looking forward with great pleasure to meeting you and with the full expectation of having the privilege of publishing your book, I am [signature]…[4]

Alfred, a 'virgin' author, was getting a personal invitation to see the head of this major publishing house as soon as possible, and a virtual guarantee from him to publish the book—unheard of! What could possibly account for such luck? As the Korzybskis later learned from Macrae himself, Macrae had had a dream in which his recently deceased wife visited him. She told him, "There is a foreign man here in New York who is writing an epoch-making book on time."[5] When he heard from Johnson about Korzybski and his book, he recalled the dream and sent the letter at once.

Mira telephoned Macrae and made an appointment for her and Alfred to see him at 3:00 that afternoon. They dressed in their finest clothes and made their way from their

Greenwich Village apartment to the E. P. Dutton & Company Building on 681 Fifth Avenue in mid-town Manhattan. Macrae escorted them into his office, pulling out his silk handkerchief and wiping the seats of the mahogany chairs for "the Count and Countess." Alfred felt himself unable to speak and left the talking and negotiating to Mira. When they left the office a little while later, they had a book deal.

Alfred assigned ownership of the book to Mira so she would receive the royalties in case of his death. The arrangement with Dutton stipulated that for the first 5000 books sold, the Korzybskis would receive 10% of the retail price for each book (30¢—based on the eventual sales price of $3.00). After that, the royalty would increase to 15%. It seemed unlikely they would become rich from book sales, but they potentially could get a nice chunk of money (30¢ times 5000 amounts to $1500 in 1921 dollars, which had the equivalent buying power of $18,000 in 2009.)[6]

Macrae wanted a completed manuscript as soon as possible. For the next few months Alfred and Mira scrambled. Until they handed over the completed work, the book title changed two more times (to *Humanity's Manhood* and then finally to *Manhood of Humanity: The Science and Art of Human Engineering*). Alfred finished reorganizing the text (including added historical footnotes from James Harvey Robinson's *An Outline of the History of the Western European Mind*); completed the three appendices to which he shifted the more technical material and side arguments; and wrote for and received permissions for all material quoted from other authors (as required by Macrae and Dutton). Alfred, more or less done with writing at the end of February, gave the manuscript to Keyser, who had agreed to copyedit it. Keyser sweated over Alfred's Polish-flavored English for another month. Alfred later claimed the book's literary style mainly belonged to Keyser. Finally on March 23, Mira delivered the completed manuscript to Dutton and signed the formal book contract. Alfred joked about it but he was obviously feeling nervous. In a letter to Burges Johnson, he wrote,

> Finally finished the M.S., Mira and myself – Buddah help the book writers; their wifes [sic], say I. It fortunately was edited by Doctor Keyser from Columbia, the world famous mathematical philosopher, and my M.S. (read it My Suicide) delivered to Dutton.[7]

Going To California

With the book now in the hands of the publisher, Mira and Alfred planned to return to Warsaw via London in mid April, only a few weeks away. If they were going to Europe, they had a lot of stuff to pack. They also had loose ends related to the book, now in production. To a few people, Alfred had indicated he thought it would be in print before they left. As soon became apparent, the process would take more time. They would be in Europe before the book came out. Alfred asked Walter to act as his U.S. representative in any book-related business. However, their plans soon changed. By the first week of April, they delayed their move to Europe once again. First, they would go to California.

Alfred told people he had been invited to lecture there. That may have been so—even though when he and Mira got to San Francisco a month later he did not have any immediate speaking engagements. More likely, their decision to go to California was at least partly a matter of money. They needed as much as they could get. They had been living on savings and, with the lousy economy in Poland their situation there would be difficult for an indeterminate period. In San Francisco, Mira could get a gallery exhibit and had hope of selling some paintings. She could also prospect for wealthy portrait clients there and in Southern California. In addition to the money motive, it would be surprising if either Alfred or Mira would have been happy being in Europe while their first 'child'—*Manhood*—was being born in the U.S. Now that they knew it was actually going to be published, they both wanted to see it to fruition. Since Alfred had never been to the far western U.S., the trip would also give him a final opportunity to see California and points along the way before returning to Poland.

They still had lots of things to do. They needed to pack for their trip West (what they didn't take they would store at the Manhattan Storage Company). According to their plan, when they returned to New York City later in the year, they would be more or less ready for the much delayed trip home to Europe.

Advance publicity for the book had begun. Alfred had given a talk on time-binding at the City Club on March 2. Some of his friends in the Time-Binding Club were preparing book reviews and related articles. Dutton was working on sales copy and book-cover blurbs, and compiling a list of whom to send review copies to. Polakov's address on Gantt's work, "Principles of Industrial Philosophy" with Alfred's commentary (which needed some editing) was due to be published in the April 1921 issue of *Mechanical Engineering*. The editorial section of the April 10 New York *World* carried a front page story by Wood with the hyperbolic headline "Man Is Not An Animal, Says Count Korzybski, Advancing Mathematical Theory Which May Revolutionize World Thought in Every Field".[8]

As they were preparing to leave, an unpleasant episode brought Alfred and Mira face to face with the antisemitism permeating parts of New York high society. Thirty-year-old Sol Abramson had been working for Alfred and Mira, helping them with the manuscript of *Manhood*. The multi-lingual Abramson was looking for work as a private secretary or traveling companion for someone among Mira's upper-crust clientele. The Korzybskis wanted to give him a letter of recommendation. Since they were leaving New York and Abramson's address was temporary, Mira suggested she could write an endorsement letter for him, including his photograph, which would also provide a forwarding address for him in care of one of the New York society ladies she knew. Mira talked to a Mrs. Stockton on the telephone, asking if the lady would allow a few letters to come to her house for a young man who had worked for them. Mira did not mention Abramson by name. Mrs. Stockton agreed to accept the letters for the young man and Mira proceeded to write the endorsement letter, dated March 21, and send it to a mailing list of prospective people who might want Abramson's services. Mira and Alfred felt happy to provide this bit of help.

About a week later, Mira got an angry indignant letter from Mrs. Stockton after some of the women in Mrs. Stockton's club had shown her copies of the letter. "You did not even tell me his name—much less show me the photograph…," wrote Mrs. Stockton. How dare Mira try to make it seem as if Mrs. Stockton was endorsing "this person."[9] In fact, Mira's letter did no such thing. The only mention of the Stockton name was at the end of letter, near the bottom, "Mr. Abramson's permanent address is: c/o Mrs. Herbert Stockton, 150 East 53rd Street, New York City."[10] There was no mention anywhere else in the letter of Mrs. Stockton, let alone any indication of an endorsement by her.

Things escalated quickly. The husband, Herbert Stockton, an attorney, sent a letter on his letterhead demanding that Mira send a notice to everyone on her mailing list saying: "By an error Mrs. Herbert Stockton's address…was given as the forwarding address for Mr. Sol Abramson's mail. …Mrs. Stockton's name should not have appeared on the letter."[11] Mira wrote back a strong letter to Mrs. Stockton while Alfred wrote a protest to Mr. Stockton. But ultimately the Korzybskis did send out a second letter indicating that Mrs. Stockton didn't know Abramson or endorse him. They provided another forwarding address. Such a "to do" over such a trivial issue made sense in a New York where a Jewish name seemed 'dirty' to some socialites worried about preserving their reputations. The Stocktons clearly did not think they were making too much of a fuss about having their name associated with someone named Abramson. At this point, Alfred and Mira had no tolerance for that kind of attitude.

Before they left, Alfred also hired Ellen Kennan, a copyeditor/proofreader in New York City, and arranged for her to get the page and galley proofs as they came from Dutton. Macrae had no problem with this but felt irritated because Alfred wanted extra copies of the proofs sent to him in San Francisco. If any situation could further delay the book that would surely qualify. Macrae couldn't understand why Alfred was in such a hurry to get out of New York before the publication. Alfred promised he would trust in his proofreader's judgment and not interfere. In spite of this, he couldn't help doing his own copyediting and trying to manage the proofreader's work by mail from California.[12]

Alfred's and Mira's friends gave them a farewell dinner. They said their goodbyes. Then at the end of April, they took the train for San Francisco with a stop in Chicago along the way. By May 8 they had arrived in a cold and windy San Francisco, moving into an apartment on 2285 Broadway provided for them by an acquaintance. Mira had a two-week long portrait exhibit at the Helgeson Gallery scheduled to start on May 18. In the first few weeks in the city, Alfred spent much of his time giving Mira whatever help she needed to prepare for the exhibit. But gradually, he began to meet the contacts he had been given and other people in the area with whom he had corresponded. He had a major concern: how to set up speaking engagements for himself along the West Coast.

"Please Drop This Time-Binding."

Soon after arriving, Alfred went to visit Professor Guido Marx of the Stanford University Department of Mechanical Engineering. Marx, well-known for his work on systematic analysis in machine design, also had a broader interest in the social responsibilities of engineers. In the spring of 1920 Marx had lectured on that subject in New York at the New School for Social Research under the auspices of Thorstein Veblen. He also gave popular lectures to the citizenship classes at Stanford and helped found the American Association of University Professors. Having corresponded with Korzybski since the autumn of 1920, he seemed naturally drawn to the notion of time-binding. Alfred had given him a copy of the manuscript which he was "reading with interest although at times not with understanding."[13]

After their meeting, Marx wrote to Korzybski and offered to put together a "smoker" gathering of academics whom he thought would have an interest in hearing Korzybski speak—exactly what Alfred had been looking for. Alfred described the May 28 meeting in a letter to Keyser:

> A friend engineer, who is a professor at Stanford [Guido Marx] got interested in Time-binding and gave me a smoker where there was about 25 professors. The audience was very mixed, engineers, philosophers, economists, lawyers, biologists, mathematicians,

linguists, and so on. It was a rather difficult task to satisfy them all. I was told later on that I did well, they were very friendly anyway. I was quiet and careful in my expressions. I explained that the speaking of this subject is so difficult that a serious exposé could be given only in writing. They understood my difficulties and were lenient to the form.

I had some gratifying moments. Few days before I met a young very promising biologist from Columbia, Calvin Bridges which is already an acknowledged authority on heredity. He read the MS. And at the smoker he made a fight for my theory and gave the explanation of the Biological App. AND EXPLAINED TO THEM THE VALUE AND APPLICATION OF THE SPIRAL THEORY...After the lecture an old lawyer, professor of Stanford and mayor of the town said that's all moonshine and nothing new...a fight began in which I did not participate, the audience was simply dying from laughter. It was the most funny thing I ever witnessed, and especially when the lawyer could not find arguments, and with desperate gesture said in a sad voice to the biologist, "Please drop this time-binding." We all rolled on the floor [with laughter] for about five minutes.[14]

Alfred got a few pieces of good news from Keyser at the end of May. Dutton had picked up Keyser's book *Mathematical Philosophy*. Korzybski had recommended the book to Macrae and felt overjoyed. Also in June the *Pacific Review* of the University of Washington would publish an article by Keyser, "Mathematical Obligations of Philosophy", which mentioned Alfred's forthcoming book. The third piece of news had perhaps the greatest importance for Alfred. In a few days, Tuesday May 31, Keyser would give the annual Phi Beta Kappa address at Columbia University on "The Nature of Man". The address, centering on Korzybski's formulation of time-binding, was subsequently published in the September 9, 1921 issue of *Science*. Keyser decided to make it the basis of the penultimate chapter of *Mathematical Philosophy*. Keyser would continue to promote Korzybski's work whenever he had the opportunity and Alfred felt deeply grateful.

Alfred and Mira, 'on pins and needles', awaited the publication of *Manhood of Humanity*, expected for the end of June. In the meantime, the San Francisco papers printed a few articles on Mira and her exhibit. The articles included some mention of Alfred. In the May 29 *San Francisco Chronicle*, the headline of another article specifically about Alfred read, "Fourth Dimension Discovered at Last! Secrets of Algebra and Soul Bared[.] New Mathematical Theory By Count".[15] On June 26, *The Boston Evening Transcript* published a four-page article based on an interview with Polakov entitled "Korzybski, Time-Binder, Upsets Darwin and Proves the Golden Rule True".[16] A couple of days later, the book went on sale.[17]

Kudos and Criticisms

Even though he felt grateful for the newspaper coverage, Alfred seemed inclined to raise his eyebrows at the purple prose of screaming headlines. But he hardly had a right to grumble about the exaggerations of headline writers. Both he and some of his friends sounded at times as if the discovery of time-binding signaled the imminent coming of the messianic age. Reading some of his letters of this period does give a sense of overreaching. For example, did Alfred actually discover and formulate a "natural law, of equal if not more importance than the law of gravitation" as he wrote to more than one friend.[18] Did the theory of time-binding indeed provide the *first* scientific understanding of wealth?[19]

Keyser had warned him about this sort of over-the-top enthusiasm which could sometimes burst through in his speech and writing. Keyser considered Korzybski's work and approach of such value, it didn't need to be goosed with exaggerated-sounding claims which might put off potentially sympathetic members of his audience. But especially in this early period of his formulating, Alfred seemed to have a particularly strong urge to help—or even to save—mankind. Sometimes this urgency—this impatience to do away with what he saw as preventable ignorance about the nature of Man—created an obstacle in the form of rhetorical excess. On the other hand, would Korzybski have gotten as far as he had or continue to develop his work further, if he hadn't considered his definition of Man of such great importance? Would he have gotten so far in stimulating the interest and enthusiasm of others? Readers' enthusiasm seems apparent not only from some of the published reviews but also from unsolicited letters Korzybski received from many individuals over the next few years when the book was still much in the public eye.

Though Korzybski may have succumbed to hyperbole at times, he remained open to criticism. This continued throughout his career. He had every intention of getting the things he was formulating as right as he could get them. He had sought criticism when he first approached authorities in the fields *Manhood* touched upon to review his manuscript (people like Moore, Keyser, Polakov, Wolf, and Loeb, amongst others). He also asked for honest commentary, critical or otherwise, from his friends and they often gave it to him. Not all their comments were laudatory. He subscribed to a clipping service—which gathered positive, negative, and in-between reviews and book notices from around the country. And a few individual readers also sent their unsolicited critical comments and reviews. Although positive reviews pleased him, he wanted people's honest opinions.

Some criticisms, he found, missed his intended points, either partially or entirely. If he could account for this by some failure of expression or lack of clarity on his part, he tried to correct it when he could. On the other hand, some of the people who missed the point seemed determined to misinterpret him or to go out of their way to nit-pick. Depending on the person or situation, he would often make an effort to communicate further to get his point across before giving up. A second broad category of individuals had legitimate questions, suggestions, factual corrections, or logical points. He saved every review and letter and appeared to try to learn from them all. He gave every personal comment or letter the utmost attention.

The protestation of Mrs. E.B. Darling, a lady from Berkeley whom he had met, provides a small example. An animal-lover, Mrs. Darling had been deeply interested in Alfred's explanations of time-binding and wanted a copy of the book. However, Korzybski's distinction between humans and animals seemed to imply to her the possible denigration of animals; she had serious misgivings. Korzybski wrote:

Dear Mrs. Darling:
I am sending under separate cover a copy of my book "Manhood of Humanity". I do not wish to hurt your feelings, kind feelings toward animals, as a soldier and farmer I know animals and love them. In my book I use sometimes an expression "beast", but this expression does not apply to animal, animals are just dear animals, "beast" is applied only and exclusively to man-animals which because man is not an animal when he wants to be an animal he becomes a "beast" in every respect LOWER than an animal. With this in mind I hope you will like the book.
Very sincerely yours.[20]

His definition of humanity and his exponential law did present problems. Humanity was defined in terms of its capacity to make progress. But how was *progress* to be exactly defined in order to be observed and measured?

Nonetheless, whatever its flaws, he continued to affirm the significance of what he had done. His law or formula did indicate an exponential, accumulative potential in humans, the existence of which he affirmed throughout his life. Others before him may have observed and commented on the phenomenon but as far as he knew, no one before him had isolated and labeled it in functional, actional, comparative terms—as he had done—and affirmed it as the necessary starting point for a deductive science of Man. For Alfred, who held the model of the exact (or mathematical) sciences as an ideal, such a science of Man should aspire to be as postulational as possible, i.e., based on initial definitions and premises comprising a theory to be elaborated deductively, tested, and revised.

To Keyser and others, Alfred could certainly admit some frustration about the limits of his own formulating. Even within the book, he had noted some of its limitations. The book "aimed to be only a sketch [p. 204]. ...Many topics have not even been broached [p. 208]." While writing the book, he had felt more directly interested in social and economic issues and reform. Now he no longer wanted to elaborate upon the implications/applications of time-binding for economics, politics, etc. Rather, he wanted to understand the *mechanism* of time-binding—*how it worked. Manhood* provided a start, but he still hadn't gotten to the core of what he wanted to understand.

Part V
Science and Sanity

"This is based on a new world outlook... We have made a <u>methodological</u> summary of what we know, practically in every field, without going into the details of it. I had to extract the <u>method</u> and 'all' I teach you is scientific method...It takes infernal work to do so, and without time-binding...I could not have produced general semantics, which is method, method, and nothing but."
—Alfred Korzybski [1]

Chapter 21
LEIBNIZ'S DREAMS

In the final pages of *Manhood of Humanity*, Alfred had presented a dream for the future of humanity which seemed to expand upon some of the old Polish ideals he had grown up with[*]:
> In humanity's manhood, patriotism—the love of country—will not perish—far from it—it will grow to embrace the world, for your country and mine will be the world. Your "state" and mine will be the Human State—a Cooperative Commonwealth of Man—a democracy in fact and not merely in name... guided ...by scientific men, by honest men who know. Is it a dream? It is a dream, but the dream will come true. It is a scientific dream and science will make it a living reality.[1]

How to bring about this dream? Korzybski made an admittedly vague proposal for "the establishment of a new institution which might be called a Dynamic Department—Department of Coordination or a Department of Cooperation" (whether wholly governmental or not, it didn't seem quite clear). Korzybski wrote: "Its functions would be those of encouraging, helping and protecting the people in such cooperative enterprises as agriculture, manufactures, finance, and distribution."[2]

However, now that *Manhood of Humanity* had been published, Alfred wasn't planning to dwell on this or any other social, economic, or political applications of the time-binding notion. He hoped others would do so. His need to figure things out in the most comprehensive way, what he called his "innate abstractness"—one of the main factors driving him to write *Manhood*—was still driving him. It led him now to explore and uncover the foundation of time-binding, its underlying mechanism.[3] Since he seemed inclined to see the broadest theory as potentially the most practical, he had confidence this might actually lead to some far-reaching social benefits.

What lay at the foundation of time-binding? It seemed to him that the very mathematical spirit he had tried to apply in developing his definition of Man, exemplified time-binding at its best. He had given this spirit—the spirit of rigorous thinking—more attention in his original manuscript. But in the editing process, he had moved it into the background. In the published book, much of his discussion of mathematics had either been deleted or moved to an appendix or footnote. Now he wanted to move time-binding to the background—as it were—and to shift his focus to this mathematical side. He felt strongly that by digging into the foundations of mathematics and the physico-mathematical sciences, he would be digging to uncover the roots of time-binding itself.

Much of the deleted material was contained in a manuscript of *Manhood* which he had loaned some time before to an acquaintance in New York City, a businessman and writer named John Martin. He could get other manuscripts in various states of revision but this was the first draft, which contained material not available in the other versions. Now in San Francisco, he urgently wanted it back. He wrote to Martin asking for its return. But Martin had loaned the draft to someone else, hadn't been able to locate the man he had given it to, and didn't seem to understand Alfred's urgency. Martin sent back a curt letter and several months of somewhat acrimonious correspondence ensued until Alfred finally did get it back.

---
[*] The motto "For your freedom and ours", used by Polish fighters in various independence movements around the world, encapsulates the universal democratic ideal long interlinked with traditional Polish patriotism. See Olszer.

Perhaps he had needed the draft. Still, he had also begun to find deeper issues in his theory, issues he simply hadn't dealt with in the first book or at least hadn't been able to treat with much clarity. He had already established that "Language no doubt is an essential instrument or vehicle of time-binding."[4] But how did it work to impede or improve progress? Perhaps there were problems with some of the language he himself had been using. How did this all relate to mathematics? Somehow, he felt, the mathematical theories of dimensions and types could be extended to "bring order in the confusion of wrong language and wrong logic in the affairs of men".[5] But how exactly? In broad terms, he knew what he was aiming for. If *Manhood* contained his "special theory", to use an analogy with Einstein's work on relativity, he was now aiming to formulate a more "general theory". But what did he need to do to get there?

Such a general theory, he expected, would have great practicality, an application to life that Russell and Whitehead, among others, had not been able to demonstrate. This was the thrust of the new book he was planning. He had already started to work on it before the publication of *Manhood*. Macrae had an option to publish it. The book would deal with the dreams and ideals of Man and the problems of human happiness from this mathematical perspective. He had hoped to be able to get it out within four to five months (it would take 12 years) and already had a title—*When Dreams Become True: The Mathematical Theory of Life*.

The title referred to Alfred's dreams but also alluded to the dreams of Leibniz. Among the many historical figures studied by Korzybski, Leibniz looms as one of his greatest conscious and acknowledged influences. Years later, Alfred would include him (spelling his name with a "t", i.e., "Leibnitz") in the list of those to whom he dedicated his second book. This was not only for Leibniz's discovery/invention (along with Newton) of the calculus, which over the years so inspired Alfred. The dreams of Leibniz—various schemes and speculations Leibniz proposed over his lifetime to advance mathematics, science, and society—stirred Alfred as well.[6]

Leibniz's Dreams

To what extent Alfred knew of Leibniz's work before meeting Keyser remains unknown. But Keyser had referred to Leibniz and his dreams in his own writings. Undoubtedly by the summer of 1921, Alfred had at least seen these references in his readings of Keyser's work. In Leibniz, Alfred sensed a kindred spirit and he went on to study Leibniz's life and work.

Leibniz was born in 1646 at the tail-end of the Thirty-Years War in Germany. Although he received a doctorate in jurisprudence and had been offered a university professorship, Leibniz spent most of his professional life in the service of German princes, first the Elector of Mainz, and then two successive Dukes of Hanover. These latter patrons deemed that the most significant work that one of the greatest intellects in human history could do, was to write a chronicle of the Hanover family. (The family now seems important mainly because of its connection to Leibniz.) In his 'spare time', among other accomplishments, Leibniz managed to invent the differential and integral calculus (independently of Isaac Newton), founded the disciplines of symbolic logic and analysis situs, i.e., topology (although he failed to develop either of these to any significant extent), and carried on extensive scientific-philosophical and diplomatic activities and correspondence throughout Europe.

Perhaps at least in part because of the era of European disharmony he had been born into, Leibniz was obsessed with dreams of universalism and unification. One of his dreams was of universal peace in Christian Europe. He had floated a scheme for unifying the Protestants and Catholics (at least in Germany) after more than a century of conflict since the start of the Reformation. The scheme never got off the ground. He also wanted to unify the various areas of knowledge. He wrote, "The entire body of the sciences may be regarded as an ocean, continuous everywheres and without a break or division."[7] He felt strongly that the sciences were the "greatest treasure of mankind".[8] In addition, his experience as a mining engineer in the Harz Mountains of Germany may have reinforced his conviction about the necessity of uniting theory and practice in order to gain the greatest benefit from this treasure.

As the Duke of Hanover's librarian he had access to texts from all over Europe and even China. As an inventor cum mathematician cum scientist he had been stimulated and encouraged by his meetings with some of the age's best "natural philosophers". These experiences fed further dreams of the unification of the sciences and scientists. While living in Paris and visiting London, he had become a member of both the French Academy and the Royal Society of London. This inspired him to work at establishing other societies in Europe for the sharing and dissemination of scientific knowledge. In this regard, he helped found the Prussian Academy in Berlin and before his death in 1716, corresponded with Tsar Peter the Great, in an effort to found a Russian Academy in St. Petersburg.

Scientific unity could be promoted in other ways too. Leibniz dreamt of a universal encyclopedia. Even at the end of the 17th Century he was worrying about the effects of the "horrible mass of books which keeps on growing" and "the indefinite multitude of authors".[9]

> …[W]ith books continuing to increase in number, we shall be wearied by their confusion…some day a great, free and curious prince, a glorious amateur, or perhaps himself a learned man, understanding the importance of the matter, will cause to undertake under the best auspices what Alexander the Great commanded Aristotle to do with the natural sciences,…namely that the quintessence of the best books be extracted and joined to the best observations, not yet written, of the most expert in each profession, in order to build systems of solid knowledge for promoting man's happiness. …such a work would be a most durable and great monument of his glory and constitute an incomparable debt which all mankind would owe him.[10]

Such a system, he speculated, could lead to new discoveries "by examining each science with the effort necessary to discover its principles of discovery, which once combined with some higher or general science (namely, the art of discovery), may suffice to deduce all the rest or at least the most useful truths without needing to burden the mind with too many precepts."[11]

Idols of the 'Mind'

A universal encyclopedia of knowledge and a general science of discovery would, in Korzybski's terms, necessarily accelerate the time-binding power of Man by helping to extend the methodology of science and mathematics to more and more areas of human life. First, however, a great deal of the 'deadwood' blocking the rate of time-binding would have to be removed from the 'tree of culture'. As Korzybski wrote in *Manhood of Humanity*:

> Metaphysical speculation and its swarming progeny of blind and selfish political philosophies, private opinions, private "truths," and private doctrines, sectarian opinions, sectarian

"truths" and sectarian doctrines, querulous, confused and blind—such is characteristic of the *childhood* of humanity. The period of humanity's *manhood* will, I doubt not, be a scientific period—a period that will witness the gradual extension of scientific method to all the interests of mankind—a period in which man will discover the essential nature of man and establish, at length, the science and art of directing human energies and human capacities to the advancement of human weal in accordance with the laws of human nature.[12]

As Korzybski was not the first to hold such a dream of scientific and cultural advancement, neither was Leibniz. Sir Francis Bacon (1561-1626), had gotten there before. Bacon had championed the move away from dry medieval scholasticism toward the modern experimental study of nature. He had proclaimed, "Knowledge is Power" and had hoped to usher in "The Great Instauration"—a golden age of science-based progress. Before Leibniz, he sought to create a universal encyclopedia of knowledge. And he too had written about a general science, an art of thinking and discovery he hoped to advance. In his 1620 work, *Novum Organum,* he had presented this new system of thought, hoping to replace or at least expand on the logic of Aristotle. This would require recognizing and dealing with,

Four species of idols [sources of error which] beset the human mind, to which (for distinction's sake) we have assigned names, calling the first Idols of the Tribe [intrinsic to general human nature, perception, etc.], the second Idols of the Den [intrinsic to each individual's idiosyncracies and training], the third Idols of the Market [related to language], the fourth Idols of the Theatre [related to doctrines and beliefs].[13]

In *Manhood of Humanity* Korzybski had quoted at length from Bacon's discussion of these idols. They seemed to summarize some of the major impediments to human understanding and successful time-binding which characterized the childhood of humanity. To clarify the mechanism of time-binding, Alfred would need to make a less 'literary', more exact formulation of how the 'idols' of the 'mind' were formed.

The Dream of a Universal Language

The dreams of Leibniz, known as a 'rationalist', in some ways extended and refined those of the 'empiricist' Bacon. But for Leibniz, a mathematician, an intrinsic part of his dream included a proposal for a "universal language" or "universal characteristic" growing out of mathematics. Alfred, as a lover of mathematics and a good mathematical 'journeyman', seemed very much in tune with Leibniz here.

As early as Pythagoras and Plato, people had wondered at the 'miracles' of mathematics and seen it as a model for other areas of thought. By the 17th century significant parts of natural philosophy, i.e., the science of mechanics and astronomy, were beginning to yield to mathematical treatment with astonishing success. It surely seemed, as Galileo commented, as if the Almighty had written the book of nature in the language of mathematics. Leibniz was convinced "there is nothing which is not subsumable under number",[14] if we only knew how to do it. Number had exactness, and exactness—the inevitablility of correct conclusions—appeared as the holy grail. Why? Because when rightly understood it led to agreement—universal agreement.

Even the simple operations of arithmetic might in a certain sense be made more exact through mechanization. In pursuit of this, Leibniz had designed and built the first four-function calculator. In other areas of mathematics, Leibniz also found more exact operations could at least be facilitated by an apt notation, such as the symbolism he designed for calculus—still used today.

Could anything like this be done for traditional logic and the even more inexact areas of knowledge and everyday language? Leibniz seemed to think so. As he put it in his 1677 essay "Preface To A General Science", his "universal characteristic" entailed developing a new language for the perfection of reason. This language would allow people to express themselves with the exactness of arithmetic and geometry. With it, arguments and errors would dissolve as conversation would come to resemble calculation. Possibility or pipe dream? Leibniz thought he could do it. But ultimately he didn't succeed in his long-term project of mathematizing everyday discourse. However, the vision did inspire a large portion of his work. His founding of the discipline of symbolic/mathematical logic, even though he was not able to carry it very far, is considered by many to be the closest he got towards the goal of a universal characteristic.

More than 100 years later, the English mathematician George Boole formulated the first system of mathematical logic, in his 1854 book, *Investigation of the Laws of Thought*. (Boole expressed delight when he learned he had in fact followed in Leibniz's footsteps.) According to Keyser, Boole's work initiated a revolution in mathematics and logic, by showing their deep relationship. Russell and Whitehead and others had built and were building upon it.

Korzybski had had many discussions with Keyser about these developments and was immersing himself in this work. He felt and knew its importance. But the work—with its high level of abstractness—seemed remote and forbidding, not anything like a universal language applicable to everyday life. For example, with the elaborate and exotic apparatus of their algebraic symbology, Russell and Whitehead had taken 379 pages just getting to the point of showing how 1+1=2. Alfred felt there was something in what they had done, and in the other books he was studying, relevant for living life. He wanted to draw it down to earth—make it practical for the man, woman, and child in the street.

This was the project he was developing in the summer of 1921, as *Manhood of Humanity* was getting publicized. He wanted, if he could, to topple the idols impeding people's ability to time-bind. He had accomplished the first step. People now had the formulation of time-binding by which they could clearly and consciously view themselves as time-binders. Mathematical logic and the exact physico-mathematical sciences seemed to hold the key for the next step—to liberate the time-binding mechanism.

In his new book Alfred hoped he could bring to life an updated version of the dreams of Leibniz, Bacon, and others. Building from the notion of time-binding and from the revolutionary new mathematics and science of the the early 20th century, Korzybski was groping to construct a methodological foundation for a science of humanity. He would continue his career of troubleshooting now on a much more general scale.

Chapter 22
"JUST WORK, WORK, WORK"

The "Great War" had scarred Korzybski both physically and psychologically. Great troubles loomed, perhaps even another more disastrous war. But despite his memories and forebodings, he seemed incapable of cynicism. He had retained his enthusiasm, warmth, earthiness—and bluntness. He had married a large-hearted woman who carried an actual golden rule with her wherever she went. Together, they deeply felt people could do better, the world could do better. After all, Alfred had clearly demonstrated (so they thought): humans, as the time-binding class of life, have at least the potential to progress.

However, Alfred also knew a good-hearted intention to help could be worse than useless if unconstrained by an accurate view of actualities. His own earlier attraction to the sort of view expressed in the *Protocols of the Elders of Zion* had come out of his deeply held concern for people's well-being (particularly in Poland) combined with an uninformed, simplistic understanding of Jewish life. His deep investment in the principle of rooting out false knowledge had required him to challenge himself once his antisemitic beliefs had come to the surface so starkly. This provided another lesson about the necessity of not taking anything for granted (least of all his own opinions), of being open to facts, and of being willing to modify his opinions in accordance with them. Doing good required a clear head.

Korzybski's committment to clarity, which he had cultivated over the years, provided the 'secret' behind his knack for solving problems of all kinds. He wanted to extract its essence and convey it to others. Now (1921) he was putting it in terms of mathematical logic. But it seemed based on an even more general orientation—a system of principles (however unclear at present) behind the physico-mathematical revolution going on around him.

These principles connected with what his father had first taught him as a child, i.e., the feel of the calculus—looking at the world, even daily life, in terms of dynamic functions, differential equations. Leibniz again—the first to use the term "function" as the name for mathematically expressed relationships between variables. Things, people, ideas were not fixed and final however they might appear. Rather, everything in the world took part in a process of growth and change. Concurrently, if things seemed confusing, an order still existed behind the confusion, an underlying network of invariant relationships that might reveal itself for someone daring enough to inquire. Function. Differentiation. Integration. This way of looking at things, part of his engineer's mentality and worldview—how could he convey it?

He felt and knew more than he could clearly say about it. He remembered the teacher who had scolded him—"If you think you know it but you can't say it, you probably don't." He now saw his first book as only an introduction to something much larger and more significant. What he was now studying, the new work in the foundations of mathematics and the recent revolution in physics, seemed to him to have come from this source of clear-headedness and rigorous thinking, the physico-mathematical and engineering 'spirit' that had fed him from childhood onwards. He was struggling now to remove the dross and confusion (his own primarily) and to more lucidly express his vision of this source—the source of the time-binding power. Somehow, he thought, there was a way of making the highly abstract and esoteric work he was now studying meaningful and applicable to everyday life.

Alfred had been corresponding with his friend Gilchrest, the Canadian who had tutored him in English at Petawawa. He wanted to know Gilchrest's opinion of *Manhood*. Later in 1921, Gilchrest wrote that he considered the book "most excellently written", but added:
> ...I do not think you have yet made the practical value of your discovery apparent to ordinary people. That may come later, in your next book. For example, I have no idea what would be your first step towards solving the problems of life or making things better. And that is the sort of advice that is most needed in the opinion of such prosaic and such dull individuals as I.[1]

Alfred could certainly agree. If he could clarify the broad system of principles behind the physico-mathematical revolution, he could provide such advice. In the meantime, he had been trying to sell some books.

Marketing *Manhood*

Manhood of Humanity never seemed in danger of becoming a huge bestseller. Macrae had anticipated an interested but limited scientifically-inclined audience. He expressed pleasant surprise as nationwide interest in the book grew through the summer of 1921 and into the fall. Published at the end of June, the first printing of 1500 copies was exhausted by the end of August. Dutton quickly had another 1500 printed with half of them bound at once. Half of these were sold almost immediately.

Publicity consisted of Dutton's marketing efforts (fliers and review copies, book store placements, and some advertisements) and whatever interest Alfred, in California, and his friends, mainly in New York City, could muster. How would they spread the word? In 1921 radio barely existed as a form of mass media. (The first commercial radio station, KDKA in Pittsburgh, had only begun limited broadcasting at the end of 1920.) Movies were still silent (though some kind of newsreel coverage could not be ruled out). Television was an inventor's novelty, and the internet, email, etc., yet undreamed. It seemed crucial to get news about time-binding and the book into print. Newspapers were the main form of daily mass media news and entertainment. Even small cities normally had more than one daily paper with editors always on the lookout for content.

Alfred, savvy about publicity, energetically made contacts and did what he could to bring his work into public awareness. Especially throughout this and the next year, he and his friends used personal contacts, letters, speaking engagements, reviews, and articles in newspapers, magazines, and journals in order to get *Manhood of Humanity* in the public eye. And as the notion of time-binding became more well-known, word-of-mouth began to take effect to some degree.

Macrae felt impressed by the ardor of Alfred and his friends. Keyser, for example, made significant efforts. Almost sixty and not in the most robust of health, he still had teaching responsibilities and was trying to finish *Mathematical Philosophy*, his magnum opus which he had been working on for years. He wouldn't let anything he didn't consider essential distract him. Although he had already edited *Manhood*, he gave the full measure of whatever spare time he had to promoting Alfred's book.

With Keyser's permission, Alfred had a local printer make reprints of Keyser's May Phi Beta Kappa address on the subject of time-binding, entitled "The Nature of Man". Alfred then privately distributed it to select individuals he met or was corresponding with. (As was typical of Korzybski, he made friends with the printer who then joined his network of "time-binders", began corresponding with Alfred and his other friends, and ended up offering Alfred a special deal for the printing costs.)

Meanwhile Keyser had an article published in the June issue of the academic journal *The Pacific Review* on "The Mathematical Obligations of Philosophy" which mentioned Alfred's new book (much of this became "Lecture I – Introduction" of *Mathematical Philosophy*). Keyser also reviewed *Manhood* for *The Bookman* (published in September) and *The New Republic* (never published) and *The New York Evening Post*. The September 9 edition of *Science*, published by the American Association for the Advancement of Science (AAAS), carried Keyser's May address on its front page. This gave Korzybski's work an obvious boost of prestige and brought it to the attention of the large number of professional scientists and engineers who saw the journal. The *Science* article was reprinted in the January 1922 *The Hibbert Journal: A Quarterly Review of Religion, Theology and Philosophy*. Keyser's elaboration on the theme, "Korzybski's Conception of Man and Some of Its Implications", appeared in the December 1921 volume of *The Pacific Review*.

Keyser's enthusiasm for Korzybski and his work was heartfelt. And he was making his promotional efforts for Korzybski do double-duty for his own work—combining the *Science* address with the December *Pacific Review* article, he formed the penultimate chapter of *Mathematical Philosophy*. (Korzybski later called this, Chapter XX, "an exceptionally deep and beautifully written contemplation"[2] and the best short discussion of time-binding he knew. Years later, he made sure to have it placed after the Appendices in the Second Edition of *Manhood*, eventually published some months after his death.) Besides his articles and review, Keyser was also making an effort to mention Korzybski's work in academic gatherings and personal conversations and meetings, whenever it seemed appropriate.

Polakov was also doing his part to push the book. Though he couldn't find consulting jobs, his severe financial woes and concomitant psychological depression didn't stop an outpouring of reviews, articles and speeches. The American Federation of Engineering Societies, under Herbert Hoover, had come out with a report on industrial waste, i.e., inefficiency—Walter's area of specialty. The report gave him an opportunity to write some articles which expanded upon his "Principles of Industrial Philosophy". *The New Republic* published one such article, "Waste", in its July 6, 1921 issue. Since the editors expunged all his references to Korzybski, Walter (and Alfred) wondered if they didn't have some kind of ill will toward Korzybski's work. They later got some confirmation of this when they discovered the editors had pitted Walter against Keyser for reviews of *Manhood* and then subsequently published a hostile review from someone else.

The July 1921 issue of *The World Tomorrow*, a progressive Christian monthly, published a piece "Ecce Homo" ["Behold Man"] by Polakov which functioned as an extended review of *Manhood*. And though Walter also seemed like the perfect person to write a review for *The Nation*, William Fielding, Alfred and Walter's friend from the "Time-Binding Club", ended up writing one for the August issue. Walter, meanwhile had a review in the August *Management Engineering* and *The New York Times* gave him a page and a half in its Sunday, September 4, issue for an article with the headline "New Theory of Man – Count Korzybski Offers "Time-Binding" as the Key". By this time newspaper, magazine and journal editors around the country were taking note and *Manhood of Humanity* was getting reviews and notices from coast-to-coast.

With Alfred and Mira planning to go to Europe, Alfred had designated Walter in the "Preface" of *Manhood* "…to act, with my authority, as my representative to whom any further queries should be addressed in my absence from America."[3] Although the Korzybskis had not yet left the country, Walter was already getting inquiries. One, from Ford Hall Forum, which had a large auditorium in Boston, asked him to speak there on time-binding on October 24. Alfred was delighted Walter had been offered this opportunity and even more delighted afterwards when he learned how it came off. Walter spoke on "Korzybski's New Law of Life" to a standing-room-only audience of over 1000 people. He spoke for over an hour, answered questions for another hour, and after his lecture got mobbed on the street outside the hall by eager listeners. Ironically, the speaker's fee barely covered his train fare, lodging, and meals and he returned home from all this adulation to his new living quarters in New York City—a maid's closet in the building where he had had his office. He had recently been evicted from his apartment for failure to pay rent. (His daughter Catherine, who had lived with him, had already moved in with a friend.)[4]

Down and Out

Alfred and Mira's situation in California seemed a little better. At least they were able to pay their bills and they had some money coming in from royalties, although the income from these was offset by their book purchases from Dutton charged to their royalty account. More or less stranded in California, they were living from hand to mouth. Their plan to return East and sail for Europe sometime in November began to seem unfeasible.

Soon after her San Francisco gallery exhibit in May, Mira went down to Santa Barbara to visit friends and hunt for portrait commissions. But while money continued to pour out for her hotel and living expenses, she was not having much luck finding lucrative commissions. Alfred referred to her as "living among the sharks".

Meanwhile in San Francisco, Alfred contemplated their prospects with some dismay. Despite book sales going reasonably well, it was becoming clear his initial hopes of selling large numbers of books (enough to accrue a significant income) wouldn't happen anytime soon. By January of 1922, Dutton would sell 2,275 books. More than 1000 copies were sold in the following year. Then sales tailed off to a few hundred per year until the last few years of the decade when sales dropped again to less than 100 per year.[5]

In 1921, paid speaking engagements were not forthcoming. Alfred had contacted a number of lecture agencies and universities with no interest in him. Although he had had a few invitations to speak around San Francisco, his first paying engagement only came in September. A San Francisco bookstore, the Paul Elder Gallery, invited him to give two lectures that, though successful, provided very little money. In a letter to a friend in New York, Alfred described their gloomy outlook, "We are always working more than we should. I am writing my next book and my wife painting. We did not have any chance to enjoy California, just work, work, work."[6]

In July, Alfred had moved to Berkeley. For one thing, he didn't need all the space of the San Francisco apartment he and Mira had rented; and besides, the move made it easier for him to use the University of California library for his research. Luella Twining (who may have been an old friend of Mira's) had a house near the campus and offered him a room for rent. Twining, a socialist and former labor organizer,[7] had gotten a copy of

Manhood as soon as it came out and become a devotee of time-binding. Alfred got permission to keep some trunks and suitcases in the old apartment and moved into Luella's house. Alfred, who needed only a bed, and a desk upon which to spread his papers and books, felt as happy as he could be, which was in fact slightly depressed. Money was still tight. And he was missing Mira. But they were both plugging away, following what Alfred referred to as their 'religion'—to keep on working.

The thought of Alfred rooming in the home of a female friend while Mira was away may bring up the question to some readers: Did Alfred (or Mira) ever 'get involved' with anyone else? Mainly as a function of Mira's need to travel for her work, this was not the first nor the last time the two of them would be living apart. But I have found no reliable indication in Korzybski's well-documented life, or in interviews and discussions with those who knew either one of them, that either of them were unfaithful in their marriage. As in any marriage, they had conflicts. Indeed, years later, their differences led them to live apart. But sexual peccadillos do not appear to have been the basis of the split. After 1938, Alfred lived at the Institute of General Semantics building in Chicago and Mira in a nearby apartment. After 1946, when the Institute and Alfred moved to Connecticut, they had, as Robert Pula put it, a "Tallulah Bankhead style marriage":

> Tallulah Bankhead, daughter of an American Congressman and Speaker of the House, actress, and owner of one of the world's best female whiskey-and-cigarette baritone voices, replied when asked in an interview if she and her then husband had separate bedrooms: 'Dahling, separate bedrooms?! Separate cities!!'"[8]

If Alfred ever did succumb to temptations—*if*—he did so discreetly. His relationships with female students and with close female associates, like Kendig and Charlotte Schuchardt, though generally warm and friendly, appear to have remained completely professional.

Sweet, Sweet Delights of Human Relations

As the summer progressed, Mira was finishing up whatever work she had found in Santa Barbara. They planned for her to rejoin Alfred at the start of September. Then they would head to southern California where they might find better painting opportunities for her. From there they planned to make their way back across the country, visiting Mira's sister in Kansas City, and earning what money they could with a few painting commissions for her and lectures for Alfred before going on to New York City, and then to Europe. In the meantime Alfred was working on publicity for *Manhood*, working on his new book project, and making friends—and a few enemies.

Soon after they came to San Francisco in May, Alfred had met biologist Calvin B. Bridges, a brilliant young colleague of geneticist Thomas Hunt Morgan in their pioneering experimental work exploring the mechanism of heredity in the fruit fly *Drosophila melanogaster*. Bridges had studied and worked with Morgan for a number of years in Columbia University's famed "fly room" where he had already made a number of major discoveries of his own, and co-authored several books and papers with Morgan. He was known as one of the brightest and most productive men in Morgan's lab. Indeed Morgan recognized this, later sharing the prize money of his 1933 Nobel Prize in Medicine with Bridges and Bridges' lab colleague, A. H. Sturtevant. Bridges—considered a major figure in the history of genetics—might have gone on himself to win the Nobel Prize but unfortunately died suddenly from a heart infection in 1938 before the age of 50.

Both Bridges and Morgan were finishing extended working visits in the Bay Area when Alfred arrived there. Bridges, in Berkeley with his family, was planning to soon return to New York. Alfred bowled him over. After only a short time, Bridges had read a draft of *Manhood* (about a month prior to the publication of the book), and became an immediate fan of Korzybski's work. The two men would remain good friends until Bridges' death.

Korzybski met Morgan around the time he met Bridges. Unlike Bridges, Morgan seems to have taken an immediate dislike to Alfred. After *Manhood* was published, Alfred learned from Bridges that Morgan often saw the book on Bridges' desk and seemed compelled to have a "daily kick at it, moral as well as Physical, he had to take it in his hands, curse it and throw it on the table".[9] Wishing to avoid a confrontation with Morgan, Alfred avoided him when visiting Bridges at the biology lab where they were working. But one day, he found himself face-to-face with Morgan, who made some snide remarks about the people who had provided supportive comments for the cover of the book. With what he described as cold politeness, Korzybski told Morgan, "[S]ome of those people THINK occasionally…if the study even of flies involves SOME thinking, therefore even a fly master should be interested in CORRECT thinking."[10] It's unlikely Alfred could have said anything to improve Morgan's estimation of him or his work. This statement certainly didn't.

Bridges was preparing to return to New York with his family. Before he left, Alfred consulted with him on a pressing concern. Alfred and Mira badly wanted to make a baby and hadn't succeeded. Although both were in their 40s (with Mira almost 50) Alfred's sperm had 'passed' whatever fertility test was done at the time. Mira was apparently fertile, as she was still having a period. Doctors examining her had said her cervix was narrowed and that this anatomical variation might make it more difficult for her to conceive. Bridges, a professional biologist and a 'progressive' in politics, had more than a passing interest in the birth control movement, eugenics, woman's rights, etc. and had apparently already done some practical consulting work on this kind of problem. When he got back to New York, he promised to make up a kit for Alfred and Mira involving a suction tube they could use for inserting Alfred's semen deeper into her womb after intercourse, thus increasing the probability of conception.

Before he left, Bridges also introduced Alfred to Cora Lenore Williams, an educator in Berkeley who would become a friend to both Alfred and Mira and a booster of his work. Miss Williams operated the Williams Institute of Creative Education, a private school located at the landmark Spring Mansion in the Berkeley hills.[11] Miss Williams' school, influenced by the progressive education movement of John Dewey and others, has been described as "a tony elementary and secondary school known for its focus on languages, poetry, music, and literature."[12] Miss Williams, who had studied and taught mathematics at the University of California, Berkeley, wanted her students to be exposed to mathematics and the sciences as well. She soon became a fan of Korzybski's work. (He gave her a copy of *Manhood* after he met her.) Miss Williams invited Alfred to speak at her school soon after they met in August. He did so and then returned several times by himself and with Mira. Inspired by *Manhood*, Miss Williams thought time-binding could be made to form the basis for a new educational philosophy and over the next year wrote several reviews and articles on the subject. Alfred felt grateful for her "push". He kept contact with her for many years. (The Williams Institute later became a junior college, and Alfred gave a number of presentations there, including seminars, after *Science and Sanity* was published.)

At the beginning of September 1921, Mira returned. Alfred had already moved out of his room at Luella Twining's and rented another apartment in San Francisco. Delighted to be together again, Alfred and Mira probably took as many opportunities as they could to use the kit Bridges had sent them. Mira had gotten a lucrative portrait commission painting members of the Spreckel family, San Francisco-area multi-millionaires known as the "sugar kings". Her work would keep them in the city for another month or so. As soon as she was done they would leave for Southern California.

In August, Alfred had met the zoologist William Emerson Ritter, who had founded the Scripps Institute for Biological Research (later to become the Scripps Institution for Oceanography) in La Jolla, just north of San Diego. Korzybski had given Ritter, who was visiting Berkeley, a copy of *Manhood*. Ritter, much interested in the theoretical framework and philosophy of biology, became fascinated with the implications of time-binding and invited Alfred to come down to La Jolla for some personal discussions and conferences at the Scripps Institute.

This seemed fine to Alfred. For the time being, he had decided to stop writing. As he had written to Luella Twining previously, he still felt "[t]he world needs a complete scientific REVOLUTION, to bring science to sanity again."[13] But the issues involved with connecting relativity, mathematical logic, etc., with the foundations of human engineering had begun to appear more complex than he had previously imagined. In relation to what he wanted to do, his understanding was not ripe. He decided for the present to do more reading, note-taking, and cogitating. Ritter, who had written a two-volume work on "The Unity of the Organism" and was writing a book on the natural history of human intelligence, seemed to have some parallel interests. Alfred was sure he could learn some things from Ritter relevant to his own research. The two men began a serious correspondence of multi-paged, theoretically-laced letters. (For Korzybski, who liked to work out his ideas in letters, this was not unusual.) Alfred was eager to get down to La Jolla for face-to-face time with the zoologist. He and Mira hoped she would be able to find some good commissions once they got to Southern California. And some speaking engagements, and other opportunities involving some income, might also arise for him.

In the meantime, in September the first public controversy concerning Korzybski's work occurred. He described the gist of it in his 1947 memoir:

There was a curious thing which happened in Berkeley. It was an ex-engineer, Mr. Smyth. Oh, he wrote whole pages in a Berkeley paper attacking my work from the point of view that everything I had to say in my *Manhood*, was taken, stolen directly from his work. As a matter of fact I never saw [his work.] ...I never knew his work, and I believe he actually produced nothing. His name is unknown. Just a crank. But the curious part of it is that that fellow Smyth, ...He somehow was friendly with some most important mathematical logician, B. A. Bernstein who is still [in 1947] in the field an important man. He's a real important man. And he backed Smyth against *Manhood of Humanity*. And they were some sort of friends and since I never met Bernstein, and since he was my enemy, and he's really an important man, personally I don't know him, but you can imagine... an important mathematician, real important, a mathematical logician in the University of California which means an important institution, and if he can be connected with a crank and because of the opinion of the crank, get against me, those are sweet, sweet delights of human relations.[14]

In response to Smyth and Bernstein's attacks, Walter Polakov wrote a letter to the editor of the Berkeley paper and Keyser wrote to Bernstein, attempting to explain Korzybski's theory. After writing a letter to the Berkeley paper as well, Alfred decided the best thing he could do would be to ignore the attacks, although he was glad Walter and Keyser had risen to his defense. In October, as he and Mira were preparing to leave the San Francisco area for southern California, Alfred's confidence was also bolstered by some distinguished visitors: Professor Mellen Woodman Haskell, Dean of the Mathematics Department at the University of California, Berkeley, and his wife; along with Florian Cajori, who held the history of mathematics chair at Berkeley, and Cajori's wife. Both mathematicians thought highly of *Manhood*. Haskell, whom Alfred had already met by means of Keyser, described how he had defended Korzybski's work against Bernstein, a former graduate student of his, at a faculty presentation. Korzybski and Cajori exchanged autographed copies of their books.[15]

Around this time in New York, Keyser and Bridges both wrote to Alfred about more 'sweet delights' from T. H. Morgan, who by that time had also returned to New York City. Keyser reported that Morgan was bad-mouthing Korzybski at Columbia faculty gatherings.[16] Morgan seemed to be pursuing some kind of personal campaign against Korzybski. Bridges wrote that Morgan had come up to psychiatrist Stuart Paton at an International Eugenics Congress in New York and upbraided Paton for having written a favorable review of *Manhood*. Bridges told Alfred he approached Paton afterwards and told him to ignore Morgan's remarks.[17]

This kind of behavior must have had at least a damping effect on Korzybski's dreams of universal agreement. He had already expressed to Polakov the hope that the Time-Binding Club might serve as a unifying core for an eventual worldwide organization of interested laypeople and, in particular, scientists. But how could the scientists of the world unite with the close-minded, petty actions of influential men like Bernstein and Morgan standing in the way? What they were doing in relation to him seemed anything but scientific in attitude. Throughout his career he would encounter others, like these two men, who seemed to take offense at some aspect of him and his work. But he was learning to become immune to petty criticisms.

The enthusiasm of friends like Keyser, Polakov, Bridges, and Williams, and of people he met like Ritter, Haskell, and Cajori, seemed sufficient to keep him from getting discouraged. He also took heart that others whom he hadn't met, including influential people in the sciences, were reading his book and finding it valuable. For example, in the fall of 1921 George Hale, the founder of the Mount Wilson Observatory in Pasadena, wrote to Mira (whom he had met through a mutual friend) about his positive impressions of *Manhood of Humanity* after a first reading.[18] In the next few years, Alfred and Mira would also meet other people who would express enthusiasm about the book, displayed proudly and prominently on their sitting-room tables, with its pages uncut and unread. He was not going to let being a 'famous author' go to his head.

Monkeying with the Octopuses
At the end of October, Alfred and Mira found themselves in a rush of packing and last minute planning for their trip to Southern California. They also busied themselves saying goodbye to friends. President Barrow of the University of California gave a party in their honor, one last time for them to see many of the people they had met at Berkeley. Finally, in the first week of November 1921, trunks and suitcases in tow, they took the train to Los Angeles.

Alfred and Mira felt exhausted when they arrived. Anticipating some time to rest, they were instead subjected to phone calls, newspaper interviews, and gatherings in their honor. But they put up with the attention. Of course, the newspaper stories could lead to confusion. Many of the stories misconstrued Alfred's claim "Man is not an animal", implying that he opposed Darwin's theory of evolution. The headline of one story about him in the Friday, November 4 issue of the *L.A. Examiner* read "Darwin Downed! Count In L. A. Denies Man Is Animal[.] World Famed Polish Nobleman and Philosopher Tells of Discoveries".[19] He certainly had no wish to down Darwin.

The couple settled into the Ambassador Hotel in Los Angeles where Mira would stay on for awhile after Alfred went south. Alfred was not expected by Ritter until the following week so they had some time to do at least a little sightseeing which included visiting the Goldwyn Picture Studios in Culver City, where they met writer/director Rupert Hughes, watched a movie being made, and got their picture in the paper once again. Alfred planned to visit with Ritter in La Jolla, and perhaps get some speaking engagements around San Diego, sell some books, and get some work done on his next book. Meanwhile Mira explored opportunities to paint in Los Angeles and Pasadena while also doing what she could to promote Alfred's work. What they thought would involve a few weeks before heading east would turn into several months. People praised Alfred's book and went to exhibitions of Mira's paintings, but paying engagements—at least for any significant amount of money—were few and far between. They would not leave Southern California until April of the following year, 1922.

On November 11, Alfred took a train from Los Angeles to the Delmar station where Ritter had arranged to meet him.[20] Soon, Alfred had settled himself and his bags into beachfront Cabin #3 at the Scripps Institute of Biological Research in La Jolla. Alfred's three-room, furnished cottage with a kitchen, bathroom, and bedroom cost him 12 dollars a month, plus a few dollars for gas and electricity. With a bus stop near the Institute, which stood on a bluff above the beach, he could get to San Diego when he wanted. One could find worse places to spend the winter.

But to begin with he was not in the best of moods. For one thing, he had arrived at La Jolla with a bad cold.[21] The parties, the packing, the rush, the newspaper interviews, etc., over the last few weeks had left him feeling tired and bothered. For all the attention he received, he didn't like being trotted out like a zoo specimen for exhibition. He disliked the exaggerations by journalists in their headlines and articles ("world's greatest philosopher", "war hero", etc.).

He also felt pressed by worries. Mira had spent most of her adult life with no fixed home. One of her friends in Los Angeles once referred to her as a "beloved vagabond". But Alfred—who had lived as a vagabond since the start of the war seven years earlier—yearned to be settled at home in Poland. Money concerned him. The question of how he and Mira were going to make ends meet once they left for Poland formed a constant nagging concern, especially since they were even having trouble making ends meet in the United States.[22]

And his efforts to write his next book—about how time-binding worked—had opened up new problems. He felt pressed to make sense of his endless reading. He struggled with his writing. How did the foundations of mathematics, relativity theory, and now Ritter's biology, among other things, all connect to each other in terms of the mechanism of time-binding? What was their practical import for living life? He could see the outline of something important ahead but it was still shrouded in a great deal of fog. As he wrote to his friend Robert Wolf, "There is a lot of troubles with ideas if we want them to be correct." [23] He was glad to finally have some time to be alone and think. He hoped his meetings with Ritter and others at Scripps would give him the opportunity to gain some added clarity.

Alfred set up his work table so he could look out to the Pacific from a window. He loved the "music of the ocean", and watching the "endless waves" helped him forget his troubles. He looked forward to a good storm.[24] He had brought with him a number of books on mathematical logic and relativity to study.

For recreation, he swam in the ocean. As he had first learned to swim in the cold water of the drainage pond of his family's farm in Poland, the chilly Pacific waters did not dissuade him. As he later recalled:

> I enjoyed in the meantime the Pacific and I bathed there and I don't know, monkeyed with the octopuses,…and I don't know what not…[25]
>
> We had a colony of seals and we were good friends and so I liked to swim with them. They didn't approve my company, but I didn't care. I did my swimming. I had to deal with all those squids, rays,… I had to be very careful not to put my foot in an abalone because they would bite my foot off...So, I swam a lot there alone, means without supervision, and I went quite far in the Pacific, but I returned somehow successfully.[26]

He would also see more than one good storm. At the end of December, when he had been at La Jolla for more than a month, he wrote good-humoredly to Keyser that:

> We had what they call here "golden rain." I was impressed as a "diamond" rain at least. We had ghastly storms for several days, and terrible muds, of course bridges have gone mails have stopped etcetc. A large piece of the shore where my cabin stands has gone several more of such storms and my cabin will go. Than I will write to you from "somewhere in the Pacific" buy buy [bye bye] in the meantime, still in America [27]

Getting carried away in a storm could not be entirely dismissed. The cabin was certainly small enough. Once, when Mira was staying with him there, it stormed while they were sleeping. The window near the bed kept blowing open. Alfred didn't want to get out of bed any more than he already had to; he held the window closed with one foot, sticking out from under the covers.[28]

Chapter 23
STRANGE FOOTPRINTS

At La Jolla, Alfred spent a great deal of his time reading, making notes, and pondering. He wanted to get to the roots of time-binding and considered the foundations of mathematics and the theory of relativity particularly relevant. Three authors in these subjects particularly managed to grab his interest at this time: Bertrand Russell and Alfred North Whitehead (who had written jointly and separately), and Arthur Stanley Eddington. The works of these men had a major influence on Korzybski's subsequent formulating. Therefore, in this chapter, I go into some detail on the 'building blocks' Alfred derived from them.

Principia Mathematica

Since Ritter didn't have Russell and Whitehead's *Principia Mathematica* available at the Scripps Institute Library, Alfred had made sure to bring a copy of Volume I (the most significant for him). He had borrowed it from Adelaide Smith, a mathematician like Cora Williams, who ran a private school in Berkeley. Miss Smith had little use for the book, while for Alfred it contained keys to what he was trying to formulate. She later let him have it for $5 and he probably felt glad to send her the check since he could then mark up the book as he liked.[1] Korzybski considered it epochal. Despite Russell and Whitehead ultimately falling short in their attempt to derive all of mathematics from logic, their three-volume work (the planned fourth volume on geometry was never produced) had a profound influence on 20th century thinkers in many fields beyond mathematics and logic. In it, mathematics had, in a sense, become conscious of itself.

In a 1949 paper, "The New Mathematical Philosophy" read at the Third Congress on General Semantics, physicist-philosopher L. L. Whyte succinctly expressed views about Russell and Whitehead which were highly congruent with Korzybski's mature attitude about those two men and their work. Whyte suggested,

> ...what Whitehead and Russell have achieved is to define the <u>form</u> appropriate to fundamental knowledge; but they did not suggest what <u>content</u> should be put into that form. They did not breathe life into the dry bones of mathematical philosophy. That is why there has so far been little general appreciation of the real nature of their achievement, which was to provide a logical technique capable of going deeper into the nature of things, and in that I include both external nature and human thought, than any previous invention of man.[2]

Koryzbski realized something similar about the nature of Whitehead and Russell's achievement soon after Keyser first introduced him to their work in 1920. And by the end of 1921, building on Keyser's suggestions in that direction, he felt he would have a chance to really 'breath some life into those bones' by showing their relation to time-binding.

A major contribution of Russell and Whitehead was their elaboration of the theory of types (Russell's creation) to deal with the paradoxes of self-reference in set theory. For example: Did Epiminedes the Cretan tell the truth when he made the statement "All statements by Cretans are false"? The theory of types posited different levels of statements or propositions, providing a way to make distinctions among statements. We make statements and can make statements about our statements—and they aren't all the same. A class of classes (set of sets) or a proposition about a proposition belonged on a different hierarchical level, had a 'higher' logical type, than a simple class (set) or simple proposition.

So a statement or a class referring to itself—Epiminedes the Cretan's statement about *all* statements by Cretans—involved a contradiction, an "illegitimate totality" forbidden by Russell's theory.

Korzybski saw that despite the ad hoc quality of the theory of types, it gave a degree of exactness to—and thus clarified as never before—a profound fact: the existence of a hierarchical ordering process of the human 'mind', reflected in its symbolic productions. He also felt the theory contained consequences of practical importance for time-binding that Russell and Whitehead hadn't explored. Their types could be seen as altered forms of the dimensions he had discussed in *Manhood of Humanity* and thought about since then. With Russell and Whitehead's help, it seemed to him he had gotten a little closer to understanding how the confusion of dimensions (types?) as depicted in *Manhood*, might even exemplify the core of faulty thinking in general. This had tremendous life implications. One didn't have to make a solid wall between logic and human behavior (was not logic made by humans?). If he was going to better understand and promote time-binding, he needed to better understand the hierarchical nature of types or dimensions. But things didn't quite fit together yet.

Qualitative Mathematics

The theory of types represented one result of the general approach of the *Principia* which formed, in Whyte's words, "...the culmination of two centuries of mathematical research, mostly in the direction of increasing abstract generality, formal definition of axioms, analysis of the basic relationships implicit in mathematical systems, and the discovery of appropriate mathematical symbolisms."

> All this work can be summarized in the concept of mathematical structure, which means a pattern of relationships with certain formal properties. By 'formal properties' one means properties like equivalence and non-equivalence, symmetry and asymmetry, and so on, which now are seen to underlie the primitive ideas of number and geometrical form.[3]

Korzybski had had the unconscious feel of this approach before he knew anything about mathematical logic. He had already accepted what Willard Gibbs, one of his intellectual heroes, had noted—"Mathematics is a language."[4] It had gradually become clear to him: in many ways, mathematics served more effectively than our everyday language at depicting the complex relations of nature. After George Boole, others had pursued the notion of *mathematizing logic (language)*, i.e., putting it into mathematical form. In doing so they had shown that formal mathematics was not limited to the study of quantity but could deal with quality as well. Thus had grown the field of symbolic or mathematical logic, which had led to research into the foundations of mathematics such as the *Principia*, elaborated into more and more exotic symbolism—highly abstract and more and more inaccessible to the layman.

By the time he got to La Jolla, Alfred—though following the field of mathematical ("symbolic") logic with great interest—was beginning to realize this was *not* his project, although he was still explaining his work in terms of 'logic'. He began to realize that from Boole's starting point he was following a path different from the one the mathematical logicians had taken: *he had begun to consider everyday language as a kind of mathematics.*

Rather than mathematizing language, he was going to find out to what extent he could "linguistisize mathematics" (a phrase he would use later in letters). At this point, Korzybski was beginning to talk about what he was trying to do as a kind of *"qualitative mathematics"*. Viewing every man and woman as a mathematician did not mean he wanted them to end up speaking in algebra. Not at all. Rather, as he eventually framed it, he was seeking ways "to impart mathematical structure to language without technicalities."[5] In other words, as he was starting to see in this early phase of his researches, he was looking for ways (as he would put it later) "to bring ordinary language closer to mathematics".[6] What did this strange-sounding reversal of the program of mathematical logic—Korzybski's reformulation of Leibniz's dream—entail in practice?

"Yes, We Have No Bananas"

Alfred recognized the importance of *Principia's* technical discussion of propositional functions—previously formulated by Russell—for what he wanted to do. With the notion of a propositional function, Russell had extended the notion of functionality to logical expressions. As Alfred saw, not just expressions in algebra or symbolic logic, but even the statements of everyday language, could be treated as functions with each term constituting a variable with no single value. What made a statement with variable terms a propositional function? Its variable terms rendered the whole expression ambiguous, indeterminate, or in a certain sense 'meaningless'. A propositional function with variable terms became a proposition only when its terms were given fixed, specific values (became constants). Until then the expression remained neither "true" nor "false". But problems could arise when indefinite propositional functions got treated as if they were propositions.

This seemed a major source of human disagreements. 'Meanings' were not in words. They existed as values assigned to words, consciously or not, by people. Every word used could have many possible 'meanings', or rather values, assigned to it by different individuals at one time, or by one individual at different times. Every individual tended to assign his own personal 'meanings' and it was easy to unconsciously assume that others intended the 'same' thing by the 'same' word. Alfred saw that in order to say anything substantive and come to further useful agreement in any discussion, the participants first had to come to some agreement on the 'meanings' of their common terms by adequately specifying them—turning their ambiguous propositional functions into definite propositions, i.e., one-valued, 'true' or 'false' statements. If those in the discussion failed to reach such agreement but acted as if they *did,* then further confusion and ultimate disagreement were likely. Alfred eventually realized there were issues here which had to be considered outside of formal logic—issues of psychology, social interaction, even physiology.

Going back to the argument at the International Labor Conference: Did "yes" always mean "yes", or did "yes" sometimes mean "no"? Samuel Gompers had broken up the meeting by answering simply "Yes!" No definite value could be assigned to the variable terms "yes" and "no" outside of the context, which included the logical level of the statement referred to. A "yes" might indeed 'mean' "no", for example as a response to a previous statement about a previous statement. The following year, the popular song "Yes, We Have No Bananas!" provided an excellent illustration of this: Do you have any bananas? "No." I'm not sure I heard you correctly, did you mean you have no bananas? "Yes, We Have No Bananas!" Keeping the levels clear was often not so easy.

Alfred had begun to see the importance of what he had started to call "multi-dimensional words" like "yes", "no", "truth", "fact", "reality", "class", "set", among many others.

Without specifically defining such a word according to a particular level of statement it referred to, using such variable terms could lead to what Russell and Whitehead had called "illegitimate totalities". Alfred would later rename them "multiordinal terms".

As Whyte noted, "…the crucial point is to achieve clarity about the structure of any system, whether that system is in the external world or in our own mind. And structure means a pattern of relationships with determinable formal properties."[7] Whitehead and Russell fully agreed on this main theme, but they differed both in personal temperament, and in the broader philosophical consequences to which they were led by their consideration of the world of science and the history of man. It was the crucial point for Korzybski as well. His interest in practical problem-solving in human relations was leading him to seek clarity about the structure of time-binding, which had to include everyday language use. Russell and Whitehead's *Principia Mathematica* was helping him to achieve clarity. In the Southern California winter of 1921-22, as Alfred incubated his new work, he was also studying the separate works of each man. Let's look first at Russell's contribution to Korzybski's inquiry.

Bertrand Russell

In Whyte's words,

Russell, with his supreme passion for logical clarity,…sought to reduce knowledge to the minimum elements of which one could be reasonably certain, the atomic or individual facts whose significance was as clear as 2 plus 2—no, much clearer than that, for Russell demanded to know what 2 and plus really meant, and to be able to express both in a language beyond vagueness and dispute. …[I]n his drive for rational clarity, objective knowledge, and emancipation from prejudice and intolerance, Russell provides an example which will always be honored by enlightened men, though the world pays only lip service to these virtues.[8]

In letters both to Russell and to others over many years, Korzybski expressed a similar view of Russell and his work. In 1921-22, Alfred was mining theoretical gems from Russell's other books besides the *Principia*, in particular *Principles of Mathematics* and *Introduction to Mathematical Philosophy*. Those who are familiar with Korzybski's work will probably recognize these gems, as I briefly review them below.

Reflexiveness and Mapping

In one instance, it was not an origination of Russell's but a reference he provided that Alfred found of inestimable value. Alfred liberally marked up the page of his copy of *Introduction to Mathematical Philosophy*, where Russell had written about reflexiveness, referring to Josiah Royce's "illustration of the map":

…[H]e [Royce] imagines [making] a map of England upon a part of the surface of England. A map, if it is accurate, has a perfect one-one correspondence with its original; thus our map, which is part, is in one-one relation with the whole, and must contain the same number of points as the whole, which must therefore be a reflexive number. Royce is interested in the fact that the map, if it is correct, must contain a map of a map, which must in turn contain a map of the map of the map, and so on *ad infinitum*. This point is interesting, but need not occupy us at this moment. In fact, we shall do well to pass from picturesque illustrations to such as are more completely definite, and for this purpose we cannot do better than consider the number series itself.[9]

Alfred *didn't* consider the map illustration merely 'picturesque'. At some point—surely after he read the work of Royce (who died in 1916)—he realized Royce's thought experiment demonstrated the impossibility of a perfect map. On the Eastern Front Alfred's life had depended on having accurate topographical maps, troop concentration maps, etc. Indeed, he had helped to draw them up with his frontline intelligence reports. He had never seen a map in a 'perfect' one-one correspondence with the actual territory it was representing. Indeed, that seemed meaningless in practice. Maps had to be revised—re-mapped—quite regularly. In his copy of Russell's book he had underlined this sentence in red from the passage above: "Royce is interested in the fact that the map, if it is correct, must contain a map of a map, which must in turn contain a map of the map of the map, and so on *ad infinitum*." It would take Alfred years to figure out the details but he knew this mapping business had importance and a deep relationship to Russell's theory of types; you can make a map of a map, a map of a map is not the original map and is on a different level than the original map, etc. Russell—who conflated "correct" with "perfect", and whose life may never have depended on having a correct geographical map—didn't seem to see the significance of these relationships.

Relations, Structure, and Order

Russell had also written about the interrelated notions of "relations" (already mentioned), "structure", and "order". Again, these terms had not originated with Russell but he had summarized much of the discussion in mathematical logic/philosophy which had made use of them. The terms "relation", "structure", and "order" began to enter into Alfred's internal mullings over the fundamentals of mathematics, logic, language, and life. For example, in his books Russell had described the different kinds of relations such as symmetrical, asymmetrical, transitive, intransitive, etc. Korzybski made major use of these distinctions in his later writing and teaching to explain how some linguistic or other representational forms might serve better than others in dealing with some kinds of relations being mapped.

In rooting around in the foundations of mathematics, Russell had also talked about the basic notion of "structure" which he defined in terms of relations. The relation of maps to a district, of a grammophone record to the music recorded, even our perceptual experience to the external world, involved 'identity' or 'sameness' of structure, as Russell put it. (In communications with Ritter and Keyser, Korzybski was already indicating some problems he was having with the implications of the terms 'identity' and 'same', although he was still using them in the way Russell and the majority of philosophers and logicians did.)

Russell had also discussed the related term "order", as in earlier-later, before-after. "Order" would also become a fundamental term for Alfred and seemed to underlie the other two. Unlike Russell, Royce had presented "order" as his main focus in understanding logic and mathematics, which he understood as the study of highly abstract types of order. All three terms "relation", "structure", and "order" would become basic related terms in Korzybski's system. In 1921-22, Korzybski still accepted Russell's definition of any particular number as the class of all classes similar to it. But ultimately this definition (focused as it was on classification and similarity) proved unsatisfactory to him as a useful way to explain numbering behavior. He eventually abandoned Russell's "class of classes" as barren and came up with an alternative definition of number based more on Royce's "order".

"My Dear Russell"

Korzybski had started writing to Russell right after *Manhood* was published, having sent Russell a copy of the book. He continued writing to Russell on an intermittent basis as his work developed. In his letters to him, Alfred always expressed his gratitude to Russell for the work in mathematical foundations. He would send Russell materials and ask for his opinion. Eventually Russell would respond, mostly to apologize for not replying to letters in a timely fashion or for not having time to study Korzybski's work further.

Prior to its 1933 publication, Korzybski had sent him proofs of *Science and Sanity*. Russell cabled back to him, "Your work is impressive and your erudition extraordinary. Have not had time for thorough reading but think well of parts read. Undoubtedly your theories demand serious consideration."[10] This testimonial was important for Alfred although he had been disappointed that Russell had not studied the book more. As subsequent correspondence years later makes clear, Russell never did take time for a thorough reading.[11] At the end of his *Introduction of Mathematical Philosophy* (1919), Russell had presented no remedy for the misleading aspects of ordinary language other than to retreat into the use of logical symbolism.[12] Russell seemed to maintain this attitude throughout his life. Thus when he wasn't 'speaking mathematically' he tended to fall into the 'traps' of ordinary language. On the other hand, Korzybski came to accept language as behavior to be used with skill in order to formulate experience of the world in a different way. Mathematicians were notable for their creative use of symbolism and there existed no inherent reason our everyday language could not be similarly amenable to purposeful change. Since Russell did not accept this, he never understood how Alfred made use of his (Russell's) work to help people make their everyday language less misleading.

There we have the crux of Korzybski's problems with Russell. The two men simply had their heads in different places. Korzybski ultimately made clear his rejection of *Principia's* logicist program to derive mathematics from logic. On the contrary, he postulated that 'logic' derives from mathematics, and that all human knowledge and language has a mathematical structure as well. Methods and symbolism from the recognized discipline of mathematics (including mathematical logic) could be searched to yield baby-like ways to change the structure of ordinary language and experience. In *Science and Sanity*, he attempted to show how the theory of types yielded to a broader theory of human evaluation, bringing Russell's work down to earth. Russell, a brilliant but impractical theoretician, didn't seem to recognize the desirability or even the possibilty of doing so and therefore didn't seem capable of recognizing the efforts of Korzybski, who had a genius for the practical, even in relation to theoretical issues.[13]

This ultimately led to some irritation on Korzybski's part. (It would become a familiar feeling, as well, in relation to a number of other mathematicians and scientists whom he found wouldn't read or listen, and who would dismiss his methods as 'trivial' or 'worthless' without giving them a genuine try.) Nonetheless, Korzybski felt a deep indebtedness to Russell for his theoretical insights (for years he kept a small photographic portrait of Russell, along with one of Einstein, on his office wall). The two men carried on an intermittent correspondence for years, eventually meeting face-to-face in 1939 when Russell, in Chicago, came for a brief visit to the Institute of General Semantics to see Korzybski there.

Afterwards, although, their correspondence remained polite, Alfred gradually began to vent more of his frustrations to Russell (it would have been out of character for him not to speak bluntly). In a lengthy letter to Russell in 1946 (perhaps the last one he wrote to him), Korzybski said:

Some of my students in London told me some amusing gossips that my Science and Sanity was so against your grain that you threw the book into the Atlantic. Should this be true, it would be sad news, because your great work in Mathematical Foundations is at the very core of a non-aristotelian revision...Well, my dear Russell, your bloody 'types' if translated...and applied in daily life do work...Your behavior and platonic verbal fictions, no matter how clever, and 'academic', are read by few 'intellectuals', but they cannot be workable, and so cannot be applied in general education. Yet your 'types' gave a formulation in crisp terms. I worked it out in a language applicable to life, and when people are trained in it in childlike terms, which applied even to 'mentally' ill it works astonishingly...[14]

In a short note, Russell told Korzybski he had heard the story too, but assured him that he had not thrown *Science and Sanity* into the Atlantic.[15]

Alfred North Whitehead

The work of Russell's *Principia* collaborator, the philosophical mathematician Alfred North Whitehead, also had great importance for Korzybski's subsequent formulating. Whitehead's synthetic metaphysical interests lay in a different direction from Russell's focus on logical analysis, despite a common interest with Russell in mathematical foundations.[16] After *Principia*, Whitehead published a book of short pieces, *The Organization of Thought*, in 1917, and two major works, *An Enquiry Concerning the Principles of Natural Knowledge* in 1919 and *The Concept of Nature* in 1920. In 1921-22, Korzybski was studying them avidly. When Whitehead's alternative rendering of the theory of relativity, *The Principle of Relativity With Applications to Physical Science,* came out later in 1922, Alfred also read it carefully and with admiration. The obscurity some found in Whitehead's later metaphysics seemed somewhat less in evidence in these books. In particular, the latter three—in which Whitehead still very much involved himself with mathematical and scientific issues—had a marked influence on the development of Korzybski's work.[17] Whitehead could at times write beautiful, clear, crisp prose. His focus on the philosophy of science combined with his broad humanism appealed to Korzybski, as well. Even Whitehead's interest in speculative philosophy was not entirely foreign to Korzybski's goals.

In his later book *Process and Reality,* Whitehead defined speculative philosophy as "the endeavor to form a coherent, logical, necessary system of general ideas, in terms of which every element of our experience can be interpreted."[18] It was becoming quite clear to Alfred that humans willy-nilly interpret their experience in terms of one or another system of general ideas. People constantly make assumptions about the nature of causality, reality, experience, etc., which they express in their everyday speech. If they are going to do this anyway, then why not do it as consciously, coherently, and as much as possible in keeping with the most accurate view of the world given by science at that date? In *Manhood* he had looked at some of the major ideas about humankind by which people ultimately interpret their experiences of themselves and their fellow humans. He had tried to show how the definition of 'man' accepted by a man could determine to a significant extent how the man saw himself and his possibilities for action. Now he was studying not just human nature but Nature as a whole. The general principles by which humans understood that broader Nature also affected what they could see and do. Could one expect people to adequately adjust to the actual world by means of an out-of-date view of the world?

In studying relativity, etc.—a product of some of the best of human time-binding efforts up to 1921–22—Alfred could see there were principles operating, broader than any particular type of logic. A new system of principles defined a new scientifically-based worldview and Whitehead was in the forefront of enunciating it. In it, the substantialness of things had dissolved. Neither 'space', 'time', or 'matter' were absolutes. 'Things' had lost their ultimate 'thinginess'. As Einstein and Minkowski had shown, the ultimate 'thing' was not 'matter', 'space', or 'time' separately but some kind of agglomeration of all three. Not 'things' but events, happenings, process appeared as ultimate, and these notions in turn could be expressed in terms of the foundational mathematical-logical notions of structure, order and relation. As Whitehead wrote in *The Concept of Nature*, "Nature is a process."[19]

Whitehead had said at the beginning of that book, "…it is possible to think of nature in conjunction with thought about the fact that nature is thought about."[20] Whitehead was doing that. Buried within Whitehead's books Alfred had found a "physico-mathematical theory of events and of objects", a theory about nature that took into consideration how nature was thought about. The sheer density of this effort seemed at least partly responsible for the obscurity of Whitehead's theory. Alfred had to work to pull it out.

The theory had something to do with Whitehead's battle against what he called "the bifurcation of nature". In principle, he rejected the dualistic notion of two entirely different realms of 'reality', one realm "the nature apprehended in awareness…[which included] the greenness of trees, the song of the birds, the warmth of the sun, the hardness of the chairs, and the feel of the velvet" and another realm "the nature which is the cause of awareness…the conjectured system of molecules and electrons which so affects the mind as to produce the awareness of apparent nature."[21] But how to explain the relation between these two versions of nature? Korzybski was beginning to understand the two systems as different, interrelated dimensions emerging out of the process of human knowing—the process of how we come to know what we think we know. It seemed essential for him to understand this process better in order to understand the mechanism of time-binding.

Whitehead had hinted that the process of human knowledge involved a process of abstraction. The concepts of time and space were, he had said, "…abstractions from more concrete elements of nature, namely, from events. The discussion of the process of abstraction will exhibit time and space as interconnected,…".[22] There was something important here but Whitehead's use of terminology seemed confusing. Whitehead seemed to be using the terms "abstract" and "concrete" in the traditional philosophical sense of conceptual generality. But then again he seemed to use the term "abstraction" somewhat more broadly. It seemed Whitehead was 'flying over' some of the most important issues that Korzybski was concerned with, taking clear sight of them, and then getting lost—at least losing Korzybski—in a cloud of unclear terminology. If the understanding of Whitehead's 'event' resulted from a process of many years of scientific formulating culminating in the theory of relativity, didn't the notion of "event" also have to be understood as an abstraction? And if so, how could it be considered 'concrete'? The linguistic usage here seemed bound to lead to confusion.[23]

Relatedly, with the terminology of "events" and "objects", Whitehead had made what seemed like a useful distinction to Korzybski. The underlying event world related to the postulated physical world of molecules and electrons and whatnot, a relativistic space-time world according to the newest understandings of science. Then there were the recognizable objects of the phenomenal world as one experienced it. As Whitehead put it, "…You cannot recognize an event; because when it is gone, it is gone.…But a character of an event can be recognized. ...Things which we thus recognize I call objects."[24] Yes,...but something seemed wrong with Whitehead's discussion: professing that we live in a world of process, rejecting in principle the bifurcation of nature into disconnected metaphysical realms, Whitehead continued bifurcating nature in practice, writing as if the phenomenal objects we recognize don't relate to the process world at all. For example, he had written:

> ...An object is an entity of a different type from an event. For example, the event which is the life of nature within the Great Pyramid yesterday and to-day is divisible into two pairs, namely the Great Pyramid yesterday and the Great Pyramid to-day. But the recognisable object which is also called the Great Pyramid is the same object to-day as it was yesterday....[W]e have no language to distinguish the event from the object. In the case of the Great Pyramid, the object is the perceived unit entity which as perceived remains self-identical throughout the ages; while the whole dance of molecules and the shifting play of the electromagnetic field are ingredients of the event....[25]

Alfred had not been to Egypt to observe the Great Pyramid in person. But he had seen the ancient monuments of Rome, recognizable objects which given long enough spans of time had certainly *not* remained the same in all respects. Did it make sense to talk about them as "self-identical throughout the ages"? Descriptions of the Coliseum from classical times did not describe the visible ruins he'd observed. And in the war, he'd seen long-standing structures, old churches, etc., that—however recognizable from before—any observer could see had *not* remained exactly 'the same object', after, say, a momentary artillery barrage. The fact that many objects *did* appear recognizably the 'same' and 'self-identical' simply meant changes resulting from their event character hadn't yet been registered by an observer. Accepting Whitehead's vision of the creative passage of nature, the terms "event" and "object" clearly referred to different dimensions of *one* process world. There seemed no inherent reason for supposing one couldn't find some language to distinguish these dimensions while still indicating the process character of everyday experience. The old philosophical terminology used by Whitehead wouldn't do.

After *Principia,* the work of Whitehead and Russell had diverged. Still, it seemed to Korzybski that what he called "Whitehead's physico-mathematical theory of events and objects" could be related to Russell's theory of types and analysis of language. Neither Whitehead nor Russell had addressed how their separate work connected. Neither man had shown much of the applicability of mathematical philosophy to living life. In order to show that applicability, it seemed clear to Korzybski he was also going to have to work out some of the theoretical issues as to how the work of the two men connected.

Eddington

Other works seemed relevant here as well. Alfred had brought to La Jolla a number of books on relativity. But he had already found one of the most remarkable books on the subject, Arthur Stanley Eddington's *Space, Time, and Gravitation*. Reading this work, Alfred had felt a confirmation of his own understanding of relativity crystallized in astonishingly beautiful prose. For Korzybski no one expressed better than Eddington the fundamental system of thought behind the revolution in physics. He had loaned the book to Miss Williams, but asked her to mail it back to him in January.

Eddington had shown quite clearly how "the relativity theory of physics reduces everything to relations; that is to say, it is structure, not material which counts."[26]

And perhaps one of the most important relations the theory of relativity had revealed was the relation of the observer to the observed. When measuring events, the frame of reference (speed) of the observer moving in relation to the frame of reference of what is observed needs to be taken into account, especially as speeds approach the speed of light. According to Einstein's special relativity, the maximum speed of light, approximately 186,000 miles per second, constitutes an unpassable limit. Strange results follow from accepting this along with the principle that the laws of physics remain invariant in every frame of reference. 'Space' and 'time' are no longer absolutes as they were considered in classical Newtonian physics. Furthermore, two simultaneous events in one frame of reference are not necessarily simultaneous in another frame of reference. And it does no good (indeed it makes no sense) to ask whether they are 'really' simultaneous or not. When the act of measurement is carefully taken into account, as Einstein did, simultaneity can no longer be understood as absolute but depends on the frame of reference which needs to be specified. Einstein's general theory got even 'weirder' with its treatment of 'space' and 'time' as inseparable aspects of an undivided matter-space-time. Newton's force of gravitation had become transformed into the curvature of the geometry of space-time.

Eddington expressed this revolutionary view of physical science with unmatched eloquence. Would it ever be possible to achieve a fully 'objective' view of the world which eliminated the factor of the observer from science? Eddington was doubtful if this even made any sense. The greatest objectivity seemed to require always taking the observer-observed relation into account. Alfred specially marked with green pencil the final passage of *Space, Time, and Gravitation* where Eddington had written the following (in later years, Korzybski made this one of the quotes he used as a coda for the end of his seminars):

...All through the physical world runs that unknown content, which must surely be the stuff of our consciousness...we have found that where science has progressed the furthest, the mind has but regained from nature that which the mind has put into nature.

We have found a strange foot-print on the shores of the unknown. We have devised profound theories, one after another, to account for its origin. At last, we have succeeded in reconstructing the creature that made the foot-print. And Lo! It is our own.[27]

Russell, Whitehead, Einstein, Eddington, and others had all found strange footprints. Alfred had too. He felt that he had made some headway in reconstructing the creature that had made the footprints—'man' the time-binder. The stuff of human consciousness seemed central to this understanding. Alfred wanted to know how the stuff worked and how it could be helped to work better. Beautiful language, poetic or philosophical paradoxes, were not enough. He had to find something workable.

Chapter 24
A VISITOR FROM MARS

Korzybski had come to the Scripps Institution for Biological Research to confer with its founder and director, veteran biologist William Emerson Ritter. Ritter who had helped start the zoology department at Berkeley had become know for his detailed studies of marine life.[1] Nonetheless, he held a very broad view of biology which emphasized the unity of organisms and their relations to their environments. In the early 1900s he had begun trying to establish a marine biological laboratory somewhere along the California coast. After several attempts to do so, he built a lab in the boathouse of San Diego's Hotel Del Coronado with help from members of the city's chamber of commerce. He soon 'struck gold': two of San Diego's wealthiest residents, newspaper magnate E. W. Scripps and his older sister Ellen Scripps, provided funds for Ritter to realize his dream to create a multidisciplinary marine biology station. In 1907, they purchased property in La Jolla, just north of San Diego, and in 1912 the Scripps Institution (in association with the University of California) was born.

Ritter and Korzybski had been corresponding since their first meeting that summer in Berkeley. They were both eager for some face-to-face discussions. Ritter had become fascinated with Korzybski's new approach to the study of Man, especially since he had been working on a book under the tentative title of "The Natural History of Intelligence." (The book finally was published in 1927 with the title *The Natural History of Our Conduct*.) Ritter had a philosophical bent and a well-developed consciousness of the role of language in scientific formulating. An article of his in the *Journal of Philosophy* had been entitled "The Need of a New English Word to Express Relation." In his book, *The Unity of the Organism*, he had stressed the need for biologists to go beyond what he called "elementalism," the study of isolated parts. He believed, "The organism in its totality is as essential to an explanation of its elements as its elements are to an explanation of the organism."[2] He called this approach "organismalism."

Discussions with Korzybski at La Jolla helped Ritter gain more understanding of the relativity revolution in physics and see its broader implications for his holistic approach to biology. In a February 1922 letter to zoologist H. S. Jennings, Ritter noted his gratitude to Korzybski for helping him realize, "...For living nature...the space-time concept will prove finally to be the death of all elementalism, including atomism as this has come down to us from Greek speculation."[3] Early on in their discussions, Ritter also realized that Korzybski's insistence on saying "man is not an animal" was not a denial of Darwin but a logical point about a more useful classification of humankind within the biological world. Ritter considered their discussions about time-binding and evolution important enough to encourage Alfred to write an article for *Science* on the matter, which Alfred began to work on. As an upshot of their talks, Alfred also got Ritter to agree not to call 'man' an animal anymore. (Ritter slipped in subsequent writings, however.)

Alfred was also learning from Ritter. One of the main things was the new term "elementalism"—which became central to his subsequent formulating. Elementalistic terms/ formulations treated as isolated and separate what might better be considered as related parts of larger wholes. But Alfred did not like "organismalism" as a term to describe terms/formulations which dealt with wholes and made explicit the relations of elements—the converse of elementalism. The term "organismalism" seemed too tied to biology. (Alfred would later come up with the term "non-elementalism," which seemed more general.)

If—as Keyser would later write—"to be is to be related,"[4] then there existed a great need for developing a way of speaking that made dealing with relations and wholes more explicit. That was becoming more clear in Alfred's studies in the foundations of mathematics. As Korzybski put it at this time, the elementalism Ritter talked about seemed associated with the old, Aristotelian, syllogistic logic. Seeing things in terms of mutually exclusive classes formalized the subject-predicate structure of everyday language and could distort an accurate, functional view of how things worked. In regards to understanding Man, the old definition of Man as Animal *plus* Spirit (M = A + S) seemed to him an example of this. Whatever actual qualities the elementalistic designations of 'animal' and 'spirit' may have stood for, this "plus," elementalistic logic surely distorted the unified functioning of a human being. On the other hand, understanding Man as a time-binder, seemed to provide a much more fitting way of talking about Man, which did not break humans into elementalistic parts.

Among the Scientists

Before Alfred had come to Scripps Institute he had had contact with individual scientists and scientific workers like Keyser, Loeb, Polakov, Steinmetz, and Wolf, among others. In San Francisco and Berkeley, the circle had expanded. At La Jolla, he extended his contacts even further throughout the U.S. scientific community.

Partly, he was reaping the fruits of previous efforts: book publicity, word of mouth from readers of *Manhood of Humanity* and from people who had attended his lectures (and those of Polakov and Keyser), book reviews, and the large number of contacts and correspondents he had begun to accumulate. Partly, it was also due to his being at La Jolla, a prestigious research center, where he could meet and mingle with the resident and visiting scientists, as a fellow scientific worker. Partly, it was due to the efforts of Ritter himself.

Since the summer, Ritter had been writing enthusiastically about Korzybski to others, including E. W. Scripps who, with his sister, had become one of the great benefactors of early 20th century American science. Although Scripps had hoped to meet Alfred, he had already left the San Diego area for the winter and was yachting off the Florida coast when Alfred arrived. The curmudgeonly Scripps—who referred to himself as a "damned old crank"[5]—had had a long-time interest in "what kind of thing this damned human animal is, anyway."[6] He read *Manhood of Humanity* with interest and liked parts of it. In letters to Ritter, he acknowledged the kind of exponential process in human history Korzybski had depicted. But Scripps didn't allow himself to express too much enthusiasm. Korzybski must be wrong about human beings' abilities to think rationally since, after all, people could believe in irrational things. As a self-declared pessimist about the human race, he rejected Korzybski's vision of human potential.[7]

Although Scripps was away, Alfred did meet Scripps' sister, Ellen. The elderly Miss Scripps seemed charmed enough by Alfred to invite him to speak at the La Jolla Community House in early December. Two months later, Alfred wrote to Keyser, "Miss Scripps had a very bad accident and broke her hip, she is about 80 so the thing is serious, and her brother has come from Florida, we probably will meet him…"[8] However, I have found nothing in Korzybski's records indicating the two men ever met face to face.

Ritter and E. W. Scripps had been instrumental in founding the Science Service in 1920 in association with the National Academy of Sciences and the American Association for the Advancement of Science (AAAS). Scripps provided an endowment and Ritter provided leadership as its President. With headquarters in Washington, D.C., the Science Service initially published a bulletin providing science stories to subscribing newspapers. When Korzybski arrived in La Jolla, they were getting ready to start the Science Service News-Letter, a science journal for general readers, finally launched in March 1922 and still in print as *Science News*.[9]

Perhaps not surprisingly, the new director of the Science Service, polymathic chemist and writer Edwin E. Slossen, soon became interested in Korzybski's work. Slossen worked for a literary journal *The Independent and The Weekly Review* and in an article, published in the February 25, 1922 edition of that magazine, he wrote a respectful review of *Manhood*, "Is There a Law of Human Progress?: Speculations on the Acceleration of Scientific Knowledge."[10]

As a result of such writings as well as Ritter's and others' communications about him, Alfred's name was becoming more widely known among scientists. For example, L. O. Howard, an entomologist at the U.S. Department of Agriculture and the President of the AAAS, mentioned Korzybski's work at the Association's conference in his end-of-year presidential address which was published in the December 30 issue of *Science*. Korzybski felt most grateful for Howard's complementary words and began corresponding with him.

Alfred was also making connections locally around La Jolla. He was meeting and talking with the resident scientists at Scripps soon after his arrival. He also gave a lecture there within the first few weeks. Some no doubt were puzzled by his presence. Others found him a positive stimulus. Alfred became especially friendly with George McEwen, a physicist and applied mathematician, who had been recruited by Ritter a number of years before and who at the time was researching ocean currents. He had a long subsequent career at Scripps Institute and the University of California as a professor of physical oceanography. Something in Korzybski's (and Keyser's) approach to mathematics resonated with him and after Keyser's book came out in 1922, McEwen collaborated with Alfred in an effort to write a joint review of it for *Science*.

With its growing reputation, Scripps Institute had an influx of scientific visitors during Alfred's time there. One of these was University of Chicago developmental biologist Charles M. Childs. After meeting Childs at La Jolla, Alfred studied his books and corresponded with him for a number of years, later acknowledging the great influence Childs' work had on him. To Alfred, Childs expressed a sensibility in his language— as did Loeb, Einstein, and others—with a consciousness of relations (avoiding elementalistic splits), characteristic of the time-binding attitude Alfred was trying to understand and make more explicit.

Along this line, his exposure to Childs' work enhanced his awareness of the biological aspects of time-binding: we 'think' with the whole of our beings as organisms. In his letters, Alfred was beginning to refer to his own approach towards mathematics as physiological. Dealing explicitly with mathematics, and other forms of time-binding, as physiological, i.e., the behavior of organisms with nervous systems, may have struck some people as weird. But Korzybski would only increase his insistence on the importance of realizing that 'thinking' does not occur in a timeless, fleshless void. If relativity had abolished infinite speeds in physics, then the speed of 'thought' was not infinite either.

The physiological gradients in primitive organisms that Childs described as time-related processes, appeared as the precursors of more elaborate nervous systems. To Alfred it made perfect sense to try to understand how organisms (including symbol-manipulating humans) gained knowledge of their environments in terms of natural processes. He had already touched on this, especially in the biology appendix of *Manhood,* and would elaborate it further in his subsequent work.

The time-dependent character of 'thought' became clear to Alfred at a gathering he attended at Scripps. Someone there had an I.Q. test that people took as a kind of party-game. Those whom Alfred regarded as the most gifted did the worst on the test. They spent the most time considering the ambiguities of the questions and attempting to understand the possible situations behind the words, and so could not respond as quickly as others with the 'correct' answers. 'Thought', taken as broadly as possible, clearly was a process. Alfred found it interesting that standard forms of logic and commonplace, even scientific, language seemed to obscure the factor of time as a consideration in thinking about thinking or thinking about anything else for that matter. In his copy of George Boole's *The Laws of Thought*, he had underlined some telling phrases from the following passage:

> It may indeed be said, that in ordinary reasoning we are often quite unconscious of this notion of time involved in the very language we are using. But the remark, however just, only serves to show that we commonly reason by the aid of words and the forms of a well-constructed language, without attending to the ulterior grounds upon which those very forms have been established...[11]

While resident at the Scripps Institute, Alfred was also meeting people and giving talks in nearby San Diego. During the summer he had exchanged letters with Dr. Edward L. Hardy. Hardy, a scholar of English Literature, teacher, and educational administrator, had become President of the San Diego Normal School in 1910. In 1921, the school was reconfigured as San Diego State Teachers College (it is now known as San Diego State University). Hardy, who remained President there until 1935, became enthusiastic about time-binding after reading *Manhood of Humanity*. At the end of November, Alfred spoke at a gathering of teachers at Hardy's home in San Diego. The two men maintained a friendly relationship and correspondence for years afterwards, with Hardy helping Alfred to edit *Science and Sanity*.

By the end of November, Alfred and Mira had not seen each other for several weeks. In the beginning of December, Alfred went to Los Angeles for a few days to spend some time with her. Mira had been staying at the Ambassador Hotel, but was hoping to make contacts and perhaps find some people whose portraits she could paint in Pasadena. The two attended a dinner with some people from California Institute of Technology (Caltech), including physicist Robert Millikan, Chairman of the Caltech Executive Council (effectively President of the school), and astronomer George Hale. Alfred provided an after-dinner speech and had meetings with both men, who seemed genuinely interested in his work.

Back in San Diego, Alfred delivered two lectures in early December. One was at the monthly meeting of the San Diego Chapter of the American Association of Engineers. A few days later, with Ritter introducing him, he gave the presentation Miss Scripps had invited him to give at the La Jolla Community House. Alfred recognized his audiences liked what he had to say. But neither his lectures nor Mira's painting commissions were progressing as they wanted. There was a great deal of interest but not much, if any, money. They decided to extend their stay in Southern California a little longer. Mira would try her luck in Pasadena. She relocated to the Vista del Arroyo Hotel there. In January she would come down to stay with Alfred and perhaps find some portrait work among San Diego socialites.

The Social Role of the Man of Knowledge

The contacts, correspondence, and mutual recognition between Korzybski and the people he was meeting in the winter of 1921-22 gives a reasonable picture of the kinds of relations he had with scientists and other brain-workers throughout his career. From the beginnings of his efforts, he saw what he was attempting to do—to found a new field, human engineering (as he was calling his efforts then)—as a scientific enterprise. Despite attempts later on by people like journalist Martin Gardner to depict him otherwise, Korzybski didn't isolate himself from, nor was he isolated by, the scientific community. He sought and received advice, approval, and criticism from many of the leading scientists and mathematicians of his day. Nonetheless, it was apparent even in La Jolla that what he was doing was outside the realm of conventional scientific categories.

Since Korzybski was trained as an engineer, he had no credentials in the academic fields his work seemed to touch upon the most. He had called it "mathematical sociology" to start with, which didn't help much. But his coinage of "human engineering" didn't fit into many people's conceptual boxes of engineering either. Figuring out what he was up to was a problem for a number of the people with whom he came in contact. It was a problem for Alfred as well. The scope of Korzybski's concerns—so general yet so practical—attracted some people but puzzled, or even repelled, others.

Korzybski's fellow Pole, sociologist Florian Znaniecki, discussed the various kinds of scientific workers in his 1940 book, *The Social Role of the Man of Knowledge*. In Znaniecki's terms, the role Korzybski had taken followed the path of the scientific "explorer", a "creator of new knowledge". "All new developments in the history of knowledge", Znaniecki wrote, "have been due to those scientists who did more in their social roles than their circles wanted and expected them to do."[12] According to Znaniecki, two broad and overlapping areas were open for scientific explorers: the discovery of new facts and the discovery of new problems. Although Korzybski had studied the facts of history—including that of scientific and technological developments—and made use of accepted facts from the scientific studies of others, he had not discovered new facts. Instead, with his theory of time-binding, he had discovered a new way of looking at what was already known. His theory led to a new set of problems.

If humans by definition 'bind time', then every area of human life—including people's personal lives—is affected by the growth or stagnation of knowledge and its applications. In studying the mechanism of time-binding, Korzybski had begun focusing on people's methods for gaining knowledge: understanding facts, formulating theories, and approaching problems. So he was interested not only in the content of what mathematicians, scientists, and other scholars had discovered but also in the pathways and pitfalls of their acts of discovery.

In addition, although he was focusing on mathematics and science, especially the exact sciences, he realized that the areas of knowledge relevant to the study of time-binding spanned the humanities and sciences. Indeed, he believed the study of time-binding and its mechanism would help achieve the Leibnizian dream of unifying the various fields of knowledge. At the start of 1922, Alfred wrote the following to H. D. Brasefield, an Oakland, California high school principal interested in his work:

> ...My aim is to unify science, and give a base for the brainworkers to unite around some constructive scientific as is possible doctrine. As a matter of fact we all speak about the "brotherhood of man" but such thing is impossible as long as we will not have a "brotherhood of doctrines". Our mental processes are so scattered between the thousands of doctrines which each one is leading somewhere else...The old system is breaking down, what next? No new doctrine is workable for the time being...What [is] the way out? To provide a new method of analysis which would show clearly the valuations and thus help all to unite toward the same end. My book makes obvious that what we need today is more the RE-EDUCATION of THE EDUCATED than the education of the masses...[13]

In an era of growing specialization, his problem was to find an audience that would consider his unifying vision on its own terms without trying to stuff it into the container of one or another different, and more limited, standard discipline. He had special hopes of gaining the interest of mathematicians, scientists, and engineers. But there was no getting around one fact—as a scientific explorer and theoretical synthesizer, it didn't seem likely the formulator of time-binding would find an adequate home in any particular academic field.

A Visitor From Mars

The start of the new year also brought some excellent news from Keyser. He had delivered the manuscript of *Mathematical Philosophy* to Macrae who was readying it for publication. Alfred wrote back with his congratulations and his own big news:

> ...Mira came to stay here with me for several weeks. Now there is a big news which you and Mrs. Keyser are the only [ones] to know (except Ritter of course). We both want very badly to have a child, when we married we think there was something but Mira fell down from an automobile and probably harmed herself in the first month, she was ill for several months and since nothing has happen. Mrs. Ritter was a practicing physician in Berkeley and litteraly "made" a baby with incubator etc etc to Prof. Lange wife, who happens to be a life long friend of Mira. Well we thought that it would be very wise to start something of this kind here. Mrs. Ritter was very enthusiastic about it, she has a friend very successful surgeon in S.D [San Diego] and few days ago they "stretched" Mira, which apparently having a splendid body and splendid health had a too little opening in her uterus. The doctors decided that the opening is small, but they only got the idea how small it was after the operation. No ordinary instrument would enter the opening was so small, finally they had to use some little thing of the thickness of a hat pin, and then they gave poor Mira a thorough stretching, and inserted a special metal mushroom which she will wear for two months. Of course all this was made under gas. Mira was two days in the hospital in La Jolla, and she came "home" today. She feels fine absolutely like if nothing would have happen. Our hopes run high, very high indeed, the metal little thing does not prevent conception. We have decided that if we have a boy his name will be Alfred Cassius K. in memory of my beloved friend whom you probably know.[14]

Mira and Alfred kept up their hopes for the next few years, even corresponding with a fertility clinic to find out if there was any other thing they could do. The clinic was run by Doctor J. R. Brinkley, who specialized in goat testicle transplants (not mentioned in his correspondence with Alfred) and was eventually revealed as a quack. He preyed on desperate people and did his best to solicit the Korzybskis' business, to no avail. Mira and Alfred were not quite that desperate.[15] Their chances of having a child had already been reduced due to their ages when they married. Eventually they resigned themselves to the realization that a child was not in their future.

In the meantime, they were together now in La Jolla. William A. Cyr, a reporter for *The San Diego Union* newspaper dropped in to interview them for a lengthy feature article on time-binding which appeared in the Tuesday morning, January 17, 1922 edition of that paper:

> I found them Sunday at the Biological Institute, in Cottage 3, their little California cottage, in a room blue with smoke, sitting comfortably about a large table littered with interesting looking papers and letters. Both the count and madame are informal and friendly at all things, with a real charm and poise.
>
> Count Korzybski I found to be a man small in stature, a bit lame, with a head clean shaven and giving the appearance altogether of a strong, frank thinker, not devoid of sentiment or in the least cold by any means. Sharp, piercing eyes, keen and expressive, a mouth twisted almost constantly with humor, compelled by instant and uninterrupted attention. And when he discussed his book, "...Manhood of Humanity, the Science and Art of Human Engineering," he became the incarnation of his exalted conception of man, possessed of the dignity and the dynamic which he believes man to have...
>
> Count Korzybski intends to remain in San Diego for several weeks yet. He is at present working on a new book which will deal with world problems in the light of man as a time-bound agent. He is to give an informal talk on his work to a group of intellectuals to be gathered by Frederick Gronberg, on Jan. 29. He spoke to a La Jolla audience on Dec. 10.
>
> Madame Korzybski is preparing to give an exhibition of her paintings at Coronado next month and probably will make portraits of prominent men and women there.[16]

Although generally pleased with the article, Korzybski could not let pass the subheading labeling him a "Russian Nobleman". He wrote a friendly but stern letter to Cyr and the error was corrected in a second article with the headline "Polish Scientist To Lecture On Nature Of Man".[17]

About 25 people from around San Diego who had read or were reading *Manhood* attended the January 29 lecture at Gronberg's Artemesia Bookstore.[18] Cyr's newspaper report of the talk summarizes well Korzybski's work to date:

> ...Count Alfred Korzybski, noted Polish scientist and soldier, held a selected audience spellbound during a two-hour discourse of his new theories at A. Frederic Gronberg's shop on Sixth street Sunday evening.
>
> Korzybski, whose book, "...Manhood of Humanity, The Science and Art of Human Engineering," has aroused the scientific world to a new concept of Mankind, proved to be in his lecture as dynamic a speaker as he is a writer and thinker. Under the fire of his enthusiasm and by the expressions of his dramatically mobile features the audience experienced no handicap from his diction or his continentalized expressions, nor were they conscious of the injuries he had received as a soldier for the armies of Russia...

Alfred started the lecture with the conclusions he had been forming about the importance of language and symbolism in relation to time-binding. By this time, he had definitely rejected positivistic 'empiricism' as a valid philosophy for understanding how we gain knowledge. No 'naked' facts exist. Any understanding we can have of so-called facts is filtered through the 'mind' of one or more human observers. These observers will perceive 'facts' in terms of some theoretical framework with accompanying language/symbolism:

> "It is obvious," he said, "that we are a speaking and thinking class of life. No human problem can be solved without some speaking and some thinking. It is therefore, of primary importance if we are speaking or thinking correctly."

One needn't conclude that reliable knowledge was impossible, however. The latest findings of mathematics and mathematical physics demonstrated methods/language by means of which reliable knowledge could be achieved/expressed:

> Only a mathematical philosophy, a mathematical logic, he declared, were valid since whatever else was proved relative by Einstein, numbers in their relations to each other always remained the same, absolute and fixed. And his theory, worked out before he had heard of Einstein and therefore entirely independent of him, he said, was the complement of it, and completely in accord with that theory.

Such methods, he argued, already applied by engineers in the limited realms of technology and construction, could be extended to human affairs:

> If a visitor from Mars should come, Korzybski showed, and on a tour of inspection should see our bridges, our skyscrapers, our subways, and other engineering feats, and were to ask, "How often does one of these collapse?" man here would say that if the engineering of these projects were correct in all respects, the material used in their construction carefully inspected, and the work well done, they would never collapse.

> Taken to our libraries the visitor from Mars, he declared, shown the histories of the world, would be appalled that the same men who could engineer non-collapsible bridges and skyscrapers could build a civilization which was collapsing at some point every year. And the reason, he pointed out, for the difference, lay in the fundamental beginnings of the logic that had built each.

The 'logic' at the basis of the non-collapsible structures was based on the power of 'simple' numbers which more exactly fit the changing relations and differentiating character of the world:

> ... Man, even the first savage, with an inherent ability to create things, that were "brand new," fixes symbols for differentiation of the things found in nature, of distinguishing one object from another of the same kind, and thus gave birth, on natural and logical basis, to mathematics. From this basis of tangible fact he had evolved the logic which enabled him to build non-collapsible bridges.

Somehow this 'logic'—he didn't (and couldn't yet) spell out how—could and should be applied to the collapsing structures of the rest of human life. (For the rest of his life, Korzybski would continue to refine this discussion on the origin and significance of numbers in the realm of human evaluation.) The remainder of the lecture returned to Korzybski's definition of Man:

> ... "The materialist has built the universe and left man out of it. The spiritualist has built a soul and left out the whole universe." Man must be treated as a whole, he emphasized, not as a bifurcated animal. A soul cannot be put in him as a flower is put in a flower pot; the soul, or reasoning faculty, or intellect, or whatever it is, cannot be detached from man and treated separately. Korzybski said he did not quarrel with either faction, those who spoke of man in terms of matter, space and time, the materialists, or those who spoke of him as energy, so long as each was consistent.

Alfred had clearly captured the interest of a wide array of San Diego residents:

> Following Korzybski's masterful talk, the privilege of questioning him was granted and a number of interesting sidelights of the theory were brought out, the crowd seeming reluctant to leave the intellectual feast he provided. Informally he and Countess Korzybski met each of the audience and exchanged brief greetings and bits of comment before the gathering broke up at a late hour. He is to hold a public lecture at the Wednesday club Thursday evening, February 16.[19]

Manhood was also still capturing the interest of people throughout the United States and elsewhere. It had just gone into its third printing. Reviews and notices continued coming in. What the clipping service didn't clip, his friends usually managed to find for him. Besides the San Diego newspaper articles, January had seen a complimentary review of *Manhood* in *Chemical and Metallurgical Engineering*. The January 1922 *Yale Review* had a friendly review from Alfred's friend Alexander Petrunkavich, a Yale University biologist who a year earlier had read proofs of the book. There was a book notice and comment in the January 1922 issue of *The Social Service Bulletin* of The Methodist Federation for Social Service. Then in February, *System:The Magazine of Business* featured complimentary comments on *Manhood* within a feature entitled "What Business Men Read Last Month". (This interest in time-binding by 'capitalist' businessmen amused the socialist Polakov.)

Despite an occasional negative review like the one in the February 8 issue of *The New Republic*, responses to the book so far generally seemed positive. Although Alfred considered *The New Republic* review malicious, he did accept negative criticism when he found something useful in it. And he found something very useful in the criticisms of psychiatrist Frankwood E. Williams, M.D. in the January issue of *Mental Hygiene* published by The National Committee for Mental Hygiene. In his review Williams wondered if Korzybski might be belaboring the obvious in his efforts at definition. He also criticized Korzybski for ignoring the contributions of psychiatry to the study of humans, although he did acknowledge,

…The expression "time-binder" is the best contribution the author makes. While there would seem to be nothing new in the conception of "time-binding", the expression itself is a happy one, so rich in imagination that one is surprised to find it in a book on "engineering"…In addition to the contribution of the term "time-binder," Count Korzybski's book will probably be useful in another way. If the book arouses interest in the science and art of human engineering…, it will be the most useful book on the subject yet printed. And if, their interest stimulated,…business men, engineers, and mathematicians wish to continue their studies, they might begin with—a number of books come to mind, but, for example,White's *Foundations of Psychiatry*.[20]

Korzybski became aware of the review later that summer and wrote to the journal for a copy. He later met Williams and considered him "a very fine man". He found the review, despite its 'scolding', "quite friendly and nice."[21] He took Williams' recommendation of White's book as a personal suggestion, obtaining and reading it as soon as he could. This was the beginning of Korzybski's serious and extensive study of psychiatry. It would lead to a unique alchemy of notions as Korzybski, 'the visitor from Mars', began to juxtapose his physiological view of mathematics with psychiatry as he delved into how time-binding works.

Chapter 25
"THE BROTHERHOOD OF DOCTRINES"

The time had come to leave La Jolla, to travel east to New York City, and from there to Poland—at last. Their friends in New York—Walter Polakov in particular—were missing the Korzybskis and eager for their return there. (Walter wrote later, saying that without Alfred to talk with, he had felt—even in Manhattan—like Robinson Crusoe.) But there were delays. Granted there was little if any money from it, but Alfred's book was still getting publicity (Dutton ran a third printing in January) and people in Southern California wanted to hear him lecture. Mira, who had more of a chance to make some significant income from her work, also took whatever opportunity she could find to speak (about her work, time-binding, and the relation between the two) and to find clients in the area for her paintings. (In 1922 the portraits she would complete—she also typically created the frames—included the one below of Alfred, which she entitled "The Time-Binder," obtained by the Art Institute of Chicago for its collection the following year.)

1922 Portrait of Alfred Korzybski with Frame
by Mira Edgerly Korzybska

Alfred was eager to see Walter and Keyser again. He had a lot to talk about with them. Letters, even the long detailed ones he was apt to write, were not the same as a tête-à-tête in Walter's studio or Keyser's apartment over tea or something stronger (Prohibition notwithstanding). Walter's and Keyser's long-awaited books had both appeared. For Alfred, each man's book represented one side of the development of the time-binding notion. While Keyser's book focused on the mathematical foundations, Walter's book emphasized the application of a time-binding, human engineering viewpoint to human affairs.

After more than a year's delay (the publisher had run out of money), Walter's book *Mastering Power Production* had finally gotten into print at the end of January. Alfred told Walter he considered it the *applied* second volume of *Manhood of Humanity*. Although written before Walter and Alfred's first meeting in the fall of 1920, Polakov's notion of "universal labor" had come extremely close to the formulation of time-binding. The book, a wide-ranging analysis of power production and its relation to socio-economic welfare, was not likely to get onto a national best-seller list. Yet the broad human framework of the book might still interest people other than power-industry engineers. Time-binding and the human engineering attitude, although not mentioned explicitly, permeated the book. Alfred wanted to promote it and Walter wanted him to write a review.

Though Alfred pushed *Mastering Power Production* to people whom he met and to lecture audiences, he wrote to Walter that he wasn't well known enough to submit a review unless it had been solicited from him by a paper or magazine. Whether right or wrong about this, it was also true Korzybski simply did not have the writing facility of Polakov, who could quickly dash off finished prose pieces and had already published many magazine articles and reviews for a wide-variety of audiences. Alfred, a perfectionist—perhaps to a fault—produced finished writing more slowly. Walter, who had already produced a number of published pieces about *Manhood*, might have perceived this as a lack of reciprocity on Alfred's part but seemed to accept Alfred's rationale. Walter's depressed mood seemed to have lifted a bit as his business, after a fallow period with almost no income, was beginning to pick up again. He was also starting on a new writing project, a more popularly oriented book with the tentative title *Life and Work*, explicitly applying the notion of time-binding to issues of labor and management—a natural next step for the industrial consultant whose last address to the American Society of Mechanical Engineers in December 1921 had been, "Making Work Fascinating as the First Step toward Reduction of Waste".

Mathematical Philosophy

At the end of February, Dutton published Keyser's book *Mathematical Philosophy: A Study of Fate and Freedom*. Keyser sent a copy to Korzybski at once. Despite being especially busy—with speaking engagements in Los Angeles and with whatever he had to do to help Mira set up a painting exhibit at the Hotel del Coronado in San Diego—Alfred had nearly completed his first reading and marking of it by March 10.[1]

He had already seen the manuscript and table of contents, having quoted from it in *Manhood*. Nonetheless, reading the completed work seemed like a revelation. The force of his response was not only a function of his gratitude to Keyser for devoting the next-to-last chapter of the book to a discussion of "Korzybski's Concept of Man". Keyser—in his discussion of "logical fate"—had revealed to Alfred an essential aspect of the *foundation* of time-binding. The formulation would help Alfred begin to unify the numerous influences he had been absorbing over the past year. The notion of "logical fate" (logical destiny) formed the nucleus of two articles he would write over the following year, and would continue to guide the development of his work thereafter.

Mathematical philosophy, as Keyser indicated in the subtitle of his book, could be viewed as "the study of Fate and Freedom—logical fate and intellectual freedom." What did this logical 'fate' or 'destiny' and the corresponding intellectual freedom consist of? As Keyser had described it:

...[I]t is in the world of ideas and only there that human beings as human may find principles or bases for rational theories and rational conduct of life,...; choices differ but some choice of principles we must make if we are to be really human—if, that is, we are to be rational—and when we have made it, we are at once bound by a destiny of consequences beyond the power of passion or will to control or modify; another choice of principles is but the election of another destiny. The world of ideas is, you see, the empire of Fate.[2]

As his discussion in his chapter on Korzybski indicated, Keyser seemed particularly impressed by Korzybski's notion of time-binding. In *Manhood of Humanity*—without having formulated it clearly himself—Korzybski had shown the mechanism of 'logical fate' at work in his discussion of the pernicious effects of specific false principles about humans and of the need to choose a new, more accurate base—time-binding—for the rational conduct of human life. What we humans think, and think about ourselves, makes a difference in how we behave. *Manhood of Humanity* provided a particularly significant example of such fate and freedom in human affairs.

In his book, Keyser—who had studied the history of mathematics for some time and had an interest in the thought processes of mathematicians—discussed various basic formulations in mathematics (postulates and postulational systems, doctrinal functions, transformation, invariance, groups, variables and limits, infinity, hyperspaces, non-euclidean geometries, etc.). Keyser demonstrated how mathematics—as the exemplar of logical fate—involved a consummate effort to make conscious and to work out the implications of particular starting principles or postulates. His chapter on "Non-Euclidean Geometry" seemed particularly clear about this.

For more than two thousand years, Euclid's geometry had been considered 'the' geometry of this world. Euclid's axioms, viewed as 'self-evident', included this postulate: through any point outside of a line, only one other parallel line can be drawn. The absolutistic nature of this assumption was finally challenged in the 19th Century by several mathematicians such as Bolyai, Lobachevski, and Riemann. These men found they could create equally consistent and valid non-euclidean geometries by postulating either no parallel lines or an indefinite number of them. The resultant revolution in mathematics entailed a greater recognition of the freedom of humans in creating their starting postulates or assumptions. The propositions of Euclid represented not 'the' geometry of this world but rather *a* geometry, one among many. Indeed, relativity-oriented physicists had found the non-euclidean geometries to more closely approximate some features of the world than the euclidean did.

Korzybski could see quite clearly: logical fate and the time-binding shift from euclidean to non-euclidean geometry exemplified a general process in human life. Man was a doctrinal creature. From our postulates, i.e., our assumptions, premises, presuppositions, expectations, etc.—often unconscious —conclusions follow. We can, however, become conscious of and revise our assumptions. In his book, Keyser had discussed mathematical thinking as a consummate effort to make conscious and to work out the implications of assumptions. It served as the prototype of rigorous thinking in any field.

Of all the mathematicians he'd encountered and read, Alfred had not found anyone other than Keyser who emphasized this application of the mathematical 'spirit' to human life—in other words to all sorts of thinking not normally viewed as mathematical. In his chapter on "Truth and the Critic's Art", Keyser had even suggested how to go about examining non-mathematical doctrines—from the Sermon on the Mount to Darwin's *Origin of Species* to "all manner of doctrinistic contentions of wise men, knaves, fanatics and fools"[3]—in terms of logical fate, i.e., postulational analysis. Interested as he was in human behavior in general, and problem-solving and trouble-shooting in all fields, Korzybski was going to pick up Keyser's 'ball' and 'run' with it. He began talking and writing in letters about "logical fate" almost immediately after his first reading of Keyser's book.

The label "*logical* fate" might lead the unwary astray here. At this time, Korzybski rather regularly harped on mathematical logic and talked of his developing work in terms of it. For example, he had just mailed a copy of *Manhood* to Eddington, writing, "My work is a trial of application of mathematical logic to life problems."[4] But as Korzybski would come to realize over the next few years, 'logical fate' was not primarily a matter of formal logic. Even now, what Keyser called 'logical fate' seemed to Alfred primarily an assertion about human psychology: to a large extent, what a human does gets 'driven' internally by his doctrines or attitudes which involve, among other things, his choice of assumptions and his willingness to analyze and revise them when needed. Formal logical follow-through has a genuine but limited part to play in this process. In seeing mathematics in such a psychological light, Keyser did not seem like a typical mathematician or mathematical logician.[5] But this was exactly the kind of illumination Alfred was seeking.

Fate and Feedback

Alfred saw huge implications in Keyser's psychological approach to mathematics, not only for mathematical/scientific practice but for understanding and dealing with problems of human behavior in general. Logical fate highlighted the role of doctrines, not only in science and mathematics but also in personal life. As part of what Korzybski was calling his physiological point of view, an individual's internally-held postulates (doctrines, beliefs, etc.) significantly determined that individual's behavior, affecting their 'emotions', physiology, etc. To *apply* this postulational approach, (a sine qua non of human engineering for Alfred) a person would have to look within, i.e., make a detailed internal self-examination of his attitudes in the manner, for example, Alfred had used to examine and challenge his own previous antisemitic views. As he had already formulated in his "spiral theory" in the Biology Appendix in *Manhood*, 'thought' influenced physiology and behavior and, thereby, subsequent 'thought'.

The notion of logical fate did not provide a fully detailed theory of psychology. But what it suggested clashed with the stimulus-response approach of environmental determinism (behaviorism) becoming more and more popular in psychology departments around the United States in the first half of the 20th century. Alfred would early and openly criticize behaviorism. Despite this, he also later sought to show the connection of his formulations to those of Pavlov (as well as to those of Freud).

Unfortunately, a psychological theory adequate for accommodating Korzybski's work did not appear until some twenty years after his death, with perceptual control theory (PCT), William T. Powers' rigorous application of feedback theory to human behavior first published in book form in 1973 in Powers' *Behavior: The Control of Perception*. According to PCT, every human (indeed every living thing)—as a negative feedback control system—controls his or her own inputs or perceptions, i.e., behaves in such a way so as to establish intended states of affairs. Circular—more exactly, spiral—causation governs its workings. Continuous signals from the environment (negative feedback) are received and compared to an intention; behavior then ongoingly gets modified as needed to produce the intended state. Simply stated: "We act to bring about (or maintain) *what we want*."[6] What we want (our intentions/purposes/goals) are arranged in a hierarchy of increasing complexity and generality. For humans, the highest levels of intention—those of what Powers calls Principles and Systems Concepts (one's basic beliefs, doctrines, self-image, etc.)—provide the most general formulations of what we want and so direct a person's general behavior in order to produce the desired perceptions—logical fate redux. If anything, the 'response' controls the 'stimulus' not the other way around.

Korzybski, who had long emphasized the importance of circular causation in human behavior (his spiral theory), grabbed onto the notion of feedback when he became aware of it in the late 1940s, calling Norbert Wiener's elaboration of it in *Cybernetics* "a turning-leaf in the history of human evolution and socio-cultural adjustment."[7] But during his lifetime, as the stimulus-response model became pervasive in academic psychology and elsewhere, Korzybski's work seemed destined to appeal mostly to those students of human behavior who rejected behaviorism.

While Alfred was pondering the implications of the premise that we are guided by our premises, he and Mira were preparing to leave their physical premises in southern California. Since Ritter had left La Jolla in mid-March for business in Berkeley and Washington, Alfred's main reason for staying at the Scripps Institute—his conferences with Ritter—had disappeared. Then too, he felt frustrated with the attitudes of many of the other biologists at Scripps, who didn't seem to get what he was driving at—except for George McEwen. Alfred had loaned him a copy of *Mathematical Philosophy* and McEwen seemed smitten. Alfred wanted to promote *Mathematical Philosophy* as much as he could. He was passing out and mailing flyers for Keyser's book, and discussing it at every opportunity in letters and in person. But given that Keyser had bestowed so much attention to Alfred's work, Alfred did not think it wise for him to submit his own review of the book to a major publication like *Science*. Instead, he and McEwen came up with a plan to write a joint review (Alfred would mainly guide and advise) that they would submit to *Science* under McEwen's name. They began to meet about the project.

Toward the end of March, Alfred also had a five-hour interview with H. L. (Roy) Haywood, an ex-minister and Freemason living in National City, just south of San Diego. Haywood had become the editor of *The Builder*, a nationally-published monthly journal for students of Freemasonry published by the National Masonic Research Society in Animosa, Iowa. Haywood, who was planning to move to Animosa, had learned about Korzybski from his friends the Gronbergs, owners of the Artemsia Book Shop in San Diego, who arranged for the two men to meet. They became lifelong friends with Roy later serving as one of the editorial readers of *Science and Sanity*. Haywood was much taken both with the notions of time-binding and of logical fate. Alfred gave him a copy of *Manhood*, which Haywood reviewed in the August 1922 issue of *The Builder*. Alfred also had a copy of *Mathematical Philosophy* sent to Haywood who read it enthusiastically and reviewed it for the October 1922 issue. For Haywood, the connection between Freemasonry and Korzybski's and Keysers's work seemed clear.[8]

By the beginning of April, Mira and Alfred's plans were set. They would head east at the end of the month. Mira had some business in Los Angeles and preceded Alfred there, staying at the Gates Hotel. Alfred left his cabin on the beach about a week later, traveling to Los Angeles with McEwen, with whom he had a number of meetings during his first week in the city. The two men read Keyser's book together and worked on McEwen's review for *Science*. Alfred also spoke at a meeting of the Southwestern Philosophical Association at Occidental College. After McEwen's return to La Jolla, Alfred and Mira busied themselves with packing and with meetings and visits with friends.

Harry Bateman of the Caltech Math department had invited Alfred to speak there in mid-April. Alfred addressed about two dozen faculty and students from the math, physics, and chemistry departments. He wrote to Keyser about his lecture and about one of the scientists he met there, Paul Epstein, who had recently come to Caltech from Europe to teach theoretical physics:

> I hope my lecture was a success. I spoke one hour and half, but nobody did want to go away, and I had to speak more. Comments of Bateman and Epstein were very favorable. Bateman is a Cambridge man. Epstein is a Polish Jew educated in Germany a friend of Einstein and a new star on the physicomathematical firmament, his discoveries in the quantum theory, I was told by Millikan are epoch making. Of course he is a relativist, but I was amazed to find his "philosophy" has not been affected at all by the theory of relativity, he still is a mixture of an absolutist and a relativist. I had to speak about the Einstein revolution as well, and I was told a complement by E. that I said things that were new to him.[9]

During this time, Alfred also made a trip to the town of Fullerton, south of Los Angeles, to tour a gasoline processing plant there run by the redundantly named Texas Gasoline Company of Texas. 'Naturally' the company had its headquarters in San Diego where Alfred and Mira had become friendly with Frank Avery, the secretary of the company, and Avery's wife Sally. Alfred and Mira met with them socially and also became interested in investing in the enterprise which had at least two processing plants, the one in Fullerton and the other actually in Texas. Alfred had a friendly correspondence with both Avery, and J. Arthur Thompson, an L.A. real estate developer, who served as the company's Vice President. Alfred and Mira had even looked into getting a bank loan, using some of Mira's stock certificates in other companies as collateral, in order to get the money needed to become stockholders. But it doesn't appear that they made the investment. They did maintain contact with the Averys, however. Within the next decade, Frank died but the Korzybskis continued to correspond with Sally, who later came east to visit them when they lived in Brooklyn. Finally on April 23, Alfred and Mira, with their 775 pounds of luggage, boarded the Atcheson, Topeka, and Santa Fe bound for Salt Lake City, through Denver, to Kansas City, Missouri.[10]

Midwest Sojourn

By April 29, they had settled in at Mira's sister Amy's farm in Lees Summit. They used the next couple of weeks to make plans. Mira was looking for some quick portrait commissions and arranging to give some presentations. She had a talk coming up at the Kansas City Women's Club on May 3 and might have a client in Cleveland. Meanwhile, Alfred was busy writing letters, working on his articles and book, and making his own arrangements for lectures and meetings around the Midwest.

At La Jolla, Alfred had met a vacationing Milwaukee pathologist, Dr. William Thalhimer, and his wife. When Thalhimer returned home, he helped arrange for Alfred to give a talk at The City Club of Milwaukee on May 16 and invited Alfred and Mira to stay at his home. On May 6, Alfred wrote to Miss Conway, the secretary of The City Club, with requests for the upcoming lecture:

> ... If possible please provide something like a blackboard for my lecture, a blackboard helps greatly the visualizing and therefore the understanding. The blackboard does not have to be large two feet square will do. In case you would have too much troubles in getting a blackboard half a dozen of sheets of heavy paper (stiff), white or grey will do also, in such case it would be necessary to provide heavy black pencil or chalk of dark blue color would be good. In such case we would nail with two nails all the papers at once and after using one sheet I would take it off like from a block.
>
> Here are some titles for my lecture select one please to your liking they mean just the same, all of them, to me. I give them in the order of my preference but you know your public better so please don't be influenced by my order. 1) The science and art of human engineering 2) Mathematical revolution and social progress 3) A new natural law 4) Mathematics and life 5) Is peaceful progress possible? 6) Can political and social sciences become exact, genuine sciences? 7) Mathematics as common sense elevated to the dignity of science...[11]

The use of a blackboard for visualizing his ideas had by this time become a staple part of his presentation method. For the remainder of his life, he would continue to stress the importance of visualization with diagrams, etc., making great use of them as a speaker and teacher. In fact he had just come up with a way to visualize logical fate—a diagram which seemed to him to make evident some aspects of the formulation that even Keyser had not made clear.[12] He would use it in his upcoming talks and articles and over the years would continue to use it and refine it. (You'll find an early form of the diagram in the next chapter.)

The suggested titles for the Milwaukee lecture indicate how the concerns of *Mathematical Philosophy* were taking up more and more of Alfred's attention. He had already abandoned the article on evolution and time-binding that Ritter had suggested he write. Now he held off working on what he had called "the big guns", an article for *Science* intended to serve as an overview of his second book. To write this he would have had to connect the various strands of what he had been studying (which now included logical fate and related material from Keyser's new book) into some kind of coherent, consistent whole. But obstacles had emerged due to "verbal difficulties".

Meanwhile, he had been invited by the editor of *The Call*, a 'progressive' newspaper in New York, to write a joint review of Polakov's and Keyser's books, with one of the titles he had suggested for the City Club talk, "Mathematical Revolution and Social Progress". Perhaps his way to at least write this review would seem clear if he just 'spit things out' in a letter to Keyser with the hope his mentor might have some suggestions for him. When Mira saw the letter, she jokingly called it Alfred's "sermon on the farm". In the meantime, he was also 'spitting things out' in his correspondence with McEwen for their *Science* review of Keyser's book, and in his various other letters, and talks with people. As he wrote to Keyser in his 'sermon', he felt sure of one thing: "Einsteinian 'joint phenomenon of the observer and the observed,' your 'logical destiny' and the theory of types and classes are three tremendous milestones which will show the road."[13]

On May 15, Alfred left for Milwaukee with Mira since she had decided to go with him rather than to Cleveland in pursuit of a questionable portrait job. The Korzybskis stayed with the Thalhimers. On the 16th Alfred spoke at the City Club which didn't use any of his suggested titles but advertised the subject of his talk as "The Manhood of Humanity".[14] Several Milwaukee newspapers published stories on it the next day. Alfred was now specifically presenting his notion of time-binding within the framework of logical fate. One of the main points he made to his somewhat 'radical' audience—Milwaukee had a socialist mayor at the time—was that social reforms that seek new solutions but start from the old premises (such as viewing 'man' as an animal) are destined by logical fate to fail.[15]

As much as the Thalhimers might have wanted them to stay longer, Alfred and Mira had to get to Chicago. Alfred had a talk scheduled at the May 19 meeting of the Chicago Chapter of the American Association of Engineers. Since Alfred also had a couple of people he wanted to see around the state of Illinois, and since Mira had friends in the city and might be able to get some business there, they decided they would use Chicago as their Midwest base of operations. They moved into a suite at the Drake, a luxury hotel near Lake Shore Drive.[16]

One of the people Alfred wanted to meet with was mathematician James Byrnie Shaw, a professor at the University of Illinois-Urbana, which lies about 130 miles south of Chicago, in East-Central Illinois. Shaw had a deep interest in the foundations of mathematics, having written a book, *Lectures on the Philosophy of Mathematics* (1918), and a review of *Principia Mathematica* that Korzybski had found inspiring and useful. He wanted to see Shaw and get his opinion about some new ideas. McEwen, who knew Shaw, had given Alfred a letter of introduction. Just before leaving Amy's farm, Alfred sent Shaw a copy of *Manhood* with McEwen's letter, requesting a meeting. Shaw, happy to receive the book and to meet with Alfred, replied promptly. He booked a room for Alfred at the University Club in Urbana. Alfred arrived there on May 24 and stayed for over a week.

Shaw proved himself a gracious host, arranging meetings for Alfred and introducing him to colleagues. Alfred felt especially grateful to meet R. D. Carmichael, another mathematician in Shaw's department who had wide-ranging interests in physics (he had already written a book about relativity), philosophy, and literature. Carmichael quickly became interested in Alfred's work. Alfred later wrote to Keyser about his time with the two men:

> During my stay in Urbana I spent all my time with Dr. Shaw and Dr. Carmichael. We had endless debates. I had two lectures before them, one was the official one before the [mathematics] faculty [which some philosophers and engineers also attended], where of course I was very modest, simple but trenchant, some of the older mathematicians wanted to trap me with silly and tricky questions. The lecture was adjudged by Shaw and C. as "masterful". It seems to me that really this lecture could be successfully reproduced before any mathematical faculty, and afterwards I had a 3 hours lecture-debate before Shaw and Carmichael. In this one I went very far and spoke about things which are still in the making and which I would not dare to speak publicly. Both S & C were very responsive and participated in the dreams…[17]

Alfred considered his trip to Urbana a success. With Carmichael, he had found a real 'fan'. A couple of months afterwards, Carmichael wrote to Alfred from his family farm in Randolph, Alabama where he was spending his summer vacation, "…I have read "Manhood of Humanity" for the third time; and I have enjoyed it more on the third reading than on either of the other two."[18] The two men would continue an active correspondence for a number of years with Carmichael eventually writing Supplement I, "The Logic of Relativity" for *Science and Sanity*.

Shaw's immediate evaluation seemed rather more restrained. As he wrote to Alfred on June 24, time-binding seemed to him, "...as old an idea as the thinking part of the [human] race itself" and a consequence of "man [as] an individual of a spiritual essence and immortal." He had more to say than Carmichael about Alfred's presentation to them of the practical application of mathematics to life:

> I think you stress entirely too much the value of mathematical logic in the discussion of your theme. Very little of your reasoning is mathematical logic. ...anyone who studies logistic [mathematical logic] in the hope that thereby he will find a method directly applicable to the discussion of the making over of human progress, will be disappointed. He may gain some sharpness of wits, he may become a better thinker, but he could do that equally well in studying other things than mathematical logic.
>
> As a philosopher, then, what do I think of your plans?...It seems certain to me that most of our action is not instigated by what we think or believe, though these will determine some features of the things we do or the manner of acting. I am of the opinion that what we desire in our inmost selves determines our action. In other words we do not act on account of reasoning...[19]

As he wrote to Keyser later, Alfred got depressed reading this. He hadn't gotten across to Shaw what he wanted to get across but he did appreciate Shaw's honesty and desire to be helpful. He knew he would have to work harder to clarify what he was trying to express. In his reply to Shaw a couple of days later he wrote:

> Many thanks for your long letter and frankness. It is impossible for me to form at once an opinion about it, generally speaking I see your point and I agree that most of what you say is legitimate in the old way. It seems that in the "new" way I will have to elaborate my problems further with more details and maybe I will be able to convince some day such important critics as you are. I value your letter greatly and it will be for me a precious and competent indication where are to be found the weak spots in my theory.
>
> There is a fundamental principle as expressed by Professor E. H. Moore which has taken strongly hold of me namely, "The existence of analogies between central features of various theories implies the existence of a general theory which underlies the particular theories and unifies them with respect to those central features." I see my way clear to show it and prove it theoretically but also experimentally. Of course only the future will show if I will fail or not.
>
> I will keep in touch with [you], and hope we will exchange our writings, my permanent address will be Fifth Avenue Bank New York City. Many thanks once more for all your kindness and also your kind wishes,
>   cordially yours[20]

Korzybski and Shaw would indeed keep in touch over the years. Shaw later became more favorably disposed towards the further developments in Alfred's work. And he helped Alfred by providing him with an amended table from his book showing the structure of mathematics, which Alfred used in *Science and Sanity* (pp. 251-2).

Mira sent a telegram to Alfred in Urbana a few days before he was ready to leave. She couldn't find some of her jewelry and thought it might have been stolen. Alfred wrote back to her advising her on what to do, how to deal with the police, etc., but there seemed little else he could do immediately so he proceeded with his plans to head north to La Salle, Illinois before returning to Chicago. He was going to La Salle to see Dr. Thomas J.

McCormack, the principal of the La Salle-Peru Township High School. The two men had begun corresponding while Alfred was still in La Jolla. Korzybski had read an article by McCormack that greatly impressed him. McCormack in turn had learned about Korzybski through reading Keyser's piece about his work in the *Hibbert Journal*. McCormack invited Alfred for a visit. Especially after McCormack finished reading *Manhood* in early May, both men felt eager to spend some time together.

McCormack, trained in science and mathematics, had a long association with Dr. Paul Carus, his wife Mary Hegeler Carus, and their Open Court Publishing Company, which had been founded in the final decades of the 19th century in La Salle with money from Mrs. Carus' father. Open Court, which published a wide range of serious philosophical and scientific books and a journal called *The Monist*, was dedicated to the rapprochement of science and religion. Since Dr. Carus's death in 1919, the enterprise, now with offices in Chicago, had been in the hands of Mrs. Carus. McCormack, had worked as an editor for Open Court and had translated numerous books on science, mathematics, and even religion. He was perhaps best known as the authorized translator of Ernst Mach's works into English. McCormack felt favorably inclined towards Korzybski's work, having in his own writings expanded on Mach's view of science as the economy of thought. By formulating progress as due to the accumulation of intellectual labor, which thereby became intellectual capital, McCormack—similarly to Polakov—had already come close to Korzybski's formulation of time-binding.

Alfred stayed with McCormack for a week before returning to Chicago on June 8. As Korzybski described it in a letter to Keyser,

> The visit ended not only in a complete theoretical understanding but also it developed into a "love affair." The whole family of Dr. McC., himself included, and myself we fell in violent love. Well they really are splendid people...I met three times the Caruses once at their home, once at my lecture in Dr. McC.'s house and once at a party they gave to us in the Carus country home...[21]

As soon as Alfred left, McCormack wrote to Mrs. Carus. Alfred had mentioned his interest in stopping at the Open Court office in Chicago to obtain some books for his research. McCormack asked Mrs. Carus to give Korzybski a discount and, surprisingly, she wrote back saying Korzybski could have whatever books he wanted for free. Although McCormack wrote to Alfred with this news, Alfred didn't find out about it until he walked into the Open Court office and was told by Catherine Cook, the office manager. He felt most grateful to both McCormack and Mrs. Carus for what amounted to a $600 gift, a substantial number of volumes in 1922. Unfortunately Korzybski had most of the books shipped to England where he and Mira expected to stop over on their way to Poland later in the year. When they ultimately didn't go, they couldn't recover the books. Open Court later graciously replenished part of Alfred's lost library.

Among the volumes Alfred managed to hold onto were McCormack's English translations of Mach's writings. In *Science and Sanity*, Alfred would include Mach on the dedication page list of those whose works greatly influenced his inquiry. It seems likely Alfred's personal friendship with Mach's authorized English translator boosted his interest and gave him extra insight into Mach's writings, which amplified Alfred's already strong sense of the importance of epistemology (the theory of knowledge) for science and had a significant impact on how Alfred eventually developed his work to apply epistemology in daily life.

In the following years, Korzybski and McCormack stayed in touch. Korzybski felt deep shock when he learned of McCormack's death in 1932, a year before *Science and Sanity*—the fruit of the labors McCormack had given early assistance to—was published.

Alfred returned to Chicago late in the evening at the end of the first week of June. He was eager to see his wife. Tired and hungry, he rushed to meet Mira whom he discovered giving a speech on his work. Alfred, sitting in the back of the room, stomach growling, had a momentary shock when Mira got stuck at a certain point in her presentation and called out to him, "Alfred, come on and finish my speech."[22] Besides this unexpected presentation, he had several more talks scheduled for June. He had lobbied to talk at an upcoming conference of engineering educators at Urbana but was unable to get a last minute slot. But other groups wanted him. He was not just giving 'boring' talks on science and mathematics. He had learned how to shape his message to draw people's interest. For example, the headline of a Chicago newspaper reported on a June 13 lecture he gave, "Count Denies Women Are Illogical".[23] With this kind of publicity, he might get a few more opportunities to speak in Chicago before heading east. Since Mira also had some clients to see around the city and in Detroit, they decided to stay in Chicago a little while longer. The Drake was beginning to seem too expensive, so they found a nearby studio to stay in more cheaply.

Haywood, had just moved to Animosa, Iowa where *The Builder* was published. He sent Alfred an advance copy of his review of *Manhood* for the August edition. Alfred was impressed with Haywood's intelligence and writing ability. Haywood was already working on a review of Keyser's book for the October edition. Alfred wondered about writing a separate, longer article on *Mathematical Philosophy* which might serve as a nice complement to Haywood's shorter piece. More than a review it would provide a kind of commentary on Keyser's book, expanding on some of the themes Alfred had been developing. At the end of June, Haywood wrote to Alfred approving the plan. Perhaps because the project was more limited, it seemed more doable than the joint review of Keyser and Polakov that Alfred had contemplated doing for *The New York Call*. He was still working with McEwen on the Keyser review for *Science*, but most of the job was in McEwen's lap at the moment. So Alfred set to work with his full energy on the article for Haywood, which would also serve as a preliminary sketch for his second book, which he now conceived of as Volume II of *Manhood of Humanity*.

"The Brotherhood of Doctrines"

Over the last year Alfred had been "sweating blood" trying to more clearly formulate the mechanism of time-binding. Now he was sweating to get this article into acceptable shape for Haywood. He and Mira, who had also been working hard, thought they both deserved a little rest and decided to take a day off on his birthday, July 3. Here is how Alfred described the day to Keyser (I can imagine a wry smile on Korzybski's face as he typed the letter the following day):

> …Yesterday was my birthday (I began 43) we decided with Mira to loaf all day, once in a year. Well - it wasn't such, we both got up with headaches, then worked at home until noon, then we decided to go lunch. Mira heard from the wife of the head of Marshall Field (you know the Field Marshall of drygoods) that the lunches there are very good, so we went there. After waiting for three quarters of an hour we did not succeed in placing our order (the place looks very rotten) disgusted we went away hungry angry etc etc. On the corner we found a "Harmony" cafeteria we went there sick angry and hungry, the food LOOKed pretty well, we made our choice, well it was so rotten that it is impossible to describe, but we were hungry and had no time because of an appointment, so we ate a

little and kept our appointment. This rotten food did not improve our headache or temper, after our appointments we decided to go to a "movie" I saw a movie the "Son of the Wolf" with a lot of snow pleinty of wolfs and dogs etc etc we thought it should be good (Jack London) we went there, there was no noise (music) no wolfs no dogs, a miserable show. So perfectly miserable we walked "home", and we went to bed and I read loud to Mira "Mathematical Philosophy, The Study of Fate and Freedom" occasionally making some remarks about the rotten fate.

Today we felt better, and your dear old letter made us happy, so the real birthday mood will prevail today. Mira of course said "Bless his heart".

Love from both to both[24]

In July, Mira had more trips around the Chicago area. Alfred worked hard on the article, to be entitled "The Brotherhood of Doctrines". (By the end of the month, he was already working on his third rewrite.) When he wasn't working on the article, he was writing letters to newspapers and magazines throughout the country asking for copies of reviews of *Manhood* and articles about him or Mira that his clipping service had not already provided them. He and Mira wanted to get back to New York soon, possibly sometime in August. They would be packing to leave for Europe and he wanted to have as complete a scrapbook as possible before he left. They didn't leave Chicago until September. Alfred was busy tuning up his *Builder* article. Haywood had come to visit for a couple of days in early August and undoubtedly made some comments. Then Mira did some editing. Finally, Alfred sent the manuscript to Keyser to edit as well. Keyser liked it, quickly sent back his comments, and Alfred was pleased. He had to leave out some of the details, but he could expand on them in a later article. Now at least he would be able to use the material about logical fate to explain the importance of Polakov's book in *The New York Call* piece he was still planning to write. He sent the completed article to Haywood on August 27, along with a request for 1000 reprints.

Alfred's review article of *Mathematical Philosophy* for *The Builder* began with a reference to the revolutionary changes that had been going on in science and mathematics. The 'Brotherhood of Man' could be advanced through the 'Brotherhood of Doctrines', an "empire of sound logic" where people guided their human affairs by means of "scientific knowledge."[25] As Eddington and others had made clear, relativity in its deepest 'philosophical' aspect epitomized the empire of sound logic because it required recognizing the role of the observer in any observation. In the article, Korzybski put it thusly, "...*all that man can know is a joint phenomenon of the observer and the observed.*"

Korzybski used the relation of the observer to the observed to roughly characterize the evolution of human knowledge according to three stages of development, one stage emerging out of the other. In the first "Absolutist" or "Pre-scientific period...the observer was everything, the observed didn't matter." In this period, humans projected their own reactions, 'thoughts', 'emotions', etc., onto the rest of the world. A second, "Mixed Absolute-Relativist" period, otherwise called the "Classical or Semi-scientific" period, emphasized the observed phenomena. It had advanced further than the pre-scientific by eliminating the grosser animistic projections of the observer. However, although it made use of logic, it assumed the subject–predicate logic used was 'perfect'. Thus, it continued to project the built-in assumptions of that logic (made by the observer) onto the observed. The third, "Relativist", "Mathematical or Scientific Period" had started with Boole's "The Laws of Thought" in 1854, which had begun the modern examination of mathematical/logical foundations. Here the interaction of the observer (in particular his logic and assumptions) with the observed had begun to be clear. As Korzybski put it,

> ...for science and life logic is as vital a factor as "facts" because, for human knowledge, there are no "facts" free from the share of the observer's mind. ...if there is such a thing as general knowledge, its foundation must be found outside of *gross* empiricism. Most probably such a thing does exist and its origin may be traced to the constitution of the human mind itself—to sound modern logic (mathematics).

Perhaps a "qualitative" mathematics could exist, where a general mathematical approach could be applied to more and more aspects of life. Alfred wrote, "...all man can know is an abstraction....some of his abstractions were false to fact;...a few abstractions...were at once the easiest to handle and were correct,...[t]hese abstractions were numbers." As he discussed at some length, "The creation of number was the most reasonable, the first truly scientific act done by man..." Mathematics constituted "...the first perfect instrument by which to train his brain, his nerve currents, in the ideal way befitting the actual universe (not a fiction) and himself a part of it."

> Now it is easy to understand from this *physiological* point of view why mathematics has developed so soundly....The biggest triumph of human thought was, and forever will be, the discovery of new mathematical methods embracing larger and larger parts of the whole—these are the milestones of man's progress.

This went along with something he had mentioned earlier—that so-called 'intuitions', 'emotions', etc., "will fall into line automatically." Qualitative mathematics will affect them since "It is a fallacy of the old schools to divide man into parcels, elements; all human faculties consist of an inter-connected whole."

Keyser's book was not mentioned until the second half of the article. Korzybski provided a lengthy quote from Keyser regarding logical fate and freedom. Korzybski emphasized its importance: "Because of this logical fate, the analyzing of these doctrines, which underly all human activities, becomes the most important—nay, the all-important—fact for all the future of man." Korzybski discussed the significance of Keyser's "new mathematical method whereby this can be accomplished" with his "theory of postulates and doctrinal functions." Korzybski then provided a list of some of the topics from Keyser's table of contents deliberately leaving out mention of "Korzybski's Concept of Man." He was getting to 'the grand finale': "The layman, the "practical" man, the man in the street, says: What is that to me?" Korzybski pointed out that even some scientists might ask this question dismissively. His answer:

> If they [the next generation] are taught false logic and false doctrines, mental cripples are produced, destined for a life of misery...It may take a still more terrible World War to whip mankind into the realization that man should use his brain and the knowledge already at hand.*

The final page "Summary" contained Korzybski's logical destiny diagram with an accompanying explanation. He did not mention the term time-binding anywhere in the piece.

He had indeed put out a dazzling display of suggestive ideas, though readers might be forgiven for feeling overwhelmed. Even now, some readers might miss how much Korzybski's views—despite some areas of agreement, i.e., the inspiration he had gotten from *Principia Mathematica*—put him at odds with the "logical positivist/empiricist" program which was coming to dominate the philosophy, particularly the philosophy of science, in the first half of

---

*Keyser's insightful little book *Thinking About Thinking* (1926) gives his own extended answer to the 'practical man's' question, "What is that to me?".

the 20th century. Korzybski's rejection of 'empiricism', his emphasis on the role of the observer and of the observer's doctrine (theory) in observation, his bringing in of a "physiological point of view", his strong emphasis on the living life applications of some seemingly esoteric notions from mathematics and science, and his advocacy of logical fate, i.e., his rejection of an assumption-free viewpoint for doing science (or living life for that matter), didn't fit well within a "logical positivist" mold (although some of Korzybski's students later tried to fit it).

Korzybski's work would appear not only *at odds with* but also *odd* to people whose view of objectivity and rationality required sharp boundaries between philosophy and science, mathematics and science, disparate fields of science, and between these various theoretical areas and practical life. Where many saw sharp boundaries, Korzybski explored murky borderlines and found unceasing connections. In his own time, only a few philosophical 'renegades' like Gaston Bachelard, Oliver Reiser, F. S. C. Northrop, and L. L. Whyte would pay serious attention to Korzybski's work.[26]

At the end of August, Alfred also sent a typed version of the just-completed article to McEwen. He wondered what happened to McEwen's review of *Mathematical Philosophy*. He hoped McEwen was not delaying just because he wanted to see Alfred's latest piece of writing. Alfred had a shock when, a few days later, he got a letter from Keyser with the news that *Science* had just published a review of *Mathematical Philosophy* by G. A. Miller from the University of Illinois. Alfred had thought that Ritter had let the editor of *Science* know McEwen was planning to submit something. But obviously, the communication had gone awry. McEwen later expressed his disappointment. Although Miller's review seemed generally favorable, it was not the blockbuster Korzybski and McEwen had hoped for. Well, Alfred couldn't do anything about it now. He and Mira were otherwise occupied. They were getting ready to leave Chicago on September 1.

Their last minute preparations to leave Chicago included arranging to leave behind some of Mira's luggage—a couple of trunks, some suitcases, hatboxes, and packages with art materials and portraits—at the Drake. This would reduce the amount of stuff Mira would have to lug since she was planning to come back to Chicago in about a month to do the portraits of the grandchildren of a Mrs. Shed. Mira didn't travel light. There was much more of her stuff in storage in New York City. The Korzybski's were anxious to get there. If they were going to Poland they had a lot of sorting and packing to do.

Chapter 26
"FATE AND FREEDOM"

Alfred would bring Mira to Poland with him as his "war bride". And Mira would bring with her 'everything' she had acquired over her years as a freelance artist. 'Everything' amounted to a lot.[1] Her belongings included clothing (much of which she had made herself); various velvets, brocades, silks, and other materials she had gathered in her travels; as well as art supplies, art work, genuine jewelry, costume jewelry, assorted tchotchkes, books, scrapbooks, photographs, written records, etc. In a later unpublished memoir, she described how she had ended up with the many trunks now in storage:

> For several years I had the custom of, for instance, being in Scotland and would suddenly discover a desirable client was on the Riviera…or Hamburg. I would buy a trunk to store my tweeds in, and buy another trunk for my other costumes, and have them…put in the Manhattan Storage…the number of trunks I had accumulated made a truckload.[2]

On their return to New York City, they had found an apartment on East 22nd Street, a couple of blocks north of Gramercy Park and the National Arts Club. But it didn't give them the space they needed to spread out and sort through all this stuff and pack what they were going to take. Luckily, within a couple of weeks they saw a sign one block away announcing "Basement for Rent". They moved in for $10 a month. They found the basement at 30 East 22nd Street a "very large, warm, and comfortable place to pack, repack and crate" their trunks and suitcases. Someone they knew, an administrator at one of the New York City hospitals, was able to get a large brass bed from the hospital for them to use. In a sub-basement area, Alfred found a nice big mahogany desk he could use for writing. They were set.

Mira called the Manhattan Storage Company and her truckload of trunks was delivered forthwith—well, actually not so forthwith. Mira called later in the morning to find out about the delay. She was told the driver had indeed arrived at the expected delivery time, taken one look at the basement apartment entrance, and decided the elegant trunks he had brought with him did not belong in such an unfashionable place. He drove his loaded truck back to the warehouse. With the second delivery later that day, the Korzybskis had over 20 trunks and several hundred bags and suitcases spread out on the basement floor.[3] When Mira decided not to return to Chicago in October, the Drake Hotel manager sent them several more of her trunks and bags which were added to the collection. Alfred's contribution to this accumulation consisted mostly of books, over 100 volumes, which could be packed tightly in trunks amongst various other items, and his minimal (compared to Mira) amount of clothing— mostly khakis, one or two suits, etc.[4]

Alfred and Mira put up lines of picture-wire across the basement ceiling so that Mira could take out her clothes to hang, examine, and sort. Meanwhile Alfred was dragging trunks, suitcases, and bags around the basement, consolidating smaller items to put into larger wooden crates which he would nail shut. It was hard work. He joked about his "rather foolish habit to hit once the nail, once my hand".[5] Their activities in the basement apartment drew some outside interest. They had met a sidewalk coffee vendor who had a lunch wagon on the street above their front entryway. They had also introduced themselves to the policeman who worked the neighborhood beat. Apparently, it was easy from their apartment to hear the two men conversing. Early one morning, as Mira related it,

> ...I heard the voice of that policeman...say to the coffee vendor in a low voice "That couple in the back look damn queer to me, I wonder if they're smugglers." The doors in our basement were so old that a mild puff and huff would separate them from the hinges. To offset that effect Alfred had put on a large brass padlock on the door, while in the rear we only stuck in an old iron fork...Alfred was at his desk when I heard a man's boots tiptoeing down the hall. I attracted Alfred's attention, held my lips tight together to indicate silence, and motioned to the back door. Very quietly Alfred went there, swung it open, and there was the policeman kneeling to get his ear to the keyhole. Alfred invited him in to enjoy the hearty laughter over glasses of wine.[6]

Alfred and Mira had initially thought they could leave for Poland within a month. But packing was taking much more time than they had anticipated. By the beginning of October, they pushed back leaving for another month or so. In the meantime, Alfred was getting more publicity and finding more interest in his work. *Manhood* continued to get reviews. Then the September and October issues of the *National Brain Power Monthly* featured a two-part article by Alfred and Walter's friend Charles W. Wood. The piece managed to discuss Alfred's work through the unlikely-sounding topic of "Let's Abolish Death: An Interview with Walter N. Polakov, America's Leading Engineer, in Which He Nearly Frightens Us to Death by Saying that Death Itself is a Habit, and that if We Choose to Do so We May Go on Living Forever Right Here on This Planet".[7]

Walter was also getting the Time-Binding Club started again with a plan to have Alfred give a weekly talk at his studio. And Alfred was not only anticipating the publication of "The Brotherhood of Doctrines" in *The Builder*, he was planning to do his own little publicity campaign by distributing, via mail and in person, the 1000 reprints of the article he had ordered. Surprises awaited. First, the National Masonic Research Society mailed him 2000 reprints instead of 1000. Then he discovered they had not printed the last page with the logical fate diagram. The Society office quickly corrected the error. They printed and sent him the 2000 extra pages. After placing the missing page inside each reprint, he started to send them out to people on his mailing list. He soon began to get thank you letters with comments, which provided grist for further formulating. When November rolled around Alfred got another surprise from *The Builder*, this time from Haywood. Publication of the article had already been delayed twice. Now Haywood's boss, who seldom interfered with editorial decisions, asked him not to publish Korzybski's piece at all. Probably having seen one of the reprints 'floating around', he considered the article too 'highbrow' and not sufficiently related to Freemasonry. There was little that Haywood, who felt his job might be at stake, could do. Alfred felt disappointed. If the original would not see print, at least he had the 'reprints' to use. (Haywood finally did manage to get "The Brotherhood of Doctrines" published in *The Builder*, but only more than a year later, in the April 1924 issue.)

"Fate and Freedom"

By the end of November, Alfred and Mira were still not fully packed. Moreover, Alfred was getting 'distracted' with invitations to speak. One of them from Henry A. Lane, president of The Detroit Mathematics Club, held particular interest. Lane wrote that most of the members in his organization of high school mathematics teachers had read *Manhood of Humanity*. Lane knew Keyser, who had told him that Korzybski "would give our Club a thought-provoking lecture."[8] Would he address their group? How could Alfred resist?

With openings to speak in January, March, or April, Alfred chose the January 11 date. Even though he would get only travel expenses and a small speaker's fee, he could use his trip to Detroit as a final opportunity to visit and speak at a few other places in the Midwest—Urbana for instance. He longed to hear the responses of people who might have some sympathy for his emerging ideas about qualitative mathematics, etc., and give him some useful comments. Alfred and Mira once again postponed their departure.

Otto Sprengler, who ran a clipping service Alfred had started to use, had already invited Alfred to speak at an ethnic German literary club in New York City. Sprengler suggested the title, "Fate and Freedom", based on the subtitle of *Mathematical Philosophy*.[9] That suited Alfred, since he was already developing related material from the "Brotherhood" article in the lectures he was giving once a week at Polakov's studio. He would use "Fate and Freedom" as the title of his upcoming Midwest lectures as well. In the meantime, he was working on writing down the 'backbone' of his presentations—unusual for him until then, since he liked to speak as extemporaneously as possible.

Significantly, in his reply to Sprengler, Alfred made a specific request to speak to the German group in English. He told Sprengler, "...[S]everal of my foreign languages have been entirely paralysed by the last acquisition namely English, so I could not for the time being lecture in German neither in my own language. For the time being I am able to express myself scientifically only in English."[10] Sprengler replied that this would not be a problem for his group. Korzybski's sense of dependence on English for his work probably served as one of the factors that would make it difficult for him to leave the United States and return to Poland to live.

Two of the ideas in "The Brotherhood of Doctrines" loomed as especially significant—"logical fate" and the view that "all man can know is a joint phenomenon of the observer and the observed". These notions interconnected—you could look at each of them in terms of the other. For example, thinking in terms of logical fate, it seemed clear that the necessity of an observer-observed relationship in any observation served as a basic postulate in the new relativistic worldview Alfred saw developing. Conversely, one of the most important aspects of what any observer contributed to his observations consisted of his framework of 'logic'(his postulates, doctrines, beliefs), i.e., logical fate.

As Alfred developed his new lecture material, he was able to bring out details he had cut or hadn't developed in "Brotherhood". More connections seemed to unfold, stimulating to be sure but also increasing the possibility of getting lost amidst the 'thicket' of formulations. When the lecture was finally published in the following year, Keyser wrote to him, "...I have read carefully your Fate and Freedom and think it excellent. It contains, however, too many [ideas]—the reader will not pause to digest so many."[11] Perhaps so, but—in a way—that could not be helped. Korzybski was trying to do something of great difficulty. He could only do his best to express his ideas as clearly as possible. He could only hope to find some sympathetic listeners.

Korzybski interwove considerations of logical fate throughout the lecture. He pointed out the circularity in human knowledge: "No matter where we start, we must start with some undefined words which represent some assumptions or postulates. We see that knowledge at every stage presupposes knowledge of those undefined words."[12] There was no getting around this, as Keyser had pointed out in *Mathematical Philosophy*: "If he [an author] contend, as sometimes he will contend, that he has defined all his terms and proved all his propositions, then either he is a performer of logical miracles or he is an ass; and, as you know, logical miracles are impossible."[13] Alfred wanted to make clear that if it wasn't possible to verbally define all your terms, at least you could try to discover your undefined terms and state them clearly. This was one of the cutting edges where traditional mathematics had begun to shift into Korzybski's 'qualitative' mathematics. In traditional 'pure' mathematics, the examination of basic assumptions had become more obvious in the work in mathematical foundations, symbolic logic, etc. In mathematical physics, basic terms and the basic assumptions behind them had also recently begun to undergo major examination. It seemed apparent to Korzybski that such analysis needed to be carried out in everyday life as well as in science.[14]

Korzybski had thus defined one of his major tasks: to uncover and revise the untenable presuppositions in science and life obstructing time-binding, i.e., the development of human knowledge and fuller human potential. He would make sure to include the diagram he had used before in "Brotherhood". To consciously make use of logical fate, as the diagram indicated, a limited role existed for logic: to discover and remove the inconsistencies (indicated by the diagonal line), between the results people said they wanted and the basic principles they professed.[15] It was becoming clear, even to him, that he had grabbed a rather ungainly 'bull' by the 'horns'.

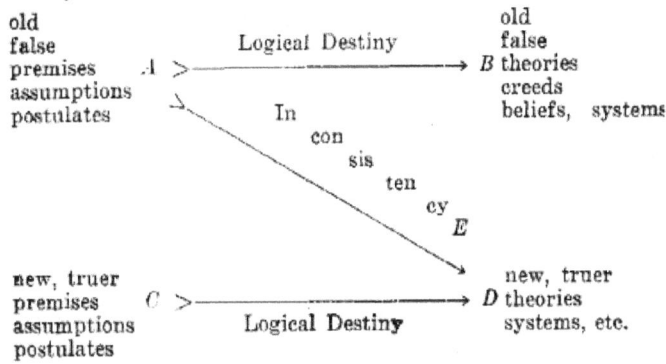

If one of the 'horns' was logical fate, the other horn was the observer-observed relation. In this new lecture, Korzybski would delve more deeply into the role of the observer (for Alfred an 'essential' aspect of relativity), and the related concepts of abstracting, and what he called the "physiological point of view of mathematics". Some of his correspondence from this time indicates how much he had been mulling over these factors.

Lionel Robertson, a friend in Chicago, had written to Alfred after getting a copy of "Brotherhood", requesting a first step in applying what he had read.[16] In his reply, Alfred indicated that, with regard to understanding the new orientation, he had no shortcuts to offer, only study. He gave Robertson a list of recommended books. One thing seemed clear, he wrote, if talking and thinking were crucial to the time-binding class of life, then *how* we talk and think had supreme significance. 'Science' was in many cases not 'scientific' because many 'scientists' had neglected this. Scientists needed to unite to investigate and revise their old doctrines. The Einstein theory provided a practical example of such revision. In the light of relativity, 'space' and 'time' in the Newtonian sense, had lost their absolutistic meanings. 'The' geometry of Euclid had become 'a' geometry. These concepts, as abstractions from events, did not and could not include everything about those events.

Alfred especially recommended to Robertson the recent works of Whitehead—*The Organization of Thought*, and in particular, *The Principles of Natural Knowledge* and *The Concept of Nature*, both of which he considered 'epoch-making'.[17] Among other things, Whitehead's treatment stressed the indivisibility of matter, space, and time, not only space and time as Einstein had formulated them.

As he wrote his upcoming lecture, Korzybski made sure to start out by acknowledging his time-binding debt to five authors in particular: Whitehead, Russell, Poincaré, Keyser, and Einstein. But his particular interest in Whitehead's work at this time is indicated by the fact that he ended up quoting from and mentioning Whitehead more than any of the others, even Keyser. He gave particular attention to Whitehead's discussion of abstractions, events, and objects from *The Concept of Nature*. From Whitehead's work, Korzybski had derived a triad of notions related to making abstractions: 1) space-time *events* "that we can not *recognize*" or experience directly, 2) *objects*, i.e., those "things which we can recognize", and 3) *labels*, i.e., words we attach to objects. There were true and false propositions and statements neither true nor false but meaningless because they contained inadequately-defined terms, or labels. Some terms represented formulations, which had what Poincaré had called "logical existence". These were defined in terms of other formulations and were "free from contradiction", such as the concepts used in 'pure' mathematics. Other concepts in science and everyday life needed to be defined in relation to some existing objects. The "central problem of all human knowledge" involved pseudo-symbols, labels that symbolized nothing, but which were taken as definite. In his lecture, Alfred said,

> As we observed before, events, in the Whitehead sense, cannot be recognized, but the things we can recognize are called objects. An event is a very complex fact, and the relations between two events form an almost impenetrable maze. Events are recognized and labeled by the objects situated in them. Obviously an object is not the whole of the event, nor does the label which symbolizes the object cover the whole of the object. It is evident that everytime we mistake the object for the event we are making a serious error, and if we further mistake the label for the object, and therefore for the event, our errors become more serious, so serious indeed that they too often lead us to disaster. As a matter of fact, we all of us have from time immemorial indulged in this kind of mental stultification, and here we find the source of most of the metaphysical difficulties that still befog the life of man.[18]

If he was unable to give Lionel Robinson an exact formula, here at least was a set of distinctions which seemed highly relevant. "Intellectual life" was "one long process of abstractions, generalizations, and assumptions…aspects of one *whole* activity…[which] materialize[s] in symbols which we call words."[19] This process eventuated in "one vast (probably infinite) system of doctrines and doctrinal functions in the making, inherently governed by logical fate." Distinguishing between events, objects, and labels seemed crucial to navigating safely within this system.

The process of 'thought' (making abstractions, generalizations, assumptions) had humble, organic beginnings. Korzybski elaborated in his lecture about this physiological point of view:

> Thought, taken in its broad meaning, is a process. Man thinks with his *whole* being;.…
> at the various stages of this process, there is a striking difference in respect to what may be called its velocity. The velocities of so-called instincts, intuitions, emotions, etc., are

swift, like a flash, while the analysis of the raw material thus presented and the building out of it of concepts and speech is slow. In this difference of velocity lies, I suspect, the secret of "emotions," etc. Unexpressed, amorphous thought is somehow very closely connected with, if not identical with, emotions. We all know, if we will but stop to reflect upon it, how very slow is the crystalization and development of ideas.

It is useless to argue which comes "first," "human nature" or "logic." Such argument has no meaning. "Human nature" and "logic" have their common starting point in the physicochemical changes occurring in man, and as such, start simultaneously. We are thus enabled to see the supreme importance of concepts, which, as before suggested, are crystals of thought. Such crystals, once produced, are permanent and they serve to precipitate their kind from out of the supersaturated solutions of the emotions.[20]

Korzybski felt some excitement. He might have too many ideas. The interconnection of concepts might indeed seem dizzying. Despite these drawbacks, the implications seemed far-reaching. But though it seemed to him his ideas had great promise, they needed to mature more. He needed to demonstrate them more conclusively. And he needed to provide better answers to sympathetic people like Lionel Robertson who wanted "some link or application to our life of the moment." It still wasn't practical enough. His approach to understanding human knowledge seemed to have wings. But he needed to show it could fly.

More Delays

By the start of December, Alfred and Mira had set their departure time for the end of January. While they continued to pack and Alfred worked on his upcoming lecture, it seemed like a good time for him to have some serious dental work done. He had neglected his teeth during the war, especially during his time on the Eastern Front. His irregular and inadequate diet then (like the loaf of bread he once retrieved from a muddy road) hardly promoted good dental hygiene. The result, as Alfred described it in a letter was "a terrible mess with my bones, jaws, teeth, etc." On December 1, he had "a hard and ugly operation where they kept me one hour and half under gas." He stayed overnight at the hospital and felt "knocked out" and unable to work for a week.[21] The exact nature of the surgery is not clear, but after Alfred had more dental work done in the following months, Henry Lane referred in a letter to Alfred's "last surviving tooth" with an unknown quantity of irony.[22] Alfred probably had at least some of his teeth extracted during this period, due to a combination of decay and gum disease. If so, he would have had to get some kind of dental bridgework done, so he could eat properly. (A 1947 letter to him from his student, dentist Louis Barrett, referred Alfred to a prosthetic dentist for emergency work. By this time Alfred had partial, if not complete, dentures.)[23] Having recovered sufficiently from the surgery, Alfred returned to work by mid-December. Alfred's lectures in the Midwest and his and Mira's return to Poland were looming as they approached the new year.

On January 9, 1923 Alfred left New York City on "The Wolverine", a fast overnight train to Detroit. He had a sleeper berth and got into Detroit on the morning of the next day (though not "on time", so he got a refund from the railroad, which reimbursed passengers for late-arriving trains). There he met his host Henry Lane.[24] He spoke on January 11 to a joint meeting of the Detroit Mathematics and History Clubs[25], then left for Urbana where on January 12 he spoke at the University of Illinois Graduate Mathematics Club.[26]

The following day, he left for Ann Arbor, Michigan where he had arranged with one of the professors to speak at the University of Michigan Mathematics department on January 15.[27] By January 20, he had returned to New York City from his 'whirlwind' tour of the Midwest, which he considered a success.

He had renewed his friendships with Professors Shaw and Carmichael at Urbana. He had also made some new friends—Henry Lane whom he finally met in person, and Louis C. Karpinski, a mathematician and specialist in the history of mathematics and cartography at the University of Michigan, with whom he would maintain a long-term correspondence. Korzybski found the reception in Ann Arbor especially gratifying. "I had a very pleasant surprise [there]. Apparently they are very interested...I had a large and very warm and able audience, after the lecture I stayed a whole day in a few conferences with some of the more interested men."[28]

Alfred was eager to get the written manuscript of the lecture published. Soon after he returned to New York, he sent it off to James McKeen Cattell, Editor of *Science*. He also had friends like Bridges and McCormack make inquiries at various publications. Lane had suggested publication in the local *Detroit Journal of Education* or in the national journal, *The Mathematics Teacher*, published by the National Council of Teachers of Mathematics, both of which had shown interest in Korzybski's lecture. (*The Mathematics Teacher*, later accepted "Fate and Freedom" for publication in its May 1923 issue.) Making these inquiries and waiting for replies took time. Besides this, Alfred and Mira still hadn't finished packing, Alfred had returned from the Midwest with a cold, and he needed more dental work. They certainly were not going to be leaving for Poland at the end of January or even sometime in February. In a letter to Keyser on February 3, Alfred wrote, "We made our minds up to sail about the 15th of March."[29] To Luella Twining, he wrote "We are sailing in about 5 weeks, that's decided for good this time."[30]

A couple of weeks later, Alfred was contacted by William B. Leeds, Jr., multi-millionaire son of a tin plate magnate. Leeds, in his early twenties, had read and re-read *Manhood of Humanity* and had developed a big enthusiasm for time-binding. He had also recently gone to the movie theatre and seen a new animated silent movie on "The Einstein Theory of Relativity" produced by Max Fleischer Studios (later to gain fame for their Betty Boop and Popeye cartoons). On February 15, Leeds wrote to Korzybski:

> ...I have been astonished...to see how plain such difficult ideas [as relativity] can be made. It has occurred to me that if the ideas in your book were to be explained in a similar simple manner as I believe they can, there would be thus rendered a very great service to the public. I should therefore like to propose the offering of 10,000 dollars for two prizes: one for the best [motion picture] scenario based upon your book, and one for the best essay dealing with the nature and significance of your concept of humanity as the time-binding class of life. Should you approve of this proposal, it would give me great pleasure to place at your disposal the sum above mentioned to be applied by you as above indicated. In such case I would suggest a meeting at your convenience for the consideration of details.[31]

Here was a huge opportunity to publicize his work. Korzybski was going to do everything he could to take advantage of it. He met with Leeds, who had a suite at the Ambassador Hotel. By March 10 they had a plan. Alfred and Mira, Keyser, Polakov, Wolf, and Alfred's friend Guy Van Amringe along with Fred Barton, who may have served as

Leeds' initial contact to Korzybski, and Barton's wife, would form a corporation, which would administer the Leeds Prizes. Alfred would serve as president and Fred Barton would manage the publicity. The corporation would find judges, administer the prizes, own the copyright of the winning film scenario, and produce the movie based on it. They hoped to get *Scientific American* magazine involved in the essay contest. But the plan had intrinsic complications. With Leeds' money completely devoted to the prizes, and apparently not to be provided immediately, Korzybski and friends needed to raise money at once for advertising, publicity, office work, film production, etc. And they had no guarantee *Scientific American* or any other publication would have any interest in the essay.

Leeds' offer quickly began to evaporate. In an initial publicity effort on March 13, copies of Leeds' and Korzybski's correspondence—along with a short notice written by Mira—were delivered to major newspapers in New York City. That evening Leeds called Korzybski asking him to have the publicity postponed. Leeds said he would take care of notifying the newspapers a few days later. That evening Korzybski wrote notes to the newspapers asking them to hold off any announcements of the prize. But there was no later notification. Would Leeds produce the money even after the contest had been conducted? Alfred was not willing to accept Leeds' offer under the increasingly doubtful conditions. By March 27, the project had ended. Alfred clearly seemed irritated. As he wrote to Roy Haywood, "We met the young man and his wife...and they were very nice and looked sincere, they were NOT. They fooled us."[32] (Leeds' promises notwithstanding, his enthusiasm had dwindled and Korzybski didn't hear from him again.) Afterwards, Alfred still entertained the possibility of forming a corporation to finance a contest and film without Leeds' help. But Wolf, and probably others as well, dissuaded him from continuing for long with the plan.

During the period of their business with Leeds, Alfred and Mira had once again delayed their trip to Poland. Now they decided to put it off indefinitely. (Those reading this may breathe a sigh of relief, as I imagine the Korzybskis may have done.) Perhaps Alfred would go to Poland by himself for a few months. They soon decided against even that, since Alfred was becoming busier. Among other things he had been getting more invitations to lecture. Perhaps after things settled down, they would be able to get their momentum going once more for the move to Poland. But although they were not going to leave the U.S. just yet, they felt determined to leave the basement on East 22nd Street as soon as possible. Alfred had come to refer to it as "the rathole". They were rushing and packing again, this time to move on April 1 to a two-room furnished suite at the Hotel Grenoble on 7th Avenue and 56th Street near Carnegie Hall.[33]

Wittgenstein

The continuing positive responses to his work (Leeds' interest, requests for talks, positive letters and reviews, etc.) indicated to Alfred that, whatever the problems so far with his formulating, he was working in the right direction. One big confirmation of this for him came at the end of February when he happened upon Ludwig Wittgenstein's book *Tractatus Logico-Philosophicus*.

Wittgenstein, a Viennese native from one of the wealthiest families in Austria, had trained in mechanical engineering and then come to England before World War I to study aeronautics at the University of Manchester. While there, Wittgenstein became interested in the foundations of mathematics and logic. He went to Cambridge to study with Bertrand Russell. He was soon teaching his teacher. Before the war, Wittgenstein returned to the continent, writing and pondering about some of the deepest issues of human life, language, and logic. With the start of the war, he joined the Austrian army, seeing action as an artillery man on the Russian front (perhaps he even fired on Korzybski), and as an artillery officer in Italy. Captured by the Italians, he finished the *Tractatus* (which he had been working on for some time) and sent the manuscript to Russell for review while still an Italian prisoner-of-war. The German version was published in 1921. An English translation by C. K. (Charles Kay) Ogden with the assistance of Frank Ramsey and an "Introduction" by Russell appeared in 1922.

Almost as soon as he discovered it, Alfred began to recommend it to friends and correspondents.[34] What did Korzybski find of value in the book? First, he delighted in its aphoristic verve, e.g., "A point in space is a place for an argument." Alfred enjoyed quoting some of his favorite passages to others. Indeed, he and Mira read from it to each other in bed. On a more substantive level, the *Tractatus* related, in part, to questions Korzybski had been struggling with: How do humans—as opposed to animals—represent the world? How do the humans called mathematicians, scientists, and engineers represent the world as effectively as they do—as opposed to when they, and the rest of us, don't? In the *Tractatus*, Wittgenstein had elaborated on the notion of representation as a picture of the world.[35] This concern for representation obviously related to language. In his later work Wittgenstein downplayed the importance of representation and became more interested in the varieties of language use or what he called "language games". He thus turned away from his early work in the *Tractatus*. On the other hand, upon encountering Wittgenstein's work, Korzybski was increasingly putting emphasis on the process and the quality of human forms of representation both in and outside of language (without denying other functions for language). This continued as a major focus for Korzybski for the rest of his life. Although he came to know of Wittgenstein's later work, it had no influence on Korzybski's subsequent formulating. However, he would recognize Wittgenstein's work in the *Tractatus* as an important inspiration.

Soon after his introduction to Wittgenstein, Alfred was describing his own work with words Russell had used in his "Introduction" to describe the *Tractatus*, "I am working myself on the line of establishing an abstract science of man, which again necessitates the compliance with *the principles of Symbolism* and avoidance of the *misuse of language*." [Russell's words in italics.][36] Korzybski would pursue this in a different way from either Wittgenstein or the group of thinkers (to become known as "logical positivists" or "logical empiricists") beginning to find major inspiration in the *Tractatus*.

For one thing, the Wittgenstein of the *Tractatus* seemed unwilling to accept what Korzybski took as a matter of course even in 1923, that the hypotheses of natural science, including biology, psychiatry, etc., might inform and set limits to philosophy as much as the other way around. Wittgenstein had written, "Philosophy is not one of the natural sciences. (The word "philosophy" must mean something which stands above or below, but not beside the natural sciences.)" [*Tractatus*, Proposition 4.111] To the extent Wittgenstein accepted this, he would probably have some reluctance to find out how the latest scientific investigations in physiology, neurology, biology, etc., might inform his philosophical concerns (and vice versa). Wittgenstein appeared to want to avoid getting "entangled in unessential psychological investigations". [*Tractatus*, Proposition 4.1121] Perhaps this was part of the appeal of Wittgenstein to logical positivists, who in general seemed inclined to want to keep their work in a 'formalistic' vein, separate from considerations of biology, physiology, psychiatry, psychology, etc.

In contrast, Korzybski didn't recognize any strict boundary separating so-called philosophy from so-called science, which separation he considered an arbitrary limitation on inquiry. Korzybski—looking at science, mathematics, and logic as forms of human behavior and thus products of human nervous systems—was becoming more and more convinced that he needed to delve even more deeply into other forms of human behavior as well. After finding Dr. Williams' *Mental Hygiene* review of *Manhood*, he had started to read in the psychiatric literature and was continuing to study the biological, physiological background of behavior. He felt that if he wanted to better understand the mechanism of time-binding, he had to do so.

Another difference emerged between Korzybski and Wittgenstein (as well as various logical positivists). According to Wittgenstein, ethical and aesthetic values were "transcendental", existing "outside the world." "…[T]here can be no ethical propositions." "Ethics [and aesthetics] cannot be expressed." [*Tractatus*, Propositons 6.41, 6.42, 6.421] Wittgenstein was not trying to denigrate values here. Rather he appeared to be emphasizing the great importance of what he judged could not be put into words. Nonetheless his position seemed to give support to a fundamental position of logical positivists: the meaninglessness and completely arbitrary nature of value judgments. This went along with their view of science and mathematics as value-free activities. The human subject (observer) could be considered as an 'intellect' apart from 'emotion'.

Korzybski rejected these assumptions. Indeed, they would become for him prime examples of the elementalism he was beginning to fight against. Values were not outside the world but an inevitable result of worldly organisms (scientific observers or otherwise) purposefully interacting in some worldly environments. Science, mathematics and any other human activity were *not* 'value-free', since 'intellect' did not exist separately from 'emotion'. Indeed there were no meaningful propositions that did not involve some considerations of human values, ethical considerations, etc. Time-binding, the relation of the observer to the observed, and the process of logical fate were entirely shot through with human values.

In the *Tractatus*, Wittgenstein seemed insufficiently aware of the logical fate of his own elementalistic language. Korzybski sensed this and Wittgenstein eventually may have sensed it too. As for the logical positivists/empiricists, many would continue in varying degrees to elementalistically isolate science from philosophy, intellect from emotion, knowledge from value, theory from practice, etc. But clearly such elementalism was not restricted to them.

Aside from that, Korzybski shared a number of attitudes with the logical positivists/empiricists, i.e., his 'anti-metaphysical' bias, a certain 'phenomenalistic' and 'nominalistic' flavor to his thinking, and his interest in the unity of the sciences and the scientific method.[37] But Korzybski was creating his own path.

Wittgenstein had stated, "The limits of my language mean the limits of my world." Keyser, in a review of the *Tractatus* published later in 1923 called this "the *nerve* of Wittgenstein's mysticism—a proposition cannot *express* its own structure or form, but can only exhibit it: the structure cannot be *said*, it can only be shown and seen. The inexpressible is the mystical."[38] While Korzybski appreciated the importance of accepting that ultimately some things cannot be said but only shown, he was not satisfied with accepting someone else's view of the limits of knowability or expressibility. He believed he could produce another language in which these issues could be analyzed further and more clearly. In March, in a draft of a biographical statement written in the third person for Haywood's publication, Alfred stated, "Logical destiny which always makes logical boundaries to a language, in this case the language and its limitations of Wittgenstein, have been surpassed by Korzybski's analysis and language."[39]

A bold claim—could he back it up? He knew that with the formulation of logical fate he had already in a way gotten to the other side of the limits Wittgenstein tended to treat as fixed. But it still wasn't clear enough. A clearer analysis and language would connect to time-binding and the difference between animals and humans. He would have loved to discuss these matters with Wittgenstein and made a concerted effort to obtain his address, even writing to Wittgenstein's British publisher. But to no avail. Still he had other incentives to stretch further. In April, he was starting a new round of lectures. For his next major piece of writing, as a preliminary to his coming book, he had decided he would write a new preface/introduction for a Second Edition of *Manhood of Humanity,* incorporating the material from "The Brotherhood of Doctrines", "Fate and Freedom", and this new material stimulated by Wittgenstein. He was stretching, pushing through the limits. Years later, after his death, Mira recalled observing his visible struggle in their apartment at the Grenoble:

> We sublet a furnished apartment on the street opposite the rear entrance of [Carnegie] Orchestra Hall in New York City. It was a small one with a sitting room, with a double brass bed in an alcove. I was sitting by the window thinking and Alfred was as usual pacing back and forth between me and the bed. He was looking at me to see if I was listening when he accidentally banged into the foot of the bed, painfully hurting his left knee. While rubbing his knee he said, "That is an object, and if a dog had a similar experience, he would be similarly pained by it, but [I need to] make clear the difference between an animal object and a human object to clear up the confusion of that…[40]

He soon would do just that.

Chapter 27
MEASURE OF MAN

Keyser had told Alfred about a curious passage he found while browsing through a *New Testament* at a funeral, a line from Paul's *First Corinthians* that especially struck him: "For he hath put *all* things under his feet. But when he saith *all* things are put under him, it is manifest that he is *excepted*, which did put *all* things under him." The quotation struck Alfred too. He wrote it down in his notebook.[1] It might seem with his inquiry into time-binding and human knowledge, he was trying to put *all* things under *his* feet. But if anything appeared certain, it was the impossibility of saying all about anything, let alone 'everything'. The quote from Paul connected to Russell's types. It related to the 'complete' map of England that Royce had written about. Such a map would have to map itself mapping itself—endlessly. In the new orientation affirmed by Alfred in "The Brotherhood of Doctrines" and "Fate and Freedom", the observer had to be included in any account of knowledge, another incomplete and endless process, since observers always could step back to observe themselves making their observations, etc. Alfred had this and other issues, i.e., the difference between man and animals, logical fate, etc., incubating in his brain as he worked on some upcoming lectures.

Henry C. Metcalf who ran "The Bureau of Personnel Management", an independent educational and consulting firm in New York City, had invited Alfred to speak to a group of businessmen and labor unionists there. On March 29, 1923 Alfred addressed them on the topic of "Fate and Freedom in Personnel Management" and the following week on April 5 on "The Implications and Applications of Man as Time-Binder". Some snippets from transcriptions of these two extemporaneous talks give a feel for what he wanted to bring to people's attention and for his down-to-earth manner of address:

…A few people come together and begin to talk. What is the talky-talk? The <u>using of terms</u>, ladies and gentlemen. To start anything we must start with the using of terms. We make a trust; again we talky-talk, using terms. Now let us see the other side. We make a strike; we begin with talky-talk, using terms again. How do revolutions happen? Talky-talk as before, using terms. A war happens. What then? Talky-talk, using terms again. A peace conference when war is over. What happens again? Talky-talk, using terms. All human life is dependent on our talky-talk and therefore we should at least know what we are talking about, and should at least know if our terms carry or if the terms are such that they carry nowhere… <u>The problems of man have to be solved in terms of man</u>…If you get clearly in your head those two terms, what is the term "term" and the term "man", you have got the key to the solution of human problems. There are plenty of mysteries to men in the universe, but when we go to the bottom of those two terms we have the key to the solution of most of them…What <u>exists in nature are neither objects nor labels.</u> What <u>exists</u> in the universe are only <u>events</u>. What we deal with are objects. What are objects? Abstractions; because you do not consider all characteristics. But we have abstracted a few, and that is what we deal with. We deal with objects which are abstractions, and when we talk we do <u>not deal with objects even, we deal with labels.</u> The whole mess can be boiled down to this; <u>the universe is filled with events, we perceive objects, and we talk in labels.</u> I want to give you the thought that you should take seriously, it is not to be passed over lightly, the mixing of a label with ten characteristics for an object with a million characteristics, and both of them for an event with an infinity of characteristics; it is a ready source of enormous errors, which we all constantly commit...All the sciences of the world are groping in the same direction. Mathematics is in the lead. There is one absolute language for the universe as far as man is concerned, and that is mathematics. Today we have a language in which in an absolute way we can deal with all problems, provided we know how to enlarge the language, to enlarge the method to embrace more subject matter. Einstein's theory of relativity is the quest for the absolute through the relative...[2]

...Mathematics does not start any more today with numbers, points, lines, and surfaces; mathematics starts today with a notion, a concept, which is purely logical—the concept of order...[3]

These examples show how Korzybski had begun to pull together various 'threads' of influence into a larger pattern more recognizable in terms of his later work. He would refer to this material again in his talk at the New School for Social Research in mid-May.

"As A Flash..."

In April, Walter Polakov had addressed a joint conference of university students and union representatives in Philadelphia. A report of the meeting and of Polakov's talk was given in the May 5 issue of *The New Student*, a national bi-weekly newspaper published in New York City by the National Student Forum, a liberal student organization. Probably as a result of the interest engendered from this talk, the Students Cooperative Association at the New School for Social Research asked Polakov, Korzybski, and friends to give a series of four talks on "Human Engineering" at the main Auditorium on West 23rd Street on successive Friday evenings in May. On May 4, Polakov had spoken on "Engineering as a Whole". The May 11 talk featured C. B. Bridges on "Biological Aspects of Human Engineering". Korzybski was scheduled for May 18 to talk on "Relativist Aspects of Human Engineering". Finally, Charles Wood's May 25 talk would wrap things up with his intriguingly titled "Witchcraft and Human Engineering".[4]

John Dewey and some other Columbia University professors founded the New School in 1919 to create a forum for the kind of 'progressive' adult education and social science research they felt they couldn't do at Columbia. Behaviorist psychologist John B. Watson, recently resigned from Johns Hopkins University and now a New York advertising executive, was one of the lecturers there in the spring of 1923 when Alfred was scheduled to speak. As far as Korzybski knew, the New School had become a "hotbed" for the views of both Watson and Dewey. Familiar with the work of both men, he anticipated a hostile reception.

As far as he knew neither man cared much for his views. Frankly, he didn't care much for theirs either. Alfred considered Dewey's philosophy okay but of limited value because of what he viewed as Dewey's relative lack of knowledge in science and mathematics. As for Watson, his behaviorism seemed exceedingly narrow. Psychology in Watson's view "must discard all reference to consciousness".[5] Korzybski—who did *not* reject the fact or the data of introspection—felt any formulation of human behavior that did so, must itself be discarded as extreme. Watson had written, "Thought can be safely left to take care of itself when safe methods of regulating behavior can be obtained. What a man thinks is only a reflection of what he does."[6] Thinking thusly, how could Watson or his followers have any use for the notion of "logical fate"? Still, Alfred wanted to succeed with what he considered an otherwise fine student and faculty audience. He felt extremely nervous about his talk.

An extra burden resulted from a 'little' conflict which had developed between him and Polakov. Since the previous fall, Walter had been very busy writing. First, he had completed a draft of a book, *Life and Work* (never published) built from some of his previous lectures and articles. Then, in December *The Call* had published his review of *Mathematical Philosophy*. In April a new journal, *The American Labor Monthly*, had been launched and featured the first of a series of four articles by Polakov on "Science and Labor". All of the articles in the series, completed in the October issue, showed Polakov's debt to Korzybski, but there was no question they had resulted from Walter's own ruminations, not only on Alfred's work but also on the material in mathematics, biology, and psychiatry he had been studying along with Korzybski. Alfred had recommended the April article to others.

That could not be said for an article by Walter in the May 1923 issue of *Management Engineering* entitled, "The Foundation of Human Engineering: Language and The New Mathematical Logic".[7] Polakov had been asked by the editor to write it and had agreed on condition that he and Alfred produce it under joint authorship. The editor seemed to have some prejudice against Korzybski and refused. Alfred and Walter agreed that Walter would publish a shortened, somewhat edited and reworded version of "Fate and Freedom" under Walter's name.[8] Even so, most of the references to Alfred's name were left out by the editor. Having seen this in print, Alfred seems to have had second thoughts about it. Especially since "Fate and Freedom" had not yet been published in *The Mathematics Teacher*. (That May edition of the journal would come out late partly due to a hold-up in the copyediting of Alfred's lecture text.)

Meanwhile, a second article by Walter for *Management Engineering* was in the works. On the Tuesday of the week of Alfred's Friday lecture, Walter had been on a consulting job in Massachusetts but had written a quick note to Alfred. He told Alfred he planned to attend the talk and also referred to this "carbon of a second paper for *Management Engineering*"[9] that he had sent and which he wanted Alfred to correct as soon as possible. Walter apologetically noted to Alfred that he had referred to Alfred's book and article in three places in the article but that the references and quotation marks had again been removed by the editor. Walter had complained.[10] The next day, Alfred wrote to him:

My dear Poly:

Received your letter from Mass. I am very glad that you may be able to attend my lecture. Until now I did not receive the carbon copy of your new article. There is one point I would like that you would insist upon the publisher namely that he should not omit this time your references to my work, I am convinced that if you see him personally or write to him he would abide to your request. It is very disagreeable for both of us if you publish first some of my work and then people will take me for a plagiator of my own work after I publish it next. This label business refer please to "The new introduction to Manhood of Humanity by A.K." "Dutton and Co." I write because you may be late and send the MS. [of the article] before we see each other. Love from both.[11]

Perhaps this letter provided the trigger for an angry outburst by Walter a few days later. When Alfred got to the New School Auditorium for his talk on the evening of May 18, about 150 people were in the audience. Walter was there too—and in a fit of rage. A few minutes before the lecture, he began cursing and yelling at Alfred: *He had helped Alfred with publicity and Alfred had treated him badly in return, Alfred had not helped him with reviews of his book, etc., etc.*

Alfred tried to appease him (which he later regretted), speaking to him in Russian and hoping to get him to at least stop yelling in English.[12] But Walter wouldn't stop. Alfred was getting upset himself. If this had been only a few years earlier in Poland, he would have slapped his friend and challenged him to a duel. But as he told Ralph Hamilton years later, "I had to glue my teeth." He went up to the speaker's platform, trembling.[13]

> ...So I was quite unhappy and very tense. It's one of the few instances of my life when I was genuinely disturbed and very, very tense. I delivered my lecture to make good in a hostile stronghold, important, which I had to, sort of, say conquer, persuade, and what not, and then that personal issue of that exceedingly, sharp, personal maladjustment of [Polakov]...[14]

> ...I was very eager to make good to that particular class in spite of Dewey and Watson, and I was eager to convey the difference between the reaction of man and dogs, cats, and so on, what are usually called 'animals'. I was struggling with myself how to convey that fundamental difference, and somehow under that stress, pressure, of necessity—I would even use the word 'emotional stress'—of conveying what I wanted to convey, as a flash, a diagram occurred to me,...[15]

> ...when I began to explain, that the process [event] level has indefinitely many characteristics that we don't know, it came in a flash. In a flash—I drew a parabola on the blackboard, and I explained that this parabola represents the process with its characteristics [represented by dots or holes within the parabola], extending without limit. And what we perceive is <u>limited</u>.[16]

Below the parabola, he drew a circle, which represented any object we perceive (including not just 'things' but anything experienced, even a bang on the knees or a toothache). And below that, he drew a figure of a label—like the ones attached to suitcases or trunks—to indicate the label (name) for the object or a description of the object. Another label drawn below this could be used to indicate a statement about the first statement, and the process could go on indefinitely. His drawing was simple with little elaboration. Each level represented an abstraction from the one above it, with some lines drawn from the parabola to the circle to the label to indicate the process of abstracting. To the side, he drew another unattached circle to indicate the "animal object". Animals also had first-order experiences (objects) but they couldn't talk about them. As Korzybski later reported on the event:

> I made the diagram on the blackboard, offhand,...to show the difference between animal and man. I was driving at time-binding. As a matter of fact, the whole of the future of GS [General Semantics] was already based on that diagram...[T]he lecture was successful. I carried my point, the difference between the reaction of a dog and the reaction of a Humpty Dumpty...When I came home and began to think about the whole problem, I began to realize more and more because my whole outlook which I already had inside of me was summarized in the most exact way in terms of [the diagram]...[17]

The diagram showed the mechanism of time-binding in its starkest, ideal form. Every individual (animal or human) gathers first-order, object level experiences. But unlike a cat or dog, which has a limited ability to convey its experience to another cat or dog, a human's world is not restricted to the circle in the diagram—the object (or objective) level. A human can communicate his experience verbally or otherwise symbolically to the other fellow. The diagram showed the pitfalls of the communication process. Problems occurred when people failed to recognize, or confused, the levels. It wasn't enough to just accept the definition of man as a time-binder. To adequately function as a time-binder, one had to stop copying animals by such confused thinking.

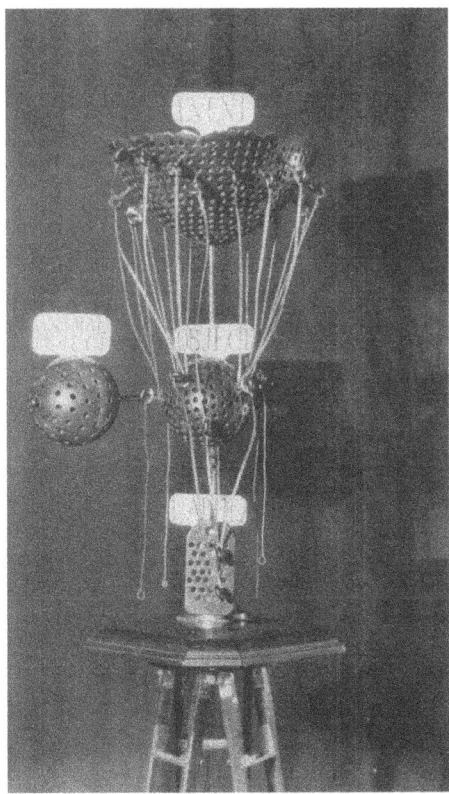

'3-D' Animal Object, Event, Object, and Label

The diagram could be used as a tool to help bring human thinking to the human level. A person could keep it in front of himself as a reference to help distinguish the levels when dealing with any problem (A statement about a descriptive statement—an inference—is not the descriptive statement; a label or description of an object is not the object; the object is not the invisible, inferred process; etc.) In order to time-bind most effectively, a person had to understand and use the mechanism correctly by recognizing and distinguishing the levels or orders in any situation. This was not a statistical approach to a science of man but one based on human potentiality.

Alfred felt overwhelmed. In some of his letters, he described his state for the next month as feeling literally ill, as if he had been knocked over by a formulational 'tsunami'. The implications of the diagram seemed endless. It brought together Russell's types *with* Royce's self-reflexive mapping *with* Whitehead's physico-mathematical theory of events and objects *with* relativity *with* organism-as-a-whole biology *with* logical fate, among other formulations. It seemed to show in an astonishingly simple way "the foundation on which all rational human activities are based."[18]

However overwhelmed he may have felt, he remained busy. The following week he attended Wood's talk on "Witchcraft and Human Engineering". He wrote to Wood, Bridges, and Polakov (with whom he seems to have patched up relations) about the possibility of getting their New School presentations into written shape for publication in a book on Human Engineering. (Although they probably met to discuss this, it never got beyond the planning stage.) Alfred was also invited back to the New School a couple of weeks later to give another talk. Later in June he gave presentations on "Fate and Freedom" in New York City at the Culture Forum and at the University Forum of America.

He had hoped to be able to have some copies of "Fate and Freedom" available at his lectures. The article had been scheduled for the May edition of *The Mathematics Teacher*. But he had only gotten the galley proofs on May 28. He corrected them at once and sent them back to the printer that day with a request for 1000 reprints, which he hoped to get quickly since he was running out of his "Brotherhood" reprints. But there was more delay from the printer and he didn't get them until mid-July.[19]

Besides his lectures, Korzybski also kept busy writing. He was now trying to integrate the new material related to the diagram into the new introduction to *Manhood*. He felt frustrated. It was not a question of 'writer's block'. He was quite capable of 'spitting things out' on paper. But coming up with something he found acceptable was another thing entirely. He wrote to Walter about his frustration:

> …I wonder if you ever are jealous of anyone. I must admit that I am sometimes a little jealous of the easiness with which you write. That's something which is apparently beyond me. I takes me years to write something and even then I find it often to be not correct. This is again the case with me now. Probably no one can accuse me of being lazy. I work 18 hours a day, yet I progress very slowly. I am still rewriting what I have already written and rewritten several times. The times are so pressing and we are in such a hurry to finish the work we began that we push, push without respite, it is the same old story with us.[20]

An Educational Appliance

Alfred had also been working on a new patent application. Soon after the May 18 talk he had decided it would be worthwhile to make a standing model of the diagram. He gathered together fiber discs, aluminum discs, gold nibs, brass castings, and violin pegs—among other materials—and by the end of June had constructed his first model. Having had some experience with patents, he got an attorney and prepared papers for the patent office with mechanical drawings of front and side elevation views. Patent application number 649,344 was filed on July 6, 1923. The beginning of an early draft of Korzybski's application reads as follows:

> To all whom it may concern:
>
> Be it known that I, ALFRED KORZYBSKI, a citizen of Poland, residing in New York City, State of New York with postal address Fifth Avenue Bank New York City, have invented a new useful educational implement (instrument) called the Anthropometer or Time-binding Differential for the demonstration of:
>
> 1) the working of the human mind and differentiating it from the parallel but inherently different working of the animal nervous and brain systems;
>
> 2) the mechanism of building up of abstractions of higher and higher orders, the numbers of possible selections of which grow according to the laws of mathematical combinations of higher order, and therefore grow extremely rapidly;
>
> 3) the mechanism and structure of human language;
>
> 4) the fundamentals of the theory of relativity of universal human interest and of extreme practical importance, showing clearly that "reality" which is made up of "events" is in fact made up of "matter," "space," and "time" indivisibly connected and can not be divided except by a mental process of abstraction, which mean[s], the emphasis of some aspects and the disregard of the others, although they are, all three, ever indivisibly present;
>
> 5) that "absolutism" which means the absence of the consciousness of abstracting is a necessary and sufficient condition for non-critical imitating of the animals and the result of the same animalistic false beliefs;

6) that [the] human mind, if it works true to its natural laws must have the "relativity point of view" which is attained only and exclusively by the consciousness of abstracting, which becomes self evident when demonstrated by this Anthropometer;

(7) that if we are not conscious continuously of abstracting (as a matter of fact we actually do abstract all the time and cannot do anything else) we unconsciously falsely believe that our words, names or labels cover all the characteristics of the object (which they do not) and that the characteristics of the object are the same in number and quality as the characteristics of the event (which they are not) and then of course we are and must be absolutists and identify our labels or words with objects, and objects with events, otherwise [in other words] do not differentiate between them, exactly as the animals do;

8) that with the consciousness of abstracting the human mind works as human (not animal) and that it must take the relativist's point of view, by dealing with abstractions as abstractions, and not as with physical, independent, existing entities, which they never are, and never "objectify" labels and symbols, which is a vicious creed, false to facts;

9) that with this consciousness of abstracting all fundamental reasons for disagreement among men vanish, and universal agreement in all problems becomes possible, just as universal agreement has been reached in this way in mathematics, or in the theory of relativity, the formulation of the laws of the universe in an invariant form, for all observers the same.[21]

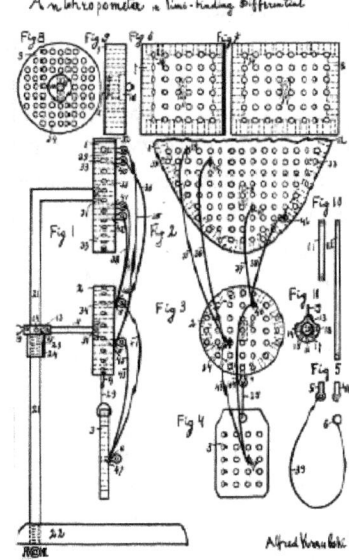

**Mechanical Drawing of Anthropometer
submitted with Korzybski's patent application**

Korzybski had called his device the "Anthropometer" (measure of man) or "Time-Binding Differential" because it showed what he considered the defining difference between animals and humans. Although it didn't numerically measure anything it did provide a qualitative standard for a person to evaluate his own 'thinking' and that of others. The model had an advantage over a simple diagram because it was not only visible but could be touched and handled repeatedly. Korzybski affirmed that people needed to do this to—quite literally— 'get a feel' for his 'ideas'. On the advice of his patent lawyers, he later somewhat revised his opening description. The patent declaration issued two years later, didn't even mention the names he had chosen for the device. There, Korzybski's invention was simply referred to as an "Educational Appliance".[22]

With the Anthropometer, Alfred now had a more intense and specific focus for human engineering. Along with the accompanying book he planned to write, he could see that the Anthropometer might eventually serve as his and Mira's entryway to a decent income from the theoretical work he had been doing. Teaching the basics of correct human symbolism with the appliance (and the logical fate diagram) would be useful anywhere humans make symbols and "talky-talk". The practical side of his work was now emerging more clearly. It involved in part, extending ordinary language use and ways of 'thought'; deriving methods and insights from various aspects of mathematics and science to help people become aware of their own roles as observers, symbolizers, 'thinkers'. Common people needed it. He knew that scientists surely did.[23]

But Alfred felt practical applications would depend on his further exploration of the "relativist" orientation to human knowledge that the Anthropometer symbolized. It had emerged not only as a flash but as a whole, a visual icon for the system he had been preparing and incubating unconsciously for some time out of "scattered bits of knowledge" from various fields. With his last two papers he had been trying to put the system, a deductive framework for a science of man, into conscious, verbal form. He was already starting to see new relationships as a result of exploring the non-verbal diagram. (He knew how much it had helped him and later promoted visualization to his students as a beneficial, non-linguistic form of representation.) But he could see there were serious scientific theoretical issues he would have to address before he could feel comfortable presenting the Anthropometer to the scientific world.[24]

The subsequent career of the Anthropometer (by the time he published *Science and Sanity*, he was calling it the "Structural Differential") in a sense covers the rest of Korzybski's work. The Anthropometer would continue to serve as one of Korzybski's major 'weapons' in his subsequent career as an epistemological knight-errant. He now had, as never before, a significant clarity about his quest. He would search the worlds of knowledge (relativity and quantum theory, colloidal chemistry, neurology, mathematics and mathematical logic, psychiatry, etc.) for whatever he could glean about how humans know what they think they know. The Anthropometer/Structural Differential would supply his main framework for organizing this knowledge about knowledge. And its practical purpose in getting people to apply this knowledge fueled his urgency to develop other devices, methods, examples, etc., for encouraging what he had started to call "consciousness of abstracting".

Over the next ten to fifteen years, Alfred put a fair amount of effort into building Anthropometers/Structural Differentials, even obtaining a small lathe to build parts. He had experimented with making round models—with a parabola-shaped bowl on top and a spherical object level—but those he produced commercially he made flat. Beautifully crafted from mahogany, they came in different sizes and designs—a desk version, a slightly larger office model, and a school set.[25] He sold some and gave away a number to friends and associates.

> In manufacturing them, of course,...I spent endless time and money on producing them. Stupidly. I have to grant that. The price of the differential, I put up about $20, but the actual cost of the differential to me was about $75 apiece. Stupidity, granted, but I cannot help it, and then decided, I spent some months brooding over them trying to find out improvements and further elaborations and this kind of stuff.[26]

In the final patent application he had written that,

> ... "reality" is made up in the rough of conglomerations of electricity in a permanent extremely complicated motion...an ever changing dance of electrons, which, as such, cannot be visually recognized. This something which we cannot recognize is called the "event"...[represented by the parabola with its broken-off top to represent its endless, indefinite extent with an infinity of characteristics.][27]

It seemed to Alfred that the speeding blades of a rotary fan provided a good visual analogy of how we abstract/create our object-level perceptions from out of this "mad-dance". Imagine that the non-rotating blades of the fan represent the actual process world. With the motor turning, we no longer see the blades but see a disk. In our general experience, we never see the 'blades', i.e., the electrons, etc., posited in physics explanations of the underlying 'reality' of objects. Everything we experience, we experience as a "a disk where there is no disk"—a phrase Alfred often later used with his students.

Alfred soon began using this example to explain our object-level experience as "a *"joint phenomenon"* of the *rotating blades and our abstracting organism.*"[28] Within the next few years, he built for himself a 'deluxe' three-dimensional differential on a standing base, which was housed in a specially-made suitcase. Just below the differential, he placed a motorized fan which made it convenient to illustrate the 'disk where there is no disk'. (A friend of his at the National Bureau of Standards in Washington, D.C. even gilded the blades.) When he went for a visit to Poland in 1929, he took this deluxe differential with him and left it in his mother's apartment where it was eventually lost during World War II.

Korzybski with 'deluxe, '3-D' model of Anthropometer
with the rotary fan, the 'disk' where there is no disk, around 1927

After the Institute of General Semantics was founded, Alfred had little time to manufacture additional differentials. Soon afterwards they were no longer available for sale. Eventually, in October 1949, the Institute made available sturdy scrolling wall-charts of the diagram lithographed by the Rand McNally Company on heavy linen map stock. By this time, Korzybski had begun to teach about the process of abstracting in another form, a diagram which made the *process*—not the *product*—of abstracting more explicit (to be discussed in more detail later.) Nonetheless, for Korzybski, the Anthropometer/Structural Differential remained an indispensable teaching tool.

For Korzybski 'intellectual' understanding of abstracting was not sufficient. Over the years, those who found the educational appliance most useful were those who actually used it—keeping it in front of them—to take any problem and 'put it up on the differential'. Those inclined to accept 'intellectual' (mostly verbal) understanding as sufficient were likely to consider such 'pains' unnecessary. For them the parts of Korzybski's work which they considered sound consisted of well-known 'platitudes' which—as Korzybski often observed—they didn't practice. For him, humankind's problems derived not so much from lack of knowledge, but rather from failure to make use of what was already known.

Korzybski got his patent for the Anthropometer on May 26, 1925. But it didn't come easily. After initial perusal, the patent office refused to consider the application further. Someone there had decided that since the Anthropometer used perforated discs and pegs, it had already been invented. It seems that some milkmen (drivers who brought milk and dairy products door-to-door to people's homes) used a system of pegs set in perforated discs to record where they had made their deliveries. The stupidity of identifying the Anthropometer with this milk-delivery record-keeping system flummoxed Korzybski. But it provided a good example of the kind of rotten thinking his device was supposed to remedy. His lawyers didn't respond to this news to Alfred's satisfaction. As a result he took it upon himself to write a blunt letter of protest to the patent office, which seemed to get the application back on track.[29]

By mid-July 1923, Mira had gone out to stay on Long Island where she had gotten some work. Alfred didn't need the entire two-room suite at the Grenoble so he moved to a smaller apartment on Grove Street in Greenwich Village.[30] Around this time, he finally got the "Fate and Freedom" reprints. He put together a mailing list and began sending copies of the lecture to friends and correspondents and at least alluding to his invention/discovery in his letters. In spite of the delays in writing, in getting to Poland, etc., his recent insight and achievement filled him with enthusiasm. With those people to whom he could do so, he looked for opportunities to explain the Anthropometer in more detail face-to-face. This was not just a function of some difficulty he might have had in containing his enthusiasm for his just-completed model. Alfred knew he had reached a new level in the development of his work. He genuinely wanted to know how people reacted to his presentation of it. How much use did the Anthropometer actually have as an educational appliance?

He described the general results of his teaching experiments to a number of people on his list. For example, in a letter to Edward McKernan, a superintendent at the Associated Press in New York, he wrote:

> Lately I have discovered a most shocking fact, that until this day even in our thinking processes we try to copy the dogs, pigs or monkeys, of course man not knowing HOW to think hates thinking, if shown in what HUMAN thought consists thinking becomes a pleasure. I tried it out on children and negroes, the change is complete in a very few hours.[31]

However patronizing this may seem to some present-day readers, did Korzybski's comment indicate racism? Probably not. Korzybski wouldn't have bothered trying out the Anthropometer on "negroes" if he didn't consider them fully human. However, in 1923 he apparently associated "negroes" with a lack of education. Korzybski probably had no exposure to black people in pre-World War I Poland, and had for the most part, up until 1923, met only 'uneducated' ones in the United States.[32] Of course, 'uneducated' black folks had come up with the story of the "tar baby" which beautifully illustrated the traps in store for those who confuse levels of abstraction (see Julius Lester's *Uncle Remus: The Complete Tales*). And Korzybski had already encountered highly educated scientists and others who, outside of their fields (or even within their fields), could demonstrate a great deal of such confusion. He would continue to meet plenty of such 'educated' people.

'A Poke In The Ribs'

Through the end of summer, Mira remained out on Long Island painting portraits. For most of that time Alfred was alone—working—in New York City. Occasionally, either Mira would come into the city for a day or two or Alfred would go out to visit her. When together, their conversation might turn to future plans and Poland. Perhaps they could leave for Europe in a few more months, perhaps early in 1924. But not yet.

First of all, Mira wanted to take whatever opportunities she could to make some money for them. And the opportunities seemed to be multiplying. President Harding had died suddenly in early August after only a little more than two years in office, amidst rumblings of scandal and corruption in his administration. Despite the rumblings, Vice-President "silent" Cal Coolidge had inherited a booming economy as President. The "rotten rich" had begun to again feel comfortable about splurging for portraits at a few thousand dollars apiece. Mira was there to oblige them.

As for Alfred, he wanted to establish his work on a firm basis in the U.S. before leaving. This included marketing Anthropometers to educators and others. To do that, he would need to manufacture more of them. More importantly, to go with it, he would also need to get into print a description of the Anthropometer and an explanation of the theory behind it. This required him to lay aside his plan to write a new introduction to *Manhood*. He would shift the material he had already written into his next book. But what that book seemed to require at this stage looked rather daunting. Before writing about the Anthropometer, he felt he first had to write something sizable on the fundamentals of methodology and epistemology.[33]

Meanwhile he continued sending out "Fate and Freedom" reprints to people who had either expressed an interest in his work or whom he thought would have an interest. He was getting a lot of positive responses from people who had already read it. He had been corresponding for two years with Lockwood de Forest II, a well-known designer and landscape painter living in Santa Barbara, California, who had originally sent Alfred a 'fan letter' after reading *Manhood of Humanity*. De Forest wrote to Alfred on August 16 thanking him for the new reprint, requesting two more to give out, and making the following observation:

> It is very curious how everything you say coincides with conclusions I have come to. I seem to have got at them from an entirely different viewpoint [as a painter and designer]. It is quite impossible to put ideas into words as in trying to do it they lose their force. Until we can discover some way in which they can be made into bullets, preferably dum dum bullets which explode inside, and shot from the best rapid fire guns, or better still lightning they will not have their full effect which should be instantaneous....No idea or machine or tool or anything else is of any real benefit to human beings until they appropriate it and use it and make it part of themselves....nothing can ever be quite clear until you can visualize it. That I think is why your work is so important. Man has to be studied as a whole, a living, vital, moving being. Is not the reason why he has never got any understanding as you state it because he has only been studying himself in parts[?][34]

This certainly struck a bell with Korzybski who wrote back on August 22:

> Dear Mr. De Forest,
> Your kind letter at hand many thanks for the friendly attitude toward "Fate and Freedom"... Once more you are right as to the words, your expression "Until we can discover some way in which they can be made into bullets, preferably dum dum bullets which explode inside etc etc" may prove to be prophetic. I have just succeeded in making such a machine gun, it is made of mahogany, ebony, brass and parchment [the Anthropometer]...[35]

At de Forest's request, Alfred sent a copy of "Fate and Freedom" to one of de Forest's son's, Alfred V. de Forest, an engineer who would soon become famous in engineering circles as one of the pioneers of non-destructive materials testing. A. V. de Forest, then working for the American Chain Company, wrote back to Korzybski with delight. He was one of many people who were finding encouragement in Alfred's work for their own innovative thinking: "I am very glad indeed to have your interesting paper....I have long thought that your questioning of premises might be very profitably applied to our engineering use of materials of construction." De Forest pointed out the confusion of dimensions then prevalent in this area:

> It is even customary to specify steel in terms of chemical analysis when the mechanical behavior is the only subject of interest. We are quite as confused as though we hired stenographers by their height and paid them according to their weight...As you point out, our definition of steel as dead leads to testing it as though it were dead, and that destroys all possibility of measuring its dynamic reactions and hidden possibilities.[36]

Such responses to his work encouraged Alfred. They fueled his desire to get on with his book. If he required additional fuel, he got it with the latest news from Walter. Early in August, Robert S. Gill, an editor with the Baltimore publishing house of Williams and Wilkins, had contacted Polakov after reading one of his "Science and Labor" articles in *The American Labor Monthly*. Gill had also just read *Manhood of Humanity* with "keen interest". He wanted to know if the Time-Binding Club, which he had seen mentioned in the book, was still meeting. (It wasn't.) He also wanted to know if Polakov had any manuscripts on Human Engineering available for Williams and Wilkins to consider. Walter mentioned Alfred's new work and went into more detail about his own two book projects on the "new line of thought". One more popularly-oriented book had the preliminary title "Observing the Observer". Another more technical book called "Engineering as a Whole" would be oriented towards engineers and businessmen. Polakov invited Gill to New York for a meeting.

A few days later, Gill came to meet Walter and Alfred. The meeting lasted several hours and led to positive results for the two friends. Alfred didn't push his new book much (just mentioning it in passing) but showed the Anthropometer to Gill, who seemed enthusiastic. When Gill got back to Baltimore he wrote to Korzybski asking if he would consider submitting his upcoming manuscript to Williams and Wilkins.[37] Since Dutton had an option on Korzybski's next book, Alfred politely deferred an acceptance. The result for Polakov was more definite. Gill would take up Walter's project "Observing the Observer", which became *Man and his Affairs: From the Engineering Point of View*, published by Williams and Wilkins in January 1925. ("Observing the Observer" became the title of the book's first chapter.) Walter got to work on it at once and by the end of the month had material for Alfred to edit, which Alfred did quite carefully. He and Keyser would both continue to work with Polakov on the manuscript into the following year.

Man and his Affairs, the first book presenting Korzybski's post-*Manhood* work, was published more than eight years before Korzybski's *Science and Sanity*. When the book came out, Walter sent Alfred and Mira a copy inscribed:
To my very dear Alfred and Myra—this 'second generation' of *Manhood of Humanity* is an inadequate token of my love and devotion
  Walter...New York...Jan. 1925

Alfred wrote back to Walter his heartfelt opinion: "...the book is really fine." He really meant it. Alfred knew how much devotion Walter had for him and his work. Despite Polakov's moods, Alfred loved him like a brother. There was no question Walter had imbibed a lot of inspiration from Korzybski. But Walter knew it and gave Alfred credit—although he had also incorporated much of Alfred's formulating as his own. Alfred did not begrudge him that. As time went on, Korzybski would observe that he had such an inspirational effect on others who might *not* have much or any consciousness of it. In the late summer/early fall of 1923, the fact that Polakov was charging ahead with this new book, and the likelihood he would get it published before Alfred's, must at the least have given Alfred a 'poke in the ribs' to keep working. When Polakov's book finally appeared it probably gave Alfred another 'poke'. As he had already told Walter, he did not want to be considered a plagiarist because others expressed his own original ideas in print before he did.

Cosmic Pipe Dreamer

Sometime in August, Mira had changed venues from the summer retreat of the New York rich on Long Island to Manchester, Massachusetts—a seaside resort town for Boston socialites—on Cape Ann, north of Boston. Exhibiting her work and painting portraits, she got a write-up in the August 24 edition of the town's *North Shore Breeze and Reminder*: "Countess Korzybska, Portrait Painter on Ivory, Impresses as of Boundless Enthusiasm".[38] Almost half of the two-column article, which took up most of the page, was about Alfred. "Speak of Count Alfred...and the fires of unified enthusiasm and belief come into the Countess' eyes." It seemed evident she was missing him. And Alfred no doubt felt likewise. In September, Mira followed her clientele to Boston. Alfred decided to join her for a prolonged visit starting the first week of October when Mira had been asked to exhibit her paintings and present a luncheon talk on "Art in relation to manhood and humanity" at the Women's City Club of Boston. Alfred came as a luncheon guest.[39]

Together in Boston for most of October, they mainly stayed at the Copley Plaza Hotel. When not together, Mira worked while Alfred met some of the people from the area with whom he had corresponded, and made arrangements to give some talks. Some of the people he spent time with included psychologist and Yiddishist Abraham Aaron Roback (then at Harvard), Harvard mathematician Edward V. Huntington, a friend of Keyser, and Harvard zoologist William Morton Wheeler, an expert on the social life of ants, who had written positively about *Manhood of Humanity*. Alfred wanted to present his views to the brightest 'minds' he could find at Boston institutions like Harvard and M.I.T. On the other hand, before his trip he had felt some hesitancy about giving a formal, scientifically-oriented lecture featuring the Anthropometer. He'd presumed that prior to speaking about it, he "... would have BEFORE to write a rather large book on many scientific [epistemological] problems which underlie the theory of the Anthropometer,...".[40] Which, of course, he had hardly begun to do.

However a few days after he got to Boston, he received a package from Catherine E. Cook, the manager at Open Court Publishers in Chicago, whom he and Mira had befriended. Miss Cook (or "Cookie" as they sometimes called her) occasionally sent complimentary books to Alfred, which she thought were 'up his alley'. This package contained the new English translation of Ernst Cassirer's two books *Substance and Function* and *Einstein's Theory of Relativity*, which Open Court had just published in one volume. Korzybski did his first reading of it at once and found "....to my astonishment and delight that Cassirer did the job for me, and of course in a much better way that would ever have been done by me."[41] Cassirer's book became one of his favorites. Reading it helped him to overcome his perfectionism about presenting the Anthropometer.

Huntington arranged a lecture for him on October 21 at a meeting of the Royce Club (a discussion group named in honor of Josiah Royce), which met at the Harvard Club of Boston. Alfred got a room there and prepared for the talk by giving a more informal presentation at Huntington's home "before [Huntington], [mathematician George] Birkoff and a few other friends."[42] Then, before the Royce Club meeting, William Morton Wheeler had a dinner in his home for Korzybski where Alfred met Dr. David G. Fairchild, a close friend of Wheeler and head of the U.S. Department of Agriculture's Plant Introduction Service. Both Wheeler and Fairchild went with Alfred to his formal lecture; so in effect, with Alfred's dinner table warm-up, they heard his presentation twice. They both seemed impressed. Alfred noticed that "Wheeler was already explaining the Anthropometer to others VERY WELL" at dinner.[43] At Korzybski's lecture, as he wrote to R. D. Carmichael,

...I went to the end of my rope, summing up "everything under the sun" merging physics and metaphysics (to the detriment of the last), and ending the whole logical SYSTEM with the law of conservation of energy! The reception was generally favorable. When I was driving home some of the very difficult (because unusual) points, a young man in my audience shouted, "that's true." I was astonished, because I was prepared that many would say just the opposite. Of course, I kept my eye on the fellow. Lately we came together quite a bit, this fellow was [Dr. Tenney L.] Davis [an organic chemist and historian of science at Massachusetts Institute of Technology].[44]

Davis had wide-ranging interests. He later wrote a classic textbook on pyrotechnics and explosives and became well known as a historian of chemistry and translator of the letters of Roger Bacon. He may have been responsible for getting Alfred his second academic speaking engagement in the area, a talk at the MIT Math Club on Saturday, October 26. An advertising poster for his talk on "The Anthropometer or The Time-Binding Differential" was prepared for display around campus. A small article in the October 26 daily student newspaper, *The Tech*, announced the event with this depiction of Alfred: "Count Korzybski is a mathematician although he does not deal in x's and y's but uses words and thoughts."[45]

Alfred left for New York by himself the following day (Mira was finishing up some business in Boston and would return in mid-November). Back at work at his desk in the studio on Grove Street, he could contemplate good news about his work. For one thing, he was continuing to get newspaper and magazine publicity. Among other periodicals, *Know Thyself*, a new 'free-thinkers' magazine, edited by Alfred's friend William J. Fielding, had an interview with him in its October issue and was planning to reprint "Fate and Freedom". The *Professional Engineer* was publishing an excerpt from "Fate and Freedom" in its November issue. In Boston, after he left, the MIT *Tech* had published a second article on Alfred's talk there, while both the *Boston Evening Transcript* and the *Boston Sunday Globe* printed interviews with him. But for Alfred, even more important than newspaper and magazine articles was the recognition of his work by mathematicians and scientists like Huntington, Wheeler, Fairchild, and Davis.

Alfred knew he had 'snared' David Fairchild when he got a letter from him early in November with an invitation to come down to Washington, D.C. to speak: "…I am very interested in your revolutionary theories and want my friends to hear them."[46] Alfred agreed to come and Fairchild arranged a lecture for him at the Cosmo Club on December 10. (Fairchild's enthusiasm may be indicated by the fact that he not only arranged for Alfred and Mira's expenses to be paid, but that he also covered the cost of producing and distributing 2000 copies of a circular advertising the event.)

When Mira returned from Boston (around November 18), she and Alfred had much to do before their trip to Washington. The Art Institute of Chicago and the Metropolitan Museum of Art in New York had each acquired a painting of hers for their collections. She was getting more publicity about her work and would do what she could to capitalize on it. She had a talk and painting exhibition scheduled on December 4 at the Art Center in New York City.

On December 5, Alfred spoke at the monthly meeting of the New York Psychiatric Society. He had become friendly with one of the group's members, Dr. Stewart Paton, and was eager to establish contacts with other people in the group, like Smith Ely Jeliffe, the editor of the *The Journal of Nervous and Mental Disease*. Since he had read the *Mental Hygiene* review of *Manhood* over a year before, Alfred had been reading widely in the neurology and psychiatry literature. Although he had so far focused most of his attention on the 'thinking' processes occurring in the exact sciences, he had come to realize that he now had to understand the 'thinking' processes involved in psychiatric disorders. He knew he could learn from psychiatrists and thought that, with the Anthropometer and his formulation of logical fate, he had some things which might have practical use for psychiatrists as well.

His book now had a sharper focus under the title *The Anthropometer, World Peace, and Modern Science*. He no long felt he had to produce a lengthy work on epistemology (since Cassirer had done that). Perhaps he could keep it relatively short. He would soon change his view about both of these things and abandon the title. But for now, the theme of the title and what he had written about it so far, would serve as the nucleus of his talks at both the psychiatric society and the Cosmo Club.

As was usual before they traveled, the day before going to Washington was a mad rush. When Mira had returned to New York in mid-November they had gotten rooms at the Grenoble again but Alfred had kept the Grove Street studio. Now, besides packing for their trip, they moved all their stuff back to the Grenoble. They took the 1:00 a.m. train from New York, arriving in Washington about six hours later on Monday morning, December 10. Alfred gave his presentation that afternoon to about 200 people at the Cosmo Club, where they stayed that night. The next day, Alfred and Mira went to stay for a couple of days with Fairchild and his wife Marian at their home, "In The Woods" in Chevy Chase, Maryland, a Washington suburb. Marian Fairchild's father, Alexander Graham Bell (inventor of the telephone), had died the previous year at his home at 1331 Connecticut Avenue in Washington. Now, the Fairchilds were closing down the mansion, where Marian's father had held weekly salons for years. They thought it would be appropriate to have one last gathering there with Alfred giving a talk as a tribute to the memory of her father. That evening Alfred spoke to about 70 friends of the Bells and Fairchilds.

He had not been happy with his New York Psychiatric Society lecture. He had tried to compress too much material into too little time. For his Cosmo Club talk, he purposely decided to limit himself and did not bring out the Anthropometer. But for his lecture at the Bell mansion, he 'pulled out all the stops'. As he described it later to W.E. Ritter:

…The event was a large beautiful and extremely solemn affair... I lectured in the little private theatre. All the memories, glorious memories were hovering around this evening. I am told that my lecture was the best I ever had. I think that this was true. I spoke for one hour and half, and after I was asked to speak for two half hours more. After, there was a reception. I looked over private papers of old Bell. It seems that he in his prophetic genius foresaw 30 years ago the latest developments. His daughter and Fairchild knowing this decided to make out of it the swan song. It was beautiful and unforgettable. After the lecture Mrs. Fairchild presented me the beloved old ashtray of G. Bell with an inscription: "In this receiver Alexander Graham Bell used to knock the ashes out of his pipe. Presented by his daughter Marion Fairchild to Alfred Korzybski, it passes in time from one cosmic pipe dreamer to another. In memory of the Swan song of 1331 Connecticut Ave. on December 11 — 1923." [47]

Chapter 28
ADVANCING HUMAN ENGINEERING

Back at his desk at the Grenoble in January 1924, Alfred could review with some sense of triumph the events of the previous year—his discovery/invention of the Anthropometer, his successful presentations, and the growing interest in his work among scientists and other members of the 'thinking class'.

After his talk at the Bell Mansion, he and Mira had stayed a few more days in Washington, where he met with Doctor William Alanson White and some of White's psychiatric staff at St. Elizabeths Hospital, the Federal psychiatric asylum White headed. White had attended all of Korzybski's talks in Washington and seemed intrigued with his views. Alfred had already begun studying White's psychiatric writings and within the next few years, White would have a major influence on the development of Alfred's work.

On their return to New York City, Mira and Alfred had stopped for several days in Baltimore. While at La Jolla, Alfred had started corresponding with H. S. Jennings, Professor of Zoology and Director of the Zoological Laboratory at Baltimore's Johns Hopkins University. Jennings wanted to learn more about the Anthropometer and organized a Korzybski lecture for interested Hopkins faculty and students on December 16. That night, Jennings held a faculty dinner for Korzybski while Mrs. Jennings feted Mira at the Jennings' home. While Alfred did not consider his presentation especially good, he did feel pleased to meet a number of people with whom he would continue to keep in touch.

This was his first face-to-face meeting with the wide-ranging Jennings, born in 1868, who had written a classic text on the behavior of lower organisms (protozoa), had contended with Loeb about "tropisms", and had begun to study the comparative roles of heredity and environment in behavior. Jennings, an original observer and thinker with deep interests in the theoretical basis of biology, had developed a great respect for the autonomy and individuality of organisms. Although clearly dedicated to the study of animal behavior, even before he met Korzybski he had commented on the excesses of Watsonian behaviorism: "If my actions are not determined by my Thought, why take Thought?....To take thought is justified because *thought determines actions*."[1] With their congenial viewpoints, Korzybski and Jennings kept up a mutually stimulating correspondence after their meeting.

Alfred recommended an article by Jennings to C. K. Ogden later in 1924. Subsequently, Kegan and Paul, the English publisher Ogden worked for, decided to publish an extension of Jennings' article as a book, *Prometheus or Biology and the Advancement of Man*, in 1925. To Korzybski, Jennings' research and writings embodied the scientific attitude that he wanted to treat more explicitly and with greater generality. Jennings, in turn, appreciated Korzybski's formulating as the herald, as he later wrote, of "a much needed intellectual revolution."[2]

Korzybski had also begun corresponding with Raymond Pearl, Jennings' colleague in the Hopkins Biology department, who had been away and unable to meet Korzybski in December. Pearl, a prolific researcher and author, pioneered in the use of statistical methods in biology, studied longevity and population dynamics, and severely criticized the scientific foundations of the eugenics movement of the early 20th century which he considered racist. Pearl became well known in the popular press of the 1920s and 1930s for his outspoken opinions. Prohibition-era newspapers were happy to run stories quoting him on the benefits of moderate alcohol consumption. The friendship of the two men (both born in 1879) continued until Pearl's unexpected death in 1940. After Korzybski's second book was published, Pearl considered Korzybski's "contribution to human thought and understanding of the very first rank of importance."[3] One of Pearl's daughters, psychologist Penelope Russianoff, became a serious student of Alfred's work in the 1940s.

Among the people in Alfred's lecture audience in Baltimore was the Russian-born mathematician and mathematical physicist, G. Y. Rainich. Rainich, a man in his thirties, had only recently come to the United States where he had gotten a position as a research scholar at Hopkins. (In 1926, he became a professor in the math department at the University of Michigan at Ann Arbor, with which he remained associated until his death in 1968.) The two men didn't begin writing to each other until later in 1924 when Korzybski sent one of his papers to Rainich. Thus began a correspondence that would continue until at least the mid-1930s. Although Rainich had had earlier interests in Leibniz's notion of a universal language and in the unification of the sciences, he appeared to have difficulties seeing the relevance of many of the far-flung fields of study Korzybski delved into. Nonetheless, he read sections of Korzybski's developing manuscript and offered incisive criticism in his area of specialty, the mathematics of relativity. Rainich was one of the people Alfred consulted to make sure that whatever he said within a particular area of technical expertise was not fundamentally mistaken. Alfred also found Rainich's general comments helpful (including his difficulties seeing what Alfred was driving at). As Alfred wrote to him, "...Some of your disagreements, very radical at that, have had the most CREATIVE influence on me. If a man like you disagrees, and yet I can stand my ground this means a genuine contribution to knowledge. In fact in several cases the more you disagreed the more I tried to cover the ground and your objections."[4] Rainich thus entered the list of those to whom Alfred dedicated *Science and Sanity*.

Although unable to attend Korzybski's lecture at Hopkins, Doctor Adolf Meyer came to the dinner given for Alfred that night. Meyer, Professor of Psychiatry and Director of Johns Hopkins Medical School's Phipps Psychiatric Clinic, was born and educated in Switzerland and Europe. He came to the U.S. in the 1890s, and began his career in medicine as a neurologist and neuropathologist. Much now considered common sense in psychiatry (but not necessarily practiced) was due to Meyer's influence. Meyer formulated the "psychobiology" school of psychiatry, which established the importance of detailed case history reports integrating biological, psychological, and social factors in order to understand an individual's behavior. Meyer coined the term "mental hygiene" and helped found the National Committee for Mental Hygiene with Clifford Beers—a layman whose best-selling memoir of confinement in an "insane asylum", *A Mind That Found Itself*, started a movement to reform state-run psychiatric institutions and provide psychiatric outpatient care in the first decades of the 20th Century. Korzybski and Meyer, who had read and responded favorably to *Manhood of Humanity*, soon began corresponding. Alfred—now friendly and corresponding with Jelliffe, White, and Meyer, among the most influential psychiatrists in America—felt inclined to think that, as he wrote to White, "Human Engineering cannot exist without modern psychiatry...".[5] He was beginning to think his own efforts might make a real contribution to 'mental' hygiene and prevention.

The Library of Human Engineering

At the start of 1924, Mira and Alfred were once again putting aside their move to Poland. Mira was lining up new work. In February, she left for Chicago—where she had several months' worth of portrait commissions—setting up her headquarters at the Drake Hotel. Meanwhile, Alfred had already unpacked the books from his trunks and was continuing with his effort to get his own second book completed. But the task he had set for himself was growing.

Alfred had found a unity in the new theories and modes of thought that had sprung up in many fields. With his expanded notion of logical fate and the Anthropometer (which he and his friends had nicknamed "the bug") he believed he had found a way of conveying that unity to others. He aimed to build a deductive system (based on the notions of logical fate and abstracting) that connected isolated areas of knowledge and had practical results. There existed no established scientific discipline for doing this but he felt that as an engineer he was as qualified as anyone to lead the effort—perhaps even more so. Under the banner of "human engineering"—the new discipline he had named in *Manhood of Humanity*—he hoped to rally the interest of brain-workers, especially scientists and mathematicians. A few short papers wouldn't do. One man alone couldn't do it. The areas of knowledge needing to be integrated seemed too vast. If his Anthropometer was to be taken seriously as an educational device in schools, he needed to produce something scientifically solid and he needed other people's help. About a year later he would write something to Ernst Cassirer which fairly summarized his attitude even at this earlier time:

> As an engineer I am trying to formulate modes of action but this involves a host of theoretical issues, some as yet unsolved, and until the scientists scrutinize the theoretical issues, it will never become a mode of action. It seems to me that the conditions of the world are deeply upset mostly [due] to the exposure (destructive) of old doctrines, which were false and at present of a lack of a general theory of <u>human</u> action,...[6]

His first idea was to get some of his friends to provide appendices for his book on the broad methodological aspects of their particular disciplines. Among others, Jeliffe, White, and Meyer could contribute something on psychiatry, Tenney Davis something on the logic of chemistry and physics, while R. D. Carmichael could provide an appendix on relativity. When he solicited their contributions, most of his friends hesitated due to the time and effort involved. Writing a succinct methodological summary of their disciplines for educated laymen and scientists outside their own fields would not be easy. Ultimately, of the people Alfred originally solicited in 1924, only Carmichael would contribute a supplement for Alfred's book. (Carmichael's "The Logic of Relativity", which he sent to Alfred within a year, became Supplement I of *Science and Sanity*.)

Carmichael definitely seemed 'on board' with Korzybski's general program. Over the last few years he had written a number of articles on the philosophy of science and the foundations of mathematics, which were published in *The Monist, The Scientific Monthly,* and *Scientia*. In these pieces, Carmichael had embraced Keyser's humanistic understanding of mathematics, emphasized the importance to exact science of postulational methods and the doctrinal function, and accepted Korzybski's schema of the development of the sciences in terms of the evolving relation between observer and observed. Korzybski suggested that Carmichael could put his essays together into a coherent book (perhaps adding one or two new chapters as well) and that Dutton might be interested in publishing it.

Alfred even suggested a title for the book, *The Logic of Discovery*, the title of one of the essay-chapters. Carmichael responded enthusiastically. By the beginning of April 1924, he had the manuscript in the mail to Korzybski who agreed to present it to Macrae. As Alfred read the manuscript, a plan evolved.

With Carmichael and Korzybski as editors-in-chief, they would launch an international "Library of Human Engineering", which at Carmichael's suggestion they also gave the Latin name "Principia Scientiae Hominis" (Principles of Human Science). Dutton had already published the first two books: *Manhood of Humanity* and *Mathematical Philosophy*. With Carmichael's book *The Logic of Discovery*, Korzybski's upcoming book now to be titled *Time-Binding: The General Theory*, and an English translation of French economist Jacques Rueff's book *From the Physical to the Moral Sciences*, they had five books to begin with. (Rueff's book had impressed both men with its call—in a somewhat more limited way than what Korzybski proposed—to apply scientific methods to human affairs, specifically economics.) The Library would have a group of associate editors from various scientific fields vetting potential books for Korzybski and Carmichael who would have the final say on publication. Korzybski envisioned adding one or two books per year focusing on the unity of method that was becoming more apparent within the exact sciences, books applying Keyser's doctrinal function, postulational approaches, and "the revision of language" to promote the development of a deductive science of man.[7]

Korzybski definitely had big ambitions for the Library. Going back to the notion of "The Department of Cooperation" he had written about in *Manhood*, he saw the Library as perhaps the "official library" and potential nucleus for a world movement of scientific workers, a "permanent congress of scientists for the revision of language and doctrines", which could have an impact on policy making and world affairs.[8] As their plan developed, before submitting Carmichael's manuscript they decided the first order of business: to get Dutton's commitment to the Library. After a number of letters back and forth with Macrae, Alfred met with him at the end of April. Further letters ensued over the next month. By the beginning of June, when Alfred went to join Mira in Chicago, the future of the Library seemed likely.

At the end of May, Alfred got additional ammunition for his campaign to persuade Macrae on the wisdom of starting the Library. Alfred had recently met Sergei Vasiliev, then living in New York, one of the sons of Russian mathematician A. N. Vasiliev. Alfred had given a copy of *Manhood* to Sergei who sent it to his father in Moscow. The elder Vasiliev read the book and sent a letter to Korzybski. A. N. Vasiliev, a respected world figure in mathematics, had a special interest in relativity and mathematical physics. He had also been involved with the late Georg Cantor in promoting the first international congresses of mathematicians. *Manhood of Humanity* inspired him. His letter had just what Alfred needed to show Macrae:

My dear Sir Korzybski,

I spent with great pleasure a whole day in reading and studying your beautiful book "Manhood of Humanity", which my son has sent to me for a while (has lent for my perusal). The main idea of the book, that the fundamental difference between man and animal is in the conscious relationship of man toward time, the past and the future, is deeply true...

...You are certainly right in seeing as the reasons for the catastrophes and the mysteries of mankind the discrepancy of the laws of growth of the necessities and the means of satisfying them.

> All these thoughts which you have so brilliantly expounded, make your book the most valuable contribution...to this old science which was called sociology, and to this new science, which after you will be called Humanology [a term used by Korzybski in a few places in *Manhood* as a synonym for "human engineering"].

As much as this may have flattered Korzybski, the letter also had a plan for a future international conference which strengthened his case to Macrae on the need for the Library:
> ...naturally you do not want to stop with this theoretical contribution, and you probably cherish the idea to lay down in fact the foundations for this institution to which you gave the modest name of a "Department of Cooperation", and which deserves to be named "The Senate of Humanity". Undoubtedly you have your own plans, but I hope you will not refuse to cooperate with other plans which lead toward the same goal, ...[9]

A few days later, Alfred received a letter of invitation from John L. Synge, Secretary of the International Mathematical Congress, to present one or more papers at the Congress scheduled from August 11 to 16 in Toronto.[10]

The confluence of events (Vasiliev's letter and the invitation) could not have been better for promoting the Library and the larger vision it represented. But over the next couple of months things began to fall apart. Korzybski had come up with a plan to use a revised version of Vasiliev's letter (with Vasiliev's permission) to make an announcement in Toronto about the need for a conference along lines Vasiliev had suggested in his letter. Vasiliev planned on coming to Toronto and would lend the needed moral and rhetorical support. Then Alfred began to question the wisdom of making such an announcement. He simply did not have the clout—the organizational or personal support—to organize anything of this sort on his own. Carmichael, involved with the organization of mathematicians in the U.S., didn't consider feasible an international congress in 1926. When Alfred learned that Vasiliev was not going to be able to come (and, as with Keyser, not coming due to health problems), he abandoned his plan to make an announcement. The best he could do was to mention the "Senate of Humanity" in the written text of the paper he delivered.

Alfred still made plans for the Library of Human Engineering (he had also mentioned this in his paper). Macrae had shown interest but clearly felt ambivalent about supporting such a project. He was not keen about having Dutton take on additional scientific books, which promised limited audiences and minimal profit for the company. To announce a series seemed even more risky. Both Alfred and Mira wrote and met with Macrae. The negotiations seemed endless. The summer, fall, and winter of 1924 came and went with no commitment from Dutton.

By January 1925, Carmichael and Korzybski agreed it would be better to simply publish their books first and then to work on establishing a library.[11] By this time Alfred and Mira were staying at a friend's rural estate in Maryland. Mira made a special trip to New York City to get Carmichael's manuscript out of their safe deposit box and deliver it to Macrae.[12] They decided Macrae's acceptance or rejection of Carmichael's book would determine the further prospects of the Library of Human Engineering at Dutton. Macrae dithered, finally sending the manuscript to a reader who was still evaluating it at the end of July. Carmichael finally got back his manuscript in October with Macrae's rejection. Alfred felt apologetic for tying *The Logic of Discovery* to the Library's fate, but Carmichael had approved of the plan and did not hold Alfred responsible for Dutton's response. (Carmichael submitted it to Open Court, which finally published it in 1930.)[13]

By mid-1925, Alfred was too involved with other things to pursue the idea of the Library of Human Engineering with another publisher. But he didn't abandon the idea and would revive it a few years later under another name.

Time-Binding: The General Theory

Alfred replied immediately to the invitation to the International Mathematical Congress in Toronto. He would present one substantial paper and began working on it at once. Since this would be his first-ever presentation at an official scientific forum, he especially wanted to have maximum impact. Although he had been struggling with the book, what he had already outlined and written for it provided what he would submit for the August Congress. His immediate goal was to≠ organize this material into suitable shape and send his abstract to the conference organizers as soon as possible. Here is the abstract he sent on June 5 :[14]

> Korzybski, A.: TIME-BINDING: THE GENERAL THEORY.
> Dependence of human knowledge on the properties of light and sound (speech). Importance of correct symbolism and its conditions."Organism as a whole" and "joint phenomenon"—two fundamental principles. Applications. The Anthropometer. The mechanism of time-binding. Confusion of types and orders. The problem of meaning, its solution. Geometrical structure of all human knowledge. Consequences. Theory of universal agreement. Its effect upon educational and scientific methods and the revision of doctrines in general. The connection between correct symbolism, postulational methods, "Doctrinal Function" (Keyser), and modern physico-mathematical developments. Deductive "natural" and "social" sciences. The deductive sciences of Man.[15]

Alfred left for the Midwest a few days later, first stopping in Urbana where he spent a couple of days with Carmichael to talk about Library of Human Engineering business. He arrived in Chicago on June 10. He and Mira hadn't seen each other for more than three months. She was finishing up her work in Chicago; he would help her wrap up her business and get things packed. In addition, he would contact some noteworthy and influential people interested in his work, whom Mira had met. Among those eager to meet him was George Lytton, Vice President and Manager of Henry C. Lytton and Sons, a major clothing store in Chicago. The Lytton Building, also known as "the Hub" had become a Chicago landmark. While in Chicago, Mira and Alfred socialized with Lytton, his wife, and G.H. Sturtevant, a friend of Lytton, associated with a large building supplies firm in Chicago. Lytton and Sturtevant were so taken with Korzybski's ideas, they got together to pay for a special suitcase/trunk for Alfred's deluxe display Anthropometer.[16] Unfortunately, Lytton died unexpectedly in 1933 and so was unable to help Alfred later on when he needed financial backing for his work.

Mira also helped arrange a talk Alfred gave to the University of Chicago Philosophy Club on June 18. The president of the club, graduate student Charles W. Morris, would go on to become well known in American philosophy as one of the founders of semiotics, the theory of signs. He had liked *Manhood of Humanity* and continued to have good things to say about Korzybski later on in his career. Alfred invited his friend E. T. Bell to attend the lecture. Bell, then a University of Washington mathematician, was teaching in Chicago for the summer. Bell had gotten his PhD at Columbia under Keyser, had been impressed with *Manhood of Humanity* when it first came out, and had been corresponding with Korzybski for about a year and a half. This was the first face-to-face meeting for the two friends. Also attending Alfred's talk was the Harvard logician, C. I. Lewis, with whom Alfred would continue to correspond.

Alfred's and Mira's time together in Chicago was darkened by their worry over the fate of their dear friend Keyser. Keyser, whose health had been iffy for some time, sent Alfred and Mira a brief note saying he was having abdominal surgery on June 16. Alfred had already lost one close mentor, Jacques Loeb, earlier in the year, which may have increased his anxiety since he and Mira were even closer to both Doctor and Mrs. Keyser. When the date came, they telegrammed Mrs. Keyser and the hospital to express their best wishes and check on Keyser's status. Keyser would experience a siege of medical troubles over the next two months including a blood clot in his leg and a second abdominal surgery. Having a rather hearty constitution, he survived but would require a rather long convalescence. One thing for sure, he wouldn't be going to the Toronto conference with Alfred.[17] Primarily because they wanted see the Keysers, Alfred and Mira felt anxious to get back to New York City and left Chicago the last week in June.

Alfred and Mira had a month to get ready for the Mathematical Congress, which they planned to attend together. After that, their plans were unclear. If he could get the book completed quickly enough, they had a chance to get to Poland reasonably soon. Meanwhile, Alfred put the finishing touches on his paper and hired a printer to print 1000 copies in the form of a 40 page booklet with a cover. He wanted a few hundred to distribute at the Congress. In addition, even though he paid for the printing himself, he got Macrae's permission to put Dutton's imprint on the title page. Dutton agree to keep a few copies in stock on sale for $2.00, an exorbitant price, which Alfred felt would discourage sales but still keep something available for purchase by the scientifically interested until his book came out. Alfred also had enough copies left over to send to those whom he wanted to have it. He had previously applied for a copyright for the diagram of the Anthropometer and he made sure to copyright the booklet which, with the patent he hoped to be granted soon, would confirm the Anthropometer as his intellectual property.

As he said later, if he had died immediately after writing his 1924 paper, discerning readers could find in it the rough skeleton of his entire work. *Time-Binding: The General Theory* began with a bold statement: "ALL HUMAN knowledge is conditioned and limited, at present, by the properties of light and human symbolism."[18] Alfred's "inquiry into the structure of human knowledge and symbolism"[19] introduced the Anthropometer to the world and also provided some fresh formulating about logical destiny. One of the main points he sought to get across: "...all human knowledge is *geometrical* [mathematical or postulational] *in structure*...",[20] involving undefined terms (postulates), "theorums" (vocabulary), and metaphysics. Thus, every word contained a world. Once one got down to the level of undefined terms, the basic philosophy or 'metaphysics of the maker of the vocabulary' would be revealed. In everyday life, most of us were 'slaves' to the makers of our vocabularies, while the power to examine ones assumptions and revise them (the postulational attitude) provided a way to master one's logical destiny:

> He who accepts uncritically the vocabulary made by X, accepts unwillingly and unbeknowingly X's metaphysics. This fact is of very great importance. If we accept the vocabulary made by X and the metaphysics made by Y, we are lost in inconsistency, the world is an ugly mess, unknown and *unknowable*.[21]

Korzybski's treatment of mathematics as a language and a form of human behavior had led him to make a startling connection of his work with psychiatry, which he now ventured to put in print. Issues of scientific controversy, personal problems and unhappiness, and even insanity showed a single mechanism at work:

> The geometrical structure of human knowledge shows that man is *extremely logical*, if we grant him his conscious and unconscious premises (language). Whoever has any doubts about all of the mentioned issues should visit an asylum, where he would *see* the working of this general theory in its nakedness. In daily life and in semi-insane cases the issues are veiled by customs, habits, overlapping vocabularies, and other doctrinal complications. It is known that "insane" people are extremely logical. In many instances "insanity"is cured by making the unconscious premises conscious.[22]

Having by this time read a great deal in the psychiatric literature and having made some initial forays into preventive education with the Anthropometer, Alfred felt confident enough to make the following claim:

> Psychiatry, as yet, has no preventive methods. The Anthropometer is such a preventive educational method against many cases of insanity and different unbalanced states, due to inherited or inhibited false doctrines.[23]

Alfred's forays into preventive education had so far included work using the Anthropometer with himself, with friends like the Fairchilds and Roy Haywood discussing personal problems (nothing very heavy), and with someone he had encountered earlier in the year. A wealthy woman in Chicago who had read *Manhood of Humanity* several times, had gone out of her way to find Mira when she learned Korzybski's wife was in town. The woman became fascinated by Mira's discussion of the Anthropometer and came to New York City specifically to see Alfred and learn more about it. In deference to Mira, Alfred agreed to meet the woman. They met three times, once at a tea party, once for a personal interview with Alfred where he explained the Anthropometer to her in greater detail, then in an extraordinary final session where the lady unburdened herself to Alfred with her story of personal tragedy and unhappy family life. When the woman returned to Chicago she saw Mira, told her about the meetings with Alfred and, as Mira wrote to Alfred, reported "a complete solution of her troubles in the 'bug', and that her whole life has been adjusted."[24]

The implications of his work seemed wide-ranging and startling. It was also clear the paper was going to 'turn off' some readers who could easily object to the torrent of formulations relating areas which many, if not most, people hadn't previously seen as related—such as mathematics and psychiatry. The content was certainly not conventional. But there was nothing Alfred could do about that. Alfred felt convinced that "Man is ultimately a doctrinal being. Even our language has its silent doctrines, and no activity of man is free from some doctrines, so that the kind of metaphysics a man has, is not of indifference to his world outlook and his behavior."[25] If so, then the examination of doctrines and their connection with human behavior, which Alfred was engaged in, would involve every field of human endeavor, mathematics and psychiatry included. Indeed, those fields would be able to 'throw light' on each other.

. The Anthropometer showed that human beings constituted "a knowing class of life". For Korzybski, this appeared a matter of urgency:

> A "knowing class of life" begins with "knowing," therefore scientific method and science is not a luxury for the privileged few; it is the very thing which differentiates "Smith's" "thinking" from Fido's "thinking." The consciousness of abstracting which is so fundamental for man, is the awareness of a faculty, and in *this* special case we can use *this* faculty only when we are aware that we have it.[26]

For Korzybski, the "scientific temper" consisted first and foremost in the ability to examine and revise one's doctrines when necessary. With the greatest urgency, he felt his work had the potential to bring the scientific temper to the masses.

His urgency about "universal agreement" may have gotten Alfred into trouble. The dream of universal agreement had long figured in his formulating and he gave it special prominence in this paper. Indeed, around this time he submitted a version of the paper to a essay contest on world peace with the title "Universal Agreement: The General Theory". For a long time before 1924, and for a significant time afterwards, Alfred seemed convinced universal peace was possible, if universal agreement could be achieved. Universal agreement in turn depended on rigorous demonstration, definition, and correct symbolism—provided for by his theory.

Alfred's emphasis on universality was not surprising given his view of knowledge. Although he was calling himself a "relativist" in 1924, he was not a relativist in the way many people understood and still understand that term. He emphasized the relativity of all observers in the abstracting process as a necessary starting point in the quest for invariant formulations true for all observers.[27] Universal agreement would be the necessary end point (the limit) of an indefinite process of scientific inquiry. And because Korzybski accepted the notion—going back at least to Socrates—that "wisdom carries its ethics with it",[28] universal peace would tend to follow.

The conclusion teetered on sloppy symbolism. 'Agreement' constituted one of the verbal *variables* Korzybski had written about. The term needed to be defined and specified according to time and place. Perhaps okay as an ideal, *universal* agreement otherwise smacked of absolutism—an illegitimate totality. Alfred's discussion of it put off some people who otherwise might have sympathized with his work.

For example, Korzybski had sent British physicist and philosopher of science Norman Campbell a copy of the *Time-Binding* booklet and Campbell wrote back early the following year. While Campbell was interested in Korzybski's work, he strongly disagreed about the possibility of universal agreement, except in what he called "the subject matter of science." In other areas of life, i.e. art, politics, religion, etc., agreement to disagree seemed to Campbell the best result possible.[29]

Alfred's hazy discussion of universal agreement had not helped to get Campbell's agreement. Yet Alfred would continue to write about "universal agreement" for some time, mentioning it in two places in *Science and Sanity* in 1933, even though it didn't figure there as a significant part of his system. Gradually, his usage of it dwindled during the 1930s, and in the last decade of his life and work, he avoided using the terms "universal" and "agreement" together in his writings. Surely his work on logical destiny and abstracting indicated some of the main sources of human disagreement and provided methods people could apply to increase the likelihood of sometimes coming to an agreement about a specific issue at a particular time and place. But as the Nazi and Communist menaces became clearer in the 1930s and 1940s, Korzybski seemed to agree that universal agreement at a given date (unless it was agreement to disagree) might be neither necessary nor desirable.

The International Mathematical Congress, Toronto (1924)

By August 3, Alfred felt relieved to get the manuscript of the Toronto address to the printer. Keyser had not been able to edit it and Alfred had struggled, rewriting it again and again. Taken as a whole, he considered it at best "not very rotten". As he was preparing

"A Short Bibliography" in "Science, Method", "Mathematics, Mathematical Philosophy, Logic", "The Theories of Relativity", "The Newer Physics", "Psychiatry", "Miscellaneous", and "Human Engineering", he seemed to be wondering at his own 'folly'. What did he think he was doing? The bibliography seemed so heavy and ponderous. Could he really expect others to take seriously the program he had embarked on and had outlined in the paper? It seemed hopeless. He did not travel to Toronto with very great expectations.[30]

Perhaps as a result, he found The International Mathematical Congress, held from August 11–16, a great success as far as his work was concerned. He and Mira stayed at Toronto's King Edward Hotel. Mira attended at least some of the sessions at the University of Toronto with him. There was a large gathering due to the concurrent annual meeting (August 6–13) of the British Association for the Advancement of Science. American scientists—including some psychologists, biologists, and others whom Alfred knew—also attended. Alfred socialized with E.T. Bell, saw his friends George McEwen and Abe Roback, met psychologist William McDougall, chatted with Arthur Eddington, and had a friendly meeting with D'arcy Thompson.

Alfred also met Giuseppe Peano, one of the founders of mathematical logic and set theory and a respected elder statesman in the international mathematics community. The two men became fast friends when Peano, who knew little or no English, discovered that Alfred spoke fluent conversational Italian. They spent a lot of time together, including a half day trip to Niagara Falls during which Peano sat with Alfred and Mira on the special train provided by the Canadian government for Congress attendees. Peano had invented Interlingua, also called "Latino sine flexione" (basically a simplified form of Latin), intended as an international auxiliary language. Alfred, who respected this effort, joined Peano's international organization to promote it—not a major commitment on Korzybski's part since it amounted to paying a few dollars for membership and receiving an occasional bulletin. Peano, in turn, became interested in Korzybski's plans and agreed to serve as one of the editors of the Library of Human Engineering. The two men continued a friendly correspondence until Peano's death in 1932.

The people in Alfred's group of presenters, Section IV– History, Philosophy, and Didactics, included two men he knew, Florian Cajori and Louis C. Karpinski. Korzybski, who had been given twenty minutes for his presentation, spent hours in his hotel room cutting things out of his printed essay and timing his talk. But when he got in front of the group, he dropped what he had prepared and spoke ad lib. The section leader gave him ten extra minutes and although he was not sure about the initial response of the audience, he later could see he had had some effect on them. Although the Section IV talks usually had 10 to 12 people in the audience, Mira counted 54 people for Alfred's talk. Twenty people immediately asked for his booklets and soon other people at the Congress were approaching him for copies.[31] This response certainly exceeded Alfred's expectations.

In general, he felt quite warmly received. Many of the mathematicians at the Congress found Alfred's work— "dealing with human life from a mathematical point of view"—an appealing novelty. But as he later discovered, the initial romance of many mathematicians —and scientists—with his work would often turn out to be platonic, i.e., they weren't willing to help him in his work in the whole-hearted way he wished.

Nonetheless Korzybski—who saw what he was doing as applied mathematical (physico-mathematical) method—appreciated whatever recognition he got from mathematicians. He felt honored by the amount of interest he got at the Congress and with the number of "friendly relationships" he made there.[32] The favorable impressions Alfred made may have led to the invitation to join the American Mathematical Society that he received the following January (1925) from R.G.D. Richardson, Chairman of the Brown University Mathematics Department and Secretary of the Society:

> Dear Count Korzybski,
>
> You have been suggested to me by a mutual friend as one who is interested in the progress of mathematics and who might well join the American Mathematical Society. I noted your presence at the International Congress in Toronto last August and this makes me venture to expect a favorable reply to the invitation which our council has authorized me to extend to you. Our new president, Professor G. D. Birkhoff of Harvard University, is joining me in recommending your name on a form which I am enclosing for your use...[33]

Alfred accepted immediately. Earlier in 1924, he had been invited to become a member of the American Association for the Advancement of Science (AAAS). He remained a member of both organizations for the rest of his life.

Chapter 29
A QUIET PLACE IN THE COUNTRY

Just before he and Mira left for Toronto, Alfred had gotten an invitation to visit with Jesse Lee Bennett, a writer whom Alfred described as an "old Maryland aristocrat", probably a few years younger than him. Bennett, formerly a journalist at the *Baltimore Sun* newspaper, lived with his mother in Arnold, Maryland, on a nonworking farm estate. This overlooked the Magothy River, about 25 miles south of Baltimore and 9 miles north of Annapolis on Maryland's Western Chesapeake Shore (near the current location of the Anne Arundel Community College). Bennett had written a book earlier that year entitled *What Books Can Do For You*. Although Korzybski liked parts of it, he detected an anti-science component, which bothered him and he wrote Bennett a letter. Bennett replied and the two men developed a friendly correspondence. Bennett, visiting New York that spring, even came to see Korzybski at the Grenoble one evening.

Bennett, known as "the philosopher on the Magothy", had made his house there, near the water, into a meeting site for literary and artistic types from the Baltimore-Washington region.[1] He found Alfred a stimulating companion and was eager to get him (and Mira) to visit. By the end of August, after Alfred and Mira had returned from Toronto, Bennett thought that Alfred might be able to stay in the farmhouse of a neighbor. But money had become 'tight' again; Alfred considered the rent beyond their budget. Then it dawned on Bennett. He had an empty nine-room farmhouse on his property. Alfred could stay there rent-free. As soon as Bennett made the offer at the end of August, Alfred—eager for a peaceful, isolated, and cheap place to work outside of New York City—said yes.

Alfred took the train to Baltimore on September 13, bringing his and Mira's baggage, while Mira stayed in New York to conduct some business with Macrae. From Baltimore, he took another train, which stopped at the Arnold station on the way to Annapolis. Jesse was waiting for him there with transportation to the farm about three miles away. The empty farmhouse where Alfred would be staying was a half mile (a 10 minute walk) from Jesse's house by the water. It took Alfred a couple of weeks of hard physical labor to get the place into reasonable shape for Mira's arrival at the end of the month.

The spartan living suited Alfred well enough. Compared to his living conditions during the war it seemed positively luxurious. It was going to be more of an adventure for Mira, who was used to living in hotels and in the mansions of wealthy clients. But it seemed to suit her too during her time there. (She also made several forays into Washington, Philadelphia, and New York City on various kinds of business during their eight months on the farm.)

Water had to be drawn from a well. An outhouse stood nearby. For heat, Jesse provided an old coal stove. Concerned that sparks from the stove could set fire to the chimney, which had wide cracks in it, Alfred separated the two and linked them with a series of metal exhaust pipes that he arranged along the ceiling.[2] For cooking, he bought a gasoline-fueled camp stove, which he placed alongside the house. For food, Alfred would go to an A & P grocery and a butcher shop in Annapolis. Once winter set in, he had supplies mailed to him special delivery and the mailman was kind enough to trudge the half mile to bring the packages to Korzybski's place. Especially important were the weekly shipments of "dark sour rye bread" from Harry Gold's Bakery in Baltimore. Jesse had beds, mattresses and pillows but Alfred and Mira brought their own sheets and blankets. There were a few cots, chairs, and a table and Alfred made more furniture out of old boxes. Jesse had a laundry he used where they sent their clothes to be cleaned. Jesse had a couple of men who worked on his property who were able to lend a hand with chores. And a man in Arnold with a truck for hire drove Alfred when he needed to go somewhere.

When Alfred first arrived, Jesse—who seemed rather extravorted—liked to see Alfred as much as possible. Once or twice a week he had what amounted to a salon with people coming down from Johns Hopkins in Baltimore, or from elsewhere, for intellectual gatherings. Korzybski certainly wasn't a hermit and seemed to enjoy these get-togethers, but he was basically there for the quiet and solitude. When Jesse and his mother left for New York City for a few months sometime in December (Jesse was editing an anthology, *The Essential American Tradition*, and had publishing business to do in the city), Alfred did not feel distressed to be left alone—just him, Mira, and the few other people around the place. Occasionally, he and/or Mira went up to Baltimore to visit friends, such as Pearl, Jennings, Meyer, or Rainich. Occasionally he went to Annapolis to shop or to look around. But mostly he worked.

He was reading and taking notes by the light of an oil lamp. It was becoming more and more obvious that the book, which he saw as an expansion of the Toronto paper, was going to take more time than the few months he had anticipated when he first got to Arnold. To many people he'd encountered, the Anthropometer and the theory behind it (at least the parts they thought they understood), seemed simple, even platitudinous—and thereby dismissible. A much more extensive account of the scientific data from many fields which supported the theory would make it harder to dismiss. Also people might be more likely to take the Anthropometer seriously if he had more detail on how to use it to train people in consciousness of abstracting and on the necessity for doing so.

He had planned to give a talk and show the Anthropometer at the annual AAAS meeting in Washington, D.C. at the end of December. But at the last moment, he decided not to go, even though he had been given a place on the program. He decided that at this point, his time would be better spent working on the book than giving another superficial 20-minute talk. If he was going to produce and sell Anthropometers and make some kind of living through this work, he would need to make the training device's usefulness much clearer by means of a definitive and exhaustive exposition. (Though Alfred stayed in Arnold, Mira did go to the AAAS meeting to confer with Carmichael and other friends of Alfred about the Library plans.)

After she returned from Washington, Mira went up to New York City in mid-January to confer with Macrae again and then went to Philadelphia for a portrait exhibition and commissions with some of Philadelphia's super-rich. With Mira away so much of the time and Jesse gone for the winter, Alfred was alone. He cherished his snow-bound isolation. He must have seemed like an odd figure to the inhabitants of this still very rural part of Maryland. Robert P. Pula, who was teaching in the area in the 1970s, reported meeting, "an Arnold native who told me that he knew an old man from there who remembered Korzybski and who reported that the locals used to refer to that fellow in the abandoned farmhouse as "the Rooshin"."[3] That would have amused the steadfast Pole.

Alfred had times when he felt dismay at the daunting task he had set for himself. But he was nothing if not persistent. The appearance of Polakov's book *Man and his Affairs* in January 1925 seems likely to have stoked the fire under his ambition. Not that he appeared jealous. Walter had produced what was basically a popularization of Alfred's latest work (with Walter's own take on it—no question of plagiarism). But Alfred had yet to publish the book with *his own* account of his newest work (he didn't count the Toronto booklet). He had to keep pushing.

Related factors fueled Alfred's persistence. People with whom he had met and discussed issues were producing articles and books that led Alfred to at least wonder about his influence on them. For example, Jennings had published an article on "Heredity and Environment" in the September 1924 *Scientific Monthly*. The article and the subsequent book based on it entitled *Prometheus*, contained a sharp discussion of misleading language in biology. If Alfred's discussions with Jennings had had an unconscious effect on Jennings' formulating, he felt glad of it. But, if so, he wanted to make sure that his own work was sufficiently known that he would be more likely to be given credit for it. (He claimed that it wasn't a matter of ego but rather of eventual income.) Besides, the analysis that Jennings provided in his article was focused on one specific area in biology. Korzybski's theory provided a more *general* analysis of misleading factors in human knowledge with the potential to affect not only biology but all of the sciences—and more—with seemingly endless applications.[4]

Further encouragement to carry on his work, despite the difficulties, came from his study of C. K. Ogden and I. A. Richard's *The Meaning of Meaning*, which Alfred had first read soon after its publication in 1923. Unlike Korzybski, the two English authors came from literary—not scientific—backgrounds. But Korzybski could see that he and they had arrived, at the very least, at a similar general area of inquiry, as indicated by Ogden and Richard's subtitle: *A study of the influence of language upon thought and of the science of symbolism*. Mira had met English playwright Halcott Glover, a friend of Ogden, in Chicago in the spring of 1924. Alfred became friendly with Glover who put him in touch with Ogden—with whom Alfred was soon corresponding. (Their correspondence would continue for at least 10 years.)

During the early part of their relationship, Alfred had some hope that he would be able to combine efforts with Ogden. This eventually didn't work out, since by 1933 Ogden had pooh-poohed the importance of time-binding and considered Korzybski's growing "non-Aristotelian emphasis as a side-issue."[5] Indeed, Ogden's mature appraisal of Korzybski's work seems to have bordered on contempt. Korzybski genuinely admired much of Ogden's work, especially his later efforts in Basic English—another auxiliary international language. However, eventually he gave up trying to get some cooperation from Ogden. He came to see Ogden as a "d…..f [damned fool]"—Korzybski didn't spell it out—for not taking his work seriously. How could one have an adequate "science of symbolism", as Ogden said he wanted, if the physico-mathematical and other factors that Korzybski brought to the fore were treated as side-issues?

The cold, quiet winter had passed. March 1925 rolled into April. The weather was warming. Mira was back. And Jesse and his mother were going to be returning home soon from New York. Alfred was nowhere close to where he wanted to be with the book. If he was going to produce what he considered necessary for a foundation of an adequate science of symbolism, a science of man, he would definitely need more time. If Polakov, Jennings, and Ogden served in various ways as positive touchstones for his efforts, Alfred also had a few negative touchstones, which inspired—no—required him to persist. These consisted of particular works and/or individuals embodying attitudes he sought to avoid. And his interest in avoiding these attitudes guaranteed that he would need more time.

One of these negative touchstones—sentimentality—was represented for him by George Santayana's book *Skepticism and Animal Faith*. Almost a year before, at the beginning of May 1924, Alfred had gotten a review copy from the publisher. By the end of that month he had written a review and submitted it to *The Monist*. The review, entitled "The Modern Lucretius", was never published. In *Mathematical Philosophy*, Keyser had written about Lucretius' early discussion of infinity, which gave a good feel for infinity but nothing workable from a mathematical perspective (that would happen centuries later with the work of Cantor and others). Similarly, in Alfred's opinion, Santayana's book seemed unlikely to produce anything workable for human affairs. With its beautiful poetic style and fine feeling, the book expressed the kind of attitude that Alfred was trying to establish in more exact terms. But with its traditional philosophical language (which seemed to Alfred more and more crucial to avoid) and without a physico-mathematical approach, Alfred considered that the reader was likely to come away with noble sentiments but no change in behavior. Granted, Santayana didn't seem interested in changing anyone's behavior. But Alfred *was* interested. From the perspective of human engineering, he didn't want humanity to have to wait until centuries later, if he could help it. Fine feelings and beautiful words were not enough. Santayana's book represented for Alfred a submission to sentimentality that he wanted to avoid in his own work.

The second negative touchstone seems difficult to label with one word. It involved a foolish fixedness, an inflexible refusal to entertain anything outside of one's habitual viewpoint with a concomitant failure to heed correction, that at its extreme could merge into serious maladjustment. Alfred had observed one aspect of such fixedness in the behavior of some scientists and mathematicians towards his own work. Alfred had no problem with those who didn't see much in it but admitted that they might be missing something and needed to study more, even if they then put his work on the shelf. But there were 'skeptics' who never questioned their own initial evaluation and simply dismissed his work as some combination of trivia and nonsense. Such skepticism seemed to him utterly unscientific, at odds with a postulational spirit of inquiry which initially demanded granting a speaker or writer his or her premises and finding out what they led to. Alfred, who accepted that a genuine skepticism required doubting your doubt, had cultivated that attitude in himself: if he encountered someone whose work held an inkling of promise in relation to his own work, he would do his best to approach it with openness.

Alfred realized that if one could close oneself to new possibilities, one could also become fixed—go down the path of fools—in another way. His experiences over the last few years with Scudder Klyce provided a sterling example of this second side of formulational inflexibility. Klyce, a man of Korzybski's age, had retired from the Navy and was living in Winchester, Massachusetts as an independent writer and scholar. Dealing with issues related to science, mathematics, language, and life in a way that mirrored Korzybski's concerns, he had maintained long and extensive correspondence with many of the most important mathematicians, scientists, and philosophers of early 20th Century America, including John Dewey,

R. D. Carmichael, and William Emerson Ritter, among others. Korzybski had learned about Klyce from Ritter and began corresponding with him in the fall of 1921, just before Klyce brought out his self-published book, *Universe*.

The two men exchanged books. Alfred found *Universe* an idiosyncratic work with a difficult style. As he wrote to Keyser "sometimes he seems sound sometimes not."[6] But he deferred definite judgment about the book until further study. Still he felt some sympathy with what he thought Klyce might be aiming at: a critique of elementalistic science that sought to renew the sense of relationship, connection, and unity of the world that had become neglected over the last few centuries by many scientific researchers focusing on minute analysis. Whatever its faults, Alfred also saw some promise in Klyce's quest for answers in people's attitudes towards language. He double-underlined in red the following passage in his copy of *Universe*: "The human race took words, mere words, far too seriously—made idols of them. The race have been highbrows:—idolaters of words, the last species of a long line of idolaters of more tangible things. …".[7]

Unfortunately, Klyce "kicked" too much at mathematicians and scientists for Alfred's liking. He felt that Klyce needed to read more, update his physico-mathematical knowledge, and root out illegitimate totalities in his formulating.[8] Alfred gave him reading and other suggestions, but Klyce didn't seem sufficiently open. The two men's correspondence, though for a time quite active and always civil, pretty much ceased after the 1925 publication of Klyces's second book, *Sins of Science*, which Alfred didn't like. Alfred gave up on trying to help him, less because of the eccentricity of his ideas, than because he didn't seem amenable to correction.[9] Klyce died in 1933 and is now more or less forgotten as a formulator.

Alfred wanted to avoid the 'sins' of Klyce. As a theoretical explorer, he had begun to link topics that few—if any—people had connected before, i.e., mathematical method and psychiatry, science and sanity. There were times when he would wonder in letters to his friends whether he had not indeed gone down the path of fools himself.[10] The apparently vast implications and applications of his latest formulations could easily be interpreted as overblown. That appearance, he knew, did not invalidate his claims. But having begun to synthesize vast areas of mathematical and scientific material for his book, he knew he would need to check whatever he wrote with recognized experts in every field of knowledge he was going to deal with. He realized that it was possible to start with something legitimate and potentially useful and move into something unsound.

Chapter 30
SAINT ELIZABETHS

At the end of January, Alfred—growing a beard and a big mustache—declared that he wouldn't shave until the the book was finished.[1] Several months later, the amount of material he'd accumulated seemed to have increased exponentially. He shaved.

Meanwhile, isolated on the farm that winter with the outhouse close-by, Alfred—who had a lifelong tendency towards constipation—tried the Battle Creek diet, using agar and mineral oil as food supplements, with apparently successful results.[2] While snowed in together, he and Mira—who had joined him in the former experiment—also tried another one with a somewhat less favorable outcome. Mira had asked Alfred a number of times to help her work with the Anthropometer and "grind a word through it" (perhaps the parabola on top reminded her of the receiving end of a meat grinder). Her metaphor for the Anthropometer indicated to Alfred that she might not actually understand it as well as he'd thought. Still, he was willing to proceed with her request by using the Anthropometer as a tool for analyzing their conversations. After about two weeks—in a continuous state of tears—she acted as if she had been put through the grinder herself. They wisely ended the exercise.[3]

Now at the end of March 1925, they were leaning towards staying on at Jesse's place for the summer. Mira could easily get to Philadelphia or to Washington for portrait work and Alfred could finish his book. But between then and mid-April, their plans changed.

Alfred had been invited to speak at Dartmouth College in Hanover, New Hampshire on April 10. On April 6, he and Mira left the farm together. They went through Baltimore and Philadelphia to New York City where they stayed together a few days before Alfred left for Hanover. Afterwards, he returned to New York for a few days with Mira and to see Polakov and perhaps Keyser. Mira had ongoing business in New York and Philadelphia and Alfred got back to the farm alone around April 15.

Waiting for him were plaintive letters from Jesse, who was still in New York, hoping the Korzybskis were going to stay in Arnold. Jesse projected the wonderful time they would have there with visitors, discussions, and consultations throughout the summer. By this time, Alfred had concluded this would *not* do. Above all else, he wanted quiet in order to work without distractions. Mira and he decided to move to Washington, D.C., partly to avoid the anticipated 'melee' at the farm and partly so that Alfred could do some research at Saint Elizabeths (the correct spelling), once officially known as the "Government Hospital for the Insane".

"Korzybski is in St. Elizabeths"

Alfred wryly recounted an incident that occurred soon after his arrival at the Government Hospital for the Insane. He had become friendly with the doctor in charge of the hospital's unit for the criminally insane. Speaking in front of a group of psychologists—some of whom were familiar with Alfred's work—the doctor had said, "Do you know that Korzybski is in St. Elizabeths?" One of the psychologists answered, "I knew he would be there, but I did not expect so soon."[4]

Alfred's story had a serious point. The mechanism of time-binding (logical fate, abstracting, etc.) worked for better or worse in everyone, himself included. Human behavior could be viewed on a continuum of time-binding power. At one end, the mathematical approach—including physico-mathematical method—showed the extreme of efficiency.

At the other end, 'insanity' represented the extreme of inefficiency. No one lived totally at either extreme. Everyone—Alfred included himself—functioned somewhere in the middle. He had already spent a lifetime getting the feel of mathematical method. Now, he thought, he should know something more about 'insanity'.

Since reading psychiatrist Frankwood Williams' *Mental Hygiene* review of *Manhood* in 1922, Korzybski had read a lot in the psychiatric literature. He had now reached a stage in his work where he felt he needed some outside direction for his studies. Perhaps more importantly, he now knew enough from his reading to realize he could no longer get what he needed to know from just reading. He did not yet have a good enough 'feel' for serious 'mental' illness though he had spent a lifetime observing people and had seen a great deal of both bizarre behavior and human unhappiness. He believed the best way to get a feel of insanity was by studying the 'insane'—observing and interacting with seriously disturbed psychiatric patients.

Alfred had written to William Alanson White, the Superintendent of St. Elizabeths asking him "whether I would be allowed to study" there:

> ...the answer was yes. Then there was a lot of red tape. To be allowed to study in St. Elizabeths I had to have the permission of the Secretary of the Interior [whose department had jurisdiction over the facility] and ... the permission of the ambassador of Poland,...So we went through all of that red tape and finally I got the permission to study.[5]

Alfred arranged to rent a house just outside the hospital's huge campus in Anacostia, an area in southeastern Washington, D.C. (He could walk to St. Elizabeths in about 10 minutes.) With Mira still away, Alfred hired a truck in mid-May 1925 and had their stuff hauled to the house. Jesse, who had been back at the farm for several weeks, felt sad to see him go.[6] Alfred felt a tinge of regret as well, not only because he liked Jesse. He had gotten used to the farmhouse and was leaving behind the four kittens he and Mira had adopted. They had slept with him and Mira and had followed them both around the property. Alfred had called the kittens his "categorists" (he had felt sorry they didn't have "dogmatists" too). But he couldn't take the "categorists" with him.[7]

For $35 a month, he had found a one-story house with a storage shed. With a peaceful setting overlooking trees and meadows, it seemed as if they were in the country, not in Washington, D.C. The woman who rented the house before them had had marital and financial problems and could no longer afford to stay there. The Korzybskis (Alfred, basically) agreed to take over the lease and let her stay rent-free in one room in exchange for doing housekeeping. She had a child, whom she said she was going to give over to the care of some relatives. Alfred anticipated they might be there for three or four months and he wanted quiet. At first, he was delighted with the place and the arrangement with the woman. But the sick and noisy child stayed with her. The woman was not doing much in the way of housekeeping either. After about four weeks of bother, the Korzybskis moved again in mid-June to another place in Anacostia, about 10 minutes north of the hospital by car.

The new place, where they remained for the rest of their time in Washington (until early 1927), was the second floor of a large house at the top of a hill with a view over the city. The house, set back from the street, was fronted by a big gated garden.[8] For $30 a month, they got three rooms with a private entrance and a screened back porch.[9] An elderly lady lived on the first floor. The place had a large backyard with stands of trees and lush growths of flowers. They liked to sit there some afternoons and drink tea.

The place seemed perfect—above all else it had the quiet Alfred craved when he was working. After they had lived there awhile, Alfred and Mira seriously discussed buying the place in the eventuality that they would stay in the United States.

Probably around this time, Mira returned from New York City with a small kinkajou she bought in a pet store there. Kinkajous, also known as "honey bears", nocturnal, arboreal animals related to raccoons, have narrow noses, long tongues, and long prehensile tails. They can grow a few feet long. As a roaming portrait painter, Mira—who had had pets as a child—wasn't able to follow her whims to have them again until after her marriage with Alfred. The kinkajou was the first, but not the last, exotic pet they would have. Alfred, who was probably already having problems with Mira's impulsive spending decisions, likely wasn't entirely pleased about their new housemate. But he indulged Mira and the kinkajou for as long as they had the creature. (It is not clear if it died or if they had to give it away before leaving Washington in 1927.) Alfred set up a large tree branch in the screened-in porch where the kinkajou could climb without risk of escaping. Otherwise, "the kink" seemed to have the run of the place. As Mira described some of the kinkajou's antics with Alfred:

> This kink selected the bathroom soiled-clothes basket for sleeping in the daytime. Alfred would be working at his desk when the kink would climb quietly up the back of his chair swinging his long prehensive [prehensile] tail around Alfred's neck for anchorage, then climbing on the top of his shaven head would get very busy licking it.[10]

Alfred commuted to St. Elizabeths every Wednesday, Thursday and Friday. (This may have changed to a more frequent basis later on.) He had a regular car ride from Philip Graven, an attending psychiatrist at the hospital, who picked up Alfred on his way. Otherwise Alfred worked at his desk at home. When Alfred first saw Dr. White at the hospital, White told him he could do pretty much what he pleased. The two men had met more than a year before and White seemed to have complete confidence in Korzybski's judgment and to fully support his study plans. He assigned Alfred a room in which to work and arranged for him to have full access to the hospital's library, pathology laboratory, staff meetings, etc. However, because Korzybski was neither a psychiatrist nor a psychologist, White told him, "The hospital is yours. Do what you damn please, but never ask my permission because I will say no."[11] Despite this, White had smoothed the way for Alfred to work at St. Elizabeths.

Soon after his arrival in Washington, Alfred had been invited by one of White's most trusted staff members, Nolan D.C. Lewis, M.D., to give a presentation on June 25 to the Washington Society for Nervous and Mental Diseases. Alfred had just moved to the second place in Anacostia and had no time to write out a paper. He entitled the talk, which he delivered from an outline, "Mathematics and Psychiatry, An Introduction to Humanology". As evident by its absence from the title, he was abandoning the term "human engineering".

An organization named "Pathfinders – Scientific Character Builders" had begun using "human engineering" to label their "positive-thinking" style educational programs. As far as Alfred was concerned, the "Pathfinders" programs had little to do with either science or engineering. After getting their materials, he protested to its director who refused to stop using the term. Since Alfred didn't want what he was doing confused with their work, he began using "humanology", a synonym for "human engineering" he had used in *Manhood*, to label his work. He would continue to do so over the next few years.[12]

After Korzybski's presentation, Dr. White addressed the audience—filled with members of St. Elizabeths' psychiatric staff—for another half hour. White highlighted what he considered some of the important points Alfred had made. Alfred felt happy with his talk and grateful to White for giving him such an introduction. For the most part, he was made to feel at home at St. Elizabeths and, from the start, received a great deal of help there.[13]

St. Elizabeths, under White's direction, had a population of around 5000 patients at the time that Korzybski arrived. Before White became the Superintendent in 1903, St. Elizabeths—which served Federal employees, military personnel, and residents of the District of Columbia—had become a dehumanizing warehouse for the insane. Since then, White had done his best to re-humanize the place. Patients no longer slept on straw pallets. He had done away with the use of straightjackets for restraint. He had opened a beauty parlor for the female patients. He had done his best to expand services to his patients and made serious efforts to provide both occupational therapy and psychotherapy. To promote research he had expanded the pathology laboratory where deceased patients and their brains could be autopsied and the possible physiological aspects of their illnesses explored. White had turned St. Elizabeths into the one of the premier psychiatric hospitals in the world.

Still, in 1925 effective treatment for seriously disturbed psychiatric patients seemed, generally speaking, somewhat limited. Sometimes patients got well enough to leave. Whether this happened as the result of any treatment was another question. Many were there for life. At least under White's regime they were treated humanely. Freudian psychoanalysis was becoming ascendant as a framework for explaining and treating psychiatric problems. Though he had helped to promote psychoanalysis in America, White was no doctrinaire advocate. He had been involved in the mental hygiene movement since its inception and had written extensively about prevention. Could Korzybski offer something useful to his staff and his patients?

As part of his study routine, Alfred would circulate to various units in the hospital where, with doctors' permission, he would read patients' charts and then interview them. In the beginning, he had trouble with only one M.D., who insisted Alfred needed to get permission from White before seeing a patient's records. As predicted, White said "No." Alfred simply got the records from another physician. Alfred never had any other problems getting records or interviewing patients during his time in the hospital.

Alfred tried to make very clear to all concerned at St. Elizabeths, his primary purpose there was to study the patients, *not* to work with them. Years later, he would give classes or do individual work with psychiatric patients (*not* his own) only if they had the permission of their psychiatrists to work with him. Many doctors not only saw no harm in sending patients to his classes, they also felt curious about what Alfred could do—even with seriously disturbed people. Psychiatrists themselves, starting with White and Graven, also studied with him. As his work developed, he realized that for a large number of people, their maladjustments seemed less medical than doctrinal, i.e., resulting from their 'philosophies' of life. Alfred definitely wanted to teach psychiatrists how to work with such people using the orientation he was developing. However, from the beginning of his time at St. Elizabeths and as he reiterated throughout the rest of his career, his only claim for his work was educational and preventive. He liked to emphasize that he never claimed to do psychotherapy.

The 'Logic' of 'Insanity'

Soon after Alfred arrived at Government Hospital for the Insane, he met the doctor who ran the women's department—a friend of Dr. White. She was interested in having Alfred study the women confined in the hospital. He wanted to study them too since he felt curious about differences between disturbances in men and women. Each unit of the hospital typically had a room where he could read patients' charts and then have conversations with them. Any female patient he intended to interview was accompanied by a female nurse acting as a chaperone, as much for his sake as the patient's. He soon confirmed the wisdom of this precaution:

> It was impossible. Perfectly impossible. What can you do with a patient, for instance, the first thing they do…they hold up their skirt. Immediately. What to do. You can do nothing about that. Of course, I was always with a nurse, and the nurse pulled the skirt down. That's not a solution. How can I talk with a patient who behaves that way? [14]

As a result, Alfred decided he was not going to have private interviews with female patients at St. Elizabeths.

Of course, he knew he also had to be careful with the male patients for reasons of his physical safety. When he went into a room to have a conversation with a psychotic man, he would have a guard nearby. In addition, as an experienced ex-fencer, he remained acutely aware of body language and the distance between himself and whomever he was talking with. He knew there could be a great element of unpredictability in a patient's reactions, even to the most innocent-seeming remarks or gestures. Surprises could happen that he might have to respond to quickly. He would later tell students of his, working with severely disturbed people, to remember to keep their distance.

Alfred had one of his most interesting patient interviews in the St. Elizabeths receiving ward. Alfred got permission to speak with a just-admitted mathematics teacher. The two men talked for a couple of hours; that is, the patient mostly talked and Alfred listened. What fascinated Alfred more than anything else was the sense he'd found his own 'insane' double, in whom the mechanism of logical fate seemed clearly evident:

> He was so clear-cut about everything he had to say except that he was 'insane' and except that everything he said had nothing to do with so-called 'reality'. But his manner, being a mathematician, his exposition to me of his 'insane' ideas were a shock to me. I could recognize myself, in my method of representation, in that insane person. [15]

Alfred was not the first person to see a kind of 'logic' in insanity. Clifford Beers, founder of the Mental Hygiene movement in America, had written earlier about a period of his own mental illness:

> Most sane people think that no insane person can reason logically. But this is not so. Upon unreasonable premises I made most reasonable deductions, and that at the time when my mind was in its most disturbed condition…During the seven hundred and ninety-eight days of depression I drew countless incorrect deductions. But, such as they were, they were deductions, and essentially the mental process was not other than that which takes place in a well-ordered mind. [16]

Alfred encountered other patients who confirmed Beers' point for him. One fellow he met had "grand parole", permission to freely move around the hospital. As Korzybski later recalled,

> [The man appeared]…quite harmless. One year he was Julius Caesar. Another year he was Napoleon, and it was a habit to address him, "Your majesty"…Whenever doctors came to America, they had to visit St. Elizabeths Hospital. It was really, and justly so,

a showplace. So a visitor came, and the doctor and I were showing him the place...that fellow [the visitor] came the year before. I did not know that. And he remembered that patient as Napoleon...and he met the same fellow who he remembered, but by this time [the patient] was Julius Caesar. And he said to the patient, "I believe I met you before, your majesty. But you were then Napoleon, now you are Julius Caesar. How come?" You know what the patient said? "Oh yes, this was by my other mother."

To Korzybski, this answer seemed "perfectly logical" however out of touch with life facts.[17] Indeed, a detachment from facts and a preference for verbalism seemed starkly evident in just about every hospital resident he saw. There was the patient born in Washington D.C., who had never left the city and who had elaborated a fictional family history based on the word "Washington". His father 'became' governor of Washington state, his brother the mayor of Seattle, and his own place of birth the state of Washington. The word had become the thing for him.

After a short time at the hospital, Alfred refined his notion of the continuum of time-binding, in terms of sanity and logical fate. A mathematician, insofar as he functioned adequately as a mathematician, didn't accept his premises as true. At best, he only considered them correct. Following up on correct premises, he abided by them—one of the main reasons why mathematics had turned out so useful for science. It allowed theories about the world to be worked out with exactness so testable predictions could be made. The theories could then be revised if necessary. If a person could function that way in the rest of his life—Korzybski didn't think that most mathematicians or scientists necessarily did—he could be considered well-adjusted or sane. An 'insane' person believed in foolish premises and abided by them with absolute conviction resulting in little or no revision and poor adaptation to life. (Alfred thought this might explain why some extremely fine mathematicians could go insane—they could carry out the implications of foolish premises better than just about anyone else.) A so-called 'normal' person might accept foolish premises as true but often didn't abide by them. This led to better, though in the long run inadequate, adaptation to life.[18]

After more psychiatrists knew about Alfred's analysis of behavior in terms of logical fate, confusion of levels of abstraction, etc., he got used to hearing the criticism that "Korzybski fancies that a human being is a piece of euclidean geometry." Alfred sometimes replied, with tongue only partly in cheek, that, "It is even worse than euclidean geometry." At St. Elizabeths he saw patients acting "like automatons, following their delusions...their premises... and they walk[ed] and react[ed] like automatons. We do the same thing except that we [so-called 'normals'] are slightly more flexible. The mechanism is the same."[19]

On one hand it seemed hopeful to see sanity as a continuum varying as a matter of degrees among individuals. Perhaps it was possible—even with some institutionalized patients—to use the methods Alfred was developing to help people become aware of and revise their faulty premises. In this way, they could move, if only a little further, along the road to greater sanity. On the other hand, it could seem disquieting to consider sanity as a relative quality. Who then could be considered completely sane? Many so-called 'normal' people certainly didn't seem to be moving along the road to greater sanity. Indeed, Alfred had seen many 'automatons' not confined to mental hospitals. Out on the streets and in their homes; working in offices, universities, government departments; leading governments; etc., they followed their delusional premises and conveyed them—sometimes with verve and great skill—to others.

Sometime in the next few years, Philip Graven would supply Alfred with a word for the vast middle group of so-called 'normal' people—the "un-sane". Alfred eventually concluded that most of us could be considered un-sane to some degree. Sanity, adequate adjustment to life facts (which included one's own potential), seemed like an art that required taking unceasing aim at a perpetually moving target. But it was important to aim. If science and mathematics, as forms of human behavior and language, provided superior means for adjustment to facts, then why couldn't they be generalized to help aim oneself towards greater sanity? Korzybski didn't expect that his connecting of "physico-mathematical methods" to psychiatry would make his next book popular. Either subject area could put off a huge portion of potential readers. Linked together, the two subjects seemed likely to drive off even more. So be it. The more patients he saw, the clearer the connection became for him.

For example, by 1925 a mental status examination had become a standard part of the hospital admitting procedure. Not uncommonly, some severely disturbed people had trouble answering questions like, "What is your name?", "Who are you?", "Where are you?", or "What day is today?" A patient might not be able to recall his name, or not know the exact city, place, day or even year. Instead he might provide vague generalities as answers. The doctor might write in the chart, "Disoriented in space and time" (Alfred would say "space-time"). Korzybski saw that, in a less obvious way, an un-sanely behaving 'normal' might also have some form of space-time disorientation which led him or her to confuse orders of abstraction: one individual/situation at one time and place incompletely specified would get mixed-up with another individual/situation or with itself at another time and place. How many kinds of 'normal' disturbances and misevaluations involved some such form of space-time disorientation?

In relativity physics, an event was not adequately specified until its space-time coordinates were given and the observational frame of reference noted. This physico-mathematical technique based on space-time ordering could be applied to life. Alfred might have remembered his own jumpiness after he first arrived in New York at the end of 1915. He had felt tension as if he was expecting artillery shells to burst near his hotel room. He had 'cured' himself by reminding himself that his hotel room in New York City in December 1915 was not an Eastern Front battlefield in 1914.

Korzybski's advocacy of physico-mathematical methods may have seemed novel to psychiatrists, but his view on sanity as a continuum was not at odds with psychiatric thinking—at least the thinking of some of the psychiatrists he met while at St. Elizabeths. One of them was Harry Stack Sullivan, a brilliant but temperamental doctor, who had worked at St. Elizabeths several years before and had then moved to the Shepherd and Enoch Pratt Hospital in Baltimore. Sullivan had written a recent paper on the "Peculiarity of Thought in Schizophrenia" and had attended Korzybski's June lecture with interest. The two men exchanged papers and began to correspond. Sullivan, relatively untrammeled by the growing orthodoxy of Freudian psychoanalysis, went on in the 1930s and 1940s to develop "interpersonal psychotherapy", one of the first of the non-psychoanalytic forms of psychotherapy in America.

Sullivan became known for his "one genus postulate", first stated in print in 1938: "We are all much more simply human than otherwise." Sullivan's postulate emphasized that,

"...all the things observed in the persons whom we call psychiatrically ill are present to lesser extents in the persons whom we call emotionally healthy."[20] As far back as 1917, Dr. White had likewise noted that, "Because of the preponderance of similarities between ourselves and others we must be prepared to see ourselves in those others, to look in the phenomena we are studying for reflections of ourselves."[21] In 1933, he stated his own "one-genus postulate" in the clearest of terms: "The difference between the so-called insane person or the criminal on the one hand and the so-called sane or normal person on the other is only a difference in quantity, a difference in the strength or weakness and the balanced relations of the various tendencies and stimuli with which he has to deal."[22] Korzybski would probably have added, 'and what a difference even a little difference can sometimes make'.

"What is Reality?"

His association with White at St. Elizabeths became probably the most important professional relationship Korzybski had—other than the one he had with Cassius Keyser. As with Keyser, Alfred held White in the highest esteem, considering him "extremely brilliant, very [well] read, very creative, very human, very warm, and very much interested in the future of psychiatry altogether."[23] A busy man, he spent a great deal of his time in his office. Although he saw patients, he had delegated most of their care to his trusted assistant, Nolan D.C. Lewis. Not only was he administering St. Elizabeths, he was editing a journal and a monograph series, and researching and writing articles and books. During this period he also served as President of the American Psychiatric Association (1924-25) and acted as a professional consultant in criminal trials.

William Alanson White

Despite his busyness, White found time to spend with Korzybski. White guided Alfred in his first-hand study of psychiatry and in his theoretical studies of psycho-biological mechanisms. In turn, White—who had had earlier difficulties with physics and mathematics in school—recognized a need to learn from Korzybski the methodological underpinnings of the latest scientific advances. Korzybski recalled:

...we spent endless hours and he was actually tutoring me in psychiatry...I was reading endlessly psychiatric books. They had a large library in the hospital. It was at my disposal. So I was reading, reading. Once I was there I made good. And I was teaching him [White] physico-mathematical stuff. I was teaching him what I knew and he was teaching me what he knew. So we were a beautiful team in this sense.[24]

In White, Korzybski recognized a 'natural'—an individual who, in many ways, professionally and personally, already exemplified the orientation he was trying to make more explicit in his writing. Korzybski could not have had a better teacher or student. Later on, he acknowledged his debt to White in *Science and Sanity*. In some of his later writings, White acknowledged Korzybski's influence upon him (see the paper "The Language of Schizophrenia", extensively quoted in *Science and Sanity*, pp. 185-187). Although it does not reference Korzybski, White's 1936 book *Twentieth Century Psychiatry*, published one year before his death, applied a physico-mathematical perspective to psychiatry and seems permeated by Korzybski's intellectual influence.

An excellent judge of men, White knew that Korzybski had many talents. As an effective administrator who knew how to delegate, White soon found a way to make official use of some of them—despite Korzybski's indeterminate status at the hospital. Korzybski reported:

...[Dr. and Mrs. White] had all the time little receptions, guests from all over the world, important psychiatrists, neurologists, etc., visiting the hospital and of course, White was making little luncheons and what not. White didn't speak any languages [except English] so usually when there was any party Mira [who had become friendly with Mrs. White] and I were not only invited but we had to take care of the guests. Mira took care of helping Mrs. White when we had plenty of people at a party in the evening, sandwiches, etc., someone has to supervise and the same with those foreign doctors, I had to just make the honors of the house. Of course, it was very pleasant, very flattering, etc., so our relationship was very, very warm and we spent endless hours in their home or they came to our home, or in his office we were talking shop,...[25]

White allowed Korzybski to sit in at staff meetings when patient's cases were discussed. Alfred recalled:

I attended practically every day what they call the staff conference. ...They brought a patient and a given doctor who was in care of this case, reported on the case, said this case should have grand parole [permission to move around the hospital freely], should or should not be released, in front of the patient, or without the patient. Then the patient was shown, the presiding doctor asking questions, and then the conference decided what to do with the patient. This was standard routine and was very, very instructive for me.[26]

At St. Elizabeths, Alfred also attended regular Washington Psychopathological Society meetings, over which Dr. White presided. (As a joke, they called themselves "the psychopaths".) Psychiatrists came from all over the Washington-Baltimore area. Someone would present a paper and a discussion would follow. Chairman White would often ask Harry Stack Sullivan to criticize the paper—something Sullivan was perhaps too good at doing. According to one biographer, Sullivan's "...angry comments, sarcasm, and scorching criticism of colleagues and students became legendary."[27] Alfred observed such behavior at the meetings. Once a paper had been 'torn apart' by Sullivan, White would often ask Alfred 'to put it together again'.

At one meeting, the psychiatrist who ran the women's department at St. Elizabeths presented a paper dealing with one of the main problems of psychiatry—also at the heart of Korzybski's work—the issue of adjustment to 'fact' and 'reality'. After her presentation, Sullivan picked and tore away at it much too harshly from Korzybski's point of view. The doctor, who by this time had burst into tears, exclaimed, "My god, if somebody could tell me what a fact or reality is!" At that point, Korzybski's turn came 'to put things together again'. He emphasized that whatever else the terms 'reality' and 'fact' represented, they existed first as words. Neither term could be given a specific meaning outside of a particular context, which had to include the level of abstraction of a particular statement containing the term. Thus, it was fruitless to get into a general theoretical, even metaphysical, argument of the type Sullivan seemed to be driving the group towards. At least some of people at the meeting probably had some familiarity with the Anthropometer. I can imagine Alfred using it there to help illustrate his point. At any rate, the woman was mollified although Sullivan appeared none too pleased.[28]

The Pathology Lab

With White's guidance, St. Elizabeths indeed seemed like the perfect place for Korzybski to learn more about some of the unfortunate extremes of human 'mental' life. White's broad knowledge of biological mechanisms, his background in medicine and neurology, and his wide experience with psychotherapy and with psychiatric patients, would not allow White to overemphasize any single cause or treatment for 'mental' disorders or to leave his compassion behind. Even as the editor of *The Psychoanalytical Review*, White was not bound to Freudian psychoanalysis but was quite open to other schools of psychotherapy, which were then developing. Furthermore, knowing intimately the infectious, toxic, traumatic, and other medical causes for some 'mental' disorders, he was not one to think of psychotherapy as the treatment of choice for every psychiatric illness. Indeed, psychotherapy often didn't seem much of a treatment even for those patients for whom it was deemed appropriate. Of all people White, the superintendent of perhaps the largest and best-run asylum in the world, knew the limitations of psychiatry in the mid-1920s. A lot was known but there was still a lot more to be known (still the case in 2011).

As a result of all this, White had adopted the organism-as-a-whole-in-an-environment viewpoint long before he met Korzybski and undoubtedly reinforced Alfred's caution about his own work. Even though confusion of orders of abstraction seemed to be a general feature observable in the broad range of psychiatric disorders (as well as in everyday misevaluations), both White and Korzybski realized that training to become conscious of abstracting was not necessarily going to reverse the confusion in everyone. Nonetheless, the preventive and therapeutic possibilities of Alfred's work for 'mental' health were still unknown.

White and Korzybski clearly shared a matter of principle (a basic postulate): any manifestation of 'mind'—sanity, insanity, or unsanity—must correlate with some neurological event(s). This meant that psychotherapy, or any form of education for that matter, must also as a matter of principle involve some kind of nervous system-brain event(s)—whether or not they could be detected or understood with 1920s-era methods and theories.

Korzybski's curiosity about the neurology of insanity and sanity had definitely been stimulated at the hospital. For example, he wondered about the people whom he had encountered with the diagnosis of dementia praecox (a term still being used, and which Korzybski favored, for what Bleuler had relabeled "schizophrenia" almost 20 years before). Alfred realized that any diagnostic label used could misleadingly objectify what might constitute nothing more than a "bundle of very loose[ly] connected symptoms."[29] Still, the symptoms in a patient with a typical form of dementia praecox seemed connected enough, however hard to explain them. What was going on in their brains? (Of course, not much was known about what happened in 'normal' people's brains either.) The illness often suddenly manifested itself in young people in their late teens or early twenties who, in the worst cases, could show a seemingly unstoppable course of deterioration. Alfred had seen one such young man in the receiving ward after the medical exam was done. The man had been a soldier. One day he simply walked out of parade formation, returned to the barracks, and went to sleep. He was court-martialed, then sent to jail, then to a military hospital, and then to St. Elizabeths. Alfred talked with him for about two hours. Their conversation seemed normal on one level, but in another way there seemed something odd about the man. As Alfred recalled, the man was "polite with a sort of grin, couldn't be any better. In the meantime he was completely dead. It is beyond description…You feel it."

> And it is a very curious thing, that deadness, what they call it, lack of affective tone, complete deadness. No feeling at all. Polite, responsive, yes, no, this way, everything coherent, *no feeling*. And [on] this ground alone he was confined. No doctor will miss this kind of thing. I couldn't miss it, a layman, so he was confined. I believe I saw him later, three, four months later, and he was completely gone. No more even coherent.[30]

If Alfred wanted to learn as much as he could about the brains of schizophrenics and other people with 'mental' disorders, St. Elizabeths seemed like the perfect place to do that too. Since the hospital had a large patient population, when one died—not an infrequent occurrence—an autopsy was done whenever possible at the hospital's state-of-the-art Blackburn Pathology Laboratory. Alfred attended every autopsy he could. He estimated that he observed about 300 during his two years at the hospital. The autopsy would be done in the lab's operating theatre, which had a balcony where medical students from George Washington and Georgetown Universities could sit and watch the presiding pathologist, either Nolan D.C. Lewis or Walter J. Freeman II, do his work while lecturing about his findings. Alfred liked to watch up close, standing near the doctor on the ground floor.

Nolan D.C. Lewis, also the director of clinical psychiatry at the hospital, had begun his medical career as a neurologist and neuropathologist but had developed his early interests in human behavior by taking additional training in psychology and psychiatry. While becoming quite involved with psychotherapy and psychoanalysis, he maintained his interests in neurology and neuropathology, and did a large number of the autopsies Korzybski observed at the laboratory. Lewis later directed the lab from 1933 until leaving St. Elizabeths in 1936, when he took a teaching post at Columbia University Medical School. He later became the Director of the New York State Psychiatric Institute and Hospital.[31] He and Korzybski maintained contact over the years, with Lewis becoming an Honorary Trustee of the Institute of General Semantics. Following his friend's final wishes, Lewis took care of the autopsy on Alfred's remains in 1950.

Walter Freeman II—trained as a neurologist specializing in neuropathology—had been recently hired by White as the lab's senior medical officer. Young Freeman was known among the medical students as a dynamic teacher. He also expanded and developed the lab facilities, including the hospital's 'brain library' where Alfred spent time studying. As Alfred recalled: "…we conserved the brains—we cut the brain apart microscopically and I don't know what not. We had a beautiful library, so to say, of brains, in jars, with histories and what not—and slices—oh, I don't know—thousands, thousands."[32] Unlike Lewis, Freeman had minimal training in psychiatry or psychotherapy, and apparently little enthusiasm for those disciplines, despite working for William Alanson White. Psychotherapy played no part in the part-time private practice in neurology Freeman established several years later, although he saw a large number of people with psychiatric complaints (at the time not out of the ordinary for neurologists). In his early practice he prescribed drugs (at that time not effective therapeutically for much more than sedation) "or suggested an exercise regime or a change in life style."[33] In 1933, he left St. Elizabeths, having already become one of the earliest advocates of various shock therapies (electrically and drug induced) for mental disorders. Sometime afterwards, he would become the chief American exponent of psychosurgery, specifically frontal lobotomy (destroying nerve tracts by swishing around an ice-pick-like instrument driven into the skull through a tear duct), which he recommended for a wide variety of psychiatric diagnoses.

To White's great credit, when Freeman and his partner were just getting started with the procedure in the late 1930s and wanted White to let them do it at St. Elizabeths, White told Freeman, "It will be a hell of a long while before I'll let you operate on any of my patients."[34] By 1949, although the procedure had become widely accepted and practiced, Lewis—who believed it was being done indiscriminately—had become one of its most vocal critics, as well.[35]

At the pathology lab, Korzybski learned from and had friendly relations with both Lewis and Freeman, who appeared to have something of an unfriendly rivalry. Ultimately, Korzybski's interests and viewpoint were at odds with those of Freeman. Even for his time and despite his apparent brilliance, Freeman demonstrated a simplistic understanding of the complexities of the brain and human behavior. Although I haven't found any documentation of Korzybski's view on lobotomy, it seems unlikely it would have differed much from that of White and Lewis. Though accepting the principle that brain and consciousness/behavior must correlate, Alfred's brain studies had already led him to conclude: "[T]here is very little correspondence in the behavior and the [macroscopic] structure of the brain [on autopsy]." (Freeman's later forays into people's brains focused on this macroscopic level although no one had demonstrated visible defects in the brains of the people, such as schizophrenics, upon whom he was doing the surgery.) For Korzybski, extending a physico-mathematical, process orientation into neurology and psychiatry meant that the main 'action' in the nervous system did not exist at the level of fiber tracts or other gross (visible) brain anatomy. More subtle, invisible, submicroscopic, organism-as-a-whole-in-environment processes had to be involved to explain mentality and behavior. How else to explain the following observation which he recounted years later?

> I remember that fellow who was quite normal in grand parole, means the garden, quite normal but low grade. And when he died and we made an autopsy, he had no brain at all. The cavity was full. It was a bag of pus. No conformation of a brain at all. And yet on the surface he somehow behaved. This was the most interesting brain I saw.[36]

Of course, something appeared visibly wrong with that man's brain, such as it was. But the coherency of his behavior while alive (walking around, smiling, saying "hello", etc.) didn't seem to match the incoherency of the 'mush' they later saw inside his skull. Something coherent must have been happening inside his skull while he was alive, in spite of the presumed loss of distinctiveness in his brain matter.

Before the explosion of molecular biology in the 1950s, colloidal science was an active area of research for trying to understand this submicroscopic realm in the life sciences. Over the next few years Alfred began to look to electro-colloidal processes in order to explain what he had seen. For it had become clear to him that neurological events—related to 'thinking','feeling', and other aspects of human activity—could *not* be understood very well just by looking at macroscopically (or even microscopically) visible brain structures. He knew that more subtle brain mechanisms *had to* exist, awaiting exploration. Alfred had begun to understand disturbed 'thinking' as significantly related to such subtle neural events (whatever they consisted of and whether or not they could be detected by the science of the day). Whatever methods could be devised to make 'thinking' less disturbed, necessarily had to change neural processes for the better as well. Indeed, he considered 'thinking' and related neural events as different dimensions of a single, ongoing process.

He had spiraled back to the spiral theory presented in *Manhood of Humanity*. Viewing 'thinking', 'feeling', 'consciousness'—in other words, *abstracting*—in neurological terms would become more and more important to the viewpoint Alfred was developing for his book. At the end of 1926, his second year at St. Elizabeths, Alfred—who had begun reading a lot of neurology—read C. Judson Herrick's *The Brains of Rats and Men* and noted the following statement, which he later quoted in his book:

> To some extent, the practice of thinking, deciding, feeling, appreciating, and sympathizing molds the personality of the thinker. Presumably, the stable patterns of cortical association are changed by the performance of these acts just as on a lower plane muscles are changed by systematic exercise.[37]

Alfred's physico-mathematical analysis of human behavior in terms of 'logic', premises, space-time orientation, neurological mechanisms, etc., may have seemed cold and overly intellectual to some. For Alfred, it was not. Indeed, at St. Elizabeths he began to undergo some deep 'emotional' changes of his own. The changes had resulted from observing and talking with patients and using the imaginative skills he had developed from his physico-mathematical training. Eventually he realized: his imaginative reconstruction of people's life situations (in terms of—and visualizing, etc.—the underlying assumptions they lived by, what and how they abstracted, etc.) helped him to reduce his own psychological 'sore spots' and thus deal with all sorts of humans and human reactions, with a minimum of upset. He described the process in detail to a seminar group at the end of 1948:

> ...I had enough imagination—mathematical training—imagination, to fancy myself in such and such a situation or with such and such impulses. My work has been done only because I was able to be my own guinea pig and my own laboratory. This is a very important thing. Now for instance with students—the number goes by the thousands, you know—in the past I knew intimately the life of every student. I imagined myself, I imagined how—imagination, engineering, mathematics, physics—how would I react under such and such conditions, how would I react under such and such impulses. I deliberately lived through all of that and it left me personally immune.*[38]

Anthropometers for Sale

The change in himself he noticed toward the end of 1925 related in particular to the Anthropometer. He had finally gotten the patent for it in May and was in the process of

---

* Korzybski insisted on the necessity of 'introspection' for a scientific psychiatry and "psycho-logics" (see *Science and Sanity*, 5th Edition, pp. xlii-xliii and 359-360).

manufacturing models for distribution and sale. Although he had found a company in Washington, D.C. to machine-make the parts, he was working on his prototypes and putting together the final products at home. He probably had one or another Anthropometer in front of his eyes for a good part of each day. At home, he would take his own model and play with the hanging strings and labels.

On his own personal set he had "many and different labels made out of ebony, box wood (white), rosewood, redwood, mahogany and walnut."[39] He would move his finger vertically to the different shapes and hues of wood representing different levels of abstraction, saying to himself, "This is not that." On the Anthropometer with three Human Objects (with labels) hanging from the Parabola, he would move his finger horizontally from the Animal Object to each of the different Human Objects, saying "This is not that", etc. This pointing reinforced the notion that humans abstract differently from animals and that every individual abstracts from any event differently than any other individual.

If verbal understanding had been enough then working with the Anthropometer would have left him, the formulator of the General Theory of Time-Binding and the Anthropometer, unaffected. Yet he strongly believed his continuous contemplation of the Anthropometer, by keeping it in view, handling it, etc., had freed his thinking-feeling (he had ceased to see these as separate) and was helping him in his continuing efforts at self-correction—he was catching himself in at least one good "Fidoism" (confusion of orders of abstraction) per week.

No, it was not just a matter of verbal, 'intellectual' understanding. He had met any number of eminent scientists who would acknowledge some aspect of his theory as something "every schoolboy knows", and then at the next moment open their mouths and violate it in practice. Rather than just being able to give verbal assent and talk nicely about it, one had to internalize the theory (get it into the nervous system deeply) to give it any usefulness. He had learned for himself that working with the Anthropometer helped to do that—indeed he didn't see how anyone could adequately apply his General Theory without using it.[40]

In the first part of 1926, he was completing the manufacture of 100 Anthropometers. As he was finishing up in May he wrote to Haywood that the apartment looked like a "regular factory".[41] He was under no illusion that he and Mira were going to make a profit on sales. On the contrary, he was prepared to sell some at cost or give some away. Until his book came out he wanted to do what he could to sustain and—even better—increase the momentum of interest in his work.

Some interest did still exist. Sales of *Manhood* though slow had not stopped altogether. There were still some articles and reviews getting published around the country that at least mentioned him and his "inspirational" viewpoint (Alfred might consider that a damning term). He had continued to do some speaking. Even his old article "The Brotherhood of Doctrines" had been 'revived from the dead' and finally gotten into print—twice. (In 1924 Haywood had finally managed to publish it in *The Builder* and it had then been republished in the July-August-September 1925 issue of *The New Orient*, Syud Hossain's New York City-based, *Journal of International Fellowship*.) In 1925, Alfred had been taken by surprise when he saw a notice announcing a "Summer School in Creative and Humanistic Education" at Olivet College in Olivet, Michigan. The theme of the 12-day conference, sponsored by (of all groups) the Fellowship for a Christian Social Order, was based on his work: "...It will be an introductory course in the Science and Art of Human Engineering...[with] Readings from Korzybski and Keyser's "Mathematical Philosophy."[42] And since he had become better known at St. Elizabeths and in the Baltimore-Washington psychiatric community, some psychiatrists had gotten interested in the possible applications of his work to their patients.

Whatever limited impact his work had made until then, he felt he had to get more people interested for the impact he wanted to make with his book. As a trial measure to accelerate interest, making a limited distribution of a preliminary batch of Anthropometers to a mainly scientific and/or already interested audience seemed reasonable. Maybe it would even help him get a publisher. With each model, he would provide a copy of his 1924 *Time-Binding* paper (to anyone who didn't already have it, since he was running short of reprints) which first described the Anthropometer. However, the 1924 paper wouldn't do by itself. He was writing a supplemental article, based on his latest discoveries, to include with it. Since 1924, new implications of the General Theory had emerged. And he had also become much more aware of the issues involved in *training* in the new orientation with the Anthropometer. He was not offering a panacea. He was learning for himself and from the experience of a few people like Haywood, how much exposure and repetition such training entailed. In this new second paper on *Time-Binding: The General Theory*, he would elaborate on the depth and width of the General Theory and provide some needed guidelines for using the Anthropometer. The two papers together would serve as his preliminary sketch for the coming book.

Time-Binding: The General Theory (Second Paper)

Alfred had another reason for writing a second paper and distributing it with the Anthropometer, even to the small select audience he intended. Since the 'cat was already out of the bag' about the Anthropometer and his General Theory, he hoped to reduce the possibility of a cheap popularizer stealing his thunder before his book was out. It was bad enough that some people already dismissed his work as platitudes and trivia. He didn't want people to actually trivialize it according to a superficial presentation. To embrace it as a fad, give it lip service, and make only limited applications might be as damaging as outright dismissal.

Writing and editing the second paper and getting it into print took up a large part of his time in 1926. On March 13, he had given a presentation at St. Elizabeths for the monthly meeting of The Washington Psychopathology Society on "The Scientific Method and Psychopathology". The material from that presentation and from his previous talk in June 1925 served as his raw material for the paper. He continued to rework it when he went to New York City in April to speak at a forum organized by Jesse Lee Bennett at the Labor Temple School. While there he attended a dinner party at Jeliffe's house in the city where he finally met C.K. Ogden in person. Then he went up to Rye, N.Y., a suburb north of the city where he stayed with Roy Haywood for a week. Haywood had by this time left *The Builder* and had moved to New York to edit *The New York Masonic Outlook*. He had been working intensively with the Anthropometer and inspired Alfred with his progress report on his self-improvements.

Probably during this trip or just after he returned to Washington, Korzybski met fellow Pole, anthropologist Bronislaw Malinowski from the London School of Economics, then in the U.S. on a trip sponsored by the Rockefeller Foundation. Korzybski attended a lecture given by him where the two men were introduced.[43] They began corresponding and subsequently developed warm personal relations. Impressed with Alfred and his work, Malinowski later became an honorary trustee of the Institute of General Semantics, a position he kept until his death in 1942.

In May, June, and July, Alfred was back in Washington writing and editing. Mira had gone to Massachusetts to paint portraits, but had stopped in New York to work with Haywood on Alfred's manuscript. Both she and Roy had concerns about the simplicity of the writing for a popular audience. They both suggested the advantage of turning the Anthropometer upside down, since they thought some people might be confused by the fact that the 'higher' levels of abstraction were below the 'lower' levels on the model. Alfred had previously considered this but decided against it. He wrote to Roy:

...<u>Granting</u> the arguments of you both, the disadvantages ... we will use [terms] "lower and lower levels of investigation or <u>deeper</u> and deeper levels["], so it goes <u>down</u>, if it does not show higher and higher order of a[b]stractions <u>it shows</u> the <u>deeper</u> levels. If we upturn th[e]n it would show the <u>higher</u> orders of abstractions but would <u>not</u> show the <u>deeper</u> levels. The event with its <u>infinity</u> of characteristics should not be turned earth way but sky way. The present structure corresponds to <u>human</u> structure, the event representing knowledge (brain) object eyes (senses) label (mouth)[.] The label <u>MUST hang</u> on to the object which is only possible in the present structure. The <u>manipulation</u> of the labels which is important [to] the training would be made very clumsy, as clumsy as it is handy now, all of which <u>hang</u> together (impossible when up) etc etc besides a very serious item that the darned thing would be <u>ugly and hard to play with</u> it would lose all of its attractiveness and simplicity. [44]

A number of years later the issue of upturning Korzybski's model of the abstracting process became a major bone of contention between Alfred and his student S. I. Hayakawa, who made the reversal a major part of his popular version of Korzybski's work in the early 1940s and thereafter.

In the meantime, Alfred had also gotten copies of his manuscript to Keyser, Bell, Carmichael, White, Sullivan, and Graven and made use of a number of their suggestions to revise it. He worked on through August, including the first two weeks of the month that he spent back at Haywood's place in Rye, supposedly vacationing. On the way back to Washington, Korzybski stopped in New York City for a brief visit with Keyser. Mrs. Keyser, who had been suffering with severe arthritis for a number of years, was recovering from a serious bout of pneumonia. Alfred worried about both her and Keyser. Nonetheless, Keyser was able to peruse and edit the final version of Alfred's paper. By September 1, Alfred had sent the completed manuscript to a local printer in Washington.

Alfred and Mira had planned to attend the Sixth International Congress of Philosophy from September 13 to 17 at Harvard. Alfred had even made a room reservation. He had planned to go to New York, hitch a ride with Walter, pick up Mira in Beverly Farms, Massachusetts where she had been working, and from there go to the Congress in Cambridge. Originally A.N. Vasiliev—the esteemed Russian mathematician with whom Alfred had corresponded since 1924—planned to attend too, having had a paper accepted there. Alfred had looked forward to meeting him in person. However, either because of ill health or financial difficulties, Vasiliev had decided not to go. (Earlier in the year Alfred had tried to get some paid speaking engagements lined up for him at various U.S. universities and other mathematics forums—with no luck.) Alfred might have made more of an effort to go if Vasiliev had indeed attended, but with the printer's proofs to deal with Alfred and Mira decided the trip to the Congress would be a waste of time and money. About a week before the Congress began, they decided not to go.

Correcting the proofs proved a major 'pain in the neck'. The original type size was too small and hard to read so the type was made larger. Subsequently 32 pages blossomed into a 54 page booklet plus cover. The final page proofs were back at the printer on October 11. Even then, the printer's 'gremlins' seemed to be working overtime. The page numbers had gotten mixed up and Alfred had to correct them by hand. But on October 21, Alfred finally had the new pamphlet. He wrote to Keyser, "I feel relieved that the thing is in print already, it has cost me so much pains, that I hardly expect that I would be able to go through it again." He would send it out with each of the limited number of Anthropometers he was making available. Until his book was published in 1933, *Time-Binding: The General Theory* (the First and Second papers)—would provide the major statement in print of Korzybski's developing work.

A Non-Aristotelian System

In the 1926 paper, Korzybski announced what he was formulating with his general theory of time-binding—a new "non-aristotelian system".† Aristotle and his followers had formed the aristotelian system of postulates and methods ('metaphysics' and 'logic') that could be shown to underlie euclidean geometry and newtonian physics, among other things. It included:

> [Aristotle's] postulate that...man is an animal, the postulate of the uniqueness of subject-predicate representation, the postulate of cause in the form [Aristotle] had it, the elementalism of "percept" and "concept," [Aristotle's] theory of definitions, his postulate of cosmical validity of grammar [the aristotelian 'laws' of 'logic'], his predilection for intensional [definitional and verbally oriented] methods, etc., etc.[45]

This aristotelian system was also at the base of what Korzybski called the "scientific, or public unconscious,"[46] the "doctrinal surrounding"[47] into which children were still getting born. It pervaded everyday language and psychology.

Although Korzybski acknowledged previous non-aristotelian formulators, no one had created an overarching non-aristotelian *system* for science and life. That was what Korzybski, nothing if not bold, proposed to do now—create a system as broad in scope as what Aristotle had attempted much earlier. He claimed that the system of related postulates and methods he was unveiling could be shown to underlie the non-euclidean revolution in mathematics and the non-newtonian physics of Einstein (and the newer quantum mechanics as well). His postulates, paralleling the aristotelian ones listed above, included the following:

> I accept man as a man, use functional [relational] representation whenever needed, expand the two-term relation cause-effect into a series, introduce organism as-a-whole form of representation in the language of time-binding, orders of abstractions, accept postulational methods as the foundation for a theory of definitions and *therefore of meaning*, which bridges the conscious with the unconscious, introduce modern "logical existence," relations, differential and four dimensional methods, use the extensional [non-verbal 'fact' oriented] methods, etc., etc., and so build up my system.[48]

Embodied in the Anthropometer, the methods (emanating from his postulates) provided a basis, he claimed, for a new applied science of humanity, or "Humanology". His forthcoming book would treat in greater detail what he could only present in outline here. (Themes noted in the above list, or covered in a paragraph or two in the paper, would require separate chapters in

---

† By this time, Korzybski had ceased the common practice of always capitalizing "aristotelian" (and some other adjectives created from proper names, e.g., "euclidean", "newtonian", etc.), probably because he was referring not primarily to Aristotle, nor even to his school of thought, but rather to a general orientation that went well beyond them. I have continued Korzybski's usage in this book.

the book to expound in detail.) He knew he would have a 'tough sell'. Drawing from and seeking to replenish the roots of numerous scientific fields, his general theory of time-binding—a non-aristotelian system—had no academic home. This hybrid creature, interdisciplinary in scope, resisted pinning down as either 'philosophy' or 'science' because it had elements of both.

Without question, his examination of the underlying assumptions in various fields could be considered from one point of view as 'philosophical'. Korzybski even acknowledged this in an offhanded way when he declared in the paper, "I...accept modern science (1926) as my metaphysics."[49] (This seems disingenuous about his own contribution. After all, he had needed to abstract from the sciences he had studied to a higher or a deeper level in order to develop his theory.) Nonetheless, he was also emphasizing here the scientific orientation of his work. 20th century 'philosophy' was becoming ever more entrenched in verbalistic speculation and 'metaphysics' detached from scientific/mathematical knowledge and practical application. True, Korzybski's questions about "the structure of human knowledge" traditionally came from the philosophical discipline of epistemology. (Of course, any view of human knowledge also implied some notion of what the world was like, a question of 'metaphysics'.) Yet as far as Alfred was concerned, these questions could no longer be fruitfully dealt with speculatively. Instead one must bring to bear on them the most up-to-date knowledge of mathematics, physics, biology, neuroscience, psychiatry, etc. If this put him outside the fold of academic philosophy, so be it. Alfred forthrightly considered his work "a branch of natural science".

But while these traditional questions from philosophy could no longer depend on the traditional speculative methods of philosophers, the work of scientists could no longer depend on a naive 'philosophy' about not having postulates, i.e., assumptions or premises. Korzybski preferred to view this as bringing not a philosophical but rather a more forthright mathematical view into all of the sciences. Indeed, in this paper he reiterated a point he had made in the 1924 one: "…owing to the fact that we must start with undefined terms…all human knowledge is postulational in structure and therefore mathematical,…"[50] The "empire of sound logic" he had announced before in "The Brotherhood of Doctrines" had too narrow a base. 'Logic' was not, after all, exactly equivalent to mathematics, nor could it provide an adequate grounding for mathematics or for the non-aristotelian revision he wanted to foment. On the contrary, mathematics (in the broadened sense Korzybski was giving it) provided the basis for any possible 'logic'. The two *Time-Binding* papers formed a clear public declaration of his liberation from Russell and Whitehead. In addition, Alfred was declaring his rejection of any form of "just the facts ma'am" positivism. No 'fact' was simple. (In a letter written in 1927 to C. K. Ogden, Korzybski suggested that his viewpoint deserved the label "postulationalism" rather than "positivism".)[51]

In the 1926 paper, he again emphasized mathematics as a language (a form of representation) and a form of human behavior continuous with daily language/behavior. The psychological processes that made mathematics so successful should be studied. Indeed, the Anthropometer and other methods he was developing had come from such a study. In the abundance of notions treated in the paper, it might be difficult to see, but Alfred's emphasis here on mathematics as language and behavior put him squarely in a minority camp of formulators about mathematics. (Gaston Bachelard would later elaborate similar views.) Not many mathematicians saw their work in this way or considered its possible therapeutic value, much less made use of it. And how many psychiatrists and others interested in 'mental' hygiene, saw mathematics as a field with significance for their field. Yet who could deny the fact of mathematics as a human activity elaborated in symbolism, an activity exquisitely suited for making postulates and their implications clear? It provided a kind of "higher psychiatry" as Korzybski put it, for "making the unconscious conscious"—what psychotherapists needed to do, if they wanted to do any good.

Korzybski's prose in the 1926 paper had vigor, as when he wrote,

...all human life is a permanent dance between different orders of abstractions. ...But as yet mankind as a whole (not a few academicians perhaps) is totally unaware of the extreme benefit as well as dangers of this "dance." [52]

The paper's guidelines on application, included a suggestive analysis (with diagram and examples) on using the Anthropometer in any kind of human decision-making. It juxtaposed two basic modes of dealing with higher order abstractions. One mode, dynamic conscious abstracting by a hypothetical "Ideal Observer" as free as possible from preconceived notions and thus creatively perceiving the world anew, starkly contrasted with its opposite, the static unconscious mode of abstracting done by a typically un-sane (perhaps even 'insane') "Smith....who habitually jumps his levels (mixes his orders of abstractions) and rather makes a business out of it." [53]

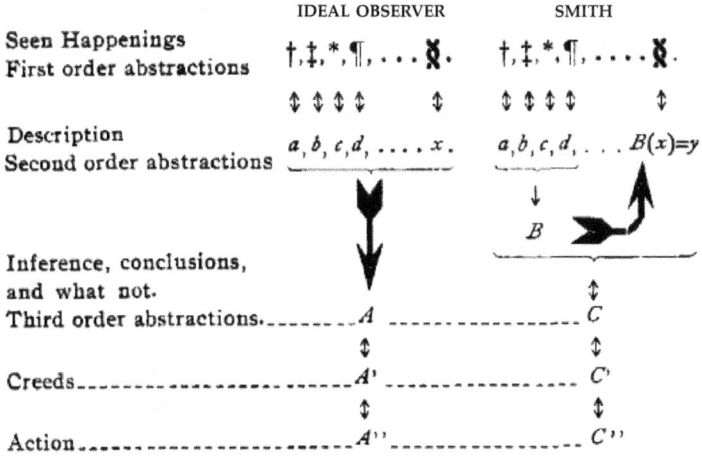

Abstracting, Ideal or Distorted

The 1926 paper, dense with interconnected formulations (some sketched in only a few words or paragraphs, some still so newly emergent that he didn't yet have distinguishing terms for them), undoubtedly put a challenge to the reader. It would require numerous readings to bear fruit in application. But Korzybski was writing as much for himself as for any presumed dedicated reader. With this 1926 supplement to his 1924 paper, he had the outline and program for his future work. (Notably, neither the noun "semantics" nor the adjective "semantic" appear anywhere in either paper.) In the last paragraph of the text he wrote, "The material presented here so roughly is being worked out in book form under the title *Time-Binding: The General Theory, An Introduction to Humanology*, to be published shortly." 'Shortly'—a variable term.

Chapter 31
"THE TRAGEDY OF MY WORK"

With Anthropometers ready and copies of the second *Time-Binding* paper in print, those willing to experiment had what they needed to give Alfred's work a trial run. At the end of October 1926, he sent out some Anthropometers, with the paper, to a few friends. Other people just got copies of the second paper. Over the next few months he began to get initial responses. Some people didn't seem to understand what he was attempting to do. Others felt they did and said, in effect—"So what?" There was much polite interest. He felt relief that at least close friends like E. T. Bell, Carmichael, Keyser, and White, considered him on the right track. Bell, for example, who had just moved from the University of Washington to the Mathematics Department of the California Institute of Technology, wrote on November 21, 1926:

Dear Korzybski:

Till now I have not had time to thank you for the generous and interesting gifts of the A [Anthropometer] and the G.T [General Theory]. I have been trying to teach the kid [Bell's young son] to use the A, and he has succeeded quite well...As he is of an essentially blasphemous and irreverent nature he has tried to teach his cat — without success.

Would it not be well to include with the A a full printed set of directions, with examples? Otherwise it is a matter of individual instruction in each case.

I am looking forward to the book on the G.T. Make it as clear as the M. of H [*Manhood of Humanity*]...[1]

Bell's friendly letter provided just one example of the respectful attention Korzybski was getting from portions of the scientific and the broader intellectual communities, mainly in America. That kind of response must have given him some sense of satisfaction and a reason for continuing the task of writing the book.

He needed encouragement because he knew the path toward favorable reception of his work had many obstacles. In his letter, Bell had inadvertently pointed to one of them: "I see that G. N. Lewis [a world-renowned professor of chemistry at the University of California—Berkeley] has used some of your ideas in his new 'Anatomy of Science'—Yale U. Press [1926]—particularly levels of abstraction."[2] Reading Lewis's repeated references to the process of abstraction in the first chapter of *The Anatomy of Science* makes Bell's conclusion seem likely. However, Lewis's book makes no mention of Korzybski or his work. (Lewis, whom Alfred didn't appear to know, could well have read and unconsciously assimilated one or more of Alfred's post-*Manhood*, pre-1926 papers since Korzybski knew people at Berkeley who would have had the papers.)

Alfred had certainly wondered about the unconscious, and therefore unacknowledged, influence he may have had on others. It seemed easy for some people to unconsciously absorb ideas from his work; perhaps because it clarified what they already knew. This seemed to have happened with H. S. Jennings and others. There is no evidence Alfred felt any animus toward these individuals or considered them plagiarists. Still, the failure to mention him as a source didn't help the spreading of his ideas. As he wrote to Jesse Bennett the following summer, he considered it one of his obstacles—"part of the tragedy of my work".[3]

Whatever intrinsic value he gave to his own work and to whatever extent he wanted to benefit science and humanity by means of it, his work was also a means for him—a matter of "the bottom line". To be forgotten would not do if he was going to have at least a fighting chance to eventually earn a decent income for himself and Mira from his writing, speaking, and teaching. Alas, in order to get adequate recognition, he was going to have to overcome the 'unackowleged influence' factor by working extra hard to promote his efforts. As he wrote to Carmichael, "The developments seem to be far beyond my original expectations, yet the lack of understanding I meet everywhere and lack of appreciation is so appalling that I am sorry some times that I started the whole d....d business. But, it is too late now to go back." [4]

On the Borderland

There were other parts of 'the tragedy of his work'. A significant part of the 'tragedy' lay in the very nature of the work itself. Starting from the notion of time-binding, he had staked out a limited, if broad, territory to study—the structure of human knowledge in relation to behavior. Moving epistemology from speculative philosophy into the realm of science, he had forthrightly outlined what the sciences and mathematics of the 1920s could contribute to the inquiry—knowledge about knowledge—and had sought to make it practical as well. His interdisciplinary discipline (the word "interdisciplinary" hadn't been invented yet),[5] on the borderland between philosophy and many specific sciences, had no established name. He had given up "human engineering" and didn't really like the term "humanology". There were certainly no academic departments in it. And he hadn't found any other "humanologists". The people he considered scientific peers were not peers in his specific work. Who else in the mid-1920s was trying to make a methodological synthesis of the sciences of the time in order to establish an empirically up-to-date and applied epistemology as a foundation for a science of man?

Psychiatry, the medical study of abnormal psychology, was important for this program. That's why he had gone to St. Elizabeths. While there, he had solidified the link he had seen between the behavior of mathematicians and scientists when working at their best, and the so-called 'insane'—extremes of behavior that many found odd to consider together.

Analysis of the methods and language used by each group had further exposed a partially hidden system of orientation that with few exceptions seemed to dominate the 'thinking' of mankind. Korzybski called it "aristotelianism". This orientation of 'aristotelian' assumptions actually preceded Aristotle and involved various forms of confusion of orders of abstraction. The logic of Aristotle and his followers, when taken as expressing self-evident laws of thought and existence, simply formalized these assumptions. The assumptions had thereby become even more bound up as a system into the unconscious everyday speech/behavior patterns of most people, including scientists and mathematicians. Alfred was attempting to replace the aristotelian *system* (not the logic) with a more general alternative orientation—a new structure, a non-aristotelian system—that kept what remained useful of the old. Good luck!

Admittedly, every significant advance in the special sciences seemed to be moving in a non-aristotelian direction. But efforts in the various sciences remained mostly scattered. So although much of what Alfred had to say could be viewed as "old stuff", what he considered original about his work was his effort to coordinate the scattered pieces of knowledge into an applied system. He had presented a program for a radically new vision for the sciences and life. He hoped it could help remove aristotelian blockages and accelerate advances in human knowledge and well-being. But if he was going to get other people to sign onto his program—other scientists in particular—he was going to have to flesh out his system in much more detail. Another part of the 'tragedy'.

He already had too much material, and more was rolling in every day: for example, the newest work in quantum mechanics. He was going to have to make sure he grasped it all well enough to show how it touched his concerns. Until the book was published, he would often lament to his closest friends that he had tackled a job that seemed beyond the strength, brain, and knowledge of a single man.

He did feel most grateful to the mathematicians and scientists who had so far been willing to comment upon and criticize the parts of his writing that touched on their areas of expertise. As he continued to work on the book, he would depend even more on such expert peer review to make sure the material he used for his synthesis was up-to-date and accurate. What would continue to disappointed him was how few of these scientists and mathematicians seemed willing to commit themselves to express much of an overall opinion about his synthesis, let alone embrace his program. Nonetheless, he could understand. How could he blame anyone for not wanting to explore this scientific-philosophical borderland with him, along unfamiliar paths that had lots of 'thorns' and 'prickles'? In the meantime, as a pioneer borderland explorer, he risked the possibility that both philosophers and scientists might just consider him an illegitimate interloper into their well-fenced, established domains.

Graven

In a certain sense, Alfred's basic thesis could be boiled down to a few seemingly simple, even childish, statements: "An event is not an object, a word (label) is not the object, and a statement about a statement is not the same statement."[6] The ramifications were not childishly simple, however. Not only did they imply a theoretical revision of all the sciences. They also led to practical techniques for the re-education of people's 'thinking' which also had psychotherapeutic implications—or at least implications for preventive mental health.

With the heavy theoretical implications of his work and its potentially far-reaching practical consequences, Alfred's two *Time-Binding* papers would simply not suffice. He had to rally enough interest in his work for laypeople and educators to even consider trying it. If it proved useful, more people would apply it and do research with and in it. He would then have a chance to make a living from it. However, because of its heavy scientific basis, he felt he first needed to gain acceptance among mathematicians, scientists, psychiatrists, etc. To do that, he was going to have to spell out the theory in much greater detail in the forthcoming book and provide empirical evidence of the effectiveness of his methods. With Philip Graven, the brilliant young psychiatrist who had been driving him to the hospital, Korzybski felt he had in hand a solution to the problem of gathering the first round of evidence.

For the last several months, Alfred had been giving Graven a private course of instruction, for several hours a day. After medical school at the University of Chicago's Rush Medical College, Graven had gone to Vienna to specialize in psychiatry and study psychoanalysis with both Wilhelm Stekel and Sandor Ferenczi. He had worked at St. Elizabeths for about a year when Korzybski arrived.[7] In addition to his work at the hospital, Graven had a private psychotherapy practice and had recently begun to apply Alfred's methods, including the use of the Anthropometer, to his patients.

Korzybski realized, "...If the preventive claims [for his work] are true there should be some direct cures in a theoretically small and narrow class of mental ills, but which in life happen to be very numerous."[8] Graven was already getting significant preliminary results. So, at least to start with, Korzybski hoped the gifted and enthusiastic young doctor, who had recently published two case studies in *The Psychoanalytic Review*, would provide an appendix on psychiatry with some case studies for the book.

He also realized that any empirical investigation of his work, case study or otherwise, would have to make allowances for the fact that it was not a panacea. And among those who might be able to benefit from it, verbal assent was not enough. Observable results would take time. From the few people who had actually made a concerted effort to apply it so far—including Korzybski himself—he had found that it could take a number of months of intensive study and work with the Anthropometer, to internalize the non-aristotelian viewpoint sufficiently to make a significant difference in a person's behavior. He would continue to emphasize this point for the rest of his career. But it was a point that many people found difficult to grasp—both those dismissing his work as platitudes and those who verbally approved it.

Building a Boat in the Middle of a Churning Sea

In addition, his theoretical difficulties seemed profound. It had become clear that if he was going to "bring ordinary language closer to mathematics",[9] he was going to have to retool ordinary language. Indeed the language would embody his system. As he had roughly expressed it in a letter to Rainich earlier in the year, most people had not gone beyond vague agreement with his "recipe for making geniuses":

> "Weaken phobias, knock out dogmatism, make the mental processes as free [as possible] from preconceived doctrines which are unconscious and which we cannot abandon" that's the general rule, a rule vaguely known but which stopped short <u>before language</u>. <u>Language was not supposed to be a doctrine</u>. My general theory goes one step deeper (lower) and recognizes that as all human knowledge has mathematical structure…And when we <u>open our mouth</u> a doctrine flies already. Let's silence ourselves by ruthless questioning, as we must come finally to some undefined terms, and to "matter" "space" "time" "continuity" "infinity" etc which as [a] starting point are a creed. Of course with [a] new conception of these entities (?) we have to reconstruct the whole d…d show." [10]

"To reconstruct the whole d…d [damned] show." This was like trying to rebuild a falling-apart, leaky, old boat while you were in it and floating in the middle of a churning sea. You could expect some discomfort. Part of the old aristotelian 'boat' involved objectifying higher order terms such as absolute "space" and absolute "time" or "thinking" and "feeling" and considering them as separate 'things' while forgetting necessary relationships. Rebuilding 'the boat' meant going all the way with the "organism as a whole" approach and abandoning such language or else using it only with awareness. At this point, Alfred had started to put quotation marks around such terms as "space", "time", "senses","mind", "perception", "conception", "thinking", and "feeling", etc., in order to flag them. To eschew these terms when formulating seriously required replacing them with "organism as a whole" forms of representation, terms such as "time-binding", "abstractions on different orders", many of the mathematical terms such as "relation", "order", "function", etc. In this case, using the new labels would help one to orient oneself to new non-verbal actualities, instead of obscuring them.

An adult had to make a concerted effort to do this. One had to consciously work to develop a habit of talking differently, not just talking about talking differently. That required a different view of language as well, since many people found it easy to objectify the term "language" and treat it as if it was entirely discrete and set off from other aspects of the process of abstracting. If no one could step outside of the process of abstracting, then the only choice a person had about it was whether to keep more or less conscious of it. In the old lingo, one's 'mind' mediated one's knowledge of anything. And it seemed all too easy for people to treat their 'minds' like 'windows' which they looked through but didn't see. Alfred was trying to get people to see the 'window' and to see, among other things, the obscuring, distorting 'dirt'—some of it linguistic—that they had gotten used to ignoring. First, he had had to look at his own 'dirty window' and he knew it could be hard work even for some of his intelligent friends like Haywood and Glover, who took him seriously.

Both men had regaled him with objections, wondering whether working with the Anthropometer was too 'cerebral' since it only dealt with "thinking" and not with "feelings". But as Alfred pointed out to each of them, one could allocate a so-called "feeling" to the "object" level of the Anthropometer just as well as a pencil or a plate. "Feelings" existed as non-verbal, lower-order abstractions. And once one opened one's mouth to talk about those "feelings", the doctrines would inevitably fly. This "thinking" associated with "feelings" could then have an effect on ongoing "feelings", etc. So, of course, you *could* work on your "feelings" (which had to involve some "thinking") with the Anthropometer. You had *better* do so if you wanted to develop your consciousness of abstracting. Alfred was not only doing this personal work on himself, he was developing a system, including the language, for doing so.

And the language of the system was still not clear and accurate enough for him because he didn't yet have enough clarity about the system. Major portions of it were only now coming into his awareness. (Was he discovering or inventing them or both?) For example, elaborating on Ritter's original usage, he had previously formulated the term "elementalism" to refer to objectifying the verbal separation of what does not exist entirely separate in the organism-as-a-whole.

Korzybski had also long seen the parallel of such organism-as-a-whole usage with Einstein's and Minkowski's abandonment of absolute "space" and "time" in favor of the more structurally correct term "space-time". He had written about it in the second *Time-Binding* paper. He was just getting to the next step—to move to a higher order of abstraction and to deliberately extend the notion of elementalism to include usages outside of biological science such as absolute "space" and "time". (He had already been doing this informally.) This then required finding a more general term than "organism-as-a-whole" to cover terms such as "space-time". (Part of what he was doing, after all, was creating a language about language.) He had to invent the term—"non-elementalism". It would take about another year before he started using it and talking about "non-elementalistic language".[11] The principle of non-elementalism consisted of remembering to distrust the verbal splitting ("elementalism") of what does not exist as split in the non-verbal world since "...there is *no* such thing as an object in absolute isolation."[12] Non-elementalism would emerge as a major premise of the non-aristotelian system.

Other formulations had begun to surface in his working vocabulary. For example, in the second *Time-Binding* paper he had referred for the first time in print to his preference for "extensional methods" and "the extensional attitude". The term "extensional" had originated in formal logic and referred to definitions given by enumerating examples or pointing to non-verbal experiences. An "intensional" definition, on the other hand, involved defining a word with other words. By the end of 1926, Korzybski had begun to extend the use of these terms to refer to a person's general orientation. An extensional attitude or orientation involved primarily orienting oneself to non-verbal 'facts'—consciousness of abstracting, sanity. An intensional attitude involved orienting oneself primarily in terms of verbal definitions—confusing orders of abstracting, unsanity, insanity. (Of course, one could use intensional definitions without necessarily behaving intensionally.)

In his paper, Alfred had related the extensional attitude to the "the principle of individualization," or the "the atomistic principle," the notion that, as he would later put it, "...the world is made up of absolute individuals, each different and unique, although interconnected [remembering non-elementalism]."[13] This principle, elaborated over the next few years, would eventually become his premise of non-identity, what Robert P. Pula called "...his [Korzybski's] forthright challenge to the heart of aristotelianism—*and* its non-Western, equally essentialistic counterparts."[14] But at the end of 1926, he hadn't quite gotten there explicitly. In the meantime, it seemed clear that mathematics provided a unique language for extensionalizing, dealing with individuals as well as relationships. In the paper, he noted how simple mathematical means could be brought into ordinary language, i.e., using numerical "indexes" to provide unique names for individuals in a category. He had already started to use them in his own speech and writing, as well as using dates (temporal indexes) with terms such as "science", e.g., "science (1926)" in the second *Time-Binding* paper. Some people considered such language an affectation, but what better way to remind oneself to see the 'window' of ones own abstracting process and not just naively 'look through' it?

Over the next year, he would also come up with a better label for the characteristic of some terms he had already formulated as "multi-dimensional"—terms like "yes", "no", and many others, whose unique context of 'meaning' included the orders of abstractions they were used on. He would now call them "multiordinal terms" which reflected the multiordinal, many-leveled abstracting process and the multiordinal nature of the world. The multiordinality of terms explained how "Yes, We Have No Bananas" could seem like fun but wasn't necessarily nonsense.

His system was growing as he worked out its implications, connected it to various scientific advances, showed relationships between formulations, and sought new structurally appropriate terms. His efforts to achieve greater generality involved dredging into his own unconscious to pass from one order of abstraction to a higher ('deeper') one, and then spiraling back with what he had found. This meant getting the living 'feel' of every generalization he came up with, i.e., translating each higher-order abstraction into a first-order, non-verbal one, i.e., a picture, an object, an action, an imagined experience, etc. Working to get the 'feel' of 'ideas' in this way—exciting and grueling work—was a procedure he later recommended to his readers and students

Pressed for Time

Every so often, Alfred would apologize/complain to one or another of his friends about the slowness with which the book was coming along. He felt a time pressure to finish it. Even his time spent working at the hospital, as necessary as it may have been for the development of his work, had seemed to him like a diversion from writing. By the fall of 1926, he was ready to leave St. Elizabeths and devote himself full-time to getting the book done.

Part of the time pressure he felt involved a pull to get back to Poland. He had been gone now for over 10 years. His mother would write from Warsaw and complain. Family business never seemed to be going well. Although he and Mira would send money, it seemed nothing much was going to get straightened out until he got back home.

On the other hand he didn't look forward to dealing with his mother on a daily basis. Also since he was formulating and writing in English and had developed a network of interested and helpful friends in the United States, he felt he had to stay in the U.S. until he finished the book. He hoped he could get it done soon. But it had become apparent; the process was simply going to take longer than the impatient part of him demanded. In the meantime, he was suspended between the U.S.and Poland.

Early in October, he went to Philadelphia for a few days to meet Mira, who was finally coming home to him after a summer of painting commissions in Massachusetts. They were planning to wrap things up in Washington over the next few months. They held the lease for the apartment in Brooklyn where Mira's sister Minnie had been living. Minnie was going to stay with sister Amy, at her farm near Kansas City. Alfred and Mira intended to move into the Brooklyn place sometime in December or, at the latest, in January 1927.

Meanwhile, just after the second *Time-Binding* paper came out at the end of October, Alfred went on a quick speaking trip to the Midwest. Ethel Dummer, a wealthy Chicago/San Diego philanthropist and child welfare advocate, had gotten interested in his work and put him in touch with psychologist L. L. Thurstone, who arranged a talk for him at the University of Chicago. Although he had a small audience, Alfred was happy to meet Thurstone and, probably even more so to meet neurologist C. Judson Herrick, whose writings he had just gotten interested in, and who attended his talk. Alfred would describe Herrick's work as a "non-aristotelian neurology". He would find in Herrick's writings some plausible mechanisms for the different forms of abstracting behavior he wanted to understand better from a neurological point of view. From Chicago, Alfred went to Detroit to give a talk sponsored by the Association of Polish Engineers of America. The high point there was meeting in the audience a boyhood friend from Poland whom he hadn't seen in 20 years. Afterwards he went to Ann Arbor for a few days to see Rainich and give a lecture before taking a train back to Washington and Mira. He considered his two-week trip a success. Many of the academics he met had wanted a copy of his latest paper and he began corresponding with Herrick, who eventually became one of the scientists who corrected his book manuscript.

Alfred had lined up a few presentations to psychiatric and educational groups around Washington for late November and early December. Then the couple would move to Brooklyn, where they planned to stay until he finished the book—soon, he hoped. And then what? Sometimes, considering the obstacles in the way, he had thought he might just finish the book and be done with the whole business, just go off somewhere exotic with Mira, say Africa, Japan, India, or China. He had talked with Mira about it and already made some inquiries about teaching possibilities in the Orient, a long route back to Poland. Alternatively, the possibilities of developing the General Theory of Time-Binding further in the U.S., or elsewhere, was dependent on getting enough people interested in applying the apparently easy-to-grasp and difficult-to-practice theory. He had severe doubts whether he and Mira would be able to do this.

Whatever his frustrations and doubts, Mira was not pressing him about the time it was taking him to complete the book, though theoretically she had the right, since she was essentially supporting them both with the income from her work. (Alfred had taken the de facto job of managing both Mira and their funds.) No, she only encouraged him. She felt only the greatest devotion to him and his work. Its success would truly fulfill her highest ideals.

Yet, the level of ardor, even utopianism, he perceived in her attitude towards his work disturbed him. In talking about it to other people, she sometimes seemed to him like she wanted to save the world. (He didn't perceive himself as a utopian.) Relatedly, his work had reached a stage where he had begun to feel that her lack of scientific background and language was making it difficult for her to accurately represent in any detail what he was doing. As his wife, people were likely to accept, as from the source, her word about his work. As a result of these factors, he was beginning to want her to limit herself in how she talked to people about it—a strain in their marriage. On the other hand he admired her intelligence, independence, and "guts"—even if he didn't like some of the things that came with them.

Some of those things included the long periods of separation her mode of work demanded. It was not only the separation itself, which he found trying. While away, soliciting the "rotten rich" for painting commissions, she had to live like them—nice hotels, the best restaurants, etc. She also tended to spend money frivolously, in his opinion, on things they didn't need. Thus the considerable money she was capable of earning (she worked hard and deserved every cent of it) tended to run through her hands once she got it, which worried him. Until he was able to earn adequate money from his work (royalties from *Manhood of Humanity* were at this point negligible), he felt they both had to hunker down, decide what they wanted together as a couple, and then work together to achieve it. Which included, for the time being, saving their money and focusing on what they had agreed upon together as most important. They were not getting any younger.

To a significant extent, Mira would eventually come to agree with Alfred about aspects of her behavior he had problems with. (Of course, there were aspects of *his* behavior that *she* had problems with as well.) Eventually, the two of them would manage to minimize the areas of conflict between them. But they were going to hit some bumps on the road before they got there.

Chapter 32
TRIAL-BY-HEADLINE

December 1926 started out on a sad note for Alfred and Mira. Ella Keyser had been ill throughout much of the year. A heart attack and bout of pneumonia that summer had left her profoundly weakened. Then in early November, Keyser wrote to Alfred, "Mrs. Keyser is again very ill—another lung and heart attack."[1] Mira sent a small gift and a week later Keyser wrote back to "Mira Khan" (his affectionate name for her), "Hearty thanks for the charming book of Pussy cat poems....I read them to Kookie Khan [their pet name for Ella Keyser]. Though she was much dejected, she smiled a little and I could see she loved them."[2] Alfred and Mira had both become very close to Ella Keyser, as well as her husband. Except for such indications of their affection and concern they didn't know much else they could do.

On November 27, a telegram came from Roy Haywood: "Keyser's Wife is Dying Wire HIM."[3] The next day Alfred wrote to Roy, "Nothing could have been more thoughtful of you than letting us know of the tragedies of Keyser. Mira went to be with him. I wanted to go but she insisted that she might be of more use than me, perhaps she is right. She probably will see you."[4] Ella Keyser died that day. Alfred apparently hadn't yet heard the news from Mira or anyone else when he wrote to Walter on the 29th, "Mrs. Keyser is on her death bed this time seemingly for good. Poor old Keyser."[5] Mira soon returned home and several days later, on December 4, Keyser sent them both a note, "Just a poor line, dear Mira and Alfred to thank you and thank you for your so tender messages and your beautiful tribute of flowers. Were your friend, Mrs. Keyser living she would join me in sending love."[6] Alfred also got a letter from Roy who wrote, "I was very glad that Mira was able to get to see Kyser [sic]. The old man will be lonelier than ever now, and I am going to make a point of seeing him as often as possible. Mira told me about the arrangements in Brooklyn. We shall all be happy to have you with us here in the city."[7]

Alfred and Mira had a few more things to do in Washington before they moved. On December 4, Alfred was scheduled to speak at a meeting of the Psychoanalytical Society of Washington. Then on December 12, he was to lecture to the parents' association of a progressive school in the D.C. area. Meanwhile he was wrapping up his business at St. Elizabeths, including his intensive teaching/consultation sessions with Graven. As a favor to their landlady, who had gone to Florida for the winter, he and Mira were also going to see if they could find new renters for their apartment. And Mira had to collect fees from some Washington, D.C. clients. As they went about their business, Alfred never imagined that he had already begun to step into what would become a serious mess.

Breakdown

Graven had been seeing another St. Elizabeths psychiatrist as a patient in his private practice and had consulted with Korzybski about him. Unbeknownst to Graven and Korzybski, Dr. Knute Houck, whom Korzybski described as "a brilliant young fellow",[8] was not simply neurotic. He had a history of severe 'mental' illness—probably some form of what is now known as manic-depressive or bi-polar disorder. While at a previous job at the Mayo Clinic, he had 'broken down', and, among other things—although he was a new psychiatrist—had decided to tell the Mayo brothers, in quite grandiose fashion, how to run their clinic. After a period of hospitalization, he appeared to recover and with his quite impressive academic, medical, and psychiatric credentials had gotten a new job at St. Elizabeths. At a meeting of the Psychopathological Society on November 27, which they both attended, Houck introduced himself to Korzybski, who recognized him as the psychiatrist patient Graven had described. Houck had heard about the Anthropometer from Graven and expressed his interest in it, ostensibly so he could use it with his patients. They made an appointment for Houck to come over to Korzybski's place to buy one (the *Time-Binding* papers came with it) the following day. He did so. Korzybski offered to help him in training himself with the device. Houck also expressed interest in Korzybski's apartment and came to look at it again a few days later with his wife Gladys. Although they both seemed tense, the couple otherwise appeared normal and wanted to rent. The Korzybskis happily informed their landlady that they had found some "young nice people" as new tenants.[9]

Houck also came to the December 4 meeting of the Psychoanalytical Society of Washington where Korzybski spoke. Korzybski didn't see him again until December 10 at the hospital, where the two men happened to bump into each other. Houck seemed overly excited about Alfred's work and Alfred found his "flight of ideas" somewhat disturbing, especially coming from a psychiatrist. He tried to calm him down, referring to the Anthropometer to do so—with seeming success. They had a similar meeting the next day, with similar results.[10]

Dr. and Mrs. Houck then attended the talk Alfred gave to the progressive school's parents' association on December 12. Alfred observed, "They both were a little too animated."[11] Houck gave Alfred a paper he had written in which he had taken off from Korzybski's discussion of space-time and introduced love as the fifth dimension! But something disturbed Alfred even more than this nonsense, which in itself he might have dismissed as idle parlor philosophy. As he recounted, it was the way the envelope containing the paper had been addressed by Houck:

> ..."to Korzybski: care of Graven." Then at a different time and in a different handwriting...[Houck] added "Count Korzybski, Dr. Graven", then he added with pencil, you [could] see the different pencils, "Count Alfred, Dr. Philip Graven." [To Alfred "this monkeying with names", suggested serious disturbance.][12]

Korzybski ran into Houck in the hospital the following day:

> [Houck] seemed to be very excited, absent minded, flights of ideas, etc. [Alfred] in conversation returned [Houck's] notes telling [him] his frank opinion about them. [Houck] destroyed them immediately. [Korzybski] stressed again this part of the General Theory and the Anthropometer, which is preventive against excitement and flights of ideas. Seemingly successfully."[13]

On December 14th, Graven asked Korzybski to see Houck who wanted to talk with him. Graven sent Houck to Korzybski's room in the hospital. At first Houck seemed excited and Alfred had to work to settle him down. Then Houck almost immediately switched into depression. He seemed to be oscillating 'up' and 'down' like a poorly regulated machine. Alfred did what he could to cheer him up and sent him back to Graven's office. A little later, Graven called for Alfred to come. Houck was lying on Graven's sofa. Korzybski described what happened next:

> ... I was very, very careful saying very little, just standard stuff. [Houck] crawled down on the floor from the sofa and put his face on my feet and sobbed. That's that. Of course, I helped him up back to the sofa, and I knew one thing, that he was breaking down completely. ...so I told [Graven] he had better give him some sleeping stuff and put him to bed.

So that's what the doctor did. He took him to an empty room [in St. Elizabeths], gave him some hypo or something and put him to sleep. And [afterwards, Houck] was told he had to go home and have a good rest.[14]

Later that day, Houck did go home. Meanwhile, after consulting with Graven, Alfred went to talk with White. Graven didn't want to officially report Houck as incapacitated just yet. However, they both thought White would want to know what was happening. Houck had been having some family troubles and was obviously going through some kind of crisis. They hoped they had seen the worst of his problems.

The next day, December 15, at 8:00 in the morning, Korzybski got a phone call at his apartment. In a "childlike voice" Dr. Houck asked Alfred, "Do you know anything?" This was not a good sign. Alfred replied, "No." Then Houck asked, "Is Gladys with you?" Alfred said, "Why should she be? Naturally, she isn't here." Houck said, "Oh, she isn't home. I don't know what happened to her." Alfred told him "Don't worry, she will come back" (although he didn't necessarily believe that). He asked Houck to meet him at Graven's office at St. Elizabeths at 10:00 a.m. and said goodbye. Two hours later, Houck, who was supposed to be on duty at the hospital, hadn't shown up. Graven searched the wards for him but couldn't find him. They called Houck's house. He answered and asked them to come over. When they got to the house they found Houck seemingly normal except for the fact that, as Alfred later described,

…[He was] sitting half-dressed in an easy chair, with one eye closed, broken eyeglasses on the table and his little son on his lap…I asked him,…"Did you break those glasses and get glass in your eye?"

—"No."

—"Why do you close your eye?"

—"Oh, I'm afraid that I will see too much."

I told him roughly, "Don't be afraid. Don't close your eyes. Don't be afraid. You will never see too much." The eye perked up and stayed up.[15]

Besides this, Houck seemed to Korzybski a little 'flat' in his expression. He told the two men about his concern that his wife had poisoned herself. Korzybski and Graven looked around the place but found nothing they thought she could have done that with. Alfred told Houck he might do well to quit psychiatry for a year, have a good rest, and take up some physical labor, say in a lumber camp or shoveling coal on a merchant ship. Graven told Houck he would definitely have to leave his job for now and go back to his family to recover. They would have someone take care of the child (a two-year old boy) until Houck's wife returned. Then Korzybski and Graven both left to go to the hospital. Though Graven may have felt embarrassed that his patient Houck had had a breakdown, the time had come to make an official report to White. White immediately made arrangements for someone to take Doctor Houck by train to his family. Korzybski and Graven headed back to Houck's place. They had only been away for a half an hour or so. But when they got there, they realized what damn fools they had been for leaving Doctor Houck and his son alone. Alfred should have stayed there and let Graven go to the hospital on his own. Years later, recounting what they found when they arrived, Alfred said, "I still feel like spitting in my face."[16] Dr. Houck had gone. He had left his two-year old son there by himself. They had to call the police. Then, all hell broke loose.[17]

Trial-by-Headline

Houck turned up three days later, disheveled and confused, in a small upstate New York town. He was brought back to Washington and placed under observation. With no sign of his wife, the police suspected foul play. But Houck couldn't provide any coherent information. Both Korzybski and Graven were brought in for further questioning. Both men had been forthright with the police and had told them everything they knew. But apparently it wasn't enough. Did Dr. Houck murder his wife? Did Korzybski and Graven know something they weren't telling? Were they shielding Dr. Houck? After about a week of such grilling, Korzybski got fed up with what he considered "the third degree" by the investigating detectives and the district attorney:

> Finally, I squashed the whole thing because I yelled at them. "Don't be damn fools, [if] Dr. [Houck] killed fifty people, not one, he is immune as far as you are concerned. The man is profoundly ill, so don't be silly about murder and shielding a murderer. He could kill fifty people. He's immune." That finally piped them down, but you can imagine what we had in the newspapers.[18]

What they—especially Alfred—had in the newspapers, could be called trial-by-headline. With newspaper space to be filled, the situation seemed ideal for sensationalistic coverage that amounted to a campaign of malicious untruth about him. There was a missing woman and no information on her whereabouts, an 'insane' doctor of the 'insane' who seemed obsessed with a strange-looking device with a funny name that no one could explain very well. (Why bother asking Korzybski when they could ask the obsessed doctor himself?) Then there was this 'exotic' foreigner Korzybski—and his wife (a Count and Countess no less), who seemed to be under suspicion by the police. Korzybski's presumed role in this affair (actually rather peripheral) provided tempting bait for a feeding frenzy by journalistic sharks.

It started with a story in the December 20 edition of the *Washington Evening Star*, which featured a panel with pictures of Dr. Houck and his missing wife, as well as a picture of the Anthropometer (taken by an enterprising photographer in Dr. White's office). Above the pictures, the headline read, "Mystery Laid To "Thought Machine"." The caption underneath read "Deep study of the "Anthropometer," designed by its inventor, a Polish count, to "diagnose thoughts" is blamed by associates of Dr. Knute Houck for his breakdown." More sensational copy appeared in the accompanying article:

> Dr. Houck, it was declared, was devoting much of this time to a device that was invented by Count Kurzypski [sic], who is a noted mathematician by profession. The device known as an "anthropometer," was supposed to register the innermost thoughts of a person and aid them in a psycho-analysis of themselves. Other physicians declared Dr. Houck had permitted the thing to prey on his mind so much that it became a Frankenstein that struck him down... Fanciful in appearance, the thing seemed to assume an eerie atmosphere as its various functions were explained, all technical and, to the layman, impossible of understanding...[19]

One can't assume that any of the physicians at St. Elizabeths actually said any of the things they were reported to have said in the article. The reporter searched out Korzybski the following day to make some inquiries and ended up apologizing for his exaggerations and misinformation. However, it was already too late. Other newspapers had picked up the story and were off and running. The story about the "thought machine", along with the photograph of the Anthropometer, spread nationwide via wire service accounts and newspaper syndicates and was embellished with each retelling.

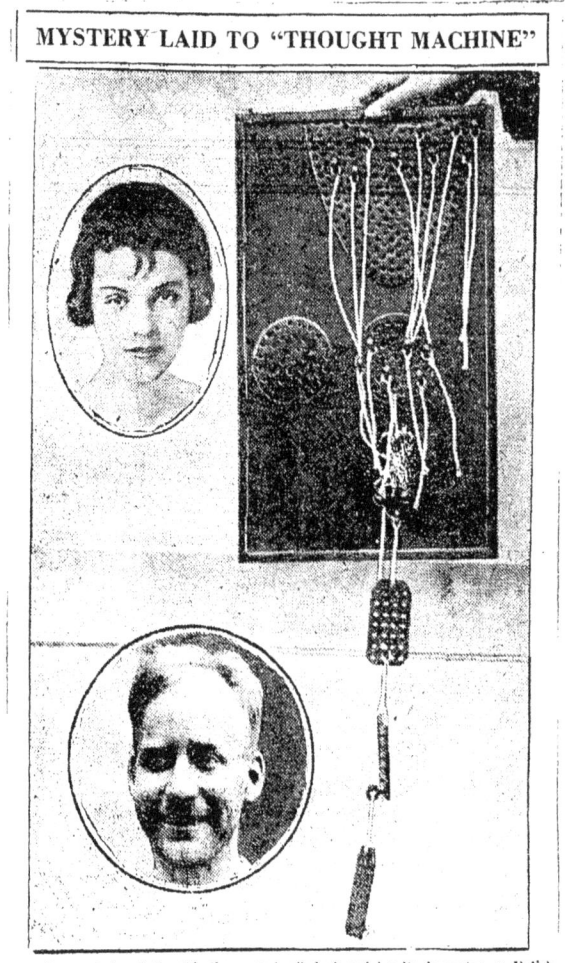

From the *Washington Evening Star*, Dec. 20, 1926

Over the following week headlines such as the following appeared in newspapers in Philadelphia, Washington, Baltimore, New York, Boston, Milwaukee, San Antonio, Detroit, Kansas City, and other major and not-so-major cities throughout the U.S: " "Thought-Machine"…believed to have unbalanced his mind",[20] "COUNT AND WIFE GRILLED IN INQUIRY [ON] MISSING MRS. HOUCK" [21] (Actually Mira was never questioned by the police), "Houck Mystery Laid To His Study of "Mind Meter",[22] " "Mind Machine" Is Blamed For Houck Mystery, Doctor and Missing Wife Believed Deranged by "Occult" Device",[23] "Mental Meter Floored Houck, Device to Measure Thoughts Is Puzzle to Fellow Alienists",[24] "Going Mad From Study Of Insane",[25] "Thought Machine Blamed for Mystery Surrounding Houcks, Doctor's Mind Affected By Too Much Concentration and Psychoanalysis",[26] "Thought Machine Sends Dr. Houck Mad".[27]

WASHINGTON TIMES
COUNT AND WIFE GRILLED IN INQUIRY
NO MISSING MRS. HOUCK

Nobility In Houck Quiz

The newspaper stories accompanying these damning headlines consisted mainly of half-truths and outright lies about Korzybski. The psychiatrists Alfred talked to agreed that Houck, and his wife, had probably sensed he was 'slipping' and grasped at Korzybski and his work in a futile effort to fend off a breakdown already in progress. So Alfred felt confident that he had no responsibility for Houck's collapse or Mrs. Houck's disappearance. But that gave him small comfort. The newspaper accounts made his work look ridiculous. He had toiled over the last few years to establish a good reputation, especially in the scientific community. Now he felt he was getting "bloodlessly murdered" by the press. He knew the power of words. Although friends like Walter told him not to feel concerned—that any publicity was good publicity—Alfred felt the future success in his work depended on his good name. He and Mira and numerous friends mobilized in order to salvage it.

By the end of December, he had already consulted some lawyers. He felt he had cause to sue one or more of the newspaper chains for libel. Since the picture of the Anthropometer was being reprinted in many of the stories, he felt he also had cause to sue for copyright violation. In the meantime, he renewed his subscription to the clipping service (which he had let run out), asked friends around the country to keep their eyes open for news stories related to the incident, and wrote to newspapers around the country to obtain multiple copies of stories about him and the Anthropometer in relation to the Houck affair. His quickly growing newspaper files would give him ammunition.

Alfred also felt heartened by the support he got from his friends. He had started to get telegrams and letters expressing outrage at the treatment he was receiving from the press. The first public sally on his behalf was a newspaper article written by Roy Haywood, which appeared in the December 27 edition of the *New York Sun* newspaper. The assistant editor of the *New York Masonic Outlook*, which Haywood edited, was A. M. Nielsen, a geography professor at New York University, who had recently gotten interested in Korzybski's work. The article, entitled "Explains "Thought Machine", Name a Misnomer, says Professor—For the Rest It's as Simple as Einstein" was written in the form of an interview with Nielsen. Accompanied by a picture (authorized by Alfred) of a woman handling an Anthropometer, it read in part:

> New York friends of Count Alfred Korzybski, Polish scientist now living in Washington, were amused and indignant at once to-day over the theory that too much toying with the Count's invention, the anthropometer, erroneously called a "thought machine," was responsible for the disappearance of young Mrs. Gladys Walter Houck of Washington and the mental unbalancing of her husband, Dr. Knutt [sic] H. Houck.
>
> "The anthropometer," said Dr. A. M. Nielsen, professor of economical geography in the New York University's school of commerce, "is no more a 'thought machine' than a blackboard in a schoolroom. It is simply a chart, a plastic diagram, that illustrates a method of thinking, and is in no sense a machine.
>
> "There is nothing occult or spiritual in it. In fact, Count Korzybski takes no stock in such things. He is an engineer with a scientific background.
>
> "It is silly to suggest that a man lost his reason over studying the Anthropometer. You may as well say that a mathematical treatise or a book on logic will drive a man insane.
>
> "The Anthropometer is made of wood instead of paper simply as a matter of convenience."
>
> ..."In a general way," he said, "Korzybski undertook to get hold of a method of thinking that underlies modern science and put it into simple form so that it would be available to the layman. The anthropometer is merely a plastic diagram that illustrates that method of thinking."
>
> With the anthropometer, he said, thoughts are analyzed and discussion and argument at an end.
>
> "Why," exclaimed Dr. Nielsen, "this thing would have a tendency to restore an insane man's sanity rather than to derange a sane man. If Dr. Houck studied the Anthropometer it was only incidental and could have had no bearing on his insanity."[28]

Alfred wrote to both Haywood and Nielsen thanking them for the fine piece. Nielsen wrote back saying that after the article appeared about 50 people contacted him expressing interest in Korzybski's work.[29] If a positive article could have that effect, what were the negative ones doing?

Unfortunately, sensational articles mentioning 'the thought machine' continued. After about a week of coverage, however, they stopped appearing with their earlier frequency. Reporters focused more on Gladys Houck, who, despite an intensive search by the police, had failed to turn up either dead or alive. On the basis of a press photograph, three men in Blytheville, Arkansas identified as Mrs. Houck a woman they saw passing through their town.[30] In a lucid moment, Dr. Houck declared the unlikelihood of that since the photo used in the papers, taken several years before, showed his wife with a different hairstyle than the one she had before she went missing. He was still convinced she was alive, somewhere around Washington, D.C. Meanwhile, detectives seemed to discount either her running away or suicide. Instead, although psychiatric consultants thought it highly unlikely, and despite no physical evidence, detectives seemed convinced Dr. Houck had murdered her.

By this time Korzybski must have felt thoroughly disgusted with the police, as well as reporters, since detectives seem to have cynically decided to use Houck's obsession with the anthropometer to further their investigation. On the day that Haywood's *Sun* article appeared, reporters and detectives converged on Gallinger Hospital, where Houck was being held, with Houck's anthropometer. *The Baltimore News* headline for December 27, 1926 read "Dr. Houck's Mind Tested In Hunt For Wife." In one of the most bizarre stories to be written about the case, the article explained how the police were planning to use the anthropometer to get Dr. Houck to psychoanalyze himself and probe his dreams for clues to his wife's disappearance. Perhaps the detectives thought they could shock or rattle Houck into making a confession. It didn't happen. The article also noted that Korzybski had met the Assistant District Attorney (this may have been the day Alfred blew up at the investigators). At any rate, the article also published a statement that Korzybski released after his meeting, undoubtedly a rebuke to both the press and police for the spate of shoddy, uncritical inferences that had been spewing forth from both camps: "The situation in regard to Dr. Houck is very complicated and very technical. To my mind, it should be dealt with by medical specialists and scientists. In this case no one else is competent to speak." I can imagine Korzybski reading this with some satisfaction, even as he may have shaken his head in disbelief at the article's description of how detectives planned to use the anthropometer to have Houck 'psychoanalyze' himself. It read: "This instrument is used for personal psychoanalysis. The person who would analyze his brain and thoughts sticks little pegs into the perforations of the figures and the resultant action tells him what he wants to know."[31] If Alfred had known a little Yiddish, it would have been appropriate for him to say, "Oy Gevalt!"

More Lies and Misrepresentations

Korzybski wrote to Adolf Meyer, "Lies and misrepresentations always leave some residues, which are not easily eliminated."[32] For one thing, he was concerned that the stories connecting him and the anthropometer to the Houcks' troubles would enter newspaper "morgues"—files of old stories kept for researchers, who could then bring up the whole mess again in future articles. For the present, he hoped to make the best of a bad situation. The promise of possible lawsuits with hefty financial payoffs cheered him. He was keeping his own "morgue" for that purpose. He also hoped to get some declarations of support from psychiatrists and scientists. Otherwise, he did not know if he would be able to continue his work. He and Mira put off their move to Brooklyn and devised a multi-pronged plan to vindicate his reputation.

The Washington Psychopathological Society met on January 4, 1927. At the meeting, Alfred requested an official statement of support from the group. (He had already gotten a letter of support from Dr. White.) There was some haggling over wording and a committee of three made up of White, Harry Stack Sullivan, and a Dr. Johnson agreed to work on a statement, approved at the Society's next meeting in March.

A few days later in January, Mira left on a trip to Baltimore, New York City, New Haven, and Boston, mainly to see Alfred's scientific friends at Johns Hopkins, NYU, Columbia, Yale, Harvard, and MIT. In February, she continued onto Detroit, where she had some connections and hoped to drum up support for Alfred. Her directives from Alfred were to inform people whom they knew about what actually had happened, and to gather letters of support from them. (Alfred had no intention of publishing any letters without additional permission but, for his personal use, wanted as many of them as possible from well-known scientists.)

Alfred also got letters of support from many other friends around the country. E.T. Bell's comments must have given him particular satisfaction:

> ...As to your work, there never has been any question in my mind that your law of time-binding is a first class discovery, first because it is true, second because it is necessary and sufficient to distinguish man from the rest of creation, third because it is simple and free of all mysticism—religious, human or scientific—, and last because it is so extremely powerful and elementary that it has been overlooked for centuries—until you stated it...As for the good opinion of men who acclaim only what is fashionable, or orthodox, or well received by the elect, it is worth not a solitary curse. That you have chosen to illustrate some of your applications of the theory by a plastic diagram may tickle the fancy of the trivial minded, but this again is a mere detail. Some who dislike your work prove thereby that they should have their noses rubbed in it.
>
> With Best Wishes — E. T. Bell[33]

Bell was right about some of the people who disliked Alfred's work. But it was encouraging to find out how many important mathematicians and scientists, like Bell, supported it.

Meanwhile, by mid-January the lack of news about Mrs. Houck seems to have led people at *The World*, the main Pulitzer newspaper in New York City, to pump up interest in the flagging story by publishing a Sunday feature comparing and contrasting her case with that of detective novelist Agatha Christie in England. Early in December, Miss Christie had gone missing. Eleven days later, authorities tracked her to a country inn, staying under the name of her husband's mistress. Presumably she had had a nervous breakdown. The headline read "Two Woman Mysteriously Vanish Here and In England." Unfortunately for Alfred, the story played up his connection with the Houck affair. The subheading began "Thought Machine Adds to Interest in Case of Mrs. Houck of Washington..."[34] In an added bit of brazenness, the article included a large photomontage of "Dr. Knute Houck, His Wife and Child, and the Thought Machine" underneath which appeared the notice "Machine Copyrighted by Alfred Kurzypski" (while infringing on his copyright). Grrrr! The story was reprinted in at least three other national newspapers owned by the Pulitzer syndicate, which seemed like the worst offender against his reputation. Korzybski discovered that Underwood & Underwood—a nation-wide purveyor of pictures to the press, provided the photographs. Perhaps he would sue them too.

It seemed difficult to counteract the potential damage that pieces like this—produced by a giant news organization—could do to his reputation. Still, Alfred felt grateful for a small protest, "Sensationalizing Science", printed on February 12 in *New York: A Four-Page Journal of Ideas for the General Reader*, a weekly paper published by New York University and edited by Harold de Wolf Fuller, an N.Y.U. professor of journalism. Though not mentioned by name, Korzybski—depicted as a victim of the prevailing low standards of 'yellow' journalism—had his dilemma summarized in the closing lines of the short piece by Fuller: "What is the foreigner [a distinguished visiting scientist] and what is respectable science to do? Bring suit for libel or submit to the trend of the times? This is a question which is now being considered."[35]

Somebody at *The World* seems to have taken note of this possibility. Indeed, Alfred and Mira later learned that a well-meaning, influential, and according to Alfred, "stupid" acquaintance of theirs had approached one of the Pulitzer brothers with complaints about the paper's coverage. Afterwards, the paper issued what amounted to a retraction.[36] A short, three-column article used one column just for its four headlines: "Sanity Specialist Still Under Cloud. Dr. Knute Houck Fails to Regain Reason Following His Wife's Disappearance. KORZYBSKI LINK DENIED. Study of "Thought Machine" Merely a Coincidence." The remaining six paragraphs of the piece contained two cursory lead paragraphs with the current non-news about Houck and his wife. The rest of the article devoted itself to backtracking on the paper's previous misrepresentations of Korzybski and his work. Alfred was not assuaged. The piece appeared in the March 1 morning edition of the paper. The story didn't appear in that day's later editions and, as far as he could find, was not syndicated in any of the other Pulitzer publications. Too little, too late.[37] Besides, Alfred felt bothered because the existence of the article provided the Pulitzers with an excuse they could use as counter-evidence in the event he sued them.

Repentance, if one could call it that, seemed short-lived at the *World* editorial offices. Perhaps the most vicious article yet appeared in the March 24 issue of *The Evening World*. The day before, Gladys Houck's remains had been found floating in the Potomac. The Pulitzer paper carried the headline, "Finding of Body Partly Clears Up Noted "Thought Machine Mystery"." The article, a libelous rehash of previous fabrications that had appeared in the Pulitzer papers, held "Kurzypski's" [sic] "thought machine" responsible for the entire affair. It also offered a new label for the affair—the "Thought Machine Mystery"—that, if it caught on, could indelibly tar his name by associating it with the fabrications about his work and the Houcks' misfortune. The final line of the piece read, "Washington believes that the "Thought Machine" brought discord and tragedy to the little home on Congress Heights." Korzybski felt infuriated but also invigorated. The stark accusatory tone and obvious falsehoods of the article, alone might provide the basis for a devastating libel suit against the Pulitzer newspaper chain.[38]

Final determination of Gladys Houck's death was soon made by an autopsy: death by drowning. However, the coroner's jury appended this with, "under circumstances unknown", refusing to come to any conclusion about how she had gotten into the water, and leaving it up to the district attorney to decide whether to prosecute Dr. Houck for murder. (He could have knocked her unconscious and thrown her into the water, for instance.) Houck was freed, however, and the case was dropped. Alfred made sure to get the full details of the findings. In a private memo, he summarized the evidence, which overwhelmingly favored suicide.[39]

So that was that. The papers had pretty much finished with the Houcks and with Korzybski too. (Korzybski hadn't finished with the papers, though.) It was time to get to Brooklyn. Mira had returned to Washington in the beginning of March. She and Alfred began to pack. They had some business problems to attend to as well. A wealthy Washington family had commissioned portraits from Mira, who had designed and purchased frames, cut the ivories, and done the major part of the painting. But the family had become uncommunicative and uncooperative. Mira was going to be out nearly $5,000 if they didn't pay.[40] Alfred helped put together letters to the family and a history of Mira's transactions with them. These eventually ended up in the hands of a lawyer when they finally had to go to court for the money.

At the start of April, Alfred wrote to their friend Sally Avery that when the church fathers gave a picture of hell, they did not know there was such a thing as moving.[41] The Korzybskis left Washington in the middle of the month. The Brooklyn apartment they found waiting for them needed cleaning and repair work. Alfred, as usual, did the carpentry.

That, and dealing with the 49 pieces of luggage that they brought with them, and the multiple trunks that they retrieved from Manhattan Storage and other places, kept them busy for another month before they had unpacked and settled.[42] The Houck business had provided a huge, unwelcome distraction from writing. Now Alfred could focus on the book again. But he hadn't let go of the possibility of one or more lawsuits for libel and copyright violation. Through the summer and fall he met with lawyers, looking for someone willing and able to take his case.

Vindication

Soon after arriving in Brooklyn, Alfred went to meet Harold de Wolf Fuller, the journalism professor who edited New York University's weekly journal, *New York*. Fuller wanted to write a more extensive article on the ethical issues related to the newspaper coverage of the Houck case. He also wanted to have it signed by as many as possible of the scientists and other figures who had sent supporting letters to Korzybski. Fuller had taken up Korzybski's grievance as part of his own crusade to raise up the level of American journalism. As he wrote in the introduction to the article, finally published in the July 23 issue of *New York*, Fuller wanted not only to "clear one individual of outrageous charges", but also to make an issue of the "widespread abuse" by the press in "sensationalizing scientific investigations". Korzybski gladly helped Fuller by proofing the article and providing the names of friends and associates who might agree to sign it and have their names published.

Twenty-five individuals—representing mathematics, biology, neurology, and psychiatry, among other fields—were able to respond in time and affirm Korzybski as a legitimate scientific worker who had been misrepresented by irresponsible journalists. The list included: E. T. Bell, C. B. Bridges, Charles Watts Burr, R. D. Carmichael, Ross McC. Chapman, Stanwood Cobb, David Fairchild, Philip Graven, H. L. Haywood, C. Judson Herrick, L. O. Howard, Smith Ely Jeliffe, Jeremiah W. Jenks, David Starr Jordan, Keyser, John T. Madden, Basil Manly, Thomas J. McCormack, William Allen Neilson, Alexander Petrunkevitch, Polakov, G. Y. Rainich, William E. Ritter, William Morton Wheeler, and Cora Williams. Alfred expressed deep gratitude to Fuller for his efforts.[43]

Although the article probably did not get seen much outside the New York City area, it had some impact and even engendered a little controversy. *Editor and Publisher*, a trade paper for the publishing industry in New York City, reprinted the text of the *New York* article in its July 23 edition under the bold headline: "Many **CHARGE PRESS FAKED IN DR. HOUCK CASE**". The subheading read: "Distinguished Scientists and Educators Issue Remarkable Statement to Clear Individual of 'Outrageous Charges' and Awaken Press to Abuses in Sensationalized Science". The article also got attention from a few New York City newspapers. A July 25 editorial in *The New York Sun* rightly took credit for its early defense of Korzybski and his work. Meanwhile, an editorial in the July 26 edition of the *New York Herald Tribune* criticized the Fuller article for painting newspapers with too broad a brush (although the *New York* article had not said that all newspapers were at fault) and took credit for not having been among those papers that had repeated rumors about Korzybski. Reading this, Fuller couldn't resist taking the *Herald Tribune* to task in the next issue of *New York* for its "calm misstatement of facts" in some of its earlier coverage about Korzybski in relation to the Houck affair.

A veteran reporter named Silas Bent also paid attention. Bent had become at least as bothered by the irresponsibilities of the press as Fuller had. He was writing a book to be published later in 1927, *Ballyhoo: The Voice of The Press*. The slang term "ballyhoo"—synonymous with "exaggerated talk", also referred to as 'baloney'—had once referred to the lurid, attention-getting claims of sideshow barkers at carnivals trying to lure gullible customers.[44] Bent's book, brimming with case examples of journalistic ballyhoo and still worth reading, provides one of the earliest examples of mass media criticism in the 20th Century. Bent devoted about a page of the book to the Houck case, summarizing Fuller's July 23 *New York* piece with little comment. Korzybski, who had had no contact with Bent, took note of the book when it appeared. For some time afterwards, Alfred was intent on referring to his newspaper 'trial' in his book to illustrate faulty abstracting and abuse of the time-binding mechanism. Friends like Haywood and William Morton Wheeler convinced him to leave it out. Korzybski likely was referring to his 'trial-by-headline', however, when he wrote his brief comments on newspapers and "other public prints" and media "stimulating morbid inclinations of the mob."[45] He made sure to include Bent's book in his bibliography.

Korzybski still wasn't satisfied. He believed various irresponsible newspapers had 'done him wrong'—having both libeled him and violated his copyright, thus threatening his future livelihood. His dueling days long over, he hoped instead to get satisfaction (significant monetary compensation from the guilty parties) by means of lawsuits against the offenders. In February 1928, he retained the law firm of Denman, Bevier & Scotti "to represent me in my intended actions to recover damages arising out of infringement of my copyright on the model Anthropometer and to recover damages for libel in articles relating thereto."[46] One of the firm's partners, Louis Bevier, personally took care of the case. Eventually Alfred accepted that, given the prevailing environment of journalistic ballyhoo, winning any libel case against the offending newspapers had too many difficulties. His best chance seemed to entail going after Underwood & Underwood, the press photo agency, for copyright violation; they had syndicated the photographs of the Anthropometer as 'thought machine' that were used to accompany many of the offending articles.

Bevier filed a bill of complaint on behalf of Korzybski against Underwood & Underwood, Inc. in the Federal District Court in New York City on April 30, 1928. A copy of the complaint with a subpoena was served against Underwood & Underwood on May 1. Although they had only 30 days to respond, their attorney didn't file their answer, a motion to dismiss the complaint, until June 29. The district judge, Julian W. Mack considered the motion on November 21 (the 'mills' of the court moved slowly), and on November 30 dismissed the complaint on the grounds that Korzybski and his attorney had failed "to state a cause of action against the defendant." Remarkable. Korzybski's attorney filed an appeal to the U.S. Circuit Court (also in New York) and, as these things go, the Circuit Court did not hear the appeal until late in the following year.[47]

The three presiding judges—Augustus Hand, Learned Hand, and Judge Swan gave their ruling on December 18, 1929: they affirmed the decision of the District Court and dismissed Korzybski's case. According to their joint opinion, the fact that Korzybski had patented the Anthropometer invalidated his claim of copyright infringement. They determined that the written material and drawings of the Anthropometer had become part of the public domain when first published by the patent office. Accordingly, they did not consider it protected by copyright. Anyone could photograph or copy the drawings and description of the Anthropometer as long as they didn't make a three-dimensional model of one.

The nature of the Anthropometer as an educational diagram illustrating a scientific formulation reduced the sharpness of the distinction the judges seemed to be making between a drawing and 3-D model. But with its dual patent and copyright, the Anthropometer sat in the rather murky legal waters between these two areas of intellectual property.[48]

The next step in the appeals process would be the Supreme Court. After consulting another lawyer, Alfred and Mira decided not to pursue the case any further. Alfred had been away from New York City from the spring of 1928 until mid-1929 and had been communicating with the lawyers by mail for much of the almost two years of litigation. He had pored over the copyright and patent laws. He probably felt tired of the business. And besides, with the recent stock market crash and declining economy, it was not a good time to be spending more money on retainer fees to lawyers for a still rather questionable outcome. Alfred tried to put a good face on things even though he also had to pay $25 in hearing costs to Underwood & Underwood. He wrote to Mira, working in Florida, that he was satisfied with the outcome: because the lawsuit was dismissed, not lost on merits, they might be able to take further action in the future. And for now they were saving bundles of money.[49]

The circuit court dismissal in *Korzybski v. Underwood & Underwood* made it a landmark case in intellectual property law for the next six decades, "cited over eleven hundred times in various court opinions" up until the early 1990s.[50] It exemplified the so-called "election doctrine" whereby having a patent precluded the ability to copyright a scientific illustration. This remained a mainstay of U.S. Copyright Office Policy until the mid-1990s. By that time, various court decisions since the 1950s had begun to reshape attitudes towards the protection of designs and illustrations. By 1995, the Copyright Office was able to reverse its previous policy and declared, "The availability of protection or grant of protection under the law for a utility or design patent will not affect the registrability of a claim in an original work of pictorial, graphic, or sculptural authorship."[51] Korzybski would have had a much better chance of winning his case in this environment—more than sixty years after he had his case dismissed.

Chapter 33
FIRST DRAFT

"When the first draft is done the back of the job is broken."[1] Korzybski would have agreed with the maxim. But getting the first draft done had turned into a monumental struggle. As the summer of 1927 slipped into autumn, he was wondering whether he or the job of the book would 'surrender' first. Alfred wrote to E.T. Bell in Pasadena, "As to my book, I [am] working like mad...if I do not get it out of my system pretty soon it will break me."[2]

At least he had a "quiet and nice" place in which to work. Alfred and Mira's penthouse studio apartment in the large, old-fashioned house at 321 Carlton Avenue in Brooklyn, convenient to New York City subway lines, consisted of one big room "like a barn" which gave the two of them plenty of space. It had a kitchen area as well as "a bath, closets, a garret and a private roof garden."[3] The metal and glass skylight helped illuminate the apartment and also contributed to the fact that, as he later noted, they "roasted in summer" and were "freezing in winter".[4] Although both Alfred and Mira would spend significant periods of time away from it, the Brooklyn apartment remained their home until 1936.

In the fall of 1927, they had settled into the "uneventful" existence, which would typify their years in Brooklyn. As he described their daily routine of the time, he and Mira were "up at 7. I prepare the breakfast, as usual, bring the papers and mail as usual, and again as usual go to my desk and work all day until late at night, day in and day out, I go very seldom out."[5] Mira had spent the summer in the Hamptons on Long Island trying to get painting commissions. The failure of her campaign had left their working funds extremely low. Since they didn't want to touch their 'sacred' savings account money, Alfred felt forced to ask both Roy Haywood and Calvin Bridges for loans to help tide them over. Neither of his friends had spare cash to lend. He and Mira were just going to have to tighten their belts for a while. Mira was probably going to have to go out soon and do some more traveling to get jobs. Meanwhile, Alfred's book appeared a long way from finished.

Alfred's voluminous correspondence vouched for the fact that he could spit out words with ease. Also, when he had to, he could produce a polished piece of writing for a deadline. Jesse Lee Bennett had asked him to write a review of Keyser's new book, *Mole Philosophy and Other Essays* for the July issue of his magazine *The Modern World*. Even with the tumult of the Houck business and the move to Brooklyn barely behind him, Alfred had come through on time with the review.

No, the slowness of the book writing came from the intrinsic difficulty of the task he had set for himself: to formulate a methodological synthesis of human knowledge circa-1927, broadly applicable to science and everyday life. He was continuing to accumulate more material, which seemed essential to his enterprise. Half in delight and half in despair, he wrote to William Alanson White that "new scientific books in every field seem to support my work, but I must stop reading and devote more time to writing as there seem[s] to be no end to it."[6] The despair seemed to outweigh the delight; in a letter he wrote to Bell:

> The slowness with which my book progresses is maddening, the more that every new neurological discovery comes beautifully my way, and also other discoveries, I still have nothing to retract but just amplify, and by Jove if I do not stop somewhere the damned book will never be published. The newer quantum messes are coming in and I do not dare even look at them.[7]

But look at them he did. The letter to Bell continued. "Do you know the papers of Heisenberg…on the phenomenological aspects of quantum theory, Carl Eckert['s] Operator Calculus…and Schrodinger's Undulatory [wave] theory mechanics…What do you think of it?"[8] Alfred also wanted Bell's opinion about the work of Dutch mathematician L. E. J. Brouwer and his colleague, German mathematician, Hermann Weyl. Brouwer had developed an approach called "intuitionism" which seemed to take a non-elementalistic, human behavior approach towards the foundations of mathematics. This, and Brouwer's questioning of the "law of excluded middle", definitely gave his work a non-aristotelian thrust that Alfred found promising. In addition to Bell, Alfred was reaching out to other mathematicians and physicists whom he hoped could help him understand these latest developments.

The Logic of Modern Physics

Among his new correspondents was Percy Williams Bridgman (1882–1961), a specialist in high-pressure physics who would eventually receive the 1946 Nobel Physics Prize for his work. Bridgman, who spent his entire professional career at Harvard, was also struggling to make sense of both relativity theory and "the new quantum messes". Very much a practical experimentalist, he described himself to Korzybski as "one of those dirty physicists, all of whose time is occupied with the highly unabstract work of discovering whiskers on the suspensions of galvanometers or rubbing dirt from electrical contacts."[9] However, what immediately attracted Korzybski's interest in Bridgman was the physicist's theoretical foray into scientific methodology with his book, published earlier in 1927, *The Logic of Modern Physics*. In it, Bridgman introduced the notion of "the operational point of view" to understand scientific formulating (this was called "operationism" or "operationalism" by others). Bridgman wrote: "In general we mean by any concept nothing more than a set of operations; *the concept is synonymous with the corresponding set of operations*."[10]

Echoing Mach's positivism and Peirce's pragmatism, Bridgman was attempting to 'clean house' in physics, to sweep away the cobwebs of "meaningless questions" which threatened to stall further progress in the science. While focusing on physics, Bridgman acknowledged the possibility of applying this approach to moral, philosophical, and social questions as well. The book would go on to have a major influence on psychology and the social sciences by means of the notion of the "operational definition".

In early July 1927 after reading *The Logic of Modern Physics*, Alfred wrote to Keyser and noted some of his problems with it. Nonetheless, Alfred was not inclined to focus on the flaws of Bridgman's work. As he told Keyser, "The book is an important event in my private life."[11] He was soon enthusiastically recommending it to others. More than anything else, *The Logic of Modern Physics* appealed to Korzybski because Bridgman's operational approach—in however limited a way—partook in the kind of "behaviouristic" attitude Alfred had found so fruitful in his own work. This was not to be confused with the narrow psychological 'behaviorism' of people like John Watson, but rather resulted from looking at all fields of knowledge—mathematics and physics included—as forms of human behavior and language.

Korzybski saw *The Logic of Modern Physics* as one of the first attempts by a working scientist to focus specifically on scientific method, especially in terms of this behaviouristic attitude. Alfred felt this attitude lay behind Einstein's achievements. Reading Bridgman helped Alfred to clarify the methodological nature of his own work. As he later put it:

> ...What Bridgman calls operational method, is exactly the method that was introduced by Einstein, but not formulated by Einstein as a method...[and] is an independent discovery. It is a further abstraction methodologically which Einstein [was] unaware of. [12]

Alfred saw his own independently developed work as more comprehensive—in terms of method—than that of either man. Einstein, not totally unaware of his own methods, wrote in a later 'philosophical' moment: "The whole of science is nothing more than the refinement of every day thinking." [13] As Korzybski saw it in 1927, Bridgman had pulled out a significant aspect of Einstein's particular "refinements" and their implications for physics. Korzybski, abstracting further, was coming around full circle by seeking to bring back this and other methodological refinements into everyday 'thinking' and living.

As background to his 'childishly simple' applications of physico-mathematical methods for daily life, Korzybski wanted his book to include, among other things, an accurate account of the worldview and epistemology of the latest physics. Perhaps Bridgman, given his methodological interests, would be willing to serve as one of Alfred's expert scientific manuscript readers. Even more, perhaps Bridgman might be open to allying himself with Alfred.

Throughout the years, Alfred had seen his scientific program—developing a science of man and a non-aristotelian revision of human knowledge—as a group enterprise. (For example, he had shelved, but not abandoned, the notion of having something like the Library of Human Engineering.) He really did not want to be working alone. Indeed, he didn't feel one man could adequately perform the necessary and ongoing tasks of scientific synthesis and non-aristotelian research and development. At this stage of the enterprise, the enormous individual effort he was making to write the book seemed necessary—like the task of lifting the artillery piece by himself on the road from Lodz—if only because he saw the 'path' of inquiry 'blocked' and in need of clearing, and he couldn't see anyone else who was doing it. (Perhaps with helpers like Bridgman, he might at least not get a formulational hernia from the strain.) Once the path had been cleared, others could travel alongside and perhaps even move ahead of him.

Over the years he had tried to get the interest of various people like C. K. Ogden, whom he had thought might closely sympathize with his goals, to work cooperatively with him. But, although he had gotten help from some, he found that most either had different goals and/or different views of cooperation—or were just too busy with their own work. He was prepared for a similar response from Bridgman. But it surely seemed worthwhile to contact him and feel him out for the possibility of getting help (he was certainly willing to help Bridgman as well, if he could). Carmichael and Keyser had both read Bridgman's book and generally agreed with Alfred's assessment of it. Keyser wrote to Alfred, "I'm giving myself the pleasure of sending your monographs [the *Time-Binding* papers] to Bridgman with a note suggesting that he <u>may</u> find them worthy of attentive reading. God only knows what the effect will be but it may be that God will never tell."[14]

A few days later, Bridgman wrote back to Keyser:
> ...I fussed over the manuscript of the thing [*The Logic of Modern Physics*] so long that I ended by wondering whether I was really saying anything of note; it is a great relief to know that you have found it suggestive.
> The monographs of Korzybski have not yet come. I shall be interested to see them and am grateful to you for sending them.[15]

Keyser shared the letter with Alfred, who wrote back to him on July 22:
> I think I understand his troubles, <u>lack</u> of language, lack of scientific psychology, scientific logic, and scientific philosophy, that's what bothers him. Can I understand him? By Jove I can. I hope he will understand me…[16]

Korzybski wrote his first letter to Bridgman on July 18 with much appreciation and some mild criticism. Bridgman, then at his summer home in Randolph, New Hampshire, replied on July 24:
> I am very much obliged indeed for your note of appreciation about my book. I shall be much interested to receive your reprints when they are available. Although I realized that our present habits of thought left much room for improvement, it had never occurred to me that psychopathic cases might be improved merely by improving habits of thought.
>
> With regard to the defects in the book,…I would be most grateful to you, if some time you could spare some of your leisure to let me know in some detail what have struck you as the most serious defects.
> Most sincerely,
> P. W. Bridgman[17]

Quantum Differences

Thus began the at-times difficult friendship of Korzybski and Bridgman. As they came to know each other better, both men communicated with unfailing directness and honesty. In addition to their correspondence, they met face-to-face a number of times. While maintaining the utmost civility, by 1934 (a year after Korzybski's book was finally published) their differences had become acute. But in the early phase of their relationship, Bridgman found Korzybski's work intriguing and quickly offered to read Alfred's developing manuscript and to help him in any other way he could. Over the next few years, he generously did so. Alfred felt much in debt to Bridgman for suggesting things to read, editing the book (particularly the mathematics and physics sections), and providing general criticism.

Although Bridgman had some minor suggestions, he never had any significant objections to Alfred's writing about physics. Indeed, one year later as he worked on editing the manuscript, Bridgman seemed astounded by Korzybski's grasp of the major new developments in the science: "I was much impressed by your chapter on the new wave mechanics; how do you manage to read so widely and digest so much? Many of your points of view I found interesting for their physical suggestiveness, apart from the special use that you make of them."[18]

Bridgman was also responsible for one of the new terms Alfred later introduced in *Science and Sanity*. Alfred was looking for a better term than "operational", "behaviouristic", or even "functional" (in the sense of "what something is doing") for the broad attitudinal perspective that he saw both he and Bridgman trying to formulate, each in his own way. Sometime over the next few years, Bridgman suggested the term "actional", which Alfred used in the book along with the other three terms. After *Science and Sanity* was published, Alfred realized he already had a better term but had not recognized it at the time—"extensional".

Bridgman's main objections to Korzybski's work related not to the physics background but to some of Alfred's non-aristotelian formulations. Although, for the most part, Alfred considered these objections wrong-headed, he still appreciated the scientist's fierce New England independence and unrestrained honesty—up to a point.

Although Bridgman had indicated his general agreement with the content of the two *Time-Binding* papers, he had wanted to learn more about the Anthropometer. About a month later Korzybski sent him one. Bridgman felt "grateful to accept it", writing to Alfred, "I shall keep it where I can often see it, and perhaps my thinking also will be wonderfully improved."

> Your letter contains many interesting and suggestive points which would require long personal discussion to treat at all adequately. There are still many difficulties for me in applying the A. to all my mental processes…The event…is the starting point for us, and it is of necessity something that we think about. But we must not think about it in words, for the moment anything verbal gets into our thinking we descend from the level of the event.[19]

Bridgman seemed to imply here that he could experience his non-verbal 'thinking','perceiving', etc., directly on the level of 'the event' itself. But according to the distinctions represented by Korzybski on the Anthropometer, whatever Bridgman or anyone else 'thought' non-verbally still had to be allocated—*not to the event level*—but rather to the 'object' level as a first-order, neurological abstraction from the event. And 'the event', for Korzybski, could *only* be inferred and definitely required symbolism and words (the accumulated science-at-a-given-date) to know anything about it. We were always 'in' the event, but any level of experience/knowledge of it always consisted of some abstraction from it.

Alfred's reply to Bridgman's concerns, written a few days later, seemed rather mild. Bridgman seemed assuaged by his reply. At least he made no further mention of the issue in his next letter to Alfred. But his perplexities about the Anthropometer and Korzybski's formulations continued to brew. Probably during one of their face-to-face conferences (either in 1930, when Alfred visited Bridgman and others at Harvard, or in 1931, when the two men both attended a AAAS meeting in New Orleans) "a dramatic moment" occurred which Alfred wrote about in *Science and Sanity*:

> …I had a very helpful and friendly contact prolonged over a number of years with a very eminent scientist. After many discussions, I asked if some of the special points of my work were clear to him. His answer was, 'Yes, it is all right, and so on, *but*, how can you expect me to follow your work all through, if I still do not know what an object *is*?' It was a genuine shock to me… The definite answer may be expressed as follows: 'Say whatever you choose *about* the object, and whatever you might say *is not* it.' Or, in other words : 'Whatever you might say the object "is", well it *is not* .' This negative statement is *final*, because it is *negative*.[20]

Examination of his extensive correspondence with Bridgman on this very topic, leaves little doubt as to which "eminent scientist" Korzybski was referring to here.

By 1934, Alfred had begun to lose patience with Bridgman in regard to a number of issues. Despite their commonalities (which Alfred had seen and had sought to bridge), what put the two men at odds could be seen in their different attitudes towards the new developments in quantum physics in 1927 and afterwards. As Korzybski related early on to Bridgman, he was ready for the new. In particular, he welcomed the developments in quantum physics, which he had started to study and which seemed to fully jibe with his understanding of the non-aristotelian viewpoint. Indeed, it seemed to him that his educational methods to promote consciousness of abstracting could help people to understand and explore the quantum realm more easily:

> …As yet we do not approach the Q. [quantum realm] with enough psychological freedom from macroscopic old prejudices expressed in the machinery of our forms of representations…I see no reason why we could not…free ourselves psychologically from the bondage of the old form of representations, and see the old facts of the Q.t. which we know already and make a happier form of representation.[21]

In contrast, in 1927 (and for a long time afterwards), Bridgman seemed to look at these developments with a tinge of regret for an earlier time when 'reality' had seemed as solid as a brick. His "blockage about the 'object'" seemed rather stubborn, despite his intellectual understanding that the underlying 'reality' postulated by quantum theory was not anything like a brick but rather more like a 'mad dance' (to use one of Alfred's favorite metaphors), where even the classical notion of causality had come into question. Bridgman wrote to Korzybski early in 1928: "Your remarks about the pathological aspects of not knowing were very interesting. I suppose perhaps that when one knows that he doesn't know the state is the most pathological; this would seem to be suggested by the constant headache, which I have when trying to get the new quantum mechanics."[22] Bridgman seemed to fear that Heisenberg's "principle of indetermination", as he called it, threatened meaninglessness in the realm of the very small.[23] Korzybski did sympathize with Bridgman's sentiment that "part of the causality concept is conditioned by our own thinking mechanism so that we can never entirely get away from it."[24] Still, the new view didn't give Alfred a headache; he relished it and the possibility of an altered notion of causality.[25] For Korzybski, the most pathological aspect of not knowing resulted from *not* knowing that one doesn't know (and from the "false knowledge" tending to fill the 'vacuum').

Alas for Alfred, by 1934 cooperation with Bridgman no longer seemed possible. Bridgman felt at odds with Korzybski, had significant disagreements with some of the basic formulations (as he understood them) in Alfred's book, and felt little to no interest in any more joining of hands. Although the men had some further correspondence, it seems to have petered out after 1936 when Bridgman sent a copy of his just-published book, *The Nature of Physical Theory*, to Korzybski.

Bridgman mistakenly understood Korzybski as wanting to make the structure of language 'identical' with experience. In the 1936 book, (without mentioning Korzybski by name), Bridgman condemned this [pp. 21-26]. Rightly so, but it had nothing to do with Korzybski's actual views. Alfred wrote back to Bridgman in a 5-page letter with lengthy commentary—not entirely critical. Alfred had read the book with great interest and could see in it a profound ambivalence about his work. Alfred still cherished Bridgman's friendship and seems to have hoped he could thrash things out with him.[26] Bridgman wasn't willing and replied dismissively:

> Now I have spent a great deal of time first and last on going over your ideas, as much as I am willing to afford in view of all my other interests, and the plain fact of the matter is that you haven't 'put it across' as far as I am concerned.[27]

Bridgman's "struggles" and "ambivalence toward changing scientific standards"[28]—perhaps accelerated by his contact with Korzybski—continued until the end of his life. Ironically, *The Way Things Are* (1959), one of Bridgman's last books, shows a startlingly significant, though apparently unconscious, korzybskian influence. Although Bridgman seemed unaware of it, Alfred had managed to 'put across' quite a bit.[29]

Badly Overdue

By the end of 1927, Korzybski was approaching a deep sense of hopelessness. His work had become both a blessing and a curse. Many areas of science and life seemed to be moving in a non-aristotelian direction. An explicit non-aristotelian system seemed to him necessary for someone to formulate. The existence of such a system might help quicken the otherwise more-or-less unconscious non-aristotelian tendencies in the culture. Alfred had started to produce such a system. If he was going to continue, he wanted to do as good a job as possible. But he truly didn't know whether he was up to it.

The book was already badly overdue. Yet his notes and writing were still in a jumble, cut into pieces that he was sorting into boxes, trying to put into a better order.[30] His project seemed like madness! Who but a madman would try to study and integrate such an abundance of diverse material? One man could not reasonably hope to master even a small portion of it. Seeking to show the connections amongst a multitude of different fields, he needed help not only in checking the separate specialty areas he referred to, but also in assessing his general system. Knowing how easy it could be to make things fit an unsound theory, he still did not entirely trust his own judgment. He was consulting with Graven, who was in the process of gathering clinical data to write up along with a psychiatry appendix. Alfred was also accumulating a number of other expert specialists willing to look at various parts of the book that touched upon their fields. Still he had no one who seemed both willing and able to competently evaluate the whole. Keyser might be one of the few who could do so, but Alfred did not want to burden his friend with too much at this point. Keyser seemed to have bounced back from Ella Keyser's death, but his health seemed delicate and he had to garner his limited energies for his own writing and teaching. Meanwhile, every blessedly cursed day brought forth more material (not just from physics) that Alfred felt compelled to deal with. Bridgman was by no means the only one who could smell something in the air.

For example, over the last year in conjunction with his work with Graven, Alfred had been digging more deeply into the psychiatric literature, especially Sigmund Freud's work in English translation. In his most recent books, *Beyond the Pleasure Principle* and *The Ego and the Id*, Freud seemed to Korzybski to be getting close to the formulation of the "scientific unconscious" as elaborated in the second *Time-Binding* paper. Alfred considered Freud's work valuable in many ways. Indeed, he would put Freud on the list of those to whom he would dedicate his book. But even in 1927, he found Freud's language "very cloudy". As Alfred wrote to Roy Haywood in early 1928, "his [Freud's] formulations are not workable."[31]

Alfred had also already begun corresponding with Trigant Burrow (1875–1950), a psychiatrist who, in 1927, had just come out with his first book, *The Social Basis of Consciousness*. Alfred also corresponded with Burrow's colleague, psychiatrist Hans Syz. Although Burrow had had an early interest in Freud's work and psychoanalysis, he had been forming his own views outside of the main psychoanalytical circles. Beside his M.D., he had gotten a doctorate in experimental psychology focused on the physiology of attention. His approach to therapy—he pioneered in group therapy and social psychiatry—developed out of his interest in the interactions among the physiological, phenomenological, interpersonal, and socio-cultural aspects of maladjustment. Burrow may have coined the word "neurodynamic" (he was one of the first to use the term) and went on to explore the role of attention and symbolism in neuroses.

Burrow had independently gotten very close to a great deal of what Korzybski had formulated in his general theory. Korzybski sought to emphasize the commonality of their work. But Burrow's understanding seemed intuitive, his language cloudy. Alfred had hopes his own work could suggest ways to bring greater formulational clarity to Burrow's efforts. Burrow didn't see it that way. In his book, *Science and Man's Behavior*, published posthumously, Burrow wrote:

I would not make all this ado about the wide disparity between...[us], were not Korzybski so determined to proselytize me on the ground that "we are saying the same thing." Perhaps we are. But do our organisms *feel* the same way?[32]

Regarding Burrow, Korzybski in later years didn't waver from the opinion he expressed to Roy Haywood in early 1928, "His [Burrow's] main thesis is that we are all insane (neurotics), do not know it and are headed for worse. I quite agree with him."[33]

The kinds of works that appealed to Korzybski, as grist for his mill, tended to share some common characteristics, no matter what their subject area. First, they were apt to have what he called a *behaviouristic* outlook (not the same as 'behaviorism'). Even in a 'seemingly' esoteric work in mathematics or physics, he looked for some acknowledgment on the author's part that knowledge, expressed through some form of language and symbolism, never 'dropped down from the heavens'—*some humans produced it*. And the process involved in developing-expressing knowledge made a difference to the knowledge produced. Acknowledgement of that, a nascent consciousness of abstracting, made a difference too.

Second, the works that especially called to Korzybski were likely to have a *comprehensive* viewpoint. To show important relationships often required bursting through the limiting box of any particular discipline or school of thought. Such working non-elementalism also tended to involve cautiousness about additive, linear approaches involving relationships among elements. 'Adding' a new element or elements could often lead to complex, non-additive results, e.g., one more guest at a party could create multiple complications. The problems of aristotelian "plus" approaches to non-linear, 'non-plus' situations had been bugging Korzybski since the early twenties when he had started his explorations in mathematical logic. The non-elementalistic issue of non-additivity/non-linearity had many theoretical and practical ramifications. Rainich had been helping him to tackle the issue on the math and physics side and he was looking for literature that would provide more examples of non-additivity in different disciplines and in daily life.

Third, the works Korzybski found most compelling were likely to show a *dynamic* attitude, dealing with their subjects in historical, process terms. The significance of space-time factors in understanding any matter of consideration could not be underestimated, as far as Korzybski was concerned. Any of the three above-mentioned characteristics would, at the very least, give someone's work a non-aristotelian direction.

Korzybski had been reading one just-published book, which had all three characteristics—*Thought and the Brain*, by French experimental psychologist Henri Piéron (1881–1964). Especially after he started reading neurologist C. Judson Herrick's writings about a year before, Alfred had more than ever been emphasizing abstracting as a psycho-physiological, neurological process (which did not eliminate the data of introspection). The lower order(s) of abstracting (non-verbal) related closely to activity in the sub-cortical areas (the thalamus, etc.) that Herrick had written about. They heavily involved the 'affective', 'feeling' aspect of people's reactions.

Both Pieron's work and that of Dr. Lewis R. Yealland as represented in his book *Hysterical Disorders of Warfare*, seemed especially relevant to understanding this 'feeling' aspect. Using a combination of electrical stimulation and verbal suggestion, Yealland had treated Great War soldiers suffering from various psycho-physiological consequences of "shell shock". Yealland's reputation would later suffer (he was depicted as a villain in novelist Pat Barker's late 20th century fictional account of British World War I soldiers, *Regeneration*). However, the apparent effectiveness of Yealland's methods impressed Korzybski. Korzybski had also become interested in the psycho-galvanic skin response (the basis of the psycho-galvanometer or "lie detector" machine) that both Hans Syz and physiologist H. B. Williams at Columbia were studying. (Alfred later recounted to his students his experiences as a test subject in Dr. William's laboratory).

From these studies, it had become clear to Korzybski that despite the great importance of language, the linguistic levels of abstracting were, in some sense, only accessory to the more dynamic, non-verbal, affective, lower-order level(s). As he wrote to Graven in October, 1927, he saw that these lower levels could and needed to be used in psychotherapy[34] : "If we stimulate by <u>ANY MEANS</u> whatsoever the "attention", we mobilize or even produce an energetic <u>tention</u> and so later we can direct the discharge of this energy in desired channels, beneficial results follow."[35] Although he was giving advice to Graven about working with patients, the recommendation 'to interest attention by any means' also reflected Korzybski's developing views on how to communicate and teach: for greatest effectiveness, the non-verbal level of abstraction needed to be used to the maximum—together with the verbal.[36]

Beside the physics, psychiatry and neurology books, Alfred was also reading the first volume of Oswald Spengler's *The Decline of the West,* which had come out in English translation in 1926. (He would read the second volume after its publication in 1928.) As Alfred later wrote, he found *The Decline of the West*, "unique and astonishing."[37] Indeed, his dark mood lightened a bit as a result of reading it in the fall of 1927. As he wrote to Florian Cajori in September:

> ....I was very lonesome in my work. I treat mathematics from a neglected point of view namely as a form of human behavior, an attitude which seems legitimate at least. I was so glad to find lately that I am not alone and that Spengler in his *Decline of the West* is also doing it. I just began to read this book a second time and find that he traces in the development of mathematics the expression of the spirit of [its] time.[38]

Given Spengler's main thesis—a variation on the theme of "logical destiny"—and the erudition with which he elaborated upon it, Korzybski's high estimation of *The Decline of the West* doesn't seem surprising. Richard J. Robertson later noted that for Spengler,

> ...The "mechanism", of history...is not physical law but destiny; that is, the playing out of consequences drawn from initial premises, as in systems of mathematics. [Spengler] made it his task, then, to outline the principles underlying the "spirit" of different cultures and detail what he saw as the evidence for them.[39]

For Spengler, this playing out of cultural premises/assumptions meant the inevitable decline of a civilization. To him, Western Civilization was already unraveling with no way out except for Mankind to continue going around in ultimately fruitless circles. Korzybski felt this profound pessimism about the future seemed justified—but only if humans could not transcend their old ways of unconscious development. As he would soon write, *The Decline of the West* provided "a great description of the childhood of humanity".[40] What appeared like a circle might then form a spiral path forward and upward toward genuine human progress. He believed his own work could help this movement. But he had to get the first draft done.

Chapter 34
"DON'T YOU SEE THE ELECTRON?"

By the end of 1927, Korzybski's general mood had sunk; he had come to feel stuck in Brooklyn. Other than an October weekend with Mira at Polakov's cabin on Long Island, he had not had a vacation in a very long time. He got another little break from his desk at the end of November when he helped Mira put on an exhibition of her work in Manhattan. But except for occasionally going to the movies with her, he had few distractions. He and Mira did get a kitten, whom they named "Sally" in honor of their friend Sally Avery. (Because of their traveling they had to give her away the following year.) The kitten provided some amusement for Alfred as he sat at his desk. He spent most of his time working there, seven days a week.

At this point he was keeping *Time-Binding: The General Theory, An Introduction to Humanology* as his working-title. Keyser had previously put forward *Suggestions Towards a Better Scientific Methodology*, which Alfred had rejected.[1] He thought his work had more value than just its suggestiveness. A little before, he had written to Jesse Bennett:

> I do not overestimate my work, it might be all wrong I am perfectly willing to grant this to anybody, but it is a new work, an attempt to build a non-aristotelian system, and attempt to build a science of man, and apply scientific method as known in 1927 to man, and no matter how fallacious, it is the first attempt of this kind, and so I have justified my existence anyway.[2]

But however "grand" his "ideas", as he wrote to Roy Haywood, "...these "ideas" will not write the book."[3]

With the start of 1928, Mira was going to have to go on the road again to make some money. He hated the long separations but, by the end of January, he was considering going away himself—specifically to Pasadena where he anticipated getting some help from E.T. Bell and others at the California Institute of Technology (Caltech). If he was ever going to produce the damn book, he had to do it soon. He had just gotten a letter from a cousin of his in Warsaw, "telling me that it is imperative that I go home, my mother is seemingly getting rather weak and the business (properties) going to the dogs." He felt "pressed like hell."[4] In a few weeks, his plans had gelled. He wrote to Philip Graven on February 11:

> The 27th of February I am sailing from N.Y. to New Orlean and from New Orlean by train to Pasadena where I will work at The California Polytechnic [sic], with such men as Bell and Bateman in mathematics and Epstein in the quantum theory. They are all world famous in their specialties...This mental solitude is beginning to affect me badly, and my nerves do not act as well as they should, I am getting too[,] something ...it looks to me as the beginnings of neurasthenia or something from over work and worry. I need some change and some cooperation of men who can understand what I am talking about, the rest make me feel rotten. I am getting downhearted and unfit to carry it alone...[5]

At the end of February after going to Washington for a few days to confer with Graven, Alfred returned to Brooklyn, said goodbye to Mira, and boarded "The Creole" of the Southern Pacific Steamship Line. With him he took some suitcases and a trunk carrying his books and a number of Anthropometers. He found the six-day ocean trip to New Orleans quite restful.

The somewhat shorter train trip got him to the city of Pasadena, just northeast of Los Angeles, more than a week after he had left New York. Whatever the discomforts of traveling and then resettling in a new place, the trip had left him feeling somewhat renewed.

Pasadena

He found a small "maid's cottage" to rent at 62 Mar Vista Street just north of Pasadena's Colorado Boulevard, within walking distance of Caltech. (On the site now sits a large condominium apartment building.) It wasn't bad at all for a "maid's cottage". It had a front parlor, a dining room with a large window toward the front that he used as his office with a large table he had for a typewriter desk, a small bedroom that he slept in, a larger guest bedroom, a kitchen, and bathroom. The owner, who lived behind the cottage in a larger house, had left some ramshackle furniture that sufficed for Alfred. He found the place easy to keep clean, sweeping and mopping it himself once a week. With electricity, hot water, a gas stove, and portable heaters, it had everything he needed.

Korzybski soon settled into a routine. Though he kept long, irregular hours, he tended to get up early. After making himself a large cup of coffee (he usually didn't eat breakfast) he would start his two-fingered pecking on the typewriter keyboard until he felt hungry, sometime around noon. Then he would often walk half a block south to Colorado Boulevard where he had found a mom and pop restaurant owned by a Swiss couple with whom he made friends. They had excellent food and took good care of him. After lunch, he often stopped at a nearby fruit and vegetable market to get grapes, oranges, pears, etc., and vegetables that didn't need cooking. There was also a nearby butcher shop where he would often stop to get either a veal kidney (which he liked to have occasionally) or his favorite—filet mignon—which he could get for 90 cents a pound. He cooked filet mignon quite often for his supper. He would fry it in a pan with lots of butter and eat it on top of a nice big piece of toasted bread.

A little more than a month after he arrived, Alfred gave a presentation at a conference held at the Los Angeles Public Library for the California Association for Adult Education. He called his talk "A New Approach in Education of Adults".[6] Although he had learned he could orient a talk on his work toward a wide range of subject matters, he had a longstanding interest in Adult Education. For a number of years, he had paid membership dues to a British group, The World Association for Adult Education. Their motto seemed right in line with his efforts: "The multitude of the wise is the welfare of the world." Clearly, if children were to be educated in his non-aristotelian approach, then their parents (though with much more difficulty) would need such education too. Although he had hoped to be able to get some paid lectures—and had written to a number of friends and contacts regarding speaking opportunities—this turned out to be one of the few presentations he gave (most of them, like this one, unpaid) during what would turn out to be a year in California. That was probably a good thing. Giving a lot of talks might have diverted him from his main job. He didn't live like a hermit (he visited people and had visitors), but, as he said, "as a rule, my life [in Pasadena] was extremely isolated."[7] He was there to write.

The new environment seemed to have somehow freed him to do it. How did he begin? Before presenting his own work "On The Mechanism Of Time-Binding" that would eventually appear as Book II, "A General Introduction to Non-Aristotelian Systems...[etc.]", he felt that, as he said, "I had to give the background, logical, physico-mathematical, all of that before I could approach my own part to have people understanding the importance of that non-aristotelian orientation. I had to give all of the background."[8] So he started writing Book I, which he would call "A General Survey of Non-Aristotelian Factors". When he had completed it a few months later, he started to write Book II, but stopped. He felt he still needed to provide more mathematical and scientific background to fill out what he had already written. This became Book III, "Additional Structural Data About Languages And The Empirical World".

Much of the material in Book III would appear intimidating to many laymen (and perhaps even to some mathematicians and scientists). Nonetheless, he felt it would be useful for all readers—and it seemed necessary to substantiate his system—to provide this more in-depth treatment. Although he needed to accurately present whatever technicalities he wrote about (thank goodness for Bridgman and others who helped him with that), his main point here was to show mathematics and science as the behavior and language of humans. He found Book III "a most technically difficult book to write" for this very reason.[9] Despite appearances, it did not deal mainly with any particular physico-mathematical problems. Rather it involved Korzybski's "...*second order* observations of the first order observations, of the first order observer, and of the relations between them, . [, etc.]"[10]

He advised his readers not to worry about grasping all of the technicalities, but to read in order to get the *feel* of mathematics and science as products of human behavior. As he wrote in the *Introductory* section of his chapter "On The Semantics Of The Differential Calculus":

> Any reader who has a distaste for mathematics will benefit most if he overcomes his semantic [evaluational] phobia and struggles through these pages, even several times. As a result of so doing he will find it simple although not always easy. It is always semantically [evaluationally] useful to overcome one's phobias; it liberates one from unjustified fears, feelings of inferiority, . [, etc.] The main point of this whole discussion is to evoke the semantic [evaluational] components of a living Smith, when he habitually uses the method which will be explained herewith.[11]

He was writing here about the feel of the calculus his father had given to him so many years before, and which, in a way, had started him on his quest. Book III also included chapters on non-linearity, geometry, various aspects of relativity theory, and quantum mechanics—all from Alfred's point of view of the behavior of "a living Smith".

Book II (the core of his non-aristotelian system and training procedures) remained the last major segment he wrote in Pasadena, completing it in early 1929. When in later years he thought back about his writing of the first draft there, he could say, "What made me and what makes me happy that I could write such a heavy book like *Science and Sanity* practically offhand."[12] Ultimately, whatever changes, additions, and other editing it got subsequently, the book published four years later substantially retained the text that—as he blithely described it— he 'offhandedly' "spit out" that year in Pasadena.

"Don't You See the Electron?"

When Korzybski first got to Pasadena, he anticipated getting help from E. T. Bell and others at Caltech. For the first month or so of his time there, he made a concerted effort to meet with as many people as he could in the Caltech community, as well as with other contacts and friends in Pasadena, Los Angeles, and Southern California. Bell, despite his busyness with his own work, certainly wanted to help his friend to do this. A few weeks after Alfred's arrival, Bell and his wife invited him to dinner along with Caltech scientist Roy J. Kennedy, a young experimental physicist shortly to be moving to the University of Washington. It was the kind of connection Korzybski had hoped for.

Kennedy—who had become known for reproducing Michelson and Morley's famous 1887 results with a refinement of their 'ether drift' experiment—became friendly and interested in Alfred and his work and would eventually help with the editing of the book. In a letter written in 1934 to Selden Smyser, a professor at a small Washington state college, Kennedy described some of his first impressions of Korzybski:

> ...My first meeting with Korzybski was at a dinner arranged for the purpose by E.T. Bell of Caltech. I was promptly impressed by the two characteristics which still seem his most salient ones, an almost complete freedom from conventionalism in speech and manner, and a rather formidable store of nervous energy. There was no subject or person he didn't feel free to discuss or evaluate for better or for worse and of course this trait is evident thruout his writing. No one could possibly call him prudish or politic. He lived in a modest cottage in Pasadena while writing his last book, and in heat of summer it was refreshing altho a bit startling to see him at his desk or answering door bell stript to the waist.
>
> In all my acquaintance with Korzybski I have never known him to exhibit a trace of fatigue. He once stopped at my office at noon; as afternoon wore on the conversation assumed more and more the character of a soliloquy and when at five he briskly departed, I was scarcely able to sit up much less reason or speak. I took him to a friend's house one evening. He regaled us with many incidents from his broad experience, and about one o'clock got around to psychiatry. After sketching the treatment of a particular case of insanity, he said that finally a test of the patient's recovery could be made in terms of his reply to a single question. "Sir", said Korzybski to our host (a man of small vitality who had by that hour become terribly stupid), "I will put the same question to you." The question was rather complicated altho it required only yes or no, and of course the wretched fellow gave the wrong answer.
>
> I have emphasized the bizarre in these few random remarks. Much could be said of the man's fine qualities, his friendliness and his impatience with bourgeois morality, but that would be superfluous.[13]

As for Bell, he seemed willing to continue advising Alfred on his manuscript, introducing him to potentially helpful people, and also trying to get a lecture opportunity for Alfred at Caltech. But Alfred had one apparent problem—Robert A. Millikan.[14]

Korzybski and Millikan, the "Chairman of the Executive Council", i.e., Caltech's president, had known each other for a number of years and had had a distantly friendly relationship. But Korzybski had gotten the sense Millikan had developed some prejudice against his work, perhaps at least in part as a result of Mira's pushing during her previous time in Pasadena several years before. And despite Millikan's admitted brilliance as an experimentalist, Korzybski definitely had difficulties with Millikan's formulating. Millikan had won the 1923 Nobel prize for measuring the charge of an electron using a cloud chamber apparatus with aerosolized oil droplets. Alfred was familiar with the work, having read Millikan's book, *The Electron*. He had read with dismay Millikan's Nobel lecture where the physicist had insisted, "He who has seen that experiment, and hundreds of investigators have observed it, has literally *seen* the electron."[15] For Alfred, this seemed "too silly for words."[16] However firmly experiments seemed to establish the existence of the electron, nothing seemed clearer than this: as a theoretical entity, *nobody* had ever seen an electron and *nobody could ever see one*. As he later wrote in his book:

> ...I have read an address by a prominent physicist in which he claims to have 'seen', and invites everybody else to 'see', an electron. He challenges his critics, and seems to feel like fighting—a quite usual result of identification [confusion of orders of abstraction]. Electrons represent *inferential entities*, and as such cannot be 'seen', but only inferred, which does not detract at all from the importance of the 'electrons'. The 'seeing' business was good enough in the infancy of science, but not in 1933. We 'see' the stick broken in water, the camera records it as broken, and yet it is not broken. We 'see' the fan as a disk, the camera records it so, but there is no disk. We 'see' a 'solid' piece of wood or stone, which under the microscope proves to have a very different structure, . [, etc.][17]

Bell knew about Alfred's feelings and indicated his concern about avoiding a fight. As it turned out, Korzybski and Millikan did fight—although they did it rather politely. Millikan sent a nice note to Alfred on May 26 inviting him to make himself "entirely at home" at the Caltech library and "in the Institute generally. I should be very glad to show you the oil-drop apparatus whenever you are about the Institute."[18] Korzybski accepted the invitation and went to see Millikan soon afterwards. In his 1947 memoir, he described what happened next:

> ...[Millikan] was very, very kind and he showed me his famous apparatus...there is a chamber with naphtha/kerosene vapors and there is an electrical apparatus which puts something, whatever, through that chamber of kerosene vapors and you see little clouds radiate and you can count those little clouds...[Millikan] asked me his usual question, "Don't you see the electron?" Well, being truthful as usual, I said, "Yes, Professor, I see a lighted cloud, but I don't see the electron, and that's all." He became my mortal enemy...and he prohibited his staff to have anything to do with me because I didn't see the electron...This in a way twisted my whole plan. The staff, of course, after Millikan gave that order, were polite and nice to me, but literally they would have no contact with me, except casual and social...Bell didn't want to have troubles with Millikan. Bell expected to have those lectures for the Institute by me. Now, this of course fell off.[19]

In fairness to Millikan, Korzybski's sense of being rebuffed by Millikan's staff may have been strengthened by Bell who told him Millikan had no use for him. Korzybski also noted at the time that Bell seemed to have fallen into a sour, cynical mood about almost everything and had an extreme concern about not imperiling his position at Caltech. Is it possible that what Bell told Korzybski was colored by Bell's bad mood and concern for Caltech politics? Even as late as November, a number of months after the incident, Alfred still reported in a letter to Keyser, "...in my face Millikan is always charming and extremely polite,...has given me the 'freedom of the tech', meaning library, club, laboratories, seminars etc. I use the library all the time, attend also important seminars but otherwise have little to do with the tech."[20] It seems impossible to know if Korzybski spoke entirely fairly in later years when he attributed some degree of malice to Millikan. At any rate, after the incident Alfred didn't want to risk his friendship with Bell by doing anything that might jeopardize the mathematician's position with his 'boss'. Alfred decided to tread lightly around Caltech.

Apart from Caltech politics, Bell also appeared to have fallen into a sour mood about the mathematics profession. Around the time of the electron incident, Alfred had been writing one of the core parts of the book—a long chapter on mathematics (or perhaps more accurately the psychology of mathematics). He showed some of it to Bell, who seemed to have a fit whenever Alfred said anything good about the field.[21] Bell's head didn't seem in the right place for him to give much help. Despite all this, the two men remained friendly and continued to visit each other occasionally.

'Ises' and Other 'Notions'

So much for plans. Alfred gave up hope of getting any special help at Caltech. He felt as alone as ever. Still, though it seemed like a never-ending slog, he was getting the book written. He found feeling settled in a place facilitated his work and he had gotten to feel sufficiently at home in his little place in Pasadena "to work like the dickens" (as he liked to say), despite that year's quite frequent little earthquakes and the Southern California native ants that seemed to impress him more than most of the native humans. As he wrote to Bridgman: "You put anything which is edible, and in a very short while you have [a] regular army invading the place. Nothing can be hidden from them, and they communicate somehow rapidly with each other. They are extraordinary."[22]

Being in Southern California, Alfred wanted to meet Will Rogers and sent a note to the "cowboy philosopher" and entertainer (1879–1935), who had a ranch in the Santa Monica hills. Korzybski, who had enjoyed Rogers' newspaper columns and books and heard him lecture, didn't consider Rogers so much as a humorist, but rather as an exceptionally down-to-earth and extensional human being who therefore often naturally said things that made people laugh.[23] On June 4, he got a letter from Rogers' office inviting him to come any afternoon for a visit.[24] Rogers would soon be traveling to cover the U.S. Presidential Nominating Conventions. So it was probably within just a few days that Dr. and Mrs. Wolfenden, friends of Alfred's who lived in Beverly Hills and had a car, drove him out to Rogers' ranch. Will Rogers' response to the visit is not known but, since he once said he never met a man he didn't like, he nigh surely must have gotten a kick out of spending an afternoon with Alfred Korzybski, another exceptionally down-to-earth and extensional horseman.

Although he did take some time out for this and other visits and visitors (both Luella Twining and Sally Avery were then living in Los Angeles), for the most part, as usual, Alfred was mainly working 18 hours a day, 7 days a week. He had hoped he could be done with the first draft by October, but decided if he was not done by then, he would stay in Pasadena until he finished. In June, he was completing an important, difficult, large, and still unwieldy chapter on what he was then calling the psychology of mathematics (this would later be divided into the two chapters of Book I, Part V, "On The Non-Aristotelian Language Called Mathematics"). From there, he decided to go on to the detailed material of Book III, and soon began working on what would become its first three chapters, making up Part VIII, "On The Structure of Mathematics".

One can get a feel of the general state of his formulating in mid-1928 from an abstract of a proposed paper he sent for inclusion in the Philosophy and History of Mathematics Section of The International Congress of Mathematics scheduled from September 3–10 at the University of Bologna, Italy. Planning to attend, he had registered for the Congress, but by the beginning of July realized he had neither the time nor money to expend for the trip. He still sent the abstract on July 3, his 49th birthday, and it was published in the Congress Proceedings:

> A. Korzybski – New York, - *Time-binding, the General theory and the generalized theory of Mathematical types. An outline of a non-aristotelian system.*
> Methodological considerations. Organism-as-a-whole verso elementalism and its parallel, space-time verso space and time. The metaphysics and method underlying the aristotelian, euclidian and newtonian systems and its too many "infinities". Mathematical methods as fundamental for a non-aristotelian system. Formulation of a non-aristotelian system. Common metaphysics and method underlying non-aristotelian, non-euclidian and non-

newtonian systems and its a few "infinities" less. Structures of languages. The General Theory of Time-binding and differential and four dimensional methods. The Theory of Mathematical Types generalized. The connection of a non-aristotelian system with a positive theory of sanity. Consequences. Applications.[25]

By this time, researching for Part X, "On The Structure Of Matter"—Book III's finale—he had just begun an intensive 'assault' on quantum physics, reading works by among others, Born, Heisenberg, Birtwhistle, and Biggs—the latter two authors having written relatively up-to-date summaries of the latest advances, which he found valuable.[26] Concurrently, as he had already assimilated relativity theory, he had started to write about it in what would become the five chapters of Book III, Part IX, "On The Similarity Of Empirical and Verbal Structures". As Korzybski saw it, Einstein's work had paved the way for the new generation of quantum physicists whose latest developments—ironically—Einstein seemed unwilling to fully embrace. Korzybski was trying to absorb a tremendous amount of material, at least enough to write about the interconnected psycho-logical, epistemological, linguistic, and methodological aspects of the new physics. As he often did, he called on his 'unconscious' processes to help him. He had been working at this for at least a month when he wrote to Bridgman on August 11:

...I use a habitual device with hard readings. I read rapidly never bothering about what I do not understand, but read repeatedly the whole and so the details begin to [dawn] upon me slowly, besides I read always this stuff in bed and sleep it over, so do not waste the hours of my sleep as my brain is digesting when I sleep.[27]

Korzybski could scarcely contain his tremendous excitement about what he was studying. The implications of quantum theory for his work struck him profoundly. As he had already written to Mira, the convergence of the different approaches of Heisenberg, Schrodinger, and Dirac delighted him. Indeed, he told her, these formulators had expressed something which he had long felt and vaguely visualized but had not had the capacity to adequately express on his own.[28] He seems a bit too modest here. In 1922 in "The Brotherhood of Doctrines" he had already formulated the principle that any observation involved the interaction of an 'observer' with the 'observed', not to be considered as entirely separate. The new quantum mechanics seemed closely connected to this. In the August 11 letter to Bridgman, he had also said:

...It appeared to me (you will judge it not me) that this new stuff is in perfect accord with the G.T. [General Theory] of mine, which if it is (GT) what it claims to be, namely a theory which gives the structure of 'human knowledge' it should embrace all scientific revolutions as well. If I do understand this new stuff, and what I say stands the <u>official professional</u> test, then these new theories are extremely useful to me. If not, well it would mean a quite serious set back to me and my work.[29]

With quantum mechanics, he realized he was on the trail of something important to his work, even if the details were not exactly clear. (As he edited and revised the book over the next few years, he would more fully formulate—in a way surprising even to him—the relationship of the new physics to his theory of knowledge.)

Other aspects of his work had already emerged in more definite form as he worked on the draft. For example, he had begun to use single quotes to flag questionable, elementalistic terms. And recently he had explicitly formulated the problems with the 'is' of identity. He was applying these linguistic revisions to his own writing in the book. He told Bridgman about these "peculiarities of language":

> ...a mathematician may die of heart failure in hearing that I call a statement twice two is four a mathematical 'notion'. The reason is that I cannot use the terms 'idea' or 'concept' etc without quotation marks and I can use the term notion. I have to <u>avoid all old elementalistic</u> terms, which makes the language very peculiar.
>
> I have also to avoid the term 'is'. This something new. When we have the emotional disturbance of 'objectification' we <u>fancy</u> that we make statements on objective level, which we never do, as all statements are verbal issues and not the thing we are talking about. If we say 'a rose is red' this is a statement where 'is' is used in the predicate sense, the other statement 'a rose is a flower' this is a 'is' of identity. Now on the objective level (where we have to be silent anyway) nothing IS nothing else except itself so all statements involving IS are unconditionally false on the objective level and remain only valid on the verbal or mathematical, in the generalized sense, level. A statement 'is not' has an entirely different character and on a 'objective level' it is unconditionally true. The rest <u>is</u> a valid 'is' by definition, it means in the construction of language but this has nothing to do with the world around us. So two and two is 4 is correct use of is. When I use the term is I try to do so only on the definition level.
>
> This is why all physical theories which tell us what IS what are fundamentally wrong, because it isn't so, and why the <u>only way</u> is to use the operational, functional, behaviouristic way of speaking not what <u>is</u> with objectification, but what happens or what something <u>does</u> (order fundamental), this seems to be the reason why the new methods mean such a tremendous departure from the old and what justifies yours and mine point of view.[30]

It seems best to read this not-meant-for-publication letter to a friend with some sympathy, i. e., not to count Korzybski's 'ises' here against him. He never advocated entirely eliminating 'ises' even in his later published work. Besides the 'is not' and the 'is' of definition, he would extend the legitimate use of 'is' to 'necessary' colloquialisms, the auxiliary 'is' (e.g., "I am going to the store."), and the 'is' of existence (e.g., "I am here."). Still, the quote shows some of the linguistic difficulties Alfred struggled with in writing his book.

The Queer Duck and the French Secretary

Korzybski had already gotten copies of one or more of his chapters to Bridgman, Roy Haywood, Bell, Graven, Luella Twining, and Mira (and perhaps a few others). But, since the early summer he had been desperately looking for someone to type for him. What an onerous job it would be if he had to personally type enough copies of the manuscript (even using carbon paper) for everyone he wanted to get it to. He also felt the need to have someone check his English to help him 'smooth' it out—he realized the book's linguistic innovations would make his prose seem odd enough without having, in addition, unnecessary non-fluencies possibly arising because English was not his native language.

When he first came to Pasadena, he had met some fans of *Manhood of Humanity*, a couple named the Witherspoons, who lived nearby. He had gone to their house several times for tea. Mrs. Witherspoon had writing and editing experience and initially had some interest in helping Alfred with the book. Perhaps she could find a typist for him. But she didn't quite seem to understand the unusual and difficult scope of what Alfred was trying to produce in the book (something both scientists and scientific laymen would find usable). Beside that, Mr. Witherspoon was having health problems, which began to occupy her attention. Alfred was going to have keep looking for help.

Another avenue of possible help opened up when he met Dr. Anita Muhl, a psychiatrist then living in San Diego who had worked at St. Elizabeths prior to his time there. Alfred had several meetings with her. She was interested in his work and knew a psychologist and pre-med student, Helene Powner, who might be able to help Alfred in exchange for private classes in non-aristotelian, physico-mathematical methods. Miss Powner didn't have the typing skills Alfred needed, though she did develop an interest in his work. She met several times with him to talk about her career decisions and health problems. Alfred gave her his *Time-Binding* booklets and taught her some of the basics of his approach to helping people. (She later wrote to him thanking him for the advice he had given her.) A friend of hers, who did have the clerical skills that Alfred needed, apparently didn't work out either.

Not until sometime in the fall of 1928 (probably November) did Alfred finally get the typing and English help he needed. Calvin Bridges, who had just come to Pasadena, provided the means for both. Thomas Hunt Morgan had been invited by Millikan to start a biology department at Caltech and had brought along Bridges, an indispensable member of his Columbia University genetics team, as a research associate. (Bridges retained his status as a research fellow with The Carnegie Institution of Washington, D.C.) Morgan, Bridges, and others moved their famous "fly room" from New York City to Pasadena for the fall term. Bridges, who died unexpectedly in 1938, worked there for the remainder of his career.

In 1928, soon after he came to town, Bridges hooked up with his old friend Korzybski who, years later, told of their time together:

...Dr. Calvin Bridges, an outstanding geneticist. He's the fly man. He was dealing with the Drosophila Melanogaster. He was already a lonesome man and he was interested very much in social problems. He didn't read much [outside of his field] and he spent all the time in the laboratory playing and observing all the time many many generations of flies, fruit flies they call it in English. It was a very important work and the main point of it was that he took care of them for a great many generations. This is the main point. So this was a sort of sacred work because the flies had to be kept from generation to generation alive to carry on eventual studies of heredity. But he was very lonesome. He was a married man with children. There was a French girl who was a perfectly good typist in English. She did some secretarial work and she followed from New York Bridges to Pasadena. To avoid some sort of scandals, I sort of protected [them] and Bridges who was a very close friend of mine came often to my cottage to advise me and eventually edited the first manuscript. The first manuscript of *S&S* I typed myself. Bridges corrected the English with me and then the French girl typed the corrected manuscript in many copies. I don't know, four, five, or six. But it was already written up and edited...[31]

As a newcomer to Caltech politics and as a 'bohemian' type who didn't seem to concern himself much with the opinion other people had of him, Bridges didn't seem prone to pay attention to any supposed ban on Korzybski:

Bridges...lived in a hotel on Colorado Avenue [Boulevard] somewhere and he also was all engrossed in his work and reading. He was a queer duck too. Completely devoted to his work and nothing but. And he was thinking more or less the way I did, and we were friends for so many years that he and I were simply like two brothers, and he was sort of a cook. He had some jalopy he bought for $50 or so because although he had a good salary, he lived, I believe, on $100 a month and $200 or so he was sending home to his wife and children. So he lived on actually $100 a month, and using his old clothes, looking like a tramp, but very serviceable. Occasionally he came to cook for himself and me, I don't know what not. We were very chummy that way, and I wrote originally offhand with two fingers, typing with two fingers the entire manuscript. Then Bridges was reading, I made everything into two copies, so he read either in my place or in his place, most of the time in my place because he had a small hotel room. Because there was no fun there, so he preferred to have the larger freedom of our comparatively larger house. So he spent quite a bit of time in my place…

I was older. He was sort of my student, so the relationship was not only friends and brothers but also that of teacher and student. We had a very, very pleasant relationship. And he was from a practical point of view very practical, hard working fellow anyway. So how much he helped me cooking, housekeeping, I don't know, but anyway he helped. When his girl came from New York, the French girl, oh, I had to, oh I don't know, had to shelter them somehow to prevent scandal. Everybody knew he was a married man and here came his girl, French girl, very expert typist, extremely fine girl just the same. She was madly in love with him. Then there was the three of us. They lived separately, means from me in town, but before they found their own places to live, I sheltered them in my house, being sort of chaperone. So I was pecking with two fingers the original manuscript, then we discussed what I have written without editing with Bridges. Then I began to edit what I have written with Bridges and still a question of English. In many ways, he was not trained physico-mathematically, and so he had sometimes objections through not understanding the physico-mathematical side. I had to explain them and I don't know [what] not. And this was a good training for me because I had to explain. It was very, very good training.[32]

By the end of September 1928, Alfred had started writing about quantum mechanics. By the first part of November, he had completed this and all the more technical parts of the book (which eventually became Book III) and began the writing of his own stuff, the general theory of time-binding, which would become Book II of *Science and Sanity*. He found that section the easiest one to do but it still took him several months more to write this, a conclusion, and the first run-through of the preface. He felt eager to get the draft done. He missed Mira and had had enough of Pasadena and Southern California.

…After the whole book was edited and finished, edited originally by Bridges. He wrote English phrases. The book was not changed. This is quite, quite, I am quite proud of it, to be able to do such thing. The amount of memory and orientation, all of which was new to the attitude, that all is human behavior, mathematics and physics is human behavior. This was written in this way. After the whole thing was edited, the first editing, it was quite smooth reading. Then I had to, after this was finished, I had to rush East.[33]

Chapter 35
ZERO HOUR

Despite whatever relief Korzybski may have felt, the effort to wrap up the first draft of the book had worn him out. At the end of December, he had 'joked' in a letter to Roy Haywood, "[I] work like an idiot and curse California for a rest. 'Is' of identity or not, it <u>is</u> a damned place in all respects."[1]

By the beginning of March 1929, he had completed the manuscript. He planned to leave in a couple of weeks. He had arranged to give a few lectures in California before traveling on to Kansas City, Missouri to join Mira, who had been visiting her sisters at Amy's farm. Then he got disturbing news. Mira had been having health problems. He might have to leave at once.

But on March 3, she sent a night letter reassuring him that, although she had sciatica, he was not to worry or rush. Alfred decided to follow through with his plans. He packed up and a week later left the Pasadena cottage and went to Los Angeles for a few days, where he gave a talk to an abnormal psychology class at the University of Southern California. Then he went to Berkeley to lecture at the (Cora) Williams Institute. From there he took the train to Misery—as Alfred jokingly spelled it—arriving a day or two later. He got a shock when he saw Mira, who looked worn and had lost weight.

Sometime in February at the farm, she had slept with a hot water bottle to stay warm and had accidentally burned her leg. Although the burn itself did not seem severe, severe leg pain—labeled "sciatica"—had followed. Mira wasn't eating much, had lost sixteen pounds, and felt weak. Whatever had set it off, the pain together with the associated symptoms seemed rather puzzling. Alfred was not beyond wondering about a psychological component to Mira's distress. They had been separated for a year, during which time Mira had been suffering from hard-to-pin-down feelings of malaise. While working in Cleveland in 1928, she had gone to the Cleveland Clinic for a check-up. The findings were not clear. She had been earning a lot of money but found it a strain to hunt for painting commissions. To Alfred she seemed generally 'nervous' and overwrought. He wondered about the effect of menopause now that she was over fifty.

They decided to carry on with their previously set plans. Alfred got a last minute invitation to speak at the Kansas City, Missouri Young Men's/Young Women's Hebrew Association (YM/YWHA) on April 1. His two-part lecture on "Time-Binding" and "An Introduction to Sanity" was preceded by a dinner. The Jewish community of Kansas City appeared eager to hear him. An article duplicated in two Jewish newspapers before the talk noted: "During the World War, Korzybski enlisted in the Russian Army and was placed in a position where he succeeded in rendering service of inestimable value to hundreds of Polish Jews who were brought before him for trial on the flimsiest of charges. He is an outspoken Zionist."[2] Alfred, in turn, also felt eager to speak to the Jewish group. Before the talk he wrote to Rainich, "I am extremely pleased and flattered by the invitation of the Zionists to lecture to them."[3]

The Kansas City Times covered in detail the YM/WHA lecture as well as an informal talk he had given a few days earlier at the home of Mr. and Mrs. J. T. Cameron, where he and Mira were staying. The article on that presentation indicates that by this time, Korzybski had brought in the map/territory analogy, one of the main unifying formulations of his non-aristotelian system, to talk about different forms of representation and language:

"...Is this map of the United States the United States? No. If it were correct would it be the United States? No. This is the human mind, this map, full of representations. What if New York came between Chicago and Kansas City on this map? Would it be a correct representation? No. But we would believe it." [Ending this quote from Korzybski's talk, the reporter added "And the map of the human mind seems full of misrepresentations."]

As often happened, Alfred entranced the reporter and others in his audience with his dynamic presentation style:

Euclid and Newton have struck out. Einstein threw a curve. And now—one, two, three, simple as that—out goes Aristotle, the Babe Ruth of philosophy. Count Alfred Korzybski is in the box. No curves. No slow balls. Simple, direct, fast ones from the long arm of his genius. One, two, three...

To compare Count Korzybski, engineer and mathematician, to a baseball pitcher is at once an affront and a compliment to his genius. See him in action. He watches all bases and keeps his eye on the home plate. He dramatizes his pitching, as a pitcher does. Finding words inadequate, he talks about chairs, with the leaves of a potted plant, with bits of paper, with his arms, legs, eyes—and last, his lips. Words? Blah! Logic? Phooey! Juggling bubbles, that is talk.[4]

From Kansas City, the Korzybskis went to Chicago for a few days, where Alfred gave another talk, "An Introduction to a Theory of Sanity", at the Institute of Juvenile Research, then at the University of Chicago. Afterwards, they saw Mira's good friend, the sculptress Tennessee Mitchell Anderson who was living in the city. Tennessee, ex-wife of author Sherwood Anderson, introduced Alfred to an acquaintence of hers, Douglas Gordon Campbell, a young Canadian M.D. interested in becoming a psychiatrist. In 1924, attending the British Association of Science annual meeting in Toronto, Campbell had heard Korzybski's presentation at the concurrent International Mathematical Congress. At the time, Korzybski's theory of time-binding and the time-binding differential/anthropometer didn't have much significance for Campbell. Nonetheless, now, Alfred invited him back to his hotel room and they talked for hours. Campbell was planning to travel with his wife to Europe in the fall and Korzybski invited him to write if he wanted to follow up on their discussion. The young physician—now intrigued—did write. Their ensuing relationship would become an important one for both men.

From Chicago, Alfred and Mira went on to Washington, D.C. Alfred likely used some of his medical connections to get Mira admitted to the Johns Hopkins University Hospital in Baltimore where, by the end of April, she was feeling much better. With Mira safely ensconced in the hospital, Alfred stayed in Washington and conferred with Philip Graven.

In the second "Time-Binding" paper, Alfred had already recognized that the confusion of orders of abstractions, which caused such problems in scientific formulating*, formed the 'cognitive' background of mental illness as well. In writing his book, the relation between science/mathematics and sanity had become even more apparent. Indeed, he had changed the working title to *Time-Binding: An Introduction to a Theory of Sanity*. In the continuum going from 'sanity' to 'unsanity' to 'insanity'—objectifications, illusions, delusions, and hallucinations all clearly seemed to involve greater and greater degrees of confused abstracting, i.e. the reversal of "the natural order of evaluation".

---

* Most obviously in the form of objectifications of higher-order abstractions.

Thus Graven's application of non-aristotelian, extensional methods to his psychiatric patients seemed more crucial than ever to Alfred. He anticipated that Graven's case studies would form a valuable appendix to the book and urged him to get over his reluctance to write. But Graven seemed unable to do so. Over the next few years as the book got closer to publication, his inability to write would become a growing source of frustration for Alfred.

While Graven was looking through Alfred's completed draft, Alfred had begun to read Graven's copy of Ivan Pavlov's *Conditioned Reflexes*, translated by Anrep, which he immediately saw as fundamental to his own work. He would soon get his own copy, as well as a copy of Pavlov's recently published *Lectures on Conditioned Reflexes*. In early 1931, he would also meet the translator of this second book, Dr. W. Horsley Gantt, who had worked with Pavlov in Russia and was just in the process of founding a Pavlovian Laboratory at the Johns Hopkins Medical School. Despite the fact that Korzybski did not reject the data of introspection, he admired Pavlov's efforts to achieve understanding of the 'mental' field on an 'objective', physiological basis. Pavlov's experiments showed how changes in 'order' and 'delay' of stimuli—both internal and external—could affect the behavior of organisms. As Alfred put it later, "Stimuli are never 'simple' and of necessity involve fourfold space-time *structure and order*."[5] It seemed to Alfred that his own work on orders of abstractions extended, and was also corroborated by, Pavlov's discoveries.

In May, Mira felt better enough to return to Kansas City to complete some business—although she still looked too thin to Alfred. Alfred returned by himself to the apartment in Brooklyn. It had been vacant since Mira had left on her travels the previous summer. The dust had been gathering and it took him several weeks to get the place cleaned, to unpack, and to begin to figure out what he needed to do to get the book in shape for publication.

In April, he had written to David Fairchild, "the d...d [damned] book is finished",[6] blithely estimating that it might take just a few more months to get it into shape for publication. But it must have dawned on him fairly quickly, it was going to take more time. For one thing, he felt he was going to have to write another chapter about Pavlov's work. In addition, in Pasadena he had begun reading the first two volumes of Jerome Alexander's encyclopedic *Colloid Chemistry*. For Alfred, the behavior of colloids appeared to provide a plausible physico-chemical basis for explaining mind-body relationships. He felt impelled to bring that into the book as well. Aside from that, although he felt generally satisfied with the draft, somehow his non-aristotelian system still seemed to be missing something. He wanted to get more reactions from his manuscript readers, including Mira. Could he make the book more readable and better organized? So, in actuality the "d...d book" seemed far from finished. This all meant more delay, which he regretted but could do little about except to continue plugging away. (As it turned out, 'a few more months' would turn into four more years of grinding labor.) He hoped the end result would be worth the effort.

Alfred also took time to go over his and Mira's finances for the last year. He estimated Mira had earned something like $100,000, over the course of their married life. 1928 had been an especially good year in earnings for her. Yet they had very little to show for it. He had tried his best to function as Mira's manager and advisor, but seeing the figures, he felt truly devastated; it seemed to him he had significantly failed. On May 21, he wrote to Mira:

My dearest one:

Today I went over our bills. In <u>1928</u> you earned no more and no less than 16,000 (<u>sixteen thousand dollars</u>). I spent for a <u>year</u>, travel, and book[s] and my living expenses <u>1600</u>, you gave Tennessee [Anderson] 500, Mother 500, Amy 500. We have in the Bank 3300 altogether 6400 so you spent in this one year <u>alone over</u> 10,000 dollars with all these months on the farm etc.

I enclose a bill.

I frankly admit that I am heartbroken and begin to have no doubt that you do not care for me as a wife should care for a husband, otherwise you simply could not throw away money like a drunken sailor. Our devotion is measured by what we are willing to do for the other fellow. I do not deny that perhaps you care for me as much as for your monkey [Mira had a pet monkey she was keeping at her sister's farm] or cat or some thing of this sort until my chloroform time comes, but no doubt you are not willing to sacrifice any of your fancies for our future independence. In fact I have given up everything I have for you and slave at my work simply to please you. I am very deeply unhappy and terribly lonesome having nobody in this world who would help me a little even. You can see clearly from the bills that my living expenses which you supply at present are not a problem to worry about, I can earn that much any old way. Your working away from me is a serious hardship for me and your throwing away money all the time makes you work the harder for nothing because very little is left out of it. Your whole help to me as you know is very little, your <u>real</u> help would be if you would not throw away money and we would go to Europe with some cash which when invested in our property or something else would establish us in independence.

Now you are not willing for one minute to take this one big help seriously, throwing money away all the time we are in messes all the time and I suffer <u>more than I can tell</u> you (I hate dramas so will not speak about it more).

You know that I suffer by your being so cold toward me but your monetary behavior shows clearly that you do not care for me, and either do not see the hell I am in, or you see it and completely disregard it. I did not nag you, you are alone again with more chances to paralyze our future by throwing away money and staying away to make it, to throw it away again. Nagging on my part won't do, I am also unable to look after every penny you throw away. You always must carry full pockets of money with you and let them go.

The issues dearest are much more serious than you think. I am unable to tell you that in letters, but I am literally heart broken because you have proven over and over again that you do not care for me. I am a plaything for you, a monkey or myself is good enough to draw some exhibitionistic attention to <u>yourself</u>. But you will not sacrifice any of your fancies for OUR future. No matter how little I spend I suffer deeply under our conditions and your behavior keeps us perfectly paralyzed and unsettled. I cannot write any more. I feel too unhappy, and too harassed by everything.[7]

Mira wrote back a few days later. She already felt distraught because her monkey had been sick and just died in her arms. She couldn't disagree with the facts Alfred had pointed out about her spending habits. She wrote, "I had the sloppiest influence of a vagabond life [and] most demoralizing influence of a highly fluctuating income…" But she was working at doing better. And she vigorously protested the implication that she did not care for him. Alfred's love and the success of his work had the highest importance in her life:

I recognize your patient pains are the most difficult pains for you to bear – I can only beg you to recognize my growing pains are the most difficult pains for me to bear and keep up my fighting courage [and] cheerfulness – against the odds of our life – if there are minor parts of my character and temperament – that leave you hungry in spots – remember there are minor parts in your character [and] Temperament that leave me hungry – Figuratively speaking [in terms of military combat] we are passing through the "zero hour" – of "going over the top"…I implore you to have more patient faith in me.[8]

Over the next few weeks their letters back and forth had a notably blunt honesty. Ultimately each wanted to resolve their problems of mutual adjustment. By the time Mira got back to Brooklyn in mid-June, they seemed reconciled. And Mira did do better over the next few years. The ensuing severe depression in the U.S. and world economy may have helped her to focus and economize—they would have no money to spare for any frivolous spending. Mira concentrated a major part of her time and attention on helping Alfred produce the book. As she said, they had reached "the zero hour". They *did*—as she wrote—'go over the top' together. Korzybski clearly would not and could not have produced what became his magnum opus without Mira. She wanted it—in a way—more than he did. She had urged him to develop his system from its inception in the notion of time-binding. She had financed his work to a significant degree. Over the next few years, her efforts with him to get the book into print became nothing less than "heroic".

It would seem natural for Korzybski to have two of his biggest past supporters, Keyser and Polakov, look at his draft. However, both men had major new developments in their lives that precluded spending much time then with his manuscript. Keyser, although now retired from teaching, was busy writing his own books. (His latest, *The Pastures of Wonder*, had just been published.) He was also busy with his personal life—he had just gotten married again. Sarah Keyser, a former pupil much younger than her new husband, taught mathematics at a private school in New York City. Alfred decided not to impose on his mentor's time and energy until the book had reached a more completed form.

Polakov also had little time to spare. He too had met a younger woman, a dancer, whom he was planning to marry soon. He was also getting involved in a new business venture. Ironically, the Soviet government—now under Stalin's brutal fist—was hiring a number of U.S. 'capitalist' companies to help industrial development in the 'communist' state. Soviet planners had a special interest in H. L. Gantt's approach to scientific management. Since Walter qualified as one of the world's leading experts in it, the Supreme Council of the National Economy hired him to lend his expertise toward implementing the Soviet Union's Five Year Plan. At the end of 1929, Polakov and his new wife Barbara would arrive in Russia. (Around this time, Stalin was initiating the forced collectivization of Soviet agriculture, which over the next few years would result in the deportation and starvation of millions of Russian and Ukrainian peasants.) Until the summer of 1931, Walter would naively try to apply his enlightened industrial management techniques to the Stalinist madhouse, with little success. Though he and Korzybski corresponded during his time in Russia, he was not in any position to provide much help with the editing of the book.

However, Russell Maddren—a globe-trotting surgeon, whom Alfred had met through their mutual friend Jesse Lee Bennett—felt eager to help. In California, Alfred had briefly seen Maddren, who had been staying with his brother in Long Beach, south of Los Angeles. From there, Maddren and his wife set off through China and Russia to Denmark—his wife's homeland. While in Copenhagen, Maddren—much taken with Korzybski's work—had even attempted to translate Alfred's 1924 *Time-Binding* paper into Danish. By the summer of 1929, the Maddrens were back in the U.S. and living in Freeport, Long Island.

One day in mid-July, Maddren picked up Alfred and Mira in Brooklyn and drove out with them to Polakov's seaside shack on Long Island. They all planned to work on the manuscript together. However, Alfred was not keen on the 'corrections' that Mira and Maddren were making. He described what happened in a letter to Sally Avery:

> We have been at the seashore…We had in mind to go there when Poly was not and invite the Maddrens and work at the reading of the MS. But Poly came, the place became too crowded so we had to go. We went to Freeport…where the [Maddrens] live and we stayed with them a few days. Mira and Dr. M were reading together the MS., cursing me out. The place was too crowded and I went back to Brooklyn and M. is still there, they are reading the MS. and making corrections and suggestions. I am back in Brooklyn, alone working as usual.
>
> When I came back from Freeport I had to go to Park Row (City Hall) you probably remember there is a movie across the post office. I went there. I was too distressed to go home and work so went to see. The story was about a fine Southern gentleman who got in troubles (women, money, etc.) He ended it all by taking poison. This cheered me up as there is always that way out when burdens get too heavy.[9]

Chapter 36
A SHORT TRIP TO POLAND

After almost 15 years away, Alfred decided to make a short trip to Poland. He was concerned about his mother and the family business. His correspondence with her, as well as with friends and relatives in Poland, held discouraging news. While Mira and Maddren continued to work on the manuscript, the time seemed right to scout the situation and see what he and Mira would be getting into when they returned to live there. Alfred and Mira had postponed their move to Poland so many times, one could easily be excused for doubting their desire to return. But they had always planned, and still intended, to do so.

He left New York City on the R.M.S. "Caronia" on August 16. In his trunk, he had his deluxe presentation anthropometer. He surely had read this announcement in his July-August copy of the *Bulletin of The American Mathematical Society*: "A Congress of Mathematicians of the Slavic Countries will be held at Warsaw, September 23–27, 1929, under the auspices of the head of the Polish government. Professor W. Sierpinski, of the University of Warsaw, is president of the executive committee of the Congress."[1] Since Alfred was going to be in Warsaw anyway, he would try to attend the Congress and give a lecture on his work, although it was already too late to submit a paper.

The trip across the ocean lasted some seven days. He spent about a week more in London waiting for the boat that would take him to Danzig. In the meantime, he looked up his friend C. K. Ogden. Korzybski recounted, "Ogden took very good care of me in showing me London and all the curiosities."[2] (I fantasize being in the next booth in a London pub listening to the two polymaths chatting over their pints.) In his short time there, Korzybski also managed to visit some of the old English castles around London.

Peace, if not quiet, prevailed in the port of Danzig when Korzybski arrived there on Tuesday morning, September 3, 1929, after four days on a steamer from London. He didn't want to get into Warsaw at night, so he spent the day wandering around the town and then took a night train to Warsaw, eight hours away.

Helena Korzybska was waiting at the station with her property manager when Alfred's train pulled into the station at 7:00 the next morning. She cried when she saw him. Alfred felt restrained, even detached. As he wrote to Mira the following day, "…she tried to do a lot of kissing but I was somehow less of the kissing kind." The manager took care of the suitcases and trunk and the three of them took a taxi to the apartment house on 66 Wilcza Street:

> Three servants were waiting at the door and then started the kissing of the hand. I was forewarned that I have to submit myself to it. I did. Women wanted to carry the big heavy suitcase. I did not let them do it but said that the janitor should do it…Mother prepared for me the parlor, so I will be fairly comfortable. She has four rooms and the furniture of her 4 rooms and my furniture of four rooms so it is terribly crowded. I recognize of course all my things. The servants are fairly long time, the maid is 3 or four years, she had already one baby at my mother's place, which mother took care of until it died, the manager is 9 years. The other are the janitors but we have not much contact with them. The manager is a kind of a better but no good butler. They all seem fairly good…the girl seems to be really good extremely hard worker and very honest, scolds the manager for

mother and scolds everybody except mother. The manager, it is too early to talk. It seems that since I came everybody begins to [behave] better, and a new spirit has entered in all of them. I behave as a family physician, am extremely quiet, and studying, have no special emotions at all.³

Except for her gray hair, Helena Korzybska—then in her early seventies—looked much as Alfred had remembered her. He seemed to have first expected to find her physically ill but after a few days he wrote to Mira that she appeared quite healthy (although he did note she tended to catch cold easily and currently had an inflammation in her vocal cords affecting her speech). Otherwise she seemed even more energetic than Mira's older sisters, who were younger than Helena. However, although he could see improvement in some ways, Alfred found his mother at least as difficult to deal with as he had found her before he left Poland:

She has changed a great deal in the favorable way, "adjustment to reality" which has been pounded into her for so many years [by Alfred in his letters to her?], yet she is as <u>impossibly aggressive</u> as ever and she only matters and her will has any value, her opinion is only right etc. When these things have nothing to do with "reality".⁴

He had a word for the behavior of hers he found so problematic—also the term he had used to summarize what he considered Mira's 'bad' habits—"infantile". In addition, her memory seemed poor. Her meticulous standards of cleanliness had dropped (the dust in the apartment seemed considerable). At this point, she seemed incapable of adequately managing her affairs. Indeed, as he had noted to Mira, there seemed around his mother "...a kind of anarchy, the usual wealthy-poor old woman and everybody trying to get something from such a person left entirely alone."⁵

The manager seemed of little help in getting her business straightened out. Alfred found him crude, uneducated, and incompetent. He even owed money to Alfred's mother. Then there was Alfred's sister, whom he probably saw more than once during his trip. He had had little contact with her even when he lived in Poland, and now after so many years she seemed like a somehow familiar stranger—a nervous wreck, suspicious of her brother's intent, though apparently unable to do much herself to help their mother manage the family property.

The property was what remained of the family fortune—about 3/4 of which, he estimated, had been lost as a result of the war. His mother still owned the building on Wilcza Street, some property in suburbs outside of Warsaw, as well as the country estate at Rudnik, where buildings had been destroyed and then rebuilt. Alfred spent three days there and it looked surprisingly good to him, given that it had served as one of the battlegrounds of World War I. As he wrote to Mira, "It looks very cheerful and the trees have grown rather large. It needs money and work and it would be a splendid thing."⁶ At this point none of the property was providing an adequate income. For example, Alfred discovered that while housing was scarce in Warsaw, the government rent control laws limited what his mother could legally collect from her tenants. As a consequence many tenants sublet their apartments to others for exorbitant prices. They were making a profit on their apartments while his mother, the owner, was losing money.

Still, many Polish families had been completely ruined in the war. The Korzybskis at least had *something* left. Helena wanted Alfred to stay. Korzybski realized he could probably straighten out the mess of family business in about a year. But he couldn't do it now. He had formulated his work in American English (or his unique version of it) and he wasn't willing to move to Poland before the book was published. He and Mira had to get the book into print and make a little money first. He hoped they could do that quickly. Then they would come to Poland, and he could sort out the family business—keeping Mother at arm's length, of course—and get himself established. He could see his work was needed just as much, if not more, in Poland as in the U.S. and he felt confident he would be able to find teaching opportunities. He was getting comfortable speaking Polish again and—preparing for his talk at the Mathematics Congress later in the month—even speaking in Polish about his work.

However, in the meantime, he began looking for some way to provide 'insurance' for what he felt was his stake in the family property. He and Mira had given Helena considerable money over the last few years—around 5,000 dollars. Alfred realized Polish law allowed them to consolidate these funds as a loan to give his mother what amounted to a second mortgage. The mortgage document, known as a "hypothec", would give them some rights in relation to the house on 66 Wilcza. As holders of this "hypothec", they would have precedence for either purchasing the house or being paid back as creditors whenever the house was sold.

Over the next few years, this may have turned out to be useful. First, Helena married her manager, thus throwing into doubt what Alfred and his sister might inherit when their mother died. Helena also defaulted on her interest payments to the Polish bank that held her first mortgage. At the end of 1932, 66 Wilcza was put up for auction. It's not clear whether Korzybski was able to use his mortgage to prevent the house from being sold at that time, although he had lawyers in Warsaw working for him. But at any rate, probably as a result of his foresight, his mother was able to continue living there. After she died in 1937, the amount of Alfred and Mira's mortgage was paid to them out of the sale of 66 Wilcza. This money was deposited for them in a Polish Bank. However, they were unable to collect their money before the German invasion of Poland in September 1939.

After World War II, Korzybski inquired about recovering this money as well as getting compensation for other property he might have inherited. But the destruction of records and the difficulties in dealing with the new Stalinist regime in Poland made getting useful information almost impossible. Most of his friends, including his lawyer, were dead. He never learned what happened to his sister. Alfred had a considerable amount of furniture and other personal belongings he had left in his mother's place at 66 Wilcza (including the beautiful anthropometer he had brought with him on the 1929 trip). After the war, he assumed that the manager who had married Mother had whatever was left of the estate. All that loss was to come. In 1929, it seemed like a good idea to arrange the mortgage. Before he returned to America he got his mother to sign the necessary documents.

His mother's condition, that of his sister, and the state of the family business seemed dismal enough. The state of more distant family and friends appeared no cheerier. Indeed, observing his countrymen on the streets, in their homes, and other places he visited, Poland in general seemed like a very sad place. A line he remembered from Zygmunt Krasinski's work *Iridion* seemed to fit what he saw in Warsaw—a city filled with "children who cannot smile". On September 29, near the end of his stay, he wrote to Keyser:

Dear dear Old Man,

I had such a hectic time day and night that outside of postcards I had no time or head to write. The Poles have done actual miracles and simply I do not understand how they have succeeded in rebuilding Poland out of NOTHING. Poland was invaded during the war three times and left nearly deprived of everything, machines, food, horses, cows, many houses destroyed, etc. We get no indemnity of any sort and so have to build everything with the hardest labor imaginable. We are also hampered by three doctrinal psychologies of the older generation (Russian, German, and Austrian) which seems to be a very serious handicap. They try to eliminate that by changing the older officers for younger who are trained in Polish doctrines. It is an infernal and slow work.

Outside of these miracles of work and organization the place is a tragic one. No one speak[s] loud, or smiles, children do not smile even, it seems that this war and the hardships have entirely ruined the nerves of the country. It is simply pathetic and once more it is proven that human nerves can only stand so much and no more. My family has been nearly entirely wiped off. Either sudden death (mostly heart) or entirely ruined. We have lost about 3/4 of our fortune but some is still left although extremely badly managed and giving very little income.

Whomever I touch of my generation or the older generation their nerves are nearly entirely shattered. There is nothing to talk about with them. But they have done wonders of work and organization just the same! I did not realize how sufferings literally annihilate not only individuals but even nations.[7]

The Congress of Mathematicians of Slavic Countries

Korzybski's attendance at the Congress of Mathematicians of Slavic Countries must have given him welcome relief from these woes. The Congress was held at his old school, the Warsaw Polytechnic. He was given half an hour of conference time to give a presentation. He spoke in Polish to an audience of from 40 to 50 people on his "Niearistotelesowy System",[8] which he considered a very clear outline of his work. He tried to get the audience to laugh as much as possible. Some of it seemed to him like confused laughter, but on the whole, as he wrote to Keyser, "It [the presentation] was received well and with interest, whatever that means."[9] For him the main point of that kind of conference, as he later pointed out, was not in any presentation. Rather it was in the opportunity to meet people and make connections. And, among others, Korzybski met many of the leading lights of the Polish 'school' of mathematical logic and analytical philosophy.

One of these was Leon Chwistek, with whom he chatted during the conference. An accomplished painter and literary critic as well as a philosopher and mathematician, he appeared to Korzybski at the time as somewhat eccentric. He delivered his paper dead drunk. A lecturer in mathematics at the University of Krakow, he was among the first to talk about "semantics" in relation to mathematics. What Chwistek intended had more to do with technical considerations of logical syntax than of 'meanings', reference, etc. (Chwistek's paper in Polish, entitled "Semantyczna metoda calkowania" in the Congress program, was translated into French for the Congress proceedings as "Une méthode métamathématique d'analyse".[10]) But Chwistek's attempt to revamp Russell's theory of types struck a chord with Alfred. After Korzybski returned to the U.S., the two men corresponded for several years. Chwistek apparently didn't think much of Korzybski's non-elementalistic attempt to develop training for sanity from physico-mathematical methods. However, it was probably through the influence of Chwistek that Korzybski began to use the term "semantic(s)" in relation to his own work, although in a different sense than how Chwistek used the term.

Korzybski also met the logicians Jan Lukasiewicz and Stanislaw Lesniewski, who did not speak at the Congress, and their younger colleague, Alfred Tarski, who presented two papers. These three men had a central place in the mathematical, "formalist" wing of Polish analytical philosophy. "Extreme rebels" against ordinary language, they considered it entirely unsuitable for "the unambiguous formulation of their ideas."[11] Instead they used mathematical logic to build new forms of logic in a highly technical and abstract symbolism.

Korzybski certainly had an interest in what they were doing (he would make direct reference to their work in his book). In particular, he noted Lukasiewicz's and Tarski's development of three-valued and many-valued logic as an important non-aristotelian advance. But Korzybski, whose earlier writings had emphasized the need for a new logic for science and life, was coming to see 'logic' per se—even this new logic—as elementalistic, i.e., too isolated from the living reactions of $Smith_1$, $Smith_2$, etc., to remain a major focus of interest for him. (He didn't denigrate its formal value.) Thus the Polish mathematical logicians, whose work he had only just encountered, had little direct influence on Korzybski's formulating.

Korzybski's work appears closer in intent to that of Tadeusz Kotarbinski and Kaszimierz Ajdukiewicz, Polish analytical philosophers of his time who were also interested in the interrelated problems of scientific knowledge, language, and method. In their general approach to language, all three men could be viewed as linguistic "reformists" according to the classification set forth in Henryk Skolimowski's book *Polish Analytical Philosophy*. Unlike the more mathematically-focused formalists, reformists qualified as "moderate rebels" against ordinary language: "The moderate rebels do not condemn ordinary language entirely but only reshape it according to their needs."[12]

Korzybski's formulating was not influenced in any significant way by the Polish reformists either, although he at least definitely knew of Kotarbinski's work.[13] Korzybski had developed his own views independently of his Polish colleagues. "It is quite clear," as Skolimowski pointed out, "that a number of other philosophers can be classified as reformists. One might even risk a thesis that most of *the* philosophers of the past were reformists; under the guise of ordinary language, they were in fact shaping their own languages to fit their philosophies."[14] Korzybski would surely agree with this. In his book he would openly state that "...a language, any language, has at its bottom certain metaphysics, which ascribe, consciously or unconsciously, some sort of structure to this world."[15] For him, perhaps the main achievement of any significant formulational advance consisted of the language it was stated in.

What then distinguished Korzybski's reformist program from these others? If everyday language had some metaphysics at its bottom, he wanted that metaphysics to reflect the most reliable up-to-date picture of the world humans had achieved. From this came his need to make a methodologically-oriented synthesis of the sciences of his time. The linguistic revision he was using and advocating in the book (a work still in progress) could help readers to reshape their everyday language and related evaluations in terms of this up-to-date scientific 'metaphysics' (basic structural assumptions about the world). Korzybski's linguistic revision had a physico-mathematical basis without literally requiring one to talk in mathematical formulas. His emphasis on application to individual personal adjustment and sanity gave a unique practical thrust to his reformist program. It brought his work closer to everyday life than the work of many, if not most, other philosophers. Indeed, Korzybski didn't see what he was doing as philosophy (although he didn't mind calling it "*an up-to-date epistemology*."[16] Scientific in intent, his general theory had serious applications for 'mental' hygiene as well as scientific formulating, which he wanted to have empirically tested.

British mathematician W. H. Young, President of the International Mathematical Union, was the special honored guest of the Congress and seemed taken with Korzybski's program. Young, a big-bearded and energetic man about Keyser's age, seemed somewhat like a fish out of water at the Congress since he didn't speak Polish. He may have fallen on Korzybski's company out of desperation for someone to talk to in English. But he also seemed genuinely interested in Korzybski's combination of mathematics and psychiatry. After hours, Alfred showed him around Warsaw, including a visit to a famous, old mead cellar (a drinking establishment serving the fermented honey drink as its specialty). The mead didn't taste very good but the two men made a connection and corresponded for some years afterwards.

Korzybski's time with Young turned out to be the high point of his visit to Poland. He had found his visit 'home' almost unremittingly depressing. He left Warsaw for Danzig on October 2, left Danzig on October 4, and about 4 days later, arrived in London.

While waiting for his ship the R.M.S. "Carmonia", which would leave for New York on October 12, he had time for more sightseeing:

...visiting different houses, oh, old stuff, and curiously enough the Tower of London, And it sounds so funny, you know, to sit on a bench, stone bench, in the Tower of London [The Chapel Royal of St. Peter ad Vincula] and behind you just two feet away is a beheaded Queen of England buried...Anne Boleyn...And I was so thrilled that I landed at the head of the London Tower because I was thinking then how the old masters of England would feel about [my work] and how in a hurry they would put me in the Tower of London. Just irony. ...that fortress is one of the oldest in Europe. Of course, I enjoyed looking at all those old buildings because I enjoyed seeing big hunks of wood where they used to do the beheading [in a small, paved area just outside the Chapel]. Looks so funny, you know, in modern days to see that old barbarian stuff. I had quite a few conversations in London with some important men who were interested in *Manhood*. Then I came back, also from the Tower, with the same kind of trip back to New York.[17]

Korzybski in London, 1929

More Bad News

Mira was waiting for him at the dock when his ship arrived in New York Harbor on Sunday, October 20, 1929.[18] He had been away for two months but, as he told one friend, it seemed as if the trip to Poland had taken 10 years off of his life. And other than Mira—whom he had missed a lot and felt happy to hug once again—what he found greeting him was an abundance of bad news.

On his desk, among the pieces of accumulated mail, was a letter from Sergei A. Vasiliev (who lived in New York City) telling of the death of his father, A. V. Vasiliev on October 6 in Moscow. Alfred felt deeply perturbed by the news. He had never met the older Vasiliev in person. But during the time of their five-year correspondence, he had developed a feeling of closeness to the Russian mathematician, who encouraged his work and inspired him with his broad, humanistic outlook. Korzybski, who had served as a conduit of communication between Vasiliev and U.S. mathematicians, informed friends who knew of or who had met Vasiliev, such as Cajori, Karpinski, and Rainich, among others. James McKeen Cattell, editor of *Science*, asked Korzybski to write an obituary, which was published in the December 20, 1929 issue. The opening of that piece indicates some of the main values Vasiliev exemplified for Korzybski—values that Korzybski aspired to for himself:

> In the passing of A. V. Vasiliev in Moscow, Russia, the world has lost one of its great scientists, great teachers, great men. To be a great scientist is one thing; to be a great scientist and a great teacher is quite another. A great teacher must ingest, digest and evaluate the works of others in many lines in order to give broad, judicial and interesting selections to students. To be at once a great scientist, a great teacher and a great man is still different—it is all too rare a combination. Besides the requisites for the first two, individual synthesis, a broad human vision and interest, effective and energetic enough to be an inspiration and guide for living and acting, are essential. A unique combination of these characteristics made the life of Vasiliev a memorable and most useful one....[19]

Another loss had occurred four days before Alfred's arrival. On October 16, Alfred and Mira's friend Edwin E. Slosson, first editor of *Science News* and first director of the *Science Service*, died suddenly of a heart attack. He too had become a supporter of Korzybski's work. And he had been charmed by Mira. He would be missed by both of them.

Four days after Alfred arrived home came more bad news—the stock market 'crashed' on October 24. The day became known in history as "Black Thursday." Five days later—on what became known as "Black Tuesday"—economic panic ensued throughout the United States. The Great Depression had arrived—not the most propitious of times to publish the kind of book Alfred and Mira were producing.

As for the book—Mira and Russell Maddren had been very busy with it. More unwelcome news, since both of them—unquestionably strong supporters of his work—had various complaints. Maddren, now back in Europe, had left notes and was also writing letters with what Alfred considered facetious and not very helpful comments, more or less picking at words. At least Mira's criticism seemed more serious. She had taken an extra copy of the manuscript and worked it over—cutting it up, rearranging and rewriting it. Alfred felt glad she had spent the time getting familiar with it but he felt frustrated by her criticism too.

She considered it "rotten", "unclear", "muddled"; he "was not true" to himself. Both Mira and Maddren seemed to have misunderstood or missed key points in his writing. As he told David Fairchild more than a year later:

> I was in a very peculiar situation, I was urged dramatically by Mira to rewrite the book, which I knew I could not do, and yet I had full evidence that if my book is misunderstood to such an extent, there must be something wrong with the presentation. Under such whipping I began to think hard and struggle with ideas, formulations and myself. To save my neck I could not see how I can improve it.[20]

Alfred brooded. In mid-November, he wrote to Sally Avery:
> Mira expects to go to Florida in January and so we are working both like hell on the revision of the MS. which means having it spread all over the place, all card tables (3) boxes shelves etc spread and no place to move or write. The main problem is the rearrangement of material, which is a messy thing and requires space and extremely close attention. I really have no head for anything now neither do I go out for a week at a time.[21]

He spent the next few months 'delousing' the manuscript, i.e., rearranging it, cutting some repetitions, and polishing the English. He also wrote the new chapters he had planned on Pavlov's conditional reflexes and on colloids. He saw these as addenda, which however necessary didn't supply anything fundamental to his non-aristotelian system. With the new year and new decade, he was still looking for some quality of underlying importance—he didn't know what—that could supply the continuity he felt but that Mira and Maddren hadn't seen.

Given his preference for a quiet setting, in December he had an unwelcome new set of distractions to make his work more difficult. His sister-in-law Amy drove from Kansas City to stay with them in their studio apartment. The two sisters soon got very busy with a major sewing project (probably to help Mira re-do her wardrobe since she had remained rather thin since her illness). Mira found comfort in Amy's presence. Though Alfred much preferred being alone with his wife he had to make the best of things. So he chivalrously slept on the sofa under the skylight while Amy slept with Mira in their bed. To reduce his getting disturbed by the two women during the day, he put up a curtain to separate his corner desk from the rest of the apartment.

The three of them would soon have to get busy preparing for a two-week exhibition Mira was giving at the Junior League starting January 6. He described what they did to Sally Avery:
> We had a hell of work at hand with Mira's exhibition, we had to redowel the frames, do a lot of carpentering and finally the packing, transportation and hanging up is always a very tiresome procedure. We finished all of that yesterday were tired to death and today my sister in law and I rest and poor Mira has to be polite at the Junior League. Imagine being polite for two weeks, that's a terrible job.[22]

Though business had been poor lately there was an outside chance she might get some local commissions and stay in Brooklyn to work. Otherwise, she and Amy would drive down to Palm Beach, Florida where she might have better luck getting portrait commissions amongst the wealthy, wintering, northern sun-seekers there.

The year had ended with more bad news when Alfred and Mira learned—probably from an article in the December 27 *New York Times*—of their friend Tennessee Anderson's unexpected death. They had visited her only months before. Another intimation of mortality. He was now on the far side of 50. Korzybski knew—if anyone did—that "all flesh is grass." The draft was done but the book was far from ready. If he was going to get it out before he died, he had to grind on. On the next to last day of 1929, Alfred wrote to Keyser:
> We as usually have little news besides working very hard. The d...d book is supposedly finished but I still have some revisions and rearrangements to make. Mira read it several times and criticized a lot, wanting it to be 'perfect' and satisfy everybody. It was hard on me, as she asked the impossible. By now she begins to see that. I am already compiling the bibliography and an index in the rough without giving the pages of my book.[23]

Chapter 37
KNOWLEDGE, UNCERTAINTY, AND COURAGE

Korzybski had been working on his second book since 1921. From 1930 until the book was finally published in October 1933, he was consumed by the effort to bring it out. Though he traveled a bit (mainly on book-related business), most of the time he could be found in the penthouse studio in Brooklyn. He spent hours upon hours there, reading and writing at his desk. (The writing would include at least a thousand letters—a conservative estimate—mostly related to the book.) Every so often he would get more dismal news from Poland, which reminded him of the need to return as soon as possible in order to sort out his mother's downward-spiraling business affairs. But what he had hoped would be a relatively short period of time (a number of months) to edit the first draft and get the book out, stretched into four more years.

Completing the book came in two broad, overlapping phases. First, he had to revise and fill in the content. He didn't consider that truly done until the fall of 1931. By then, with the substance of the book fairly well in shape, the next phase—further editing, finding someone to publish it, and seeing it into print—had become the major focus.

Mira's and Maddren's criticisms notwithstanding, Korzybski didn't consider what he had written as too bad. Granted the English needed polishing, some of the lengthy chapters needed splitting up, and some of the material could be rearranged. Nonetheless, the first draft had the basic 'skeleton' and most of the 'flesh' he thought the book required.

But he had to agree it lacked something. A few additional chapters, on colloids and on conditional reflexes, filled in some gaps. But more fundamentally, the integrating sense of the non-aristotelian system that he had in his head hadn't come through in the manuscript as he had wished. In February, he was struggling with this issue when he had a breakthrough. He wrote at once to Mira, in Florida with her sister:

My dearest one,

At least I have something really important to tell you and for a year or so [for] the first time they are rather cheerful.

I HAVE SOLVED AT LEAST the problem of the difficulties I had with myself and <u>readers</u> of my MS. You and other had often a feeling of lack of continuity in the book, I COULD NOT RECONCILE myself to this discontinuity, to me it had continuity, yet somehow it must not have been apparent to the reader.

The solution is <u>structure</u>. The whole book is written from the point of view of structure and I did not make it quite clear. In reading the MS. at present at each page I eliminate here and there some silly word like 'natural'…etc. and add <u>structural</u> instead. The whole book is getting <u>NEW VIGOR AND NEW GENUINE CONTINUITY</u>, and it looks really cheerful.

But by Jove it takes some pains to make such one step and see finally the 'flood of light'…[1]

Korzybski defined *structure* as a complex of *relations* consisting of multi-dimensional *order*. Each term—"structure", "relation", "order"—could be circularly defined in terms of the other two (perhaps along with "difference", "dimension", etc.). Eventually one reached the un-speakable, non-verbal level, which meant that these terms represented the basic assumptions, the bare-bones metaphysics, of the worldview Korzybski was trying to elucidate: accepting the world and everything in it—ourselves included—as a world of structure, relation, order. Structure (relation, order) had no opposite; although it could be obscured by ignorance.

Although he continued to add to the conditional reflex material for the rest of 1930, "structure" became that year's main formulational theme in "replenishing" the book. (He used this term because he wasn't doing much rewriting, but rather adding a word here and there to the text or appending additional remarks to what he had already written.) As an experiment he took his *Time-Binding* essays and inserted "structure", "structural", "structurally" throughout these texts where they seemed suitable. The result impressed him favorably. He wrote about 12 pages on structure for the first chapter of the book. This eventually became a separate chapter "On Structure" and would lead off "Part II, General On Structure". (He also wrote new material on the related notion of "relation".) Although he had referred to the notion of structure in the first draft, he now proceeded to go through the manuscript adding "structure", and the rest wherever they fit. Doing this made it seem to him as if a new book had emerged. By emphasizing structure, the formulational unity of the work had became much more apparent.

In March, Mira (with her sister) returned from Florida. She had had a dearth of portrait business down there (her wealthy patrons were getting tighter with their money). She hoped to do better at Newport, where she planned to go with Amy in a few months. When Alfred showed his new material to her, Mira was pleased. She agreed that it provided some of the continuity that had been lacking in the book. Alfred was pleased too, but he was beginning to feel spent from his labors in the higher realms of abstraction. His 'head' had gotten restructured too with the rewriting and he needed a break.

He spent most of April arranging his tools into a nice little machine shop with lathes, motors, etc., in his corner of the apartment. For several weeks he kept happily busy supplementing, fixing, and redesigning equipment so he could more easily do minor wood and metal work, e.g., make anthropometer parts, fix Mira's jewelry, or make small metal pieces like a multi-shelved equipment caddy he made out of sheet metal added to a small child's wagon.* Alfred had unsettling news near the end of April when he learned of the sudden death of his good friend Jesse Lee Bennett, who had had a heart attack while fighting a fire that broke out on his Arnold, Maryland farm. Despite this blow, overall Alfred felt restored by the time away from his desk. He had hoped to present a complete paper on his work as a "theory of sanity" at the First International Congress on Mental Hygiene in Washington, D.C., being held in May. But even with William Alanson White as the conference organizer, he couldn't get onto the program. Alfred attended anyway and managed to participate as one of the discussants of a paper given by Dr. Franz Alexander on "Mental Hygiene and Criminology". Korzybski's brief remarks were enough to get a number of psychiatrists interested in what he was doing, including Swiss psychiatrist M. Tramer, who began to correspond with him and helped edit the book, and American psychoanalyst

---

* The caddy was eventually retrieved from a junk shed in Connecticut by GS writer Robert R. Potter, who gave it to me [BIK]. With a new paint job, it sits by my bedside and works quite well as a nightstand, holding books, tissues, and other such paraphernalia—probably what Korzybski used it for—and still rolling easily from place to place, although it could well be at least 80 years old now.

Abraham A. Brill, translator of Freud's and Jung's work, who later became an honorary trustee of the Institute of General Semantics. Korzybski's edited remarks were published along with Alexander's paper in the *Proceedings of the Congress*, published in 1932.[2]

Back at his desk, Korzybski continued replenishing the book through the summer. Mira had gone to Newport and he had no distractions. He took another break in September, when he went to Detroit to give a lecture and to Ann Arbor to see Rainich. Then he drove back with Sally Avery through Canada (including Toronto and Montreal) to Newport where he visited Mira, who was planning to come home shortly. After a few days with her, he went on to Cambridge, Massachusetts for several days, where he met with Bridgman, Huntington, Wheeler, Birkhoff, and other Harvard academics interested in his work. Perhaps his most noteworthy meeting was with Alfred North Whitehead, whose writings he so greatly admired, despite their—to him—lingering aristotelianism. Alfred returned to Brooklyn in mid-October and wrote to Keyser :

> The main shock, and a joyful one was my meeting with Whitehead. Huntington to whom you introduced me some years ago is always much a helpful and charming man. Knowing that I will visit him he tried to get Whitehead but he was out of town. Then he telephoned in my presence trying to arrange a meeting between us. Well Whitehead knew about me and my work, and was seemingly eager to meet me and invited me for an hour chat to his home. Knowing about my work he asked a lot of very pertinent questions which apparently I answered to his satisfaction. I had the temerity to explain to him the generalized theory of types.
>
> Of course all my impressions may be mistaken, the more that some results are so unexpectedly simple and solve completely some of the most difficult problems we had in the past, that in short conversations there is always the danger that I may make a fool of myself, although given time I can always make good.[3]

Whatever trepidations Alfred may have had in the fall of 1930, he felt far enough along with his new, structurally-informed work to present it in three papers which were accepted for presentation at the October 25 meeting of the American Mathematical Society in New York City. He thought he would have 10 minutes for each paper (he had hoped to have 30 minutes altogether to give an overview of his entire system) but the time was shortened to 15 minutes total—hardly enough time to even skim the surface. The abstracts of "On structure", "A generalized theory of mathematical types", and "A non-aristotelian system" were published in the *Bulletin of the American Mathematical Society*.[4] They contained the basic framework of his work—a system linking knowledge, uncertainty, and courage.

Knowledge

Keyser had stated the basic structural-relational premise: "To be is to be related."[5] The premise of non-elementalism—"There *is no* such thing as an object in absolute isolation."[6]—could be viewed as a corollary. One important example of non-elementalism related to human knowledge. The classical interpretation of 'objectivity' tended to treat knowledge as if it existed in absolute isolation from human observers/formulators in their contexts of time and place. This view had to go.

Korzybski had accepted that "...*all we know is a joint phenomenon of the observer and the observed,*..."[7] One could no longer study how people know what they presume they know (epistemology) without scientific understanding (at a given date) of the 'physical', 'neuro-biological', 'psycho-social', 'linguistic,' etc., factors affecting human observers. Over the past decade, the observer-observed relation had remained the constant focus of Korzybski's scientific, epistemological research on the process of abstracting in science, maladjustment, and daily life.

Korzybski's new emphasis on structure gave him greater clarity about the relations between the inferred process universe and the different levels of abstraction. As he replenished the book in 1930, he realized that as a multiordinal term, "structure" could refer equally to any of the different vertically arranged levels of the Anthropometer—the presumed structure of the process world (represented by the parabola), the implied structure of the nervous system, the structure of non-verbal 'objective' level experience (the circles), the structure of a language in its representational aspects (the various hanging labels), etc. Structure was also shown in the horizontal differences between different human abstractors and between human and animal abstractors. Within a few months of his October presentation, he had changed the name of the Anthropometer (a name he had grown to dislike) to the "Structural Differential".

With his more conscious structural viewpoint, his non-aristotelian system seemed more coherent to Korzybski as a *system of interrelated formulations*. He continued to work out the implications as he revised. For example, he got more explicit about one of his basic assumptions about the structure of the world, i.e. *non-identity*.

Non-identity involved the complete denial of 'identity'—defined as the 'absolute sameness' in *'all'* aspects of any two things. 'Identity' could never be found in the world inside or outside our skins. No two individuals labeled with one name under a category were exactly the 'same' in *all* respects. Furthermore, since we live in a process universe, anything humans dealt with on the 'object' levels—an iron bar, an apple, a toothache, etc.— represented a space-time event. So even to say that "something is identical with itself", i.e., absolutely the same in *all* aspects of itself from one moment to the next, seemed invariably false to facts. (Korzybski made sure to point out that this didn't have to lead to "metaphysical shivers". If 'absolute sameness' in *'all'* aspects didn't exist in this world, neither did 'absolute difference': "In a world of only absolute differences, without similarities, recognition, and, therefore, 'intelligence', would be impossible."[8])

Regarding 'identity', when things changed—in the view of Aristotle and his followers—their underlying 'substance' still remained 'the same'.[9] Things which existed in the world remained 'the same' for all. Different humans could have 'the same' 'mental' experience of those things. Knowledge consisted of finding the 'essence' of a thing's underlying nature or substance, which could be expressed in a definition. This quote from the beginning of Aristotle's *On Interpretation* epitomizes what could be called the aristotelian "essentialist" approach:

> Spoken words are the symbols of mental experience and written words are the symbols of spoken words. Just as all men have not the same writing, so all men have not the same speech sounds, but the mental experiences, which these directly symbolize, are the same for all, as also are those things of which our experiences are the images.[10]

With the assumption that 'mental experiences' were the same for all, Aristotle had set the horizon for his program. One could conclude that different people's differing forms of language and symbolism did not affect their 'mental experience' in any significant way (for if it did, 'mental experience' would surely not be the 'same' for all). This radical separation between symbolism and mental experience reduced the need to question or change basic assumptions and the language or symbolism expressing them. Aristotle's metaphysics—which posited the 'fixed' nature (according to our categories) of the things which our mental experiences depicted—remained intact. Attention stayed focused on studying and classifying things according to their 'essential' nature and coming to reliable conclusions and agreement through the use of logic.

The premise of non-identity—fundamentally non-essentialist—significantly diverged from Aristotle's metaphysical emphasis on fixed substances. Its process view had been foreseen in the poetical teachings of the pre-Socratic Greek philosopher Heraclitus: "Everything flows and nothing abides; everything gives way and nothing stays fixed. You cannot step twice into the same river, for other waters and yet others go ever flowing on."[11]

Non-identity could be stated in terms of the "principle of individualization" or the "atomistic principle" which Korzybski had mentioned in the second *Time-Binding* paper. Briefly, it postulated "...the absolute individuality of events on the un-speakable objective levels, ...".[12] Leibniz had recognized the significance of this in what he called his principle of the "identity of indiscernibles":

> There is no such thing as two individuals *indiscernible* from each other. An ingenious gentleman of my acquaintance, discoursing with me, in the presence of her *Electoral Highness the Princess* Sophia [Electress of Hanover, mother of George I of England, and one of Leibniz's patronesses] in the garden of *Herrenhausen*, thought he could find two leaves perfectly alike. The princess defied him to do it, and he ran all over the garden a long time to look for some; but it was to no purpose. Two drops of water, or milk, viewed with a microscope, will appear distinguishable from each other. ...To suppose *two* things *indiscernible*, is to suppose the *same thing* under *two names*.[13]

However, in referring to this in terms of "the identity of indiscernibles", Leibniz seems to have reduced the full impact of his insight. He was not able to abandon 'identity' altogether, retaining the notion as legitimate in the realm of propositions and 'necessary' truths. Wittgenstein also seemed to have noted problems with 'identity' in his *Tractatus Logico-Philosophicus*: "Roughly speaking, to say of *two* things that they are identical is nonsense, and to say of *one* thing that it is identical with itself is to say nothing."[14] (Korzybski had underlined this proposition in red in his copy of the *Tractatus*.) But the practical import of this did not seem clear in Wittgenstein's work either.

As far as Korzybski knew, he was the first to explicitly state the principle of "non-identity" (the denial of 'identity') as a basic system premise, exploring its implications and attempting to apply it in science and daily life. In mathematics and 'logic', the assumption of 'identity' could be done away with. It no longer seemed necessary to interpret "A = A" or "1=1" as "A is 'identical' to A" or "1 is 'identical' to 1." Instead the " = "sign could be taken to symbolize equivalence, which depended on an agreement by some humans to ignore differences when they didn't make a difference.

> If we take even a symbolic expression 1=1, 'absolute sameness' in *'all'* aspects is equally impossible, although we may use in this connection terms such as 'equal', 'equivalent',. [etc,.] 'Absolute sameness in all aspects' would necessitate an *identity* of different nervous systems which produce and use these symbols, an *identity* of the different states of the nervous system of the person who wrote the above two symbols, an identity of the

surfaces ., [etc.,] of different parts of the paper, in the distribution of ink, and what not. To demand such impossible conditions is, of course, absurd, but it is equally absurd and very harmful for sanity and civilization to preserve until this day such delusional formulations as *standards of evaluation*, and then spend a lifetime of suffering and toil to evade the consequences. This may be comparable to the spending of many years in teaching and training our children that one and one *never* equal two, that twice two *never* equal four . , [etc.,] and then they would have to spend a lifetime full of surprises and disappointments, if not tragedies, to learn, when they are about to die, that the above statements are always correct in mathematics and very often true in daily life,...[15]

This seemed difficult to deny and, for some people, equally difficult to accept. One world-renowned 'philosopher' would later 'report' that Korzybski had claimed here that "1=1 must be false because the two sides of the equation are spatially distinct."[16] Whoa! This misinterpretation was subsequently quoted with authority by others as representing Korzybski's views. He got used to having his views distorted like this and often said "I say what I say. I do *not* say what I do not say."

He would also say that in a world of structure, whatever you say something 'is' *is not* it. This led him to advocate avoiding the "is of identity". It could mask discernible differences between different individuals placed under a single category. It could also obscure important temporal changes in a single individual. This didn't mean for Korzybski that all versions of the verb "to be" must be eschewed or that we should somehow stop using categories or classifications—the latter impossible for abstracting nervous systems. However, to remain conscious of abstracting when speaking, people somehow had to remember that any individual thing labeled within a classification/category is not exactly the same in all respects to any other thing so labeled. A label is not the thing labeled. A map is not the territory.

Beside non-identity, the premise of non-allness characterizes any map-language. In the asymmetrical relation between a territory and a map, a territory always contains *more* than what any map of it could represent. So a map-language about some object-territory cannot cover 'all' of the territory it represents. In this light, it appeared futile to try to capture the ultimate 'essence' of any object of knowledge with any particular verbal/symbolic formulation. No finite human abstraction can finalistically cover the apparently infinite field of possible knowledge, represented on the Structural Differential by the parabola—the 'ultimate' territory. However, the fruitlessness of an aristotelian search for 'essences' clearly did not do away with the possibility of any reliable knowledge. Indeed, Korzybski could see that *structure constitutes the sole content of knowledge*. As he put it in the chapter "On Structure":

> If words *are not* things, or maps *are not* the actual territory, then, obviously, the only possible link between the objective world and the linguistic world is found in *structure, and structure alone*. The only usefulness of a map or a language depends on the *similarity of structure* between the empirical world and the map-languages. If the structure is not similar, then the traveler or speaker is led astray, which, in serious human life-problems, must become always eminently harmful,. [etc.] If the structures *are similar*, then the empirical world becomes 'rational' to a potentially rational being, which means no more than that the verbal, or map-predicted characteristics, which follow up the linguistic or map structure, are applicable to the empirical world.[17]

Further exploring these notions, Korzybski formulated the centrality of *identification* to faulty habits of abstracting. 'Identity', as the *absolute sameness in all aspects* of two or more different individuals (things), does not exist in the world. However, it is possible to *identify*—to attribute 'identity' or 'sameness' (overemphasize similarities while ignoring important differences) to different individuals and/or to one individual from one time to another. Identification, equivalent to confusing orders or levels of abstractions (stratified both horizontally and vertically), constituted the chief 'idol' to be knocked down through the use of the Structural Differential. (See below.)

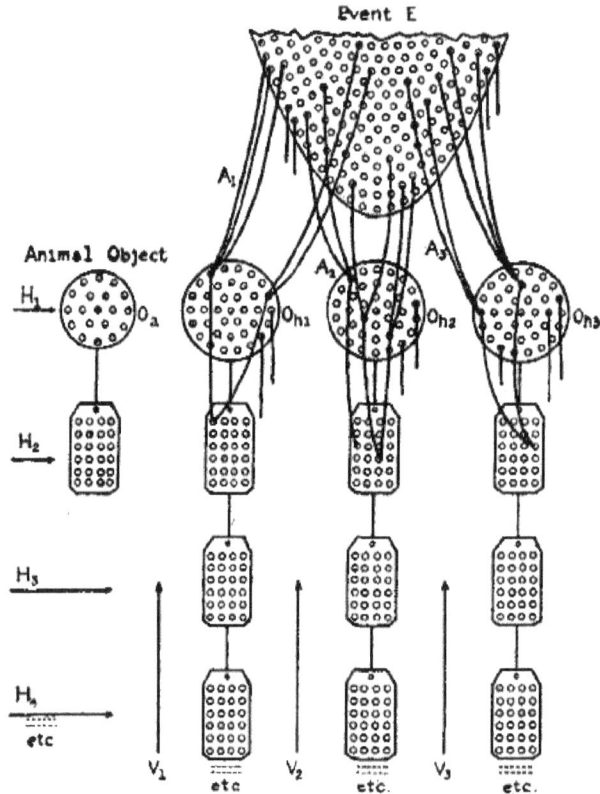

Structural Differential, Vertical and Horizontal Stratifications, *S&S*, p. 396

With each individual observer, each successive horizontal level of abstraction represented a mapping of the previous level: the object level served to map or provide some similarity of structure to some event level 'territory' but *is not* the event level and does not cover *all* of that event territory; a lower order verbal description mapped a particular object level experience but *is not* that object level territory and does not cover all of it; a statement about the previous statement mapped the previous statement but *is not* the 'same' as that statement, i.e., an inference is not a description; et cetera. When you didn't distinguish these levels, you identified. When you didn't distinguish your abstractions from those of other observers (other vertical levels), you identified too. You talked and acted as if your map 'was' the territory, and could represent 'all' of the territory.

Beside non-identity and non-allness, there was another significant characteristic of the mapping/modeling/abstracting process—*self-reflexiveness*. You could always make another map about your current map, another statement about the last statement, and go on indefinitely. As Josiah Royce had pointed out, someone in England attempting to produce a 'perfect' map of England would have to include 'all' of the details of England including himself producing the map of England. And in order to be complete he would have to produce a map of himself producing the map of himself producing the map of England, etc. (The artist Norman Rockwell made a picture of this kind of self-reflexive process in his 1960 painting, *Triple Self-Portrait*.) This process, infinite in extent, could never be completed. There could be no final, complete map, no last word.

As a corollary of self-reflexiveness, the existence of a map always implied a map-maker at a date. You could look at the Structural Differential as a highly abstract portrait of yourself the mapmaker—abstractor, knower, etc.—at any given moment. The parabola's broken-off edges (visual et ceteras)—sometimes also put on the last hanging label—self-reflexively indicated the incompleteness of any abstractions, including the best scientific knowledge at-a-date. Awareness of this could prevent you from treating any particular abstraction as final. You could best approach the seemingly infinite universe by becoming conscious of abstracting, acknowledging the finitude of your abstractions at a date and indefinitely continuing to explore beyond their limits. In this way, you'd more likely continue abstracting afresh instead of staying stuck in your model of the moment.

'Knowing'—the "end-product" *effect* (at a given date) of this self-reflexive process—"must be considered also as a causative psychophysiological factor"[18] in an individual's and others' ongoing behavior because of the spiral structure of human knowledge and action. (Linking of the 'last' label to the parabola indicated this circular or spiral structure of human knowing.) Self-reflexively acknowledging this spiral character of map-making, and studying the mapmaker, including yourself, could lead to a new level of responsibility in knowing and living. To bring self-reflexiveness into conscious practice in this way involved a different, more conscious use of language.

The Language Filter

For centuries, thinkers had already questioned aristotelianism on many fronts. Tearing down the separating wall between experience and language that Aristotle had bolstered if not erected, Korzybski ranks among the boldest of those who challenged aristotelian metaphysics and its assumptions about language and symbolism.

In 1924 Korzybski had written, "All human knowledge is conditioned and limited, at present, by the properties of light and human symbolism."[19] Since then it had become even clearer to him that if there were no 'facts' free from the share of the observer's 'mind', then language and other symbolic media were not neutral. For good and for ill, language served as a major 'filter' for human knowledge. Understanding the structure of knowledge required exploring the structure of representational language and its relation to human action. A non-aristotelian revision of the sciences and life required linguistic revision—a new consciousness of what language does with us and what we can do with language.

Of course, it was important not to consider 'language' elementalistically. As a product of human nervous systems and a form of human behavior, no language existed entirely separate from the 'culture' and 'consciousness' of the individuals who used it with others. Humans in societies created their languages, and their languages in turn also affected them. Although not the sole determinant of 'thought' and behavior, it appeared to Korzybski that an individual's language and related evaluations had tremendous power to channel his ongoing actions.

Any language could be said to have structure, indeed multiple levels of structure. Korzybski had particular interest in the *implicatory* aspects—the implications, presuppositions, and assumptions a language might 'entice' us to project upon the world. Humans tended to act according to the way they mapped the world—'logical' destiny. Without consciousness of the mapping effects related to their language, people could react to words, and whatever experiences they processed verbally, like Pavlov's dog salivating to the sound of a bell. One could change the way one responded to the world by finding some ways to circumvent language (to the extent this could be done, e.g., through silent observation, visualization, etc.). One could also change the structure of one's language. Contemplation of and practice with the Structural Differential encouraged both of these methods. In addition, Korzybski contended that the use of *non-elementalistic terms* and various other changes in the structure of everyday language (taken from the simplest of mathematics) could promote greater consciousness of abstracting and a more up-to-date outlook. People could learn to use language more consciously to orient themselves more extensionally (according to 'facts') and thus more sanely.

For example, in order to promote a non-elementalistic outlook, it helped to purposefully—and with understanding—use non-elementalistic terms like "abstracting", "time-binding", etc. Much mathematical terminology had a non-elementalistic character as well, and could be carried over, when appropriate, into everyday speech. (He recommended Keyser's *Mathematical Philosophy* for suggestions in this regard.) Korzybski created other non-elementalistic terms in the book by connecting two terms with a *hyphen* whenever he wanted to make certain relationships explicit. For instance, 'logic' (which he now saw as an aspect or part of mathematics) seemed to him a highly significant product of human nervous systems, involving and affecting human behavior. Therefore Korzybski felt it necessary to link 'logic' to the study of 'psychology' (human behavior) and came up with the new term "psycho-logics" to make that linkage explicit—although the usage and its significance seemed difficult for many logicians, philosophers, mathematicians, and psychologists to accept. In addition, when using a term with potentially elementalistic or other misleading implications in a given context, Korzybski decided to use *single quotes* (more common in British usage) as a kind of warning to 'watch out' and not objectify the term. Thus 'thinking', 'feeling', 'matter', 'substance', 'language', etc., might be used with single quotes. He applied such *single quotes* to terms he found consistently elementalistic or otherwise problematic, like 'psychology', 'logic', and 'philosophy'. Some 'psychologists', 'logicians', and 'philosophers'—among others—may have considered it silly or felt offended, but Alfred felt he had a useful point to make.

In the book he also used indexes to highlight individuals within categories. For example, as he wrote about it later in his introduction to the second edition of the book, 'houses' could include a variety of buildings, some with termites or hidden structural flaws, which had to be examined extensionally as individuals—house$_1$ was not house$_2$, etc. One didn't want to simply buy a definition, which was what advertisers tended to try to sell.[20] Korzybski also made extensive use of temporal indexing or dating to bring out the awareness of space-time processes. For example, when he knew the book would definitely get into print by the end of 1933, he made sure to emphasize that his statements about science referred to 'science 1933'—a move that probably irritated some readers. But he wanted to make the point that he was not in a position to legislate for 'science' for 'all' time. Of course, he didn't expect his work to go out of date by 1934. Still, he wanted to acknowledge, as part of his non-finalistic outlook, that readers in 1934 or 1974 or 2024, etc., would have to check out what he said in 1933 and possibly revise it.

Throughout the book he had made many statements with lists of examples that he completed by writing "etc." (et cetera). He was writing "etc." so many times that he decided to create a non-aristotelian extensional punctuation where a period would represent the "etc." combined with whatever other punctuation was used with it (for example, "etc.," would be represented by " .,". Some people treated this punctuation as a quirk on Korzybski's part and undoubtedly many people ignored it. A proper reading of the book required attending to it. For Korzybski, who later referred to it as "junior infinity", the use of "etc." was a tangible reminder of non-allness. He would say that the extensional punctuation (with "etc." as a period) could help put a stop to a "a period and stop attitude".

He had to go through the manuscript quite carefully to expunge any uses of 'is' that smacked of identity. (Some years after the book was published someone sent him a letter excoriating him for retaining some such 'illegitimate' 'ises'. He spent a number of hours combing through the given page references before he concluded that his critic was not correct.) He also got rid of any uses of the term 'same' without quotes. If he was serious about non-identity, he had to apply it in his writing.

Korzybski also emphasized the multiordinality of terms, which was based on the multi-leveled, self-reflexive structure of the human nervous system and its mappings—the fact that we could map our maps and react to our reactions. Awareness of multiordinality could increase a person's vocabulary tremendously and also opened up a large and relatively unexplored (because previously difficult to talk about) field for students of human behavior. It now made sense to talk about 'positive' second order reactions such as "curiosity about curiosity, attention of attention, analysis of analysis, reasoning about reasoning… knowing of knowing…evaluation of evaluation…"; morbid second order reactions such as "worry about worry, fear of fear…pity of pity...belief in belief…conviction of conviction,…ignorance of ignorance"; and reactions where "the *second order reverses and annuls* the first order effects" in a constructive way such as "inhibition of an inhibition…hate of hate…[and] doubt of doubt… ."[21]

Korzybski used certain terms so often that he introduced a number of abbreviations which he used throughout the book. *A* for aristotelian, *E* for euclidean, *N* for newtonian (and $\overline{A}$, $\overline{E}$ and $\overline{N}$ for their '*non*' counterparts), *el* for elementalistic, *non-el* for non-elementalistic, and *m.o* for multiordinal.

Uncertainty

Uncertainty was built into the abstracting process. Perhaps the most 'certain' (least uncertain) knowledge came when we learned how a map *did not fit* a given territory:

> All knowledge is hypothetical, in which…[t]he most important facts must be *negative*. When the [linguistic and empirical] structures do not match, then we learn something quite definite about the empirical structures.[22]

> Because words are never the things we speak about, the sole link between languages and the objective world being structural, the only 'positive' facts about this world are of the old 'negative' character.[23]

Around the time Korzybski was writing this, Karl Popper in Vienna was developing related notions while writing what would become his first book, *Logik der Forschung*, to be published in 1934. Popper's book, later published in English as *The Logic of Scientific Discovery* (1959), was his opening volley in the theory of knowledge and scientific methodology. His work centered around the importance of falsification (disconfirmation). According to Popper, a theory that couldn't conceivably be tested and shown false was not scientific. The best tests of a theory applied the most rigorous, potentially falsifying challenges to it. We could learn something definite when a theory did not pan out. A successful scientific theory, one with better predictivity than others at a given date, had simply better survived attempts to test it.

A minimal 'maybeness' pertained to even the best, nigh certain scientific theories. As Popper wrote in the closing pages of his book:

> The old scientific idea of *episteme*—of absolutely certain, demonstrable knowledge—has proved to be an idol. The demand for scientific objectivity makes it inevitable that every scientific statement must remain *tentative for ever*. It may indeed be corroborated, but every corroboration is relative to other statements which, again, are tentative. Only in our subjective experiences of conviction, in our subjective faith, can we be 'absolutely certain'.[24]

I have found no evidence that Korzybski was ever aware of Popper. Popper apparently didn't know or think much of Korzybski's work (according to Stuart A. Mayper, chemist, korzybskian scholar/teacher, and former editor of the *General Semantics Bulletin*, who studied with Popper at the University of London).[25] Nonetheless, their complementary views both pointed to an uncertaintist perspective.

With similarity (not 'sameness') of structure providing the sole link between different levels of abstracting, one could only have varying degrees of similarity of a map with a territory, giving varying degrees of predictability. You could not have a 'perfect' map. But you could strive for maximum probability of predictability in a map at a given date. In 1931, Korzybski formulated this in terms of a "general principle of uncertainty":

> ...on objective levels we deal structurally with absolutely individual stages of processes and situations and by necessity we speak in higher order abstractions and generalities and use many multiordinal terms (without the use of which no speaking is possible), so *any possible statement* about the objective levels must be only probable in different degrees, which introduces a fundamental and entirely *general $\bar{A}$ principle of uncertainty.* Heisenberg's restricted principle in physics appears only as a special case.[26]

The implications of this for Korzybski seemed profound. For one thing, it resolved the problem of "indeterminism" brought to the fore by the development of quantum physics. Many scientists and philosophers were 'reeling' from the replacement of classical, two-valued determinism with statistical approaches for understanding the submicroscopic world. Many had leaped to assuming the end of causality and perhaps the loss of confidence in scientific knowledge. Many, like Bridgman, appeared to despair or rail at this conclusion. Einstein, for example, accepted the findings of quantum physics but rejected the fundamental nature of the statistical approach (although he had helped develop it). He continued to embrace classical determinism, searching for hidden variables behind the probabilities of quantum physics. He could never accept that 'Herr Gott' might play dice with the universe.

Korzybski agreed with Einstein: indeterminism was not a scientific option. He argued that 'indeterminism' would involve a denial of structure or relations, an inherently contradictory viewpoint since, as he wrote to William Alanson White in early 1931,

...the language of causation which in a subtler analysis requires series (mathematics) is a characteristic of human rationality and [as such] has little to do with the world, but it is also the foundation of relations and structure and a non-aristotelian system. If empirical data lead us to indeterminism verbally, such language is in structure non similar to the world and our nervous system and simply should be changed to another language which retains determinism.[27]

Here was another echo of Leibniz. One of Leibniz's guiding principles had been that of "sufficient reason"—"nothing happens without a sufficient reason why it should be thus rather than otherwise."[28] According to Leibniz's 17th-century scientific 'faith', anything that happens exists within the compass of potential human understanding and knowledge. Korzybski could be seen to have held an updated form of Leibniz's principle: any knowledge—'scientific' or otherwise—involved a search for structure. Determinism provided the test for structure. But for Korzybski, determinism must involve probabilities.

Unlike Einstein, Korzybski did not see causality as at odds with chance. He embraced the fundamental role of probabilities in our knowledge of anything. Accepting the generalized uncertainty of all statements (not only the statements of quantum mechanics) did not require abandoning the search for knowledge and predictability. It did require abandoning the "one cause, one effect" determinism, which seemed based upon two-valued 'certainty'. This had to be refashioned into a probabilistic, many-valued determinism which would require a many-valued logic of probability in which two-valued logic remained as a special case.† (Korzybski argued for such a probabilistic logic, but didn't develop one himself.) Second-order certainty of degrees of uncertainty remained. "If so, then invariably and always *so*" had to give way to "If so, then probably *so*, which could depend upon multiple factors, e.g., x, y, z, etc." Knowledge and uncertainty existed together, inexorably intertwined.

Even with some degree of uncertainty, reliable knowledge remained possible. Indeed, under some circumstances—when developed through a scientific approach—higher order abstractions (also known as generalizations or inferences) could provide the most reliable knowledge possible at a date. Some people later got the notion that Korzybski was against making generalizations. This conclusion could not have come from a careful reading of his book. "It is no mystery that when we want to look further into the past and future we need higher and higher order abstractions."[29]

Linking knowledge with uncertainty also related to a conscious recognition—at the heart of non-elementalism—of the importance of non-additivity. "As a structural fact, the world around us is *not* a 'plus' affair, and requires a functional [relational] representation."[30] Yet it was especially easy to misrepresent complex, non-additive, nonlinear processes, relationships, organizations, etc. as 'plus' affairs. Since the early 1920s—long before the formal development

---

† Korzybski only rejected the *universality* of two-valued, either-or 'logic' as a general *orientation*. Within a multi-valued orientation, either-or distinctions sometimes appeared appropriate. As he wrote to Keyser soon after the book was published, "... mathematics in the main (1934) (only) would be impossible if today $1 + 1 = 2$ and tomorrow $1 + 1 \neq 2$. So when we want sharp tools we use two-valued orientations, but that's VOLITIONAL. I try to establish some sharp tools for efficiency in human orientations, and once in a while I must use two-valued orientations..." [*AK Collected Writings*, p. 186]. He had already made this point in *Science and Sanity* [Korzybski 1994 (1933), pp. 94, 195, 405, 760–761], and continued to do so in later writings. Still, petty criticism about his supposed rejection of two-valued 'logic' would also continue.

of systems theory, 'chaos' theory, 'complexity' theory, etc.—Korzybski had been concerned with this additive or plus tendency in people's evaluating, reflected in their language. The addition of one 'small' factor in a situation didn't necessarily lead to the 'same old thing'. One mother and one father 'plus' one small baby involved a whole new, complex set of relations as a couple became a family. An uncertaintist perspective, informed by non-additivity, could prepare one to expect the unexpected and thus reduce undesirable shocks from the new.[31] Korzybski devoted an entire chapter of the book "On Linearity" to the ramifications of this. After the book was published, "*New factors: the havoc they play with our generalizations*" became a prominent focus of his teaching and writing.[32]

Interestingly Leibniz had written that, "Those great principles of a *sufficient reason* and of the *identity of indiscernibles*, change the state of metaphysics. That science becomes real and demonstrative by means of these principles; whereas before, it did generally consist of empty words."[33] Korzybski's parallel principles of *structure* and of *non-identity*—with their attendant redefinition of knowledge in terms of structure, generalized uncertainty, probabilistic ∞[infinite]-valued determinism, non-additivity, etc.—seemed to Korzybski to change the state of 20th-century metaphysics, epistemology, etc., into something real and demonstrative, and of potentially great human significance—a foundation for a science of 'man'.

Courage

Alfred and Mira had indeed reached the 'zero hour' and were 'going over the top'. The Great Depression had settled in. They had seriously started to look for a publisher and publishers seemed leery. They had to face up to selling a big and demanding book at a time when many people were going to think twice about buying any book at all. And the book was going to ask a lot more from its readers than just an investment of money. Alfred wasn't just espousing another 'philosophy'. He had 'taken the aristotelian bull by the horns'. To show how the non-aristotelian orientation worked in practice, he had changed the structure of the language in his book in all the ways noted above. He and Mira had to gather up the courage to proceed and persist in their project despite these difficulties.

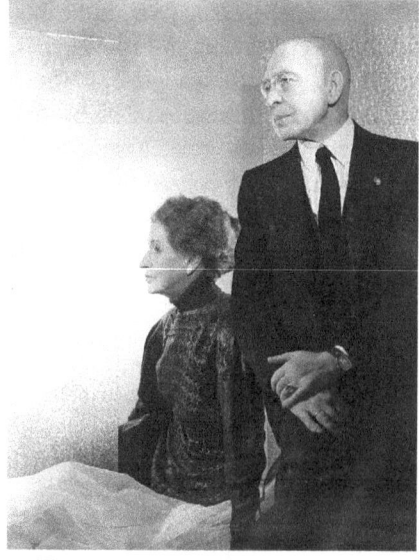

Mira and Alfred, probably circa 1930

Readers would have to have courage too. The hefty book, both in size and content, would look daunting to many. Regarding intimidating content, despite its appearance otherwise, it was not about the technical details of science and mathematics but rather about the psycho-logical, evaluational aspect of science and mathematics as human behavior, among other forms of human behavior. Alfred made this point explicitly and did his best to encourage readers who were not professional scientists or mathematicians. He had written the book in such a way that reading it would teach the reader how to read it. A reader was going to be required to learn a new way of talking. One who approached the work with sympathy and effort (reading it at least twice) would more likely begin to look at things differently, talk differently, and begin to deal with problems differently. He or she would have to work at it. An unsympathetic reader who refused to go along, even tentatively, with what Korzybski suggested would likely find the book—as a number of people did—repetitious and trivial, when not puzzling. But Korzybski had seen enough evidence, from working on himself and other people and from hearing Graven's reports on patients, to indicate that his system provided a valuable self-help approach to 'mental' hygiene and better problem-solving, a method for dealing with fears in what were becoming increasingly fearful times.

Embracing uncertainty with knowledge—and knowledge with uncertainty—made it possible to develop courage and find stability in one's personal life despite difficult and changing circumstances. Ignorance and, even more, ignorance of ignorance and false knowledge encouraged by various kinds of identification, could breed serious maladjustments. "When we live in a *delusional* world, we multiply our worries, fears, and discouragements, and our higher nerve centres, instead of protecting us from over-stimulation, actually multiply the semantic [evaluational] harmful stimuli indefinitely. Under such circumstances 'sanity' is impossible."[34]

For sure, Korzybski expected to 'catch some hell'. He was not aware of anyone else in his time, who had done quite what he had. Some critics later seemed to behave as if he didn't even have the right to attempt something Aristotle had done over 2000 years before, i.e., to formulate "a *general method* for 'all' scientific work."[35] But Korzybski felt that whatever his own inadequacies—which he was ready to attest to—he had as much right as anyone else to aim for a 20th century version of this: an *applied* update of how we know what we think we know. He wanted his work to be judged on its merits. He thought he had developed something important and he had to carry it through. In keeping with the thrust of his work (consciousness of abstracting, etc.) he made a point not to claim perfection or finality. Indeed, in the book he was modestly stressing the limitations of his work (despite its generality of application), recommending research, and inviting corrections and suggestions. Nonetheless, the notion that he had come up with "a *general method* not only for scientific work, but also life,…"[36] was going to be too much for some skeptics to ever swallow. Korzybski's reach would exceed their grasp. There was nothing to be done at this stage except to get the book into print and then deal with whatever 'hits' would come his way.

Chapter 38
"GENERAL SEMANTICS"

At the start of 1931, Korzybski still lacked one main formulational piece for the book—a label for his own approach more specific than "non-aristotelian". The work of a number of other individuals could be called non-aristotelian too. What he had attempted to formulate strained the conventional vocabularies of every discipline he drew from and required new terminology, including a new name. His theory encompassed, or at least intersected with, 'psychology', 'philosophy', 'logic', etc., but couldn't exactly be encompassed by any one of those fields. He had eliminated "human engineering" and "humanology" as choices. The "general theory of *time-binding*", while broadly descriptive, didn't quite get to the way he was looking at human behavior. He liked "general anthropology" and considered it fitting, but his friend C. K. Ogden didn't. Alfred deferred to Ogden. He mentioned the term in the book, but continued to look around for another way to describe the discipline he was forming.

He needed a name for his basic subject—*what* he was studying. As much as he wrote about language, he was actually focused on a particular holistic (non-elementalistic)—and more general—view of human behavior. Any use of language (mathematics included) inevitably involved a related, non-verbal response. It was this non-verbal response that concerned him:

> ...the psycho-logical reaction of a given individual to words and language and other symbols and events *in connection with their meanings,* and the psycho-logical reactions, which *become meanings and relational configurations* the moment the given individual begins to analyse them or somebody else does that for him." [1]

This non-verbal reaction, by necessity psychophysiological, involved an organism-as-a-whole functioning *with and as* a nervous system in an environment. Electro-colloidal correlates had to be involved. As much as he admired Pavlov's work, Korzybski did not want to neglect the importance of the so-called 'subjective' or 'introspective' dimension of the individual's response—a direct fact for the individual, which had to be inferred by others. A suitable name for this form of non-elementalistic reaction would also have to do away with the elementalistic separation of 'emotion' from 'intellect', 'thinking' from 'feeling'.

A General Theory of Evaluation

Evaluation seemed like it would do the job since it implied some 'cognitive' effort connected with values. "Evaluation", unlike "cognition", non-elementalistically implied 'feeling' operating together with 'thinking'. Korzybski's work constituted a general theory of non-elementalistic evaluation. As he would emphasize some years later:

> Abstracting by necessity involves evaluatiing, whether conscious or not, and so the process of abstracting may be considered as a *process of evaluating stimuli*, whether it be a "toothache," "an attack of migraine," or the reading of a "philosophical treatise." [2]

In Korzybski's usage, evaluating *did not* require language. Both animals and pre-verbal human infants evaluated—had evaluational reactions—as much as any linguistically-capable adult human did. The difference between animal and human evaluating was roughly indicated in the greater stratification and variety of human reactions connected with symbolism/language. Even when human symbolism/language was involved, evaluation was not mainly a matter of words:

> Our actual lives are lived entirely on the objective levels [represented by the circle on the structural differential], including the un-speakable 'feelings', 'emotions' . , [etc.,] the

verbal levels being only *auxiliary*, and effective only if they are translated back into first order un-speakable effects, such as an object, an action, a 'feeling'., all on the silent and un-speakable objective levels.[3]

As a term equivalent to 'evaluational', he decided to use the adjective 'semantic', without the final "s", as a modifier to other words, as in "semantic (evaluational) ills", "semantic (evaluational) blockages", "semantic (evaluational) flexibility", etc. In the first half of 1931, perhaps due to his long mulling over of Pavlov's reflexology, he had begun formulating about evaluation in general in terms of "semantic *reflexes*". But by August he decided the implications of the term "reflex" (two-valued, on-off, etc.) couldn't adequately cover the variety and complexity of human evaluation—no matter how often people seemed to indulge in "knee jerk" responses. The more general term "reaction" covered reflexes as well as more complex states of behavior. The term "semantic reaction(s)", which he abbreviated as "$s.r$", referred to the non-elementalistic and un-speakable reactions to words, symbols, and other events he had been concerning himself with.

Now he had a name beside "evaluation" for the behavioral focus of his work: "The *non-el* study of the $s.r$ becomes an extremely general scientific discipline. ...The present work is written entirely from the $s.r$ point of view;..."[4] As for the name of his work, he would call the general study of semantic reactions, *general semantics*. He added a long section "On semantic reactions" which became the largest part of Chapter II, "Terminology and Meanings". Then he went through another round of replenishing the manuscript., changing mentions of 'thought(s)' and 'feeling(s)' to "semantic reaction(s)"or "$s.r$"and putting in "semantic," and "semantically" where they seemed to fit to emphasize his evaluational thrust.

Korzybski had derived his choice of terms from the Greek root, *semainein* (to *mean*, to *signify*). He had wanted to give a historical nod to pioneers in the study of 'meaning'— Michel Bréal, Ogden and Richards, Lady Victoria Welby, logicians like Chwistek, etc.— although he hadn't been influenced by any of them in any significant way. Their studies were mainly concerned with more or less elementalistic linguistic and symbolic meanings. 'Meanings' or significations could certainly be 'stretched' to include the non-verbal, neurological, evaluative responses to events—including language and other symbols—that Korzybski was interested in. But the term 'semantic(s)' had so much historical baggage related to linguistic meanings, the history of words, etc., that many people would find it hard to put that aside in considering Korzybski's use of *semantic reaction* and *general semantics*. As a result, the principle of least effort tended to operate. Many people, supporters and critics alike, would confuse Korzybski's work with the more elementalistic studies of verbal and philosophical "semantics". (In the first few years after the book came out, Korzybski may have added to the confusion himself—at times casually using "semantics" to refer to his own work.)

Nonetheless, in the book, he had made it abundantly clear: any $s.r$, i.e., semantic (evaluational) reaction, constituted an un-speakable, psycho-logical response to an event with "a number of aspects, an 'affective', and an 'intellectual', a physiological, a colloidal, and what not."[5] It *was not* words, although any response to words or symbolism necessarily involved $s.r$. One could go through the text and find numerous examples (almost any reference to $s.r$) where he explicitly differentiated "language" from the "$s.r$" connected with it. Discussing the different forms of identification, he made sure to note that one form of it involved "the identification of our $s.r$ and states with words..."[6]

Insofar as he was dealing with issues of language, Korzybski had thus taken an organismic tack radically different from the approach of the verbally-oriented "semanticists". Language related to general behavior because, "In different people, through experience, associations, relations, meanings, and $s.r$ are built into some symbol."[7] At a relatively 'low' order of response, say "For the infant, a cry or a word becomes semantic magic. In Pavlov's language, a word governs a conditional reflex."[8] Unless this mechanism was understood, adults also seemed likely to respond to language in a similar reflex manner. This was why Korzybski harped so much on the importance of people retraining themselves with the structural differential and consciously using his terminology and the various linguistic devices he had proposed, if they wanted to change their $s.r$ for the better:

> We do not realize what tremendous power the structure of an habitual language has. It is not an exaggeration to say that it enslaves us through the mechanism of $s.r$ and that the structure which a language exhibits, and impresses upon us unconsciously, is *automatically projected* upon the world around us. This semantic power is indeed so unbelievable that I do not know any one, even among well-trained scientists, who, after having admitted some argument as correct, does not the next minute deny or disregard (usually unconsciously) practically every word he had admitted, being carried away again by the structural implications of the old language and his $s.r.$[9]

Many of the people, some of them 'followers', who insisted on calling Korzybski's work "semantics", exhibited this kind of mechanism. Their continued use of the old terminology led to an abundance of confused $s.r$ and became an obstacle to understanding and using Korzybski's system. Korzybski would end up expending considerable effort trying to correct the confusion. For one thing, soon after the book came out he began writing about "neuro-semantic" and "neuro-linguistic" factors, reactions, issues, etc., (see his 1934-1935 "Outline of General Semantics"). Appending "neuro-" to "semantic" and "linguistic" gave these terms a more explicit, organism-as-a-whole connection to evaluation. His use of the two terms, usually side by side, indicated somewhat different but related aspects of evaluation with the neuro-linguistic realm a subset of the neuro-semantic. This new usage would lead to some new and fruitful formulating—by 1940 he had begun to explicitly talk about human cultures in terms of *neuro-linguistic* and *neuro-semantic environments*. Neuro-semantic environments, for example, included not just linguistic factors as such but any of the media later explored by Marshall McLuhan and other "media ecologists". In the 1930s, after the book was published, Korzybski also devised a non-verbal practice he called "semantic relaxation" or "neuro-semantic relaxation." This form of muscular manipulation used to reduce 'emotional' tensions would be hard to understand for anyone who, in regard to Korzybski's work, insisted "semantics" had to have something directly to do with language and an elementalistic approach to linguistic 'meaning'.

"A theory of 'meaning' is impossible."

In the book, he had written a great deal about 'meaning' and of his own "non-elementalistic theory of meanings".[10] But by the late 1930s, the conflation of his work with verbalistic "semantics" had become serious enough for him to begin to pull away from talking about his work in such terms:

> ...a theory of 'meaning', or still worse, a theory of 'meaning of meaning', being verbalistic, must be elementalistic and non-similar in structure to the structure of the world and of ourselves." (1938)[11]

I introduced the term General Semantics to indicate a general theory of values, a <u>general theory</u> of <u>evaluation</u> of facts, relations, 'feelings', etc., not of meanings by mere verbal definition." (1939)[12]

By 1941, he would devote several pages of his book's "Introduction to the Second Edition" to "Perplexities in Theories of 'Meaning'" noting their hopeless inadequacy. In 1942, in his "Foreword" with M. Kendig to *A Theory of Meaning Analyzed*, he would go further and decry,

…'Cheshire Cat Theories of Meaning'. You know the cat with a head and no body which kept appearing and disappearing, and which Alice found quite bewildering, even in Wonderland. Something drastic must be done about 'that cat',…

….General semantics formulates an empirical natural science based on the action and reaction of the human nervous system. It is a general theory of evaluation involving the nervous system-in-an-environment, and it has very little, if anything, to do with 'meaning' in the academic sense.[13]

With this statement, he had indeed come to the point of doing something drastic. Over the next few years, the conflation of his work with linguistic semantics—especially by some of his 'popularizers'—became a major irritant to him. As the Third Edition of his book was being prepared in 1947, Korzybski wrote a preface in which he attempted to separate his work from "semantics" and theories of 'meaning':

My work was developed entirely independently of 'semantics', 'significs', 'semiotic', 'semasiology', etc., although I know today and respect the works of the corresponding investigators in those fields, who explicitly state they do not deal with a general theory of values. Those works do not touch my field, and as my work progressed it has become obvious that a theory of 'meaning' is impossible…, and 'significs', etc., are unworkable. Had I not become acquainted with these accomplishments shortly before publication of this book, I would have labeled my work by another name, but the system would have remained fundamentally unaltered.[14]

A theory of 'meaning' is impossible. Until the end of his life, he would continue to emphasize this point, in print and in his seminars and presentations.[15] He had long since stopped using the word 'meaning' without single quotes. He preferred using terms with more non-elementalistic associations like "orientations", "methods", and "evaluations" in discussing the issues he was dealing with in his work.

He also began to fully treat the term "semantic(s)" as the troublesome 'trigger' for misevaluating his work it had become. He had introduced the term "general semantics" to emphasize that his work constituted a theory of non-elementalistic evaluation. So, in "What I Believe", a credo he wrote in 1948, he put "evaluational" in parentheses whenever he referred to "semantic (evaluational) reactions" or "neuro-semantic (evaluational) environments". In his final paper, "The Role of Language in the Perceptual Processes", which he was editing at the time his death, he made a further transition from this "evaluation in parentheses". After introducing "semantic (evaluational) reaction", "neuro-semantic (evaluational) environments", etc.; he quickly switched to just writing about "evaluations", "neuro-evaluational reactions", "evaluational reactions", "neuro-evaluational environments", etc., for most of the rest of the paper. In this final work, he thus showed he didn't need to use the term 'semantic(s)' in his serious formulating—despite the somewhat well-recognized name of his discipline by then (1950).

In his 1934-1935 "An Outline of General Semantics", Korzybski would criticize the confused and self-contradictory uses of the term 'identity' in psychiatry, 'philosophy', 'logic', and mathematics. Ironically, the criticism turned out equally pertinent to the name he chose for his work and his initial attempt to extend 'semantic(s)' and 'meaning' to cover non-elementalistic evaluation:

> ...It is necessary to stress here, that it is an unreasonable practice and harmful to mankind, if specialists utilize a common term which implies humanly undesirable orientations, and make out of it a technical term, even if they give it a special meaning. Such unreasonable practices only introduce difficulties in human orientations, make the understanding of scientific issues difficult to the layman, and worst of all, this only facilitates harmful orientations. General Semantics suggests that specialists particularly should be more careful in their choice of common words for their technical terminology, because a technical definition will not alter the folk-meaning, and corresponding living human neuro-semantic reactions. In General Semantics the folk-meanings can no longer be neglected.[16]

In his later work, Alfred did his best to follow this advice in relation to his own work and thus to correct his initial mistake of not doing so. To be charitable to Alfred, it seems well to remember something he sometimes said: 'It's damned difficult to talk sense.' He never stopped revising his system and, at the time of his death, seemed well on the way to retiring "semantic reaction". Perhaps if he had lived longer, the next step would have been to find another name for his system to replace "general semantics". Certainly after his death, people's automatic, undelayed reactions to the terms "general semantics" and "semantic reaction" became a neuro-evaluational obstacle for teachers of his work who were trying to convey his non-elementalistic approach to others.

But things looked different at the end of 1931. Alfred had just finished replenishing the manuscript with "semantic reactions", "s.r", etc. Various people were reading the manuscript and he had begun to get it professionally edited. The damned book did indeed seem 'done'. Now he and Mira had to decide what to do about getting it into print. Meanwhile, he was ready to present his work to the world. He was writing a summary paper to present at the American Association for the Advancement of Science (AAAS) winter meeting at Tulane University in New Orleans. He would go there to announce the birth of *"general semantics"*.

'Won't you have a seat?'

The AAAS meeting would run from December 28, 1931 until January 2, 1932. Alfred had hoped to give two, or even three, presentations of his work if he could: one to the AAAS Psychology Section, under the title "A Non-Aristotelian System. A General Introduction to a Theory of Sanity"; one to the Medical Section, on "A Psycho-Physiological Theory of Sanity and its Dependence on Physico-mathematical Sciences"; and one at the joint meeting of the AAAS Mathematics Section and the American Mathematical Society. Basically he planned to write one paper, which he could then modify according to the audience. But he was too late submitting his titles and abstracts to the Psychology and Medical sections. So he ended up with just one paper to give on the subject of "A Non-Aristotelian System and its Necessity for Rigour in Mathematics and Physics". Although he had anticipated it would take only a few days to write, it actually took him three weeks. He sent advance copies of the manuscript to a number of mathematicians, some of whom would be attending the conference. The paper, a sharp summary of his work, would later appear as Supplement III of Korzybski's book. His abstract, published the following year in the *Bulletin of The American Mathematical Society*, read as follows:

This paper gives an anthropological approach to the subject. Identity, a fundamental, false to fact, postulate of the aristotelian trilogy (the aristotelian, euclidean, newtonian systems), establishes elementalism; an non-aristotelian system rejects "identity," becomes non-elementalistic. The inter-relation between the non-aristotelian, non-euclidean, non-newtonian systems (called non-systems) is given, also the essential differentiation between the un-speakable objective levels (ordinary objects, processes, action, functionings, immediate feelings, etc.) and verbal levels, establishing *structure*, defined in terms of relations or multi-dimensional order, as the only link between the two worlds. Structure becomes the only content of "knowledge." Semantic definition of number and mathematics in terms of relations explains why mathematics gives structure-knowledge. There is *one name* for happenings on the un-speakable levels and "mental pictures," a partial mechanism of identification. The two-valued aristotelian logic is a limiting case of a general many-valued logic of probability. Two-valued logic does not apply to processes, the objective world, the foundation of mathematics, the theory of infinity, etc. The many-valued logic covers all 1931 human needs, mathematics and mathematical physics included. (Received November 27, 1931)[17]

The last time he had traveled to New Orleans (on the way to Pasadena in 1928), Korzybski had taken a boat. He had found the trip inexpensive and relaxing and he decided to travel that way again to the conference at the end of December 1931. On board he had an experience, which he related in the book (p. 423–424) and later recounted in seminars and in 1947 when he was recording his memoirs:

I deliberately wanted to be alone and have peace for three, four days, so I went by ship from New York. Deliberately. Left alone and rest. And on the ship I had the differential in my cabin. And I happened to have a card table, a ship card table, perfectly lousy, ricky, ricky [rickety], and I had a ship chair, complete wreck. Merely stuck together somehow. I had to be very careful with the table and with the chair. But we went along somehow.

Once a fellow sufferer of the ship visited my room. Oh he was sitting on my berth, and I was sitting on the chair, and he asked "What is the differential?" I tried to explain to him. This actually happened. And I was performing by extension. I show, never mind talking, I show. The fellow is sitting on my bed. I went to the door and I pretended, I come in and the visitor tells me—this is all pretending, playing a game—"Won't you have a seat?" Now I am explaining to him in the meantime. I say, 'If I take your word as an actuality the seat, the chair, then...if I take your word as granted, I will sit on the chair, the word chair, with great security no matter what the damn thing is. Chair is a perfectly good solid word, so I sit on the word with great security.

In the meantime, I was standing, speaking that way, shaking, literally shaking the chair. The chair was falling apart. One of those ship chairs. Few wooden pieces somehow connected and some canvases. You know that kind of stuff. Very flimsy. The chair was falling apart and the chair was already a derelict without my knowledge. And then big, loud, with energy, I said, "And then if I sit with great security on the word...," and I actually with great elegance sat on the derelict which collapsed underneath. Completely collapsed. The table, you see, was so lousy that I couldn't even get out of the chair.

What happened? Did I fall down? Unconsciously I didn't trust the chair. I didn't sit down on the term there. I was sitting on an actual silent level business. Instinctively I didn't trust and I didn't fall down. In the meantime, say if I had fallen down, even if I would have been hurt, I would not be frightened.

The frightened business is worse than the hurt. Experiences of the war, for instance, show that. If a soldier gets a big fright unexpectedly, he may break down. If he expects horror and gets that, he does not break down, and there's another thing. You know from the first war and has probably been verified in this war [World War II]—psychiatry reports on that. If the fellow is wounded, he does not break down mentally because he is too busy suffering physically. He hasn't time for elaboration. These are extremely important things and with me, I am cautious without being conscious of it. The best example I can give is that chair on the ship. I had thousands of cases like that of my own during a lifetime. [He went on to recall some of his 'Oh, how extraordinary!' moments as a young man.] Yes, how extraordinary. It's a delayed reaction all right. ...if you get the feel no matter what happens [that] you are observing, 'oh, that's what happens,' 'oh, quite interesting.'[18]

In New Orleans he saw Bridgman, who had been invited to give that year's keynote Willard Gibbs Lecture, at some joint sessions the Mathematical Society had with the American Physical Society. Alfred also saw Birkhoff, Bell, and Carmichael (who had all read his paper ahead of time), and a number of other mathematicians he knew. They attended his 15 minute talk. Alfred considered his "not too rotten presentation" well received. However, after his talk a Jesuit professor of mathematics came up to him and told him that,

...I destroy the very foundation of 'religion' and I should abandon it or I will get in trouble with the church and get on the index. Among others he said "You certainly will not deny that everything is identical with itself." I asked him if he ever heard of modern physics, and as he admitted that he teaches it, I said "I certainly will deny that a submicroscopic process is ever 'identical' with itself." He said nothing to that, but on his face he exhibited the most bewildered and horrified attitude.[19]

Korzybski may have actually agreed with the Jesuit mathematician that the foundation of 'religion', or at least Catholicism 1931, was incompatable with his non-aristotelian views. He would have had to modify this opinion at least a bit if he had been able to see the work of Bernard Lonergan, a Jesuit whose major work *Insight*, was published in 1957. Lonergan brought an appreciation of modern scientific method into Catholic philosophy. Korzybski would surely not have disagreed entirely with Lonergan's statement from that book: "*Thoroughly understand what it is to understand, and not only will you understand the broad lines of all there is to be understood but also you will possess a fixed base, an invariant pattern, opening upon all further developments of understanding.*"[20] The anti-clerical Korzybski was not going to abandon his work for fear of getting into trouble with the Catholic church. He had anticipated major opposition from there, but—as it turned out—his main opposition came from another quarter—some quite 'irreligious' intellectuals, philosophers, and scientific spokesmen whose 'idols' his work would threaten.

Chapter 39
A MONKEY ON HIS LAP

Korzybski finished writing his book with a monkey on his lap. Actually two monkeys probably shared his lap as he worked during the winter of 1931-32. First, sometime in the fall of 1931 he and Mira got a female 'ringtail' monkey (a capuchin). They named her Kiki Netouche, and spent weeks constructing an elaborate six-foot wide cage of steel fencing material for her. It had a 14-inch opening with a 'door' going up and down on a rod, and an inside shelf upon which Mira installed a warm, woolen nest for Kiki to sleep on. With a soft belt they could put around her middle and attach to a six-foot leash of steel chain, they could have some control over her movements when she was out. Mira loved the animal. Korzybski, probably despite his better judgment, loved her too. As Mira recalled many years later:

> I used red woolen cloth as a cape for my shoulder and a piece of the same material on my writing desk and it fascinated me how she behaved as if that color and wool was her "isle of safety." When I would be writing at my desk, which I now have in the library here [Mira's apartment in Chicago], I would have her sit on a piece of red flannel. She would draw marks on a piece of paper, giving me the feeling that she was trying to copy me. Later on, Alfred and I found great entertainment in putting a piece of red flannel next to my pillow and with Alfred's head on my right shoulder we would chortle with delight at her response to playful teasing.[1]

In October 1931, soon after they got her, Alfred wrote about Kiki to E.T. Bell: "[Kiki Netouche] is the wildest most selfish lively little beast one can imagine, she does everything to us but we are not allowed to touch her hence her name."

> Kiki was a famous Parisian cocotte, a typical infantile type. Her pet spot is on the top of my head and probably from this simian reaction I get some glimpses of the semantic reactions. In the meantime she is the wisest little thing you can imagine. She learns everything in 2–3 trials which is better than many many 'humans'. Jokes apart one learns a great deal in watching day after days such a delightful little animal. She is the more charming that her little face is a copy of an old southern Negro, her temper is just of a Brooklyn gangster. I build for her a 'royal cage' with a Waldorf-Astoria roof garden on the top where she goes for her exercises.[2]

Then, while Alfred was away in New Orleans at the end of the year, Mira "had an illegitimate child", as he joked to Roy Haywood in a January 1932 letter, "and got another monkey (babe) which looks and acts like a rat so now we have two monkeys."

> But by Jove in watching monkeys one understands better what I mean when I say 'copying animals in our nervous reactions'. The bigger Monkey 'Kik[i] Nitouche' is so disgustingly human and clever as to be shocking.[3]

Korzybski's notion of 'copying' in our nervous reactions—and his emphasis on *not* copying animals—became one of the theoretical formulations some found difficult to grasp. To some it seemed to disparage animals, which Alfred clearly had no intention of doing. (He once wrote to an editor acquaintance "Imagine calling humans = animals, how grieved the poor beasts must be!")[4] Korzybski's warning *against* copying animals also did "*not* necessarily include conscious copying."[5] He studied reports about animal behavior most carefully, and in his lectures frequently illustrated some point about human behavior with examples from

Kohler's *The Mentality of Apes* and similar material. (He might insist '*man' is not an animal*, but he didn't deny that we descended from a mammalian line known as primates.) He had certainly learned a great deal throughout his life from interacting with animals and studying their behavior; now he had new 'teachers', Kiki and the other monkey, known at various times as 'Kiki no. 2.', "the monk", or simply "the monkey". From one or the other of them, Alfred copied a gesture—making a behind-the-back upward 'scoop' with the hand, and then a forward throwing motion. He made a point to teach it to his students in subsequent years:

> There is another extremely important gesture—without talking. I speak from personal experience. To train a monkey—you know I wrote *S & S* with a monkey on my lap—now to train a monkey to be clean is practically impossible. They may be darlings—they are—but try to train them to be clean. You can train a horse, a cow to be clean, a dog, a cat, but not a monkey. One monkey happened to be born that way. I didn't do it. I am not guilty, but that monkey happened to be born somehow clean, and so when he had to evacuate he did it in his hand, from behind. You understand? Do I have to give you a diagram? (laughter) He did it in his hand and then threw it in my office on the walls. (laughter) This is the gesture, which is very, very useful to you, because we do the same thing with labels. We throw labels, and particularly medical men and psychiatrists when they talk to you; oh, paranoia (throw), oh, dementia praecox (throw). Labeling and I advise you to learn that gesture which I learned from a monkey who was so clean that he evacuated in his hand and threw it in my office on the wall. You like it? (yes) We are so accustomed to throwing labels on each other, this is a tragic thing, we are so accustomed to throwing labels on each other. Are we not? When you throw labels remember the monkey. If you would learn that 'fact' alone, be conscious when you are throwing around labels.[6]

Alfred would certainly need to remember this for himself, given what was thrown in his direction in the years after the book was published—not only from critics, but also from some people who fancied themselves as students of his work.

Whatever trouble they got themselves into and whatever messes they made for Alfred and Mira, the monkeys also provided great amusement during a time of otherwise difficult drudgery. For instance, one day, probably in 1933, Lily MaDan, the secretary Alfred and Mira hired to help them complete the production of the book, "brought in a young sparrow, just learning to fly, which she rescued from a cat about to pounce on it." Mira recalled:

> We clipped one wing so that it could not fly out the high window we had…We scattered bird seed on a space beside Kiki's cage. Then it happened. Curiosity brought Kiki down from [her] cage and out of the open door, and the seed scattered stuck to [her] moist feet. For reasons of [its] own, the sparrow had preferred picking them from the bottom of this foot that Kiki held up, which of course tickle[d] [her]. Seeing is believing…Kiki gently, very gently put her…hand over the back of the sparrow and held it quietly there while [she] gobbled up the seeds [from her other foot] for herself.[7]

Kiki, unfortunately, died only a few years later—probably sometime in early 1935, as indirectly indicated by condolences written to Mira by Barbara Polakov in June 1935. Kiki's demise, which Mira wrote about in her memoirs, was unexpected:

> [One day] I noticed her walking on the floor, she limped badly on one side. The next day I bought a small animal case and took her to Philadelphia where a personal friend was Director of the Zoo. She died that night there, and I have her heart preserved. The Doctor reporting that the rib had pierced one of her lungs due to my ignorance in not feeding her the vitamins she would have gotten had I fed her cod liver oil.[8]

They may have had the other monkey with them for another two years. But after the book was published, Alfred and Mira had to hustle to support themselves and to get Alfred's work 'off the ground'. Their lives became increasingly busy with travel and other complications. Having the monkey to care for simply became too much for either one of them to handle. Eventually Walter and Barbara Polakov, who had returned from Russia by mid-1931, agreed to take "the monk". They had more space and were more settled than Alfred and Mira, having bought a little farm in Fairfax, Virginia near Washington, D.C. where Walter was working for F.D.R.'s administration. Early in 1937, Barbara Polakov, then in New York City, wrote to Mira about her anticipation of having the monkey:

Dear Edgy,
Of course, Poli's told me of the monk and I've been practically sleepless nights thinking of the fun I'll have with it! He's also told me the monk is a more playful rascal than Kiki N° 1. No matter what I say and how I say it, it will all hail down to this: I'm just all gaga over the thought of having him. The above can also be said for: at the prospect of seeing you-all. ...[9]

Several months later, Walter wrote to Alfred, "Kiki$_{[2]}$ is very mischievous – a hore [whore?] and fun all in one."[10] Alfred missed the monkey. Early in the following year, 1938, as he was packing to move to Chicago where the Institute of General Semantics was being set up, he wrote to Walter, "How is the monkey? Ask him to report on his health. The more I know humans the more I like monkeys."[11]

Publishers and Editors

Early in 1931, although Alfred was still fine-tuning the formulations ("semantic reactions", etc.), the book seemed sufficiently done for him to begin looking in earnest for a publisher. He wasn't the only one impatient to get the book out. Keyser, who had just had another of his own books—*Humanism and Science*—brought out, gently gibed Alfred in a letter: "I hope you will publish your new book soon——I was born in 1862—I hope to read your book before I go over to the great majority..."[12]

Alfred felt obligated to give the first pass on the book to John Macrae of E. P. Dutton. Given that Macrae had sought him out in order to publish *Manhood of Humanity*, Alfred had great initial confidence Macrae would take this new work. But this time around, the deepening economic depression made Macrae as well as other publishers rather faint-hearted about this difficult-to-categorize and rather imposing-looking book. Macrae received two manuscripts from Korzybski in early March. Dutton had sold 18 copies of *Manhood* over the last year[13] and Macrae did not exactly seem full of enthusiasm although he did respect what Alfred had done, pondering over it and giving it to one of his editors to evaluate as well. He wrote the rejection letter himself on April 28:

My dear Count Korzybski,
I have given both human and inhuman consideration of a very deep nature to your new manuscript...
...I regret to tell you that I must decline to publish this new manuscript solely on the ground that I cannot afford to publish it. If I undertook to publish your new manuscript it would bring me, in my judgment, an actual loss of something like $2000...
...We might find five hundred people to buy the book but actually I do not know where we can reach five hundred people who would read it...[14]

Alfred felt irritated. Although he wasn't expecting to have a huge bestseller, he did have confidence his work had value and believed, once properly edited, the final book would gradually find an audience, begin to sell and, he hoped, continue to do so for a long time. He disagreed with Macrae's gloomy projection. He estimated he had an audience of around 10,000 people who might want to read his book.[15] Neither he nor Macrae had any way of actually knowing how many people would eventually become interested in and buy the book. But Korzybski's assessment turned out more correct. By the time of his death in 1950, the book published in 1933 had sold almost 20,000 copies. Now (2011) the book is in its Fifth Edition. Dutton would certainly have made some profit if Macrae had shown more faith in Korzybski's work. But Alfred wasn't going to let this rejection discourage him. He would do whatever he could to find another publisher.

At least one positive thing resulted from his contact with Macrae. Alfred got in touch with one of Dutton's long-time literary editors, George Moreby Acklom, whom he had met back in 1921. Alfred had been looking for some professional editing advice and Acklom, who felt positively disposed towards the book, agreed to help spruce up Korzybski's prose for a fee. So around mid-1931, Acklom perused the manuscript, as did a young literature professor at Columbia, whom Alfred also paid to edit the manuscript. By this time Alfred was juggling multiple copies among multiple other readers as well, but somehow managed to keep order over the relative stages of editing of the different copies. This particular phase of the book production—paying literary editors to bring his writing closer to standard English—led to a dead end. As far as he was concerned, these editors "ruined the ms. completely. ...literally eliminated the main things I wanted to say...I had to eliminate really whatever they did. It was really a good lesson for me. I must say, for instance, that in my work I cannot stick to grammar in the orthodox sense."[16]

For example, there were certain passages he had kept deliberately vague in order not to say something clearly false if put in more definite terms. In order to achieve the right amount of precision, he had also qualified statements in various other ways that might not suit a literary stickler. He liked to split infinitives, to more specifically modify a verb. He also liked to use double negatives, pointing out that to say "I am not a non-drinking person" and "I am a drinking person" had entirely different implications.[17] His use of new terms and of devices like the indexes, dates, single quotes, hyphens, extensional punctuation, etc., also didn't lie within the bounds of certain ideals of either acceptable formal or idiomatic English. Beyond these conscious decisions of style, his English—however fluent—was permeated with the syntactical forms of his first language, Polish. (Mary Morzinski's study, *Linguistic Influence of Polish on Joseph Conrad's Style* seems applicable to Korzybski's as well as Conrad's prose.)

All of these elements of style rankled the literary editors. It became very clear he would not be able to accept their corrections when they not only corrected his own writing, but also passages he had quoted from Bertrand Russell and Alfred North Whitehead.

> The structure of their language [Russell and Whitehead's] is different, [like his own] more or less of a mathematical character, logical, mathematical. And so ultimately I had to, after all their corrections, I had ultimately to eliminate the falsifications and go ahead with Mira to correct, oh, say, smooth up the English.[18]

Korzybski found more useful another way Acklom helped. Knowing the publishing business as he did, he composed a query letter that Korzybski would use as the basis of his campaign to find a publisher. Korzybski edited the letter, and in August 1931, had a typist 'crank out' multiple copies, which he sent to a number of U.S. publishers, most of whom were located in New York City. He also had letters of recommendation from some of his prominent friends and an analytical table of contents, which he would send to those publishers who expressed interest. Although he got a few rejection letters immediately, many wanted to know more. Korzybski had subsequent meetings with a number of editors at Holt, Knopf, Macmillan, and Simon & Schuster, among other publishing firms. Some requested a manuscript. Alfred was still awaiting final responses from a few of them well into the summer of 1932.

One of the publishing companies he contacted in August 1931 was Brewer, Warren & Putnam Inc. Korzybski's query letter was directed to partner Joseph Brewer, who definitely had an interest in the book. Years later, Brewer recounted his first encounter with Mira and Alfred. Though he didn't accurately recall some minor details, his account gives an impression of how Korzybski and his work were perceived by Brewer and his colleagues in the publishing world:

> I was sitting in my office one day in 1930 [correspondence indicates the actual year as 1931] doing whatever it is that book publishers do, when I was told that the Countess Korzybska was in the reception room asking to see me. Whereupon in swept Mira in a flurry of furbelows, for she always wore a sort of fancy dress with hats, cloaks, scarves etc. After a little social conversation she proceeded to enquire about our firm and to tell me about her husband and a book he had written to be called *Science and Sanity* [that title wasn't actually chosen until the middle of 1932]. Well, publishers are often faced with cranks and this all sounded suspicious. But still, you never know and you don't want to risk turning down out of hand a work of genius. And so I agreed to look at the manuscript if submitted.
>
> Mira, it seems, had been sent to case the joint and to see if our firm looked suitable as a possible publisher for the magnum opus. Apparently we passed inspection for a few days later Alfred himself appeared with a typewriter-paper box of manuscript. His appearance, with his limp, his shaved head, his piercing eyes and his accent raised again the crank suspicions. But his warm smile and gracious manner allayed them and we began to discuss his work. I had not heard of the *Manhood of Humanity* but I did know about I. A. Richards and *[T]he Meaning of Meaning* and had long been interested in psychology and linguistics. Thus what Alfred said about his book sounded eccentric perhaps, but just not crankish. The upshot was that I undertook to read the manuscript.
>
> This was no easy task for besides my unfamiliarity with much of the subject matter—especially the mathematics—this was by no means a finally revised text. And it was a not too well typed carbon copy on almost onion-skin paper. Nevertheless, I persevered with it even over weekends in the country and became fascinated by it. I talked to my partner, Edward Warren, and after reading some of it, he agreed that it was not crank stuff and was an important work as I had suggested. We discussed it over a period of time and finally came to the conclusion that while it was something that we should like to publish and would be proud to do, we just did not have the know-how nor the equipment to handle such a book to good advantage. We were a young firm whose experience had been exclusively with current fiction, non-fiction and art books. This would be an expensive book to produce and we simply had no idea of how a book of this character could or should be marketed. It needed a knowledge of special outlets and sales methods to handle it with any hope of success and we felt it would not be fair to the author nor to us to undertake it.[19]

Brewer wrote a rejection letter to Alfred at the end of October 1931. However, he remained fascinated by the book and its author. For his part, Korzybski felt grateful for Brewer's interest and advice. (Brewer had provided a printer's estimate of production costs for the book, which Alfred and Mira found useful since they were beginning to consider the possibility of publishing the book themselves.) Brewer recalled: "Alfred understood our position and I believe respected us for it since he was convinced of our sympathy for the work. Out of our consultations and discussions Alfred and I developed a warm friendship that lasted throughout his life."[20]

The Dartmouth-and-Oxford-educated Brewer, in his early thirties, became a frequent visitor to Carleton Avenue. He discovered that Alfred also belonged to the 'brewer' family. As he described,

> In those early days I saw a good deal of him and Mira. I went fairly frequently to the apartment on top of an old house in Brooklyn. There was a large studio-like room with a monkey in a cage for Alfred's behavioral observations, work space and equipment for his studies and for his secretary's typing, filing, etc. I wish I could remember her name [Lily MaDan] for she was an integral part of the menage. She was an odd, tall girl, very New England spinster in appearance but a bright, warm person devoted to Alfred and Mira. This was still Prohibition time and Alfred used to make his own very strong beer. [He used a small still sent to him by Sally Avery.] Coming up the stairs to the apartment there was often a pervasive aroma of malt and hops. Alfred would discourse learnedly about the varieties of hops and how they were to be selected if the beer was to be as he liked it. I spent many merry evenings there drinking the beer and discussing revisions of the manuscript plus a multitude of other topics including Mira's lovely miniatures, her reminiscences of their subjects and Alfred's reminiscences of Poland and the War.[21]

Brewer left the publishing business after Brewer, Warren & Putnam, Inc. went bankrupt in 1933, shortly after publishing *The Pastures of Heaven*, a book of short stories by John Steinbeck. Brewer, a Michigan native with an interest in higher education, became the President of Olivet College in Olivet, Michigan in 1934. In the following years, Brewer kept contact with Alfred, who came to Olivet several times to lecture.

The International Non-Aristotelian Library Publishing Company

As they continued to seek a publisher in the fall of 1931, Alfred and Mira also decided to reconstitute the old dream of the Library of Human Engineering under a different name. Alfred's forthcoming book would be the first of a series of titles in The International Non-Aristotelian Library, which he would edit along with one or another of his interested friends. They also anticipated organizing (or having someone else organize) an International Non-Aristotelian Society, which could encompass a network of university and professionally-associated study groups they hoped to encourage. Along with the Library, such an organization might help to accelerate various non-aristotelian trends they could see developing in the U.S. and elsewhere. Of course, the Library would require an additional commitment from any publisher taking on Alfred's book. He seems to have seen this as a selling point. But it's not clear that any of the publishers he approached felt likewise.

By the summer of 1932, although one or two publishers were still considering his manuscript, it was appearing less and less likely anyone would take on the book and the Library, as Alfred had wanted. A few publishers seemed willing to consider accepting the book if Korzybski could guarantee the production costs by means of advance sales. Under such terms the book would sell for as much as $10 (about $160 in 2010 terms).[22] This would surely have put off most potential readers, even without the severe economic depression that had 1932 in its grip. Since they wanted as wide a readership as possible, Alfred and Mira found the price unacceptable. Should they publish the book on their own?

Before deciding to do so, Alfred wrote for estimates from a number of book printers, as well as from publishers he knew who did their own printing. One of these, The Science Press Printing Company, owned by psychologist James McKeen Cattell and family, published the AAAS journal *Science* as well as a number of other publications and books. Korzybski had seen their work. James Cattell's son Jaques, who managed the company, sent Korzybski a figure of a little over $3000 for printing 2000 copies of an estimated 800-page book. The company could also take care of distribution and shipping for a percentage of each book ordered. The Korzybskis weighed the possibilities before them. At the end of September 1932, they made a final decision to publish the book themselves under the rubric of The International Non-Aristotelian Library Publishing Company. The Science Press Printing Company would produce it. They had already chosen the title.

Chapter 40
SCIENCE AND SANITY

Over the last six years, Philip Graven had worked with from 300 to 400 patients using Korzybski's methods combined with psychoanalysis. At the beginning of 1932, Graven agreed to write up some of his case notes for a paper to be presented at a scientific conference that year. Graven tended to get bogged down in details, and—despite his protestations—seemed to Alfred to have a serious writer's block. He never produced the paper. But in the meantime, Alfred had written a theoretical introduction for it, which he entitled "Psychophysiology". This seemed to him like a good title for his book as well—for a good part of 1932 he would call it *Psychophysiology: A General Introduction to a Theory of Sanity and General Semantics*. Alfred had sent his article to a number of people—including neurologist C. Judson Herrick—who liked the article, which may have reinforced Alfred's preference for the book title. Certainly bringing neurological considerations into the practical epistemology he had developed could be said to add a psychophysiological component. But he eventually decided not to use that uninviting and perhaps misleading name.

In February 1932, Arthur F. Bentley had contacted him. Bentley, an Indiana-based, interdisciplinary-oriented, political scientist and independent scholar, was writing a book to be published later that year called *Linguistic Analysis of Mathematics*. Bentley had an interest in both Chwistek's and Korzybski's work, and would devote part of a chapter of his book to Korzybski. The two men corresponded mainly from 1932 until 1935. Part of their back and forth discussion in 1932 included consideration of a title for Alfred's book.

Bentley initially suggested *General Semantics: A Theory of Logic and Sanity*. But, as Korzybski pointed out, the notion of 'logic' seemed too limited and elementalistic to describe his system. He preferred *General Semantics: An Introduction to a Theory of Sanity and Non-Aristotelian Systems*. However, that might seem rather too mysterious to an innocent reader and he narrowed in on *Psychophysiology*. By the beginning of June, he had second thoughts about that title and returned to the working title he had kept for several years, *A General Introduction to a Theory of Sanity and Non-Aristotelian Systems*. Bentley suggested *General Semantics: A Non-Aristotelian Theory of Sanity and Knowledge*. A little later that month, he suggested *A Theory of Sanity: Presented in a Non-Aristotelian System of Science*, perhaps too unwieldy and with too much emphasis—being written by a non-psychiatrist—on a *theory* of sanity. A few days later, Bentley came up with *Knowledge and Sanity: A System of Non-Aristotelian Semantics*. Alfred and Mira 'chewed' on this for a while. Alfred wrote back to Bentley on June 27:

SCIENCE and SANITY
———
A General Introduction to
NON-ARISTOTELIAN SYSTEMS
and
GENERAL SEMANTICS

My wife and I rather like this title, it has many advantages over the older titles. I would avoid the 'theory' of sanity yet keep the word sanity, which [seems] even more correct. The words Gen. intr. would allow me to use the title GENERAL SEMANTICS (simply put) for my next book.[1]

Bentley liked the title and others did too. By November, when the galley proofs with the book's title page were going to be printed, Korzybski had dropped the first "General". The final title became *Science and Sanity: An Introduction to Non-Aristotelian Systems and General Semantics*. If the subtitle might seem obscure or even mislead some readers, the main alliterative title seemed snappy and clear. It not only caught the book's main theme but also ended up catching many people's attention.

The Science Press Printing Company

In late August 1932, Korzybski traveled to the Science Press Printing Company in Lancaster, Pennsylvania to meet Jaques Cattell and George M. Houck, the associate manager in charge of the company's composing room, who would supervise the composing process—everything involved with typesetting the book prior to printing it. Korzybski felt just about ready to give the go-ahead to the company but wanted first to meet both men in person, and get a good feel for the actual operation. Then they could begin the process of getting the book into production as soon as possible—a matter of seemingly endless details.

He had finally decided to have Books I, II, and III in one volume rather than two. They were estimating the entire book might amount to something like 800 pages. This meant that the high quality paper Alfred wanted had to be thin enough to avoid making the book too unwieldy to handle. Beside the paper, he had to pick a typeface (Bodoni) and type size for the main text and for the different headings and parts.

To get everything into one volume he decided to put Book III, the more technical section of the book as well as the "Supplements" in a type size smaller than the main text in the rest of the book. (This probably guaranteed that Book III would become the least read part of the book by people who tended to get put off by the appearance of mathematical formulas and technicalities—a pity.) Supplements I and II—R. D. Carmichael's "The Logic of Relativity" and philosopher (Alfred preferred calling him an "epistemologist") Paul Weiss's "The Theory of Types"—had been approved by their authors and ready to publish since the end of 1930. The third Supplement would be Alfred's New Orleans paper. Phillip Graven had agreed to write a fourth Supplement for the book on Psychiatry and General Semantics. It probably wouldn't be very long (since Graven didn't seem to like writing) but it still wasn't ready and Alfred was beginning to feel some urgency about Graven getting it done.

Alfred and Mira had also decided to 'salt' the book with a large selection of quotations they had collected which would precede the various sections, books, parts, and chapters. As he would write in the "Preface":

> ...I have done so to make the reader aware that, on the one hand, there is already afloat in the 'universe of discourse' a great deal of genuine knowledge and wisdom, and that, on the other hand, this wisdom is not generally applied and, to a large extent, cannot be applied as long as we fail to build a simple system based on the complete elimination of the pathological factors [identification in its various guises].[2]

Of course, this entailed more work for Alfred who, despite his dislike for 'red tapes', dutifully wrote many letters to authors and publishers in the first few months of 1933 asking as a courtesy for permissions to quote.

As the epigraph for the book he chose the fable of the Amoeba from Appendix E of Ogden and Richard's *The Meaning of Meaning*. The quotation had Ogden's characteristic literary flair (even flamboyance) and playfulness and caught some of the concerns Korzybski shared with Ogden, Lady Welby (who had first written about "linguistic conscience"), and others in the field of 'semantics'. However, within a few years, as confusion between 'general semantics' and 'semantics' grew, it didn't help to feature Ogden's fable so prominently in his book. He dropped it in the 1941 Second Edition of *Science and Sanity*, replacing it with a long quote, "A Voyage to Laputa", from Jonathan Swift's *Gulliver's Travels*. This remained as the book's epigraph in all subsequent editions.

The volume would need a strong, sewn, cloth binding and Alfred and Mira spent some time picking it along with its color—a nice deep blue. (Blue in various shadings would for many years continue to serve as the distinctive color of the International Non-Aristotelian Library.) Both he and others would later refer to the book as "the blue peril". He'd joke that copies needed such a strong binding to remain intact from falls—in case they got pitched from high-story windows by exasperated readers.

There were several major steps in the printing process. In the 1930s, although books had long been mass-produced, the process remained very much a dirty, mechanical one. An operator entered the text of the manuscript on a keyboard, whose output—holes punched in a paper tape—controlled a hot-metal typecasting machine which would form metal type from a hot lead alloy poured into molds for the characters. Working at the keyboard could be hot, sweaty work. The type produced this way was then sequenced in lines of text. After hardening, the type for each line was arranged either by hand or machine into trays known as galleys. Pages printed from these on a flat proof press were known as galley proofs. A certain amount of proofreading—including grammatical and spelling corrections—was done by the printer during the initial, mechanical typesetting phase, as well as after the galley proofs were printed.

As they were run off in parts, galley proofs would be sent to Alfred, and whomever else he wished, for proofreading. He wanted twenty-five copies printed beside the standard two he would otherwise get. Alfred had already written to a large number of people, mainly those who had already read the manuscript, like William Morton Wheeler and H. B. Williams, asking them to read the proofs. (He got a shock when he got a reply to one of these requests informing him of the death of his long-time friend and supporter, Thomas J. McCormack, the high school principal who had translated Mach's work into English.) Alfred was to mark any errors he or his other readers found. According to the contract, Korzybski would pay for one half the total of the printing job when the galley proofs were all done. He would have to pay extra for any errors he wanted to correct that were not due to the printer.

Back at Science Press, changes would be made from the corrected galley proofs and the type would be laid out to produce page proofs (designed to have the intended appearance of the completed book) for final review. Any changes required at this stage would be expensive for Alfred—if they were due to his, not a printer's, errors. With the page proofs, Alfred would pay for another quarter of the job. The final payment would be due after the book was printed. The book would be run off on a letterpress in signatures of 16 or 32 pages, collated, sent to the bindery to be bound, and then shipped back to the Science Press Printing Company for the final step of receiving the paper jacket.

Alfred sent Science Press most of the manuscript in late September 1932 along with detailed written instructions to the printer, a copy of *Rules for Compositers* and the shorter *Oxford Dictionary*. (He had decided to use British spelling and grammatical conventions, which seemed more suitable for the international audience he intended for the book.) He had seen many serious scientific books marred by typos, unattractive layout, unreadable type, poor illustrations, bindings that fell apart, cheap paper, and general unattractiveness, etc. To get the book done according to his standards, he knew he would have to attend to the smallest detail. Some of the printers would come to consider him a difficult customer.

His urgency about having the job done right was accentuated by news he was getting about his mother's increasingly tangled affairs in Poland. His loss of potential income from his mother's poor management of the family properties was accentuated by her marrying her manager. Now Alfred and Mira were in danger of losing the thousands of dollars they had invested in his mother's real estate. As soon as his work became well enough established, he and Mira would be able to get to Poland where he hoped to straighten out his mother's business. For his work to become well established, the book had to do its job. He was not ashamed of its contents. But, in addition, the book had to look and feel as good as possible to readers.

By the end of October 1932, as the galley proofs began to come out, problems emerged. He found many mistakes, a large number made by the printer, which he marked in red ink while marking in blue/black the relatively few he was responsible for. One of the things he found distressing: a proofreader was correcting his grammar and punctuation—somewhat excessively, he thought. The proofreader, for example, didn't seem to think he used enough commas and had inserted quite a few more. He was certainly willing to let it slide a bit if the proofreader wanted to put more commas in the text *he* had written. But the proofreader was also correcting the grammar and punctuation of the quotations he had included. No one had any right to put extra commas in material that he (Alfred) didn't write. He had carefully checked the quotations for accuracy with the originals before sending them to the printer. The printer's unnecessary 'corrections' would make extra work for him since he had to correct the corrections.

He also noticed problems with alignment, appearance, spacing, size of type, and frank typos, etc. For example, the infinity symbols used throughout the book had been put in the wrong type size. In his initial instructions, he had also made a special point about the dashes above the letters in the abbreviations for non-aristotelian, non-euclidean, and non-newtonian ($\bar{A}$, $\bar{E}$ and $\bar{N}$). These dashes had to have an adequate length and just the right height above the letter (hard enough to achieve). He had approved samples, which looked right. But the galley proofs didn't. Moreover, a few of the 'non-' dashes had been placed underneath the letters like so: $\underline{A}$.

In addition, the extensional punctuation, which used a period as an abbreviation for *et cetera (etc.)* combined with other punctuations, seemed problematic. Again, Alfred had approved some samples but in the proofs the spacing of this punctuation looked inconsistent. He wrote to George Houck about the problem (mistakes in his typing marked out with Xs):

> There is a serious trouble about the blooming 'etc.' (., ,. And others). The worse of it is that it is a purely <u>artistic</u> affair and rigid rules cannot be given. XXXX 'etc', after all stands for a <u>word</u> and so the <u>period</u> which stands for the three letters XXXX e t c should <u>not crowd upon the last letter of the word</u>. Here comes the difficulty as letters differ in structure besides the roman and italics also differ. I enclose two galleys (No. XX 17 and 18) which please keep as they will be missing from the lot which I will return, and you will see what I mean. (The passages are marked read [red?] ink). Thus 'institutions.,'

the period looks crowded upon the 's'. Similarly with 'harmful,.' The ',' looks crowded. 'Adjustment,.' , and 'verb.;' particularly this last looks very crowded. 'Breathing.,' looks less crowded than 'mechanics.,'. [3]

He wanted the things he had specifically asked for, as they appeared in the samples he had approved—a 'difficult' customer, indeed.

Science Press had produced all of the galley proofs (except for the front matter, preface, bibliography, and the index—which Alfred had not yet provided) by January 1933. Alfred and Mira paid for half of the printing job as originally contracted. He was working as fast as he could to consolidate the corrections from his readers so that the page proofs could get started. (William Morton Wheeler was especially helpful in finding little mistakes that needed to be corrected.)

By February, although he was still working on the galley corrections for Book III, page proofs had already begun to arrive. It would take at least several weeks to proofread these. In the meantime, Graven still had time to complete his psychiatric supplement. Alfred wrote to him with an urgent request to send it, along with a letter, for publication in an advertising circular Alfred was planning. Alfred and Mira's savings were being tapped out. They needed to generate some income as soon as possible and wanted to send out a mass mailing of the circular in the next few months to begin generating some pre-publication book orders.

The circular would include portions of letters from a number of scientific figures who had read the manuscript and/or galleys; a specimen page from the book; the Table of Contents; an insert announcing the formation of the International Non-Aristotelian Library and Society; and an order form. Some of his friends had also agreed to produce volumes for the Library and the titles with their names would be listed in the announcement and later in the front matter of the book , e.g., *Non-Aristotelian Methods As Neuro-Psychiatric Prevention* by M. Tramer, *Non-Elementalistic Genetics* by C. B. Bridges, *Non-Elementalistic Reflexology* by W. H. Gantt, *The Evolution of Rigour* by E. T. Bell, *Identification In Physics* by R. J. Kennedy, *From Aristotelian to Non-Aristotelian Physics* by B. F. Dostal (a mathematical physicist at the University of Florida whom Korzybski had met in New Orleans in 1931), *Non-Aristotelian Power Analysis* by Polakov, and Korzybski's own next planned volume to be titled *General Semantics*. Philip Graven had committed himself to write a volume on *Non-Aristotelian Psychotherapy* (later changed to *Non-Aristotelian Neuro-Psychotherapy*).

The pre-publication price would be $5.50 (postpaid). After the official publication date, which he hoped would be soon, anyone who wanted one could still get an "educational discount" price of $5.50 if they ordered directly from Science Press. Indeed, that's how he expected most people to obtain the book. He didn't anticipate many bookstore sales and set the bookstore price at $7.00. The discounted price was the lowest Alfred felt he could go without giving the book away. That way he and Mira would be able to make at least a small profit from sales, which eventually turned out to be the case.

By March, Alfred had gotten written statements from most of the people on his list of manuscript and proof readers who, at the very least, all approved of the material they had seen in relation to their own specific disciplines, and agreed to have their comments made public in the circular. The group included anthropologist Bronislaw Malinowski; biologists C. B. Bridges, C. M. Child, H. S. Jennings, and Raymond Pearl; botanist David Fairchild; pavlovian psychiatrist W. H. Gantt; educators E. L. Hardy and Cora Williams; entomologist W. M.

Wheeler; ophthamologist Willam H. Wilmer; mathematicians E. T. Bell and Bertrand Russell; neurologist C. J. Herrick; physicists B. F. Dostal, P. W. Bridgman, and Roy J. Kennedy; physiologists Ralph Lillie and H. B. Williams; and psychiatrists John A. P. Millet, M. Tramer, and W. A. White—and Graven. (Their comments would later also be printed in the back of the Second Edition.) Alfred was preparing the statements and the other circular material to send to The Science Press, which was going to print it. But he still hadn't gotten anything from Graven.

Waiting in Suspense

Alfred had spent a huge amount of time and effort cultivating Graven. Graven's comments and the psychiatric case histories he had accumulated over the last six years could prove invaluable in showing the practical application of Alfred's work. Yet it seemed more and more likely that Graven was not going to be able to come through with the material when Alfred needed it. Alfred had last heard from him in the middle of January. In the next month and a half, he wrote a number of letters to him; Graven made no reply. This was following an all too familiar pattern. On March 7, Alfred sent him the following telegram message:

> Your silence is extremely distressing and harmful to me Must know immediately whether I can depend on your supplement or not stop. Shall I use your first letter for extracts stop. Can I expect a translation of Tramers letter stop am awaiting urgent decisions from you over one month.[4]

On the following day, Graven sent a telegram to Korzybski:

> Letters Forthcoming Stop Am Seeking Greater Verbal Clarification Of Event Necessary For Any Desired Application Of Structural Differential [5]

Korzybski, who rightly may have felt puzzled and distressed to read this, wrote back to Graven at once, answering with great patience. It seemed to him Graven was getting stuck, once again trying to get a finalistic answer to a question full of 'metaphysical' difficulties nobody could answer definitively. For Korzybski's purposes it seemed enough to say that the 'event' represented "a process, a sort say of wriggling jellfish which means a FOUR-dimensional affair...If you try to go beyond that you are lost completely as you touch unsolved physico-mathematical problems which for practical purposes is entirely unnecessary."[6] Two weeks went by with no response from Graven. Korzybski wrote to him again on March 24:

> The way you treat me is genuinely painful, and I do not understand it at all...Do you realize that not knowing where I am with you and that anxiety in which somehow you persist inflicting on me, by the way you treat me, are at present simply devastating under the terrific pressure of work and of responsibilities. You always made me believe that my work meant something to you and that we are friends.[7]

Was the psychiatrist going to produce the supplement and send in the material for the circular or not? On March 31, Graven sent another telegram:

> Your Last Letter Anything But Clear Stop Am Head Over Heels In Unrelenting Effort Stop Its Big Thing Stop Does It Appear In That Form In Index Stop I Regret That You Ignored Overlooked The Unsettled And Very Urgent Aspect To Which Your Attention Was Directed In Telegram
> Graven[8]

Alfred wrote back immediately in a long letter, emphasizing again what he needed.[9] No reply. He sent another letter on April 3. He was ready to send the circular materials with his readers' statements to the printer. He was giving his friend an ultimatum: Graven should either drop him or answer him.[10]

About a week later, Graven finally sent his letter for the circular, and the translation of Tramer's letter, with no other comment or news. Graven's letter included the following:
> ...By direct clinical application, I have found the non-aristotelian principles workable in this enormous group [the mentally disordered]. My observations cover a period of about six years. I shall have a great deal to say about these observations in contributions to medical and scientific journals.[11]

Alfred, still at this late date, was hoping for Graven to write up some of these observations for the supplement as he had promised. He wrote to Graven. Was Graven working on the supplement? How far along had he gone?, etc., etc. No reply. Alfred wrote again on April 15—are you going to produce the supplement, yes or no? About a week later he sent Velda Graven a telegram—was Philip ill? A few days afterwards on April 24, he finally got a telegram from Philip: "Very Overworked Discussed Matters With Carmen Haider She Will Phone You End Of Week."[12] On April 28, Carmen Haider, a mutual acquaintance, wrote to Alfred suggesting a meeting. Alfred had no time to spare and Mira arranged to meet with her. The news from Philip: he was not going to write the supplement.

In the subsequent correspondence between the two men, Graven never seemed to acknowledge that he had kept Alfred waiting in suspense for weeks because he couldn't bring himself to say he hadn't done—and didn't feel able to do—what he had promised.[13] If only this had been communicated clearly in a timely fashion, it would have been okay with Alfred.[14] Korzybski considered his own word binding. Graven's approach to communicating with his friend about his inability to follow through with the supplement—an approach of vagueness, avoidance, and delay—must have seemed puzzling to Alfred. Nonetheless, the two men managed to patch up their differences. Graven helped edit the unfinished parts of *Science and Sanity* over the next few months and seemed timely in his responses. Over the following few years the two men kept in contact. But Korzybski soon began to direct his attention to other interested psychiatrists who seemed more willing and able to follow through with commitments they had made about developing applications of his work.

The Final Push

The circular kit (with Philip Graven's comments, among others) was quickly composed and edited, then printed in final form in May. Alfred ordered 25,000 copies with related stationary including mailing envelopes and return envelopes for orders. By the end of May, Alfred and Mira, and whomever else they had helping them, had already sent out 10,000 advance order kits to a special list of people: educators from a list supplied by Cattell, psychiatrists, subscribers to the journal *Mental Hygiene*, and Korzybski's personal mailing list. Preparing the mailing had to have taken several furiously-working people at least several days to do, even if they worked for twelve-hours or more at a stretch. After all, they would have had to take breaks to eat and go to the bathroom. No doubt it helped to have address stickers run off ahead of time. Science Press received the first order only a few days after the mailing. And by the end of June, they had received 100 advance orders—barely enough to pay for the postage, but a good sign nonetheless.

Alfred needed some good signs because it was beginning to look as if the book was not going to come out in time for autumn reviews. He had sent back the last corrected page proofs of the main text in May. In June, Science Press started printing the book, but informed him it was going to take longer than they had initially estimated to complete the job, even with the parts they already had. Besides, Alfred was still working on the page proofs of the Notes and References, the Bibliography, and some of the front matter, as well as finishing up with the Index. And he hadn't finished writing the Preface.

The studio at 321 Carleton Avenue had become a buzzing publisher's office. Korzybski supervised the work of Lily MaDan, their secretary/typist who had turned out to be a talented illustrator; Eunice Winters who was reading proofs and working on the bibliography; and Harvey Culp, a young science student who read the mathematical proofs and was preparing the index. Alfred had wanted to attend the AAAS meeting in Chicago, but was too busy with these final, crucial parts of the book. Mira went in his place, taking plenty of circulars to help drum up some interest.

Korzybski in his corner of the apartment in Brooklyn

In early July, Alfred sent in the manuscript material and instructions for typesetting for the rest of the book's front matter, index, book jacket and spine design. Except for the preface, which he was still working on, every other part of the book was now in the last stage of getting printed for the actual book or being typeset for galley or page proofs before being sent to Korzybski for 'delousing'.

The preface was still giving him problems. To grab potential readers, he considered it one of the most important parts of the book. He wanted to use it to introduce his work and set the theme of the book succinctly and in the broadest, most accessible terms. He felt nervous about doing this adequately. He had come up with two analogies for identification: one, as a 'lubricant contaminated with emery sand' that 'gunks up' the mechanisms of human evaluating; and two, as an 'infectious agent' spread by misevaluating humans, which makes general sanity impossible. Korzybski was proposing a system, a practical method to filter out the 'emery sand', to immunize people from the 'infection':

> The present work is written on the level of the average intelligent layman, because before we can train children in non-identity by preventive education, parents and teachers must have a handbook for their own guidance.* It is not claimed that a millennium is at hand, far from it; yet it seems imperative that the *neuro*-psycho-logical factors which make general sanity impossible should be eliminated.[15]

---

* Plenty of people would wonder at Korzybski's apparently high regard for the 'average intelligent layman', but he never retracted this statement.

Given his trepidations about the preface, he asked Ralph Lillie, the Fairchilds, and William Morton Wheeler to have a look at what he had written. Apart from a few suggestions, they all thought he had done a good job. He accepted their advice (which included not to make any mention of the Knute Houck case) and on August 2, along with some already proofed items, he mailed the manuscript of the "Preface" to the printer.

At this point, other than some proofs that still had to be produced and edited, the book was being printed. Alfred was anxious to have the job done as quickly as possible. The more time he had to look at things, the more things he was finding that needed correcting. The printer had somehow managed to produce new mistakes in the proofs. Would the printer also introduce mistakes into the final copy? Indeed, that turned out to happen, though given the size and complexity of the book such mistakes seem relatively few. For example, Alfred wrote to George Houck at the end of August instructing him to have a line from G. E. Coghill's *Anatomy and the Problem of Behaviour* added to the preface's introductory quotes: "When new turns in behaviour cease to appear in the life of the individual its behaviour ceases to be intelligent." The printer entered Coghill's initials as "C. E." instead of "G. E." which Alfred had spelled correctly.[16] Such a mistake was not the sort of new turn in behaviour Korzybski had wanted to encourage with the quote. Unfortunately, he failed to catch the error in the final proofreading of the "Preface". It got printed in the book (and only indicated in the Fifth Edition's "A Note on Errata", long after Korzybski's death).

He was still finding a few of his own mistakes as well. In early September, George Houck couldn't find the final proofs of some pages of front matter that Korzybski thought he had already sent. When Alfred looked over some earlier proofs of the copyright page, he found two glaring errors he had previously missed. He wrote to Houck at once: "If this blessed delousing will not stop soon, you will have no customer but a corpse of A. K. at hand."[17]

At the end of September, the books were getting bound. The first week of October he got 12 books from the bindery. He was told to be careful handling them—the glue still might need to dry more. For international copyright purposes (the law seemed most unclear), Alfred had decided to have one date as the U.S. and International Publication date. To make this official, he sent some books to a man in Toronto who would telegram him when the book went on sale there. The man in Toronto telegrammed him on October 10. Alfred sent off another telegram at once:

October 10, 1933

To Doctor Jaques Catell
   Science Press
       Lancaster, Pa.
   Book Science and Sanity published today in United States
   Please distribute at once
                    Alfred Korzybski[18]

Part VI
Words Are Not Enough!

*"**Knowledge**...some are satisfied when they hear it, some when they see it, and others stop when they have a Greek word for it; only too few go beyond the word."*
—DAGOBERT D. RUNES[1]

Chapter 41
WHAT HAD ALFRED WROUGHT?

'You can ride a tiger; try to dismount.' As Korzybski once noted to a seminar class, he knew this from personal experience—literally—although he had learned it from a young bull, not a tiger. As a boy of eighteen or nineteen, he had impulsively jumped a fence and grabbed the bull by the tail to impress a young lady visiting his family's farm in Poland. The bull ran and Alfred couldn't let go for fear of getting gored or trampled. The bull threw him off anyway and turned to attack him. Because of the bull's flat forehead and widely spaced horns, Alfred escaped a goring by managing, again literally, to grab the bull by the horns. He tried to wrestle it to the ground as the bull pummeled him with its forehead. The bull threw him off, he slipped and fell, and he was only able to save himself by kicking the bull in the nose with the heel of one of his boots, which he wore with spurs attached. The girl, calling for help, attracted workers who ran and fended off the bull with pitchforks while Alfred scrambled back over the fence to safety.[1]

By the time *Science and Sanity* came out in the fall of 1933, Alfred had been hanging on to a figurative bull by the tail for 13 years. He had leaped over the fence (encouraged by his 'girl') by writing *Manhood*. Once he had grabbed hold of the definition of man as time-binder he hadn't let go until, in the new book, he had pinned down and elaborated—to some extent anyway—how time-binding worked. Maybe he hadn't let go yet. Still he and Mira could now rightly feel somewhat pummeled by the tremendous effort they had both put forth. Alfred felt "thoroughly tired."[2]

It had taken him 12 years to bring together material from anthropology, biology, chemistry, epistemology, general history, history of science, logic, mathematics, neurology, physics, psychiatry, psychology, physiology, etc. With his reading, his massive working correspondence, as well as his research at St. Elizabeths, and his years of work with Graven, among other things, the writing of the book had dragged on. Just the amount of reading he had done seems staggering. A student of Alfred's in the mid-1940s, W. Benton Harrison, once "...brashly asked him whether he had read all the books included in the bibliography of *Science and Sanity* (619 in the first edition, 100 additional in the second). With a quick look of surprise and even scorn, he replied 'Certainly—and studied all of them and many articles not included'."[3] Had it been worth it? He thought so.

A System of Systems

He had a system, a set of related formulations focused on how we know what we 'think' we know. One of the quotations he had put at the start of his Preface came from the Talmud: "Teaching without a system makes learning difficult." He had accepted that. Without the system, much of the data used in *Science and Sanity* could be considered "old hat" and many of its insights "commonsensical" or even "trivial". Alfred had already admitted as much in the book, "One is amazed to find that 'everything has already been said', and that, to a large extent, these important, separated statements were *inoperative*."[4] But if he had a sound system it would generalize the un-systematized data and wisdom of others and thus make it teachable as a method to promote time-binding. As he noted,

One of the human tragedies can be found in the fact that *wise epigrams* do not work. It takes *a system* which often expresses similar notions; but they must be expressed in a *unified language* of different structure to make them workable.[5]

Korzybski's unified language of "abstracting", etc., necessarily had *greater generality* and this seemed key; it made his work a system in a sense that went beyond just a set of related formulations.*[6] It gave his non-aristotelian system—a theory about theories, a system about systems—generativity; it could be consciously used to construct new theories for a 'scientific' adult age—a new operating system for world culture, a foundation for a science of man. Even he felt astonished.

"Nothing So Practical"

Korzybski accepted what psychologist Kurt Lewin would later write: "There is nothing so practical as a good theory."[7] From the time that he had called his work "human engineering", he had aimed it towards practicality. His general theory of evaluation ("general semantics"), as the "modus operandi" of the non-aristotelian system, provided an *applied* epistemology, a generalized practical *method* for dealing with problems in science and life.

Some people seemed to conclude that Korzybski's reach had exceeded his grasp. While writing the book he had often wondered so himself—one of the reasons he had sought out some of the best mathematicians and scientists of the day to critique what he had written. He had certainly taken on an ambitious project. Abstracting through the 'lenses' of "time-binding", "abstracting", etc., he had formulated one very simple and very general mechanism—"identification"—behind "the quarrels between two lovers, two mathematicians, two nations, two economic systems ., [etc.,]"[8], and a general method for dealing with them.

Leibniz, in expressing his dreams of 'universal agreement', etc., had imagined the possibility of somehow algebraizing 'thought': with a 'perfect' language, involving some kind of impersonal, formulaic, and step-by-step procedure (an algorithm), people could sit down and say "Let us calculate" in order to settle a dispute or work out a problem. But Korzybski, in pursuit of Leibniz's dreams, had produced something different.

Rather than a 'logical' algorithm, the 'methods' he produced that embodied his theory (involving the Structural Differential and other techniques and devices) seemed closer to a set of psycho-logical heuristics—behavioral guidelines to get more extensional and to reach agreement with others at a particular time and place. Even in mathematics, you couldn't have a 'perfect language'—at least one inherently free of all ambiguity—as Leibniz seemed to suggest. Considering any language as a joint product of abstracting human nervous systems, each individual would inevitably abstract differently and give different values to words and other symbols. Even in mathematics, agreement had to be worked at by people in a given context.[9] Korzybski's approach to agreement and method—non-formulaic and personal—reflected this.

---

* Korzybski was presenting his non-aristotelian system as not only more general—at a higher level of abstraction—than any specific theory of the modern age, it also seemed more general *as a system*: it subsumed the more limited aristotelian system that underlay specific theories of the old and waning 'childhood' stage of at least 2000 years of Western science and civilization (and perhaps of so-called 'primitive' cultures and Eastern civilizations as well).

To follow his heuristic approach, you would have to internalize a set of standards and use them to self-reflexively inquire into your own reactions (linguistic or not) and those of others—i.e., 'put them up' on the Structural Differential. From there, new possibilities could emerge for modifying your reactions and adjusting to the reactions of others.

Despite the fact that Korzybski would sometimes describe his work in terms of 'mathematical', 'physico-mathematical', or 'scientific' method, he wasn't teaching mathematics or science per se. (Perhaps talking about a generalized scientific *attitude* or *approach* might have seemed clearer.) What he taught boiled down to an *extensional orientation* or *attitude*, how to habitually orient yourself towards 'facts'. It wasn't limited to mathematicians and scientists although perhaps they demonstrated aspects of it especially clearly when working at their best. At any rate, with his system and methodology he believed an extensional attitude no longer had to be 'caught' by means of haphazard, unconscious learning. It could be taught. He liked to joke that as a very unreasonable fellow he felt educators should be educated and 'scientists' should actually behave scientifically. An extensional orientation, learned explicitly, could even help 'scientists' behave more 'scientifically' in their work. And a 'scientist' no longer had an excuse for compartmentalizing himself, leaving extensional behavior in his laboratory or office when he hung up his white coat and became a 'man in the street'. In this sense of 'scientific method', scientists and ordinary people could learn to apply it in their daily lives.

A Theory of Sanity

Korzybski's focus on behavior and everyday life had turned his work into a theory of sanity, an inevitable consequence for him of his non-elementalistic, non-aristotelian system. The importance he gave to this theory of sanity was indicated by the numerous times he referred to it and discussed it throughout the book. A thoroughly sane individual, according to Korzybski, followed an extensional orientation, adjusted him/herself to life-'facts', showed consciousness of abstracting, avoided identification, had fully conditional reactions, etc. On the continuum from sanity to insanity, most of us could be considered somewhere in the middle, i.e., *un-sane*. The standards of 'rationality' he had developed thus merged with those of psychological health.

Thus, in addition to educators and those wishing to become more 'scientific' problem solvers, Korzybski's work had implications for psychiatrists and psychotherapists. As he later noted, "...all existing psychotherapy, no matter of what school, is based on the partial and particular extensionalization of a given patient, depending on the good luck and personal skill of the psychiatrist."[10] Korzybski asserted that a psychotherapist no longer had to depend upon good luck alone, that his methods provided a standard by which to develop therapy/counseling skills. He had no interest in supplanting psychiatrists or in doing psychotherapy himself. He referred to his work as preventive and educational with his main thrust that of helping the legion of the un-sane, the bulk of humanity not under psychiatric care. But at this stage, he certainly wanted to see what results psychiatrists would get with their patients by using it, or by using him to educate their patients. As Graven's work indicated, some people diagnosed as 'medical' cases seemed able to positively respond to such education alone. More psychiatric corroboration would perhaps make it easier for so-called normal people to see that Alfred had something of value for them.

With the vast scope and potentially momentous consequences of his work—which he spelled out in some detail in the book—some people failed to notice Korzybski's humility. Nonetheless, writing and speaking with consciousness of abstracting as a standard required a basic epistemological modesty—what Robert P. Pula would call "epistemodesty"—that Korzybski sought in his habitual means of expression. Throughout the book readers could find statements like this:

> In the present work, each statement is merely the best the author can make in 1933. Each statement is given *definitely*, but with the semantic [evaluational] *limitation* that it is based on the information available to the author in 1933. The author has spared no labour in endeavoring to ascertain the state of knowledge as it exists in the fields from which his material is drawn. Some of this information may be incorrect, or wrongly interpreted. Such error will come to light and be corrected as the years proceed.[11]

In his published writings, Korzybski continued to practice the epistemodesty he 'preached'—with his use of "etc." and related extensional punctuation, as well as modifiers, qualifiers, dates, indexes, etc. As part of this modesty, he had to directly acknowledge his work as limited—despite its great generality. Because general semantics could be applied wherever humans evaluate (everywhere), did not mean he had a theory of everything.[12] As a consequence, he could not and never did claim his work as a panacea.[13]

Eager For Research

Korzybski considered his work scientific. The last thing he wanted anyone to do was to view what he had produced as a 'philosophy', which by 1933 he saw had become predominantly a field of detached verbalism and intensional speculation. (He preferred to call 'philosophers' who did what he considered valuable work, "epistemologists".) What he had developed, in his view, constituted a new and applied empirical science of evaluation.[14] He felt eager for research of all kinds since his claims for his system and methodology would stand or fall on reports of experiments.[15]

What kinds of experiments? Korzybski gave a number of suggestions in the book.[16] Statistical studies, e.g., comparing a control group with a group receiving general-semantics training, could supply some useful data. But this kind of statistical research ("the method of relative frequencies") could yield only limited understanding about human potentialities, which his work had focused upon. To investigate how species-wide mechanisms of abstracting (from identification to consciousness of abstracting) worked in individuals, required research methods that studied individuals. (Such methods are discussed in Philip J. Runkel's book *Casting Nets and Testing Specimens: Two Grand Methods of Psychology*.)

Sophisticated studies could wait. To research the mechanisms of time-binding (abstracting, etc.) directly, any individual could begin to observe them operating in him/herself. Alfred needed people to study the book, put their arguments aside, and experimentally do what he advised (using the various neuro-linguistic and neuro-evaluational techniques, i.e., working with the Structural Differential, etc.). As he would say, a knee jerk reflex wouldn't operate if you didn't tap the tendon but argued about it instead. You had to do it. Part VII, "On The Mechanism Of Time-Binding"—which made up all of Book II—was full of suggestions for how to train yourself in Korzybski's extensional methods (in particular Chapter XXIX, "On Non-Aristotelian Training"). The extensional practices seemed so simple, even baby-like. But doing them, he already knew, was not necessarily so easy.

Someone with a nervous system deeply "canalized" (entrenched in habit) in the old elementalistic, aristotelian orientation would have to "sweat blood" for a good while to get anywhere with them. How much sweating and how much time would depend on the depth of their old habits, among other things. Then they could see what extensional practices made possible.

So before anything else he needed to get people (including pivotal scientists, educators, and psychiatrists, among others) interested and willing to train themselves in his work, apply it, and begin to see what they could do with themselves, their students, and patients using his methods. Years later, behavioral researcher Runkel[†] would come up with a name for this type of exploratory research, "the method of possibilities", an important—although often too easily dismissed—form of experimentation. A personal trial could indicate the possibility of bringing something about. Alfred had already seen a number of 'unlikely' results in Graven's patients and in some of the people he had worked with, such as individuals stopping 'panic attacks' through the persistent practice of dating and indexing. Such results didn't seem so unlikely to him anymore. He hoped psychiatrists and psychotherapists would publish case studies and educators would file reports of their research. Then, once enough people experienced the possibilities of extensional training, other types of more elaborate research could follow.

Korzybski did not see himself as an especially gifted writer. But he felt he had produced a book, which—however imperfect—he and Mira didn't need to feel ashamed of. Nonetheless, having written the book was not enough. At best, it provided—yes—*only a map*, a blueprint for a vast, multi-faceted program of personal-socio-cultural restructuring. The program had promise and needed publicity, support, and research. Having 'ridden the tiger' this far, they were not going to dismount now.

---

† See *Casting Nets and Testing Specimens: Two Grand Methods of Psychology*. Runkel, a close co-worker of William T. Powers in Perceptual Control Theory, studied Korzybski's work early in his career and felt influenced by it, as did Powers. [P. J. Runkel, Personal communication to BIK. See also Powers and Runkel.]

Chapter 42
REVIEWING REVIEWS

Korzybski clearly knew he could no longer carry on with no one but Mira at his side. He didn't have the energy, knowledge, money, or time to do it. Others would need to make applications in various fields (especially mental hygiene, psychiatry, psychotherapy, and education) and do research. An ideal situation, however unlikely, would involve either some group or agency within the U.S. government or some foundation (or both) getting interested in promoting his work. Or perhaps some kind of university position was possible. With adequate funding, he and Mira wouldn't have to scramble for money and he could focus his attention on training people and promoting applications and research with, and in, his methodology.

The International Non-Aristotelian Library had the potential to play a significant role in getting a general non-aristotelian movement off the ground. *Science and Sanity* was just the first volume. For the Library program to happen as originally planned, a number of Alfred's friends—like Calvin Bridges—who had put their names to various "Volumes In Preparation", would have to come through with their books, preferably soon. For various reasons, they didn't. Bridges, for example, unfortunately and unexpectedly died at the end of 1938. Korzybski's work had inspired him to begin consciously reformulating basic biological notions in non-aristotelian terms. Who knows what effect his promised volume on *Non-Elementalistic Genetics* could have had on future developments in biology and on Korzybski's work if he had lived long enough to produce it.

The first edition's longer list of "Volumes" with authors "to be announced later" provides a fascinating list of other titles that never saw the light of day, such as *Principles of Non-Aristotelian Political Science*, *Non-Aristotelian Comparative Religion Analysis*, and *From Infantile to Adult Civilizations*, among many others. In subsequent editions of the book (the second and third published in Korzybski's lifetime) the list was revised. Eventually, some monographs and books actually did get published as part of the Library, but the extensive publication program originally envisioned by Korzybski never materialized. Even as he was getting *Science and Sanity* to press, he had hoped to produce "a brief and simplified book for school use" to be titled *General Semantics*.[1] But the next—and as it turned out final—17 years of his life, despite their successes, required Alfred to do quite a bit of hustling in order to get his work established to the extent it did. As a result, despite a great deal of other writing, he never produced that book. (Although *General Semantics Seminar 1937, Olivet College Lectures*—in its First Edition published by Olivet College with the shortened main title of *General Semantics*—comes close to the kind of brief and simple presentation Korzybski intended for the book he never wrote.)

Along with their long-term plans for the work, Alfred still hoped he and Mira could move to Poland to live, as soon as his work was going well enough in the U.S. The Poles needed his work as much as any group of people did and he thought he would get a good reception there since it seemed to him to fit in so well with the national culture. After his mother's death in 1937, he may still have held out the hope of at least going back there to lecture and perhaps to repair some of the mess in which his mother left family business affairs—even if he didn't live there. But his work in the U.S. would become more involving by that time and the Nazi invasion of Poland in 1939 and the start of World War II ended the possibility of even a visit to his homeland.

At the end of 1933, the world already seemed to be getting crazier. The German people had elected Hitler as Chancellor of Germany earlier in the year and his Nazi party had begun to consolidate its dictatorship in Germany and to persecute German Jews, political opponents, and others. Korzybski found the "mass psychopathology of the Hitler movement" highly disturbing. If a revolution in Germany couldn't extinguish it, he was already predicting another war.[2]

He had come to see the situation in Russia as equally bleak. In *Science and Sanity*, Korzybski had restrained the expression of his negative views about communism. He still had some radical friends who may have continued to see the Soviet Union, despite 'setbacks', as a promising laboratory for the development of a 'new man'. But if Korzybski had once felt willing to at least stay open about the Soviet experiment, by this time he had no illusions about Stalin's regime: "...[T]hrough a purely Tartar fanaticism they have subjected tens of millions to terrible sufferings, and killed outright millions."[3]

The political-economic situation in the U.S. seemed somewhat more hopeful to Korzybski. President Franklin D. Roosevelt's first year in office had started off well. In his March inaugural address he had made his memorable multiordinal statement "...the only thing we have to fear is fear itself." Alfred liked Roosevelt but he wondered how the "New Deal" policies could work if guided by outdated evaluating. He hoped some of his contacts could help him to get someone or other in the Roosevelt administration to take an interest in his work. Polakov was working as a consultant for the Federal Government's new Tennessee Valley Authority project and would do what he could. Perhaps Doctors White and Graven at St. Elizabeths—and others—could put in a good word (or more) for him where it mattered. He would try to take advantage of any contact he could find within F.D.R.'s administration to promote his work, which he felt could help the administration.

Whatever the long-term possibilities, at the end of 1933 Alfred and Mira were nearing financial depletion. They badly needed immediate income. They still owed money to Science Press and would not completely clear up this bill for another two years. They had not paid their rent for a number of months and even had an outstanding bill at the food store. Mira was trying to sell some of her paintings and to get new commissions. Alfred was scrambling in various ways to sell books, get reviews, and generally promote his work. By the beginning of December, almost two months had passed since publication, and he had not seen a single review.

First Reviews

In fact, the first one had already been published in September 1933 in *The Collecting Net*, a subscription newsletter "devoted to the scientific work" at the biological research stations at Woods Hole on Cape Cod and Cold Spring Harbor on Long Island. Ralph Lillie, a University of Chicago physiologist who had helped edit *Science and Sanity* and had great regard for Korzybski and his work, wrote an informative and complimentary notice based on his reading of the manuscript. Lillie began, "This interesting and original book deserves careful study by all who are concerned with science and its applications." Alfred didn't know about it until mid-December when Lillie wrote to him sending along a copy.

By this time, other reviews began to trickle in. Alfred and Mira had been working for months to try to get the proper attention for the book. Responses from the circular mailing in May had included a number of requests for review copies, which they began to send out as soon as the book had been published. Given their tight budget, Alfred felt constrained about the number of copies they could distribute. But despite his insistence that they must focus on more scientific journals (psychiatric and educational included), they had sent a number of copies to more literary-focused magazines and to philosophical journals as well. Given that he had no budget for advertising, he was eager for publicity wherever he could get it.

However, he had limits. He refused—politely—to send a review copy, as requested, to *The Catholic School Digest*, whose review may or may not have been bad. He also refused another request, from a biologist who wanted to review the book for *The Christian Century*, a popular, non-denominational, liberal Christian magazine. The man sent another review he'd already written along with some other pages from the magazine. Korzybski wrote back to him and politely refused to send a copy noting, "I must strictly depend on scientific journals for reviews." However, when he got a request for a review copy from Rabbi Felix Levy, who wanted to put something about it in the Year Book of the Central Conference of American Rabbis (representing the Reform movement of Judaism), Korzybski wrote back saying he would gladly send a copy. Alfred's biases against religion, especially Christianity, may have unduly cut off his work from exposure to potentially interested readers. His personal opinions aside, nothing in the system he had developed made it inherently odious to religious people *not* inflexibly committed to fundamentalist views.

Surprisingly, one of the first and—in Korzybski's opinion—one of the best reviews of *Science and Sanity* appeared in a daily newspaper, *The Knickerbocker Press*, in Albany, New York. The paper ran a two-page feature article by A. Ranger Tyler, its new literary editor, in its Sunday, December 10 edition. Tyler had already written to Alfred in early November after 'inheriting' the book from the paper's previous literary editor who had received the review copy. The book immediately 'grabbed' him, as he frankly told Korzybski in his letter,

> I can not adequately express my joy at finding someone attempting the fundamentals of sanity. My work as a newspaperman—when I am not reviewing books—gives ample evidence of the stranglehold of what you term Aristotelian semantic reactions have on a woefully large majority of otherwise personable human beings. Walter Pitkin [an acquaintance of Korzybski] gropingly felt the situation in his amusing "A Short Introduction to the History of Human Stupidity," but he was simply being a reporter.[4]

Even after only about a month of reading, Tyler was already analyzing news issues (for himself) in terms of orders of abstractions.[5] He even admitted to Korzybski to have become a bit manic in relation to the book, "My wife thinks I dream orders of abstraction, etc."[6] He started writing the article at the beginning of December as he finished his first reading.

Korzybski appreciated the headline, "Can Human Nature Be Changed? Yes, Author Reveals" and the sub-heading, "Basic Shift in Methods of Thought on Scientific Lines, Suggested in Epoch-Making Book". In the article itself, Tyler had written, "I stake my reputation on the belief this is the most significant book of the century, so far."

> Let us be frank. While the book is written for the comprehension of the "average educated layman," most readers of any degree of education will find it difficult, especially at first to understand. The divergence from our customary channels of thought is responsible for this...Anybody with the willingness to understand can gain great value from the book. It is naturally of particular significance in the work of educators, teachers, and psychiatrists, because it offers the first suggestion of how to teach children to think as they were "constructed" to think and how to eradicate the confusions that usually are found at the bottom of mental ills.[7]

After the review was published and he felt more at ease to express himself, Korzybski told Tyler about his amazement at the fact that Tyler had managed to write about aristotelian and non-aristotelian systems, non-identity, semantic reactions, and abstracting, among other formulations in more or less everyday language without introducing fallacies about his work.[8]

In the young newspaperman (who admittedly had a biology degree and had taught math at a boy's prep school), Korzybski appears to have found his ideal 'average intelligent layman'—actually an all-too-rare, more or less extensionally-oriented and generally sane individual. As he later wrote to Tyler: "...you 'knew it' all by yourself, and I only happened to <u>formulate</u> what you felt instinctively yourself. The depth of understanding [in the review and subsequent letters] shows that. You could not <u>absorb</u> organically that much from one reading, unless you had it."[9] To Korzybski, Tyler seemed to belong to that small group of 'naturally' extensional non-aristotelians who found in general semantics a clearer language and method for doing better what they were already inclined to do. The much larger group of 'aristotelians' would need a great deal more training and drilling, whatever their verbal assent, to orient themselves differently. Over the next year, Korzybski and Tyler met in person and maintained a steady correspondence. Alfred would confide to him quite a lot in this early period of getting his work established. (The two men stayed in contact for a number of years afterwards and Tyler was one of the few people to have papers presented at both the First (1935) and Second (1941) American Congresses on General Semantics.[10]

In the first six months after publication, other newspaper reviews, articles, and editorial pieces appeared in the *Mansfield [Ohio] News-Journal*, the *Binghamton N.Y. Press*, the *Cincinnati Enquirer*, the *Wilmington [Delaware] Evening Journal*, *The New York Post* and *The Brooklyn Daily Eagle*. In early February 1934 an Associated Press reporter interviewed Korzybski, which led to a whole new round of articles in newspapers around the country, which made use of the syndicated piece. Finally *The New York Times*, whose editors had initially seemed resistant to covering the book, on February 11 carried a sizable and friendly review by Korzybski's old acquaintance George Moreby Acklom. Although containing some errors (Acklom referred to Alfred as 'Dr. Korzybski...'a psychiatrist') and mildly critical, Korzybski probably couldn't have expected anything better.[11] In general, the newspaper coverage of the book (mainly positive, if not laudatory) indicated a rather remarkable public interest for such a seemingly 'heavy' book.

Perhaps the most important initial review for Korzybski was the personal one he awaited from Cassius Keyser, who—occupied with his own writing and various health issues—had had limited time and energy over the past few years to help with the evolving manuscript of Korzybski's opus. And although Korzybski had occasionally seen the "dear dear old man" and had tried his best to keep Keyser up to date via letters, he had shied away from imposing too much on his friend. After the book's publication, Keyser surely must have gotten one of the first of the complementary copies Alfred sent to various friends and helpers. What would Keyser make of it?

Toward the end of 1933, Alfred had begun collecting statements about the book for possible use in his campaign to interest foundations in his work. Mira saw Keyser in the beginning of December by which time Keyser had finished his first reading. Would he write a recommendation? Keyser agreed. In a few days he sent Alfred a letter with his statement enclosed:

> I have read Korzybski's Science and Sanity attentively and critically from lid to lid. Though I do not find myself in full agreement with the author at every point, I am bound in candor to say that as a whole this work is a tremendous and timely drive in the right direction. It is undoubtedly and beyond all comparison the most momentous contribution that has ever been made to our knowledge and understanding of what is essential and distinctive in the nature of Man...bearing...upon...the whole of our human methodology for gaining, communicating, and utilizing knowledge at any stage and upon any level.[12]

At the beginning of his trials to get publicity and establish his work, seeing Keyser's response—combined with the Lillie and Tyler reviews, which he had just received—buoyed up Korzybski tremendously. He wrote to Lillie a few days later:

> ...I rush this letter not only as an acknowledgement and expression of my gratitude, but also to send you a statement of Prof. Keyser...The letter of Professor Keyser made me very happy not only because it is really splendid but particularly because Prof. Keyser has done so much for putting my first book before the public, as he devoted his most important Phi Beta Kappa address to a review of the book, and in some cases was criticized for it and his health did not allow him to see the Ms or the proofs of the new S+S so he read an entirely new book to him. Personally for about 12 years I labored under a definite and permanent longing that the dear Old Man should not be ashamed of this new work, to have such an appreciation is of course a great deal of happiness to me.[13]

Soon afterwards, Keyser extended what he wrote for a review later published in the April 1934 edition of *The New Humanist*. The review, entitled "The Foundations of the Science of Man", discussed *Science and Sanity* in terms of its aim, means, principles, terms, and major theses. The review showed the mathematician's remarkable capacity as a careful, analytical reader. By January, Keyser had almost completed another still more extensive review article for *Scripta Mathematica*, when he was hospitalized for some problems related to his old surgeries. He wasn't able to finish it until April. As he explained to Korzybski, he felt the lack of criticism in the *New Humanist* review might lead readers to dismiss it. Keyser had not only tightened up and elaborated what he had previously written but added a critical section of "Queries, Doubts, and Reservations". This piece, entitled "Mathematics And The Science Of Semantics" published in the May *Scripta* qualifies as one of the best reviews of *Science and Sanity* ever written—and one of the clearest short introductions. As the late Keyser/Korzybski scholar Elton S. Carter, pointed out, "Cassius J. Keyser [was] rare indeed among the critics of general semantics, not because he praised *Science and Sanity*, but because he exhibited ample evidence of knowing what he was talking about."[14] Korzybski wrote to Keyser in June after he had read the *Scripta* review and addressed some of Keyser's queries, doubts, and reservations. He felt grateful to Keyser and considered the criticisms mild.[15]

Some 'Philosophers' Respond

Throughout 1934, *Science and Sanity* continued to generate much interest. Alfred and Mira were filling the pages of their scrapbook with clippings of new reviews (as well as other articles and materials related to Alfred and his work). Only a few reviews seemed downright dismal. Two of the worst came from one man, Ernest Nagel—a student of John Dewey and a respected Columbia University philosopher of science. In the February issue of *The Journal of Philosophy*, Nagel panned the book. In a shorter review note for the August 1 *New Republic*, Nagel wrote "Writing as much as Mr. Korzybski does, he is bound to say good things occasionally. But most of the book consists of irrelevant material taken from mathematics, physics, chemistry, biology and psychiatry." It bothered Korzybski that what

Nagel seemed to disagree with were Nagel's own misrepresentations. How could Nagel have possibly come to the conclusion, as he wrote in the February review, that Korzybski believed "..hypotheses contrary to the fact are meaningless (e.g., p. 168)"? Huh? Such a misleading account of his work could do real harm. How many people would accept Nagel's judgment and as a result not bother to take Korzybski seriously? Alfred wrote a protest letter to the *New Republic*, but in the October 24 issue the editor chose instead to print rejoinders to Nagel by Polakov and Robert H. Allen, a journalist whom Alfred knew. In his reply to these, written from Warsaw and published at the end of the year, Nagel wrote:

> ...While I respect very highly the men who endorse "Science and Sanity," I must differ with them in their evaluation of it; moreover, I am not convinced that they have all undergone the same labor with the book that I have...it is my considered opinion that "Science and Sanity" has no merit whatsoever,...[16]

Perhaps the only serious review rivaling Nagel's in nastiness was published in the July 21, 1934 *Journal of the American Medical Association*. Like Nagel, the anonymous reviewer—possibly Morris Fishbein, the *Journal's* editor—considered the book worthless. The review began disparagingly, "In spite of its title, this book is neither scientific nor sane; it is merely ponderous." It continued with various misstatements about the book such as "It is the first volume of a series of books dealing with non-Aristotelian logic" [a fairly common error about Korzybski's work] and "Since he points out that mental adjustment is a purely linguistic matter [*he most definitely had not pointed that out!*], the author would seem to be well adjusted, but to the psychiatrist there seems to be little of value in the book." Korzybski wrote to Fishbein protesting the misrepresentation and prejudicial remarks. Many psychiatrists were finding a great deal of value in his work. The April *Psychiatric Quarterly* had called *Science and Sanity* "a source book of ideas and inspiration." Dr. William A. White, although too busy as usual, had already written a friendly, if superficial, review published in the July issue of *Mental Hygiene*. (The book would later receive positive reviews in a number of psychiatric journals.) A paper on Korzybski's work had just been respectfully presented more than a month before at the 90th Annual Meeting of the American Psychiatric Association in New York City. Other psychiatrists, besides Graven, were becoming students of his work. Fishbein wrote back refusing to make any correction and the two men carried on an unpleasant correspondence until October when Korzybski seems to have given up.

However much he felt irritated about the Nagel and *JAMA* reviews, Sidney Hook's more positive treatment of *Science and Sanity* in the March 10, 1934 *Saturday Review of Literature* may have bothered him more. He had started to correspond with Hook in the middle of 1933 and had initially seemed willing to consider Hook, a student of Dewey who taught at New York University, as one of those 'philosophers' doing valuable work in epistemology. But Hook, though more friendly, treated Korzybski's work much as Nagel and the *JAMA* had—as a work of 'philosophy' or 'logic'—and missed its applied, experimental nature. Restating Korzybski's views in elementalistic, 'philosophical' language, Hook distorted them. Like Nagel, he had read the book and continued to 'hum his own humming' as Korzybski sometimes characterized poor readers or listeners who jumped to and stuck to their own incorrect conclusions about what a writer or speaker said. Korzybski had repeatedly referred to semantic [evaluational] reactions as non-verbal in nature—psycho-logical, organismal responses to words, symbols, and other events. Korzybski apparently hadn't repeated this often enough for Hook to get it—for in his review Hook identified semantic reactions with language. Nonetheless, this didn't stop him from criticizing Korzybski for his "repetitiousness". Not understanding what Korzybski meant by identification as an organismal response, Hook had no trouble declaring that John Dewey— in his work on 'logic'—had actually already "worked out" Korzybski's "fundamental position". According to Hook, still a Marxist in 1933, "Social and economic problems have no more to do with the interpretation of the law of identity than "the flowers that bloom in the spring, tra-la." "[17] Decently enough, Hook had sent a copy of the review to Korzybski about a month before it was printed. Korzybski quickly wrote back and cordially attempted to correct the misinterpretations. But subsequently, the final published piece gives no indication that Hook re-evaluated what he wrote in response to Korzybski's suggestions. Writing to Tyler on March 16, Korzybski located part of the problem in Hook's approach to reading, an approach common to many readers, not only 'philosophers':

...Physiological mechanisms require relaxation before they may work, and reading at first critically inhibits responses. I had a real body-blow. Sidney Hook a very gifted, learned, honest, etc., 'philosopher' wrote a review of my book for the Saturday Review of Literature, the review is very friendly etc., but...he has missed the whole thing because as a philosopher he starts to read critically, and this inhibits the working. And so it goes.[18]

Despite Korzybski's general feelings about academic 'philosophy' he was not badly treated by all 'philosophical' reviewers. For example, the October 1934 edition of *The Personalist* had a brief, intelligent overview of the book by H. B. Alexander, a wide-ranging humanist professor who had made forays into lexicography and anthropology and helped found Scripps College, an innovative school for women in Southern California. Alexander commended Korzybski's "critical language consciousness and conscience" which came "from a 'semantics' deeper-set than any verbal contrivance of experience." Korzybski wrote to him to thank him for the kind review.

Though he didn't write a review, another 'philosopher', Oliver Leslie Reiser became a supporter of Korzybski's work and helped publicize it at the end of 1934. Reiser had studied and taught both psychology and philosophy at Ohio State University before becoming a professor of philosophy at the University of Pittsburgh. He seemed ready for Korzybski when they first became acquainted—probably sometime in 1930 after Korzybski read an article by Reiser and sent him a complimentary note. The two men corresponded for several years before the publication of *Science and Sanity*. In a May 1933 letter to Alfred, whom he addressed as "Count Korzybski" he said "There was a time when I depended [on] the tradition[al] (aristotelian) "laws of thought" (e.g. in my 'Humanistic Logic') but in recent years I have moved away from this position."[18b] Clearly, general semantics had 'grabbed' him and he came to see Korzybski as a possible herald of a new era of human 'thought'.

During those first years of their relationship, Reiser seemed to be emerging consciously as a non-aristotelian epistemologist. While *Science and Sanity* was being prepared for publication, Reiser agreed to have his name announced as the prospective author of *From Primitive Religious To Modern Scientific Structural Assumptions*, one of the 'Volumes In Preparation' mentioned in *Science and Sanity*. Over the next year, Reiser studied *Science and Sanity*, sent Alfred copies of his published papers, and the two men corresponded with more frequency. Korzybski could still see some 'shades' of elementalism and identification in Reiser's formulating. But he respected the 39-year old 'philosopher', whom he saw as good non-aristotelian material and bluntly asked Reiser in a June 29, 1934 letter:

> Why do you insist in printing all the stuff you have ever written instead of tackling a fundamental analysis of so called 'fundamentals' and do some constructive real work? I have read everything you have written and frankly consider that you are a <u>most gifted and informed</u> man for a 'philosopher', but why in the Dickens do you bicker with 'philosophers' for 'philosophers' instead of applying your great gifts and knowledge to <u>human orientations</u> and methods and disregard professional 'philosophers' as everybody else does.[19]

Reiser told Korzybski that he was finding it somewhat difficult to leave behind these trappings of the culture of academic 'philosophy'. Nonetheless he was working at it and presented one result of his efforts at the 94th Annual American Association for the Advancement of Science (AAAS) meeting, held in Pittsburgh at the end of December 1934. His paper, entitled "Modern Logic and Non-Aristotelian Logics", discussed general semantics in the context of various developments in logic, although he *did* explicitly note, "Korzybski's system should not be described as a non-Aristotelian <u>logic</u>. All existent logics, Korzybski argues, are elementalistic...The science of the adjustment of man to his environment is a psycho-logic, and this should be a non-Aristotelian <u>system</u> rather than a logic."[20]

Reiser's paper, one among some 1,500 talks given, drew remarkable attention from the press. It was not only mentioned but written about at length in articles around the U.S. Watson Davis, the Director of the *Science Service* and editor of the nationally-distributed *Science News Letter* (which also had a press service) had written an article devoted to Reiser's presentation and on the "new mode of thinking" of Korzybski and others. Davis's article, dated December 28, was picked up by papers like the Buffalo, New York *News* and *Buffalo Evening News*, the Houston, Texas *Press*, and *The Washington Daily News*. The *Pittsburgh Post-Gazette* and *The Bulletin Index* ("Pittsburgh's weekly newsmagazine") had separate stories on Reiser's talk. The notion of non-identity especially seemed to grab reporters. This headline for the Davis article appeared in one paper: *"Einstein Theory" of Logic Offered: That a Thing Is Not Always Itself* [21]. As a follow-up, in its January 12, 1935 edition, Watson's weekly *Science News Letter* printed another article on Reiser's talk, "New Mode of Thought Urged To Replace Aristotle". Reiser had definitely made a big publicity splash for Korzybski and himself. Afterwards, Alfred asked Reiser to submit a paper for the upcoming First American Congress for General Semantics which Reiser did, entitled "A Non-Aristotelian System and General Semantics".

The two men remained in contact for many years. Reiser, now neglected as a 'philosopher', taught at the University of Pittsburgh and published many articles and books until his death in 1974. He would write some excellent things related to general semantics in the course of his career, including the 1940 book, *The Promise of Scientific Humanism* and the 1958 *The Integration of Human Knowledge*. In his 1989 book *Logic and General Semantics: Writings of Oliver L. Reiser and Others*, Sanford Berman commented that Reiser, in the 1940 book, "presented the most complete analysis of Aristotelian and non-Aristotelian logic and thought ever written by a student of general semantics."[22] Robert Pula recommended Reiser's writings with some qualification, noting "...a residual mystical inclination, some unconscious identifying, hankering after 'absolutes', etc."[23] in Reiser's 1958 book.

Korzybski certainly noted this tendency over the years. In early 1935, soon after Reiser's success at the AAAS meeting, Korzybski wrote to him, "You see for many reasons I do not deal with 'philosophers', and you are the <u>only</u> one in the 'sem. family'. There is endless work to be done by a man like you, but this work to be effective must be RADICAL with no compromise."[24]

Reiser never seemed to become radical enough for Korzybski. He continued writing about Korzybski's work in terms of 'logic', 'semantics', and 'philosophy', as those terms were commonly and elementalistically employed. In subsequent years, Korzybski spoke bluntly to his friend the 'philosopher' whom he didn't want to see "flounder in a rarified atmosphere of verbalism which has nothing to do with so-called realities."[25]

Chapter 43
'SCIENTISTS DON'T READ'

Korzybski saw himself as a scientific worker and, despite the radical nature of his work as a gadfly in scientific borderland, he experienced remarkable acceptance by the scientific community at large throughout his career. Even before publication of *Science and Sanity*, he had gotten a good sense of this. A significant number of respectable scientists and mathematicians had helped him with the research and editing. It gratified him that these (mainly) men—with whatever corrections they'd suggested—found acceptable his treatment of their particular specialties. And just before the book came out, he got another significant confirmation of his status in the scientific community.

At the end of August 1933, he received an envelope from the Washington, D.C.–based AAAS. Very busy with the final production of the book, he had allowed the unopened envelope, which he assumed might be a bill about overdue membership fees, to get buried on his desktop among other papers and mail. When he finally got around to opening the letter he was surprised to see an official notification: "I have the honor to inform you that you have been elected Fellow of the American Association for the Advancement of Science. Respectfully yours, Henry B. Ward, Permanent Secretary." The back of the membership card, included the definition of "Fellowship" from the "(Bylaws of the AAAS, Art. II)": "*Section 4.* All members who are professionally engaged in scientific work, or who have advanced science by research, may be elected by the Council to be fellows on nomination or on their own application." Replying to Henry Ward, Korzybski expressed his "deep appreciation for this honour." The life-long honor might serve a useful purpose as well, if it helped him in his quest to find more scientists willing to cooperate with him.[1]

If enough scientists got inspired to jump into the non-aristotelian trenches, a great deal could be accomplished. For one thing the social sciences might move considerably forward. But even in the so-called physico-mathematical sciences, progress often seemed inhibited because of inadequately addressed linguistic, epistemological issues. Perhaps, as he suggested in the book, applying his methods could even help resolve such impasses as the esoteric controversy about the status of transfinite numbers in mathematics, to pick only one example. He believed that a consciously non-elementalistic, non-aristotelian revision—a methodological unification—of the sciences could result in unexpected breakthroughs through cross-fertilization of disciplines formerly seen as disconnected.

For such a non-aristotelian revision of the sciences and life to happen, polite interest or even general agreement would not suffice. A large enough number of individual scientists would need to get interested enough to *study* and *apply* what he was advocating and, as he realized even in 1933/34, they would first of all have to *adopt* and *integrate* it, to some degree, into their personal lives.* That requirement would always remain a snag—perhaps *the* snag—for many scientists, as well as others, trying to make sense of Korzybski's work.

---

* If you have trouble distinguishing between orders of abstractions (in other words, lack consciousness of abstracting) in your personal life, how can you possibly become optimally conscious of abstracting in your profession?

Some scientists would respond as Max Born did, after Korzybski had sent him a letter early in 1933 asking for permission to quote from his writings. Alfred briefly explained the subject of his book and offered to send Born a copy when it came out.[2] Born—friendly, though interestingly 'closed', considering his role as one of the founders of quantum physics—wrote back in German:

> I thank you for your nice letter and am glad that you have drawn inspirations from my book about Einstein's Theory of Relativity. Indeed I really am interested in epistemology but absolutely cannot understand what this has to do with sanity (mental health). I'm afraid that we will not be able to communicate with each other over this point. Because I am very concerned with not drawing more conclusions from insights into physics than it is absolutely certain. The application for medical problems seems to me too bold.[3]

Nonetheless, other scientists found Korzybski's work initially appealing. Visiting Baltimore and Washington in the first part of November, some weeks after the book was published, Alfred had a chance to gauge the response of many of his scientist friends, some of whom had at least read his manuscript or parts of it and consequently had received complimentary copies. While he found a great deal of interest, he ruefully noted that despite the fact many hadn't read the completed book, they seemed to think they 'knew all about it'.

There were also a few men like the Harvard zoologist William Morton Wheeler who had already written to Alfred in late October to say he was reading the book and had realized he missed a great deal of value while correcting the proofs—having lost the trend of the reasoning while editing Korzybski's English. As he was getting "a better understanding of the [non-] A system", it was now making a "profound impression" on him. Wheeler also reported that two of his colleagues at the Harvard Biological Institute and the Comparative Zoology Museum, G.H. Parker and T. Barbour had bought *Science and Sanity* and were taking their copies to bed with them.[4]

Later in November, Alfred (with Mira) went to Boston to see Wheeler and Bridgman and to meet with a number of other Harvard scientists. After he returned, he wrote about his trip to Keyser:

> Dear Dear Old Man,
>
> Please excuse the delay in answering your dear old letter of Nov. 16 but I was lecturing at Harvard and came home only yesterday home [sic]. It seems the lectures were a success. I [had] a large and very mixed audience at a biological seminary [probably arranged by Wheeler at the Biological Institute] in which many specialists attended. I had a two hour lecture at the home of [E.V.] Huntington [where Alfred and Mira stayed as guests] with Birkhoff and also E.B. [Edwin Bidwell] Wilson, [Harlow] Shapley, [L.J.] Henderson, etc., two two-hours lectures at the psychopathic hospital to doctors, one to the astronomical group at the home of Shapley, and one to neurologists at the home of a prof. of physiology and anatomy. One never knows but it seems that all these specialists have been genuinely electrified. I gave hell to Birkhoff and Veblen (at the Nat. Academy dinner), and I think I got under their skin a little. We had a very nice and long dinner with Sheffer. I saw Whitehead twice and he was kind enough to invite us to his seminar. [Korzybski had already sent an extra copy of *Science and Sanity* to Huntington, who had delivered it to Whitehead's home.] I attended also one lecture of Sheffer. I was amazed that both lectures were aiming the same direction.

The widespread interest among these scientific workers encouraged him:

> As a rule I am not optimistic about my lectures, but this time I believe that I really made good. I had other important conferences with [Henry] Murray (Clinic of abnormal Psychology) and anthropologists and physiologists, and we fell on each others' necks, it looks really that perhaps my work may have after all some value. It is so peculiar that discussing the problems from so many angles with specialists all of them should find an advance in their fields.

But he also experienced some shocks or at least frustrations at Harvard. Whitehead, for example, seemed deeply concerned with the kinds of problems Korzybski had dealt with in his book. In his seminar, as Alfred wrote to Keyser, "Whitehead said "Identity is a horrible idea, no one seems to know what it means"." Had Whitehead even glanced at the preface of *Science and Sanity*? Alfred commented:

> The trouble with Whitehead is that he has no use for anthropology and psychiatry, otherwise he would know that 'identity' represents a <u>misevaluation</u> which makes the optimum adjustment impossible
>
> ...With Whitehead of course there is no discussion, he listens very attentively and sympathetically but he will not read. Personally to me this is a drama, but this cannot be helped. He told me that Wheeler 'knows more about philosophy and logic than the whole department'. I utilized this and Wheeler promised to convey to Whitehead many points of my work.[5]

Another jolt for Alfred involved his friend Percy Bridgman, who hadn't done more than glance at the book and seemed unlikely to read the whole thing. Since he had read parts of the manuscript, he seemed to assume he already understood Korzybski's work and it was becoming more and more apparent to Alfred that he didn't. Alfred's meeting with the physiologists and neurologists also left him surprised and dismayed at what he perceived as their generally antiquated outlook.[6]

After he got home Alfred also wrote to mathematician E. B. Wilson, who had attended the talk Alfred gave at Huntington's home. The letter explained his work a bit more and asked for Wilson's help in trying to get Alfred's message across to scientists. Could Wilson write an endorsement statement for him for the foundations or perhaps even write a review for a scientific journal? Wilson replied several weeks later saying that despite his interest in the talk, he could make neither heads nor tails of Korzybski's aim or message. He had also spent a few hours with *Science and Sanity* but, as he wrote to Korzybski, "I do not find your book intelligible any more than I found your talk intelligible."[7] Wilson admitted that he thought the fault was probably in him but until he had more time to adequately study Korzybski's work he could not say anything about it. Korzybski found Wilson's response worrisome but expressed his gratitude to Wilson for his honesty and hoped he would continue to reserve judgment until he had further time to study and apply the material in the book.

Around this time, Korzybski got some other more annoying reactions. He had written to some book clubs to explore the possibility of them carrying his book. Not surprisingly, *Science and Sanity* seemed too specialized a volume for *Book of the Month Club*. But it just seemed wrong for the *Scientific Book Club* editor to reject it as over the heads of the majority of his members without having a look at the book itself.[8]

The wildly varying reactions to his work would continue to bother Korzybski. On the one hand, he had received enough positive responses from people like Keyser, Wheeler, and Dr. Wilmer, the famous Johns Hopkins ophthalmologist, to reassure him of the value of pursuing his plan to get scientists behind him. On the other hand, he felt bewildered by either the lack of interest, the lack of comprehension, or the closed-minded dismissal by a number of others. If he could only get Einstein, one of his great inspirations, on his side.

"Dear Professor Einstein"

By the end of 1933, the mathematical physicist—a world-famous, living symbol of science—was residing in the United States, a Jewish refugee from Nazi Germany. His public endorsement could give Korzybski a powerful entering wedge into the awareness of other scientists, foundations, various state and federal agencies, the general public, and others who could further support his work. But although Einstein had become the object of great public interest, he had also become beset—as Korzybski knew—with the attempts of many people to get his attention for their causes or projects. Jewish scholars trying to escape Europe wanted Einstein's support to get into the United States. Various Jewish groups and individuals saw Einstein as a leader—in spite of his lifelong detachment from Jewish culture and religion. Einstein may have mainly wanted to be left alone to pursue his research. Still, Korzybski would see if he could get Einstein's attention and interest.

At the end of November 1933, he sent the physicist a copy of *Science and Sanity* with a one-page letter, which summarized his work:

Dear Professor Einstein:

I am taking the liberty of sending to you my new book Science and Sanity as an evidence of my deeply felt homage and gratitude for your great work.

Methodological investigations have disclosed quite unexpected results; namely that elementary physico-mathematical methods as particularly embodied in your's and Minkowski's work, are essential for sanity. ...

When he hadn't gotten any acknowledgement by mid-January of the following year, he sent another letter asking if Einstein had received the book. If not, Alfred offered to send another copy. At the end of the month, Einstein wrote back in German thanking Korzybski for the book, which he had indeed gotten. At least Einstein (unlike Max Born) seemed to be reserving his judgment:

I received your book already some time ago and thank you cordially. My workload with duties and correspondence is so immense, that I could only dedicate little (time) to your work, in any case much too little to allow myself a judgment concerning it. I hope to perhaps be able to still catch up with it.[9]

Over the next year or two, Korzybski made efforts at further contact with Einstein through mutual acquaintances. In the late summer of 1934, Alfred's good friend and supporter, botanist David Fairchild, was staying at the resort town of Watch Hill, Rhode Island where Einstein had also gotten a cottage for a summer of relaxation and sailing. Alfred did not shy away from suggesting to his friend David that developing a friendship with his "backdoor neighbor" Einstein might also benefit Alfred. Fairchild had met Einstein on the beach and chatted with him, but it seemed clear to Fairchild that Einstein mainly wanted to be left alone. Fairchild did not want to impose on the physicist. So that was that. Korzybski also knew a number of other people who knew Einstein, including a mathematician who seemed close to Einstein and who also seemed enthusiastic about Korzybski's work. But her relationship, however close, never seemed to work out for Korzybski's benefit.

Over the next decade, Korzybski would occasionally contact Einstein with a reprint or a note. In late 1939, more than a year after the founding of the Institute of General Semantics, Korzybski wrote to Einstein asking him if he would accept a position as an Honorary Trustee. It took Einstein some time, and a second letter from Korzybski, to respond, which he finally did on January 17, 1940 in an ornately polite letter written in German:

Dear Sir,
With great regret I don't see myself in the position to accept your kind offer because I see myself unable to accept a moral responsibility of any kind for publications that currently appear under the topic of 'Semantic'.[10]

Even after getting turned down like this, Korzybski continued on occasion to write quite cordially and collegially to Einstein with, apparently—from comments in Korzybski's letters—no response. By 1947, a few years before his death, Korzybski had ruefully come to conclude that Einstein was not able or willing to see the human import that Korzybski had derived from his work. He recalled an interview with Einstein he had seen a number of years before. Einstein was asked "What will your theory mean to the world?"

Einstein had no answer. He smiled only and said, "Let them discover." "Let them discover." And curiously enough, this is rather funny, curiously enough when it was discovered, then Einstein does not agree. Oh, the tricks of human nature.[11]

Evidently, Einstein did eventually at least peruse *Science and Sanity*. In the early 1950s, some time after Korzybski's death, Harry Weinberg, one of Alfred's favorite students—was vacationing with his wife Blanche in upstate New York. They had taken out a boat on Lake Saranac and noticed a small sailboat in the distance with two white-haired figures, one of whom looked familiar—like Albert Einstein. The Weinbergs got themselves over to the other boat. They had indeed found Einstein who was sitting with a woman (his sister?) who looked startlingly like the scientist. Weinberg introduced himself as a student of Korzybski and asked permission to take a photograph, which he was allowed to do. He understood that Korzybski had once sent Doctor Einstein a copy of *Science and Sanity*. Had Einstein read it and what did he think of it? Einstein replied in his heavily German-accented English, "Dot's ah krrrazy boook!"[12]

Coghill

Korzybski's relationship with biologist George Ellett Coghill (1872–1941) helped him put into perspective his efforts to connect with other scientists. For people like neuroscientist C. Judson Herrick, who wrote a biography of Coghill, and evolutionary biologist Julian Huxley, Coghill qualified as a major—though rather unacknowledged—scientific figure. Shortly after Coghill's death, Huxley said, "His death is a devastating loss to science. In my opinion Coghill stood among the twenty outstanding biological scientists of our time, although so few people were cognizant of his work that perhaps not many others would agree with me."[13]

Korzybski had started to correspond with Coghill in 1933, after reading his book, *Anatomy and the Problem of Behavior*. To Korzybski, Coghill's approach to biology ably embodied the dynamic, structural approach he had sought to lay bare in his non-aristotelian system. Coghill, then a primary researcher at the Wistar Institute of Anatomy and Biology in Philadelphia, also served as President of the American Association of Anatomists and had spent a lifetime of teaching and research in zoology, embryology, histology, and anatomy. His pioneering studies on the relation of so-called 'function' and 'structure'—which Coghill considered inseparable in living organisms—had focused on the embryology of behavior and associated bodily apparatus. Coghill had used the simplest research tools— a human hair at the end of a wood splinter—to tickle embryos of the amblystoma, a type of salamander, at different stages of development. Then he observed and described what they did and made generalizations about their development in relation to their behavior. Coghill tickled Korzybski too, who used a number of quotes from Coghill's book in *Science and Sanity*.

Coghill had read most of *Science and Sanity* by January 1934 and wrote to Korzybski:
> ...At least I have read Science and Sanity as far as the mathematical part, which I am taking in small doses...
>
> It was a pleasure to follow your analysis and interpretation of the nature and problem of sanity. The presentation is clear and forceful. It should do a great deal of good—an inestimable amount if the book is sufficiently studied. It should be studied by all teachers of children, and all parents particularly.
>
> My own interpretation of the scientific method seems to me to be directly in line with your ideas of abstraction and identification; and my concept of the relational nature of scientific data seems to be an expression of Einsteinian relativity. In the reading of the book I could see why you liked the methodological part of my address before the Anatomists [in *Anatomy and the Problem of Behavior*].[14]

Coghill clearly got what Korzybski had wanted to get across. Indeed, he already had a broadly, non-elementalistic viewpoint before he read *Science and Sanity*. Perhaps it had some connection with the fact that in his student days, he had enjoyed studying the calculus for fun. As a solitary researcher, Coghill had little day-to-day contact with other scientists, but he would do what he could to help promote Korzybski's work including arranging a lecture for him at the Wistar Institute (which he managed to do in 1935). Korzybski, in turn, felt able to confide in the scientist. He wrote back to Coghill the next day:
> I am struggling with enormous odds, scientific, commercial, religious ('aristotelian'), etc., I knew that my path will be a thorny one, but I did not realize to what extent the scientific world having established for themselves a monopoly of 'wisdom' do not feel like their duty to be scientific in all concerns. As I see it we generally still depend on 'philosophers' to do the methodological work for us. I suggest that we abandon these hopes and do it ourselves. This is of extreme importance for education, as this is more transmittable than mere technicalities, as necessary as they are: besides it is more workable.[15]

In the following month, Korzybski would further reveal to Coghill what he had begun to formulate as his problem with the 'scientific community' at large and, given that, where he wanted to help direct it if he could. He was asking Coghill for assistance:
> ...Methodology deals with general human orientations and so directly with life problems...Your great work differs so fundamentally from other similar works that I believe that the work as such would advance much further if all research men would be educated to its importance, and this can be done only in methodological papers. Assuming that you are interested in your work as work not as a personal issue (I am convinced of that), I am certain your work as work would benefit if you could or would educate methodologically large numbers of students...Under the present practice of science we are inefficient, we do not realize that some laboratory facts, no matter how important, are less important than new and reliable methodological papers which explain non-commercial and non-patented semantic [evaluational] processes by which you have achieved such important results.[16]

While Coghill wanted to help Korzybski, he had begun to suffer from serious heart troubles and furthermore was coming into a period of conflict with the administration of the Wistar Institute which forced him to retire at the end of 1935. Coghill couldn't follow through with the kind of writing or teaching that Korzybski suggested for him to do. But as a particularly sympathetic reader, he did give valuable advice for promoting GS to scientists, which Korzybski ended up following.

Coghill wrote back to Korzybski on March 3: "...Your presentation of the problems you are facing have run back and forth through my mind in many ways. Whether the result will prove to be constructive remains to be seen." He mentioned the possibility of writing a review for *Science*, although he didn't think his present state of health, combined with his natural slowness in writing, would lead to his getting this done quickly. (It turned out he didn't write the review.) Based on his observations of some fellow workers who were trying to read *Science and Sanity*, he told Korzybski:

> ...My impression is that the chief obstacle before the reader, particularly the experimental scientist, is the size of the book. I believe that relatively few experimentalists are great readers. Philosophers are; and they will probably read the book–for books are their bread of life. But when an experimentalist faces a book of nearly 800 pages he is likely to say to himself: "well, I would like to read that book: I must some time", and he puts it back on the shelf with all good intentions but no results–probably ever.
>
> I am of the opinion that your field of action now is to re-state parts of the book–not so much parts of the book as the ideas you have developed there–piece by piece, so to speak–and publish a series of articles in various magazines. In all these articles you would of course refer to the full treatment of the subject in S&S. By this means you could get your ideas instilled in the minds of readers and at the same time stimulate a desire to read more in the book itself.
>
> In the same respect, other books of the non-A series should be relatively short...A series of short books along the lines which you have advertised, if written for particular classes of readers, –teachers in public schools– physicians– psychiatrists– etc. would I believe be read. S&S would stand as the opus magnum of the series, or the main source, and the smaller books would lead out into various fields of thought and practice with specific applications in each case.
>
> To come back to my own situation– your book has been much help to me, and your evaluation of my work has been most stimulating. But my health is such now that I must watch my step...
>
> I mention this personal side of my life so that you will not judge my slowness too harshly.[17]

By June, 1934 Korzybski had concluded he was going to have to follow Coghill's advice. He had just attended, as an invited guest, the Ninetieth Annual Meeting of the American Psychiatric Association in New York City. Reginald St. Elmo Murray, M.D., a psychiatrist at the Veterans Hospital in Lyons, New Jersey, had gotten interested in his work and written a paper on it called "The Semantic Differential in Mental Hygiene". As the title might suggest, Murray's grasp of the book seemed rather limited. Despite at least one prior face-to-face meeting, back and forth correspondence, and some editing on Korzybski's part, Murray presented 'semantic' reactions as responses to words only, a significant mistake that many others would make as well. From Korzybski's point of view, Murray's style of expression seemed rather florid and the paper came across more like a church sermon than a scientific talk.[18] Still, with considerable resistance from the psychiatry meeting organizers (who, given his status as a non-psychiatrist, seemed loath to give him any time on the program), Korzybski got 10 minutes to serve as a discussant for Murray's paper. Before the meeting, Alfred wrote to many of his psychiatrist friends inviting them to come to the talk. The paper delivered on June 1, the last day of the meeting, drew a lot of interest, not only from the attending psychiatrists but also from the press. An Associated Press reporter wrote a piece about the presentation that included interview comments from Korzybski and had national distribution.

Korzybski appreciated the interest and the publicity but, as he told A. Ranger Tyler, he found the meeting depressing:

> It seems that a fairly large number of psychiatrists are interested in my work, some of the really important very much so, but they are very slow. There were some really fine papers of an "inspiring" character for the profession, but these do not give workable means, and so they are quite useless for any immediate activities. My wife attended the meetings with me, she was quite happy because "every important paper went my way." I was frankly very depressed, because out of a 20 year sentence (the average for all pioneers in human problems) I have served only six months, and so I will die before anything will happen if it goes this way.[19]

Since the theory of sanity and mental hygiene had become so central to his work, he needed the cooperation of psychiatrists, who as a group seemed as reluctant to read the book as the experimentalists Coghill told him about. He decided to produce a brief outline of the initial remarks he had written for Murray's paper. In the "Outline" he would distill the main points of *Science and Sanity* that most readers seemed to be missing, and with this perhaps entice others to open the book and read. He would either get it published as an article or print it himself as a pamphlet.[20] In any case, such a piece could help "to eliminate my wasting a life time of personal education of people by letters."[21] He wrote to Coghill shortly after the psychiatric association conference, "My difficulties become clearer everyday and it seems that only lectures (which I cannot get) and articles (which nobody wants to print or read) would do."[22]

In this initial stage of figuring out how to promote his work, George Ellett Coghill's support and advice seemed priceless. But Coghill was not going to be able to help with much else. He had a major physical collapse at the end of June 1934. He couldn't even respond to letters from Korzybski until January 1935. In May of that year, he got Korzybski to lecture at the Wistar Institute. After Coghill was forced to retire from Wistar at the end of 1935, the two men stayed in touch. In 1939, Coghill agreed to serve as an Honorary Trustee of the Institute of General Semantics, a role he continued until his death in July 1941.

My Work is Preventive and Educational

The multi-faceted nature of Korzybski's work opened up multiple possibilities for misinterpretation. Each reader could approach his system like a blind man standing before an elephant, groping around, and prematurely identifying the beast in terms of whatever part he *didn't* find useful. To some 'educated' laymen, intimidated by equations and other scientific trappings, it might seem like he was teaching mathematics and science, although he was not so much interested in the technical details as in the method and mode of human behavior they demonstrated. To some mathematicians and physico-mathematical scientists, his background review and examples from math and physical science might seem obvious, even trite. And why was he dragging in the other stuff from psychiatry, biology, etc.?

Some psychiatrists, on the other hand, might puzzle about the physico-mathematical stuff. He wanted to help people solve problems in living. But his ultimately simple methods could get lost in what might seem like a forest of technicalities which provided their rationale. On the other hand, his methods could be dismissed as trivial. Or, as he would encounter more and more frequently as his work became more widely known, they could get neglected by enthusiasts more interested in talking and theorizing than in doing. In his "Outline", he was emphasizing this last point especially: general semantics involved physiological, "neuro-semantic", "neuro-linguistic" mechanisms that had to be worked to be useful.

As he wrote and re-wrote his outline, sending out drafts to friends like Tyler and Keyser for editing suggestions, his eagerness to find people applying and researching his work—or interested in doing so—bubbled to the surface. In August, Mira had gone to Newport to paint. Alfred, as usual, chained to his desk in Brooklyn, sent out a form letter to several dozen psychiatrists, psychologists, and educators around the country who had ordered his book:

August 16, 1934

Dear __ ,

I am preparing a paper on General Semantics giving some data on experiments in psychotherapy and education. I wonder whether you have had an opportunity to experiment yourself, and if so, with what results? I would be very grateful if you could give me some data.

With Appreciation,
Yours Very Sincerely,[23]

For some time he had been getting interesting and positive reports from Joseph C. Trainor, a psychology instructor at Washington State Normal School in Ellensburg, Washington. Trainor clearly appeared smitten with general semantics. The school's library had ordered a copy of *Science and Sanity*, which Trainor had already read once by the time he wrote what looks like his first letter to Korzybski at the beginning of November 1933. By the start of 1934, Trainor had ordered his own copy of the book and started on his third reading (he was reading it aloud to his wife this time). Like Tyler, Trainor had some physico-mathematical background and seemed to take naturally to Korzybski's work. It provided him with a conscious framework and language for an orientation that before then he'd been struggling towards unconsciously on his own.

He already had begun restructuring his beginning psychology and social psychology courses according to non-aristotelian principles. He made a copy of a structural differential out of wall-board to use in his classrooms. Even though Trainor had unintentionally violated his copyright, Korzybski didn't get upset when he found out. He told Trainor—a young man he seemed eager to encourage—to destroy his copy once he received the hand-made mahogany differential Korzybski sent to him. Trainor also experimented with teaching non-aristotelian principles to his young son. In addition, he started a non-aristotelian study group in Ellensburg with Seldon Smyser, another teacher at the Normal School, who had been corresponding with Korzybski since mid-1933. Over the next year, Trainor gathered data from his psychology classes, where he was bringing general semantics into the lectures and drilling his students in Korzybski's methods, including the use of the structural differential. Student writings and interview comments, as well as pre- and post-course intelligence and personality testing (using paper and pencil tests) indicated remarkable improvements in I.Q., mental health, and problem-solving measures.

In a study he presented the following year (1935), Trainor measured a mean increase in I.Q. test scores from 137 to 173 in an experimental group of sophomores in his Beginning Psychology class. They received extensional training according to the guidelines given in Chapter XXIX of *Science and Sanity*. With 30 students in his reported test group, Trainor was the first to admit, "It is impossible in an experiment as limited in scope as this, or with so many factors unmeasured, to give a highly detailed explanation of the results obtained in the usual cause-and-effect formula." However, given the dramatic changes he observed and measured in his students, he concluded, "[f]urther and extensive research is imperative and its advisability would seem to be indicated by the results given."[24]

Korzybski was also hearing about the research of Harold M. Potts, a principal in the Olympia, Washington public school system, who had also gotten interested in general semantics after contact with Trainor, probably from participation in the Ellensburg non-aristotelian study group. Potts found a teacher in his school, whom he called a "natural non-aristotelian" to work with. The two studied *Science and Sanity* together and then designed a classroom plan to train a group of mentally retarded children ranging in age between 12 and 17 years old with I.Q.s ranging from 56 to 80 on the Binet-Simon Individual test. The children received lessons in general semantics from one half to one hour per day for four months and then a lesson every two weeks for a total of seven months. In his report "Some Results of Extensional Training of "Mentally Retarded" Pupils", also presented in 1935, Potts detailed a "typical example of classroom procedure in abstracting" which began as follows: "The teacher writes upon the blackboard the word rain, as a symbol of an event taking place outside at the time and under observation of the children in the class. They are then asked to tell all that they know about the rain." Remarkably. by the end of the lesson "[t]he class [of retarded children] began to see the infinite nature of an object [rain]." Among the results of training noted by Potts:

...5. The method seems to impress them almost immediately, tending to enhance interest and sound curiosity, eliminating feelings of inferiority, hopelessness, inertia, etc., and this is reflected in the general orientations of the pupils.

6. Restlessness, etc., due probably to some extent to their incapability of solving their own problems by intensional methods and language, disappear and marked calmness, hopefulness, careful self-reliance, etc., make their appearance.

7. The value of knowing that an event has extensionally an infinite number of characteristics, from which our nervous system abstracts only the object, has an unconscious effect upon the pupils over a period of time. It has been eight-months since this method was first applied and at the present time when a new center of interest is started they consciously try to discover or explore the many-sided (infinite-valued) aspects of any event without overt urging.

8. They do not feel inferior to others, because they know that, although some know more about an object or a situation than they do, nevertheless no one knows 'all' about the simplest things, and they enjoy field trips and experiments to discover new data...[25]

Extensional training appeared to benefit both college students and retarded children. This was just the kind of research Korzybski wanted to see. He would mention the work of both men in his "Outline". But obviously much more needed to be done.

It seemed less and less likely that Philip Graven would come through with publishing any of his case studies, although Alfred continued to correspond with him and encourage him. He referred to Graven's unpublished case studies in the "Outline". Clearly Alfred was going to have to begin cultivating other psychiatrists—a number of whom he had already met—who might be more likely to write and publish about his methods.

Among this group, John G. Lynn—a young psychiatrist who had recently begun his psychiatric residency at McLean Hospital, a prestigious private mental hospital in Waverly, Massachusetts near Boston—had gotten terribly excited by Korzybski's work. Lynn, who didn't seem to have a problem with writing, began a program of treatment for two of his patients with alcohol-abuse problems and in the following year presented a case report on the men, "Preliminary Report of Two Cases of Chronic Alcoholism Treated By the Korzybski Method". Korzybski and Lynn would have a great deal of contact over the next few years and Korzybski would visit McLean, among other psychiatric hospitals, to observe and give presentations on his work.

Korzybski didn't object to 'psychologists' (he would usually place the term in quotes) doing research related to his work. For a number of years he had remained friendly with psychologist Abraham Roback, who later wrote about Korzybski in his 1952 *History of American Psychology*. After the publication of *Science and Sanity*, psychologists like Gardner Murphy and Henry Murray had also begun to express interest in Korzybski's theories. Nonetheless, he seemed to esteem psychiatry much more than 'psychology'. In the coming years, he would focus more of his attention on psychiatrists. Why?

For Korzybski in 1934, psychology—having only recently emerged as a scientific discipline separate from philosophy—still generally seemed not quite scientific enough. Elementalism seemed rampant in the profession, with behaviorism ascendant (a dead end as far as Korzybski was concerned), while psychologists mainly ignored the vast area of human activity, science and mathematics, that he had come to consider as basic for understanding human behavior. On the other hand, although psychiatrists also seemed to have ignored science and mathematics as behavior, they somewhat made up for this lack by their study of insanity. And as physicians, psychiatrists necessarily had training in medicine. So however poorly they did so, psychiatrists tended to connect their work to other sciences, such as biology, chemistry, etc. As a branch of medicine, psychiatry was also inherently oriented towards application. And their casework with individual patients gave psychiatrists an extensional push to gather data and notice the differences between generalizations about behavior and what they might see in an individual. Despite Korzybski's attitude toward 'psychology', many more psychologists would become interested in his work. (Although, as far as I know, no psychologist would seriously take up his suggestion to replace the term "psychology" with "psycho-logics".)

Korzybski's personal aim was not to reform psychology or psychiatry (he hoped he might inspire others in those fields to do so). He didn't aim to do psychotherapy either. The region overlapping mental hygiene and education, which he considered inseparable, would constitute his main teaching arena. As he often emphasized throughout his career, he saw general semantics as primarily 'preventive and educational'. But demonstrating prevention could be difficult. Getting psychiatrists to use his methods could test the power of his educational approach for ameliorating even so-called 'psychiatric' problems, many of which he felt convinced had their origins in semantic (evaluational) factors—not traditionally considered medical. Any resulting 'cures' could thus help substantiate the case for prevention. Conversely, educators like Trainor and Potts could also help to show the link between education and adjustment. In the late summer of 1934, Korzybski was to meet one of the most important people among those who would help him in his quest to demonstrate this link and develop his work in education for sanity.

Kendig

On a Wednesday afternoon, August 8, 1934, Marjorie Mercer Kendig rang the doorbell at 321 Carleton Avenue in Brooklyn. Reading *Science and Sanity* for the first time only a few months before, she had gotten excited and phoned Korzybski to make an appointment. Now here she was to see him. She had just finished her course work at the Columbia University Teachers College, Department of Higher Education, with only her final thesis paper to complete in order to graduate with a Masters Degree in Higher Education (which she received the following July, 1935). In only a matter of days, she would be heading for Kansas City, Missouri to begin her new job for the fall term as the Head of Barstow School, a private academy for girls with about 500 students ranging from nursery school to college preparatory age. She entered the old brownstone building and began climbing the four flights of stairs to the Korzybskis' 'penthouse' studio. Looking up, she saw a "round-faced, shaven-head, khaki-clad" figure—Alfred himself—"beaming" down at her from the top bannister. She was seeking his help in what she was planning for Barstow—a one-woman revolution in education. She would only realize many years later that the main 'revolution' for her—a slow, internal one—would take place within her self.[26] At this point in 1934 at the age of 42, Kendig (as she liked to be called) had already reached an outer level of competence in her chosen field of education. She seemed mainly focused on changing the world around her—or at least the small piece of it at Barstow, she had just been charged with directing.

Born in 1892 in Utica, New York, Kendig—the sickly, only child of an apparently distant father and a possessive mother—got an unusual, informal early education. Her mother liked to read aloud to her for hours at a time from literary classics like Scott, Dickens, Thackeray, etc. As a result she had grown up with "a relatively high oral vocabulary without the slightest notion of how words and sentences look." (She only learned to read and write at the age of 10.)[27] While she was still a child, her family moved first to Brooklyn, then to an apartment on Sutton Place in Manhattan, a prestigious New York City address. She entered Vassar College in 1911 at the age of 19, graduating in 1915 (a few years after one of her favorite poets Edna St. Vincent Millay) with a Bachelor of Arts degree, having focused on history, chemistry, French and economics. She began work in the publishing business at Scribner's, moving from the advertising to the publication department and then into editorial work. After the U.S. entry into the 'Great War' in early 1918, she volunteered for a Nurses Training Camp at Vassar becoming ill during the influenza epidemic near the end of her training at New York City's Presbyterian Hospital (where she ended up being hospitalized herself). With the end of the war that winter, she didn't continue with nursing but reentered the publishing business, working throughout the nineteen-twenties first at Doran and later at Consolidated Magazines Corporation where she became Director of the Department of Educational Information, until 1931.

Looking back many years later (in the late 1960s/early 1970s) Kendig saw her younger self (from her childhood into at least the early 1930s) as a rather alienated person. She had participated to some extent in the revelries of the "roaring twenties", but although she appeared immersed in the literary mileu surrounding F. Scott and Zelda Fitzgerald, the "Crowd"—as it was called—didn't involve her much.[28] Indeed, by 1931 (as she described herself later) she felt "very alone, against the world and afraid." She had become a workaholic with a tough outer shell she used to protect herself from powerful feelings of fear and anger, etc., that she had learned to suppress as a child. As she said later, "I wasn't happy. I just wasn't unhappy as long as I drove myself." And by 1931, despite her professional success, life within the 'smart set' of the New York publishing world no longer seemed enough for her. She felt drawn to the world of education. "For years I had been asking 'What's wrong with education?' and what could we do to develop 'intelligence' — if we gave up defining it as inborn and unchangeable."[29] Her questions and dissatisfactions had much in common with Korzybski's pre-1914 malaise about society and science.

Kendig left New York City in 1931 to study and work in Europe for the next two years. She had already read Ogden and Richards' *The Meaning of Meaning*. Then she met C.K. Ogden in Nice, France at an international meeting on Progressive Education. She went to England for a brief time to study with him, reading his *Basic English* and other works. Under Ogden's guidance, she then went to Geneva, Switzerland where she took courses at the University of Geneva, Switzerland with Piaget and others while working as Assistant to the Director of the American College for Women in Geneva. As a result of her studies, she became more and more convinced that the answer to her questions somehow involved the relations of 'language', 'thought', and 'behavior'.

After returning to New York City and stumbling into a brief and unhappy marriage, she enrolled in 1933 into the Masters program in Higher Education at Teachers College, Columbia, training to teach at the college level. Her degree was in problems of instruction in institutions of higher learning. When she read *Science and Sanity* in April 1934, she felt that she had found a basic key to her long-standing quandaries.

At their first meeting, Kendig and Korzybski talked for hours. It was a fateful day for them both. In Korzybski, Kendig had found a mentor who provided her with a specific approach for the practical reformulation of education and improvement of 'intelligence' in the way that she had long envisioned. She intended to make 'language' (as she understood Korzybski's formulation of it) the central focus of all the teaching at her school. As she would come to say over the next few years at Barstow, "Every class is an English class." (She would later somewhat modify this emphasis on the centrality of 'language' per se as she developed a better understanding of general semantics).

Conversely, in Kendig, Korzybski found a highly intelligent student who would shortly become one of his most hard-working and dedicated co-workers. After her time at Barstow, Kendig would devote the rest of her life to helping Korzybski while he lived, and promoting his work long after his death (she died in 1981). Of course, when they first met in August 1934, neither of them knew this.

Kendig, circa 1940-1941

But Korzybski nigh certainly knew that Kendig's work at Barstow could help him immensely in applying, researching, and promoting his work. Kendig had superb educational credentials. She was intent on applying and testing his general semantics in the most rigorous manner she could. In her position as Head of Barstow School, she was planning to turn the entire school, not just one classroom, into a test laboratory for Korzybski's methods. He certainly felt more than willing to help her.

One of the first things he did was to provide a topic for her thesis paper. As he usually did with people he met, he put her in touch with a number of his other contacts, friends, and associates. She soon learned more about Trainor's and Potts' classroom research. She decided to write a research proposal on the effects of general-semantics training entitled,"A Proposed Research Investigation Valuable in the Improvement of Teaching on the Junior College Level: Application of a Method for Scientific Control of the Neuro-Linguistic and Neuro-Semantic Mechanisms in Learning". Her paper laid out in detail the rationale and protocol for a controlled two-year study on the effects of general-semantics training on "academic success, and increased 'emotional' stability and 'social' and 'individual' adjustment." The actual study never got done (over the next few years at Barstow, she had her hands full with many other things) but the paper sufficed for completing her Master's Degree requirements.[30]

Things Look Up

Mira came home from Newport in September. With whatever portrait work she had found, she and Alfred were financially surviving, but not thriving, in the closing months of 1934. As for the family property in Poland, Alfred now had only dim hopes of recovering anything from it. And a year after publication of *Science and Sanity*, he and Mira still had only minimum income from the book. By the end of the year, sales had reached about 500 copies—not exactly a best seller. Alfred had also given some lectures with minimal remuneration. And neither the Roosevelt government nor any grant-giving foundations had so far shown interest in supporting his work.

Still, by the end of the year, the overall response to the book showed promise. Given the book's rather limited distribution and Alfred and Mira's inability to pay for advertising or other marketing, the large number of reviews and other newspaper and magazine articles about his work seemed remarkable. They were filling up the pages of their scrapbook. And reviews and articles continued to come in—as they would for a number of years to come.

So far he had heard and seen only a few truly bad reviews. But other than Keyser's *Scripta Mathematica* review (which he cherished) and perhaps Tyler's early newspaper review, most of the positive reviews seemed tepid and had left him feeling rather tepid himself. He couldn't complain about the recognition. But, as he wrote to Trainor, the responses of 'grand, grand' from people who had not seemed to study it in any depth were not what he wanted.[31]

Reading what he called the "splendid" new review of *Science and Sanity* by Markus Reiner in the October 1934 edition of *The Psychoanalytical Quarterly* surely must have buoyed up Alfred's mood. Reiner, a Palestinian Jew living in Jerusalem, only had psychoanalysis as a side interest. As an engineer and applied mathematician, he had helped found and name a new branch of mechanics—rheology, the study of flow and deformation of complex materials under stress. After the founding of the state of Israel, he became a professor at the Technion, the Israeli Institute of Technology, in Haifa, where he taught for many years. Regarding his 1934 review of *Science and Sanity,* Kendig later wrote in the *General Semantics Bulletin*, "No reviewer-critic who tackled the book cold (i.e., without training) has surpassed Reiner's grasp of the basic formulations and clarity in expounding them."[32] With responses like Reiner's, Korzybski felt encouraged. He'd had good responses to his lectures too. And he felt heartened that Lynn, Trainor, Potts, and Kendig (among others) had begun to use and research his work.

It also did him good to know that his old friend Walter Polakov supported his work. Walter had finished his first reading of the book earlier that year and was doing his best to push it. Walter had written a review for *The New Republic*, which had instead published Ernest Nagel's short but dismissive book note. The magazine later published Walter's reply to Nagel, more than twice as long as Nagel's notice, for which Alfred felt grateful.[33] At a regional conference of the *Progressive Education Association* held in New York City in late November, Walter also gave a presentation on "Science's Contribution To The Social Sciences" which featured Alfred's work and later got published in the monthly journal of the association.

And earlier in the year while still working for the Tennessee Valley Authority, Walter—on the lookout for non-aristotelian trends for his friend—had informed Alfred about the theoretical research of Vytautus A. Graicunas and Lyndall F. Urwick on a manager's span of attention or control. Graicunas had published a short paper, "Relationship in Organization", in 1933, now considered a classic of management. According to him and his colleague Urwick—who wrote another 1933 paper on the subject, "Organization As A Technical Problem"—the number of relationships an executive would have to deal with, increased dramatically as he or she added assistants or major functions under his or her control. According to an equation involving exponential growth that Graicunas formulated, each addition of an assistant or function beyond about four would result in a sharp rise in complications. This could increase the likelihood for confusion and failure. Granted, other factors might increase or mitigate the complications. Nonetheless, in 1934 Polakov had begun to apply this in his consulting work. Korzybski considered it extremely significant and later made it the subject of a 1943 paper, "Some Non-Aristotelian Data On Efficiency For Human Adjustment" which included Polakov's summary of Graicunas' and Urwick's original articles. Korzybski also came to impart the span of control as an important formulation in his seminars since it highlighted for him the havoc that could result in human affairs if people ignored non-additive factors.

A year after the publication of the book, thanks to Walter and other readers, reviewers, and supporters with varying levels of enthusiasm, a great deal of interest had been stirred up. The potential for his work seemed promising. But there was no getting around it, Korzybski was going to have to meet more people, give more lectures, and publish more articles, if he wanted to sell more books, to get general semantics into the scientific and general culture—and to make a living.

Chapter 44
ON THE ROAD

In 1934 Joseph Trainor, with his colleague Selden Smyser, started planning for a conference on general semantics at the Washington State Normal School, which they eventually scheduled for March 1 and 2, 1935. They would call it the First American Congress for General Semantics. Meanwhile, after Kendig had been at Barstow School for several months, she asked Korzybski to come to Kansas City to work with her students and teachers. She and Korzybski arranged for an extended visit by him starting at the end of January 1935, continuing through most of February. From there he would travel to Ellensburg, Washington for the Congress, On the way home afterwards, Alfred would engage in as many paid presentations as possible. He was taking *Science and Sanity* on the road.

"The Horror of Hitlerism"
In the latter part of 1934, Korzybski had been busy writing. In September, he worked on and sent out a letter to co-workers like Kendig and Trainor. The letter emphasized the extensional practices he felt people must make habitual in order to apply his work. (Kendig, who recognized the letter's importance, later included it in Korzybski's *Collected Writings*.)[1]

He also intended to finish the "Outline of General Semantics". He planned to present it at the Ellensburg Congress and then use it for further publicity. For this purpose, he had sent drafts of it to some of his friends for editing, including Philip Graven. Korzybski's reaction to some of Graven's comments, related to the topic of "Hitlerism", demonstrated some of Korzybski's concerns about the state of the world at the time. It may also partly explain his further falling away from the already strained relationship with Graven.

Throughout 1934—though under the gaze of foreign governments and the international press—Germany, in its second year under Nazi rule, had further descended into barbarity. On June 30, in "the night of the long knives", elite SS storm troopers, who had pledged their special loyalty to Hitler, murdered Ernst Roehm and the other leaders of the SA Brown Shirts, a Nazi party militia that had formed from the street thugs who had served Hitler during his rise to power. When President Paul von Hindenburg died in August, Hitler became President of Germany as well as Chancellor. The German military establishment, which had been concerned about encroachments on their leadership by Roehm and the SA, seemed assuaged by Hitler's purge of them. Every German soldier was asked to swear an oath of personal allegiance to Hitler. His power seemed complete.

In the meantime, political opponents, Jews, Romany (Gypsies), and other German ethnic minorities, the mentally ill, and mentally retarded, as well as overt homosexuals, among others, were beleaguered by increasingly harsh Nazi laws. German Jews remained the special targets of the Nazi government. Seven to eight percent of the German Jewish population had already fled the country by the end of the year. Like the kind of semantic (evaluational) infection Korzybski had written about in *Science and Sanity*, antisemitism—including government-sponsored discrimination against Jews—had become widespread throughout not only Germany, but Eastern and Central Europe, including Poland. Alfred had followed the news of all this and felt deep concern, making references to the problems of Hitlerism and Germany in his "Outline" draft— references which Graven found objectionable.

As already noted, Korzybski had long felt an almost indefinable sense of connection with Jews and Jewish culture. This connection became clearer earlier in the year, when he read an article that appeared in the Spring 1934 issue of the *American Scholar*, "The Essence of Judaism" by Hans Kohn, a Prague-born, Jewish historian and political scientist then teaching at Smith College. The article presented a bold contrast between Hellenism, the static, 'space' orientation of Greek civilization (more or less equivalent, in Korzybski's terms, to 'aristotelianism') and Judaism, the dynamic, 'time' orientation of Jewish civilization. To Korzybski, the Nazis represented an extreme example of the first. Whereas, the orientation Kohn depicted as 'the essence of Judaism" seemed to Korzybski like what he was aiming for with 'non-aristotelianism'. He had already recommended the article to Graven in August[2] and referred to it again in a letter to the psychiatrist on September 29, partially quoted below:

...I know you associate often with people who praise Hitler. [In 1934 America, this was by no means an anomaly, and Graven's German-speaking wife apparently had strong positive feelings towards the new German regime.] But also you do not read carefully reports from the world (I DO STUDY THEM). Hitler happens to be a sick man,...on his nerve[-]shaken masses he has succeeded of imposing his conditions. Even now Germany is a victim of this illness as the world enmity and fear will doom them as an outstanding nation. They base their whole movement on falsified 'science'. I write about it because one cannot profess Gen. Sem. and not perceive the horror of Hitlerism. You know he hates the Jews. All of us as persons have perfect right to select their friends, but these personal attitudes should never be generalized. This issue is fundamental for us and between us. PLEASE read carefully in the American Scholar, Spring, 1934 an article by Kohn 'The Essence of Judaism'. With some revision of language what he says is profoundly true, but applies not only to Jews but many individuals in every nation...Remember please the issue is sharp either 'space-binding' etc., Greek and animalistic, or 'time-binding', Gen. Sem. and human and sane. We are up against these issues dear Philip, it is better to be forewarned.[3]

On October 10, Graven wrote back to Alfred:

To put it mildly, I do think your comments regarding Hitler were exceedingly biased, unfair, unkind. He merely represents a reaction to gangster diplomats of Europe. Look what they did to our Wilson. It is regrettable to hear you voice such jingoist petty politics.[4]

Korzybski responded quite mildly to his friend but firmly reasserted his position about the unique semantic (evaluational) status of the Nazis, who seemed to him to be consciously but perversely using linguistic, evaluational manipulations (propaganda) to further their pathological political aims. The two men discussed this and other business in letters over the next month. Finally, on November 15, Korzybski wrote to Graven, that among his other editorial helpers with the "Outline" draft, "...all approved the inclusion of the German tragedy in it (really human tragedy)."

Dear Philip you do not want me to be scientifically dishonest. I would feel this way if I would disregard one [of] the most serious tragedies on human record. I know through personal connections and friends you feel differently...As the author of G.S. I have a further vision, quite clear which as yet is not explained in writing, as it is extremely long to write, but the movement of Hitler...[is] definitely culturally retrogressive, anti-semantic, anti-world culture, etc., a very long list, and in all honesty, I as a student of individual and group behaviour cannot disregard this...What I will do however is change the term 'hitlerism' which may be considered by some 'offensive' and make a serious human sentence out of it, which could not be considered 'offensive' or anything else,...[5]

Korzybski had deferred to his friend by taking some of the 'juice' from his article (probably to its detriment). Nonetheless, Graven still seemed offended, asserting without irony: "I must accuse you of talking sheer rubbish whenever you open fire on the Germans and poor little [H]itler...I do not believe you can be fair to the Germans in one sentence, nor in a chapter..."[6] Graven didn't seem open to reconsidering his stand.

By the following year (1935), after he began his intensive period as an itinerant lecturer, Korzybski had stopped giving way to Graven's opinion. He was beginning to make public his views about Hitler and Germany—even predicting a second world war. In August 1935, while he was in Berkeley giving a three-week seminar at the Williams Institute, a local paper carried the following story:

Count Sees Germans As Menace To Peace

"A sick nation of 66,000,000 people led by a sick man will plunge the world into another war!"

Thus Count Alfred Korzybski, world-renowned "human engineer," now lecturing at Williams Institute in Berkeley, characterizes Germany and her Fuhrer, Adolph Hitler, and predicts another conflagration as the result of Germany's determination to turn backward on the path of human progress.

The distinguished Polish scholar whose recent book, "Science and Sanity," is acclaimed by many of the world's foremost scientists as the last word on "the true nature of man," analyzes Germany's persecution of the Jews in psychological terms:

"The Jews have always had a sense of the time process. They were dynamic, drivers, time-binders. Jesus, Freud, Marx, Einstein—all were conscious of the fourth-dimensional time-world.

"Hitler is avowedly Aristotelian, and in constant opposition to Jews because of a fundamental antagonism. The Greek or Aristotelian, was a static orientation.

"Einstein was the first to catch up with the modern world. Germany which considers itself scientific, disowns him!"...[7]

This open expression of views, unpopular at a time when most Americans seemed isolationist, would have made it more difficult for Alfred to avoid discussing the topic with his friend. And as time went on, he became even more vociferous. By 1937, he was more urgently sounding the alarm against Hitlerism, publicly suggesting that concerned psychiatrists ought to get involved in fighting it—a theme he would continue to develop.[8] Perhaps not surprisingly, the frequency of Alfred's correspondence with Graven gradually dwindled until the two friends eventually ceased having contact. Graven's early attitude toward Hitler seemed to have demonstrated something Korzybski noted in the "Outline", and which he often repeated elsewhere: "...even one identification, can ruin a human life, a science, or a social, etc., system."[9] Or a friendship.

Gypsy Teacher

1934 ended for Korzybski with a flurry of activity. He visited the Boston area for a couple of weeks in October to confer with John Lynn and other psychiatrists at McLean Hospital, as well as various people at Harvard and around Boston, including Miriam Van Waters, a woman teaching general semantics to some of the inmates at the Massachusetts Reformatory for Women. Then in November he made a quick trip to Lancaster, Pennsylvania to The Science Press headquarters to pay off the main part of the balance he still owed the printer. In mid-November he and Mira attended a daylong meeting of the National Committee for Mental Hygiene, topped by an evening banquet given at the Waldorf-Astoria Hotel in Manhattan. The program for the day focused on the mental hygiene needs of children, with speakers calling for educational curricula and research. They seemed to be asking for just the kind of thing Trainor, Potts, Kendig, and others were in the process of doing with his work.

The meeting may have served as the location for the following, related by Korzybski in 1947 to Charlotte Schuchardt [Read] who took notes:

> A Situation. New York? 15 years ago? Important Psychiatric Meeting of foreign & USA psychiatrists, Meyer included. MEK [Mira] was with AK [Alfred]. [Adolf] Meyer of course was a god. MEK 'knew better' than AK. When we sat down to talk at table, Meyer brought a chair to me, pushed me down, said (in front of great specialists,.) 'Don't talk now, we are all baffled by GS let the Countess explain it.' MEK burst into speech with the most [psychiatrically] idiotic stuff although the feeling was OK. 'From an artistic point of view'. Of course the national and international authorities were 'convinced' GS was 'all bunk'.[10]

Few people knew the extent to which Mira had helped with Alfred's work (not only supporting him financially but also making publishing decisions with him, and serving as a major editorial sounding board throughout the writing process). Yet Mira's explanations of his work to others had often seemed inadequate to him. He seemed to have held her, as his wife, to a higher standard than he held other people. This complex of factors, suggested in the story above, would become a significant issue in Alfred and Mira's relationship over the next few years, during which time he and Mira would again be separated for long periods of time—always a strain for them both.

At the end of January, Alfred would be leaving home to visit Barstow School, attend the Congress, and make other presentations. He would spend much of the next three years on the road: from 1935 into early 1938, Korzybski would crisscross the United States by train a number of times, giving many lectures and beginning his signature training-seminars. He would present to a variety of groups including children, college students, teachers and other professionals, as well as mental hospital staff and patients. He would continue to develop and refine his formulations and methods in significant ways as he seriously involved himself with helping individuals to adopt an extensional orientation in their lives. He would give several papers at conferences and publish one of them, plus an important review, in a psychiatry journal. His work would begin to gain an unprecedented level of public recognition (some of which became a mixed blessing). He would find crucial supporters who would help him launch the final, institutional phase of his work.

The next few years would also tax him personally. He would have to deal somewhat helplessly from afar with his mother's increasing disability and distress and then with her death. In 1936—after what seems like a precipitous move that he and Mira would make from their long-time Brooklyn apartment to Cambridge, Massachusetts—his relationship with Mira would come close to the breaking point. And during these years the great depression would continue and he would watch the world move closer towards an apocalyptic war he could predict but do little to prevent.

During this period, Korzybski's whirlwind pace gave the impression of a traveling road show. He gave lectures and taught seminars wherever he could, preferably for at least his expenses. He was looking for sponsors and trying to develop interest in his work so ultimately he wouldn't have to continue moving around as an itinerant, gypsy teacher.

By the end of 1937, plans—spearheaded by two of Korzybski's psychiatrist students—would be set in motion for an Institute of General Semantics to be formed in Chicago. From May 1938 on, the Institute would give him—if but little rest—a home base to work from and a small staff of people to help him teach, develop, and promote his work. But at the end of January 1935, the future of his work seemed hidden behind a giant question mark, as he said goodbye to Mira and headed west—first stop, Kansas City, Missouri.

Tears for the Human Cauldron

Soon after he arrived in town, a feature story about him appeared in the January 23, 1935 morning issue of the *Kansas City Times*. The newspaper account gives a plausible portrayal—in keeping with other accounts and private letters of the time—of Korzybski's appearance and state of mind. "The man who is so pessimistic that he has become an optimist stirred the human cauldron in a visit with friends at the Barstow school last night and laughed. It was so funny so tragically funny." The newspaper article continued:

> The whole world has been fooling around near the animal level because of assumptions based on the stupid definitions of words. And there was Count Alfred Korzybski, bald and dramatic, who has laid the foundation for a new start in a book,..."I am an optimist because I have reached the climax of pessimism and am ready to do something about it," he said. "The old way of thought is hopeless, but there is another way. I am an optimist because I am so pessimistic that I doubt the doubts."
>
> With a cane in one hand, wielded in the manner of the Polish nobleman, he took a few strides around the room. He is lame as a result of wounds received when he was a staff officer in the Russian army. Stupid, wasn't it? By the way, there is an incident in connection with war which proves even Count Korzybski retains a few of the animal reactions...You know the experiments of Pavlov with his dogs. A bell would ring, food would be produced and the dog's saliva would flow. After a time the saliva would flow at the ringing of the bell, regardless of the food. Bell—saliva, Count Korzybski likes to repeat the formula, bell—saliva; it explains so much of human response here on the near-animal level.
>
> The animalistic response retained by Korzybski is tears. Whenever he thinks about the war, the tears flow. Last night he demonstrated. He started thinking of horrors, blinked his eyes a few times and there, sure enough, were tears. Purely mechanical. He explained that all the time he was thinking he was in a perfectly happy state of mind.
>
> The Korzybski attitude, however is not so simple as that. He called it simple as he sat laughing at the abject horror in the human cauldron; but his hearers had to take a few long breaths and look blank from time to time.
>
> "Don't call me 'high-brow!" he exclaimed. "A child can understand it. We teach it to 5-year-old children."[11]

Barstow School

As its Head Mistress and Education Director at Barstow School for Girls, Kendig had set out to teach it to children—to center the entire curriculum around evaluation and language. Before the First American Congress for General Semantics scheduled for early March, she had an entire month to see how Korzybski could stir up the cauldron at her elite Mid-Western school. She had made up a work schedule for Alfred soon after his arrival:

January 21, 1935

Alfred Korzybski - -

Call at office each morning and at 4:15 for communications, will be left on big table. This is our clearing-house.

Please write out stuff for press. They wish a typed handout with each interview.

There is an exhibit of Polish art at Nelson Gallery and Museum this month—make tie-up.

See Calendar of events on Bulletin board in hall outside the Study Hall.

You will lecture to faculty every Monday and Wednesday evening: January 30, February 4, 6, 11, 13, 18, at 7:30, beginning lecture Tuesday night, January 29.

You will work with a group of 8th Grade girls every morning from 11:30 to 12:10, beginning Monday, January 21, with Ruth Faison Shaw till Friday, January 25. After that, alone (with an observer) every morning throughout the visit; Ruth will explain cases and so will I. Having you with her first will make a natural transition which must always be considered in any work with young people in School.

Monday at 4:00 o'clock, Ruth Shaw will talk to a group of 12 most intelligent (Honor Roll) Juniors and Seniors and they will try out Finger Painting. This will give you an orientation.

I will outline other work with girls later.[12]

Among other things, Alfred appreciated the opportunity to directly work with Ruth Faison Shaw, whom he had met earlier in New York City. Her book, *Finger Painting: A Perfect Medium For Self-Expression* had come out in October 1934 and it immediately grabbed his interest. A North-Carolina-born teacher, Miss Shaw had opened a school for American and English children in Rome in 1922. While there, in the latter part of the decade, she had discovered/invented finger painting. As she later wrote,

It all began, in the most natural way in the world, with a little boy at the school who smeared the bathroom wall with iodine. All the children liked to "smear"—"smearing" with the hands is a primary impulse, a way of having fun and of learning. So I went about the task of compounding a suitable medium [non-toxic earth pigments on moistened sheets of special paper] with which they could smear to their heart's content without damaging results.[13]

The technique she evolved provided a means for personal symbolic expression not requiring verbal facility, which had surprising, beautiful, and sometimes therapeutic results for young children—and also adults. Korzybski believed Miss Shaw's work involved "important semantic [evaluational] factors which are quite unique". He had been recommending her book to others since he had read it and wanted her to give a presentation at the upcoming Congress on "the semantic aspects of finger painting".[14] But she couldn't comply because she was continuing from Kansas City to other Mid-Western towns as part of a tour to promote her book. Korzybski would continue to have an interest in finger painting and refer to Ruth Shaw's work in his seminars for some years to come.

As Kendig realized when she invited Ruth Shaw to Barstow, finger painting could be used to introduce general semantics to even the youngest children there. Years later, in a 1961 talk, Kendig described the process:

...No one in my school was allowed to ask the child, 'What is it?'...They made a finger painting, and you said well 'tell me about it'. Or what does it represent to you? Or what do you call it...And you can begin...de-identification by the way your teachers speak to the child....I always remember this one little child who made a finger painting, she was probably five. And it was just some brown and some green, and she'd just done this. And we said tell us about it, and what do you call it. She said 'it's Jo-jo in the park.'... Well she had a dog named Jo-jo...in the old days, at least, the teacher would have said, 'well that's not a picture of a dog.' We just said, well you were in the park with Jo-jo? Yes. Then of course it occurred to us that Jo-jo in the park was the way she was petting Jo-jo...But if someone had said 'what is it,' and 'but that doesn't look like a dog to me,' well see what you've done.' [15]

An Educational Experiment

Korzybski left Barstow at the end of February. He did not have great expectations for Kendig's chances of making any significant change at the school. He considered the atmosphere in Kansas City too hidebound and parochial to keep her from 'breaking her head'. But over the next few years he would stay in close contact and do what he could to help her.

Kendig hired two new staff members. The new English teacher Sarah Michie, with a PhD in English philology and linguistics, began to implement a year-long program for the eighth grade that Kendig had wanted to get started. Dona Worral Brown—who had a Masters degree in English language and linguistics—became Kendig's administrative assistant. As described in an article she later wrote for *The Modern Language Journal*, Dr. Michie's work at Barstow did not appear especially korzybskian.[16] She left after a year to take a university post. Mrs. Brown, who had become much interested in general semantics, took over her position at Barstow.

Kendig wanted to reform the teaching at all grade levels. As she said in a 1940 talk on "New Approaches to Education", given before a group of Vasser alumnae:

At Barstow I was convinced of the harm done by the 'old' verbalistic education, and equally convinced of the actually maladjustive tendencies of the 'new' progressive education, centered on the student's own experience without supplying him with a system and method of evaluating his own experience in the light of the socio-cultural-scientific race experience. In applying General Semantics in our developmentally organized program, I found a satisfactory blending of the best features of the 'old' discipline and the 'new' experiential progressive education."[17]

Initially she and Mrs. Brown worked on remedial programs for individual students and in teacher training. All teachers were asked to study *Science and Sanity* and Korzybski returned to Barstow in mid-October of 1935 to give a five-week-long seminar to the faculty (three evening lectures per week plus private conferences with each teacher). Mrs. Brown, who had been studying general semantics with Kendig, considered this a benefit. But many of the other teachers didn't respond very well, as she described many years later:

Korzybski had come to give a "short" seminar and stayed and stayed. The situation was certainly 'caviar to the general' of Kansas City. The good people were already suffering from the shock of the new. The faculty was in rebellion. They didn't want to 'waste time' on Korzybski's lectures and on reading *Science and Sanity*. Furthermore, the parents were baffled by the cachet of Marjorie Mercer Kendig. She was a beautiful and intelligent woman, but one who didn't fit into their image of a schoolmarm.[18]

At the end of 1935 at an AAAS meeting in St. Louis also attended by Korzybski, Kendig presented a paper to a joint psychology and education session describing her overall approach and initial efforts at Barstow. The paper, entitled "Language Re-Orientation of

High School Curriculum and Scientific Control of Neuro-Linguistic Mechanisms for Better Mental Health and Scholastic Achievement", also described further plans for the yearlong program for the eighth grade, which she wanted to become the school's basic high school and college preparatory course. After replacing Dr. Michie in 1936, Mrs. Brown began implementing this more korzybskian program. (She reported on some of her procedures and results in a paper presented at the 1941 Second American Congress on General Semantics.)[19] She also began an elective course for juniors and seniors, and College Board training classes—all based on general semantics.

Case reports and class records of all students from the eighth grade and above were kept and updated frequently. Students also took semi-annual standardized tests given through the Educational Records Bureau, which the school had joined when Kendig became head. Barstow students could thus be compared "with 1,500 other individuals at the same grade level, and [the] class performance with performances in 145 other private schools." When they began testing in 1934, Barstow placed as "the lowest school in the lowest quartile." Within four years, the school score had climbed to "the bottom of the top percentile".[20] Test results included remarkable increases in many students' I.Q. scores, which led Kendig to later write and publish a paper questioning the fixedness of I.Q.[21]

Despite her observed and measurable success with students, by the fall of 1937 Kendig's time at Barstow had come to an end. As Dona Brown reported:

> ...The board of trustees decided that there must be a change at the top. The school was losing money and was not the kind of harmonious place in which learning and the arts could flourish. Kendig was kept on as educational advisor in absentia for one year. The new principal, I think, tried to make our program work. (Kendig, at least, gave her the benefit of the doubt.) But eventually it was the end of the line for me and the entire faculty. She tried the next year with an entirely new set of teachers, but she failed miserably [with carrying on Kendig's program]...The whole experiment was over and the issue closed.
>
> Many years later, after Korzybski had died, Kendig asked me if I thought our program at the school had taken off. My answer was "yes" and "no." We simply did not have the resources and the financial support that such a program needed to make it fly. Or perhaps we tried to do too much in too short a time.[22]

In a short 1983 biography written after Kendig's death, Charlotte Schuchardt Read summarized Kendig's experiment at Barstow School thusly: "It was an ambitious, brave attempt, unequalled before or since then. In later years other teachers have dreamed of such a possibility, but no one else has so far attempted such a far-reaching re-orientation of an entire school."[23]

The First American Congress for General Semantics

On February 16, Korzybski gave a presentation at a regional conference of the Progressive Education Association in Kansas City. Several days later, having finished his lectures at Barstow School, he left for Lawrence, Kansas, about 40 miles to the west, where he gave a presentation at the University of Kansas on "Language and Mental Hygiene". From there he took a train to Seattle and thence 100 miles southeast to Ellensburg, arriving on February 28, a day before the start of the First American Congress for General Semantics. This gave him a little bit of time to meet Joseph Trainor and the other organizers, check out the environs of the Washington State Normal School, and have a look at the papers being presented—a number of them to be read by Trainor or others, since many of the authors were not attending in person.

Korzybski, happy to at least have had his expenses paid, had minimum expectations about the Congress. Once there however, he felt pleasantly surprised at the place, the people, and the program. As he jokingly recalled years later, "I expected an old barn and 2 [and] 1/2 members, the half being myself. That's all I expected. Now I found a beautiful little college. Very well organized. A beautiful hall. Lecture hall, and something like 150 people, and they had a very nice program then."[24]

Trainor and Potts presented their papers on their classroom research. Selden Smyser, talked on "Subverbal, Verbal and Superverbal Logics". Also present, Professor E. O. Sisson of Reed College spoke on "Basic Technique of Language". Papers, read by others, included ones by W. Burridge, M.D. (Dean of the Medical Faculty and Professor of Physiology at King George's Medical College in Lucknow, India); Cassius Keyser (an excerpt from his *Scripta Mathematica* review of *Science and Sanity*); geneticist Harry H. Laughlin; John Lynn (case reports on his two alcoholic patients); Roderick Macdonald (a Harvard biologist and friend of the Korzybskis who had just become director of the Philadelphia Zoo); William Malisoff (editor of the *Philosophy of Science* journal); social worker Sydney Maslon; businessman Charles Owen; Oliver Reiser; W. E. Ritter; University of California Education Professor C. E. Rugh; A. Ranger Tyler; penology researcher Miriam Van Waters; University of Kansas psychologist Raymond H. Wheeler; and Cora Williams. Korzybski gave three addresses pulled from his "Outline"—one to an audience of students and faculty on "The Significance of General Semantics" at the start of the Conference on Friday morning, March 1; one that evening to an audience of physicians on "The Relation of General Semantics to Medicine"; and the last, on "Education and General Semantics", the following afternoon to an audience that included the Yakima Valley Schoolmasters Club. The variety of general-semantics applications and research presented at the Congress, and the interest engendered there—so soon after the appearance of *Science and Sanity*—seemed to him quite remarkable.

Korzybski felt especially delighted to have Burridge's contribution at the Congress, having encountered Burridge's four books *Excitability: A Cardiac Study*, *A New Physiology of Sensation*, *A New Physiological Psychology*, and *Alcohol and Anaesthesia*, in the latter part of 1934. Since then he had been enthusiastically recommending them to 'one and all' as important for the electro-colloidal outlook which they presented and which he considered essential for a more process-oriented understanding of medicine and nervous system functioning. Korzybski continued to recommend the books in subsequent years. Burridge also had an invited paper at the 1941 General Semantics Congress. Korzybski's enthusiasm notwithstanding, after 1935 the colloidal point of view (until then a quite lively focus of bio-medical research) suffered a severe decline in fashion from which it has not recovered.

The Congress received quite extensive press coverage—and not only from the Normal School's *Campus Crier* and the Ellensburg *Evening Record*. In the first few days of March 1935, one could find stories on the Congress with headlines such as the following in local newspapers—nationwide and coast-to-coast: "Most People 'Unsane,' Polish Scientist Says", "Average Man Beset by Fears, Semantic Congress Hears" (*New York Herald-Tribune*, March 2); "HAS AID TO HAPPINESS Polish Scientist Introduces New Light on Semantics. Alfred Korzybski Says Man Can Be Immunized Against Vicious Propaganda" (St. Joseph, Mo. *News-Press*, March 2); "SEMANTICS HELD 'WAY TO GENIUS' Polish Scientist Avers Present Tutoring "Manufactures Morons"—Lives by Inference" (Spokane, Washington *Spokesman-Review*, March 3).

Korzybski with Robert McConnell (President of Washington State Normal School) on his right and Joseph Trainor on his left at the First American Congress for General Semantics, March 1935.

After the Congress, Korzybski seemed to be flying high. From Ellensburg he returned to Seattle where he had two days of lectures and meetings at the University of Washington, organized by Dean Uhl of the School of Education. An article on his visit in the *University of Washington Daily* included the following, "Almost 60 years old, the Count, mathematical philosopher, author, lecturer and World War veteran,...explained that he had slept just nine hours during the last 10 days, but that he was used to hard work."

The "Strolling Around the Town" section in the following week's March 11 *Seattle Times* contained this snippet:

> Aside from the astonishing subject matter of addresses by Count Alfred Korzybski, Polish mathematical philosopher, who was in Seattle last week, two things are notable in his speaking. One is the count's fine grasp of blunt Anglo-Saxon terms, his fine sense for injecting them as punctuation. The second is his constant and energetic smoking, for which he uses—or abuses—an amber cigarette holder.
>
> Two friends spent a hectic two hours before one of Count Korzybski's addresses, in escorting him on a frantic trip to a pipe hospital. The cigarette holder suffered a breakdown, and until an expert overhauled it, the count's lecture itself was in jeopardy.
>
> The evening Count Korzybski left for San Francisco, the amber holder disappeared. The count was philosophical about it, naturally enough, but friends were happy to hear the next day that the holder had been found in the count's suite at the Hotel Edmond Meany and had been rushed on its way to its owner.[25]

It took Korzybski another month to get home. From Berkeley, where he gave five lectures at the Williams Institute, he traveled to Los Angeles to spend a few days there and in Pasadena, where he met in person his friend R.B. Haseldon, curator of manuscripts at the Huntington Library, with whom he had been corresponding for several years. Haseldon, who had developed a considerable interest in Korzybski's work, seemed full of fun. He had invented a cocktail which he called "The Korzybski" with the following formula, as reported third-hand later on in a newspaper snippet:

"...You take a large cocktail shaker and place therein: 3 parts gin, 2 parts applejack, 3 parts dry vermouth, 1 part sweet vermouth. Stand this in the refrigerator for one hour, then drink and note results. Better still, have someone note the results for you. You soon reach the nonverbal level, where one can point, but cannot utter."[26]

In addition to seeing friends in Southern California, Korzybski had wanted to get a paid lecture or two, but only managed an informal talk at Haseldon's home, before returning east. After a stop in Kansas City, he went on to lecture in Chicago and at the University of Michigan–Ann Arbor, and finally at Olivet College in Olivet, Michigan (where his friend Joseph Brewer had recently become President) before getting back to Brooklyn by the second week of April. Mira had literally counted the days until his return. He felt very tired but considered the trip a great success.[27]

Chapter 45
SEMINARS

Tired as he felt, Korzybski took little time for rest. He had more lectures scheduled almost immediately. On April 20 he gave his second lecture at the Galois Institute of Mathematics, run by Hugh Gray Lieber and Lillian R. Lieber of the Math Department of Long Island University in Brooklyn. Alfred and Mira had met the Liebers early in 1934 when they invited Alfred to speak soon after the opening of the Lieber's institute. They had founded it as a vehicle to make mathematics more enticing to high school and university students as well as the general public. For many years, the Liebers organized frequent lectures there and published a series of books on mathematics, logic, and physics written by Lillian in 'free verse' form and illustrated by Hugh's playful drawings. Their work, influenced by Keyser, who often lectured at the institute, developed a wide and devoted audience drawn to their humanistic approach to science and mathematics. Their writings, which continued into the early 1960s, included *The Einstein Theory of Relativity* (1936), *The Education of T.C. MITS (The Celebrated Man In The Street): What Modern Mathematics Means To You* (1942), *Infinity* (1953) and *Human Values and Science, Art and Mathematics* (1961). The Leibers remained lifelong friends and supporters of Korzybski.

A few days after the Galois lecture, Korzybski gave another talk at the Columbia University Sociology Department. Then in early May, he lectured at the Wistar Institute of Biological Research in Philadelphia, where he had a chance to meet his friend George Coghill in person (Coghill, in poor health, would leave Wistar at the end of the year). Korzybski would give more lectures that year and throughout the rest of his career. However, he was about to begin a new phase in the presentation of his work—training seminars.

Alfred's old friend and student, psychiatrist Douglas Gordon Campbell, had called him from Chicago and invited him to give concurrent seminars there starting May 20—two weeks at Northwestern University and four weeks at the International House of the University of Chicago. Alfred accepted. Campbell had been at the University of Chicago since 1931 and had become not only Assistant Clinical Professor of Psychiatry there but also the head of psychiatry at the University Student Health Service and an attending physician at the Cook County Psychopathic Hospital. Both he and his colleague at the Health Service, Charles B. Congdon, had read *Science and Sanity* and had begun to use general semantics with their clinic and private patients. They were eager to see what Korzybski could do.

When Alfred arrived for the Chicago seminar he found that the two psychiatrists had packed the audience with their patients, not only the mildly neurotic but also a number of seriously disturbed ones, some brought directly from hospital confinement. The results of the Chicago seminars astonished not only the two psychiatrists but Alfred as well. Even with some of the most deadened and disturbed individuals there, he seemed to be able to get through and bring some life, although that hardly represented a cure. Campbell and Congden became enthusiastic boosters of his work.

Over the next few years, Korzybski would work quite a bit with seriously disturbed people. He gave a number of his subsequent seminars to groups of patients in mental hospitals selected to participate by their psychiatrists. Since he considered his work educational and preventive and was not a psychiatrist himself, he preferred teaching the psychiatrists and working himself with the unconfined and so-called normal un-sane. Still, given the continuum of sanity, there was going to be an overlap and when he first began teaching he did not always succeed in maintaining the clear boundaries he would insist upon later. From 1938 on, he did his best to screen out seriously disturbed students and would allow those under psychiatric care to attend Institute of General Semantics seminars only if they had permission from their psychiatrists.

Seminars

Not working with the seriously disturbed, but teaching the everyday un-sane would become the central focus of his work. The seminar format would give him the chance to do what he couldn't do in one or even several lectures—not just to get people's attention and interest, but to begin to train them towards consciousness of abstracting. Many interested people had not read *Science and Sanity*, and of those who did, many seemed to miss the meat of it. In his seminars, which could extend over a number of days and even weeks, he would have time to cover his system 'deductively'—i.e., showing the systemic interconnections between the formulations—while also providing lots of examples along the way, with the ultimate goal of helping as many students as possible by "rubbing in" what he felt they needed in order to deal better with their life difficulties. He was not there just to expound theory. He wanted results.

After the first two seminars in Chicago, he returned briefly to Brooklyn and then left for an intensive schedule of teaching he had lined up for the remainder of 1935:

* July 29 to August 20 – a seminar in Berkeley at Cora Williams Junior College;

* August 27 to October 13 – two seminars in Los Angeles organized by Vocha (Bertha) Fiske, a former teacher for Cora Williams, presently working in the California Department of Education who had attended Korzybski's March lectures in Berkeley; and

* October 16 to November 22 – a seminar for teachers at Barstow School.

During this time, he established the basic structure for the many subsequent seminars he would give. Eventually, he found he could cover what he wanted to cover in about 40 hours of lecture. And over the next 15 years, he would continue to develop both the content and presentation of his seminars (which, of course, were not entirely unrelated.)

Regarding content, throughout his subsequent teaching career Korzybski would find new examples and stories, and new demonstrations to illustrate his points. He would also continue to develop his formulations, which—as a visualizer—he liked to diagram. Over the years he would thus develop a collection of blackboard notes consisting, in large part, of such diagrams, which he used in each seminar to represent the significant formulations he wanted students to remember and use. For him the diagrams had great significance since he wanted to encourage what he called 'eye-mindedness' in his students.

Regarding his presentation, in the beginning period of his seminar-giving he would start with the basic formulations, what he called "the baby stuff". In time, as he expected students to have read his work, or various popularizations of it, he found it more effective to move this material towards the end of the seminar. By providing more preliminary background to show the complexities involved, this order might reduce people's tendency to dismiss 'the baby stuff'.

In his seminars, Korzybski became known for his "footnotes"—digressions wherein he expanded on a topic, provided an example, or made a connection with something else he considered important. This led to his "peculiar style of lecturing". Kendig, who attended many of his seminars, would describe it as,

> ...a non-linear method of developing his exposition of non-aristotelian orientations by going round and round in widening circles, turning back to some example given at the beginning to illustrate a mechanism of his later lectures. He used shocking examples from his study in mental hospitals, from psychiatry, from his own experience with deeply maladjusted people, criminals, etc., to (as he called it) 'get under the skins' of the class, to 'shake them up'. He used examples from daily life, from the history of science, from mathematics. At times he was elegant, crisp, suave—at others, humorous, discursive. Often his face, his hands, conveyed as much as his words and diagrams. One educator said he was 'the most powerful and effective teacher' he knew, 'a master of pedagogy'. Another said he was 'the worst, should study pedagogy'. People were seldom neutral about him, what he did, or how he did it. The more he shook their complacency, irritated them by 'rubbing in' the method, the more they learned. He insisted that anyone who wished to, could enroll for a seminar. 'Because a general method of evaluation,' he said, 'has to work with anybody in any human activity or it's no good.' Professors, doctors, psychiatrists, artists, researchers, young college students, businessmen, social workers, laborers, etc., all sat in the same classes. This may all sound chaotic; it was effective.[1]

Korzybski acknowledged that the quality of his lectures could vary and sometimes suffer, especially if he felt preoccupied with something pressing or if he hadn't sufficiently planned. Until the end of his life, he sought to improve the quality of his presentations. For this purpose, he came to have an assistant sitting close by him and taking notes, who could give him a 'flap' during the lecture to remind him of where he had left off if he got lost in his order of presentation after an extended footnote. The assistant's notes also helped him to review what he had covered in the course of the day's talk. In a day-long teaching session, say for six hours with a break for lunch, he would do a mid-day 'course correction' looking over the assistant's notes, checking off the diagrams he had discussed, deciding whether to move on to another topic or to spiral around again for another turn on a subject he felt needed more elaboration. An end-of-day recap with the assistant helped him review the day's performance.

As Kendig said, some people liked his teaching style and some didn't. One who did, Goddard Binkley—at the time a 23-year-old pre-med student—took several seminars in Chicago with Korzybski in 1942 and 1943. For him, "General Semantics had a distinctly purifying, immensely stimulating, and thoroughly therapeutic effect on my feelings, thoughts and general attitude towards life and the world." He described his impression of Korzybski lecturing:

> I looked and listened with rapt attention as Korzybski talked and gesticulated, absorbed in his every expression, gesture and movement. He constantly illustrated his concepts with diagrams and symbols and sometimes, little mechanical devices, like a small electric fan or a match box. His talk was punctuated with small quick movements of his hands and fingers, pointing for emphasis, making quotation marks in the air, and, most characteristic of all, indicating an "et cetera, et cetera," with a quick ripple-like motion of his hand. He was a short heavy-set man with a large, totally bald head. He wore rimless glasses with thick lenses. He spoke deliberately with a deep Polish accent. He conveyed great understanding, warmth, and love for—but sometimes an irritable impatience with—his fellow human beings.[2]

Extensionalize

From the start, Korzybski considered what he was doing as training. He aimed at "extensionalization", i.e., getting his students to 'think' in terms of 'facts' about themselves and their problems. He had used the term, "extensionalization"—the name of a process or an act—once in his 1934 "Outline", and he used it again in 1935. Indeed, by the end of that year, he had turned it into a verb—"to extensionalize".

In November, after his last seminar of the year, he stayed in the Midwest to conduct further business in Chicago with Campbell and Congden, and to prepare two papers for presentation at the 97th annual, end-of-year meeting of the AAAS in St. Louis, where Kendig was also presenting.[3]

The first paper, which he gave at the Psychology Section meeting on December 31, had the potentially tongue-tying title of "Neuro-Semantic and Neuro-Linguistic Mechanisms of Extensionalization: General Semantics as a Natural Experimental Science". The paper, as its title suggests, focused especially on neurological and psychiatric aspects of Korzybski's developing work. His paper seems to have impressed not only some of his professional listeners (it was published the following July in the *American Journal of Psychiatry*), but also a newspaper reporter attending. The next day's *St. Louis Globe Democrat* included the following report of Korzybski's talk at the end of a general article on the conference:

"Science of Man."
The possibility of establishing a "science of man" was discussed yesterday before a subsection on psychology by Count Alfred Korzybski of Brooklyn, N.Y.
[The article quoted almost exactly from the last paragraph of Korzybski's paper.] "The white race has come to a real impasse, the actual conditions of life are shaped by extensional science while our inner orientations and language remain intensional," he stated. "Increasing maladjustment must follow, as it actually does. Either we return to primitive states and abolish extensional science and then perhaps survive, or we bring about our orientations to conform with the actualities of our lives, in other words extensionalize them."[4]

Korzybski gave his second paper, originally titled "Extensionalization in Mathematics, Mathematical Physics, and General Education: General Semantics" two days later on January 2, 1936 to the AAAS Mathematics Section. It surely qualifies as one of his most succinct presentations of his work—general semantics stripped down to its roots in mathematical method. Whatever the response of the mathematicians to the paper, the notion of "extensionalization" had certainly captured Korzybski's attention. Over the next few years, he wrote two more papers with that main title and different subtitles for AAAS mathematical venues, although other than abstracts they never appeared in AAAS publications. (Korzybski later changed the 'subtitle' of this first "Extensionalization in Mathematics,..." paper from "General Semantics" to "Paper I – The Extensional Method" and eventually published it himself along with the others in the series.)

The two St. Louis papers had importance beyond their general emphasis on extensionalization. In *Science and Sanity*, Korzybski had used Indexes, Dates, Quotes, Hyphens, and Etc., but he had not summarized them sharply as part of a single mechanism. Although the 1934 "Outline", referred in general terms to "linguistic extensional devices" it said nothing specific about them. For the first time, in the St. Louis papers, Korzybski used "extensional devices" as the common summary term for Indexes, etc., which he then listed and discussed. In retrospect, it may seem obvious to us to do this. But to create a common term for them, Korzybski had to take himself to another, higher level of abstraction in order to clearly enough see the similarities of the different devices. The common term made them more usable and teachable. And the extensional devices served as essential tools for the work of extensionalizing his seminar students, the ultimate purpose of his teaching.

Laboratory Work

The group format of the seminar allowed Korzybski to introduce his work to more than one person at a time. It also allowed students, often 40 or 50 per class, to observe and interact with and so to learn from each other. But the intellectual, i.e. verbal, understanding of general semantics that could be gained from seminar lectures was not enough. Individual students typically needed individualized help to apply the extensional method to their personal lives—what Korzybski referred to as the "laboratory work".[5]

From his first seminar in Chicago, Korzybski offered this "laboratory work"—in personal interviews—to all of his seminar students. He came to see the personal interview as a necessary part of his teaching. As the process for the interviews evolved, a student would provide a written history of him/herself and whatever he/she wanted to work on. Reading this statement let Korzybski begin to visualize the person's life situation, which included how the person talked about things. Then in one or more sessions, Korzybski would work to help the student extensionalize his problems and himself.

Throughout his life, Korzybski had worked as a translator. The interviews seemed much like a job of translation: how to translate his student's personal problems from intension (verbal definitions in which they had gotten 'stuck') to extension ('facts'). Sometimes another form of representation could help someone change his/her approach to a situation. For example, to someone who had a rough time with "Papa" and "Mama", Korzybski might suggest referring to them instead in the third person, as "Mr. and Mrs. Jones", or, when addressing them directly, to do so by first name, e.g., "Richard and Darlene"—with the parent's permission, of course. So 'simple' a change could often make a significant difference in a habitually sticky relationship between an adult child and his or her parents.

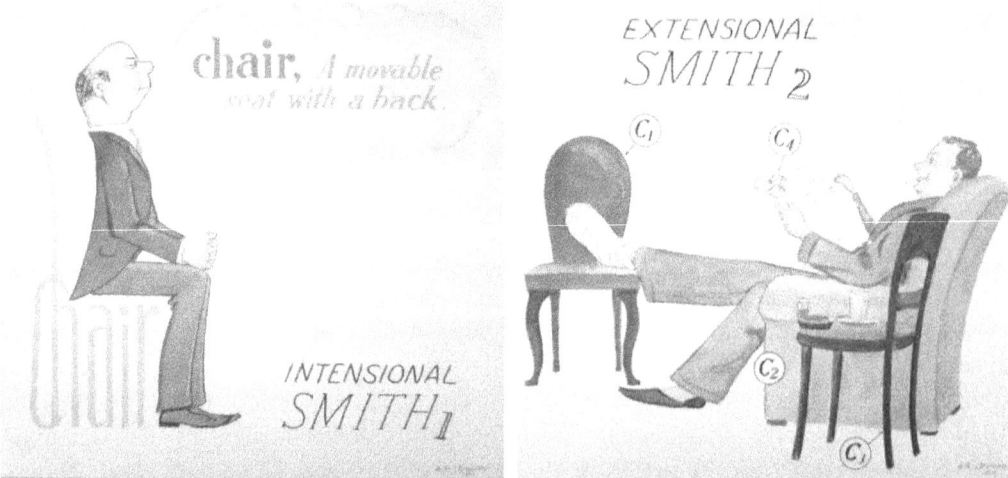

'A Chairy Tale' of Intensional Smith$_1$ Versus Extensional Smith$_2$,
Watercolor and Ink drawings for Korzybski by A.B. Stewart, 1940

Using the extensional devices provided a major way to translate a problem situation—to newly represent it—in extensional terms. Korzybski would tell seminar classes about former students he had helped in this way (leaving out identifying information). There was, for example, the case of "the boy out the window". One of Korzybski's early, seminar students had related that, as a five-year-old boy, he had been picked up by his nanny—who supposedly loved him—when she couldn't get him to stop crying. She held him out of the fifth-floor window and told him she would drop him if he didn't stop. He stopped. This single occurence appeared to have shaped his whole life into adulthood. He had troubles with anxiety, with trusting people, with women, etc. In the interview sessions, Korzybski worked with him on dating and indexing. "It took me a long time to make him date his experience. Date the experience, yet what happened twenty-three, [twenty-]four years ago, is not what happened today."[6] The man had to 'sweat'—practicing for about two years—but eventually he no longer suffered from the anxiety that had plagued him most of his life. He was not "the boy out the window" anymore.

Students needed to do more than make a superficial change of words; 'words' in isolation were not enough. The associated neuro-semantic (evaluational) reactions *were not* verbal. To challenge the unspoken assumptions behind problems, new assumptions, new behavior, feelings and experience had to arise as well. Korzybski might do something as simple as getting a student to actually pinch his finger. Saying "I am pinching my finger" was not the same as pinching his finger. A student had to pinch his finger to experience this. Students had to remind themselves of the un-speakable level often. He wanted them to handle the structural differential, to keep it in sight, and to point to it and use it to make sense of a situation or problem. He wanted them to use their hands to make kinesthetic gestures for the devices whenever possible. If the hands weren't available for doing single quotes, you could use your toes. As Korzybski roughly formulated it, these methods bridged the predominantly verbal 'cortical' region of the brain with the 'thalamic'—the pre-verbal, lower-order-of-abstraction, 'sensory'-'emotional' region where people lived, suffered, and could experience deep change. He had tested everything on himself.

To demonstrate a point to a student, he might ask her to play with a simple toy like the spinner sparkler one could buy at Woolworths. (Korzybski would end up with a collection of these in his desk drawer.) Held in the hand, you made the toy's little wheel spin by pumping a spring-loaded slider at the base. The wheel might make sparks but the main point for Korzybski was that by cutting or replacing the wheel to make a fan-shape, you could spin it and see 'a disk where there is no disk'. Campbell had used one of these with a priest who heard voices. The priest was taken with the realization that he could perceive something that 'wasn't there'—that just as his nervous system had constructed the 'disk', it had constructed the voices as well. He played with the device quite often. His auditory hallucinations eventually stopped.

Korzybski's job, as he saw it, required 'holding up a mirror' to his students so they could honestly look at themselves and their reactions. Such self-reflexiveness could apply in the most literal sense. For example, if he saw a deadness in the facial expression of a student, he might ask him or her to practice actually holding up a mirror to look at themselves.

Personal interviews for students were included in the tuition fee. Initially, even after the founding of the Institute of General Semantics, Korzybski tried to see everyone that he could and scheduled the interviews concurrently with his course of lectures. Eventually as the exhausting—for him—character of the interviews became more apparent, he had them scheduled to begin only after he had completed the lectures. He stressed the optional nature of the interviews as well. He found those claiming to be satisfied with their lives might be less likely to come or, if they did, less likely to seriously use it to apply general semantics to personal issues. More's the pity. Korzybski didn't consider it likely that anyone—even a well-trained mathematician or mathematical physicist—could master a general extensional approach to life unless he had first worked to apply it to himself. If a student felt he didn't have any significant personal problems to work on, one couldn't justifiably conclude he didn't have any.

Korzybski would later estimate that about "Ten percent of every class got nothing out of it. Some became my enemies for life." As Kendig phrased it, "When you touch the fundamental verbalisms around which an individual has organized his life pattern, it may be too disturbing for him to face."

> Some 'got it' quickly and as easily fell back into old habits of thinking-feeling. They use the words but not the method. 'They "refused" to work at themselves, he said. Some learned general semantics 'intellectually' (i.e., verbally, 'cortically') knew all the principles and terminology and techniques, but simply could not apply them, change their evaluations, their living reactions. Some 'got it' very slowly, over the years. It apparently had no effect on their lives, their work, and then—something happened.[7]

As to how slowly this 'something' might happen, Kendig quoted a letter that research psychiatrist Charles J. Katz wrote to Korzybski in April 1950 (not having heard yet of his death on March 1 of that year):

> Dear Count Alfred :
>
> I think I owe you a little apology, a vote of thanks, and an explanation. As you recall it was in the summer of 1939 that I first became aware of General Semantics. At that time your and my good friend Dr. ___ [deceased] . . . took me with him to your Seminar. I could 'get' the cortical aspect [verbal] but for some reason the thalamic portion [change in living, feeling] seemed to elude me. However in this last month something apparently has happened. I begin now for the first time to 'feel' that general semantics has something I need and which can help. What the explanation is I do not know—all I can give you is the answer my small son (thirty-four months) gives me—when I ask him why he does this or that, he simply says, 'Well I did it'... just to let you know that sometimes it takes a little while for things to sink in, I remain,
> Semantically yours [8]

From the time he began teaching until the end of his life, the personal interviews with students took a tremendous toll on Korzybski's time and energy. They took up not only the hours of interview time—often with a large portion of a seminar's participants—but the hours of personal follow-up as well. He encouraged his students to write to him in detail to let him know how they were doing. He, in turn, would respond to these letters with his detailed analysis, advice, and encouragement. (Korzybski's large correspondence with students, their letters to him, as well as their autobiographical statements, were destroyed or returned to the students soon after his death. A small number of letters were retained in the Institute files with students' permission, their names cut out from the letters.) After the founding of the Institute of General Semantics, a number of the Institute trustees tried to convince Korzybski to stop providing interviews. Korzybski refused. Although he readily admitted their taxing nature, he felt compelled to provide a laboratory wherein he could help his students learn to apply what he taught—the main point, after all.

The Alka-Seltzer Case

With his students, Korzybski was willing to do what he thought it took to get results. He would later recount an interview at one of his early seminars with an anxious and withdrawn college teacher in her late twenties who hallucinated a skeleton. She told Korzybski that a teenaged boy had molested her when she was three. Her mother had told her about it when she was in her teens. The little girl had been left alone with the boy for only a few minutes. The mother returned before he had time to do any physical damage. Sitting at his desk across from the young woman, Korzybski guessed her skeleton hallucination had something to do with her early childhood experience. He kept various items on the desk and happened to see the long glass cylinder of an Alka-Seltzer bottle in his field of vision:

....It occurred to me, which is quite natural, that she felt a 'bone' between her legs, bone. No harm done, except fear. You understand that the fear was there all right, a little child having a bone between her little legs, and it occurred to me that eventually that hallucination of a skeleton, bone, may have originated from that, to her, fearful experience...

I explained to her that the male organ is more or less like an Alka-Seltzer bottle, and I had it on my desk. I explained to her that this is possibly the combination of the memory of a bone between her little legs, then I showed her the Alka-Seltzer bottle and made her handle the Alka-Seltzer bottle.

...It is beyond description, the terror, the horror, when she had to handle the Alka-Seltzer bottle. This was confirming, so to say, my guess, that it may be the origin of the skeleton, the bone between her leg. The terror and horror she exhibited handling the Alka-Seltzer bottle. It means, I hit the nail on the head. I made her overcome that horror or fear. She had to, through skirts and everything, it means between her legs use the Alka-Seltzer bottle, poke herself with it—still worse trouble, horror, terror; my god, I have seen such terror only on the battlefields.

Well, I used to have some fruit [on my desk], I had a banana—yes, we have no bananas—well, I had a banana...I explained to her that the male organ is more or less like the Alka-Seltzer bottle. Then I explained the male organ is not as stiff as the bottle and then I picked up the banana and explained to her that a banana in this direction may feel like a bone, but this way it is flexible and what not. I made her actually handle the banana. Still worse horror. I didn't have any pity, I wanted her to overcome the hallucination of that skeleton which ruined her life, because she was ruined in the head here. She put still more horror, suffering, handling the banana. Of course I was explaining to her the whole situation, the origin of her hallucinations, to make her conscious of it, why the hallucinations happened.

Then I took her to the college museum where there was an actual skeleton. It happened to be a male skeleton. She was a small thing, frightened to death; she cuddled to me, I put my arm around her and she had to play, get acquainted—I called the skeleton her 'boyfriend'. And I had to protect her and make her get acquainted with the skeleton. And because she was protected, like a little child she began to poke her fingers in the eyes of the skeleton, handle, handle. I simply wanted to eliminate the hallucination of that skeleton; so she had to inspect the skeleton. I explained to her, among others, that the skeleton has no Alka-Seltzer bottle there; that muscles, nerves hurt, the bones don't hurt. And I took her little hand; she had a very little hand. My hand is very strong; I hurt her, deliberately—you know how you can hurt squeezing the hand too hard. I deliberately hurt her. She didn't wince even; paid no attention to it. I ask her to shake hands with her boyfriend the skeleton; see whether the skeleton can hurt her. I was hurting her deliberately. She shook the hands and inspected the hand of the skeleton; naturally the skeleton didn't hurt her.

That's all there is to it; she had to inspect and get acquainted with the skeleton. I called him deliberately her 'boyfriend', and she was left with orders to go daily to the college museum to shake hands with her 'boyfriend', which she did for months. Do you know, the hallucination disappeared. On my part it was, if you wish, extensional guessing. It was nothing but guessing, but it did work. It took her about six months visiting daily her 'boyfriend', shaking hands with him, the skeleton. Do you realize that after six months of daily performance not with me; I explained of course that she has to do it alone—the hallucination disappeared. A medical man may know what it means if we can eliminate hallucinations. Hallucinations are extremely serious; it means a person who has hallucinations is very seriously ill. Well after six months hallucinations disappeared.

She was in a way a beautiful young woman, but shy, afraid of life, retired, afraid of men, I don't know what kind of a mess she had. I have seen her later; she became a beautiful young woman. She was an ugly duckling at first; then she became very popular with the college fellows, then she became more and more popular with the college fellows, she changed physically from an ugly duckling to a beautiful young woman and hallucinations disappeared. It was only one meeting remember, and the performance of what I described apparently did the trick. Oh, by now she is married woman with babies and so on; but even when I was having my seminar she already was changing and becoming more interested in life, not skeletons. She was losing the fear of men, she became more and more attractive, even in the three weeks I carried on the seminar...She had to perform, perform. If she would have never been forced to become acquainted with a skeleton, she would not have overcome the hallucination.[9]

Neuro-Semantic Relaxation

At the first seminar in Chicago, during the first personal interviews he gave there, Korzybski made an interesting and, for him, pivotal discovery. He conducted the interviews in his hotel suite, which had a narrow table where he sat across from a student during a session. He heard more than one tale of woe. "The carpet after a few hours", he said, "was wet from tears."[10] Seeing the 'unhappiness' frozen on a student's face, he often felt impelled to reach across and touch it in a gesture of comfort. He hated to see such a face "tense as hell".[11] He wanted to relax it. And the student's face seemed to invariably soften and relax. If the student began to 'make a face' again during the session, Korzybski would quietly reach across once more to relax him. It seemed to make a difference in the student's attitude, at least during the session. Afterwards, accompanying the student to the door, he would often pat him on the back, shoulder, or arm, making a more or less instinctive gesture of connection, reassurance, and calm as they said goodbye. More than one student returning for a second interview would ask Korzybski to repeat what he had done to relax them. Korzybski began to wonder about what had happened, to consider what he had done with so little plan.

He realized he had done this kind of thing most of his life, first with horses. He wouldn't get on a horse, even one he knew, without approaching it first and making a friendly physical contact. And having trained wild horses, he had learned how to relax a skittish one this way too. What had worked with horses had worked with people as well. At St. Elizabeths he remembered that upon finishing an interview with patients there (not the kind of consultative interview with students he had just started to do) he would sometimes give them a farewell pat which seemed to leave them in a somewhat brighter mood.

Now his students were coming back to him and asking him to purposefully repeat "his friendly grasp of their arm, or gentle shake-up of [their] distorted, worried face."[12] He now began to consciously experiment with what he had first done in an off-handed kind of way. His students began to do it to themselves as well and a new technique evolved, which he came to call "semantic relaxation" or "neuro-semantic relaxation".

The label would make no sense to those who continued to restrict the term 'semantic' to the realm of verbal 'meaning'. But since for Korzybski, evaluation or 'semantic reaction' related to *non-verbal* organism-as-a-whole-in-an-environment responses, he came to feel that dealing with the musculature in this way had critical importance in reducing 'emotional' tension and thus in becoming more extensional. He came to believe the technique had its main effect not on the tension of the voluntary musculature, which we can feel, but on the involuntary, insensate musculature of the blood vessels, which affected the blood pressure. (He had some confirmation of this from the effects which the procedure seemed to have on normalizing the blood pressures of students who practiced it regularly.) A few years later, he would write in his "Introduction To The Second Edition" of *Science and Sanity*:

> We are never aware of this particular steady kind of 'emotional' tension, which involves hidden fears, anxieties, uncertainties, frustrations, etc., and through nervous mechanisms of projection colour harmfully our attitudes toward the world and life in general. Such conditions result in defensiveness, which is no defense, but a wasteful, useless drain on the limited nervous capacities.[13]

Korzybski later became fond of Dave Breger's 1944 cartoon which showed a tough-looking drill sergeant, hands on hips, yelling at a group of frightened looking recruits: "You, on the end! Wipe that opinion off your face!" Whatever its mechanism, semantic relaxation seemed to help students wipe their opinions off their faces. It became a regular part of the seminar training (usually put at the tail-end of Korzybski's lectures). First, he would explain the origin and theory of the technique and demonstrate it with a male volunteer. Then the class would break up into small groups (men and women separated) where they would practice on themselves with the help of one of Alfred's assistants.

Although Korzybski saw it as primarily a self-help method, it could be done by a practitioner on someone else as well. Korzybski became quite adept at applying the technique to others with quite noticeable effects. Goddard Binkley, who later studied with F. M. Alexander and became a well-known teacher of Alexander's technique of postural education, described his experience with Korzybski:

> ...Stripped to my shorts and seated on a chair facing Korzybski who was also seated on a chair, he gently took fleshy parts of my body in the palm of one hand, flexed the palm with straight fingers and then, gently pulling the flesh-muscle away from the bone, shook it gently and released his hand. This procedure he followed on all the more fleshy parts and in a different way on the face and hands. ...Afterwards, when I walked down the street from the Institute to my car, I felt light, free and floating, as though I'd shed a hundred burdens.[14]

A few of Korzybski's students would write about the technique and develop it further, but after his death it fell into disuse, without the research Korzybski seemed to think it deserved.[15]

Chapter 46
"SHOOT ALL THE MOTHERS!"

One day—probably in late May or early June 1935, while Alfred was away doing his first seminars in Chicago—Kiki Netouche had begun to drag herself along the floor of the Korzybskis' Brooklyn studio apartment. Something wasn't right. Mira bundled her up at once and rushed with her to Philadelphia to get help from their friend, zoologist Roderick Macdonald, who as noted before had taken over as head of the Philadelphia Zoo. Macdonald and the veterinarians there couldn't do anything to save the poor monkey who had somehow fractured a rib and punctured a lung. Kiki died at the zoo that night. Mira felt heartbroken. Barbara Polakov wrote to her: "Dear Bereaved One, Walter and I read with great regret of your Kiki's departure to a better (at least we hope so) world."[1] Still, Mira had the other monkey. And Alfred would be back soon.

But not for long. After briefly returning home in July, he had gone off again for his seminars in Berkeley, Los Angeles, and Kansas City, which finished at the end of November. From there he went to Chicago. At the end of the year, he went to St. Louis to deliver his extensionalization papers at the AAAS meeting. He then returned to Chicago where he had more business with Campbell and Congden. And there, in mid-January 1936, he got disturbing news from John Lynn about Mira, whom he hadn't seen for months.

Mira had felt terribly unhappy with Alfred away so long. She not only missed him but worried he was driving himself too hard—working too much, not sleeping or eating enough, and drinking too much. To some extent she may have been right about these things but the worrying certainly didn't do her any good. In such a state, she had not been taking care of herself either, had not been eating enough, and was losing weight, looking 'thin', and not feeling well at all. Lynn, the young psychiatrist at McLean Hospital who had become an enthusiastic student of general semantics, had arranged medical tests and examinations for her at a Boston hospital. On January 16, Lynn sent Alfred the following telegram: "Imperative To See You In New York January Eighteenth And Nineteenth Stop Two Weeks Ago Discovered Countess Has Cancer Of Intestines As Yet She Does Not Know Stop." The same day Alfred got a telegram from Mira, then back in Brooklyn; her only urgency seemed to be about Alfred's business with the Chicago and Boston-area psychiatrists, not about herself.[2]

Alfred got back to Brooklyn as soon as he could. With Alfred home again, Mira seemed better. She started to eat more and even showed a fondness for sweets, not typical for her. But she and Alfred agreed she should go to Boston for more tests. By the end of February, having received a thorough examination at Massachusetts General Hospital, she was given a clean bill of health.[3] So much for the 'intestinal cancer'. The alarming diagnosis that Lynn had shot off in his telegram to Alfred turned out to be completely wrong.

Cambridge

Whatever other interests Alfred had with the Chicago and Boston-area psychiatrists, he was after financial support. It did not appear that book sales and seminar income alone were going to allow him to continue his work in the way he wanted. He had become increasingly convinced he would require extra funding, either private (foundation or otherwise) or government-based. Since the mental hygiene benefits of his work seemed more and more obvious, getting the support of psychiatrists could help him to attract such funding.

Among psychiatrists, he had detected a growing conscious need for what he felt he could provide with his work. He had read with great interest a 1933 booklet published by the National Committee for Mental Hygiene, *Psychiatry in Medical Education*, which emphasized the need for psychiatric instruction in basic medical education. This confirmed his own view that, as he wrote in the paper he delivered to the AAAS Psychology Section, "...medicine which neglects psychiatry represents nothing more than glorified veterinary science." He had gone a step further in that paper with a challenge to psychiatrists:

> All human psycho-logical reactions ultimately represent problems of *evaluation*, and all psychopathological mechanisms, problems of *misevaluation*. How can psychiatry and psychotherapy become *scientific* and so more *efficient* if psychiatrists neglect General Semantics which discloses the mechanisms of "normal function" and the general factors of evaluation which made science what it is.[4]

Some psychiatrists had taken up his challenge—at least to the extent of paying attention. Despite the fact that the *American Journal of Psychiatry* had not reviewed *Science and Sanity*, Korzybski's St. Louis paper grabbed the notice of the journal's editor, Clarence B. Farrar, M.D. with whom he was corresponding. Farrar would publish the paper in the July 1936 issue. This, the first of a number of appearances by Korzybski in that journal, seems especially remarkable given Alfred's lack of psychiatric, medical, or higher academic credentials.

Older and esteemed psychiatrists like White, Paton, Meyers, and Jeliffe had already endorsed his work. (Jeliffe's complimentary review of *Science and Sanity* was published in the September 1935 issue of the *Journal of Nervous and Mental Disease*.) Now at the start of 1936, with Campbell and Congdon in Chicago and Lynn in the Boston area, he had three close and enthusiastic students (other than Graven) among the younger generation of psychiatrists.

Campbell and Congdon, already established in psychiatry as teachers and clinicians, and Lynn, still in his residency, all felt excited about the results they were getting with the 'semantic method', as Congdon referred to it. By early 1936, the three psychiatrists were in contact with each other. Korzybski's work gave them a theoretical framework and set of techniques for a more directive approach to therapy. As psychiatrists they were becoming educators, teaching their patients how to examine, challenge, and change their attitudes, beliefs, language, etc. The three men represented a pioneering korzybskian tributary feeding a larger stream just emerging at that time in psychotherapy—it would not have a name until the final decades of the 20th Century—the *cognitive-behavioral* approach.

Over the next few years Campbell, who had already published a number of articles in psychiatric journals, would produce additional articles on general semantics. Congdon never wrote anything for publication that I have been able to find, although he remained an accomplished speaker active in the field of general semantics throughout the 1940s. And Lynn—as it turned out—would soon move onto other things.

But at the start of 1936, Lynn was bursting with enthusiasm for Korzybski and his work. He had given a number of presentations on general semantics to the medical staff of McLean Hospital and by late May had also designed a very ambitious and intensive Korzybski-inspired, post-graduate study program for himself. He wanted to study "human symbolic functions...in the language of primitives, children, mathematics, dreams, etc." and "the pathological, neuro-physiological processes mediating these language functions."[5]

The program, which he planned to start later that year at Harvard, included not only neurology and anthropology coursework, but also logic and scientific method as well as tutorials in mathematics starting with trigonometry and analytical geometry, calculus, and probability. The psychiatric resident certainly seemed to have been bitten hard by a korzybskian bug. He was friendly with both Mira and Alfred and was writing to both. He had helped Mira with her medical issues. Both Korzybskis had visited him and he had visited them in Brooklyn.

Alfred had also gone a number of times to McLean where he lectured and sat in at staff meetings. The distinct differences from psychiatric staff meetings he had attended elsewhere impressed him. For one thing, at his first meeting, a doctor gave a patient's history, then came a pause, and everyone stood up. Alfred did too. What was up? The patient being discussed was entering the room and this was the normal show of respect MacLean doctors gave to patients. The language used at the hospital impressed him even more:

> ...The doctors never used 'feeling', never used 'thinking', 'emotion'—never; the only word they used at all occasions was the word 'evaluation'. Evaluation. And this was apparently a tradition at McLean. They didn't get it from me. But I was learning among others—oh, my work was already done; so I didn't get the benefit out of it—but I got the benefit by watching the tremendous application of the word 'evaluation'; how it covers practically every field of human endeavor. And you can speak in terms of evaluation at any level...what entirely new atmosphere a hospital has using the word 'evaluation', instead of the old 'psychological' lingo.[6]

Both Lynn and his colleagues in Chicago wanted to find a way to support Korzybski in his work. Lynn wrote to him in March 1936:

> It is essential that we organize a group. Call it the Semantic School of Psychiatry if you will—but no advertisement as of yet—not until we have the facts [i.e., more research]. Several individuals working together talking the same [s]emantic language stimulating each other are bound to produce much more than having them scattered about working alone.
>
> Furthermore, if we could start such a group here or in Chicago we could then be in a position to have you with us as adviser-leader. This would give you much needed security [and] also recognition limited at first but bound to spread as our work progresses and becomes known...it would be a tremendous help to both of us if you could come [and] live in Cambridge. I could help with the transportation expenses. However, I believe it is essential that we get together somewhere here or in Chicago – Campbell feels the same.[7]

On April 1, Alfred informed Dr. Lynn that he and Mira had indeed decided to move to Cambridge. The Korzybskis had already spent a great deal of time in Boston that year and had even rented a place to stay. Alfred had met with Dr. Kenneth Tillotson, the Psychiatrist-In-Chief at McLean Hospital and, through Lynn and Tillotson, had gotten in contact with Dr. Gregg, a psychiatrist associated with the Rockefeller Foundation. So there seemed some promise that Lynn's boosting and research at McLean might give Alfred a lever for connecting with more psychiatrists and perhaps getting foundation support. Korzybski's numerous connections at Harvard also had some influence on the decision. He still had hopes of "saving the skin of Bridgman as a personal friend" and of "giving hell to the mathematicians and physicists" there. He also wanted to "try to interest [Rudolph] Carnap" the logician and philosopher of science then at Harvard. Perhaps he could manage to give some seminars there as well.[8]

Since they were going to be moving, Alfred didn't have much time for lecturing or giving seminars, although on April 9 he did give a two-hour lecture at Marlboro State Hospital, a psychiatric facility in Marlboro, New Jersey. His audience, a mixed group of about fifty people, included staff doctors, administrative personnel, patients, and some of their friends and relatives. Dr. Graves, the chief psychiatrist at the hospital had started a GS class for patients the previous July. As a result, GS had an enthusiastic following there. The hospital newsletter reported on Korzybski's lecture:

> To many present it was a memorable occasion. The speaker had a dashing and colorful personality. His energy was unbounded. Within the two hour period he gave clearly and forcefully a succinct account of his system...As pointed out by the Count, our difficulties, both personal and public, are caused by false knowledge...Following dinner at the home of Dr. Graves the Count returned in the evening to his residence in New York City.[9]

The Korzybskis had a lot of packing to do. Vagabonds both, Alfred and Mira had spent a good part of their lives in transit. Nonetheless, as a couple, they had lived in their Brooklyn studio apartment longer than anywhere else. The studio had seemed less than ideal—too hot in summer, too cold in winter, and by now not large enough to keep Alfred and Mira from feeling they were encroaching on each others' space. Still they had become somewhat rooted there. Now they were pulling up their roots once more. Alfred related how he and Mira got all of the trunks they had kept at the Manhattan Storage Company. Many of the trunks and the items inside—books, papers, clothing, etc.—had gotten ruined during the years of storage and had to be thrown out. Alfred was given a release to sign: "I have no claim against Manhattan Storage from the beginning to the end of the world." He wrote a polite letter to the director of the company objecting to "the beginning to the end of the world" stuff: "I cannot sign that paper...How do I know that my ape ancestors didn't store some coconuts with your ape ancestors?"[10] In reply, he got a very polite business letter stating that the release simply contained the standard legal language in use throughout the United States. He wasn't planning to make a claim against the company but, as he reported later, he refused to sign the form.

By June 1, they had finished packing and were in the process of moving themselves and their stuff, along with their remaining pet monkey whom Mira had come to call "Kik", to their new address.[11] A small item appeared in the *Boston Evening Transcript* of Friday, June 12, 1936 under the title "Summer Notes":

> Count Alfred Korzybski and Countess Korzybsk[a] have taken a house at 11 Story Street in Cambridge. From the first of July until the middle of August, the Count will conduct seminars on general semantics at Northwestern University. Countess Korzybski will spend part of the summer on the North Shore, fulfilling commissions for portraits.[12]

As it turned out, Cambridge would not provide the place of opportunity they had hoped. To start with, it didn't seem that Alfred was going to be able to do much more with P. W. Bridgman. Alfred had written a long letter to him responding to Bridgman's new book, *The Nature of Physical Theory*, which seemed in large part a critical response to Korzybski's work (without mentioning it by name). Bridgman wrote back just before Alfred and Mira's move, declaring his unwillingness to spend any more time considering Korzybski's ideas. That was that. Alfred wasn't going to "save the skin of Bridgman as a friend" because Bridgman had little interest in engaging with him anymore. Still, he knew other people at Harvard who seemed more open to his work. And the interest of John Lynn and the psychiatric community in the Boston area showed tremendous potential. But this didn't work out either.

A Worried Letter

The move to Cambridge seemed full of sunshine and promise. Alfred had a budding seminar career, a coterie of close professional students in psychiatry and education, and increasing possibilities for getting serious financial support. Yet in his personal life as well as his work, fog and darkness had rolled in. He had sailed into dangerous waters.

To produce the work of his two books, he'd labored for years with a dogged determination bordering on obsessiveness. Since then, he had worked with an equally ferocious intensity to show the potential of his work and to promote and teach it. But his tendency to make heroic effort habitual had led to habitual personal strain. His persistence in pursuing his vision at times crossed the line into blind rigidity. While holding up a mirror to Mira and to some of his students, he had failed to sufficiently hold up a mirror to himself. He was heading into potentially serious troubles for his health, his work, and his marriage. Alcohol may have played a part.

For most of his life, even during prohibition when he brewed his own ale, Alfred 'had not been a non-drinker', as he sometimes phrased it. And Mira was not a teetotaler and did not disapprove of moderate drinking. But according to her (and I give her statements some credence), Alfred's alcohol use started to become a problem for him—and her—around 1931 as he felt increasing pressure to complete *Science and Sanity*. At this time he started drinking to relax and to help him sleep. Apparently he sometimes drank alone. Mira would observe the results. More than once she had come home to find him intoxicated or difficult to arouse from an afternoon nap. Sometimes, intoxicated, he would break into tears before her from the burdens he felt he was carrying. Sometimes, thus disposed, he would harangue her about her faults. Although he would apologize afterwards, this kind of behavior recurred. She had hoped things would change after the book came out, but they didn't. During the period from the publication of *Science and Sanity* until the move to Cambridge in 1936, it's not clear how much or how frequently he drank or how often he became seriously intoxicated. (In letters he wrote to Mira later that year, Alfred briefly acknowledged "drinking troubles" which he assured her were over.) But even when he didn't drink or at least was not visibly drunk, she found him more and more tense, impatient and critical. Life with the man she so loved and idolized had become increasingly thorny.

Although his alcohol use apparently made the problems between Alfred and Mira worse, it seems likely they would have arisen whether or not he drank. For Alfred had come to focus primarily on what he perceived as Mira's negative qualities while ignoring or downplaying her virtues. He consistently told her he had done what he did for her, and continued to work so hard primarily for her benefit. He also never hesitated to say he would not have written his two main works without her support and encouragement. But he seemed to have forgotten the extent to which her active help—not only financial and moral support—had contributed to them as well. Mira had served for years as the main sounding board for Alfred's formulating. Her innocent, intuitive questions, reflections, and advice nigh undoubtedly helped him to develop his work from the beginning. But at this point, Mira—progressively more conscious of the quality of her own intelligence (quite different in style from Alfred's)—had gotten into a seemingly un-winnable position with him.

She had always regretted missing out on a college education and considered that she had a sloppy 'thinker'. To put this right, she had aspired to learn as much as she could from her husband. Thus, she considered herself his student as well as his wife—as did he. By 1936, this probably was not the best way for either of them to look at their relationship, since Alfred seemed to have difficulty pulling himself out of the role of the teacher whose job it was to find her faults and correct them.

Alfred agreed with Mira about her sloppy 'thinker'. She had once confused Buffalo with Albany and he grabbed onto this verbal slip. 'Buffalo-Albany' became a term he used to refer to what to him seemed her habitual tendency to confuse map-territory relations, her disregard (as far as he was concerned) for hard facts. For years he brought up 'Buffalo-Albany' to her when they had a disagreement. Among his ongoing and repeated criticisms (in letters and conversations with her)—besides her non-extensional 'Buffalo-Albany' ways—were the inexact manner with which she talked about his work to others, and her tendency for dramatic self-presentation in public (what he referred to as her 'Sarah Bernhardt' style) which he considered damaging to his scientific reputation. He had trouble considering the possibility that he might at times overgeneralize about these, making mountains out of molehills.

Certainly, given her lack of formal education, particularly in science and mathematics, she was not going to be a scientific expositer of Alfred's work. But having already become familiar with his assessments of her, I felt surprised by the extent of the mismatch I found between his evaluations of her and what I gathered about her as I read their personal correspondence, as well as some of Mira's other writings. I was struck with her talent for astute observation, her gift for apt metaphor for sizing up a situation or person, and her general playfulness with language and life. I was also repeatedly struck with the depth of her personal application of the extensional methods she had learned from Alfred, her concerted efforts to understand herself and her relationships, her openness to criticism, her hunger for knowledge, her original elaborations of Alfred's formulations, and her often wise advice to him. Even more striking was Korzybski's apparent blindness to much of this. He loved her dearly. He may have been right about a great deal in regard to her faults (she agreed with him about these to a remarkable extent). But he seriously underestimated her for years. After the move to Cambridge the problems in their relationship began to come to a head.

In the last week of June, with boxes still unpacked, he left for the seminar he was giving at Northwestern University from July 1 to August 15. After Mira saw him off at the train station, she was feeling especially miserable, alone, and cut off. The period around the move had been tense. She felt disturbed by whatever he said before he left. Despite her confused feelings, she missed him. She began to write to him almost immediately. Not having heard much from him (he may have sent one letter a few days after he left) she began to feel more concerned. In a way she considered general semantics as much her child as it was his. She worried he was going to drive himself too hard, drink too much, lose control, and as a result compromise the success of his seminars and the possibilities for getting financial support. Still not hearing from him, she wrote a letter to John Lynn on July 8, detailing the history of their troubles, including Alfred's use of alcohol, and pleading with Lynn (and Campbell and Congdon) to be on the alert. It was the first time she had revealed these problems to anyone. Lynn forwarded the letter to his colleagues in Chicago.[13]

Within a day of this, Mira got a letter from Alfred, who had been extremely busy. Everything was going fine in Chicago. She seemed relieved. Perhaps she had worried needlessly. Indeed, in his lectures—the transcriptions of which I have seen—he seemed well-organized and in tip-top form. The seminar had many interested participants and he was asked to come back the following year. But perhaps Mira's letter did have some effect. The seminar organizers, Campbell and Congdon, having been forewarned by her letter (which Alfred didn't know about) may have kept an extra-vigilant watch on him to try to keep him in line. At any rate, from this point forward, Mira and Alfred settled down to a somewhat regular and congenial exchange of letters.

Case #46

He was away for much longer than either of them expected. Although the seminar finished in mid-August, Alfred remained in the Midwest until the end of November. At the end of September he had visited Topeka, Kansas where he lectured at the Menninger Clinic; otherwise he had been shuttling between Chicago and Kansas City to work and consult with Campbell, Congdon, and Kendig. But mainly his work with Kendig had kept him from returning home.

Kendig was having significant problems, not only with the culture of the Barstow School, which seemed resistant to the changes she was trying to bring about. She also had more personal issues. Soon after she encountered his work, Kendig had become one of Korzybski's most stalwart students. Like Mira, who had started much earlier, she was discovering that earnestly applying extensional methods to herself involved a certain amount of suffering. Since the previous year she had been doing extensive 'laboratory work' with Korzybski via personal interviews and letters. As far as I know, there is no remaining record of this work; the exact and detailed nature of the inner conflicts she was dealing with at the time remain unknown. But from Alfred's letters to Mira, a general picture emerges: she seemed to have dredged up and to be struggling with some serious unresolved problems going back to her childhood (perhaps related to sexual abuse). Clearly, by the summer of 1936 she seemed to be undergoing a major serious internal reorganization. And Alfred, as he wrote to Mira, was seriously concerned for her sanity. In fact, he worried that Kendig was going to have a complete psychological collapse.

Even before he had completed the Northwestern seminar, he had been traveling to Kansas City to work with her and she, apparently, was coming up to Chicago as well. Mira had for a long time been the only person who knew that Kendig was the one he had referred to in letters and discussions with others as case number 46. Without going much into specifics, he inundated Mira with news about 46's problems, his worries about her impending breakdown, etc. This constituted a major part of his letters while he was away. Mira did not like to hear about the nitty-gritty details of the evaluational housecleaning of Kendig's (or any of his other student's) psyche. She also worried about Alfred getting in over his head since he had no official psychotherapy training or credentials. (Although Mira didn't mention it, Korzybski had certainly stepped onto dangerous ground, in this early phase of his teaching career, by referring in his letters to 46 and other of his students as "patients".) According to Mira, it wouldn't look good for Alfred if Kendig—a well-known student and advocate of his work for education and mental hygiene—had to be hospitalized for a nervous breakdown. By late July, Mira was already warning him to be careful, to consult with his psychiatrist students, and perhaps to stop pushing Kendig so hard. (The possibility cannot be eliminated that Korzybski may have inadvertently helped precipitate the 'crisis' Kendig was going through.)

Although he did end up following Mira's advice by consulting in a limited way with Congdon and Campbell (apparently with Kendig's permission), he seemed to bristle at the fact that Mira had dared to give him advice:
> Many thanks for your advises about 46, I have spent a great deal of concentration on this subject, from every angle. It's a most tragic situation all together and I have taken into consideration every single angle imaginable. Please dearest UNDERSTAND that as far as insanity is concerned, you have a complete misunderstanding. I am using my best judgement I ever had, because the issues at hand are the most serious any MD ever faced. 46 KNOWS the whole problem. Her situation is difficult everyway, my situation is also extremely difficult, but I am sane, she is not, and you do not understand INSANITY at all.[14]

I find it hard to read this and not to conclude that Korzybski was overreaching. I doubt that he had taken every imaginable consideration into account. Mira, from the evidence of her advice to him, did not seem nearly as benighted about human behavior as he implied. Unquestionably Kendig was going through difficult times in the summer and fall of 1936. And it seems likely that Alfred did greatly help her to deal with some significant-for-her life issues. It seems clear she later felt indebted to him. She would devote her life to promoting and developing his work. But Korzybski's estimation of Kendig's general sanity seems questionable. Before she met Korzybski, Kendig had already shown herself capable and successful in the worlds of business and education. She had friends, a social life, and had married—although this had ended in divorce. (Of course, none of these preclude a person from having a serious psychiatric condition.) Even while this apparent crisis was going on she was running a school, apparently successfully despite problems. Later in life (even a short while later) she would function as a highly competent administrator, editor, and teacher at the Institute of General Semantics. People who knew her over extended periods considered her an exceptionally well-balanced individual. She was known as a wise and warm person to her friends, and a loving wife to her second husband. Since Korzybski's judgment about people was hardly perfect, she may have not been in as serious a condition as he seemed to think at the time.

In any event, by the end of October 1936, Kendig seemed to have passed some kind of crisis point and to be on the way to restoration of her personal balance. Perhaps Korzybski helped her to do that—and sooner than would have happened otherwise. (But perhaps she would have eventually done so on her own without the extensive intervention on his part.) At any rate, Alfred began to consider returning home.

A Beautiful Home

While he'd been unloading the burdens of his work in his letters to her, Mira was writing to him about her manifold doings in Cambridge. Given her level of upset when he left, her letters showed a surprising cheeriness. She'd unpacked their things, bought some needed furniture (cutting costs where she could as she respected his concern for saving pennies), and rearranged the place in a way she hoped would provide a welcoming sense of home to Alfred when he returned. Doing this, she felt in herself a level of domesticity that surprised her. The growing discord with Alfred in Brooklyn had left her feeling anything but homey, but she realized part of the problem there may have been the cramped studio space without enough room for two such independent people to get out of each other's way. This was not going to be a problem on Story Street. When she unpacked during the summer, with much of the contents of their suitcases and trunks laid out in the open, there seemed to be almost as much space to move about as before. Both she and Alfred would have rooms of their own to work in. By the fall, having almost fully unpacked, furnished, and cleaned the place, she hoped the physical order she'd made might bring a new order of relationship between her and Alfred.

Kik the monkey had something to do as well with keeping up Mira's spirit. Mira tried to keep the little monkey on a leash when uncaged but from her reports to Alfred, she seemed to give the monkey a fair amount of freedom to roam around the house. Mira had always loved monkeys (her nickname was "Monk" for a reason) and enjoyed observing the animal as it explored. It was a smart, playful monkey. It liked to drink from the bathroom and kitchen faucets and had started to learn how to turn the spigots on and off. A few times a day it would run up to Mira when she sat or lay on the couch and would hug her around the neck, nibble on her ear, and playfully dance on her belly. It also liked to play "hide and seek" getting chased or chasing Mira around the room in fun. With all this, the monkey seemed relatively well behaved. Mira had trained it to respond to a few voice commands such as "no" when it was getting into some of Alfred's things or "cage" to go into its cage. Mira confusedly referred to it with both feminine and masculine pronouns. But whether boy or girl, Kik was apparently a lot cleaner than naughty Kiki—or had somehow learned better hygiene—since there's no indication from Mira's letters that she ever had to clean any walls the monkey decorated.

That summer and fall, she planned to do some painting and had made a few forays to Nantucket and north of Boston to explore possibilities for commissions. But having only a short walk to the Harvard campus, a major objective of hers—besides getting the house in shape—lay in another direction: to make use of the educational opportunities of Cambridge. Her regret at not being able to attend college, and the exigencies of making a living had fed a lifelong ambition to make up for her lack of formal education. It was one of the things that had attracted her to Alfred. She had made her 'sloppy thinker' more meticulous and gotten it better furnished under his tough, sometimes merciless tutelage. She now seemed more eager than ever for further study on her own.

The celebration of Harvard's Tercentenary (300th anniversary) then in progress gave her a great opportunity. She made it her business to attend many of the special public lectures and presentations provided during the summer session. During the two-week Tercentenary Conference of Arts and Sciences in early September she reveled in the scholarly feast, which included lectures by Whitehead, Eddington, and Einstein, among others. Friends of Alfred attending the Conference, such as G. Y. Rainich, and Hugh and Lillian Lieber, seemed genuinely glad to see her and to enjoy her company and conversation. During her short time in Cambridge, she was managing to get quite a boost to her intellectual self-worth after having come to feel so low about herself. During the summer session, sitting in a lecture hall while waiting for a speaker, she had written to Alfred "If I do say it, I am gaining an increased respect for my own thinker – that is after the hard, endless work you have put on it."[15]

She had already met a number of Harvard people who seemed to respect her as a person with some intellectual ability. Chief among these were mathematician E.V. Huntington and his wife who had befriended the lonely Mira and invited her for dinner in their home. At the end of July they asked her to come with them on a trip to their summer cottage in the Berkshire Mountains of Western Massachusetts. She brought Kik with her on the trip (the Huntingtons loved the monkey) and ended up staying two weeks. During that time she became quite friendly with both husband and wife, reveling in the good relations they seemed to have with one another. Huntington had been writing a paper on symbolic logic. He invited Mira to read it, tutoring her on the subject, which she found both flattering and helpful since she was deeply interested in the relation of different kinds of notation to people's formulating processes.

By the middle of September, feeling stimulated by all this input she decided to put some of her thoughts into writing. Her main purpose was to clear up for herself some GS-related topics she'd been wondering about. She ended up with a number of longhand pages. To make them more readable she got them typed (at this point she couldn't type well enough to do it herself). The typed notes amounted to around 18 pages. For a little additional charge, the not-very-busy typist mimeographed a few extra copies for Mira, who decided she wanted Alfred, the Huntingtons, and a few other people to look at them. As she wrote to the Huntingtons on October 9, she didn't want anyone to take what she wrote too seriously. It was a "purging" so to speak of some things she was trying to get out of her system and she only wanted to know if it might contain any inkling of a usable idea.[16]

Up until then she had not written much, other than letters. One could find a lot to criticize if one wanted. Experimenting with hyphens and underlining, she overdid them. She misspelled words. She wrote incomplete sentences and long ones with confusing or absent punctuation. But despite these flaws, her 1936 writings sometimes also showed originality and raw vigor with a quality like free verse. (Remember, she had spent some time with Gertrude Stein.) And having studied and worked to get GS into her gut, she did have some significant things to say about learning and applying it. Here are some snippets from a page she wrote, addressed to a supposed student of general semantics—truly reminder notes to herself:

> When one is enmeshed in an Aristotelian civilization,...I grant you combined with the habits of one's own education and language – one has to be constantly vigilant – just as one has to be in transforming the energy used in an un-useful physically pleasant habit – say – from childhood of biting one's nails – to the higher transformed useful pleasure in the energy of cultivating beautiful nails.
>
> To transform personal "emotional" wastes of energy in connection with living out uncongenial conditions – one has only to call into activity, onto the job, one's unique human faculty or function – because of our cortex – that is – of being the observer and the observed, in one organism; the sculptor and the clay, in one organism; the organism and the organizer, in one organism:– of being humanely impersonal about the most personal goings-on inside one.
>
> It makes of life a "grand adventure" if one can have as an intimate companion, one who is also so oriented, but, with those who are not, it makes for tolerance, poise, patience, and master of a situation, by making it clear to the other fellow in extensionalizing the situation, what characteristics the other fellow has left out of consideration, as it helps one to discover what one's self has left out, and when that is done, fight for dominance is stopped and co-operation is begun. Widely different biological and sociological inheritances, and life-habits can be adjusted and just the differences, united enlarge each the other's life, constructively.[17]

She surely had inklings of some good ideas here and in the other pages she sent special delivery to Alfred on October 9. She had written a bit about a GS evaluational compass and among other things had worked out some novel ways of relating some of the main GS formulations to each other in diagram form. Alfred wrote back the following day:

> Dearest One:
> Received your special delivery with enclosures of the article of Norris and your own. Please do not add to my burdens by spending money on typing, mimeography, etc., perfectly worthless verbal masturbation the distribution of which does definite harm to my whole work...Please do not get discouraged, STUDY SERIOUSLY S+S without adding your fancies to it, try to understand PLAIN ENGLISH following your "beloved" Oxford, with which you only play. Dearest I have enough professional troubles, for pity sake do not add family troubles to it. Write long hand all you want to, but do not waste money on typing mostly worthless or harmful material. I am terribly tired dealing with "mental aberrations", PLEASE do not add to my burdens. All my love[18]

'All my love' indeed! On his side, he did have some justifiable grounds for concern. What Mira—as his wife—said or wrote might gain more attention and be judged more critically as a representation of him and his work than something said by almost anyone else. It seemed reasonable to ask her to be careful. But his blatantly patronizing attitude and nearly total dismissiveness towards her written efforts surely seem excessive. He did love her, but unfortunately he had also developed a fixed set of disapproving attitudes toward her that would stay fixed for a number of years and that would lead to much pain for both of them. And Mira had reached a point in her life, much to her chagrin, where she wasn't going to accept the resulting treatment.

"Shoot All The Mothers"

The following event probably took place around this time. I heard Dr. Campbell relate the story in person many years afterwards at the 1979 Korzybski Centennial celebration:

> ...I knew one very well-to-do man who was impressed by Korzybski and GS, and suggested that we meet his mother, who was very wealthy, and that she might endow an institute, which was what I hoped would happen. Korzybski was somewhat difficult to manage in those days, to put it mildly. I didn't know how he would behave at a North Shore reception that was being given in his honor. However, he agreed to go. We went to this event and he behaved superbly with all the charm of his aristocratic background.
>
> Well, she started questioning him about the increasing problems of juvenile delinquency and what did he think about it and wasn't it bad and so forth, and what could we do as a group to combat juvenile delinquency in Chicago? He held himself in control quite well, which was a lot for Korzybski, and it was at this point that I was beginning to get a little anxious as to what might come out.
>
> He began to talk about the juvenile delinquent being a product of a family situation, with defects in the parenting of the children and particularly the failure of the American mother to do her job properly. He went on and she said, "Yes, but now tell me what would you do to prevent further problems of delinquency?" He said, "I would shoot all the mothers," [Laughter] So with that --[Laughter]--the party broke up rather quickly and--[Continued Laughter]--and the Institute was not financed by this famous family,...[19]

No one can know for sure why Korzybski made his 'little joke', but I'll take a stab at an explanation. Korzybski would openly admit that, although he was usually polite, decorum and respectability were not qualities he had much use for. It seems likely to me he said what he said to take the wealthy lady 'down a notch'. If she and the people at the party couldn't laugh it off and instead felt offended by his jest, he wouldn't have wanted their money. Perhaps he had had a little too much to drink as well. In any case, it might have served him better to keep his mouth shut.

Mira found out about what happened, probably from Campbell or from John Lynn, who was in communication with Campbell. She did not take the news lightly. Indeed, combined with the verbal slap Alfred had given her about the material she had sent him (the intent of which she felt he had misunderstood), she became increasingly upset and angry.

Alfred was continuing to write to her, reporting on his work with 46 and others, as if nothing else had happened. By the end of October, Mira had stopped writing regularly to him. She had tired of his scolding and the seemingly endless number of letters about his 'sick' students. He had put off returning to Cambridge for months. She was waiting for him to show some concern in something besides his work, i.e., in her and their home life. She also hoped he would recognize that he had some responsibility for problems regarding both his work and their relationship. She was communicating with Campbell, Lynn and others in an attempt to explain her concerns and to give some justification for the earlier material she had sent to them. But her attempts to explain her actions to Alfred's friends and colleagues simply backfired. Alfred went to Campbell, who made things worse by sharing some of the material Mira had sent—including the July letter to Lynn containing Mira's worries about Alfred's drinking. Alfred became furious and angrily wrote to Mira accusing her of broadcasting their private lives and "killing" his work. Mira in turn wrote an angry missive entitled "All Mothers Should Be Shot" excoriating Alfred for his shooting of "silly-slogans that don't fit and have torn M.E. psycho-logically as successfully as explosive bullets could physically."[20] As Mira would say, they had gotten themselves into a very vicious circle.

While Congdon seems to have kept himself out of the fray, Campbell had gotten himself into the unenviable position of mediating between Alfred and Mira and in that role had made more of a mess of things. Meanwhile Lynn, still a psychiatric resident and—as Mira had concluded—rather naive, was making the bad situation even worse by hatching serious doubts about both Mira's and Alfred's sanity and sharing his suspicions with Campbell and Congdon. Lynn, who earlier had so confidently sent a telegram to Alfred announcing Mira's 'cancer', didn't seem to question the soundness of these psychiatric 'diagnoses' either.

In early December Alfred finally returned to Cambridge. Mira was not at home. She had checked into a hotel (probably boarding the monkey with the veterinarian who had previously taken care of it). Initially, Alfred didn't know where she had gone. His only contact with her was through Dr. Lynn with whom she was checking in by phone every day. It took some cajoling on Alfred's part to break the impasse with her, which he finally managed to do. As far as he was concerned, Mira had had a 'breakdown', which he attributed to Dr. Lynn's influence. To Alfred, the psychiatrist seemed to be showing signs of serious disturbance himself. Lynn was apparently presenting his concerns about Korzybski's sanity to others at McLean Hospital and around Boston. Alfred's reputation in the Boston area seems to have sustained serious damage.

Within a month, the storm had passed. He and Mira were seeing each other and talking and had managed to patch up their relationship. Clearly, Mira had come to feel peripheral to Alfred's work—not an inaccurate assessment. But underlying all that, her undying devotion remained. The extremity of her upset seemed partly due to that devotion and her assessment that Alfred was not living up to his own teachings. Although she realized she had made some serious mistakes as well, his stubborn resistance to seeing her point of view bothered her immensely. "Donk", for Donkey (rhyming with Mira's "Monk")—the nickname they both used for him in letters—seemed at times a quite fitting name for Alfred. By this time, Mira had concluded that her efforts to be helpful had made a mess of things and she didn't want to have anything more to do with the 'semantic family' or to be involved in Alfred's work. She decided it would do her good to take a long trip to South America to travel and paint and get some distance to sort out their relationship. She brought Kik to the Polakovs who had agreed to keep the dear monkey (Alfred was just too busy to care for the high-maintenance pet by himself). By the end of January, Mira was on a ship on her way to Argentina. She would spend most of 1937 and 1938 there, especially in Buenos Aires, and would travel to Brazil (Rio de Janeiro) and Trinidad as well, before getting back to the United States at the end of 1938.

What happened to Dr. Lynn? Indications from Alfred's letters to him, and to Campbell and Mira, suggest that by the spring of 1937 he was struggling with some serious adjustment problems of his own. He left McLean Hospital around that time. By the fall, he had apparently improved enough to get married. Korzybski got a wedding invitation in August. He was in contact with Lynn over the next year but in March 1938 still felt uncertain enough about the psychiatrist's stability to ask him "...not to do further harm to me..., as you did before by propagating sick attitudes toward my work,..."[21] Lynn didn't seem to take offense at Alfred's scolding. Letters he wrote to Alfred later that year, show an unreservedly friendly tone. Alfred's letters also appear congenial. They seem to have dated their problems. By 1940, Lynn was in New York doing research at a neurological institute and training in psychoanalysis. He continued with an occasional friendly letter to Korzybski for at least a couple more years. However, his great involvement with and ambitious plans for GS had gone kaput.

Chapter 47
ONE WEARY MAN

The troubles with Mira and with Lynn had not only disturbed Alfred's personal life. They also seemed to him to have reduced his prospects for establishing his work around Boston—and perhaps elsewhere too. He wondered whether the whole unfortunate business had harmed Campbell's and Congdon's opinion of him. Campbell visited him in Boston and reassured him otherwise. In a March 3, 1937 letter to Kendig, Campbell wrote,
> I saw Alfred in Boston and was delighted to find him very much better in every way—healthy, hard at work and self-controlled. Lynn [at this time apparently still working at McLean], Congdon and myself are continuing to have unexpectedly good results with G.S., and while we cannot share some of Alfred's propagandizing and proselytizing tendencies there is no doubt we are more and more enthusiastic. I believe that I shall soon be able to announce some form of permanent subsidy for him, perhaps making it possible for him to locate in Chicago.[1]

Until whatever Campbell was planning came through, Alfred would indeed be hard at work. (Then again, when was he not hard at work?) From February 17 until March 20, he gave a seminar for a group largely composed of Boston-area academics at the Baker Library of Harvard Business School which had become a center of human relations studies under the direction of Professors Elton Mayo and F. J. Roethlisberger. The two men had pioneered the study of motivating factors in workers' behavior in their famous "Hawthorne Experiments", at the Western Electric Hawthorne Works in Illinois. Roethlisberger, who attended the seminar along with Mayo, had previously read *Science and Sanity*:
> [Korzybski's book] although difficult to read, seemed to me to be saying something important. What I think attracted my interest was the way he put epistemology to work, so to speak. Boiled down, his approach seemed to me to be *applied epistemology*.
>
> At this time there was considerable interest in comparing the way a child thinks (Piaget) with the way a primitive thinks (Levy-Bruhl) and with the way a neurotic thinks (Freud). Only a genius or a nut would have tried to compare the way a mathematician thinks (Russell and Whitehead) and the way a neurotic thinks (psychiatry). Korzybski was such a man.
>
> Because he took such an extreme position, which at that time did not fit well into any discipline, Korzybski never gained any academic post or much recognition. His field was neither strictly philosophy, mathematics, linguistics, semantics, psychiatry, nor mental health. It was a brilliant one-man synthesis of all these things which he called general semantics to differentiate it from ordinary semantics (e.g., Ogden and Richards, *The Meaning of Meaning*).[2]

Man The Unknown

By mid-February, Mira had reached Argentina. Although she and Alfred had just experienced the biggest blowup they had ever had in their relationship, they kept in frequent contact throughout her time away. Mira wrote more often than Alfred, who at times didn't feel he had much new to tell her other than the fact that he was working very hard and worried about her health. He needn't have worried. Even in this early part of her time away, she had begun to feel better. She was gaining weight as well as perspective, was beginning to meet people, and working out plans for getting painting commissions among the social elite of Mar del Plata and Buenos Aires.

Mira felt just as concerned about Alfred's health, given his tendency to push himself. His report that he was drinking very little, repeated often in his correspondence throughout the year, must have reassured her. He also wrote to her in February that he was trying a pill Lynn had suggested to him—benzedrine sulfate, a form of amphetamine just starting to get widely prescribed as an 'energy booster'. Rather promiscuous prescription of the drug continued through the 1960s, when its addictiveness and damaging side effects became more widely understood. Korzybski confirmed the energizing effect of the drug on himself in his letter to Mira. It's intriguing to wonder how long he continued to take it and what effect it might have had on his behavior. I've found no direct evidence of long-term amphetamine use by him. His astounding capacity for work in later years could have been explained by amphetamine use. On the other hand, his exceptional endurance had been noted by others, long before he had the opportunity to take the drug.

On March 7, as his Harvard seminar was going on, Alfred's friend and mentor William Alanson White died. White had been Alfred's first and main teacher in psychiatry through his writings, the hours of personal discussion, and through the opportunity he had given Alfred to study at St. Elizabeths. White had grasped the importance of bridging psychiatry with the physico-mathematical sciences. Despite the press of his own affairs he had consistently attended to Alfred's peculiar efforts along that line. Alfred would always remain grateful to White for his encouragement. And White had also learned from Alfred. Traces of Korzybski's influence appeared in the last book White had published, his 1936 *Twentieth Century Psychiatry*.

In 1937, the wave of psychiatric interest in Korzybski's work that White had helped start was continuing to gather momentum. The January 1937 issue of the *American Journal of Psychiatry* had carried Douglas Campbell's article "General Semantics: Implications of Linguistic Revision for Theoretical and Clinical Neuro-Psychiatry". The May issue of that journal included Alfred's review of *Man, The Unknown*, the 1935 best-seller by Nobel Prize-winning medical researcher Alexis Carrel.

Alfred and Mira had read Carrel's book soon after it came out and Alfred had begun recommending it to his seminar students. In his two St. Louis papers he had referred to Carrel's discussion of the role of language in science and medicine. Carrel had criticized the regrettable tendency of scientific/medical "schemata" to emphasize 'abstract' "universals" over the 'concrete' individual and thus to objectify verbal fictions.

Korzybski's laudatory 1937 review, written a year previously, emphasized Carrel's mid-decade survey of the various specialties providing knowledge about humans. Carrel saw a pressing need for a future synthesizing effort to develop "the science of man" which would—according to Carrel—reduce the dangers of over-specialization by emphasizing "the human being in his entirety."[3]

>...[m]odern civilization absolutely needs specialists. Without them, science could not progress. But, before the results of their researches are applied to man, the scattered data of their analyses must be integrated in an intelligible synthesis.
>
>Such a synthesis cannot be obtained by a simple round-table conference of the specialists. It requires the efforts of one man, not merely those of a group. A work of art has never been produced by a committee of artists, nor a great discovery made by a committee of scholars. The syntheses needed for the progress of our knowledge of man should be elaborated in a single brain.[4]

Such a synthesis would constitute the basis of an over-arching "superscience":
This superscience will be utilizable only if, instead of being buried in libraries, it animates our intelligence. But is it possible for a single brain to assimilate such a gigantic amount of knowledge?...It seems that such an accomplishment is not impossible. In about twenty-five years of uninterrupted study one could learn these sciences. At the age of fifty, those who have submitted themselves to this discipline could effectively direct the construction of the human being and of a civilization based on his true nature.[5]

Korzybski pointed out that the world didn't have to wait for another 25 years. He had already produced at least the foundation of the kind of synthesis Carrel had envisioned. Carrel's dream of a science of man—expressed in the old language—seemed unworkable if Carrel and others continued to neglect the foundational issues that Korzybski had already brought to the fore (evaluation, extensionalization, neuro-linguistic and neuro-semantic environments, etc.). Despite this criticism, Korzybski appreciated Carrel's 1935 diagnosis of the degenerating condition of modern civilization. But in subsequent years, Korzybski would have to qualify his enthusiasm.

After retiring from Rockefeller University in 1938, Carrel would return to France. In 1941 he became an official in the Nazi collaborationist Vichy government. His French Foundation for the Study of Human Problems would oversee demographic and eugenics research in Vichy France. Although Carrel himself was never directly implicated in any crimes against humanity, his Vichy association and his espousal in *Man The Unknown* of eugenics and the use of "poison gas" in dealing with criminals and the criminally insane, would taint him as a proto-Nazi.[6] By 1941 his reputation had already begun to slip. Korzybski, in a footnote in that year's "Introduction to the Second Edition" of *Science and Sanity*, made a brief, apparently critical reference to Carrel and his book while discussing "führers" in different fields "fancying that they represent 'all' of the *human* world!"[7]

Carrel would remain a 'mixed bag' for Korzybski. In subsequent seminars until the end of his life, while openly stating his qualms about Carrel's political sympathies and mystical Catholicism, Alfred acknowledged the man's contributions as a great physician-scientist. He would still refer to some of Carrel's findings and would use a statement from *Man The Unknown*—not included in his review—as one of the quotes on self-reflexiveness with which he typically ended his lectures: "To progress again, man must remake himself. And he cannot remake himself without suffering. For he is both the marble and the sculptor."[8]

Olivet

In April, Korzybski traveled to Olivet, Michigan. His friend Joseph Brewer, President of Olivet College, had asked him to return there to give an extended seminar, a series of fourteen, two-hour evening lectures from April 22 to June 18. As Brewer later noted, almost the entire school community of faculty and students had attended Korzybski's previous two introductory lectures in 1935. "The reactions varied from anger through confusion to enthusiasm but there was no indifference. This acted as a sort of ferment in the institution..."[9] Brewer, who was developing a reputation as one of the most innovative small-college leaders in the United States, now wanted to add more korzybskian yeast.

On April 19, about the time of Alfred's arrival at Olivet, his friend William Morton Wheeler collapsed and died of a heart attack on a Cambridge subway platform. The 72-year-old entomologist and professor emeritus of zoology at Harvard, had felt enthusiastic about Korzybski's work from the first time the two men met in 1923. Subsequently, Wheeler provided major help to Alfred in editing *Science and Sanity*. Although retired from teaching, just prior to his death he had continued to work at Harvard's Biological Laboratories and Museum of Comparative Zoology. He had also continued to write and had gained broad respect as an exceptionally well-read and wide-ranging scientist-humanist. Alfred would miss his friendship and steadfast support.

At Olivet, President Brewer had gotten funds from an anonymous donor to sponsor Alfred. Arrangements were made to transcribe the lectures and have them published. The lectures were open to all 35 of the faculty and all 265 students—although the students were limited to a first come, first serve basis. Between 75 and 100 people, mostly students, attended. Since he considered the effects of his lectures cumulative, Korzybski discouraged causal drop-ins and had attendance taken. Towards the middle of the seminar, he began offering interviews (as usual, on a voluntary basis) for interested group members who wanted to clear up confusions and get help making personal applications. The *Olivet College Echo*, the campus newspaper carried reports of the lectures for the general college community.

The transcript, under the title *General Semantics*, was edited by Korzybski and made available in a limited First Edition by the Olivet College Book Store, soon after the seminar in 1937.[10] Later plans to republish it were delayed during Korzybski's lifetime. A Second Edition, published by the Institute of General Semantics, came out in 1964 under the title *General Semantics Seminar 1937: Olivet College Lectures*, with a Third Edition in 2002.

The *Olivet College Lectures* provides the closest impression so-far-in-print of how Korzybski talked while teaching. In his "Foreword to the Second Edition" Joseph Brewer noted,

> Re-reading the Olivet Seminar now [1963], it is extraordinary to find how the rhythm, tone and flavor of Korzybski come through. To those who knew him, it is easy in going through this text to visualize his gestures and especially his mobile features, the quizzical expression succeeded by a warm, broad smile, his eyes shifting quickly from an amused twinkle to a penetrating intensity.[11]

At this point in his teaching career, Korzybski had been giving seminars for two years. He had developed a facility for conveying his work in simple terms. As Homer J. Moore Jr., editor of the 2002 Third Edition, pointed out, "In this early presentation, [Korzybski] gives a complete outline of his system with the training methods needed to apply it."[12] Brewer wrote that, "Those who have attended later seminars [as Brewer did] will recognize the basic pattern that was set here. Korzybski sought constantly to refine and improve and enrich the presentation to make it more effective, and to adapt it to the particular group present, but the fundamental method and content are here."[13]

Nonetheless, the presentation in the *Olivet Lectures*—like earlier seminars (notes and transcripts of which I have seen)—seems more linear than that of seminars Korzybski gave in subsequent years. The twenty-eight total hours, which his fourteen two-hour lecture periods gave him, afforded less time than he would have liked to elaborate stories, relate his own personal experiences, give examples from current events, make digressive 'footnotes', or do much in the way of demonstrations—although he did his best to include these aspects. He also couldn't assume that many students had much familiarity with his work, which he could expect of later seminar students who had various popularizations or some of his own articles to read, if not *Science and Sanity*.

In the first lecture he noted the background of his work in mathematics and psychiatry, the importance of *predictability*, and the centrality of *evaluation* and *values*—the latter two forming the core subject matter of general semantics. GS was for use in solving life problems. He compared it to algebra. Reading a book on algebra was not enough to learn how to solve algebra problems; a technique had to be learned, and then applied. Similarly, with GS: "...it is just like another kind of algebra; it exists and its only value is to help the solution of life's problems. But, we have to have a technique. You must master the technique before you can apply it and solve the problems." Nonetheless, Korzybski emphasized that he was not there to solve his students problems for them: "It is my business to give you a *method* to *solve your own problems*."[14]

Part of this orientation involved an attitude of minimum expectations, learning not to expect too much. (This *did not* mean not having goals or not working toward them.) In *Science and Sanity*, he had briefly noted the "semantic shocks" resulting from unjustified expectations (p. 472). Since then he had been elaborating an "extensional theory of happiness" or "happiness formula" that he presented at Olivet. From then on, this would become a permanent part of his seminar content.

He draw a small circle E_1 on the blackboard to represent minimum (extensional) expectations. A middle-size circle labeled 'F' stood for facts—whatever happened irrespective of expectations. On the opposite side, an even larger circle E_2 represented maximum (intensional) expectations.

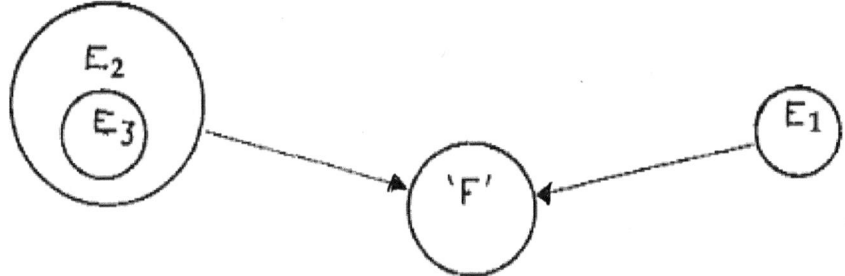

Extensional Theory of Happiness

He advised his class to get in the habit of starting out with minimum (extensional) expectations E_1, since maximum (intensional) expectations E_2, when disappointed, led easily to cynicism, bitterness, and frustration, labeled E_3:

> ...If you expect, say 'nothing', in the actual living, bumping against facts, impact with the environment, you will find the facts better than you expected. You will be encouraged. You will not be cynical; you will not be bitter; etc. Life then will be happier for you as living protoplasm reacting to the impact of the environment. Expect the minimum. That is [expectation$_1$ (E_1).] That is the new extensional infiinite-valued expectations based on maximum probability.[15]

At Olivet, he also began to pull away from his previous informal usage of the term "semantics"—by itself—to refer to his work, declaring in the lectures, "the old semantics is now dead"[16] and more consistently referring to his work as *general semantics* (or simply as "G.S."), a "general theory of values and evaluation". In presentations over the next two years, he would move towards completely abandoning the shortcut use of 'semantics' to label his work. *General Semantics*—despite the suggestion of its name to many—wasn't any kind of 'semantics' at all, as people usually interpreted the latter term.

Many Olivet students and faculty felt inspired and changed as a result of Korzybski's lectures and interviews. For example, one of the main points he emphasized in his lectures (as he would continue to do) was the importance of people considering themselves in neurological terms in order to become more extensional about themselves. This might lead to a number of practical consequences such as the following: if right or left-handedness depended on some 'innate' structuring of an individual's brain, naturally left-handed people should not continue trying to force themselves to write, etc., with their right hand just because they had been told to do so as children. Continuing to do so could create many difficulties in functioning. In personal conferences, Korzybski had advised a few such probable 'lefties' to try switching their handedness. They noticed remarkable changes in making the switch.

One young man reported on the vastly improved legibility of his writing, his greater ease in expressing himself, and a significant reduction in a stammering problem. These changes occurred within a few weeks of making the change. He did have an initial period of difficulty during the transition when he felt unable to exert much pressure while writing with his left hand. During this time, he noticed a great deal of tension in his right hand, which seemed to be reproducing the left hand's writing motions. He also experienced strange sensations in his head, which passed after a few days.[17] Korzybski considered his 'simple' advice about laterality as part of his general-semantics instruction. (This wouldn't make much sense to someone who viewed his work as mainly about words.)

Olivet College's assistant librarian, Helen L. Evans, was also one of the 'left-handers' helped as a result of switching to her left hand (she eliminated a speech block). She got to know Korzybski fairly well during the time of the seminar, attending all of his lectures and helping him by serving as a chaperone during his interviews with the women students. She came to see him as a valued friend and corresponded with him afterwards.[18]

A few days after the seminar ended in mid-June, Joseph Brewer sent a letter of appreciation on behalf of the Olivet Board of Trustees to Korzybski, who was staying in Chicago. Brewer soon followed this with a detailed personal letter reporting on the beneficial effects of the seminar on the college community as a whole and on various individual students and faculty participants. Both letters were published as addenda for the 1964 Second Edition of the *Olivet Lectures*.

Despite Korzybski's general success at Olivet, there were grousers. Prior to the seminar, Olivet's Registrar and Dean of Men—although he attested to having no personal complaints about Korzybski or his work—had objected to Brewer about Korzybski's visit. The Dean, who had had to deal with various epidemics of campus rumors in the past, considered it "extraordinarily dangerous to harbour a person of the Count's spectacular and compelling personality" which he felt might engender more rumors.[19] Brewer didn't consider this a legitimate reason for not inviting Korzybski. What small community like the Olivet College campus wasn't subject to a certain amount of gossip-mongering?

Indeed, hearsay about Korzybski may have been promoted by a faculty couple, a philosophy/psychology instructor and his wife, a drama teacher. The two harbored resentments against both Brewer and a number of their fellow faculty members. When Brewer terminated their contracts the following year, they filed a complaint with the American Association of University Professors. Their charges against Brewer and a number of Olivet teachers also included a number of accusations against Korzybski: his lectures were "virtually compulsory" (he took attendance) and were characterized by "gutter" language (he talked frankly about sex) and the violation of "all known forms of logic and clear discourse" (he discussed the limitations of the aristotelian orientation). The philosophy teacher attended only the first lecture while his wife wrote, "I had better use for my time than to listen to the lewd stories of a half-intoxicated man." The two recounted stories that they said some students had told them about Korzybski's inappropriate behavior. Brewer compiled a folder full of responses to these claims from a number of students, faculty, and administrators. They unanimously disputed every one of the couple's allegations about Brewer, Korzybski, and others. Korzybski also responded with a 15-page letter, which must have taken him several days to write, refuting point-by-point the claims made against him. Neither the Olivet College Board of Trustees nor the American Association of University Professors found any basis for further investigation. The couple's complaints were dismissed. Despite these problems, there is no indication Brewer ever regretted his decision to sponsor Korzybski. Indeed, Korzybski was welcomed back to Olivet. After giving another seminar at the Chicago Campus of Northwestern University from July 7 to August 20, he returned to the Olivet campus to use the library there and gave two lectures between September 20 and October 5.[20]

One Weary Man

By August 2, Alfred wrote to Walter Polakov, "Most probably an institute for General Semantics will be financed in Chicago. In the meantime, 'I don't know, let's see.'"[21] He had been invited to give a seminar to the GS class at Marlboro State Hospital from November 18 to December 12. By that time, the plans for an institute had become more definite. After the Marlboro seminar, he planned to return to Cambridge and begin packing at once for the move to Chicago.

Without question Mira's absence continued to affect Alfred. Every so often they would end up writing to each other about the issues that had led to her leaving. These continued as sore spots for both of them. Alfred didn't seem able to acknowledge how his own attitudes and behavior may have contributed to the troubles in their relationship. And Mira, while admitting her mistakes, no longer felt willing to take all of the responsibility for their vicious circle. Her attempts to correct what she saw as his misevaluations of her behavior and motives met with fierce resistance from him. She had an intense interest in general semantics and demonstrated her life-use of it in her letters. She had suggestions for making his work easier and for promoting it. But as far as he was concerned, she didn't know a thing about it. He treated her thoughts about GS as so much 'blah, blah, trah, trah'; if she would only just pipe down, listen to him, and do what he told her, everything would be all right. Although none of their fundamental differences had gotten resolved, her time away had left her feeling stronger in dealing with him. Still, she would try her best to accommodate his wishes. She recognized his burdens and didn't want to add to them. She missed him and she wanted to come home.

He missed her too and, as he wrote to her at the end of the year, desperately missed having the personal life away from his work that he knew he could only have with her. But he felt that at this point, it would be better for both of them if she remained in Argentina, letting him pack and move to Chicago by himself. And he wanted her to stay away until he had established the Institute and set up a home for them. She reluctantly agreed.

Although his work seemed to be progressing quite well and was apparently going to get funded, a sad, lonely, even pessimistic tone came forth in his letters from this time. On December 10, he wrote to Helen L. Evans:

> Am after the hospital seminars a sadder and older man. It's pathetic how similar seminar-reaction[s] are in hospitals of confined "insane" and colleges of non-confined un-sane. As long as the seminars lasted, everything went well, but the results will be except a few cases just as effective as on the majority of the Olivet group,... Please realize that the main value of G.S. is preventive, not trying to "cure" "incurable" cases.[22]

A week later he wrote to her again,

> "Lonely", well if anyone knows the meaning of this word it is me. I am always lonely even in crowds and with students as they usually are so far off the mark.[23]

While working with him during the Olivet seminar earlier in the year, Helen had already observed those qualities in him. In a letter to him near the end of the seminar, she wrote:

> June 9, 1937
>
> Count Korzybski —
>
> I am aware you do not want either gratitude nor compliments, but from my studies and your conferences so much has been gained it would be strange if I had remained entirely unaware of the 'mind' and personality responsible for such a work.
>
> Your courage in facing before-hand the obstacles that General Semantics has to meet, and in meeting your own personal problems is clear in the lines of suffering in your face. The fact that you understood and experienced so much probably accounts for the confidence you are able to inspire in others.
>
> The enclosed is a feeble attempt to paint your portrait in outline as it has appeared to me. Please accept it without sentiment.

The next page contained the following poem. After the date and the title, the script suddenly slanted to the left (unlike the letter) in a way that appeared to have been written by someone writing left-handed:

> <u>Portrait in Outline</u>
> One can but guess the depth or breadth of mind
> Whose sad, ironic certainty predicts our woe
> Before we speak, so keen to find
> Some common thing to ease the flow
> Of thought — awaken thus an unresponsive world;
>
> One weary man who sits alone, with tender hand
> Upon the pulse of sodden lives we meet...
> Eager to give, content to feel, like a strand
> Of Polish music in some sunlit street
> Against our smug, complacent faces hurled.[24]

Part VII
The Institute

"...one man's effort is not enough."
—ALFRED KORZYBSKI[1]

Chapter 48
THE INSTITUTE OF GENERAL SEMANTICS

At the start of 1938, with Mira still in South America, Alfred was in Cambridge by himself packing their stuff when he got a newspaper death notice in Polish along with a formally addressed letter from Boleslaw Olszewski, his friend and lawyer in Warsaw, dated January 2. Alfred's mother had died.[1]

Whatever sadness he felt, he experienced significant relief as well. His mother Helena's prolonged illness, her helplessness and complaining, her disastrous business dealings, and the troublesome marriage to her manager Pawlowski had led to a great deal of grief for Alfred. He could leave that behind now. There were still the matters of recovering his and Mira's mortgage money on the house at 66 Wilcza St. and his (and his sister's) inheritance. Olszewski would work on it.

In the meantime, his mother's death broke another thread in the cord of connection drawing him back to Poland. Even after the publication of *Science and Sanity*, he and Mira had still planned to eventually return there to live. Future visits might still be possible. But Mira and he were no longer young—he was heading towards his 59th birthday. With this new venture in Chicago, he was committing them to remain in the United States. A sign of this commitment—soon after the move to Chicago, he began the process of becoming a U.S. citizen (accomplished in 1940).[2]

Alfred informed Mira about his mother's death and details of the move. He anticipated leaving Cambridge around February 1 (he managed to leave by the middle of the month.) In Buenos Aires, Mira had a law firm draw up a document giving Alfred power of attorney to represent her in any business done in Poland. The document gave her and Alfred's address as Dearborn Lodge, 1347 North Dearborn, Chicago. The North Dearborn apartment, which Alfred had used during his previous stays in Chicago, would be their official residence until he got the Institute of General Semantics established and could find a residence for them. As to when Mira would return to their new city and home, the date became somewhat open-ended. She had recovered her equanimity, had gotten painting commissions, and seemed to be enjoying herself in South America. But she missed Alfred and was eager to return. Alfred didn't want her to come back until he had gotten things more firmly established in Chicago.

The Tyranny of Words

To say the least, Korzybski's time in Cambridge had not turned out very well. Still, he was not leaving Cambridge with a complete sense of failure. Although he had lost a number of long-time friends and boosters in 1937—including Cora L. Williams, who died in December—he had also found new friends and supporters in Cambridge, even as he was preparing to leave. One new friend, Porter Edward Sargent—a Boston-area writer and the publisher of the well-known *Handbook of Private Schools*—had read *Science and Sanity*, become very enthusiastic, and introduced Korzybski to Harvard anthropologist Ernest Hooten. In a letter to Kendig on January 28, Sargent wrote:

> Hooten...has had two sessions this week of three hours with Korzybski, has devoted his leisure time to reading the book, and in a recent address at the Harvard Club talked Korzybski in the aftermath of his address.[3]

People were also getting excited about Stuart Chase's book, *The Tyranny of Words*, just published in January. Chase, by then a popular non-fiction writer and social critic, had decided to examine his tools—i.e., words. By studying 'semantics', he hoped to learn "how words behave, and why [verbal] meaning is so often frustrated."[4] Chase had become aware of Korzybski's work as early as 1935 and had studied it, as well as the writings of Malinowski, Ogden and Richards, P.W. Bridgman, and others. In 1937 Chase began corresponding with Kendig, Korzybski, and Walter Polakov; the latter had guided Chase through *Science and Sanity*. Chase's resulting book emphasized the commonalities amongst the various formulators he had investigated. Without question *The Tyranny of Words* drew a lot of interest to the works of these men. But whatever use the book may have served as a simple introduction to their writings, Chase's melding of their different approaches obscured the uniqueness of the individual formulators. Chase's purposeful neglect of the "subjective", psycho-logical, inner life of the individual—as if this could be neatly separated from the "objective relationships between the individual and the outside world"—especially shortchanged Korzybski.[5] Chase's treatment of general semantics contained a number of other subtle and not-so-subtle misrepresentations. (An early reviewer, Henry Hazlitt, who had not read *Science and Sanity*, argued that Chase misinterpreted the other formulators as well.)[6]

In late 1937, when Polakov saw excerpts in *The New Republic* from the soon-to-be-published book, he wrote to Alfred: "[Chase] must be spanked."[7] He felt bothered by, among other things, what he saw as Chase's apparent animosity towards higher-order abstractions. As Korzybski had emphasized repeatedly—apparently not enough—science is not possible without them. Once the book was released, Walter wanted to give it a favorable review but felt he couldn't since, in his opinion, it didn't do justice to Korzybski. He wanted Alfred's opinion on the matter.[8] Alfred replied that, given his limitations, Chase hadn't done such a bad job: "I sincerely suggest do not give Hell to Chase, neither try to explain your semantics [in any possible review]. I suggest praise his book, although you may suggest he did not go far enough."[9] As Korzybski told his first Institute of General Semantics seminar class later that year: "[*The Tyranny of Words*] is a fine first attempt [at popularization]. Not sharp; not good enough. Superficial, but the best there is, just the same."[10] (Korzybski may have been too generous in his assessment of the benign impact of the book, since many of its readers appeared to incorrectly conclude that it accurately represented Korzybski's work.)

At the start of 1938, *The Tyranny of Words*—the first popular book dealing in a significant way with Korzybski's work—had no competition. Widely publicized and reviewed, its publication marked the beginning of a new level of public recognition for Korzybski. The *Reader's Guide to Periodical Literature*, a widely-recognized index of 'popular' magazines in the U.S. and Canada, provides a rough indication of popular print media attention to a topic. Korzybski had received a surprising amount of newspaper and magazine coverage over the years. However, prior to 1938, the *Reader's Guide* had only one reference to him or his work—his 1929 *Science* obituary of Vasiliev (in Volume VIII, published in 1932). With Volume XI, covering the period from July 1937 to June 1939, things changed. There were five articles directly related to *The Tyranny of Words* listed under "Stuart Chase". Most of the articles listed under "Semantics" (used for the first time as a heading) also related to Chase's book. Many of these articles at least mentioned Korzybski. Another article was listed under the heading "Korzybski". "General Semantics" was not used as a heading at all.

Over the remainder of Korzybski's life, subsequent editions of the *Reader's Guide* (published every few years) would index a respectable number of articles directly related to his work (listed mainly under "Semantics" or his name—never as "General Semantics").

As the year began, Alfred got more good news. George Houck from The Science Press wrote to tell him that out of the 2000 originally-bound copies of *Science and Sanity* only about 240 copies remained.[11] The Science Press awaited instruction from him as to when to bind the 1000 additional books they held in storage. He told Houck to hold off until they were down to 100 copies. *Science and Sanity* may not have qualified as a bestseller but it was selling.[12]

The Institute of General Semantics

For several days in March, Korzybski lectured to the medical staff at Peoria State Hospital, Peoria, Illinois. His presentation there marked the end of his career as an independent, itinerant teacher. For the next twelve years—until his death on March 1, 1950—he would carry on his work under the auspices of the organization, the Institute of General Semantics (IGS), which he and a few of his closest students were in the process of setting up in Chicago. The state of Illinois incorporated it in May as a non-profit institution for "Linguistic Epistemologic Scientific Research and Education".

Besides Korzybski, the Director of the Institute (the position he kept until his death), the founding trustees included Campbell, Congdon, Kendig, and Cornelius Crane. Kendig, having moved to Chicago to work with Korzybski, took the role of Executive Secretary and Education Director. Korzybski was named President of the Institute Board of Trustees and Crane, heir to a plumbing-fixtures manufacturing fortune, the Vice-President. Crane had had a number of personal consultations with Korzybski over the last year or two, which had helped him. Enthusiastic about general semantics, he had pledged a total of $50,000 to be paid out to the Institute in semi-annual portions of $10,000 each on the first of July and January of each year until mid-1940. He had indicated he might give additional money after that, but hoped the Institute by then would have begun to generate income on its own from seminars, book sales, and additional fundraising. (Alfred had wanted Crane's pledge in writing, but Crane never got around to doing so.) Korzybski got Crane's first check on July 1, 1938. The Institute was ready for business.

Korzybski had signed a personal lease for a little apartment to house the Institute. These quarters, at 1330 East 56th St. on the outskirts of the campus of the University of Chicago, had a large reception room or parlor for lectures, a dining room serving as a library, and two bedrooms for Korzybski's and Kendig's offices. Pearl Johnecheck, a young woman with a secretarial background who had studied with Korzybski and helped out at previous Chicago seminars, would serve as his office manager and confidential secretary. Pearl, who planned to become a psychiatrist, attended morning pre-med classes at the University of Chicago, and then worked at the Institute 'part-time'—in other words from around 1:00 in the afternoon until some indefinite evening hour. She seemed to be one of the few people whom Korzybski could relax around—it doesn't appear she had any significant 'emotional' problems that he ever had to deal with. He could depend on her to keep mum about his personal student files and private correspondence. Pearl, Alfred, and Kendig constituted the initial Institute staff, along with one or more clerical workers.

Pearl Johnecheck,
circa 1940

The humble first home of the Institute seemed a far cry from the headquarters for anything like an "International Non-Aristotelian Society"—Korzybski's 1933 vision of a center for a world-wide movement of institutions of learning with the aim of reducing misevaluation in science and life. Still, the new Institute provided a partial fulfillment of Korzybski's earlier dream. With its location in Chicago—a major, centrally located U.S. city and university center—Korzybski would no longer *have* to travel to teach. He could focus on working with so-called 'normal' people rather than institutionalized ones. (He was no longer referring to students as "patients".) And he wouldn't have to go it alone. He could develop his work further with the help of others. He looked forward to the fructifying effect of students from different professions coming to the Institute for assistance in applying GS in their fields. He also wanted to write more and to encourage others to write. The Institute would be able to serve as the conduit for further publishing, another old dream going back to the early 1920s when he first envisioned "The Library of Human Engineering".

1938 certainly seemed like a good time for starting an institute dedicated to educating people about the perils of human evaluating—and what they could do about it. In March, 1938, just prior to the founding of the Institute, Nazi Germany had marched troops into Austria and annexed it. In May, while the Institute was being incorporated, Hitler and Mussolini declared their eternal friendship. Hitler was threatening Czechoslovakia over the Sudentenland, the German-speaking portion of Czechoslovakia bordering Germany. Both the British and French leaderships seemed prepared to appease Hitler in the belief they could thus prevent a wider conflict. Meanwhile in Asia, Imperial Japanese forces carried on with their brutal invasion of China, having recently accomplished that rampage of atrocities and mass murder now known as the "Rape of Nanking", in China's then-capital city. An atmosphere of concern, even fear, hung in the air.

On July 6, the Institute sponsored its first Korzybski seminar. (He wrote to Mira that he felt so extremely nervous about doing it—believing so much depended on its success—that on the first night, he untypically soaked his bed clothes with sweat.)[13] The seminar ran for six weeks, until August 17 (although the personal interviews with Korzybski continued afterwards). Thirty-nine students met with Alfred twice weekly in the evenings—convenient since many of them were graduate students at the University of Chicago and/or taught at other institutions. Tuition was twenty dollars.

It seems unlikely that Korzybski—an inveterate newspaper reader—would have missed the following story, which made headlines midway through the seminar. On July 18, Douglas Corrigan had landed his single-seater plane in Ireland after supposedly trying to fly it from New York City to Los Angeles. He claimed that with the cloud cover beneath him and a stuck compass directing him, he had flown east when he thought he was traveling west. With "dumb luck" he ended up in Dublin instead of Los Angeles. Corrigan became a celebrity. His new nickname—'Wrong Way Corrigan' also became a favored label for anyone addled by a severe map-territory mismatch. (Suspicions remain that Corrigan—a seasoned airman—had indeed known what he was doing and faked his trans-Atlantic blunder in order to evade punishment from aviation authorities who had refused his initial flight plan to Europe.) This story didn't just provide a lighthearted sidelight to more serious news. Korzybski was probably not the only person wondering about the 'Wrong Way Corrigans' who seemed to be running the governments and institutions of the world.

He felt he was in a position to help those who wanted to do something besides simply lament 'wrong-way' evaluation. In his first lecture he told the class, "Fear is ruling the world today. Why that fear? Because we have no rational means to be rational. It practically amounts to a world neurosis. In [general] semantics we will find means with which we can deal with these problems."[14] On August 1, he was telling this first Institute of General Semantics seminar class:

> I wonder if you have ever thought of the extreme dishonesty etc. going on in the world. Can you trust a Mussolini or a Hitler or a Jap? Can we depend on their promises? Can we have dependability; predictability? Do you realize the anti-human, anti-civilized [forces] depending on lies and treachery? You can see how personal issues spread to wider issues. This has spread across the world. <u>Fear</u> is the result, and <u>fear is at the bottom of all neuroses</u>. Is this class here only because of scientific curiosity? No. You want to get at some of these mechanisms. Lack of predictability and dependability is at the bottom of life today. ....[15]

Dishonesty, lack of predictability and dependability not only characterized the extreme behavior of Hitler, et al., but also of more benign leaders. For example, after the annexation of Austria the situation for European Jews, especially those directly under Nazi rule in Germany and Austria was becoming desperate. While this first IGS Seminar was taking place, an international League of Nations conference called by President Roosevelt, was being held in Evian, France to discuss the fate of German and Austrian Jewish refugees. Delegates from nation after nation bemoaned the fate of the Jews. None of them, including the U.S., made even a tiny opening in their restrictive immigration policies (except for the Dominican Republic). At Evian the map had replaced the territory it was supposed to represent. The words of concern expressed there substituted for the policies actually needed.[16]

Korzybski felt perpetually peeved by this kind of behavior, again demonstrated a few months later in September by British Prime Minister Neville Chamberlain and French Prime Minister Edouard Deladier. The two leaders went to Munich for a conference with Hitler and Mussolini. There the British and French leaders acceded to Nazi demands to annex the Sudentenland in return for which Hitler promised to cease all further aggression. (Czech government representatives were not invited to participate in the deliberations dividing up their country.) Chamberlain returned to England with a piece of paper in hand, signed by Hitler. He declared to a cheering throng "I believe this is peace for our time." Korzybski felt sheer disgust. (Several months afterwards, at the end of January 1939, he wrote to his friend R. B. Haseldon, "Since the Armistice I have never been so depressed as because of the latest Deladier-Chamberlain performances.")[17] Korzybski felt confident that Chamberlain's policy of appeasing the Nazis through negotiations and concessions wouldn't work. He definitely expected Hitler to break his promises. Indeed, Nazi Germany soon invaded and annexed the remainder of Czechoslovakia in the spring of 1939. Predictability. Korzybski had already predicted a second world war coming.[18] Feeling that the world desperately needed what he had to teach, he knew of nothing else to do but to work harder.

Seminars and Scholars

Even before finishing his first evening seminar, Korzybski had begun a second, week-long course which went from August 15 to August 20—the Institute's first "Intensive" seminar. The twenty-four attendees included nine people who had studied with Wendell Johnson, a Professor of Speech Pathology and Psychology at the State University of Iowa, who had been presenting general-semantics material in his speech hygiene course. Johnson had become interested in Korzybski's work—and had been privately studying with him—as a result of his own lifelong stuttering problem

Johnson had taken his interest in finding a remedy for stuttering quite far—to the extent of getting a PhD in clinical psychology and speech pathology in 1931. In the fall of 1936, while convalescing from an emergency appendectomy, he started reading Korzybski's 'blue peril', which a friend had just given him. Johnson recalled in a 1956 article:

> As soon as I recovered sufficiently to hold this massive tome I began to read it—and I have never been the same since. My convalescence lasted about two weeks and by that time I was so thoroughly enmeshed in what I found in *Science and Sanity*, that I ended up spending the greater part of my reading time for the next year or so reading and rereading, evaluating and re-evaluating Korzybski's complicated document. I satisfied myself that it is not a book about which one can be glib.[19]

Soon afterwards he met Korzybski in Chicago and began to work with him privately. "I had never before encountered a teacher quite like him and he had never had a student who stuttered as I did, and so between the two of us we licked the platter of our mutual interests."

> ...By 1936 I had the feeling that I had pretty much exhausted the possibilities of gaining substantial benefit from the existing theories of stuttering and the current methods treating it...
>
> Coming to *Science and Sanity*...I was motivated to gain from the book anything I could that might be helpful. I found a good deal that was intriguing...There is nothing in *Science and Sanity* about stuttering, as such, except one sentence which I believe to be in error, but the book generally is about the processes of abstracting, and I recognized it therefore, as being peculiarly relevant to the particular problem with which I was concerned...It seems to me that stuttering is similar to many other human problems that involve anxiety-tensions, and to the degree that this is so the possibility exists that the field of general semantics holds promise for the improvement of our understanding of a number of other human problems in addition to that of stuttering.[20]

Korzybski soon met another individual with great promise. From September 8 to 15, he gave a special course mainly devoted to one-on-one individual training for Wilma Lloyd, a psychologist working with the Progressive Education Commission on Secondary School Curriculum. Three other individuals also attended for several days. One of them, Samuel Ichiye Hayakawa would play a significant role in generating interest in Korzybski and his work, although Korzybski and others would ultimately come to consider his contribution a mixed blessing.

Hayakawa, a Canadian citizen of Japanese descent, had gotten his PhD in English and American literature at the University of Wisconsin in 1935 for his work on Oliver Wendell Holmes (published as a book with Howard Mumford Jones in 1939)[21]. He had also done work in lexicography. At the time he met Korzybski, he was about to return to his job as an English professor at the University of Wisconsin Extension Department in Madison. He had just come from a summer course in Linguistics at the University of Michigan. People there had heard of Korzybski but knew little about his work. Hayakawa, who had done some reading, gave a few presentations and felt curious to find out more. He wrote to Korzybski, who invited him to visit. Hayakawa later reported what happened when he met Korzybski that first day:

> Korzybski greeted me with great cordiality. "So you are Hayakawa! You have been lecturing on general semantics at the University of Michigan and you don't know a goddam thing about it!" I couldn't take offense at this greeting. It was warmly meant—and I was certainly in no position to disagree. I laughed and he laughed and we were on good terms at once.[22]

In Hayakawa, Korzybski recognized a man who had a special ability to write with ease. And Hayakawa found in Korzybski's work the fresh and integrative point of view for teaching English he had been looking for. Hayakawa's few days at this 1938 seminar appeared to give impetus to his ongoing interest in developing a vitalized approach to language instruction. He had been reading various writers on what he called 'semantics', such as Bloomfield, Bridgman, Ogden, Richards, Sapir, and others. General Semantics, with its emphasis on the total behavioral response of the individual, seemed to him to provide an important and practical unifying approach to these other studies.

Over the next year he would write an introductory text-book, *Language in Action*, using 'general semantics' as his framework for bringing together these various other, related approaches to understanding words and their 'meanings' in human communication. Initially, he had the book mimeographed and published privately as a textbook for classes at the University of Wisconsin. It was soon picked up as a text by other universities. In 1940 he produced a second revised book, giving discounted copies to the IGS, which agreed to be listed as the publisher. Korzybski recommended the book to his friend David Fairchild. Fairchild told another friend, an editor at Harcourt, about it. Harcourt and the Book of the Month Club published it at the end of 1941 and it soon became a huge success both as an English textbook and for general readers. The book in its Fifth Edition, with the title *Language in Thought and Action* (renamed in 1949), remains in print. By now, it has sold over one million copies. By the mid-1940s, differences between the two men would emerge as a major source of trouble for Korzybski. However, at the beginning of their relationship, Korzybski felt delighted with Hayakawa's interest in his work.

In these early days of the Institute, as GS was becoming better known, Korzybski wanted to focus on teaching professionals in different fields how to train their own nervous systems, achieve some kind of improved adjustment for themselves, and *then* to apply GS to their work, teach it, and write about it. Some people were already confusing Korzybski's educational work with psychotherapy—although there was no denying some overlap. He welcomed the interest of students of speech and language instruction like Johnson and Hayakawa because—for one thing—it clearly showed that GS could not be isolated within the bounds of therapy.

However, the prominence of such students in the early days of the Institute may have encouraged an equally mistaken view. Many people had trouble understanding that GS *was not* another school of speech or language study but provided a general methodology dealing with problems in any human activity involving evaluation (not exclusively a linguistic matter). One could get a glimpse of the discipline's generality in the Institute's first copyrighted publication. Earlier in the year, Hansell Baugh, a librarian of the University of Pennsylvania Medical School, had started putting together a volume of papers from the 1935 Congress at Ellensburg, Washington. Korzybski and Kendig corresponded with him for several months to assist with the editing. The book, entitled *General Semantics: Papers from the First American Congress for General Semantics* came out in October and included papers relating GS to mathematics, logic, psychology, linguistics, education, sociology, biology, and psychiatry. The printing of around 200 copies sold out within a year (it was reprinted in 1940).

Korzybski had several more seminars scheduled in 1938. He found the pace grueling but deemed it necessary if the Institute was to get a large enough core of professionals working to apply the discipline. For some time, the Institute would continue to experiment with different formats for delivering the twelve or so lectures of two or more hours each that Korzybski considered necessary for conveying the basic content. (This didn't include the additional time needed for students' personal interviews with Korzybski.) Formats included bi-weekly evening, Saturday, and longer continuous courses. After that first August intensive, Korzybski gave a number of other intensive courses over the next year, including a Holiday Intensive that winter which ran from December 26–31. Success with the intensives led Korzybski and Kendig to judge that format particularly useful for busy professionals and Korzybski delivered at least one, usually more than one, every subsequent year of his life. The Winter Holiday Intensive became an annual IGS tradition, usually starting a day after Christmas and continuing through the first few days of the New Year. Korzybski's lecture time—in whatever format—gradually increased over the next two years from about twenty hours per course to from thirty-six to forty hours, which would become his standard.

At the lectern, Autumn 1938

Cornelius Crane

After the September intensive, Korzybski had a break of a few weeks prior to the seminar starting October 10. He traveled to Ipswich, Massachusetts, north of Boston for discussions with Crane at Castle Hill, the country estate of Crane's mother. Crane had ideas for developing the Institute. No doubt Korzybski had some things to tell him as well. Korzybski felt a responsibility towards Crane as the Institute's main donor. Both he and Kendig had tried by means of letters to keep Crane informed of Institute goings-on. But some things were probably best said face-to-face.

Crane, then in his early thirties, was wealthy enough to have never needed to work for a living and had made a career for himself as a philanthropist and patron of science. His main accomplishment so far had involved leading a sailing expedition around the Pacific islands in the late 1920s, which had collected archeological artifacts and biological specimens for Chicago's Field Museum of Natural History. In the late 1930s, Crane was providing financial support to a number of individuals besides Korzybski, including George Devereux, a Hungarian-born anthropologist who had done field research among the Mohave Indians and became known as a pioneer in applying psychoanalysis as a framework for anthropological research. Korzybski, initially impressed with Devereux's brilliance and interest in GS, agreed to have him work at the Institute. Crane acted as if Devereaux's salary was to be taken out of the Institute's operational funds, rather than from a special fund for that purpose (as Alfred had understood the arrangement). Korzybski sought to dissuade Crane of that notion but the issue soon became moot because it turned out that Devereux's and Korzybski's personalities didn't mix well. Korzybski dismissed him early in 1939. Later in 1939, Crane was paying to get psychiatrist N. E. Ischchlondsky's books translated from German into English. Ischchlondsky had worked with Pavlov and written on the confluence of Pavlovian reflexology and psychiatry. Crane again asked Korzybski to dispense payments through the Institute and Korzybski, perhaps foolishly, agreed to do so.

Cornelius Crane

Korzybski's visit to Castle Hill in the fall of 1938 seemed to go well, with Crane enthusiastic about him and the work of the Institute. Crane's extended family, with whom Alfred got better acquainted, seemed enthusiastic too. Indeed, in a few months, Crane attended the Holiday Intensive Seminar with his wife Cathalene and his adopted teenage daughter from his wife's previous marriage—also named Cathalene (later, the mother of actor Chevy Chase). Crane, despite his enthusiasm, had a number of criticisms which he expressed in a letter to Alfred written on the first day of the Intensive. The letter clearly shows he felt uncomfortable with the out-of-the-ordinary nature of general semantics; he expressed his distress upon hearing people talking about "the new cult" that he was interested in.

Korzybski's demeanor and lack of concern for social conventions didn't help: "I believe your foreign accent, shaven head, work clothes, constitute a bizarre general impression which may be beneficial and attractive if your conduct is at all times stable, suave, "gentlemanly", etc." He then went on with three more pages of complaints about Korzybski's speech and behavior which he considered ungentlemanly, unscholarly, and suspicious—including the fact that Alfred kept a roll of toilet paper on his desk to blow his nose with. Some of the criticism seemed apt. For example, Crane wanted him to do better about keeping his fingernails clean and washing his hands before doing the hands-on work of 'relaxing' a student. Korzybski seemed unlikely to do anything about most of Crane's concerns other than shrug them off as petty. Still the letter definitely showed Crane's ambivalent feelings towards Korzybski and the Institute. Alfred was going to have to watch his step.

Crane had also invited Douglas Campbell to Camp Hill to participate in the discussions with Alfred. Campbell had recently left Chicago for New York City with his wife Berta (Bertha) Ochsner, a well-known Mid-Western dancer-choreographer. Among other things, Campbell planned to do psychoanalytical work with Karen Horney. He would remain in New York for a year. Whether his work with Horney did him any personal good seems hard to say. By 1940 after a twenty-year marriage, he would leave Berta, move to San Francisco, and marry Marian Van Tuyl, a dancer with whom Berta had worked in Chicago. Since 1937 Campbell had published a number of articles on psychiatry and general semantics in professional journals and given numerous presentations and courses on GS. Then, in 1942 Berta killed herself.[23] Afterwards, Campbell's writing and work in general semantics virtually ceased (although he did remain on the IGS Board of Trustees for a number of years). Perhaps he felt embarrassed to do more than maintain minimal contact since Korzybski and others at the Institute knew Berta and likely knew the circumstances of her death. (Years after Korzybski's death, Campbell—who died in 1983—made a kind of return to the Institute by agreeing to become an honorary trustee. He reminisced about his old friend Alfred at the Korzybski Centenary Celebration in New York City in 1979.)

Mira Returns

The death of his friend Calvin Bridges on December 27, at the age of 49 after a brief illness, was sad news for Alfred. Still, on the whole, 1938 had concluded positively—both for the Institute and for Alfred personally. Crane's support seemed reasonably secure. Alfred's work and the Institute were getting national publicity. *Time Magazine* had featured an article on him and the Institute under "Education" in its November 21 edition. He also had another paper accepted and presented in abstract (since he couldn't appear in person) at the December 29th AAAS Mathematics Section meeting in Richmond, Virginia: "General Semantics: Extensionalization in Mathematics, Mathematical Physics, and General Education. Paper II: Thalamic Symbolism and Mathematics". And Mira had returned home.

Her ship, coming from Trinidad, had docked in New York City in November. The private apartment Alfred had rented for them around the corner from the Institute was still filled with unpacked boxes. He had not spent much time there, and had even sublet the apartment for a while, sleeping on his office floor. Now he had to unpack and get the apartment ready. He asked Mira to delay coming to Chicago and she spent the month in New York and Boston, visiting friends. When she arrived at the end of the month, one can assume a warm welcome from Alfred who had genuinely missed her. In their letters, they had seemed to come to some kind of agreement as to how to renew their relationship.

But some things would have to be different. Alfred had made clear in letters that he did not want her to be involved with his work or the Institute. Given her interest in general semantics, she would find this difficult but would do her best to comply. (Alfred did relent on this a bit, since over the next year and a half he allowed her to attend three of his seminars.) Although he still expressed some desire for a personal life with her, he had told her that he hadn't initially anticipated the degree to which the Institute would dominate his time. He didn't expect this to change anytime soon. Mira had said she understood this. Ever hopeful, she believed that despite Alfred's conditions they would be able to share some kind of decent life together.

Chapter 49
GROWING PAINS

The next $10,000 check from Crane was due on January 1, 1939. Alfred had already wondered to Mira about Crane's reliability. He couldn't have felt totally surprised when the check didn't come on time. He waited about a week before sending several letters and telegrams to Crane at his New York City address. He wrote to Douglas and Berta Campbell, also in New York, asking them to try to contact Crane. Shortly thereafter, in the middle of the month, the check finally arrived. Alfred felt relieved. Nonetheless, he didn't relish depending so much on his benefactor's whims.

No one understood the tenuous nature of the Institute's existence better than Alfred. On the surface, things looked good. For a small, recently founded, non-profit educational organization representing a strange new hybrid—to some mongrel—discipline without academic affiliation, the Institute of General Semantics was doing remarkably well. Korzybski finally had some decent, though insufficient, help. His work was getting publicity and gaining students and supporters. Science Press had bound the last 1,000 copies of the First Edition of *Science and Sanity*, which was selling well (about 100 books per month). In the long run, he felt sure the Institute could thrive based on his ability to "deliver the goods". But he didn't know of any organization like his that could function on book sales and tuition income alone. Crane had promised three more semi-annual payments of 10,000 dollars, which would get them through the end of 1941. By that time, they would have taught enough students and developed enough momentum and publicity to be able to mount a decent fund-raising campaign. In the meantime, the Institute's survival depended on Crane keeping his original commitment.

The insecurity Korzybski felt about Crane's largesse was only one of the pressures under which he was operating. There was also the pressure of his and Mira's personal finances. If his berating of Mira from time to time about money seemed excessive, he genuinely worried about the fact that they did not have a large amount of savings. This meant they would have to count their pennies—even with an anticipated income from his Institute salary of $5,000 per year, the royalties and profits from his books, what his mother's estate owed them for the mortgage of the house on Wilcza Street, and whatever Mira would be able to earn from her painting. In letters to Mira, to whom he seemed more likely than anyone else to reveal his dark and gloomy side, he told her more than once that he considered them both quite 'old'—she had just had her 67th birthday and he would soon be 60—and they would need money soon enough for their final hospitalizations and funeral expenses. In the meantime, before he coagulated, he felt he had no choice but to push ahead with his work as hard and as far as he could. If for no other reason, he wanted to make sure Mira would continue to have food to eat and a roof overhead if he died before she did.

Since the publication of *Science and Sanity*, his dealings with other people and their concerns had increased with his efforts to publicize and teach his work. The founding of the Institute brought a new level of complications as the number of people and relationships he dealt with multiplied. As Gracuinas would have predicted, his problems had seemed to increase exponentially. He was juggling an expanded set of complicating responsibilities: to his chief funder Crane, to his co-workers, to the Institute-as-a-whole, to Mira, to his students, etc.

His sense of obligation to his students introduced extra complicating factors, especially his insistence on the necessity of personal interviews with them, which involved a serious enlargement of his work. But he saw no way out. His request that former students then write and report on their ongoing progress added to his workload. He also had mail from non-students seeking his help or advice, people who had either read his books or had read or heard something about his work (Chase's book and the *Time* article already had a major impact here). Either he, Kendig, or Pearl had to reply. Then, he had visitors to the Institute—sometimes the obscure and sometimes the well-known like Bertrand Russell, I. A. Richards, and Kurt Lewin.

Some walk-in visitors he couldn't turn away. For example, the previous November he had received a surprise telephone call from his friend Bronislaw Malinowski. The ailing anthropologist had come through Chicago on his return from the Mayo Clinic, where he had just gone through a complete medical workup. Alfred invited him to come to the Institute. The two men talked shop and Alfred gave his friend a manual relaxation session, then called in Kendig to meet him. When Alfred stepped out for a few minutes, Malinowski told Kendig that he considered Korzybski's work the most important of the century. Alfred undoubtedly felt pleased with the visit.[1] He may not have considered such an unplanned event as a burden, but it did take time, which seemed more and more scarce.

In early January 1939, he got another surprise—this time burdensome. The managing company of 1330 E. 56th St. wrote to Korzybski demanding that he stop giving lectures in the Institute apartment. One of his neighbors in the building had complained. The seminars constituted a major income source for the Institute, which didn't have enough money to rent an extra hotel room or lecture hall just for that purpose. Alfred surveyed the other tenants, some of whom hadn't even been aware of the Institute in their building. They wrote letters of support for Korzybski. But the letters didn't help. If Alfred wasn't going to stop giving his seminar lectures on the Institute premises, then the Institute was going to have to move. The change would not be entirely unwelcome. After all, the cramped apartment had turned out rather less than ideal. Korzybski and his small office staff couldn't avoid getting in each others' way. And when Alfred closed the door of his windowless office for privacy—say to conduct an interview—his hot and inevitably smoke-filled room was not exactly conducive to semantic relaxation.

Within a few months, he had found an entire house to rent located on their current street, but a block further west in the direction of the University of Chicago campus. In terms of space, the peculiarly numbered building at 1234 East 56th Street seemed much better. It had a downstairs reception area and a dining room they could use for a library. Another large room that could hold at least 60 people would work very well for lectures. There were four or five rooms upstairs that could be used for offices and/or bedrooms, as well as a large garret for storage trunks. It definitely had the extra room they needed and, since they would have the whole building to themselves, no neighbors to bother. On the other hand, the oil-heated building, in disrepair, needed a fair amount of maintenance and would require a full-time janitor. And at $175 a month, it was certainly going to cost more than their present rental. A special board of trustees meeting had been called on March 31 to take advantage of the fact that Crane, then living in New York City, had come to town. What did he think? At the meeting, he approved of the move and a week later, when the prospective landlord wanted a commitment on a five-year lease, Crane sent a telegram to Alfred in which he agreed to guarantee it for that period of time.

IGS Headquarters in Chicago at 1234 E. 56th St.

At the meeting, Crane still appeared highly committed to the Institute. For one thing, he told Alfred that he was planning to get additional life insurance for himself in which he would name the Institute as his beneficiary. In addition, he might be willing to provide more money after the last of his promised semi-annual payments (there were three more to go). He also strongly urged a number of measures designed to bolster the Institute.

First, he wanted some plans in place for the Institute in case of Korzybski's unexpected death. Who was competent to fill in as Director? Korzybski assured Crane that, if necessary, C. B. Congdon would be able to carry the Institute mission forward with Pearl and Kendig's guidance and assistance. Second, Crane had become a strong advocate of gathering a list of well-known academics, professionals, government officials, etc., as honorary trustees of the Institute. (The original idea had probably come from Kendig.) Crane believed such a list would be useful for Institute fundraising. The Honorary Trustees would have no official duties but would agree to have their names associated with Korzybski and get listed as supporters of the aims and program of the Institute of General Semantics. Within the next nine months, letters of invitation would get sent and an initial group of distinguished world scientists, intellectuals, and professionals would agree to be listed. Third, Crane offered additional material help. Kendig was in serious financial straits. She had made $5,000 to $12,000 a year in previous jobs. But now she was getting a salary of $2,400 from the Institute from which she had to pay her rent and living expenses as well as send money to support her ailing mother, who had a mortgage on a farmhouse in Connecticut. She didn't think she would be able to continue working for the Institute unless she got more money. But losing her at this point would seriously disrupt Korzybski's efforts to keep the Institute going. Her background in publishing, education, and research, and her strong work ethic and organizational abilities had made her indispensable. Crane said he would donate an extra $1,000 to the Institute for the next two years to supplement her income. He sent the first check for Kendig in April. With the general enthusiasm he showed at the board meeting, and the additional money he was providing for Kendig, could Crane's reliability still be in doubt?

In mid-May, the Institute moved to the new address. Alfred and Mira also moved to a new apartment, still close, which they would keep for another year before letting the lease run out. Alfred's long working hours, combined with the increasing disability he experienced due to his war injuries, made sleeping at the Institute more convenient. He had a bedroom right next to his upstairs office. Mira had found a painting studio to rent at 161 East Erie Street on Chicago's Near North Side, about eight miles north of the Institute. Over the following year, she would make her living quarters there as well. Alfred and Mira still saw each other, talked on the telephone, and—she more than he—wrote letters. She also attended a few Institute seminars. From the evidence of letters into the next year, their relations seemed congenial enough. But since Mira had returned, the pattern of distancing by Alfred seemed clear. He worked almost constantly with the result of far too little contact for Mira's liking.

Two weeks after the move, Alfred and Pearl left for a short trip to Los Angeles on a slow train. (He figured a slightly longer ride, away from everyday business, would give him a little 'vacation' and a chance to work on a third "General Semantics: Extensionalization..." paper he was planning for an upcoming AAAS meeting.) Vocha Fiske had organized a Los Angeles Society for General Semantics. She had at least sixty people there eager to hear Korzybski. He gave three introductory lectures on GS, another one on GS and psychotherapy, and one on GS and education over a weekend (June 2, 3, and 4), in addition to having personal interviews with interested attendees. With whatever fees he received (besides paid expenses), he considered the results quite positive. His lectures, which were transcribed and later printed by the Los Angeles Society, seemed exceptionally good. He returned to Chicago immediately, getting back about five days later. Both he and Pearl felt exhausted. So did Kendig, who had been left to supervise the Institute where they were still unpacking and developing a daily routine. Almost at once, they had to prepare for another intensive seminar among innumerable other tasks. As Alfred wrote to Crane, "Everybody is fooled and surprised because the Institute is run so well. Nobody realizes that we can do that at the price of killing ourselves, with practically no help."[2]

The pace of seminars for 1939 (seven in all) did seem rather killing. The first, from February 5 to 11, had been a special tete-a-tete seminar given for psychiatrist George S. Stevenson, Director of the National Committee for Mental Hygiene, who had become very interested in Korzybski's work. (A psychologist from Canada participated as well.) Then Alfred taught a March-April evening seminar series, before giving the Los Angeles lectures in early June. After his return, he had another Intensive scheduled in June, to be followed by another June-July evening series. An Intensive followed in August, then after a long break, the second annual Holiday Intensive. He found the teaching load—including interviews—exhausting. If they could reduce the number of seminars for 1940 (which seemed possible), he would have more time to write, attend to long-term planning, fund-raising, etc.

Long term plans and fund-raising—for what? From the beginning of the Institute, Korzybski had wanted to focus on training professionals in different fields who would be able to teach and apply GS in their own areas. Physicians and psychiatrists were important groups for him, as were educators from elementary to college levels in different specialties. He and Kendig foresaw senior students running separate IGS divisions for the purpose of training the professionals in their fields in extensional methodology. The first area to be developed would be psychiatry. A senior psychiatrist such as Congdon, well-trained in GS by Korzybski, could serve as the Medical Director of a Psychiatry Division of the Institute supervising the in-depth training of other psychiatrists, physicians, medical students, social workers, nurses, and counselors. This division would develop therapy staff and facilities. Korzybski could continue his introductory, in-depth seminar courses including personal interviews. However, he would be able to refer those who wanted or needed more long-term personal application work, or even psychotherapy, to others more suited to do that. An education division could train GS-oriented teachers from different subject areas, as well as teachers who would teach GS, including some who might teach at the Institute. Such an extensive program would free Korzybski's time for focusing on just the teaching he wanted to do, for his own creative writing, and for directing other people's writing and research. Of course, this plan—which Kendig outlined in September 1939—would require significant grant money to get started. And they would need more time, planning, and money to get the grants. Still, they certainly intended to get out from under the staggering work-load they had been carrying, in order to develop the IGS into a powerful educational force with adequate staff and a program that might make optimal use of Korzybski's, Kendig's, and others' creative energies. In the meantime, they would have to keep up with the brutal pace they had set so far—one damn seminar after another.

Chapter 50
THE AUGUST INTENSIVE

The eclectic mix of students likely to attend an IGS seminar might include artists, businessmen, college professors, college students, engineers, doctors, housewives, lawyers, psychiatrists, salesmen, scientists, secretaries, writers, and an occasional mystic. In that regard, the 1939 August Intensive seminar—which ran from August 25 to September 2 (the personal interviews continued until September 6)—had a typical group. However, a number of notable participants also made this one of the more remarkable groups in the history of Korzybski's Institute seminars. For one thing, S.I. Hayakawa, Wendell Johnson, Irving J. Lee, and Elwood Murray all attended. These men would soon become known as major academic interpreters and popularizers of Korzybski's work.

August 1939 Intensive Seminar,
Group photo with Korzybski

Hayakawa, the man with the bow tie seated on the ground on the left, had just taken a job in Chicago at the Armour Institute of Technology (later to be named the Illinois Institute of Technology). He had registered as a seminar student and had gotten a tuition scholarship. He brought his wife Margedant as a guest. An examination of the seminar attendance record shows that both missed more than half the sessions, much more than any other students in the class. Neither of them had a personal interview or participated in the semantic relaxation session. Hayakawa himself sat in at later seminars, although he often fell asleep when he felt bored, a habit he apparently kept when—many years afterwards—he became a U.S. Senator. He never did sit through a complete seminar, and he later proudly admitted that he never had a standard interview with Korzybski to work on his own personal adjustment.[1] In a later video interview, he did recall experiencing semantic relaxation at some time or other from Korzybski's hands, which definitely impressed him.[2]

As for Margedant Hayakawa, she recalled years later that Korzybski terrified her from the first time she met him—he struck her as an 'authoritarian personality'. Later, although Korzybski sometimes invited her to come to classes or see him for an interview, she always managed to avoid doing so.[3] Her negative initial reaction to Korzybski may have influenced her husband. But at this point, he appeared very enthusiastic about Korzybski and GS. He had already had two articles about GS published. He had also just finished the draft of the first experimental edition of *Language in Action*. Korzybski and Kendig did some editing of it during the seminar and felt very enthusiastic about Hayakawa as well.

Wendell Johnson (standing in the third row from the front at Korzybski's lefthand side) also attended the August Intensive with his wife Edna. Johnson was becoming another major academic exponent of Korzybski's work. In relation to GS, 1939 had already turned out to be a very productive year for him. In the Spring, the IGS had published his booklet *Language and Speech Hygiene: An Application of General Semantics*, as the first in its series of *General Semantics Monographs*. It had started as the course outline of Johnson's University of Iowa speech hygiene class. With a great deal of editing by Korzybski and Kendig, he then expanded it into a short practical treatise on general semantics. (In 1946, he presented his further development of this monograph material in *People in Quandaries: The Semantics of Personal Adjustment*. Published by Harper & Brothers, the book provides a highly-readable and still valuable introduction to Korzybski's work.) In the latter part of 1939, Johnson was continuing to be productive in his teaching and application of GS. He had already begun supervising speech-pathology graduate research related to his GS-inspired "diagnosogenic" theory of stuttering.[4] For the 1939 Fall semester, Johnson would begin teaching a regular three-credit course in "General Semantics", the first university course offered anywhere under that name. (He continued to teach a course in "General Semantics" at Iowa for over two decades.) At this August seminar, eight of the other participants (besides his wife) were either colleagues of his or students, who said he had gotten them interested in attending.[5]

Irving J. Lee, a 29-year-old assistant professor of public speaking at Northwestern University, had preceded his attendance at the August Intensive with what he described as a 'six-months battle to digest everything Korzybski had put into print.'[6] Lee (in the group picture standing behind Kendig on the far left of the third row) had worked for a number of years as a high school social studies teacher before beginning his graduate studies in Speech and Social Psychology at Northwestern, where he had already begun to gain a reputation as an exceptionally talented teacher. Although he had gotten his PhD only a year before, he had already been appointed Chairman of the Northwestern School of Speech. His interest in GS seemed to have sprung naturally from his interest in public speaking, rhetoric, and social/behavioral science. On his registration form for the seminar, Lee wrote that he was "...interested in those modes of analysis by which a speaker can make his assertions more 'meaningful' to audiences and vice versa." Within two years, he would write the book *Language Habits in Human Affairs* with a foreword by Korzybski. Korzybski would come to consider him one of his finest students. Before his untimely death in 1955, he had become one of the most accomplished writers and teachers in GS, writing many more articles and books and inspiring general readers, as well as a new generation of general-semantics teachers and researchers in the field of Speech Communication.

The last of this group of four was veteran speech professor Elwood Murray (standing on the far right of the back row). Unlike Hayakawa, Johnson, and Lee, whose works developed a popular audience, Murray's influence remained primarily within academia. Born in 1897, Murray had grown up on a Nebraska farm and had already had a varied career as a school teacher and debate coach before getting his PhD in Speech with a minor in Psychology at the University of Iowa in 1931. His graduate school experience seems emblematic of the direction he took in his career. He had intended to do his work in rhetoric. But after he wrote an article on Aristotle that upset his chief advisor on the subject, he switched his topic to Speech Pathology and did research on "Disintegration of Breathing and Eye Movements in Stutterers". He would remain interested in those areas of communication traditionally the purview of rhetoric, but he would take a decidedly behavioral/social science approach to studying them—something relatively new in the field of speech at that time. Since 1931, he had served as Professor of Speech and Dramatic Arts and Chairman of the Department of Speech at the University of Denver.

Murray had learned about Korzybski from someone in his department. Having read *Science and Sanity* before the course, he wrote on his registration form that he wanted to know how he could apply GS "[f]or personality adjustment of speakers, [and was] also interested in [using it for] improving technics in human relations for a technological age." Kendig noted after the seminar, "[as] a person [Murray] benefited from the seminar and seems pretty well 'sold' on General Semantics although puzzled about how to translate his own former work into the system of evaluation."[7] He managed to do so quite well. He would soon integrate general semantics into his teaching and writing. Many of his graduate students would pursue GS-related research. On a personal level, Murray maintained a close, helping relationship with Korzybski and the Institute of General Semantics over the rest of Korzybski's life. Murray's relationship with the Institute continued throughout the course of his long career at the University of Denver and after his retirement from active teaching in 1962 (he briefly served as Director of the Institute from 1967 to 1969). Murray would become an important pioneering figure in getting the academic Speech discipline to evolve into the interdisciplinary science-art of Communication. Korzybski's work would remain one of his main sources of inspiration.

Several other participants in the August Intensive seem worth mentioning here. It was the second seminar for Alvin M. Weinberg, then teaching mathematics and working as a research assistant in biophysics at the University of Chicago where he had just finished his PhD work. (In the group picture, you can see him in the second row sitting on the right, next to Pearl.) He would later become the Director of the Oak Ridge National Laboratory and a major figure in physics research, scientific administration, and public policy in the United States. As a graduate student he had consulted with C. B. Congdon at the student health service about depression and his lack of success with girls. Congdon eventually sent him to the Institute where he attended Korzybski's first 1938 seminar. Thereafter he wrote an article for *The American Physics Teacher* on "General Semantics and the Teaching of Physics", published in April 1939. In his autobiography, he recalled his studies with Korzybski with a curious combination of obtuseness and appreciation:

> Korzybski was a roly-poly, bald Pole who looked like a football linebacker. I would listen intently as he explained what was in *Science and Sanity*, but to no avail. Perhaps if I could read *Science and Sanity* I could understand what he was driving at—but again, it was all

too obscure. So, although I attended Korzybski's seminars for two years..., I can't say that Korzybski's seminars cured my malaise. (Marrying my wife Marge in 1940 did do the trick!) Still, Korzybski's basic thesis—that the structure of language has much to do with our psychological perceptions—seems to me to make sense.[8]

In 1963, many years after Korzybski's death, Weinberg agreed to become one of a new second group of Honorary Trustees of the Institute. Kendig later reported, "In accepting election, [Weinberg] indicated that doing so was by way of acknowledging 'my intellectual debt to Korzybski'." He also gave the Alfred Korzybski Memorial Lecture in 1966.[9]

Twenty-five year old William Seward Burroughs II from Clayton, Missouri, grandson to the inventor of the Burroughs Adding Machine, labeled himself as a "student" on his seminar registration form. (In the picture, you can see him in the front row, the man on the right in the light jacket and dark tie, seated on the ground directly in front of Weinberg.) One of the future creators of what became known as the Beat movement of mid-20th Century American literature, he had graduated from Harvard in 1936 with an English degree. Since then he had studied anthropology and hoboed around America and Europe. He had already read *Science and Sanity* and noted on his registration form that he was interested in the "interrelations of language and cultures". A rapt student with perfect attendance at the thirty-five hour seminar, he said many years later that he "...was very impressed by what [Korzybski] had to say. I still am. I think that everyone, everyone, particularly all students should read Korzybski. [It would] save them an awful lot of time."[10]

A thirty-one year old instructor in philosophy and logic from Harvard, Willard Van Orman Quine, also attended (seen in the picture standing at Korzybski's righthand side). Quine—who would come to be considered one of the most important American philosophers of the mid-to-late 20th Century—didn't agree with Burrough's assessment of their teacher. He had corresponded congenially with Korzybski before coming to the seminar. He would continue to do so intermittently for several more years. But, as he later indicated in his autobiography, he had long held serious "reservations" about Korzybski—and Cassius Keyser—ever since he had read Keyser's chapter on "Korzybski's Concept of Man" in *Mathematical Philosophy*.[11] Quine came to the seminar in order to humor his friend Edward F. Haskell, then a University of Chicago anthropology graduate student, who shared a common interest with Quine in the unity of science. (Haskell would later become known as a maverick formulator in that area.) Haskell had already attended a seminar and had spoken enthusiastically about Korzybski to Quine. Concerned about what he called the "uncritical following"[12] that *Science and Sanity* had developed at Harvard, Quine felt curious to see the man for himself. On his registration form he wrote that he had read the book. Yet it seems clear from what he wrote in his autobiography that he had actually only read "samples"—and rather carelessly at that. According to Quine, Korzybski nonsensically claimed on page 194 that '1 = 1 is false' because of the spatial difference between the two sides of the equal sign. (The nonsense actually consisted of Quine's assertion that Korzybski said that.)[13] By the time the seminar began, Quine had already sized up Korzybski as a quack. However, he presented a front of polite interest.

Korzybski, for his part, welcomed Quine's presence. He had given Quine a tuition grant to attend the seminar and also gave him class time to make a presentation on mathematical logic. In a letter to Crane after the seminar, Kendig wrote,

Quine was the high point of the seminar. He was a great inspiration to A.K. and his being here has very important implications for the I.G.S...As a result of his conferences with A. K. and the material presented in the seminar he will base his future work on the extensional method...Quine was most enthusiastic in his parting comments on the seminar and the great value of General Semantics.[14]

Some enthusiasm! Quine's letters to others dripped with contempt for Korzybski and his work.[15] In his published writings, Quine never stopped disparaging Korzybski (see *Word and Object*, *The Time of My Life*, and *Quiddities*). Korzybski seems to have eventually caught on to Quine's true attitude toward him and the extent to which the philosopher had gotten himself entangled in verbalism about issues they had both explored. Korzybski was probably thinking of Quine when he referred in a later seminar to an important mathematical logician who had tried to refute Heraclitus—as Quine did indeed try to do. As Korzybski explained, the nameless logician argued that contra-Heraclitus, you *could* cross the same river twice since the river 'is' "running water" and you are crossing again into 'running water'.[16] This seems like a fairly close paraphrase of Quine's consistent view of the matter and a good example of orientation by definition rather than fact.

The August Intensive had its mystic too. Ralph M. deBit (in the picture, the short man at the far right of the third row) described himself on the registration form as a lecturer and writer of books such as *Textbook of the Sacred Science*, *Universal Will*, and *The Way To Life*. Born in 1883, he had grown up in a small town in Kansas as a Bible-toting Christian literalist. At the age of eighteen he had gone out west and worked for several years at an Idaho lumber camp, before forestry school, marriage, and work as a ranger in Idaho's Bitteroot Mountains. A number of anomalous and inexplicable experiences there impelled him to leave his job at the end of 1910; he didn't know exactly what he was looking for, but he had embarked on a 'spiritual' quest. He moved with his family to Spokane, Washington, the nearest big city. When he saw a poster for a lecture on the Bhagavad Gita being given by a teacher named A. K. Mozumdar, he decided to attend. At the lecture—as related in *Vitvan,* Richard Satriano's biography of deBit—Mozumdar, a short Hindu man in his thirties dressed in suit and tie, had just started to speak when he jumped off the podium, ran up to deBit, rapped him on the legs with the thin wooden cane he'd been using as a pointer, and shouted: "Where have you been? What has kept you? I have been waiting for you."[17] He told the rest of his audience to go home.

DeBit had found what he was looking for too. For the next seven years he studied with Mozumdar who had founded a "Society for Christian Yoga" in Spokane and was seeking to connect various so-called "Wisdom Teachings" from Eastern and Western religious traditions. In 1918, deBit left to teach on his own after years of studying and working with Mozumdar, who had given him the Sanskrit name, Vitvan ("one who knows"). DeBit moved to New York City, lecturing there and in other places on his own and for the Theosophical Society, before moving to Los Angeles where he founded "The School of the Sacred Science", later building an ashram in Colorado. He was able to support his family with his teaching but felt increasingly dissatisfied. Having read widely, he saw the need to integrate what he was teaching with the outlook and findings of modern science. In 1937, one of his sons on vacation from college handed him a copy of *Science and Sanity* and told him he ought to read it. DeBit started to leaf through the book and then began to read:

The boy protested, "I didn't mean that you must read it now, Father." But Vitvan was totally immersed in his reading. That evening he did not come to supper and the light in his room burned through the night. Late the following afternoon he finished the book. He could not contain his excitement. "I've found it!" he said. "Here is the key. This man has shown me the way. It is possible now, with this system, to correlate the Ancient Gnosis with modern scientific findings; to formulate a new articulation suitable to present the Wisdom Teachings on a level comparable to our present state of development."[18]

On the registration form for the 1939 August Intensive, he wrote that he became interested in general semantics "In response to a life long search" and expected "to use *Science and Sanity* as a text-book for my own School and in public work." He felt tired of what he called "meta-fizzling" in esoteric teaching and knew his encounter with GS meant he was going to have to reorient what he taught and the way he taught, but didn't know exactly how he would do it.

Satriano recounted what deBit/Vitvan experienced in his first personal interview with Korzybski, whose motto was "I don't know, let's see." (Like everyone who had a personal interview with Korzybski, Vitvan would have been asked to write an autobiographical statement that Korzybski would read beforehand.):

...When Korzybski arrived at the office where Vitvan awaited him he took one look at Vitvan, seized him by the shoulders and pulled him to his feet. Then he ran him head first into the wall. When Vitvan had sufficiently recovered to speak he said, "What in the name of God was that all about?" "God is a word without a referent, sir," said Korzybski. "I bumped your head because you are soft. Sentiment is repugnant in you. The job you must do can only be done if you get hard. You must get hard." Vitvan said later, "He knew where and how I had been functioning. The heart center was my direct contact with anyone I taught. He knew that I had to get tough if I was going to make the next steps up available to my students. He used example most effectively." ...At the seminar's conclusion Vitvan bade goodbye to Korzybski, whom he was ever afterward to refer to as Blessed Count Alfred.[19]

DeBit eventually changed the name of his school to "The School of the Natural Order", integrating GS into his teaching. By 1956, after a couple changes of address, the school had relocated to a ranch in the Snake Valley just below Mount Wheeler in the high desert of Eastern Nevada, near the small town of Baker. Although deBit/Vitvan died in 1964, as of 2011 the school still exists there as a non-profit, educational organization. Although what the school teaches may seem rather esoteric to some, those who run it do encourage their students to study GS.

One other person attending the 1939 August Intensive deserves special mention, a thirty-year old dancer/modern dance educator from Milwaukee named Charlotte Schuchardt (seen in the group picture, sitting next to Hayakawa in the front), whom Korzybski had invited to participate without tuition as a guest. She had first met Korzybski when she attended his 1936 Northwestern University Seminar. She subsequently moved to Boston, where she worked for two years as the secretary of the Mathematics Department at MIT. After this she worked for a year as a secretary for Porter Sargent. Charlotte, who had studied zoology and physical education in college, had a masters degree in dance education from the University of Chicago and still had great interest in doing something with dance. On her seminar application she wrote about how she hoped to apply GS to her professional work: "Cortico-thalamic evaluation seems closely related to genuine movements in Dance. I would like to work along this line."

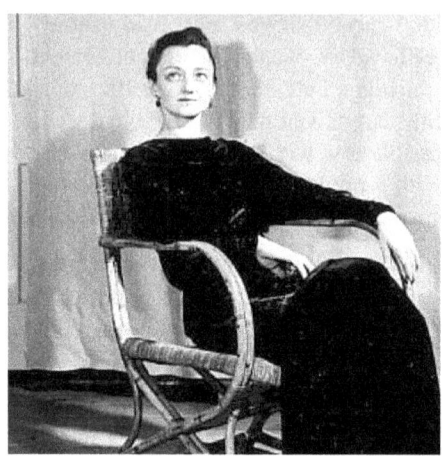
Charlotte Schuchardt, circa 1940

Korzybski may have already asked her to come work at the Institute, which she did within the next few months, working there part-time for the next few years while continuing to pursue a dance career. She would in due course become one of Korzybski's most trusted co-workers, first as a secretary and editorial assistant, then a few years later as his confidential secretary and as a seminar instructor (she would assist and eventually teach the semantic relaxation sessions). He later appointed her as his estate and literary executor. After his death, she fulfilled those roles and also served the IGS for many years as a teacher[20], editor, trustee, and Executive Director. Until her death in 2002, she remained one of the most important continuators of Korzybski's work.

Chapter 51
NOTHING TO DO BUT CONTINUE

On September 1, the day of Korzybski's last August 1939 Seminar lecture, World War II began with the German invasion of Poland. He had seen it coming. English translations of *Mein Kampf* had become readily available by the start of 1939 and he had been telling his students to prepare themselves by reading the book for insight into German intentions. The week the seminar started, newspapers had covered the visit to Moscow of German Foreign Minister Ribbentrop. A few days before Korzybski's first lecture, Ribbentrop and the Soviet foreign minister Molotov—with a smiling Stalin behind them—had signed a Nazi-Soviet non-aggression pact (also known as the Hitler-Stalin pact) leaving both nations free, for a start, to aggress against Poland. At his first lecture on August 25, Korzybski predicted how the war would begin. A writer from the *Chicago Daily News* attended, and the next day reported what Korzybski said (Kendig's notes from the lecture confirm the newspaper account):

> ...Never in the history of the world has civilization been so seriously menaced by the threat of paranoic rulers....Hitler and his henchmen have been outwitting their opponents with the cleverness of the monkey or the paranoic...It is not their intention to 'declare war' on Poland. They intend to send in a 'police force' to protect the 'German minority'.[1]

The Nazis did just that. On August 31, the SS collected a bunch of German convicts, dressed them in Polish uniforms, and staged a phony assault by them on a German radio station in the town of Gleiwitz near the Polish border. After a brief broadcast in Polish, the SS 'recaptured' the station, marched the hapless convicts outside, and machine-gunned them down, leaving their Polish-uniformed corpses as evidence of the 'attack'. The Nazis now had an excuse to 'defend' Germany from Polish 'aggression' and 'protect' the German minority in Poland.

Early in the morning of September 1, a German battleship fired the first shots of the war on the Polish garrison in Danzig. This was followed in a few hours by a Blitzkreig attack from the west: one and a half million German troops and two thousand tanks streamed into Poland while the Luftwaffe sent in waves of aircraft for strafing and bombing runs. Polish civilians were deliberately targeted along with Polish troops. The British and French governments had signed a common defense pact with Poland but although they both declared war against Germany on September 3, they failed to help the Polish forces. Then on September 17, the Soviet Union attacked Poland from the east, as Stalin and Molotov had agreed to do in the secret protocol that accompanied the 'non-aggression' pact. By the end of the month, the Nazis and Soviets had divided the country. The Soviets accepted a smaller portion of Poland, east of the Bug River in exchange for the Baltic states (including Finland) which they wished to take over. The remnant of the Polish army was scattered, captured, or driven out. The brutalizing of Poland by both Germans and Russians was well underway.

On top of his dismay at the onset of a worldwide war and the general sorry state of homo sapiens (whom he said should be called "homo the sap"), Korzybski felt terribly distressed at the fate of his ravaged homeland. He had suddenly been cut off from friends and relatives and other contacts in Poland. But through his connections with various Polish organizations in the United States and the free remnant of Europe, he would do his best to learn what was happening there in forthcoming years. Otherwise, there was nothing to do but continue along the path he'd been treading. Democracy had to be defended. He didn't want the barbarians to win. He felt he had something important to offer in the fight against them. The survival of democracy presupposed intelligence—a quality the leadership (governmental, business, academic, etc.) of the so-called free world seemed to seriously lack. Without such intelligence—not just facts crammed in school—things indeed looked hopeless. The dire situation called for a system of standards and a set of methods for developing effective practical education for intelligence in a sufficient number of individuals to make a difference that could make a difference.[2] That's what he was selling. He would be working even harder to deliver the goods.

One good he would have to deliver very soon was a second edition of *Science and Sanity*. Almost 3,000 books had been sold, orders continued to come in, and the second printing of the first edition would soon be exhausted. By the end of the August seminar, Science Press reported they had only 140 copies left.[3] It didn't seem necessary to revise the text. Despite a great deal of new scientific knowledge, the methodological data he had based his work upon hadn't significantly changed. So the main part of the second edition could be run off from the existing printer's plates. However, he wanted to add some new front material. Since 1933, he had refined some of the formulations, devised new ones, and learned a great deal about applications from teaching seminars and working with individuals. It seemed time to put his work into a fresh framework for the coming decade. He had new books to add to a supplementary bibliography. He had some things to say about the war. He also wanted to deal with the growing confusion between 'semantics' and 'general semantics'. He had gotten clearer about the inadequacy of talking about 'meaning'. To emphasize his work as a theory of human *evaluation* he would have to disassociate it from the work of Ogden and Richards, for example. The epigraph he had taken from their book *The Meaning of Meaning* would have to go and he needed something to replace it. In addition, he now had a chance to revise the listings for the International Non-Aristotelian Library, both the "Volumes In Preparation" and those whose authors were to be announced later. He hoped to get Campbell, Congdon, Polakov, and others to commit themselves to books they would write.

But this was getting a bit ahead of things. He had other more immediate priorities. First he and Kendig were putting together a memorandum on the first two years of the Institute. Since its founding, Korzybski had taught 250 students in 11 seminars (the Holiday Intensive at the end of December would make 12). Kendig was compiling a list of the academic institutions and the various fields represented by the students, as well as a summary of the sales statistics and geographical distribution of the first edition of *Science and Sanity*. Korzybski wrote a brief description of other GS courses, new publications, and the results and mechanism of training. A description of the various formats of the IGS seminar and a tentative schedule for 1940 were also included. On the opening page, they decided to put a picture of the front of the Institute building and another of the August Intensive group. With a list of monographs, articles, and books for sale by the Institute and an order form insert in the back, they basically had an Institute brochure for the interested public. It could also be sent, along with a press release, to scientific journals and the general press.[4]

A preliminary version of the memorandum had been prepared for Institute board members for the annual meeting originally scheduled in October. Korzybski was also sending copies to those he was in the process of inviting to become Honorary Trustees (a list of whom was included in the final version of the memorandum). On October 20, Kendig sent a copy of the memorandum to Cornelius Crane along with a brief note asking him when he could come for another meeting, which they had decided to defer until some time in December when both he and Campbell presumably could attend.

Crane had communicated little since attending the March 1939 board meeting, although they did get the expected $10,000 check from him by the second week of July. Otherwise Korzybski had heard nothing from him since getting a letter in mid-August. (Crane wrote then that he might consider giving more money to the Institute after July 1940.) Korzybski did his best to keep Crane informed about Institute doings. In August he sent a financial report that Crane had requested. In September, Kendig sent a long newsy letter. On October 26, Korzybski got a typed letter signed by Crane in New York City, perhaps stimulated by the note and memorandum Kendig had just sent:

Dear Alfred:

I have been thinking over the matter for several months and have decided to resign as Vice President and Trustee of the Institute of General Semantics.

This decision has nothing to do with the scientific side of the work, but is a purely personal matter. I will be glad, if you wish me, to continue the same financial arrangement with the Institute until the first of July, 1940, but thereafter the Institute must do its own financing.

With best wishes for the continued success of your work, I am,

Sincerely yours,
Cornelius Crane

P.S. I will be glad to receive any publications you put out from time to time.[5]

Although Korzybski knew a lot about Crane's personal problems (having counseled him in the past), he couldn't know what Crane meant by "a purely personal matter." But the letter didn't bode well. Concerned about the influence on others if it appeared that Crane was suddenly dropping the Institute, he wrote back asking Crane to at least hold off his resignation until after July 1, 1940. He also asked Crane to maintain his connection to the Institute in other ways. For one thing, he wanted Crane to become an Honorary Trustee. Crane had promised two more endowment checks. Until they could get some other funding sources, Korzybski felt very concerned about how they were going to tide over the Institute after July 1. As a consequence, as he told Crane, he was adding more seminars to the 1940 schedule—for a total of seven once again—in order to make more money (so much for more time to attend to other Institute business). He still wanted to have a regular board meeting Crane could attend, to personally take care of the matters surrounding Crane's resignation.[6]

Crane replied that he would be glad to become an Honorary Trustee. But he would not be able to attend any forthcoming meeting and didn't think it would harm the Institute for his resignation to go ahead. Indeed, he wrote, "I must make it a condition of sending the Institute any further funds, that the Board of Trustees send me before the end of 1939 an official acceptance of my resignation."[7]

Kendig sent a copy of Hayakawa's new book to Crane at the end of November and a newsy note to him at the beginning of December. A week later, Korzybski wrote to him again—more news (a list of eighteen prominent men had already agreed to become Honorary Trustees) and an expression of his concern for Crane:

Speaking to you as my student and, I hope, my friend, I am sort of worried about you. I believe you are in the midst of some personal difficulties and I would like to help you, if we ever have a chance to get together again, which somehow you seem to evade.[8]

Regarding the business of Crane's resignation, Douglas Campbell couldn't get to Chicago just then, so Korzybski, Congdon, and Kendig would have to hold a meeting before Christmas to act on it. Would Crane write a formal resignation that could be placed in the minutes? Korzybski hoped Crane would reconsider and make his resignation effective in mid-1940 rather than at the end of the year.

Crane had not yet responded when Korzybski, Congdon, and Kendig met for their truncated Board of Trustees meeting on December 19. Their main business was to pass a motion to accept Crane's resignation with regret "to take effect on June 30, 1940, or at any other date which Mr. Crane might indicate as more acceptable to him." As part of the motion they urged Crane "to withdraw his resignation and remain on the active board." Korzybski also announced Crane's "acceptance of the invitation to become an Honorary Trustee at whatever time his resignation may take effect."[9] Campbell had been very busy studying for specialist board exams, but if his presence as a Trustee was needed later, he'd be in Chicago since he planned to attend the Holiday Intensive from December 27 to January 2.

At the end of December 1939, a great deal occupied Korzybski besides his problems with Crane. Among other things, in September he had submitted an abstract for a paper accepted for the December meeting of the American Mathematics Society at Columbus, Ohio. The abstract was for the third and last of his series "General Semantics: Extensionalization in Mathematics, Mathematical Physics, and General Education". He had developed a new formulation for Paper III on "Over/Under Defined Terms". Without the use of extensional methods, most terms could be considered as over-defined by intension or verbalism while under-defined by extension or fact. He hoped to print this together with the first two papers as the second IGS monograph. He made a quick bus trip to Columbus before Christmas to make his presentation. (He must have done it from notes because only the abstract remains.) He immediately returned to Chicago, just in time to start the Holiday seminar, and had no time to deal with the letter from Crane, dated December 23, he had just received. In no uncertain terms, Crane said he would send no further funds until he received an official letter accepting his *immediate* resignation both as an active Board Trustee and Honorary Trustee. Although he was still seeing people for interviews, Korzybski called a Trustees meeting (including Campbell) for January 3, the day after his last lecture. That very day he sent Crane a personal note as well as the official letter. He had done what Crane had asked. He hoped Crane was not making a complete break with him and the Institute. But as the days progressed, the next check did not arrive.

Chapter 52
"RECOGNITION BUT VERY LITTLE MONEY"

Crane had bolted from his commitment to the Institute. Even by January 5, 1940, that had become increasingly, disturbingly clear. Dr. Ischclondsky, passing through Chicago on his way from New York City to Los Angeles, called that day to report on a recent conversation he'd had with Crane, having finally bumped into the philanthropist after not seeing him for several months. Pearl took notes over the phone. Crane had told the psychiatrist that he would continue to provide the money—to be disbursed by the Institute—for the translation of Ischlondsky's book. Not very reassuring. Crane, whom Ischlondsky admittedly didn't know very well, seemed more "correct", i.e., formal, than the psychiatrist had recalled from previous meetings. Crane also mentioned financial problems. He would have "to restrict all his financial obligations because for 1940 it is all filled up." Ishchlondsky opined that Crane might become more agreeable in the future and advised that "the Institute should not break contact with him."[1]

But Crane, not Korzybski, was breaking the contact. Although both Korzybski and Kendig would continue to write to him, Crane would no longer communicate directly with either of them. He turned over that job to his lawyer who sent his first letter to Korzybski at the end of January.

A small item with the headline, "Sues for Divorce", in the *Chicago Daily Tribune*, of Tuesday, February 20, soon clarified Crane's "financial obligations": "Mrs. Cathalene Parker Browning Crane filed suit in Circuit court yesterday for a divorce from Cornelius Crane... The Cranes were married Oct. 15, 1929, at Newark, N.J. ...She charges Crane deserted her Feb. 1, 1936." The clipped article went into Korzybski's file folder of Crane-related items and correspondence, along with this *Daily Tribune* article from two days later: "Mrs. Cathalene Parker Crane was granted a divorce yesterday from Cornelius Crane,...Under terms of the agreement...she is to receive $25,000 a year for life, regardless of possible remarriage, and her daughter, Cathalene, 16 years old, is to receive $5,000 a year for life."[2]

The correspondence between Korzybski and Crane's lawyer went back and forth for several months. Finally in April, the lawyer sent a contract and release for Korzybski to sign, which formalized what he had already told Korzybski in previous letters. Crane and/or his lawyer seemed concerned about the guarantee Crane had signed for the rent on 1234 E. 56th Street; the Institute lease extended until 1944. The lawyer wanted Korzybski to agree to Crane giving the Institute just $10,000 more—$8,400 to get doled out monthly for the next four years in $175 increments for paying rent, with the small remaining difference to be paid forthwith to the Institute. In addition, he wanted Korzybski to release Crane of any other obligations to the Institute. According to the lawyer, this contract simply confirmed Crane's original commitment to the Institute.

Korzybski politely but firmly refused to go along with this. From his point of view the lawyer had not represented things accurately. As he had already told Crane, he had never wanted Crane to pay the rent. He had asked him to sign a guarantee simply to make it easier to get a long-term lease from a reluctant landlord. As for what Crane had previously agreed to do, it was true: he had not committed himself in writing. But he had clearly stated at board meetings, and implied elsewhere, that he would give semi-annual payments of $10,000 to the Institute until July 1940. Korzybski felt that these commitments had legal standing. As Korzybski saw it, Crane had a binding obligation to give the Institute $10,000 immediately (the amount past due from January 1), with an additional final payment of $10,000 for July 1, 1940. Crane had also promised a yearly supplement to Kendig's salary and Korzybski expected him to make good on that promise at least one more time as well. Altogether, Korzybski expected Crane to honor his commitment to give the Institute $20,750 more.

The Institute's attorney, Samuel Clawson, had joined the Board of Trustees to replace Crane. He would continue negotiations with Crane's attorney. And Alfred would continue to write to Crane about the Institute and its doings. He still hoped to persuade Crane to follow through on his initial obligation. And he hoped to do this sooner rather than later, for the very existence of the Institute was now in peril.

Even with Crane's contributions, the Institute had been operating very close to the bone. The Institute's earned income, mostly from Korzybski's seminars, averaged a bit less than a third of what it needed to survive. Without Crane's two remaining payments, the projected income would only suffice to pay the rent and some of the operating expenses for the rest of the year. How was Alfred going to get the money for other operating costs as well as for salaries—the main expense? Clearly, to maximize income he would have to keep to the grueling schedule of seven seminars for the year. Furthermore he would have to cut costs by letting go clerical staff other than Pearl Johnecheck and Charlotte Schuchardt, who both supposedly worked 'part-time'. He and Kendig also would have to take half salaries. He had already started to draw money from the Institute savings-account reserves. In order to keep a positive balance there, he would have to borrow money from Mira and his hardly ample private accounts.

A private appeal was made to some of Alfred's closest students who might have financial means to help. A number of them stepped forward. One, Frances Hall Rousmaniere Dewing, began to give a substantial monthly donation. Mrs. Dewing, as Korzybski addressed her in letters, had studied with Josiah Royce and in 1906 was one of the first women to graduate from Radcliffe with a PhD (in philosophy and psychology). She and the rest of her family had definitely become enamored with Korzybski's work. Her husband, Arthur Stone Dewing—a retired professor of corporate finance at Harvard who had also studied with Royce—had already attended one seminar. Their daughter Mary— a social worker studying anthropology at the University of Chicago—had attended three. As for Mrs. Dewing, although she lived in Newton, Massachusetts, she was staying in Chicago to attend Korzybski's 1940 January-February evening seminar. She soon returned to attend his next evening seminar as well, which ran through the month of April. The financial crisis, which began at the start of 1940, would last until the end of 1941. Without the Dewings' support, Korzybski might have had to close the Institute. With it and the additional donations of others, Korzybski was able—in a piecemeal fashion—to fill the gap left by Crane's withdrawal. Mrs. Dewing also paid a salary for Anne Cleveland, a young woman who had grown up with her daughter and with whom she felt close. Anne had gone to some seminars already and Mrs. Dewing seemed to feel she needed some personal direction that Alfred could give her. Anne would continue to work as a secretary at the Institute for several years.

A Good Name

If a good name was better than riches, then things were not going too badly for Korzybski in the Spring of 1940. In March the Institute presented, to the press and public, its progress-report/pamphlet, "A Memorandum", which showed the impressive first two years of IGS accomplishments. Among other things, it contained the list of men who had so far agreed to become Honorary Trustees of the Institute, which gave a sample of the support Korzybski had garnered among academic and professional workers. The list included notables such as: Thurman Arnold, Gaston Bachelard, Maxim Bing, Abraham Brill, Ross McC. Chapman, George E. Coghill, Arthur Stone Dewing, Franklin Ebaugh, P. H. Esser, David Fairchild, Clarence B. Farrar, William Healy, Lancelot Hogben, Earnest Hooten, Smith Ely Jeliffe, Edward Kasner, Cassius Keyser, Nolan D.C. Lewis, Ralph S. Lillie, Bronislaw Malinowski, Adolf Meyer, Winfred Overholser, Stewart Paton, Raymond Pearl, William F. Peterson, Roscoe Pound, George S. Stevenson, M. Tramer, Walter L. Treadway, and Richard Weil, Jr. Some of them he knew. Some he hadn't met in person. But personal friend or not, their support seemed eager and heartfelt. The group included a law professor, an Assistant U.S. Attorney General, a business executive, a professor of finance, a professor of philosophy, two anthropologists, three mathematicians, five biologists, and sixteen medical doctors. A professor of pathology, a public health administrator, and fourteen psychiatrists comprised this latter group. The psychiatrists included some of the most revered and respected names in the profession.

Among those on the list, anthropologist Bronislaw Malinowski did not seem exceptional in his enthusiasm for Korzybski and his work. He expressed this in a letter he wrote to Korzybski on December 20, 1939, which also gave a sense of his own (and Alfred's) feelings at that time about the unfolding war and the fate of their beloved Poland:

Dear Alfred,
Of Course I accept the honour of being associated with you [and] your work as Hon. Trustee. I'd be glad to act as OfficeBoy, if you needed one—though I'd not be an efficient O.B.
I fully agree with your sentiments ab. the Anglo-Saxon world [and] also the importance of Science and Sanity—both in abstract [and] concrete sense in our crisis.
I am pessimistic as you are, but a fight is better than a fall into the void of defeatism. Were I not so old I'd still go back there just to get smashed up or smart. But alas for both of us only the spirit remains! And Spirit is at a discount now.
...We shall meet soon, as I may be in Chic and shall ring you up at once...[3]

Richard Weil, Jr., President of the Bamberger department store chain, having studied *Science and Sanity*, had corresponded with Korzybski for about a year. In his own 1940 book, *The Art of Practical Thinking*, he was introducing Korzybski's work to a business-oriented audience:

I have said that Korzybski is a genius. If you are the average reader, to whom I originally addressed myself, you must, for a time, take my word for this. If it be only a short time, which is what I hope for, it will be simply until you have implemented yourself in the armory of thinking to the point where you can read Korzybski with understanding and yourself take his measure. If it be for a longer time, posterity, as is its custom, will perform this service for you, posthumously: that is, long after you will be unable [sic] to reap the benefits.[4]

Gaston Bachelard's 1934 book *Le Nouvel Esprit Scientifique*, which Korzybski had gotten, already showed the French epistemologist as a compatible formulator. Since he had written that book, Bachelard had come to know Korzybski's work and to give it considerable importance. The following excerpt (part of a larger discussion of Korzybski and his work) comes from the English translation of Bachelard's 1940 book *La Philosophie du Non: Essai d'une philosophie de nouvel esprit scientifique*. (A translation of this done by a student of Korzybski's, G. C. Waterston, was published in the U.S. in 1969 as *The Philosophy of No: A Philosophy of the New Scientific Mind*.):

> Those of us who are trying to find new ways of thinking, must direct ourselves towards the most complicated structures. We must take advantage of all the lessons of science, however special they may be, to determine new mental structures. We must realize that the possession of a form of thought is automatically a reform of the mind. We must therefore direct our researches towards a new pedagogy. In this direction, which has attracted us personally for a number of years, we shall take as our guide the very important work of the non-Aristotelian school, founded in America by Korzybski, which is so little known in France... The psychological and even physiological conditions of a non-Aristotelian logic have been resolutely faced in the great work of Count Alfred Korzybski, *Science and Sanity*,...[5]

The large number of psychiatrists on the Honorary Trustee list didn't get there by accident. Korzybski had targeted psychiatrists as an audience for a number of years, since he felt that his extensional method and theory of sanity had important, though still undeveloped, implications for their work. The willingness of so many important psychiatrists to associate themselves with him by serving as Honorary Trustees surely must have gratified him, as did the invitation he received—unusual for a non-psychiatrist—to give a presentation at the upcoming conference of the American Psychiatric Association from May 20 to 24 in Cincinnati, Ohio.

Sanity Update

He considered his conference paper an important project. Entitling it "General Semantics, Psychiatry, Psychotherapy and Prevention", he managed to get an extra ten minutes to present it (over the usual twenty minute allotment for such papers). Douglas Campbell, also presenting a GS-related paper, and Adolf Meyer were picked to discuss his paper afterwards. Korzybski had already been working on the various changes and additions to the front matter for the Second Edition of *Science and Sanity*. With new copies of the book no longer available, back orders were accumulating. Getting out a new edition seemed urgent. His paper for the psychiatric conference would serve as a prototype for the main job he needed to do for the Second Edition—a new Introduction.

In both, he would present an updated picture of his work with the refinements and sharpened formulations he had developed since 1933. In the psychiatry paper he would include more detail about the preventive, educational work he and his students had done with groups and individuals, giving a number of examples to show the application of his evaluation-oriented epistemology to personal problems that psychiatrists were apt to view as strictly medical. (These, as well as a number of other illustrative examples, plus a couple of diagrams, and a table showing the differences between aristotelian and non-aristotelian orientations all got deleted from the abridged version of the paper published in the September 1941 *American Journal of Psychiatry*.) He also addressed the role he thought psychiatry and general semantics should play in the developing war-related complex of world problems.

Only a few days after the invasion of Poland the previous September, Korzybski had sent letters to the Polish government-in-exile, and to British and U.S. government officials—including President Roosevelt—explaining that role:

> Today newspapers everywhere, except in Germany call Hitler a mad man, etc., ...Name-calling, to which politicians and newswriters are making us so accustomed, will, of course, be ineffective in the long run. The Institute of General Semantics suggests that the respective governments stop calling names, and call experts. By experts, in this case, we mean competent professional psychiatrists...to sit as a <u>sanity</u> tribunal. After studying all the available data, furnished by the governments, this psychiatric tribunal would, without doubt, technically speaking, unanimously establish the 'insanity' of Hitler, Goering, Goebbels, etc. ...We in the Institute feel that if such a professional verdict of psychiatrists would be published and distributed by governments, it would stop the 'insanity' of the present situation. This would become the most powerful <u>verbal</u> weapon to break the spell of Hitlerism. It is not realized what a profound psycho-logical effect such a diagnosis would have on the people, particularly in Europe...The Institute of General Semantics is willing to offer all the professional help eventually needed, but we are not in a position to undertake such activities on our own.[6]

As he later noted he "received only *two* polite acknowledgements" to these letters.[7] Still, he would repeat the suggestion and elaborate upon it throughout the duration of the war and afterwards.

One of the things he would emphasize both in the psychiatry paper and the "Introduction to the Second Edition" was the importance of *"New factors:* [and] *the havoc they play with our generalizations."*[8] If medicine and the behavioral/social sciences needed psychiatry, then psychiatry, in turn, needed GS. In particular, the new factors—as he had formulated them—of "our neuro-semantic (neuro-evaluational) and neuro-linguistic *environments as environment"*[9] seemed to him crucial for psychiatrists and governmental leaders to take seriously.

In his paper for the psychiatric conference, Korzybski recommended the expansion of the sanity tribunal he had suggested in his earlier letter to leaders. The Germans under Hitler showed a notable ability to use *"pathological verbal distortion"* and other propagandistic and psychological methods as part of its 'war *of* nerves' against the allies. (Korzybski would soon refer to this in his "Introduction to the Second Edition" as the Nazi 'war *on* nerves'.) The 'sick' Nazi, Fascist, and Japanese governments at least intuitively understood the importance of shaping the neuro-linguistic and neuro-evaluational environments, even if they didn't formulate exactly in those terms. To this end, the Nazis, et al, purposely employed psycho-logical methods against their enemies. As he saw it, the governments of the so-called free world needed to marshal their psychiatrists and other experts in human behavior—including advisors in GS—to consciously counteract these methods and fight back with their own explicit neuro-evaluational, neuro-linguistic means.[10]

Korzybski estimated that something like five hundred people attended his talk and he felt happy with his reception at the conference. As he wrote to Crane soon afterwards, he found the people he met there "very warm and friendly and interested." Despite this, the bad war news weighed painfully upon him, though it also seemed to goad him to continue his hard work. As he noted to Crane (trying to goad him as well):

> The first World War ruined me financially, very considerably, and I was also injured physically, for which I am still paying the price. The recent annihilation of Poland deprived me of the rest...I have seen too many dead and dying, too much destruction and suffering, not to realize what it all means for the future hence my investigations of factors of proper evaluation, predictability, sanity, etc., ...You may understand at present, judging by facts, why the work of the Institute is now, more than ever, of such extreme human importance.[11]

"Do You See Red?"

As Alfred was putting the finishing touches on his presentation in early May, grim news continued to come out of Europe. Poles who had escaped to the West had already told of the widespread destruction inflicted on their country by both Nazi and Soviet invaders.[12] In Scandanavia, the Germans were wrapping up a spring offensive against Norway and Denmark and moving into Luxemburg, Holland, and Belgium, which soon fell. In June, Alfred got his U.S. citizenship and may have quietly celebrated by going out to eat at a fish and chips place with Mira.[13] As the month progressed, when he was not teaching or writing, the news of the fall of France absorbed him. In an astonishingly short period of time, the Germans—moving down from Belgium—had simply gone around, and to some extent through, the major portion of the "Maginot Line", the extensive series of defense fortifications the French had built along the German and Italian borders with great confidence that they could hold back the Nazi advance. By the end of June, Germany occupied the northern half of France while a collaborationist French puppet government was establishing itself in the south with its capital in Vichy. Korzybski expressed his disgust in part 1 of section H of the "Introduction" which he entitled 'Maginot Line Mentalities':

> Present day scientific researches and historical world developments show there is no doubt that the old aristotelian epoch of human evolution is dying...I doubt if in the whole of human history there is a more accentuated illustration than the tragic and sudden collapse, in the summer of 1940, of the French government and army, and eventually of French culture and 'democracy'...We test the freshness or deterioration of fishes by smelling the head end, and as we know at the date of this writing, the head ends of the French 'democracy' have a putrid odor...The 'Maginot line mentality' will become a historical classic, and will be applied quite appropriately to other than military fields. It means a thoughtless, self-deceptive, etc., 'security' in antiquated systems as matched by modern methods of 1940.[14]

However demoralized he may have felt, he didn't mope. His typical style of coping consisted of staying busy and getting busier, working as hard as he possibly could. He was teaching an Intensive Seminar and trying to finish his "Introduction to the Second Edition". In June, one of his tasks in relation to that included writing to a number of scholars, luminaries, and others whom he knew, for examples of over/under defined terms in their fields. In July he started an evening seminar and in August another intensive. By the end of that month, he finished the first draft of the Introduction and began editing it with Kendig, Charlotte, and Pearl. Meanwhile, the main text for the new edition of the book was being printed.

With all this activity, he only saw Mira occasionally, talked with her on the phone perhaps once a week, and wrote an occasional letter (she wrote to him more often). Pearl and to some extent Charlotte, had become significant intermediaries between the two of them. Mira was becoming quite friendly with them. While she found the infrequent contact with Alfred unsatisfactory, she kept busy with other things. She was living and painting in her studio apartment on the Near North Side. In July, she had gone to Kansas City to visit her sisters. Minnie now had a room in a rest home that seems to have functioned much like an "assisted living facility". Amy was thinking of giving up her farm and joining Minnie. When Mira returned from her trip, she busied herself with elaborating her notes from the IGS seminars she had audited with Alfred's permission. For years, she had had a tremendous involvement with Alfred's work. She had always given it the highest importance. Now despite the troubles of recent years between them, despite her promises to not involve herself with the Institute and with his work, she had gotten re-engaged.

On August 16, Mira sent a blue presentation folder to Alfred. The first of the twenty-six collated pages, obviously the title page, had the following in large type at its center: "When <u>Where</u> and <u>How</u> do <u>you</u> see RED? ask ME one of the Million". The word "RED" was printed in red. As she later explained to Alfred, she was not presenting this as anything more than her rough ruminations. In a note to him that accompanied the manuscript, she wrote that a wealthy woman she had met in the course of her work had gotten interested in GS through discussions with her and had paid to get Mira's crude typing neatly mimeographed. Mira also gave copies to one or two friends, besides this woman and Alfred. On the bottom right of the title page was typed "Copyright 1940" with "Mira Edgerly" below that. On the bottom left, was typed "Witness:". with a blank line below it.

Inside were the results of Mira's ponderings as she had studied her seminar notes and considered the war in Europe and Asia. GS, for her, gave a new and important slant to the age-old theme, "the pen is mightier than the sword". The opening page shows a deep and heartfelt understanding of her husband's work and a clear talent for expressing it, albeit in an amateurish way:

"The Pen is Mightier than the Sword"
"Whose Pen?"
Read and see for yourself.

This pen, with which my hand is making these dark marks on this white paper; these word-marks, as <u>objects,</u> or as recorded language is of no living-value to any living-being. For, what is under my hand is
neither edible...clothable...sleepable...sit-onable.

I ask you to eat, to dress, to sleep or to sit-on this piece of paper: What then is <u>it</u>, in <u>any</u> pen that is mightier than the sword?

It is in the fact that when, and only when <u>these pen-marks</u> are taken as <u>tools for communication,</u> these tools which I now am using and with which I am now trying to convey what is going-on inside my skin to inside your skin; namely, their <u>living</u>-value to <u>you</u> depends entirely on how much alive you are to the <u>neurological processes involved</u>. These pen-marks are an extension onto this paper of what is going on inside my skin and its <u>living-value</u> to you, inside your skin, is entirely in proportion as to how your <u>living nervous system reacts</u> to those pen-marks and what you make out of them, inside your skin...[15]

When he read the manuscript, Alfred 'saw red' alright. On August 18, he wrote to C.B. Congdon:

Dear C. B.,

I am deeply distressed by my wife's latest episode in mimeographing. It looks to me very similar to the episode she had around 1936. ...This episode lasted for a pretty long time, and as you know, did endless harm to me and my work.

After her South American trip she seemingly recovered. Now seemingly she has another episode which most probably will be more harmful to our work and me than the first one.

The enclosed latest verbalistic outburst I am afraid shows clearly the symptoms of another forthcoming episode. I am afraid I made a mistake to let her attend my seminars, in spite of the fact that I insisted on her attending as a student, not as a wife. It seems that it only supplied her with material for some worthless verbalism. By now I know that my direct dealing with her leads nowhere.

I did my best for 21 years and I admit I see no results.

I will be very grateful to you if you would see her, diagnose her case, and give her some stern advices which perhaps would be more effective than whatever I may say...

...I telephoned to my wife, roughly telling her the content of this letter, asking her to stop distributing her mimeographed episodes, and I am sending to her a copy of this letter. My seeing her personally would do no good and I believe should be avoided.[16]

Alfred not only phoned Mira, he apparently visited her the previous day. Neither conversation could have been a happy one. In a note dated then—Saturday, August 17—Mira wrote: "Doubtless you had a taste of the flood – I had over the phone – after you left – today." Above this she had copied down the following limerick, which seems easy to read, in this context, as a testament of the shame she must have felt:

"How happy is the moron,
he doesn't give a damn.
I wish I were a moron,
My gosh, perhaps I am."[17]

Alfred finished his letter to Congdon with further complaints about Mira's spending habits and the trouble her 'episode' had caused him. He already had a mixed reputation in the academic/scientific community around Chicago and was not totally unconcerned about what people might think.

Allen Walker Read could testify to the academic resistance of many at the University of Chicago. An English language scholar and lexicographer, he would not attend his first Korzybski seminar until the 1941 Winter Intensive, but he had already become one of Korzybski's most solid students and supporters. Born in Minnesota in 1906, Read grew up in Iowa where his father worked as the one-man science faculty of Iowa State Teacher's College in Cedar Falls. With a love of the English language inspired by H. L. Mencken's *The American Language*, Read had decided to follow in his father's footsteps and take up an academic career studying English *as a scientist*. With a 1926 M.A. in English from the University of Iowa, he taught English at the University of Missouri before being awarded a Rhodes Scholarship for study at Oxford University from 1928 to 1932 where he specialized in descriptive linguistics and lexicography. His extensional attitude and down-to-earth interest in how people talk had already led him in the late 1920s to collect material, i.e., men's room graffiti, that others did not consider suitable for academic study in English. His resulting book on 'nasty' words, *Lexical Evidence From Folk Epigraphy In Western North America: A Glossarial Study of the Low Element in the English Vocabulary* had to be privately published in Paris in 1935 in a limited edition of 75 copies. (It was reprinted in 1977 by Maledicta Press under the title, *Classic American Graffiti*.) In 1932, Read had come to work at the University of Chicago as a research associate and as an Assistant Editor of the *Dictionary of American English*. He first heard of Korzybski in 1936, read *Science and Sanity* at that time, and found that Korzybski's system provided a congenial, scientific orientation for his own studies. "It struck me as exemplifying the rigorous intellectual discipline that I was looking for."[18] Read had left Chicago for England in 1938 on a Guggenheim fellowship. Unable to stay there when the war started in the fall of 1939, he returned to the U.S. where he finished out his fellowship in 1940 by studying at the New York City Public Library. He returned to Chicago in 1941, to become a colleague of S. I. Hayakawa at the Armour Institute of Technology as an instructor of English. He would also come to know Korzybski and become friends with Kendig, and Charlotte Schuchardt (whom he would marry in 1953).

Allen Walker Read[19]

Even before his return to Chicago, Read had had a chance to observe the responses to Korzybski in the academic community there:

...Intellectual interests were very much polarized by the new young president, Robert Maynard Hutchins, and by his henchman Mortimer Adler. They espoused the "Great Books" movement, which seemed to many of us to be backward-looking and in opposition to experimental science...[20]

Korzybski...was not much accepted by the University community. There were several reasons for this. He was regarded as "over-eager"—pushing his own worth too zealously. Then he used the word "non-Aristotelian" to describe his work, and the defenders of Aristotle's greatness took offense. Any amount of explaining that Korzybski respected and even venerated Aristotle did not suffice. Furthermore, Korzybski did not come up from a specialized discipline, as one is supposed to do, but burst forth as a full-blown generalist. And he was scornful of the traditional philosophers. I have even heard him use the callow word-play "foolosophers," and no wonder the foolosophers boycotted him.[21]

Mira certainly did not want to give ammunition to the 'foolosophers'. She had not intended her missive to be taken too seriously—even with her mention of 'copyright' on the first page and of the 'publisher' in the text. She had only given copies to a few interested friends and to Alfred. But Alfred did have a certain point in believing he couldn't afford to have her playing around like that. People would tend to judge her—as his wife—by different, more stringent standards and would, in turn, be likely to judge him by her behavior.

Mira regretted what she had done. But Alfred's severity disturbed her. She felt he was making too much of the whole thing—to the point of gross unfairness. She felt, as she told him, that he had still not acknowledged his own part in their ongoing vicious circle. Since she had returned from South America at the end of 1938, Mira had felt increasingly cut off from Alfred by his request not to involve herself with his work and with the Institute. Since the founding of the Institute, and especially with the beginning of that year's financial crisis, he had become even more single-focused on his work. As a result he had almost no time left for her and she yearned for more contact. Besides, his request for her to not get involved with his work had become impossible for her to follow. She had always felt interested, and her attendance at the seminars (with his permission) had awakened her interest still further. She had also felt unduly constrained by his request for her to avoid communicating with people at the University of Chicago and others whom she knew, who were somehow connected to his work. Now, Alfred trusted her even less.

Mira felt she couldn't win. When she tried to explain and to document her side of things to Congdon, Alfred accused her of broadcasting their private life again. (Congdon may have talked to Mira a few times and received some letters from her but otherwise seems to have wisely avoided getting himself caught in the middle of the dispute.) Alfred also complained about her spending habits over the last year. In 1939 he had agreed to her spending extra money in order to set up her painting studio/apartment. This amount was over and above the regular amount Alfred was giving to her as a monthly stipend for her rent and daily expenses. (She got extra money as well from Alfred's book royalties, which he considered her due.) She had intended to pay back this 'loan' within the next year and she did. She felt Alfred had no right to complain.

With all their problems, they didn't stop communicating. When Mira wouldn't answer the phone for fear of a tirade from Alfred, he would write to her. Pearl would also call or come by to take her to the bank, give her news of the Institute, or drop off something Alfred wanted her to see. In the first week of October Pearl dropped off a draft of Alfred's "Introduction" for Mira to read. Alfred wanted to rub in the point, as he wrote in a letter to her then, that she had very little understanding of what serious writing entailed. He would not dare to publish anything he had not painstakingly edited first. This, the tenth draft, still didn't satisfy him. (By this time, the text of the Second Edition was already printed and the "Introduction", the manuscript of which he finally sent off to Science Press in mid-November, remained the chief thing to be done.)

Mira could admit that Alfred had some reasonable points to make about her behavior. But did he have to be so hard on her? He threw up to her things she had previously said and done that he might better have forgiven and forgotten. He blamed her for other things too. For example, he wrote to her that her 1936 'broadcast' had been responsible for their current financial mess by planting a seed of alienation in Campbell and—through him—in Crane. But did responsibility for what happened in 1936 lay solely on Mira's shoulders? And how could he know that Crane's withdrawal from the Institute had anything much to do with that whole sorry episode? Worrying about money and how he was going to keep a roof over either of their heads, Alfred seemed too distressingly busy as 1940 came to a close, to be able to hear Mira's side of things. It didn't help that he wasn't feeling well. What seemed like a bad cold turned into pneumonia. It laid him low and lingered on into the spring of 1941, though for the most part he kept on working.

The Institute's problems at the end of the year were not due to lack of recognition. The response of the psychiatric and mental health communities had been outstanding. New university courses incorporating GS continued to get organized. Articles about Korzybski and his work were being published in professional journals, magazines, and the daily press. The 1940 version of Hayakawa's *Language in Action* had gotten favorable reviews.

In June a short book by Aldous Huxley, *Words And Their Meanings*, had come out which gave more attention to Korzybski's work. Huxley, a resident of Los Angeles, had first read *Science and Sanity* in 1938. He wrote then to his brother Julian:

"Have you read Korzybski's *Science and Sanity*? If not, I think you shd—in spite of the fact that the author is maddening and his book 800 pp long. For he does seem to have said things about 'Semantics'—the relation of words to things and events—which are of the highest importance. And incidentally he seems to have read practically everything."[22]

In Los Angeles, the movie world had also discovered Korzybski. In 1939 screenwriter and producer Robert Lord had read *Science and Sanity*, written some articles about it in *Rob Wagner's Script*, a Los Angeles-based magazine along the lines of *The New Yorker*, and had attended the 1939 Winter Intensive seminar. Lord was helping the Institute with a monthly donation and, along with some of Korzybski's other Los Angeles students, may have been one of those responsible for getting a number of Hollywood actors and actresses interested as well.

Korzybski's work figured prominently in Oliver Reiser's book *The Promise of Scientific Humanism*, published at year's end. Topping the 1940 publicity for the Institute, the national magazine *Newsweek* published an article "A Healer of Mental Muddles" with a photograph of Korzybski in the "Education" section of its December 30 issue.

Unfortunately all this publicity had so far not translated into adequate funding and Korzybski was struggling just to keep the Institute afloat. As he wrote to Mrs. Dewing, "...we have got more recognition than could possibly be expected, except that most of the people we are dealing with are of very limited means, so we have recognition but very little money."[23] As for the muddle between him and Mira, it seemed anything but healed. By the beginning of 1941, Mira wanted no more of her no-win situation with Alfred. She decided to leave Chicago.

Chapter 53
QUESTION MARKS

On January 2, 1941, Korzybski finished the lecture portion of the Holiday Intensive, a seminar notable not only for the presence of his old friend Joseph Brewer, but also for two exceptional students, Francis P. Chisholm and Harry L. Weinberg, each of whom would become important general-semantics teachers.

Chisholm, an English instructor at Syracuse University, had already attended the June 1940 seminar with his wife. He had a particular interest in the implications of general semantics for graduate school training in the humanities. Korzybski would develop a high regard for Chisholm and his talents. Within a few years, Chisholm was teaching an introductory course in general semantics at the Institute—a job few people had in Korzybski's lifetime.

Weinberg—an industrial research chemist from Philadelphia—had first read *Science and Sanity* in 1939 and as he later wrote, "swallowed it whole—the book, the line, the thinker." He and his wife Blanche—anticipating imminent U.S. entry into the war and the possibility of Harry getting drafted (as it turned out an accurate prediction)—had quit their jobs in 1940 to take a four month, thousand-mile-long canoe trip together. As Harry wrote:

> Neither of us had ever been in a canoe before and so our progress at first was slow. Even slower was my reprogress through *Science and Sanity*. Each morning I would read a page or two and spend the rest of the day thinking about them while paddling. I like to think that my understanding and my biceps improved at about the same rate.[1]

Attending Korzybski's Holiday seminar improved his understanding still further. After the war he began his next career as a teacher of speech communication and GS. Korzybski would declare him one of his most gifted students.

The Holiday seminar had gone well for other reasons. R. F. Hedin, a surgeon who ran the Interstate Clinic, a multi-disciplinary medical practice in Red Wing, Minnesota, attended with his wife. Impressed with what he had absorbed at the seminar, Hedin not only decided to add a psychiatrist to his staff but also invited Korzybski to come to Red Wing to give a seminar. The Hedins and another attendee, independently wealthy Red Wing artist and photographer John Anderson, also donated money to the Institute. Both the Hedins and Anderson probably came to Korzybski at the suggestion of Charles Biederman, a painter/sculptor friend of Anderson, who had spent time in Red Wing and had attended one of the Institute's earliest seminars in August 1938. (Biederman, profoundly affected by Korzybski, had begun work on a non-aristotelian theory of art and art history, later published in the 1948 book, *Art As The Evolution Of Visual Knowledge*.)

While Korzybski was giving his final lecture on January 2, Kendig was having meetings and making plans for the coming year. In a January 5 memo to Korzybski, she reported on the two-hour meeting she had with Irving J. Lee, who had gotten very busy. Besides his regular teaching, he had just had an article published on "General Semantics and Public Speaking" in the December 1940 *Quarterly Journal of Speech* and was in the midst of giving a series of talks around Chicago to men's and women's groups. As he told Kendig, he also planned to meet with an official from the Rosenwald Fund, an educational foundation, to see if he could get money for the Institute. He would present GS as a method for dealing with race prejudice and antisemitism.

Lee also told Kendig perhaps his most exciting news: he had just signed with Harper & Row to write a book based on the material from the "Language and Thought" course he'd begun at Northwestern in the Spring of 1940. (Kendig and Alvin Weinberg, among others, had served as guest lecturers.) He'd contracted to deliver a manuscript to the publisher in April. Lee showed Kendig the chapter outlines of the book, to be called *Words Are Not Enough!: An Introduction To General Semantics*.[2] (It seems unfortunate he later changed this catchy and quite fitting title to the more academic and restrictive one of *Language Habits In Human Affairs*.) He would write it in less than five months while teaching his regular course load. Along with Hayakawa's *Language In Action*, Lee's book would for many people provide an entry to Korzybski's work more easily accessible than *Science and Sanity*. Korzybski unhesitatingly promoted the work of both men in private letters and in Institute announcements, although it seems clear that Lee had especially impressed Korzybski. He read Lee's manuscript and Lee asked him to write the foreword, which he did in August, commenting that,

> ...Its theoretical foundations are solid, presented in a common-sense practical language. Besides, from his long study the author gives a wealth of examples which are very illuminating and important. For years I have been hoping that a student of general semantics would write just such a book. I am satisfied that Dr. Lee has done it. In my own work I shall have to keep his book on my desk as a handbook that I may benefit from his erudition and examples.[3]

After the book came out in December, Korzybski told Mrs. Dewing, "It really is a very workable and remarkable book. Lee is one of my best students, and for the time being, if I coagulate he is the best man at present we could have as the head of the Institute."[4]

A Congress and a Book

In her January 5 memo, Kendig also reported to Korzybski about a long phone conversation she had with Elwood Murray about a Congress on General Semantics they hoped to hold sometime that year at the University of Denver. As early as 1939, Kendig had thought about having a symposium in 1943 to celebrate the tenth anniversary of the publication of *Science and Sanity*. But now it seemed that enough students had come through Korzybski's seminars—and experienced personal results, made professional applications, and done sufficient research—to justify pushing up the time to the present. The publicity and interest engendered by a Congress on General Semantics might give a critical nudge to Crane and could also lead to new funding opportunities.

But another more immediate push existed for holding such an event now—U.S. entry into the war seemed more likely than ever. If they were going to have it, they needed to get going without delay. Murray, who had infused the University of Denver Speech department with a strong korzybskian flavor, believed the University would support such an event and could cover the costs—including Kendig's and Korzybski's travel and other expenses—from the conference fees. Murray had initially wanted to limit papers to the field of education, but Kendig and Joe Brewer had convinced him to open the Congress to all fields from which they could possibly draw papers. During their phone conversation, Murray asked Kendig to provide names of possible presenters and a small number of invited speakers—besides Oliver Reiser, whom he wanted to have for an opening address on the broader cultural framework of Korzybski's work. He also wanted Korzybski on the "advisory committee". Kendig felt assured enough to give Murray the go-ahead over the phone without getting Korzybski's permission first. Murray had gotten Kendig on the program of the Rocky Mountain Speech Conference in Denver from February 13-15. Once there she would stay an extra day to meet with him and solidify plans. In the meantime, Murray would put together a prospectus.[5]

At their February meeting in Denver, the plans gelled. By the beginning of March, work had gotten underway on the Second American Congress on General Semantics, scheduled for August 1-2 under the auspices of the University of Denver. As the central theme of the Congress program they chose: "General Semantics and Methodological Foundations For Cultural Integration In Our Time". Murray, the General Chairman of the Congress, would take care of the arrangements in Denver while Kendig, the General Secretary, would "secure the papers, organize and direct the program, etc."[6] University of Denver Chancellor Caleb Gates, Jr. agreed to serve as Honorary President of the Congress. A slew of dignitaries (predominantly IGS Honorary Trustees) agreed to serve with Korzybski on the General Advisory Committee. A sponsoring committee from the University and the City of Denver, as well as program and organization committees were also formed. Writing in 1943, Kendig gave a sense of the flurry of activity required to bring it off:

...The decision to hold the Congress at the University of Denver in August, 1941, was not made until March first of that year. The announcement of the Congress and call for papers were sent out in April to some two thousand persons or institutions known to be interested in the subject.

Citing these dates suggests the conditions under which the program was organized and the papers produced. For both the organizers and the contributors to the Congress, it was a race against time in the midst of world chaos, accelerating insecurity and disintegration of national morale. Our temerity in attempting to organize the Congress in four months, and those the busiest for the majority of the contributors (75 percent were in academic life), has been justified by developments. Had we aimed at an 'ideal' program 'completely' representative of those applying general semantics and doing allied work, had we taken a year to secure papers and arrange the program as common sense and the experience of others said we should, there could have been no Congress on General Semantics until after this war. By August, 1942, many of the contributors were in the armed forces, or otherwise engaged in war work, and travel conditions alone would have prevented the holding of a congress.[7]

Korzybski probably felt glad that he didn't have to do more than advise Murray and Kendig as they planned the Congress. He had enough else to keep him occupied. At the end of January, he started teaching an evening seminar, which ran until February 27. Beyond the immediate exigencies of teaching and the day-to-day business of the Institute, he also *had* to get out the Second Edition of *Science and Sanity*, to fulfill the large accumulation of back orders. Having just received the publisher's proofs of the "Introduction to the Second Edition" in early February, he was editing and adding to it. (He would finish it in March although further correction of proofs would continue afterwards.) He was also working on the "Supplementary Bibliography of the Second Edition", the new book jacket, and editing the proofs of the rest of the new front matter. A new page of the volumes in the International Non-Aristotelian Library listed one already published (*Science and Sanity*), those in preparation (including the upcoming Lee and Hayakawa books) and a revised list of the books whose authors would "be announced later". Of the fifty-seven titles listed on that page only the three noted above ever got published. (Korzybski could be called naive but he believed in aiming high.)

He also selected a new opening epigraph for the book in place of the 'Fable of the Amoeba' he had used in the First Edition. The new epigraph, placed after the dedication page, consisted of several related passages from Chapter II of Part III of *Gulliver's Travels* by Jonathan Swift. They described Gulliver's visit to the flying island of Laputa and his experience with some of its well-to-do but rather odd inhabitants. Although adept in mathematics and music, they indulged so ceaselessly in high-order abstractions and had so little practical sense that they had to hire individuals called "flappers" to remind them to pay attention to what was going on around them.*[8] As with Swift, fierce indignation at human folly had long torn Korzybski's heart. He probably couldn't have chosen a better parable to illustrate the message of his book. Whether they recognized it or not, many if not most people (including mathematicians and scientists) seemed more or less in need of an extensional 'flapper' to bring them 'down to earth'. Indeed, as he was finishing the "Introduction to the Second Edition", the whole world seemed in need of flapping. With this Second Edition, Korzybski was taking another opportunity to flap people and, even more, to emphasize how they could *flap themselves*.

In the "Introduction" he sought to cover not only the formulational refinements he had made since 1933, but also aspects of the original text of *Science and Sanity* he felt needed special emphasis. After the brief introductory section A. on "*Recent developments and the founding of the Institute of General Semantics*", he devoted a lengthy Section B. to "*Some difficulties to be surmounted*" wherein he hoped to clarify some of the formulational blockages that seemed to prevent some people from understanding his work.

This section concluded with part 5. "*Methods of the Magician*". Korzybski had long had an interest in stage magic, employing simple tricks in his teaching to dramatically demonstrate mechanisms of misevaluation to his students. A brilliant young psychiatrist from California, Douglas McGlashan Kelley, who had attended Korzybski's 1939 holiday intensive seminar, had stimulated his interest in magic still further. Korzybski would come to see Kelley as another of his most gifted students. As an undergraduate Kelley had already developed professional level skill as a stage magician. He had used magic as an adjunct to his psychiatric and educational work. In 1940, in the *Journal of Occupational Therapy and Rehabilitation*, he published an article on "Conjuring as an Asset in Occupational Therapy". Korzybski referred to it in part 5, while pointing out: "A scientific study of magic with its methods of psycho-logical deception is most revealing, as it shows the mechanisms by which we are continually and unknowingly being deceived in science and daily life."[9]

Korzybski would come to see the various forms of misdirection Kelley discussed as a good basis for understanding the psychology of deception the Germans and Japanese had been using so successfully in their war propaganda. And Kelley suggested in his Congress paper that: "At present the most efficient methods which we have of actively overcoming such misdirection are the principles involved in extensional evaluation and Korzybski's non-aristotelian system."[10] Korzybski very likely had read this by the time he completed the "Introduction". In Section D, where he counterpoised "Old Aristotelian Orientations" to "Non-Aristotelian Orientations", he had added "Methods of magic (self-deception)", under the first and "Elimination of self-deception" under the second. He considered it important. In later teaching and writing he would often refer to Kelley's work on magic and other writings of his as well.

---
* At least the residents of Laputa had sense enough to know they needed flappers.

The "Introduction to the Second Edition 1941" contains more material than I intend to elaborate here—much of it refinements Korzybski developed in papers published after 1933, which I've already covered. Perhaps the most important contribution of the "Introduction" consisted of the fact that Korzybski's digest of the developments in his work would now be available alongside the original text of *Science and Sanity*. Those who took the time and effort to read carefully would be able to see the continuing evolution of his formulating.

In some cases the innovations presented in the "Introduction" consisted of new packaging to clarify what he had already treated in the original text. The prime example of this consists of his discussion of the neuro-linguistic devices (indexes, dates, etc., quotes, and hyphens) that he had used throughout the book. Korzybski held that using them—along with slight hand motions when appropriate—modified the structure of people's language and could help nudge their evaluating in an extensional direction. Based on the non-aristotelian principles he had elaborated, the devices provided a means of 'self-flapping'. After 1933, he had explicitly written about the extensional devices in articles, but readers of the "Introduction" of this new edition could now find his filled-out treatment of them in one place in *Science and Sanity*. Since he hadn't discussed them in one place in the original text *as extensional devices*, he considered this summary under one term a development of major significance in his work.[11]

The "Introduction" also contained extensive discussion of the World War which the United States had not yet entered. Korzybski's distress and anger about the continuing Japanese army assault against the Chinese and about the madness of Nazi German exterminationism, etc., appeared evident if restrained. The final sentence of the "Introduction to the Second Edition"—followed by his initials and the place and time-signature, "Chicago, March, 1941"—hints at his urgency: "A non-aristotelian re-orientation is inevitable; the only problem today is when, and at what cost."[12]

In addition to the new front matter, Kendig had suggested they include as back matter the scientific opinions he had obtained about the First Edition (previously printed as a promotional booklet in 1933). Science Press had to reformat this material which then needed further editing. He also was arranging to have the Front Matter, including the "Introduction" and "Supplementary Bibliography" of the Second Edition, printed as a sixty-page booklet, which the Institute would then be able to sell and distribute separately. Additionally, the Institute was obtaining and editing statements about professional applications from some of Alfred's students to include in a thirty-two page promotional booklet, which would also contain selections of reviews of the First Edition. With all this to occupy Alfred and the Institute staff—besides the ongoing seminars and the Congress planning (soliciting and selecting papers, organizing the program, writing and editing the program pamphlet, etc.)—he could still write to Marian Van Tuyl, Douglas Campbell's new wife, on April 6: "All the material for the second edition is already in the printer's hands, and we expect the book out in two or three weeks."[13] That was not going to happen.

Question Marks

When would the book be published? Would Crane come through with some money? How to close the Institute money gap in the meantime? And how would the Congress go? With these question marks as background, Korzybski once again took to the road.

First, from May 29 to June 2, he gave an intensive seminar at Dr. Hedin's Interstate Clinic in Red Wing, Minnesota. He had most of the Institute staff come along since an overwhelming amount of other time-dependent work, especially related to the Congress, continued to need at least some of his direct attention. Korzybski probably would have preferred not going at all. But the Hedins made the situation somewhat more appealing by moving out of their home, staying with the Andersons, so Korzybski and his staff could have their cook as well as the run of their place. Korzybski found the seminar group an interesting one to work with. It included not only the Hedins and physicians from his clinic (and their wives), but also John Anderson and his wife Eugenie, Eugenie's sister Mary (who would marry Charles Biederman at year's end), other physicians and educators, as well as Isadore Fankuchin, a pioneer x-ray crystallographer and explorer in what would become known as "molecular biology". The psychologist Charlotte Buhler and her psychiatrist husband Karl also attended a number of sessions. On June 9, Alfred was still in Red Wing doing post-lecture interviews, and only got back to Chicago a little before the June 16 start of the next intensive seminar scheduled at the Institute. July provided a break from seminars but not from the intense pace of work as preparations revved-up for the Denver Congress on August 1 and 2.

Kendig arrived in Denver and set up an office on campus about a week before Korzybski got there, a day or two before the Congress began. About 300 attended, including University of Denver students and pre-registered people from around the country. The Program started on Friday morning, August 1, with some opening introductions and short addresses by Korzybski and others. Korzybski also spoke from notes to the entire Congress group in two general sessions, with material taken from his still unpublished "Introduction". He entitled his first talk, after dinner on Friday evening, "Non-aristotelian Methodology: Neuro-linguistic and Neuro-semantic Factors in a Disintegrating Culture". On Saturday night after the closing banquet he gave another talk to the general group entitled "Non-aristotelian Orientation: Neuro-social Integration without Regimentation". Some 70 authors, most of whom attended the Congress, presented around 90 papers during two very full days in four concurrent sessions on: Psychosomatic Problems, Medicine, and Psychotherapy; Education; Speech and Speech Arts; and Public Affairs.

One notable Congress contributor, engineer and anthropologist Benjamin Lee Whorf, had just died on July 26 at the age of 44. Korzybski had recognized him (and to some extent his mentor Edward Sapir) as an important non-aristotelian formulator. Through studying the Mayan, Aztec, Hopi, and other Native American languages and cultures, Whorf had come to conclusions similar to Korzybski's about the relations of language, perceptual processes, and other behavior. Whorf referred to his theoretical framework as "the point of view of linguistic relativity".[14] Whorf's invited paper, "Languages and Logic: Chemical Compound or Mechanical Mixture, a Sentence Hides within its Structure Laws of Thought Profoundly Important to the Advance of Science", was read at the Congress and later printed in the Congress papers. Whorf appeared to not have had much exposure to Korzybski's work except through unreliable secondary sources. Whorf expressed concern to an editor in 1940 about having his work confused "with things like the recent popular stultification of a similar subject by Mr. Stuart Chase..." Earlier in 1941 he had written in a letter that, "For the immediate future, probably the loose-thinking 'semanticists' à la Stuart Chase, will introduce many popular clichés and make [the] term 'semantics' a hissing and byword, so that it will cease to be used by serious scientists."[15] Korzybski was coming to conclude that too. Whorf's agreement to participate in the Congress indicated a willingness to make a more direct connection to Korzybski and his work despite his hesitancy about popularizers like Chase. In his paper, Whorf had referred to the "far off event" in linguistic science of "a new technology of language and thought." Korzybski and his students were already demonstrating that such a technology was not so far off after all. Whorf's early death at this pivotal point of connecting with Korzybski was a lost opportunity for the work of both men.

Korzybski felt unwell in Denver's high altitude but at least one of the questions hanging over him had been answered very nicely: he felt very good about the Congress, which even got national publicity in an article in the August 11 issue of *Time Magazine*.[†][16] As he wrote to Cornelius Crane a couple of months later,

...The congress was a genuine success, the papers were mostly important and the attendance large. The great psychiatrist Dr. Adolf Meyer of Johns Hopkins attended the Congress, presented a paper and participated in many discussions of medical papers. At the opening of the Congress he introduced me at length in such a way that some of the audience were moved to tears. I admit that the Congress, and the unqualified warm approval of Meyer made this one of the happiest events of my life.[17]

Korzybski probably did not find out until later about the death on July 23 of his friend George E. Coghill, among biologists one of his strongest advocates. Coghill, already an honorary trustee of the Institute, had last written to Korzybski in April when he agreed to serve on the advisory committee of the Congress.

Korzybski's work would have figured prominently in Coghill's uncompleted book. *Principles of Development in Psycho-organismal Behavior*, "designed to present a psychological and philosophical synthesis of his studies on organismic development and the significance of mentation in these vital processes."[18] From remaining notes, Coghill's friend and biographer, the neurologist C. Judson Herrick, paraphrased his views about "...the emergence of the specific human type of adjustment...by the process which Count Korzybski calls time-binding—the conscious blending of the past and future into the *now* of present experience."

As he [Korzybski] so passionately argues, this is the badge of our humanity. Our ability to forecast the future in terms of the past is the secret of our superiority over the brutes in control of the forces of nature, including social forces and, most important of all, the course of our own cultural development.[19]

Korzybski and Kendig returned home from Denver and left almost immediately for an August 11 to 23 seminar at State College, Pennsylvania, during which Kendig assisted. Emmett Betts, the head of the Pennsylvania State College Reading Clinic, was sponsoring it and even offering it to students as a two-credit Graduate Education course under the title, "Psychology of Reading". Ora Ray Bontrager, a professor of teacher training at the State Teachers College in California, Pennsylvania, and Director of the Reading Clinic there, helped organize the Penn State Seminar and also attended it—his third with Korzybski. Bontrager had not been able to attend the Denver Congress but had his paper "Re-education in Reading: A Report of Applications of General Semantics in Remedial Work in Reading" presented there.

[†] Regrettably, the *Time* article started with a by-this-time common mistake: "Last week 200 sworn enemies of Aristotelian logic gathered at the University of Denver..."

(It remains one of the best analyses of reading problems I've ever encountered.) Bontrager, trained in mathematics and psychology and a seasoned educator, had absorbed a great deal from Korzybski and was becoming a friend and ally.

Wisely, Korzybski had agreed to cancel another intensive at the Institute, scheduled to start August 26. Soon after returning home, however, he gave a presentation at the Unity of Science Conference at the University of Chicago in the first week of September. (He had written a complaint to Charles Morris, the Conference organizer, when he saw the preliminary program after coming back from Denver: it bothered him that he had been put in a little section on 'Language'—and scheduled to speak last, besides. After some back and forth, Morris agreed to at least change the name of Alfred's section to 'Language and Personal-Social Orientation'. He also included Adolf Meyer on the program at Alfred's request.)[20] A week later Alfred began teaching another intensive, with the lectures running from September 8 to 15 (the personal interviews as always extended the actual seminar work for Alfred beyond the final date). For several months, he had intermittently noted to Mira his ongoing sense of exhaustion. By the middle of September, he felt dead tired.

The Second Edition of *Science and Sanity* (already printed in July) still hadn't been issued.[21] Korzybski had held back the official publication date because of the unresolved business with Crane. In the acknowledgements at the end of the "Introduction", he had wanted to add another paragraph expressing his gratitude for Crane's initial interest in and financing of the Institute. With Crane's obligations unfulfilled, Korzybski didn't feel he could do that. However, sometime in September, he had to make a decision. He simply couldn't wait any longer. On October 1, the Institute issued an addendum to its publication list announcing the availability for sale of the separately printed booklet of the "Introduction To The Second Edition" with "Supplementary Bibliography". The notice also announced the availability of the Second Edition starting on November 1. Neither the booklet nor the limited number of books getting bound for the publication date would contain any acknowledgement to Crane. That bothered Korzybski (not just for sentimental reasons) and he was going to use this missing acknowledgement in a final October 28 appeal to Crane.

...People know that you started to finance the Institute. Suddenly you stopped paying. People know that we are broke, and have been struggling along for two years. Naturally everybody asks the simple question, 'What is wrong with the Institute or with Crane? I know of course what is 'wrong', but could not tell because you were my student... For historical reasons I have to give credit to you in my new edition for your interest and original financial help in starting the Institute. You and I have definite obligations toward the staff for our salaries. Besides, I have definite moral obligations toward the trustees and honorary trustees to carry on the work of the Institute. I feel my obligations very strongly. What I publish must adequately represent the facts of the situation and so depends on your clearing up your relationship with the Institute. In the most realistic way possible it is today a question of your name, Crane, against my name, Korzybski, and my reputation for fulfilling my obligations, which I did and am doing in spite of handicaps. Let us be clear on this subject: it is a question of your name or mine, and I can not damage my work to protect you...Something must be done about it very quickly, so please answer this letter promptly.[22]

Korzybski would have to wait a bit longer to see how this would work.

"To Transform Myself"

During a large part of 1941, the question of what would happen with Mira remained another significant unanswered one for Korzybski—and for Mira too. He not only still considered her—probably unfairly—as a loose cannon in relation to his work, but he worried about her personally. However, he was too consumed by work to see her or talk to her much. He still didn't appear to have forgiven her for her last 'broadcast' and seemed more likely to scold her than to 'make nice' whenever they saw each other or otherwise communicated. Not that they did that much.

During this period Pearl and Charlotte may have had more direct contact with Mira than he did. As much as Mira liked them, she found that arrangement utterly inadequate. She felt lonely. She missed the intellectual stimulation of the years she had spent as Alfred's main muse and audience, and sometime amanuensis. She still felt vitally interested in his work (perhaps even more so) and in the fate of the Institute. Indeed, the advancement of his work and the success of the Institute seemed as important to her—in her own way—as it did to him. She agreed with him that she would not be able to take the hothouse atmosphere and intense pressures of the day-to-day work there. Still she had hoped and continued to hope for some sense of "everydayishness" with Alfred: a sense that they could at least have some regular time together, however little, during which they didn't necessarily have to deal with his students' or the world's neuroses—and, more importantly, where he wasn't ruthlessly dissecting her 'floppy thinker'.

For Alfred, however, "everydayishness" had become a nasty word. He felt it would kill him faster than overwork. He would have his 62nd birthday in July and he didn't know how long he had to live. (Despite the appearance of extraordinary energy that others saw, he could feel the diminishment of his vitality. The effects of his war injuries had worsened as he aged.) He felt he had to make the most of whatever time he had left by working as hard as he could. Mira could understand that to some extent. For her the greatest sin for anyone consisted of not making the fullest use of their potential. (She also didn't consider it the wisest management of one's energy to work to the point of sickness, which Alfred often seemed on the verge of doing.) Given that Alfred didn't want Mira to involve herself with the Institute at all, his almost total involvement with work, and his still quite negative feelings toward her, what was she to do?

Over the winter of 1940-41, her sister Amy had come up to stay with her. In early February, Amy had returned to Kansas City. As the end of the month drew near, Mira felt she needed some time to consider what she was going to do with the rest of her life. The studio lease ended in October and, if she wasn't going to have much contact with Alfred, she felt no compelling reason to stay in Chicago. She had just had her 69th birthday. Her painting didn't engage her. She wanted to get away from the "rotten rich". She was looking for something—solace, connection. She had a few friends in Chicago. She had also made new contacts in a few of the Jewish synagogues near where she lived, and had gotten counsel from some of their rabbis. In spite of this, the city had begun to feel intolerable to her. On February 28, 1941, she wrote a note to Alfred to let him know she was going away for a few months and included a forwarding address of a friend in New York City. She then got on a Trailways bus for Washington, D.C. and other parts east. A young woman friend of hers, a doctor of engineering, would stay in her studio while she was away.[23]

Mira spent March and probably most if not all of April in Washingon, where the Smithsonian Institute had taken one of her paintings, a portrait of Señora Helena Udaondo de Pareyra Iraola, a member of a prestigious Argentine family. She had gotten in touch with Ruel Tolman, the Acting Director of the Smithsonian's National Collection of Fine Arts, and Charles Greeley Abbot, the Smithsonian Secretary, who were interested in the possibility of having an installment ceremony for the portrait in the fall. (This apparently never took place.) Mira also saw old friends from her times of living and working in the nation's capitol. She kept Alfred and Pearl informed of her doings and they, or at least Pearl, wrote to her about what was going on at the Institute.

At the end of April, Alfred finally found time to respond to a letter Mira had written to him in November 1940, in which she had summarized the ups and downs of their relationship from her point of view. Among other things she pointed out that his letters and other communications with her had come to take on "in their repetitive descriptions of your evaluation of me, a close resemblance to gramophone records."

> For me, they are the antithesis of practicing what you preach in "S [&] S" pp. 328-9 – in being an extensionalized "impassive observer", etc. It is our failure in being exemplars of Gen. Sem. that breaks my heart [and] disturbs me now. But one has only to read the life of a Galileo to learn what kind of citizen [and] husband some "geniuses" can be.[24]

In Alfred's eight-page April 27, 1941 reply to Mira's November letter, he still seemed full of anger. Mira had given her letter to Congdon (with permission for him to read it), instructing the psychiatrist to then deliver it to Alfred. Although Korzybski hadn't hesitated about presenting his side of their dispute to Congdon, he seemed furious that Mira had sought to reveal her side of the story to him. Alfred considered this another of her 'public' broadcasts of their personal problems. Alfred went on to make a number of points about Mira's misevaluating ways: for example, her inexact reference, "impassive observer", which mixed the quoted passage's mention of *emotionally impassive* with *impartial observer*. This constituted for him one more example of her 'Albany-Buffalo' disregard for facts, habitual map-territory confusions, etc. He may have been technically correct here, as he was perhaps about a lot of the behavior he complained about to her. Nonetheless, he comes across as doing the sort of petty picking he often found so distasteful in others. A great deal of his letter seems to exemplify what Mira had written about—his failure to apply his own work to himself and his relationship with Mira. To this observer, who at least *aspires* to impartiality, Mira was holding up a very accurate mirror to Alfred, as few if any others could do.

By early May, Mira had gotten to New York City. She decided not to respond to the details of Alfred's letter but simply reported to him on what she'd been doing. He wrote back with another copy of his letter asking her to respond in detail to its points. She replied that she didn't want to continue contending with him. To her, a life like that was not worth living. She wanted more than anything to be of help to, and at peace with, him. If she couldn't find a way to stay in Chicago to do that, then she would move to Washington, D.C., where the distance between them might make their unwanted estrangement more tolerable to her. She would be coming home shortly and they could discuss things then.

While still in the East she went to see more old friends. On May 29, she wrote to Alfred from Cambridge where she was visiting the Huntingtons. She had experienced a revelation:

...Mrs. Huntington took me with her to exercise the dogs – on a farm on the top of Bellemount. We were reminiscing our relationship – from the first – the dinner Prof. H. gave you [at the end of 1923] – to demonstrate the anthropometer – to a chosen group. And of my coming "dancing in" with the anthropometer on my arm – playing with the strings of "our child" and Mrs. H. noticing the expression on your face. This is the first time in 21 years [I've had] that new angle of perspective – and if I had not found a new evaluation – I was going to arrange a plausible "accident." As I saw it – the least of service I could be to you [and] your work was not to be a burden to you – by my existence. Whereas – the genuine service now – is to transform myself.[25]

This previously unknown and somewhat painful glimpse of herself, as Alfred must have seen her, struck her with a special force—perhaps because it came from a palpably kind and loving friend, her Coo-coon, as she called Mrs. Huntington. It helped her to realize—as she hadn't before—that if she was going to have any success in getting along with Alfred, she would have to sublimate her tendencies toward pushing and dramatics that had helped her so much in obtaining her painting clientele and in working with them. (The pushing had also served as a major motivating force for Alfred in developing his work.) She wasn't willing to assent to every one of Alfred's complaints against her. He had some responsibility as well for the problems in their relationship. But she seemed even more willing now to make greater allowances for some of his points and more willing to bend (even if she considered him wrong) in order to make things work with him. She would find it a difficult balancing act. He could 'be' a stubborn "Donk".

Beyond that, she felt ready for a change. Her lack of formal education had bothered her for a long time before she met Alfred. Her years with him whet her appetite for learning. Living with Alfred had also given her a rather significant brush with many of the works he had studied. And she had studied everything he wrote. But the necessity of getting painting commissions had meant she usually had little time for sustained study on her own. Now she wanted to remedy what she considered her still significant lack of scientific and general knowledge and her 'floppy thinker'. She yearned to read more deeply not only in mathematics and the sciences, but also in history, anthropology, psychiatry, literature, etc. The Huntingtons had seen that yearning. As going-away gifts they had given her copies of David Smith's *History of Mathematics* and E.T. Bell's *Men of Mathematics*. In the Bell book they wrote: "To Mira...who appreciates the exactitude of pure mathematics no less than the fundamentals of human relations." The books became prized additions to her growing library. She would read them both, marking them carefully as she had learned to do from Alfred. Perhaps through her studies she could eventually become useful again to Alfred in his work, at least as another pair of eyes and ears able to bring his attention to some salient bit of knowledge from some book, article, or lecture he might otherwise not see or hear.

With a renewed sense of purpose, she returned to Chicago in early June on another Trailways bus. She was still considering the possibility of either staying at the Institute or moving to Washington. In a somewhat blunt and negative-sounding letter that Alfred wrote to her on July 12, he quashed the idea of her staying at the Institute. If she wanted to go to Washington and hang around the parlors of the rotten rich, "masturbating salivary glands"‡ with them, he wouldn't stop her. That certainly wouldn't have any appeal to her.

---

‡ "Masturbation of the salivary glands" was one of Alfred's favorite pejorative terms for detached verbalism: 'I have to refer to speaking as compared with making noises. I called some manners of speaking after Stanley Hall, "masturbation of the salivary glands". Well, we do a lot of this masturbation—verbalizations that are meaningless. I wonder if you are getting the importance of this.' [Korzybski. 2002 (1937), p. 31.]

But he had another suggestion, which did:

...You could take a little one-room apartment somewhere close to the Institute and see me, say once a week, by appointment. You could even attend courses at the University where you would hear a lot of useless verbalism, read in the library and so on, provided you would not gossip about the Institute.[26]

Within a couple of months, she did exactly that. A small apartment across the street from the Institute became available in September. By the end of that month, she had moved in. By the end of the year, she had gotten a kitten, whom she called "Kitten-Kat". She would reside in Apartment 7 at 5551 Kimbark Street, for the rest of her life, largely in pursuit of the learning that she hadn't been able to get until then. Alfred would pay her rent and give her a monthly allowance with extra money for special expenses, books, courses, etc. He would say his main reason for continuing to work so hard was to support her education.

"Mira's Heaven" with Kitten-Kat[27]

So at the end of the year, one important question for both Alfred and Mira seemed to have gotten answered—at least tentatively. Mira had gotten settled in a new home with a new purpose for herself and a fresh willingness to try to make her relationship with Alfred work. Her new situation seems to have provided some relief for Alfred as well. In his own way, he seemed to want to recover something positive from their relationship too. But resolution of their deeper problems would take quite a while longer. For one thing, Alfred wasn't going to change the pace of his work. He therefore simply wouldn't have much time to devote to normal domestic life. Mira would do what she could to adjust to that. To complicate things, he would continue for some time to remain hypercritical and distrustful of her. She would have to deal with that too. But at this point she seemed better able to stand up to him than ever before. In regard to their relationship, she also seemed more flexible than him. She loved him and wanted him to succeed. She hoped she could help him to soften some of his hard edges—for his sake as well as hers.

Debt Paid

At the end of November 1941, one of the biggest questions and sources of stress for the last two years—the unfinished business with Cornelius Crane—began to look like it would get resolved. Korzybski had just gotten the registration certificate from the U.S. Copyright Office for the newly published Second Edition of *Science and Sanity,* when he heard from Crane's lawyer. He sent a telegram on November 27 to Congdon: "We are making settlement with Crane and must have trustee meeting."[28]

On December 11, Korzybski wrote to Francis Dewing, "[W]e are in a business conversation with the lawyer of Crane, and eventually Crane. Nothing is settled yet, but most probably some settlement will happen."[29] Despite this promising news about Crane, Korzybski confessed to feeling rather "disorganized" due to the events of the previous four days: the Japanese had attacked Pearl Harbor on December 7; the U.S. in turn declared war on Japan, and Nazi Germany declared war on the U.S. The country, which had been supporting England for about two years through the Lend Lease program, had officially entered as a combatant nation on the side of Allied forces in World War II.

Besides the negotiations with Crane, a number of other important items were dealt with at the Trustees meeting of December 19 (which, it turned out, Congdon couldn't attend). It seemed desirable to have a larger number of board members. A committee was appointed to rewrite the Institute bylaws so this could be done. Kendig's status was changed as well. She was elected as a regular member of the board (a change from her ex-officio status). Her title of "Executive Secretary" of the Institute was dropped although she would continue as Secretary of the Board of Trustees. In addition to the position she held as Educational Director, the board confirmed a new role for her, Associate Director of the Institute. This certainly fit the responsibilities she already fulfilled. She had become indispensable to Korzybski in running the Institute.

One of the ways she hoped she could help reduce the burden of work on both her and Korzybski was presented at the board meeting, when she announced the appointment of S. I. Hayakawa, Wendell Johnson, and Irving Lee in their new function as honorary Fellows of the Institute. In October, as a result of an earlier brainstorm of hers, she had written to the three men, inviting each of them to accept a position as an IGS Fellow, intended not only to honor them for their contribution in forwarding GS in their teaching and writing, but to also "enlist their help in planning future developments, especially in the matter of setting and maintaining standards for workers in the discipline." After the Denver Congress, she and Alfred had begun to feel increasingly bothered by the problem of critiquing papers submitted by some of the "eager and sincere students of GS (often college professors) whose grasp of the discipline and use of language in conveying it were unacceptable." She hoped that "in getting the Fellows to criticize such writings, we could 'soften the blows' for these writers and relieve Alfred of the odium of being considered an inflexible dictator."[30] The three had accepted, were confirmed as Fellows of the Institute at the board meeting, and met with Kendig during the Holiday seminar for further planning. They decided with her to appoint future Fellows on the basis of unanimous agreement of the existing Fellows and began working at once on some of the writings that had been submitted to the Institute.

The meeting agenda also listed a report on another plan intended to ease Korzybski's burden. Some of his students in Chicago had formed a committee to start a "Society for the Study of General Semantics", which would have as a major purpose promoting "the welfare of the IGS by plans for financial support." Financial support seemed crucial for many reasons, among them the following. For some time, Mira had been pushing the notion to Alfred that he ought to write a third, more popularly-oriented book. Although he often seemed to pooh-pooh her suggestions, he also often eventually took them up—as he did this suggestion. But he would need time to write it, time which he so far had been unable to find. The next-to-last item listed on the Agenda for discussion at the Trustees meeting, referred to his hoped-for book: "...Discussion of a possible three year plan for financial support of IGS and the need of financial stabilization to facilitate Count Korzybski's writing his new book in that period."[31] Financial support and stabilization remained devoutly to be wished for.

At least the Institute had reached the point of getting out of its deep financial hole. In the last few days of 1941, Crane paid up his outstanding debts, which allowed the Institute to disburse outstanding salaries to Korzybski's staff and repay Korzybski for the money he had loaned it, which had nearly exhausted his and Mira's personal savings. In addition, the settlement left sufficient money for the Institute to cover rent until 1944. Korzybski felt grateful and appended a "Special Acknowledgement" to the "Acknowledgements" page specifically thanking Crane. This would appear in all future printings of the Second Edition.

But the Institute remained far from financially secure. For one thing, seminar attendance would remain an ongoing problem over the next few years since the pool of potential students had suddenly shrunk. Many were entering the armed forces. Even those who remained civilians seemed more likely to have priorities other than coming to an Institute of General Semantics seminar. At least the Institute now had the Second Edition of *Science and Sanity* to sell. Surely, they would have to do something about fund-raising. The war would make that more of a challenge. 1942 didn't look like it was going to provide a good time for rest.

Chapter 54
WAR WORK

Korzybski began a three-weekend seminar in Los Angeles on February 14. He had written about the trip to Crane, saying, "I am personally convinced that for nuisance sake Los Angeles will be bombed."[1] Indeed, he arrived there in time to experience the most remarkable episode of 'bombing' on U.S. soil in World War II.

Increasingly affected by his war injuries, traveling had become more bothersome. And although financially the Institute would come out slightly ahead, the considerable expenses and the time away from home made him wonder about the worthwhileness of the trip. But the group of Los Angeles students who organized this weekend series and another intensive in March, had been insistent. (Another group of students in San Francisco had organized a two-weekend seminar in Berkeley to follow in April.) Things seemed to be going well enough, though with the lectures and the personal interviews and whatever other appointments he had, he felt extremely pressed for time—in other words, not so different from his usual slave-driving of self.

In his suite at the Wilshire Arms Hotel, the site of the seminar, Alfred had the parlor that served as his bedroom and office with a fold-up bed in the wall and a table for his desk. The actual bedroom had two beds for Kendig, who accompanied him on the train trip, and Charlotte, who'd be coming out in a few weeks to replace Kendig as his assistant. A dinette and small kitchen added to the comforts of the place. He felt happy to have a small electric heater for his room to supplement the room heat. (He tended to get cramps in his legs if he didn't stay warm enough and it could get surprisingly chilly in Southern California at this time of year.) He felt grateful that to teach he didn't have to commute farther than the lecture room in the hotel, since he tended to get breathless—apparently related to his 'busted gut', i.e., hernia—when he walked too much or otherwise overexerted.

With a great deal of ongoing Institute business to take care of, Kendig returned to Chicago a few days after Charlotte's arrival on February 26. Charlotte just missed by a day the 'Battle of Los Angeles', which had begun and ended on the morning of February 25.

A few days before, a Japanese submarine had surfaced off the Santa Barbara coast and shelled an oil facility there, about 100 miles north of Los Angeles. Although only minor damage occurred, Southern California—which had oil depots, airplane factories, and shipping facilities galore—had gone on alert. Then, in the early morning hours of February 25, something or things happened in the sky. Who and how many saw whatever happened does not seem clear. Police had reports of from one to 100 unidentified objects—Japanese aircraft?—flying along the coast from Santa Monica to Long Beach. Sirens blared to signal a blackout. Anti-aircraft batteries began firing (over 1,400 rounds) into the sky at the invaders. The ruckus likely awakened Korzybski in his downtown Los Angeles hotel room. Perhaps he looked outside to see the 'light' show as did many people in Los Angeles.

Before the alert was over, five hours later, according to a newspaper account, "Thirty persons, twenty of whom were Japanese, were arrested; two persons were killed in traffic accidents during the blackout and at least two houses were damaged by shells which had failed to explode in the air. Shrapnel which fell like hail in some sections broke windows and caused other minor damage."[2] Nonetheless, if there had been Japanese planes—if there had been any planes at all—they didn't seem to have dropped any bombs.

No one in authority seemed to know what happened—or rather 'everyone' in authority seemed to be saying that different things had happened. While Henry Stimson, the U.S. Secretary of War, praised the successful military and civilian defense of Los Angeles, Navy Secretary Frank Knox declared that the whole thing had resulted from "a false alarm".[3] Korzybski seemed confident, based on reports from one of his students involved in Los Angeles area civil defense, that the Japanese Imperial Air force had made its presence known. But after the war, the Japanese denied any wartime mission at this time to Southern California. One thing seemed clear: a little over two months after the attack on Pearl Harbor, people had gotten very nervous. And shooting into the sky at unidentified flying objects, with different authorities giving different stories, was not going to do much to reduce the nervousness or improve wartime morale.

Questions of Morale

Even before the attack on Pearl Harbor, the U.S government had set up an Office of Civilian Defense to plan and coordinate federal and local government efforts to mobilize and protect civilians during wartime emergencies. Efforts included local organizations for blackouts, fire brigades, first aid, etc., with strong efforts to get civilian volunteers. The Chicago area office had distributed Block Roster Cards to local residents. Korzybski dutifully filled out his card. The question at the bottom asked for "Day and Hours Available for Civilian Defense Assignment". Korzybski wrote, "Working on National Morale, unless in case of real emergency, have no time to spare."

He had already addressed the issue of morale in an interview he gave to a reporter from *The Washington Post*, published in that paper two days after the Pearl Harbor attack. Among other things, he pointed out that German propagandists had been using naive, isolationist, and sometimes fascistically-inclined congressmen as outlets for their material, which was getting sent out as mailings to constituents (postage paid by U.S. taxpayers) and published in the Congressional Record. Investigations were underway but the fact that these German propaganda efforts had happened with so little public attention seemed worrisome. The general public and the government needed to wake up to the importance of public attitudes—as the German and Japanese governments certainly had done. He also reviewed his by-now long-repeated view of the need for the U.S. government to employ "a board of eminent psychiatrists and other experts to plan and guide reconstruction of human values now being ravaged by Nazi and other evil influences." As part of its job, the board could provide factual, expert opinions, not concocted lies, as the basis for counter-propaganda against the Nazis. He felt convinced that behavioral experts would legitimately be able to find Hitler and his minions psychiatrically disturbed. (At about this time Korzybski was recommending Erich Fromm's newly published book *Escape From Freedom* for its analysis of "The Psychology of Nazism" and related issues.) The newspaper article concluded,

> As a long range measure, Count Korzybski believes it essential to prepare to deal with the effect of the last few decades of war and chaos on the minds of the people of the world.
>
> "Here is a thing more deadly than any epidemic you can imagine," he explained. "We set experts to work on sanitary measures, safety measures; we put scientists in laboratories to study cancer and the common cold. We must have no less vision in grappling with the deterioration of values, which, I seriously assure you, concerns the sanity of the whole race."[4]

For Korzybski, the role of the news media seemed critical for the more short-range bolstering of public values necessary to win the war. As a somewhat lonely, early proponent of recognizing and doing something about the German and Japanese threats (when that view was not popular), he had long expressed contempt for the editorial policies of *The Chicago Tribune*. Under the direction of its isolationist and fervently anti-Roosevelt publisher and owner, Colonel Robert J. McCormick, the newspaper had given strong support to the "America First" movement, which became a shelter not only for those with sincere anti-war sentiments but also for Nazi sympathizers.[5]

Korzybski could feel much better about the *The Los Angeles Daily News*. Its owner-publisher-editor Manchester Boddy, a founding member of the Los Angeles General Semantics group, had converted the former tabloid paper into a formidable journalistic presence in Los Angeles with a circulation of over a quarter of a million.[6]

Starting on November 24, 1941, *Daily News* writer Edwin Green, who had taken several seminars with Korzybski, began producing a weekly column, "General Semantics and Human Affairs " for the paper. His column ran for over a year until the spring of 1943, when he left Los Angeles on an army assignment. He sat in as a guest at Korzybski's L.A. weekend seminar; in March, while Alfred was teaching the intensive and doing interviews with students, the two men collaborated on five of Green's weekly columns in the form of a series of interviews with Korzybski on the general theme of building wartime morale. The first interview, published on March 9, started,

> Count Alfred Korzybski, director of the Institute of General Semantics and famous authority on human behavior, considers the daily newspaper "an instrument of tremendous power" for counteracting the effects of enemy propaganda. "Our people do not realize what a magnificent educational weapon their press can be in the battle for a sane world," said Korzybski.[7]

To put the content of the five interviews in a nutshell, Korzybski contended that improving morale to counter enemy propaganda would require the cooperation of the government, press, and public. Clear and honest factual education could best counter enemy propaganda based on falsification and distortion. This would include conveying an understanding of the neuro-psycho-social mechanisms of behavior and deception being exploited by the enemy, an honest presentation of facts about the enemy (basically gangsters as Korzybski saw them), and a recognition of what the Allied nations were fighting for (in short, democracy against gangsterism).

In the final interview, published on April 6, Korzybski emphasized that Nazi and Japanese psychological warfare had made the term "honest propaganda" seem like an oxymoron. "It therefore becomes necessary to exclude this word 'propaganda' from the context of our war effort." Instead he argued for the "morale building potency of plain facts and figures"—not a surprising suggestion coming from Korzybski. Politicians, journalists, and others needed to consider the effects their communications might have on personal, social and national morale:

> The test of a public utterance,...could well be the question: "How will the issue affect the way we get along with one another?" Applying such a test to a great deal of the verbalism being put on the air and into print would serve as a counter-attack against the misleading information and defeatist arguments now actively sabotaging our war effort.[8]

Korzybski's concern for morale extended to the Allied soldiers now mobilizing to fight on all fronts. He still carried daily reminders of his time on the Eastern Front in the First World War. He wondered about the costs some of his students would undoubtedly bear for their wartime service in this one. He had his Kipling—*Barrack Room Ballads and Other Verses*—close at hand, with the line from "Arithmetic on the Frontier" that he and Mira had written out in the front or end pages of their multiple copies: *The flying bullet down the Pass, That whistles clear: "All flesh is grass."* How could these men and women, especially those in combat, best cope with the stresses of those flying bullets and everything else they would experience? Since the First World War, Korzybski had had a vital, personal interest in preventing and dealing with "shell shock", which would become known as "battle fatigue" and "traumatic neurosis" during this war. From a preventive point-of-view, he had long rubbed-in the importance of minimizing expectations, and he believed those prepared for the possible horrors of their wartime experience would more likely deal adequately with whatever horrors they might actually encounter. During and after the war, Korzybski and some of his students would continue to explore how extensional methods could help people cope with post-traumatic stress problems.

Many of Korzybski's students would soon be called into military service. I'll note only a few. Douglas Kelley got commissioned as a second lieutenant in the U.S. Army Medical Corps. He would go on to use korzybskian principles and extensional methods in group psychotherapy for psychiatric casualties in the European Theater, publishing a paper on this after the war. Irving Lee would enter the army that summer as a lieutenant in the air corps, stationed at the School of Applied Tactics in Orlando, Florida where he worked developing training aids. Allen Walker Read would be inducted into the army that summer as well, assigned to work in the Military Intelligence Service in New York City. He got an appropriate job for a lexicographer, working on an *American Military Definition Dictionary*, English-Foreign language dictionaries, and on military phrase books. Harry Weinberg went to war in the Merchant Marine service. As he later wrote, since the seminar he took with Korzybski in December 1940,

> ...I more or less neglected my study of general semantics until one September morn I found myself aboard an ammunition ship headed for Guadalcanal with a copy of *Science and Sanity* in my duffel bag. Naturally, since I had been a chemist, the obvious position for me aboard ship was that of chief pot washer and potato peeler.[9]

In the long run, even such apparently mundane and unrelated wartime duties could further work in general semantics. Weinberg's meditations about seeing the sunrise and on related issues while peeling his daily quota of potatoes, would eventually lead to a paper published after the war, "Some Functional Patterns on the Non-Verbal Level". The paper led to: Irving Lee offering him a graduate assistantship at Northwestern; an eventual PhD in speech communication; and a new career for Weinberg as an instructor in speech and general semantics at Temple University. He eventually wrote one of the best books ever written on GS, the 1959 *Levels of Knowing and Existence*, which incorporated parts of his original paper. Other students, like Kelley, were able to make more direct wartime contributions to GS application and research. But on the whole, the war took many of Korzybski's students out of significant contact with him and pretty much out of the immediate picture in terms of developing his work. But then again, the war disrupted many important things.

Although Korzybski would give six seminars in 1942, the number of students and demand for seminars began to diminish. In 1943, the Institute would hold four seminars and in 1944, just three. With fewer students, the Institute would continue struggling at the edge of financial survival—not so great for Korzybski's morale. It seems ironic because by this time the impact of his work had begun to register even more thoroughly on public consciousness. The growing recognition probably served as a major factor in bolstering Korzybski despite the wartime difficulties.

More Publicity and Reviews

Korzybski had made an impact on many people. One of them was Robert Heinlein, a new writer in the nascent field of science-fiction writing. Heinlein—who attended a seminar in Chicago in 1940—had first attended Korzybski's 1939 lectures in Los Angeles. That year John W. Campbell, the editor of *Astounding Science Fiction*, published Heinlein's first story in that magazine along with those of A. E. Van Vogt and Isaac Asimov. What would be called "The Golden Age of Science Fiction", which roughly spanned the next two decades, had begun. The genre was becoming widely popular. Korzybski would serve as a significant influence on some of its principal figures, such as Heinlein (one of the first to mention or make use of Korzybski in his work), Campbell, Van Vogt, H. Beam Piper, and Reginald Bretnor, among many others—more and less well-known. Their work, in turn, would help to further publicize Korzybski's work.

The publication of the Second Edition of *Science and Sanity* at the end of 1941 provided another opportunity for fresh publicity. Undoubtedly, the concurrent appearances of Hayakawa's and Lee's popularizations, as well as the reviews those books received, also drew attention to their primary source. New reviews of the Second Edition began to come out in 1942 in both popular and professional publications and continued over the next several years. They varied from the laudatory (psychiatrist Hervey Cleckley's review for the April 1943 *Journal of Mental Hygiene*) to the respectful but questioning (Howard P. Becker in the April 1942 *American Sociological Review*) to sincere misconstrual (Kenneth Burke's comments in his 1945 book *A Grammar of Motives*) to sheer ad hominem (philosopher Max Black's nasty, brutal, and short attack in the April 1943 *North Central Association Review*).

In this latter review, Black very skillfully said little if anything of substance about the book, decrying its "faintly crazy tone" and concluding, "the volume is perhaps a little too large to be conveniently used as a missile." Korzybski (unusually for him) bothered to protest to the editor of the publication almost a year later, writing in his typical blunt and direct fashion,

> In my protest I can say nothing worse than that a reviewer should <u>read</u> honestly what he reviews, not glance through a book, pick here and there some few words taken out of context, falsify important issues, and just personally abuse the author. Is that the 'intellectual' standard of integrity of Max Black, Professor of Philosophy at the University of Illinois? If so, fortunately this is not the standard of scientific men anywhere. Professor Black may not believe in honesty, but certainly he should be able to read understandingly; if not, he should be silent. In science we do not follow the notorious legal motto: 'If you have no case, abuse the opponent'.
>
> ....Under such conditions it would be only fair to education and human adjustment, and even science, if the editors of your Quarterly would decide to publish a review of <u>Science and Sanity</u> by a responsible person, who at least would read understandingly and honestly the volume for review, as honest criticism is always useful.

Professor Black ends his review '...with the parting comment that the volume is perhaps a little too large to be conveniently used as a missile.' Even here the reviewer mis-evaluates, as in cases of some frivolous reviewers this admittedly heavy book used as a 'missile' may not be so 'convenient' (if we want to be 'lazy'), but it may nevertheless be very effective to knock in some sense, perhaps even honesty, and anyway some respect for heavy work.[10]

The editor, in reply, seemed apologetic. Korzybski also sent a copy of his protest letter to Black as well as a cover letter in which he told the philosopher, "It was a painful protest for me to write, because somehow I can not reconcile myself to the lack of intellectual integrity of a reviewer who does not read the book he reviews."[11]

Black, apparently unchastened, replied to Korzybski with a short note, "...I am not in the habit of replying to personal abuse and I do not propose to depart from that practice in this instance. My professional reputation can take care of itself. ...As for the review itself, I am content to have readers check its accuracy by comparison with your original text."[12] That, so it seemed, 'was' that. But, as we shall see, Black had not finished with Korzybski.

It didn't cheer Alfred that much of the criticism of his work seemed beside the point, although not usually as egregiously as in Black's review. But he had an attitude toward such criticisms much like that of his friend E.T. Bell, who wrote a short notice for the Second Edition in the October 1942 edition of *The American Mathematical Monthly*. After briefly describing the contents, Bell wrote,

There is nothing to add to the notice of the first edition, except one general observation: any book that was ever worth reading has been cordially damned by at least two persons. With this in mind, the author may see fit to exhibit in his third edition a select anthology of the fatuous things that have been said about general semantics, and his contribution to it, in the eight years between the two editions. Such an exhibition would be more illuminating to serious students than a hundred pages of laudatory remarks."[13]

Bad reviews or not, over the next few years the demand for *Science and Sanity* seemed extraordinary for such an apparently daunting book. With the Second Edition in print, at least 1,500 books per year were being sold—over four times the average yearly rate of sales for the first edition. By the end of the war, approximately 8,000 copies had gotten into circulation, with from a quarter to a third of individual orders coming from people in the armed forces.[14] Despite the financial and operating difficulties that the war had brought on, the Institute of General Semantics still seemed to fill a crying need. Somehow, it was going to hang on.

Boosters

Two projects intended to boost the strained personal and financial resources of the Institute had begun. One, the "Institute Fellows" program was described in the last chapter. The other, a separate membership organization for individuals interested in GS, was being formed by some of Korzybski's Chicago-area students. Both projects eventually became enmeshed in problems Korzybski found difficult to handle. However, at the start of 1942 both seemed full of promise.

An executive committee for the membership organization had formed and held a dinner meeting at the end of January, inviting all those interested to attend.[15] At the meeting Korzybski, Hayakawa, and Lee spoke about their recently published books. Group organizers hoped to publish a periodical, have meetings in Chicago and elsewhere with

GS-relevant speakers and discussions, and provide financial support to the Institute. While Korzybski was teaching on the west coast, the committee put together a prospectus for the new organization, to be called the "Society for General Semantics". They formulated by-laws and plans for a publication. A dinner meeting for a public unveiling of the Society was scheduled for the Electric Club in Chicago on April 24. Korzybski could not get back in time to attend but he felt vitally interested and supportive of the organization and its plans.

Both he and Kendig had long wanted a general-semantics journal but hadn't had the time or resources to bring it about. Among other things, the new Society would make a journal possible at last.The initial issue, *etc*, subtitled "The General Semantics Bulletin", edited by Gordon L. McKnight, did double-duty as the "Prospectus" of the new Society for General Semantics.[16] It consisted of six stapled pages on newsprint. It included a "Statement and Preamble" (including organizational by-laws) by the ten-member executive committee; three pieces by Hayakawa, Johnson, and Lee on "How to Write on General Semantics" based on their critiques of writings submitted by several students; "Letters from A. K." consisting of excerpts from two recent letters he had written; "News Notes" interspersed among the issue's six pages; and a reprinting of "Politics and Magic", one of Ed Green's recent *Los Angeles Daily News* interviews with Korzybski.[17] S. I. Hayakawa was announced as editor in October 1942, but Volume I, Number 1 of the print journal with a cover—now named *ETC.: A Review of General Semantics*—was not published until August 1943.

In that initial issue of *etc*, the executive committee had announced giving financial support to the Institute as one of the Society's main purposes. Accordingly, with three levels of paying membership ("Charter" - $10, "Sponsoring" - $25, "Foundation" - $100), the organizational by-laws stipulated that the Society would retain only five dollars from any dues paid. The remainder would go to the Institute. Thus, in exchange for membership, which included the promised quarterly journal, people would be able to support the 'parent' Institute, although the two non-profit organizations remained legally separate. Over the next year, Society for General Semantics organizers would solicit memberships, begin to sponsor lectures and programs, and start to connect to general-semantics study groups getting formed around the country. For his part, Korzybski allowed his staff to provide a great deal of clerical help to the new organization. And he shared with the society one of the Institute's most precious resources—the large mailing list he had begun accumulating even before the founding of the Institute. To Korzybski, the new organization certainly looked like a promising development for the growth of the discipline he had founded.

" Something drastic must be done about 'that cat' "

On January 7, Korzybski's old friend and Institute Honorary Trustee, psychiatrist Stewart Paton died at the age of 76. Paton, also a trustee of the Carnegie Institution in Washington, D.C, had taught at Johns Hopkins, Princeton, Yale, and Columbia Medical Schools, had written books, and had been on the forefront of the mental hygiene and social psychiatry movements. He had known Korzybski since the early 1920s and had remained a strong advocate of his work, starting with *Manhood of Humanity*. It seemed inevitable—the 'old guard', a generation of prominent scientists, medical men, intellectuals, etc., who had backed Korzybski were leaving the scene.

On May 16, soon after Korzybski's return to Chicago, he had to cross off another Honorary Trustee from the list of the living. His friend and intellectual ally, anthropologist

Bronislaw Malinowski—then teaching at Yale—dropped dead of a heart attack at the age of 58 in his home in New Haven, Connecticut. Alfred put the obituary and death notices in a special folder. The two men had corresponded and had occasionally visited with each other since 1926 when they first met. Malinowski had remained one of Alfred's most stalwart supporters. In writing *Science and Sanity*, Korzybski had made use of his friend's work, seeing it as an important non-aristotelian effort. And in 1933 Malinowski included this in his comments about *Science and Sanity*,

> The functional or relational conception of matter, mind and, finally, of human culture, seems to be gradually crystallising from all attempts at scientific synthesis. Count Korzybski's work contributes to these efforts in no mean measure. I am perhaps biassed as a countryman, but to me this Polish attempt at synthesis seems to rank as one of the most important.[18]

One of Malinowski's last shows of support was his signing onto the Advisory Committee for the 1941 American Congress on General Semantics. Now in May 1942, Kendig and others, including Alfred, were up to their necks in work trying to bring out the volume of Congress Papers. Having in hand a written record of the wide range of application and research being done in GS would aid the Institute in seeking foundation and other funding.

Preparing the Papers had begun soon after the Congress when the Institute began taking pre-publication orders. As the General Editor, Kendig had originally hoped to get out a volume in January 1942. However, the realities of getting manuscripts in shape and of editing them and other materials going into the volume, along with the uncertainties related to printers and paper, moved the publication date further and further ahead. By January 1942, not one but two volumes were being planned in hope that at least the first one would get into people's hands that summer. These volumes were envisioned as the first two issues of a new Institute journal, *The General Semantics Review: The Yearbook of the Institute of General Semantics*. But the Society's plans for a quarterly soon made such an Institute journal seem redundant. It didn't look as if they were going to get anything out before sometime in 1943. They would do better to just get the whole thing done as soon as possible within a one-volume book. As Consulting Editor, Wendell Johnson had begun to do major work helping Kendig edit all of the papers. Hayakawa helped edit the language and literature-related papers, while Congdon, McNealy, and Hervey Cleckley read and advised on the papers in medicine and psychiatry. Of the three Institute Fellows, only Irving Lee—who had two papers in the volume—didn't get involved. Drafted in July, he couldn't do much on behalf of the Institute until his release from the military in 1946. Korzybski read and discussed most of the papers with Kendig and did serious editing of some of them—besides his other work which included teaching, personal interviews and other writing.

Despite the delay in publication of the Congress Papers to 1943, the IGS did publish three of the papers in 1942 as *General Semantics Monograph III, A Theory of Meaning Analyzed* with a "Foreword" by Korzybski and Kendig. In recent years, students of speech and language had come to take center stage among the advocates of Korzybski's work. However important, this emphasis on language was tending to obscure the broader aspects of the discipline, which the completed Congress Papers volume would cover. (For example, one of Alfred's students, May Watrous Niles had made a Congress presentation on the use of GS techniques—primarily the non-verbal 'semantic relaxation' method—in physical therapy.) Even though the articles in the monograph had language as their focus, this "Foreword" provided an opportunity for Korzybski—with Kendig—to disassociate his work from theories of linguistic 'meaning', with which it had gotten confused.

The first paper, by Thomas Clark Pollock, at that time a professor and department chairman of English education at New York University, presented "A Theory of Meaning Analyzed: A Critique of I. A. Richards' Theory of Language". John Gordon Spaulding, an English professor at Stockton Junior College who had attended two seminars with Korzybski, provided a more detailed analysis of the problem with Richards' approach in "Elementalism: The Effect of an Implicit Postulate of Identity on I. A. Richards' Theory of Poetic Value". Finally, Allen Walker Read wrote about his alternative non-aristotelian approach in "The Lexicograper and General Semantics".

To Korzybski and Kendig these papers demonstrated the necessity to get beyond non-neurological, disembodied, and de-contextualized 'Cheshire Cat Theories of Meaning' (alluding to the disappearing character from Lewis Carroll's *Alice's Adventures in Wonderland)*: "...the authors of the papers in this monograph have made a fine start towards building up a body for the grinning Cheshire Cat – not verbally twisting the tail of a non-existent cat." Korzybski himself seemed almost at the point of altogether abandoning the 'cat'— the notion of 'meaning'—as a useful category for discussing what he was concerned with:

> ...Under scrutiny a theory of 'meaning of meaning'* would have to be a biological theory of evaluation based on the empirical data of modern science, which can not be handled within the limitations of aristotelian methods. An organismal, relational approach to evaluation is needed. Various Cheshire Cat theories of 'meaning' have bewildered us long enough. They can not be revised from within the aristotelian system, although their inadequacies can be profitably analyzed.
>
> *Unfortunately the authors of a volume with that title did not produce anything of the sort - just a promising title.[19]

The Foreword proceeded to deal with the issues of unconscious assumptions in science and life and the mechanism of logical fate (with a revised version of the old diagram from Korzybski's early-1920s papers, "The Brotherhood of Doctrines" and "Fate and Freedom", that Korzybski would use in his subsequent teaching). "It is useless to try to build new adequate 'cortical blueprints', theories, etc., (T_2), while we are still at the mercy of our unconscious assumptions (P_1), and expect such 'blueprints' to work."[20] From there, Korzybski and Kendig elaborated on some of the main faulty assumptions underlying the aristotelian orientation ('errors of <u>commission</u>') and some of the non-aristotelian factors which the aristotelian orientation left out ('errors of <u>omission</u>').

In a little over six pages, Korzybski and Kendig provided one of the sharpest, most succinct presentations ever made on the non-aristotelian foundations of his work. They forthrightly reiterated what he had often said: Korzybski's non-aristotelian system was not entirely new. They did claim as new, the resulting "revised <u>methodological synthesis</u> which could be imparted even in elementary education."[21] The conclusion stated what Korzybski was finding more and more important to emphasize: "The reader is advised not to confuse the traditional 'Semantics' (aristotelian theories of 'meaning', etc.) with <u>General</u> Semantics (the <u>modus operandi</u> of a non-aristotelian system)...[which] has very little, if anything, to do with 'meaning' in the academic sense."[22]

Korzybski and Kendig didn't complete the writing until June 1942. As far as I know, Korzybski only published one other piece of writing with another person as co-author. However, he always depended on editing from others. In this case, Hayakawa served as a special editor for this joint effort with Kendig. The monograph came out in mid-to-late August.

1942 seemed like the time for Korzybski to make brief but fundamental explications of his work. While teaching two seminars that summer and fall, he had another piece of writing to complete, his own review of *Science and Sanity* for *The Humanist*, the journal of *The American Humanist Association*. Several years before in Chicago, Korzybski had met the editor of *The Humanist*, Edwin Wilson. Wilson had a friendly but flippant attitude towards Korzybski (reflected in a later memoir he wrote about him). It seems that Wilson felt put off by Korzybski's quite openly-expressed view that Wilson suffered from an occupational disease of those in the humanist camp: sentimentality. Wilson described how,

> When [Korzybski's] new edition of *Science and Sanity* was published in the early forties he sent an autographed copy to me with the admonition to "read the book", a tome of close to a thousand pages [Wilson exaggerated a bit here], "rapidly the first three times through; it will mean more each time." There was also a copy to review in *The Humanist*. "Who actually," I thought, "will read this all the way through even once, let alone three times?"
>
> Of one person I could be sure, Korzybski himself. So I asked him to give me an article review of his own book giving in 3,000 words the basic concepts of General Semantics for novices. He did it in a very useful article, later reprinted in some quantities, which we were glad to do.[23]

Korzybski's article "Science, Sanity, and Humanism", published in the Winter 1942 volume of *The Humanist*, nicely complemented Korzybski and Kendig's "Foreword". While the "Foreword" had focused on the non-aristotelian foundations, this new article concentrated on giving a very condensed explication of the aims, methods, and techniques of the non-aristotelian modus operandi, general semantics.

To his humanist audience, Korzybski wanted to rub in that,

> ...The aims of "Science and Sanity" were humanistic, but the author, being an engineer and a mathematician by training, was interested in producing something not sentimental, but workable...The present author, knowing the results of his predecessors [like Michel Breal and, in particular, Lady Welby], took an *engineering* point of view in the sense that theories should be *workable* and *teachable*, with practical results, even on the level of elementary education. This led to the next step; namely, his formulation of a general theory of *evaluation*, which has very little to do with "meaning" as such, but deals with the organismal neuro-semantic reactions of an organism-as-a-whole-in-an-environment, involving psycho-somatic issues."[24]

Korzybski described the origins of his inquiry in the following questions:

> "Why is it that bridges built by engineers as a rule do not collapse, and even if they do collapse, errors of calculations can be found immediately?" "Why is it that human structures such as social, political, and economic structures collapse sporadically, and all we have to show historically for our pains are wars, revolutions, slaughter, ruin, etc?"... "What do the engineers *do* when they build a bridge?"...The same question was asked in connection with ...[p]oliticians, priests, philosophers, educators, etc., the specialists in collapsible structures,...[25]

He then roughly outlined what resulted from his attempt to answer these questions: his serious investigations which led to an explicit formulation of a non-aristotelian revision of human knowledge: "The main aim of a non-aristotelian system is exactly to systematize and formulate modern scientific methods in a form which would be applicable to daily life."[26]

The editor had made one change, which may have irritated Korzybski—substituting double quotes throughout the review for Korzybski's usual use of single quotes as "safety devices" around elementalistic and other terms he wished to flag. Otherwise, given the necessary sketchiness of Korzybski's account of his own work, his review—as he might put it—didn't seem too bad. With little room for necessary details, he at least included enough to stimulate some readers to inquire further. He certainly emphasized the need to refer to his book and other sources. There was no way to get around the difficulties involved in learning to orient oneself extensionally. For those wise enough to notice, he neatly summarized the hard-won knowledge he had gained from his years of working to help individual students extensionalize themselves.[27]

"Some Non-Aristotelian Data on Efficiency for Human Adjustment" or Overworked Like Hell—As Usual

Alfred worked with great efficiency. Within the limited human and financial resources of the Institute—especially now with the war going on—he had a systematic way of dealing with problems, and achieving goals, and he got things done. Key for this: he knew how to delegate work, and he had co-workers whom—though insufficient in number—he could trust. Nonetheless, he habitually seemed to have too much to get done. For example, he was inundated with letters. He certainly tried to have Kendig and others deal with whatever correspondence he didn't have to touch. However, people were constantly writing to him and the Institute—some students, some not—requesting advice, referrals, or other help that no one else could deal with. He encouraged his seminar students to write to him and report on how they were getting along and he responded with care and concern to every one of them who did so. His typing skill and speed had deteriorated over the years and he dictated his letters whenever he could—to his trusted confidential secretary Pearl or to Charlotte if there were privacy issues—but sometimes he had to type them himself, which he disliked. Then there were his seminars, not so bad to prepare for and give, but followed by the 'killing job'—especially if he had a large class— of conducting personal interviews. But given the importance he gave to students' personal applications (the 'meat' of his work), he felt he had to continue to offer them.

And then, unexpected events that created new problems—sometimes significant ones—could be expected to happen. Such an event happened on December 16, as Alfred was gearing up for the Holiday Intensive that would start in a little more than a week. Institute trustee and lawyer, Samuel G. Clawson, died suddenly of a heart attack at the age of 46—an especially heart-rending loss given that he left a wife and 28-month old twins, a son and daughter. Clawson, a student of Korzybski's work, had ably provided the Institute with legal advice throughout the negotiations with Cornelius Crane and had helped with other matters as well. A specialist in tax law, Clawson had served as one of the prosecutors in the Federal case against Al Capone, which put the Chicago crime boss in prison. (Korzybski, fascinated by the case, had gotten the story first-hand from Clawson.) Clawson's renown resulted in national coverage of his death. As if Clawson's death was not bad enough, I can imagine Korzybski scowling and shaking his head as he read the obituaries in *The Chicago Daily News* and *The New York Times* which both repeated "...[Clawson] was appointed a member of the board of trustees of the General Semantics Institute, an organization devoted to the study of words."[28] Now Korzybski and

Kendig were going to have to scramble to find a replacement for him on the board. Within a couple of months they got Lee R. LaRochelle, another relatively young Chicago-area lawyer. (Unfortunately, in 1947, he too would die of a heart attack.)

It's not surprising then that Korzybski, himself constantly skirting on the edge of too much to deal with, had long had great personal interest in the work of V. A. Graicunas, discussed earlier, who had quantified the long-noted reduction in a manager's ability to adequately manage as the number of assistants or tasks increased; leading to increasingly poor and confused management and ultimate failure. British management writer Lyndall F. Urwick had included Graicunas' original paper, with his own further development of it, in his 1937 book, *Papers on the Science of Administration*. Korzybski had been presenting this material to his seminar classes and recommending the book to all of his readers. Now at the end of 1942 and the first couple of months of 1943, he was working on what he considered an important introductory/expository essay to the original note Polakov had written to him about Graicunas' work. His essay and Polakov's note would go into the Congress Papers as the final article, an appendix of the volume that would take up the whole of the final "Part IV": "Some Non-Aristotelian Considerations".

In their "Foreword", Korzybski and Kendig had put the following on their list of faulty aristotelian assumptions: "The belief that the principle of additivity (in mathematics called linearity) can adequately account for all the relations involved in the fields of science and life processes, which is implied in the three-letter word, and."[29] Graicunas' work opened up for consideration many of the practical aspects of *non-additivity* that Korzybski had long tried to get across to his students and that he worked to apply in his own life. In the article, entitled "Some Non-Aristotelian Data on Efficiency for Human Adjustment", he expanded upon the importance of non-additive, non-linear relationships in everyday life—even beyond the particular management/administrative applications Graicunas had emphasized:

> If in personal life we undertake or have to carry too many responsibilities, interests, involvements, etc., the complexities often grow beyond the capacity of *one* human brain to manage them adequately, and human tragedies, disorganizations, etc., follow, very often culminating in maladjustment and even neurosis or psychosis.
>
> Many times a single painful event in childhood or even later in life distorts the attitudes and colors the whole life. Thus, the 'addition' of a single factor results in unnecessary complexities which are certainly not additive, but spread all through life in some geometrical ratio.[30]

Korzybski demonstrating the Graicunas diagram at the August 1947 Institute seminar.

The Graicunas "Span of Control" diagram and this material on non-additivity would continue to have an important part in Korzybski's seminar teaching on how to manage oneself.[31]

Chapter 55
POLAND FIGHTS

Since the start of the war, Korzybski had followed with great personal interest the news from every front; he had students just about everywhere that American soldiers were stationed. But he had a special concern for what was happening on the Eastern Front in Europe, especially in Poland. By January 1943, the news had become rather grim. He had gone to the Chicago Arts Club for a luncheon meeting of the Chicago Chapter of the American Friends of Poland. Michael Kwapiszewski, the minister plenipotentiary of Poland to the United States, talked to the group on the situation in Poland. The January 31 issue of *The Chicago Sun* gave a brief account of his presentation:

> A phrase which brought sighs was his mention of the systematic extermination of Polish culture which the Nazis have undertaken for the three years past. "Men of science and learning have been exterminated," he said. "All schools except primary have been closed. For the first time in 600 years Cracow University, founded in 1364, has been closed and looted." [1]

There seemed little Korzybski could directly do. In letters to various influential individuals, he continued to ask for governmental support to bring together experts in human behavior (including those trained in his methods) to deal with war-related issues of morale, propaganda, etc. He remained adamant about the need for the allied powers to support investigating the sanity of Germany's rulers and publicly advertising the results. But no one seemed to take this seriously. He was willing to offer his services if someone did.

Since the beginning of the war he had kept in touch with a number of Polish organizations connected to the Polish government-in-exile in London and to the Polish Underground. These groups included the Polish Labor Group, which two times per month published a newsletter *Poland Fights*, with news and reviews. This group also published a series of pamphlets, which Alfred obtained, on various activities of the Polish Underground. He also received publications from the Polish Information Center, the American Friends of Polish Democracy, *Tygodnik Polski: The Polish Weekly* published in New York City, and another weekly *The Polish Review*, among others. These, along with his daily consumption of other newspapers and magazines, radio reports, and material Mira and others found, kept him more informed than most people about the Germans' "criminal destruction of Poland". As indicated by letters to Mira at this time, this news distressed him terribly.

As with other Poles of the 'progressive' stripe, the fate of Jews at the hands of the Nazi Germans seemed to him linked with the fate of Poland, where the Nazis were committing the major portion of their attempted genocide of the Jewish people. Reports of the Nazi mass exterminations tended to get buried in the back pages of America's leading newspapers, but those looking for this news could find it. Korzybski sought it out and, unlike many, did not consider it beyond belief. He filled file folders labeled "Jewish", "Jewish Problem", and several labeled "Poland", with newspaper and magazine clippings, pamphlets, and other materials about the outrages in his homeland. Mira, who also felt an affinity with Jews and Judaism, gathered such material for him too. She received regular bulletins from a number of Chicago synagogues and occasionally went to their programs, if not their religious services. I don't know if Alfred ever attended any of these functions, but at least he got the synagogue bulletins from her, which he marked and filed.

Regarding the fate of the Jews, since the mid-1930s he had contemplated writing a fundamental article on 'the Jewish Question'. From a civilizational point of view, a non-aristotelian analysis of this had long seemed essential to him. Antisemitism seemed to him basic to the Nazi German ideology, which he had railed against for a decade. (Nazi/Fascist promotion of *The Protocols of the Elders of Zion*, with which he had profound familiarity, qualified as the perfect paranoid projection of Germany's own program of world conquest.)

He had also spoken publicly and positively about the Jewish role in the development of a higher, non-aristotelian civilization (although he habitually misconstrued the notion of 'the chosen people' as understood in traditional, normative Judaism). In the summer of 1938, at the first Institute of General Semantics seminar, he had told his students:

...A gifted race called the Jews had extremely good organization among themselves; high culture. They established a doctrine that they were 'chosen people', by which they meant really that they were a superior race, according to what they saw around. Others did not like them. Then in about 300 years what did they establish? A rabbinical institution, which was strictly a brain institution. The rabbis were taken care of, and all they did was think for the race. The institution, as such, is sound. The rest in the world keep the thalamus throbbing, but not thinking. We are undoing the historical tragedy. The Jews applied thousands of years ago the scientific method of today. Applied scientific method to verbiage; tremendous spread of words. Later turned out to be the Talmudistic movement. They had the guts and the institution to do it thousands of years ago.[2]

Alfred had had many Jewish students whose difficulties seemed bound up with the painful history of antisemitism—a history that now pressed in upon both them and him with un-speakable enormity. Some of them had urged him to write about these issues, but lack of time and money had prevented him from doing it—so far. As 1943 progressed, he felt he had to do something.

In April, news had already begun leaking out of Poland about what was happening in the Warsaw Ghetto. The last remaining Jews there—who had not yet been sent to Treblinka, a German-run death camp in Eastern Poland—were engaging in pitched battle with their Nazi tormentors with help from the Polish underground. Korzybski undoubtedly read the sparse newspaper accounts of the uprising, only about a half-hour walk north from where he had once lived on Wilcza Street. By mid-May, the Warsaw Ghetto had been destroyed along with most of the Jewish fighters there. Only a few ghetto residents escaped. Those who remained were captured and sent to their almost certain deaths. The July 5 issue of *Poland Fights* had more details about "The Battle of the Warsaw Ghetto". The report began, "The 35,000 Jews [more like 40,000-50,000] remaining in the Warsaw ghetto took up arms in an heroic struggle against annihilation by the Germans." Alfred underlined the rest of the opening paragraph in red pencil: "They did not fight for their lives, for their fate was known in advance. They fought to let the world know that they died as soldiers of the fighting Polish Underground."[3]

Some of Alfred's clippings reflected an interest in how Jews in America were responding to the news from Europe. One could see in these accounts a mixture of despair, resignation, and resolve to do something—along with a profound confusion of goals and means. The American Jewish community, however small, had many groups and interests. These groups had difficulty working cooperatively to influence the U.S. government to do anything to aid the Jews of Europe. Many of the leaders of the major Jewish organizations, like the Reform Rabbi Steven S. Wise, who had connections with the Roosevelt administration, seemed profoundly hesitant to speak out for fear of encouraging more antisemitism, already rampant in the U.S.

Other groups and individuals appeared less willing to go along with F.D.R.'s policy of "rescue through victory"—the idea that nothing could be done for the Jews being slaughtered in Europe except for the allies to win the war against Germany. For example, Peter Bergson (Hillel Kook) and a small group of other Palestinian Jews, who had come to the U.S. as colleagues of Vladimir (Ze'ev) Jabotinsky in the Revisionist Zionist movement, were working along with people like screen-writer Ben Hecht, and Congressman Will Rogers, Jr. to publicize to Americans the terrible news from Europe. They sought to mobilize public opinion to push the Roosevelt administration into some substantive action. Alfred's February 25, 1943 copy of *The Sentinel*, a Chicago "weekly newspaper devoted to Jewish Interests", carried a dramatic full-page advertisement by the Bergson group with the headline "For Sale to Humanity 70,000 Jews Guaranteed Human Beings at $50 a Piece..." The Romanian government, at this time in the Nazi camp, had actually expressed its willingness to save these Jews—then in concentration camps—and deliver them to Palestine for that price. With "Action—Not Pity" as their motto, the Bergson group, at this time calling itself the "Committee For A Jewish Army Of Stateless and Palestinian Jews", was lobbying American Jews and the American People-as-a-whole to prod their government to do something. Korzybski had a clipping about the Bergson group's dramatic pageant, "We Will Never Die," which came to Chicago in May for one performance at the Chicago Stadium. As evidenced by later clippings in his personal files, over the next few years Korzybski followed the efforts of various groups associated with Bergson like the New Zionist Organization of America. Korzybski had clipped a full page ad from that organization out of the *Chicago Daily News* of 4-17-44. Its headline pleaded "OPEN THE DOORS OF PALESTINE". I have not found any specific statements by him about Bergson or the Revisionist Zionists. However, it seems to me that given his sympathy for Zionism, his preference for blunt honesty, and the way that he followed reports about Bergson, et al, in the papers, he probably looked favorably upon their efforts.

If he could do little else, Korzybski as a Polish nobleman could show his solidarity with the Jewish people. In May, while the Germans were finishing their 'liquidation' of the Warsaw Ghetto, Korzybski decided to have the Institute issue a mimeographed edition of "The Essence of Judaism", the 1934 article from *The American Scholar* he had long recommended. This version included a foreword of some four pages by Korzybski where he stated, "We reprint here the article of Professor Hans Kohn, who deals with the 'space' versus 'time' orientations, because this article is unusually valuable for getting a glimpse of modern scientific trends."[4] To Korzybski it made sense that Nazi Germany would demonize the Jews, whose tradition, to him, represented an unusual, early, non-aristotelian outcropping of Western culture. The 'beastly' Nazis, on the one hand, had raised 'lebensraum'—the space-binding, power-based conquest of territory for German dominance over lesser 'races'—as their supreme ideal. On the other hand, Jewish culture—more consciously 'time-binding' in its basic orientation—elevated progress not through 'space' but through 'time', knowledge, and 'history'; and was an exemplar for "creative individuals all over the world, who have a 'feel' for life, [and] have also a 'time' process orientation in some degree, as there is no sanity in science or life without it."[5] Mimeographing provided the least expensive way of making Kohn's "unusually valuable" article, with Korzybski's commentary, available for distribution. (Never published elsewhere in Korzybski's lifetime, Kendig nonetheless gave the article, with Korzybski's "Foreword", the place of significance it deserved in Korzybski's *Collected Writings*.)

The Need for Funds

As midyear approached, Korzybski could do very little to help the Jews or anyone else in his besieged homeland. He had little time or money to donate to any efforts like Peter Bergson's. The Institute was barely scraping by financially. It was getting harder to get students. He would give only four seminars that year, with smaller class sizes. In addition, the Institute had just expended a great deal of time and money to publish the *Papers from The Second American Congress on General Semantics*, finally coming out at the end of July. After much delay, Kendig had completed the final major job of writing the contributors' biographies earlier in the year. They had gotten page proofs from the printer in April of 1943.

The struggle to produce the Congress volume definitely seemed worthwhile. In an "Acknowledgment" dated May, 1943, Alfred had written:

...My words of appreciation can not convey the depth of my feelings of gratitude for the Congress and to the Congress contributors and those responsible for this volume. In many ways, this Second Congress with all the empirical data and the whole atmosphere was an unique experience for me. After the struggle to formulate a non-aristotelian system, to see that it does actually work in practice was a sort of fruition of a lifetime's work. So once more I want to express my deep-felt thanks to those who contributed to that memorable occasion.[6]

Nonetheless, despite the back orders for the volume, it would take some time to recover the Institute's investment.

Another significant burden on the Institute was the Society for General Semantics and its new publication, now called *ETC.: A Review of General Semantics*. S. I. Hayakawa, who had been appointed editor, was working furiously on getting out Volume I, Number 1 of the journal. (Scheduled for June publication, it finally came out in August.) Although the Society existed as a separate organization, helping it and Hayakawa had definitely taxed Korzybski's already reduced and over-worked secretarial staff. (Korzybski, who took seriously his role as a "Consulting Editor", also contributed to the journal's first issue. He wrote a letter to the editor on the significance of the new journal's title, and a foreward to an article on "Science and Values" by Edward L. Thorndike, that he had gotten Hayakawa to reprint. Hayakawa had also reprinted Korzybski's early post-Manhood article, "The Brotherhood of Doctrines".)

Besides the Congress Papers, the Institute was adding to its record of solid work and accomplishment with an expanding offering of general-semantics related articles and books. These included a new Institute publication for seminar students on *The Technique of Semantic Relaxation* by Charlotte Schuchardt, who by then had taken on a significant part of the teaching of that activity at Korzybski's seminars. With even greater impact, as Kendig pointed out in her letter, over two hundred thousand copies of Hayakawa's *Language in Action*, several thousand of Lee's *Language Habits in Human Affairs*, and many copies of Johnson's *Language and Speech Hygiene*, had gone into circulation. *ETC.* was widening public interest in general semantics as well. Hayakawa, Lee, and Johnson, among other students of Korzybski, were writing articles and becoming well-known in their respective fields. Hayakawa, in particular because of his book, had become a national figure and was locally known as well because of a regular column he'd begun writing for the *Chicago Defender*, Chicago's weekly newspaper for the Black community.

Interest in general semantics or 'semantics', not all of it enthusiastic, was becoming widespread in the broader intellectual community. In the Fall 1942 issue of the marxist Journal, *Science and Society*, Margaret Schlauch had written an extremely critical piece, "Semantics as Social Evasion", based on her misinterpretations of Korzybski's work. English professor and literary theorist Herbert J. Muller also misconstrued Korzybski's work, but came out more favorably towards it in his book *Science and Criticism: The Humanistic Tradition in Contemporary Thought* (published in March of 1943):

> ... *Science and Sanity* can equip [the critic] with a sounder grammar and vocabulary. Unlike the positivists and the totalitarian reformers, Korzybski points to a principle of flexibility, not a fixation, as a solution to our problems. He leaves room for the necessary criticism and supplement of his thought..."[7]

In more popular American culture, 'semantics' had become pervasive. A newspaper review described the late 1943 movie *Lost Angel* starring six-year-old child actress Margaret O'Brien. The movie concerned "a group of scientists who take over a foundling child and attempt to educate her in lore and knowledge, forgetting altogether the human equation. She is taught semantics, music, Napoleonic history, Chinese economics and the higher sciences and arts."[8] As Allen Walker Read would write in his 1948 article "An Account of the Word 'Semantics'": "The great popular vogue of the word *semantics* can be traced to the ferment caused by the works of Alfred Korzybski."[9] But already by 1943, the term had slipped away from any korzybskian moorings it might have had and was likely to be used to refer to a mishmash of Korzybski's work with that of others, or to indicate detached verbalism, verbal quibbling, or the intentional use of words to mislead and deceive. It had become clear to Korzybski that it confused people for students of his work to refer to it as 'semantics'. As a result, he was emphasizing even more strongly the importance of explicitly distinguishing between 'semantics' and 'general semantics'.

Despite the significant public interest, with wartime asperities prevailing the Institute was going to have difficulty surviving for very much longer. The income from seminars (Korzybski taught 37 of them from July 1938 to the end of 1943), and from books (even with greatly increased sales of *Science and Sanity*), could not cover expenses. The Institute continued to get financial help from various individuals. In April, it received $1,000 from the Society for General Semantics, which had pledged $5 from every individual's membership dues. None of this sufficed. The Institute was going to be drawing on cash reserves soon. Without a significant infusion of more money, it would not be able to continue past 1944—let alone carry on the kind of program Korzybski and Kendig had envisioned but had not yet been able to carry out. In October Kendig wrote to Charles Congdon, who had been elected President of the Society and was still on the Institute Board of Trustees:

> Some days ago I sent you the Financial Report which was submitted at the Annual Meeting. I call your attention particularly to the Forecast for 1943-44. You will notice that we had an operating deficit of over $6,000 for 1942-43 and forecasted operating deficit of $13,500 for 1943-44. If we don't make up this $20,000 early in 1944, we shall have exhausted all our reserve funds by the end of the fiscal year. That would be goodbye to the Institute. The immediate objective must be to raise some $20,000, in order for us to plan to go on.[10]

They would require even more money to carry out the long-term plans, first elaborated in 1939, to make the Institute a center for training leaders in different professions as well as competent teachers of GS. With sufficient funds, Korzybski could be freed from the incessant burden of having to give one basic seminar after another, as others could give them too. This would give Korzybski the time to do more creative work and writing and to do in-depth training of leaders. In the meantime, Korzybski and everyone else at the Institute were going to have to carry on as they had been doing and muddle through. Kendig worked on her appeal, "Letter to the Students and Friends of The Institute of General Semantics", throughout the fall. She had a final version in December, which got sent out to the Institute mailing list in January 1944.

A Serious Curmudgeon

Reading Korzybski's personal correspondence with Mira throughout 1943 makes it hard not to put him in the category of 'serious curmudgeon'. He wrote to her, talked to her by phone, went out with her occasionally, and saw her at the seminars she was continuing to attend. She mainly spent her time reading, reading, reading; taking time from her studies to send him clippings, letters with suggestions for his work and the Institute, outlines from books she read and lectures she attended, and love notes. He made use of many of her suggestions—eventually—and appreciated a great deal of what she sent him, including book and lecture notes, when he had time to read them thoroughly. But 1943 was still characterized by phone blowups by him, as well as letters scolding her for what he considered irresponsible verbalizing or for her 'Sarah Bernhardt ways' in public or for interfering with his students and staff at the Institute. How much actual justification he had for his complaints seems hard to say. I have the distinct impression that much of it actually had little to do with her behavior and more to do with his unhappiness with the state of the world, and the pressures he felt from his unending work and financial worries.

As the person who, for all their troubles, remained the closest to him, Mira served as the target of choice for Alfred blowing off steam. It still bothered her but she seemed to have a better ability now to not let it bother her too much. She seemed to realize that he had no one else to complain to. Then too, at times he seemed to be softening. He sometimes would write to her without vituperation—simply confessing his tiredness with the endless work, the constant interruptions from former students dropping in or writing letters for advice, the seemingly endless exhausting personal interviews which accompanied the seminars and which he also provided—for a fee—for former students on request, problems with trustees and with staff, and his vicarious suffering from the war and the conditions in Poland, etc., etc., etc. She loved him. She felt grateful for the fact that he was supporting her in a way that finally was allowing her to get some of the education she had missed most of her life. And she seemed more cognizant than before that his almost complete dedication to work and consequent lack of 'everydayishness' with her *did not* reflect any lack of love or concern for her. He reiterated that he was doing it all for her. And she believed him. Even considering this, at times it was not easy to be married to Alfred.

In spite of this, it would be a mistake to think that Korzybski was perpetually boiling over in a bad mood. He may have had, as he frankly admitted at times, a rather pessimistic outlook on life, but he did not seem much inclined to let himself succumb to depression. He had always had the ability to bury himself in whatever task he had taken for his work. And he seemed to find it congenial to take a stoic attitude towards the whips and scorns of life. Indeed, he scorned the scorns. He could somehow often laugh at himself or at least make a wry joke out of his pains and troubles. And there was always one damned thing after another to provide such 'comic' material. Here, in a February 1944 letter to Douglas and Marian Campbell, he described his general condition and gave an account of one of those 'damned things' that happened toward the end of 1943:

> I know that Kendig is keeping you informed of our official doings because I read the copies of her letters. Here I may tell you a few of my private news. I am overworked and imposed upon by a great many students. In connection with endless administrative duties, editorial work, writing, lecturing, and personal interviews. Sometimes I doubt if a Missouri army mule, even in sunny Calif...I am sorry, I mean Italy, would stand all of that. But somehow I stand it. My old war injuries, and particularly hernia, bother me quite a lot. Dear old McNealy looked me over physically thoroughly and found me in good shape, but he believes that an operation on my hernia would be too late for me now. You know my sweet disposition about monkeying around with doctors. Well, I can tell you a funny story of what I would call a 'modern medical treatment'. As you may know, I have rubber soles on my shoes and my stick has also a rubber end, the three of them being slippery like hell on wet surfaces. Well, just the day before the intensive seminar, which means more than 6 hours a day for 2 or 3 weeks, last August I slipped in my office, fell down and cracked a rib. Pearl telephoned to McNealy describing how I feel, being an Adam when something interferes with my rib. The telephone diagnosis was 'cracked rib', and McNealy suggested we call a doctor who supposedly was pretty good, to come and bandage me. We called him, he came, and did really a lousy job (5 bucks please). I did not feel that I could lecture all day under those conditions of pain I had. The Old Faithfuls, Charlotte and Pearl, decided to take care of me. I had to sit on the bed without a shirt, but the rest of me intact; they got a mile of adhesive tape, sat on each side of me and put their feet in the remaining ribs, and started to make a mummy out of me, bandaging me as far as they could. They certainly made a good job, and I went through the seminar and interviews with flying colors. Being a vital fellow, I am a 'hairy ape'. You can imagine what fun I had when the damn tape was taken off. When it was taken off Dr. [Samuel] Rosen of New York was here with his wife and I had an interview with them the same night. Dear old Mrs. Rosen laid on the sofa and went to sleep; dear old Rosen (M..D. and an old student) felt it his professional duty to take the bandages off the hairy ape. But after hours of pulling hair by hair I had enough of professional help, and under the alibi that his wife needs to go to bed for good, I begged the professional to leave me alone, which ultimately they did. Then Charlotte and Pearl began to soak me in benzine and instead of pulling hair by hair, they pulled them out in bunches, which was much easier for them <u>and me</u>. Ultimately it was a happy performance. You probably know my biblical inclinations, and so you realize my appreciation of the monkey-business the almighty did to poor Adam. By this time, in spite of the work on the seminars and interviews, I was recovered.
>
> The old staff, Kendig, Charlotte, Pearl, Anne and Mrs. Williams [Kendig's secretary], stick with us at the Institute. It is really a joy and help to deal only with old students. There is so much in it, no matter with how many of their god damn 'mamas' I have to struggle, so far successfully.[11]

Chapter 56
TIME TO TRY NEW THINGS

If the fund-raising letter motivated people to help, the Institute's financial problems would have better chances of resolution. Korzybski maintained that the Institute, if it survived, had a useful function to serve in "breaking the hold of aristotelianism". He penciled in those words below the last paragraph of a later mimeographed version of an April, 1944 memorandum that he wrote to Kendig "about his future-work program." The paragraph read,

> Please remember that my age and war injuries are getting to be a handicap and I have only a few years left for constructive work. And yet I feel that I still have something to contribute for the future of mankind. These few years should be spent in the most constructive way for the future, by preserving the Institute as a center for the training of <u>future</u> <u>leaders</u>, so that there will be some capable people able to carry on. Knowing the difficulties, I do not believe that without a special center such training of leaders can be accomplished, and I believe this should be the main immediate aim of the Institute.[1]

They would do what they could. But 1944 was going to be a tough year. With registrations for seminars at their lowest point, Korzybski would only give two Institute seminars this year—plus lectures at the end of February at the Menninger Psychiatric Clinic in Topeka, Kansas and lectures at a University of Denver Workshop in August. Given the hobbling state of Institute finances and Korzybski's goal to develop leaders, it seemed like a time to try new things.

The IGS Seminar-Workshop

One way to develop new leaders would be to open up Korzybski's seminars. For one thing, Kendig had long noticed that,

> ...The people who came to [Korzybski's] seminars got a great deal out of them, and they were moved, and something happened inside of them, inside of their skins. But they got some very peculiar notions that they took away in their notebooks—I used to look in their notebooks sometime. So I thought, well, I asked him if I could just have a few sessions afterwards, after the seminars, and find out what was inside their heads,...I thought it might be nice if we could straighten out at least some of their verbalisms, as well as their semantic reactions.[2]

For a number of years, Korzybski had provided time slots during his seminars for guest lecturers such as Dr. William Peterson, a University of Chicago physician and an Institute Honorary Trustee who had authored a multi-volume work on the influence of weather on health and behavior. Johnson, Hayakawa, Lee, and others had also lectured on non-aristotelian applications in their work. Why not bring in these kinds of presentations—and what Kendig wanted to do—after Korzybski had introduced the system? These extensions to Korzybski's seminar would emphasize participant practice and the variety of applications of the system—a workshop. After all, application remained the main thrust.

By February, the first IGS "seminar-workshop" (Kendig's term for the new format) was being planned for that summer. As Kendig wrote in a promotional letter she sent out a few months later, "At this time it seems to us that increasing competence of 'old students' is of equal or greater importance than enlarging the number of IGS students. The seminar-workshop program was organized to suit this situation."[3] After this first one in 1944, the

IGS would continue the Seminar-Workshop—with ongoing transformations—as a yearly offering usually given for three weeks every summer. (Elements of the workshop were integrated into Korzybski's shorter intensive seminars as well.)

This first one was supposed to go from July 6 to 28, but having to rearrange the schedule to accommodate the guest speakers allowed them to finish two days early. Korzybski first gave the seminar, his 36 hours of lecture-demonstrations on the basic formulations. Then while he saw individuals for interviews, the other students participated in the workshop sessions (another 50 hours), which included group discussions with Kendig on applying GS, as well as lecture sessions and other activities in areas of special interest led by various advanced students such as Congdon, Hayakawa, Johnson, and Bontrager. Raymond W. McNealy, M.D., Institute trustee, surgeon and medical school professor discussed "General Semantics and Medical Education". Wilbur E. Moore, head of the Speech Department at Central Michigan College of Education, gave presentations on "New Patterns for Debate", and "Non-verbal Electrical Tests of Extensionalization". (He had been doing research on the effects of extensional training on galvanic skin resistance using 'lie-detection' instruments). Korzybski also had some sessions with those who had attended previous seminars to deal with theoretical and practical questions related to people's attempts to make applications. Francis Chisholm, who gave several workshop presentations, assisted Kendig in organizing and running the entire seminar-workshop.

Some Students

Three first-time students at the seminar-workshop illustrate a variety of responses to Korzybski's work. David Harold Fink, a psychiatrist then living in Detroit, had published a book, *Release From Nervous Tension* in 1943. One chapter, "Words Are Triggers To Action" made generous use of general semantics although he made no mention of it or Korzybski. In writing his book, Fink seems to have been mainly influenced by Chase and Hayakawa, whose books he did mention. (He would also mention Wendell Johnson in later editions.) What he got out of the seminar-workshop seems hard to say since little changed in subsequent editions of his book and I've found no correspondence between him and Korzybski. (Mira did read Fink's book and made notes about the chapter for Alfred.) Pooh-poohed by some academic psychiatric reviewers, Fink's book would become a self-help bestseller, going through numerous editions over the next several decades and selling hundreds of thousands of copies. Fink wrote about the importance of becoming aware of words as directive maps, which entailed emotional reactions of all kinds. Human progress, social and individual, involved the process of making better, more scientific word maps. Undoubtedly, works like Fink's, derived in part from Korzybski's work (without directly referring to it), did much to bring a few of Korzybski's basic notions into more common usage.

A second student, Alabama native Annie Goulding Dix, taught English and Journalism at the Richmond Professional Institute of the College of William and Mary. A fellow teacher had given her a copy of *ETC.*, something about it grabbed her, and she immediately signed up for the 1944 summer seminar-workshop. A kindly intelligent woman with little pretense, she was willing to do the simple-sounding stuff Korzybski suggested and found it more than eye-opening. As she recounted years later in a memoir, she "found [general semantics] of more value to her students than any other subject she had taught." It became a central part of her teaching repertoire for the remainder of her career—although she would have to learn how to deal with the reactions of some of her colleagues:

"What is new in all of this?" say some of my learned friends. "It's all old stuff; everybody knows it. It's too obvious." So they will not waste their time with it. I am reminded of the story in the Bible of Naaman, the Syrian captain, who came to the prophet Elisha to be cured of his leprosy. Elisha said, "Go and bathe seven times in the River Jordan." Naaman was insulted by such trivial treatment, and went away in a rage. His servants said to him, "If he had told you to do some big thing, you would have done it. Why not try what he says?" So he put his pride in his pocket and went back to do the thing that was so trivial that it was insulting. And, lo and behold, he was cured!

Ann felt willing to experiment with what she was learning at the seminar-workshop:
I remember the first time I consciously tested the efficacy of language usage as suggested by General Semantics. It was during my summer with Korzybski in Chicago in 1944. I was in the Loop in Chicago. It was dinner time and I was hungry. I looked at menus in the windows of restaurants. One was appealing, except that it had carrots, food that I had hated since I was a child. Korzybski had recently discussed the obvious fact that all things change. The ancient Greek philosopher, Heraclitus, put it this way: "No one can step into the same river twice." You come nearer to communicating what you mean if you mentally date your comments. For example: myself 1944 is not myself 1914. So I consciously brought my distaste for carrots out into the open. "As a child, I didn't like carrots. I still don't like them." Now to test the General Semantics suggestion, I said to myself: "Annie Goulding (as my mother called me in 1914) didn't like carrots. Now, I am Ann (as my friends call me in 1944.) Those two persons are not the same." So putting my distaste in my pocket (as Naaman had put his pride), I went into the restaurant and ordered the dinner with the carrots.

And, lo and behold, they were delicious.

Thus I discovered that, to speak truth in any judgment or evaluation, the **tense** of the verb is very important. In this case, only the **past** tense: "I hated" carrots or "used to hate carrots," was true. By testing for current facts, I saw that my use of the **present** tense: I "hate carrots" was false. Many changes had occurred in those past thirty years. I had no current opinion. I had only been quoting the opinion of that little girl of long ago.[4]

In 1947, she would become a professor at the New Jersey State Teachers College (now Montclair State University), where she worked until her retirement in 1962. Afterwards, she continued teaching adult classes in GS. She wrote only a few articles for *ETC.* and the *General Semantics Bulletin*. But one of them, "Avoiding The Dangers Of Semantic Adolescence", presented in 1951 as a paper at the First Conference on General Semantics at the University of Chicago, provides one of the clearest accounts of some of the dangers and challenges involved in internalizing a non-aristotelian orientation.

Beware of merely talking about general semantics without applying its principles in practice. The highly verbal individual who finds in general semantics a new and exciting philosophy is in danger of keeping it forever on the verbal level, thus increasing the very futility that its discipline hopes to correct. ...general semantics has not served its purpose until it enters into the language and evaluative habits of the individual. It is this that concerns me as a teacher,...Our beginners—be they young or old—need to be constantly reminded of what Korzybski said: that extensional orientation is a lifetime process. The exhilaration that comes with the beginning of awareness is not the end but only the beginning, and the growing or adolescent stage will not always be easy. But the maturity we seek is worth the effort.[5]

A few years after her seminar with Korzybski, Ann would move to New York City and marry another student of Korzybski, Adlerian psychiatrist Joseph Immanuel Meiers—a Jewish refugee from Latvia. Both Ann and Joseph Meiers exemplified the quiet maturity and good humor of Korzybski's best students. They didn't become famous, but as relatively uncelebrated leaders they positively affected many people's lives. (The couple became life-long friends of Charlotte Schuchardt Read and Allen Walker Read, living a few blocks from them on the upper Westside of Manhattan near Columbia University.)

A third notable student at this first IGS seminar-workshop was a twenty-three year old 'firecracker' from Miami, Florida named Ken Keyes, Jr. He had joined the Navy in the summer of 1941. As he had hoped by enlisting early, he was able to live at home while 'sailing a desk' in a Naval Intelligence censorship unit in Miami. By 1944, he was serving as chief petty officer in a Naval Intelligence photo lab on the 'U.S.S. DuPont', his name for the building in downtown Miami where he had his office. Ken and his wife, Roberta Rymer Keyes, already the parents of two, had become very enthusiastic about general semantics and its possibilities for reforming childhood education.

They (mainly Ken) began corresponding with the Institute in 1943 on the stationary of an organization they had just founded, "The Society for Educational Research—a non-profit group devoted to the formulation and dissemination of objectives and methods for 20th Century education". With considerable financial resources (both Ken and Roberta had wealthy parents) they had already in 1944 bought 45 acres of property south of Miami for a non-aristotelian educational experiment they planned. Using general semantics as the core they were "hoping to set up and run a demonstration project in which five orphans from each race of humankind could grow up in loving harmony together."[6] Life eventually prevented the project from happening.

Although Korzybski and Kendig provided encouragement, there seems more than a whiff of utopianism in Keyes' letters. His 'semantic adolescence' seems clear from a note he wrote to Korzybski at the seminar: he had not prepared a personal history for his interview because "there are no personal problems of personality maladjustment, relations with people, etc., that I am aware of at the present time."[7] (Years later, Keyes would write extensively about his own personality problems after he *did* become aware of them.) In his interview, he wanted to talk with Korzybski about the work he and his wife were planning. It seems likely that Korzybski indulged him. Without question Keyes could get things done. He had already demonstrated talents as a businessman, inventor, and photographer, among other things. He had access, probably through his work, to people with graphic design and printing skills. Although he wasn't able to stay until the end of the workshop, he had agreed to prepare for seminar participants a professional-looking print handout of Korzybski's blackboard diagrams—which he did. Korzybski and Kendig greatly appreciated his work.

The young man seemed very serious about changing the world with general semantics. Soon after the seminar-workshop in September 1944 he changed the name of his organization to "The Institute for Non-Aristotelian Research and Education". Over the next year and a half, he continued to correspond with Korzybski and Kendig about the organization's projects. He formed a study group in Miami, gave seminars; and sent professional-looking graphic mockups to Korzybski with cartoons and illustrations for a handbook he was producing, as well as for a journal for an association of GS teachers he wanted to establish.

In June 1945, Korzybski wrote to him, bluntly advising him to 'put on the brakes':
> Your experience in teaching GS is not long enough or good enough...I am not trying to discourage you. Your ambitions are praiseworthy, but certainly for success you have to slow down and give yourself more time to digest the whole thing in your organism more.[8]

After leaving the Navy, Keyes with Roberta and their two children, would put aside his institute and its long-term educational projects for the more immediate business of making a living. Then in 1946, their institute got permanently shelved after he contracted polio. But, despite becoming significantly disabled, he—and Roberta—would help Korzybski afterwards in a most important way.

The Process of Abstracting

The July seminar-workshop was notable for more than its new structure. Korzybski also produced a mimeographed handout for an important new visualization, to use with the structural differential, for conveying the *process* of abstracting. As a partly iconic, visual (and kinesthetic) representation of Korzybski's system, nothing had seemed to match the differential as a training device—once students understood the distinctions and relationships represented. There was the rub. Some basic and persistent misunderstandings of the differential by students had vexed him for several years. The origin of Korzybski's new diagrammatic formulation of abstracting came from his attempt to deal with some of these issues, particularly brought to the fore by Hayakawa's work.

He described part of the problem in a May 24 letter to Robert Lee Durham, President of the Southern Seminary and Junior College in Buena Vista, Virginia, who had sent a letter asking about some fundamental issues related to identity and identification:
> You know from Science and Sanity the structural differential. On top there is the event, then comes the 'object', and then follow higher and higher order abstractions. On a printed page the 'higher' go 'down'. A great many students are somehow confused because higher and higher abstractions in a diagram go physically lower and lower on a printed page. In the lithographed edition [1939] of Hayakawa's Language in Action the differential was given the way it was in Science and Sanity, from the top of the page down, which was correct. He was pestered by his students on this subject. Somehow he did not know the answer, so in the printed text edition of his book on page 96 he turned around the differential and put in print: 'Start reading from bottom UP'. Why in the dickens then do it, when normally you read from up down? The answer is the unconscious assumption trained in us in a pre-scientific orientation; namely, the earth is flat and so 'up' and 'down' have absolute value, while on a spherical earth they have only relative value.[9]

In the later editions of his book, Hayakawa had further compounded the problem of reversing the Structural Differential by renaming it "The Abstraction Ladder", a metaphor that *reified* the unconscious assumption of absolute 'up' and 'down' and obscured the *process* aspect of abstracting. Hayakawa's ladder metaphor effectively eliminated the circularity of human knowledge, the important connection between the highest and lowest levels in the process. In subsequent editions of the book, Hayakawa even used a picture of a ladder with a little man seemingly stranded at the top.

The structure of a representation could radically change what got expressed. Korzybski had long warned his students about the dangers of translating the non-aristotelian system into the old elementalistic distinctions and terminology. To a significant extent, Hayakawa had so far—and would continue—to do exactly that. Korzybski had advised speaking in terms of "evaluation".

But in *Language in Action*, Hayakawa continued to talk about 'meaning' without quotes (easier to forget about a 'meaning-maker'). Korzybski had built his terminology distinguishing different *orientations* (extensional versus intensional), from the prior distinction between extensional and intensional *definitions*. He had rejected the distinction of 'denotation' and 'connotation' as elementalistic and confusing, since it depended on what he considered a faulty distinction between 'objective' and 'subjective' factors. But Hayakawa built his discussion in terms of 'extensional meaning' or 'denotation' and 'intensional meaning' or 'connotation'. Hayakawa wrote:

> The extensional meaning of a word or expression is that which it points to (denotes) in the extensional [physical] world...[it] cannot be expressed in words, because it is that which the words stand for...The intensional meaning of a word or expression, on the other hand, is that which is suggested (connoted) in the mind.[10]

If one accepted Korzybski's contention that any definition (extensional or intensional) evaluated—by someone—had a neurological context, one could not continue to distinguish 'denotation' from 'connotation' in the way Hayakawa had done. Using Hayakawa's elementalistic terms in quotes, *any* 'meanings' had to exist 'in the mind', i.e., 'inside someone's head'. Talking about 'denotation' and 'connotation' in the way Hayakawa did, implied a sharp distinction between 'objective' and 'subjective' factors that didn't exist, even if most people felt familiar and comfortable with those terms.

Hayakawa's presentation of 'general semantics' had other related problems, including: his under-emphasis of non-verbal levels of abstracting; his emphasis on individual words rather than statements to illustrate different levels of verbal abstraction (potentially very misleading since determining the level of abstraction of one word compared to another required a larger context); his under-emphasis on the constructive as well as the 'leaving out' aspects of abstracting; his failure to connect mapping to the process of abstracting; his relative neglect of self-reflexiveness and complete neglect of multiordinality; his neglect of the elementalism/non-elementalism distinction and his persistent use of elementalistic formulations (e.g., talking about 'affective', 'informational', 'directive' and 'pre-symbolic' dimensions of language as if these could exist as entirely separate forms); his persistence in formulating elementalistically in terms of 'meaning' (he could have remedied this somewhat by using quotes but in the book he had neither discussed nor used single quotes or hyphens as safety devices); his interchangeable use of 'semantics' with 'general semantics' long after Korzybski had warned him and others about the confusion it caused; et cetera.

According to Kendig, as early as 1943 "as he said at the time, [Korzybski] was 'struggling how to put his finger on'—how to convey to a writer—the hidden confusions in a manuscript about poetry and science."[11] She nigh surely was referring to Hayakawa as the writer and to his article "Poetry and Science" published in 1942 in the *English Institute Annual*, which he reprinted in the Summer 1944 volume of *ETC*. After grappling with these issues for about a year, Korzybski presented his new diagram to the first summer seminar-workshop class. With a revision of it in 1946 (to bring in feedback interactions and interplay among the levels) and further explanatory text then and in 1950, the diagram became a centerpiece of his teaching in seminars and in his writing until the end of his life. Using it as an adjunct to the Structural Differential, he wanted to make as clear as possible the notion of *abstracting as a neurological process*.

TIME TO TRY NEW THINGS

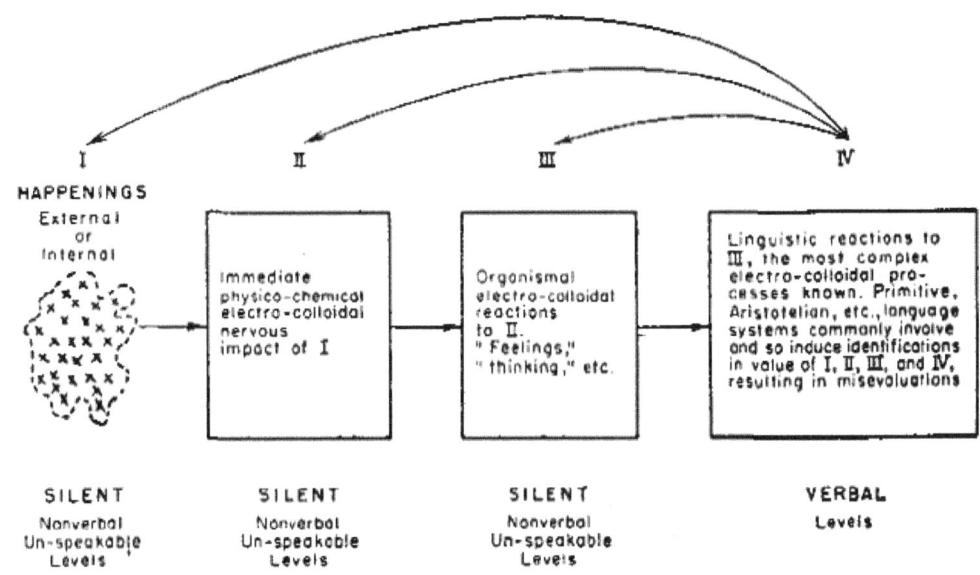

The Process of Abstracting

'A Deaf Ear'

Hayakawa had gotten some *pieces* of general semantics but had insufficiently grasped the *system* that connected them. You could get to some useful places by climbing his ladder. He had skillfully translated Korzybski's new vision into the old elementalistic language that people could use without getting too discomforted. But at a certain point, you would have to kick away the ladder after you had climbed it, in order to understand and make use of Korzybski's more comprehensive and radical approach.

Korzybski was becoming more concerned about Hayakawa's lapses, especially since Hayakawa had come to appear to more and more people as a major spokesman for his work. At this point, he had written to Hayakawa about some of these issues in a friendly way. Despite these differences there seemed little rancor between the two men in the summer of 1944. They still seemed like friends. But trouble had been brewing.

As early as 1940, Kendig had written a memo to Alfred discussing some of these issues. It had bothered them that Hayakawa had never had a personal interview with Korzybski, nor attended a complete seminar (and as noted before, typically fell asleep when he sat in on Alfred's lectures). He later explained he got bored hearing Korzybski repeating the 'same' things he already 'knew'.[12] So much for 'Lecture$_1$ is not Lecture$_2$, Lecture$_2$ is not Lecture$_3$, etc.'—the form of which Hayakawa had enthusiastically praised as "the most simple, most general, and most efficient of the rules for extensionalization."[13] But Hayakawa didn't follow his own rules, as he admitted in a 1990 interview with Roy E. Fox:

> SIH: I'm not conscious of approaching some things with a non-Aristotelian point of view.
>
> RF: So to carry general semantics around with you all the time is not something you would advocate?
>
> SIH: That's right. To carry it around with you all the time, you'd have to be more obsessed than I have ever been.[14]

Up until 1944, Korzybski had mainly decided to overlook such things in consideration of the young professor's merits. On December 2, 1943, he had written a two-page report recommending Hayakawa for a Guggenheim Fellowship.[15] There's no evidence that Korzybski's appreciation of Hayakawa's talents as a teacher, writer, and editor was anything other than entirely genuine. He had agreed to having Hayakawa put the Institute as the nominal publisher of the 1940 second lithographed edition of *Language in Action*—despite the abstraction ladder. Korzybski had helped Hayakawa get a commercial deal with the Book-of-the-Month Club through his contact with David Fairchild. Despite its flaws, he had spoken well of the book, and of Hayakawa, in public and in private letters. The Institute had promoted the book and reprints of Hayakawa's articles on its publication list, had promoted his work in seminars, and had honored him by making him an Institute Fellow. Korzybski had expressed delight with his appointment as Editor of *ETC*. He seemed to think the problems with Hayakawa could be resolved with suggestions and corrections. But it didn't all depend on Korzybski.

Hayakawa had developed some disparaging notions about Korzybski and some grandiose ones about his own relation to Korzybski's work. Whatever the reasons, his attitudes toward Korzybski seemed to make Hayakawa impervious to any of Korzybski's efforts to get through to him. These attitudes are revealed in detail in two remarkable documents—one, an interview-memoir of the Hayakawas conducted in 1989 and later by Julie Gordon Shearer (publically available on the internet from the University of California, Berkeley) and the 1990 Fox interview, published in *ETC*. in 1991.

Margedant Peters Hayakawa noted in the Shearer interview that she had felt an instant aversion to Korzybski when she first met him.[16] Despite a number of friendly gestures and invitations to come to seminars and have an interview with him, she assiduously avoided such contacts. Both she and her husband soon came to look at Korzybski in terms of her initial snap judgment: he 'was' in their view a dogmatic and demanding dictator who encouraged unquestioning, cultish followers.[17] By the end of their lives, the Hayakawas did not hesitate to cast aspersions about Korzybski's 'nuttiness', his supposed failure to develop his work after writing *Science and Sanity*, his discouragement of student's contributions to the development of general semantics, etc. I'm not sure they exactly qualify as lies because the Hayakawas apparently accepted them as innocent truths. The notion that Hayakawa and his wife might be projecting their own issues onto Korzybski and identifying him with their projections never seemed to occur to either one of them. Hayakawa seemed to see every action of Korzybski—every comment and suggestion—as an unreasonable demand for obedience.[18] Perceiving Korzybski thusly and given his own significant drive for power (he later became a controversial university president and then a U.S. Senator) he seemed determined to put himself in the role of "disobedient and disloyal son."[19] I can imagine a likely reply from Alfred: "I am not your father!"

The Hayakawas still maintained a veneer of pleasantness with Korzybski in 1944. However, Hayakawa's resentments would become overt, at least behind Korzybski's back, within the next few years. Much of what he said and did influenced other people's attitudes toward Korzybski. Much of this eventually got back to Korzybski and his colleagues at the Institute. Hayakawa's misunderstandings and hostility became not only a significant source of personal pain for Korzybski but a major source of the problems that would occur between the Institute and the Society for General Semantics. And Hayakawa's influence would help perpetuate misunderstandings about general semantics that continued long after Korzybski's death.

Hayakawa's behavior in relation to Korzybski from 1944 on seemed consistent with attitudes he expressed much later: he believed that he—and to a lesser extent Johnson and Lee—had made Korzybski famous and that Korzybski felt jealous of him because of that. In the *ETC.* interview with Fox, he remarked:

S.I.H.: When my *Language in Action* became a Book-of the-Month Club selection, that made him furious!....

R.F. [Interviewer Roy Fox]: "So Korzybski thought your book was incomplete? or inaccurate?"

S.I.H.: [Laughing] Just unfair competition! He wanted people to buy his book and not mine![20]

At bottom, probably even by 1944, Hayakawa had very mixed feelings about Korzybski, his work, his colleagues, and the Institute. He gave little value to the Institute courses, which he considered 'religious indoctrination'.[21] Korzybski's more dedicated students seemed suspect too: "I'm sure there were people who made a kind of cult out of it, and I'm sure Korzybski encouraged it."[22] In short, the Institute didn't seem academically respectable to him.[23] To believe this in 1944, he would have had to ignore the fact of Korzybski's many students from academia who were making use of his work in university courses around the country. However, Hayakawa's discomfort with Korzybski's work may eventually have had some self-fulfilling effects on the attitudes of academics with whom Hayakawa interacted and influenced.

As he indicated in the Shearer interview, the Society for General Semantics, *not the Institute*, represented the future of general semantics for him. Hayakawa believed he had done more than anyone else to make Korzybski and general semantics famous. *ETC.*, which he later claimed to have founded and took credit for naming, constituted for him the main reason for the existence of the Society.[24] And, as far as he was concerned, *ETC.* existed as his ballywick. He didn't intend to have Korzybski interfere with the editing of the journal.[25] He seemed determined to become *the* major figure in 'semantics'. He—not Korzybski—would use *ETC.* to define the field and determine the direction of the discipline.[26]

At the beginning of the year, the problems with Hayakawa that had remained quiescent for so long began to blossom—quietly at first. In January, Kendig had suggested Francis P. Chisholm as a new Institute Fellow. Hayakawa rejected him. According to the rules they had set up, the appointment of a new Institute Fellow needed unanimous approval of the existing Fellows, so there was nothing else Kendig or Korzybski felt they could do. This surely must have bothered them. They both considered Chisholm to have a solid grasp of the non-aristotelian system-discipline and a gift for communicating it. It surely must have grated on them to have Hayakawa, about whom they already felt some qualms, turn down such a capable individual.

There were also inklings of problems with the editing of *ETC.* Korzybski and Kendig were listed as "Consulting Editors". Korzybski certainly saw his role as more than symbolic but Hayakawa seemed lax in consulting with either him or Kendig. Korzybski was contributing pieces to the journal—mostly forewords and commentaries on articles, as well as letters and reviews. He had wanted to see the Tables of Contents of upcoming issues. He had comments and suggestions for Hayakawa, who was not communicating with him about these things as he wished. Hayakawa had also begun publishing some material that Korzybski found questionable.[27]

Now Hayakawa was planning to publish "Newtonian Physics and Aviation Cadets", in the Spring 1944 issue of *ETC*. Korzybski had seen the article by Anatol Rapoport, a mathematician then in the Army Air Corp stationed in Alaska, and liked it a lot: it seemed to provide an exceptional example of the power of hidden assumptions and the usefulness of uncovering them. Korzybski had written a foreword to another article by Jerome Alexander and wanted to do something similar with the Rapoport piece, but didn't know what was going on with the new issue due to come out soon. He wrote to Hayakawa on March 6, in part to get some information and to make some suggestions about the journal.:

> Where in hell did you get the article of Rapoport? It is an extremely fine article, just the kind of stuff we want to publish in ETC. Please let me know the history of this article, how you got it...This article is most important for our work and in many ways a justification for it.
>
> ...I am not happy, and neither is Kendig, that you do not let us know about your plans for every next issue of ETC. We have so much fretting to do and guessing what you might do as an editor. For instance, do you plan to publish in the same number the article of Alexander as a leading article in the next issue (I didn't see the proofs yet)?...please don't torture me in guessing what you will or may do as an editor. I have plenty of guessing to do altogether; I want to know what is going on. And believe me, if I am prevented from advising you about ETC. it will not be for the good of ETC. and yourself.[28]

But Hayakawa seemed to have already turned a deaf ear to Korzybski and his concerns.

Autumn News

Korzybski, who followed the news closely, must have been aware of the debacle occuring in Poland, even as the war seemed to be coming to an end. D-Day, the successful invasion of Normandy in June, had marked another turning point. Germany was getting squeezed from all sides between British and American forces from the west and the Soviets from the east—small comfort for the Poles. In August as the Soviet army reached the eastern suburbs of Warsaw, it stopped. Stalin had decided to let the Germans level Warsaw. The Germans focused their remaining forces and weaponry on defeating the Polish Home Army, which had begun an uprising in Warsaw. A quarter of a million citizens in the Polish capital were killed before the uprising was over in October. Before the Germans withdrew from the city, they destroyed as much of it as they could and exiled a large portion of its population. Whatever agony Korzybski may have felt (and I guess that he felt a great deal), he kept it inside. There was nothing he could do about the situation in Warsaw. And the situation at home, as always, required his attention.

The Institute had gotten even more short of help in June when Pearl Johnecheck came down with a serious infection, either measles or scarlet fever. As 1944 advanced into autumn, she developed some kind of rheumatic heart condition. She could no longer continue her studies or her work at the Institute. She would do what she could do to help and would remain in close contact with Mira (with whom she had grown close), Alfred, and the other people at the Institute. But by the next year, she would be hospitalized before beginning a slow recovery in the last half of 1945. Charlotte Schuchardt, still hoping to develop a career in dance, had been working as Korzybski's editorial assistant and as the main instructor of the seminar-workshop 'neuro-semantic relaxation' sessions—besides myriad other office and organizational duties. Now she took over Pearl's job as Korzybski's confidential secretary and Institute office manager.

The shortage of money also remained a pressing concern. A report at the end of 1944 would indicate that they were $10,000 short of their $20,000 short-term fundraising goal. They would need $10,000 more in pledges soon just to allow them to continue operating until the end of 1945 at what had become their normal, bare-to-the-bone level—with little extra for new programs, additional staff, etc.

Before the summer seminar-workshop, Kendig had applied for a grant from the Field Foundation to fund the IGS project in leadership training, which she and Korzybski had been hoping to develop for a number of years. She had an interview in New York with the foundation's executive director, Maxwell Hahn. The foundation, a charitable trust started by *Chicago Sun* publisher Marshall Field III, had a special interest in programs related to fighting racial prejudice. Kendig had tried to focus her conversation with Hahn on Korzybski's work in relation to prejudice and social tensions. Kendig had arranged and annotated for Hahn a selection of reviews, articles, and reprints. She also had Elwood Murray send materials about the many general-semantics related programs at the University of Denver and elsewhere, including a course on "Minority Problems in Denver". Even with this impressive array of materials and courses, the Field Foundation turned down Kendig's grant application in October. She would continue to try to get grant money from them, to no avail.

Despite the Institute's struggle to survive, 1944 saw a surprising amount of public interest in Korzybski's work. *Life* magazine commissioned Fred Rodell, a law professor at Yale who had done some popular writing, to write an article on GS and politics with Korzybski's collaboration (Korzybski and Rodell would be listed as co-authors). Rodell, as well as a *Life* photographer, came to see Korzybski before the summer seminar. Eventually, *Life* decided not to carry the article, entitled "A Word to the Wise". and sold it to *Liberty* magazine, which published it in its November 4 edition. To Korzybski the article seemed like a mishmosh due to faulty editing, but without question it brought publicity.

Korzybski's books were selling like never before. *Manhood of Humanity* had completely sold out. With continuing demand for it, the Institute put out a call for used copies. It was listed as "temporarily out of print" on the Institute booklist. It would remain 'temporarily out of print' for the next six years. E.P. Dutton no longer had an interest in continuing with it. Mira, who had long reminded Alfred of the importance of time-binding for his ongoing work, urged him to begin writing an introduction to a new edition. The International Non-Aristotelian Library Publishing Company would publish it. He worked on it in fits and starts until the end of his life, but with other projects, various interruptions, and the exceptionally demanding standards for publication that he had come to impose on his own writing, he never completed it. (The second edition, with additional material by him and others, came out in 1950, a few months after his death.)

The demand for *Science and Sanity* in 1944 seems even more remarkable. The Institute sold four times as many copies as were sold in any previous year since the original publication of the book, just a little over 10 years before. They had already had to do some reprintings of the Second Edition. Later, in the spring of 1945, the book became unavailable for a number of months due to labor problems and paper shortages.

Even with the reduced demand for his seminars, Korzybski and the people at the Institute remained extremely busy. In August, Korzybski had gone with Kendig to Denver where they both lectured as part of the University of Denver's summer workshop in improved communication, based on general semantics. While there, Korzybski spoke to the psychiatrists' group at Fitzsimmons Hospital. Meanwhile at the Institute, Francis Chisholm began giving a six-session evening course, "Introduction to General Semantics", over three weeks in August. Chisholm had left his position at Syracuse University and was going to begin teaching at Stephens College in Columbia, Missouri in the fall. About 40 people attended his course, which was transcribed and published by the Institute that winter as *Introductory Lectures in General Semantics*. Chisholm had been working at the Institute over the summer and seemed to Korzybski and Kendig like the kind of leader they wanted to encourage and develop. Kendig, whose professional background included curriculum development and educational research had long seen the need for a "so-called standard course which [could] be used in 'controlled experiments.'" Chisholm had begun researching and designing such a course or at least an outline/syllabus that could serve to standardize courses in this way.[29]

Much of these Institute doings were reported in an Autumn 1944, *General Semantics Newsletter* written by Kendig and sent out near the end of the year along with another fund-raising notice. The newsletter noted an additional bit of promotional news for the Society for General Semantics. The Society had consolidated its business office with the editorial office of *ETC.* at the Illinois Institute of Technology (formerly the Armour Institute), where Hayakawa worked. The item noted that Karl Hauch, the Society's Secretary-Treasurer, would be glad to receive membership applications and renewals. Given the difficult wartime circumstances, the Society for General Semantics, at the end of its first membership year, seemed to be doing rather well, which promised to add to the Institute coffers too. The Institute had managed to survive for another year.

Chapter 57
"RELEASE OF ATOMIC ENERGY"

Despite the fact that Hayakawa's work in *ETC.* had begun to get more bothersome, Korzybski had continued to send in contributions and Hayakawa continued to publish them.[1] Korzybski's contributions (forewords and reviews of articles and books from the fields of psychiatry, education, biology, physics, etc.) provided updates to the background research material he had used in *Science and Sanity*. They also reflected an issue that had pulled on his attention for some time. The authors of these articles and books were pointing out the need for explicitly acknowledging the value orientation of the sciences, the need for integration among different areas of study, and the need for application of scientific attitudes and approaches to social problems. Although they pointed out such needs, these authors for the most part failed to indicate practical means for fulfilling them. Korzybski considered it important to point out that his methodology, explicitly dealing with neuro-evaluational and neuro-linguistic issues, provided that missing factor of application. As he had written to Keyser in the fall of 1943,

> Under separate cover I am sending to you the first issue of ETC: A REVIEW OF GENERAL SEMANTICS. On my insistence the first number of the ETC opened with Thorndike's 'Science and Values'. Please note my foreword. I endorsed that article thoroughly and yet does it work? It does not. And it takes our particular training to make it workable. We are in an empirical field and we count the results. In the next issue of ETC we are publishing, also with my foreword, the presidential address of Langmuir, and a paper of Bell on Greek mathematics. The difficulties again are the same; we can say 'fine, fine, fine' and no doubt they are fine. As an engineer I ask 'does that work?' and the answer is unfortunately 'no'. We need a whole discipline as shown in forty hours of seminars, the extensional method as I call it, to make it work. We are having results, which as far as I am concerned, is all that matters.[2]

Perhaps more than anything else Korzybski wanted to get across to people this message of application. As he would often say, with every seminar he learned something more about how to do this—especially in regard to the obstacles related to students' preconceived attitudes and corresponding psycho-logical difficulties. He also felt concerned about the obstacles involved in conveying his work to individuals (not just his students) from different groups: individuals within a particular group might share common 'problematic' attitudes. In 1945, he found new opportunities to address two of the main groups he had long sought to influence: mathematicians and psychiatrists.

"Mathematics as a Way of Life"

For several years, Korzybski had been corresponding with Jekuthiel Ginsburg, a mathematician at Yeshiva University in New York City. In 1932, with some mathematician friends, including Cassius Keyser, Ginsburg had founded the journal *Scripta Mathematica*, devoted to the history and philosophy of mathematics with an extra emphasis on humanistic and educational aspects of the discipline. Ginsburg had a special interest in conveying the excitement of mathematics to beginning students and non-mathematicians.[3] He was known for addressing such groups by asking each audience member to take an 8 1/2 by 11 inch piece of paper and use a scissors to cut a hole in it big enough to pass a piano through. (By the end of the session he would demonstrate how to do it.)[4] *Scripta Mathematica* became known for its articles geared to a general audience. Ginsburg had probably met Korzybski through Keyser, and in late 1944 invited Korzybski to lecture to the Friends of *Scripta Mathematica* group on January 31 and February 1 at the Horace Mann Auditorium at Columbia University's Teachers College. For Korzybski, his two lectures on "Mathematics as a Way of Life" gave him an opportunity to return to some of the core issues which had originally inspired him. He gave a summary of his work geared to the group of mathematicians and mathematics educators and interested laypersons who attended. They received him with polite interest, even enthusiasm.

One of those listeners, Edward Kasner—Keyser's successor as Adrain Professor of Mathematics at Columbia—had long admired Korzybski and his work, starting with *Manhood of Humanity*. Kasner had already served for several years as an Honorary Trustee of the IGS. He considered Korzybski a "gifted" thinker of "keen intellect" and "broad humanitarian interest."[5] Korzybski, in turn, had loved Kasner's 1940 book *Mathematics and the Imagination* (written with James Newman), which he recommended highly to his seminar students.

I haven't found any copies of Korzybski's 1945 lectures but some notion of what he talked about can be gathered from a letter he wrote to Kasner several months later. Some people would continue to think Korzybski was advocating some complicated plan to get people to 'talk in mathematical logic', and thus to convert everyday speech into some kind of formal and esoteric jargon. But, as he wrote to Kasner, what Korzybski was proposing as 'the mathematical way of life' had little if anything to do with the formal side of mathematics:

> In this connection I feel like quoting Herman Weyl from his 'Mathematical Way of Thinking' published in SCIENCE of November 15, 1940...: 'Indeed, the first difficulty the man in the street encounters when he is taught to think mathematically is that he must learn to look things much more squarely in the face; his belief in words must be shattered; he must learn to think more concretely.'
>
> Here I would introduce a fundamental correction: Instead of saying 'more concretely' it should be said 'in terms of facts'. This is a serious correction because our 'feelings', 'imaginations', etc., are matters of facts yet they hardly could be called 'concrete'.[6]

For Korzybski, 'thinking' in terms of facts was closely connected with the human capacity to generate numbers. The modus operandi of the non-aristotelian orientation boiled down to practices as 'simple' as using the extensional devices which he had taken for the most part directly from mathematical notation. Their apparent simplicity was deceptive. Even for those who saw the mathematical connection, it was much more difficult to actually *use* these 'simple' devices in daily life—even for mathematicians.

> ...Hardly anybody could admire your work and the works of men like Einstein, Weyl, and others, more than I do. But, frankly speaking, these works do not give a modus operandi for how to bring about the wisdom you formulate on the level of elementary education.[7]

A highlight of his *Scripta* lectures for Korzybski was seeing Keyser face to face after many years apart (although the two men had continued to correspond). In a letter to Keyser later that year, Korzybski wrote:

...Yes, dear Dear Old Man, years are going on, and you and I are still not going into the second childhood. We still are struggling, so far for the good.

I hardly can tell you how I enjoyed seeing you in New York after years and years of absence. I must admit that I was amused when you were still shy of my hugging you and giving you a kiss.

Hell with your shyness; any time I would see you I would hug you and kiss you and give you my love, no matter what kind of violet you will play. Tell your lady she should not be jealous, as I am only an old man. Give to her our best.[8]

Korzybski remained in New York City to give a seminar at the New York University Faculty Club from February 3 to 14. It went very well. As he wrote to Kasner, "It was a fine and lovely group of around fifty-five students, mature, mostly professional. They were very receptive, and because of it, my delivery was unusually satisfactory, as I hear."[9] Some of the participants had formed a New York Society for General Semantics. Eleanor Wolff and the other organizers of the group got Major Irving J. Lee, then in New York, to lecture to them after Korzybski left. A few months later, they sent $300, the receipts from Lee's lecture course, as a contribution to the Institute.

February 1945, New York University Seminar, Korzybski and Kendig standing.

In the spring of 1945, world developments certainly seemed more promising than they had seemed in quite some time. Although Franklin D. Roosevelt had died on April 12, his worthy successor Harry S. Truman competently carried on the duties of a wartime president. By this time, the Nazi regime in Germany was finished. Hitler committed suicide at the end of April. Although the war with Japan was continuing, VE (Victory in Europe) Day was declared on May 8 with the unconditional surrender of Germany one day before. People were already being demobilized from the armed services.

Things were looking up for the IGS too, with increased demand for programs now that people were coming home from the war. The Institute was planning not only the second annual summer seminar-workshop, but also another introductory course by Chisholm, and in the late fall both an introductory and an advanced seminar with Korzybski in San Francisco, in addition to his regular Holiday Intensive. It looked as if, with the increased seminar income, the Institute would be able to squeak by for another year. (Although it would still not have enough money to get Korzybski off the treadmill of giving one seminar after another with little time for creative work or the development of the new programs he hoped for.)

Even with the war coming to an end, Korzybski did not seem exactly full of bubbly cheer. A good deal of his dampened mood may have resulted from accumulated fatigue and a sense of his own increasing physical limitations. On May 4, he wrote to Douglas Campbell,

> As to my health, I just carry on, thoroughly paralyzed by lack of help. With Pearl ill, Ann [Cleveland] married, what is left here of the old staff are Kendig and Charlotte, and the rest are accidentals, mostly lousy and hard to get these days. I do not accomplish as much as I should. My war$_1$ hernia is bothering me more and more. I am too old to have an operation and the g.d. diaphragm trouble here and there affects my breathing and so eventually even my heart., which still is in very good shape. I am all right at the Institute and lecturing, but I have difficulties traveling or delivering lectures elsewhere. I may still survive for a while.[10]

Alfred's relationship with Mira seemed to have passed a milestone the previous year. Except for a brief flurry of upset then, regarding an autobiography she had written for *Who's Who*, Alfred finally seemed to have come to grips with Mira's gifts and the benign nature of her sometimes careless (to him) previous manner of public expression. By 1945, from the evidence of their ongoing correspondence, he had ended his recriminations. The two maintained a loving relationship until the end of his life. Having attended eight seminars and having steeped herself in reading and study for several years, Mira had come to a deeper appreciation of her own educational gaps and the true measure of Alfred's achievements. She seemed at last to feel comfortable with a quiet role in the background of Alfred's work. She read, attended lectures, sent him notes, and offered suggestions, which he often heeded. She could see he appreciated her intelligence, her dedicated personal application of extensional methodology, and her help. In turn, she also came to realize that ultimately, he had done his work and continued to do it—as he had told her—primarily for her sake.

Alfred and Mira, circa 1945-1946

Now, Alfred had serious concerns about her health. In 1944, she had begun to have significant attacks of crippling pain in her arms, hands, knees, etc. It had hobbled her at times and though the attacks seemed to pass she had had to stop painting altogether. Both she and Alfred had concerns about the prognosis of what was diagnosed as "transient arthritis". How were they going to pay for her care and possible treatments? Another worry developed at the beginning of the year—she had serious gum infections that required surgery, tooth extractions, and extensive denture work. At least she was now getting these problems dealt with.

Her physician had referred her to Dr. Dick, an arthritis specialist and director of medicine at nearby Billings Hospital, associated with the University of Chicago. Dick was interested in Mira's case and found her such an observant and helpful patient that he offered her free treatment in exchange for her willingness to serve as a 'guinea pig'. Dick arranged for the hospital to cover the cost of her treatments and even of her dental surgery. He had admitted her to the hospital for several weeks in April but finally released her at the beginning of May as her symptoms subsided and she felt antsy about getting back home.

When she collected her mail from the janitor of her building, she—and then Alfred—got shocking news. A letter from Walter Polakov postmarked May 2 from Washington, D.C. had the following short note inside: "Dearest Edgy and Alfred, Barbara shot herself on the 26th. Polly". Walter wrote a more extensive note dated April 27:

Edgy dear:

Yesterday at 1:07 p.m. Barbara committed suicide by blowing her brains out. I was serving dinner. She could no longer endure, I suppose, the memories of her youth and childhood as she turned out to be again an invalid. T.B. returned full blast under war conditions. I need not tell you more. You can understand the unsaid. I grew so much a part of her and she of me. Not a thought and emotion were separated. No action without mutual agreement.

Walter Polly
Washington

P.S. I am returning to Fairfax, Virginia[11]

What could either Alfred or Mira do to console their longtime friend? Not much. At least they had remained in contact with Walter and Barbara—however sporadically—over the last few years and they would continue to do so with Walter.

"Release of Atomic Energy"

On August 6 and 9, U.S. planes dropped atomic bombs on the Japanese cities of Hiroshima and Nagasaki. On August 15, two days after Korzybski began his lectures at the IGS's 1945 Summer Seminar-Workshop, the Japanese Emperor Hirohito announced his country's unconditional surrender. Korzybski told his students that the world had forever changed.[12]

The fateful bombings had resulted from the accelerating acceleration of war technology. They signaled that human history had reached a clear new chapter based on a simple 'secret'—exponential growth. The fission bombs depended upon harnessing a chain reaction, an exponential function, within the uranium atom. Several years before, only a few blocks from the IGS's 1234 E. 56th Street address, physicist Enrico Fermi and his team of scientists and technicians had built a crude atomic reactor in a squash court underneath the grandstand seats of the University of Chicago's Stagg Field Stadium. On December 2, 1942 they achieved history's first self-sustaining controlled nuclear fission reaction there and demonstrated the key to the tremendous power later unleashed by the Hiroshima and Nagasaki bombs. Fermi's reactor produced an exponential release of neutrons from uranium 235 nuclei struck by other random neutrons released in the process of radioactive decay. When the amount of uranium reached a critical mass the release of more nuclei resulted in a chain reaction. Cadmium rods inserted into the reactor kept the chain reaction in check and could stop it. The exponential process and the enormous amounts of energy released, had the potential to take a controlled form for peacetime atomic power plants or, in the form of bombs, could yield a devastating force. Over the last several years, the U.S. government had rallied scientists and engineers in a tremendous top-secret effort to build such bombs (in the hope they could beat the Nazis at that game). The multi-centered enterprise, with some initial research done in New York City, was known as the Manhattan Project. With the Hiroshima and Nagasaki blasts, the Manhattan Project secret suddenly became public knowledge. The general public had a definite interest in both the principles and the details involved in atomic research—all to the good from Korzybski's point of view.[13]

During the 1945 seminar, Korzybski wrote a short article "Release of Atomic Energy", in which he registered some of his main concerns about the new world situation. The technical control of chain reactions in the atomic realm would lead to disaster, unless the concurrent development of beneficial social chain reactions involving the general release of time-binding energies took place. As he had emphasized in *Manhood of Humanity*, the growth of human ethical-social-political-economic life had to catch up to the exponential growth in the more limited exact-science/technical realm. As he had harped on even more since the publication of *Science and Sanity*, humans could only consciously marshal their time-binding energies through the extension of what he called "scientific method" or an extensional orientation into all areas of society and life. In the article he wrote,

> The releasing of atomic energy is the attempt to solve one of the greatest mysteries of the universe. It took endless patient research work, but what guided the research workers? It was the physico-mathematical method, common to them. Dealing with human beings, who are also mysterious and confusing, it is found in general semantics that the physico-mathematical method can also be applied in solving the complex individual and group human evaluations. Our experience shows that the application of physico-mathematical methods to life orientation helps people, and can be taught even in elementary schools, which involves a revision of our educational methods. The 'great books' of the thomists, Mortimer Adler, etc., have to be supplemented and to a large degree supplanted by *atomist* studies.[14]

Korzybski pointed out that, "One of the consequences of the latest discoveries is that the old methods of warfare become obsolete."

> ...In the future a few aeroplanes and a few hundreds of atomic bombs would eliminate a New York, a Chicago, a Paris or London, or a new Berlin and a new Tokyo. Scientific discoveries do not remain secrets. It means that any aggressor at a very cheap price will be able to conquer continents, and be annihilated himself.
>
> This fact alone requires new kinds of social and government control. One of the human consequences may be that devastating wars will cease to happen, as no nation wants to deliberately suicide...The atomic bomb, one of the most world-shaking discoveries ever made, is due to the application of physico-mathematical methods. The utilization of atomic energy in a constructive way will benefit you and me. This discovery as connected with education affects our human adjustment to a universe now better understood. But it will not be a simple task to make the necessary revisions of existing economic, political, sociological, educational, etc., theories. The obstacles are serious, and it will require concerted and strenuous efforts to change the dogmas canalized in our nervous systems for hundreds or thousands of years.[15]

Korzybski provided an example of these kinds of dogmas in the American acceptance—with the Japanese surrender—of the continuation of the Emperor Hirohito's symbolic rule. Korzybski felt concerned about the strong possibility of prolonging the atavistic Shintoist orientation, which he felt needed to be removed as an active element from Japanese culture.

He concluded the article, eventually published in the Winter 1946 [1945-1946] issue of *ETC.*, by saying,
> Another irony of fate, emphasized even in newspapers, is that some dictators helped our victory through their racial, religious, and political persecutions. The atomic energy release has been accomplished by mathematical physicists of many nations, many of whom are refugees from Nazi and Fascist intolerance, and continued their work in free countries. It is good to be free, but our freedom depends on infinite-valued flexibility, essential to science, and away from Nazi and Shinto ritualism. Scientific method is the only solution for a new system of education. The main lesson we should learn from the latest scientific discoveries is that we are entering a new world, and to comprehend it and adjust ourselves to it requires those infinite-valued orientations which are at the foundation of the brilliant achievements in the exact sciences.[16]

"A Veteran's Readjustment"

One of the first tasks in this new world would be to clean up the detritus of the old one. Most significant perhaps was the debris of wartime experiences, which could haunt men and women coming home to civilian life from military service. Some of them had witnessed horrendous scenes of devastation, destruction, and death. Some of them had personally heard "the flying bullet down the pass that whistles clear," had learned indeed how "flesh is grass." And some, traumatized by their experiences, found it hard to assimilate and move beyond them later in peacetime surroundings. If wounds from psychic trauma continued to bleed into their civilian life, they might get a diagnostic label; in this war, e.g., "battle fatigue", "combat exhaustion", and "combat neurosis".

Korzybski knew from personal experience what it could be like to cope on the battlefield and afterwards. He considered it a matter of great concern. All through the war he had gotten letters from soldiers and flyers from around the world, not all of them his personal students, reporting on their experiences and asking for his help. One letter from an American fighter pilot in England, dated May 5, 1943, covers the issues of the sanity of fighting men rather well. After thanking Korzybski for *Science and Sanity*, which he had found enlightening, he noted that returning soldiers, however sound in body, might be "...warped and twisted in their minds, rendered less than 'human' because they found battle 'not what they expected it to be.'"

> I have made every effort to avoid the false identifications in this matter of battle, identifications I have observed in many of my fellow pilots. I have sensed, up until recently, how I must avoid certain sure pitfalls—and with the tools you have given me, I am even more confident of myself—but that solves the problem for me alone.
>
> Why don't you apply yourself to this particular aspect of sanity and write a pamphlet specifically designed for soldiers? I realize that the aim of general semantics involves a complete reorientation of the individual's outlook, but I think specific local applications of the system can be applied usefully.[17]

Some of Korzybski's students, like Douglas Kelley and Elwood Murray had been working on just that.

Kelley, who had become a Lieutenant Colonel in the Army Medical Corps, served as Chief Consultant in Clinical Psychology and Assistant Consultant in Psychiatry to the European Theatre of Operations. He worked with psychiatric casualties from "combat exhaustion" in army hospitals in England prior to the D-Day invasion of Normandy and in Belgium afterwards. He and his associates devised a program of treatment involving intensive but brief classes and group counseling sessions based primarily on Korzybski's educational approach. Kelley also trained non-psychiatrist medical officers, who served in aid stations, exhaustion centers, and Army hospitals. There is some evidence (although statistical data were lost) that the use of these methods with thousands of troops may have had something to do with the apparently reduced number of psychiatric casualties during the D-Day invasion as compared with previous Allied invasions in North Africa and Italy.

As described in a 1946 memorandum written to Vice Admiral Louis E. Denfield by Captain James A. Saunders, Ret. USN, a student of *Science and Sanity* who worked on the U.S. Senate Committee on Naval Affairs:

The methods used by Doctor Kelley were briefly as follows:

By means of pictures, charts and lectures the men [receiving treatment for combat exhaustion] were instructed in the structure of the human nervous system, the manner in which it functioned and the relationship between events in the external world and the human nervous system. He taught them physico-mathematical methods of evaluation, including the use of the extensional techniques of thinking. The men who were able to understand and use the new methods of evaluation were able to reevaluate their combat experiences and overcome their psychoneuroses. They were also able to use the new methods of evaluation and make appropriate adjustments to the new experiences they encountered in combat in the European Theatre of Operations.[18]

Kelley wrote a paper on this work, "The Use of General Semantics And Korzybskian Principles As An Extensional Method of Group Psychotherapy In Traumatic Neurosis", eventually published in *The Journal of Nervous and Mental Diseases* in 1951. In his paper, Kelley described his classes in sufficient detail for others to test it by replicating his work.

At the IGS seminar-workshop, the war had just ended when some of the students put on a skit "G.I. Joe Comes Home" for a near-the-end-of seminar celebration party. But even before the end of the war, G.I. Joes had been coming home, some of them with significant problems of adjustment. Elwood Murray had had a Pacific war veteran in one of his general-semantics classes at the University of Denver. The veteran "discharged from the army because of his 'nervous disability' " was—as Korzybski described him—"the only survivor of a Japanese bombing of a group of fifteen of his buddies." Murray's evening class consisted of one lecture a week for ten weeks. The veteran struggled to apply what he was learning and wrote an end-of-term paper that Korzybski, who was in contact with both Murray and the veteran, considered of exceptional value in demonstrating what was possible from explicitly using extensional methods. In the summer of 1945, Korzybski wrote up his commentary on the veteran's paper as a case study in the application of his work. He put this together with the veteran's paper as an article, which he entitled "A Veteran's Readjustment and Extensional Methods". In it he recounted a number of his own wartime experiences and how he dealt with them.

In a Foreword eventually published with the article, Douglas Kelley provided a useful summary :

War produces a series of situational stresses which result in the development of profound changes in an individual's psychosomatic structures. Korzybski's paper demonstrates many excellent examples of these changes which are best understood in terms of Pavlovian conditional systems. The veteran's reaction to rice and maggots, his aversion to special noises, his fear of low-flying aeroplanes, and his basic feelings of irritability and resentment are born of a conditioning, the like of which civilization has previously never experienced. No human being can conceive of a more adequate mechanism for twisting human emotion and for developing organismal responses to specific stimuli than is achieved in an active battle zone.

Following the development of primary symptoms we find, as Korzybski puts it, the occurrence of second-order reactions 'such as fear of fear, nervousness about nervousness, and worry about worry.' General semantics, as a modern scientific method, offers techniques which are of extreme value both in the prevention and cure of such reactive patterns.[19]

By 1945, Korzybski had become even more insistent that many of the problems psychiatrists dealt with could not be viewed as simply medical. Specialized psychiatric approaches overlapped considerably with the educational and preventive general methodology of evaluation—physico-mathematical in structure—he had formulated. If more psychiatrists and others realized this, it would enhance psychiatric, medical and educational practice. Korzybski had been writing to many of his psychiatrist friends about this and in the following year published a memorandum he had written, "Some Excerpts From Letters To Psychiatrists...". In the "Veteran's Readjustment" paper, he noted:

The importance of non-medical, scientific methodological training for extensionalization must be emphasized here. In our work we are striving for neurological thalamo-cortical integration through scientific method alone, which occurs empirically, if the students are willing enough to co-operate and work. This particular veteran did co-operate, and took his retraining seriously. Without medical help in the narrow sense, he did improve steadily, and probably will recover completely. He is probably not psychiatrically ill but just naturally disturbed. We will have to deal with large numbers of such cases with a very restricted number of available psychiatrists. In our records we have a number of similar communications from all battlefronts about the benefits derived from studying extensional methods through *Science and Sanity*, etc., which might be called 'bibliotherapy.'

In many ways, such results should be expected because modern extensional methods are *prior* to any science, medicine and psychiatry included. ...[20]

Korzybski submitted the article to *ETC.* at the end of the year and felt dismayed when the journal's Editorial Committee turned it down. Korzybski was told that although Congdon and Hayakawa liked it, one or more psychiatrists who were consulted felt that the paper 'stunk'. Korzybski wrote a 'protest' letter to Wendell Johnson, one of the journal's editorial associates, which may have had some effect since the piece finally got published in the Summer 1946 issue of *ETC.*, (Volume III, No. 4). *The American Journal of Psychiatry* also published part of the article in the "Clinical Notes" section of its July 1946 issue (Vol. 103, No. 1).

War's End

Pearl seemed to have passed the worst part of her illness. She got married in November 1945 and Alfred, of course, felt delighted at such good news. The end of the year had turned into a busy time for him. Before the Holiday seminar, now an annual event, he and Kendig had gone to San Francisco in late October to give two seminars. Earlier in the year, the United Nations had been founded there, taking over the mantle from the defunct League of Nations as the new international body for promoting world peace. Korzybski wondered how much good it would actually be able to accomplish.

At the end of 1945, the world seemed rather far from the adulthood of humanity—not anywhere close. And it didn't seem likely to get much closer in Korzybski's lifetime. The Allied nations had won the war, but he only needed to think of the millions dead, injured, and homeless to get further confirmation that the old aristotelian system remained intact as the 'thought' system that ruled the world—'logical fate' with a vengeance.

The fate of Poland remained a particular sore spot for him. I imagine him with tears in his eyes when he looked at pictures of his devastated homeland, now under Stalinist control. The front cover of his October 11 copy of *The Polish Review* showed before and after pictures of the "Royal Castle" on Castle Square, about a forty-five minute walk from his family's old apartment house. (The Royal Castle had served as the seat of the Polish King and Sejm (Parliament) before the 1795 partition.) The Nazis had deliberately leveled the iconic building shortly after putting down the 1944 Warsaw Uprising. In the foreground, a small human figure stood next to a piece of the toppled pillar of King Zygmunt III lying on the ground. The advancing Soviet Russian army had waited on the other side of the Vistula while the retreating Germans—as their final punishment for Polish resistance—destroyed as much of the rest of Warsaw as they could. When the Russians entered the city in January 1945, most of Korzybski's hometown lay in ruins.

Warsaw's Castle Square as it looked in August 1939 (above) and as the U. S. House Foreign Affairs Sub-Committee found it in August 1945 (below).

The fate of the Jews after the war remained another sore spot. By the end of 1945, the stories and pictures of death-camp survivors, and of those who hadn't survived, had already had a number of months to seep into public consciousness. The meticulous German engineering of genocide had begun to be openly revealed at the Nuremburg War Crimes Trials, which started in November. Douglas Kelley had begun working as Psychiatrist at the Nuremburg Jail earlier in the year, examining and interviewing many of those who would go on trial. (He would leave after the first month of the proceedings and shortly thereafter write a book, *22 Cells in Nuremberg*, about his experiences.) It was becoming clear that the Nazi Germans and their helpers throughout Europe had succeeded in murdering, largely in organized industrial fashion, about six million European Jews, one third of all of world Jewry. Of course, the Nazis had targeted other groups as well, but the sheer number of Jewish victims and the systematic way in which the Germans killed them—simply for the fact of their 'Jewishness' as the Nazis defined that characteristic—beggered the imagination. It would take some time, indeed years, for the greater import of the atrocities to sink in—and even then...

Whatever his horror at what had happened, the Nazi atrocities certainly didn't take Korzybski by surprise. In 1941, in the "Introduction to the Second Edition" of *Science and Sanity*, he had predicted that Nazi Germany under Hitler would try to destroy the Jews. At the end of 1945 many survivors waited in displaced person camps in Europe while various Jewish organizations tried to lift the British ban on Jewish entry into Palestine or to sneak Jews into Jewish Palestine despite the ban. The Palestinian Jewish community seemed on the way to forming a state, which Korzybski had long supported—having declared himself sympathetic to Zionism in the 1920s. For several years he had been telling many of his Jewish friends and students, and also close friends like Cassius Keyser, that he sincerely believed "world problems can not be solved without solving the Jewish problem,..." And, as he wrote in 1944 to a German Jewish emigre psychiatrist Richard D. Loewenberg, "...the Jewish problem can not be solved on racial or territorial grounds alone...there is nothing else for us to do than to put every kind of international problems on a strictly non-racial neutral impersonal scientific basis, and that's what we are trying to do."[21]

Korzybski had been trying to figure out the relation of Jews and Judaism to him and his work for quite some time—at least since 1920, when he became conscious of the antisemitism he had absorbed and succumbed to, however superficially, by that time. He had had to work to overcome it in himself. (Perhaps this provided one reason for his heightened sensitivity and early recognition to the dangers of Hitlerism.) But he clearly hadn't figured out a solution to what he called "the Jewish problem" even now—except in these most general terms. He had recognized strong non-aristotelian elements in the Jewish tradition and he strongly felt that somehow both Jews and Gentiles would have to come to terms with what that meant in more detail—as would he.

Chapter 58
"SHOOT YOURSELF!"

Korzybski's Holiday Intensive Seminar ran from December 27, 1945 to January 9, 1946. He had a full class of thirty-five students. Notable among them was a French Canadian psychologist from Montreal, Joseph Samuel Anselme Bois (pronounced "Bwa"), already becoming well-known in Canadian psychology and management consulting circles.

Born in 1892, Bois graduated from Laval University in Quebec and became a priest in the Catholic Church, where he served for twenty years before his dismissal "for preaching that with love, all will be good." As Bois put it, "This translated as 'love, and do what you want.' They thought I meant free love, not God-love."[1] Afterwards, he studied psychology at McGill University in Montreal, getting his PhD in 1936 at the age of 44. In 1939, he came across *Science and Sanity*. It changed his life—challenging to the roots the thomistic-aristotelian philosophy he had studied to enter the priesthood. Eventually he embraced the non-aristotelian revision Korzybski offered. He spent the war years as the head of Research and Information for the Canadian Army, where his work involved morale building, organizational research, and publishing the Canadian Army weekly magazine, *Khaki*, in English and French. Having recently left the service at the time of the Holiday seminar, he worked as head of psychological services for a Canadian management consulting firm. At the Holiday seminar, as Bois later wrote:

> For two hours, from midnight until 2 A.M., [Korzybski] spoke to me in his office, after his closing lecture. I didn't have time to remain for the workshop, and he consented at this late hour to comment on the biography I had submitted to him.[2]

Despite not spending much personal time with Korzybski, Bois became one of Korzybski's most important continuators. Starting in 1947, he began lecturing at Institute seminar-workshops with Korzybski's full approval. Bois would come to view Korzybski as one of that group of men called in French "les grand couers"—great hearts.[3] Teaching and developing the non-aristotelian system and discipline became the main focus of Bois' long life of writing and teaching.

"Shoot Yourself"
Another attendee at this 1945-46 Winter Holiday Seminar, Richard T. McClaughry, never became well known, but he left a record of his interview with Korzybski notable for its personal honesty, likely detail, and rarity. Although Korzybski's individual work with his students constituted a major part of his efforts, few independent records exist of what happened in these interviews. The autobiographical statements of students and Korzybski's follow-up correspondence with them were, as he had requested, returned to them or destroyed upon his death to protect their privacy. Only a few students' letters—with their permission—remained in the archives, with their names cut out. McClaughry wrote an account of his interview with Korzybski in an article written for the *Reader's Digest*—never published, but discovered by his son among his papers many years after his 1973 death. With his son's permission, I present his story here.[4]

At the age of thirty, McClaughry had a successful marriage and a promising career when tragedy struck. Soon after his wife gave birth to their first child, a healthy boy, he received a fateful phone call at work. His wife had just died from a blood clot. With that call, his world began to fall apart. He became depressed. Though not very religious to start with, he became a militant atheist. Within a year, he was seeing a psychiatrist who advised him to get married in order "to face the future and provide a home for my infant son." The marriage broke up six months later. He sent his son to live with relatives, fired his psychiatrist, quit his job as an advertising account executive, and had a heart attack (considered "psychosomatic") in short order. While recovering, he read an article about Korzybski and his seminars and decided that he might learn something helpful.

Then living in Detroit, he attended the September intensive seminar in 1941. In his own words, here are his first impressions:

> I'm not sure yet why I actually went. Largely, I think, because my physician had forbidden me even to think of work during the period, and time hung heavy on my hands. I didn't expect much—in that length of time and for that price [$50]. (I had already spent thousands on psychiatry.) I was nine-tenths convinced in advance that Korzybski had to be an imposter and a fake. Perhaps, like most cynics, I had developed a morbid pleasure in exposing the "stupidities" of others, and went to Chicago to match my intellect against anyone who dared to believe in anything.
>
> At any rate, I went. My first sight of the man I proposed to challenge somewhat jarred my preconceptions. I had expected either a "long-haired intellectual" or a suave and urbane Hollywood "faith healer" type. Instead I saw a man of sixty [sic] who looked more like a Polish wrestler than anything else. Head like a billiard ball—either completely bald or completely shaved, I never knew which. A round, flat, Slavic face. A short, squat, powerful body, with tremendous shoulders. A baffling accent, at times incomprehensible to my Mid-Western American ears. A tremendous grasp of a staggering range of academic subjects, including mathematics, the physical sciences, languages, history, philosophy, psychology and psychiatry. He was capable of Falstaffian humor and Jovian wrath. Though Bertrand Russell, who should know, once referred to his erudition as "extraordinary", I have never, before or since, heard any lecturer or teacher answer so many questions with a simple and unequivocal *"I don't know"*.
>
> I am happy to say now that any ideas I may have had of pitting my "intellect" against Korzybski's disappeared quickly. I attempted just one confrontation, only to feel ten seconds later as if I had been picked up by a giant and shaken like a child. From then on, I kept my mouth shut, and listened.

This 'confrontation' may have been the encounter that his son described to me in a letter:

> I lived with my father during high school, 1950-1954. The only artifact I have from him is his cherished copy of S&S, carefully underlined by me when I read it 40 years ago.
>
> Here's the one anecdote [my father] told me back then about attending AK's seminar...
>
> At an early lecture AK mentioned *"zat famuz Greek general who conquered z'vurld"*.
>
> My father, long used to being the brightest boy in the class, piped up "Alexander the Great."
>
> AK paused, looked quizzically at my father, and feigning deafness said *"Vot?"* [Korzybski was probably not feigning as he definitely had a hearing deficit – BIK]
>
> My father said, "ALEXANDER THE GREAT."
>
> AK, looking even more puzzled, said *"VOT?"*
>
> My father, now getting very embarrassed, shouted **"ALEXANDER THE GREAT!"**
>
> AK pondered this a moment, then said, *"It duss not matter."*
>
> That was the only time my father sought to supply AK with missing information.[5]

McClaughry found the seminar exhilarating and valuable. He convinced his estranged second wife to come to the upcoming 1941-42 Holiday Seminar with him. Perhaps they could find some means there to restore their marriage. But, as he wrote, "her reactions were different than mine, and the project failed."

By this time, America was at war, so shortly after my divorce decree became final, I enlisted in the Army. Three and one-half years of military service, including two and one-half overseas, wiped out what progress I had made toward personal re-orientation. After demobilization, I decided to attend one more seminar at the Institute as a last resort, not so much because I thought a third series of lectures would reach me with anything new, as because I hoped contact with Korzybski might give me back the will to try again.

This was the 1945-46 Holiday Intensive—the last one he would ever attend. He came to believe that his interview there with Korzybski saved his life.

The seminar was as expected. But at the end of each seminar, it was Korzybski's practice to grant a two-hour private interview to each student, based on a written, confidential autobiography submitted in advance. I had submitted autobiographies twice in the past, but I now realized that they had been less than candid. This time I determined, cost what it might, to be brutally honest about myself in my paper, in order to get from Korzybski the help I desperately needed.

I got more than I bargained for.

Korzybski's face was like stone when I entered his office for my scheduled interview. The room was in darkness, except for a pool of light in the far corner of the room, where the man I had come to see sat at his desk, waiting. He motioned me to a chair, without greeting. As I sat down, he picked up and glanced briefly at the document I had mailed him, sentences in which, I could see from across the desk, had been heavily underlined.

Alfred Korzybski in his Chicago office, 1944[6]

"Well", he said finally, after what seemed an interminable silence, *"you're paying me to tell you what's wrong with you. You are <u>not</u> paying me to make you like it."*

"You are an alcoholic."

I winced. Though I knew I had frequently drunk to excess, I worked in fields in which heavy drinking was laughed at. Neither my psychiatrist nor I had seen this as a basic problem. Furthermore, those were the days when the term "alcoholic" was still an insult, not a diagnosis. I reacted accordingly.

"That isn't what my psychiatrist said," I retorted belligerently. "He said. ..."

"I don't care what your psychiatrist said", Korzybski interrupted. *"If anyone can read this revolting mess"*—here he picked up and waved the document I had sent him through the mails—*"and not see alcoholism in every line, I'd like to know how. You're not a misunderstood genius. You're not a pathetic victim of Fate. You're an alcoholic, and the sooner you realize it, the better."*

I tried to protest again, but he talked right through me.

"How long do you think you're going to last, the way you're going?" he asked, again waving my paper.

I answered with what I thought was cynical bravado. "I don't know", I shrugged, "six months, maybe."

He shook his head sadly. *"No, not six months; thirty years, with each year more miserable than the one before. Most alcoholics don't die young, though everyone wishes they would. They just keep on stumbling along, a nuisance to everyone else and a misery to themselves."*

"Now, I'm going to tell you what you can do about it", he continued, *"and you're not going to like that, either."*

"From where you sit right now, you have only three choices. First, you can go on as you are; that's probably what you will do. You think you've had a hard life so far. Let me tell you what you can expect, if you continue in your present direction."

Korzybski prided himself on his ability to speak to the senses and the emotions as well as to the intellect. During the next thirty or forty minutes, he more than proved his point. It was not a temperance lecture. It was a detailed, statistically-based description of a typical case of alcoholic disintegration.

I didn't just hear what he said. As he talked, I felt the things he talked about actually happening—and to me. As if in a motion picture, I saw myself fighting a hopeless battle against alcoholic odds...the progressively more severe and more prolonged drinking episodes and their aftermaths...the humiliation and degradation...the friends lost...the jobs thrown away...the lies and excuses used over and over again until finally worn out...and only finally the jail, the mental hospital and the dishonored grave. At times, in considering these possibilities in the past, I had managed to see myself in an heroic role: Man against Fate. There was nothing heroic in Korzybski's picture. Instead of Prometheus defying the lightnings, I saw only an increasingly revolting parody of a human being condemned by his own stupidity to a revolting end. I felt this just couldn't be a true picture of me and my future; yet, when I looked at myself through Korzybski's eyes, that's what I saw.

"Now", he said at last, *"that's one choice you can make. Fortunately, a much better choice is available."*

"Shoot yourself."

I gasped. It was no time for jokes.

He wasn't joking.

"That's right," he repeated. *"Shoot yourself. I'm not sentimental about suicide. There are a lot of people moving around on the face of the earth who would be better off dead, and you're one of them. Why drag out the misery and disgrace I've just told you about for thirty years, when you can get it all over in thirty seconds? Get a revolver...load it... put it to your temple...pull the trigger. In two or three days, you'll be buried and forgotten, and the whole human race, including you, will be better off."*

He paused a moment, and then resumed in a more reflective tone. *"There would be a third choice—for some people—but, on second thought, I don't believe it's worth mentioning to you. You have no religion. That's out. You've tried psychiatry long enough to prove yourself untreatable. You've attended my seminars three times and are worse off now than when you started. Obviously, I can't help you. Frankly, I don't know anyone who can—or anything."*

He paused again. Then he said: *"There is something called 'Alcoholics Anonymous'. They seem to get results, in some cases. I don't know how. I wish I did. Their number is in the phone book."* He thought again. *"But, no—even they have to have something left to work with, and you're too far gone. You can call them, if you want to, but I can tell you right now that if you do you'll just be wasting their time and yours."*

I made one last attempt at self-defense. "But I have shown some ability in some things", I protested.

He looked at me with heavy scorn. Then he said something which I have tried to remember, ever since.

"Oh, I admit you have ability," he snorted. *"But, will you kindly tell me: WHAT GOOD IS ABILITY WITHOUT CHARACTER?"*

He left that thought trailing in the air. Then he suddenly looked at his watch and stood up.

"Well, old man, that's it. I said in the beginning that you have three choices, but actually you have only two: continue on your present course or shoot yourself. Even you ought to be able to see which is better."

...The man across the desk spoke with the cold, impersonal tones of a judge pronouncing sentence.

"I'm sorry, but that's it", he said. *"The only thing you can do that makes any sense at all is: SHOOT YOURSELF"*.

I tried to interrupt, but he continued remorselessly, with chilling pauses between each sentence.

"Now—your time is up."

"There's the door."

"Walk out of it."

"Don't come back."

"And don't bother to let me know how you come out—because I don't care."...

...That...ended the interview.

Obviously, I didn't shoot myself. I left Korzybski's office feeling like a whipped cur, but in a few minutes my mood changed to towering rage. Whom was he calling an alcoholic? Maybe I had drunk too much, at times, in the past—but always for good reason. Now

"SHOOT YOURSELF!"

I would drink only with control, like a gentleman, and ultimately throw my detractor's likes back in his teeth! Less than two months later, I awoke on the floor of a Chicago North Clark Street rooming house, completely unable to remember where I had been or what I had done for the past ten days!

My first thought was: "My God! Everything he said was true. The only thing I can do that makes any sense is shoot myself!"

Alcoholics with schizoid tendencies desperately avoid committing themselves to courses from which there is no withdrawal, as Korzybski well knew—and death is so final. On the heels of my first thought came a second. Even if Korzybski _had_ said that AA wouldn't work for me, I could always try that _first_, and then shoot myself afterwards, if AA didn't work. At least it would postpone my awful decision.

So I phoned the local AA office for help, in what I thought was defiance of Korzybski's advice. I couldn't have called under better auspices. Much of the alcoholic's characteristic arrogance and conceit had already been beaten out of me. I was intensely aware of the gravity of my situation. And it was my _own_ idea, upon which hung my last chance to salvage some shred of self-respect as well as my life. It was my last chance to prove that, in this respect at least, I could be right and Korzybski wrong. If I was being manipulated by a superior mind—and I was—I didn't realize it at the time.

Twenty-one years have passed since then. It would be nice to be able to report that an "instant miracle" occurred when I joined AA, and that my life since February, 1946, has been one of mounting triumph. It hasn't. There has been progress, mixed with set-backs and reverses. After six years of uninterrupted sobriety in AA, I took a "refresher course" in drinking, after which it took me seven desperate years to get solidly back on the AA program. (I thought "just one drink" wouldn't hurt!) Now an additional eight years of abstinence have ensued. I have not, during those twenty-three years, pitched a no-hit game nor become a Hollywood celebrity nor even a business tycoon. I have kept from becoming a public charge, I have stayed out of jails, mental hospitals, and gutters, I have helped raise my own son and two step-[children] and I have developed a quiet faith in "something" that gives [hope].

In retrospect, I cannot find adequate words with which to express my gratitude to Alcoholics Anonymous and its members for the help I have received from them. Yet, in my heart, my greatest gratitude goes to general semantics and Alfred Korzybski. Without the good fortune of exposure to general semantics and Korzybski _before_ I attempted AA, I do not believe I could have accepted the religious over-tones and basic common sense of the AA program—though others have. In my personal approach to AA—and AA insists that each member must build his own "individual" program—I found a surprising correlation between the principles of general semantics and the practices of AA. For me, general semantics provided the theory, Korzybski the goad, and AA the way of life. I needed all three to stay alive.

I never saw Korzybski again after that day in 1946. I did write to him, after I thought I had become well-established in AA, telling him how things were going. From his prompt and encouraging reply, I learned that I had done and was doing exactly what he hoped I would do. I corresponded with him thereafter until he died.

I shall never forget my last two hours with him, painful as they were at the time. I particularly try to remember, not always successfully, his reference to the valuelessness of ability without character. My feelings about Korzybski, who had his faults as well as his virtues, is still: "There was a man. When comes such another, into my life, at least." And I still believe that the man who told me to shoot myself saved my life.

Chapter 59
A MATTER OF CHARACTER

On the Eastern Front in 1914 and 1915, Korzybski had more than once escaped death. Since then, although he had taken a rather matter-of-fact view of his own mortality, he had seized the gift of life that fortune had given him and had worked to make the most of it. By the beginning of 1946, he knew that the largest part of his life was over. He had little if anything to regret. He had produced his work. He believed that he had done what he set out to do. He had helped many people. He had gotten a measure of recognition from many of those whose opinions he cared about. He had taught others who would carry on his work as best they could. Mira had a roof over her head. Still, if he was ready to die at any time, he was not ready to quit. The last four years (and two months) of his life were not years of retirement. The accumulated fatigue of his endless work had combined with his war injuries to slow him down from his former, seemingly endless vigor. Yet he still felt reasonably healthy and creative. He was not walking into the sunset quietly even if he did need more support from his cane.

A 'New Type of Thinking'
At the start of 1946, people still struggled to make sense of a world made topsy-turvy by the atomic bomb (that term first mentioned in a 1914 H.G. Wells story). Some parents had initially turned to their children—at least those who read science fiction—to learn about the effects of radiation, etc.[1] Korzybski felt that his work provided definite means to help people deal constructively with this new world situation; he was not going to shy away from offering it.

In early December 1945, he wrote to Jekuthiel Ginsburg, who had invited him to lecture again for Scripta Mathematica in New York City:

> When we were discussing the last time the titles for the two lectures somehow you were not too enthusiastic about the word 'non-aristotelian'. I did not object, but this was <u>before</u> the release of atomic energy. Today we do not need to be shy about this term, as it is crucial for the future of all of us, science, mathematics, education and even sanity. It is simple to speak about the application of physico-mathematicial method, but one has to extract out of it the essential non-aristotelian epistemology which so far no one has done except in General Semantics. All success we have with the non-aristotelian re-orientation is due to this extremely simplified and natural physico-mathematical method and epistemology. I enclose a report of a disturbed veteran and how in ten hours of class training he was helped. And so it goes.[2]

A number of prominent public figures had also expressed their post-war urgencies about the role of education in human life in 'the atomic age'. Brock Chisholm, a Canadian veteran of World War I and a psychiatrist who had served as the Director General of the Canadian Army Medical Corps during World War II, had given the William Alanson White Memorial Lecture in Washington, D.C. in the latter part of 1945. The lecture, "The Psychiatry of Enduring Peace and Social Progress" presented a case for psychiatry to take up a broader social and preventive role in "overhauling the educational system." Chisholm, who would go on to head the newly-born World Health Organization, had already become a controversial figure in his battle against "poisonous certainties" by scolding Canadian parents for telling their children that 'there is a Santa Claus.' His White lecture was published in the February issue of the journal *Psychiatry*, then edited by Harry Stack Sullivan. Sullivan wrote a heartfelt editorial pointing out the need for psychiatry as a profession to "proceed responsibly with a cultural revolution" as Chisholm had envisioned. Although Korzybski felt concerned about Chisholm's brashness, he welcomed both men's pieces. In May he wrote a congratulatory letter to Sullivan, later mimeographed and distributed by the Institute of General Semantics, making clear that his own work provided specifics lacking in Chisholm's and Sullivan's more general statements.[3]

Einstein was also speaking out. At the end of May, Elwood Murray received a telegram from the physicist that he passed on to Korzybski. Reading it must have both buoyed and annoyed Alfred:

> Our world faces crisis as yet unperceived by those possessing power to make great decisions for good or evil. The unleashed power of the atom has changed everything save our modes of thinking and we thus drift toward unparalleled catastrophe...We need two hundred thousand dollars at once for nationwide campaign to let the people know that new type of thinking essential if mankind is to survive and move toward higher levels. This appeal sent you only after long consideration of immense crisis we face...[4]

On June 23, the Sunday *New York Times Magazine* published an article by Einstein about the unprecedented dangers of the atomic bomb. "Science has brought forth this danger," he wrote, "but the real problem is in the minds and hearts of men. We will not change the hearts of other men by mechanisms, but by changing *our* hearts and speaking bravely."[5]

Einstein certainly seemed on the right track in proposing the necessity for a new way of 'thinking', a change in people's 'hearts' and 'minds'. But without exploring and making use of the *mechanisms* by which it operated, Korzybski didn't know how that change could happen. Korzybski must have appreciated the tweaking that Elwood Murray gave the physicist in a reply to his telegram:

> Here is a slight token of support for your telegraphed appeal...I am especially interested in the methods of this new type of thinking you would teach. I would be glad to have any materials you might refer me to on this. In these respects, have you ever investigated the work of Alfred Korzybski, and the <u>general</u> scientific methods he has formulated which are applicable to the immense problems of inter-personal relations. [6]

Einstein had no methodology or materials for teaching the 'new type of thinking' he called for. Korzybski, and colleagues like Murray, did. Korzybski didn't think socially responsible scientists should ignore that. He would take whatever opportunity he could find to apprise people of his work. Some people would find that bothersome. But Korzybski's sense of urgency matched Chisholm's and Einstein's.

In his article, Chisholm had written: "We must at whatever cost prevent our children and their children from being as we have been, but freedom from the tyranny of these faiths and fears is not to be gained in one generation. ..." On the contrary, as Korzybski wrote in a commentary on Chisholm's article,

> This freedom might be achieved <u>provided</u> psychiatrists and mathematicians, and the respectively inter-connected scientists, could and would snap out from their professional 'shell of isolationism', improve their methods, and clarify their nomenclature and formulations as suggested by General [William] Menninger to psychiatrists. This would

be an epoch-making step. ....Co-operation of different specialists in various fields is indispensable if anything is to be accomplished. The solution of the problem is to unify methodology. If there is a 'mortal sin' in this world, destructive to us all, it is the mutual ignorance of learned specialists of the work of other specialists, and their mutual apathy and self-centered indifference to the unification of methodology.

...Einstein, speaking as a layman, says: 'The real problem is in the hearts of men'. In general semantics we formulate it workably and so differently: 'The real problem depends on <u>human evaluations,</u> and <u>any</u> evaluation depends on different conscious or unconscious assumptions, premises, postulates, creeds, dogmas, prejudices, guesses, and what not, which, when <u>acted upon,</u> by necessity result in <u>some</u> methodology.'[7]

A Matter of Character

Before anything else, the methodology had to be applied by people to themselves. Korzybski's concern for people found particular expression in his extensive and painstaking individual work with his students to help them do just that.

Each student presented a different set of difficulties for him to troubleshoot. He was not always the stern taskmaster that he may have seemed with Richard McClaughry. Each student (including the 'same' student at different times) required a different approach in order to help them extensionalize, i.e., face facts and find options, in a way he felt they could handle. He found the work absorbing. But although he worked at minimizing his expectations about what he could accomplish, his individual work with students took a toll on his organism-as-a-whole. Especially after the block of interviews he would do after a seminar, he typically felt exhausted. Nonetheless, he had to teach in his personal way if he was going to continue working, and to get others to carry on with his work, in the way he intended. It was a matter of character.

Indeed, the rhetorical question to McClaughry—"What good is ability without character?"—had great significance for Korzybski. Not just incidentally, the question sounds 'aristotelian'. Years before, Korzybski had read Aristotle's *Nicomachean Ethics* and had noted connections with his own aims and work. The Greek term *ethikos* translates roughly as 'character'. Aristotle's work, supposedly written for his son Nichomachus, consisted of a treatise on personal character development in terms of virtue or human excellence—a notion that he had carried forth from an earlier stream of 'thought' in classical Greek culture. Aristotle's book in turn had a profound effect on later formulators, perhaps in a round-about way on Korzybski too. However non-aristotelian his applied epistemology, Korzybski could definitely be called 'aristotelian' in this sense—his deep concern with developing human excellence, both personal and group, in terms of what seemed to him most characteristic of human life, time-binding.*

Early in February 1946, Korzybski described the aim of his work to Irving J. Lee, talking very much in terms of the by-now-ancient sense of character, virtue, and human excellence. Lee's private seminar—a refresher with Korzybski—took place over a period of more than a week, soon after Lee's return from military service. Altogether, the two men spent nine sessions together (two to three hours each time), so that Lee could catch up with developments in Korzybski's work that he had missed while he was away, e.g., the newest

---

*Conversely, Aristotle's notion of human nature ('man is a rational animal', etc.), though not equivalent to Korzybski's, still showed prefigurings of time-binding, as Korzybski noted in the margins of his copy of the *Nichomachean Ethics*—along with instances of Aristotle's elementalism, etc.

'baby-like' extensional device, chain-indexes. Lee later spoke about how Korzybski related the core of his work to character development:

...At one of these sessions, I said, "Now, Alfred, you have been thinking about this stuff for a very long time. Can you tell me, in a nutshell, what are you trying to do? What is the objective of all this reading and studying and talking and sweating that you go through day after day, year after year? What are you after?"

...I never could call on him in those sessions without being forced to take notes. If I came without a pencil and paper, he invariably found a pad and pencil, and "take some notes" was the continuous refrain. Well, I have gone over those notes many times and in answer to that question, this is almost a verbatim account of what he said when I asked him, "Alfred, what are you trying to do, in a nutshell?"

...He said, "Irving, we are trying to produce a new sort of man...A man who will have no new virtues, but we will know how to describe him and, maybe, we will know how to create him..."†[8]

More than 2000 years had passed since Aristotle. Perhaps Korzybski's new man would have no new virtues, but based on the understanding of humans as time-binders and more recent knowledge of how we know what we say we know, the old virtues would need re-formulating in order to be described in terms of a broader—and epistemologically non-aristotelian—approach.

Korzybski himself never made a formal analysis of *Nichomachean Ethics*, but a non-essentialist, non-elementalistic approach seemed to require 'fuzzifying'—even dissolving—the apparently distinct boundaries among the virtues delineated as ideals in Aristotle's book: the boundaries between the intellectual virtues corresponding to various theoretical realms ('intuition', 'philosophy', science and mathematics); the rigid boundaries between the various forms of theoretical knowledge (no longer 'unchanging truths') and contingent practical knowledge; and the boundaries between various forms of practical knowledge. Theoretical knowledge could be seen as a development of everyday 'common sense'. And simple (but not necessarily easy) lessons of practical wisdom could be extracted—as Korzybski did—from a study of physico-mathematical methods. The walls between the other intellectual virtues and productive—i.e., engineering/technical—knowledge would also have to be bridged or fall away. Reviewed from such a 'non-aristotelian', non-elementalistic perspective, Aristotle's intellectual virtues represented not entirely separate realms, but rather different aspects or stages in a unified process of abstracting (in the korzybskian sense of that term).

Furthermore, since the process of abstracting necessarily involved evaluating, no human abstracting process could be said to exist entirely separately from factors of value, emotions, personal character, etc. In this way, the so-called moral virtues had as much relevance to science and other intellectual endeavors as to the rest of human life. Conversely, one would need various kinds of intellectual excellence, good sense—i.e. sound evaluation—to do 'good'. So the elementalistic walls between Aristotle's types of intellectual virtue and his types of moral virtue would have to come down too. From a korzybskian point of view you could still read *Nichomachean Ethics* with profit, but you would have to put in a lot of quotes, hyphens, etc.

---

† Korzybski told Lee that he had already basically described the 'new sort of man' in *Science and Sanity*.

For Korzybski, as much as for Aristotle, the personal character development he sought to spark in his students had to involve a student's conscious cultivation of new habits in the desired direction. This required persistent effort. Korzybski knew this not only from his experience with students, but also from his experience of working on himself. "I am the same kind of moron as the rest of you," Alfred told Charlotte Schuchardt, who by this time was managing the Institute office and had become his confidential secretary, editorial advisor and—beside Kendig—his more or less indispensable right-hand woman. "[I]t's the method that does the work, for me as well as for you."[9] But the method wouldn't work without the student supplying the sweat.

The sweating might start with preliminary reading: *Science and Sanity*, or at least Francis Chisholm's *Introductory Lectures on General Semantics* or Lee's *Language Habits in Human Affairs*. Then, attending 30 to 40 hours of Korzybski's lectures—along with additional workshop experiences or presentations from others—provided an experience far richer than anything a student could hope to get through reading the books alone. For those who chose to put themselves on 'the firing line', the two to four hours of personal interview with Korzybski could give them an extra boost of motivation and a useful new tack on how to apply the general extensional methods to their own particular problems. Some students might be in for rough times and unpleasant surprises. As a student continued working, barriers awaited to emerge. But, as Korzybski indicated to Richard McClaughry, he considered his job that of helping students to face facts and learn how to continue facing facts about their lives. And as he told McClaughry, his students were *not* paying him to make them like it. (He realized that if he was doing his job adequately, some of his students would probably not like *him*, either).

Both Aristotle and Korzybski would agree about this: intellectual interest and assent were not enough to cultivate the virtues they espoused. Aristotle, long before, had noted:
> We are right then in saying, that these virtues are formed in a man by his doing the actions; but no one, if he should leave them undone, would be even in the way to become a good man. Yet people in general do not perform these actions, but taking refuge in talk they flatter themselves they are philosophising, and that they will so be good men: acting in truth very like those sick people who listen to the doctor with great attention but do nothing that he tells them: just as these then cannot be well bodily under such a course of treatment, so neither can those be mentally by philosophising.[10]

Practical wisdom had to be applied—not just talked about.

Beyond Lip Service

As Korzybski had put it in "A Veteran's Re-Adjustment," "Learning must be *in deed* and not mere lip service, and this is the main difficulty."[11] David Levine was finding out for himself about philosophising lip service in relation to GS. Born in Boston in 1929, the precocious 16 year old from Norfolk, Virginia, had completed one year of high school before passing a test to enter the University of Chicago as a sophomore in 1945. To make extra money, he got odd jobs waiting tables and washing dishes before starting to work at the Institute as an errand boy for Charlotte. Soon afterwards, Kendig invited him to take Francis Chisholm's 1945 summer introductory course. He found it an eye-opening experience, particularly the schema of "logical fate" which he applied in his math and philosophy courses with "favorable results." (He later recalled that the premises-conclusions diagram helped him to get an "A" in his philosophy class—and the philosophy professor found it useful too.) Around this time, he met Korzybski and heard him speak, although the two did not get to know each other until two years later. When David talked to Kendig about further studies, she got him a second-hand copy of *Science and Sanity*. David took two weeks off from his classes to read the book. He felt "stunned" by the time he finished it and immediately began the first of what would become many re-readings.[12]

David worked at the Institute in Chicago for only about a year. He wouldn't have an opportunity to take a seminar with Korzybski until 1948. However, he definitely seemed 'besotted' with GS, a condition he described in an article published in 1953:

> The organization of a University of Chicago chapter of the Society for General Semantics gave me an opportunity during 1946 and 1947 to verbalize in large quantities about general semantics. Such intense over-verbalization about GS seems to be the 'standard' reaction to an introduction to GS. While such verbalization may be 'standard,' later I found it empirically to be an extremely unprofitable expenditure of time and energy. My only time-binding comment here is, that if you must run off at the mouth about GS to any chronic degree, then for pity sake relax, preferably with a drink in one hand, and make up your mind you're not going to accomplish a hell of a lot. I emphasize relax, because if you get too 'deadly serious' in your verbal escapades, I find through personal experience you may actually injure yourself as well as others.
>
> On the campus of U of C a great deal of 'neurotic' over-verbalization about GS probably wouldn't distinguish you from the rest of the denizens, but if a fellow in the 'outside world' who has a reasonably responsible position to fill engages in intense verbalization, 'crusading,' 'lecturing,' etc., it may cost him his job, his family's peace of mind, etc., and in general could get him the unsavory reputation of 'crack-pot.'[13]

Such crusading might repel potential students, preventing them from taking Korzybski and his work seriously. If they did get interested, over-verbalization would divert them from the necessary personal work involved in the discipline. Admittedly, this very aspect of Korzybski's teaching, his focus on "the personal adjustment of his students" might bother others. As Allen Walker Read noted years later:

> ...More and more [Korzybski's] purpose came to be to have an impact on the society of his time. To accomplish this, the whole person must be involved, with the reactions of the nervous system restructured. For the academic intellectual, this intrusion into his personal life arouses antagonism. Most of us have resistances to assaults on our ways of evaluating. Some people cannot stand it and have left seminars in the middle of them.[14]

Korzybski had carefully studied the issue. "In every seminar I learn something about the difficulties which my students confront when they try to apply GS to life, which helps me in formulating new approaches, and in fact the discovering of new mechanisms which are perhaps crucial."[15] A major part of the problem was that mastering extensional methodology required more than reading a book or attending a lecture. Internalization required practice. Many if not most people could benefit from the personal guidance of a teacher—the more individualized the better. This was the main reason he insisted on continuing his work with students in personal interviews.

At this point, looking to the future when he would no longer be around, Korzybski felt more than ever the need to develop a core of qualified people to carry on his work. Such people definitely would need to have an adequate verbal understanding of the non-aristotelian formulations. More importantly, they would need to have adequately internalized the extensional methods of GS. Such individuals would be in a position to apply and teach the work in the way he intended. Over the first part of 1946, he and Kendig developed a new program to do this (as part of the larger IGS development program they had long hoped for). They announced it in the first item on page one of the Summer 1946, *IGS Student Newsletter*:

> DEMAND GROWS FOR APPROVED WORKERS IN GS as indicated by many items in this letter. To designate those whose qualifications and training in General Semantics in their own line of work have been approved by Korzybski, the Trustees are creating the title *Associate of the Institute of General Semantics*. Teachers, physicians, lecturers and all other workers in any field who wish his approval and official recognition of their competence are invited to qualify for appointment as an 'Associate.' In general, they will be expected to take some refresher training in the Non-A discipline and have a conference with Korzybski. Other qualifying procedures will not be subject to standard routine but will vary with Korzybski's evaluations of the individual's status in personal mastery of the discipline...[16]

(Because of continuing limitations of money and personnel over the next few years, this plan never took off.)

Whether they became Associates or not, additional educational material could provide guideposts for students wishing to develop in the direction of the new man and woman that Korzybski had envisioned. People would find stories of personal experience valuable. He had acquired a large file of autobiographical statements and correspondence from the students who had seen him for interviews. He also had materials from students of his students, like the veteran who had taken Elwood Murray's class in Denver, upon whom the "Veteran's Re-adjustment" paper had been based. As an educator and not a psychiatrist nor psychotherapist, he didn't feel he would get taken seriously by writing standard clinical-sounding case studies. Instead, Alfred would provide some commentary as he had done in the "Veteran's" paper, but the material would basically consist of students' self-reports on the struggles, successes, and failures of their ongoing self-reeducation.

Many of the letters he got from students—briefly recounting positive and/or negative results—wouldn't do. Without knowing more details about the students' lives, a reader would have trouble understanding what they were talking about. In February, Korzybski had received, about a week apart, two letters from one person; they exactly suited his purpose. A reader wouldn't need much else than these letters to get a good sense of the process of struggle and internalization that this student—whom he renamed $Smith_1$—depicted. Korzybski got permission from $Smith_1$ to publish the letters along with Korzybski's reply to him, wrote a brief commentary to introduce them, and had the document mimeographed. He began to distribute the $Smith_1$ document "Letters on Non-Aristotelian Retraining" to select people as an example of how serious students could benefit from working to apply this 'new type of thinking' to themselves. (The $Smith_1$ letters were published in the *General Semantics Bulletin* in 1951 and republished in Korzybski's *Collected Writings*.) Korzybski prepared a second set of letters from another student, renamed $Smith_2$, later in the year and made plans to prepare a series of such pieces from his personal correspondence with students. But various disruptions and projects that became more pressing made it impossible for Korzybski to devote the necessary time before he died to carry out what he called "The $Smith_n$ Series of GS Life-Histories."[17]

Chapter 60
SNAFU

The U.S. Army acronym for "situation normal—all fucked up" had originally referred to any confused outcome resulting from an "excess of Army rules and routine", then had expanded to include any complication resulting from human stupidity, and by 1946 had entered civilian usage and could refer to any "snarled", "haywire", "ruined", or "fouled up" state of affairs.[1] The human stupidity behind any particular snafu might not be apparent. There was also the factor of plain bad luck—all the disturbing factors in the universe that could defeat human purposes. But one could probably safely assume human stupidity—or at least the general tendency toward opacity in human thinking-feeling—as a factor in most human messes. 'Snafu' might well serve as a one-word label for the human condition and rather neatly summarized the world's post-war situation.

Snafus. Across the former battlegrounds of Asia and Europe, people tried to piece their lives together, struggling with wartime injuries, psychic traumas, loss of loved ones and possessions—as poverty, hunger, and disease all continued to take their terrible toll. In China, the civil war between Chiang Kai-shek's Nationalist Chinese government and the Communist "Red Chinese" guerillas under Mao Tse Tung had resumed in full. In Europe, as noted by now-former British Prime Minister Winston Churchill in a March speech at a small Missouri college, "...an iron curtain" had "descended across the continent." Franklin D. Roosevelt (perhaps too agreeably) and Churchill (more reluctantly) had both acquiesced to Stalin's hegemony in Eastern Europe at Yalta in early 1945. Now the Stalinist sealing off of Poland and East Germany behind this iron curtain—with other countries soon to follow—seemed much worse than what even Churchill had previously feared.

Snafus. In the United States, the country was straining in 1946 with consequences of the peacetime "reconversion" of the wartime economy: food shortages, inflation, and high unemployment. Crippling strikes by autoworkers, miners, and railroad workers had only been averted by President Truman's threats of severe government action. A nationwide housing shortage had set in. The depth of this shortage in Chicago created multiple snafus for the Institute of General Semantics. Since the end of the war, out-of-town people coming to IGS seminars even had trouble finding temporary lodging, with some participants having to book a different hotel room every night. And regarding housing, the Institute got very bad news in March. The owner of 1234 East 56 Street was selling the building and the new owner wanted to live there. The Institute would have to move by August 1.

Where Shall We Go?

As Korzybski neared the end of the last seminar he would teach in Chicago (an evening one which ran from February 26 to March 27), he wrote to Frances R. Dewing:

> ...Where we shall go, to New York or San Francisco, we really don't know. In both places our old students and friends are working for us looking for a place with as yet unknown results. There is one thing certain, that no one of us wants to remain in Chicago, and are willing to move to the far East or far West, but no middle West anyway.[2]

Several years before, Mira had suggested a fund-raising campaign to buy the Institute building. At that time she told Alfred "I would be sick to the bone if I had to move from here, or you had to move from 1234 before we coagulate."[3] Now, they didn't have the option to buy and Alfred *had* to move. Furthermore, wherever the Institute would go, he and Mira couldn't afford to have her leave her comfortable apartment across the street. Besides, she was getting free medical care at nearby Billings Hospital. Still, Mira took the bad news about the move rather well. She even suggested printing cards to hand out to seminar students to elicit their help in finding a new place in New York City.[4]

Alfred had time to ponder where the Institute would go while in New York in mid-April to present an intensive seminar for The New York Society for General Semantics and then to give his Scripta Mathematica lectures. Kendig went with him, and seemed especially harried. Just before they left for New York, her mother—in Cambridge, Massachusetts—had died after a long illness. Kendig felt so pressed by Institute business, including the seminar arrangements, that she didn't go to the funeral.[5]

Charlotte remained in Chicago. A few years before, with Korzybski so desperate for help, she had decided to stop teaching dance or going to dance classes for one year in order to devote herself full-time to work at the Institute. One year had turned into several. Now if she stayed with the Institute, it might doom her dance career for good, simply due to lack of opportunity wherever they might end up. (At this point, she had reached her late thirties, but she may have been able to continue for years in modern dance—especially teaching.) She decided she would stay with the Institute.[6] Now, she had a lot of things to do including getting files, books, and other Institute materials into storage in Chicago and setting up a small, short-term transitional office in Kendig's apartment. (The Institute would maintain this Chicago office well into 1947.)

Korzybski's New York seminar and lectures went well. The large and lively seminar group included Princeton historian Erich Kahler—a friend of Einstein and Thomas Mann—who seemed favorably impressed with Korzybski. Another seminar attendee, Robert K. Straus—a grandson of Isidor Straus, one of the founders of Macy's Department Store—gave the Institute money to fund a working fellowship for one or more students to train with Korzybski for up to a year. During a time of extra expenses, this and other students' donations would give the Institute a little monetary cushion to get more help and even begin some new projects.

Korzybski and Kendig returned from New York in May. They continued preparations to leave, but as July began, they still didn't have a place—not even for the summer seminar-workshop, which remained on the schedule. In "a brief historical survey" of the Institute, which Charlotte wrote 42 years later, she recalled, "That we had to move was perceived by us as a catastrophe, and indeed the process was exhausting."[7] Perhaps she especially felt that way—she had major responsibility for the logistical details of the move.

Promising Developments

Korzybski didn't seem worried about the move—at least not in the letters he wrote at the time. Despite the Institute's problems, he could see many promising developments for his work. More people than ever were ordering *Science and Sanity*, which had finally gotten into print again in February. Science Press was already looking for paper (still in scarce supply) for another printing. Meanwhile, new articles about GS continued to appear. Elwood Murray and two co-authors, Wilson Paul and Frederick Sorenson, had written, "A Functional Core for the Basic Communication Course", about their University of Denver curriculum for the April *Quarterly Journal of Speech*. "Human relations", they wrote, "[are] the core of the

Basic Communications Course with General Semantics as the principal method for training in appropriate evaluative reactions."[8] Another article, "General Semantics and The Science of Man", by Charles L. Glicksberg had come out in the May *Scientific Monthly*—"really a splendid paper" by Korzybski's standards.[9] Glicksberg had just become a Professor of English in the Department of Education at Brooklyn College, where he would go on to a long, distinguished career as a teacher of literature and creative writing. A prolific writer, he had already produced several articles and reviews for *ETC.* since 1943 and had another article, "General Semantics in English Teaching", published in February in *The English Leaflet*, a journal for English teachers. Glicksberg, who had attended the 1945 New York seminar, was invited to teach at the upcoming seminar-workshop, wherever it would be held.

Korzybski's work had also gotten favorable mentions in some recently published books. In *A Nation of Nations*, social critic/historian Louis Adamic devoted several pages in a chapter on "Americans from Poland" to Korzybski, describing him so: "Picturesque, patently honest, immensely learned, often witty, [he] is still essentially an engineer. He uses engineering and mathematical terms; they are constructive, they mean what they say."[10] University of Chicago philosopher Charles Morris in *Signs, Language and Behavior*, his new book on semiotics, briefly noted, "The work of A. Korzybski and his followers, psycho-biological in orientation, has largely been devoted to the therapy of the individual, aiming to protect the individual against exploitation by others and by himself. ..."[11]

Korzybski's name had turned up in the U.S. Congressional Record as well. This came about primarily through the efforts of James A. Saunders, a retired U. S. Navy Captain, who had worked for a number of years as liason officer with the U.S. Senate Committee on Naval Affairs—soon to get incorporated into the Senate Armed Services Committee. A long-time enthusiastic student of *Science and Sanity*, Captain Saunders had made explicit use of korzybskian methodology in his work for the Committee, making note of it in reports published in the *Congressional Record* as far back as 1940. Most recently he had made use of GS in a March 13, 1946 report published in June by the Naval Affairs Committee, entitled "A Scientific Evaluation of the Proposal that the War and Navy Departments be Merged into a Single Department of National Defense". The report recommended preserving institutional structures of the different armed services that had already proved effective. Part VI of the report, "Methods Employed in Making the Evaluation" included *Science and Sanity* and other GS references. The report may have had some influence in helping the Navy and other armed service branches to maintain some relative independence when in 1947 the cabinet level Department of the Navy, along with the other armed services, got absorbed into the newly created Department of Defense.

By mid-1946, Saunders had corresponded with Korzybski and Kendig, but had not met them in person. Nonetheless, on the strength of his letters and his Congressional reports, they invited him to lecture on his committee work at that summer's seminar-workshop. At the end of the year, he also attended Korzybski's Holiday Seminar. Korzybski seems to have found Saunders a helpful influence and a commendable teacher. In 1947 Saunders got appointed to the IGS Board of Trustees and also for several years taught at the IGS seminar-workshops—in 1948 serving as chief administrator and lecturer of the workshop sessions and in 1949 lecturing on GS and problem solving. He began teaching General Semantics at the Graduate School of the U.S. Department of Agriculture in 1947 and—at least into the late 1950s—continued giving that course and others in the Washington, D.C. area. Saunders, a central figure in stimulating GS-related activities in Washington, D.C. throughout the 1950s, doesn't seem to have published any articles or books of his own. But a student of his, Frank Reed Eldridge a Washington, D.C. diplomat and intelligence officer, published a book, *General Semantics*, in 1949 with his wife Kathleen Tamagawa Eldridge, based on Saunders' course lectures. (When Eldridge joined the Central Intelligence Agency in 1951, he was asked to cease his leadership activities with the Lemma Society, the local GS group.)[12]

Partly through Saunder's influence, Korzybski's work caught the attention of others in the Navy. After the August seminar, Saunders wrote a lengthy memorandum to his Naval Academy classmate Vice Admiral Louis E. Denfeld, then Chief of Naval Personnel (soon to become an Admiral and Chief of Naval Operations).The memo suggested incorporating GS into various aspects of Naval operations and training.[13] Apparently Denfeld got interested. Captain Karl Poehlmann, attached to Denfeld's office, attended Korzybski's Holiday seminar—on orders—and got deeply interested. Korzybski and Kendig both met with him privately during and after the seminar. The Office of Naval Research had a section exploring various kinds of medical, behavioral and social science research pertaining to human relations, instruction of officers, psychological warfare, combating propaganda, etc. Poehlmann believed that GS, providing a kind of 'master map', could play an important role in guiding such research.[14] Perhaps the Institute could provide some training for the Navy. If this took off, a contract to do GS training throughout the Navy could do a lot to ensure the survival of the Institute.

Korzybski was willing to devote a lot of time and attention to such a project, which he believed could have world-changing effects.[15] The kind of project he envisioned—a long shot—ultimately didn't work out. However, Korzybski's work still had notable influence in the Navy. Either Saunders or Poehlmann may have had something to do with the strongly GS-flavored 1949 edition of *Naval Leadership*, a manual for Naval Academy midshipman published by the U.S. Naval Institute. Part I of the book, "Psychological Principles", particularly Chapter 1 "Science and Human Relations", was described in a subsequent *General Semantics Bulletin* as "an excellent example of general semantics-in-action. [The unknown author's] account of scientific attitudes and methods applied to the problems of leadership is written in a lively, down to earth fashion, refreshingly free of 'rehashing'."[16]

Interest in Korzybski's work was not limited to the United States. In June, he had received two separate letters of invitation to speak at the Second International Summer Conference of the Netherlands-based International Society for the Study of Significs, from August 24 to August 31. The Dutch Significs circle—to some extent influenced by the work of Lady Victoria Welby—had started as a discussion group among psychiatrist Frederik Willem van Eeden (who had met Lady Welby), L. E. J. Brouwer (founder of the non-aristotelian, intuitionist school of mathematics), and Brouwer's teacher, mathematician Gerrit Manoury, among others, in the early 1920s. These individuals—and those who joined them later—had some interest in more 'holistic' (i.e., non-elementalistic) living, and in practical approaches to problems of symbolism, the foundations of mathematics, the unity of science, etc. At least some of the younger members of the circle had carefully studied Korzybski's work, seeing a connection to their concerns. Psychiatrist P. H. Esser had published two articles on Korzybski in Dutch journals just prior to the Nazi invasion. Korzybski felt that, for the most part, neither Lady Welby nor her Dutch followers went far enough. But he did recognize their aims as similar to his. He particularly admired Brouwer's work and felt deeply honored to be invited to speak to the group.

Dr. W. M. Kruseman, the Assistant Secretary of the organization, and one of the editors of its journal *Synthese*, wrote that he and his colleagues had read *Science and Sanity* "with great interest and approval."

> ...They would welcome your visit as an opportunity to establish and to further a regular scientific contact between your Institute for [sic] General Semantics and our International Society for the Study of Significs. They would be delighted if, on this occasion, you would be willing to read on a special subject (e.g. on "Everyday language with regard to the Structure of our nervous system").[17]

In a letter written a few days later, E.W. Beth, University of Amsterdam professor of mathematical logic, apologized to Korzybski: the Conference's organizing committee only had enough money to offer him free food and lodging. They could not pay for his travel expenses.[18] The Dutch organization had only recently reconstituted itself after years of Nazi occupation and they undoubtedly had a quite limited budget. But apart from the question of money for a trip to the Netherlands, going there was not an option for Korzybski, given the impending move and the seminar-workshop scheduled at the time of the conference. However, his work was represented by E. A. Pritchard, an American educator living in New York with an interest in GS. Pritchard hadn't studied with Korzybski or even met him. The two men corresponded briefly but Pritchard wasn't able to see Korzybski before leaving in early August. Despite some reservations, Korzybski decided to cooperate with him since no one else was going to represent the Institute. In addition to a talk Pritchard prepared, he read Korzybski's latest version of the "Silent and Verbal Levels" handout written in July, and organized a booth of GS publications.

In the fall, Pritchard visited Korzybski and reported on the conference, having found a great deal of interest. With at least one other presentation by a Dutch student of *Science and Sanity*, a whole conference day had been devoted to GS. The GS booth was always crowded. (Given that it was the only booth there, Korzybski likened this to the increased public interest when a new animal gets brought for exhibition to a zoo.)[19] Over the next few years, Korzybski continued to correspond and exchange publications with members of the Dutch Significs group. However, although subsequently invited, he couldn't attend further conferences either.

Through the influence of Esser, a small significs group—and with it a pocket of interest in Korzybski's work—continued in the Netherlands for a number of decades after Korzybski's death. Esser, who was made an Honorary Trustee of the Institute, seems instrumental in having founded a Methodology and Science Foundation in Haarlem, which operated at least throughout the 1970s. Its journal, *Methodology and Science*, had a "Special Korzybski Issue" in 1977 (Volume 10, No. 2). *Synthese*, although still (2011) getting published in the Netherlands, has become a philosophy of science journal and seems to have little if any connection to its earlier roots in the now apparently defunct Dutch Significs Movement.

A Helping Hand

Robert Upjohn Redpath Jr. hadn't yet met Korzybski and colleagues when he found a place for the Institute in July. With a long dormant but recently revived interest in Korzybski's work, he had decided to help when he learned that the Institute could use a location around New York City—if not for a permanent home, then at least for a place to hold the summer seminar-workshop.

Science and Sanity had gathered dust on Bob Redpath's bookshelf for years. A highly successful, 39 year-old insurance underwriter working in New York City, he had first gotten the book in 1935 on the recommendation of a former Yale classmate, the writer Wilder Hobson. Hobson told Redpath at the time that he considered Korzybski's book the "only revolutionary thinking he had come across in the twentieth century." Redpath skimmed through it quickly—an error, he later realized: "I...made the mistake of looking at some of the chapter headings in the latter part of the book and, in my then profound ignorance, putting it away unread on the shelf."[20] With so many 'foreboding' terms, he assumed he needed to know advanced mathematics and science to get much out of it.

> ...I later told Korzybski that I regretted that I came to the study of his work with so little knowledge of mathematics. He said in effect that the *content* of knowledge in any area, including those, was so small a proportion of the to-be-known that I need not waste time in acquiring more content or feeling myself handicapped by the lack of it. Instead, the important skill to acquire was the *feel* of the mathematical-scientific *way* of thinking.[21]

An omnivorous reader with a hungry curiosity, Redpath had probably gotten a little of that feel already, even from his cursory 1935 reading. In a 1949 letter to Yale psychiatrist Clements C. Fry, who was consulting with him about possibilities for mental hygiene research at the University, he recalled his return to studying GS:

> In the fall of 1945,... I was lucky enough to be confined for a period of ten days and started the book at the very beginning. I studied it during my train rides to New York, while waiting in business offices, etc., over a period of six months. I have never read a book that so enormously enlarged my understanding of the potential that may accrue to man through applying certain general methods of evaluation, some of which are admittedly still untested.[22]

In Redpath's effort to help the Institute, he found the Indian Mountain School in Lakeville in Northwestern Connecticut. The private school had classroom as well as food and lodging facilities available in August. The Institute quickly made arrangements with the school. The seminar, at least, was no longer in limbo. Korzybski, Kendig and Charlotte—understandably stressed by the exigencies of moving—felt most grateful. All of them would form a close bond with Redpath over the next few years.

Leaving Chicago

Korzybski felt glad to be leaving Chicago. At least that's what he told Ken Keyes a year later. Perhaps some 'sour grapes' were involved. Although the Institute building itself seemed just about 'perfect', he had come to feel disgusted with the city itself:

> ...the whole lot of us was disgusted with Chicago, mis-administration due to politics [Chicago had remained an American stronghold of machine 'boss' politics]. We were plain disgusted, and that endless dirt. Did you ever live in Chicago? There [was] a 16th of an inch of black dirt everyday over the furniture. You can imagine that. It was due

to soft coal in the manufacturing all around. It was a simply impossible place. Even the water happened to be plain mud. Couldn't drink that water. It was a perfectly impossible city, so we were in a way glad to move.[23]

The Institute's proximity to the University of Chicago, along with whatever connections it had made there, didn't provide any significant incentive for the Institute to stay in Chicago either. Some students and faculty had shown interest in Korzybski's work and studied with him. A campus chapter of the Society for General Semantics had gotten organized. But there also remained a fair amount of unfavorable talk on campus about Korzybski, GS, and the Institute. Ed MacNeal, a University of Chicago student at this time, who had attended an Institute seminar, later noted a joke going around: "Do you know the difference between *ceramics* and *semantics*? Semantics is *crack*pottery."[24] However, perhaps surprisingly to some, Korzybski had corresponded and established cordial relations—at least on the surface—with University President Robert Maynard Hutchins, and the Dean of Humanities, Richard McKeon. Neither man seemed particularly hostile and had given at least a positive nod in his direction.

McKeon, a philosopher and Aristotle scholar, had even given a number of talks in which he dealt with Korzybski's work. Both Mira (taking extensive notes for Alfred) and Kendig had attended some of those sessions. In a letter to one of Korzybski's students, Kendig observed:

...During the Fall [1943] Quarter, [McKeon] taught a public course on 'Semantics and Modern Thought'. I attended some of his lectures and although he misinterpreted parts of S&S, he showed a respectful attitude and it was also evident that he had really seriously studied the book and his misinterpretations were honest mistakes. I had a very pleasant little meeting with him after one of the lectures. I heard favorable comments on me afterwards; also, Count Alfred had written him a very good letter, to which I understand, he reacted favorably.[25]

Hutchins, an educational reformer and promoter of "the Great Books" program with Mortimer Adler, had made a small but friendly contribution to Korzybski's "Introduction to the Second Edition 1941". Korzybski had written to a number of people in 1940, including Hutchins, asking for examples of over/under defined terms in their fields:

...The most extensional answer was given by that brilliant jurist, Dr. Robert Maynard Hutchins, who sent to me his Convocation Address of June, 1940 with a letter, which he has kindly given me permission to quote, as follows: 'I am afraid you will feel that all the words I use are examples of the errors you are attacking. Here is my last Convocation Address, with a sample in every line.' Such a judgement is profoundly justified whenever language is utilized. This address is a splendid piece of work, and it implies the intuitive recognition of the fundamental neuro-linguistic difficulties we are up against.[26]

Korzybski later wrote to Hutchins, "I repeat that in spite of your official 'aristotelianism', which is very unpopular and controversial, you are not an aristotelian in the vulgar sense, but you just protest against the abuse of Aristotle, with which we are in full sympathy."[27] Maybe. But in spite of polite nods in either direction, there remained considerable distance between the Institute and 'aristotelians' (official or not) at the University. Nothing much had developed as a result of Korzybski's and others' efforts to connect—nothing that contributed any urgency to staying in Chicago.

The fact that the Society for General Semantics had its center of activity in Chicago also did not provide a compelling reason for the Institute to stay in the city. Indeed, the Society had become a source of increasing frustration to Korzybski and his co-workers. As an organization, the Society had fallen seriously short in regard to two of the major activities for which it was founded (as set out in its 1942 Charter and By-laws): "to secure financial support", and to secure "wider recognition for the Institute of General Semantics as a center of training, study and research." Among people who had an interest in GS and made inquiries and/or who wanted to help the Institute, there seemed to exist a great deal of confusion about the distinction between the two organizations. Mail to one often was addressed and got delivered to the other. Some believed that a significant amount of their membership fees to the Society, as publicly announced, was going to support the Institute. They wondered why the Institute was sending out additional fundraising appeals. Korzybski, Kendig, and Charlotte all perceived a lack of communication and cooperation from Society leadership on various issues. They believed both organizations could benefit by working together more. In spite of persistent efforts—including letters, and memos—to try to resolve their issues with the Society and to work together with it, things just seemed to get worse.

The failure to contribute any significant financial support to the Institute seemed mainly a result of the measures originally set out to do so. As specified in its by-laws, the society was to retain only $5 from any membership fee category (basic annual participating membership started at $10). Wendell Johnson, who served as the Society President from mid-1945 to mid-1947, wrote in 1947,

> ...from April of 1942 to June of 1945, the arrangement had secured only $2258.00 for the Institute, and the Society was in arrears to the extent of $166.75 (paid November 29, 1945). At the same time these payments had involved such a severe drain on Society funds that by 1945 it had become clear that the very continuation of the Society was being seriously endangered.[28]

Not only continuation but also growth had importance to Johnson and others involved with running the Society. In addition to publishing *ETC.*, the Society had in April 1945 started to publish a free, more-or less monthly newsletter for members entitled $Quotes_n$—each issue would get sequentially numbered. Among other activities, the Society was also organizing lecture series and attempting to bring a number of study groups around the country under its wings as local chapters. To help do all these things, the Society had hired Anne Coleman (the former Anne Cleveland who had worked at the Institute) in 1945 as a full-time Business Manager. Later that year, she needed an assistant. Salaries, office expenses, etc., had stretched the Society's meager income. If the Society was going to continue to exist—and to grow—something had to change in its arrangement with the IGS.

In February 1945, the Society board had prepared a proposed revision to the by-laws that would change membership categories, fees, and the amount of money given to the Institute.[29] According to its own by-laws, such a revision would require a vote by all Society members, but no vote was taken. Nonetheless around July—soon after Wendell Johnson became President—the Society sent out a new membership invitation brochure. The brochure simply announced the new membership fees as an accomplished fact, including a range of $4 to $9 per year to become a basic Participating Member. One could reasonably expect a larger number of people—paying the reduced $4—to join; according to Society bylaws, it would not have to contribute any of this to the Institute. (Not surprisingly, over the next six months, the society's membership more than tripled.)³⁰ Korzybski undoubtedly saw the brochure.³¹ It seems astonishing that anyone on the Society board could expect Korzybski to ignore this 'little' change.

At the end of 1945, Korzybski had gotten another surprise from the Society—Wendell Johnson's Editorial in *ETC.* as the Society's new President. Johnson announced plans to encourage the teaching of general semantics in schools and colleges, to organize local chapters, start a 'Semantic[s] Book Club', provide financial support for scientific research dealing with 'semantic' problems, conduct more lecture series, etc. The several-page editorial notably omitted mentioning either the Institute or Korzybski, whom Johnson had not consulted. So much for securing "wider recognition for the Institute". Korzybski, who had promoted the Society from its beginning, believed Johnson's editorial violated the Society's own By-laws (which had not been changed) and compromised those of the Institute. Furthermore, if the Society was going to carry out its programs without consulting and coordinating with Korzybski and his colleagues, it seemed more likely to pull income and interested people away from the Institute—helping to keep the Institute financially strapped.

If not destitute, the Institute at least qualified as seriously short of money. From July 1945 to May 1946, about 75 percent of the Institute's earnings still came mostly from participants' fees from Korzybski's seminars and consultative interviews—along with publication sales and other services. Only about 25 percent of Institute operating income came from donations. For such a "non-profit pioneering Institution" as the IGS, Kendig wanted that ratio closer to 50-50.³² Without a serious fundraising campaign, Korzybski would have to continue with the never-ending round of seminars he'd done for so long to keep the Institute going. He would not have the freedom to do the writing he wanted or to focus his teaching on advanced training to develop competent teachers of the methodology and to train leaders in various fields who could apply it.

The Institute had demonstrated it could do serious fundraising on its own. In the summer of 1945, an 'emergency' campaign had quickly raised enough money to hire Francis Chisholm for a year to do special educational projects. (Chisholm decided to decline the position and instead joined the English faculty at the State Teachers College–River Falls, Wisconsin, where he spent the rest of his academic career.) Nonetheless, Korzybski and his colleagues had considered it better to work with the Society. In the fundraising letter sent out in 1944 (sent again in 1945), they had purposely promoted membership in the Society as a way to support the Institute—given the Society's founding mission to do so. In so promoting the Society, the Institute had held back a full-blown fundraising campaign of its own. Johnson's editorial came as a definite blow.

Perhaps Johnson's neglect of Korzybski and the Institute resulted from distraction. He had completed the manuscript of a book on 'the semantics of personal adjustment' in the fall of 1945. *People in Quandaries*, to be published by Harper & Brothers, expanded on Johnson's monograph published a few years before by the Institute. The book included his own development of GS formulations and applications in psychotherapy and speech pathology (stuttering) with material he'd amassed on teaching GS and an appendix on research. Publication had gotten delayed due to post-war paper and labor shortages. Distraction and preoccupation—how else could one account for Johnson writing to Science Press in March to ask them for permission to quote from *Science and Sanity*?

Korzybski finally got the note in May. Having known Korzybski for so long and having had his own monograph published by the Institute, Johnson surely must have known that Science Press was not the publisher and that he actually needed to contact Korzybski directly. A quandary to ponder—no doubt. Korzybski demonstrated no interest in pulling away from Johnson. He had continued to write enthusiastically to others about Johnson's teaching and research. When Johnson's book came out later in the year, Korzybski wrote a congratulatory letter to him and had the book placed on the Institute's list of publications for sale. Korzybski invited him to lecture at the upcoming seminar-workshop. And Johnson was later invited to join the Institute Board of Trustees. Nonetheless Johnson's detachment seemed indicative of a general attitude among leaders of the Society—an attitude epitomized by Hayakawa, as Editor of *ETC.* perhaps the group's most prominent figure.

With Friends Like These...

Hayakawa's standoffishness had continued, as had his failure to consult his "Consulting Editors" Korzybski and Kendig, and the increasing lack of rigor in his own writing and in the general content of *ETC*. Korzybski's pleasure at seeing his "Veteran's Re-Adjustment" paper in the summer 1946 issue of *ETC.*, must have quickly deflated when he also saw the five-page "Terms in General Semantics: A Glossary" by Hayakawa and Anatol Rapoport. Among other misstatements from Korzybski's point of view, the two men continued presenting 'general semantics' as a kind of 'semantics'. Korzybski felt seriously nettled. He later wrote to Hayakawa:

> Practically every 'definition' misses the main point and trend of my life work. For instance, what is said in the glossary about the use of the term 'semantic' in my 'General Semantics', i.e, in a new theory of values, is entirely misleading, for reasons explained before. Such initial common errors must lead automatically to further more aggravated misinterpretations,...
>
> Unfamiliarity with a new discipline might be historically forgivable, but what is unprecedented among serious individuals is that the authors should undertake such misevaluations in my lifetime without ever consulting with me, although they lived then only a few blocks away from the Institute. I saw the glossary only after it had been printed and distributed to the public. Such behavior may seem unbelievable, but it is all there, in print, a public document of misinformations.[33]

It didn't help Korzybski that Rapoport had become Assistant Editor. (He would remain in that role—or later "Associate Editor"—for several decades.) Rapoport looked up to Hayakawa as his mentor in 'semantics'/'general semantics' and the two became close friends. He surely qualified as one of the people least likely to help Hayakawa modify his misconceptions about Korzybski. Indeed, Rapoport probably helped amplify and solidify many of Hayakawa's negative attitudes.

Anatol Rapoport was born in Russia in 1911. His parents, who had consciously rejected their Jewish roots, raised their son as an atheist and socialist. He remained a dedicated leftist all his life. Coming to the U.S. with his family in 1922, he pursued a career in music as a young man, studying piano in a conservatory in Vienna from 1929 to 1934. He toured Europe, the U.S., and Mexico as a concert pianist in the mid-1930s, before realizing the unlikelihood of his success in that career. Disdainful of business as a bourgeois capitalist pursuit, his growing interest in science and mathematics led him to enter academic life. He applied to the University of Chicago and after only a short time as an undergraduate passed a comprehensive exam and entered graduate school to study mathematics in 1938, obtaining a PhD in 1941. (With an interest in applying mathematics to biology and sociology, he would later become well known for his contributions to mathematical game theory.) In 1938, he also joined the Communist Party, U.S.A. Although he resigned from the Party—on orders from its leadership—when he joined the U.S. army in 1941, he continued to admire Joseph Stalin for some time afterward and maintained his loyalty to the Soviet Union as a model of democracy until sometime around mid-1948, when the so-called Lysenko affair, which banned the study of genetics in the Soviet Union, finally burst his Bolshevik bubble.[34]

Rapoport's deep ambivalence about Korzybski and his work began when he first encountered *Science and Sanity* in 1943 or 1944 during his wartime army air force service in Alaska. Someone loaned him a copy of the book.

> My first impulse was to dismiss Korzybski as a crackpot. [This or similar epithets about Korzybski—often attributed to 'others'—often came up later in Rapoport's writings.] I was reading Hegel's *Science of Logic* at the same time, and the "non-Aristotelian system" constructed on a "law of non-identity" looked to me like an impertinent and awkward imitation. I could not see how anyone could take Korzybski seriously. But Hayakawa evidently did, as I was told by a Red Cross girl who had read *Language in Action* and talked the G.S. lingo. I recalled what I had heard about that book, borrowed it from her, and was enchanted.
>
> My attitude toward Korzybski changed from contempt to anger. If this was what the man meant, why didn't he say so... Why couldn't Korzybski write lucid prose like Russell's or Hayakawa's?... Why could not Korzybski be at least logically rigorous? If he was not a crackpot (this previous impression of mine was now vigorously shaken), why was he so repetitive, verbose, pugnacious, redundant and self-congratulatory, manifesting all the symptoms of crackpot delusions?[35]

Rapoport never did shake off that impression, although he felt enough of a pull from Hayakawa's work to inspire him to send in his first article to *ETC.*, which Hayakawa published in 1944. (Korzybski liked the article.) Later that year, his first encounter with Korzybski reinforced his negative attitude even further. While on leave he went to Chicago, where his parents still lived, and visited the Institute while Korzybski was lecturing. He was invited to sit in and found Korzybski's lecture dull, his demonstrations unimpressive.

> ...To the extent that the lecture had a topic, it was that "things are not what they seem," something Longfellow had said in a sentimental poem a century earlier. Bored by the lecture, I scanned the audience and recognized Hayakawa...He was the man I really wanted to meet....
>
> After the lecture, I introduced myself and was cheerfully greeted. Hayakawa insisted on introducing me to Korzybski, to whom, he said, he had spoken about me. We went to Korzybski's study, where he, too, greeted me with disarming warmth. It was embarrassing. I had formed an unflattering opinion about Korzybski's intellect...Korzybski's first remark to me made the situation definitive: "You have read *Science and Sanity*...how many times?"
>
> I made some noncommittal remarks about rereading certain portions and started half-hearted attempts to engage him in a substantive discussion about his assumptions, lines of reasoning, and conclusions. It was useless...[36]

As a result of this initial meeting he wrote elsewhere, "I decided to write him off. But I didn't. The basic idea of what he called "general semantics" stuck with me."[37]

What stuck with Rapoport seems hard to fathom, given his condescending attitude toward Korzybski. However, as Rapoport struggled away from the communism he still embraced in the mid-1940s, 'general semantics'—at least Hayakawa's version of it—probably served as a lifeline to a saner viewpoint and to somewhat more moderate views on science and values in human life. He eventually did express a number of useful things in doing so. But, like Bertrand Russell, he seemed most comfortable in the theoretical realm; when it came to practicing a 'scientific approach' in his own personal conduct—certainly in relation to Korzybski—Rapoport appeared quite remiss.

For their part, as reflected in correspondence, Korzybski and his colleagues remained unfailingly cordial and often complementary to Rapoport, even when later honestly confronting differences. They liked his early *ETC.* articles, in 1945 inviting him to lecture on one of them, "The Criterion of Predictability" at the Institute Holiday seminar—which he did. But although Korzybski invited him numerous times to attend a seminar, Rapoport stayed away. He never attended more than a few of Korzybski's lectures. He spent little personal time with Korzybski or any of the people from the Institute. Yet based on this limited experience, he felt comfortable—after Korzybski's death—alluding in public print to Korzybski's 'demagogic' personality, his incompetence as a teacher, and the 'cultism' of "Korzybski-ites", an unspecified group of people whose distinguishing mark may have amounted to the fact that they had more respect for Korzybski than he did.

In addition to the barely veiled personal attacks from the early 1950s on, Rapoport until the end of his life consistently pooh-poohed Korzybski's originality, the scientific status of his system, and its practical value. Korzybski's individual work with students seemed to him no better than the faith healing of primitive medicine men. He found Korzybski's terminology irritating. He saw the extensional devices and the structural differential as gimmicks. Of the latter he wrote in 1975, "I have always remained in the dark about the point of this demonstration."[38]

Whatever faint praise he gave, it seems clear from private letters that he came to find Korzybski insufferable. In 1956 he wrote to Russell Meyers [who most probably sent the letter to Kendig, since a copy of the letter got into Kendig's files]:

> We [Rapoport and others from the Society for General Semantics]...were able to stem the tide of contempt which kept pressing against g.s. prestige in academic circles. We knew this contempt was rooted in A.K's buffoonery and in his complete negation in his personal conduct of all the principles he preached. On the other hand, those of us who enjoyed the respect of honest scientific workers were sometimes successful in explaining why AK's vision was important and just what his peculiar contribution had been.[39]

As a man in his mid-sixties, Rapoport wrote in 1976: "Korzybski's lasting achievement consisted in pointing out the dangers of [a severely polluted semantic environment] at the time when its toxic effects were just becoming manifest."[40] In theory, Rapoport seemed to genuinely appreciate this. But for most of his life, he never appears to have questioned the toxic effects of his own public misrepresentations and downgrading of Korzybski and his work. (To Hayakawa's credit, he appears to have never descended to disparaging Korzybski in public print as Rapoport did.) In his autobiography published in 2000, Rapoport—approaching his nineties—admitted with hardly veiled irony that "I now take perhaps somewhat unjustified exception" to the view in academic circles of Korzybski as a crank.[41] Did it entirely escape him that his own decades-long denigration of Korzybski may have helped to promote that view?

Until the summer of 1946, Rapoport seems to have kept his misgivings about Korzybski to himself. But then, he confessed,

> ...When the Institute moved to Connecticut, there was no longer any necessity, dictated by decorum, for either Hayakawa or me to maintain personal contact with Korzybski, and we talked about him freely. Our talks were not centered on Korzybski's baffling excursions into neurophysiology (Hayakawa didn't give a damn about the colloidal level and things like that). We talked about the man himself...[42]

"Ahh," as Korzybski might have put it, "those 'sweet', 'sweet' human relations."

A Model Seminar-Workshop

Korzybski, who usually didn't give titles to his seminar lectures, called his first one on August 12, "SNAFU," Situation Normal — All Fouled Up (he considered this more 'polite form' "the more serious form, not the physiological one.") The term seemed to him "a supreme generalization of thousands of years of misculture" summarizing "the whole trend of our so-called civilization."*[43] Fortunately, the term did not sum up the seminar-workshop itself; it went far better than anyone could have reasonably expected. They had only known in mid-July—just one month before the start of the seminar—that it would not be held in Chicago, Denver, or New York but at the Indian Mountain School in Lakeville, Connecticut. Neither the extended workshop staff nor registered students had much time to adjust travel plans, yet this didn't seem to affect seminar attendance. The setting at the school proved ideal; the intensified interaction of staff and students learning, eating, and living together for several weeks encouraged a GS-permeated atmosphere—a model for subsequent seminar-workshops for many years to come.

1946 IGS Summer Seminar-Workshop group
at the Indian Mountain School, Lakeville, CT

---

* Ralph C. Hamilton, one of the seminar-workshop participants, noted what Korzybski said at the start, "When you look at this snafu, all you can do is laugh...To get all tragical and desperate about it is to get into dramatics and role-playing and conflicts. We can cope only by saying 'What is going on? How can we fix it?'" [Ralph C. Hamilton in letter to Bruce Kodish, 11/17/2005.]

The workshop lineup of lecturer/presenters seemed more than adequate in both quantity and quality: Douglas Kelley assisted Kendig with workshop administration and dazzled participants with his presentations on military 'mental' hygiene and rehabilitation, the Nuremburg Nazis, the nervous system, magic, and the Rorschach test; speech professor Wilbur Moore, once again demonstrating the psycho-galvanometer, presented his research showing how GS training decreased student's measurable signal reactions to words; Lou LaBrant of N.Y.U. spoke about her 'genetic approach to language'; Charles Glicksberg discussed his use of GS in high school and college English classes to teach creative writing; May Watrous Niles discussed her use of GS techniques to deal with the psycho-somatic side of physical therapy; Allen Walker Read presented the history of the word 'semantic(s)'; Ray Bontrager detailed his extensional analysis of reading difficulties ('Ninety-five percent of the teaching of reading' he said, 'concerns maps, minus territory.'); Captain Saunders lectured on his GS-derived system for evaluating national policy problems for the Senate Committee on Naval Affairs; plus a number of other presentations, panels, etc. Of course, Charlotte taught neuro-semantic relaxation in small groups; while Kendig did a workshop on writing, led group discussions, and administered the whole thing. Korzybski seemed in top form. Robert Redpath, having found the seminar location for the Institute, spent four days as a guest, attending three of Korzybski's lectures; he later wrote to a friend, "...Korzybski's teaching methods impressed me."[44]

Twenty-seven year-old Ralph C. Hamilton, who had taken a bus from his parent's home in Wooster, Ohio to attend the seminar-workshop, later recalled his first impressions of Korzybski and colleagues:

> Kendig knew how the program was supposed to proceed and was determined to see that it did. Charlotte, on the artistic side, [was] energetic [and] capable in administration... Korzybski surprised me. Not at all academic; vigorous; direct; pragmatic; focused on application; humorous; possessed of a vast background of experience and learning. His personality reminded me—and subsequent acquaintance strengthened the impression—of Winston Churchill.[45]

**Korzybski with Douglas M. Kelley, M.D.
at the 1946 Summer Seminar-Workshop**

Hamilton—born in Manila, the son of Presbyterian missionaries—had spent much of his early years overseas, coming back as a teenager to his hometown of Wooster, Ohio to attend the last two years of high school. Having already 'fallen from grace' by becoming agnostic at the age of 13, he majored in physics and mathematics at church-associated Wooster College. He graduated in 1941 just in time to enter the Army Signal Corps that October, serving in England and North Africa. In his last year of college, he had read *The Tyranny of Words*. "The notion that words and language shape our 'thinking' and don't necessarily correspond to 'facts' was a light turning on." The light stayed on during his time in the Army.

> When I got home...I bought a copy of *Science and Sanity* and dug in. More revelations. ... Came up bemused; dived in again and went through the book a second time. The next step was obvious, get in touch with IGS and go there for a seminar...What I got from the seminar was [a] deeper grasp of GS, especially in application, and hope for my own development. This was strengthened by my interview with AK at the end of the seminar. He analyzed my personality, gave suggestions of measures to take—by way of coming down from the fascinating heights of theory and grubbing about in day-to-day experience.[46]

Hamilton received no profound revelations about himself, but felt he had gotten something tremendously useful from Korzybski and company, and spent the next year in GS-related study, including writing an article on GS for John Campbell's *Astounding Science Fiction* (subsequently rejected). He would return for the 1947 seminar and then come to live at the Institute and work with Korzybski.

At this seminar, a number of new Institute staff members helped Kendig administer, including: Thomas Leonard, a student assistant who had just started working for the Institute a few months before (he would stay on for about a year); Elizabeth Kirkpatrick, Kendig's new assistant, a graduate of Earl English's GS-flavored School of Journalism at the University of Missiouri (she would leave early in the spring to get married); Hansell Baugh serving as seminar librarian, a professional librarian who had edited the *Papers from the First American Congress on General Semantics* (he would soon leave his job in Atlanta to work at the Institute where he stayed until mid-1948 taking care of the library, orders, registrations, general correspondence, mailing lists, etc.); and Guthrie E. Janssen, who flew in from Tokyo to attend the seminar.

In 1943 the Institute had begun getting cables from Egypt ordering dozens of copies of *Science and Sanity*. Letters soon followed from Janssen, a 1938 graduate of the University of Illinois, teaching English at the American University in Cairo. Janssen was teaching GS to third-year journalism and social science students with much enthusiastic response: one student, Anthony M. Economides, wrote a monograph entitled *A Non-Aristotelian Study of Philosophy* as his 1945 Bachelor of Arts project, eventually published in 1947 by the Institute. In 1944, Janssen began working for NBC (National Broadcasting Company) as a correspondent in Egypt, Greece, and the Far East (becoming one of the first foreign journalists to enter recently atom-bombed Hiroshima). He had corresponded with Kendig about plans to study with Korzybski.

During the seminar the plans gelled; he received the Straus Fellowship, which provided money for him to work for approximately a year at the Institute, starting September 2, although his fellowship soon nearly ended precipitously. On November 11, returning from a speaking engagement in Illinois, he was seriously injured in a plane crash near Cleveland, Ohio. Back at the Institute by March 1947, his main work involved preparing *Selections from Science and Sanity*, consulting closely with Korzybski who wrote in his *Author's Note*, "I personally am most grateful to Guthrie Janssen for his considerable painstaking work,..."

When Janssen completed his Fellowship at the end of September 1947, he worked on the staff of the Institute until April 1948 when he married another student of Korzybski, dermatologist Guila Beattie. As Korzybski often did with people he felt affection for, he gave them nicknames—'Jan' for Janssen and "the Beat" for her 'because she can't be beat'. The couple briefly lived in New York City, before moving back to Lime Rock and then Lakeville, where they remained in close touch with Korzybski and the people at the Institute (the couple named their son, born in November 1949, Alfred Guthrie Janssen).

A talented writer, Janssen wrote a number of significant GS-related pieces including: an important paper in 1949 on the political implications of time-binding (published in the *General Semantics Bulletin* in 1951); a moving memorial article after Korzybski's 1950 death; and two interesting books published later in 1950, *Basic Human Engineering Handbook* and *A Salesman's Handbook Course in Human Engineering*, both mainly based on Korzybski's work. Then, within a few years, Janssen disappeared completely from the GS scene with the last trace I found of him in the IGS archives, an August 1954 edition of *You: The Magazine for Everyone* edited by him. Despite its brevity, Janssen had a brilliant, productive GS-related career.

Lime Rock

In mid-September, done with the seminar-workshop and interviews, Korzybski, Kendig and two new Institute staffers moved to the Lime Rock Lodge in Lime Rock, a Northwestern Connecticut village too small to have a post office of its own, located about five miles east of Lakeville, the nearby 'big' town with a post office. Korzybski felt bereft without his desk, most of his books, papers, and records. Meanwhile, Charlotte had returned to Chicago with Guthrie Janssen to check up on the materials in storage, on the two Institute employees still working at the makeshift Chicago office, and on Mira. Then they loaded up the Institute's 1938 Ford with as many suitcases they could fit for the drive back to Connecticut. The question remained: where would the Institute go?

Even with no home for the Institute, expenses accumulating, and money getting low, Korzybski wasn't one to get morose. As usual he kept busy working. He had just finished his initial editing of an outstanding presentation on "General Semantics Utilized As An Auxiliary To Psychotherapy" for a forthcoming book on *Brief Psychotherapy: A Handbook for Physicians On The Clinical Aspects of Neuroses* sent to him by Bertrand S. Frohman, an internist/psychiatrist from Beverly Hills, California. Frohman had completed most of the book with his wife Evelyn when he encountered *Science and Sanity*. He later told Korzybski, "We relabeled the manuscript "incomplete", set it aside, and dug in for a period of study and application of General Semantics." This resulted in delaying publication until they had revised the entire book.[47] (It finally got published in early 1948.) Korzybski offered minor comments to tighten up the language; but what he read tremendously impressed him. Frohman, someone he had not personally met, had finally produced the book that Alfred for so long wanted to see from one of his psychiatrist students. Already extensionally oriented, as he said, by "instinct", Frohman had made himself one of Korzybski's most careful students.

Besides this, Korzybski was finishing up an article on "General Semantics" that the *Encyclopedia Britannica* had asked him to do for *Ten Eventful Years*, an upcoming 1947 supplement. *Nelson's Encyclopedia* (later renamed *The American People's Encyclopedia*) based in Chicago had also just invited him to submit an article; for starters he would send them what he had written for the *Britannica*. All of this interest in his work must have bolstered his mood, as the success of the seminar-workshop surely had done.

Within the first few weeks of October, the Institute had a new home. Kendig sold her mother's property in Pound Ridge, New York and bought the Barnum House, a run-down, 100 year old mansion on White Hollow Road across the creek from the Lime Rock Lodge. Built by a relative of circus showman P.T. Barnum, the large three-story house with attached garage had several acres of garden and grounds. It needed a great deal of work but would give Kendig a place to live and store her possessions, now scattered amongst a number of places, and would provide a home for the Institute—and for Alfred and Charlotte as well—until they could relocate closer to 'civilization'. Kendig would charge the Institute a nominal rent.

While awaiting remodeling to be done, they rented a small office across the street from the Lime Rock Lodge but did much of their work from their temporary living quarters at the Lodge, which had begun to feel very "small and inconvenient", as Korzybski wrote to Ken Keyes: "You can imagine the beauty of the situation, carrying the main work here in Lakeville, where we have to spread correspondence on beds and reorganize the whole thing every evening and morning, never being able to put our hands on anything."[48] They would move into the house in December. Within a year, they had transferred most of the files, records, inventory, library, private furniture, etc., from Chicago. Kendig also had to move antiques and furniture from her mother's place. Though the stay there was planned as only a temporary hiatus, the Institute remained in the old house in Lime Rock (with a Lakeville post office box) for 39 years.

The house's location had benefits but seemed far from ideal. They had no space in the house for giving seminars, although they did have the use of the Lime Rock Lodge, Indian Mountain School, or the numerous nearby private schools and inns as seminar venues—of course with the added inconvenience. New York City was fairly easy to reach 100 miles away. They were even closer to Hartford, New Haven, Poughkeepsie, etc., yet far enough from city life to make them feel at times more isolated than they would have liked. In the Litchfield Hills (part of the foothills of the Berkshire Mountains) overlooking Salmon Creek, the springtime and fall could seem beautiful, as could the winter with its new fallen snow. But the weather often became forbidding. Winters could get very cold, too cold to start the car, and sometimes socked them in with major blizzards: the snow too deep to drive through and, once melted, leaving the long driveway to the road a muddy impasse. Summers could get very hot and Korzybski noticed a peculiar dampness throughout much of the year, which he attributed to the low valley they lay in, and which he believed promoted the muscle cramps that sometimes kept him from sleeping.

New home of the Institute, December 1946—in the Lime Rock district of Lakeville, Salisbury Township, Litchfield County, Connecticut. Korzybski's office (✓) on second floor.

The old house itself, though adequate, also had its share of problems. Something always seemed to need maintenance or to break down, like the hot water tank that stopped working the following spring and had Charlotte dreaming of hot baths. The basement had room for files, cabinets, and the book/publication inventory but could get damp and even flood if the sump pump didn't work, so water damage remained a constant threat, with things more than once having to get moved out. The place in general could seem jam-packed with people and stuff. A large front room, alongside the first floor parlor off the front entry hall, got turned into the main office where Kendig, her secretary, and Hansell Baugh all had desks. Behind stood a room filled with clerical desks and files; a dining room actually occasionally used for dining; and at the back of the hall, a little closer to the stairs to the second floor, Charlotte's desk. (Kendig and Charlotte would have cherished the quiet and privacy of separate offices but there simply didn't exist any convenient place to spare for them.) In back, they had a large kitchen with a long center counter and behind this an attached garage. On the second floor, Kendig and Charlotte had front bedrooms across the hall from each other. Behind the stairs, Korzybski had his office, directly across from which, behind Charlotte's room, stood his bedroom with its own bath. Further back and across the hall from each other, two "Horror Rooms" were filled with Institute stuff that had nowhere else to get plunked, apparently in such quantity and disorder that people were later simply warned to stay out. In the rear of the second floor stood a separate hall bathroom and more storage, as well as the back stairs, utility spaces, etc. The third floor held the library, a small bedroom, a bathroom, and a couple of spare rooms for storage. Korzybski wrote to Mira the following year that although he and his housemates got along with each other, they all felt very crowded, working and living 'hanging on each others necks'.[49]

Korzybski didn't consider the move to Connecticut necessarily permanent. New York City or a similar more urban environment would suit the Institute better, if they could come to afford it. There was also the issue of Mira. He wouldn't have wanted her to stay in the Lime Rock house so close to Institute goings-on. And given her arthritis and general health, he didn't think the weather there would suit her. With the Institute in New York, they could get an apartment for her in the city where he could see her at least once a month and where she could have reasonable access to necessary medical care. In the meantime, Mira seemed reasonably comfortable in her Chicago apartment, with free medical care at Billings providing an added inducement for her to stay put. And in the meantime, Kendig's house would serve as his and the Institute's home. (Some hope of moving revived in 1949, with a potential buyer for the house, but this ultimately didn't work out.) Over the next few years, traveling for both Alfred and Mira became more difficult and although they stayed in close contact by letter, supplemented occasionally by telephone calls (not so good for Alfred because of his deafness), they would only see each other a few more times before he died. One might note with irony, even a tinge of sadness, that the couple—now reconciled with each other—were forced by circumstances to live so far apart. The old house in Lime Rock would become Korzybski's final home.

Chapter 61
"I DON'T CARE A DAMN ABOUT THOSE YAHOOS..."

Gulliver's Travels, Jonathan Swift's book for 'children and philosophers', remained one of Korzybski's favorites. "This little book", he had written early in 1946, "is old but today more alive than ever."[1] Having spent a lifetime wrestling with human folly in many forms, Korzybski seemed particularly taken by the book's depiction of the yahoos—greedy, short-sighted man-creatures used by Swift to represent humans, capable of 'reason' but far from behaving 'reasonably'. By the end of 1946 and start of 1947, the continued yahoo-like behavior of some of the leadership of the Society for General Semantics, crossed a threshold he could no longer discount nor delay confronting.

Antics With 'Semantics'

First, at the beginning of November, he, Charlotte and Kendig received what they all considered an outrageous mailing from the Society for General Semantics office, dated November 1. This included a new proposed Society Constitution and By-laws, which the Governing Board of the Society wanted members to approve or disapprove, sending in their ballots by November 15. The new by-laws, just approved by the Society Board, made only one mention of the Institute: "Article VII, Relationship to The Institute of General Semantics" stated "Financial contributions from Society funds shall be made to the Institute of General Semantics by two-thirds vote of the Governing Board." This provision would mark a significant formal change in the relationship between the Institute and the Society and between the Institute and Society members, many of whom had joined the Society because they wanted to support Korzybski and the Institute. How could a regular voting member of the Society (basically anyone who had paid dues) be expected to necessarily know enough to make an informed vote on the proposed re-structuring, without a copy of the pre-existing constitution and by-laws, and in such little time?

This bad news wasn't completely surprising given the previous lack of responsiveness of Society leadership to efforts to improve coordination between the two organizations. Wendell Johnson, the President of the Society, had not informed Korzybski that this was in the works. As an added irritant, the brief time frame for voting gave Alfred, Charlotte, and Kendig very little chance to do anything that could have a palpable effect on the outcome of what they considered a very problematic vote.

On November 15, Korzybski, Charlotte and Kendig—as voting members of the Society—all X'd in their ballots at the line that said, "I disapprove the Constitution and By-Laws as submitted November 1, 1946." Korzybski sent a protest telegram, and Charlotte and Kendig sent separate protests with their ballots, to the Society Board of Directors. None of them pulled any punches, as indicated by this paragraph from Kendig's lengthy response:

> I disapprove your methods of securing approval on two counts: Asking for a vote without documenting the content and intent of the proposed changes violates accepted parliamentary practice. More important, by 'putting it over' on the membership you violate the democratic spirit you profess—now and since the beginning—in running this membership association. The suppression of history by the 'democratic and responsible leadership' postulated distorts evaluations and rigs a 'yes' vote in good fascistic style.[2]

This surely must have stung Wendell Johnson when he read it. As President, he had presided over what had and hadn't happened. To some extent, he did later acknowledge the problems that the Society reorganization posed for the Institute in his Editorial "Report of the Retiring President of the Society for General Semantics", in the Spring 1947 Volume of *ETC*. But as far as the Institute was concerned, the damage had already been done. The new Society Constitution and By-laws overwhelmingly passed, just as Kendig had suggested it would, by a vote of 271 to 13. The Institute, in tenuous financial shape, was clearly going to have to restructure itself in order to survive. Still, Korzybski and his colleagues hoped the two organizations could find some way to cooperate more in the future "in setting up a mechanism of intercommunication, for consideration and evaluation of plans, policies and pronouncements before taking action."[3] As Kendig had pointed out in her protest letter, "In the wider public relations aspects of the general semantics movement, the Institute and the Society are not and can not be separated in the 'public mind'—identified as they are by the use of the term general semantics."[4]

Unfortunately, in the short run, Korzybski would soon feel the need to protest to the Society again—this time about the Society's public representations of 'general semantics'. Korzybski probably received the circular announcing the Society's 1947 Chicago lecture series sometime at the beginning of January 1947, as he was finishing up his Holiday seminar. He had nothing to say about the six publicized lectures, planned from January 31 until April 4, which looked like an interesting mix of speakers and topics: Thurman Arnold on "Symbol and Reality in Public Affairs", Wendell Johnson on "How to Become What We Might Have Been", Irving Lee on "It's Not Fun To Be Fooled", S.I. Hayakawa on "The Semantics of Modern Art", Anatol Rapoport on "Music and the Process of Abstraction", and Hugh and Lillian Lieber on "The New Realism in Art and Science". But Korzybski could not abide the way the circular depicted his work. Perhaps the most egregious distortion for him was in a boxed insert with the following text, that he considered a 'masterpiece' of confusion:

> **Semantics**...The study of how people act, with and under the influence of words and other symbols.
> **General Semantics**...A system for applying the findings of semantics to every-day life.[5]

These 'definitions', following the viewpoint Hayakawa had pushed for some time in *ETC.*, now permeated the Society's public portrayal of Korzybski's work. Korzybski had had enough. The circular grossly and glibly misrepresented both the origin and scope of his formulations. He had certainly *not* based his work on the findings of any kind of 'semantics' commonly understood in relation to language and 'meaning'. As he told Karl Poehlmann at the start of the year,

> If I would have investigated language, 'thinking', I would have written a perfectly rotten book on 'psychology'. ...The secret of my work is that I did not investigate 'thinking' or 'speaking'. I investigated time-binding.[6]

Certainly words and symbols had importance in this investigation, but as he later pointed out to Ken Keyes, "...we humans are human just because we can intercommunicate somehow, not only linguistically, and the future generations can benefit by the experience of the past generation."[7] *Not only linguistically.* He repeated some version of this point in published writings, private letters, conversations, lectures, etc.; describing GS as a theory of *evaluation* "dealing with the inner life of the individual, on the silent levels."[8]

He felt he had some justification asking Hayakawa and others to stop promoting the confusion of 'general semantics' with 'semantics'. His requests didn't seem to matter. His choice of terminology in 1931, using 'semantic' as a synonym for 'evaluational' and 'general semantics' as the overarching name for his system, had now come back to haunt him.

In some distress, he spent at least a month working on a protest letter "To the Editor of ETC.", carefully choosing each word about both the offending circular and his accumulated backlog of objections to ETC. editorial policy.[9] He also referred to the Society's uncooperative attitude in relation to the Institute, and the Society's preemption of Institute functions without consulting him. So as to not appear as if he condoned serious distortions of his work, he also resigned as "Consulting Editor" of ETC., as did Kendig. He sent the letter in March, requesting that Hayakawa publish it in the next issue of the journal. Soon afterward, something else added fuel to Korzybski's ire: a copy of a recently written article by Hayakawa distributed by the Society. The *Encyclopedia Britannica* had rejected as too technical Korzybski's article on general semantics for their volume *Ten Eventful Years*. They eventually contacted Hayakawa who produced a piece "Semantics, General Semantics"—as usual not notifying or consulting with Korzybski, and as usual presenting 'general semantics' as a system of 'semantics', albeit in a category all its own as "the most ambitious and most controversial,...of all the systems of semantics." Hayakawa published his Britannica piece as the lead article in the Spring 1947 issue of ETC. Korzybski was not happy.[10]

His protest letter never got published in ETC. In the 1990s, it did become public as Appendix V (5), in *Alfred Korzybski Collected Writings*, along with other documents pertaining to the difficulties between the Institute and Society. In 1947, only a few individuals saw Korzybski's letter, mainly trustees of the Institute and the leadership of the Society, which included Hayakawa and Rapoport. Wendell Johnson, as indicated by his subsequent editorial as the Society's retiring President; Irving Lee, who became the Society President that summer; and Francis Chisholm, an Associate Editor of ETC., all sought to make peace with Korzybski. But appearing to defer to Hayakawa, more and more the dominant influence in the Society, the three men didn't seem to fully get what bothered Korzybski. The issue boiled down to the integrity of his work and how it would get represented by those presumed by the public to know it. In July, Guthrie Janssen wrote to W. Benton Harrison,

...[M]any seem to feel AK's reactions are based on some sort of personal pique against Hayakawa. Well, it just isn't so. And that's categorical. From what I have heard I am sure AK feels that with Hayakawa writing articles like this [the Britannica piece] his establishment as an 'authority' on GS will retard the advancement of the discipline for God knows how many years."[11]

As both Hayakawa and Rapoport later indicated, they seemed to consider Korzybski the main obstacle to the advancement of GS. But Korzybski's desire to maintain standards in the presentation and development of his work didn't mean he wanted unquestioning obedience to him as the ultimate authority, as the two men would at times insinuate. Ralph Hamilton would later observe,

Now and then someone would say "I agree with you," or the Montessori method of teaching, or Einstein's relativity, or whatever. And AK would say, with a dismissive wave of the hand, "Agree—not agree; that doesn't matter. Observe; study the facts, and maybe you can make a new formulation, or verify an old one; and others can <u>verify</u> your work." Sometimes the notion of doing original work on one's own rather flummoxed the agree-er."[12]

When Korzybski found a student doing original work that also represented his own work accurately, it delighted him. Harry Weinberg had returned to the Institute to attend Korzybski's Holiday Seminar and had given a lecture there on the topic of a paper he wrote while on shipboard during his wartime Merchant Marine duty. Korzybski reviewed the paper, later published in the Spring 1947 *ETC.*, and referred to it when he wrote this recommendation for Weinberg in April:

> I consider Harry L. Weinberg one of the most gifted students I have had, with exceptional creative capacities and outstanding potentialities as a high-grade teacher . . . In his recent paper on General Semantics, 'Some Functional Patterns on the Non-verbal Level', . . he actually made some original contributions to my work. . . I can recommend him highly as an expounder of General Semantics and [modern] scientific method.[13]

Members of The Institute

The Society, having officially cut loose from its former responsibilities to the Institute, now unfortunately seemed in competition with it for people's attention and money. As Korzybski wrote in his March "Protest" letter,

> ...today I am afraid to promote the Society or <u>ETC.</u>, lest those who are interested in my work become monopolized, not only financially, but with harmful, incompetent dilutions of the discipline which amount to misinformations and misrepresentations of its fundamentals by <u>commission or omission</u>.[14]

Perhaps the Institute and Society could work out ways of coordinating their separate functions. Perhaps even Hayakawa and others in his camp could come around in their treatment of him and his work—at least insofar as to take his input into account before publishing definitive articles on 'general semantics'. But in the meantime, the Institute seemed in immediate financial peril—again. Both Korzybski and Kendig had stopped drawing their salaries and Kendig was spending her own money, as she put it "like a drunken sailor", in order to get the house and property in shape.[15] Later in the year, Korzybski got upset when he found out Charlotte had stopped cashing her salary checks.[16]

In spite of the difficulties, moving to Connecticut had also opened up new possibilities. A group of people outside of Chicago (many but not all in the New York City area), felt sympathetic to Korzybski in his problems with the Society and had an interest in contributing to the Institute's survival and development. At a Trustees meeting at the end of 1946, Douglas Kelley was appointed the fourth Fellow of the Institute on the basis of his work using GS in wartime psychiatry (the three existing Fellows, including Hayakawa, still had to approve of him). Kelley, beginning a teaching stint at the Bowman Gray Medical School Psychiatry Department, also was appointed Institute Director of Research (his work in this area didn't end up amounting to much) and with two other men, John Jacobs from Denver and Bob Redpath, was voted in as a Trustee of the Institute.

At the 1947 Annual Meeting of the Institute Trustees in May, the existing Board changed the By-laws of the Institute to allow for a total of sixteen Trustees and voted in eight additional members including: three from the New York City area—W. Benton Harrison; Marian Tyler Chase, the wife of Stuart Chase; and Marion Harper of the McCann-Erickson Advertising Agency—as well as Irving Lee and Wendell Johnson, both of whom were somewhat sympathetic to Korzybski's concerns despite their involvement with Hayakawa and the Society; Elwood Murray; Delaware Supreme Court Judge George B. Pearson; and Captain James Saunders. Given the existing situation with Hayakawa, the IGS Board also changed its

By-laws so new Institute Fellows no longer had to be confirmed by a unanimous vote of existing Fellows. Four new Institute Fellows—Ray Bontrager, Francis Chisholm, Elwood Murray, and Allen Walker Read—were appointed by Korzybski and Kendig and confirmed by the Trustees at the May meeting. While the initial group of Fellows had been chosen in 1941 for their publication of GS articles and books, the emphasis now was on Fellows who had shown exemplary competence in teaching and writing with the kind of rigor Korzybski had come to prize and who had demonstrated their interest in serving the Institute.

The Institute now had the personnel. It had a general plan to make clear its role as the world center of authority and training in Korzybski's non-aristotelian extensional discipline. Now, what about funding?

At the next Trustees meeting in July, a finance committee was appointed to develop a membership/fundraising plan, and in August the committee approved materials and prepared for an all-out membership drive. Kendig and others had no illusions that this could substitute for other kinds of fundraising, but they hoped the membership drive would make a significant dent in their immediate need for money. Guthrie Janssen, whose Korzybski Fellowship was coming to an end, agreed to stay on as an Institute employee to administer the membership campaign. Membership benefits would include tuition and book discounts, a newsletter, special mailings of Korzybski's and others' writings unavailable elsewhere (Korzybski would no longer submit his writings to *ETC.*), and a "General Semantics Yearbook" that they intended to get into publication. Along with an information sheet and a reply card, the initial membership invitation letter signed by Bob Redpath went out to the Institute mailing list in August, leading to immediate good results, and also fomenting a minor crisis, as a result of the following passage:

> Note we are offering you membership in the Institute of General Semantics, not the Society. When the Institute was incorporated its original by-laws provided for a membership structure. This was not acted upon because in 1942 the Society was formed 'to secure financial support and wider recognition for the Institute'. Last winter in adopting a new constitution the Society abandoned this aim and formal connections with the Institute. This means that to keep in touch with Korzybski's work and support it you should become a member of the Institute. We feel sure you will want to. Because of a severe drain on money reserves in the past year occasioned by having to move from Chicago the Institute badly needs your help NOW to keep going while we put long term programs into effect. The membership plan makes it easy for you to help.[17]

By October, 300 people had become members, contributing a total of $6000. New members received a special mailing, a copy of Korzybski's unpublished *Britannica* article, "General Semantics: An Introduction To Non-Aristotelian Systems"along with a personally signed letter from Korzybski, dated August 1947, which read in part:

> Dear Students and Friends:...
>
> 'Young birds,' wrote Tolstoy, '...know very well when there is no longer room for them in the eggs', nor '...can the fledgling be made to re-enter its shell.' It often happens that the beak of the little bird is too soft or the shell is too hard, and the result is a rotten egg, utilized sometimes in political debates.
>
> ...Our human shell of habits and prejudices is very hard and our old aristotelian beaks are not strong enough for us to emerge to mature and fuller life. In my work I tried to forge a method to break through the confining shell, but one man's effort is not enough. My co-workers and I need your help, now.

We live in a period of socio-cultural spasms, and we as individuals must unite in a concerted effort toward more maturity, to bring about the eventual 'manhood of humanity'.[18]

Until the first issue, in 1950, of the promised IGS yearbook, the *General Semantics Bulletin*, the Institute sent a series of at least 12 special mailings to members consisting of articles by Korzybski and others not available in *ETC*. Over the next few years, the membership program would account for about 25% of the Institute's income. With few other major contributions, this and other income wasn't enough to allow them to begin the training program Kendig had envisioned and to free Korzybski as they had wished, but it did allow the Institute to keep going.

The aforementioned minor crisis had to do with Irving Lee, now an Institute Trustee, who had also just gotten elected as President of the Society. Lee did not approve of the invitation letter, feeling that it misrepresented the facts of the relation between the Institute and the Society and would lead to conflict. He and Francis Chisholm, representing the Society, met on August 31 with the Institute representives: Bontrager, Kendig, and Robin Skynner (a British medical student who had just attended Korzybski's summer seminar and would later become a well-known psychiatrist). The five of them hashed and thrashed out the Institute's main difficulties with the Society, but the meeting seemed curiously unproductive. (Bontrager wrote a memorandum for Korzybski later published in *Collected Writings*.) Lee appeared conflicted—more or less defensive about Hayakawa's actions and editing as well as Society decisions that the Institute had found problematic. He suggested he might resign from the Institute Board. Kendig said she would regret that and Lee ultimately didn't do it. Otherwise the meeting ended with nothing solid, only a general sense of commitment among those attending about the need to reconcile the two organizations.[19] Lee and Chisholm pushed through a resolution at a November Society Board meeting to "earnestly request" that Korzybski withdraw his resignation as Consulting Editor of *ETC*. Lee, as Society President, officially wrote to him with this request, and Korzybski—although the 'injured party'—agreed to continue having his name listed in *ETC*., where it remained until his death (although he would no longer offer anything for publication there).[20] The Society became more careful in its discussion of general semantics in subsequent circulars. And attempts at reconciliation from both sides would continue over the next two years.

Hayakawa seemed unmoved by any of this. It didn't seem to matter to him what the Institute did or didn't do. Korzybski's complaints seem likely to have constituted for him (and Rapoport) more evidence of authoritarianism. One might expect Hayakawa, who had written about the ethics of time-binding, to at least acknowledge the lapse on his part for not consulting with Korzybski before having the *Britannica* article published. I've seen no evidence he did so. In the Autumn 1947 edition of *ETC*., he *did* print a long, civil but critical letter to the editor by Guthrie Janssen that critiqued the content of the article in some detail. But Hayakawa's headline for Janssen's letter, "Hayakawa's Article Censured", doesn't seem accurate, while striking a resentful, censorious tone of its own. Hayakawa's subsequent behavior on and off the pages of *ETC*. doesn't indicate that he ever took seriously Janssen's (and Korzybski's) concerns, persisting in his private view of Korzybski as an embarrassment to academically respectable 'semanticists' like himself, continuing in his public treatment of Korzybski's work as an extension, however brilliant, of linguistic semantics.

"The Most Appalling Scandal of the Year"

Academics overly interested in conventional respectability would probably not find Korzybski easy to take. He had plenty of idiosyncrasies to sneer at, from his blunt manner of speech, to the khaki clothes he favored, to the rolls of toilet paper he unashamedly kept on his desk for nose blowing. Other things made him easily misunderstood, like his profound hearing loss, which made conversations with him difficult. Since he had only a degree in engineering, those inclined to do so could easily mistake his remarkable erudition in dozens of subjects as bogus, the profundity of his aims and broad scope of his concerns as arrogance, his claim to have formulated the first—as far as he knew—non-aristotelian *system* as ridiculous, and his claim to have developed a practical methodology that could help one understand and ameliorate "the quarrels between two lovers, two mathematicians, two nations, two economic systems., [etc.,]..."[21] as absurd. Careless interpretations of his lectures or writings might easily follow, confusing his taking of all human knowledge as "within his scope"—certainly legitimate for a worker in epistemology—with "taking all knowledge as within his competence," which he never pretended.[22] Korzybski often said, "I say what I say. I do *not* say what I do not say." He would also repeat that he 'offered no panaceas' but many people still came to the conclusion of one seminar student who commented, "You seem to say that every human problem can be solved by general semantics." Korzybski replied "Every thing I say is limited, limited, limited!"—a statement (or something like it) he repeated often.[23]

By 1947, one could clearly see the divide about Korzybski among academics, exemplified by varying reactions to a spring seminar he taught at Adams House, Harvard University from May 30 to June 7, sponsored by The Boston Society for General Semantics and the Semantics Workshops Associates, a GS-based, Boston consulting group. On the one hand, a number of faculty from Harvard and other universities who felt favorably inclined towards Korzybski's work signed on as honorary sponsors, including: John B. Fox, Assistant Dean; F. J. Roethlisberger of the Business School; Ernest Hooton and Clyde Kluckhohn of the Department of Anthropology; Norman T. Newton, Professor of Landscape Architecture; Roscoe Pound, University Professor; Arthur Stone Dewing, Emeritus Professor of Finance; Joseph G. Brin, Professor of Speech Correction and Edward A. Post, Professor of English, both of Boston University; Dr. William Healy, Emeritus Director of the Judge Baker Guidance Center; Porter Sargent, Educational Advisor; and Professor Emeritus Alfred D. Sheffield of Wellesley College. Forty-two people registered for the seminar, about half of them Harvard students, graduates, or faculty. Among the rest, students or faculty from MIT, Boston University, Andover-Newton Theological School, and Radcliffe also attended. Two Harvard Assistant Deans, J. L. Rollins and John B. Fox, who had attended a seminar with Korzybski in 1939, hosted a supper for him at the Harvard Faculty Club before his evening lecture on June 5. Obviously, if the Boston-area can be taken as typical of other places, Korzybski didn't lack serious academic support

On the other hand, there were also people at Harvard like philosopher/logician Willard Quine. On a conscious level, Quine seemed to have gained nothing from his seminar with Korzybski except contempt. On May 2, he ended a long letter to Rudolf Carnap with this comment:

> ...In closing let me try to be the first to pass along to you the most appalling scandal of the year. For a week at the end of this month Korzybski is to lecture at Harvard, in Harvard. The senior common room of Adams House will be his temple. He will put on his regulation 40-hour show.
> With best regards...[24]

The opinions of influential academics like Quine, however few, undoubtedly would shape how others viewed Korzybski. Korzybski, who eventually got wise to the extent of Quine's hostility, didn't seem to care—much. How much did it pay to worry about the yahoos?

"I Have Done My Job"

Alfred did worry about Mira, who at the start of 1947 had begun having problems with arthritis again. He and Charlotte—who had begun addressing her letters to Mira "Dear Edgy" instead of "Dear Countess"— stayed in touch mainly by letter and telegram. Pearl Johnecheck Scofield, still in Chicago, would see Mira when she could and also wrote to Alfred. In July, he heard from Pearl, now a mother, that she and her husband and son planned to move to Tucson, Arizona at the end of the year (largely because of Pearl's health). Devoted to Mira, Pearl wanted to take her with them since Mira seemed to her rather isolated, unhappy, and now unsafe on her own. The weather in Arizona might also ameliorate her arthritis problems. They would need money from Alfred to build a small cottage for her near the house on the ranch property to which they planned to move. Alfred didn't consider this a good move for Mira for a number of reasons, not least of which the cost—around $7000—more than they could afford. Mira seemed eager to go. He told her to hold off on making any decision about moving until he came to Chicago, which he planned to do after the August seminar (he ended up coming with Charlotte in November). When Pearl did move, Mira didn't.

Later in the year, he and Charlotte contacted Evelyn Garlick, who had done secretarial work for them at the Institute in Chicago. They asked Evelyn and her husband to keep tabs on Mira. In addition, the janitor of Mira's building and his wife helped her with shopping and checked up on her frequently. And she was getting taken care of by some new doctors at Billings Hospital, who seemed to be doing a conscientious job. Regarding her problems, Mira seemed as stoic as Alfred did about his. She kept busy, reading a great deal and sending him books, newspaper articles, cartoons, etc., that she thought he might find useful. She also provided a sympathetic ear to him, as one of the few people in the world to whom he could vent his feelings. He wrote to her in August, expressing what was not an isolated sentiment:

> ...I know you 'love' mankind and this can not be helped. Personally I don't care a damn about those yahoos and in many ways I am sick of them. Do not forget I am a world war veteran and the originator of my work. I have done my job, let others carry on if they want to. In my two books I gave all the credit to you, and privately, between you and me, I did my work and carried on uniquely because I want you independent and being taken care of.[25]

About his own health, he let Mira know that he felt in not-too-bad condition. He did have his aches and pains, his muscle cramps, his g...d... hernia, his heart 'misbehaving' if he exerted himself too much, his various cold 'bugs' when he got run down from fatigue. Still, he considered himself healthy enough, with some possibility for creative work left, if he didn't have to squander his time struggling to keep the Institute afloat. Mira sent him encouraging notes—whatever value his work had for advancing civilization (and she believed it had considerable value), the eventual 'manhood of humanity' didn't seem likely until long after her and Alfred's coagulations. Alfred agreed with her. He seemed quite aware of his own mortality. He noted to Ken Keyes in early July, "People die like hell at my age" [and younger and older acquaintances and friends too].[26] The deaths of Kurt Lewin and Cassius Keyser may have served as additional reminders that he needed to get on with his work while he still could.

Lewin had unexpectedly coagulated on February 12, at the age of 56. Alfred read about it in *The New York Times* and considered it, "a real loss, as he was very creative."[27] The two met in person at least once and carried on a cordial correspondence over several years. While writing *Science and Sanity*, Korzybski had despaired about the scientific state of 'psychology'. When Lewin's *Principles of Topological Psychology* came out in 1936, Korzybski began recommending it to his students, seeing it—whatever its faults—as a pioneering non-aristotelian effort. By 1947, Lewin's ongoing research served as one of the main factors convincing Korzybski that an adequate science of human behavior had indeed begun to develop.

Perhaps Lewin in turn had begun to see the relevance of GS to social psychology. He had used an illustration from *Science and Sanity* in one of his papers,[28] had responded to Korzybski's request for examples of over/under-defined terms for the "Introduction to the Second Edition" of *S&S*, and had agreed to serve on the organizing committee of the 1941 GS Congress in Denver. Lewin probably learned more about Korzybski and his work while at the University of Iowa, where he carpooled with Wendell Johnson. Lately, as Director of MIT's new Research Center for Group Dynamics, Lewin had been involved with the Office of Naval Research and just a few days before his death sat beside Korzybski's student who worked there, Navy Captain Karl F. Poehlmann, at a meeting of the Navy Advisory Panel on Human Relations.

Whatever lost possibilities Lewin's death represented, Korzybski and others at the Institute would retain a deep interest in his work. In the next few years, Kendig would attend workshops at the National Training Laboratory (NTL) set up by some of Lewin's students in Bethel, Maine and would introduce the NTL "T-Group" method of group discussion at the Institute seminar-workshops. When the first posthumous selection of Lewin's papers, *Resolving Social Conflicts*, came out in 1948, Korzybski grabbed it up, studied it carefully, and made notes for a review in which he planned to deal with an important topic of the book, a topic he had long wanted to write about—Jews and antisemitism. Korzybski never managed to get the review in shape to publish, but he did put the Lewin volume on a short list of books he recommended and that the Institute sold.

On May 8, another death occurred with undoubtedly much greater significance for Alfred. His friend and mentor, the 'dear dear old man' Cassius Keyser died just a week short of his 85th birthday. Over the last few years, the two had only occasional contact by mail and had last seen each other at one of Alfred's lectures for *Scripta Mathematica*. Elton Carter, a student of Irving Lee and of Korzybski (at the 1949 summer seminar-workshop), wrote his 1950 doctoral dissertation on Keyser, and many subsequent articles relating Keyser's work to that of Korzybski. In one such article, Carter noted the "fundamental similarities... between Keyser's and Korzybski's <u>Gedankenwelts</u>"('thought' worlds)[29] and their common concern for the humanistic aspects of science and mathematics in the pursuit of human excellence, which Korzybski had devoted himself to turning into a practical methodology for living. Of all the mathematicians/scientists whom Korzybski personally knew, Keyser more than any other served as his best friend, greatest influence, most enthusiastic supporter, and ablest critic. As a tribute to his friend, in the upcoming Second Edition of *Manhood of Humanity*, Korzybski planned to add Keyser's Chapter XX on time-binding from *Mathematical Philosophy* to the book's appended material and to express more explicitly than he had before his indebtedness to Keyser for the mathematician's help in the book's editing.[30]

Looking Back

Korzybski had begun to look back over his life and work. Recent events had likely stirred reminiscence: the Institute's abrupt and traumatic move to Lime Rock after its years in Chicago; his concerns over the Society, the fate of the Institute, and misinterpretations of his work; Mira's ill health and his own aches and pains and increasing age; and the recent deaths of friends. He had other reasons too for looking back. *Manhood of Humanity*, long out of print, had sat on the to-do list for several years. Mira had long stressed to him the significance of time-binding and, perhaps as a result of this, he had begun to more strongly reconnect to the importance of his earlier formulation as the foundation of everything he had done since 1921. The two encyclopedia articles he had written, as well as Guthrie Janssen's work on *Selections from Science and Sanity*, which involved conferences between the two men, had also forced Alfred to review and reassess his lifework starting with *Manhood*. Now he, Kendig, and Charlotte had begun to plan for a Second Edition, for which he still had to write a new introduction. But work on *Manhood* would have to wait.

Over the last year, the rate of sales of *Science and Sanity* had zoomed, and by the end of April 1947, the supply of the Second Edition was nearly exhausted.[31] Back orders would soon start to accumulate at the Institute (now that Science Press was going out of business as a distributor, the Institute had taken over that role). Enough had happened since 1941, over the last few years in particular, to justify putting out a Third Edition with a new Preface. That now topped his writing list. Although he could spit out something fairly quickly, getting it into publishable shape involved a much slower process for Korzybski. Completing the Preface, now gestating, couldn't wait too long if he wanted to get *S&S* back in print anytime soon. But it too would have to wait a little longer since he had gotten very busy by mid-year.

Korzybski had decided to go to Georgia to visit Ken and Roberta Keyes during the period between the early June ending of the Harvard intensive seminar and the August 16 start of the seminar-workshop. Although the Keyeses had abandoned their previous plans for a GS-based foundation and school, Ken had gotten interested in writing Korzybski's biography and had been bugging Alfred for months to come down to record his memoirs. Korzybski, although somewhat reluctant, finally agreed to go. As he wrote to Vocha Fiske just before the trip,

> Dear DD:
> Too rushed to write. It is about midnight and Charlotte and I have to leave in the morning for Warm Springs to visit Keyes, and of all things to work day & night on my g-d biography. I am so damned sick of myself, and to have to shout into a transcriber is a poor sense of vacation to me, but the bosses (Charlotte & Kendig) 'decreed' and so poor me has to obey.[32]

On June 24, Guthrie Janssen drove him and Charlotte to New York City to catch the Atlanta train. In Atlanta Ken and Roberta met the two and drove them to Warm Springs where the Keyeses now lived. Ken, severely stricken with polio early in 1946, seemed indomitable. Although his legs were completely paralyzed and his arms showed only a flicker of activity, he was now up and about in a wheelchair. He and Roberta had moved to Warm Springs with their two children, buying a house a couple of blocks from the famous Warm Springs Foundation where Ken was receiving therapy.

With the Keyeses paying for Alfred's and Charlotte's trip and rooms at the Warm Springs Hotel, Alfred spent the next two weeks recounting his life into Ken's Audograph recorder, filling up 36 acetate discs. Ken also recorded Korzybski's "Historical Note on the Structural Differential", took photographs of Alfred, and movies of him and Charlotte. Roberta Rymer

Keyes' transcription of the recorded biographical material amounted to 499 typed pages, taking her close to 300 hours to do.[33] Without question, Ken Keyes, Jr. had a deep interest in GS. Over the next two years, he wrote a popular book based on some of Korzybski's methods, *How to Develop Your Thinking Ability*, published by McGraw-Hill in 1950. Over the next five decades, he wrote a number of other books on nutrition, futurism, and personal development. "I never got around to writing the biography, though", he confessed in his own 1989 autobiography.[34] He eventually lost the biographical recordings, but Roberta's transcription, an invaluable account of otherwise undocumented aspects of Korzybski's life (especially from its first half in Europe), became a valuable source for this book.

Alfred's 68th Birthday with the Keyses

On July 9, Korzybski and Charlotte hurriedly packed to leave Warm Springs with Ken and Roberta, who drove them to Atlanta for a jarring train ride back to New York City. Before returning to Lime Rock, they stayed for about a week in Greenwich Village near Washington Square Park at the genteel, though somewhat rundown, old Albert Hotel (both Robert Louis Stevenson and Thomas Wolfe had once stayed there). Exhausted from the trip, they could "hibernate" at the Albert while Alfred got a new eyeglass prescription filled, his dentures refitted, and tried to finish the "Preface To The Third Edition". Although she appreciated some aspects of country living, Charlotte definitely felt the advantages of life in New York City, with its many delicatessens, restaurants, shops, museums, plays, etc., all within a short walk or ride by taxi, bus, or subway. Korzybski appreciated being away from the many distractions of the Institute house in Lime Rock; he could just concentrate on writing.[35] Over the next two years, he would return to New York City with Charlotte, now his amanuensis and chief editor, for a number of extended stays to write.

As soon as they returned to Lime Rock and unpacked, Alfred and Charlotte had to get ready for the summer seminar-workshop to be held again at the Indian Mountain School starting August 16. Despite counting as Alfred's 57th seminar since the founding of the Institute, he still had to prepare—making notes to himself before his presentations, having his assigned student-assistant take notes during the presentation, and reviewing these with the student after the lecture. The assistant could also remind him when he 'got lost in a footnote' and needed a cue for where he had left off in the main body of his talk. Despite the reappearance of much material from one seminar to the next, he continued reshuffling it, as well as adding new formulations (e.g, chain indexing within the last couple of years), demonstrations (he may have started doing the 'Atomic Mousetrap' demo this year to illustrate exponential functions), and stories and examples from the news, his reading, etc. He would note important books for students to read; this year he recommended Philip Frank's newly published biography, *Einstein: His Life and Times*, which he considered beautifully written and important for understanding his own work.

The stories Korzybski told—not to entertain, he would emphasize, but to make a point—might offend some people. By this time, he had begun telling the following one from the March 1947 *Reader's Digest*. Some white African planters suddenly faced a strike by their native workers. When the planters asked the leaders to explain the reason for the strike, the leaders said they were doing it because the planters ate Negroes. The astonished planters vehemently denied it and called for their native cook to clear up the mess. As Korzybski would tell it:

'Did you ever cook a Negro for me?' one planter asked. 'Of course I did,' replied the cook. 'What? How did you serve it? Fried, or boiled, or what?' The cook answered, 'Oh, they were chopped to pieces.' And the planters, who had ordered the pancake mix picturing 'Aunt Jemima' on the box, could not persuade the workers that they didn't eat Negroes.[36]

After all, didn't the cans and boxes of food from America always come with a picture of the contents inside? Alfred began to use the story in his lectures, not to show the foolishness of African natives compared to other ' more enlightened' people, but as a particularly stark example of identification, to which everyone seemed prone—whether in such gross or in more subtle forms. (Korzybski subscribed to Harry Stack Sullivan's dictum: "We are all more human than otherwise.")

One would hardly know that the Institute had gotten to its lowest financial ebb from the appearance of the people-packed seminar. A number of previously attending students had returned, including Ralph Hamilton, whom Korzybski asked to work at the Institute after the seminar ended on September 5: 'Go home, arrange your affairs and come back to IGS to work as an unpaid 'dogs body' [to get room and board, living at the Institute]; You will get the benefit.' Ralph went home to Ohio, bought a car, packed some belongings, and drove back to the Institute to start working there that month.[37]

Nineteen-year old Texan, Delphus David Bourland, Jr., now a Harvard undergraduate, had come for his first Institute seminar-workshop. As a student several years before at Culver Military Academy in Indiana, he had gotten enthralled by A. E. Van Vogt's 1945 serial, "The World of $\bar{A}$", in *Astounding Science Fiction,* and more enthralled when he realized there actually existed an Institute of General Semantics—*not* located on Korzybski Square in the City of the Machine as in Van Vogt's story, but in Chicago. Bourland had found a copy of *Manhood of Humanity* in the school library, read it, and had also written to the Institute for a copy of *Science and Sanity*, then out of print; he had to wait impatiently, getting Institute reprints in the meantime. When he finally did get his copy, it qualified as major news. A Culver English teacher whom he liked asked him at a pre-class meeting, "What are you doing these days, Bourland?" He replied "I finally got my copy of *Science and Sanity*!" "Oh," said the teacher, "I had trouble with that book; I couldn't get beyond 50 pages." Bourland decided that whatever else he would do, he would get past the first 50 pages; but he got nonplussed when he saw the 51-page "Introduction to the Second Edition." He decided that he wouldn't count it, which, as he later said, "significantly [de]creased the minimal read."[38]

By the time Bourland got to the 1947 seminar, he had read the book a couple of times, feeling more enthusiastic than ever about GS. He later recalled Korzybski's lectures as interesting and coherent (feeling that his prior preparation allowed him to get more out of the course than others who hadn't read Korzybski's works carefully or had read only one or more popularizations). Altogether, Bourland would attend five seminars with Korzybski. He returned for the 1948 seminar-workshop as a "student assistant"; then for Korzybski's February 1949 short seminar at Yale; then, while taking a leave from Harvard for the year, as the second and, as it turned out, last recipient of the Straus-funded Korzybski Fellowship, he attended Korzybski's 1949 summer seminar-workshop and the 1949-1950 Holiday seminar. Korzybski and his work obviously had a great impact on him.

In September, Korzybski had the "Preface to the Third Edition" to get done, as well as the ever-waiting introduction to the Second Edition of *Manhood*, a Credo someone had asked him to write for an Indian publication, and continued work on Janssen's *Selections from Science and Sanity*. However, he had distractions too—new people at the Institute. Ralph Hamilton was supposed to function as his personal 'secretary' or assistant to supplement Charlotte, taking dictation for non-personal letters (Alfred still dictated to Charlotte his letters to Mira), reading scientific books and journal articles that Alfred wanted him to pull the 'gist' from, organizing the library, and generally freeing up Charlotte to give more attention to the thousand and one details of administering the Institute with Kendig. Eventually Ralph, whom Alfred liked, would become a great help, but of course both men had a normal beginning period of mutual adjustment to get through. Another person, Surindar Singh Suri had come to the seminar from India, and had, with Alfred's permission, stayed on at the Institute for further study. Alfred found him a brilliant fellow but also a burden, as one more person living at the Institute he had to deal with, with non-additive effects. (Suri shortly left, eventually going to study at the Northwestern University department of philosophy.)

On October 10, Alfred could finally write to Mira,

> My preface, together with endless other materials, instructions to the printer, and so on, has finally gone to the printer yesterday. Last night we had a little 2-hour celebration after office-hours, for that finishing job. Today I took it easy, but tomorrow I have to start and finish my 'Credo' for that Indian publication, about which you know. Charlotte is the 'slave-driver', and I suspect that she is in love with Ghandi [sic], Tagore, etc., and that is why she is driving me so hard. Personally, I feel like going to bed and sleeping for a week, but of course there is no chance for it.[39]

The new Third Edition of *Science and Sanity* would have a new cover as well, which had to be designed, proofed, etc. With everything else, including a new printer, the Third Edition would not appear until the following May. Korzybski's five-page "Preface To The Third Edition 1948", provided not only a pithy summary of his work, but for those who could read between the lines, a clear record of his and the Institute's struggles with Hayakawa and the Society, that had come to a head over the last year. Hopefulness and pessimism seemed to naturally go together for Korzybski. In his October 10 letter to Mira, he had told her, "Yes, we both know a great deal about life and people. Neither you nor I have a very cheerful outlook. I am glad you remember how for years I insisted that human progress is extremely slow, and some situations can not be remedied short of decades."[40] Both hopefulness and pessimism seemed reflected in the Preface, starting with the two introductory quotes he chose from Charles Saunders Peirce*:

> If thinkers will only be persuaded to lay aside their prejudices and apply themselves to studying the evidences . . . I shall be fully content to await the final decision.

> For the mass of mankind . . . if it is their highest impulse to be intellectual slaves, then slaves they ought to remain.

---

* Alfred had told Ken Keyes, "Peirce has been a real and very important pioneer who originated new trends in mathematics and mathematical logic, and with William James established 'pragmatism'...If you read the suggested book of Peirce [*Chance, Love, and Logic*] and some of the bibliography given there, you will get a glimpse of what a 'system' has to offer. Peirce in his lifetime was not popular, but today he is a foundation of the scientific progress we have achieved." [AK to Ken Keyes, Jr., 9/11/1945. IGS Archives.]

Korzybski began by noting that despite new scientific discoveries since 1933, "...the fundamental *methodological* issues which led even to the release of nuclear energy remain unaltered, and so this third edition requires no revision of the text." Interest in and application of GS had continued to spread since the founding of the Institute, exemplified by the 1941 American Congress and by Douglas M. Kelley's World War II experiences in battlefield psychiatry.

> I must stress that I give no panaceas, but experience shows that when the methods of general semantics are *applied*, the results are usually beneficial, whether in law, medicine, business, etc., education on all levels, or personal inter-relationships, be they family, national, or international fields. If they are not applied, but merely talked about, no results can be expected.

Notably, he returned to his work's origin in *Manhood's* 1921 definition of 'man', its development "[t]hrough the discovery of factors of sanity in physico-mathematical *methods*," and its implications for cultural evolution in the shift from an aristotelian to a non-aristotelian system of orientation.

He then devoted more than a page to what had become a significant issue for him in his conflict with Hayakawa and the Society: the confusion between 'semantics' and his use of 'semantic' as a modifier referring to 'evaluation'.

He ended the "Preface" with a call to action that managed to give both a sober warning and a hopeful note:

> It is not generally realized that with human progress, the complexities and difficulties in the world increase following an exponential function of 'time', with indefinitely accelerating accelerations. I am deeply convinced that these problems cannot be solved at all unless we boldly search for and revise our antiquated notions about the 'nature of man' and apply modern extensional methods toward their solution. ...
>
> We *need not* blind ourselves with the old dogma that 'human nature cannot be changed', for we find that it *can be changed*. We must begin to realize our potentialities as humans, then we may approach the future with some hope. We may feel with Galileo, as he stamped his foot on the ground after recanting the Copernican theory before the Holy Inquisition, *'Eppur si muove!'* The evolution of our human development may be retarded, but it cannot be stopped.

Maybe he did care about those yahoos, just a little.

"Lonesome for him"

Mira's problems labeled "transient arthritis"—pains in her neck, arms, hands, knees, etc., that made using her hands as well as walking difficult at times—would shift in area or from one limb to another, would wax and wane, come and go. Unfortunately, throughout this year, the pains didn't stay gone. Evelyn Garlick had written to Alfred and Charlotte that Mira now seemed shaky on her feet. Mira wrote to him not to worry—it wouldn't help her and would only unnecessarily tax his precious time and energy. But he worried anyhow.

In the second week of September 1947, at Mira's behest, her sister Amy, still remarkably mobile, came from Kansas City to check up on her and help out for a while. She got Mira to go to an osteopath whose treatments of manual traction to her neck gave her at least some temporary relief. Alfred wanted Amy to stay, at least until his upcoming trip to Chicago. But Mira seemed better and at the end of the month Amy wrote to Alfred that she was going home.

Meanwhile, Mira's doctors at Billings Hospital wanted her to come in for more tests and experimental arthritis treatments and they got a bed for her by the second week of October. By whatever combination of rest, medication, etc., the arthritis seemed generally better by the time she came home on October 22. But she felt and looked awful, according to Mrs. Garlick, and was readmitted to Billings a few days later with a diagnosis of pleurisy and lobar pneumonia, most likely picked up during her prior hospital stay. Mrs. Garlick visited her and kept Alfred and Charlotte informed. On October 27, Alfred telegraphed her doctor asking him to telegraph back on her status. And he wrote to Mira in the hospital: he was giving two lectures for *Scripta Mathematica* in New York on November 3 and 10 and, with Charlotte, would come to visit immediately afterwards.

> I am enclosing a newspaper reprint from the Waterbury Republican, with some pictures which may cheer up the 'Mother of a new civilization'. How I wish I could put my fingers in your beautiful gray hair and shake you up. I am confident it would shake the damn bugs out of you...
> [handwritten]   All my love and Devotion
> Your Donk[41]

Alfred's letter improved her mood, antibiotics her lungs. Her doctor telegrammed back: she was out of danger. Within a week, she had returned home, sending a November 3 telegram to Alfred at the Horace Mann Auditorium of Teachers College, Columbia University, where he was giving the first of his two-lecture series on "Mathematical Method As A Way Of Life" for The Society of Friends of *Scripta Mathematica* and The Yeshiva Institute of Mathematics: "Alfred Dearest Home Well And Happy Again All Love From Mira."[42] Given the challenge of conveying his aims and work under what he felt as severe time limitations, receiving her telegram at the lecture hall likely gave him a mood boost for his presentation that evening. This was the third year in a row he had addressed Jekuthiel Ginsburg's group and for some weeks he had been reading and preparing for this talk, "On the Structure of Mathematics and Human Evaluation", and the next one scheduled a week later on November 10, "General Semantics as Applied Physico-Mathematical Method". As before he wanted to convey as best he could his vision of the role of mathematics in human life and its potential, if looked at from his peculiar point of view, to promote human sanity.

In order to show how to 'mathematize' human life, he first needed to humanize mathematics. The character of mathematics, its remarkable effectiveness in dealing with the world, and yet its humble human origins, were the focus of his November 3 talk. What he sometimes referred to in seminars as the 'miracles' of mathematics were the products of behaving human nervous systems in time-binding association with one another. In notes, probably dictated to Charlotte for what appears to be his November 3 talk, he said, "...The foundation of math. is the psychology [psycho-logics] of mathematizing and number,...Mathematical foundation has nothing to do with the world, but with human beings, the makers of mathematics."[43] (In recent years, Korzybski had recommended Jacques Hadamard's book, *The Psychology of Invention in the Mathematical Field*, as a contribution to the foundation of mathematics in this sense.)†

---

† Korzybski considered his own discussion of the psycho-logics of mathematics—as a form of language use uniquely similar in structure to the world and the human nervous system [*S&S*, Part V]—central to his system and potentially significant to the foundation of mathematics as well. See his definition of *mathematics* in terms of linguistic-symbolic human behavior [*S&S*, pp. 253, 277] and of *number* in terms of relations rather than classes [*S&S*, pp. 258–259, 438]. See also his discussions of 'infinity' and the 'infinitesmal' in *S&S*, Chapters XIV, XV, and passim.

About 450 people attended his first lecture, as Charlotte wrote to Mira on November 6.[44] For his second lecture on November 10, Alfred felt "particularly pleased" as he later wrote to Jekuthiel Ginsburg, "that numerically the audience did not dwindle."Among those in the audience, "...Mrs. Keyser came; she seemed to be heavily hit by her husband's passing. So was I; when I mentioned his name at the lecture I could hardly speak, and when I saw her we hardly could speak also."[45]

This second lecture focused more specifically on his work and was taped and later transcribed and distributed by the Institute of General Semantics. Whatever interest Korzybski stimulated in the audience, ultimately his approach to mathematics and physico-mathematical science as forms of human behavior with methodological implications for non-mathematicians, seemed bound to puzzle many. Whether mathematically inclined or not, they might have had trouble seeing how much of what he talked about—the nervous system process of abstracting, the Aunt Jemima story, the behavior of psychiatric patients in mental hospitals, even the various extensional devices (that Korzybski took bodily from mathematics and mathematical physics)—what all this had to do with what they thought of as 'mathematics'. 'Logical fate' explained a lot. Korzybski had a warning for skeptics inclined to think that his physico-mathematically inspired approach could not deal with the human factor:

...Do not have a criticism, so to say, about my work, that 'Korzybski fancies that humans are like geometry; there is a difference between geometry and a human being.' I didn't find it that way, because I have found that humans, even 'insane' are extremely logical provided you trace their premises, except their premises have no realization in actuality. So that's the main point, not a problem of logic. From some premises, some consequences follow.[46]

These lectures would constitute Korzybski's last major venture specifically addressing a mainly mathematically-oriented audience.‡

Alfred and Charlotte remained in New York City at the Albert Hotel for another week. They had some meetings with people, including Kendig, who had attended the final lecture; but they mainly stayed because the high demand for places on the train to Chicago prevented them from leaving; they had to wait until some ticket-holders cancelled their reservations. Finally on Tuesday evening, November 18, they were able to leave New York, getting into Chicago around noon the next day and staying for a little over a week. Mira had offered to have them both stay with her. But, as they planned their visit, Alfred didn't want to burden her and thought a nearby hotel would be better. Charlotte had business to do in Chicago with the Institute's bookkeeper still there, and with the warehouse where they still had Institute stuff stored. And Alfred had some people to see. But while Charlotte made a side trip to visit her parents in Milwaukee, Alfred would stay with Mira. They had ample time to spend together and Alfred's visit appeared to serve as a balm to them both.

Alfred and Charlotte returned by train to New York, and from there to Lime Rock. Alfred sent a telegram to Mira on December 1, "Arrived Safely Saturday. Are Submerged. Happy About Visit. All Love. Alfred."[47] Mira wrote a short note to him the next day:

---

‡ Given his abiding interest in the foundation of mathematics, mathematical logic, etc., it's disappointing that he didn't have anything to say here—or anywhere else apparently—about logician Kurt Godel's 1931 theorem of mathematical incompleteness. (Korzybski, though not a mathematical logician, got the quarterly journal of the Association for Symbolic Logic and recommended it to his students.) Perhaps he had at least heard of Godel's work, the importance of which by this time had begun to get recognition in the mathematical logic community and among other mathematicians. The implications of Godelian incompleteness on Korzybski's formulations about mathematics, etc., and the implications of Korzybski's work for Godel's, both remain to be explored.

"My dearest one – What comfort and courage your visit [and] your telegram gave your devoted Mira."[48] Two weeks later in a short note, Evelyn Garlick's husband Sayres wrote to the Institute: he had dropped in to see Mira who answered the door and, except for some difficulties with her hands, seemed fine. A dietition from Billings was visiting her too. Garlick wrote, "I judge she is in the clear and all is well."[49] The next day, Mira wrote a one-page letter to Charlotte, including at the bottom, "Alfred's visit made me lonesome for him."[50]

Chapter 62
"WITHOUT PUBLICITY THERE IS NO PROSPERITY."

By the late 1940s, Korzybski and general semantics—sometimes in the guise of 'semantics'—had gained a remarkable niche in public awareness, remarkable given the forbidding appearance—at least to some people—of Korzybski's major work. References to Korzybski or to one of his popularizers, such as Stuart Chase, appeared in unexpected places. In a 1947 Dixie Dugan comic strip, preserved in an IGS scrapbook, one of Dixie's 'acquaintances' sees Dixie, whom she's never liked, approaching. The woman tells her companion, "Here comes Dixie Dugan. Watch me tear her apart...I've just read *The Tyranny of Words*."[1] In 1949, Guthrie Janssen sent Alfred a cartoon clipped from an unspecified, undated Boston church publication.[2]

"Surely you don't expect to win this argument by supporting it with two-value Aristotelian abstractions such as Count Korzybski exposed fully two decades ago."

Books, Books, and More Books

References to Korzybski also continued to appear in numerous books in a wide variety of fields. A number of them he welcomed; not the case with other books by would-be critics and so-called advocates who addressed his work extensively, but with varying degrees of error.

Among the critics, Barrows Dunham in his 1947 *Man Against Myth* devoted considerable space to debunking a 'straw' version of Korzybski, conflating his work with that of other 'semanticists' in a chapter on the myth "That All Problems Are Merely Verbal". Also conflating Korzybski with 'the semanticists', Richard M. Weaver in his 1948 *Ideas Have Consequences* criticized Korzybski for degrading 'the power of the word'. Korzybski surely agreed with Dunham in this: all problems *were not* merely verbal—although linguistic and other evaluational issues had some importance in dealing with any problem. Korzybski also had some common ground with Weaver, for one thing agreeing that 'ideas' have consequences, having for years explored with his students the application of logical fate, writing as far back as 1921, "Humanity is a peculiar class of life which, in some degree, determines its own destinies; therefore in practical life *words* and *ideas* become *facts*—facts moreover, which bring about important practical consequences."[3] Dunham's and Weaver's mistaken ideas about Korzybski would undoubtedly have consequences, misleading those who accepted them to dismiss Korzybski's work. What could Korzybski do? He simply didn't have time to deal with all the inaccurate portrayals and non-constructive criticism by people who didn't adequately study his work. At seminars when someone would object to what they misconstrued as his views, Korzybski would repeat as often as needed, "I say what I say. I do not say what I do not say."

In 1949 another faulty critique of his views appeared, a particularly interesting one because it lacked the hostility one might otherwise expect, given the writer's history with him. Early that year, philosopher Max Black, then at Cornell University, wrote to the Institute asking for permission to quote from *Science and Sanity* for a chapter on Korzybski's work. Although Korzybski had strongly protested Black's scurrilous review of *Science and Sanity* five years earlier, he wrote back to the philosopher giving permission in a remarkably congenial manner; he also said he would appreciate seeing the chapter proofs.

Black's book, *Language and Philosophy: Studies in Method*, appeared later that year with its final chapter on "Korzybski's General Semantics". Although mainly critical and mainly missing the mark in regard to what he criticized, Black had matured enough to treat Korzybski and his work with the kind of consideration they deserved. Allen Walker Read would comment:

> In a way it is refreshing to find the degree of respect that he accords GS, and it is the sort of attempted criticism that [should be] welcome. Black thinks he is devastating in two directions: in his first part he discovers the circularity of knowledge and attributes it as a shortcoming of Korzybski, and in the second part he discovers that abstraction is a multi-ordinal word (though earlier in the essay he seemed to understand and praise the doctrine of multi-ordinality) and claims that this is a shortcoming in general semantics.[4] *

Misrepresentations by supposed advocates of his work would bother Korzybski much more than those from misguided critics. In 1949, Korzybski read and responded to the pre-publication proofs of books by two such advocates, S. I. Hayakawa and Anatol Rapoport.

Hayakawa had revised *Language In Action*, renaming it *Language In Thought And Action* (a retreat into elementalism from the previous restrictive-though-functional title). Hayakawa noted in his "Foreword", "My deepest debt in this book is to the General Semantics ("non-Aristotelian" system) of Alfred Korzybski", indicating his subject area—and by implication that of Korzybski—as "Semantics...the study of human interaction through the mechanism of linguistic communication."[5] He sent a version of the new "Foreword" to Korzybski in early June (the publisher later sent some galley proofs related to 'the abstraction ladder'). The two men corresponded into the next month, with Korzybski again frankly stating his concerns about his work getting misinterpreted as a result of Hayakawa's depictions of it.[6]

---

* Max Black's respect for Korzybski and his work continued to grow. In a letter to Elwood Murray, Kendig noted the following regarding Black's 1958 "write-up of general semantics in the last edition of the *Encyclopedia Britannica* ["Semantics, General"]": "Certainly this is not a very laudatory statement, but it does represent progress towards some sort of appreciation of Korzybski and his contribution. It might be interesting to mention here that on the day that Korzybski died Max Black went to his class in (I think it's called) 'Linguistics and Logic' and said, 'We will take a holiday today in honor of a very great man who died this morning.' This was reported to me by one of his students." [M. Kendig to Elwood Murray, 11/15/1960. IGS Archives]

Although Korzybski had long suffered Hayakawa's indifference to his concerns, he had been willing to forgive a lot. Even as late as 1948, in the front matter of the first printing of the Third Edition of *Science and Sanity*, he had continued to include *Language in Action* in the list of books, "By Other Publishers" under non-aristotelian "Volumes Already Published". Korzybski had certainly shown willingness to overlook a great deal in other people's writings about his work. Stuart Chase had continued to marry general semantics with semantics in the discussion of the communication field in his 1948 book *The Proper Study of Mankind*, a popular survey of the state of the social/behavioral sciences. Irving Lee seemed to do similarly in his anthology called *The Language of Wisdom and Folly* that appeared early in 1949. Although dedicating the book to Korzybski and including Korzybski's "Fate and Freedom", Lee had changed his original, descriptively accurate subtitle from "Readings on the Relations of Language, Fact and Human Evaluation" to "Background Readings in Semantics". (Lee's book with its earlier subtitle is noted under "Volumes in Preparation" on the International Non-Aristotelian Library page of the first printing of the 1948 Third Edition of *Science and Sanity*.) Their books showed that neither Chase nor Lee seemed sensitive to Korzybski's growing problem with having his work linked to 'semantics'. But neither Chase nor Lee shared the public status of Hayakawa as a major spokesman for GS. Korzybski knew the power of public perception and misperception if anyone did. He had good reason to feel concerned about Hayakawa's book and found it very unsatisfactory when it came out later in 1949. Despite Korzybski's pleas, Hayakawa did not—perhaps at this stage he could not—retreat in this or in later writings from his elementalistic language, emphasis on 'semantics', 'abstraction ladder', etc.

Korzybski seemed even more upset seeing the proofs of Anatol Rapoport's upcoming first book, *Science and the Goals of Man*, presumably based on Korzybski's work. Rapoport wrote to him about it in July 1949 and had the publisher, Harper and Brothers, send him a copy of the galleys. Korzybski studied them that fall and felt flummoxed. How could Rapoport write, "We are time-binding animals"[7], if he had read *Manhood of Humanity*, where Korzybski had said over and over in various ways that 'man...is not an animal' (p. 192)? And if Rapoport considered Korzybski (not Hayakawa) as the foundational writer in general semantics, how could he have written that the "...abstraction ladder is represented by Korzybski in his so-called "structural differential" "[8], implying that for Rapoport the 'abstraction ladder' constituted the primary model of abstracting?

Reading Rapoport's galleys, it must have finally dawned on Korzybski the extent to which Rapoport, for several years now the Associate Editor of *ETC.*, had fallen under Hayakawa's spell. Before this time—despite some problems Alfred had with an *ETC.* article by Rapoport on "Dialectical Materialism and General Semantics" in early 1948—he had generally liked Rapoport's articles in *ETC.*, complimented him on his writings, tried to get him to come to seminars (to no avail), and had generally seen him as a rising star worth cultivating. As late as September 1949, Korzybski wrote to Rapoport, congratulating him on his "unusually fine article" on "Mathematical Biophysics, Cybernetics, and General Semantics" in that Spring's *ETC.* and asking for reprints.[9]

Regarding Rapoport's book, both the publisher and Rapoport wanted Korzybski's comments; he hemmed and hawed, working with Charlotte on notes for a response, until finally in November he wrote to the publisher, who expected some kind of blurb:

> Thank you for sending me the galley proofs of Anatol Rapoport's SCIENCE AND THE GOALS OF MAN. I have read them carefully three times, and am very sorry to say I have no comment to make which you could use. I am writing to Dr. Rapoport separately, and will send a copy to you.[10.]

But Korzybski didn't write to Rapoport, deciding to remain silent. He had already spent a great deal of time on Rapoport's book and had more pressing things of his own to work on. Given the depth and number of his objections to the book and the unlikelihood of having any impact on Rapoport, whom he now considered 'inaccessible', spending more time composing a letter seemed futile.[11] Shortly before his death, Alfred told Dave Bourland about his disappointment with Rapoport, "who had *such* promise for contributions he could make to the field of general semantics, considering his background, his intelligence,...doing damage to everything that I tried to present."[12]

From Korzybski's point of view, other books published in 1948 and 1949 gave much more satisfactory accounts of his work, starting with physician Bertrand S. Frohman's *Brief Psychotherapy: A Handbook for Physicians on the Clinical Aspects of Neuroses*, which had finally come out in January 1948. Frohman sent a signed book at once to Korzybski, who read and reread it—as indicated by the markings in his copy. Korzybski wrote his kudos to the book's publishers, Lea and Febiger and, on February 18, to Frohman:

> I am deeply grateful to you for your inscribed copy. As I said to the publishers, that such a book was a dream of mine which has just materialized. I know it's a strong statement, but just the same it's true, and I hardly can fully express my gratitude to you. ...I intend to make your book an obligatory textbook for all my students and I feel it should have a world-wide distribution and eventual translation into a number of languages.[13]

Korzybski meant every word of this. He gave copies inscribed by him with marked enthusiasm to Charlotte, Kendig and Mira, writing in Mira's book: "Dearest – The first textbook of Sanity from professional point of view based on GS – to the 'Mother of future civilizations' yours as ever March 1948 Alfred". Korzybski wanted to do whatever he could to promote Frohman's book and followed through by having it for sale on the Institute's publication list and by getting 2000 advertising circulars from the publisher for the Institute to distribute with special added promotional wording: "This new text utilizes General Semantics, the Non-Aristotelian system of orientation, formulated by Alfred Korzybski. The application of General Semantics to problems of personal maladjustment is described in a special section."[14] Korzybski also worked on a review of the book but never completed it; had he lived longer he probably would have done so.

The two men found each others' work compatible for good reasons. Frohman found in Korzybski's work a conscious approach to his 'natural' mode of evaluating. (He is still known today, as perhaps the first person, in the early 1930s, to apply the term "bruxism" to tooth grinding and to explain it as a stress-anxiety symptom.) Korzybski provided a basic language for what Frohman had already been doing. And Frohman's work exemplified for Korzybski the application of his extensional methods to psychiatry, an application he had long hoped to see in book form.

Penelope Pearl [later Russianoff], a clinical psychologist and the daughter of Korzybski's friend Raymond Pearl, attended several seminars with Korzybski and also saw Frohman for personal help. In her 1988 book *When Am I Going To Be Happy: How To Break The Emotional Bad Habits That Make You Miserable* (dedicated to Korzybski, among others), she described Frohman's extensional approach to get her "off my tall kick," the "crippling" obsessive self-consciousness she had developed growing up as an especially tall girl ("by age fourteen, I was six-foot-two and weighed under one hundred pounds."):

> One day Frohman said to me: "Every time I ask you something, you manage to turn it around into something wrong with you. Your height. Your personality. Your intelligence. It's as though you're driving along at night and your headlights are supposed to be shining on the highway so you can see where you're going. Instead, you've got them pointing backward so that they are blinding you. You can't see anything but your own failings. You don't see anything else that's going on around you. You don't really see other people. You're so absorbed in what a man might think about your height that you don't give yourself the right to judge *him*. It's highly possible he's not perfect. What is it that you might not like about *him*? Turn those headlights around so that you can see something besides yourself."
>
> Flash of insight! Suddenly I had this vivid image of myself careening along a highway in a blinding glare of self-absorption. Bertrand Frohman's words were literally a turning point in my life. I turned the lights around and instantly saw with crystal clarity exactly where I was. ...I woke up the next morning and said to myself: "All right. I'm not a cuddly little blond and I never will be. So I'm going to start living my life as what I am. I am going to stop rejecting myself."...My new attitude must have communicated itself. After a lifetime of rejections by men, actual or self-inflicted, I started dating fairly often and also began making a number of just plain friends, who coincidentally happened to be men.[15]

Frohman definitely seemed like a person after Korzybski's heart. Penelope Russianoff described his "very direct way of dealing with the issue of motivation."

> Psychiatrists do not ordinarily make house calls, But, as Frohman once explained it to me, a bedridden woman had pleaded with him to come to see her. As soon as he entered her bedroom, she handed him a box of matches. "Open it," she said. He did, and inside he found a dozen or so burnt match sticks. "Every one of those," she announced defiantly, "stands for a therapist who failed me." Frohman took out one of the unused matches. He lit it, blew it out, put it back in the box, and said, "That'll be one hundred dollars." Sometimes we have to be jolted into knowing whether we want to change or keep on clinging to our negativity.[16]

Although not now well-known, *Brief Psychotherapy* notably appears as one of the earliest books in the fields of brief and 'cognitive' psychotherapy. The book remains highly readable for its down-to-earth language, large number of interesting case studies, and the remarkable extent to which Frohman, both explicitly in the GS section and implicitly throughout the book, utilized Korzybski's insights to discuss the psycho-somatic issues and adjustment problems frequently confronted by general medical doctors, psychiatrists, psychotherapists, and other health professionals. Well received when it came out, the book went into a second printing only a few months after first appearing. Tragically, Frohman developed serious health problems over the next two years and died in December 1949 while still in his fifties. Given his talent, his enthusiasm for Korzybski's work, and Korzybski's enthusiasm for his, he seemed likely to have become well-known promoting his korzybskian approach to psychotherapy. Instead, both his name and his book sank into obscurity.

In 1948, another new GS-related book, A.E. Van Vogt's *The World of Ā*, intrigued and bewildered Korzybski. He wrote to Mira in March, "Do not buy it, because I am sending a copy to you. I read the damn thing three times, and I simply cannot make out what he is driving at; if you can, I would appreciate your opinion."[17]

Van Vogt's 1945 three-part serial about the adventures of the body-switching, memory-swapping Gilbert Gosseyn ('go sane') in John W. Campbell's *Astounding Science Fiction* magazine, had already become a big hit. Campbell called it a "once-in-a-decade classic" and Van Vogt revised the story for Simon and Schuster, which brought it out in early 1948, making it the first post-war science fiction hardcover book offered by a major publisher. The early magazine stories had already drawn some people to general semantics, David Bourland for one. The novel, known in subsequent paperback editions as *The World of Null-A*—still in print—and two sequels by Van Vogt, presented the prospect of a $\bar{A}$ civilization and would introduce many more to Korzybski's work in following years.[18] It would also confuse some people about Korzybski's work; for one thing, Korzybski never talked about 'Null-A'.[19]

Another 1948 book, William Vogt's conservationist call-to-arms, *Road to Survival*, devoted an opening chapter to korzybskian methodology and its application to ecological problems. Chosen as an August 1948 selection by the Book-of-the-Month Club, *Road to Survival* especially addressed the problems of population growth and land use. Vogt, Chief of the Conservation Section of The Pan American Union, had developed an interest in GS at least a year or two before, and had applied it in a 1947 article on "River Resources Development in Latin American Economic Life", that the Institute sent out as its February 1948 mailing to members. Despite some negative reviews at the time depicting Vogt's book as a product of Neo-Malthusian hysteria, *Road to Survival* became widely popular as one of the pioneering documents of the environmental movement that would sweep the United States and elsewhere over the next half century. Whatever the merits or demerits of his detailed analysis, Vogt's concern for the land certainly had the sympathy of Korzybski, who had a deep interest in soil conservation, etc., from the days of his childhood in Poland growing up on his family's farm. Korzybski included *Road to Survival* on the list of books available at the Institute that he recommended for students of general semantics

In October, Charles Biederman's long-awaited, lavishly illustrated, 710-page, *Art as the Evolution of Visual Knowledge,* appeared. Some people might feel puzzled to find 'general semantics' linked with 'art'. But when Biederman gave a copy of his book to Korzybski signed, "To my teacher Alfred Korzybski I dedicate this volume [signed] Charles Biederman", he didn't exaggerate; his attendance at Korzybski's 1938 seminar had a profound influence on his art and his theory of art. Biederman had taken as his motto, "Nature is not words,"[20] and had presented the function of art as a series of statements about and means of orientation towards 'reality', pointing to the ultimate possibility of a merger of 'art' and 'science' with other aspects of human culture. John W. Barnes and Joan Waddell Barnes, husband and wife students of Korzybski, wrote an extensive 18-page review of Biederman's book, which the Institute printed and distributed as its April 1949 membership mailing.

Students, Classes and Groups

Korzybski had long understood the truth behind the statement later attributed to Russian physicist Yakov Zel′dovich: "Without publicity there is no prosperity."[21] Korzybski's name and work had received a lot of publicity by the end of the decade and after years of struggle the Institute of General Semantics, if not prosperous, would at least for a time get financially in the black.[22] Although cartoons, books, as well as newspaper and magazine articles had some role, ultimately the main credit for whatever public interest existed in Korzybski's work resulted from the unremitting efforts of Korzybski and his colleagues at the Institute and the resultant chain reaction set off by their numerous students.

By the late 1940s, Korzybski had imparted his work to thousands of people from a wide range of academic fields in the sciences, humanities, and arts and from many professions at more than fifty seminars and other lecture presentations. He had counseled and corresponded with many of his students, as well as with a significant number of other intellectual and professional figures—some well-known—from around the world. Close colleagues of his at the Institute, such as Charlotte, Kendig, Francis Chisholm, and Guthrie Janssen, had given additional presentations and classes. Considerable demand existed for Korzybski's books and other writings of his on the Institute's publication list. Many of Korzybski's students and correspondents were now doing research, writing articles and books, and teaching classes that made significant use of the non-aristotelian extensional discipline he had founded. Wendell Johnson, Elwood Murray, and Irving Lee had supervised graduate research significantly influenced by their work with Korzybski. Murray, in particular, had built a significant portion of the University of Denver Speech Communication Department curriculum around a korzybskian core. Institute Workshop staff members, including O. R. Bontrager, head of the Reading Clinic and Teacher Training at the Pennsylvania State Teachers College; lexicographer Allen Walker Read, lecturer in English Linguistics at Columbia University; and visual artist Harry Holtzman, at the Katherine Dunham School of Dance and Theatre (later at Brooklyn College) were applying GS in their courses. (Holtzman, invited by Kendig to teach a popular workshop session on "Non-Verbal Abstracting in the Visual Field" at the 1947 IGS Summer Seminar, had impressed Korzybski and would return to teach at subsequent seminar-workshops for a number of years.) As a result of the writing, research, and teaching activities of students of Korzybski, students of his students, or those self-taught from reading *Science and Sanity* and other works—those directly or indirectly influenced by Korzybski influenced many others as well.

For some time, people had written to the IGS asking about academic institutions offering "accredited courses in General Semantics or...training in the methodology as embodied in the teaching of various subject matter courses." In response to these inquiries, in January 1948, Kendig produced a memo for distribution on "Institutions Offering Work in General Semantics: A Pro-tem Reply and Incomplete List".[23] She hoped to later get funding to do a more detailed and thorough investigation, but in the meantime the four-page list she put together might surprise those who considered GS solely in terms of language study. Besides a number of English and Speech professors offering courses, other teachers included: Frank L. Verwiebe at Hamilton College and Frederick H. Binford of Lemoyne College, who used GS in their physics and math courses; Gene V. Chenoweth, who conducted a GS course at the Arthur Jordan Conservatory of Music; and Janice V. Kent at Radford University who applied GS in her art education classes. David Bitzen of the University of Southern California Divinity School used *Science and Sanity* as a text in his pastoral counseling courses, as did A.P. Guiles of the Andover-Newton Theological School. Douglas Kelley at Bowman Gray School of Medicine and Hervey M. Cleckley, author of *The Mask of Sanity*, at the University of Georgia Medical School introduced korzybskian methodology in their psychiatry teaching. Douglas E. Wade, College Naturalist at Dartmouth, used GS in his work in ecology. Milton Konvitz, Director of Research and Associate Professor of the New York State School of Labor and Industrial Relations at Cornell University, wrote to Kendig that "he requires the reading of two General Semantics texts in his course called 'Patterns of Thought'."

At Harvard, anthropologist Clyde Kluckhohn required either *Science and Sanity* or "one of the other General Semantics texts in his first year course." Also at Harvard, Norman T. Newton, Associate Professor of Landscape Architecture at the Graduate School of Design, had introduced GS "in his various courses, especially 'Construction I' a required course for students in Architecture, Design, etc." Around the time Kendig produced her memo, the Institute sent out Newton's article, "A Non-Aristotelian Approach to Design" as its third membership mailing. Newton had attended a number of seminars with Korzybski, lectured at IGS workshops, and not long after Korzybski's death, in the "Preface" of his 1951 book *An Approach to Design*, would write,

> I feel a special debt to the memory of Alfred Korzybski, that great and warmly human friend in whose tremendous life-work the attentive student can find implicit what I suspect Korzybski himself was unaware of—a solid basis for a twentieth-century attitude toward the creative arts.[24]

Universities didn't have a monopoly on GS courses. For example, the Dover, Delaware Public Schools held a GS "Teacher Training Program" over the entire 1947-1948 school year, which combined discussion groups with a series of lectures by James A. Saunders, Madeline Semmelmeyer, Ray Bontrager, and Kendig.

An indication of the widespread diffusion of GS could be seen in the number of study groups and local societies that had already formed or were forming. Groups had already existed for some time in Boston, Chicago, Detroit, Iowa City, Los Angeles, New York, Pasadena, St. Louis, St. Paul, etc. International groups had also formed or were forming in, among other places, Montreal, England, and Australia. The Society for General Semantics continued making efforts to organize these and other groups under its auspices. In a nod to the expanding interest both in the U.S. and abroad, the Society Board voted in March 1948 to change the name of the organization to the International Society for General Semantics, a change ratified by a mail-in membership vote in May. Korzybski, Kendig, and Charlotte (who between them ran the Institute on a day-to-day basis) had concerns about the Society trying to 'take over' the Institute's role in relation to these groups, as well as other functions. But there seemed little the Institute could do except make connections, offer support, and solicit memberships among the various local groups. And they believed that perhaps efforts to coordinate with the Society could still succeed. Despite the negative and hardly negligible influence of Hayakawa, Korzybski had supporters on the Society Board. Among them, Bontrager, Elwood Murray and Irving Lee, the outgoing President, had done their best to conciliate between the Society and the Institute. And Francis Chisholm, elected President in June, seemed quite intent on finding a way for the two organizations to cooperate more closely regarding local groups and other issues.

Chapter 63
"WHAT – ME WORRY?"

Unless a lot of people mistook GS for 'Group Sex', there seemed little danger that *Manhood of Humanity* or *Science and Sanity* would follow the Kinsey report onto the 1948 bestseller list. Nonetheless, with interest in GS rising, with the proliferation of GS study groups and courses, with numerous books—both pro and con—being written, there actually existed a demand for Korzybski's books. The unavailability of both of his books at the start of 1948 added to the demand, and the pressure Korzybski and his colleagues felt to get them out again as soon as possible. The delayed appearance of the Second Edition of *Manhood of Humanity*, promised for several years, seemed sure to frustrate the waiting list of people who had already ordered it. *Science and Sanity*, out of print now for nearly a year, had around 1000 back orders. People, especially university instructors, were eager for *Selections from Science and Sanity* as well. Publishing these last two books as soon as possible was at the top of the IGS to-do list. But the delay of *Manhood of Humanity*, Korzybski's first book, especially frustrated him. Its theme of time-binding had begun to play an explicit part in his formulating once again, but the writing of a new Introduction, the main bottleneck to getting out *Manhood's* Second Edition, would not go easily.

'Cool' Warrior

Two presentations he gave in January 1948 reflected Korzybski's renewed interest in time-binding. Almost as soon as he'd finished the Holiday seminar, he and Charlotte headed for New York City where he gave a lecture at Hunter College on January 9 for the New York Society for General Semantics: "Time-Binding and Human Potentialities: A New Foundation For Human Relations". The lecture—recorded, transcribed, and later reprinted in *Collected Writings*—provided an overview of his lifework, seen through the lens of time-binding. He had broached this in writings over the past few years, starting with his ill-fated 1946 *Encyclopedia Britannica* article. But the Hunter College presentation seemed his most in-depth attempt—since his post-*Manhood*, pre-*S&S* writings—to connect later formulations with his earliest work. In the Hunter lecture, he also alluded to an issue he hoped to explore further in his Introduction to *Manhood*, the relationship between time-binding and democracy :

> ...What will work in our world, a dictatorship or some kind of democracy?...From a time-binding point of view a dictatorship of whatever kind simply won't work, and eventually won't last; it twists the time-binding of humans, and so humans themselves. And a democracy, however imperfect, after all permits us humans to behave like humans in the time-binding sense.
>
> These issues are so complex; we have not begun to analyze them fully.[1]

The U.S. government had recently released captured German documents on the Nazi-Soviet pact, which divided up Poland between the two totalitarian powers just prior to the start of World War II. Reading of this in the *New York Times* had gotten Korzybski exercised; he ordered copies of the government document and sent one to Mira, to whom he wrote: "I was nagged many times for what I had to say about the Soviets in S&S; I always classified the Soviet Bigwigs as collaborators of Hitler and many people somehow did not like it. But here it is in black and white."[2] His disdain for Stalin (still firmly in power) and the Soviet system seemed apparent when he and Charlotte returned to the city at the end of January for his talk at a luncheon given in his honor at the Chatham Hotel celebrating the 10th anniversary of the founding of the Institute of General Semantics, the 15th anniversary of the publication of *Science and Sanity*, and its to-be-hoped-soon forthcoming Third Edition. *The New York Times* and *The New Yorker* magazine covered the event.[3] His short luncheon talk, "Understanding Human Potentialities", elaborated on the relationship between time-binding and democracy, focusing on the relations between the Western democracies and the Soviet Union.

While he might *not* have seen democratic socialism as an oxymoron, he clearly indicated the incompatibility of democracy with Stalin's communist government. Consequently, he saw that the Soviet Union had to fail, though perhaps at great human cost to its own subjects and to the citizens from democratic nations who opposed it. The Soviet leadership (Stalin, et al.) accepting the inevitability of 'class struggle' and seeking to encourage conflict around the world, appeared inherently aggressive—and inaccessible to boot. Korzybski didn't see discussions and negotiations changing them.

> ...We must, therefore, stand firm and be prepared for eventualities. We will find no 'salvation' in wishful 'thinking' of any sort. For survival we must have predictability; this requires thorough anthropological and socio-cultural studies as to why the Soviet leaders behave as they do. We can then have some measure of prediction as to what they will do and be prepared for it.[4]

Korzybski's distaste for the Soviet system and its leadership seems even clearer from a detailed nine-page letter he wrote on February 6 to Anatol Rapoport in response to the galleys of an article, "Dialectical Materialism and General Semantics", that Rapoport had written for the upcoming Winter 1948 issue of *ETC*. The article showed that Rapoport, though no longer a Communist party member, had remained a Soviet fellow-traveler—albeit one beginning to have second thoughts. In the article he sought to show how "the general semanticist of today can trace his philosophical geneology both to the dialectical materialist, Engels, and to the 'empiro-criticist', Mach." Stalin, he wrote, "has shown a semantic awareness to a far greater extent than his colleagues. He has also definitely stated that in his opinion the East-West conflict is not inevitable." In the end, Rapoport appeared to have some criticism of Marxist orthodoxy, but wrote as if it could somehow be reformed by an infusion of general semantics.[5]

Korzybski wouldn't stand for this. He had no problem getting linked with Mach, but otherwise took strong exception to Rapoport's geneology:

> If I may be frank, since childhood I rebelled against the 'facts' of our civilization but I never had any use for DM [Dialectical Materialism], as I judge by 'facts'. To link my work with DM is not only false to fact but genuinely harmful to my work; [p. 2]. ...please do not link GS with DM; it has nothing to do with, and in fact is a protest against DM.[6]

The term "Cold War" had recently come into popular usage, and the policy of "containment" to counter the Soviet Union (including a build-up of U.S. and allied military strength) had begun to get formulated. Korzybski's anti-Soviet views qualified him as a cold warrior, or at least a 'cool' one—focusing as he did on opposing anti-democratic dictatorships of any type, whether 'communist' politburos or 'capitalist' cartels, rather than on communism per se. The basis for his disdain for the Soviet system seems perhaps most clearly represented in his concern about the persecution of Russian geneticists and the twisting of biological research by Stalin's 'Tsar' for Soviet biology, T. D. Lysenko. Beginning to get significant news coverage in the West, this issue had caught Korzybski's attention by early 1948 (he had started to clip newspaper articles) and confirmed his views about the incompatibility of dictatorship with optimal time-binding and its expression in the healthy pursuit of knowledge.

"What I Believe"
In February, back at the Institute, Korzybski had as his most immediately pressing task getting out *Selections from Science and Sanity* and the Third Edition of *Science and Sanity*. That month, he finished his 7-page "Author's Note" to *Selections* mainly "dealing with the misinterpretations of *general* semantics and confusions with semantics."[7] (As it was going to press, Korzybski added a note on Allen Walker Read's paper "An Account of the Word 'Semantics'", published in August 1948, since it provided supporting data for his efforts to differentiate his work from 'semantics'.) By the beginning of April, the Institute announced publication and began taking orders for the initial limited printing run of 3000 copies of *Selections*. As an "experimental" production, it had a plain, blue, thick paper cover showing only the title, so production remained relatively simple. The 274-page volume, with later additions (an index produced by David Bourland that summer and some extra text from *S&S* put in several decades later) stayed in print for many years and provided an easy-to-handle format of Korzybski's work for use by university classes and reading groups, perhaps more inviting to those who felt leery about tackling "the blue peril" itself.

The publication of *Selections* came in time to provide a kind of 'parting gift' for its compiler Guthrie Janssen, who got married that month to Guila Beattie and was leaving his employment at the Institute. Jan and Beat were moving to New York City and would be missed. (Although in the fall they ended up returning to Lime Rock to live and would continue involvement with Korzybski and the Institute.) Besides his editorial work, Janssen had served as the Institute's membership secretary. These duties would be taken over by Maxine K. Mallach, affectionately known as 'Mac', a young woman from Lime Rock, who had started working at the Institute in June 1947. Before the war, she had studied at the American Acadamy of Dramatic Arts in New York City, then served as a sergeant in the WACs (the Women's Army Corps) in New Guinea. After the war, she worked for a business in New Canaan in Southwestern Connecticut before starting as a typist and office assistant at the Institute, an easy walk from her home where she lived with her parents. Having shown exceptional competence in dealing with IGS office intricacies, she soon became Kendig's assistant and the seminar registrar before taking over Janssen's duties as membership secretary as well. With great fondness for Korzybski and esteem for his work, Mac would continue working devotedly for the Institute, over a span of four decades, playing a pivotal role in keeping the IGS operating during some later lean and rather difficult times.

Real pressure existed to get out the Third Edition of *Science and Sanity* as soon as possible. A letter from Mira on January 16 reflected the wide interest and demand for the book:

Alfred my dearest one: –

How a great idea makes strange people kin, to which add this strange coincidence. This noon I was struggling to open the front door and get food bag in when a young woman did both for me and carried the heavy bag up to Apt. *When lo and behold* I saw S&S on her arm. She lives in small apt. just south of this on the alley; is librarian in science library * that smallish bldg Charlotte will remember near lily pond at a 59th St. entrance. It seems that there are 4 copies of 1st Ed. And 4 copies of 2nd ed. and always a waiting list for S&S. The last one of the list was so disappointed that when later a copy came in she grabbed it to satisfy her curiosity and was enthralled at the combination of my being your wife and the beautiful things here. Her husband is a butcher and apparently has had a very limited existence. She offered to bring any books from that library, [I] immediately remembered two on arthritis. Such eager young people are a pleasure.[8]

In March, pretty much done with *Selections*, Alfred, Charlotte, and others worked on page proofs for the Third Edition's new and revised front material and on its new jacket cover, which would include a quote from his 'credo', "What I Believe", that he was in the process of finishing:

The progress of modern science, *including the new science of man as a time-binder*, has been due uniquely to the freedom of scientists to revise their *fundamental assumptions*, terminologies, undefined terms, which involve hidden assumptions, etc., underlying our reflections, a freedom prohibited in 'primitive sciences' and also in dictatorships, past and present.[9]

He had written "What I Believe", at the invitation of Indian author/editor Krishna M. Talgeri for a book *The Faith I Live By*, a "symposium" of essays with a list of invitees besides Korzybski that included Gandhi, Nehru, and Montessori, among others. The book seems never to have gotten published. Nonetheless, Korzybski would make good use of the essay; besides using a quote from it for the *S&S* cover, he would later have the essay printed for distribution to Members of the Institute in September 1949 and include it in the content to add to the Second Edition of *Manhood*. As he wrote in a letter to Members that accompanied that September 1949 mailing, "What I Believe" was "really a summary of my whole life work. ..."[10]

The essay touched briefly, even impressionistically, on major themes in his work, connecting them to the overarching theme of time-binding. Topics included: discussion of his personal background and purposes in developing the notion of 'time-binding'; understanding not statistical averages but human potentialities within a theoretical 'deductive' framework as the sine qua non for an applied 'science of man'; the consequent importance of studying human reactions at their best and worst; time-binding and dictatorships; adequate versus inadequate linguistic and grammatical structures and the necessity of developing an adequate "unified terminology of *evaluation*" for a science of man; the overwhelming importance of "*non-verbal*, or what I call *silent levels*" and a working "*consciousness of the differences between*...the silent and the verbal levels, [as] the key and perhaps the first step for the solution of human problems"; the role in human knowledge of "*relations, as factors of structure*" and of postulational methods; religions and sciences; the importance of inferential knowledge; and the significance of "self-reflexive and circular mechanisms" as "*the uniquely human types of reaction* which made our human achievements possible." He concluded by discussing the historical importance for humans of becoming conscious of their capacities as time-binders: "...this consciousness may now mark a new period in our evolution."[11]

By the end of April, the Institute had reprints of Korzybski's new "Preface To The Third Edition 1948" to send as its latest mailing to members. And by the end of May, the Institute received its first copies of the Third Edition, although most of the 5000 books from this first printing would be stored with a firm in New York City. Science Press, the book's printer, had changed ownership and management and, under the new name of Business Press, would no longer serve as the Institute's distributor. The Institute office processed orders, printed shipping labels, and sent them to the New York firm, which did the wrapping and shipping. 1,000 back-ordered copies went out immediately and the remaining books sold quickly, approximately 4000 over the next year, a quarter of the total copies sold since the book's original 1933 publication. By the end of 1948, Charlotte was scrambling to arrange a second printing, which included getting a new printer and getting the printer's plates shipped from Business/Science Press, etc. (The second printing, ready by May 1949, sold equally quickly, requiring a third printing in 1950.) Mira wrote to Alfred, telling of her pride and delight at seeing a copy in the window of a nearby bookshop. Unlike many of the delayed projects and unmet deadlines that had plagued the Institute since its inception, the publication of the Third Edition of *Science and Sanity* had come through as announced at the January luncheon.

"What - Me Worry?"

Meanwhile planning had begun for the anticipated big event of 1948, the Third Congress on General Semantics, first announced in the fall of 1947. A postcard to members in February gave the dates and location, October 29 to 31 at the University of Denver, and included a request for getting abstracts to Kendig by March 1. In March, Kendig made another call for papers and announced a Pro Tem Committee for the Congress, with herself and Douglas Kelley as Co-Chairs, Korzybski consulting, and Hansell Baugh assisting them. In April, she took a whirlwind trip for the Institute to Washington D.C.; then to Denver for several days of planning with Elwood Murray and others at the University of Denver; then back to Lime Rock by way of Chicago, where she stopped to see Mira, and met with a number of people from the ISGS to promote—if she could—cooperation with the Institute. She returned to Lime Rock exhausted, but the plans for the Congress seemed well under way. Almost immediately, however, things began to unravel.

It came down to a manpower shortage. Guthrie Janssen had just left the Institute. In a little more than a month, Hansell Baugh, another highly productive member of the IGS staff, would leave. The relative isolation of Lime Rock had begun to wear on him. In April, he had gone on vacation to New York City and the city's attractions grabbed him and wouldn't let go. By the time he left the Institute at the start of June, Kendig—awash in contributor's papers to evaluate—was beginning to drown under them and the growing wave of other programming and planning details. She had committed herself to teach in the first two weeks of Elwood Murray's five-week Basic Communication Workshop "Evaluation in Communication" at the University of Denver starting July 26 and then would have to rush home for the mid-August IGS seminar-workshop being held in Millbrook, New York. When would she have time to work on the Congress? With Douglas Kelley going to England to represent the Institute for a mid-August International Congress on Mental Health, delaying the Denver Congress until sometime in 1949 seemed inevitable. The delay, until an as-yet-uncertain date the following summer, was announced in early August; although to keep some momentum going, the Committee decided to hold a Congress Colloquium for planners and participants in Chicago over the same weekend in October for which they had planned the Congress.

They met on Saturday evening, October 30, at Abbot Hall on the Chicago Campus of Northwestern University where, after introductions from Kendig, Douglas Kelley, the moderator, explained what the program committee was looking for in papers, i.e., rigorous applications of non-aristotelian methodology. Elwood Murray spoke on the arrangements in Denver and suggested a general theme, "A Method of Integration Without Regimentation". Each of seventeen people intending to present, gave three-minute summaries of their papers. Although successful, Kendig found her weekend in Chicago fraught with tension: she and Kelley had met with Institute Trustees there and she also conferred with Francis Chisholm and the ISGS Board of Directors on the long sought and frustrating issue of better coordination between the two organizations. After returning to Lime Rock, she collapsed into bed for two days.[12]

Several months earlier, in July, when the October Congress still seemed imminent, Korzybski had come to New York City with Charlotte to get away from the hubbub of the Institute in order to put together an Introduction to the Second Edition of *Manhood*—but he couldn't complete it. The trip had started off badly. After their arrival at the train station, a stranger had picked up Alfred's bag (borrowed from Ralph Hamilton) containing his papers and his copy of *Manhood*. Visits to the police proved fruitless in getting it back. Then, once they got down to work, Korzybski found the process of formulating the Introduction painful and difficult. They had nice rooms on the 12th floor of Hotel 33 on West 51st Street, a new place for them, across from Radio City Music Hall. Neither of them seemed to have gotten out much; although Charlotte, more mobile, had various items of business to do around town. Alfred spent much of the time in his room reading, mulling, and then talking over the proposed content while Charlotte took notes. He was reading a number of books on Russia, among them, John Fisher's *Why They Behave Like Russians* and David Shub's new biography *Lenin*, which soon took a prominent place on his recommended reading list for students. Shub, a writer for the Jewish Daily Forward in New York, had participated in the early Russian socialist movement and had known Lenin before 1917. His portrait of Lenin left no doubt that the Stalinist dictatorship of 1948 constituted a logical extension of Lenin's earlier regime and vision. Both derived not only from Marxism, but also from the heritage of the older Russian autocracy. The book reminded Korzybski of his own days living as a subject of the Tsarist regime, and jogged his formulating about dictatorship from the perspective of time-binding.

By the time he and Charlotte returned to Lime Rock in early August, after rather agonizing efforts, he had a lot of notes Charlotte had taken and, however inadequate, a tentative first draft. Although the front matter of the recently released Third Edition of *Science and Sanity* had listed a 1948 Second Edition of *Manhood* under "Volumes Already Published", the delay of the Congress removed some of the incentive for producing the Introduction so quickly. Korzybski must have felt a measure of relief.

Charlotte described some of Korzybski's process of working in a letter to Kendig on August 5, just before their return. Alfred had apparently responded somewhat gruffly to something Kendig had said to Charlotte (probably in a phone conversation) that Charlotte, in turn, had conveyed to him. Charlotte didn't want Kendig to take his reaction personally:

> He is so wrapped up in 'thinking' that nothing else makes the slightest impression on him. I can barely talk to him myself. He says that his present evaluation of Manhood, introduction, rather, is the most difficult thing he has written since Manhood, more difficult than writing S&S. He now has to include them both in his evaluation. It has been very painful for him, and I get kicked out regularly when he wants to be alone. It is a most frustrating and painful procedure all the way around. No talking, pleading, cajoling, considerations of the seminar [scheduled to start in one week], etc., etc., make the slightest

bit of difference. Perhaps that is 'what it takes'. Perhaps if you and I were like that we would get some creative work done. Well, this is just by way of sympathies, not really trying to be an explanation, but trying to point out that persons – you or I – or situations – the Institute, the seminar – etc., just don't matter in this instance, and while feelings of bitterness, etc., may be justified from one point of view, from Alfred's point of view they are un-understandable to him, at least at present. Present things that you and I and others would be deeply concerned in, simply do not enter his consciousness particularly.[13]

Still, whatever his creative agonies and apparent gruffness, he was managing to maintain at least a pinch of humor. On July 30, Charlotte wrote a letter to Kendig, including in the envelope a postcard with the by-then ubiquitous image (non-copyrighted) of the big-eared, gap-toothed smiling boy that *Mad Magazine* would later take as its mascot "Alfred E. Neuman" in the 1950s. The card had "to MK from AK [and] CS" written on its back. Charlotte ended the letter by referring to the boy's by-this time equally ubiquitous catchphrase underneath the picture: "Didn't you love the little 'What – Me Worry' card? A. says to send to all our trustees."[14]

Maybe he had gotten beyond worry, but he certainly seemed to have serious concerns about completing the Introduction and getting out the Second Edition of *Manhood of Humanity* without further delay. It would take up a major part of his time and effort during his remaining lifetime. Over the next year and a half, he would have several more sojourns in New York City at Hotel 33 for concentrated work on it with Charlotte. He would produce many more drafts of the Introduction and his fussiness about making it as good as possible reflected the importance he gave to it—even as it increased the book's delay. His concern about clarifying his own intellectual legacy against the background of growing misrepresentations of his work, including those by students—e.g., getting past the confusion of his work with 'semantics'—probably added impetus to his struggles here. Not surprisingly, more than he had ever done since the earliest days of his work, he would emphasize time-binding in his presentations and writing; stressing its foundational importance to his work, its connections to his subsequent formulations and those of others, and its unexplored implications, particularly in human relations and politics.

Chapter 64
HARDLY A DAY OFF

Korzybski took hardly a day off; then only, it seems, when forced by exhaustion or illness. He was mainly speaking for himself, when he told Ken Keyes in 1947, "We just work and work and work. No rest for the wicked, Saturday or Sunday."
> ...We have some years ago discovered that once a week we simply have to take one day off completely. Simply we are dull the next week, and unfortunately as far as I am concerned, it turns out that I never have a Saturday or Sunday. When the weekend comes, then I have to start on something else to work, but occasionally I am just dead. Naturally.[1]

Such devotion to work in his later years was not anything new, of course. From his childhood on the farm at Rudnik when he was told "Alfred, do it!", he had always devoted himself with extra measure to whatever task he had set before him. In his final years he continued to push himself as hard as ever, though age had perhaps mellowed his intensity.

Home At Work

Ralph C. Hamilton, living at the Institute for most of the time from September 1947 until January 1949, working as a personal assistant to Korzybski, gained a unique view of his mentor. Ralph, a veteran of World War II in his late twenties, had enough background and maturity to meet Korzybski as more of an equal than either of two younger men, Dave Levine and Dave Bourland, who filled similar roles for shorter periods after him. For its intimate feel of Korzybski's daily life, I'll quote extensively from Ralph's recollections [2]:

> I lived at the Institute. My room was on the third floor. It was a room-and-board arrangement. Charlotte did the cooking. I washed the dishes – often fixed my own breakfast, sometimes lunch. Dinner was usually in AK's office en famille – AK, Kendig, Charlotte, me... I had some minor chores about the house – keeping the kitchen kerosene water heater fueled, some snow shoveling in winter, going shopping weekly with Charlotte, etc. I ran off mailings and related material on the third-floor mimeo machine, took care of the library, read and wrote reviews on books—mostly scientific—sent to AK for review, had "consultations" and "junior seminars" with AK in his office when he had some issue he wanted to get off his chest, typed his letters (he dictated directly to the typewriter), provided technical or scientific comments, if asked, on matters he was interested in—in fact saw him daily or twice daily.

> He kept a police whistle on his desk. One blast, Charlotte. Two blasts, me. He used to say, "I hate that whistle. But I have to use it."

> Occasionally, some oddball, weirdo, or interested person found the Institute and wanted to talk. When any showed up on the front walk or at the door, I was summoned by Kendig or Charlotte and he was handed to me for interview. I was usually able to spot, in something he was concerned about, an aspect where GS could be applied. And he generally went away happy. This happened perhaps three or four times during my stay there.

> During the '48 winter seminar, I think it was, Douglas Kelley remarked to me, "You're keeping him alive. He needs someone to talk to." And he explained that in contrast to the Chicago scene, there were no scientifically trained people around Lakeville AK could talk to, except me. I have doubts that the matter was that vital.

> Anyway, I became a sort of technical assistant and commentator. He would give me a scientific article, have me read it, and then talk to me about it, partly for my benefit, partly

to get his notions about it formulated and clarified. My main duty during seminars, was to take full notes of AK's lectures. He would review the notes each night to see if he'd said the necessary and if anything more was needed; this was an education in itself.

During this time I was not otherwise employed; did have some time to work on my own stuff. I was not paid by IGS. We had agreed that being steeped in a GS environment, including daily "lectures" from AK, plus room and board, were fair exchange for my services. And Kendig and Charlotte, because I was a singer, encouraged me to further community relations by joining the Lakeville Methodist Church choir and taking part in other musical choruses, oratorios and such. I was a soloist at the church.

Korzybski had gotten somewhat overweight by this time, though not markedly so. Still, except for an occasional cold, he seemed generally healthy and vigorous.

Regarding his mobility, Ralph didn't see any marked change since 1946, but he had probably become less active. Limited by his war-damaged left leg, Korzybski stayed mainly on the second floor, only occasionally coming down to the ground floor for a party or other event. Using his cane, he seemed to have little trouble crossing between his room and office.

He seemed to enjoy his food. For their dinners in his office, Charlotte would run up and down the stairs with the Eastern European food she had cooked that Alfred liked—kasha, potato pancakes, sausage, etc. Ralph recalled Korzybski patting his stomach at the end of such a meal saying, "I et too much but it was good", then looking over to Ralph and saying "Skinny, you must eat." A fairly constant smoker, who knew it wasn't good for him, Korzybski at least wasn't one of those people Ralph had known who would light up the next cigarette with the embers of the previous one. He used a cigarette holder and lit up about once every hour or so. Ralph, not a smoker himself, didn't recall the brand. (Dave Bourland recalled it as *Lucky Strike*.) Alfred normally kept a glass of rum-and-water on his desk (he liked *Ronrico*), sipping from it occasionally, the frequency of refill depending on his mood of the day. Once in a while, he would appear to get a bit clouded toward day's end with a slight slurring of speech, but Ralph recalled "no change in interests, values, concerns." Ralph recalled Guthrie Janssen once joking that when Korzybski said 'I speak of cases...,' *Ronrico* was what he had in 'mind'. (But Korzybski was not the only person at the Institute—as he put it—'*not* a non-drinker'.)

Regarding Korzybski's daily routine and working habits, Ralph noted:
AK was usually at work in his office by 0900 or earlier, and kept at it, often until well after dinner. He worked slowly, taking pains that everything was just right; pausing now and then to hold forth to me on the meaning and implications of whatever it was; sometimes with applications to me personally—sort of "counseling." His work consisted of correspondence; study of some scientific development with respect to its own field and to GS; preparation and editing of articles, etc., etc. He was not much involved in day-to-day business such as administrative details (Charlotte), membership, relations with trustees, planning programs, overall finances (Kendig), etc.; but was kept briefed. Routine, business, promotional and other correspondence was mostly handled by Kendig, Charlotte, and their assistants according to responsibilities listed above. AK took care of correspondence with his friends, scientific connections, media, etc.

Korzybski still did some of his own two-fingered typing, sometimes having to bandage his fingers to protect them when they got raw. But he had Ralph type his letters (except for personal ones to Mira or more confidential ones to students, which Charlotte continued to type). Ralph would sit at the typing table in front of Alfred's desk and sometimes they might get done 6 to 10 letters per day if they contained brief responses to something. With other 'heavy' letters to E.T. Bell or to Kelley for example, they might do one or two per day. Alfred might dictate for a while, then at some point stop and give Ralph a 'junior seminar', before saying "Continuity" so that Ralph would read back what he had written so far and they could go on.

Korzybski saw educating Ralph as an important part of their work together. When Ralph first arrived at the Institute, Alfred arranged with Doctor Overholser, an Honorary Trustee of the Institute and the Superintendant of St. Elizabeths Hospital, to have Ralph go down there for a few days for a supervised tour of the place. Alfred told Ralph, "You will find yourself" among the psychiatric patients there. After Ralph returned, he reported he had actually done so. Later, when Ralph would abstract an article or book for Alfred and give a report on it, Alfred seemed as interested in Ralph's process as in the reported content. He might give Ralph a gentle scolding, "You don't read. Remember this when you read, study the author."

Ralph observed that the amount of work to be done at the Institute seemed tremendous:
> AK and the staff were, each of them, riding a formidable backlog. There were not enough hands, or heads knowledgeable in the underlying theme of IGS ("Linguistic Epistemologic Scientific Research & Education"); not enough hands to run the ship, not enough funding. AK used to say, "We ought to be funded by the Government."

Nonetheless, Korzybski plunged and plugged ahead. Ralph "likened his passion for getting every detail right to a cowboy leaping from his horse to wrestle a mouse to the ground. It could get trying. Without this focus to a tremendous overall drive he would not have produced his work." Ralph found him slow as a reader, marking just about everything he read. His work model in writing, as he stressed to Ralph, was: "First spit it out, then go back and fix it up." Having eaten very little breakfast, Korzybski would have lunch and then continue working in the afternoon. After dinner, he would usually either go back to work, if he had something pressing to do, or retire to his room.

Despite the amount of work, Ralph and Alfred had many conversations:
> We had all kinds of conversations: scientific, political, reminiscences about his youth in Poland, WWI, selling war bonds in the US, the moment of inspiration when the conception that became GS occurred to him, personal stuff, etc., etc. He was a one-way "conversationalist." His hearing had been blasted during the war and he had great difficulty hearing what you were saying (especially when he had something important to say) and that double barrier was sometimes impassable. But that was minor. I would not have missed any of those conversations.

Among the topics of conversation was the U.S. Congress: "Ah, that filibuster! It's short of criminal! Saunders approves it, I say it should be prohibited."

> As to opinions, he used to say, "In the old, 'democratic' way, everyone has a 'right' to his opinion. In the new way, scientifically, no one has a 'right to his opinion—if he has not studied the matter and informed himself."

Working daily with Korzybski for over a year typing letters; 'delousing' his writings; chasing down some piece of scientific data for him; helping him with seminar preparation, note-taking, diagramming, demonstrating, etc., gave Ralph Hamilton a great deal of data for some strong impressions about Korzybski's output and personality. Regarding Korzybski's output (his lectures and writings):

AK had a feel for, an insight into the existence and importance of basic levels of process, submicroscopic ('nanotech') and sub-conscious. He lived in a multiordinal, multidimensional world, of structure and function, misrepresented by our language and A [aristotelian] orientations. I think it was this that gave his prose, written and spoken, its convoluted and often labored approach. He was trying to convey his "take" on things to his readers and hearers. And it was this that made diagrams and models (e.g., Structural Differential) and such visualizations necessary in his seminars and lectures. Such means enabled him to show several levels, dimensions, etc., at once: the structure of things...Mathematics too, is, or represents, multidimensionality, e.g., matrices, simultaneous equations, etc.

Alfred's analytical ability and what he called 'feel' seemed especially noteworthy:
You studied the data, you explored the structure involved, you visualized it and so on, until you had the feel. You could fly by the seat of your pants. You could feel the relations, patterns and structures involved...AK applied his "feel" to people too. He looked from his office window once and saw, some 80 yards away, a couple headed for the Institute. At that distance he couldn't see who they were. He watched them for a couple of seconds and said to Charlotte and me, "That man is in love with that woman." I knew who they were. He was right. And from such "feel" he derived his caring for the people he worked with; his ability to see "where they were at." Which was sometimes uncomfortably acute.

Ralph noted the force of Korzybski's personality:
The first impression you got on meeting AK was vigor and directness and openness. These came with courtesy. If you hit it off, the courtesy grew into consideration and, over time, caring. He cared about anyone associated with him, and spiced it with an impish humor. "Warm" was the word most used at IGS. Robert Heinlein described him: "He had gusto." (Said of a character representing AK in the tale "Blowups Happen.") If you didn't hit it off, and he still had dealings with you, you soon found out. And if you needled him he was quite ready to lower the boom without malice.

Regarding Korzybski's 'impish' humor:
On one occasion, at his desk, anent something he and Charlotte had been reading, AK (glancing sidelong at Charlotte), remarked to me "But you know, human bodies really ugly." CS: "Now don't start that." AK (grinning at me): "You go out to the beach and look at the people. Ugly!" And so on, for a couple minutes. Charlotte, in a sort of resigned protest, walked out and sat on the steps outside the office door, while AK, still grinning, continued in this vein a bit. This was blaspheming part of Charlotte's creed: beauty of the human body. With her dancing and related work, she aimed at perfecting the human form, in motion and rest. And AK in the role of Puck, mischievous but benign. Kendig could smile at this. But sometimes the mischief came her way, and it was her turn to protest. And Skinny got his share too. But, I wasn't inclined to protest...As Charlotte strove...to develop beauty in the human form, so AK, you might say, strove to develop sanity. He kept at it in the face of what he saw at the beaches and hospitals and governments—manhood, as Lewis Carroll put it, involved in ambition, distraction, uglification and derision.

Ralph recounted what happened near the end of 1948 when, deciding to leave his 'informal' unpaid Institute job, he told Korzybski. (Ralph would stay in touch and later, over the next year and into 1950, worked pro tem for the Institute for pay):
...I began to see that I'd done what I could at IGS, and IGS and AK had done what they could for me. More, at that point, would on my part be a surfeit with relatively little, by comparison, application in work. I knew AK would not take to my leaving and would vigorously try to persuade me to stay; and that I wouldn't have much success in

explaining my view, by reason of the one-way communication I've described. I left a note on his desk saying how much benefit I'd gained, how much I appreciated it, and how, regretfully, I must get a job and get to work. I would leave on such a date. Two blasts on the police whistle soon followed, and, bracing myself, I reported to the mentor. He asked, "How have I failed you?" I said I didn't think he had; that I was much more capable now of doing the job I needed to find. He doubted it; asked me to cite how I would perform; how I would use my hands (always a big point with him) in talking to those I had to deal with; etc. Not much reassured, he gave me advice: act more extensionally, get in more direct contact with people, drop the theorizing and integrating for now—all sound, all valid. And shrugged his shoulders and sighed, and wished me well.

Yale

By this time, Mira had gotten less steady on her feet; but otherwise, under the care of her doctors, she seemed to be managing fairly well with a visiting nurse coming twice a week (she would soon have a young woman helper staying with her as well). She had hoped Alfred and Charlotte would be coming to Chicago to visit her before the end-of-year Holiday Intensive. Alfred, continuing to worry about her wellbeing, had hoped so too. But as it turned out, coming to Chicago would have to wait. Recovering from the flu, he still felt weak and didn't feel up to rushing to get to Chicago then. Instead he decided to make another trip to New York City with Charlotte in early December to deal with publishing issues and to work on a writing project of some importance to him—a review of the recently published *Resolving Social Conflicts: Selected Papers on Group Dynamics* by the late Kurt Lewin, whose physico-mathematical way of 'thinking' Korzybski felt very much in synch with.[3]

AK with Charlotte Schuchardt in New York, December. 1948

The book, edited by Lewin's widow Gertrude, dealt with issues related to changing the cultures of groups and societies (e.g., Germany) in the direction of democratic values; conflict resolution; and psycho-social problems of minority groups using the example of Jews coping with antisemitism—all topics of great interest to Korzybski. (However seriously he took the review, he couldn't get it into adequate shape before having to return to Lime Rock, and ultimately it never got published.) While still in New York, he thought he could go out to see Mira in January even though he would really have to rush, since he'd been invited to give a seminar at Yale University at the start of February. But it would turn out that January would have too much going on with too little time for a visit to Chicago.

While 1948 had been Korzybski's least busy year in number of presentations, his 1949 schedule already included many seminars, lectures, and talks, some connected with the upcoming Third Congress on General Semantics in Denver. In addition to all else, he would have to continue working to finish the Introduction to the Second Edition of *Manhood*, and otherwise preparing the book for print, advising on other Institute publications of his works, other writing projects, etc. When was he going to see Mira?

On December 31, mid-Holiday Intensive seminar, heavy rains overflowed the creek between the Institute and the Lime Rock Lodge, inundating the Lodge and requiring them to evacuate it with everything and everyone to the Indian Mountain School in Lakeville, where they still managed to have a New Year's Eve party that night and continue the seminar the next day. The Institute appeared unaffected by the rains. But early the next morning Kendig got a nasty surprise: the Institute basement had filled up overnight with four feet of water. A laborer had borrowed the Institute sump pump and, after returning it, failed to plug it in. They had a huge mess to clean up with water-logged books, files, pictures, trunks, etc. In his lecture that day, Korzybski—who normally devoted seminar time to talking about organizational and management issues—used the incident as an example of 'the eternal need for supervision' to make sure that 'little things' that might lead to heavy consequences got done, even while respecting vertical-horizontal structure in an organization and so working to avoid Graicunas-style overload.*

In January 1949, after the 'Flood Seminar', the Institute had some important personnel changes. Werner von Kuegelgen, whose wife Fritzie had done secretarial work for the Institute, began working as IGS accountant and sales manager. A German who had spent the war years in Berlin as an economist on the Price Control Board, von Kuegelgen had come to the U.S. and Lime Rock in August 1948, where Fritzie, an American citizen, and their three children had arrived two years before. The Institute accounting, sales procedures, etc., greatly disrupted during the move from Chicago, still needed major overhauls. Von Kuegelgen, who had a doctorate in Economics as well as practical experience in accounting and financial management, would get the IGS books, etc., into very efficient shape over the next year. Meanwhile, Ralph Hamilton, who had already moved from the Institute in November, was phasing out of his job as Korzybski's assistant; although over the next year he would still occasionally meet with Korzybski and do editing work for the Institute. Meanwhile, 19-year-old David Levine, who had been working at the Institute as a general assistant since the fall, picked up some of Hamilton's duties. After getting his Bachelor's degree from the University of Chicago in June 1948, Levine had gone to work at the ISGS office until getting laid off because of slumping Society finances. He had immediately called the Institute and asked Kendig if she had work for him. She offered him a working scholarship at that summer's seminar-workshop at Millbrook and after the seminar offered him a complete "support package" in exchange for work at the Institute. He had worked in the office, and had started to type and do research for Korzybski. Now at the end of January, Kendig asked him to come to Yale as part of the IGS staff to help Korzybski with his seminar there.

---

* Ralph recalled that in this final part of what became known as the *Flood Seminar*, "AK seemed to have shed 20 years. He was vigorous; high-spirited; his face looked much as it does on the back cover of S&S, 4th edition. He spoke with verve, élan and wit – astonished us all." [Ralph C. Hamilton to Bruce Kodish, 11/17/2005.]

The invitation to lecture at Yale that Korzybski had received from F. S. C. Northrop, Sterling Professor of Philosophy and Law, reflected a genuine interest in Korzybski's work among both students and professors there. The Yale student organization provided a generous honorarium for Korzybski and expenses for him and his staff. A distinguished list of professors, including Northrop, had signed on as Honorary Sponsors. Robert Redpath obtained a grant from the Blue Hill Foundation for student scholarships and 65 people, mostly Yale students, registered to attend the seminar, which ran from Tuesday to Sunday, February 1 to 6. Redpath helped organize the event with Fred Sanborn, another Korzybski student and 'Yalie'. Besides the seminar (totaling 27 hours of lecture by Korzybski), an evening Colloquium was held over three successive nights with an average attendance of 150. Various professors held forth on their interpretations and applications of Korzybski's work with Korzybski responding afterwards.

On the preceding Saturday, Levine, Kendig, Charlotte, and von Kuegelgen (who would be attending his first seminar) drove down to New Haven from the Institute with Korzybski. Levine "...watched in fascination as Korzybski came down the stairs from his second floor office, to get into Kendig's automobile for the trip.":

> He held onto the railing with a "death grip" and moved slowly, in obvious pain. But there was a determined expression on his face and an aura of confidence about him...I thought to myself, "Neither heaven nor hell would keep this fellow from his seminar at Yale." We got him safely buckled into his seat in the front passenger's [side]. Korzybski was wearing his usual khakis and a warm, lined trench overcoat that gave him a distinctly military air. His heavy cane was perched on the back seat, ready at hand. I traveled with Charlotte in her little coupe.[4]

On Monday, January 31, the day before the start of the seminar, a luncheon organized by Robert Redpath was held in Korzybski's honor at the Yale Faculty Club attended by about 15 professors, including faculty sponsors and colloquium speakers.[5] F. S. C. Northrop, a former student of Whitehead's, was among those who met Korzybski there and Korzybski greeted him with great enthusiasm. Northrop belonged to that select group of philosophers whom Korzybski would designate with a more honorable title—for him—an up-to-date 'epistemologist'. Philosophical commentator Bryan Magee, who studied with Northrop in the 1950s, would note his genius for teaching and considered him as a polymath, "in the same class as Bertrand Russell and Karl Popper."[6] But Northrop would not become nearly as well known as either of those two men. Northrop had immersed himself deeply in the sciences and in comparative socio-cultural history, and in particular had a deep concern for the epistemological and cultural implications of the relativity and quantum revolutions in mathematical physics. In a time when philosophy and other academic disciplines seemed to be moving towards more and more minute analysis and specialization, Northrop's interest in and talent for synthesis led him to transcend disciplinary boundaries in a way that probably helped put his work increasingly in the shadows of academic fashion.

Korzybski had been aware of Northrop's work for a long time, including Northrop's first book, the 1931 *Science and First Principles* listed in the bibliography of *Science and Sanity*. In his 1947 book, *The Logic of the Sciences and Humanities*, Northrop had attempted to establish a common epistemological framework for all forms of knowledge that included aesthetic experience and theoretical science and that had a place for values and value judgments. As Northrop recounted, Korzybski gave him a "warm and enthusiastic report on the merits of this same book. He told me that the only trouble with the book was that I packed so much into each sentence that only an informed reader paying attention to the meanings of words appreciates what is being said."[7]

As with many of those contemporaries whose works he admired, Korzybski seems to have known Northrop's work much better than Northrop knew his. (Northrop continued to refer to Korzybski's work as a kind of 'semantics'.) But Northrop was interested and open to learning more. Korzybski had known about the luncheon in advance and worked for some time on the short speech that he gave there describing his own work (recorded and later published in the May 1949 issue of the *American Journal of Psychiatry*). He began with a tribute to the late Yale mathematical physicist, Willard Gibbs, whom he considered "one of the greatest scientists this country has ever produced."[8] This impressed Northrop, who also admired Gibbs:

> This made it immediately clear to me that [Korzybski] was not one of those nominalistic semanticists who think the meanings of all concepts reduce to inductively given particulars [e.g., Hayakawa's Bessie the Cow_1, Cow_2, Cow_3, etc.] One cannot know and understand Gibbs' work without recognizing the important role of what I term concepts by postulation as well as nominalistic particulars in scientific knowledge."[9]

Dave Levine, who took care of the microphone, speaker, and recording equipment for Korzybski's lectures and took notes for Korzybski, described his performance in the sessions at Yale as a "tour de force...His personal remarks were kept to a minimum (much to our relief) but he sprinkled his talk with touches of humor and little 'stories' that captured his audience, made them laugh, and made them listen...I was amazed at Korzybski's stamina."[10]

Seminar attendee Thomas A. Gleeson, a graduate student in meteorology would agree with Levine's assessment. Gleeson had already read *Science and Sanity* twice, had been working to make applications to himself and his work, and felt that, as he later wrote to Korzybski, "this seminar seemed tailor made for me. I had, I believe, a grounding in GS from S&S, etc. that seemed to be a definite prerequisite to the course."

> The course served to enhance a non-verbal 'feeling,' a perspective for the subject; and this was due to the stresses, intonations, gestures, etc. imposed on the verbal subject material. Thus my curiosities were satisfied, I filled a notebook completely, —and now the 'photograph' of the blackboard diagrams is framed on an easel on my desk in lieu of a model of the structural differential, as a constant reminder of the methodology.[11]

Yet Korzybski had his problems. After the first full day of lectures Charlotte wrote to Mira about how things were going: "Edgy dear...The Count is doing very well. I haven't seen him so full of pep for a couple of years. The program is quite a killing one, but he seems to be enjoying it."[12] With the large class and short amount of time, Korzybski couldn't personally meet all of the students, as he preferred to do. In addition, as Charlotte wrote: "Many of them don't know S&S which makes it difficult. But the Count is giving good lectures."[13] Many of the Yale students—as well as faculty—seemed primed with non-useful preconceptions about Korzybski's 'semantics'. Gleeson noted a "bull session" he had late into the second night with five or six of the students who "were rather unfamiliar with GS, not to mention S&S":

> They were, to put it mildly, quite unreceptive to the subject matter of the lectures. They appeared not too well equipped to attack GS more generally, but rather picked at details in the lectures, (a practice you warned against, I believe, as a deterrent to the learning process). My arguments on the pro side were somewhat limited, for I had learned from previous experience how inadequate arguments can be in like circumstances. So I just listened.[14]

Regarding the colloquium, Korzybski had his difficulties too—especially so on the second night when social psychologist Leonard Doob gave a talk focusing on Korzybski's work as an approach to language and 'semantics'. Korzybski found Doob's questions to so misconstrue his work, that he struggled to answer without contradicting and embarrassing Doob. He wanted to be polite but apparently felt irritated enough to ask Doob if he had read *Science and Sanity*. Doob, as he later wrote to Korzybski, felt miffed. The next day in class, Korzybski mentioned in passing his discouragement with the session, though not mentioning Doob by name. His critical comments got back to Doob. The two men corresponded after the seminar and existing letters show that they not only honestly discussed what happened—including 'hurt feelings', etc.—but also expressed genuine admiration for each others' work. Much later, Doob's 1952 textbook *Social Psychology* devoted several pages to Korzybski and GS as a school of "semantics" of "interest to social psychology along with Ogden and Richards."[15] If his understanding of Korzybski's work remained superficial, at least he gave what he did understand of the extensional devices, etc., some honorable mention, and made some applications, however tentative, in subsequent parts of the book.

In his letter to Korzybski, Thomas Gleeson observed how easy it seemed for Doob and others to have "missed the point" about Korzybski's work:

> Which only reminded me of difficulties I'd had in the past in trying to answer acquaintances who'd asked me what GS is. I never did succeed in answering them well 'in just a few words,' partly because of my poor presentation perhaps, but also, (and this is more to the point,) because a new orientation cannot be imparted 'in just a few words.' Finally, I just tell them, "Read the book." Others have balked at this task, saying they haven't the 'time.' The latter have often been content to read, Language in Action, or a similarly less adequate presentation. After reading such a popularization they have made such remarks as, "I knew this stuff all the time! Why all the fuss about calling it 'General Semantics?'," or, "Would you say General Semantics is a branch of pragmatism or empiricism?", or , "I guess you could sum it all up by saying, 'Don't make generalizations,' couldn't you?," (quite a generalization in itself,) etc.[16]

Since driving wasn't allowed on the Yale campus, colleagues had to use a wheelchair to take Alfred around in a timely fashion from the campus residence where he was staying to the lecture hall. After their return to Lime Rock, *Time Magazine*, one of a number of periodicals that had sent reporters and photographers to cover Alfred's visit to Yale, ran a story on him, "Always The Etc." in the "Education" section of its February 14 edition. Somewhat flippant in tone, it had a number of factual errors; for example, according to the article Korzybski had spent most of his time at Yale in the wheelchair and in addition used the wheelchair to 'whisk' around the halls of the Institute. Still, as Charlotte wrote to Mira, the article could have been a lot worse. Mira for one, felt delighted to see it. The coverage of Alfred's work in the national weekly—a much deserved sign of recognition—seemed to her like a wonderful valentine.[17]

Cooper Union

The Introduction to the Second Edition of *Manhood of Humanity* now became the focus of Korzybski's attention once again. If he could get it to the printer—along with the other manuscript changes—no later than the first week of June, they had a chance of having the book available for the Third Congress on General Semantics scheduled for July 22 to 24 in Denver. In the interim, he had to prepare for a presentation on "Time-Binding–The

Foundation for General Semantics" on Monday evening, March 28 at the Cooper Union in New York City, to open a series of "Five Lectures on General Semantics" scheduled to run at Cooper Union through the end of April. On April 11, Lillian Lieber from the Department of Mathematics of Long Island University would speak on "Modern Logic"; followed by a talk on "Pictures and Meaning" two days later by her husband Hugh; Hayakawa, speaking on "Semantics, General Semantics", was scheduled for Monday April 18; and the series would wrap up on April 25 with a presentation on "General Semantics and Abstract Art" by Martin James from the New York Society for General Semantics.

Korzybski had been generating a lot of material on time-binding for the *Manhood* Introduction that he could use for his lecture. He usually spoke extemporaneously even when he had a written speech; but perhaps because he had so much material for the lecture and didn't feel confident about the organization, he asked Guthrie Janssen to summarize his presentation outline and typed notes into a more condensed and polished written text they could use as a press release. Janssen prepared a typed triple-spaced text within 24 hours, just in time for Alfred and Charlotte's departure for New York City on the Saturday before the lecture. Korzybski may have used this as a template to further organize his talk.

Janssen's summary, unfortunately, was not included in Korzybski's *Collected Writings*. Janssen deleted a lot of material, but tried to stay as close as possible to Korzybski's words and outline; and one can see Korzybski's hand—indeed his handwriting—on earlier typed manuscript versions. An examination of these and Janssen's final version shows Korzybski's lecture as an account of his work from the viewpoint of time-binding, including a foray into his personal history, applying the time-binding notion to himself to show some of the important influences that led to his work. He emphasized that he built GS from his study of time-binding and its mechanisms, not from studying 'thinking' or 'language' or 'semantics' as such. He discussed the importance of exponential laws for time-binding, Graicunas' work, dictatorships, and the relationships among these.[18]

On the evening of the lecture, a nice turnout of perhaps 200 people was expected; 800 showed up. The publicity from the *Time* article may have increased Korzybski's draw. Having gotten another head cold, he wondered later "how I lasted the lecture."[19] Nonetheless, those attending seem to have found his presentation memorable. Eugene Garfield, who would become well known in library/information science as the developer of the Science Citation Index, wrote in 1953:

> Many years ago, I attended a lecture by Alfred Korzybski, the founder of General Semantics. I am sure that the large audience in attendance at Cooper Union Hall in New York will never forget Korzybski's dramatic technique in getting across the idea that association-of-ideas techniques can lead to poor semantic adjustments. Korzybski had placed a huge placard on the stage which was an enlargement of the familiar Aunt Jemima pancake flour box. Aunt Jemima remained on the stage all the time Korzybski spoke.[20]

Garfield would note his interest in general semantics and time-binding as one of the influences that drew him into the field of scientific documentation and would put *Manhood of Humanity* as one of the 18 books on his "Basic List of Works In Documentation".[21]

Jan Sand, a writer for the online magazine *Ovi*, also attended Korzybski's lecture but seemed to have a less satisfying experience, which he wrote about it in a 2007 column:

> ...I first encountered non-Aristotelian thought in a science-fiction story by A. E. Van Vogt titled "The World of Null A" wherein someone adept in non-Aristotelian concepts

could instantly transport himself through space merely by thinking the proper thoughts. A tempting but, unfortunately, unattained so far capability.†

Like most philosophical tracts Korzybski's book covers a broad spectrum of human cognition and is frequently such a tangle of words and concepts that it presents a virtual jungle of linguistic density that could easily daunt the casual explorer. I once, long ago, attended a lecture by Korzybski at the Cooper Union auditorium in New York City in the hopes that he might lead me through easy paths into reasonable comprehension of his ideas. His lecture remains only a faint memory and the only outstanding characteristic of his presentation that still remains is that his Polish accent was so dominant that the words flew through my mind like a panicked flight of exotic birds leaving behind only the memory of disturbing squawks and violent passage. I left the lecture still puzzled and frustrated. Nevertheless, there is value in his viewpoint.[22]

Incommunicado

With the Cooper Union lecture out of the way, Korzybski originally intended to stay in New York for a couple of weeks to devote his full attention to *Manhood*, and then to go to Chicago for about a week to see Mira. However, by the second week of April he again decided to put off his visit. Recovering from the 'bug', he was resting and sleeping a lot, and he hadn't gotten a lot of work done. (Charlotte was recovering from a cold too, so they had both slowed down.) Charlotte was stuffing him with vitamins and felt somewhat concerned about his vulnerability to colds. She didn't worry that he had a serious illness but it seemed clear he suffered from overwork. She wrote to Kendig that in her opinion he could do with a long rest, somewhere with a warm climate like New Mexico or Arizona—clearly a pipe dream. With the Congress coming up, he felt more hard-pressed than ever to get *Manhood* out. A good long rest anywhere seemed out of the question. He and Charlotte would remain in New York, 'holed up' at Hotel 33 for most of the next three months.

Supposedly 'incommunicado' in order to work on *Manhood*, they had plenty of interruptions. In addition to visitors, they had to deal with a steady stream of correspondence—as well as occasional phone conversations—with Kendig. The Institute had entered an especially hectic period, only partly due to the looming Congress and its mounting details of contributor's papers, program organization, and general conference arrangements. Kendig had primary responsibility for managing all this, but Korzybski and Charlotte served as consultants. However much it distracted them, if Kendig needed their input they needed to respond.

A huge distraction came in early April with a sudden offer Kendig got for the sale of her house. Since the end of 1948, a man who was planning to buy the Lime Rock Lodge and the nearby Old Mill building had indicated interest in buying her house to live in with his wife and six children. Kendig would have a chance to recover her investment in the house and to make a small profit besides. Charlotte and Alfred both told her earlier in the year that she should do it if she could. The Institute's contract with her to rent the house had ended in September 1948 and it was now paying her on a month-to-month basis. She didn't feel she had much financial security and when the man finally agreed to her asking price after months of dickering, she felt tempted but also faced a dilemma. Where would the Institute go?

---

† But Van Vogt's character could transport himself through the universe solely because he had an extra brain designed for that purpose, not because he was adept in non-aristotelian 'thinking'.

Some trustees and other Institute supporters already had suggestions or made offers to help move the Institute to other states. Kendig didn't consider any of these options viable, since a number of Institute personnel whom she considered essential for present operations lived in Lime Rock or Lakeville and would not find it easy to move. Even if the Institute moved somewhere relatively close-by in Connecticut or upstate New York, Kendig didn't think they could afford to lose the Lakeville post office address for the immediate future. And even a local move promised to disturb plans for the Congress and the general activities of the Institute to some extent. She had to decide what to do. If she sold the house, the Institute would have to move by May 15. After a considerable flurry of activity on her part in the first week of April, including a 13-page memorandum on the issue that she wrote and sent out to Trustees for their advice; she declined the offer. She couldn't see disrupting the Institute's affairs solely for her personal benefit. The Institute of General Semantics would remain at the house in Lime Rock until the early 1980s.

With the issue of the house settled, Kendig could focus on the Congress. She needed all the help she could get. Unfortunately for her, David Levine would be leaving the Institute in a few months to return to graduate school, just as he had gotten really useful to her. With the complex administrative details of the Congress accumulating, she needed a competent person at once, and hired E. Lindley Gates, a former newspaper reporter with editing skills, for the job. "Lynn" Gates, in his late twenties, had served in the Navy from 1942 to 1946, and then returned to reporting, and had opened a duplicating and direct mail business in Johnstown, Pennsylvania before coming to the Institute. Besides helping Kendig with administrative tasks, he would soon take charge of the production end of Institute publications, among other jobs. David Levine got to know him and described him as,

...a hard-drinking fellow, a habit he had developed to keep in step with the other "drinking" reporters...[but] He seemed able to hold his liquor without showing much, unless you knew what to look for...He had a slow gentle way about him, very thoughtful, and very careful about the way he interacted with people. Kendig took an instant liking to him.

He shortly became a valuable member of the Institute staff...Lynn later, in the early nineteen fifties, became very much attached to Kendig, and they were married. Although Lynn was Kendig's junior by over a score of years [29 years], they seemed to bridge that gap very well and were very obviously fond of one another.[23]

Also in April, David Bourland, taking time off from his undergraduate studies at Harvard, began working at the Institute as an assistant. Given his legal status as a minor (he would have his 21st birthday in June), the Institute required his parent's permission for him to work there. He had a variety of jobs to perform including emptying garbage cans, filling kerosene heaters, maintaining the Institute car, and taking care of the library. He would soon begin helping with the Congress, taking care of some of the Institute correspondence and editing publications, as well as assisting Korzybski in upcoming seminars.

Meanwhile in New York City, Charlotte and Alfred were getting done whatever they could in relation to *Manhood*—other than the Introduction. Getting everything else to the printer as soon as possible would increase their chances of having the rest of the book ready to print while they worked on that last, most difficult part. They might still get the book out in time for the Congress. They were including three new appendices with material Alfred seemed likely to refer to in his Introduction: his paper on Graicunas' work, his "Author's Note" from *Selections from Science and Sanity*, and his credo "What I Believe", which—though written the year before—needed some finishing touches. The book would end with Keyser's final chapter from *Mathematical Philosophy*, "Korzybski's Concept of Man". They were planning to print "What I Believe" as a separate booklet as well, so at the very least they would have that ready for the Congress. For the cover, they would continue with the blue color originally used for *Science and Sanity* that had become an IGS tradition. As the cover graphic behind the text, they were using a vertical spiral expanding at the top, inspired by some art work that Mira had sent to Alfred in January—an old portrait by her of the two of them to which she had added a spirally ascending 'whirlwind' in the background. Alfred had used the spiral in Appendix II of the First Edition to model how the exponential process of time-binding operates, and further discussed the 'spiral theory' of time-binding in *Science and Sanity*. Over the last few years the development of cybernetics, with the notion of feedback and the increasing recognition of exponential functions and non-linear processes in this and other areas, seemed to him to corroborate his spiral theory. Putting a spiral on the cover definitely seemed fitting as symbol for his work.‡

Mira's new 'spiral portrait' of herself and Alfred, 1948-1949

On April 21 Charlotte (and Alfred) wrote to Kendig:

The [Graicunas] diagram arrived this a.m. with your note. Thanks. I can imagine how overwhelmed you must be, and our sympathies. At this front, we are ploughing ahead. At this moment we are finishing all the laborious details for the printer, Manhood with all corrections, paper selections, etc., various instructions to the printer, etc., etc. (and if there has been a comma or period missed it isn't our fault!) Anyway, in a few minutes I hope to take it all* in hand over to the printer, or rather the NY office, which fortunately is only a few blocks away.

*all, alas, but the new introduction, which we have now to settle down to finish. But I feel hopeful, determined, and grim. You and I know what is still ahead. However, we do nothing but work. The 'g-d delousing' seems never to end.[24]

To finish the new introduction—indeed. They already had lots of notes along with several drafts, unsatisfactory as they seemed to Alfred, and as they began to work they developed a somewhat satisfactory outline of important points to cover after the opening section.[2]

‡ Accompanying Mira's 'spiral portrait' was a note to Alfred, which said in part: "January 16 + 17, 1949 The spiraling recognition of your work is the most precious of birthday gifts to your loving Mira." [MEK to AK. MEK Archives, Box 22, Folder 2.]

They ploughed ahead. Through reading and research—including self-observation, Korzybski had developed an understanding of the role of unconscious processes in creation and discovery, which he consciously applied to his own creative work. His process of writing involved a lot of preliminary out-loud formulating, spitting things out on the typewriter, and multiple rounds of editing, re-writing, and that 'g-d delousing'. During any part of this process—even after mostly completing a piece of work—he might return to talking out various issues in order to refine what he wanted to say. And he liked to have someone to talk things out to. During the writing of his two books, Mira had fulfilled that role, which long since had descended to Charlotte. His formulating might lead into areas that would never reach print; although some interesting digressions could also lead to new and important insights to bring out. As she took dictation, Charlotte helped Alfred to corral his formulating with queries, questions, and doubts. If only they could eliminate the 'g-d distractions'.

May started out with a huge one—a surprise dropped on them by Hayakawa. Annual election time for the International Society had arrived and Hayakawa had decided to run for the Presidency against Francis Chisholm, the current President running for re-election. Chisholm had been planning with Kendig to get the two organizations working more in synch by bringing them together as divisions within a "foundation for G.S. with possible advantages public relations-wise, better opportunities for securing financial and other support for the G.S. program of training, publication, directing rigor and developing of discipline, etc."[26] They had gotten a general consensus from both organizations to pursue this plan at the October 1948 joint meeting in Chicago, with Kendig and Kelley representing the Institute and six representatives from the Society Board, including Hayakawa and Rapoport who together stood in sole opposition to the project. Within his next term, Chisholm hoped to begin working out the details to bring the general plan into fruition. By becoming President, Hayakawa sought to maintain the status quo. Understandably so; since his control over the day-to-day management of the ISGS office in Chicago (observed by David Levine who had worked there in 1948), his autonomy in running *ETC.*, and his ability to present general semantics there in whatever way he saw fit, seemed unlikely to continue under a new organizational structure.

The ISGS election ballots didn't get sent out to members until the end of the month, with a due date for returning them by June 24. But Hayakawa had already started campaigning in early May, sending letters to various leaders of the major local GS societies explaining his reasons for running. His May 9 letter to Robert L. Read of the Los Angeles group seemed particularly revealing. Read, a supporter of Chisholm and friendly with Korzybski, conveyed Hayakawa's letter to the Institute (a copy of an excerpt of this and other Hayakawa letters and related correspondence is in the IGS 1949 scrapbook). Kendig, Korzybski, Charlotte, and others likely read it with dismay. Hayakawa wrote:

...The Society, because it is not run by the Institute, is acquiring prestige and scientific acceptance for general semantics. ETC. is being ever more widely quoted as an authoritative source of information and theory, and is being regularly abstracted by the technical journals of psychology, education, etc. This is happening because we have succeeded so far in avoiding the public relations errors that IGS has a genius for...I can hardly tell you how often...I have been made heartsick by AK's unconscious sabotage of general semantics.

Also Kendig. Also the whole Institute. AK telling dirty stories before strange audiences not yet oriented to his ways; Kendig infuriating women's clubs; AK talking to the American Sociological Society and the American Psychiatric Assn. as if they were school children. There is an incredible list of worse than faux pas extending back for decades...The latest is Yale, where I should not be surprised if AK hasn't done as much harm as good for GS. For example, he kept calling Professor Leonard Doob—a very big bigshot in the social sciences—Professor Boob. This little joke has probably cost us the support of the Social Science Research Council for the next twenty years...The Society is run, and has been run, on the right track. It must continue following such policies as we have evolved. ...I do not need to tell you, of course, that none of the foregoing beefs reduces in any respect my enthusiasm for general semantics and my determination to see it operative on a wider and wider scale, to the enhancement of Korzybski's prestige and fame which he richly deserves.[27]

Dealing just with Hayakawa's claim that Korzybski called Leonard Doob 'Professor Boob' at Yale: how could Hayakawa have known, if he himself didn't directly hear it? He didn't. So did someone else who did hear or thought he heard it tell Hayakawa? Or did someone who heard the story from someone else who heard it from someone else..., etc., etc., etc.? David Levine, who did attend as Korzybski's assistant, recalled no such remark.[28] In the Yale lecture transcripts, Korzybski criticized Doob's colloquium presentation without referring to him by name (p. 132). Whether or not Korzybski called Doob 'Boob' (I surmise not), what justified Hayakawa repeating this story about Korzybski in order to influence the election? What happened to the ethics of time-binding Hayakawa had written about?

It's hard to say how upset Korzybski got as a result of Hayakawa's negative campaigning and the possible negative election outcome for the Institute. However by this time, Hayakawa's behavior couldn't have totally surprised him. At any rate, he and his colleagues at the Institute hoped to counteract Hayakawa's campaigning with some of their own. They sent copies of Korzybski's 1947 protest letter to a number of people among the leadership of the large local GS groups in Los Angeles, New York, and Boston, asking them to oppose Hayakawa and vote for Chisholm. (The Chicago group seemed split about 50-50, from a rough survey Kendig took.) The presidents of the three other groups, who strongly supported the Institute and the plans for its unification with the Society, sent out letters to their chapter members in support of Chisholm. But by the end of June it seemed clear that despite their efforts, Hayakawa was going to win. Most of the 1800 or so International Society members who could vote had neither studied with Korzybski nor read his books nor knew of the controversies between the two men. Hayakawa, as the editor of *ETC.*, and the nationally known author of a popular book supposedly based on Korzybski's work, was going to win what amounted to a popularity contest. Chisholm threw in the towel on July 1 with a letter to the Executive Secretary of the ISGS. Chisholm still hoped that greater cooperation between the two organizations was possible. But any plans for unification had effectively been dashed. For better or worse, the separation of the two organizations—with their at times competing functions—that Hayakawa wished to preserve, would remain in effect for many years to come.

With this going on, Charlotte and Korzybski continued working on *Manhood*. Alfred, wanting to get every detail of fact as correct and up to date as he could, wondered what had happened to Walter Polakov. He planned to refer to him in the Introduction, but hadn't heard from his old friend for quite some time. Charlotte wrote to Mira to find out if she knew whether Walter was even alive or not. If not, Alfred would have to write 'the late

Walter Polakov'. Mira wrote back that she had last heard from Walter about a year before when he was living in Berkeley on a $100 a month pension from the United Mine Workers Union. As far as she knew he was still alive. Alfred would have to go with that until he heard otherwise.

By the middle of May, Charlotte wrote to Kendig:

> I don't know what to say about Manhood. If only A. did not think he had to say 'everything' in a nutshell, if only he would not have the feeling that this is the most important thing he has ever written and would not worry so much about it, it would be so much easier. It is still very rough. I suppose if we do come back right away that would be the end of it. If he would only write 4 or 5 pages and not try to say so much. Well, I just try to do the very best I can, and I must say, he does too. It has possibilities of being very good, if it ever gets done.[29]

Two weeks later, she gave Kendig this 'progress' note about "the intro. situation":

> Sometimes I am pessimistic, sometimes optimistic. Right now I am rather optimistic. Needless to say, the book will not be out before the Congress. But we will have the Credo reprints anyway. About the book, the printer did some changing of dates, but of course I can't get too angry because we haven't finished our job I suspect (he is supposed to call me this pm) some time the first week in June would be the deadline for the intro. Whether true or not, I'll tell them to give us the date of, say, June 6. Then maybe it will be ready soon after.
>
> In A.'s words, whatever we have written so far is lousy. Besides, it isn't put together right. If A.'s present mood keeps up, I believe he will be psycho-logically ready to put it together later today or tomorrow. It is the structure that bothers. We can go on adding, cutting out, revising, talking about, but very soon that has to stop and it has to be clinched into a structure. I just honestly don't know what to say, as sometimes I think we should return immediately to Lime Rock, as there must be so many things there to be done, and for your sake; then it seems rather a pity, when so much money has been spent, and time consumed, and the possibility, if not the probability, of being so close to the end and finally getting it done – I just don't know what to do. I know A. wants very much to finish in a few days. And I hate to squelch that, even if I actually do have doubts. We cannot stay here indefinitely. I rather hope that the printer's date will spur the energy for the final spurt. However, if you believe it is urgent for us to return now, let me know.[30]

Several days later, she wrote:

> Our dear MK –
>
> A note while sitting glued to my chair. We do nothing but work at Intro. for past days, every waking moment. At last it is getting a satisfactory structure [and] A. is enthusiastic. I also believe it has fine possibilities. Hope we can finish tonight putting together.
>
> A. says we will finish this week. I have my doubts, knowing the process of de-lousing.[31]

Charlotte managed to get out of the hotel more than Alfred, but she also managed to cajole him to leave his room occasionally for some recreation. On June 7, she wrote that Allen Walker Read, the President of the New York Society for General Semantics, of whom both she and Alfred had become very fond, "went with us to Hamlet yesterday. A. sort of enjoyed it, but not as much as I had hoped. Anyway, it was a good thing for him to get out." One day past the printer's deadline date, they still seemed far from completing the introduction:

> If we can just get it written...so that it is in a semi-final form, I will be happy. No one I suppose has been more set in strong hopes of seeing Manhood than I; that is, I have had my heart set on it, as have you too, and Alfred. The psycho-logical difficulties have been great, and I shall ask for no more now than to have it in a somewhat finished form,

to which he can go back relatively easily in Lime Rock after the seminar. This would mean a tremendous lot for him, and also will help to clarify his speech for the Congress. I believe he expects to finish it pronto, however, and I have not mentioned anything otherwise to him.[32]

The Third Congress on General Semantics

Charlotte and Alfred returned home in mid June. Even though they hadn't finished the Introduction, at least they had gotten far enough along—with several more drafts and a structure that had gelled—to have it near the semi-final form Charlotte had hoped for. They could return to it in the fall. With most of the other new material for the Second Edition of *Manhood* in proofs, the book seemed well on its way to publication, but unfortunately not in time for the upcoming Congress. They had also started the somewhat simpler process of getting Alfred's 1924 and 1926 *Time-Binding* papers photographed for reprinting in a booklet, as well as setting up for the production of lithographed Structural Differential wall charts on heavy linen-backed map stock—both the booklet and wall chart to be ready for sale later that year. Now back in Lime Rock, Alfred and others prepared for the upcoming Third American Congress on General Semantics at the University of Denver and a very busy next few months.

On July 3, he had his 70th birthday. They gave a little party for him at the Institute. Mira sent a note. He planned to see her shortly and telegrammed ahead to her. On July 8, Charlotte and he would leave on the New York night train with a next day afternoon stopover in Chicago so that they could visit with Mira at the station for a few hours, before traveling on to Denver. Arriving on July 10, they would then have a day and a half to 'rest' before things started up with the short pre-Congress intensive seminar Alfred was teaching at the University.

When they did finally arrive at their Denver Hotel, which Charlotte described in a note to Kendig as an "old people's home", Alfred seemed "all right." Charlotte had felt concerned about his health. He had been having a lot of colds, seemed a little rundown, and had not responded well to the high elevation on his previous trips to Denver. She had already wondered to Elwood Murray when they were planning things, if Alfred should minimize his time in the mile-high city. Perhaps Alfred was taking on too much by teaching the pre-Congress intensive. There was nothing she could do about it now. Alfred seemed intent on fulfilling everything they had planned.

After they arrived, Charlotte just wanted "to sleep and sleep" but she didn't have time for much rest.[33] She was assisting Alfred in his short seminar at the University 'barracks' where Elwood Murray had his office. The afternoon and evening course ran from Tuesday, July 12 to the following Tuesday, July 19 with a break for the weekend and a 'whopping' tuition fee of $18. The fifty or so students were supposed to have read *Science and Sanity* or *Selections from Science and Sanity* ahead of time, but it's a good guess many of them didn't. Alfred and Charlotte had prepared a class handout of "Books And Articles Referred To By Korzybski In His Lectures"—a short list of works of significance for him. The list might confuse those who viewed Korzybski's work in terms of 'semantics', but seemed a good example of the wide scope of Korzybski's actual concerns:

Lenin: A Biography by David Shub

Topological Psychology and *Resolving Social Conflicts* by Kurt Lewin

'The Mathematical Way of Thinking' by Dr. Hermann Weyl, *Science*, Nov. 15, 1940.

'Qualifications of a Research Physicist' by Dr. Albert W. Hull, *Science*, June 12, 1931.

'Two Modes of Social Adaptation and Their Concomitants in Ocular Movements' by Trigant Burrow and Hans Syz, *Journ. Of Abnormal and Social Psychology*, April 1949.

The Nature of the Physical World by A. S. Eddington[34]

Before the course ended, that scope would—with any luck—begin to make sense to the students who hadn't known much about general semantics. Given the limited time Korzybski had for presenting the material or for getting to know the students (no personal interviews), when the seminar finished, he considered it "very successful."[35]

Korzybski and Charlotte had only a couple days break before the start of the Congress on Friday July 22. Kendig had flown in on July 16. With Dave Bourland and Lynn Gates to help her, Elwood Murray, and Douglas Kelley, they managed to pull off a well-organized and highly successful event. Kendig had a lot of issues to contend with. For one thing, she had worried that Hayakawa and others might boycott the Congress, but both he and Rapoport came and presented papers, as did Chisholm. Peace seemed to prevail despite the recent unpleasantness of the ISGS election. 300 people registered for the Congress with 75 presentations given over the Congress's three days.[36]

Korzybski helped start out the Congress with his keynote address at the opening general session on Friday morning. His talk was entitled, "Implications of Time-Binding Theory for Human Progress in A Free Society Versus Stultification by Dictatorships of Human Time-Binding Potentialities". At least in his outlined notes (according to Charlotte, he diverged from them in his actual talk), he began by discussing how the notion of time-binding emerged from his early life experiences and how the development of his later work (in a way summarized in the structural differential) came out of time-binding—the structural differential representing the fundamental difference between animals and humans. Time-binding progress depended "on our freedom to revise our higher order abstractions in conformity with study of facts." Dictatorships, in basic opposition to human time-binding potentialities, kept people infantile, clinging to authority, unable to think for themselves, fearful, and isolated from others. To the contrary,

> With a realization of time-binding, we realize we are not 25 or 50 or 75 years old. We are millions of years old. All dependent on each other. Time-binding involves feelings of responsibilities, duties to ourselves and others, duties to future generations. What do we want to leave as a legacy to our children? If we are conscious of ourselves as time-binders, we take pride in doing our part in carrying forward the best wisdom of the race and enlarge on it, for the benefit of future generations. This involves serious obligations and moral issues.
>
> In closing, I want to quote some wisdom from Shakespeare which applies to us here very directly: 'To thine own self be true, and it will follow, as the night the day, thou canst not then be false to any man.' But before we can be 'true to ourselves' we have to know ourselves, and this is the chief aim of general semantics. I will end with a quotation by Robert Browning [he had gotten this from Mira and planned to use it in his introduction to the Second Edition of *Manhood*]:
>
> 'Tis time new hopes should animate mankind, new light should dawn.'
>
> I hope you are feeling as encouraged and hopeful as I do when I see this splendid group here, carrying on so constructively and helping to realize more fully our potentialities as time-binders.[37]

Over the next three days, the Congress featured several general sessions plus separate sectional meetings on Education; Socio-Economic Issues; General Semantics in a Communication Program (with enough papers for two panel discussions on the University of Denver's use of GS to unify its curriculum); Theoretical, Methodological and Linguistic Issues; Speech and Clinical Psychology; "An Organismal Approach to the Liberal Arts Curriculum" (another University of Denver panel on applying GS); Psycho-Somatic Issues and Applications; Education Applications; Education and Communication: Special Applications; A Panel on Methods and Materials for General Semantics Study Groups and Adult Education; and a Round Table on the Arts as Communication.[38] The surprising number, variety, and quality of presentations over just one weekend, pleased Korzybski; the surfeit of stimulation must have set participants' heads abuzz. Kendig intended to produce a volume of Third Congress papers. This never happened, probably due to subsequent financial and manpower issues at the Institute, but a number of the papers were subsequently reprinted in the *General Semantics Bulletin* and *ETC*.

A Bequest To His Fellow-Sufferers

At Sunday night's closing banquet at one of Denver's mountain-view restaurants, Korzybski was presented with a check for $1,837 raised over several months by the Alfred Korzybski Fellowship Fund Committee, intended to pay for tuitions and stipends for working Fellowships with Korzybski at the Institute.[39]

Korzybski's scheduled banquet speech followed, beginning with a couple of stories, before the meat of his presentation: the text of the "Bequest of Pavlov To The Academic Youth of His Country", written shortly before Pavlov's death in 1936. At the end of 1944, Korzybski had sent it to Hayakawa to print in *ETC*. In his 1947 'Protest' letter to Hayakawa, he had referred to it again, writing "Whoever will read that 'testament', whenever he finds the word <u>scientific</u> or <u>science</u>, he should substitute <u>life</u>, since the advice of this epoch-making man applies to both science and life."[40] He repeated this admonition to the banquet audience, then read "Pavlov's Bequest" aloud (in *italics* below). Since it described so well the path he himself had followed, Korzybski was turning it into his own bequest to them:

What can I wish to the youth of my country who devote themselves to science?

Firstly, gradualness. About this most important condition of fruitful scientific work I never can speak without emotion. Gradualness, gradualness and gradualness. From the very beginning of your work, school yourself to severe gradualness in the accumulation of knowledge.

Learn the ABC of science before you try to ascend to its summit. Never begin the subsequent without mastering the preceding. Never attempt to screen an insufficiency of knowledge even by the most audacious surmise and hypothesis. Howsoever this soap-bubble will rejoice your eyes by its play it inevitably will burst and you will have nothing except shame.

School yourselves to demureness and patience. Learn to inure yourselves to drudgery in science. Learn, compare, collect the facts!

Perfect as is the wing of a bird, it never could raise the bird up without resting on air. Facts are the air of a scientist. Without them you never can fly. Without them your 'theories' are vain efforts.

But learning, experimenting, observing, try not to stay on the surface of the facts. Do not become the archivists of facts. Try to penetrate to the secret of their occurrence, persistently search for the laws which govern them.

> *Secondly, modesty. Never think that you already know all. However highly you are appraised always have the courage to say of yourself – I am ignorant.*
>
> *Do not allow haughtiness to take you in possession. Due to that you will be obstinate where it is necessary to agree, you will refuse useful advice and friendly help, you will lose the standard of objectiveness.*
>
> *Thirdly, passion. Remember that science demands from a man all his life. If you had two lives that would be not enough for you. Be passionate in your work and your searchings.*[41]

Korzybski then proceeded with his own commentary on this. He told those assembled in the restaurant:

> Never forget that <u>gradualness</u>. About the third bequest, <u>passion</u>, sometimes I wonder whether today some of that passion of which he [Pavlov] speaks is lacking, and among some young men and women there is some cynicism, bitterness, or frustration creeping in, which are a serious handicap for further knowledge. Never lose that <u>wonder about the world and ourselves</u>, that capacity to 'see the old anew', as the great Leibnitz said, which has led mankind to its great achievements so far. Never allow that <u>hunger to know</u> to become too satisfied, for our human race is young and still immature, and there are many thousands or millions of years ahead in which to continue our search for structure, which is all we will ever know, since the silent levels will never be the same as the structure in which we will represent them.
>
> Here today, I am happy that we have taken another step forward. I am proud and honored that we can share this forward step together.
>
> I am grateful to Miss Kendig, who is so largely responsible for this congress and to Dr. Kelley and to Miss Schuchardt, who has helped me. I am also grateful to Dr. Murray, Dr. Larson [an associate professor in the Department of Speech Communication], Chancellor [Alfred C.] Nelson [Honorary Congress President] and the University of Denver, and the Denver students of general semantics.
>
> I may end with a quotation by the great physician, Dr. Alexis Carrel: 'To progress again man must remake himself. And he cannot remake himself without suffering. For he is both the marble and the sculptor.' My best wishes and thanks to you, Fellow-Sufferers.[42]

At the Castle

At the end of the Denver Congress, the Mutual Broadcasting System gave Alfred a one-minute radio spot to explain his work. He barely had time to declaim the five-sentence description he had written for the Introduction to the Second Edition of *Science and Sanity*, which began: "General semantics is not any 'philosophy', 'psychology', or 'logic', in the ordinary sense."[43] The August 1 edition of *Time* magazine had another feature story about him as well. Mira must have felt thrilled to hear and see these acknowledgements of his work in the national media—despite their brevity and, in the case of the *Time* article, inaccuracy as well. The *Time* Education feature entitled "Always Either-Or" depicted Korzybski at the Congress depressed at the state of the world. The accompanying photograph of him labeled "Semanticist Korzybski" had the subtitle: "*A hopeless count.*"[44] Charlotte sent a corrective letter to the editor, which *Time* didn't publish.

Mira undoubtedly also felt thrilled when a few days after the Congress ended, Alfred and Charlotte, on their way back to Lime Rock, stopped in Chicago to see her. They stayed for at least a week, with Charlotte probably taking the opportunity to visit her parents nearby in Milwaukee.

Back in Lime Rock by the second week of August, they scrambled to prepare for the annual summer seminar-workshop. They had to rent a truck to schlep Korzybski's special chairs, typewriters, and the myriad other things they needed, to the seminar site 35 miles north of the Institute—"The Castle" in Great Barrington, Massachusetts. Occupied during the academic year by Barrington School, a posh private institution for girls, the castle was built at the end of the 19th Century for the widow of a San Francisco railroad baron. David Levine, who came to attend as a student-staff member, described it as,
> ...complete with battle crenellations on the gray masonry, ivied walls, a classic Greek 'temple' out on the back lawn, and a nine-hole golf course,...It was a perfect, self-contained world with sleeping quarters for thirty or forty "students", a grand piano, and a conservatory where the seminars were held. We dined out on the enormous side patio, near the kitchen.[45]

The seminar-workshop, advertised with the theme of "Time-binding and the Improvement of Human Evaluation, Communication, Social Relations and Scientific Advance", ran from Sunday August 14 to September 6, with private interviews given by Korzybski after he finished his course of lecture sessions. 65 students registered, with 45 staying for the full workshop. "The group", as the report published by the Institute later put it, "was typical of other courses in one respect, what a student called their 'stimulating un-homogeneity.'"[46]

Korzybski's 57th course since the founding of the Institute seemed like one of his best ever. Stoked by the recent Congress, he seemed in excellent humor. Before his first lecture, testing the microphone, he said "One, two, three, testing. Then after three comes four. Then five." Kendig chimed in to suggest to him that they ring a bell for the latecomers not yet in the lecture hall. Korzybski replied, "How about a pistol?"[47] His 40 hours of lectures, replete with stories, diagrams, and demonstrations, took up about a third of the entire seminar-workshop. As he had done for a number of years, he made sure to have a showing of Jules Masserman's film "Experimental Neuroses in Cats", since he felt the movie had relevance for neurotic humans as well as experimenter-crazed cats. He also had David Levine set up the box of mousetraps and candies for the chain reaction demonstration. David remembered the 'explosion': "...it was spectacular! One got the feel all right!"[48]

As part of the workshop, Kendig was beginning to integrate group dynamics (based on Lewin's research) into the curriculum. In the month before the Congress, she had attended the National Training Laboratory in Bethel, Maine. Along with three of the seminar students who had also studied there, she led a workshop panel discussion on group dynamics and instituted small group discussion sessions (based on the Bethel "T-groups") with a facilitator to encourage group members to examine their own processes of interaction. These self-reflexive sessions would become a regular and fascinating part of Institute seminar-workshops for years to come. Kenneth G. Johnson, a teacher at later Institute seminars, recalled some of the things he heard during sessions he 'led'. Once, after a long, uncomfortable pause someone interjected, "I love the silence. I just enjoy sitting here whether anyone is talking or not. Don't you?" Another observed, "Have you noticed—we're more in the here-now today than we were yesterday."[49]

Korzybski had invited George Kingsley Zipf to give a lecture about his work; Zipf's presentation at Great Barrington became a high point for Korzybski. Zipf, University Lecturer at Harvard (which meant he could teach whatever he wanted), had started out in the fields of English and Philology. After getting his doctorate in Comparative Philology and Linguistics, he had written two books, *The Psychobiology of Language* and *National Unity and Disunity: The Nation as a Bio-Social Organism*, along with numerous articles before his latest book, *Human Behavior and the Principle of Least Effort: An Introduction to Human Ecology* (*HBPLE*), published at the start of 1949. In *HBPLE*, Zipf indicated his aim to develop "an objective science of society that may be used as a frame of reference for an empiric system of ethics," and recognized Korzybski as one of a group of figures whom he considered to be working with him along that line. He appreciated Korzybski's brilliant analysis of the way that "intangible and trite verbalistic behavior" led to "enormous intellectual confusion."[50] (Korzybski, in turn thought highly of *HBPLE* and by July had it added to the list of books recommended by him available for sale by the Institute.) Dave Bourland had become a student of Zipf at Harvard and probably helped get his teacher even more interested in Korzybski's work. Zipf's paper for the July Congress, "General Semantics and the Principle of Least Effort: Toward a Synthesis," appeared as a genuine effort of integration. Indeed Zipf wrote that "if the synthesis is to succeed, it will be General Semantics either in its present structure or altered with the evolution of time and further experience that will absorb the Principle of Least Effort, not the reverse."[51] Zipf wrote to Korzybski after his seminar-workshop presentation expressing regret that he couldn't stay longer at Great Barrington. But the two men remained in contact. Korzybski soon invited Zipf to become an Honorary Trustee of the Institute and Zipf accepted, getting voted in at the meeting of the Institute Trustees on December 9. In his paper and lecture, Zipf had sought to express "an intimation of what I feel profoundly is the next great step that General Semantics may be about to take." Unfortunately, he didn't have the opportunity to integrate his work with that of Korzybski. After receiving a Guggenheim Fellowship in January 1950, he became ill during the summer and died at the age of 48 in September 1950.[52]

In her report on the 1949 seminar-workshop, published in the first *General Semantics Bulletin*, Kendig wrote this summary: "With this course [at Great Barrington] we felt we had now evolved the most fruitful sort of pattern."

> Looking backward, we found we had come a long way from the early Seminars in the old Chicago Institute building when people came to two or three lectures a week for many weeks, or every day for one week of intensive lectures. Students' obvious needs for review, practice, and conferences on applications germinated the workshop program. It began in 1943 with a few days of review and drill, a few talks on applications by old students after the Seminar and little opportunity for the informal group learning which living together affords. We have come a long ways, too, from the summer of 1946, when we moved the Seminar-Workshop and ourselves from Chicago to Lakeville on two weeks' notice and improvised our first 24-hour living and learning program at the Indian Mountain School.[53]

More Work To Do

With the seminar done in early September, Korzybski and the Institute staff returned to Lime Rock. The atmosphere of bedlam after the Congress while preparing for the seminar had ceased, but the small staff still seemed mightily busy, if not overwhelmed, with work. Mac Mallach had been joined in June by a new office assistant Henrietta Vandervoort. "Miss Van", as she was called, managed the 8,000-name student and general mailing lists and stencils, and did the general correspondence filing as well as secretarial work for Charlotte. As 1949 was drawing to a close, she may have helped to keep Charlotte and Kendig sane—and thus everyone else as well. Like many people in the U.S., their nerves were probably a little on edge anyway. On September 23 came ominous news: President Truman confirmed that Stalinist Russia had exploded an atomic bomb. In China, with Chiang Kai-shek's Nationalist forces forced to retreat to Taiwan, the Communists under Mao Zedong had won the Civil War. On October 1, Mao declared a "People's Republic" in Mainland China.

Still, they had good news at the Institute of General Semantics. Dave Bourland had just received the Korzybski Fellowship, which he had applied for in June. He would draw a stipend from the Institute and, along with his ongoing duties, would take on a few more responsibilities, and also presumably get more time to study with Korzybski. Among other things, along with Ralph Hamilton, he began working as an Assistant to Kendig, editing the Institute's new publication, the *General Semantics Bulletin* (*GSB*)—with Lynn Gates in charge of production and cover-design.

Given its currently dicey relationship with the International Society and lack of control over *ETC.*'s editorial content, it seemed time for the Institute to bring out its own regular publication. *GSB* would serve as a more rigorous korzybskian alternative to *ETC.*'s watered-down approach. (In fairness to Hayakawa, he would continue to publish articles by more korzybskian writers like Allen Walker Read, Sam Bois, Ray Bontrager, etc., along with articles that people at the Institute would consider unsuitable from a non-aristotelian point of view.) Also by consolidating important articles into the *GSB*, the Institute could stop sending them out as separate mailings, and in that way save time, effort, and money. The first *General Semantics Bulletin* (*Numbers One & Two*)—a double issue for "Autumn-Winter 1949-1950" published for 'Members of the Institute' "for information and inter-communication among workers in the non-aristotelian discipline formulated by Alfred Korzybski" with "news, views, comments, group activities, work-in-progress reports, research and applications, etc." and intended "to appear three or more times per year"—was ready for the printer by the end of February 1950. Korzybski would naturally know and have a say about whatever was going into this first issue, but he was not much involved with the editing or production.

Besides working directly with Alfred, Charlotte had other business needing her attention. For example, she was managing the production of the Institute's two newest major publication items: Korzybski's *Time-Binding: The General Theory, Two Papers 1924–1926* with an introduction by Kendig, as well as the Structural Differential wall charts. By the end of October, both were produced and ready for official announcement and sale by the Institute. Charlotte also had a great deal of correspondence to catch up with—for one thing, correspondence with Ken Keyes (partly on behalf of Korzybski). Since 1947, Charlotte had been keeping tabs on the various aspects of Keyes' proposed biography of Alfred and sending information and loaning materials to him that she hoped would facilitate his work on it. Keyes had just moved, started a new job, and finished his first book—*How To Develop Your Thinking Ability*, set to be published in 1950. It wasn't clear how much progress he had made on the biography. Not much it turned out; though by this time his wife, Roberta had finished transcribing the recording of Korzybski's 1947 memoir—not a small task in itself. Charlotte did what she could to help him and at the end of October, she wrote to fill him in on some important information she thought he should have for the biography:

> Probably you have been reading about the many books recently published on 'The Life of Chopin'. If you do not get the Sunday New York Times, I call your attention to the Book Review Section of October 16th. I mention this because of your interest in Alfred's biography. I also wonder if you are acquainted with the publication, Poland of Today,...

The issue of October 1949 is dedicated to the Centenary of Chopin's Death. Alfred believes it is a socio-culturally important issue and would also be helpful in understanding the Poland of seventy years ago, into which Alfred was born. We do not have any extra copies, or we would be glad to send you one.[54]

Korzybski had his own backlog of correspondence, also the *Manhood* Introduction to finish, and in October a new project that fell into his lap—an invitation to speak at a psychology symposium at the University of Texas in Austin. He couldn't refuse. The psychology department there had gotten a grant from the National Institute of Mental Health to conduct an ongoing symposium on "Perception: A Focus for Personality Analysis". Speakers would individually lecture in Texas from October 1949 until June 1950, each presenting a different aspect of the topic, which would constitute their contribution to a published book of the proceedings. Beforehand, they would each get a theoretical outline of the symposium by the organizers, Professors Robert R. Blake and Glenn V. Ramsey, who presented the first paper on "Perceptual Processes as Basic to an Understanding of Complex Behavior". Each speaker would also get summaries of the preceding speakers' presentations and would have the opportunity to revise their contribution for the book after all invited papers had been presented. Those invited included a number of significant and rising figures in the behavioral sciences. (One of the contributors, James G. Miller had only recently suggested "behavioral sciences" as a general integrating term for the life and social sciences). Besides Miller, the invited speakers included: Clifford T. Morgan, Frank A. Beach, Ernest R. Hilgard, Jerome S. Bruner, Wayne Dennis, Urie Brofenbrenner, Norman Cameron, Carl R. Rogers, George S. Klein, and Else Frenkel-Brunswik. Korzybski—the only non-academically connected, non-psychologist/non-psychiatrist in the bunch—was to give his presentation in the last week of January (the date later moved to early April). He would get an honorarium and travel expenses for the trip to Texas for both him and Charlotte. By means of his applied epistemological approach, Korzybski could probably have said something useful about any area related to "functional determinants of perceptual processes", but his specific assignment focused on 'the effect on perceptual processes of the language system". He considered the invitation a great privilege and his contribution something worth sweating over. On the way back from Texas, he planned to stop in Chicago, where the GS group there wanted him to speak and he could also visit Mira. He would write his contribution, with Charlotte's help, mainly over the first two months of 1950. But now as the end of the year approached, along with the annual Holiday Intensive, he wanted to see if he could get further along, even done, with the Introduction to *Manhood*. This meant another trip to New York City in November.

By this time, Mira had gotten fairly hobbled and pretty much housebound. She didn't feel stable walking alone outside and needed help in the apartment as well. The young woman who had lived with her had left some time before. Mira wrote to Alfred about a 24-year- old medical student, Albert William Kneller, who had just started staying in the spare bedroom where Charlotte usually slept during visits. In exchange for the room and a small stipend, "Dr. Bill"—as Mira called him—was helping her with cooking, cleaning and other chores and would accompany her on those increasingly rare times when she left the apartment. Alfred, of course, felt concerned but with the help she received from her doctors, neighbors, etc., and now Dr. Bill, Mira still seemed to manage.

And despite her problems she seemed to maintain a positive outlook. She continued to write to Alfred often—little notes with memories of their earlier times together, references to his work, and interesting things she heard on the radio or read about. For instance, she had found this reference to time-binding in a collection of essays, *Reflections On Our Age*, newly published by UNESCO: Julian Huxley's essay "A Re-definition of Progress", referred to "the present culmination of life in the emergence of man—the microcosm, the time-binders with brain and mind capable of annihilating the sequence of events and tying them together in the unity of consciousness;..." As Mira noted, there was no direct reference to Alfred or his work.[55] Mira's stream of references, suggestions, links, and leads both great and small had continued to exert an influence on the content of Alfred's formulating. And if in his general mood he also seemed more mellow, perhaps even more hopeful—in spite of all the messes and problems he continued to observe or personally had to deal with—perhaps a little bit of Mira's somewhat sunnier disposition had also gradually rubbed off on him. But she probably wasn't trying to give him a subliminal message when she sent him a volume called *Sunspots in Action*, which she thought he might like to read. He telegrammed her on Thursday, November 17:

Thanks Your Letters. Grateful For Sunspots. Am Going To New York Friday To Work On Manhood. Will Be At Thirty-Three West Fifty-First Street, As Before, Love Alfred[56]

Within a few days he and Charlotte were back at Hotel 33. Sometimes he just sat in his room alone, silently contemplating, visualizing what he still had left to say in the *Manhood* Introduction. Then he would talk things out with Charlotte, wrestling to get what he wanted into words; then having finally gotten something written, both of them would delouse it; and then the whole process would begin again. Over the past two years, as they had worked on the Introduction, Korzybski no doubt spent a fair amount of time contemplating the arc of his life's work from its beginnings to the present. He sought to express *that* in the Introduction. The delay in getting it finished probably inspired frustration, but he knew the writing and editing process had to take its course. Earlier in the spring, also at Hotel 33, as he and Charlotte had worked away, he had jokingly said as she took notes, "This new introduction by Korzybski has been edited by me, as it was not finished."[57] He surely intended this as a joke and not a prediction. Until the piece seemed good enough for publishing, he and Charlotte would have to push on with steady work. He wanted to get it done. So this extended period away from the distractions of Lime Rock seemed necessary. They stayed in New York for four and a half weeks.

Throughout this period, Charlotte kept Mira filled in on their progress. And as he sometimes did, Alfred would pencil-in short notes to Mira at the end of Charlotte's letters. Just as Mira had pushed Alfred to write the book in the first place, she had 'nagged' him for years about the importance of time-binding when he had placed it to the side. Mira's impetus had helped him to get re-engaged with the notion, and there was no one more eager than her to see the Second Edition in print once again.

A little more than two weeks into their stay, Charlotte wrote to her that Alfred had caught another 'bug', a chest cold, but otherwise he felt alright and was working hard. As Charlotte told her, the Introduction had a good structure in spite of that eternal—or infernal—delousing. They felt very anxious to have it done. Other than Alfred inviting 25 people up to their rooms for a December 7 cocktail party for Charlotte's birthday, they didn't appear to socialize or go out much. One visitor, Dr. Wolf, a student of Alfred's from the last summer seminar, came socially but also examined Alfred and prescribed some quinine, which seemed to help his cold. Wolf also told them about a friend of his, photographer Lotte Jacobi, who had photographed many writers, artists, and scientists in Weimer Germany and, as a Jew, had escaped to the U.S. before World War II and was now living in New York. She was interested in Alfred's work and wanted to take his picture. Alfred didn't object, Charlotte contacted her, and Lotte Jacobi came to Hotel 33 sometime during the next few weeks to do so.

Alfred Korzybski, December 1949 (Photographed by Lotte Jacobi)

Charlotte and Alfred had gone through at least several more drafts and had gotten the Introduction into what Charlotte considered pretty good shape. But they still hadn't finished it by the next-to-last week in December when they had to get back to Lime Rock. With the Holiday Intensive at the Sharon Inn starting on December 26, they needed several days to prepare and on Christmas had to get themselves and the seminar stuff moved to the Inn, even though it was only a few miles away. So they returned on December 21. When they got home they found that Kendig had been admitted to the Sharon Hospital, apparently due to exhaustion. Typical of her, she had already done the seminar planning, assigned tasks to the staff, and left a memo with the details for Alfred and Charlotte. She was out of the hospital in a few days. She would stay at the house but was able to participate in the seminar, coming over for part of the day and having lunch and dinner at the Inn with Alfred, Charlotte, and the others. Thank goodness they had a small group. The seminar went well. Alfred did a good job, seemed jovial and sharp, even if he no longer paced the room nor made points by brandishing his cane or stamping it on the floor. On December 22, just before the seminar started, he had sent out a special invitation letter to friends and trustees to attend the New Year's Party, which might indicate his mood:

Dear ____
As this half-century draws to a close, I want to share with you our hopes for the years to come. I wish that our whole 'semantic family' could toast together the New Year, and the New Era...[58]

In the seminar group photograph he looked rather worn and tired. He, Kendig, and Charlotte could all use a good rest. That wasn't going to happen. As a compromise perhaps, as soon as they had gotten back from New York, he had Charlotte write to Mr. McKee from the GS group in Chicago to cancel the lecture he was supposed to give there. It's quite likely that also at his impetus, his University of Texas presentation got moved back from the end of January to April 3. The Intensive was over on January 3. He had several more days for personal interviews with students, and then he and Charlotte had to get rolling on the paper for the Texas conference. The Texas paper would put *Manhood* on the back burner for now.

With Mira's birthday on January 16, and her and Alfred's 31st wedding anniversary on January 17, 1950, a flurry of congratulatory telegrams and notes in the mail went back and forth for several days between Chicago and Lime Rock. The Institute staff drank with Alfred to Mira's birthday and their anniversary. Mira and Dr. Bill toasted to her and Alfred on glasses of orange juice. Alfred sent a handwritten note to Mira:

January 17, 1950

Dearest,

Pardon pencil but I want a carbon copy. Many thanks for your notes and wire. We had a very warm 'burstday party' and anniversary for you. Yes, our union has perhaps had a world influence, thanks to you. Without you I certainly would never attempt my work. In my two books, as you know I give full credit to you and am so happy that I can provide for your life security.

Charlotte and I are sweating over the paper for Texas, certainly she did the main 'sweating' and did really a splendid work, you will have a copy. Otherwise no news except that damn sweating day and night, which is no news.

With my Devoted best wishes Donk [59]

Chapter 65
FAREWELL

> "The teacher who walks in the shadow of the temple, among his followers, gives not of his wisdom but rather of his faith and lovingness. If he is indeed wise he does not bid you enter the house of his wisdom, but rather leads you to the threshold of your own mind."
> ——Khalil Gibran, "On Teaching", *The Prophet*[1]

About 60 people from around the United States and Canada came to Connecticut for the memorial service at the Institute on Saturday, March 4, 1950. Since she could not come, Mira sent in her stead, an arrangement of flowers molded in the shape of a five-pointed star. One of her nicknames, "The Wonder Star", had come from the variable star discovered in 1905 that astronomers had named "Mira".[2] The flower star—indicating Mira's presence—was placed at the head of the plain open coffin where Alfred's corpse lay wearing his glasses and the khaki attire he had favored.

As they gathered, guests heard some of the music Alfred loved best: recordings of the *Sixth (Pathetique) Symphony* of his favorite composer, Tchaikovsky; *Asa's Death* by Grieg; and *Siegfried's Funeral March* from Wagner's *Die Gotterdammerung* (which Korzybski liked in spite of its Nazi echoes). Then Ralph Hamilton sang Hugo Wolf's *Weyla's Song*.

Kendig and Charlotte wanted Bob Redpath to conduct the service. Kendig had told him,
> ...both Charlotte and I believe that you will do it simply and with dignity, and that he would have liked you to do it. You may not know all that there is to know about GS but you will give the feeling that you have for him, and that he sensed. And that is what we want.[3]

Redpath read passages from Khalil Gibran's *The Prophet* (extracts from "On Teaching" and "Farewell to the People of Orphalese"); Proverbs 3:13-18; Chapter 13 of First Corinthians (which to Redpath seemed to fittingly "refer to the faith-love that underlay the personality [of Alfred] and the effort towards mankind underlying his whole life-work)"[4]; Erwin Schrodinger; Ivan Pavlov; and, from Korzybski's own writings, *Manhood of Humanity* and the "Preface to the Third Edition" of *Science and Sanity*.

The quote from the Preface to Schrodinger's book *What is Life?* seemed to Redpath an especially fitting description of Korzybski's lifework:
> We have inherited from our forefathers the keen longing for unified, all-embracing knowledge. The very name given to the highest institutions of learning reminds us, that from antiquity and throughout many centuries the <u>universal</u> aspect has been the only one to be given full credit. But the spread, both in width and in depth, of the multifarious branches of knowledge during the last hundred years has confronted us with a queer dilemma. We feel clearly that we are only now beginning to acquire reliable material for welding together the sum-total of all that is known into a whole; but, on the other hand, it has become next to impossible for a single mind fully to command more than a small specialized portion of it.
>
> I can see no other escape from this dilemma (lest our true aim be lost forever) than that some of us should venture to embark on a synthesis of facts and theories, albeit with second-hand and incomplete knowledge of them.[5]

The service closed with the playing of the fourth movement (a funeral march) of Tchaikovsky's *Manfred* that Korzybski had often enjoyed listening to in the evening hours with friends. In a statement that Redpath read beforehand to those assembled, Charlotte had written:
> ...Usually when we played music in the evenings,...he said, 'Let's end with a funeral march.'...[Alfred] particularly loved the dramatic poem 'Manfred' by Byron and the music which Tchaikovsky composed to it...Manfred, the hero of Byron's poem seemed to Alfred as one who was ceaselessly and passionately in quest, searching, searching, and who refused ever to surrender; and while listening to the music Alfred used to make a large question mark in the air with his hand : 'Why, why, what is it all about?' Toward the end of the symphony, the music comes to a climax, and the death of Manfred is at hand, and then follows the beautiful, solemn and peaceful finale.[6]

Soon afterwards, an autopsy—as Korzybski had arranged for— was done by an associate of his long-time friend, Doctor Nolan D. C. Lewis, at that time Director of the New York State Psychiatric Institute and Hospital. (Lewis was ill and could not come to do it himself.) Korzybski had observed many autopsies Lewis conducted at St. Elizabeths Hospital when both worked there in the mid-1920s. Both men had an interest in the relations—even sketchier in 1950 than now—between brain, behavior and consciousness. Dr. Lewis, who had looked at and handled many human brains, later reported the observations of Korzybski's brain:
> It showed some of the normal shrinkage due to the age of the man, but it had a very rich blood supply which is significant and a complex convolutional arrangement which will be very important to study in detail, as it is the brain of a great scientist.[7]

Alfred's cremated remains were buried in a little cemetery in Lime Rock, in a simple grave, marked with the $\bar{A}$ (non-A) symbol representing the non-aristotelian system he had formulated and taught. (Alfred's beloved Mira, without whose urgings and help he would never have produced his work, died four years later. As both had wished, her remains were buried next to his.)

Ernest R. Schaefer, a Yale University art student whom Bob Redpath found, had already made a death mask and casted both of Korzybski's hands. With the help of those notably large and supple hands, Korzybski had done his job; now he himself was done. Others would have to carry on.

Death Mask of Alfred Korzybski
by Ernest R. Schaefer of Yale University School of Art

NOTES
Preliminary Note on References

In 1993, Charlotte Schuchardt Read, the original executor of Korzybski's literary estate (appointed by Korzybski), asked me to succeed Bob Pula, whom she had appointed to become literary executor after her retirement or death. At that time, I agreed to take over that role from Bob under the circumstances of his unwillingness or inability to serve; I also began getting instruction from Charlotte as to what the job involved. By the time of Bob's death in 2004, the Executive Director of the Institute of General Semantics (IGS) had assumed the job, somewhat later arrogated by the IGS Board of Trustees. Under those circumstances, I've tried my best to provide guidance. Certainly, as the person actually designated by Charlotte to assume Bob's place as executor of the Korzybski literary estate, I've continued to have a keen interest in the materials that constitute that legacy—an interest which only increased after I decided to write this book, the content of which has greatly depended on these materials, which include: Korzybski's published works, correspondence, personal records, photographs, notebooks, tapes and other recordings, manuscripts, scrapbooks, etc., held at one time at the IGS offices or stored at the Alfred Korzybski Archives and the Mira Edgerly Korzybska Archives at Columbia University's Butler Library Rare Book and Manuscript Collection in New York City.

In addition to the already microfilmed materials at Columbia, I have made use of other materials there that have not been microfilmed or digitized, as well as non-microfilmed materials that were held at Read House, the IGS center in Fort Worth, Texas from 2005 to 2009. (The previously-scattered materials gathered and organized there included letters, files, notes, and manuscripts of Korzybski and a few from his wife Mira Edgerly Korzybska; unpublished transcripts and notes of Korzybski's lectures and seminars; various audio recordings and films of Korzybski and his associates; original photographs, scrapbooks, artifacts, additional microfilms, library books and journals including Korzybkski's personal library books and journals marked by him; and the archives of some of Alfred Korzybski's close associates and of some later important korzybskian teachers and workers.) The IGS sold Read House and rented a smaller nearby space in Ft. Worth in the Fall of 2009, with plans to leave Ft. Worth, which it eventually did. Regrettably, prior to that final move from Texas in 2010, several officers of the IGS Board of Trustees inexplicably decided to throw out a large portion of these irreplaceable archival materials—apparently not realizing the time-binding consequences this entailed. Shortly afterwards, in May 2010, I was informed of their actions by some observers at the Ft. Worth office. As a result, a few individuals managed to salvage a small portion of the material before it got sent, along with everything else, to the Ft. Worth dump. (Luckily, in the course of my research, I had already obtained copies of the majority of the documents from those archives that I've used for this book.) Nonetheless, the total loss to the literary estate and for the possibilities for research—seems inestimable; the loss includes a vast amount of historical material, covering the final 12 years of Korzybski's life, as well as much of the history and records of the previous 73 years of the Institute of General Semantics. As a scholarly resource, the fate of the remaining now-orphaned-and-disorganized material—scattered among several individuals, including myself—appears unclear.

In the following reference notes, I've used abbreviations or shortened phrases, which I will now explain, to designate and distinguish frequently-mentioned sources. In the reference notes below, "**AKDA**" refers to what I've labeled the Alfred Korzybski Digital Archives, a digitized version of the thousands of documents and letters on scores of microfilm rolls, covering over 20 large boxes of original material, housed in the Alfred Korzybski Archives at Columbia University. (The AKDA was made from a second set of microfilms that Charlotte Schuchardt Read kept for the literary estate.) I could not have provided the details of factual narrative in this book without the close and careful study of these materials, which mainly cover the period of time from late 1915 to 1938, and which also include some of Korzybski's personal scrapbooks as well as scrapbooks from the Institute of General Semantics. The raw digitized pdf files (one pdf for each microfilm screen) were given to me on two DVDs in 2005 by then IGS Executive Director, Steve Stockdale. To be of much use, these raw files required further digital processing by me. I collated the individual pdfs into larger files that correspond to the numbered microfilm rolls at Columbia and (for the most part) their corresponding hard-copy boxes of documents. I have further annotated a large proportion of these expanded pdf documents, which I hope to make available for the future use of other researchers interested in Korzybski's life and work. In the notation below, "AKDA 11.388" refers to the document numbered 388 in the sequence of digitized pages of microfilm roll number #11. "**IGS Archives**" refers to material from the now dismantled Fort Worth archives. I have specified non-microfilmed material from the Mira Edgerly Korzybska Papers at Columbia ("**MEK Archives**") by box number and date. I have labeled documents from the several boxes of non-microfilmed material in the Alfred Korzybski Archives at Columbia as "**AK Archives**", with box number and date. In addition, Ralph C. Hamilton (a personal assistant to Korzybski from 1947 to 1949) shared with me his collection of copies of selected letters from Korzybski and some of his associates from 1933 to 1950. I have labeled material from this collection as from the "**Ralph Hamilton Papers**". With such frequent use of their names in referenced correspondence, I have abbreviated Alfred Korzybski as "**AK**" and Mira Edgerly Korzybska as "**MEK**". Dates are given numerically, in order of Month/Day/Year: July 3, 1933 would appear as "7/3/1933".

As the following documentation may suggest, I have taken great pains to represent the facts of Korzybski's life and work as accurately as possible. When I say that Korzybski or someone else thought or felt something in particular, this is based on written or otherwise recorded statements by them. I have worked to make it clear when I am offering my own or other people's conclusions and interpretations. For readability, I have lightly edited quotes from Korzybski's letters and unpublished writings.

Epigraph

1. Marcus, et al. 2001.

Preface – Does Korzybski Matter?

1. Qtd. in Mordkowitz 1985, p. 58. **2.** See Drew. See also "Outdated charts may be blamed in sub crash". Associated Press, Jan. 15, 2005. **3.** Pula 1994, p. xvii. **4.** Korzybski 1947, p. 408. This unpublished memoir of Korzybski provides a major source of information about his life and attitudes. **5.** Korzybski 1947, p. 23. **6.** Korzybski 1947, p. 420. **7.** Korzybski 1947, p. 29. **8.** Korzybski 1947, p. 31. **9.** See Kendig 1950, p. 4. **10.** Korzybski 1947, p. 482. **11.** I took this configuration of terms from my mentor and friend the late Robert P. Pula, who used "Knowledge, Uncertainty, and Courage" as the summary title for one of his definitive articles about Korzybski's work.

Language Note and Pronunciation Guide

1. Korzybski referred to single quotes used in these ways as "safety devices" *not* "scare quotes". As I remember Bob Pula once saying, "If you say something differently, you say something different."

Part I – Final Day

1. Kipling, "Arithmetic on the Frontier", in *Barrack Room Ballads and The Vampire and Other Verses.*

Chapter 1 – "We Only Coagulate"

1. Korzybski 1947, p. 412. **2.** The name of Charlotte's cat and many other details of daily life at the Institute of General Semantics in Connecticut were initially supplied by Ralph C. Hamilton, who worked for a time as a personal assistant to Korzybski, and by David Linwood [Levine] who also worked at the Institute for a time assisting Korzybski. Institute office memos, letters, and scrapbooks from this period of time corroborated their information as well as providing many other personal details. **3.** Kendig 1950, *General Semantics Bulletin* 3, p. 9. **4.** Korzybski 1947, p. 40. **5.** Korzybski 1947, p. 23. **6.** M. Kendig to Robert U. Redpath, Jr., 3/27/1950, IGS Archives. **7.** Ibid. **8.** M. Kendig, "Memorandum Re D. David Bourland, Jr", 3/27/1950, IGS Archives. **9.** Von Kugelgen, Memorandum - "Conference with AK on February 28th, 1950,' 3/1/1950, IGS Archives. **10.** D. David Bourland to Alfred Korzybski, 2/28/1950, IGS Archives. **11.** M. Kendig, Memorandum - "Circumstances of AK's Death", 3/27/1950, IGS Archives. **12.** D. David Bourland to M. Kendig, 3/13/1950. IGS Archives. **13.** D. David Bourland qtd. in Klein 2000, p. 344. **14.** Dr. Loren T. Dewind to Charlotte Schuchardt, 1 March 1950, IGS Archives. **15.** David Linwood [Levine], personal correspondence. **16.** Ibid. **17.** Ralph C. Hamilton, interview with author, November 2005. **18.** Clarence B. Farrar to M. Kendig, 3/2/1950. IGS Archives. **19.** "Comment: Alfred Korzybski". 1950. The *American Journal of Psychiatry* 106 (11). Reproduced in *General Semantics Bulletin* 3, p. 32. **20.** David and Miriam Fairchild to Kendig and Schuchardt, 3/2/1950. IGS Archives **21.** Erich Kahler to M. Kendig, 3/25/1950. IGS Archives. **22.** G. C. McKinney to M. Kendig and C. Schuchardt, 3/5/1950. IGS Archives. **23.** Blanche and Harry Weinberg to M. Kendig and C. Schuchardt, 3/3/1950. IGS Archives.

Part II – Beginnings

1. Qtd. in *Sayings of the Sages of the Talmud*, p. 9.

Chapter 2 – Young Alfred

1. Davies 1982, p. 28. **2.** Davies 2005, p. vi. **3.** Qtd. in Davies 1982, p. 524. **4.** Note on the Polish Nobility: Although the szlachta were disappearing as a class by the time of Korzybski's birth, their culture had become inextricably linked with Polish national culture. The culture of the szlachta also left an enduring mark on Korzybski. Nobility-related norms had gradually filtered into all levels of Polish society to become the basis of what Szczepanski called "the traditional Polish personality ideal". Among other things, this ideal consisted of "readiness for the defense of the Catholic faith, readiness for the defense of the fatherland, a highly developed sense of personal dignity and honor, and full-blown individualism, an imposing mien, chivalry, intellectual brilliance, and dash." [Szczepanski, p. 167] Brought up in the late 19th Century among what was left of the Polish aristocracy (and from one of its most ancient families), it is not surprising that Korzybski's personal behavior as an adult reflected this ideal in action (although he had fairly early abandoned the Roman Catholic faith as a value worth defending). By the time he began his work in America, Korzybski had generalized the szlachta ethic: He had come to accept the potential 'nobility' of every human. And in tending to consider everyone as his 'noble' equal and himself as theirs, he also tended to treat everyone (whatever his or her credentials, rank, or fame) with equal respect—and equal directness. This appears to have bothered some individuals who may have considered themselves deserving of special deference. **5.** This difference between the written forms of the two Slavic languages, Polish and Russian, points to a deep cultural divide between Poles and Russians that had begun almost 1000 years before. In the year 965, Mieszko I, recognized as the first Polish king, had converted from paganism to Roman Catholicism. This made Poland the easternmost bastion of the Catholic faith. A few decades later, Prince Vladimir of the Kievan Rus (forerunners of the Russians) converted to Eastern Orthodox Christianity. Facing East, the Russians remained somewhat disconnected from the rest of Europe for much of their history. By contrast, Miezko's conversion helped point Polish society toward the West. The Catholic Church brought its institutions (including its educational framework) to Poland. Polish scholars wrote in Latin and then chose Latin script for Polish writing rather than the Eastern Cyrillic alphabet. Facing West religiously and linguistically left the Poles more open to the humanistic intellectual, and social movements that were taking shape there, i.e., the Renaissance, the Scientific Revolution, etc. It also allowed for Polish influence in the rest of Europe. **6.** Korzybski's father's family, the Korzybskis, belonged to the extensive Habdank Skarbek clan of nobles. Originally, they had been the Habdanks of Korzybie (located near Plock, about 60 miles west of Warsaw). [Korzybski 1947, p. 116] Korzybski related the legend of his first Habdank Skarbek ancestor who "…was elected as a special envoy to a German prince…to consider the question of war and peace."

> …After all the possible arguments always with the stiff-necked Polish nobleman…that little prince took my ancestor to a cellar full of barrels of gold [treasure]…showed him the gold in the cellar and said, 'We will beat you with gold'. And the ancestor took his golden ring of some sort from his finger, threw it in the barrel of gold…and said, 'We will beat you with iron, not gold'. The [polite] German prince said 'Thank you' in German…Habe Dank from which the name Habdank…And when he came back to Poland…and a war between Germany and Poland started…the Germans were beaten with iron. His generic name and crest became Habdank or Abdank. Because it had to deal with that famous gesture…it was connected with treasure. Skarbek in Polish means treasure… So Skarbek and Habdank became synonymous. Later on it [Habdank] became a crest for endless connected families… [Korzybski 1947, p. 9-10]

According to Korzybski, the W-shaped emblem, constituting the "core" of his heraldic crest, supposedly represented a "broken up, flattened" barrel [of treasure?]. [Korzybski 1947, p. 9.]

Habdank Skarbek Crest (Korzybski Branch)

7. Korzybski 1947, p. 385. **8.** Korzybski 1947, pp. 386–7. **9.** Korzybski 1949, p. 10. **10.** Korzybski 1947, p. 71. **11.** Korzybski 1947, pp. 58-59. **12.** Korzybski 1947, p. 61. **13.** Korzybski 1947, pp. 62-63. **14.** Korzybski 1947, pp. 415-417. **15.** Korzybski 1947, pp. 475-476. **16.** Korzybski 1947, p. 23. **17.** AK "Manhood Notes". n.d. [probably 1948], Transcribed by Charlotte Schuchardt, IGS Archives. Besides Alfred Korzybski's own recollections, factual details about both of his parents and Alfred's early life were gleaned from an article in Polish on Wladyslaw Korzybski in the *Polish Biographical Dictionary*, Volume 14 (1968-9) published by the Polish Academy of Sciences, Institute of History. **18.** Korzybski 1947, pp. 370-371. One can picture young Alfred, watching the workmen and starting to make crude measurements of his own. Years later, Korzybski penciled an asterisk in the page margin beside the following passage of his personal copy of A.S. Eddington's 1920 book *Space, Time and Gravitation: An Outline of the General Relativity Theory*, where Eddington wrote: "But the relativist, in defining space as measured space, clearly recognizes that all measurement involves the use of material apparatus; the resulting geometry is specifically a study of the extensional relations of matter. He declines to consider anything more transcendental." [Eddington 1920, p. 16] In the bottom margin below another asterisk, Korzybski expanded on Eddington's point and his penciled note could well have been describing his experience as a boy at Rudnik: "When "Rel." [the Relativist] becomes a psychobiologist he recognizes that this conclusion is merely an elaboration of primitive man and small child as they measure both space and time without appeal to either measuring rule or clock, but with their steps, arm movements, fingers, etc." **19.** Korzybski 1947, p. 384. **20.** Korzybski 1947, p. 25. **21.** Korzybski 1947, p. 461. **22.** Korzybski 1947, p, 416. **23.** Korzybski 1947, p. 39. **24.** Korzybski 1947, p. 41. **25.** Ibid. **26.** Korzybski 1947, p. 425. **27.** Korzybski 1947, pp. 447-448. **28.** Korzybski 1994 (1933), p. 140. Active atheists would probably have a problem with Korzybski's openness on the question of "G. O. D". When asked whether or not he believed in God, he would spell out the letters and ask his questioner, "What do you mean by 'Gee Oh Dee'?" His late-life speculations about a 'supreme power' sounded like the views of a rather broad-minded agnostic: "Suppose we do discover some day an 'almighty'...A 'supreme power' is there – no two two's [buts?] about it. But we don't know the character. We can only discover the *structure*, never the *it*." [AK Manhood Notes of 4/17/1949 taken by Charlotte Schuchardt. "AK- Re.: We being the 'builders of our own destinies'." IGS Archives.] **29.** Korzybski 1947, p. 450. **30.** Korzybski 1947, p. 52. **31.** Korzybski 1947, p. 53.

Chapter 3 – A Good Engineer

1. "Warsaw University of Technology - University History", Warsaw University of Technology (Polytechnika Warszawska), http://eng.pw.edu.pl/University/History (accessed on 10/21/2010) **2.** Korzybski, "American Men of Science Application, 1948". IGS Archives. **3.** Korzybski 1947, p. 52. **4.** Korzybski, "American Men of Science Application, 1948". IGS Archives. **5.** Korzybski 1947, pp. 44-45. **6.** Korzybski 1947, p. 32.

Chapter 4 – To Rome

1. With no surviving personal records from the time, and only Korzybski's uncertain memories from years later and a few historical facts to go by, here's how I established the time-range of 1902–1904 for Alfred's sojourns through Europe and his time in Rome. Korzybski recalled graduating in 1902. In 1947 he indicated that while in Rome he had an audience with Pope Leo, one or two years before Leo's death. Leo died in July 1903. If two years before, in 1901, Alfred was still attending the Polytechnic, he would have had to have gotten to Rome and met Leo there sometime in 1902, after his graduation—one year before Leo's death. Alfred would have had to reside in Rome for sufficient time to do everything that he did there. Sometime later, he left Rome to travel to other parts of Italy (probably during the first half of 1903). He reported returning to Rome soon after the start of the new Pope's reign. Pope Pius's coronation took place in August 1903. This would place Alfred in Rome in the latter half of 1903. After he finally returned home to Poland, he got into trouble with the Tsarist authorities.Wladyslaw Korzybski, still alive, intervened on his behalf. From Alfred's return until his father's death in October 1904, enough time would have had to elapse for those events to take place. Therefore Alfred would have had to return home to Poland in late 1903 or early 1904. [Korzybski 1947, pp. 453, 466. See also Pula 2003c (1996), pp. 57-58] **2.** Schuchardt 1950a, p. 34. **3.** Ibid. **4.** Korzybski 1947, p. 474. **5.** Korzybski 1947, p. 458. **6.** Korzybski 1947, p. 424. **7.** Korzybski 1947, p. 455. **8.** Korzybski 1947, pp. 460-462. **9.** Korzybski 1947, pp. 460–463. **10.** Korzybski 1947, p. 469. **11.** Korzybski 1947, p. 471.

Chapter 5 – Sick of Everything

1. Davies 2001, pp. 234–235. **2.** Schuchardt 1950a, p. 34. **3.** Korzybski 1947, p. 476. **4.** Ibid., pp. 54–55. **5.** Ibid., pp. 71–72. **6.** Davies 2005, p. 273. **7.** Davies 2005, p. 274. **8.** Korzybski 1947, p. 485. **9.** 'I was influenced by Fichte and Hegel. Spinoza did not influence me – he was not hard enough.' AK to Charlotte Schuchardt, 5/31/1949. "Notes on *Manhood of Humanity*". IGS Archives. **10.** Korzybski 1994 (1933), p. 86. **11.** AK to Alexsander Wundheiler, 7/9/1934. AKDA 27.478. **12.** Ibid. **13.** AK to Arthur F. Bentley, 4/25/1932. AKDA 7.688. **14.** Korzybski 1947, p. 56. **15.** AK to Scudder Klyce, 3/12/1922. AKDA 8.431.

Part III – The Great War

1. "Let The Dead Be Heard - By A Polish Soldier". AKDA 34. 529.

Chapter 6 – Germany Must Be Beaten

1. East Prussia (by the early 21st Century, part of Northeastern Poland with a small bit under Russian sovereignty) had long been a German island in the midst of a Slavic sea. In the 13th Century, the Teutonic Knights, a ruthless group of crusaders from the German lands, had been invited by a Polish prince to come and help him in his war against the original Prussians, a pagan tribe on the Polish frontier. The Poles soon regretted this move. For the Teutonic Knights proceeded to brutally wipe out these original inhabitants—taking the Prussian name for themselves. They then captured most of the Baltic coast of Northern Poland including the port of Gdansk and colonized the area with ethnic Germans. The Poles, who had already been fighting German princes to the west, now had a German enemy to the north as well. In 1410, a newly unified Polish kingdom under King Jagiello defeated the Teutonic Knights at the battle of Grünwald and eventually recaptured Northern Poland and part of Prussia. A small Prussian principality was allowed to remain as an ethnic German enclave, though it came under Polish domination. In the early 17th Century, a Polish king granted rule of Prussia to the Hohenzollern family, descendants of Teutonic Knights from the German town of Brandenburg. Then for over a century, the Hohenzollerns sought to gain Prussian independence and join it to the other German lands. At the end of the 18th Century, under the leadership of Frederick the Great and his successor Frederick Wilhelm II, they finally succeeded in doing so by destroying Poland via the infamous partitions. Northwestern Poland, Pomorze, became West Prussian Pomerania. Wielpolska or "Old Poland", the heartland of the first Polish kings, became an extension of Brandenburg lands east of Berlin. Southwestern Poland became Prussian Silesia. The partition of Poland made Prussia the largest and most powerful of the German states. This led the way, in the latter part of the 19th Century, to the newly unified—and Prussianized—authoritarian German state. **2.** Pognowski 1998, p. 26. **3.** Pognowski 1998, p. 89. **4.** Sweetman, p. 45. **5.** Korzybski 1947, pp. 75–76. **6.** Ibid., p. 76. **7.** Korzybski 1947, p. 75. **8.** Ibid., pp. 76–77. **9.** Olechowski, p. 51; Watts, p. 45. **10.** Korzybski 1947, p. 79. **11.** Ibid., p. 82. **12.** Ibid.

Chapter 7 – On the Eastern Front
1. Korzybski 1947, p. 128. See John Sweetman's *Tannenberg 1914* for a historical account of the battle of Tannenberg. Aleksandr Solezhenitsyn's well-researched novel *August 1914* provides a compelling sense of what it must have felt like on the Russian side. One can imagine Korzybski as a minor character here, riding in on horseback and finding Russian Second Army stragglers after it was already too late with the battle lost. **2.** Korzybski 1947, pp. 133-135. **3.** Ibid., pp. 135-136. **4.** Ibid., pp. 130-132. **5.** Ibid., pp. 88–89. **6.** Ibid., p. 86. **7.** Ibid., p. 104. **8.** Ibid., p. 98. **9.** Ibid., 91–96.

Chapter 8 – Battle and Retreat
1. Korzybski 1947, p. 116–120. **2.** Ibid., pp. 120–123. **3.** Ibid., pp. 109–110. **4.** Ibid., pp. 100-102. **5.** Ibid. p. 115. **6.** Ibid., p. 111. **7.** Ibid. pp. 111–112. **8.** Ibid., p. 115. See Norman Stone's book *The Eastern Front: 1914–1917* for the history of the WWI Eastern Front battles and, in particular, for important details about the battles of Plock and Lodz which Korzybski participated in. **9.** Korzybski 1947, p. 125. **10.** Ibid., p. 125; "Artist and war hero wedded in Washington". *The Philadelphia Record*, Feb. 8, 1919. IGS Archives. **11.** Korzybski 1947, pp. 125-126. **12.** Ibid., p. 127. **13.** AK - 1948 Biographical Form for the 8th Edition of *American Men of Science*. IGS Archives.

Chapter 9 – At the Disposal of the Minister of War
1. Korzybski 1947, p. 304. **2.** Ibid., pp. 304-305. **3.** Ibid. p. 304. **4.** The microfilmed copy of Korzybski's 1915 pocket calendar makes it possible to specify the times for his presence there."Kalendarz". AKDA 2.27-2.37. **5.** Korzybski 1947, pp. 148, 216. **6.** AK to V. Molodoy, Unsent letter, 12/16/1924. AKDA 15.733. **7.** Korzybski 1947, p. 148.. **8.** Korzybski 1947, p. 152–153. **9.** AK to V. Molodoy, Unsent letter, 12/16/1924. AKDA 15.733.

Chapter 10 – Oh! Petawawa
1. Press pass for representing L'Agence De Presse Nord-Sud in America, issued in Petrograd. AKDA 5.29. **2.** Korzybski 1947, p. 155. **3.** http://www.town.petawawa.on.ca/history/index.asp **4.** Korzybski 1947, p. 472. **5.** Ibid., p. 163. **6.** Ibid., p.165. **7.** Alfred Korzybski Scrapbook. AKDA 3.324. **8.** Korzybski to V. Molodoy, Unsent letter, 12/16/1924. AKDA 15.733. **9.** "The Popular Song of Petawawa". AKDA 32.3. **10.** Korzybski 1947, p. 262. **11.** "An enjoyable private dinner was given on board the Steamer "Oiseau" on the evening of July 28th..." Unknown newspaper. n.d. AKDA 32.13. **12.** On the Eastern Front, a Russian offensive the previous March at Lake Narotch in Lithuania had failed miserably at the cost of huge casualties. In the summer of 1916, around the time of Alfred's party, General Brusilov had masterfully managed a Russian offensive in Galicia, where his forces made a significant breakthrough into Austrian territory. However, with tremendous losses on both sides and severe shortages of supplies, Brusilov couldn't sustain the campaign. **13.** AK to Lt. Consitt, 2/15/17. AKDA 32.19. **14.** AK to Capt. Maloney, 2/22/1917. AKDA 32.15.

Chapter 11 – 1917
1. Korzybski, Patent Application "Wheel Red Cross". AKDA 35.874 **2.** Pauly 1987, pp. 43-44. **3.** Korzybski 1947, p. 170. **4.** Ibid., p. 171. **5.** Ibid., pp. 172-173. **6.** Scrapbook of Alfred Korzybski. AKDA 3.324. **7.** Recruiting Notice, AKDA 32.63. **8.** AK to N.Y.C. Army Recruiting Station, 9/15/1917. AKDA 32.63. **9.** Chief of Military Intelligence Section, War Department to AK, 9/18/1917. AKDA 5.52. **10.** I derived my account of

Korzybski's work at the United States Horse Shoe Co. from his correspondence files on the company dated Nov. and Dec. 1917. AKDA 32.136-225. **11.** An old nursery rhyme reflects the potential importance of a 'little thing' like a horseshoe nailhole:

> For want of a nail, the shoe was lost;
> For want of the shoe, the horse was lost;
> For want of the horse, the rider was lost;
> For want of the rider, the battle was lost;
> For want of the battle, the kingdom was lost;
> And all for the want of a horseshoe nail.

See "Engines of Our Ingenuity, No. 1541: History and Horseshoe Nails" by John H. Lienhard. University of Houston College of Engineering. http://www.uh.edu/engines/epi1541.htm (accessed on 10/25/2010).

Chapter 12 – "Buy Liberty Bonds and Work Like Hell."

1. Unnamed Newspaper article on Gasiorowski in Cleveland, Feb. 18, 1918. AKDA 37.378. **2.** Korzybski 1947, p. 177. **3.** Letter from Polish Military Commission to "To Whom It May Concern". AKDA 5.122, 32.257. **4.** Korzybski 1947, p. 178. **5.** Ibid., p. 180. **6.** Ibid. **7.** "Polish Legion Seeking Men". *The Globe* (Toronto), 5/13/1918. AKDA 1.10. **8.** "Poles Determined To Stay In War". *The World* (Toronto), 5/13/1918. AKDA 1.12. **9.** Korzybski 1947, p. 181. **10.** Ibid., p. 182. **11.** "Polish Legion Receives Flag From Allies". 6/19/1918. AKDA 1.19; "White Eagle of Poland Again In Thick of Fray" by Walter Duranty, *New York Times*, 6/23/1918. AKDA 37.383. **12.** Korzybski 1947, p. 190. **13.** Letter from Polish Military Commission to "Whom It May Concern", 8/5/1918. AKDA 5.122. **14.** AK to Taylor Allderdice, 7/28/1918. AKDA 34.519. **15.** AK to Sloane Gordon, AKDA 34.514. **16.** "Soldiers Make Pleas To Miners for Coal". *Pittsburgh Gazette Times*, 6/5/1918. AKDA 37.387. **17.** AK to J.T. Miller, undated [Aug. 1918]. AKDA 32.405; J.T. Miller to AK, Aug. 20, 1918. AKDA 32.404. **18.** Other newly-formed Federal agencies included the War Industry Board, The National War Labor Board and the Railroad Administration. See Clements. **19.** Whatever justification greater governmental control of the economy may have had during wartime, the USFA—as well as the other new agencies—had to deal with a hodgepodge of private companies, unions, and individuals that had various levels of resistance to government intervention in their affairs. The agency's efforts fell short of fully nationalizing the U.S. fuel economy. But among other things, it promoted conservation (the agency promoted the shift to Daylight Savings Time, which congress passed into law in March, 1918) and fuel productivity and distribution, especially that of coal (World War I-era America was highly dependent on coal for heating people's homes, fueling industry, producing munitions, etc.). The USFA was disbanded in 1919, briefly revived at the end of that year to deal with the nation-wide effects of a coal miner's strike, and then finally abolished in 1920. See "Records of the U.S. Fuel Administration (USFA). Administrative History". The National Archives. Washington, D.C. – http://www.archives.gov/research/guide-fed-records/groups/067.html (accessed 10/25/2010). **20.** Korzybski 1947, p. 191. **21.** Ibid., p. 188; T. Yurkowski to AK, 10/17/1918. AKDA 32.380 **22.** George L. Neuhoff, Jr. to AK, 10/18/1918. 32.374. At the Library of Congress website, you can download two versions of the song "Danny Deever", including one by baritone Arthur Middleton that Korzybski probably heard: Go to http://lcweb2.loc.gov/diglib/ihas/loc.natlib.ihas.200031148/default.html **23.** "Addresses Coal Miners in Three Languages". *Bluefield Daily Telegraph*, Sept. 1, 1918. AKDA 32.509. **24.** Korzybski 1947, p. 191. **25.** United States Fuel Administration, Speakers' Daily Report, Sept. 28, 1918. AKDA 32.470. **26.** *Cumberland Evening Times*, Sept. [30], 1918. AKDA 1.34. **27.** Crosby, p. 60. **28.** "'Flu' Cancels Fuel Meetings". *Cumberland Times*, 10/4/1918. AKDA 1.39. **29.** Telegram, AK to Yurkowski. AKDA 5.247. **30.** "Speakers' Daily Report", Nov. 10, 1918. AKDA 32.445. **31.** Korzybski 1947, pp. 196-197. **32.** Watt, p. 61. **33.** *San Antonio Light*, Thursday, November 7, 1918. AKDA 1.39. **34.** "War Talks To Be Resumed". *U.S. Miners,* Number 1, Cumberland, Maryland, Nov. 9, 1918. AKDA 1.45. **35.** Korzybski 1947, p. 196.

Chapter 13 – A Veteran of the Great War

1. "Ideal Democracy. Officer of Polish Army Says U.S. Is Department Store for Europe to Copy". Unnamed Newspaper (Eagle Pass, Maverick County, Texas). 11/12/1918. AKDA 1.45. **2.** AK to Woodrow Wilson, Undated letter, (1918). AKDA 5.91. **3.** Alfred Korzybski, "Facts For Declaration of Intention [to 'renounce allegiance to The Present Government of Russia'], U.S. Dept. of Labor, Naturalization Service", n.d. [probably Dec. 1918]. AKDA 5.35. **4.** Alfred Korzybski, "Application for Appointment to Position of Special Agent of the Dept of Justice", 12/9/1918. AKDA 5.39 **5.** See Patterson, Michael Robert. **6.** See "Flanders Field and Replies to

Flanders Field" at http://www.nbc-links.com/miscellaneous/FlandersField.html (accessed on 10/26/2010) for a number of poems written in response to McCrae's. **7.** AK to H. Flanders Dunbar, 12/4/1934, AKDA 32.940. **8.** Ralph C. Hamilton, Interview. **9.** Korzybski 1947, p. 499. **10.** I 'know' Korzybski said this about his baldness but can't find the reference now. I guess that every biography written has at least one of these. Here's one of mine. **11.** Kipling, p. 77. In the line "all flesh is grass", Kipling was quoting the Bible— Isaiah 40:6—the metaphor going back to the Book of Psalms (see Psalm 90 for example). **12.** "Be conscious!" Korzybski wanted students to stop dragging themselves through life, inattentively, passively, unconsciously. In one lecture he gave at the 1948-49 Holiday Intensive Seminar, he drilled the point home:

> ...Do you know that with us humans, we have such a thing as consciousness—do you know that—do you understand the word 'conscious'? Are you fully conscious that you are conscious? No. Great many of us are just a flop—not conscious of anything [he purposely mumbled this to simulate the attitude of 'half-assed' awareness he was criticizing]. Well it isn't on the human level. Be conscious! If you want to relax, relax consciously. Otherwise [in other words]—it means be conscious of your possibilities as well as your shortcomings, as well as taking care of the environment; because we are a product not only out of our own organismal possibilities but we are also connected with the environment. There is no way out—no way out; therefore let's not look for utopias. The secret of your own adjustment lies in you, nobody else. Not in a doctor or me. [*Alfred Korzybski: 1948-1949 Seminar,* (mp3-20b, 8:07); p. 220 (in the written transcription)]

Chapter 14 – Mira

1. Korzybski 1947, p. 199. **2.** Edgerly Family Records. AKDA 20.673. In later life, both Alfred and Mira treated the earlier date of birth as the actual one. **3.** "Mrs. Frederick Burt" (Mira Edgerly), portrait photograph 1914 by Arnold Genthe. Library of Congress, Prints & Photographs Division, Arnold Genthe Collection: Negatives and Transparencies, [reproduction number, LC-G432-0545], http://www.loc.gov/pictures/item/agc1996003605/PP/ **4.** C. S. Read 1955, pp. 53-54. **5.** For Gertrude Stein's reference to "Myra [sic] Edgerly" in *The Autobiography of Alice B. Toklas*, see Stein, pp. 118-119. **6.** Korzybski 1947, p. 201. **7.** C.S. Read 1955, p. 56. **8.** Korzybski 1947, p. 208. **9.** Ibid., p. 208. **10.** Ibid., pp. 200, 202. **11.** Ibid. p. 202. **12.** The fact of Mira's first marriage is not mentioned in Charlotte Schuchardt Read's biographical account of Mira or in Korzybski's 1947 autobiographical statement. I first discovered it by chance while looking through old *New York Times* archives. See "Sculptor To Wed Artist". *New York Times*, Jan. 30, 1914 and "Mira Edgerly Weds. She Becomes Wife of Frederick Burt At Quiet Wedding".*New York Times*, Feb. 2, 1914. **13.** Wedding Announcement, *Washington Herald*, 1/17/1919. AKDA 1.51. **14.** "The Club Fellow and Washingon Mirror". Jan. 22, 1919. AKDA 1.55. **15.** Qtd. in Simon, p. 339. **16.** Ralph C. Hamilton, Personal Interview. **17.** Korzybski 1947, pp. 199, 208. **18.** Ibid., p. 204. **19.** Ibid. **20.** C. S. Read 1955, p. 55. **21.** Korzybski 1947, p. 210.

Chapter 15 – "Let the Dead Be Heard"

1. "Tells of Poland's Needs. Count Korzybski Makes Plea for Funds to Carry on Relief Work". *Washington Post*, 2/3/1919. AKDA 1.55. **2.** "Let the Dead Be Heard by a Polish Soldier". AKDA 34.529. **3.** Tom Jones Meek to AK, 3/28/1919. AKDA 5.124. **4.** http://www.swarthmore.edu/library/peace/CDGA.A-L/leaguetoenforcepeace.htm **5.** Alfred Korzybski Polish Language Resume'/Autobiography (trans. by Zahava Sweet). n.d. [probably 1919] "...President Taft...invited me as a member and speaker of an association [promoting a] League of Nations. The invitation I didn't throw away, but I didn't take part in that company because I didn't want other nations to ride on my patriotism, for unknown and unclear goals."AKDA 37.510-511. **6.** *Washington Times*, May 25, 1919. AKDA 1.76. **7.** National Arts Club membership. AKDA 32.676. **8.** "Jews Robbed, Murdered And Driven From Homes In Polish Pogroms".*New York Herald*, May 26, 1919. Korzybski Scrapbook. AKDA 1.73. **9.** Polish intolerance, i.e., antisemitism, in the years leading up to and including World War II, has loomed large in many people's awareness since that time. To a great extent some confusion has resulted from the Nazi Germans' choice of Poland as the main killing field for their slaughtering of Jews. Germans, not Poles, initiated the genocide of World War II. Indeed, the German Nazis considered ethnic Poles "subhuman Slavs" and murdered about three million of them as well as three million Polish Jews. Certainly Polish antisemitism did exist. But the fact remains that Jews had lived in Poland for centuries, under conditions of acceptance and autonomy unknown elsewhere on the planet. If the treatment of its Jewish population provides an index of the tolerance of a nation, the Poles throughout much of their history deserved very high marks. During the time of the Crusades, and from the thirteenth to the sixteenth centuries, pograms and persecution against Jews grew throughout the rest of Europe. Meanwhile, the Poles invited Jews to come and stay in peace. "As early as 1264, The Charter of Jewish Liberties [The Act of Kalisz] allowed Jews in Poland to set up a system of self-government with exclusive jurisdiction over religious and cultural issues." [Pogonowski, p. 14] As a result the Jewish people thrived:

> It has been estimated that as many as eight million Jews lived during the first century of the Christian era (*Encyclopedia Judaica*, vol. 13, pp. 866-903). By A.D. 1000, the world's Jewish population may have dwindled to considerably less than 500,000, or fewer than one for every sixteen living in the first century. The revival of the population to its earlier peak of eight million was achieved by 1880, and occurred almost entirely within the historic lands of Poland. [Pogonwoski, p. 13]

This revival of the Jewish people in Poland was not an accident, but resulted to a great extent from conditions created by humanistic sources deep within Polish culture. (This discussion about the Jews of Poland and general Polish attitudes towards them has relevance for understanding Korzybski's evolving attitudes towards his own 'Polishness', towards 'Jewishness', and the relation of both to his work.) **10.** Telegram - AK to MEK, 5/26/1919. AKDA 34.491. **11.** Telegram to AK, 5/31/1919. AKDA 34.492. **12.** Telegram - MEK to AK, 6/1/1919. AKDA 34.494. **13.** AK to Glenn Plumb, 8/20/1919, AKDA 32.743. **14.** Korzybski, "The Profiteers and How To Fight Them". AKDA 5.42. **15.** See Sowell 2005. **16.** See Will Eisner's *Fagin the Jew* (2003). **17.** IGS Library-Ft. Worth, Texas. **18.** IGS Library-Ft. Worth, Texas. **19.** Transcription of 10/31/1919 Meeting of "The New Machine". AKDA 32.646. **20.** *The Merchant of Venice*, Act I, Scene III **21.** Ibid. **22.** Davies 2005, p. 71. **23.** Overman Committee. See U.S. Congress, Senate, Committee on the Judiciary, 1919. *Bolshevik Propaganda...*, p. 135. The entire Overman Committee Report can be downloaded from Google Books. **24.** Carlson, p. 204. For more on Boris Brasol's reprehensible career see Joseph W. Bendersky's *The Jewish Threat*, John Roy Carlson's *Undercover*, Albert Lee's *Henry Ford and the Jews*, and Steven G. Marks' *How Russia Shaped The Modern World*. **25.** See Blobaum, ed., *Antisemitism And Its Opponents In Modern Poland*. **26.** W. S. Mackay [?] to AK, 11/5/1919. AKDA 32.610-611. **27.** John D. Costello to Mira Edgerly-Korzybska, Nov. 1, 1919. AKDA 32.593 **28.** Korzybski 1947, pp. 197-198. **29.** Korzybski. *Manhood of Humanity and Its Universal Language*, Unpublished First Draft, p. 40. AKDA 4.52. **30.** Korzybski 1947, p. 198. **31.** Bill to Polish Mechanics, 25 Lutego (February) 1920, (trans. by Zahava Sweet). AKDA 37.65. **32.** Polish Mechanics Poster, (trans. by Zahava Sweet). AKDA 37.143.

Part IV - Time-Binder
1. Keyser in "The Nature of Man" in *Mole Philosophy and Other Essays*, p. 211.

Chapter 16 – "Binding Time"
1. Ferguson to AK, July 26, 1920. AKDA 32.555. **2.** Korzybski 1949, p. 59, 59a. (Mp3-5c, 5d.) **3.** Korzybski 1947, p. 213. Paul Strand and Charles Sheeler's 1921 movie short, *Manhatta,* viewable on YouTube.com shows the boiling, steaming city of New York much as Korzybski must have seen it from atop the Woolworth Building in 1919 (or early 1920), complete with the people 'down below' looking like 'vermin' and streetcars looking much like 'caterpillers'. **4.** I originally obtained the Ferguson quotes from *The Revolution Absolute* in Michael Lane's short book, *Charles Ferguson: Herald of Social Credit* [p. 35]. Lane provides a nice introduction to this neglected social theorist. Curious readers can now download Charles Ferguson's otherwise hard to obtain book *The Revolution Absolute* from GoogleBooks at << http://books.google.com >>. Type the book title into the search box. You can find more information on Ferguson and Social Credit on Lane's webpage at http://www.alor.org/TriumphofthePastBooks.htm **5.** Korzybski 1947, p. 215. **6.** "Manhood & Credo Notes by CS [Charlotte Schuchardt]", (1948/1949). IGS Archives. Mira recalled Alfred's nighttime insight as coming after a two-day long, tea-drinking discussion in Washington, D.C. soon after their marriage. See Charlotte Schuchardt Read 1955, pp. 54-55. While the insight may well have come after a marathon discussion/tussle with Mira (with lots of tea), evidence from Korzybski's prior writings and letters, makes Alfred's account here—that it happened in Missouri—more likely. **7.** *The Manhood of Humanity and its Universal Language*. AKDA 4. **8.** Korzybski 1921, p. 1. **9.** Draft of letters to Charles Armour and the Blackstone Hotel manager, N.d. (probably early May 1920), AKDA 32.569. **10.** *The Manhood of Humanity and its Universal Language*, p. 34. AKDA 4. **11.** Korzybski 1950 (1921), pp. lxii-lxiii. **12.** Ibid., pp. 110-111. **13.** Ibid., pp. 147-148. **14.** Ibid., p. 115. **15.** Ibid. **16.** Ibid, pp. 132-133. **17.** Ibid., p. 198. **18.** "Tradition", in Wigodor, pp. 782-783. **19.** Merejkowski, p. 345. **20.** George Boole. Qtd. in McHale, p. 123. **21.** Korzybski 1921, p.111. **22.** "All creation is a mine, and

every man, a miner... In the beginning, the mine was unopened, and the miner stood *naked*, and *knowledgeless*, upon it. Fishes, birds, beasts, and creeping things, are not miners, but *feeders* and *lodgers*, merely. Beavers build houses; but they build them in nowise differently, or better now, than they did, five thousand years ago. Ants, and honey-bees, provide food for winter; but just in the *same way* they did, when Solomon referred the sluggard to them as patterns of prudence. Man is not the only animal who labors; but he is the only one who *improves* his workmanship. This improvement, he effects by *Discoveries*, and *Inventions*." [Lincoln 1915. Aso available at http://showcase.netins.net/web/creative/lincoln/speeches/discoveries.htm]. Lincoln gave another version of this speech in February 1859 [Lincoln 1989, pp. 3-11]. Lincoln appeared devoted to this subject but the lecture was generally not considered a success [Holzer, pp. 19-20, 210]. **23.** Ibid. **24.** George, p. 507. **25.** Note from MEK to AK, nd. AKDA 5.69-70.

Chapter 17 – Dear Dear Old Men
1. Korzybski 1947, p. 216. **2.** The Hilltop Club, "Purposes, Principles, Procedures". AKDA 32.697. **3.** Carter 1953, p. 134. **4.** Korzybski 1921, p. 222. **5.** Cassius J. Keyser to George Brett, 9/21/20, AKDA 6.624-625. **6.** Keyser, "Mathematics as a Career". In *Mole Philosophy & Other Essays*, p. 105. Although enthusiastic about Frege's and Russell's work, Keyser's broader view of the unity of mathematics and logic (with mathematics as the overarching framework) was not refuted by the subsequent failure of their program. **7.** Keyser 2001 (1922), p. 412. **8.** George Boole, p. 1. **9.** Mary Everest Boole, "Indian Thought and Western Science in the Nineteenth Century: A Letter to Dr. Bose", in Vol. 3, *Collected Works*, p. 952-953. Frege and Russell had helped popularize the notion of the separation of logic/mathematics from psychology. Mathematics, according to this fashionable view, did not reveal anything about human thinking. Following Frege, "psychologism" became a term of disapproval wielded against those like Keyser and Korzybski who *did not* accept that mathematics/logic was completely 'objective' and independent of human 'minds'. **10.** AK to C. J. Keyser, 8/8/1920. AKDA 4.539. **11.** C. J. Keyser to AK, 10/9/1920. AKDA 4.342-343. **12.** C. J. Keyser to AK, 12/3/1920. AKDA 4.754. **13.** "AK Personal Notebook...Early 1920s". AKDA 37.778. **14.** Korzybski 1947, p. 43. **15.** AK to Phillip Graven, 12/1/1927. AKDA 19.675. **16.** Korzybski 1921. p. 211. **17.** AKDA 4.349. **18.** AKDA 11.453-456. **19.** "Korzybski: Pole, Artilleryman, Logician", by R. H. Allen. *Boston Evening Transcript*, Saturday, Oct. 27, 1923. AKDA 2.667. **20.** Cora L. Williams to AK, Sept. 24, 1921. AKDA 6.478. **21.** See Pauly 1987. **22.** Loeb 1912, p. 62. **23.** Korzybski 1921, p.233. **24.** Korzybski 1921, pp. 250–251. **25.** Korzybski 1994 (1933), p. 291. **26.** AK to R.D. Carmichael, 4/29/1924. AKDA 14.759; AK to William Morton Wheeler, 3/30/1924. AKDA 14.632.

Chapter 18 – Alfred and the Jews
1. AK to C.J. Keyser, 8/16/1920. AKDA 32.719. **2.** Bendersky, p. 141. **3.** IGS Archives. **4.** See, for example, Kurt Lewin's "Self-Hatred Among Jews" in *Resolving Social Conflict*, pp. 186-200. Korzybski remained fascinated by the phenomenon of antisemitism and the related Jewish 'self-hatred'. He not only had open files containing material on these topics but also kept other, more hidden, samples of antisemitic material—hidden, perhaps, because their more visible presence might be misunderstood as endorsement. (I found the advertising brochure for the infamous 1934 hate tract *Jews Must Live* by Jewish antisemite Samuel Roth—with Korzybski's red pencil underlinings and handwriting: "Keep for me"—'filed' inside Korzybski's marked-up copy of the *Protocols*. The *Protocols* itself was tied and wrapped inside an unmarked package of brown butcher paper tucked deep inside some IGS file drawers, that I doubt anyone had looked through for at least 60 years.) When Lewin's book—with antisemitism and Jewish self-hatred as major topics—came out in the late 1940s, Korzybski considered it an important event. **5.** "Jewish Population of the United States (1654-2006)", Jewish Virtual Library, http://www.jewishvirtuallibrary.org/jsource/US-Israel/usjewpop1.html **6.** Note from Overman Committee report, in "AK Personal Notebook, Early 1920s". AKDA 37.720. **7.** Advertisement for *The Cause of World Unrest*. AKDA 37.769. **8.** "The Protocols Come to America". Jewish Virtual Library, http://www.jewishvirtuallibrary.org/jsource/anti-semitism/protocols1.html **9.** "Count Korzybski To Speak at 'Y' Monday Evening". *The Kansas City Jewish Chronicle*, 3/29/1929. AKDA 3.319. **10.** Overman Committee Report. See U.S. Congress, Senate, Committee on the Judiciary, 1919. *Bolshevik Propaganda...*, p. 381. **11.** "Jewish organizations" in "AK Personal Notebook, Early 1920s". AKDA 37.720. **12.** "Hebrew literature". AKDA 34.747-749. **13.** Notes on Gottheil's *Zionism* in "AK Personal Notebook, Early 1920s". AKDA 37.762-763. **14.** AK to C. B. Bridges, 3/31/1929. AKDA 22.146; AK to G.Y. Rainich, 3/31/29. AKDA 22.145. **15.** Korzybski 1921, p. 234. **16.** Maimonides quote from Friedlander, trans. p. 267 in "AK Personal Notebook, Early 1920s". AKDA 37.764. **17.** See *Science and Sanity*, p. 404 and 406. **18.** Korzybski's "Foreword to "The Essence of Judaism" by Hans Kohn" in Korzybski, *Collected Writings*, pp. 401-404. **19.** Kahler, p. 1. **20.** See "Hitler And Psychological Factors In His Life" in Korzybski's "Introduction To The Second Edition 1941" of *Science and Sanity*, p. lxxiv. **21.** As Chaim Potok later wrote:

...The notion of chosenness...is an assumption of responsibility, not superiority. That the notion of chosenness may have been the basis for various theories of national and racial superiority indicates to me nothing more than that all ideas are potentially corruptible when taken up by small minds. That does not mean that those with great minds should cease thinking...Judaism is one configuration of thought and action. There are many others. Judaism is the responsibility of the Jew. As such, it makes no claim to being the only source of salvation for the world. Its sole criterion for the worth of one who is not Jewish is whether or not he observes the universally applicable Noahide Code. Such observance, in the Talmudic terminology of approbation, makes the non-Jew worthy of the world-to-come. Some of the rabbis of the Talmud went even further: a moral non-Jew is more worthy in the eyes of God than a sinful high priest. [*The Conditions of Jewish Belief*, pp. 175-176]

Chapter 19 – The Time-Binding Club
1. AK to Harvey O'Higgins, 8/8/1920. AKDA 4.539. **2.** The last letter from Polakov to Korzybski that I found in the IGS Archives (non-digital) was dated June 20, 1947—ten years after the presumed year of his death as given in Wren 2001, p. 238. I have been unable to adequately determine the actual date of Polakov's death which obviously had to have occurred after this letter was written. **3.** "Jews of Prominence In The United States", Compiled by I. George Dobsevage, in *American Jewish Year Book*, Vol. 24 (1922-1923), pp. 109-218. American Jewish Committee Archives, http://www.ajcarchives.org/AJC_DATA/Files/1922_1923_5_SpecialArticles.pdf **4.** Daniel Wren's 1980 article "Scientific Management in the U.S.S.R., With Particular Reference to the Contribution of Walter N. Polakov" provides many details of Polakov's career and early life. D. J. Kelly's 2004 article, "Marxist Manager amidst the Progressives: Walter N. Polakov and the Taylor Society" analyzes in more detail Polakov's work and ideas in relation to the beginning of the scientific management movement. **5.** See Polakov 1925, p. 205–227. **6.** Best, p. 88. **7.** Polakov to C. L. Boone, Sept. 13, 1920. AKDA 6.615. **8.** Polakov 1925, p. 60. **9.** Korzybski 1921, "Appendix III, Engineering and Time-Binding", p. 262. **10.** Polakov 1921, p. ix. Qtd. by Korzybski in typed notes, AKDA 4.365. **11.** AK to Lincoln Steffens, 1/28/22. AKDA 8.589. **12.** AK to Luella Twining, June 5, 1922. AKDA 8.205. To place the deeds of Morgan and Rockefeller, whatever their greedy machinations, on a similar scale with those of the two Soviet leaders seems arguable. By this time, Lenin and Trotsky (as Korzybski would acknowledge) already had the blood of millions of Russians on their hands. Despite Alfred's perhaps-skewed 1922 perception of 'capitalists' like Morgan and Rockefeller, he was not an admirer of the Soviet system. **13.** Keyser to AK, 3/17/1924. AKDA 10.362. **14.** See "Summary Of Remarks by Alfred Korzybski" in "Understanding Human Potentialities, Key To Dealing With The Soviet Union" in *Collected Writings*, p. 640. **15.** Ralph Hamilton, Interview, Oct. 2005. **16.** "Korzybski, Time-Binder, Upsets Darwin and Proves The Golden Rule True" by Lincoln M. Schuster. *Boston Evening Transcript*, Wed., June 22, 1921. AKDA 3.13. **17.** Walter N. Polakov to Robert S. Gill, 8/6/1923. AKDA 10.31. **18.** Polakov to AK, 10/6/1920. AKDA 4.362. **19.** "Science and Labor" by Walter N. Polakov in *American Labor Monthly*, April 1923. AKDA 3.171. **20.** Robert B. Wolf to AK., 12/3/1920. AKDA 6.610. **21.** Robert B. Wolf to AK, 10/27/1920. AKDA 4.320 **22.** Polakov to AK, 4/11/1921. AKDA 5.439. **23.** Korzybski 1921, p. 259. **24.** AK to Charles Steinmetz, 9/12/1920. AKDA 4.808. **25.** AK to Charles Steinmetz, 10/9/1920. AKDA 4.357. **26.** Charles Steinmetz to AK, 10/26/1920. AKDA 4.319. **27.** Charles Steinmetz to AK, 12/21/1920. AKDA 6.607. **28.** Charles Steinmetz to AK, Feb. 1, 1921. AKDA 6.598 **29.** Korzybski to Charles Steinmetz, Ap. 7, 1921. AKDA 5.418 **30.** Steinmetz Obituary by Walter N. Polakov in *The Nation*, 11/7/1923. AKDA 3.202. **31.** Polakov to AK, June 20, 1947. IGS Archives. **32.** Keyser in "Man and Men" in Keyser 1927, p. 189 and Polakov in "Maggots In The Cheese" (a Review of Keyser's *Mathematical Philosophy*) in *The Call*, Dec. 10,1922. AKDA 3.162.

Chapter 20 – Manhood of Humanity
1. "New Theory As To Man". *New York Times*, Sunday, Jan. 16, 1921. AKDA 3.1. **2.** E. P. (Edward Payson) Dutton had opened a bookstore in Boston in the mid-19th century. He soon expanded his bookstore business to New York City, where he also began a publishing firm which specialized in religious books for the Episcopalian Church. In 1885, John Macrae started his career there as an office boy. By 1901, when E.P. Dutton & Company was incorporated, Macrae had become Vice-President and subsequently helped the company acquire the famous "Everyman's Library" and American publishing rights to British authors like W. H. Hudson, G. K. Chesterton, and A. A. Milne. By 1920, Dutton had become a major New York publishing house with Macrae running it. (He would become company president in 1923 and owner, with his two sons, of the publishing wing, when it separated from the bookstore business in 1928.) "About Us – Dutton – Penguin Group (USA)". http://us.penguingroup.com/static/html/aboutus/adult/dutton.html (accessed on 8/22/2006).

3. Korzybski 1947, p. 218. 4. John Macrae to AK, 1/4/1921. AKDA 6.606. 5. Korzybski 1947, p. 219. 6. Samuel H. Williamson, "Seven Ways to Compute the Relative Value of a U.S. Dollar Amount, 1774 to present". *MeasuringWorth*, April 2010. www.measuringworth.com/uscompare/ (accessed 10/29/2010). 7. AK to Burges Johnson, 3/23/1921. AKDA 5.354. 8. "Man Is Not An Animal, Says Count Korzybski..." by Charles Wood. *New York World*, 4/10/1921. AKDA 3.2. 9. Miriam Stockton to MEK, 3/29/1921. AKDA 4.373. 10. MEK to "To Whom It May Concern" (Endorsement letter for Sol Abramson), 3/21/1921. AKDA 4.369. 11. Herbert Stockton to MEK, 3/30/1921. AKDA 4.375. 12. John Macrae to AK, 4/29/1921. AKDA 11.531. 13. Guido Marx to AK, 5/19/1921. AKDA 11.493. 14. AK to C.J. Keyser, 5/29/1921. AKDA 11.466. 15. "Fourth Dimension Discovered at Last!...". *San Francisco Chronicle*, 5/29/1921. AKDA 1.103. 16. "Korzybski, Time-Binder, Upsets Darwin...". *Boston Evening Transcript*, 6/26/1921. AKDA 3.13. 17. John Macrae to AK, 6/27/1921. AKDA 11.273. 18. AK to William J. Fielding, 4/24/1921. AKDA 11.548-550; AK to Basil Manly, 6/13/1921. AKDA 11.369. 19. AK to William J. Fielding, 6/12/1921. AKDA 11.387. 20. AK to Mrs. E.B. Darling, 7/13/1921. AKDA 11.226.

Part V – Science and Sanity
1. Korzybski qtd. in Mordkowitz "Listener's Guide to Alfred Korzybski's 1948-1949 Intensive Seminar", *General Semantics Bulleting* 52 (1985), p. 58.

Chapter 21 – Leibniz's Dreams
1. Korzybski 1921, p. 199-200. 2. Ibid., p. 200. See pp. 200-203 for more detail on Korzybski's Dynamic Department proposal. 3. AK to C. J. Keyser, 6/20/1921. AKDA 11.335-338. 4. AK to V. S. Sukthankar, 6/12/1921. AKDA 11.388. 5. AK to Keyser, 6/6/1921. AKDA 11.409-411. 6. Indeed, he noted twice in *Science and Sanity*—the book that was finally published 12 years later—that the system presented in it implied a theory of universal agreement that would allow "the dreams of Leibnitz" to become "a sober reality." Korzybski 1994 (1933), pp. 52, 287. 7. Leibniz 1979 (1951), "The Horizon of Human Knowledge [After 1690]", p.73. 8. Ibid, "Precepts For Advancing The Sciences And Arts" [1680], p. 33. 9. Ibid., pp. 29–30. 10. Ibid., p. 32. 11. Ibid., pp. 39-40. 12. Korzybski 1921, pp. 44-45. 13. Bacon qtd. in Korzybski 1921, pp. 42. 14. Leibniz 1979 (1951), "Towards A Universal Characteristic [1677]", p.17.

Chapter 22 – "Just Work, Work, Work"
1. Gilchrest to AK, 10/24/1921. AKDA 11.727. 2. Korzybski qtd. in Schuchardt [Read] 1950b, "Editor's Note", p. x. 3. Korzybski 1921, p. xiii. 4. Polakov to AK, 10/6/1921. AKDA 12.66. 5. The 5000th copy of *Manhood of Humanity* was finally sold sometime between May 1934 and April 1935. But Alfred and Mira got very little benefit from the subsequent 15% royalty increase. After the publication of Alfred's second book, *Science and Sanity* in 1933, interest in *Manhood*—which had virtually no sales in 1932 and 1933—began to increase. But with only 10 to 30 orders per year, Dutton had little incentive to continue with another printing. With several hundred sheeted copies of the book still sitting in a warehouse, Dutton only bound the books when an occasional order came in. By 1944, these were gone. *Manhood of Humanity* was out of print. Meanwhile, the Institute of General Semantics had been promoting and selling the book. Korzybski bought the printer's plates and obtained the copyright from Dutton but the IGS was unable to get it back into print until the fall of 1950. "Copyright Folder and Business Correspondence with Dutton about *Manhood of Humanity*". AKDA 31. 6. AK to Beatrice Irwin, 7/18/1921. AKDA 11.164. 7. "Strike Leaders Facing Defeat". *New York Times*, 3/8/1910. 8. Pula 2003c, p. 64. Alfred's and Mira's separation after 1946 had to do with exigencies of finance and health, beyond the control of either of them. By this time, they had resolved their marital conflicts. Up until Alfred's death, they remained in frequent contact, and hoped to find some way to live closer and see each other more often. 9. AK to C. J. Keyser, 10/7/1921. AKDA 12.92. 10. AK to Keyser, 10/7/1921. AKDA 12.92. 11. "Berkeley Private School Attracts Wide Attention". *Berkeley Daily Gazette*, 8/16/1921. AKDA 1.129. 12. http://www.berkeley-heritage.com/berkeley_landmarks/spring_mansion.html (accessed Oct. 16, 2006). 13. AK to Luella Twining, 7/18/1921. AKDA 11.172. 14. Korzybski 1947, pp. 226–227. 15. AK to C. J. Keyser, 10/24/1921. AKDA 11.756. 16. C. J. Keyser to AK, 10/11/21. AKDA 6.425. 17. C. B. Bridges to AK, 10/4/1921. AKDA 6.445. 18. "[Korzybski] has certainly done a great service by defining so clearly and emphatically the chief characteristic of man—his time-binding capacity. I can appreciate this in some measure, though I cannot claim competence to follow all his reasoning or to estimate the probable practical bearing of his conclusions. If applied literally, they would apparently involve revolutionary changes, but whether these are feasible or even in all respects desirable is another matter." George Hale to MEK, 10/21/1921. AKDA 6.471.

19. "Darwin Downed! Count In LA Denies Man Is Animal[.] World Famed Polish Nobleman and Philosopher Tells of Discoveries". *L.A. Examiner*, Friday, November 4, 1921. AKDA 3.46. **20.** Telegram, W. E. Ritter to AK, 11/9/1921. AKDA 11.747. **21.** AK to Luella Twining, 11/12/1921. AKDA 11.702. **22.** AK to Amy Edgerly Rush and Minnie Edgerly Russell, 12/22/1921. AKDA 11.581. **23.** AK to Robert Wolf, 11/12/1921. AKDA 11.710. **24.** AK to Cora Williams, 11/12/1921. AKDA 11.711. **25.** Korzybski 1947, p. 224. **26.** Ibid., p. 423. **27.** AK to C. J. Keyser, 12/22/1921. AKDA 11.595. **28.** Korzybski 1947, p. 224.

Chapter 23 – Strange Footprints
1. AK to Adelaide Smith, 6/5/1922. AKDA 8.204. Years later, Russell visited Korzybski, then in Chicago, and autographed the book for him. **2.** L. L. Whyte 1951, p. 44. **3.** Ibid., p. 46. **4.** Rukeyser, p. 279-280. **5.** Korzybski 1994 (1933), p. 50. **6.** Ibid., p. 69. **7.** L. L. Whyte 1951, p. 46. **8.** Ibid. **9.** Russell 1919, p. 80. **10.** B. Russell to AK (Telegram), 4/7/33. AKDA 25.551. **11.** In 1939 Russell wrote to Korzybski "I should like very much to know about the semantic definition of number that you mention [in a previous letter to Russell]." If Russell had read with any care either the page proofs or the published copy of *Science and Sanity* that Korzybski sent to him, then he would not have missed Korzybski's suggested improvement upon Russell's definition of number, discussed in detail in Chapter XVIII of *Science and Sanity* and mentioned in various places throughout the book. B. Russell to AK, 1/14/1939. IGS Archives. **12.** Russell 1919, p. 205. **13.** Philosopher Bryan Magee who got to know Russell toward the end of the great mathematical philosopher's life, called him a genius for theory who "treated practical problems as if they were theoretical problems. In fact I do not think he could tell the difference." Magee 1999 (1997), p. 210. **14.** AK to Russell, 7/27/1946. IGS Archives. **15.** B. Russell to AK, 8/9/[1946] IGS Archives. **16.** As Whyte put it :

> Whitehead...had a rich sense of the role of the religious, aesthetic, and moral elements in human experience. Indeed I think that it is fair to say that most of his energies from 1910 to his death in 1947 were devoted to the attempt to bring his mathematical and scientific knowledge into harmony with the qualities and values of personal experience. His attempt at a synthesis centered round one philosophic idea, that of the creative passage of nature, the time process which somehow transcends the apparent separation of individual entities, and carries the whole on into new forms of existence. [L. L. Whyte 1951, p. 46.]

17. AK to Harrington Emerson, 11/26/1922. AKDA 9.269. **18.** Whitehead (*Process and Reality*, Part I, Chapter I, Section I) in Whitehead 1961, *Alfred North Whitehead: An anthology.* Eds., F. S. C. Northrop and Mason W. Gross, p. 567. **19.** Whitehead (1920) 1964, p. 53. **20.** Ibid., p. 3. **21.** Ibid., p. 31. **22.** Ibid., p. 33. **23.** See Whiteheads discussion of Cleopatra's Needle. Ibid., p. 171.

> We cannot well miss Cleopatra's Needle [a London landmark, one of a trio of ancient Egyptian obelisks standing in London, Paris and New York City], if we are in its neighborhood; but no one has seen a single molecule or a single electron, yet the characters of events are only explicable to us by expressing them in terms of these scientific objects. Undoubtedly molecules and electrons are abstractions. But then so is Cleopatra's Needle. The concrete facts are the events themselves—I have already explained to you that to be an abstraction does not mean that an entity is nothing. It merely means that its existence is only one factor of a more concrete element of nature.

24. Ibid., p. 169. **25.** Ibid., pp. 77–78. **26.** Eddington 1920, p. 197. **27.** Ibid., p. 200-201.

Chapter 24 – A Visitor from Mars
1. Ritter's 1893 doctoral dissertation was entitled "On the Eyes, the Integumentary Sense Papillae, and the Integument of the San Diego Blind Fish". Pauly 2000, p. 291. **2.** W. E. Ritter, *The Unity of the Organism*, Vol. I, p. 24. **3.** "Now, and particularly in the last year, has come some real, even though slight, understanding of relativity as interpreted by Einstein and its bearings on the problems of living nature. For what I have been able to get from this…I am much indebted to Count Alfred Korzybski, who, as you know, is spending some months with us here." W.E. Ritter to H.S. Jennings, 2/23/1922. AKDA 6.160. **4.** Keyser 1927, p. 94. **5.** Scripps qtd. in Pauly 2000, pp. 204. **6.** Ibid., p. 206. **7.** "…I am bound to believe that man is mythological (perhaps mystical) and at the same time brutally beast. Thus with a sad heart I am prevented from receiving to myself an offering of hope. Perhaps Korzybski is but another of those dreamers of which his race [the Slavs] has been so prolific." E. W. Scripps to W. E. Ritter, 8/29/1921. AKDA 6.206. Ritter shared this correspondence with Korzybski. Alfred appeared amused by Scripps' concern with the question "What is a dollar?" and by Scripps' efforts to convince Ritter that he (Scripps) had already come up with many of the ideas in *Manhood*.

8. AK to C.J. Keyser, 2/2/1922. AKDA 8.570. 9. Pauly 2000, pp. 210-211. See also "Smithsonian Institution Archives, Finding Aids to Personal Papers and Special Collections: Record Unit 7091, Science Service, Records, 1902-1965, Historical Note" at http://siarchives.si.edu/findingaids/FARU7091.htm#FARU7091h (accessed 1/17/2011). 10. Edwin E. Slossen, "Is There a Law of Human Progress?: Speculations on the Acceleration of Scientific Knowledge". *The Independent and Weekly Review*, 2/25/1922. AKDA 3.80. 11. George Boole, p. 173. 12. Znaniecki, p. 164. 13. AK to H. L. Brasefield, 1/5/1922. AKDA 8.691. 14. AK to C. J. Keyser, 1/14/1922. AKDA 8.647-8. 15. AK to Dr. J. R. Brinkley, 8/12/1923. AKDA 13.302; AK to Ray P. Martin (Brinkley Jones Hospital), 8/21/1923. AKDA 13.275; Dr. J. R. Brinkley to AK, 10/29/1923. AKDA 13.182. See Brock for more on the career of J. R. Brinkley. 16. "Count Korzybski, Native of Warsaw, Now San Diego Visitor...". *The San Diego Union*, 1/17/1922. AKDA 3.71. 17. "Polish Scientist To Lecture On Nature Of Man". *The San Diego Union*, 1/25/1922. AKDA 3.71. 18. Fred Gronberg to AK, 1/10/1922. AKDA 8.640. 19. "Holds His Audience Spellbound For Two Hours". *The Sun Dial*, 2/11/1922. AKDA 3.87. 20. *Manhood of Humanity* review by Frankwood Williams, M.D. in *Mental Hygiene*, Vol. VI, No. 1, Jan. 1922. AKDA 3.122-123. 21. Korzybski 1947, p. 233.

Chapter 25 – "The Brotherhood of Doctrines"
1. AK to C.J. Keyser, 3/10/1922. AKDA 8.460. 2. Keyser 1922, p. 5. 3. Ibid., p. 151 4. AK to A. S. Eddington, 4/5/1922. AKDA 8.361. 5. See Keyser's chapter on "The Psychology of Mathematics" where he wrote that:
> ...It is indeed obvious that the whole literature of mathematics may be read and interpreted as a commentary upon the nature of the human mind...A normal human mind is such that, if it begin with such-and-such principles or premises and with such-and-such ideas and if it combine them in such-and-such ways, moving from step to step in such-and-such order, it will find that it has thus passed from darkness to light,—from doubt to conviction. Obviously such a proposition is not mathematical; it is psychological—it states a fact respecting the nature of a normal human mind. Such interpretations of mathematical literature are psychologically very illuminating; the possibility of making them is so evident, once it is pointed out, that I should have refrained from mentioning it except for the fact of its being commonly overlooked and neglected. [Keyser 2001 (1922), pp. 412-413]

6. Robertson, p. 230. Korzybski would have felt delighted to know that his work influenced Powers, who wrote the following to me on 11/17/2009:
> "...when I was in high school, a hopeless SF [science fiction] addict, I read A. E. van Vogt's *The World of Null-A* and was intrigued to find that the chapter quotes were from a real book, *Science and Sanity* by our mutual friend. I rushed to the library and read the whole thing, and from then on, the word was not the object and the map was not the territory. I took courses in General Semantics in college from Lee and Hayakawa. These experiences had a definite influence on my thinking when the development of PCT [Perceptual Control Theory] began, in around 1953." Comment on "Historic Breakthrough Promises Major Progress Throughout the Life Sciences", [http://korzybskifiles.blogspot.com/2009/11/historic-breakthrough-promises-major.html]

7. Korzybski qtd. by M. Kendig in "Book Comments", *General Semantics Bulletin* 1 & 2, p. 46. 8. "Introduction by the Editor of "The Brotherhood of Doctrines". *The Builder Magazine*, April 1924, Volume X – Number 4 in *Alfred Korzybski Collected Writings*, p. 53. 9. AK to C. J. Keyser, 4/23/1922. AKDA 8.326. 10. "775 pounds of luggage", Jas. B. Duffy (Atcheson, Topeka and Santa Fe General Passenger Agent) to AK, 5/11/1922. AKDA 8.214. 11. AK to Margaret Conway, 5/6/1922. AKDA 8.285. 12. AK to V. S. Sukanthar, 5/10/1922. AKDA 8.277. 13. AK to C. J. Keyser, 5/13/1922. AKDA 8.254. 14. *City Club News*, 5/12/1922. AKDA 1.290. 15. *The Milwaukee Leader*, 5/17/1922. AKDA 3.102; *The Wisconsin News*, 5/17/1922. AKDA 3.99. 16. "Drake-A-Day". AKDA 3.110. 17. AK to C. J. Keyser, 8/27/1922. AKDA 9.54. 18. R. D. Carmichael to AK, 8/14/1922. AKDA 7.377-8. 19. J.B. Shaw to AK, 6/24/1922. AKDA 7.450-452. 20. AK to J.B. Shaw, 6/26/1922. AKDA 8.124. 21. AK to C. J.Keyser, 6/8/1922. AKDA 8.188. 22. AK to T. J. McCormack, 6/8/1922. AKDA 8.189. 23. "Count Denies Women Are Illogical". *Chicago Evening American*, 6/14/1922. AKDA 3.112. 24. AK to C. J. Keyser, 7/4/1922. AKDA 8.90. 25. This and subsequent quotes in this chapter related to "The Brotherhood of Doctrines" come from that article, found on pp. 39–54 of *Alfred Korzybski Collected Writings*. 26. Korzybski's views here seem more or less compatible with those of a number of epistemologists/philosophers of science whose work became prominent after his death (David Bohm, N. R. Hanson, Thomas Kuhn, Michael Polanyi, and others). See Harold I. Brown, *Perception, Theory and Commitment: The New Philosophy of Science*.

Chapter 26 – "Fate and Freedom"

1. AK to Scudder Klyce, 12/9/1922. AKDA 9.286-7. **2.** MEK., Autobiographical Memoir (Unpublished), p. 38, IGS Archives. **3.** AK to Scudder Klyce, 12/9/1922. AKDA 9.286-7; AK to Harvey O'Higgins, 12/7/1922. AKDA 9.300. **4.** AK Personal Notebooks. AKDA 37. **5.** AK to Harvey O'Higgins, 12/7/1922. AKDA 9.300. **6.** MEK, Autobiographical Memoir (Unpublished), p. 42, IGS Archives. **7.** "Let's Abolish Death...". AKDA 3.140-141. **8.** Henry Lane to AK, 11/22/1922. AKDA 7.279. **9.** Otto Sprengler to AK, 11/26/1922. AKDA 7.255. **10.** AK to Otto Sprengler, 11/9/1922. AKDA 9.223. **11.** C. J. Keyser to AK, 7/21/1923. AKDA 7.37. **12.** "Fate and Freedom", *Alfred Korzybski Collected Writings*, p. 15. **13.** Keyser 1922, p. 152. **14.** "The few first words with which mankind started its vocabulary were labels for pre-scientific ideas, naïve generalizations full of silent assumptions, objectifications, of non-existents,...Our daily speech and in very large measure our scientific language is one enormous system of such assumptions." ["Fate and Freedom", in *Alfred Korzybski Collected Writings*, p. 18.] **15.** Logical Destiny diagram from "Fate and Freedom", in *Alfred Korzybski Collected Writings*, p. 29. **16.** Lionel Robertson to AK, 11/19/1922. AKDA 7.277. **17.** AK to Lionel Robertson, 11/25/1922. AKDA 9.269. **18.** "Fate and Freedom", in *Alfred Korzybski Collected Writings*, p. 17. **19.** Ibid., p.20. **20.** Ibid, pp. 19-20. **21.** AK to R.D. Carmichael, 12/7/1922. AKDA 9.301. **22.** Henry Lane to AK, 3/8/1923. AKDA 7.143-5. **23.** Louis G. Barrett, D.M.D. to Alfred Korzybski, July 10, 1947. IGS Archives. **24.** AKDA 9.433. **25.** AKDA 3.166. **26.** AKDA 3.167. **27.** AKDA 3.166. **28.** AK to J. B. Shaw, 1/22/1923. AKDA 9.445. **29.** AK to C. J. Keyser, 2/3/1923. AKDA 9.474. **30.** AKDA 9.484. **31.** William B. Leeds to AK, 2/15/1923. AKDA 9.556. **32.** AK to Roy Haywood, 3/26/1923. AKDA 13.589. **33.** Ibid. **34.** On February 24, he wrote the following to Jesse S. Reeves, a political scientist he had met during his talk at the University of Michigan at Ann Arbor:

...It [Tractatus Logico-Philosophicus] is of enormous importance as a trial of the establishing [of] a LOGICAL language, in which arguments would be impossible, and only errors could be corrected. He claims in many instances finality, I do not think so, but he said there more than any other writer I know of. I have already in two readings found some mistakes, but in general I am amazed on the bigness of this work. It seems to me that you may enjoy studying an example of this new stuff. There is no doubt that he is on the right track. I feel very enthusiastic about it because my own thoughts were developing in the same channels, and he has saved me considerable amount of time through his work, my lecture ["Fate and Freedom] deals with the same subject but yet in [a] more general and further going way. The book as the beginning is a marvel, but I don't believe that finality can be attained even theoretically, IT seems to me that I am able to prove that finality is NOT in the nature of things and therefore theoretically impossible. [AK to Jesse S. Reeves, 2/24/1923. AKDA 9.511]

35. The following passages (among others) were underlined in green for special emphasis in Korzybski's well-marked copy of Wittgenstein's book:

2.1 We make to ourselves pictures of facts....

2.12 The picture is a model of reality....

2.15 That the elements of the picture are combined with one another in a definite way, represents that the things are so combined with one another. This connexion of the elements of the picture is called its structure, and the possibility of this structure is called the form of representation of the picture....

2.16 In order to be a picture a fact must have something in common with what it pictures.

2.161 In the picture and the pictured there must be a something identical in order that the one can be a picture of the other at all.

2.17 What the picture must have in common with reality in order to be able to represent it after its manner—rightly or falsely—is its form of representation.

36. AK to Joseph Roe (NYU dept of Industrial Engineering), 3/9/1923. AKDA 9.530. **37.** See Leszek Kolakowski, *The Alienation of Reason: A History of Positivist Thought*, Chapter One, for more on 'the rules' of phenomenalism, nominalism, etc. in 'positivistic thought'. **38.** C.J. Keyser, "Fundamental Thinking". *Literary Review*, August 18, 1923. IGS Archives. **39.** AKDA 13.591-3. **40.** MEK, Autobiographical Memoir (Unpublished), p. 43, IGS Archives.

Chapter 27 – Measure of Man

1. AK to R.D. Carmichael, 9/20/1922. AKDA 9.70-71; AK Notebook, n.d. AKDA 37.799. Korzybski later quoted the passage in *Science and Sanity*, p. 753. **2.** Korzybski, "Fate and Freedom in Personnel Management". AKDA 13.390-395. **3.** Korzybski , "The Implications and Applications of Man as Time-Binder". AKDA 13.396-401. **4.** AKDA 3.177. **5.** Watson 1914, p. 7. **6.** Watson 1917, p. 54. **7.** Polakov, "The Foundation of Human

Engineering: Language and The New Mathematical Logic". *Management Engineering*, May 1923. AKDA 3.181-18. **8.** AK to C. E. Drayer, 8/16/1923. AKDA 13.284. **9.** W. N. Polakov to AK, 5/15/1923. AKDA 13.538. **10.** W. N. Polakov (correspondence with editor of *Management Engineering*), AKDA 7.86,7.87,7.90. **11.** AK to W. N. Polakov, 5/16/1923. AKDA 13.536. **12.** AK to W. N. Polakov, 5/21/23. AKDA 13.512. **13.** Ralph C. Hamilton to Bruce I. Kodish, letter dated "17 Nov. [20]05" (sent March 8, 2006), p. 9. **14.** Korzybski 1947, p. 308. **15.** "Historical Note on the Structural Differential [1947]", *Alfred Korzybski Collected Writings*, p. 593. **16.** Ralph C. Hamilton to Bruce I. Kodish, letter dated "17 Nov. [20]05", p. 9. **17.** Korzybski 1947, p. 310-311. **18.** AK to H. L. Haywood, n.d., probably 7/28/1923. AKDA 13.381.**19.** AK to Henry Lane, 7/16/1923. AKDA 13.417. **20.** AK to W. N. Polakov, 6/29/1923. AKDA 13.457. **21.** Korzybski Patent Application. AKDA 35.602. **22.** See "Patent Application", *Alfred Korzybski Collected Writings*, pp. 31-38. **23.** AK to C. J. Keyser, 7/14/1923. AKDA 13.422. **24.** AK to Adolf Meyer, 12/29/1923. AKDA 13.35; AK to Stewart Paton, 1/7/1924. AKDA 13.31. **25.** Anthropometer Accounts, AK Notebook. AKDA 37.837-838. **26.** Korzybski 1947, pp. 309-310. **27.** AKDA 35.591. **28.** "Time-Binding: The General Theory (First Paper)" in *Alfred Korzybski Collected Writings*, p. 68. **29.** Korzybski 1947, p. 2. **30.** AKDA 13.380. **31.** AK to Edward McKernan, 8/4/1923. AKDA 13.342. **32.** Korzybski later wrote about the "white race" as what he mainly knew; what he said about it seems mainly uncomplimentary. See *Science and Sanity*, pp. 302, 304. **33.** AK to R.D. Carmichael, 1/23/1924. AKDA 14.450. **34.** Lockwood de Forest to AK, 8/16/1923. AKDA 10.47–45. **35.** AK to Lockwood de Forest II, 8/22/1923. AKDA 13.271. **36.** A. V. de Forest to AK, 8/28/1923. AKDA 10.67. **37.** Robert S. Gill to AK, 8/10/1923. AKDA 10.29. **38.** "Countess Korzybska, Portrait Painter...". *North Shore Breeze and Reminder*, August 24 edition. AKDA 3.195. **39.** "Personals - Countess Korzybska Speaks". *Boston Evening Transcript*, 10/4/1923. AKDA 3.198. **40.** AK to W. E. Ritter, 11/10/1923. AKDA 13.170. **41.** Ibid. **42.** AK to R.D. Carmichael, 1/23/1924. AKDA 14.450. **43.** AK to W. E. Ritter, 12/29/1923. AKDA 13.43. **44.** AK to R.D. Carmichael, 1/23/1924. AKDA 14.450. **45.** "Count Korzybski Speaks Tonight". *The Tech* (MIT Student Newspaper), 10/26/1923. AKDA 3.206. **46.** David Fairchild to AK, 11/8/1923. AKDA 10.175. **47.** AK to W.E. Ritter, 12/29/1923. AKDA 13.43-44.

Chapter 28 – Advancing Human Engineering
1. H. S. Jennings, qtd. in Polakov 1925, p. 178. **2.** "Scientific Opinions about the First Edition", in Korzybski 1994 (1933), Fifth Ed., p. 784. **3.** Ibid. **4.** AK to G.Y. Rainich, 7/23/1932. AKDA 29.54. **5.** AK to W.A. White, 1/5/1924. AKDA 13.17. **6.** AK to Ernst Cassirer, 4/28/1925. AKDA 16.456. **7.** AK to E.T. Bell, 4/26/1924. AKDA 14.74. **8.** AK to William Morton Wheeler, 5/16/1924. AKDA 700-701. **9.** A. N. Vasiliev to AK, 3/28/1924. AKDA 14.157-151; Translation by AK of Vasiliev letter. AKDA 13.623-626. **10.** J.L. Synge to A.K, 5/29/1924. AKDA 15.127. **11.** AK to R.D. Carmichael, 1/7/1925. AKDA 16.194. **12.** AK to C. J. Keyser, 1/14/1925. AKDA 16.209. **13.** R.D.Carmichael to AK, 10/10/1925. AKDA 17.231. **14.** AK to John L. Synge, 6/5/1924. AKDA 15.157. **15.** Qtd. in *Abstracts, the International Mathematical Congress, Toronto, Canada, Aug. 11-16, 1924*. AKDA 3.247 **16.** AK to R.E. Sturtevant, 8/2/1924. AKDA 15.283. **17.** AK to R.D.Carmichael, 8/3/1924. AKDA 15.287. **18.** "Time-Binding: The General Theory (First Paper)" in *Alfred Korzybski Collected Writings*, p. 59. **19.** Ibid. **20.** Ibid., p. 74. **21.** Ibid., p. 75. Interestingly, Korzybski's emphasis in this paper on what he called "undefined terms" was later taken up by J.L. Synge, the secretary of the Mathematics Congress, who saw Korzybski's paper, and may have attended his talk. Synge, who had a long and distinguished career afterwards as an applied mathematician, invented a game called "Vish" based on the 'vicious circle' which results from attempting to define every term one uses. Eventually as Korzybski pointed out you will reach the level of undefined terms, where the words start 'doubling back' on themselves. As Synge put it "In defining some word [with other words], you are bound to use a word whose final definition you are seeking." [J. L. Synge, *Science: Sense and Nonsense*, p. 23] **22.** "Time-Binding: The General Theory (First Paper)" in *Alfred Korzybski Collected Writings*, p. 75-76. **23.** Ibid., p. 76. **24.** AK to R.D.Carmichael, 5/3/1924. AKDA 13.751. **25.** "Time-Binding: The General Theory (First Paper)" in *Alfred Korzybski Collected Writings*, p. 77. **26.** Ibid., p. 72. **27.** AK to T. Percy Nunn, 8/27/1924. AKDA 15.378. **28.** AK Notebooks circa 1920. AKDA 37.774. **29.** Norman Campbell wrote to Korzybski:
> ...I was much interested in your work, and your main ideas are certainly striking and original. But I fear I am rather a sceptic of very wide-sweeping generalizations and am not quite the right person to appreciate their value fully. It seems to me in particular that your conception of "universal agreement" is radically different from mine. I think that universal agreement is possible in only a very narrow range of human affairs, those namely which form the subject matter of science. Outside that range, in everything which concerns art or politics or religion or indeed the daily life of mankind,

I am much more impressed by the diversity than the similarity of human nature. It seems to me that the solution of human antagonisms (which are the source of most of the evils of this world) will come when it is recognized that on very many things we must agree to differ and come to some practical compromise on our differences. An attempt to discover laws in what is essentially irregular is, in my opinion, the main fallacy in most philosophies. I fear therefore that though I shall always read your writings with interest and enjoyment, we can neither of us look to the other for support in our particular outlook." [Norman R. Campbell to AK, 2/14/25. AKDA 17.78.]
30. AK to R.D.Carmichael, 8/3/1924. AKDA 15.287. **31.** AK to R.D.Carmichael, 8/17/1924. AKDA 15.347, 348 **32.** Korzybski 1947, p. 230. **33.** R.G.D. Richardson to AK, 1/27/1925. AKDA 3.263.

Chapter 29 – A Quiet Place in the Country
1. "Author Stricken Fighting A Fire". *New York Times,* April 22, 1931. **2.** MEK, Unpublished Memoir, pp. 36-38. **3.** Pula 2003c, p. 72. **4.** AK to R. D. Carmichael, 10/24/1924. AKDA 15.614. **5.** C. K. Ogden to AK, 1/23/1933, in Gordon 1990a, p. 37. **6.** AK to C. J. Keyser, 12/29/21. AKDA 11.574. **7.** Klyce 1921, p. 6. **8.** AK to Scudder Klyce, 3/12/1922. AKDA 8.431. **9.** AK to P. W. Bridgman, 10/14/1928. AKDA 20.191. **10.** AK to C. J. Keyser, 11/10/1925. AKDA 15.40.

Chapter 30 – Saint Elizabeths
1. AK to R. D.Carmichael, 1/29/1925. AKDA 16.274. **2.** AK to C. J.Keyser, 4/4/1925. AKDA 16.411. **3.** AK to Ethel Dummer, 1/28/1926. AKDA 18.205. **4.** Korzybski 1947, p. 244. **5.** Ibid., p. 235. **6.** J. L. Bennett to AK nd. AKDA 16.504. **7.** AK to E.T. Bell, 11/22/1924. AKDA 15.684; MEK to John Macrae, 1/12/1925. AKDA 16.214; AK to C.J. Keyser, 1/16/1925, AKDA 16.216; AK to J. L. Bennett, 5/25/1925. AKDA 16.505. **8.** AK to Helen Hastings, 11/2/1925. AKDA 15.29. **9.** AK to George Lytton, 6/13/1925. AKDA 16.547. **10.** MEK, Unpublished Memoir, p. 47-48. **11.** Korzybski 1947, p. 236. **12.** J.F. Wright to AK, 8/29/1924. AKDA 15.470; AK to J.F. Wright, 9/29/1924. AKDA 15.471. **13.** AK to David and Marian Fairchild, 7/5/1925. AKDA 16.622. **14.** Korzybski 1947, p. 237. **15.** Korzybski 1949 ("1948-1949 Holiday Seminar"), p. 111. **16.** Beers, p. 54. **17.** Korzybski 1947, p. 240–241. **18.** AK to C. J. Keyser, 7/11/1925. AKDA 16.638. **19.** Korzybski 1949 ("1948-1949 Holiday Seminar"), p. 2. **20.** Chapman, pp. 140-141. **21.** W. A. White 1917, p. 30. **22.** Qtd. in Perry, p. 184, from W. A. White, *Crimes and Criminals* (New York: Farrar and Rinehart, 1933), p. 31. **23.** Korzybski 1947, p. 255. **24.** Korzybski 1947, pp. 255-256. **25.** Korzybski 1947, p. 255. **26.** Korzybski 1947, p. 244. **27.** Chapman, p. 55. **28.** Korzybski 1949, p. 382-383; Korzybski 1947, pp. 257-258. **29.** Korzybski 1947, p. 237-238. **30.** Ibid., pp. 247-248. **31.** "Dr. Nolan D.C. Lewis dies at 90; Psychiatrist was leader in field" by Walter H. Waggoner. *New York Times*, 12/19/1979 **32.** Korzybski 1949, Lecture II (4A), p. 41. **33.** Valenstein, p. 134. **34.** Ibid., p. 145. **35.** Ibid., p. 254-255. **36.** Korzybski 1947, p. 248-249. **37.** Herrick, p. 18. Qtd. in *Science and Sanity*, p. 386. **38.** Korzybski 1948-1949 Intensive Seminar Transcription, p.122. **39.** AK to H. L. Haywood, 5/31/1926, AKDA 18.401. **40.** AK to H. L. Haywood, 10/17/1925, AKDA 15.9; AK to T. H. Stevens, 1/[?]/1926, AKDA 18.200. **41.** AK to H. L. Haywood, 5/3/1926. AKDA 18.334. **42.** "Summer School in Creative and Humanistic Education" at Olivet College. AKDA 3.265. **43.** AK to Malinowski 5/31/26. AKDA 18.417. **44.** AK to H. L. Haywood, nd. AKDA 18.467. **45.** "Time-Binding: The General Theory (Second Paper)", in *Alfred Korzybski Collected Writings*, p. 98. **46.** Ibid., p. 108. **47.** Ibid., p. 127. **48.** Ibid., p. 98. **49.** Ibid., p. 98. **50.** Ibid., p. 116. **51.** AK to C. K. Ogden, 7/26/1927. AKDA 20.513-512. **52.** "Time-Binding: The General Theory (Second Paper)", in *Alfred Korzybski Collected Writings*, p. 113. **53.** Ibid., p. 137–139.

Chapter 31 – "The Tragedy of My Work"
1. E.T. Bell to AK, 11/21/1926. AKDA 18.110. **2.** Ibid. **3.** AK to J.L. Bennett, 8/7/1927. AKDA 20.582–580. **4.** AK to R.D. Carmichael, AKDA 18.466. **5.** Websters, p. 630. **6.** AK to Edwin E. Slossen, 1/7/1927. AKDA 19.525. **7.** Philiip S. Graven to MEK, 1/23/1927. AKDA 18.55. **8.** AK to Miss E. Leona Vincent, 6/25/1927. AKDA 20.505. **9.** Korzybski 1994 (1933), p. 69. **10.** AK to G. Y. Rainich, 1/8/1926. AKDA 18.187–191. **11.** AK to Trigant Burrow, 12/17/1927. AKDA 21.534. **12.** Korzybski 1994 (1933), p. 50. **13.** Ibid., p. 254. **14.** Pula 1994, p. xvii.

Chapter 32 – Trial-By-Headline
1. C. J. Keyser to AK, 11/1/1926, AKDA 19.121. **2.** C. J. Keyser to MEK, 11/8/1926. AKDA 18.46. **3.** H. L. Haywood to AK, 11/27/1926. AKDA 18.93. **4.** AK to H. L. Haywood, 11/28/1926. AKDA 18.701. **5.** AK to Vladimir (Walter Polakov), 11/29/1926. AKDA 18.698. **6.** C. J. Keyser to AK and MEK, 12/4/1926. AKDA 18.80. **7.** H. L. Haywood to AK, 12/4/1926. AKDA 18.731. **8.** Korzybski 1947, p. 248. **9.** AK to Mrs. Guerdrum, 11/9/1926. AKDA 18.725. **10.** Korzybski provided a brief account with dates of his interactions with Houck in a memorandum

to Dr. White. AKDA 19.189–193. **11.** Korzybski Memorandum to William Alanson White. AKDA 19.189–193. **12.** Korzybski 1947, p. 249. **13.** Korzybski Memorandum to William Alanson White. AKDA 19.189–193. **14.** Korzybski 1947, p. 249–250. **15.** Ibid., pp. 250–251. **16.** Korzybski 1947, p. 252. **17.** I put together this account of Houck's breakdown from Korzybski's 1947 autobiographical memoir, Korzybski's memo to Dr. White, and a letter he wrote to Roy Haywood on 12/28/1926 [AKDA 19.587]. **18.** Korzybski 1947, p. 253. **19.** *The Washington Evening Star*, 12/20/1926. AKDA 19.330. **20.** *Philadelphia Evening Public Ledger*, Tues 12/21/1926. AKDA 19.317. **21.** *Washington Times*, 12/23/1926. AKDA 19.296. **22.** *The (NY) World*, 12/24/1926. AKDA 19.276. **23.** *(NY) Evening World*, 12/24/1926. AKDA 19.273. **24.** *The Milwaukee Journal*, 12/24/1926. AKDA 19.272. **25.** *Boston Post*, 12/24/1926. AKDA 19.265. **26.** *The Florida Times Union*, (N.Y. World News Service), 12/25/1926. AKDA 19.271. **27.** *Chicago Herald and Examiner*, 12/24/1926. AKDA 19.257. **28.** "Explains 'Thought Machine', Name a Misnomer, says Professor—For the Rest It's as Simple as Einstein". *The New York Sun*, 12/27/1926. AKDA 19.244. **29.** A. M. Nielsen to AK, 1/4/1927. AKDA 19.550. **30.** "Say They Saw Mrs. Houck". *New York Times*, 12/27/1926. **31.** "Dr. Houck's Mind Tested In Hunt For Wife". *The Baltimore News*, 12/27/1926. AKDA 19.243. **32.** AK to Meyer, 1/14/1927. AKDA 19.505. **33.** E.T. Bell to AK, 2/6/1927. AKDA 19.645. **34.** *The World*, 1/16/1927. AKDA 19.228. **35.** "Sensationalizing Science". *New York: A Four-Page Journal of Ideas for the General Reader*, 2/12/1927. AKDA 19.226. **36.** AK to Sally Avery, 4/1/1927. AKDA 19.369. **37.** *The World*, Tuesday, 3/1/1927. AKDA 19.227. **38.** AK to the editor or secretary of the *New York Masonic Outlook*, 3/30/1927. AKDA 19.368. **39.** Note for *New York American* Washington Correspondent. AKDA 19.372. **40.** "Statement about the facts in the Everett case". AKDA 20.419. **41.** AK to Sally Avery, 4/1/1927. AKDA 19.369. **42.** AK to Sally Avery, 5/27/1927. AKDA 20.459. **43.** AK to Fuller, 6/29/1927. AKDA 19.354. **44.** Wentworth and Flexner, *Dictionary of American Slang*, p. 17. **45.** Korzybski 1994 (1933), p. 556-557. **46.** Copy of AK Contract with Denman, Bevier, & Scotti, 2/15/1928. AKDA 36.271. **47.** "United States Circuit Court of Appeal for the Second Circuit [-] Alfred Korzybski, Complainant-Appelant, against Underwood & Underwood, Inc., Defendent-Respondent [-] Transcript of Record". AKDA 36.225-236. **48.** Appelate Decision in AK v U & U in Report of U.S. Circuit Court of Appeals for Second Circuit, affirming decree dismissing bill of complaint for failure to state cause of action. AKDA 36.220-223; See also AKDA 36.237-238. **49.** AK to MEK., 1/30/30. AKDA 22.468. **50.** Pressman and Klein, p. 63. **51.** "Registrability of Pictorial, Graphic, or Sculptural Works Where a Design Patent Has Been Issued...Policy Decision and Amendment of Regulations". U. S. Copyright Office, Docket No. 95-3, *Federal Register*, March 24, 1995 (Volume 60, Number 57). http://www.copyright.gov/fedreg/1995/60fr15605.html (accessed 1/24/2011).

Chapter 33 – First Draft

1. Barzun and Graff, p. 384. **2.** AK to E. T. Bell, 8/24/1927. AKDA 20.608. **3.** AK to H. S. Sullivan, 10/9/1927. AKDA 20.699. **4.** Korzybski 1947, p. 269. **5.** AK to Sally Avery, 10/13/1927. AKDA 20.704. **6.** AK to W. A. White, 9/28/1927. AKDA 20.667. **7.** AK to E. T. Bell, 10/20/1927, AKDA 20.723. **8.** Ibid. **9.** P. W. Bridgman to AK, 11/13/1927. AKDA 21.13. **10.** Bridgman 1927, p. 5. **11.** AK to C. J. Keyser, 7/9/1927. AKDA 20.541. **12.** Korzybski 1947, p. 48. **13.** "Physics and Reality" in Einstein 2000, p. 247. **14.** C. J. Keyser to AK, 7/13/1927. AKDA 19.16. **15.** P. W. Bridgman to C. J. Keyser, 7/18/1927. AKDA 19.2. **16.** AK to C. J. Keyser, 7/22/1927. AKDA 20.557. **17.** P. W. Bridgman to AK, 7/24/1927. AKDA 19.28. **18.** P. W. Bridgman to AK, 11/18/1928. AKDA 21.281. **19.** P. W. Bridgman to AK 9/24/1927. AKDA 19.62. **20.** Korzybski 1994 (1933), p. 35. **21.** AK to P. W. Bridgman, 9/26/1927. AKDA 20.665. **22.** P. W. Bridgman to AK, 1/29/1928. AKDA 21.29. **23.** P. W. Bridgman to AK, 3/18/1928. AKDA 21.113. **24.** P. W. Bridgman to AK, 1/29/1928. AKDA 21.29. **25.** AK to P. W. Bridgman, 3/28/1928. AKDA 21.795. **26.** AK to P. W. Bridgman, 5/15/1936. IGS Archives. **27.** P. W. Bridgman to Korzybski, May 31, 1936, qtd. in Walter, p. 155. **28.** Walter, p. 197. **29.** *The Way Things Are* clearly demonstrates Bridgman's assimilation of much of what Korzybski conveyed to him during the period of their active association and correspondence. Nonetheless, Bridgman's single, brief 'put-down' comment about Korzybski's work in that book [Bridgman 1959, p. 33] shows his continued conscious misapprehension of it. Bridgman's failure to appreciate what he got from his friend Alfred provides a prototypical example of what Korzybski called "the tragedy of his work". [See Lucier.] **30.** AK to Sally Avery, 10/31/1927. AKDA 20.738. **31.** AK to H. L. Haywood, 1/2/1928. AKDA 21.571. **32.** Burrow 1953, p. 295. **33.** AK to H. L. Haywood, 1/2/1928. AKDA 21.571. **34.** AK to Philip S. Graven, 10/20/1927. AKDA 20.720. "I wrote to you some time ago asking about the psychogalvanic experiments. Did you put your hands on it? I have a very definite feeling that there is a great deal which could be done by improving the psychoanalytical technique. See Pieron (*Thought and the Brain*) particularly part IV the affective regulation of mental life, its role and mechanism. There you will find a definite <u>energetic</u> treatment (he does not connect it with psychoanalysis, this connection is mine). He ascribes to attention definite energetic characteristics, quite justly I think. This of course is strictly connected with transfer [transference ?]." **35.** Ibid. **36.** "The main point is to <u>interest "attention"</u> by <u>any means</u> and this is why we should resort to <u>every possible</u> instrument, which is always a <u>lower order abstraction</u>, and therefore <u>affecting</u> lower centers, and <u>acting</u> by lower centers and so having maximum effect on the thalamus etc and the affective. This is why I suggested Blackboards, toys etc. Now I go further and suggest galvanometers, MIRRORS and even electrical treatment." [Ibid.] **37.** Korzybski 1994 (1933), p. 47. **38.** AK to Florian Cajori, 9/25/27. AKDA 20.661. **39.** Robertson, p. 101. **40.** Korzybski 1994 (1933), p. 49.

Chapter 34 – "Don't You See the Electron?"
1. C. J. Keyser to AK, 9/16/1927. AKDA 19.47. **2.** AK to J. L. Bennett, 8/6/27. AKDA 21.586. **3.** AK to H. L. Haywood, 1/29/1928. AKDA 21.641. **4.** AK to H. L. Haywood, 1/2/1928. AKDA 21.571. **5.** AK to Philip Graven, 2/11/1928. AKDA 21.701. **6.** "A New Approach in Education of Adults". *Los Angeles CA Herald*, 4/20-21/1928. AKDA 3.316. **7.** Korzybski 1947, p. 492. **8.** Ibid. **9.** Ibid. About Book III, one of my editorial readers, Jim French, wrote: "I doubt that anyone would agree with this, but I actually think that Korzybski would have done better to make Book III, Book II, as he originally planned. I can't justify that opinion too rationally, but I think it would have been better for his work to do that, though he would have lost a lot of the "popularizers" and other readers right there, presumably." **10.** Korzybski 1994 (1933), p. 569. **11.** Ibid., p. 574. **12.** Korzybski 1947, p. 492. **13.** Roy J. Kennedy to Selden Smyser, 1/21/1934. qtd. in Kessler, pp. 14-15. **14.** AK to MEK, 3/31/1928. AKDA 21.799. **15.** Millikan, p. 58. **16.** AK to MEK, 3/31/1928. AKDA 21.799. **17.** Korzybski 1994 (1933), p. 696. **18.** R. A. Millikan to AK, AKDA 21.189. **19.** Korzybski 1947, pp. 264-265. **20.** AK to C. J. Keyser, 11/1/1928. AKDA 20.208. **21.** AK to MEK, 5/15/1928. AKDA 20.17. **22.** AK to P. W. Bridgman, 7/7/1928. AKDA 20.67. **23.** Korzybski 1947, p. 31, p. 410. **24.** Zula [Shand?] (Will Roger's secretary?) to AK, 6/4/1928. AKDA 21.188. **25.** Korzybski Abstract, Congresso Internazionale Dei Matematici, Sept. 3-10 1928. AKDA 3.319. **26.** Probably a bit later, Korzybski read the clarifying works of German theoretical physicist Arnold Sommerfeld, whom he considered "a very great man". While in Pasadena, he noted that the Caltech physics students were recommending Sommerfeld to each other to help make sense of quantum theory. When he finally read Sommerfeld he understood the appeal, since he found a man after his own heart: "[Sommerfeld had] a lot of footnotes, and he explained in one of them that the best way to understand something is to be told why something is said, so that the fellow will know why such and such a statement is made. Then the statement becomes more understandable. I follow this example so I have always a lot of footnotes, even in my talking. In writing I try to avoid them, which I cannot do casually." [Korzybski 1949 ("1948-49 Holiday Intensive Seminar Transcript"), p. 7.] **27.** AK to P. W. Bridgman, 8/11/1928. AKDA 20.93. **28.** AK to MEK, 7/18/1928. AKDA 20.71. **29.** AK to P. W. Bridgman, 8/11/1928. AKDA 20.93. **30.** AK to P.W. Bridgman, 8/11/1928. AKDA 20.93. **31.** Korzybski 1947, pp 265–267. **32.** Ibid., 490–491. **33.** Ibid., pp. 492–493.

Chapter 35 – Zero Hour
1. AK to Roy Haywood, 12/22/1928. AKDA 20.29. **2.** *The Kansas City Jewish Chronicle*, 3/29/1929. AKDA 3.19–20. **3.** AK to G. Y. Rainich, 3/31/1929, AKDA 22.145. **4.** *The Kansas City Times* (Kansas City, MO.), 3/28/1929. AKDA 3.320. **5.** "Discussion of Mental Hygiene and Criminology" in *Alfred Korzybski Collected Writings*, p. 162. **6.** AK to David Fairchild, 4/26/1929. AKDA 22.190. **7.** AK to MEK, 5/21/1929. AKDA 28.84. **8.** MEK to AK, 5/25/1929. AKDA 28.85. **9.** AK to Sally Avery, 7/20/1929. AKDA 22.282.

Chapter 36 – A Short Trip to Poland
1. "Notes", *Bulletin of the American Mathematical Society*, No. 35, Vol. 4 (July-August 1929), p. 583. http://www.ams.org/journals/bull/1929-35-04/S0002-9904-1929-04782-7/S0002-9904-1929-04782-7.pdf (accessed 1/26/2011). **2.** Korzybski 1947, p. 272. **3.** AK to MEK., 9/5/1929. AKDA 28.50. **4.** AK to MEK, 9/9/1929. AKDA 28.48. **5.** AK to MEK, 9/5/1929. AKDA 28.50. **6.** AK to MEK, 9/18/1929. AKDA 28.44. **7.** AK to C.J. Keyser, 9/29/1929. AKDA 22.316. **8.** Korzybski, Notes in Polish for his talk at 1929 Congress of Mathematicians in Warsaw. AKDA 34.845 **9.** AK to C. J. Keyser, 9/29/1929. AKDA 22.316. **10.** Congress Program. AKDA 34.833; McCall, p. 391. **11.** Skolimowski, pp. 173, 175. **12.** Ibid., pp. 173–174. **13.** Korzybski 1947, p. 274. **14.** Skolimowski, p. 175–176. **15.** Korzybski 1994 (1933), p. 89. **16.** Ibid., p. 554. **17.** Korzybski 1947, p. 279. **18.** AK to the Gravens, 9/29/1929. AKDA 22.314; AK to Sally Avery, 10/23/1929. AKDA 22.372. **19.** "Alexander Vasilievitch Vasiliev (July 2, 1853–October 6, 1929)". *Science*, December 20, 1929, Vol. LXX, No. 1825, pp. 599–600. Reprinted in *Alfred Korzybski*

Collected Writings, p. 157–158. **20.** AK to David Fairchild, 10/28/1931. AKDA 23.449. **21.** AK to Sally Avery, 11/15/1929. AKDA 22.392. **22.** AK to Sally Avery, 1/6/1930. AKDA 22.448. **23.** AK to C. J. Keyser, 12/30/1929. AKDA 22.443

Chapter 37 – Knowledge, Uncertainly, and Courage
1. AK to MEK, 2/11/1930. AKDA 28.112 **2.** Discussion of "Mental Hygiene and Criminology" by Dr. Franz Alexander at First Interrnational Congress on Mental Hygiene, Washington, D.C., May 1930. Published in *Proceedings of the Congress*, Vol. 1, pp. 784-786. (New York, 1932). Reprinted in *Alfred Korzybski Collected Writings*, pp. 159–163. **3.** AK to C. J. Keyser, 10/19/1930. AKDA 22.648-9. **4.** "On structure", "A generalized theory of mathematical types", "A non-aristotelian system". Reprinted in *Alfred Korzybski Collected Writings*, p. 182. **5.** Keyser 1927, p. 94. **6.** Korzybski 1994 (1933), p. 61. **7.** Korzybski, "The Brotherhood of Doctrines" in *Alfred Korzybski Collected Writings*, p. 43. **8.** Korzybski 1994 (1933), p. 165. **9.** 'Identity' was implied but not directly mentioned in Aristotle's works. Along with the laws of contradiction and the excluded middle—which Aristotle *did* explicitly advance—what became known as the aristotelian law of identity (*A* is *A*) constituted one of the traditional "laws of thought". These 'laws', interpreted as more than just basic 'logical' rules, implied deeply-rooted structural assumptions about the world. **10.** Aristotle, "De Interpretatione" in McKeon, p. 40. **11.** Heraclitus (Philip Wheelwright translation), qtd. in Lakoff and Johnson 1999, p. 359. **12.** Korzybski 1994 (1933), p. 93. **13.** Leibniz 1979 (1951), "Mr. Leibniz's Fourth Paper; Being an Answer to Dr. Clarke's Third Reply", p. 228-229. **14.** Wittgenstein 1921, Proposition 5.5303 **15.** Korzybski 1994 (1933), p.194–195. **16.** Quine 1960, p. 117. **17.** Korzybski 1994 (1933), p. 61. **18.** Korzybski 1994 (1933), p. 12. **19.** Korzybski, "Time-Binding: The General Theory (First Paper)" in *Alfred Korzybski Collected Writings*, p. 59. **20.** Korzybski 1994 (1933), p. lxv. **21.** Ibid., p. 440. **22.** Ibid. p. 324. **23.** Ibid., p. 365. **24.** Popper, p. 280. **25.** Stuart A. Mayper, Personal communication. **26.** Korzybski 1994 (1933), p.760. **27.** AK to W. A. White, 2/4/1931. AKDA 23.246. **28.** Leibniz 1979 (1951), p. 222. **29.** Korzybski 1994 (1933), p. 483. **30.** Korzybski 1994 (1933), p. 605. **31.** Korzybski believed that a basic study of permutations and combinations could help give a feel for the complexities that arise from increasing the number of elements in a situation. Later, in his seminars, he would recommend Stanley Jevon's chapter "On The Variety of Nature" from *The Principles of Science* as a good introduction to this. **32.** See "Introduction to the Second Edition", Korzybski 1994 (1933), p. lv-lvii. **33.** Leibniz 1979 (1951), pp. 228–229. **34.** Korzybski 1994 (1933), p. 481. **35.** Ibid., p. li. **36.** Ibid., p. lii.

Chapter 38 – "General Semantics"
1. Korzybski 1994 (1933), p. 24. **2.** "The Role of Language in the Perceptual Processes", in *Alfred Korzybski Collected Writings*, p. 686. **3.** Korzybski 1994 (1933), p. 35. **4.** Ibid., p. 25. **5.** Ibid., p. 23. **6.** Ibid., p. 456. **7.** Ibid., p. 513. **8.** Ibid., p. 512. **9.** Ibid., pp. 90–91. **10.** Ibid., p. 9. **11.** "General Semantics: Extensionalization in Mathematics, Mathematical Physics, and General Education. Paper II: Thalamic Symbolism and Mathematics", in *Alfred Korzybski Collected Writings*, p. 260. **12.** "General Semantics and You", in *Alfred Korzybski Collected Writings*, p. 273. **13.** Korzybski (and M. Kendig, his coauthor here) provided a footnote for 'Chesire Cat Theories of Meaning'*: "* To paraphrase Doctor Preston. See George H . Preston, Psychiatry for the Curious, Farrar & Rinehart, 1940, p. 7 ", in "Foreword with M. Kendig, A Theory of Meaning Analyzed". *General Semantics Monographs, Number III* (1942). Reprinted in *Alfred Korzybski Collected Writings*, p. 371, p. 379. **14.** "Preface To The Third Edition", in Korzybski 1994 (1933), p. xxxiv. **15.** See "Author's Note" (1948) in *Selections from Science and Sanity*. Reprinted in *Alfred Korzybski Collected Writings*, p. 620. **16.** "An Outline of General Semantics", in *Alfred Korzybski Collected Writings*, p. 204. **17.** Abstract of "A non-aristotelian system and its necessity for rigor in mathematics and physics". *Bulletin of The American Mathematical Society*, Vol. 38 (1932), p. 36. Reprinted in *Alfred Korzybski Collected Writings*, p. 182. **18.** Korzybski 1947, pp. 405-408. **19.** AK to W.M. Wheeler, 7/16/1933. AKDA 24.78. **20.** Lonergan, p. xxviii.

Chapter 39 – A Monkey on His Lap
1. MEK, Autobiographical Memoir (Unpublished), p. 49. IGS Archives. **2.** AK to E. T. Bell. 10/28/1931. AKDA 23.458. **3.** AK to Roy Haywood, 1/13/1932. AKDA 23.517. **4.** AK to G. M. Acklom, 8/7/1931. AKDA 24.693. **5.** Korzybski 1994 (1933), p. 36. **6.** Korzybski 1949, p. 345, (mp3 – 32C & 32D). **7.** MEK, Autobiographical Memoir (Unpublished), p. 53. IGS Archives. **8.** Ibid., p. 49. **9.** Barbara Polakov to MEK, 1/4/1937. IGS Archives. **10.** Walter Polakov to AK 1937. IGS Archives. **11.** AK to Walter Polakov, Jan. 18, 1938. IGS Archives. **12.** C. J. Keyser to AK, April 15, 1931. AKDA 23.14. **13.** E. P. Dutton Statement of Royalties to AK & MEK from 5/1/30 to 4/30/1931.

AKDA 31.158. **14.** John Macrae to AK, 4/28/1931. AKDA 24.677. **15.** AK to Tramer, 5/29/1931. AKDA 23.328. **16.** Korzybski 1947, p. 281. **17.** Ibid., p. 280. **18.** Ibid., p. 281 **19.** Brewer, pp. 377-378. **20.** Brewer, p. 378. **21.** Ibid. **22.** Inflation Calculator, accessed on 6/5/2010 at coinnews.net/tools/cpi-inflation-calculator/

Chapter 40 – Science and Sanity
1. AK to Arthur F. Bentley, 6/27/1932. AKDA 7.552. **2.** "Preface To The First Edition 1933", Korzybski 1994 (1933), p. xci. **3.** AK to G. M. Houck, 10/28/1932. AKDA 2.483. **4.** AK to Philip S. Graven (Telegram), 3/7/1933. AKDA 30.393. **5.** Philip S. Graven to AK (Telegram), 3/8/1933. AKDA 30.392. **6.** AK to Philip S. Graven, 3/8/1933. AKDA 30.391. **7.** AK to Philip S. Graven, 3/24/1933. AKDA 30.390. **8.** Philip S. Graven to AK (Telegram), 3/31/1933. AKDA 30.389. **9.** AK to Philip S. Graven, 3/31/1933. AKDA 30.383. **10.** AK to Philip S. Graven, 4/3/1933. AKDA 30.381. **11.** AK to Philip S. Graven, 4/11/1933. AKDA 30.380; Circular for First Edition of *Science and Sanity*. IGS Archives. **12.** Philip S. Graven to AK (Telegram), 4/24/1933. AKDA 30.376. **13.** Philip S. Graven to AK, 5/15/1933. AKDA 30.370. **14.** AK to Philip S. Graven, 5/5/1933. AKDA 30.371. **15.** "Preface To The First Edition 1933", Korzybski 1994 (1933), p. xci. **16.** AK to George M. Houck, 8/22/1933. AKDA 2.213. **17.** AK to George M. Houck, 9/9/1933. AKDA 2.203. **18.** AK to Jaques Cattell, 10/10/1933. AKDA 2.176.

Part VI – Words Are Not Enough!
1. Runes, p. 80.

Chapter 41 – What Had Alfred Wrought?
1. Korzybski 1949. **2.** AK to Jean Rennie nee Huggins,10/10/1933. AKDA 26.232. **3.** Harrison, p. 408. **4.** Korzybski 1994 (1933), p. 408. **4. 5.** Korzybski 1994 (1933), p. 767. **6.** The often neglected discussions of doctrinal functions and system-functions in *Science and Sanity* seem especially pertinent here; consult the index of *Science and Sanity*. See in particular pp.144 ff. **7.** Lewin 1951, p. 169. **8.** Korzybski 1994 (1933), p. 761. **9.** Korzybski 1994 (1933), p. 134. **10.** "Introduction to the Second Edition 1941" in Korzybski 1994 (1933), p. lx. **11.** Korzybski 1994 (1933), p. 142. **12.** Korzybski 1994 (1933), pp. 143-144. **13.** Korzybski 1994 (1933), pp. xxxi,10, 561. See also Mayper 1979 (1977), pp. 26, 38 and Allen Walker Read 1984, pp. 16–17 for further discussions of what some people saw as Korzybski's lack of modesty. **14.** "Introduction to the Second Edition", Korzybski 1994 (1933), p. xli. **15.** Korzybski 1994 (1933), p. 532. **16.** See Kenneth G. Johnson's "Korzybski on Research: Suggestions from *Science And Sanity*" in *General Semantics Bulletin* 51 (1984): 43–53.

Chapter 42 – Reviewing Reviews
1. AK to C. M. Child, 2/28/1933. AKDA 25.351. **2.** AK to Robert H. Allen, 10/26/1933. AKDA 27.160. **3.** AK to A. Ranger Tyler, 11/26/1933. AKDA 27.188. **4.** A. Ranger Tyler to AK, 11/ 2/1933. AKDA 27.178. **5.** A. Ranger Tyler to AK, 12/1/1933. AKDA 27.197. **6.** A. Ranger Tyler to AK, 12/7/1933. AKDA 27.215. **7.** A. Ranger Tyler. "Can Human Nature Be Changed? Yes, Author Reveals". AKDA 2.688. **8.** AK to A. Ranger Tyler, 12/12/1933. AKDA 27.223. **9.** AK to A. Ranger Tyler, 1/3/34. AKDA 27.254. **10.** See Tyler's "The Place of General Semantics in Journalism" (1935) and "Newspapers, Education and General Semantics" (1941) in the volumes of the First and Second American Congresses on General Semantics. **11.** Acklom, "The Cleavage Between Science and Human Activities". *New York Times*, Feb. 11, 1933. **12.** C. J. Keyser to AK, 12/9/1933. AKDA 34.329. **13.** AK to Ralph S. Lillie, 12/14/1933. AKDA 27.225. **14.** Carter 1955, p. 66. **15.** See E. L. Gates, "Keyser And Korzybski: Letters About Keyser's Reviews of *Science and Sanity* And Comments, April-June 1934" in *Alfred Korzybski Collected Writings*, p. 183–188. Also see Elton S. Carter 1955. **16.** See Ernest Nagel. "Review of Science and Sanity", *Journal of Philosophy*, February 11, 1933. AKDA 2.692; "Review of Science and Sanity", *The New Republic*, August 1, 1934, AKDA 2.719; and "Mr. Nagel Answers", *The New Republic*, December 26, 1934, AKDA 2.719. **17.** Hook, "The Nature of Discourse", *Saturday Review of Literature*, 3/10/1934. AKDA 2.695. **18.** AK to A. Ranger Tyler, 3/16/1934. AKDA 27.392. **18b.** O.L. Reiser to AK, 5/29/1933. AKDA 33.362. **19.** AK to O.L. Reiser, 6/29/1934. AKDA 33.378. **20.** O.L. Reiser. "Modern Logic and Non-Aristotelian Logics", AKDA 33.399. **21.** "Einstein Theory" of Logic Offered: That a Thing Is Not Always Itself". Houston, Tex. *Press*, 12/28/1934. AKDA 2.735. **22.** Berman, p. ix. **23.** Pula 1996 "General Semantics Seminar-Workshop Bibliography. Revised, Updated and Annotated". Accessed 6/7/2010 at www.generalsemantics.org/index.php/component/content/article/18-learning-center/105-biblio-pula.html **24.** AK to O.L. Reiser. 1/10/1935. AKDA 33.385. **25.** AK to O. L. Reiser, n.d. [1948 or 1949]. Ralph Hamilton Papers.

Chapter 43 – 'Scientists Don't Read'

1. AK to Henry Ward, 9/24/1933. AKDA 24.160. 2. AK to Max Born, 2/24/1933. AKDA 35.121. 3. Max Born to AK, 3/7/1933. AKDA 25.383. Translated by Max Sandor. 4. William Morton Wheeler to AK, 10/30/1933. AKDA 34.197. 5. AK to C. J. Keyser. 11/26/1933. AKDA 26.278. 6. AK to C. J. Keyser, 12/16/1933. 26.306. 7. E. B. Wilson to AK, 12/16/1933. AKDA 34.355. 8. Kirtley F. Mather to AK, 9/19/1933. AKDA 34.248. 9. AK to Albert Einstein, 11/29/1933. AKDA 32.968; Albert Einstein to AK, 1/29/1934. AKDA 32.966. Translated by Max Sandor. 10. Albert Einstein to AK, 1/17/1940. IGS Archives. Translated by Max Sandor. 11. Korzybski 1947, pp. 48–49. 12. Pula 2001b. pp. 48–49. After her husband's death, Blanche Weinberg told this story to my friend and colleague Robert P. Pula who related it to me a number of years before he wrote it down. 13. Julian Huxley, qtd. in Herrick 1949, p. 6. 14. G. E. Coghill to AK, 1/17/1934. AKDA 32.882. 15. AK to G. E. Coghill, 1/18/1934. AKDA 32.878. 16. AK to G. E. Coghill, 2/21/1934. AKDA 32.889. 17. G. E. Coghill to AK, 3/26/1934. AKDA 32.899. 18. AK to David Fairchild, 8/16/1934. AKDA 25.126. 19. AK to A. Ranger Tyler, 6/4/1934. AKDA 27.464. 20. Korzybski presented "An Outline of General Semantics: The Application of Some Methods of Exact Sciences to the Solution of Human Problems and Educational Training for General Sanity" in 1935 at the First American Congress for General Semantics. He had it published in 1938 in *General Semantics: Papers from the First American Congress for General Semantics*, edited by Hansell Baugh. He later had it reprinted as a pamphlet sold by the Institute of General Semantics. It was later reprinted in *Alfred Korzybski Collected Writings*, pp. 189–224. 21. AK to A. Ranger Tyler, 7/10/1934. AKDA 27.473. 22. AK to G. E. Coghill, 6/10/1934. AKDA 32.871. 23. AK to Professor H. M. Johnson, 8/16/1934. AKDA 25.128. 24. See Trainor's report "Experimental Results of Training in General Semantics Upon Intelligence-Test Scores" in Baugh 1938, p. 60. I understand that 140 and above is now considered at the "genius" level. Perhaps the high before-and-after scores of Trainor's students has something to do with the particular kind of test scale he was using in 1934/1935 (the Detroit Intelligence Test, Advanced Form); in 1939, Wechsler introduced a new scale which then became the standard. 25. Potts, pp. 63–64. 26. M. Kendig, personal notes,11/22/1965. IGS Archives. 27. Kendig to Henri Laborit, 2/20/1968. IGS Archives. 28. In a September 30, 1970 letter to her life-long friend Priscilla Sheldon, whom she had met at the Nurses Training Camp, Kendig wrote:

> ...I found *Zelda* [by Nancy Mitford] as fascinating as you described -- and pathetic, too. Yes, the book was full of ghosts of my life in the 20's and 30's. Slightly, in one way or another, my life touched many of (the) persons in the Fitzgeralds' saga...Actually, though, I recall all too well the Fitzgerald Epoch, I was not much in touch with the "Crowd," but that is hardly the important thing about the book as a tremendous production and its evocation-impact personally. [Kendig qtd. in Priscilla Sheldon, "A Tribute to M. Kendig, Memorial Gathering, January 10, 1982". *General Semantics Bulletin* 50, pp. 17–18]

29. M. Kendig, personal notes, 8/6/1965. IGS Archives. 30. Kendig 1935. "A Proposed Research Investigation Valuable in the Improvement of Teaching on the Junior College Level: Application of a Method for Scientific Control of the Neuro-Linguistic and Neuro-Semantic Mechanisms in the Learning Process" (Paper presented to complete the requirements for Master's Degree, Department of Higher Education, Teachers College, Columbia University, July 1935.), in Baugh 1938. 31. AK to Joseph C. Trainor, 7/25/1934. AKDA 33.598. 32. Kendig, "Introduction" to Markus Reiner "*Science and Sanity*, A 1934 Review", reprinted in *General Semantics Bulletin* 28 & 29 (1961/1962), p. 119. 33. Walter Polakov, "Was Korzybski Irrelevant?" in "Correspondence", *The New Republic*, Oct. 24, 1934. AKDA 2.719.

Chapter 44 – On the Road

1. "Letter to Co-Workers", in *Alfred Korzybski Collected Writings*, pp. 729–735. 2. AK to Graven, 8/16/1934. AKDA 30.199. 3. AK to Philip Graven, 9/29/1934. AKDA 30.164. 4. Philip Graven to AK, 10/10/1934. AKDA 30.156–159. 5. AK to Philip Graven, 11/15/1934. AKDA 30.134. 6. Philip Graven to AK, 11/23/1934 AKDA 30.130. 7. "Count Sees Germans As Menace To Peace". *Oakland Post-Enquirer*, 8/9/1935. AKDA 2.792. 8. "Hitler Called "Sick Boy"; Rulers' Mental Test Urged". *Asbury Park, New Jersey Evening Press*, 11/24/1937. AKDA 2.877. 9. "An Outline of General Semantics", in *Alfred Korzybski Collected Writings*, p. 213. 10. Memo, "BIOG.", 4/16/1947. IGS Archives. 11. "This Is All A Mistake". *The Kansas City Times*, 1/23/1935. AKDA 2.742. 12. Barstow School Agenda for AK, 1/21/1935. AKDA 34.315. 13. Shaw 1947, p. 5. 14. AK to Ruth F. Shaw, 2/6/1935. AKDA 33.441. 15. Kendig, "Talk in Los Angeles", 1/18/1961. IGS Archives. 16. "A New General Language Curriculum for the Eighth Grade", *The Modern Language Journal*, Vol. XXII, No. 5 (February, 1938): pp. 343–346. AKDA 2.894–895. 17. Kendig. "New Approach To Education Outlined Before Vassar Alumnae", Press Release, April 1940. AKDA, IGS Scrapbook 1.188–189; Kendig's March 1937

address to the Barstow School community, "This Living Barstow (reprinted in *General Semantics Bulletin* 50) provides a good overview of Kendig's educational vision for the school. **18**. Dona Brown 1983, p. 36. **19.** Dona W. Brown 1943. "The Use of General Semantics in Teaching the Language Skills in the Eighth Grade", in M. Kendig, ed., *Papers from the Second American Congress on General Semantics*, pp. 524–527. **20.** Kendig, "General Semantics 1961: Historical Perspectives, Trends and Criticisms", Unpublished paper. IGS Archives. **21.** Kendig, "On The Nature And Constancy of The I.Q". *Educational Method*, Vol. XIX, January, 1940, No. 4. IGS Archives. **22.** Dona Brown 1983, pp. 36–37. **23.** Charlotte Schuchardt Read, "Marjorie Mercer Kendig Gates: A Biographical Sketch". *General Semantics Bulletin* 53, 1983. p. 51. **24.** Korzybski 1947, p. 284. **25.** "Strolling Around the Town". 3/11/1935, *Seattle Times*. AKDA 2.784. **26.** "Punk and Incense". *Trenton N.J. Advertiser*, 3/27/1938. AKDA 2.833. **27.** AK to P. Graven, 4/13/1935. AKDA 30.58.

Chapter 45 – Seminars
1. Kendig 1950, "A Memoir: Alfred Korzybski & His Work" in *Manhood of Humanity*, Second Edition, pp. xxx–xxxi. **2.** Binkley, pp. 6-7. **3.** AK to Jacques Cattell, 11/26/1935. AKDA 35.238. **4.** "Phases of Research in Different Fields Occupy Scientists. New Developments Are Discussed at Joint Meetings". *St. Louis Globe Democrat*, 1/1/1936. AKDA 42.72. **5.** Korzybski 1947, p. 327. **6.** Korzybski 1947, p. 405. **7.** Kendig 1950, p. xxxii–xxxiii. **8.** Charles J. Katz, M.D. to AK, 4/4/1950. IGS Archives, quoted in Kendig 1950, pp. xxxiii–xxxiv. **9.** Korzybski 1949, pp. 358–361. **10.** Korzybski 1947, p. 289. **11.** Ibid. 12. **12.** Schuchardt 1943, p. 1. **13.** Korzybski 1994 (1933), p. lx. **14.** Binkley, p. 8. **15.** For more on neuro-semantic relaxation see Wendell Johnson 1938 and Wendell Johnson 1946. Also see *The Technique of Semantic Relaxation* by Charlotte Schuchardt [Read] (1943) and the 1941 paper by May Watrous Niles, "Use of General Semantics Techniques In Physiotherapy", pp. 183–186 in *Papers From The Second American Congress On General Semantics* (1943) edited by M. Kendig.

Chapter 46 – "Shoot All the Mothers!"
1. Barbara Polakov to MEK, 6/6/35. IGS Archives. **2.** Telegram John Lynn to AK, 1/16/1936; Telegram MEK to AK, 1/16/1936. IGS Archives. **3.** AK to Graven 2/26/1936. AKDA 30.26. **4.** Korzybski 1936, "Neuro-Semantic And Neuro-Linguistic Mechanisms Of Extensionalization: General Semantics As A Natural Experimental Science". *American Journal of Psychiatry* 93 (1), July 1936: pp. 31–32. Reprinted in *Alfred Korzybski Collected Writings*, pp. 229–230. **5.** "Note for Dr. Tillotson on Educational and Research Program of Dr. John G. Lynn", 5/28/1936. IGS Archives. **6.** Korzybski 1949, Intensive Seminar transcript, pp. 54-55. **7.** John G. Lynn, IV to AK, 3/25/1936. IGS Archives. **8.** AK to Oliver Reiser, 5/27/1936. Ralph Hamilton Papers. **9.** *Marlborogram* Newsletter, April 1936. AKDA 2.826. **10.** Korzybski 1949, Intensive Seminar transcript, p. 155. **11.** AK to Philip Graven, 6/1/1936. AKDA 30.8. **12.** "Summer Notes". *Boston Evening Transcript*, 6/12/1936. AKDA 2.833. **13.** MEK to John G. Lynn, 7/8/1936. MEK Archives, Box 17. **14.** AK to MEK, 8/14/1936. MEK Archives, Box 17. **15.** MEK to A.K, 7/20/1936. MEK Archives, Box 17. **16.** MEK to Huntingtons, Oct. 9, 1936. MEK Archives, Box 17. **17.** MEK, n.d. MEK Archives, Box 17. **18.** AK to MEK, 10/10/1936. MEK Archives, Box 17. **19.** "Douglas Gordon Campbell, MD: An Interview with Helen Hafner, Mary Morain and David Waggoner, MD". *General Semantics Bulletin* 47: 65-66. **20.** "All Mothers Should Be Shot". IGS Archives. **21.** AK to John G. Lynn, 3/3/1938. IGS Archives.

Chapter 47 – One Weary Man
1. D. G. Campbell to M. Kendig, 3/3/1937. IGS Archives. **2.** Roethlisberger 1977, pp. 71–72. **3.** Carrel 1935, p. 47. **4.** Carrel 1935, p. 47. qtd. by Korzybski 1937, in *Alfred Korzybski Collected Writings*, p. 250. **5.** Carrel 1935, p. 285. Qtd. by Korzybski 1937, in *Alfred Korzybski Collected Writings*, p. 251. Carrel had received a copy of Korzybski's first *Time-Binding* paper in 1925, and wrote to Korzybski: "I shall take your reprint on "Time-Binding" with me to France, so that I may have an opportunity of reading it with the care it deserves." [A. Carrel to AK, 5/25/1925. AKDA 17.135.] Given his discussion in *Man The Unknown* of the "science of man", etc., it appears likely that he did just that. **6.** Carrel 1935, pp. 318–319. **7.** Korzybski 1994 (1933), "Introduction to the Second Edition" of *Science and Sanity*, p. xliii–xliv. **8.** Carrel 1935, p. 274. **9.** Brewer, "Forward to the Second Edition", *General Semantics Seminar 1937: The Olivet College Lectures*, p. viii. **10.** Rough editing by Korzybski of the Olivet Lectures transcript consisted of about 200 hours of work, which still didn't seem good enough for him [AK to Cornelius Crane, 7/11/1939. IGS Archives]. **11.** Korzybski 2002 (1937), p. viii. **12.** Homer J. Moore, Jr. in Korzybski 2002 (1937), p. iv. **13.** Brewer in Korzybski 2002 (1937), p. viii. **14.** Korzybski 2002 (1937), p. 5. **15.** Korzybski 2002 (1937), p. 89–93. In the original diagram, published in the First Edition of the Olivet Lectures, Korzybski used "E_1" to label the smaller, minimum expectation circle, and "E_2" to label the larger, maximum expectation one. This original labeling, which I've used, got reversed in

NOTES

later presentations of the diagram, and in subsequent editions of the book after his death. **16.** Korzybski 2002 (1937), p. 6. **17.** Ronald Leipholz "Report of the Change from Right-handedness to Left-handedness", May 30, 1937. IGS Archives. See also "Addendum for 1964 Edition", in Korzybski 2002 (1937) for Brewer's report on the seminar's effects on various Olivet students and faculty. **18.** Helen L. Evans to Joseph Brewer, 4/25/1938. IGS Archives. **19.** Olivet Dean of Men to Joseph Brewer, 1937. IGS Archives. **20.** Olivet College "Flory" Folder. IGS Archives. **21.** AK to Walter Polakov, 8/2/1937. IGS Archives. **22.** AK to Helen Evans, 12/10/1937. IGS Archives. **23.** AK to Helen Evans, 12/17/1937. IGS Archives. **24.** Helen Evans to AK, 6/9/1937. IGS Archives.

Part VII – The Institute
1. Korzybski, "Letter to Students and Friends", August 1947 in *Alfred Korzybski: Collected Writings*, p. 585.

Chapter 48 – The Institute of General Semantics
1. Boleslaw Pobog-Olszewski to AK, 1/2/1938. AKDA 38.440. Translated by Teresa Grabiec Silverstein, October 16, 2008. **2.** IGS Memo dated 7/22/1938 - "As citizenship—what procedure?" IGS Archives. **3.** Porter Sargent to Kendig, 1/29/1938. AKDA 42.75. **4.** Chase 1938, p. 7. **5.** Chase 1938, p. vii. **6.** Hazlitt, "On the Importance of Meanings: Stuart Chase Attempts to Popularize Recent Studies in the Relationship of Words, Thoughts and Things". *New York Times Book Review*, 1/23/1938. AKDA 2.863–864. **7.** Walter Polakov to AK, 11/29/1937. IGS Archives. **8.** Walter Polakov to AK, 1/5/1938. IGS Archives. **9.** AK to Walter Polakov, 1/15/1938. IGS Archives. **10.** Korzybski, "Transcript of July, 1938 IGS Summer Seminar", p. 65. Unpublished. IGS Archives. **11.** G. M. Houck to AK, 1/27/1938. AKDA 35.290. **12.** AK to G. M. Houck, 1/30/1938. AKDA 35.289. **13.** AK to MEK, 7/26/38. MEK Archives, Box 17. **14.** Korzybski, 'Transcript of July,1938 IGS Summer Seminar', p. 4. Unpublished. IGS Archives. **15.** Ibid., p. 53. **16.** Dwork and Van Pelt. *Holocaust: A History*, p. 124. **17.** AK to R. B. Haseldon, 1/30/1939. Ralph Hamilton Papers. **18.** Korzybski 1937, pp. 20, 54, 143. **19.** Wendell Johnson 1956 'I Knew Korzybski When' in Kessler, p. 7. **20.** Ibid., pp. 8-12. **21.** *Oliver Wendell Holmes: Representative Selections*. **22.** Hayakawa 1979, p. xiii. **23.** See Wilson, Hagood and Brennan. Cambria Press, p. 50.

Chapter 49 – Growing Pains
1. AK to MEK, Nov. 13, 1938. MEK Archives, Box 17. **2.** AK to Cornelius Crane, 6/20/1939. IGS Archives.

Chapter 50 – The August Intensive
1. See Shearer, "Avoiding Korzybski's Seminars", p. 134. **2.** S. I. Hayakawa video interview, http://thisisnotthat.com/video/MP-stade.html **3.** Shearer, "Avoiding Korzybski's Seminars", pp. 132–133. **4.** In 2001, master's degree research done in 1939 by Mary Tudor and supervised by Wendell Johnson became the subject of sensationalized newspaper accounts of supposed ethical abuses, which eventually resulted in a lawsuit filed against the University of Iowa by alleged victims of the study. Whether any ethical abuse occurred remains a matter of controversy. An account, with documentation, of the Tudor study and lawsuit, written by Johnson's son Nicholas can be found at "The Wendell Johnson Memorial Homepage" at http://www.nicholasjohnson.org/wjohnson/, accessed on Feb. 2, 2009. **5.** Participant Applications, Intensive Seminar, Aug. 1939. IGS Archives. **6.** Irving J. Lee Biographical Sketch in Kendig 1943, p. 562. **7.** M. Kendig to Cornelius Crane, 9/2/1939. IGS Archives. **8.** Weinberg, Alvin. p. 4. **9.** Kendig, "Alvin Weinberg Biography", *General Semantics Bulletin* 34 (1968), p. 15. **10.** William Burroughs. "Press Conference at Berkeley Museum of Art, November 12, 1974". Internet Archive audio. http://www.archive.org/details/BurroughsPressConf **11.** Quine 1985, p. 59-60. **12.** Ibid, p. 140. **13.** Ibid., p. 139. Also see Quine 1960, p. 117. **14.** Kendig to Crane, 9/2/1939. IGS Archives. **15.** See Creath. **16.** Korzybski 1949, pp. 144-145. **17.** Satriano, p. 24. **18.** Satriano, pp. 75-76. **19.** Satriano, pp. 79-81. **20.** After Korzybski's death, Charlotte gradually moved away from teaching Korzybski's method of neuro-semantic relaxation and incorporated the sensory awareness teachings of Charlotte Selver and Elsa Gindler into the IGS seminar-workshop curriculum, leading groups in non-verbal awareness, i.e., training in conscious listening, seeing, touching, moving, etc.

Chapter 51 – Nothing To Do But Continue
1. AK quoted in "Hitler's 'Insane' Cleverness Likened to That of Monkey". *The Chicago Daily News*, Saturday, Aug. 26, 1939 by Gene Morgan. AKDA 41.17. **2.** Korzybski. *Five Lectures on General Semantics*. Los Angeles Society for General Semantics, June 1939. Unpublished. IGS Archives. **3.** Kendig to Crane, 9/2/1939. IGS Archives. **4.** "A Memorandum on the Institute of General Semantics", in *Alfred Korzybski Collected Writings*, pp. 277-293. **5.** Cornelius Crane to AK, 10/26/1939. IGS Archives. **6.** AK to Cornelius Crane, 10/31/1939. IGS Archives. **7.** Cornelius Crane to AK, 11/12/1939. IGS Archives. **8.** AK to Cornelius Crane, 12/8/1939. IGS Archives. **9.** Minutes of Trustee Meeting, December 19, 1939. IGS Archives.

Chapter 52 – "Recognition But Very Little Money"

1. Transcript labeled "Telephone Conversation. Report of Ischlondsky On Crane. (Rough semi-verbatim report)", 1/5/1940. IGS Archives. **2.** Cornelius Crane files, IGS Archives. **3.** Bronislaw Malinowski to AK, 12/20/1939. IGS Archives. **4.** Weil 1940, p. 71. **5.** Bachelard 1940, p. 108. **6.** AK to President Franklin D. Roosevelt, 9/7/1939. IGS Archives. **7.** "Introduction to the Second Edition 1941" in Korzybski 1994 (1933), p. lxxvii. **8.** Ibid., p. lv. **9.** Ibid., p. lvi. **10.** "General Semantics, Psychiatry, Psychotherapy And Prevention", *American Journal of Psychiatry,* Vol. 98 (2), September, 1941. p. 213. Reprinted in *Alfred Korzybski Collected Writings*, p. 306–307. **11.** AK to Cornelius Crane, 6/3/1939. IGS Archives. **12.** "Poles Gather Data On 'Pillage' By Foes", *New York Times*, Jan. 19, 1940. **13.** MEK to AK, 6/13/1940. AK Archives, Box 22, Folder 6.491. **14.** Korzybski 1994 (1933). "Introduction To The Second Edition 1941", p. lxix. **15.** "When Where and How do you see Red?" AK Archives, Box 22, Folder 4. **16.** AK to C.B. Congdon, 8/18/1940. IGS Archives. **17.** MEK to AK, 8/17/1940. AK Archives, Box 22.6.467. **18.** Allen Walker Read. "Changing Attitudes Toward Korzybski's General Semantics". *General Semantics Bulletin* 51, p. 12. **19.** Allen Walker Read having tea at "The Honeypot", Pevensey Bay, England, July 11, 1954. Photograph by Charlotte Schuchardt Read. IGS Archives. **20.** Allen Walker Read. "A Personal Journey Through Linguistics" in Allen Walker Read 2002, p. 307. **21.** Ibid., p. 309. **22.** Aldous Huxley to Julian Huxley, July 22, 1938. in Smith 1969, p. 436. **23.** AK to F. Dewing, 9/10/1940. IGS Archives.

Chapter 53 – Question Marks

1. Weinberg, p. xii. **2.** Lee's book was listed as *Words Are Not Enough!* in preliminary 'Front Matter' page proofs of the Second Edition of *Science and Sanity*. IGS Archives. **3.** Korzybski, "Foreword" *Language Habits In Human Affairs*, p. x. **4.** AK to F. Dewing, 12/11/1941. IGS Archives. **5.** Kendig Memorandum to AK, 1/5/1941. IGS Archives. **6.** "Introduction", *Papers From The Second American Congress on General Semantics*, p. xv. **7.** Ibid., pp. xv-xvi. **8.** See Swift, qtd. in Korzybski 1994 (1933, 1941), p. vi. **9.** Korzybski 1994 (1933, 1941), p. xlviii. **10.** Douglas M. Kelley, "Mechanisms of Magic and Self-Deception: The Psycho-logical Basis of Misdirection; An Extensional Non-Aristotelian Method for Prevention of Self-Deception" in Kendig, *Papers From The Second American Congress On General Semantics*, p. 59. **11.** AK to Charlotte Schuchardt, Notes transcribed by C.S., 5/24/1949. IGS Archives. **12.** Korzybski 1994 (1933, 1941), p. lxxxi. **13.** AK to Mrs. Douglas Campbell, 4/6/1941. IGS Archives. **14.** Whorf, in *Congress Papers*, p. 44. **15.** Whorf qtd. in Penny Lee 1996, p. 16. **16.** "New Kind of Sense". *Time Magazine*, 8/11/1941. **17.** AK to Cornelius Crane, 10/28/1941. IGS Archives. **18.** "Biographical Memoir of George Ellet Coghill" by C. Judson Herrick. *National Academy of Sciences Biographical Memoirs, Vol. XXII*: (251-273) 1942, p. 252. **19.** Herrick 1949, p. 215. **20.** Pearl Johnecheck to Charlotte Schuchardt, 8/27/1941. 'CS Private' file, IGS Archives. **21.** AK to MEK 7/28/1941. AK Archives, Box 22, Folder 6.349. **22.** AK to Cornelius Crane, 10/28/1941. IGS Archives. **23.** MEK to AK, 2/28/1941. AK Archives, Box 22, Folder 6. **24.** MEK to AK, 11/21/1940. AK Archives, Box 22, Folder 6. **25.** MEK to AK, 5/29/1941. AK Archives, Box 22, Folder 6. **26.** AK to MEK, 7/12/1941. AK Archives, Box 22, Folder 6. **27.** Drawing by MEK in 3/5/1942 letter to AK. AK Archives, Box 22, Folder 6. **28.** AK to C.B. Congdon, 11/27/1941. IGS Archives. **29.** AK to Francis R. Dewing, 12/11/1941. IGS Archives. **30.** "Memorandum on the Institute Fellows", M. Kendig to Russell Meyers and Marjorie Swanson, Oct. 4, 1956. IGS Archives. **31.** "Notes on Order of Business and Agenda For Trustee Meeting December 19, 1941", 12/18/1941. IGS Archives.

Chapter 54 – War Work

1. AK to Cornelius Crane. 12/24/1941. IGS Archives. **2.** "Los Angeles Guns Bark at Air 'Enemy'". 2/26/1942, *New York Times*. **3.** "West Coast Raided Stimson Concedes. Differing From Knox's 'False Alarm' Statement". 2/27/1942, *New York Times*. **4.** "Expose Hitler's Insanity to German People[,] Authority Urged to Counteract Propaganda[.] Expert on Semantics Says Europeans Have Horror of Such Ills" by Dillard Stokes. *Washington Post*, 12/9/1941. IGS Archives; AKDA 41.180. **5.** See Avedis ("Arthur") Derounian's 1943 book, *Under Cover: My Four Years in the Nazi Underworld of America*. New York: E.P. Dutton, Inc., pp. 396-39. Derounian wrote under the pseudonym "John Roy Carlson". **6.** "Two-Man Show". *Time*, Monday, Nov. 23, 1942. (http://www.time.com/time/magazine/article/0,9171,773937,00.html). **7.** Green-Korzybski Interview articles, AKDA 41.406. **8.** Green-Korzybski Interview articles, AKDA 41.407. **9.** Harry Weinberg 1959, p. xiii. **10.** AK to The Editor, *The North Central Association Quarterly*, 2/22/1944. IGS Archives. **11.** AK to Max Black, 3/11/1944. IGS Archives. **12.** Max Black to AK, 3/13/1944. IGS Archives. **13.** E.T. Bell. Review of *Science and Sanity* (Second Edition), *The American Mathematical Monthly* 49 (8), Oct 1942. AKDA 41.170. **14.** Institute of General Semantics Newsletter, August 1945. AKDA Scrapbook 4.137. **15.** "Letter from Pro-Tem Committee About Forming A Society" in *Alfred Korzybski Collected Writings*, p. 795. **16.** See Bernard Chalip,

"How Et Cetera Was Named" in *ETC.*, Vol. 41, No. 2 (Summer 1984), p. 206. **17.** "Prospectus of the journal ETC. and Society for General Semantics, Preamble, By-Laws, etc.", *Alfred Korzybski Collected Writings*, pp. 799-806. **18.** Bronislaw Malinowski, "Scientific Opinions About The First Edition, 1933", in Korzybski 1994 (1933), p. 784. **19.** Korzybski and Kendig, "Forword to a Theory of Meaning Analyzed", in *Alfred Korzybski Collected Writings*, p. 371, 373. **20.** Ibid., p. 375. **21.** Ibid, p. 373. **22.** Ibid, p. 379. **23.** Edwin Wilson, "I Knew Korzybski When..." in *Semantika*, Vol. 2, No. 2 (February 1956), pp. 26–27. **24.** Korzybski, "Science, Sanity, and Humanism", in *Alfred Korzybski Collected Writings*, pp. 383. **25.** Ibid., pp. 383-384. **26.** Ibid, p. 386. **27.** Ibid, p. 385. **28.** Samuel Clawson Obituaries. AKDA 41.210. **29.** Korzybski and Kendig, "Forword to a Theory of Meaning Analyzed", in *Alfred Korzybski Collected Writings*, p. 378. **30.** Korzybski, "Some Non-Aristotelian Data On Efficiency For Human Adjustment", in *Alfred Korzybski Collected Writings*, p. 392. **31.** Korzybski wrote:
> In human life one of our difficulties is that we are 'both the marble and the sculptor', as Carrel says, and so we are both the managed and the manager of our personal lives, the supervised and the supervisor, the co-ordinated and the co-ordinator. Perhaps one of the main sources of a great many maladjustments is exactly that self-reflexiveness and circularity which we do not know how to manage simply because we don't know that there are non-aristotelian methods to do so. ["Some Non-Aristotelian Data On Efficiency For Human Adjustment", in *Alfred Korzybski Collected Writings*, p. 394.]

Chapter 55 – Poland Fights
1. "Events of Week". *The Chicago Sun*, 1/31/1943. AKDA Scrapbook 41.214. **2.** Transcript of IGS 1938 Summer Seminar, p. 69. IGS Archives. **3.** "The Battle of the Warsaw Ghetto" in *Poland Fights*, 7/5/1943. IGS Archives. **4.** Korzybski, "Foreword to 'The Essence of Judaism' by Hans Kohn", in *Alfred Korzybski Collected Writings*, p. 403. **5.** Ibid. **6.** "Acknowledgment by Alfred Korzybski", in M. Kendig, ed. *Papers from the Second American Congress on General Semantics*, p. vi. **7.** Muller, p. 104. **8.** " 'Lost Angel' at Capitol Exhilarating". *Washington, D.C. News*, 12/31/1943. AKDA Scrapbook 41.374. **9.** Allen Walker Read, 'An Account Of The Word "Semantics",' in *Word* 4 (2), August 1948, p. 88. Reprinted for private distribution by the Institute of General Semantics. **10.** M. Kendig to C. B. Congden, 10/12/1943. IGS Archives. **11.** AK to Douglas and Marian Campbell, 2/1/1944. IGS Archives.

Chapter 56 – Time to Try New Things
1. "Memorandum From Alfred Korzybski to M. Kendig About His Future-Work Program", April,1944. (Mimeographed IV/1945). IGS Archives. **2.** M. Kendig, "Talk in Los Angeles, 1/18/1961, Unpublished. IGS Archives. **3.** Kendig promotional letter, 5/19/1944. AKDA, IGS Scrapbook 4.13. **4.** Annie Dix Meirs 1995, pp. 61-62. **5.** Ann Dix Meiers 1952, p. 277. **6.** Keyes 1989, p. 16. **7.** Ken Keyes, Jr. to AK, nd. I.G.S Archives. **8.** AK to Ken Keyes, 6/21/1945 qtd. in letter of Ken Keyes, Jr. to AK, 7/5/1945. IGS Archives. **9.** AK to Robert Lee Durham, 5/24/1944. IGS Archives. **10.** *Language in Action* (1940), p. 27 **11.** Kendig, Foreword to Korzybski's "An Extensional Analysis...", in *Alfred Korzybski Collected Writings*, p. 565. **12.** Fox, p. 247, Shearer, pp. 79, 126-127. **13.** *Language in Action* (1940), p. 103-104. **14.** Fox, p. 245. **15.** AK to H. A. Moe, 12/2/1943. Ralph Hamilton Papers. **16.** Shearer, p. 132. **17.** Shearer, pp. 133, 134. It appears that Margedant Hayakawa also avoided Korzybski because both she and her husband believed 'he was a lech'. S. I. later "recalled": "...he [Korzybski] offered private and rather intimate "semantic massages" to some women he found especially attractive." [Haslam,. *In Thought and Action: The Enigmatic Life of S. I. Hayakawa*, p. 109.] Disturbing: that S. I. Hayakawa could so blithely accept and repeat as 'fact' what most likely existed as hearsay or as his and his wife's projection; there is no evidence of any inappropriate incidents that he or she directly observed or reliably knew about. Doubly disturbing: Hayakawa's biographer, Gerald Haslam, seems to accept as 'fact', this unflattering gossip about Korzybski that Hayakawa 'recalled'. (Myths and misinformation about Korzybski and his work abound. Haslam—who studied with Hayakawa—uncritically repeats in his book [and thus may help perpetuate] other unfavorable canards, projections, and unsubstantiated opinions about Korzybski and his work, from Hayakawa and others; I think a key to the *enigma* of Hayakawa lies therein.) If I had found any reliable evidence of inappropriate sexual conduct on Korzybski's part (or of other such egregious activity), I would have openly dealt with it in this biography. I didn't find any. **18.** Shearer, p. 81–82. **19.** Shearer, p. 78. **20.** Fox, p. 247-248. **21.** Fox, p. 248-249. **22.** Fox, p. 248. **23.** Shearer, p. 130. **24.** Shearer, p. 121, 123. **25.** Shearer, p. 126. **26.** Shearer, p. 123-124. **27.** Korzybski had already written a friendly note to Hayakawa about one such questionable piece. [AK to S.I. Hayakawa, 1/18/1944, Ralph Hamilton Papers.] **28.** AK to S.I. Hayakawa, 3/6/1944, Ralph Hamilton Papers. **29.** *General Semantics Newsletter*, Autumn 1944, AKDA Scrapbook 4.79.

Chapter 57 – "Release of Atomic Energy"
1. In the *Discussion* section of *ETC*'s 1944-1945 Winter issue, Hayakawa had reprinted an article, "Semantics, General Semantics: An Attempt At Definition", that he had originally written for the *Dictionary of World Literature*. In the article, Hayakawa defined 'General Semantics' under the term 'Semantics', which from Korzybski's view—at this point in the development of his work—confused the two disciplines. Hayakawa also referred to the extensional devices as 'semantic devices'—an inaccuracy in terms of Korzybski's usage, which Korzybski believed, increased the confusion. Perhaps most bothersome, Hayakawa had written this original article, had it published, and then reprinted it in *ETC.*, without consulting Korzybski at any step. See Korzybski's 'Protest letter to the editor of *ETC.*' in *Alfred Korzybski Collected Writings*, p. 820. **2.** AK to C. J. Keyser, 10/6/1943, IGS Archives. **3.** Jekuthiel Ginsburg Obituary, 10/8/1957. *New York Times.* **4.** "Paper and Piano Puzzle Explained", 10/10/1957. *New York Times.* **5.** Kasner, "Foreword" to the Second Edition of *Manhood of Humanity*, p. xv. **6.** AK to Edward Kasner, 5/15/1945. IGS Archives. **7.** Ibid. **8.** AK to Cassius Keyser, 9/22/1945. IGS Archives. **9.** AK to Edward Kasner, 5/15/1945. IGS Archives. **10.** AK to Douglas Campbell, 5/4/1945. IGS Archives. **11.** Walter Polakov to MEK, 4/27/1945. AK Archives, Box 22, Folder 3. **12.** Billie Jane Baguley (who attended the 1945 Seminar-Workshop). Personal Communication with author, Sept. 2005. **13.** By 1947 mousetrap models of the chain reaction in an 'atomic bomb' began to get written about in journals and even the popular media. Korzybski read about "Atomic Mousetraps" in *Science News* and decided that he had to have one in his seminars to demonstrate the important notion of chain reactions, which he wanted students to realize as ubiquitous in science and life. For him it wasn't sufficient to explain 'concepts' like this; they had to be seen, heard, and felt to 'get under the skin'. The demonstration he used in his 1948-1949 Winter Intensive seminar involved an array of mousetraps set up in a large box with a glass front (for viewing) and a closed top (for protection) with a hole in it. The traps were set and arranged on the floor of the box in columns of about five traps arranged in cross-rows of 10 or so in close proximity. Two hard candies, representing 'neutrons' had been balanced on the spring of each trap. Then Ralph Hamilton, one of Korzybski's assistants at the time, dropped another single 'neutron' candy (raspberry flavored, by the way) through the hole in the top of the box to trigger one trap below, which sent its two 'neutrons' flying within the box. Each one set off another two 'neutrons', and so on. Within a few seconds the whole 'bomb' of about 50 mousetrap 'atoms' had exploded with dramatic results. [This description of the IGS Atomic Mousetrap demonstration came from interviews with Ralph Hamilton and David Linwood [Levine], both of whom assisted Korzybski at seminars in the late 1940s.] **14.** Korzybski, "Release of Atomic Energy (August 1945), Etc.: A Review of General Semantics*, Vol. III (2), Winter 1946. Reprinted in *Alfred Korzybski Collected Writings*, p. 537. **15.** Ibid., p. 537-538. **16.** Ibid., p. 538. **17.** Copy of a letter to A. Korzybski from an American fighter pilot. IGS Scrapbook 2.228, AKDA. **18.** "Brief Resume of Facts, Conclusions and Recommendations Contained in Memorandum to Vice Admiral Louis E. Denfield, U. S. Navy, Dated 27 September 1946". IGS Archives. **19.** "Foreword by Lt. Col. Douglas M. Kelley" in *Alfred Korzybski Collected Writings*, p. 541. **20.** Korzybski. "A Veteran's Re-adjustment and Extensional Methods", in *Alfred Korzybski Collected Writings*, p. 542-543. **21.** AK to Richard D. Loewenberg, Feb. 3, 1944. IGS Archives.

Chapter 58 – "Shoot Yourself!"
1. Qtd. in Gary David, "About the Author" in Bois 1996, p. xxiv. **2.** Bois, 1950. "The Alfred Korzybski I Knew", p. 20, in *General Semantics Bulletin* 3 (1950), pp. 20-21. **3.** Ibid., pg. 21. **4.** Excerpts from R.T. McClaughry's 1969 unpublished article, '"SHOOT YOURSELF," He Said—and Saved My Life!' Used with permission of John McClaughry. **5.** John McClaughry to B. I. Kodish, Feb. 4, 2009. **6.** The sign on the lower left corner of Korzybski's blackboard had a Walter Winchell quote from the November 1942 issue of *Reader's Digest* which read as follows:

> When a private at Randolph Field comes to a noncom with a complaint, he is handed a mourning-bordered card which says: "Your trials and tribulations have broken my heart. They are unique. I have never heard of anything like them before. As proof of my sympathy, I give you this card which entitles you to one hour of condolence."

Chapter 59 – A Matter of Character
1. See Martha A. Bartter's *The way to ground zero: The atomic bomb in American science fiction* and Alexei and Cory Panshin's *The world beyond the hill: Science fiction and the quest for transcendence.* **2.** AK to Jekuthiel Ginsburg, Dec. 1, 1945. IGS Archives. **3.** "Copy of a letter to Harry Stack Sullivan, M.D., May 1946",

Alfred Korzybski Collected Writings, pp. 899-903. **4.** Einstein Telegram as Chairman, Emergency Committee of Atomic Scientists. AKDA, Scrapbook 41.449. **5.** Albert Einstein, in an interview with Michael Amrine. "The Real Problem Is In The Hearts of Men". *New York Times*, 6/23/1946. **6.** Elwood Murray to Albert Einstein, 6/12/1946. AKDA, Scrapbook 5.241. **7.** Comments by Alfred Korzybski to "Excerpts From the William Alanson White Memorial Lectures, Second Series by Harry Stack Sullivan and Major-General G. B Chisholm". AKDA, Scrapbook 5.8-14. **8.** See "The Semantic Man: An address delivered by Irving J. Lee at the first conference on General Semantics, Chicago, Ill.", 6/22/1951. Unpublished. (Thanks to Sanford I. Berman for providing me with a copy of this paper.) See Sanford I. Berman, "Irving J. Lee: 'The Semantic Man'", in *General Semantics Bulletin* 18 & 19, 1955, pp. 22-25. Also see Steve Stockdale "Snooping Around the Time-Binding Attic, Part 2, in *ETC. A Review of General Semantics*, Fall 2002, pp. 338-339. **9.** C.S. Read. "Alfred Habdank Skarbek Korzybski: A Biographical Sketch. p. 9. **10.** *Nichomachean Ethics*, Book II, Section IV, p. 32. **11.** Korzybski, "A Veteran's Re-Adjustment and Extensional Methods" in *Alfred Korzybski Collected Writings*, p. 547. **12.** Personal Interview–David Linwood [Levine] with Bruce Kodish, conducted on May 11, 2005. **13.** Levine, David A. "A Student's Progress Report on Some Applications of Korzybskian Methodology". *General Semantics Bulletin*, 10 & 11, Autumn-Winter 1952-1953, p. 63. **14.** Allen Walker Read 1984, p. 17. **15.** AK to C. B. Congdon, 2/6/1946. IGS Archives. **16.** *IGS Student Newsletter*, Summer, 1946. AKDA, Scrapbook 4.246. **17.** Notes on "The Smith$_n$ Series of GS Life-Histories". IGS Archives.

Chapter 60 – SNAFU
1. Wentworth and Flexner, pp. 493–494. **2.** AK to Mrs. Arthur Dewing, 3/22/1946. IGS Archives. **3.** MEK to AK, 10/20/1943. AK Archives, Box 22, Folder 3.212. **4.** MEK to AK, 4/4/1946. AK Archives, Box 22, Folder 3.7. **5.** Kendig to W. Benton Harrison, 4/15/1946. Ralph Hamilton Papers. **6.** Charlotte Schuchardt Read, an interview with Louise Boedeker, 4/11/1997. *Sensory Awareness Foundation Newsletter*, Summer 2000, edited excerpt reprinted in *Time-Bindings: An IGS Newsletter*, Vol. XX, Nos. 2 & 3, Spring & Summer 2002, pp. 4-5. **7.** Charlotte Schuchardt Read 1988, p. 64. **8.** Qtd. in *IGS Student Newsletter*, Summer 1946. IGS Scrapbook 4, AKDA. **9.** AK to Jerome Alexander, 5/20/1946. IGS Archives. **10.** Adamic, p. 304. **11.** Morris, p. 283. **12.** Robinson and Creef. "Introduction", p. xxx in Tamagawa. **13.** Memorandum – Captain James A. Saunders (U.S. Navy, Ret.) to Vice Admiral Louis E. Denfeld, 9/27/1946. IGS Archives. **14.** Kendig, "Report on Talk with Capt. K.F. Poehlmann, 10 to 12:30 PM Dec. 29, 1946". IGS Archives. **15.** AK to Captain Karl F. Poehlmann, 1/21/1947 with "Some Notes Taken At An Interview January 4, 1947 [between A. Korzybski and K. Poehlmann] by C. Schuchardt". IGS Archives. **16.** "Items Biographic and Bibliographic: News of People, Their Writings, Activities, Comments, etc", *General Semantics Bulletin* 4 & 5, p. 68. **17.** W.M. Kruseman to AK, 6/14/1946. IGS Archives. **18.** E.W. Beth to AK, 6/17/1946. IGS Archives. **19.** AK to Ken Keyes, 11/2/1946. IGS Archives. **20.** Robert Redpath, Jr. to Clements C. Fry, in Redpath 2007c (Vol. III – Letters), p. 76. **21.** "What Korzybski's thinking-methodology have contributed to me", 6/1/1950. In Redpath 2007b (Vol. II – General Semantics and Tributes), p. 76. **22.** Robert Redpath, Jr. to Clements C. Fry, in Redpath 2007c (Vol. III – Letters), p. 76. **23.** Korzybski 1947, p. 335. **24.** MacNeal, p. 47. **25.** M. Kendig to Eleanor Parkhurst, 3/3/1944. Ralph Hamilton Papers. **26.** Korzybski 1994 (1933), p. lxviii. **27.** AK to Robert Maynard Hutchins, 9/24/1941. IGS Archives. **28.** Wendell Johnson, "Editorial – Report of the Retiring President of the Society for General Semantics", *ETC.* Vol. VI, No. 3 (Spring, 1947), p. 232. **29.** "Charter and By-Laws of the Society for General Semantics, Proposed Revision, February 1945". AKDA 41.561 [IGS Scrapbook]. **30.** Wendell Johnson, "The Society for General Semantics", *ETC.*, Vol. III, No. 2, p. 140. **31.** "Benefits of Membership in the Society for General Semantics". AKDA Scrapbook 41.564 **32.** Kendig, *IGS Student Newsletter*, Summer 1946, p. 8. AKDA, IGS Scrapbook 5.42–49. **33.** "Korzybski's 'Protest Letter' to the Editor of ETC", March 1947. Reprinted in *Alfred Korzybski Collected Writings*, p. 820. **34.** See *Certainties and Doubts: A Philosophy of Life* where Rapoport revealed his admiration of Stalin and devotion to the Soviet Union during the late 1930s and a good part of the 1940s. **35.** Rapoport 1976. p. 352. **36.** Ibid., pp. 352–353. **37.** Rapoport 2000, p. 80. **38.** Rapoport 1975, p. 385. **39.** Anatol Rapoport to Russell Meyers, 4/18/1956. IGS Archives. **40.** Rapoport 1976, p. 365. **41.** Rapoport 2000, p. 79. **42.** Rapoport 1976, p. 354. **43.** Korzybski, 'SNAFU' lecture transcript, 8/12/1946. IGS Archives. **44.** Robert Redpath, Jr. to Ross Runnels, 9/3/1947, in Redpath 2007c (Vol. III – Letters), p. 173. **45.** Ralph C. Hamilton to Bruce I. Kodish, 11/17/2005. **46.** Ibid. **47.** Bertrand S. Frohman to AK, 2/21/1948. IGS Archives. **48.** AK to Kenneth S. Keyes II, 11/2/1946. IGS Archives. **49.** AK to MEK, 10/10/1947. AK Archives, Box 22, Folder 1.

Chapter 61 – "I Don't Care A Damn About Those Yahoos…"
1. Comments by Alfred Korzybski to "Excerpts From the William Alanson White Memorial Lectures, Second Series by Harry Stack Sullivan and Major-General G. B Chisholm." AKDA, IGS Scrapbook 5.8-14, . **2.** M. Kendig Protest letter to SGS Board, 11/15/1946. AKDA, Scrapbook 41.577. **3.** Ibid. **4.** Ibid. **5.** From "New Viewpoints" circular in AKDA, IGS Scrapbook 5.78-8. See also *Alfred Korzybski Collected Writings*, p. 825. **6.** C. Schuchardt. "Some Notes Taken At An Interview January 4, 1947, A. Korzybski and K. Poehlmann". IGS Archives. **7.** Korzybski 1947, p. 311. **8.** Korzybski, March 1947 "Protest Letter to the Editor of *ETC*" in *Alfred Korzybski Collected Writings*, Appendix V (5), p. 818. **9.** Charlotte Schuchardt to MEK, 4/17/1947. AK Archives, Box 22, Folder 1. **10.** AK to C. B. Congdon, 5/9/1947. IGS Archives. **11.** Guthrie Janssen to W. Benton Harrison, Jr., 7/31/1947. Ralph Hamilton Papers. **12.** Ralph Hamilton to Bruce Kodish, 3/13/2007. Personal correspondence. **13.** Korzybski, qtd. from 1947 letter in Note on *Levels of Knowing and Existence*, in *General Semantics Bulletin* 38-39-40, p. 61. See also "Charlotte Schuchardt Read, "Harry L. Weinberg, Ph.D. 1913-1968" in *General Semantics Bulletin* 35, p. 64. **14.** Korzybski, March 1947 "Protest Letter to the Editor of *ETC*" in *Alfred Korzybski Collected Writings*, p. 821–822. **15.** M. Kendig to Vocha Fiske, 7/4/1947. Ralph Hamilton Papers. **16.** AK to MEK, 8/13/1947. AK Archives, Box 22, Folder 1. **17.** Robert Redpath, member solicitation letter, nd. AKDA Scrapbook 5.174. **18.** Letter from Korzybski to new IGS members, August 1949. *Alfred Korzybski Collected Writings*, p. 585. **19.** O. R. Bontrager, "Memorandum to Korzybski on meeting with president of the Society and Institute representatives on 31 August", 9/4/1947. Supplementary V (6) in *Alfred Korzybski Collected Writings*, p. 827–831. **20.** "Letter of the Society President [Irving J. Lee] to Korzybski", 11/17/1947. Supplementary V (7) in *Alfred Korzybski Collected Writings*, pp. 833–835. **21.** Korzybski 1994 (1933), p. 761. **22.** Communication scholar Neil Postman—Editor of *ETC.* for 10 years from 1976 to 1986 (when it was still published by the ISGS, not the IGS)—made this claim years later in an error-ridden essay entitled "Alfred Korzybski" in his book *Conscientious Objections*: "Korzybski's thought *was* grandiose in that he took all knowledge to be within his scope [p. 138]….[I]n taking all knowledge as within his competence, Korzybski's reach exceeded his grasp [p. 145]." As with Hayakawa, many people presumed Postman to know a lot more about Korzybski and his work than he actually did. Unfortunately, like Hayakawa, Postman seemed to presume this too. **23.** Ralph Hamilton to Bruce Kodish, 11/17/2005. For examples of Korzybski's "epistemodesty" see Korzybski 1994 (1933), pp. 10, 43–44, 142–144. **24.** Quine qtd. in Creath, p. 412. **25.** AK to MEK, 8/15/1947. AK Archives, Box 22, Folder 1. **26.** Korzybski 1947, "AK Biographical Material", p. 496. **27.** AK to Karl F. Poehlmann, 2/17/1947. IGS Archives. **28.** Lewin, "Regression, Retrogression, and Development", in *Field Theory in Social Science*, p. 89. **29.** Carter, "Keyser's Gedankenwelt And General Semantics", in *General Semantics Bulletin* 38, p. 137. **30.** Korzybski 1947, "AK Biographical Material", p. 222. **31.** Charlotte Schuchardt to Ken Keyes, Jr., 4/29/1947. IGS Archives. **32.** AK to Vocha Fiske, 6/23/1947. Ralph Hamilton Papers. **33.** Ken Keyes to AK, 7/18/1947. IGS Archives. **34.** Keyes, *Discovering the Secret of Happiness: My Intimate Story*, p. 22. **35.** Charlotte Schuchardt to MEK, 7/12/1947. AK Archives, Box 22, Folder 1. **36.** Korzybski 1949, Draft Transcript, 1948-1949 Holiday Intensive Seminar, p. 1. **37.** Interviews with Ralph Hamilton, 11/21/2005 and 11/28/2005. **38.** Video Interview of D. David Bourland by Steve Stockdale, Part I of III, May 26, 1997. Accessed at http://thisisnotthat.com/video/MP-ddb-csr.html on Jan. 5, 2010. **39.** AK to MEK, 10/10/1947. AK Archives, Box 22, Folder 1. **40.** Ibid. **41.** AK to MEK, 10/27/1947. AK Archives, Box 22, Folder 1. **42.** MEK to AK, 11/3/1947. AK Archives, Box 22, Folder 1. **43.** AK Notes for Scripta, nd. IGS Archives. **44.** Charlotte Schuchardt to MEK, 11/6/1947. AK Archives, Box 22, Folder 1. **45.** AK to Jekuthiel Ginsburg, 12/15/1947. IGS Archives. **46.** Korzybski, "General Semantics As Applied Physico-Mathematical Method", Transcription of a tape recording of Scripta Mathematica lecture, 11/10/1947. IGS Archives. **47.** AK to MEK telegram, 12/1/1947. AK Archives, Box 22, Folder 1. **48.** MEK to AK, 12/2/1947. AK Archives, Box 22, Folder 1. **49.** Postcard from Sayres Garlick to Institute of General Semantics, 12/15/1947. AK Archives, Box 22, Folder 1. **50.** MEK to Charlotte Schuchardt, 12/16/1947. AK Archives, Box 22, Folder 1.

Chapter 62 – "Without Publicity There Is No Prosperity."
1. "Here comes Dixie Dugan", AKDA, IGS Scrapbook 6. **2.** Guthrie Janssen to AK, III/3/1949. IGS Archives **3.** Korzybski 1950 (1921), p. 47. **4.** Allen Walker Read qtd. in "Book Comments To Come" in *General Semantics Bulletin* 1 & 2 (Autumn-Winter) 1949-1950, p. 48. **5.** Hayakawa 1949, "Foreword", p. v. **6.** AK to S. I. Hayakawa, 7/8/1949 in "Two Letters from Alfred Korzybski to S. I. Hayakawa" in *Alfred Korzybski Collected Writings*, p. 840. **7.** Rapoport 1950, p. 143. **8.** Rapoport 1950, p. 155. **9.** AK to Anatol Rapoport, 9/19/1949.

IGS Archives. **10.** AK to Richard B. McAdoo, 11/27/1949. IGS Archives. **11.** Charlotte Schuchardt to Anatol Rapoport, 6/1/1950, IGS Archives. In her letter to Rapoport, Charlotte included these notes: "Re: SCIENCE AND THE GOALS OF MAN by Anatol Rapoport, Notes made by Charlotte Schuchardt in November 1949 in conversation with Alfred Korzybski, preparatory to writing letter to Rapoport", IGS Archives. **12.** Korzybski qtd. by D. David Bourland. Video Interview with Steve Stockdale, 5/26/1997, Part 3 of 3. http://thisisnotthat.com/video/MP-ddb-csr.html **13.** AK to Bertrand S. Frohman, 2/18/1948. IGS Archives. **14.** Advertising Circular for *Brief Psychotherapy*. IGS Archives. **15.** Russianoff, p. 51-52. **16.** Russianoff, p. 61. **17.** AK to MEK, 3/25/1948. AK Archives, Box 22, Folder 1. **18.** I opine that Van Vogt did a much better job of demonstrating a non-aristotelian, extensional orientation in a subsequent book, *The Voyage of the Space Beagle*, which didn't mention Korzybski or GS. **19.** "Null", in Van Vogt's (*not* Korzybski's) usage for the bar above the A, referred to the 'empty set' in set theory, implying 'nullity', 'denial', and 'without value'; thus suggesting an outright rejection of aristotelian 'logic', etc. In contrast, Korzybski's usage of the bar above the A represented *non*, the $\bar{A}$ standing for '*non*-aristotelian', where the *non-* indicated a system 'broader than', 'extending', and 'going beyond" but *including* aristotelian 'logic', etc., as a special case. If some readers of Van Vogt's fiction, enticed to further GS study, failed to get beyond the terminology and related assumptions of Van Vogt's books, it seems unfair to blame Van Vogt too much for their mistake. He was writing fiction, after all. Nonetheless Van Vogt's terminology may have misled some people—once again demonstrating 'the power of the word'. **20.** Neil Larsen, Dec. 2000. "Charles Biederman: A Brief History". http://www.charlesbiederman.net/biography.html **21.** Rothstein and Sudarshan, p. 115. **22.** M. Kendig to Ken Keyes, Jr., 11/11/1949. Ralph Hamilton Papers. **23.** Kendig, "Institutions Offering Work in General Semantics: A Pro-tem Reply and Incomplete List". AKDA, IGS Scrapbook 5.218. **24.** Newton, p. x.

Chapter 63 – "What – Me Worry?"
1. Korzybski, "Time-Binding and Human Potentialities: A New Foundation For Human Relations", *Alfred Korzybski Collected Writings,* p. 630. **2.** AK to MEK, 1/23/1948. Box 22, Folder 1, AKDA **3.** "Talk of the Town", *The New Yorker*, Feb. 7., 1948 and "Guide For U.S. Seen In Soviet Behavior", *New York Times*, 1/29/1948. AKDA, IGS Scrapbook 41.480. **4.** "Understanding of Human Potentialities, Key to Dealing with The Soviet Union" in *Alfred Korzybski Collected Writings,* p. 642. **5.** Rapoport 1948. **6.** AK to A. Rapoport, 2/6/1948. IGS Archives. **7.** Korzybski. "Author's Note" to *Selections from Science and Sanity* in *Alfred Korzybski Collected Writings,* p. 615. **8.** MEK to AK, 1/16/1948. AK Archives, Box 22, Folder 1. **9.** Korzybski, "What I Believe", in *Alfred Korzybski Collected Writings,* pp. 655-656. **10.** Korzybski, "Letter to Friends and Members", September 1949. *Alfred Korzybski Collected Writings,* p. 663. **11.** Korzybski, "What I Believe". *Alfred Korzybski Collected Writings,* pp. 643-663. **12.** Kendig to Elwood Murray, 4/ 9/1949. IGS Archives. **13.** Charlotte Schuchardt to M. Kendig, 8/5/1948. IGS Archives. **14.** Charlotte Schuchardt to M. Kendig, 7/30/1948. IGS Archives.

Chapter 64 – Hardly A Day Off
1. Korzybski 1947, pp. 420-421. **2.** Ralph's observations were gathered in number of phone interviews and letters between 2005 and 2009. After an initial phone conversation in October 2005, I mailed him an extensive list of questions to prime the pump for later discussions. Most of the material quoted here is from a remarkable 20-page letter stimulated by these questions that he began writing soon after our first contact. (Although dated November 17, 2005, Ralph's letter was postmarked March 8, 2006.) The material in this letter-memoir was supplemented by interviews (Nov. 21, 2005), (Nov. 28, 2005), other letters (Mar. 7, 2006; Mar. 13, 2007), and phone conversations (Dec. 30, 2009). I remain in contact with Ralph, who has become a friend. **3.** Charlotte Schuchardt to Kendig, 12/17/1948, IGS Archives. **4.** David Linwood [Levine] 2005, "Institute of General Semantics – 1945 to 1950: A Personal History". Unpublished. **5.** Charlotte Schuchardt to Kendig, 2/5/1949. AK Archives, Box 22, Folder 1. **6.** Magee 1997, p. 130. **7.** Northrop, Letter to Editor, *General Semantics Bulletin* 8 & 9 (Winter Spring 1952), p. 95. **8.** Korzybski, "On General Semantics and Physico-Mathematical Method", *Alfred Korzybski Collected Writings,* p. 667. **9.** Northrop, Letter to Editor, *General Semantics Bulletin* 8 & 9 (Winter Spring 1952), p. 95. **10.** David Linwood [Levine] 2005, "Institute of General Semantics – 1945 to 1950: A Personal History". Unpublished. **11.** Thomas A. Gleeson to AK, 2/21/1949. IGS Archives. Gleeson went on to a distinguished career in meteorological research and education becoming an elected Fellow of the American Meteorological Society. **12.** Charlotte Schuchardt to MEK, 2/3/1949. AK Archives, Box 22, Folder 1. **13.** Ibid. **14.** Thomas A. Gleeson to AK, 2/21/1949. IGS Archives. **15.** Doob 1952, pp. 115-119. **16.** Thomas A. Gleeson to AK, 2/21/1949. IGS Archives. **17.** MEK to AK, 2/13/1949. AK Archives, Box 22, Folder 1. **18.** Korzybski. "Cooper Union Address", Unpublished. IGS Archives.

19. AK to Kendig, 2/3/1949. IGS Archives. 20. Garfield 1953. "Librarian Versus Documentalist". [http://www.garfield.library.upenn.edu/papers/librarianvsdocumentalisty1953.html]. Accessed on 3/26/2010. 21. Garfield. nd. "Basic List of Works In Documentation". [http://www.garfield.library.upenn.edu/papers/6.html]. Accessed on 3/26/2010. 22. Sand 2007. "IS". [http://ovimagazine.com/art/2387. Accessed 3/26/2010]. 23. D.A. Linwood [Levine]. Institute of General Semantics –1945 to 1950 – A Personal History. Unpublished. 24. AK & Charlotte Schuchardt to M. Kendig, 4/21/1949. IGS Archives. 25. AK Manhood Notes, ND. IGS Archives. 26. M. Kendig in "Memorandum to IGS Officers and Trustees of Finance Committee on Proposed Sale of IGS Building". 4/2-3/1949. IGS Archives. 27. "Excerpt from a letter from S.I. Hayakawa to Robert L. Read", 5/5/1949. AKDA, IGS Scrapbook 6.218-220. 28. David Linwood [Levine] to BIK, Personal Communication. 29. Charlotte Schuchardt to Kendig, 5/13/1949. IGS Archives. 30. Charlotte Schuchardt to Kendig, 5/27/1949. IGS Archives. 31. Charlotte Schuchardt to Kendig, 5/31/1949. IGS Archives. 32. Charlotte Schuchardt to Kendig, 6/7/1949. IGS Archives. 33. Charlotte Schuchardt to M. Kendig, 7/12/1949. IGS Archives. 34. "Books and Articles referred to by Korzybski in his Lectures". IGS Archives. 35. AK to MEK, telegram, 7/22/1949. AK Archives, Box 22, Folder 1. 36. The printed Congress *Program Notes* seemed as remarkable for its distancing from the term 'general semantics' as for its emphasis on the Congress theme of 'time-binding'. Its opening page, *Historical: On General Semantics and Korzybski's Works*, devoted much space to explaining what 'general semantics' *was not*, reflecting how problematic the confusion of 'general semantics' with 'semantics' had become for Korzybski and others at the Institute. (On the day he left for Denver, Korzybski had written bluntly to Hayakawa about the latter's role in that confusion.) [AK to S.I. Hayakawa, 7/8/1949. *Alfred Korzybski Collected Writings*, pp. 837-841.] The opening paragraph of the *Program's* "Theme and Organization of the 1949 Congress" rather significantly expressed Korzybski's and others' growing estrangement from the term 'general semantics' which could easily have been crossed-out without any significant loss of comprehension:

> The work of the Third Congress will stress the General Theory of Time-Binding as a foundation for a science of man, and applications of the non-aristotelian methodology derived from this functional definition of man as a time-binding class of life. It will stress the implications of Time-Binding and the non-aristotelian methodology of General Semantics for organization and integration, without regimentation, of human progress on the various personal, social, scientific levels of sane development. It will stress the criteria of sane progress on the dynamic bases of human time-binding potentialities when released from static statistical thinking and orientations of current aristotelian modes of evaluation. It will stress the extensional methods as generalized physico-mathematical method, its implications for concrete creative thinking on non-verbal levels as distinct from our ingrained aristotelian methods of verbal thinking by definition from which stem many blockages in personal and social adjustment and scientific advance. [*Program Notes - Third Congress on General Semantics*, "Theme and Organization of the 1949 Congress". AKDA Scrapbook 6.205.]

37. Korzybski, "Implications of Time-Binding Theory for Human Progress in A Free Society Versus Stultification by Dictatorships of Human Time-Binding Potentialities". Unpublished Notes of Keynote Address at 1949 Congress. IGS Archives. 38. See Third Congress program sections and scheduled presentations in *Alfred Korzybski Collected Writings*, pp. 774-782. Except for a Friday evening reception, which he had to attend, Korzybski had the freedom to go to the sessions that interested him. The presentations underlined or otherwise marked in his copy of the Congress Program indicate what he might have attended—or at least what interested him. These included: Allen Walker Read's presentation on "Linguistic Revision as a Requisite for the Increasing of Rigor in Scientific Method" (Korzybski marked-up a draft of his paper); Francis Chisholm's "Positive Training for Maturity"; George K. Zipf's "General Semantics and the Principle of Least Effort: Towards a Synthesis" (Korzybski also marked up a draft version of this); and Guthrie Janssen's "A Time-Binding Measure for Democratic Action", which represented a more worked-out version of the political theory that Korzybski had pointed toward over the last few years. (A version of Janssen's paper, "Time-Binding: Functional Basis of Democracy" was published in the 1951 *General Semantics Bulletin* 6 & 7). A few other notable presentations marked in Korzybski's program included: "Executive Training and General Semantics" by Sam Bois (so impressive to Korzybski and his colleagues that only a few months later they distributed it to IGS members); "Some Neglected Considerations of Order in Current Reading Methodologies" by Ray Bontrager; "General Semantics as Applied in a Course in Municipal Affairs" by W. Donald Fletcher of the Coro Foundation; "The Semiotic versus the Idiotic in Patent Law and Practice" by Cecil Kent; "On the Varieties of Research in General Semantics" by Irving Lee; "Therapeutic Techniques for the Loss of Abstract Ability in Patients with

Cortical Damage" by Lawrence LeShan, who had taken some seminars with Korzybski; "Semantic Dilemmas in Neurology, Psychology and General Semantics" by neurosurgeon Russell Meyers, who only just met Korzybski at the Congress and would later become friendly with Kendig, and teach at IGS seminar-workshops; "Admitting the Patient to the Medical Team" by physical therapist May Watrous Niles; and "Some Functional Patterns on the Non-Verbal Level: Laughter at the Comic" by Harry Weinberg, Korzybski's prize student who by this time had become an "Instructor in Public Speaking and General Semantics" at Temple University. [Third Congress Program (personally marked by AK). IGS Archives.] Papers read at the Congress included: "The Why and Wherefore in Everyday Life: An Application of Extensional Devices" by Ken Keyes; "The Island of Phenomena" by Korzybski's old friend P. W. Bridgman; 'Philosophical' Interpretations of Physical Theories, Discussed from a Semantic Angle" by Einstein biographer Phillip Frank; and "The New Mathematical Philosophy" by scientific philosopher Lancelot Law Whyte, author of *The Next Development in Man*. Korzybski, who considered cybernetics "a turning leaf in human evolution and socio-cultural adjustment", [Qtd. in Book Comments on *Cybernetics* by M. Kendig in *General Semantics Bulletin* 1 & 2, p. 46.] probably felt disappointed that Norbert Wiener declined his personal invitation to attend or even to provide a paper to get read by someone else. (Anthropologist Gregory Bateson, with whom Korzybski had exchanged articles, also got invited, but finally didn't attend or contribute a paper.) **39.** "Report on the Alfred Korzybski Fellowship Fund", *General Semantics Bulletin* 1 & 2 (Autumn-Winter 1949-1950), p. 27. **40.** "Korzybski's Protest Letter to the Editor of *ETC.*", *Alfred Korzybski Collected Writings*, p. 824. **41.** Pavlov's "Bequest" qtd. from Dec. 1943 *Scripta Mathematica*, in Notes of AK Third Congress Banquet Speech. IGS Archives. **42.** Notes of AK Third Congress Banquet Speech. IGS Archives. **43.** The full descriptive quote from *Science and Sanity* that Korzybski chose for his one-minute radio broadcast, goes as follows:

...General semantics is not any 'philosophy', or 'psychology', or 'logic', in the ordinary sense. It is a new extensional discipline which explains and trains us how to use our nervous systems most efficiently. It is not a medical science, but like bacteriology, it is indispensable for medicine in general, and for psychiatry, mental hygiene, and education in particular. In brief, it is the formulation of a new non-aristotelian system of orientation which affects every branch of science and life. The separate issues involved are not entirely new; their methodological formulation *as a system* which is workable, teachable and so elementary that it can be applied by children, is entirely new. [Korzybski 1994 (1933), pp. xxxviii-xxxix]

44. "Always Either-Or". *Time*, 8/1/1949. AKDA Scrapbook 41.494. **45.** David Linwood [Levine], "Institute of General Semantics – 1945 to 1950 – A Personal History". Unpublished. **46.** "1949 Seminar-Workshop: A Report". *General Semantics Bulletin* 1 & 2, p. 38. **47.** Korzybski, "Rough Draft of First Lecture, 8/14/1949. IGS Archives. **48.** David Linwood [Levine] to Bruce Kodish, 8/12/2008 email. **49.** Kenneth G. Johnson. "Group Process Notes". IGS Archives. **50.** Zipf 1949, pp. 481-482. **51.** Zipf 1952, p. 7. **52.** Zipf's name remains widely mentioned in reference to a kind of pattern he observed in the relation between rank and frequency of occurrence among a wide variety of phenomena, including word usage in texts, populations within and among cities, distribution of economic power and social status, etc. This relation became known as "Zipf's Law"—not a designation that Zipf himself used. Zipf's books, long out of print, remain mainly unread. His "principle of least effort" remains an often-downplayed-if-not-dismissed curiosity and his vision of integrating it with Korzybski's work remains largely unexplored. Besides Zipf's Congress paper eventually published in the *General Semantics Bulletin*, a few preliminary efforts to relate the principle of least effort to general semantics include the articles of Bourland 1950, Saunders 1958, and Payne 1967, all published in the *General Semantics Bulletin*. **53.** "1949 Seminar-Workshop: A Report". *General Semantics Bulletin* 1 & 2, p. 40. **54.** Charlotte Schuchardt to Ken Keyes, Jr., 10/25/1949. IGS Archives. **55.** MEK to AK, 10/7/1949. AK Archives, Box 22, Folder 1. **56.** AK to MEK, 11/17/1949. AK Archives, Box 22, Folder 1. **57.** Charlotte Schuchardt, "Editor's Note" to Second Edition of *Manhood of Humanity*, p. v. **58.** AK "1950 New Years Party Invitation", 12/22/1949. IGS Archives. **59.** AK to MEK, 1/17/1950. AK Archives, Box 22, Folder 1.

Chapter 65 – Farewell
1. Gibran, p. 64, qtd. in "Memorial Service for Alfred Korzybski, Four March 1950", *General Semantics Bulletin* 3 (1950), p. 14. **2.** David Linwood [Levine], personal communication. **3.** Qtd. in Redpath, Vol. II. p. 69. **4.** Redpath, Vol. II. p. 71. **5.** Schrodinger, p. vii, qtd. in "Memorial Service for Alfred Korzybski", *General Semantics Bulletin* 3 (1950), p. 14. **6.** "Memorial Service for Alfred Korzybski", *Ibid.*, p. 13. **7.** Qtd. in Schuchardt 1950, p. 40.

LIST OF PHOTOGRAPHS AND ILLUSTRATIONS
(In order of appearance, with *page numbers* in *bold italics*)

Alfred Korzybski lecturing at the August Intensive Seminar, 1940, *6*; Korzybski's desk, March 1, 1950, *22*; The Little Master, *26*; Alfred and his sister Adrianna, *28*; Alfred at the Realschule in Warsaw, 18 or 19 years old, *34*; 66 Wilcza, *45*; A young man in Warsaw, *47*; Somewhere on the Eastern Front, probably early 1915, *66*; Artillery Demonstration, 1916, *75*; Korzybski in San Antonio, November 1918, *95*; Mira Edgerly, Portrait by Arnold Genthe, *103*; Alfred and Mira, Wedding Day, *105*; 1920 Doodle – Chain Reaction ($Y=2^x$), *126*; Mira's 1921 portrait of herself and Alfred, *131*; Cassius J. Keyser, *134*; Walter N. Polakov, *148*; 1922 Portrait of Alfred Korzybski with Frame by Mira Edgerly Korzybska, *198*; "Logical Destiny" ("Logical Fate"), *215*; '3-D' Animal Object, Event, Object, and Label, *227*; Mechanical Drawing of Anthropometer submitted with Korzybski's patent application, *229*; Korzybski with 'deluxe, '3-D' model of Anthropometer with the rotary fan, the 'disk' where there is no disk, around 1927, *231*; William Alanson White, *262*; Abstracting, Ideal or Distorted, *273*; 'Mystery Laid to "Thought Machine"', from the *Washington Evening Star*, December 20, 1926, *286*; 'COUNT AND WIFE GRILLED IN INQUIRY [ON] MISSING MRS. HOUCK', *Washington Times*, December 23, 1926, *287*; Korzybski in London, 1929, *325*; Structural Differential, Vertical and Horizontal Stratifications [S&S, p. 396], *334*; Mira and Alfred, probably circa 1930, *340*; Korzybski in his corner of the apartment in Brooklyn, *363*; M. Kendig, circa 1940-1941, *392*; Korzybski with Robert McConnell (President of Washington State Normal School) on his right and Joseph Trainor on his left at the First American Congress for General Semantics, March 1935, *404*; 'A Chairy Tale' of Intensional Smith$_1$ Versus Extensional Smith$_2$ (Watercolor and Ink drawings for Korzybski by A.B. Stewart, 1940), *410*; Extensional Theory of Happiness, *433*; Pearl Johnecheck, circa 1940, *441*; At the lectern, Autumn 1938, *445*; Cornelius Crane, *446*; IGS Headquarters in Chicago at 1234 E. 56th St., *451*; August 1939 Intensive Seminar, Group photo with Korzybski, *454*; Charlotte Schuchardt, circa 1940, *460*; Allen Walker Read, *473*; "Mira's Heaven" with Kitten-Kat, *487*; Korzybski demonstrating the Graicunas diagram at the August 1947 Institute seminar, *501*; The Process of Abstracting, *515*; February 1945, New York University Seminar, Korzybski and Kendig standing, *523*; Alfred and Mira, circa 1945-1946, *524*; Castle Square in Warsaw, Poland, August 1939 and August 1945, *530*; Alfred Korzybski in his Chicago office, 1944, *534*; 1946 IGS Summer Seminar-Workshop group at the Indian Mountain School, Lakeville, CT, *557*; Korzybski with Douglas M. Kelley, M.D. at the 1946 Summer Seminar-Workshop, *558*; New home of the Institute, December 1946—in the Lime Rock district of Lakeville, Salisbury Township, Litchfield County, Connecticut with view of Korzybski's office on second floor, *561*; Alfred's 68th Birthday with the Keyses, *573*; Cartoon – "Surely you don't expect to win this argument...", *580*; AK with Charlotte Schuchardt in New York, December 1948, *599*; Mira's new 'spiral portrait' of herself and Alfred, 1948-1949, *607*; Alfred Korzybski, December 1949 (Photographed by Lotte Jacobi), *620*; Death Mask of Alfred Korzybski by Ernest R. Schaefer of Yale University School of Art, *623*.

BIBLIOGRAPHY

Adamic, Louis. 1944,1945. *A Nation of Nations.* New York: Harper & Brothers.

Adler, Mortimer J. 1978. *Aristotle for everybody: Difficult thought made easy.* New York: Macmillan.

"Allen Walker Read Obituary". 2002. *New York Times* (October 18). Reprinted in *General Semantics Bulletin.* 69–70 (2003): 93–94.

Allen, Frederick Lewis.1972 (1940). *Since yesterday: The 1930s in America, September 3,1929 – September 3, 1939.* New York: Perennial.

———. 1964 (1931). *Only yesterday: An informal history of the Nineteen-Twenties.* New York: Perennial.

Allen, Frederick Lewis and Agnes Rogers. 1947. *I remember distinctly: a family album of the American people, 1918-1941.* New York: Harper.

Ansky, S. 2002. *The enemy at his pleasure: A journey through the Jewish Pale of Settlement during World War I.* Ed. and trans. Joachim Neugroschel. New York: Henry Holt and Company.

Archibald, Raymond Claire. 1938. *Volume I: A Semicentennial History of the American Mathematical Society, 1888–1938.* New York: American Mathematical Society.

Aristotle. 1911. *Nichomachean Ethics.* Trans. D.P. Chase. New York: E. P. Dutton.

Aronson, Virginia. 2000. *The influenza pandemic of 1918. (Great Disasters: Reforms and Ramifications Series.)* Philadelphia: Chelsea House Publishers.

Axelrod, Alan. 2006. *Patton: A biography. Great Generals Series.* New York: Palgrave Macmillan.

Bachelard, Gaston. 1968 (1940). *The philosophy of no: A philosophy of the new scientific mind.* Trans. G. C. Waterston. New York: The Orion Press.

Bailey, Richard W. 2004. "Allen Walker Read, American scholar". *ETC.: A review of general semantics*, 61(4): 433-437.

Baldwin, Neil. 2001. *Henry Ford and the Jews: The mass production of hate.* New York: Public Affairs.

Bartter, Martha A. 1988. *The way to ground zero: The atomic bomb in American science fiction.* New York: Greenwood Press.

Barrow, John D. 1992. *Pi in the sky: Counting, thinking, and being.* New York: Oxford University Press.

Barzun, Jacques and Henry F. Graff. 1970 (1957). *The modern researcher. Revised edition.* New York: Harcourt, Brace & World.

Baugh, Hansell, ed. 1938. *General Semantics: Papers from the First American Congress for General Semantics.* New York: Arrow Editions.

Bayer, Piotr Pawel. 2000. "Polish nobility and its heraldry: An introduction". http://www.szlachta.org/heraldry.htm

Beam, Alex. 2001. *Gracefully insane: The rise and fall of America's premier mental hospital.* New York: Public Affairs.

Beers, Clifford Whittingham. 1917. *A mind that found itself: An autobiography.* Fourth Edition. New York: Longmans, Green and Co.

Bendersky, Joseph W. 2000. *The Jewish threat: Anti-semitic politics of the U.S. Army.* New York: Basic Books.

Bent, Silas. 1927. *Ballyhoo: The voice of the press.* New York: Boni and Liveright.

Benson, Jackson J. 1984. *The true adventures of John Steinbeck, writer: A biography.* New York: The Viking Press.

Best, Gary Dean. 2005. *Peddling panaceas: Popular economists in the New Deal era.* New Brunswick, NJ: Transaction Publishers.

Biernacik, Stan Z. 1998. "Haller's volunteers will always be remembered". *Polish American Journal.* Reprinted at http://www.geocities.com/hallersarmy/journal.html

"Big Bertha: How she won her wicked reputation. Legends and traditions of the Great War". http://www.worldwar1.com/heritage/bbertha.htm

Binkley, Goddard. 1993. *The expanding self: How the Alexander Technique changed my life.* London: STAT Books.

Blobaum, Robert, ed. 2005. *Antisemitism and its opponents in modern Poland.* Ithaca, NY: Cornell University Press.

Bois, J. Samuel. 1996. *The art of awareness: A handbook of epistemics and general semantics*. Ed. Gary David. Fourth Edition.Santa Monica, CA: Continuum Press & Productions.

Boole, George. 1916. *George Boole's collected logical works. Volume II, The laws of thought (1854)*. Chicago and London: The Open Court Publishing Company. (Full title: *An investigation of the laws of thought on which are founded the mathematical theories of logic and probabilities*.)

Boole, Mary Everest. 1931. *Collected works*. Ed. E. M. Cobham with Preface by Ethel S. Dummer. London: The C. W. Daniel Co.

Born, Max. 1968. *My life and my views*. New York: Charles Scribner's Sons, New York.

Bourland, D. David, Jr. 1950. "Preliminary notes on 'foci of synthesis': General Semantics and the principle of least effort". *General Semantics Bulletin* 1 (Autumn-Winter 1949-1950), pp. 7-21.

Bowen, Ezra, ed. 1969a. *This fabulous century: 1940–1950*. Alexandria, VA: Time-Life Books.

———. 1969b. *This fabulous century: 1930–1940*. New York: Time-Life Books.

Brasol, Boris L. 1920. *Socialism vs. civilization*. New York: Charles Scribner's Sons.

Brasol, Boris L., ed. and compiler; trans. Natalie de Bogory [names not included in publication]. 1920. *The protocols and world revolution, including a translation and analysis of "Protocols of the meetings of the Zionist men of wisdom"*. Boston: Small, Maynard & Company.

Breál, Michel. 1900. "Language the educator of the human race" in *Classics in semantics*, pp. 185–194. Eds. Donald E. Hayden and E. P. Alworth. New York: Philosophical Library (1965).

Bretnor, Reginald, ed. 1974. *Science fiction: Today and tomorrow*. New York: Harper & Row.

Brewer, Joseph. 1976. "A reminiscence of Alfred Korzybski". *ETC.: A review of general semantics*, 33 (4): 377–379.

Bridgman, P. W. 1959. *The way things are*. Cambridge, MA: Harvard University Press.

———. 1936. *The nature of physical theory*. Princeton, NJ: Princeton University Press.

———. 1927. *The logic of modern physics*. New York: The Macmillan Company.

"Brief History of Intellectual Discussion of Accelerating Change". www.accelerationwatch.com/history_brief.html (accessed 6/1/2006)

Brock, Pope. 2008. *Charlatan: America's most dangerous huckster, the man who pursued him, and the age of flimflam*. New York: Crown.

Brown, Dona W. 1984. "M. Kendig at the Barstow School For Girls". *General Semantics Bulletin* 50 (1983): 35–37.

———. 1943. "The use of general semantics in teaching the language skills in the eighth grade, 1936–1938 at the Barstow School". in *Papers from the Second American Congress On General Semantics*. Ed. M. Kendig. Chicago: Institute of General Semantics.

Brown, Harold I. 1977. *Perception, theory and commitment: The new philosophy of science*. Chicago: Precedent Publishing, Inc.

Buckley, Kerry W. 1989. *Mechanical man: John Broadus Watson and the beginnings of behaviorism*. New York: The Guilford Press.

Bugajski, Janusz. "Poland". The World Book Multimedia Encyclopedia, Mac OS X 2002 Edition. World Book, Inc.

Burrow, Trigant. 1984. *Trigant Burrow – Toward social sanity and human survival: Selections from his writings*. Ed. Alfreda S. Galt. New York: Horizon Press.

———. 1953. *Science and man's behavior: The contribution of phylobiology*. New York: Philosophical Library.

Campbell, Douglas Gordon. 1981. "An interview held with Helen Hafner, Mary Morain and David Waggoner". (held at the 1979 Korzybski Centennial Conference in New York City.) *General Semantics Bulletin* 47 (1980): 63–75.

Carlson, John Roy [Avedis ("Arthur") Derounian]. 1943. *Under cover: My four years in the Nazi underworld of America*. New York: E. P. Dutton (available at http://spitfirelist.com/books/under-cover-my-four-years-in-the-nazi-underworld-in-america/).

Carter, Elton S. 1955. "On Keyser's 'Queries, Doubts, and Reservations'" in "Special Supplement, Elton Carter: Collected Papers on Keyser - Korzybski - Polya". *General Semantics Bulletin* 38, 39, 40: 142–143. Reprinted from *General Semantics Bulletin* 16 & 17: 66–67.

Carter, Elton S.. 1953. "Cassius Jackson Keyser: A Biographical Sketch and Comments on *The Rational and the Superrational* by Cassius Jackson Keyser". in "Special Supplement, Elton Carter: Collected Papers on Keyser - Korzybski - Polya" in *General Semantics Bulletin* 38, 39, 40 : 133–134. Reprinted from *General Semantics Bulletin* 10 & 11 (Autumn-Winter 1952-53): 84-85.

Chapman, A.H. 1976. *Harry Stack Sullivan: The man and his work.* New York: G. P. Putnam's Sons.

The Chicago manual of style. 15th Edition. Chicago and London: The University of Chicago Press.

"Chronology of Alfred Korzybski's life" in *Alfred Korzybski Collected Writings 1920–1950,* pp. 907–908. Englewood, NJ: Institute of General Semantics, 1990.

Clark, Wallace. 1922. *The Gantt chart: A working tool of management.* With appendices by Walter N. Polakov and Frank W. Trabold. New York: The Ronald Press.

Clements, Kendrick, ed. "Thomas Woodrow Wilson". Miller Center of Public Affairs. University of Virginia http://millercenter.org/president/wilson

Clendenning, John. 1985. *The life and thought of Josiah Royce.* Madison, WI: The University of Wisconsin Press.

Clute, John and Peter Nichols, eds. 1995. *The encyclopedia of science fiction.* New York: St. Martin's Griffin.

Cohn, Norman. 1996 (1967). *Warrant for genocide: The myth of the Jewish World Conspiracy and the protocols of the elders of zion.* London: Serif.

The condition of Jewish belief: A symposium compiled by the editors of Commentary Magazine. 1966. New York: The Macmillan Company.

Conway, Flo and Jim Siegelman. 2005. *Dark hero of the information age: In search of Norbert Wiener, the father of cybernetics.* New York: Basic Books.

Cooksey, Elizabeth B. 1997. "George Boole: The Man Behind "And/Or/Not" ". *Libraries & Culture* 32 (1), Winter. Austin, TX: University of Texas Press.

Creath, Richard, ed. 1990. *Dear Carnap, Dear Van: The Quine-Carnap correspondence and related work.* Berkeley and Los Angeles: University of California Press.

Crosby, Alfred W. 2003. *America's forgotten pandemic: The influenza of 1918.* Second Edition. New York: Cambridge University Press.

"D. David Bourland, Jr. (1928–2000), In Memorium". 2003. *General Semantics Bulletin* 69–70: 141–145.

"D. David Bourland, Jr., Obituary". 2003. *General Semantics Bulletin* 69–70: 139.

Davies, Norman. 2005. *God's playground: A history of Poland in two volumes. Volume II, 1795 to the present.* Revised edition. New York: Columbia University Press.

———. 2001 (1984). *Heart of Europe: The past in Poland's Present.* Second Edition. Oxford: Clarendon Press.

———. 1998 (1996). *Europe: A history.* New York: Harper Perennial.

———. 1982. *Gods playground: A history of Poland in two volumes. Volume I, The origins to 1795.* New York: Columbia University Press.

Davis, Martin. 2000. *Engines of logic: Mathematicians and the origin of the computer.* New York: W. W. Norton

Derry, Gregory N. 1999. *What science is and how it works.* Princeton, NJ: Princeton University Press.

Dolan, Edward F. 1996. *America in World War I.* Brookfield, CT: The Millbrook Press.

Doob, Leonard W. 1952. *Social psychology: An analysis of human behavior.* New York: Henry Holt and Co.

Douglas, A. Vibert. 1957. *The life of Arthur Stanley Eddington.* London, New York: Thomas Nelson and Sons, Ltd.

Doxiadis, Apostolos and Christos Papadimitriou, Alecos Papadatos, Annie Di Donna. 2009. *Logicomix: An epic search for truth.* New York: Bloomsbury, USA.

Drew, Christopher. 2005. "Submarine crash shows Navy had gaps in mapping". *The New York Times*, Jan. 15.

———. 2005. "Danger zone that wasn't and a sub's hidden peril". *The New York Times*, Sun. Jan, 23.

Dwork, Debórah and Robert Jan van Pelt. 2002. *Holocaust: A history.* New York: W. W. Norton.

Eco, Umberto. Trans. James Fentress. 1995. *The search for the perfect language. (The Making of Europe).* Oxford UK & Cambridge USA: Blackwell Publishers.

Economides, Anthony M. 1947. *A non-aristotelian study of philosophy.* Lakeville, CT: Institute of General Semantics.

Eddington, Arthur S. 1928. *The nature of the physical world.* New York: The Macmillan Co.

———. 1920. *Space, time, and gravitation: An outline of the general theory of relativity.* Cambridge (UK): Cambridge University Press.

Edmonds, David and John Eidinow. 2001. *Wittgenstein's poker: The story of a ten-minute argument between two great philosophers.* New York: Harper Collins.

Einstein, Albert. 2000. *Albert Einstein in his own words.* New York: Portland House.

Eisner, Will. 2005. *The plot: The secret story of the protocols of the elders of zion.* New York: W.W. Norton & Company.

———. 2003. *Fagin the Jew.* New York: Doubleday.

Eldridge, F. R. [1949]. *General Semantics.* Based on a series of lectures given by Capt. J. A. Saunders at the Dept. of Agriculture Graduate School. Privately Published.

Elsner, Henry. 1967. *The technocrats: prophets of automation.* Syracuse, NY: Syracuse University Press.

Feferman, Anita Burdman and Solomon Feferman. 2004. *Alfred Tarski: Life and logic.* Cambridge, U.K.: Cambridge University Press.

Feinberg, Barry and Ronald Kasrils, eds. 1969. *Dear Bertrand Russell...: A selection of his correspondence with the general public 1950–1968.* Boston: Houghton Mifflin.

Feldman, Ruth Tenzer. 2004. *World War I: Chronicle of America's wars.* Minneapolis: Lerner Publications Company.

Ferguson, Charles. 1918. *The revolution absolute.* New York: Dodd, Mead and Company.

Figes, Orlando. 1997. *A people's tragedy.* New York: Viking.

Fink, David Harold. 1962 (1943, 1953). *Release from nervous tension.* New York: Simon and Schuster.

Flowers, Charles. 1998. *A science odyssey: 100 years of discovery.* New York: William Morrow and Co.

Fox, Roy E. 1991. "A Conversation with the Hayakawas". *ETC.: A review of general semantics*, 48 (3), Fall 1991, pp. 243-250.

Frank, L. K., G. E. Hutchinson, W. K. Livingston, W. S. McCulloch, and N. Wiener. 1948. "Teleological mechanisms". Special Issue, *Annals of the New York Academy of Sciences,* Volume 50 (4): 187-277. Eds. Roy Waldo Miner and Lothar Salin. New York: New York Academy of Sciences.

Frank, Philipp. 1947. *Einstein: His life and times.* Trans. George Rosen and Ed. Shuichi Kusaka. New York: Alfred A. Knopf.

Frohman, Bertrand S. 1948. *Brief psychotherapy: A handbook for physicians on the clinical aspects of neuroses.* Philadelphia: Lea & Febiger.

George, Henry. 1929 (1879). *Progress and poverty.* New York: The Modern Library.

George, William H. 1938. *The scientist in action: A scientific study of his methods.* New York: Emerson Books.

Gessner, Teresa. "[Paderewski:] Patriot, composer, piano virtuoso, philanthropist, statesman". http://wings.buffalo.edu/info-poland/classroom/paderewski/tg.html

Goldman, Eric F. 1960 (1956). *The crucial decade—and after: America, 1945-1960.* New York: Vintage Books.

Goldstein, Rebecca. 2005. *Incompleteness: The proof and paradox of Kurt Gödel.* New York: W.W. Norton.

Gordon, W. Terrence. 1990a. "Semantic pioneers revisited". *ETC.: A review of general semantics*, 47 (1), Spring 1990: pp. 36–43.

———. 1990b. *C. K. Ogden: A bio-bibliographical study.* Metuchen, N.J., & London: The Scarecrow Press, Inc.

Gottheil, Richard J. H. 1914. *Zionism. "Movements in Judaism" series.* New York: Jewish Publication Socieyty of America.

Graven, Philip S. 1925. "A case of smoke phobia". *The Psychoanalytic Review*. XII (2), April: 180-190.

———. 1924. "A series of clinical notes on headache". *The Psychoanalytic Review*. XI (3), July: 324-328.

Grauerholz, James and Ira Silverberg, eds. 1998. *Word virus: The William S. Burroughs reader.* New York: Grove Press.

Haber, Molly Nelson. 2004. "Thomas E. Nelson: A biography". *General Semantics Bulletin* 71: 70–73.

Harrison, W. Benton. "Some personal memories of Alfred Korzybski and his times". *ETC: A review of general semantics*, 34 (4), August 1977: 405–409.

Haslam, Gerald W., with Janice E. Haslam. 2011. *In thought and action: The enigmatic life of S. I. Hayakawa.* Lincoln, NE: University of Nebraska Press.

Hayakawa, S. I. 1979. *Through the communication barrier : on speaking, listening, and understanding.* New York: Harper & Row.

Hayakawa, S. I. 1949. *Language in thought and action.* With Basil H. Pillard. New York: Harcourt, Brace and Company.

———.1947. "Semantics, General Semantics". *ETC.: A review of general semantics*, Vol. IV, No. 3 (Spring, 1947), pp. 161–170. Reprinted from *Ten Eventful Years, Encylopedia Brittanica* (1947).

———.1941a. *Language in action: A guide to accurate thinking, reading and writing.* New York: Harcourt, Brace.

———. 1941b. *Language in action: A guide to accurate thinking.* Book-of-the-Month Club. New York: Harcourt, Brace.

———.1940. *Language in action: A second draft.* Chicago: Institute of General Semantics.

———.1939. *Language in action.* Madison, WI: College Typing Company.

Hayden, Donald E. and E. P. Alworth, eds. 1965. *Classics in semantics.* New York: Philosophical Library.

Herrick, C. Judson. 1949. *George Ellett Coghill: Naturalist and philosopher.* Chicago: University of Chicago Press.

Hersh, Reuben. 1999 (1997). *What is mathematics, really?* New York/Oxford: Oxford University Press.

Heydel-Mankoo, Rafal, 2000. "Almanach de Polska: The titled families of Poland". http://www.geocities.com/polishnobles/intro.html

"History of Petawawa". http://www.town.petawawa.on.ca/history/index.asp

Hobson, J. Allan and Jonathan A. Leonard. 2001. *Out of its mind: Psychiatry in crisis, a call for reform.* Cambridge, MA: Perseus Publishing.

Holzer, Harold. 2005 (2004). *Lincoln at Cooper Union: The speech that made Abraham Lincoln president.* New York: Simon and Schuster Paperbacks.

Howard, Michael. 2002. *The First World War.* Oxford: Oxford University Press.

The Institute Calendar. 1950. *General Semantics Bulletin* 1&2 (1949–1950): 35

Jevons, W. Stanley. 1958 (1873). *The principles of science: A treatise on logic and scientific method.* New York: Dover Publications, Inc.

———. 1883. *The elements of logic: A textbook for schools and colleges.* Recast by David J. Hill from Jevon's *The elementary lessons in logic.* New York, Cincinnati, Chicago: American Book Company.

Johnson, Kenneth G. 1984. "Korzybski on research: Suggestions from *Science And Sanity*". *General Semantics Bulletin* 51 (1984): 43–53.

Johnson, Wendell. 1946. *People in quandaries: The semantics of personal adjustment.* New York and Evanston: Harper & Row.

Kahler, Erich. 1967. *The Jews among the nations, with an appendix The Jews and the Arabs in Palestine by Albert Einstein, Erich Kahler, and Philip K. Hitti.* New York: Frederick Unger Publishing Co.

Kasner, Edward and James R. Newman. 1967 (1940). *Mathematics and the imagination.* New York: A Fireside Book (Simon and Schuster).

Kelley, Douglas M. 1951. "The use of general semantics and korzybskian principles as an extensional method of group psychotherapy in traumatic neuroses". *The Journal of Nervous and Mental Disease*, Vol. 114, No. 3.

———. 1947. *22 cells in Nuremberg: A psychiatrist examines the Nazi criminals.* New York: Greenberg.

Kelly, Diana J. 2003 "Socialism in scientific management: Walter Polakov and the Taylor Society". *Journal of Industrial History,* UK (September): 61-75.

Kendig, M. 1950. "A memoir: Alfred Korzybski & his work". *General Semantics Bulletin* 3: 3–11. Reprinted in *Manhood of Humanity.* Second Edition (1950), pp. xvii–xxxix.

Kendig, M., ed. 1943. *Papers from the Second American Congress on General Semantics (University of Denver, August, 1941): Non-aristotelian methodology (applied) for sanity in our time.* Chicago: Institute of General Semantics.

Kendig, M. 1937. "This living Barstow". *General Semantics Bulletin* 50: 38–44.

Kessler, John, ed. 1965. 'I knew Korzybski when –'. *Semantika: A monthly publication of articles on semantic and related subjects.* 2 (2), February. St. Louis, Mo.: Privately Published.

Keyes, Ken. 1989. *Discovering the secrets of happiness: My intimate story.* Coos Bay, Oregon: Love Line Books.

Keyser, Cassius J. 2001 (1922). *Mathematical philosophy: A study of fate and freedom.* Honolulu, Hawaii: University Press of the Pacific.

———. 1927. *Mole philosophy & other essays.* New York: E. P. Dutton & Co.

———. 1926. *Thinking about thinking.* New York: E. P. Dutton & Company.

———. 1925 (1916). *The human worth of rigorous thinking.* Second edition, enlarged. New York: Columbia University Press.

Kipling, Rudyard. n.d. *Barrack-room ballads and the vampire and other verses.* Philadelphia: David McKay Company.

———. n.d. *Barrack-room ballads.* New York: Little Leather Library Corporation.

Klein, Jeremy. 2000. "An interview with D. David Bourland, Jr". *ETC.: A review of general semantics*, 57 (3). Reprinted in *General Semantics Bulletin* 69–70 (2002-2003): 147–150.

Klyce, Scudder. 1925. *Sins of science.* Boston: Marshall Jones Company.

———. 1921. *Universe.* Winchester, MA: Scudder Klyce

Koch, Christof. 2004. *The quest for consciousness: A neurobiological approach.* Englewood, CO: Roberts & Company.

Koch, Howard. 1970. *The panic broadcast: Portrait of an event.* Boston-Toronto: Little, Brown and Company.

Koen, Billy Vaughn. *Discussion of the method: Conducting the engineer's approach to problem solving.* New York/Oxford: Oxford University Press.

Kohn, Hans. 1934. "The essence of Judaism". *The American Scholar*, Vol. III (2), Spring: 161–170. Reprinted with "Foreword" (1943) by Alfred Korzybski in *Alfred Korzybski Collected Writings*, pp. 399–414.

Kolakowski, Leszek. 1968. *The alienation of reason: A history of positivist thought.* Trans. Norbert Guterman. Garden City, NY: Doubleday & Company, Inc.

Korzybski, Alfred. 2002 (1937). *General Semantics seminar 1937: Transcription notes from lectures in general semantics given at Olivet College.* Third Edition., Ed. Homer J. Moore, Jr. Brooklyn, NY: Institute of General Semantics.

———. 1994 (1933). *Science and sanity: An introduction to non-aristotelian systems and general semantics.* Fifth Edition. Preface by Robert P. Pula. Englewood, NJ: : Institute of General Semantics.

———. 1990. *Alfred Korzybski Collected Writings 1920–1950.* Collected and arranged by M. Kendig. Final editing and preparation for printing by Charlotte Schuchardt Read with the assistance of Robert P. Pula. Englewood, NJ: Institute of General Semantics.

Korzybski, Alfred. 1971. "Letter from Alfred Korzybski to William Benjamin Smith". Eds. Robert P. Pula and Charlotte Schuchardt Read. *ETC.: A review of general semantics,* 28 (2): 139–149.

Korzybski, Alfred. 1950 (1921). *Manhood of Humanity.* Second Edition. Lakeville, CT: The International Non-Aristotelian Library Publishing Company.

Korzybski, Alfred. 1949. *Alfred Korzybski: 1948-1949 Holiday Intensive Seminar* (mp3 audio) with Listener's Guide (in PDF). Ft. Worth: Institute of General Semantics. Accompanying Rough Draft Transcription (unpublished) by Ralph C. Hamilton and David Levine. IGS Archives.

Korzybski, Alfred. 1947. *Biographical material.* Recorded by Kenneth Keyes, July 1947. Transcribed by Roberta Rymer Keyes. Indexed by Robert P. Pula. Unpublished.

Korzybski, Alfred. 1945. "A veterans readjustment and extensional methods", in *Alfred Korzybski Collected Writings*, p. 541–551. Englewood, NJ: Institute of General Semantics (1990).

Korzybski, Alfred. 1937. *General Semantics: Olivet College.* (First Edition of Olivet College Lectures). Olivet, MI: Olivet College, The Book Store.

Korzybski, Alfred. 1921. *Manhood of humanity: The science and art of human engineering.* New York: E.P. Dutton.

"Korzybski (Habdank Korzybski), Jozef Karol Wladyslaw (1839-1904)", in *Polish Biographical Dictionary*,Volume 14 (1968-9), pp. 184-185. Warsaw, Poland: Polska Akademia Nauk – Instytut Historii (Polish Academy of Sciences, Institute of History).

Krzywicki-Herburt, George (Jerzy). 1967. "Polish Philosophy", in *Encyclopedia of Philosophy*, Vol. 6, pp. 363-370. Ed. Paul Edwards. New York: Macmillan/Free Press.

Lakoff, George and Mark Johnson. 1999. *Philosophy in the flesh: The embodied mind and its challenge to western thought.* New York: Basic Books.

Lane, Michael. 2002. *Charles Ferguson: Herald of social credit*. Chidlow, Western Australia: The Australian Heritage Society.

———. 2002b. "Charles Ferguson." http://www.socialcredit.com/subpages_history/ferguson.htm.

Lee, Albert. 1980. *Henry Ford and the Jews*. New York: Stein and Day.

Lee, Irving J. 1994 (1941). *Language habits in human affairs*. Second Edition. Ed. Sanford I. Berman. Concord, CA: ISGS (in cooperation with the IGS).

Lee, Irving J, ed. 1949. *The language of wisdom and folly: Background readings in semantics*. New York: Harper & Brothers.

Lee, Penny. 1996. *The Whorf theory complex: A critical reconstruction*. Amsterdam/Philadelphia: John Benjamins Publishing Co.

Leibniz, Gottfried Wilhelm. 1979 (1951). *Leibniz Selections*. Ed. Philip P. Wiener. New York: Charles Scribner's Sons.

Leonard, Jonathan Norton. 1929. *Loki: The life of Charles Proteus Steinmetz*. Garden City, NY: Doubleday, Doran & Company.

Levine, David A. "A Student's Progress Report On Some Applications Of Korzybskian Methodology". *General Semantics Bulletin* 10 & 11, Autumn-Winter 1952-1953.

Levitt, Jesse. 2004. "In memoriam: Allen Walker Read (1906–2002)". *ETC.: A review of general semantics*, 61(4): 438–443.

Lewin, Kurt. 1951. *Field theory in social science: Selected theoretical papers*. Ed. Dorwin Cartwright. New York: Harper & Brothers.

———.1948. *Resolving social conflicts: Selected papers on group dynamics*. Ed. Gertrude Weiss Lewin. New York: Harper & Brothers.

———. 1936. *Principles of topological psychology*. New York and London: McGraw-Hill Book Co., Inc.

Lewis, Gilbert N. 1926. *The anatomy of science*. New Haven, CT: Yale University Press.

Lincoln, Abraham.1989. *Abraham Lincoln: Speeches and writings 1859–1869*. Ed. Don E. Fehrenbacher. New York: The Library of America.

Lincoln, Abraham. 1915. *Discoveries and inventions: A lecture delivered by Abraham Lincoln in 1860*. San Francisco: John Howell.

Linwood [Levine], David A. 2005. "Institute of General Semantics – 1945 to 1950 – A Personal History". Unpublished.

"List of Korzybski's Seminars and Lectures, 1935–1950" in *Alfred Korzybski Collected Writings*, pp. 723–728. Englewood, NJ: Institute of General Semantics, 1990.

Loeb, Jacques. 1912. *The mechanistic conception of life: Biological essays*. Chicago: The University of Chicago Press.

———. 1906. *The dynamics of living matter*. New York: The Columbia University Press.

Lonergan, Bernard J. F. 1958 (1978). *Insight: A study in human understanding*. New York: Harper & Row.

Lucier, Omer. 1960. "Bridgman and Korzybski: Comments and comparisons". *General Semantics Bulletin* 24 & 25, 1959:101-105.

Mach, Ernst. 1919. *The science of mechanics: A critical and historical account of its development*. Trans. Thomas J. McCormack. Chicago: The Open Court Publishing Co.

———. 1910. *Popular Scientific Lectures*. Trans. Thomas J. McCormack. Chicago: Open Court.

———. 1906. *Space and geometry in the light of physiological, psychological and physical inquiry*. Trans. Thomas J. McCormack. Chicago: Open Court.

MacNeal, Edward. 1994. *Mathsemantics: Making numbers talk sense*. New York: Viking.

Marcus, Y. B. and Nissen Mangel and Eliyahu Touger, trans. 2001. *Tehillim [Psalms] Ohel Yosef Yitzchak with English translation*. New York: Kehot Publications Society.

Marks, Steven G. 2004. *How Russia shaped the modern world: From art to anti-Semitism, ballet to bolshevism*. Princeton, NJ: Princeton University Press.

Magee, Bryan. 2001 (1998). *The story of philosophy*. New York: Dorling Kindersley.

———. 1999 (1997). *Confessions of a philosopher: A personal journey through Western philosophy from Plato to Popper*. New York: The Modern Library.

———. 1988 (1987). *The great philosophers: An introduction to western philosophy*. Oxford/New York: Oxford UP.

Mauldin, Bill. 1947 (1945). *Up front*. New York: Bantam Books.

Mayper, Stuart A. "Tarskian Metalanguages and Korzybskian Abstracting". Haarlem, The Netherlands: *Methodology and Science, Special Korzybski Issue*, Vol. 10, No. 2, 1977, pp. 102-129. Reprinted in *General Semantics Bulletin* 46, 1979: 26-53.

MacHale, Desmond. 1985. *George Boole: His life and work*. Dublin: Boole Press.

McCall, Storrs. 1967. *Polish logic 1920–1939*. Oxford (UK): Oxford University Press.

McKeon, Richard, ed. 1941. *The basic works of Aristotle*. New York: Random House.

Meiers, Annie Dix. 1995. *Scenes from My Life*. Privately printed.

Meiers, Ann Dix. 1952. "Avoiding The Dangers of Semantic Adolescence". *ETC.: A review of general semantics*, 9 (4) Summer 1952: 273-277.

"Memorial Service for Alfred Korzybski, Four March 1950". 1950. *General Semantics Bulletin* 3: 13–15.

Merejkowski, Dmitri.1928 (1931). *The romance of Leonardo Da Vinci: The gods resurgent*. Trans. Bernard Guilbert Guerney. New York: Random House.

Merz, John Theodore. 1948. *Leibniz*. New York: Hacker Press.

Michener, James A. 1983. *Poland: A novel*. New York: Fawcett Crest.

Millikan, Robert A. 1924. "The electron and the light-quant from the experimental point of view", Nobel Lecture, May 23, 1924. http://nobelprize.org/nobel_prizes/physics/laureates/1923/millikan-lecture.html

Mordkowitz, Jeffrey A. 1985. "Listener's guide to Alfred Korzybski's 1948-49 Intensive Seminar". *General Semantics Bulletin* 52: 51-76.

Morris, Charles. 1946. *Signs, language and behavior*. New York: Prentice-Hall.

Morzinski, Mary. 1994. *Linguistic influence of Polish on Joseph Conrad's style,* Vol. III, Conrad: Eastern and Western perspectives, general editor: Wieslaw Krajka. Eastern European Monographs No. CDXII (Boulder, CO). Lublin, Poland: Maria Curie-Sklodowska University.

Muller, Herbert J. 1956 (1943). *Science and criticism: The humanistic tradition in contemporary thought*. New York: George Brazillier, Inc.

Newton, Norman T. 1951. *An approach to design*. Cambridge, MA: Addison-Wesley.

Noble, Ralph A. 1933. *Psychiatry in medical education*. New York: The National Committee For Mental Hygiene.

Northrop, F. S. C. 1949. *The logic of the sciences and the humanities*. New York: The Macmillan Company.

Ogden, C. K. and I. A. Richards. 1947 (1923). *The meaning of meaning: A study of the influence of language upon thought and of the science of symbolism*. New York: Harcourt, Brace and Co.

Olszer, Krystyna, ed. 1981. *For your freedom and ours: Polish progressive spirit from the 14th Century to the present*. New York: Frederick Unger.

Olechhowski, Gustav. 1916. *Poland and Prussia*. Copenhagen: Egmont H. Petersens.

Ottaviani, Jim and Leland Purvis. 2004. *Suspended in language: Niels Bohr's life, discoveries, and the century he shaped*. Ann Arbor, MI: G.T. Labs.

Page, Curtis Hidden and Stith Thompson. 1929. *British poets of the nineteenth century*. Chicago, New York, Boston: Benj. H. Sanborn & Co.

Panshin, Alexei and Cory Panshin. 1989. *The world beyond the hill: Science fiction and the quest for transcendence*. Los Angeles: Jeremy P. Tarcher, Inc.

Patterson, Michael Robert. "In Flanders Field[s], Lieutenant Colonel John McCrae". Arlington National Cemetery Website [private]. http://www.arlingtoncemetery.net/flanders.htm (Accessed 4/4/2006).

Patterson, William H., Jr. 2010. *Robert A. Heinlein: In dialogue with his century: Volume 1 (1907-1948): Learning curve*. New York: Tor Books.

Parker, Kelly A., "Josiah Royce", *The Stanford Encyclopedia of Philosophy* (Summer 2005 Edition). Ed. Edward N. Zalta. http://plato.stanford.edu/archives/sum2005/entries/royce/

Pauly, Philip J. 2000. *Biologists and the promise of American life: From Meriwether Lewis to Alfred Kinsey*. Princeton, NJ: Princeton University Press.

———. 1987. *Controlling life: Jacques Loeb and the engineering ideal in biology.* New York: Oxford University Press.

Paulson, Ross Evans. 1983. *Language, science, and action: Korzybski's general semantics – a study in comparative intellectual history,* Contributions in Intercultural and Comparative Studies, Number 9. Westport, CT: Greenwood Press.

Payne, Buryl. 1967. "Abstracting, identification and the principle of least action". *General Semantics Bulletin* 32: 63-65.

Peirce, Charles S. 1958. *Values in a world of chance: Selected writings of Charles S. Peirce (1839–1914).* Ed. with an introduction and notes by Philip P. Weiner. New York: Doubleday Anchor.

———. 1923. *Chance, love and logic: Philosophical essays.* International Library of Psychology, Philosophy and Scientific Method. Ed. with an Introduction by Morris R. Cohen. New York: Harcourt, Brace.

Perl, William R. 1989. *The Holocaust conspiracy: An international policy of genocide.* New York: Shapolsky Publishers.

Pemberton, William H. 1984. "Remembrance of Douglas Gordon Campbell: 1902–1983". *General Semantics Bulletin* 50 (1983): 167–168.

Perry, Helen Swick. 1982. *Psychiatrist of America: The life of Harry Stack Sullivan.* Cambridge, MA: Belknap.

Pine, Eli S. 1975. *How to enjoy calculus.* Hasbrouk Heights, NJ: Steinlitz-Hammacher.

Poincaré, Henri. 1913. *The foundations of science: Science and hypothesis, The value of science, Science and method.* Authorized trans. George Bruce Halstead. New York: The Science Press.

Pogonowski, Iwo Cyprian. 1998 (1993). *Jews in Poland: A documentary history.* New York: Hippocrene Books.

———. 1993 (1987, 1988). *Poland: A historical atlas.* Revised edition. New York: Barnes & Noble Books.

Polakov, Walter N. 1925. *Man and his affairs: From an engineering point of view.* Baltimore. Williams & Wilkins.

———. 1921. *Mastering power production: The industrial, economic and social problems involved and their solution.* New York: The Engineering Magazine Company.

Popper, Karl R. 1959, 1968. *The logic of scientific discovery.* New York: Harper & Row.

Potts, Harold M. 1935. "Some results of extensional training of "mentally retarded" pupils", in *General Semantics: Papers from the First American Congress for General Semantics*, pp. 62-65. Ed. Hansell Baugh. New York: Arrow Editions (1940).

Powers, William T. 1973. *Behavior: The control of perception.* New York: Aldine De Gruyter.

Powers, William T. and Philip J. Runkel. 2011. *Dialogue concerning the two chief approaches to a science of life: Word pictures and correlations versus working models.* Ed. Dag Forssell. Hayward, CA: Living Control Systems Publishing.

Pressman, David and Jeremy Klein. 1991. "The Korzybski lawsuit: A major legal precedent". *ETC.: A review of general semantics*, 48(1), Spring: 62–63.

Prior, A. N. "Polish Logic", in *Encyclopedia of Philosophy*. 1967. Vol. 4, pp. 566–568. New York: Macmillan/The Free Press. See also in this source, articles on Ajdukiewicz, Chwistek, Kotarbinski, Lesniewski, Lukasiewicz, Tarski and Twardowski.

Province, Charles M. nd. "George S. Patton, Jr. U.S. Army 02605, 1885 – 1945" (Patton biography). San Diego, CA: The Patton Society. http://www.geocities.com/pattonhq/homeghq.html

Pula, Robert P. 2003a. "Partners: Charlotte Schuchardt Read (1909–2002); Allen Walker Read (1906–2002)." *General Semantics Bulletin* 69–70: 95–103.

———. 2003b. "Biographical accounts of Charlotte and Allen Read from the *General Semantics Bulletin*". *General Semantics Bulletin* 69–70: 129–134.

———. 2003c. "Alfred Korzybski, 1879–1950: A bio-methodological sketch". *General Semantics Bulletin* 69–70 (2003): 49–92. Reprinted from Polish-American Studies LIII (2), 1996 Autumn.

———. 2001a. "General Semantics and the restructuring of Polish society for the 'third' millennium". Zlota Ksiega. Opole: Uniwersytet Opolski-Instytut Filologii Polskiej.

———. 2001b. "The impact of Korzybski at the planetary level : The view from 2000". Alfred Korzybski Memorial Lecture at the Yale Club of New York City, Friday, November 3, 2000. *General Semantics Bulletin* 65–68 (2001): 43–55.

———. 1994. "Preface to the Fifth Edition 1993" in *Science and sanity: An introduction to non-aristotelian systems and general semantics* by Alfred Korzybski. Fifth Edition, pp. xii–xxii. Englewood, NJ: The Institute of General Semantics.

———. 1980. "Korzybski's Polish Matrix." *General Semantics Bulletin* 47: 36–54.

Pyke, Catherine. 2007. "The soul as steersman of our lives: Hartley Burr Alexander". *Scripps Magazine* 79 (1), Spring 2007: 26–27. Clairmont, CA: Scripps College.

Quine, W. V. O. 1985. *The time of my life*. Cambridge, MA: MIT Press.

———. 1960. *Word and object.* Cambridge, MA: MIT Press.

Raleigh, Donald J. "Russo-Japanese War". *The World Book Multimedia Encyclopedia*, Mac OS X 2002 Edition. World Book, Inc.

Rapoport, Anatol. 2000. *Certainties and doubts: A philosophy of life.* Montreal: Black Rose Books.

———. 1976. "What I think Korzybski thought—and what I think about it". *ETC*, Vol. 33, No. 4 (December 1976): 351-365,

———. 1975. *Semantics.* With the collaboration of Leo Hamalian. New York: Thomas Y. Crowell Company.

———. 1953 (1969). *Operational philosophy: Integrating knowledge and Action.* San Francisco: ISGS.

———. 1952. "What is semantics", *ETC.: A review of general semantics*, Vol. 10, No. 1 (Autumn 1952), pp. 12-24. Reprinted from *American Scientist*, Vol. XL, 123-135 (Jan. 1952).

———. 1950. *Science and the goals of man: A study of semantic orientation.* New York: Harper & Brothers.

———. 1948. "Dialectical materialism and general semantics". *ETC.: A review of general semantics*, Vol. V, No. 2 (Winter 1948), pp. 81–104. Presented before the University of Chicago Chapter of the Society for General Semantics, Dec. 3., 1947.

Read, Allen Walker. 2002. *Milestones in the history of English in America.* Ed. Richard W. Bailey. Publication of the American Dialect Society. No. 86. Annual Supplement to *American Speech*. Durham, NC: Duke University Press.

———. 1984. "Changing attitudes toward Korzybski's General Semantics". The Alfred Korzybski Memorial Lecture, 1983. *General Semantics Bulletin* 51: 11–25.

———. 1980. "Formative influences on Korzybski's General Semantics". Presented at the Centennial Conference on General Semantics in New York, 10/27/1979. *General Semantics Bulletin* 47 (1980): 55–62. Reprinted (abridged) in *Alfred Korzybski Collected Writings 1920–1950*, pp. xxi–xxiv.

———. 1977 (1935). *Classic American Grafitti.* Waukesha, WI: Maledicta Press.

———. 1948. "An account of the word 'semantics'. *Word*. Vol. 4, No. 2, August, 1948. Reproduced by the Institute of General Semantics for private distribution to Members of the Institute, Nov. 1948.

Read, Charlotte Schuchardt. 1988. "The Institute of General Semantics: A Brief Historical Survey". *General Semantics Bulletin*, Number 54, 1988/9: (62-68).

———. 1984. "Marjorie Mercer Kendig Gates: A biographical sketch". *General Semantics Bulletin* 50 (1983): 47–57.

———. 1981. "A personal perspective". (Presentation at the 1979 Korzybski Centennial Celebration, New York City). *General Semantics Bulletin* 47 (1980): 30–34.

———. 1955. "Mira Edgerly Korzybska: A biographical sketch". *General Semantics Bulletin* 16 & 17: 53-56.

Redpath, R. U., III, ed. 2007a. *A compilation of the writings of Robert Upjohn Redpath, Jr. Volume I: Family, extramural pursuits and work.* Privately Published.

———. 2007b. *A compilation of the writings of Robert Upjohn Redpath, Jr. Volume II: Letters.* Privately Published.

———. 2007c. *A compilation of the writings of Robert Upjohn Redpath, Jr. Volume III: General Semantics and tributes.* Privately Published.

Reid, Constance. 1993. *The search for E. T. Bell, also known as John Taine.* Washington, D.C.: The Mathematical Association of America.

Reiser, Oliver L. 1958. *The integration of human knowledge: A study of the formal foundations and the social implications of unified science.* Boston: Porter Sargent Publisher.

———. 1943a. "Historical-Cultural significance of non-aristotelian movement and the methodological contributions of Korzybski". In *Papers from the Second American Congress on General Semantics*, pp. 3–10. Ed. M. Kendig. Chicago: Institute of General Semantics.

———. 1943b. "From Classical Physical to Modern Scientific Assumptions". In *Papers from the Second American Congress on General Semantics*, pp. 69–78. Ed. M. Kendig. Chicago: Institute of General Semantics.

———. 1940. *The promise of scientific humanism: Toward a unification of scientific, religious, social and economic thought.* New York: Oskar Piest.

———. 1930. *Humanistic logic for the mind in action.* New York: Thomas Y. Crowell Company.

Robertson, Richard J. 2003. *Perception of reality and the fate of civilization: Ordinary people as virtual pioneers in critical times.* Xlibris Corporation.

"Records of the U.S. Fuel Administration (USFA). Administrative History". The National Archives. Washington, D.C. http://www.archives.gov/research/guide-fed-records/groups/067.html

Ross, George MacDonald. 1984. *Leibniz.* Past Masters Series. Oxford: Oxford U Press.

Royce, Josiah. 1914. "The principles of logic" in *Royce's logical essays*, pp. 310–378. Ed. Daniel S. Robinson. Dubuque, Iowa: Wm. C. Brown Company (1951).

———. 1908 (1899). *The world and the individual. The Gifford lectures. First series. The four historical conceptions of being.* New York: Macmillan.

Ritter, William Emerson. 1919. *The unity of the organism or the organismal conception of life,* Volumes I and II. Boston: Richard G. Badger, The Gorham Press.

Roethlisberger, F.J. 1977. *The elusive phenomena.* Ed. George F. F. Lombard. Boston: Division of Research, Harvard Graduate School of Business Administration.

Rucker, Rudy. 1982. *Infinity and the mind: The science and philosophy of the infinite.* Boston: Birkhäuser.

Rukeyser, Muriel. 1942. *Willard Gibbs.* Garden City, NY: Doubleday, Doran & Co., Inc.

Runes. Dagobert D. 1959. *A dictionary of thought: From my writings and my evenings.* New York: Philosophical Library.

Runkel, Philip J. 1990. *Casting nets and testing specimens: Two grand methods of psychology.* New York: Praeger.

Russell, Bertrand. 1964 (1903). *Principles of mathematics.* Second Edition. New York: W. W. Norton & Company, Inc.

———. 1919. *Introduction to mathematical philosophy.* London/New York: Allen & Unwin/Macmillan.

Russell, Bertrand and Alfred North Whitehead. 1910. *Principia mathematica. Volume I.* Cambridge: Cambridge University Press.

Russianoff, Penelope. 1988. *When am I going to be happy: How to break the emotional bad habits that make you miserable.* New York: Bantam Books.

Sayings of the sages of the Talmud. 1994. Jerusalem: Koren Publishers.

Saunders, James A. 1958. " 'Brain' tool and least effort (letter)". GSB 20, p. 87.

Schuchardt [Read], Charlotte.1950a. "Alfred Habdank Skarbek Korzybski: A biographical sketch". *General Semantics Bulletin* 3: 33–40.

———. 1950b. "Editor's Note" in Alfred Koryzybski, *Manhood of Humanity.* Second Edition, 1950 (1921). Lakeville, CT: The International Non-Aristotelian Library Publishing Company.

———. 1943. *The technique of semantic relaxation.* Chicago: Institute of General Semantics.

Schroeder, Michael. 1997. "A brief history of the notation of Boole's algebra". *Nordic Journal of Philosophical Logic* 2 (1): 41–62.

Sharp, William Henry. 2007. *Alfred Korzybski: Time-Binder.* Privately Published.

Shaw, Ruth Faison. 1947. *Finger-painting and how I do it.* New York: Art for All, Inc.

———. 1934. *Finger Painting: A perfect medium for self-expression.* Boston: Little, Brown, and Co.

Shearer, Julie Gordon. 1994. "From Semantics to the U.S. Senate, Etc., Etc." An oral history of S. I. Hayakawa and Margedant Peters Hayakawa based on interviews with the Hayakawas and others conducted in 1989, 1992 and 1993. Regional Oral History Office, The Bancroft Library, University of California, Berkeley. http://content.cdlib.org/view?docId=hb5q2nb40v&brand=calisphere (also accessed via http://www.calisphere.universityofcalifornia.edu/).

Shorter, Edward. 1997. *A history of psychiatry: From the era of the asylum to the age of Prozac.* New York: John Wiley & Sons.

Shub, David. 1948. *Lenin: A biography.* Garden City, NY: Doubleday & Co.

Sickels, Robert. 2004. *The 1940s. American Popular Culture Through History*, Series Editor, Ray B. Browne. Westport, CT: Greenwood Press.

Simon, Linda. 1991. *The biography of Alice B. Toklas.* Lincoln, NE: Bison Books.

Simpson, Joanne Cavanaugh. 2000. "It's all in the upbringing - Pioneers in scholarship [John B. Watson]." *Johns Hopkins Magazine* (April). http://www.jhu.edu/~jhumag/0400web/35.html.

Skolimowski, Henryk. 1967. *Polish Analytical Philosophy.* New York: The Humanities Press.

Smith, Grover, ed. 1969. *Letters of Aldous Huxley.* New York: Harper & Row.

Solezhenitsyn, Aleksandr. 1972. *August 1914.* New York: Farrar, Straus and Giroux.

Sowell, Thomas. 2005. "Is anti-semitism generic?" *Hoover Digest*, 2005, No. 3, pp. 143-150. Stanford,CA : Hoover Institution on War, Revolution and Peace (Stanford University).

Stein, Gertrude. 1962 (1945). *Selected writings of Gertrude Stein.* Ed. Carl Van Vechten. New York: Vintage Books.

Steinsaltz, Adin. 2005. *We Jews: Who are we and what should we do?* San Francisco: Jossey-Bass.

Stone, Norman. 2009 (2007). *World War One: A short history.* New York: Basic Books.

———. 1998 (1975). *The Eastern Front: 1914–1917.* London: Penguin Books.

Stockdale, Steve. 2002. "Snooping around the time-binding attic, Part 2: Wendell Johnson, Francis Chilsholm, Russell Meyers, Ray Bontrager, Irving Lee, Samuel Bois". *ETC: A Review of General Semantics*, 59 (3), Fall 2002: 330–340.

Strausz-Hupé, Robert and Stefan T. Possony. 1954 (1950). *International relations in the age of the conflict between democracy and dictatorship.* Second Edition. New York: McGraw-Hill Book Co., Inc.

Sweetman, John. 2002. *Tannenberg 1914.* London: Cassell & Co.

Synge, J. L. 1951. *Science: Sense and Nonsense.* London: Jonathan Cape.

Szczepanski, Jan. 1970. *Polish Society.* New York: Random House.

Swift, Jonathan. 1938 (1726). *Gulliver's Travels.* Ed. with Notes and Commentary by Arthur E. Case. New York: The Ronald Press Company.

Taleb, Nassim Nicholas. 2007. *The black swan: The impact of the highly improbable.* New York: Random House.

Tamagawa, Kathleen. 2008 (1932). *Holy Prayers In A Horse's Ears: A Japanese American Memoir.* Ed. and with an Introduction by Greg Robinson and Elena Tajima Creef. New Brunswick, NJ: Rutgers University Press.

Teachout, Terry. 2002. *The skeptic: A life of H. L. Mencken.* New York: HarperCollins.

Thurman, Kelly, ed. 1960. *Semantics.* Boston: Houghton Mifflin.

Torrey, E. Fuller. 1984. *The roots of treason: Ezra Pound and the secret of St. Elizabeths.* New York: McGraw-Hill.

"The Town of Petawawa", "History", "Different Yet The Same". http://www.petawawa.ca/index.php?option=com_content&task=view&id=461&Itemid=88

U.S. Congress, Senate, (Overman) Committee on the Judiciary. 1919. *Bolshevik Propaganda: Hearings Before A Subcommittee of the Committee on the Judiciary.* Sixty-Fifth Congress, Third Session and Thereafter. Pursuant to S. Res. 439 and 469, February 11, 1919 to March 10, 1919. Washington, D.C.: Government Printing Office. http://books.google.com (type in Bolshevik Propaganda, U.S. Congress).

U. S. Copyright Office. 1995. "Registrability of pictorial, graphic, or sculptural works where a design patent has been issued." *Federal Register*: March 24, 1995 (Volume 60, Number 57). Washington, D.C.: Library of Congress. www.copyright.gov/fedreg/1995/60fr15605.html

Valenstein, Elliot S. 1986. *Great and desperate cures: The rise and decline of psychosurgery and other radical treatments for mental illness.* New York: Basic Books.

Van Vogt, A. E. 1992 (1950). *The voyage of the Space Beagle.* New York: Collier Books.

———. 1976. *The best of A. E. Van Vogt.* New York: Pocket Books.

———. 1974 (1948). *The players of Null-A.* New York: Berkley Publishing.

———. 1970 (1948, 1945). *The world of Null-A. Revised.* New York: Berkley Publishing.

———. 1948. *The world of $\bar{A}$.* New York: Simon and Schuster.

Waggoner, Walter H. 1979. "Dr. Nolan D.C. Lewis dies at 90; Psychiatrist was leader in field". *The New York Times*, Dec. 19.

Walaszek, Adam. 1998. " Polish immigrants in the USA and their homeland 1914 – 1923." (Presented during the XVIII Historical Congress in Montreal, Canada, August 1995.) *Drustvena istrazivanja: (Croatian) Journal for General Social Issues*, Vol.7, No.1-2 (33-34), January 1998, pp. 89–108. http://hrcak.srce.hr/index.php?show=clanak&id_clanak_jezik=32593&lang=en

Walter, Maila L. 1990. *Science and cultural crisis: An intellectual biography of Percy Williams Bridgman (1882–1961).* Stanford, CA: Stanford University Press.

Watson, John B. 1917. "Practical and theoretical problems in instinct and habits" in *Suggestions of modern science concerning education*. Ed. Ethel S. Dummer. New York: The Macmillan Company.

———. 1914. *Behavior: An introduction to comparative psychology*. New York: Henry Holt and Company.

Watt, Richard M. 1979, 1982. *Bitter Glory: Poland and its fate 1918–1939*. New York: Barnes & Noble Books.

Weinberg, Alvin M. 1994. *The first nuclear era: The life and times of a technological fixer*. Woodbury, NY: American Institute of Physics.

Weinberg, Harry L. 1959. *Levels of knowing and existence: Studies in general semantics*. New York: Harper & Row.

Welby, Lady Victoria 1911. "Significs". *Encyclopedia Britannica*, 11th Edition, Vol. XXV (mimeographed excerpt). IGS Archives. Reprinted in *The Language of Wisdom and Folly*, ed. Irving J. Lee.

———. 1903. "What is meaning?" in *Classics in semantics*, pp. 211–220. Eds. Donald E. Hayden and E. P. Alworth. New York: Philosophical Library (1965).

Wentworth, Harold and Stuart Berg Flexner, eds. 1960. *Dictionary of American slang*. New York: Thomas Y. Crowell.

White, William Alanson. 1936. *Twentieth century psychiatry: Its contribution to man's knowledge of himself*. New York: W. W. Norton & Company. (Reprinted by Arno Press, New York, 1973)

Whitehead, Alfred North. 1961. *Alfred North Whitehead: An anthology*. Eds., F. S. C. Northrop and Mason W. Gross. New York: The Macmillan Company.

———. (1920) 1964. *The concept of nature: The Tarner Lectures delivered in Trinity College November 1919*. Cambridge: Cambridge University Press.

"Who's Who at IGS." 1949–1950. *General Semantics Bulletin* 1 & 2: 31, 64.

Whyte, Lancelot Law. 1951. "The new mathematical philosophy". *General Semantics Bulletin* 4 & 5 (Autumn-Winter 1950-1951): 44-47.

———. 1950 (1948). *The next development in man*. New York: Mentor Books.

Wigodor, Geoffrey, et al, eds. 2002 (1989). *The new encyclopedia of Judaism*. New York: New York University Press.

Williamson, Samuel H. "Seven Ways to Compute the Relative Value of a U.S. Dollar Amount, 1774 to present", *MeasuringWorth*, April 2010. www.measuringworth.com/uscompare/

Wilson, John with Thomas Hagood and Mary Alice Brennan. 2007. *Margaret H'Doubler: The Legacy of America's Dance Education Pioneer*. Cambria Press.

Wirtualna Polska (Polish internet encyclopedia). http://www.encyklopedia.wp.pl/index.html

Wittgenstein, Ludwig. 1974 (1921). *Tractatus logico-philisophicus*. Trans. D.F. Pears and B.F. McGuinness. London/New York: Routledge Classics.

———. 1922. *Tractatus logico-philisophicus*. Trans. C. K. Ogden. With an Introduction by Bertrand Russell. New York/ London: Harcourt, Brace/Kegan Paul, Trench, Trubner & Co.

Wren, Daniel A. 2001. *The History of Management Thought*. Fifth Edition. New York: Wiley.

———. 1980. "Scientific management in the U.S.S.R., with particular reference to the contribution of Walter N. Polakov". *The Academy of Management Review* (pre-1986). Academy of Management: 5 (Jan. 1980), pp. 1–11.

Wyman, David S. and Rafael Medoff. 2002. *A race against death: Peter Bergson, America, and the Holocaust*. New York: The New Press.

Zamoyski, Adam. 1987. *The Polish way: A thousand-year history of the Poles and their culture*. London: John Murray.

Znaniecki, Florian. 1968 (1940). *The Social Role of the Man of Knowledge*. New York: Harper Torchbooks.

Zipf, George Kingsley. 1952. "General semantics and the principle of least effort: Toward a synthesis". *General Semantics Bulletin* 8 & 9 (Winter-Spring 1952), pp. 7-15.

———. 1949. *Human behavior and the principle of least effort: An introduction to human ecology*. Cambridge, MA: Addison-Wesley.

Index

A

Abstracting, Abstractions 210, 215, 223 *See also Knowledge; Maps, mapping; Structural Differential.*
"...all human life is a permanent dance between different orders of..." 273
and evaluation 342
'concrete' v. 'abstract' confusion 186, 636
confusing orders or levels 273, 334. *See also Identification.*
consciousness of 246, 273, 380
Hayakawa's ladder 513, 515
lower order(s) of (non-verbal) 302–303
process of 186, 513
triad of notions related to making 216
uncertainty and 337
unified language of 367
'window' analogy 278
Acklom, George Moreby 352–353, 374
Adamic, Louis
   A Nation of Nations (1944, 1945) 547
Adams, Henry 131
Adjustment (sanity) 9
Agnosticism 33, 42, 628
Agreement 167
   major source of human disagreements 181
   to disagree 247, 640
   'universal' 247, 635, 639
Ajdukiewicz, Kaszimierz 324
Albert Hotel, New York City 573
Alcoholics Anonymous 536–537
Alcoholism 534–537
Aldrich, Mildred (writer) 106
Alexander, Franz 329
Alexander, H. B. 377
Alexander, Jerome 16, 316
   Colloid Chemistry 316
American Association for the Advancement of Science (AAAS) 191
   AK's membership 249
   AK's 1933 election as Fellow of 380
American Federation of Labor (AFL) 94
American Humanist Association 499
American Journal of Psychiatry 21, 529
American Mathematical Society
   AK elected to membership 249
American Society of Mechanical Engineers 113
Ames, Adelbert 18
Anderson, John 476, 481
Anderson, Tennessee Mitchell 315, 327
Animals 160. *See also Space-Binding.*
   copying animals in our nervous reactions 349–350
   difference between humans and 7, 122, 130
Annapolis, Maryland 250
Anne Arundel Community College 250
Anthropometer. *See Structural Differential.*

Antisemitism 111–113, 631–632, 633
   Mendel Beilis case 115
      The Fixer (Bernard Malamud) 115
   "Blood Libel" 115
   Brasol, Boris 115–117, 632
      The Protocols and World Revolution 116
   Coughlin, Charles E. ("Father Coughlin") 116
   DeBogory, Natalie 116
   "Fagin was a Jew" 113, 632
   Ford, Henry
      The Dearborn Independent (antisemitic newspaper) 116
      The International Jew (book based on *The Protocols of the Elders of Zion*) 116
   Houghton, Harris 116, 117
   in Post-War America–1920 115, 143, 157. *See also Bolshevik Propaganda, Senate Committee on.*
   in pre-World War II Europe 115, 395
   Korzybski and 111–113, 115–117, 141–147, 157–158, 169, 395–397, 531, 632, 633
   pogroms 111–112
   'Protocols of the Elders of Zion' 115
      concoction of Ochrana (Tsarist secret police) 115
      Warrant for Genocide (Norman Cohn) 115
      The Plot (Will Eisner) 115
   Nazi German 503, 504. *See also Germany, Nazi.*
   in "Social Credit" movement 116
Aristotelian (A) assumptions, orientation, system 271, 275, 331, 335
   "laws of thought" 643
   non-aristotelian revision of 567–568
   subsumed under non-aristotelian system 367
Aristotle 271
   AK's similar aims 341, 542
   Nicomachean Ethics 540–542
   on 'identity' 331–332
   On Interpretation 331
Arithmetic 167
Armour Institute of Technology 454. *See Illinois Institute of Technology.*
Arnold, Maryland 250
Assumptions 214, 272, 638
Atheism 33, 628
Atom 36
Atomic bomb 125, 303, 525–527, 538, 650
   mousetrap models 650
Atomistic principle. *See Individualization.*
'Aunt Jemima' 574, 604
Austria 24, 52. *See also Germany, Nazi.*
Autopsies 265
'Average intelligent layman' 363, 373–374
Avery, Sally 203, 291, 309, 330

B

Bachelard, Gaston 211, 272, 468
   Le Nouvel Esprit Scientifique (1934) 468
   The Philosophy of No (1969 [1940]) 468
Bacon, Francis
   baconian method 123–124
   Novum Organum (Francis Bacon) 167
   on idols 167

INDEX

Baltimore, Maryland 250
Barbour, T. 381
Barstow School (private girl's academy in Kansas City, Missouri) 391
   Kendig's educational experiment at 402–403
   Kendig's educational vision and program for 646
Bateman, Harry 203
Battle Creek diet 255
Battle of Grunwald (First Battle of Tannenberg in 1410) 629
Battle of Tannenburg (1914) 56, 629
Baugh, Hansell 445, 559, 592
Becker, Howard P. 494
Becquerel, Henri 36
Bedkow, Poland 24
Beers, Clifford 240, 259
   A Mind That Found Itself 240
'Behaviorism' 202
Beheading 124, 325
Bell, Alexander Graham 237
Bell, E.T. 133, 244, 248, 274, 290, 306, 307, 308, 495
Bendersky, Joseph
   The Jewish Threat 115–116
Bennett, Jesse Lee 250–251
   What Books Can Do For You 250
   The Essential American Tradition 251
   death of 329
Bentley, Arthur F. 356
   Linguistic Analysis of Mathematics 356
Bent, Silas (journalist, mass media critic) 293
   Ballyhoo: The Voice of The Press (1927) 293
Bergson, Peter (Hillel Kook) 504
Berman, Sanford I. 11
   Logic and General Semantics: Writings of Oliver L. Reiser and Others, 1989) 378
Bernardine (friend of AK in Rome) 42
Bernstein, B. A. (mathematical logician) 175–176
Beth, E.W. 549
Biederman, Charles 476, 481
   Art As The Evolution of Visual Knowledge (1948) 476, 585
"Big Bertha" (German World War I howitzer) 56–57
Binford, Frederick H. (physicist, educator) 586
Binkley, Goddard 408, 415
Birkoff, George D. 236, 249, 330
Bismarck, Otto Eduard Leopold von 52
Bitzen, David (pastoral counseling educator) 586
"Black Hundreds" 115
Black, Max
   1943 Review of *Science and Sanity* 494–495
   Language and Philosophy: Studies in Method (1949) 581
   on Korzybski's death 581
Bloch, Jan *See World War I, prediction of.*
Boddy, Manchester (publisher, *Los Angeles Daily News*) 492
Bohm, David 637
Bois, J. Samuel (Joseph Samuel Anselme) 12, 532
Bolshevik Propaganda, Senate Committee on 116
   report of 117, 144, 145
   Simon Wolf, testimony of 145
Bolsheviks, Bolshevism 85. *See also Russia, Soviet.*
   fear of spread beyond Russia 115
   Korzybski's attitude toward 96
Bontrager, Ora Ray 482–483, 586

Boole, George 48, 130, 135, 168, 180, 192, 209
   Investigation of the Laws of Thought 168, 192
   "The Social Aspects of Intellectual Culture" 130
Boole, Mary Everest 135
Born, Max 381
Bourbon Family 40
Bourland, D. David 19
   background and early education 574
   seminars with AK 574–575
   working at IGS 606
   receives Korzybski Fellowship (Sept. 1949) 617
   AK in loco parentis 19
   wedding plans with Virginia McMullen, February 1950 19–20
   final interview with AK 20, 21
   formulator of E-Prime. *See English, E-Prime.*
Brasefield, H. D. 193
Bréal, Michel 343
Breger, Dave (cartoonist) 415
Bretnor, Reginald 494
Brewer, Joseph 431, 432. *See also Olivet College.*
   first encounter with Mira and Alfred 353
   visits to Alfred and Mira's apartment 354
   became President of Olivet College (1934) 354
Brewer, Warren & Putnam Inc. (publishing firm) 353–354
Bridges, C. B. (Calvin Blackman)
   first meeting with AK 159
   friendship with AK 173–174, 175
   "Biological Aspects of Human Engineering" (1923) 224
   editing first draft of *Science and Sanity* 312–313
   death in 1938 447
Bridgman, P. W. (Percy Williams) 382, 418, 419
   career in physics 296
   The Logic of Modern Physics (1927) 296
   importance for AK 296–297
   operational point of view 296
   AK's debt to 298
   interest in AK's work 297–298
   help editing *Science and Sanity* 298
   friendship and disagreements with AK 298–300
   face-to-face meetings with AK 298, 299, 330, 348
   Korzybski's influence upon 300, 641
   The Nature of Physical Theory (1936) 300, 419
   The Way Things Are (1959)) 300, 419
Brill, Abraham A. (psychiatrist, translator of Freud/Jung) 330
Brinkley, J. R. 194
'Brotherhood of Man' 209
Brouwer, L. E. J. 296, 548
Brown, Dona Worral (Kendig's assistant at Barstow School) 401, 402
Brusilov, Aleksey (Russian general) 629
Bugs and skunks 76–77
Buhler, Charlotte 481
Buhler, Karl 481
The Builder (Freemason journal) 202, 213
Burke, Edmund 24
Burke, Kenneth
   A Grammar of Motives (1945) 494
Burridge, W. (physician, physiologist)
   work on colloids 403
Burroughs, William Seward II 457

Burrow, Trigant 301–302
    "Two Modes of Social Adaptation and Their Concomitants in Ocular Movements" (with Hans Syz, 1949) 612
Byron, George Gordon
    "Manfred" (epic poem) 623

C

Caesar (AK's horse in Rome) 41
Cajori, Florian (mathematician, historian of mathematics) 176, 248
Calculus, differential/integral
    getting the feel of the 30, 169
California Institute of Technology (Caltech) 192, 203, 274, 304
Campbell, Douglas G. 315, 406, 417, 426, 427, 430, 447
Campbell, John W. 494
Campbell, Mrs. Patrick 104
Campbell, Norman 247, 639–640
Canadian Car and Foundry Company 73, 74
Cantor, Georg 48, 242
Capital, intellectual 207
Capitalists 128
Carmichael, R. D. 205, 243
    The Logic of Discovery 241
    "The Logic of Relativity," Supplement I, *Science and Sanity* 205, 241, 357
Carnap, Rudolf 569
Carrel, Alexis 430–431, 614, 646, 649
    Man, The Unknown (1935) 430–431
Carter, Elton S. 375
Carus, Mary Hegeler 207
    gift to AK 207
Carus, Paul 207
Cassirer, Ernst 236, 237, 241
    Substance and Function and Einstein's Theory of Relativity 236
Categorists and Dogmatists 256
Catherine E. Cook 236
Catholicism 33, 41–42, 348, 532
Cattell, James McKeen 326, 355
Cattell, Jaques 355, 357
Causality
    circular (spiral) 140, 202
    implications of Heisenberg's principle 300
Cavalry school (Roman) 41
Chain reaction 125. See also Atomic bomb, mousetrap models; Exponential Growth.
Chain-indexes 541
Chairs 347–348, 399
Chamberlain, Neville. See Germany, Nazi: Munich Conference.
Character 536, 540–541, 542
Chase, Stuart 439
    The Tyranny of Words (1938) 439, 580
    The Proper Study of Mankind (1948) 582
Chemistry 35–36
    organic 35, 36
Chemistry-Binding 124. See also Time-Binding.
Chenoweth, Gene V. (music professor) 586
Chesire Cat (*Alice's Adventures in Wonderland*) 345, 498
Chicago 441, 550–551
    housing shortage post-World War II 545
Chicago Defender 505

Childhood of humanity 166–167
Childs, Charles M. 191
China 441, 545, 617. See also Japan, Imperial.
Chisholm, Brock 538–539, 539
Chisholm, Francis P. 476, 517, 520, 608–609
    Introductory Lectures in General Semantics (1944) 520
    1949 re-election bid for ISGS presidency 608–609
Chopin, Frederic 33, 618
Christ 42–43
Christie, Agatha
    1926 disappearance of 290
Churchill, Winston 545
Chwistek, Leon 323, 343
Clawson, Samuel G. 500
Cleckley, Hervey 494
    The Mask of Sanity 586
Cleopatra's Needle 636
Cleveland [Coleman], Anne 466, 524, 552
"Coagulate" (AK's term for "die") 16. See also Colloids,.
Coal mining 90–92
    Mexican miners 94
Coghill, G. E. (George Ellett) 364
    Anatomy and the Problem of Behaviour 364
    scientific work 384–385
    interest in *Science and Sanity* 385
    advice to Korzybski 386
    deteriorating health 386, 387
    death 482
"Cold War" 589–590
Colloids, Colloidal Behavior 139
    nature of life and consciousness 16, 267, 316
Communication (academic field). See Speech Communication.
Communism 247, 589–590, 617
Comte, August 130
Conditioned Reflexes. See Pavlov, Ivan.
Congdon, Charles B. 406, 417, 451
Congress of Mathematicians of the Slavic Countries - Warsaw, Poland, September (1929) 320
Connaught, Duke of (Governor General of Canada) 75, 104
Consciousness 101, 224, 631,
Conspiracy theorists 115–116
Control theory 140
    Feedback, negative 140, 201–202
    Powers, William T. 201–202, 370, 637
        Behavior: The Control of Perception (1973) 201
    Perceptual Control Theory (PCT) 201–202
Cook, Catherine E. ("Cookie") 207, 236
Coolidge, Calvin 233
Correspondence
    method of handling used at IGS 16–17
    records of AK's 82
Corrigan, Douglas "Wrong Way" 442
Crane, Cornelius 440, 445–447, 449, 450–451, 463–464, 465–466, 474, 483, 487–489
Culp, Harvey 363
Curie, Marie and Pierre 36
Cybernetics. See Control theory; Wiener, Norbert.
Czechoslovakia. See Germany, Nazi: Munich Conference; Germany, Nazi: Annexation/Invasion of Czechoslovakia.

INDEX

D

Dabo, Leon (U.S. painter) 88
Daffodil (cat of Charlotte Schuchardt) 16
Damrosch, Walter (music composer) 90
    "Danny Deever" (song from Kipling poem) 90, 630
Danzig (now Gdansk, Poland) 39, 320, 461.
Dating 261, 279, 336-337. *See Extensional devices.*
Davies, Norman 44, 115
Davis, Tenney L. 236, 241
Davis, Watson 378
Deception 479
Defense Mapping Agency 8
de Forest, Alfred V. 234
de Forest, Lockwood, II 233-234
DeKruif, Paul 139
Deladier, Edouard. *See Germany, Nazi: Munich Conference.*
Delayed reaction 348
"Delousing" 18, 363
Delusions 341
Democracy 49, 462
Democritus 35
Denfeld, Vice Admiral Louis E. 548
De Rerum Natura (Lucretius) 130
Determinism
    two-valued, classical 338
    indeterminism, denial of structure with 338-339
    probabilistic, many-valued 339
    test for structure 339
Detroit Mathematics Club 213
Devereux, George 446
Dewey, John 224
Dewing, Arthur Stone 466
Dewing, Frances Hall Rousmaniere 466
Dewing [Morain], Mary 466
Dialectical Materialism 589
Dictators 527
Differences 331. *See also Sameness and similarity.*
Discovery 166, 273
Dmowski, Roman (Polish nationalist leader) 85
Doctrine 200, 246
Doob, Leonard 603, 609
    Social Psychology (1952) 603
Dostal, B. F. 360
Douglas, C. H. 114, 116
Dover, Delaware Public Schools' GS "Teacher Training Program" 587
Drake Hotel (Chicago) 205, 241
Dr. Dick 525
Dueling 40-41, 78-79
Dunham, Barrows
    Man Against Myth (1947) 580-581
Durham, Robert Lee 513
E.P. Dutton & Company 155-156, 634
Dutton, Edward Payson (E.P) 155, 634

E

Eddington, Arthur Stanley 111, 179, 209, 248
    Space, Time, and Gravitation (1920) 187
    The Nature of the Physical World (1928) 612
Edgerly, Mira. *See Korzybska, Mira Edgerly (MEK)*
Edgerly, Sam (father of MEK) 102
Edgerly, Rose Haskell (mother of MEK) 102
Education 194
    preventive 246
Eeden, Frederik Willem van 548
Einstein, Albert 111, 216, 297, 310
    education at Swiss Polytechnic 34
    1905 papers 48-49
    residence in U.S. 383
    AK's attempts to get Einstein's attention 383-384
    Einstein's 1946 appeal for a 'new type of thinking' 539-540
    Einstein's eventual 'review' of *Science and Sanity* 384
Eldridge, Frank Reed and Kathleen Tamagawa 548
    General Semantics (based on lectures by James A. Saunders, 1949) 548. *See also Saunders, James A.*
Elementalism, elementalistic 189, 278
    terms 189-190, 277, 311
'Emotions' 210
'Empiricism' 195
    AK's rejection of 210
Engineering
    professional training of AK 35
    ethos of making things work 38
    human engineering 125, 241
    methods 196
English 311, 322
    English Minus Absolutisms (EMA) 13
    E-Prime (English minus all forms of the verb "to be") 20
Epistemology 237. *See also Knowledge; Methodology.*
    applied, up-to date 17. *See also 'General Semantics' (GS).*
    importance for science and life 207, 538
    "epistemodesty" 369, 652
    and 'intellectual' virtues 541
    informed by up-to-date science 272, 330-331
Epstein, Paul 203
Escape From Freedom (Erich Fromm, 1942) 491
Esprit de corps 55
Essentialism, essentialist 279, 331
Esser, P. H. 549
Etc.: A Review of General Semantics 505, 617. *See Hayakawa, S. I. See also Society for General Semantics.*
    founding by Society for General Semantics 496
    Kendig and Korzybski as "Consulting Editors" 505, 517, 568
    Korzybski's contributions (1943-1947) 521, 529, 567
Etc. (Et cetera). *See Extensional devices.*
    as "junior infinity" 337
    special punctuation for 337
Ethics
    'aristotelian' 540
    character 540-541
    non-essentialist, non-elementalistic approach 541
    virtues and knowledge 540-541
Euclid 48, 200
Euclidean geometry 200, 260
Evaluation (as term combining 'thinking' and 'feeling') 17, 20, 342-343, 418, 540
    un-speakable (non-verbal) nature of 342-343
Evans, Helen L. 434
    "Portrait in Outline" of AK (poem) 436

Events 186–187, 216, 223–224, 226
Excluded middle, law of 296
Exponential growth 125–127
  in human history 190
  'secret' of the atomic bomb 525
Extensional. *See also Intensional.*
  attitude, orientation 278–279, 347–348, 368
  definitions 278
  devices 13, 336–337, 409–410, 411, 480
  extensionalization, to extensionalize 409
  methods 279

F

'Fact(s)' 264, 335, 337
Fairchild, David (botanical explorer) 21, 236
  first meeting with AK 236
  enthusiasm and support for AK's work 237–238
  contact with Einstein 383
Fairchild, Marian Bell (daughter of Alexander Graham Bell) 21, 237
Fankuchin, Isadore 481
Farrar, Clarence B. (Editor, *Am. Journal of Psychiatry*) 21, 417
Fear 348
Ferguson, Charles 113, 119, 123–124
  The Great News 113
  The Revolution Absolute 114, 119, 122
Fermi, Enrico 525
Field Museum of Natural History 446
Finger Painting. See also Shaw, Ruth Faison.
  'semantic' aspects of 400–401
Fink, David Harold 510
  Release From Nervous Tension (1943) 510
First Corinthians 223, 622
Fishbein, Morris 376
Fiske, Vocha 452
Flappers. *See Gulliver's Travels.*
Fox, Roy E. 516
Frame of reference 188
France 442–443
Philip Frank
  Einstein: His Life and Times (1947) 573
Franz Ferdinand (Archduke, heir of Austro-Hungarian throne) 50
Franz Josef (Emperor of Austria and King of Hungary)
  AK's encounters with 28, 39
Freeman, Walter II 265–266
Freemasonry 202
Freud, Sigmund 301
  The Ego and the Id 301
  Beyond the Pleasure Principle 301
Frohman, Bertrand S. 560
  Brief Psychotherapy: A Handbook for Physicians on the Clinical Aspects of Neuroses (1948) 560, 583–584
Fuller, Harold de Wolf 290, 292

G

Galois Institute of Mathematics (Long Island University) 406
Gantt, H. L. 113
  Organizing for Work 113
  The Gantt Chart: A Working Tool of Management (by Walter Clark, Walter N. Polakov and Frank W. Trabold, 1922) 149

Gantt, W. Horsley (Pavlovian researcher) 316
Gardner, Martin 193
Garlick, Evelyn 570
Gasiorowski, Waclaw (Polish novelist) 85–86
Gates, R. Lindley "Lynn" 606
Gdansk, Poland. *See Danzig.*
Generalizations 469
General Semantics Bulletin (GSB) 13, 18, 567, 617
General Semantics Congresses
  First American Congress for General Semantics (Ellensburg, Washington, March 1935) 402–404
  Second American Congress on General Semantics (University of Denver, 1941) 477–478, 481–482
  Third Congress on General Semantics (University of Denver, 1949) 592–593, 611–614, 654–655
'General Semantics' (GS) 9, 13
  alternative names
    "General Anthropology" 17
    general theory of time-binding 17, 654
    "human engineering" 125, 241
    "humanology" 257, 304
  application, importance of 521
    learning to apply 542, 543–544
  basic subject of 342
  birth announcement of 346–347
  character development and 542–544
  confused with "semantics" 17, 439–440, 462, 506, 564–565, 654
  courses and teachers 546, 547, 586–587
  epistemology, up-to-date and applied 17, 310, 324, 429, 538. *See also Epistemology.*
  foundation for a science of man 340, 430–431
  general theory of evaluation 17, 433
  heuristic approach 367–368, 433
  interdisciplinary nature 275
  "modus operandi" of the non-aristotelian system 367
  not a non-aristotelian logic 378, 578
  origins of inquiry 499
  popularizing 19
  and psychotherapy 406–407
  scientific enterprise 369
    research and evidence 276, 369–370, 388, 389, 390, 393, 520
  study groups 548, 587
  system of interrelated formulations 331, 366–367
  theory of sanity 368
Genthe, Arnold (art photographer) 103
  As I Remember 103
Geometry
  euclidean 48, 200
  four-dimensional 48
  non-euclidean 48, 200
George, Henry 130
  Progress and Poverty 130
George Patton, Colonel and Mrs. 110
Germany
  Prussian 24
  Teutonic Knights 628
  destruction of original Prussians 628
  East Prussia 56, 628
  expansionism 49, 52, 504, 628–629

INDEX

Germany (*continued*)
  World War I
    two-front strategy 52
    U-Boat attacks on shipping 72
Germany, Nazi. *See also Hitler, Adolf.*
  Hitler election (1933) and Nazi takeover
    AK's response 372
  SA Brown Shirts (pre-1934 Nazi party militia) 395
  1934 consolidation of Nazi rule and persecution of 'untermenschen' 395
  1938 Austrian Annexation 441
  Munich Conference (1938) 442.
  Annexation/Invasion of Czechoslovakia 441, 442–443
  1939 invasion of Poland 461
  Nazi "war on nerves" (propaganda and psycho-logical warfare) 469
  "criminal destruction of Poland" 502
  antisemitism and Nazi ideology 503, 504
  attempted extermination of the Jewish People 531
  1945 surrender of 523
  Nuremburg War Crimes Trials 531
Gibbs, Willard 36, 180, 602
Gibran, Khalil 622
Gilchrest 73, 170
Gill, Robert S. 234
Ginsburg, Jekuthiel 521–522, 538
Gleeson, Thomas A. 602–603, 653
Glicksberg, Charles L. 547
Glover, Halcott 252
Godel, Kurt 133, 578
Gompers, Samuel (President of Am. Federation of Labor) 94, 96, 117, 181
Goodima, Captain 74
Gordon, Sloane 89
Graicunas, Vytautas A. *See Urwick, Lyndall*.
Graven, Philip (psychiatrist student of AK) 257
  private course of instruction with AK 276
  AK's desire for help from 301, 315–316, 356
  'writer's block' of 362–363
  early sympathy toward Hitler and Nazi Germany 396, 397
  end of contact with AK 397
"The Great Instauration" (Francis Bacon) 167
Great Pyramid 187
Great Britain 442–443
Great Depression (Economic) of 20th Century 318, 326
Green, Edwin 492. *See Los Angeles Daily News.*
Greko (AK's Italian fencing teacher) 40
Grenoble Hotel 219, 237, 239
Grieg, Edvard
  "Asa's Death" 622
Group Dynamics 615
Grove-Korski, Julian 139
Guide for the Perplexed (Maimonides [Moshe ben Maimon]) 146
Guiles, A.P. (pastoral counseling educator) 586
Gulliver's Travels (Jonathan Swift)
  "A Voyage to Laputa" (new epigraph for *Science and Sanity*) 358, 462, 479
  "flappers" 479
  "yahoos" 563

H

Habdank (Abdank) Skarbek (Korzybski family clan) 627
  family heraldic crest 627
Hadamard, Jacques
  The Psychology of Invention in the Mathematical Field 577
Hale, George 176, 192, 635
Hamilton, Ralph C. 12, 21, 558, 574, 600, 622, 650
  work at IGS 575, 595–599, 600
  relationship and conversations with AK 597
Handedness 434
Hanover family (German noble patrons of Leibniz) 165–166
Hanson, N. R. 637
Happiness, extensional theory of 433
Harding, Warren G. 233
Hardy, Edward L. (President, San Diego State Teachers College) 192
Harvard University Tercentenary (1936) 424–425
Haseldon, R.B. 405
  "The Korzybski" cocktail 405
Haskell, Mellen Woodman (Dean, Mathematics Department at The University of California, Berkeley) 176
Hayakawa, Margedant 454–455, 516, 649
Hayakawa, S. I. (Samuel Ichiye) 17, 270, 443–444, 454–455, 505
  Language in Action (1939, etc.) 444, 455
  as editor of *ETC.: A Review of General Semantics* 496, 505
  problematic presentation of 'general semantics' 514, 554, 650
  lapses 515, 565, 568
  AK's support for 516
  hostility towards AK 516–517, 649
  Language in Thought and Action (1949) 17, 444, 581–582
  successful 1949 bid for presidency of International Society for General Semantics 608–609
Hayek, Friedrich 151
  The Road to Serfdom (1944) 151
Haywood, H. L. (Roy) 202, 213, 269, 270, 282, 311
Hazlitt, Henry 439
Hedin, R. F. 476, 481
Heinlein, Robert 494
Hellenism 396
Heraclitus 332, 511
Herrick, C. Judson 267, 280, 482
  The Brains of Rats and Men 267
"Hilltop Club" 132, 132–133
Hindenburg, Paul von 395
Hiroshima and Nagasaki, atomic bombing of 525
Hitler, Adolf 52, 372, 395–397
  suicide 523
Hitlerism 395–397. *See also Germany, Nazi.*
Hitler-Stalin pact 461
Hobson, Wilder 550
Holtzman, Harry 586
Hook, Sidney 376–377
Hooten, Ernest 438
Horney, Karen 447
Horses 26–27, 41, 56, 62, 67
Horseshoes 629–630
Hotel 33 (West 51st Street, New York City) 593, 605, 619
Hotel Del Coronado (San Diego, CA) 189

Houck Affair (Knute and Gladys) 282–294
  nervous breakdown of Dr. Knute Houck, St. Elizabeths psychiatrist 282–285
  disappearance of Gladys Houck, wife of Knute 284
  AK's role as sympathetic onlooker 282–284, 287
  inept police investigation with Knute Houck suspected of murder 285, 289
  remains of Gladys Houck found 291
    autopsy findings 291
  sensational news stories about AK and his 'Thought Machine' (Structural Differential) 285–287, 290–291
  AK's reputation, defense and support of 287–288, 289–290, 292–293
  AK's lawsuit for damages (Korzybski v. Underwood & Underwood, Inc.) 293–294
Houck, George M. (Science Press) 357, 440
Howard, L. O. 191
Hull, Albert W.
  "Qualifications of a Research Physicist" (1931) 612
Human action, general theory of 241
Human engineering 125. *See also* Library of Human Engineering
  abandoning the term 257
  and psychiatry 240
  series of four talks by AK and friends (May 1923) 224
The Humanist 499
Human nature 217
Humanology 257, 271, 304
Humans
  difference between animals and 7, 122
  differences between different kinds of enterprise 122
Huntington, Edward V. 235, 330, 381
Hutchins, Robert Maynard 551
Huxley, Aldous 475
  Words And Their Meanings (1940) 475
Hyphens 336. *See Extensional devices*

I

Identification 311, 334, 367, 397
'Identity'
  AK's criticism of use of term 346
  AKs denial of 331, 332
  does not exist in the world 334
  Heraclitus on 332
  'is' of 310, 333, 337
  Leibniz on 332
  Quine on 457–458
  'sameness' 183
  symbolic equivalence in contrast with 332–333
  view of Aristotle 331–332, 643
  Wittgenstein on 332
Idols 167, 348
Ignorance 341
Illinois [formerly Armour] Institute of Technology 520
Imagination 267
Indeterminism. *See Determinism.*
Indexing 279, 336. *See Extensional devices.*
Indian Mountain School (Lakeville, Connecticut) 550
Individualization, principle of 279, 332. *See also Non-identity.*
'Infinity', 'Infinitesmal' 577

Inflexibility 253
'Insanity'. *See also 'Sanity'.*
  logical fate and 260
  'logic' in 259–260
  mechanism of 245–246
  recognizing yourself in the insane 259, 597
Institute of General Semantics (IGS) 475
  efforts to establish 429, 435
  incorporation in Chicago, Illinois (May 1938) 440
    as non-profit institution for "Linguistic Epistemologic Scientific Research and Education." 440
  first headquarters, at 1330 East 56th St. 440–441, 450
  aims 441, 462
  Board of Trustees 447, 450–451, 463–464, 488–489, 506, 566–567
  publicity 447, 449, 475, 482, 519, 546–549, 585–586, 603, 614
  correspondence 450, 596–597
  second headquarters, at 1234 East 56th St. (1939-1946) 450–451
  "Honorary Trustees" 451, 463, 467, 509
  long term plans 452, 506–507, 544
  fund-raising and financial struggles 452, 465–466, 476, 483, 488–489, 506–507, 509, 519, 523, 552–553, 566–567
  IGS Fellows 488, 495, 566, 567
  Associates of IGS (approved workers in GS), plans for program to train 544
  fellowship to study with Korzybski funded by Robert K. Straus 559, 567
  forced to move from Chicago in 1946 545–546
  leaving Chicago and relocation of headquarters to Connecticut (1946) 550–551, 552, 557, 560, 560–562
  location in Lime Rock, Connecticut
    Barnum House bought by Kendig; rented for nominal fee from her 561
    location and weather 561
    as office and residence 562
    aborted sale in 1949 605–606
  becomes a membership organization in 1947 566–568
  celebration of 10th anniversary of the founding of the Institute of General Semantics (Chatham Hotel, NYC, Jan. 1948) 589
IGS publications (1938-1950)
  General Semantics: Papers from the First American Congress for General Semantics (Hansell Baugh, ed., 1938) 445
  Language and Speech Hygiene: An Application of General Semantics. General Semantics Monograph I (Wendell Johnson, 1939) 455, 505
  A Memorandum on the Institute of General Semantics (AK, 1939/1940) 462–463, 467
  General Semantics Monograph III, A Theory of Meaning Analyzed with a "Foreword" by Korzybski and Kendig (1942) 497–499
  "The Essence of Judaism" (Hans Kohn, 1934), with "Foreword" by Alfred Korzybski (IGS reprint, 1943) 504
  Papers from the Second American Congress on General Semantics: Non-Aristotelian Methodology (Applied) for Sanity in Our Time (Kendig, ed., 1943) 497, 505

IGS publications (1938-1950) *continued*
   The Technique of Semantic Relaxation (Charlotte Schuchardt, 1943) 505
   Introductory Lectures in General Semantics (F. P. Chisholm, 1944) 520
   membership mailings 567-568
   A Non-Aristotelian Study of Philosophy (Anthony M. Economides, 1947) 559
   Selections from Science and Sanity (1948) 559
   Structural Differential wall charts (1949) 617
   Time-Binding: The General Theory, Two Papers 1924-1926 (1949) 617
   General Semantics Bulletin (GSB) 617
IGS Seminars (1938-1950)
   by AK, 18, 441, 443, 445, 446, 447, 452, 454-460, 476, 478, 481, 482-483, 490, 494, 505, 509, 523, 529, 532, 569, 573, 611-612, 620
   by others 520, 523
   seminar-workshops 509-510, 523, 557-559, 615
   staff members 586
Intellectual life 216
'Intelligence' 392, 462
Intensional. *See also Extensional.*
   definitions 278
   orientation, attitude 279, 347-348, 458
International Labor Conference, League of Nations 114, 117-118, 181
International Labor Organization (I.L.O.) 117-118
International Mathematical Congress (1924) 243, 244, 247-249
International Non-Aristotelian Library 354, 371
   proposed volumes for 360, 462, 478
International Non-Aristotelian Library Publishing Company 355
International Society for General Semantics (ISGS). *See Society for General Semantics.*
International Society For The Study of Significs. *See Significs.*
Introspection 224, 267, 342
'Intuitions' 210
I.Q. (Intelligence Quotient) 388-389, 402, 645
Ischchlondsky, N. E. 446, 465
'Ises' 311, 333
I.W.W. (Industrial Workers of the World) 96

J

Jabotinsky, Vladimir (Ze'ev) 504
Jacobi, Lotte 619
Janssen, Guthrie E. 559-560, 568, 592
   edited *Selections from Science and Sanity* (1948) 559
   marriage to Guila Beattie 560, 590
   Basic Human Engineering Handbook (1950) 560
   A Salesman's Handbook Course in Human Engineering (1950) 560
Japan, Imperial 441
   Russo-Japanese War (1904-1905) 44, 46
   "Rape of Nanking" by Japanese Imperial Army 441
   Japanese attack on Pearl Harbor, Hawaii (1941) 488
   Hiroshima and Nagasaki bombings 525
   1945 surrender 525
   Emperor Hirohito 525, 526

Jeliffe, Smith Ely 237
Jennings, H. S. (zoologist) 239, 252
   "Heredity and Environment" article (Jennings, 1924) 252
   Prometheus or Biology and the Advancement of Man (1925) 239, 252
Jesuits 33, 41
Jews, Jewish culture/civilization 111-113, 115-117, 141-147, 503. *See also Antisemitism; Zionism, Zionists.*
   AK's sense of connection with 396, 502-503, 531
   "Chosen people" notion 147, 633-634
   dynamic 'time' orientation 396
   Jews of Poland 113, 631-632
   as middleman minority 113
   refugees 442
   special targets of the Nazi government 395, 502, 531
Johnecheck, Pearl (First IGS office manager and confidential secretary for AK, 1938-1944) 440-441, 451, 466, 508, 518-519, 529
Johnson, Burges (writer, friend of MEK) 103, 155
   As Much as I Dare 103
Johnson, Kenneth G. (korzybskian scholar/teacher) 615
Johnson, Wendell 443, 454, 552-554, 571
   controversial research 647
   "diagnosogenic" theory of stuttering 455
   People in Quandaries (1946) 455, 553-554

K

Kahler, Erich 22, 147, 546
Kansas City, Missouri 122
Karpinski, Louis C. (mathematician, historian of mathematics and cartography) 218, 248
Kasner, Edward 133, 522
   Mathematics and the Imagination (with J. Newman, 1940) 522
Kelley, Douglas McGlashan 479, 493, 527-529, 558, 566, 592-593
   "The Use of General Semantics And Korzybskian Principles As An Extensional Method of Group Psychotherapy In Traumatic Neurosis" (1951) 528
   22 Cells in Nuremberg (1947) 531
   on deception and magic 479, 558
Kendig, M. (Marjorie Mercer) 16. *See also Barstow School.*
   early life and unusual schooling 391
   publishing career 391
   New York City milieu in 1920s 391, 645
   studies in education with Ogden and Piaget 391
   Masters degree course and thesis at Columbia University Teachers College 391, 393, 645
   first meeting with AK (1934) 391, 392-393
   as Head of Barstow School, 1934-1937 (private girl's academy in Kansas City, Missouri) 391, 392-393
   "This Living Barstow" (M. Kendig's March 1937 address to the Barstow School community) 646
   "Language Re-Orientation of High School Curriculum and Scientific Control of Neuro-Linguistic Mechanisms for Better Mental Health and Scholastic Achievement" (M. Kendig, 1935 presentation at A.A.A.S meeting, St. Lous, MO.) 401
   as educational advisor in absentia at Barstow School, 1937-1938 402
   AK's concerns about 422-423

Kendig, M. (*continued*)
  Education Director and Assistant Director at the Institute of General Semantics (1938-1950) 440, 451, 452–453, 488, 507, 546, 558, 592–593, 620
  mother dies 546
  buys Barnum House (becomes IGS home) in Lime Rock, Connecticut 561
  introduces NTL "T-Group" method of group discussion at IGS seminar-workshops 571, 615
Kennedy, Roy J. 307
Kent, Janice V. 586
Keyes, Ken Jr. 512–513
  How To Develop Your Thinking Ability (1950) 617
Keyes, Ken Jr. and Roberta Rymer 617
  GS educational projects 513
  Ken stricken with polio (1946) 572
  AK biography project 572–573
Keyes, Roberta Rymer 512–513
Keyser, Cassius J. 48, 133–137, 194, 199, 522–523
  early life and education 133
  The Plane Geometry of the Point in Space of Four Dimensions (doctoral dissertation) 133
  Science and Religion: The Rational and the Superrational (1914) 133
  The New Infinity and the Old Theology (1915) 133
  mathematics, approach to 133, 135, 633, 637
  The Human Worth of Rigorous Thinking (1916, 1925) 133
  as AK's mentor 135
  close friendship with AK and MEK 135
  first wife Ella 135
  updating AK, help in 136
  editing help with *Manhood of Humanity (MoH)* 136
  promotion of *MoH* 159, 170-171
  writings on time-binding and *MoH* 170–171
  Mathematical Philosophy: A Study of Fate and Freedom (1922) 133, 194, 199–201, 242, 253, 336
    "Korzybski's Concept of Man" chapter 199
    theory of postulates and doctrinal functions 210
    AK's review article of 208, 209–210
  health 245
  Thinking About Thinking (1926) 210
  Mole Philosophy and Other Essays (1927) 295
  promotion of AK's work 297–298
  Pastures of Wonder (1929) 318
  AK's desire not to burden 301, 318
  second wife Sara 135, 318
  anticipation of AK's second book 351
  Humanism and Science (1931) 351
  opinion and reviews of *Science and Sanity* 374
  death 570–571
Keyser, Ella 135
  illness of 270
  death of 282
Keyser, Sara 135, 318
Kiki Netouche (one of Alfred and Mira's pet monkeys) 349–350, 416
Kiki no. 2 (their other pet monkey) 350–351, 424, 428
Kind Hearts and Coronets (1949 movie satire of Edwardian English high society) 104

Kipling, Rudyard
  Barrack-Room Ballads 98–99
  "Danny Deever" (poem) 98
    Walter Damrosch song of 90, 630
  "Arithmetic on the Frontier" (poem) 101
Kirkpatrick, Elizabeth 559
Kluckhohn, Clyde 587
Klyce, Scudder 253–254
  Universe 254
  Sins of Science 254
  the 'sins' of 254
Kneller, Albert William 618
Knowledge 8. *See also Abstracting* and *Epistemology*.
  bluffing about 31
  evolution of human 209–210
  false 146, 246, 300
  geometrical (mathematical) structure of 246
  involving a search for structure 339
  joint phenomenon of observer and observed 209
  "knowledge is power" 167
  language as 'filter' 335–337
  lies and misrepresentations 289
  possibility of reliable 196, 333
  self-reflexiveness and 335
  spiral structure of 335. *See also Time-Binding*, "spiral theory" of
  structure of 245, 272
  uncertainty and 337–341
  universal encyclopedia of 166, 167
  virtues and values 540–541
Knox, Frank 491
Kohn, Hans 147, 504
  "The Essence of Judaism" 147, 396, 504
Konvitz, Milton 586
Korzybska, Adrianna (AK's sister) 28–30
  AK's 1929 reunion with 321
  unknown status after World War II 322
Korzybska, Helena Rzewuska (AK's mother) 44–45, 279–280, 304, 359
  early life 28
  demandingness 28
  AK's perception of 104, 321
  AK's Post-WWI correspondence with 99
  AK's 1929 Warsaw reunion with 320–321
  property manager of 320, 321
    marriage to 322, 359
  death of 438
Korzybska, Mira Edgerly 317. *See also Korzybski (Alfred and Mira)*.
  year of birth, uncertain 102
  early life in Illinois, Michigan, Kansas City, MO., San Francisco 102
  self-education as portrait painter 103, 104
  Guatemala, travel as teenager to 103
  career as painter in British Isles and Europe 104
  friendship with Gertrude Stein and Alice B. Toklas 104, 106
  friendship with Mildred Aldrich 106
  first marriage 105
  wealthy clientele 106, 175
  studio at Stoneleigh Court (Washington, D.C.), 1918-1919 102

INDEX

Korzybska, Mira Edgerly (*continued*)
  meeting AK 102, 104–105
  courtship and wedding with AK 105–106
  Countess, title as 106
  admiration of Alfred and his work 131, 235, 281, 484
  encouragement and help to AK 106, 108, 131, 132, 270, 280, 420, 570, 572, 618–619
  altruism of 104, 106
  'Sarah Bernhardt' style 421, 485–486
  industriousness 104
  'intellectual' style 105, 108
  money management 106, 281
  trunks and belongings 212
  AK's disapproving attitudes toward 420–421, 426, 485
  dissatisfactions with AK 484, 485
  as portrait painter,
    earnings 102, 106
    specializing in portraits on ivory 102
    painting methods and problems 107
    painting exhibits 172, 237, 327, 485
    need to search for portrait commissions 175, 192, 235
    painting career, waning and end of 484
  portrait of AK ("The Time-Binder", 1922) 198
  health problems 21, 314–315, 524–525, 570, 576–577, 599, 618, 622
  friendship with Charlotte Schuchardt [Read] 103
  self-education efforts of 421, 424–426, 486, 487
  on AK's death 21
  "The Wonder Star" at AK's memorial service 622
  death in 1954 623
Korzybski, Alfred 194
  brief biography 9–10
  pronunciation of name 13
  family background of titled nobility (Counts) 25, 28, 626. *See also* Habdank (Abdank) Skarbek Clan.
  influence on others 10
    unacknowledged 274
  inventions 36, 47, 68–69, 80–81, 107
  as multi-lingual speaker 31, 33, 39 , 73, 74, 91
  as networker 132–133
  reading habits 137
  speaking skills 87, 89, 91–92, 100, 315
Korzybski, Alfred (boyhood, education, early manhood)
  boyhood athletics 32
  career dreams 30, 33–34
  getting the "feel of the differential calculus" as a small child 30, 169
  "the little master"
    supervising workers 25–26
    lifesaver in medical emergencies 25
  training horses 26–27
  education at Warsaw realschule (scientific-technical high school) 31
    study-habits 32, 36–37
    Latin and Greek, lack in early education 32, 33–34
  at Warsaw Polytechnic 35–38
    chemical vs. mechanical engineering as profession 35, 89
    final examinations 37
  travels throughout Europe 39
  in Rome (1902–1904) 39–43, 628

  dueling 40–41
  "Maladetto Pollaco" (Accursed Pole) 40–41
  anti-Tsarist underground activities 44, 49
  sentenced to Siberia 44
  during first Russian Revolution (1904-1905)
    property management 44–45
    teacher at girls' school 46
    advice to striking peasants 46
  pre-World War I activities
    focus on study, reading 48, 50
    legal career 47
    love life of 39, 40, 48, 104
    management of family's properties 47
    mood 47–50
    pet bulldog 47
Korzybski, Alfred (World War I Service/Activities)
  support of Tsarist Russia and Allies 52–54
  Second Russian Army Headquarters Intelligence Department Cavalry 54–55, 68
  'private with a string' 54
  "Translator of the General Staff" 55
  artillery experience 56, 73, 74–75, 76, 78
  Battle of Tannenberg 56, 629
  spycraft and intelligence work 57–60, 61–63
  retreat from Plock 61–63
  Battle of Lodz (1914) 63–65
  bomb-making by 68–69
  in St. Petersburg (Petrograd) 69
  Bodyguard Heavy Artillery Regiment, assignment to 70
  Petawawa, Canada, 'Junior Inspector' of ammunition for Russian Military Commission 72–79
    English, study of 73
  chief loading inspector, Brooklyn waterfront 81, 81–82
  French-Polish Military Commission, organizing and recruiting work for 86–88
  U.S. Fuel Administration
    traveling speaker, West Virginia and Maryland coal-mining towns 90–93
    coal-mine production inspector, Texas 93
    U.S.F.A. delegate to Pan-American Labor Conference (Nov. 1918) 94
  press coverage during war 95
  wartime afflictions and injuries. *See Korzybski, Alfred (health)*.
  view of United States post-WWI 97, 99
  renouncing Russian, gaining Polish citizenship 97
  post-war personal finances 99, 100
Korzybski, Alfred (life with Mira)
  first meeting 104–105
  companionability 104
  courtship 105
  differences in education and 'thinking' style 105, 106
  wedding (Jan. 17, 1919) 105, 105–106
  newlyweds in Washington, D.C. 106–108
  unwarranted speculation about 106
  sex life 106, 173, 174, 194
  marathon conversations 107
  Poland, plans to go to 106, 114, 156, 212, 213, 214, 217, 219 279, 280, 320, 359, 371, 438
  AK's work for Hanover Trust Company (Boston bank) 111

Korzybski, Alfred (life with Mira) *continued*
  MEK in Washington and traveling for work; AK in New York at National Arts Club 111. *See also* Ferguson, Charles; "New Machine"; "Social Credit" movement.
  AK delegate for Poland at League of Nations International Labor Conference 114, 117–118, 181
  AK's work for Polish Mechanics Company 118–119
  visiting MEK's sister in Missouri, April 1920. *See also Manhood of Humanity*.
  Greenwich Village (NYC) residence, 1920-1921 138
  periods of travel and separation in married life 173, 635
  1921 travels in California 157, 172–173, 176–177, 281, 318, 398, 420–421
  attempts to have a child 194
  Midwest travels (1922) 203–211
  return to New York City (1922) 212
  residing in rural Maryland (1924-1925) 250–251, 252
    work together with the Anthropometer 255
  living in Washington, D.C. (1925-1927) 255, 256–257
    pet kinkajou (1925-1927) 257
  finances 280, 295, 316–317, 329, 372, 393, 449
  residence at 321 Carleton Ave., Brooklyn, New York (1927-1936) 280, 291–292, 295, 354
  1928 year apart (MEK traveling for work, AK to California to write *Science and Sanity* first draft) 304
  return to Brooklyn (May/June 1929) 316, 318
  AK's 1929 trip to Poland) 231, 320–327
    Korzybski family property 321–322
  AK and MEK as team to produce Alfred's work 318
  loans to AK's mother 322
    second mortgage for 66 Wilcza 322
  pet monkeys 317, 349–351
  visit to Harvard (Nov. 1933) 381–382
  move to Cambridge, Massachusetts (1936) 418, 423
  serious marital conflict 426–428, 429
  "Donk" and "Monk" 427–428, 577
  Mira's long trip to South America (1937-1938) 428, 429–430, 435, 438
  Chicago (1938 move) 438, 447–448
    living arrangements (1938-1946) 452, 487
  Alfred becoming U.S. citizen 438
  "Do you see RED?" incident, 1940 471–472, 474, 475
  MEK's 1941 trip in Eastern U.S. 484–486
  lost property in Poland after World War II 322
  gradual reconciliation 487, 507, 524
  long-distance relationship when IGS forced to move from Chicago in 1946 545-546, 562, 570, 599, 603, 605, 607, 611, 614, 618, 621
  Alfred to Chicago to see Mira 578, 611, 614
Korzybski, Alfred (itinerant teacher, 1934-1938) 395, 398–399
  1935 lectures and seminars 400, 401, 403, 404–405, 406–407
  at Barstow School 399–402
    AK's interest in finger painting 400
  efforts to get funding for his work 416–417, 418, 426
  1937 Seminar at Harvard Business School 429
  1937 Olivet College Seminar 431–435
  other 1937 seminars, lectures 435
  Peoria State Hospital, March 1938 440

Korzybski, Alfred (at IGS, 1938-1950)
  IGS Director and Board of Trustees President 440, 449, 500–501
  first seminar at IGS 441–442
  almost total involvement with work 484, 595–597
  mixed reputation, concerns about 472–473
  intended third book 488–489
  "future-work program" (1944) 509, 523
  World War II responses/activities
    close following of news 502
    concern for fate of the Jews 502–504, 531
    critique of 'Maginot line mentality' 470
    suggestion of sanity tribunal for Hitler, et al. 469, 502
    taking it personally 470, 502
    "Working on National Morale" 491–493
  1947 trip with Charlotte Schuchardt to Keyeses in Warm Springs, Georgia to record memoirs 572–573
  publicity about his work 580–587, 588
  students and co-workers 586–587
  'writing forays' to New York City with Charlotte Schuchardt 573, 593–594, 599, 605–611, 619–620
  last seminar 620
Korzybski, Alfred (death, March 1950) 16, 20
  obituary notices 21
  reactions to 21–22
Korzybski, Alfred (memorial service, etc.) 622–623
  Mira's inability to come due to ill health 622
  death mask 623
  autopsy 623
  cremation and burial 623
Korzybski, Alfred (as teacher)
  academic respectability 568, 569–570
  AK's seminars, group format 410
  assessments of AK's pedagogy 408
  atomic mousetrap demonstration of chain reaction 573, 650
  attention, important to interest by any means 303, 642
  content and presentation 407, 573
  development of seminar format 407
  follow-up with students 412–413
  footnotes 642
  Graicunas "Span of Control" diagram. *See* Urwick, Lyndall.
  neuro-semantic relaxation 414–415
  non-linear style of exposition 407–408, 573
  presentation style 315
  "recipe for making geniuses" 277
  stories, use of 574
  student responses to 412, 533–537
  teaching load at IGS 18
  translating problems 410–411
  use of an assistant 408, 573
  visualization with diagrams 204, 215, 226, 407, 514
  work with individual students (personal interviews, etc.) 19, 246, 410, 410–413, 450, 534–537, 597
    Alka-Seltzer case 413–414
    "Boy out the window" case 411
Korzybski, Alfred (working methods) 228, 596–597
  creative 'agonies' 593–594, 596
  footnotes 642
  methods for developing formulations 100, 175, 222, 279
  as a reader 597

skill with typewriter 305, 596
writing, 'spitting things out' 204, 306, 597
  "delousing" 18
Korzybski, Alfred (basic attitudes and personality) 10, 101
  ambition and sense of limitations 161, 269, 276, 277, 300-301, 304, 341, 368-369, 569, 652. *See also Epistemology: "epistemodesty".*
  attention to detail 21, 83-84, 596, 597
  "Be conscious!" philosophy of life 101, 631
  'behaviouristic' outlook 296, 298, 302, 311
  boldness 40, 366
  committment to clarity, 169, 178
  complaints, attitude towards 650
  comprehensive viewpoint 302
  'curmudgeon' 507
  curiosity 30
  'decorum' and 'respectability' 426
  devotion to self-education 31, 32
  direct manner and independence 76
  dynamic, multidimensional viewpoint 302
  engineering attitude 30, 81
  energy and enthusiasm 18, 21, 159-160, 597
  ideal of noble gentleman 76, 626
  inventiveness 36, 81
  ironic acceptance, attitude of 31-32, 57
  kindness 21
  sense of mortality 101, 538
  systematic habits 82
  openness 565-566
  optimistic pessimism 399, 575
  outspokeness 87
  persistence 420
  sense of humor 46, 327, 507-508, 567, 572, 598
  sentimentality, disdain for 109, 169, 188, 253
  troubleshooter 9, 19, 38, 168
  'visitor from Mars' 196
  work on self 143-147
Korzybski, Alfred (motivation and aims of work) 9, 99, 164, 164-165, 194, 241
  concerns with foundations of science and mathematics 30
  "the dreams of Leibnitz" 167, 635
  interest in psychiatric disorders 237
  lifetime mission 10
  management/human relations, interest in 26, 81-82, 83-84
  mathematics as ideal 38, 164
  as scientific explorer 193
    contact with scientific community 193
  scope of concerns 193
Korzybski, Alfred (attitudes and opinions)
  anti-communist 588-590
  anti-fascism 395-397
  air travel, aversion to 68
  animals, love of 27, 47, 349, 351
  on Catholic church and creed 33, 41-42
  commercialism, disdain of 150
  cooperative economics, interest in 112
  criticism, attitude and responses to 79, 160-161, 175-176, 197, 206, 214, 240
  as a 'liberal' 49
  military esprit de corps, appreciation of 55

Polish patriot 44, 119
private opinion, attitude toward 107, 597
on profiteering 72, 74
progress, vision for human 576
religious views and views on religion 33, 628
  anti-clericalism 147, 373
"the rotten rich" 233
Korzybski, Alfred (health) 490, 508, 524, 570, 596
  alcohol and other drug use 75, 420, 430, 596
  dental problems 217
  hearing loss 100
  post-traumatic stress 73, 100
  tendency toward constipation 255
  wartime afflictions and injuries 65, 66, 66-67, 99-100, 169, 490, 508
Korzybski, Alfred (hobbies and recreation)
  beer-making during Prohibition 354
  horse training (1890-1916) 26-27, 67
  machine tools 329
  musical training and taste 18, 33, 623
  taste in literature 18, 73, 91, 563
Korzybski, Alfred (books by).
  See Manhood of Humanity.
  See Science and Sanity.
  General Semantics Seminar 1937: Olivet College Lectures 371, 432-434, 646
  Selections from Science and Sanity (1948) 590
Korzybski, Alfred (some notable lectures/presentations) 172, 192, 282, 314, 315, 483
  "The Relationship of the Polish Youth Toward the Clergy, and the Clergy toward Polish Youth." 41
  Toronto rally for French-Polish Army (May 1918) 87
  on behalf of the Polish Relief Committee (1919) 109
  lecture at San Diego, CA bookstore (January 29, 1922) 195
  at The City Club of Milwaukee (May 16, 1922) 204-205
  "Fate and Freedom", 1922/1923 lectures to NYC German literary club and to Mathematics and History Clubs in Detroit 213-214, 217
  at Bureau of Personnel Management, NYC (March/April 1923) 223
  talk on "Relativist Aspects of Human Engineering" at New School (May 18, 1923) 224-227
  at the MIT Math Club (Oct. 1923) 236
  at the Royce Club, Harvard University (Oct. 1923) 236
  meeting of the New York Psychiatric Society (Dec. 1923) 237
  at the Cosmo Club, Washington, D.C. (Dec. 1923) 237
  at closing of Alexander Graham Bell Mansion (Chevy Chase, MD. (Dec. 1923) 237-238
  at The International Mathematical Congress, Toronto (1924) 247-249
  "Mathematics and Psychiatry, An Introduction to Humanology", to Washington Society for Nervous and Mental Diseases (June 1925) 257-258
  on "The Scientific Method and Psychopathology" for Washington Psychopathology Society (March 1926) 269
  "A New Approach in Education of Adults", LA Public Library (1928) 305
  to Congress of Mathematicians of Slavic Countries on 'Niearistotelesowy System' (1929) 323

Korzybski, Alfred (some notable lectures/presentations) *continued*
  at American Mathematical Society, Oct. 1930 meeting in New York City ("On structure", "A generalized theory of mathematical types", and "A non-aristotelian system") 330
  discussant at First International Congress on Mental Hygiene in Washington, D.C. (May 1930) 329
  at American Mathematical Society/AAAS meeting, Dec. 1931 in New Orleans, Louisiana 346-348
  discussant for paper on his work at American Psychiatric Association meeting (June 1934) 387-388
  First American Congress for General Semantics, three addresses (1935) 403
  at the annual, end-of-year 1935-1936 A.A.A.S meeting in St. Louis 409-410
  to American Psychiatric Association meeting, May 1940, Cincinnati, Ohio 468-469
  1945 Scripta Mathematica lectures on "Mathematics as a Way of Life" 522
  1946 Scripta Mathematica lectures 546
  invitation to speak at the Second International Summer Conference of the Netherlands-based International Society For The Study Of Significs (1946) 548-549
  1947 Scripta Mathematica lectures on "Mathematical Method as a Way of Life" 577-578
  "Time-Binding and Human Potentialities: A New Foundation For Human Relations" (Hunter College, Jan. 1948) 588
  "Understanding Human Potentialities" (Chatham Hotel, Jan. 1948) 589
  seminar and presentations at Yale University (Feb. 1949) 599-603
  on "Time-Binding-The Foundation for General Semantics", at the Cooper Union in New York City (March 1949) 603-605
  Korzybski's banquet speech at the Third Congress on General Semantics (Denver, CO., July 1949) 613-614
  invited paper to 1949-1950 University of Texas Clinical Psychology symposium on "Perception: A Focus for Personality Analysis" 18, 618, 621

Korzybski, Alfred (notable articles, unpublished)
  pre-World War I writing, 50
  "Let the Dead Be Heard" by "a Polish Soldier." (1919) 109-110
  "The Profiteers and How to Fight Them" (1919) 112-113
  "The Implications and Applications of Man as Time-Binder." (1923) 223
  "Fate and Freedom in Personnel Management" (1923) 223
  "The Modern Lucretius", 1924 review of Santayana's *Skepticism and Animal Faith* 253
  Time-binding, the General theory and the generalized theory of Mathematical types. An outline of a non-aristotelian system (abstract to International Congress of Mathematics - Bologna, Italy, 1928) 309-310
  "The Smith n Series of GS Life-Histories" (1946) 544

Korzybski, Alfred (notable articles/papers)
  "The Brotherhood of Doctrines" 208, 208-211, 213, 268
  "Fate and Freedom" (1923) 214-217, 218
  Time-Binding: the General Theory (First Paper, 1924) 244-247

Korzybski, Alfred (notable articles/papers) *continued*
  Time-Binding: The General Theory (Second Paper, 1926) 269, 280
  Obituary of A. V. Vasiliev - (*Science*, December 20, 1929) 326
  "A Non-Aristotelian System and its Necessity for Rigour in Mathematics and Physics" (1931)–Supplement III of *Science and Sanity* 346-347
  "Letter to co-workers" on non-aristotelian training (1934) 395
  "Outline of General Semantics" (1934-1935) 344, 346, 387, 388, 389, 395, 396-397, 403, 645
  "Neuro-Semantic and Neuro-Linguistic Mechanisms of Extensionalization: General Semantics as a Natural Experimental Science." (1935) 409
  "Extensionalization in Mathematics, Mathematical Physics, and General Education: General Semantics [Paper I: The Extensional Method]" (1936) 409
  Man, The Unknown by Alexis Carrell- A Review (May, 1937 in *American Journal of Psychiatry*) 430
  "General Semantics: Extensionalization in Mathematics, Mathematical Physics, and General Education. Paper II: Thalamic Symbolism and Mathematics." (1938) 447
  "General Semantics: Extensionalization in Mathematics, Mathematical Physics, and General Education: Paper III, Over/Under Defined Terms." (abstract, 1939) 464
  "General Semantics, Psychiatry, Psychotherapy and Prevention" (1940), publ. *American Journal of Psychiatry* (Sept. 1941) 468-469
  Foreword to *Language Habits in Human Affairs* by Irving J. Lee (1941) 477
  "Foreword" with M. Kendig to *A Theory of Meaning Analyzed* (GS Monograph III, dated June, 1942) 345, 497-499
  "Science, Sanity, and Humanism" (1942) 499-500
  "Some Non-Aristotelian Data on Efficiency for Human Adjustment" (1942-1943) 394, 501
  Foreword to "The Essence of Judaism" by Hans Kohn (1943) 147
  contributions to *ETC.: A Review of General Semantics* (1943-1947) 505, 521
  "Release of Atomic Energy" (1945) 526-527
  "A Veteran's Readjustment and Extensional Methods" (1945) 528-529
  "Letters on Non-Aristotelian Retraining: Correspondence with $Smith_1$" Feb. 1946 (published 1951 in *General Semantics Bulletin*) 544
  Encyclopedia Britannica article (unpublished there) on "General Semantics" (1946, distributed to IGS members in 1947) 560, 565, 567
  "What I Believe" (written in 1948) 591
  American People's Encyclopedia article on "General Semantics" (published in 1949) 560
  "The Role of Language in the Perceptual Processes" (1950) 18, 618, 621

Korzybski v. Underwood & Underwood (landmark case in intellectual property law) 293-294
Korzybski, Wincenty Andrzej (AK's grandfather) 29
Korzybski, Wladyslaw (AK's father) 29-30
  general in Russian Ministry of Ways & Communications 29
  engineering mentality 29

INDEX

practical idealism of 29
soil restoration at Rudnik 29-30
   author of *Melioracje Rolne* (*Agricultural Amelioration*) 29
teaching Alfred 30
career hopes for Alfred 35
retirement and illness 34
saving Alfred from exile in Siberia 44
death of 44
Kotarbinski, Tadeusz 324
Kruseman, W. M. 549
Kuegelgen, Werner von (IGS accountant and sales manager) 19, 600
Kuhn, Thomas 637
Ku Klux Klan 143
Kwapiszewski, Michael 502

L

LaBrant, Lou 558
La Jolla, California 177, 189, 191
Lake, Amy Edgerly (MEK's oldest sister) 103, 327, 484
   farm in Lees Summit, Missouri 122
Lake, Rush C. 103, 122
Lakeville, Connecticut 16, 560
Lane, Henry A. 213, 218
Language 165, 192. *See also Terminology.*
   as a kind of mathematics 180-181
   bringing ordinary language closer to mathematics 277, 279
   changing the structure of one's 336-337
   dating (temporal indexing), use of 336-337
   "etc." (et cetera), use of 337
   GS and 483, 497-498
   habitual language, power of 344
   hyphens, use of 336
   implicatory aspects 336
   indexes, use of 336
   labels 216, 223, 226
      'throwing' of 350
   metaphysics 324
   'monkeying' with names 283
   multiordinality of terms, conscious use of 337
   non-elementalistic terms, use of 336
   non-elementalistic view of 335
   retooling (restructuring) ordinary language 277-278
   single quotes, use of 336
   "talky-talk" 223-224
   universal 167
LaRochelle, Lee R. 501
Lavoisier, Antoine-Laurent 35
League of Nations 107, 109-110, 114
   conference on Jewish refugees from Germany and Austria (Evian, France -1938) 442
League to Enforce the Peace 110
Learning
   and 'lip service' 268
   exposure and repetition 269, 277
Least effort, principle of 343, 655
Ledochowski, Count (AK's religious instructor) 33
Leeds, William B. Jr. 218-219
   'Leeds Prizes' for essays and movie scenarios on time-binding 219-220

Lee, Irving J. 454, 476-477, 568
   Language Habits In Human Affairs (1941) 477
   The Language of Wisdom and Folly (1949) 582
Leibniz, Gottfried Wilhelm 38, 48, 165-166, 167-168
   dream of a 'perfect' language 367
   "identity of indiscernibles" 332, 340
   principle of "sufficient reason" 339, 340
Lenin, V. I. 85, 593
Leonard, Thomas 559
Leo XIII (pope) 42
Lesniewski, Stanislaw 324
Levine (Linwood), David 12, 21, 542-543, 600, 602, 615, 650
Lewin, Kurt 570-571, 615
   Principles of Topological Psychology (1936) 571, 611
   Resolving Social Conflicts (1948) 571, 599, 611
Lewis, C. I. 244
Lewis, G. N. 274
   Anatomy of Science (1926) 274
Lewis, Nolan D.C. 262, 265, 266, 623
'Liberal' 49
   classical 49
Liberty Bonds (World War I) 90
Library of Human Engineering 241-244
   "Principia Scientiae Hominis" (Principles of Human Science) 242
   continuation of old dream of 354, 441. *See International Non-Aristotelian Library.*
Lieber, Hugh Gray and Lillian R. (husband and wife mathematics educators) 406
   The Education of T.C. MITS (The Celebrated Man In The Street): What Modern Mathematics Means To You (1942) 406
Lillie, Ralph 372
Lime Rock, Connecticut 16, 560-562
   Lime Rock Lodge 561
Lincoln, Abraham 130, 632-633
   "Lecture on Discoveries and Inventions" 130, 632-633
Linguistic Influence of Polish on Joseph Conrad's Style (Mary Morzinski) 352
Linguistic reform
   AK's view 324
Lodz, Poland 24, 63-64
Loeb, Jacques (physiologist) 16, 138-140, 146
   depicted in Sinclair Lewis novel, *Arrowsmith* 139
   friend and mentor of AK 140
   influence of work on AK 139-140
Loewenberg, Richard D. 531
'Logic' 217
   and mathematics 135
   as elementalistic (in AK's view) 324, 378
   limitations 192
   mathematical ('symbolic') 48, 165, 168
      mathematizing logic (language), program of 180
   two-valued (either-or), usefulness of 339
"Logical fate" ("logical destiny") 199-202, 214, 215, 498
   diagram 215
   Spengler and 303
Logical Positivism (logical empiricism) 210-211, 220-221

London, England 320, 325
Lonergan, Bernard 348
Lord, Robert 475
Los Angeles Daily News 492
    Edwin Green's column "General Semantics and Human Affairs" 492
    interviews with Korzybski 492
Los Angeles Society for General Semantics 452
Lost Angel (1943 Margaret O'Brien movie) 506
Lucretius (Classical Roman Poet-Philosopher) 130, 253
Lukasiewicz, Jan 324
Lynn, John G. 390, 416, 417–418, 427, 428
Lytton, George 244

M

Mach, Ernst 207. *See also* McCormack, Thomas J.
Mackensen, August von (German general) 63, 65
MacNeal, Ed 551
Macrae, John (publisher, E.P. Dutton Co.) 242, 243, 351–352, 634
MaDan, Lily (AK's secretary/typist during production of *Science and Sanity*) 350, 363
Maddren, Russell 318–319
    work with MEK to edit *Science and Sanity* manuscript 319
'Maggots in the cheese' 77, 154
Maginot Line 470
Malinowski, Bronislaw 269, 450, 467
    death 496–497
Mallach, Maxine K. (long-time IGS secretary) 590, 616
Management
    self 649
    project 113
    scientific 113
    span of attention or control. *See* Urwick, Lyndall F.
Manhattan Project. *See* Atomic Bomb.
Manhattan Storage Company 212, 419
Manhood of Humanity 124, 164–165
    working titles 124, 155, 156
    assessment by AK 131, 132
    MEK's 'spiritual' satisfaction with 131
    publishers, seeking 135, 155. *See also* Macrae, John.
    polishing by Keyser 136
    discussion of mathematics in 137
    "human engineering or mathematical sociology" 148
    publishing history 635
    book sales 172, 268, 351, 519
    publicity 155, 157, 159, 170–172, 213
    reviews and notices 197, 213
        Frankwood E. Williams review in the January issue of *Mental Hygiene* (National Committee for Mental Hygiene) 197, 221
    Second Edition 519, 588, 603, 605, 606–607
        AK's work on 'Introduction to the Second Edition' 17, 572, 588, 593–594, 607–608, 610–611, 619–621
Manoury, Gerrit 548
Maps, mapping. *See also* Abstracting, Abstractions.
    map/territory analogy of abstracting 8, 315
    map is not the territory 333
    map covers not all the territory 334
    self-reflexiveness of mapping (Royce) 182–183, 223, 334–335
        map-maker at a date implied 335

Marlboro State Hospital (psychiatric); Marlboro, New Jersey 419
Marx, Guido 158
Masserman, Jules
    "Experimental Neuroses in Cats" 615
Mass Media
    1921 state of 170
    criticism. *See* Bent, Silas and Fuller, Harold de Wolf.
    publicity for AK 236
"Masturbation of the salivary glands" 486
'Materialism' 196
Mathematics 124, 224
    and imagination 267, 522
    and logic 135, 168
    as a "higher psychiatry" 273
    as language 37, 125, 180
    as physiological 191
    definition of 577
    everyday language as a kind of 180, 277
    exemplar of logical fate 200
    foundations of 577
    intuitionism 296
    'linguisticizing mathematics' 180–181
    methods, discovery of new 210
    "miracles of" 38, 167
    notation 167
    psychological approach 135, 201, 637
    qualitative mathematics 181, 210
    terminology, non-elementalistic character of 336
'Maybeness' 338
Mayo, Elton 429
Mayper, Stuart A. (korzybskian scholar/teacher) 338
McClaughry, Richard T. 13, 532–537, 540, 542
McCormack, Thomas J. (educator, writer and translator of Ernst Mach) 206–208, 358
McCormick, Robert J. 492
McCrae, John D. 98
    "In Flanders Fields" 98–99
McDougall, William 248
McElroy, L. E. (President, the U.S. Horseshoe Co.) 83
McEwen, George 191, 202, 211, 248
McKeon, Richard 551
McKinney, G. C. 22
McKnight, Gordon L. 496
McLean Hospital 417–418
McLuhan, Marshall 344
McMullen, Virginia 19
McNealy, Raymond W. 508, 510
'Meaning'
    Cheshire Cat theories of 345, 498, 643
    pioneers in study of 343
    AK's abandonment of theory of 'meaning' 344–345
'Meanings' of words 181
Measurement 30, 627
Media ecologists 344
Meiers, Ann [Annie Goulding Dix] 11, 510–512
    "Avoiding The Dangers Of Semantic Adolescence" (1951) 511–512
Meiers, Joseph Immanuel 512
Mendeleev, Dmitri 35

'Mental' disorders 264
"Mental hygiene" 240, 324
The Mentality of Apes (Wolfgang Kohler) 350
Mentally retarded children, GS training of 389
Mental status examination 261
Metaphysics
  language and 324
  scientific 272
Metcalf, Henry C. 223
Methodology. *See also Epistemology; Extensional: attitude, orientation; Scientific method.*
  deduction 124
  induction 123–124
  physico-mathematical 123–124, 125, 246, 261, 368, 538
  role in scientific education 385
  unification of 539–540
Methodology and Science (Dutch journal) 549
Methodology and Science Foundation (Haarlem, Netherlands) 549
Meyer, Adolf 240
Michie, Sarah 401
Miller, Joseph T. (U.S. Fuel Administration) 89
Millikan, Robert A. 192, 307–308
Military Intelligence Department, U. S. Army (MID) 115
Moisiev, Colonel 71
Monkeys. 317, 349–351
Moore, E.H. 132
Moore, Wilbur E. 510, 558
Morgan, Thomas Hunt 173–174, 312
Morris, Charles W. 244
  Signs, Language and Behavior 547
Muhl, Dr. Anita 312
Muller, Herbert J. 506
  Science and Criticism: The Humanistic Tradition in Contemporary Thought (1943) 506
Multiordinality 279, 598. *See also Self-reflexiveness.*
  of terms 117–118, 181–182, 279.
Murray, Elwood 454, 477–478, 528–529, 546–547
  "A Functional Core for the Basic Communication Course" (Murray, et al, 1946) 546
Murray, Reginald St. Elmo 386

N

Naaman and Elisha (Biblical story) 511
Nagel, Ernest 375–376
The National Student Forum 224
National Arts Club (New York City) 111
National Brain Power Monthly 213
National Masonic Research Society 202, 213
National Training Laboratory (NTL) 571, 615
Nature 223
Navy, U.S.
  interest in AK's work 547–548
  Naval Leadership (1949 edition) 548
Nazis (National Socialist German Worker's Party) and Nazism 247. *See also Germany, Nazi*
Negroes 232–233
Nelson, Thomas E. (korzybskian scholar/teacher) 18
Neuro-linguistic environments, factors, reactions, etc. 344
Neurology 264–267

Neuro-semantic [evaluational] environments, factors, reactions, etc. 344
"New Machine" ("Technarchy") 113-114. *See also Ferguson, Charles.*
The New Student (newspaper of National Student Forum) 224
New School for Social Research 224
Newton, Norman T.
  An Approach to Design (1951) 587
New York: A Four-Page Journal of Ideas for the General Reader (NYU Weekly) 290, 292
New York City 123
New York Psychiatric Society 237
New York Society for General Semantics 523, 546
New York University 290
Nicholas, Grand Duke (Commander-in-Chief of the Tsarist Army General Staff) 53, 58, 68–69
Nicholas II (last Russian Tsar) 49, 53
Nicomachean Ethics (Aristotle) 540–542
Nielsen, A. M. 288
Niles, May Watrous 497–498, 558
Non-additivity (non-linearity) 302, 339–340
  practical aspects 501
Non-allness 333, 334
Non-aristotelian ($\bar{A}$) assumptions, orientation, system 271, 275, 367, 473, 500, 538
Non-Elementalism, non-elementalistic 190, 278. *See also Elementalism.*
  non-additive/non-linear implications 302
  premise of 330
  terms 13, 277, 336
Non-essentialism, non-essentialist 332
Non-euclidean geometry 200
Non-identity. *See also Identification; Identity.*
  AK's premise of 279, 331
  and symbolic equivalence 332–333
'Normal' 260–261
Northrop, F. S. C. 211, 601–602
  The Logic of the Sciences and Humanities (1947) 601
  Science and First Principles (1931) 601
Northwestern University 455
Number(s) 196, 210
  as class of classes (Bertrand Russell) 183
  in terms of relations (Korzybski) 577.

O

Objectification 311
'Objectivity' 188, 330
Objects 186–187, 216, 223–224, 226
O'Brien, Margaret 506
Observer and the observed. *See Relation, observer-observed*
Ochsner, Berta (Bertha) 447
Ogden, C. K. (Charles Kay) 220, 239, 252, 320, 343
  The Meaning of Meaning: A study of the influence of language upon thought and of the science of symbolism (written with I. A. Richards) 252, 462
Olivet College (Olivet, Michigan) 354, 431–435
  early interest in AK's work 268
Open Court Publishing Company 207, 236
Order 183, 224
"Organismalism" 189–190
Over/Under defined terms 464

P

Paderewski, Ignacy Jan 85
Palestine, Palestinians 504, 531
Palmer, A. Mitchell 144
Parker, G.H. 381
Pasadena, California 192
   AK's year there writing *Science and Sanity* (1928) 304–313
   earthquakes and native ants 309
Pasteur, Louis 36
Paton, Stewart 237
   death 496
Patton, George S. and Beatrice Ayer 110
Paul of Tarsus 223
Pavlov, Ivan 316, 622
   Conditioned Reflexes 316
   Lectures on Conditioned Reflexes 316
   "Bequest of Pavlov To The Academic Youth of His Country" (1936) 613–614
Peano, Giuseppe 48, 248
Pearl, Raymond 239–240
Peirce, Charles Saunders 575
Permutations and combinations 643
pessimism 399
Petawawa, Canada
   Canadian Army base and proving ground 72–73
   Russian Q.F. (Quick Firing) 3-inch field guns 73
   minor annoyances 76
   "The Popular Song of Petawawa" 76–77
   grand party hosted by AK 77–78
Peterson, William 509
Petrunkavich, Alexander 197
'Philosophy' *See also* Aristotle, Bachelard, Bacon, Campbell (Norman), Leibniz, Peirce, Dewey, 'Logical Positivism', Northrop, Popper, Reiser, Russell (Bertrand), Santayana, Wittgenstein, Whitehead, Whyte, etc.
   AK's discomfort with term and frustration with academic 'philosophers' 324, 369, 385, 473
   AK's comments on Fichte, Hegel, and Spinoza 628
   Polish philosophers, AK's relation to 324
   philosophers of science (post-korzybskian) 637
   speculative 185, 272
Phipps Psychiatric Clinic (Johns Hopkins Medical School) 240
Physics. *See also* Quantum theory; Relativity.
   newtonian 271
   statistical mechanics 36
   thermodynamics 36
Piéron, Henri (French experimental psychologist) 302
   Thought and the Brain 302
Pilsudski, Josef 54, 95
Piper, H. Beam 494
Pittsburgh, Pennsylvania 87–89
Pius X (pope) 42
Planck, Max 48
Plants. *See Chemistry-Binding.*
Plock, Poland 61–63
Plumb, Glenn 114
   "Plumb Plan" 114
Poehlmann, Captain Karl F. 548, 571
Pogroms. *See Antisemitism.*

Poincaré, Henri 136–137, 216
   The Foundation of Science 136
Polakov, Walter N. 146, 148–150, 198–199, 213, 351, 525
   AK's formulational 'brother' 148
   expert in power plant operations and in industrial engineering and management 149
   career as a consultant to businesses and governments 149
   co-worker of H. L. Gantt 149
   credo of rendering rigorous service 149
   interest in waste reduction (increased productivity by making work fascinating) 149, 199
   "Universal Labor", notion of 150, 199
   Marx, reverence and criticism of 149, 151
   financial woes (1921) 171–172
   promotion of AK's work 171–172
   Mastering Power Production (1921, 1922) 149, 199
   "Engineering as a Whole" May 1923 talk at New School 224
   "Science and Labor" Series of four articles for *American Labor Monthly*, 1923 225
   "The Foundation of Human Engineering: Language and The New Mathematical Logic" Article in May 1923 *Management Engineering* journal 225
   conflict with AK 225–227
   Man and his Affairs: From the Engineering Point of View (1925) 234–235, 252
   second wife, Barbara 318, 350, 351
      death of 525
   as industrial advisor in Soviet Union with Barbara (1929-1931) 318
   return from Soviet Union (1931) 351
   farmstead in Fairfax, Virginia 351
   post-*Science and Sanity* help to AK 376, 394, 439
   introducing AK to Graicunas and Urwick's work 394. *See also* Urwick, Lyndall
   work for the Tennessee Valley Authority 394
   1949 whereabouts 609–610
Poland, history of
   partition (1795) 24
   role of szlachta (nobility) 9, 25, 113, 626
   Jews of 113, 631–632
   under Tsarist Russian domination 24, 44, 49
   1904 protests in Warsaw 45
   1905 general strikes 46
   effects of 1905 Russian Revolution on 45, 49
   cooperative movement in 112–113
   geopolitical role in World War I 52–54
   World War I devastation 70, 78, 99
   independence 85, 87, 88, 97
   Second Polish Republic
      established (Nov. 11, 1918) 95
      (interwar period) 97, 99
   AK's 1929 impression 322–323
   1939 invasion by Nazi Germany and Soviet Russia 461–462, 588
   Warsaw Ghetto uprising (1943) 503
   Warsaw Uprising (1944) 518
   Stalinist sealing-off post-World War II 545
Polish language 24, 627
Polish culture 164, 502, 618, 626

INDEX

Polish nationalism 29, 44, 52, 54, 85–88, 90, 24
Poland Fights 502
Polanyi, Michael 637
The Polish Review 502, 530
Polish Mechanics Company 118–119
Polivinov, General A. A. 69–70
Pollock, Thomas Clark 498
Ponzi, Charles 111
Popper, Karl 338
    The Logic of Scientific Discovery (1934, 1959) 338
Popularization 269
Positivism 272
Post, Emil 133
Postman, Neil 569, 652
Post-Traumatic Stress Disorder 73, 527–529
Postulationalism 272
Potter, Robert R. (GS writer) 329
Potts, Harold M. 389
    research on effects of GS instruction on retarded children 389
Powers, William T. *See Control Theory*.
Powner, Helene 312
Predictability, maximum probability of 338
Prince Radizwill 41, 42, 43
Principia Mathematica (Russell and Whitehead) 48, 133, 136, 168, 179–182
Pritchard, E. A. 549
Profiteering 72, 112–113
Progress 207, 303
Propositional functions 181
Propositions 181, 214–215
'Protocols of the Elders of Zion'. *See Antisemitism.*
Proverbs (3:13-18) 622
Psychiatry 237, 246, 258
    AK's focus on 390
    interest of psychiatrists in AK's work 417–419, 430, 583
    limitations of 264
    potential role in wartime 469
Psychiatry in Medical Education (National Committee for Mental Hygiene, 1933) 417
Psychoanalysis 258
Psycho-galvanometer ("lie detector") 303
'Psychology' 390, 570–571
    Psycho-logics 267, 336, 390
    postulational approach 201
Psychotherapy 264
    cognitive-behavioral 417
    overlap with education 258
Pula, Robert P. (korzybskian scholar/teacher) 8, 11, 378

Q

Quantum theory 48
    AK's attitude towards 299–300, 310
Quine, Willard Van Orman 457–458, 569
Quotes 13, 277, 336, 626. *See Extensional devices.*
Quo Vadis (Italian theatrical production of Henryk Sinkiewicz novel) 42–43

R

Racism 232–233
Rainich, G. Y. 240
Ramsey, Frank 220

Rapoport, Anatol 518
    ambivalence about AK and his work 555–557
    devotion to the Soviet Union and admiration of Stalin (late 1930s-late 1940s) 554–555, 589, 651
    "Dialectical Materialism and General Semantics" (1948) 589
    Science and the Goals of Man (1950) 582–583
Read, Allen Walker 11, 472–473, 493, 498
    "An Account of the Word 'Semantics'" (1948) 506, 558
    English Minus Absolutisms (EMA) 13
Read, Charlotte Schuchardt 11, 625. *See also Charlotte Schuchardt.*
Reader's Guide to Periodical Literature 439–440
Reading 8, 482–483
    AK's advice on 137, 215–216
    importance to AK of general literacy 44
'Reality' 264
Redpath, Robert Upjohn, Jr. 11, 550, 558, 567, 622–623
"Red Scare" of 1920 America 144
Red Wing, Minnesota 476, 481
Regeneration (Pat Barker) 303
Reiner, Markus 393–394
Reiser, Oliver Leslie 211, 377–379
    The Promise of Scientific Humanism (1940) 475
    The Integration of Human Knowledge (1958) 378
Relation 183, 189
    basic structural-relational premise of $\bar{A}$ system 330
    observer-observed 188, 204, 209, 214, 215
Relativity theory 49, 187–188
    general theory of 100, 111
    The Einstein Theory of Relativity (Max Fleischer Studios silent movie, 1923) 218
Remington arms factory 72
Rennenkampf, Paul von (Tsarist-Russian general) 56, 63
Representation, form of 149
Research Center for Group Dynamics, MIT 571
Richards, I. A. 252, 343, 498. *See also Ogden, C.K.*
Richardson, R.G.D. 249
Ritter, William Emerson 175, 189, 190, 191, 202
    The Natural History of Our Conduct 189
Roback, A. A. (Abraham Aaron) 146, 235, 248, 390
Robertson, Lionel 215
Robertson, Richard J. 303
Roehm, Ernst 395
Roethlisberger, F. J. 429
Rogers, Will 309
    AK's 1928 meeting with 309
Rome, Italy 39–43
    ancient monuments of 187
    Pincio Garden 40
    University of 39
Roosevelt, Franklin D. 442, 469, 504, 523, 545
    AK's response to FDR's first year of office (1933) 372
Rontgen, Wilhelm Conrad 36
Rosen, Samuel 508
Rosenwald Fund 476
Royce, Josiah 182–183, 466

Rudnik (AK's family's estate in Poland) 24, 46, 47, 58, 66, 321
   poorly-draining clay soil 25
Rueff, Jacques
   From the Physical to the Moral Sciences (1922) 242
Runkel, Philip J. 369, 370
Russell, Bertrand 48, 136, 179, 181, 182–185, 216, 220. See also Principia Mathematica.
   Introduction to Mathematical Philosophy 182–183
   Principles of Mathematics 182
   number as the class of all classes 183
   personal relations with AK 183–185, 636
Russell, Minnie Edgerly (one of MEK's sisters) 103
Russianoff, Penelope (Pearl) 240
   When Am I Going To Be Happy: How To Break The Emotional Bad Habits That Make You Miserable (1988) 583–584
Russia, Tsarist 24–25
   Russian language/culture 627
   role in partition of Poland (1795) 24
   domination of Poland 24, 44, 49
   Ochrana (Tsarist secret police) 44, 115
      provokatsiya (provocation), practice of 115
      See also Antisemitism.
   Gendarmes (Tsarist uniformed security police) 45, 59–60
   anti-Tsarist underground 49
   Russo-Japanese War (1904–1905) 44, 46
   1905 Revolution 44–46, 49
      constitutional reforms of 1905 49
      regression towards absolutism 49
   World War I military performance 53–54, 56, 57, 68, 69–70, 629
      Second Army 54
      Stavka (Tsarist-Russian General Staff Headquarters) 61
      Ministry of War 69–70
   'February' 1917 revolution 80
   abdication of Tsar, 1917 80
Russia, Soviet
   1917 "October Revolution" (Bolshevik) 85
   Stalin's Five Year Plan 318
      agriculture, forced collectivization of 318
   Stalin's regime, AK's 1933 opinion of 372, 593
   Hitler-Stalin pact 461
   1939 invasion of Poland 461
   Lysenkoism 589–590
   explodes atomic bomb, 1949 617
Rzewuski (family of AK's mother) 28

S

Sachanow, Colonel 72
Saint Elizabeths ("Government Hospital for the Insane"), Washington, D.C. 255, 258
   Pathology Laboratory 265
   male patients 259
   staff meetings 263
   women's department 259
Saint Peter 43
Sameness and similarity 331. *See also Identity; Non-Identity.*
San Diego, California 189, 192
San Diego State Teachers College (San Diego State University) 192
'Sanity'
   continuum of 260–262, 315
   "un-sane" as term 261
   logical fate and 260
   relation between science/mathematics and sanity 9, 315
   theory of 368
Santayana, George 253, 546
   Skepticism and Animal Faith 253
Sargent, Porter Edward 438
Saunders, Captain James A. 547–548, 558
Schaefer, Ernest R. 623
Scheffer, Reinhard (German general) 63
Schlauch, Margaret 506
Schoenbrunn Park (in Vienna) 39
The School of the Natural Order 459
Schrodinger, Erwin
   What is Life? (1944) 622
Schuchardt, Charlotte 11, 16, 459–460, 466, 508, 519, 542, 558, 614, 620-621, 647. *See also Read, Charlotte Schuchardt*
'Science'
   AK's critique of 175, 215
   as the economy of thought 207
   dating of term 336–337
   higher or general science 166, 168
   late 19th Century 35–36
   pre-World War I (early 20th Century) 48–49
   unification of 166, 193, 194
Science Press Printing Company 355, 591–592
Science and Sanity 9
   titles, early alternate 17, 165, 237, 242, 273, 304
   project of 164–165, 251
   as Volume II of *Manhood of Humanity* 208
   some milestones in development 204–205, 222, 226–228, 244, 245
   'positive and negative touchstones' for AK 252–254
   research at St. Elizabeths 255–256, 258–267
   Time-Binding papers as preliminary sketches 269, 271
   originality of 275
   basic thesis 276
   first draft
      producing 295, 300–301
      to Pasadena, CA to write (1928) 304–305
      purpose and development of Books I, II, and III 305–306, 309, 313
      linguistic difficulties in writing 311
      editing help from C. B. Bridges 312, 313
   1929 working title 315
   insertion of material on Pavlov's work and on colloids 316, 327, 329
   editing by MEK and Russell Maddren 326–327
   "structure" as major unifying term for 328–329
   completing book, two broad phases of 328
      fine-tuning the formulations 328, 328–341, 342–348
      finishing production 328, 351–355, 356–364
   abbreviations in book 337
   extensional punctuation for "etc.", use of 337
   aims of work 341, 499
   sympathetic and unsympathetic readers 341
   search for publisher 351–355
   AK's prose style in 352, 598
   paid literary editors, failure of 352

Science and Sanity (continued)
   initial printing estimate 355
   decision to self-publish 355
   final deliberations on title 356
   epigraph for First Edition 357
   quotations , 'salting' the book with 357
   Supplements 357
      proposed supplements 241
      Graven's 'case studies and supplement on psychiatry' 301, 315-316
      Graven's 'writer's block' 361-362. *See also Graven, Philip.*
   typesetting 358
   binding ("the blue peril") 358
   proofreading ('delousing') 358-360, 362-363, 364
   manuscript and proof readers (partial listing) 360
   pre-publication advertising circular 360-361, 362
   "Preface To The First Edition" 1933 363-364
   October 10, 1933 publication 364
   effort to produce 366
   one reader's experience with 550
Science and Sanity (reviews and publicity, First Edition) 372-379, 393-394
   Keyser's opinion and reviews 374
Science and Sanity (sales) 352, 393, 440, 449, 462, 495, 506, 520, 546, 572 588, 592
Science and Sanity (Second Edition, 1941) 462, 478-480, 483, 572
   "Introduction to the Second Edition 1941" 462, 468-469, 470, 474, 531
   new epigraph 358, 462, 479
   "Special Acknowledgement" 489
Science and Sanity (Third Edition, 1948)
   AK's "Preface to the Third Edition 1948" 572, 573, 575-576
   production 575, 590-591
Science and Sanity (Fifth Edition, 1994)
   "A Note on Errata 364
Science and Society (journal) 506
Science Fiction 538
   influence of AK's work 494
Science Service 191
'Scientific method' 246-247, 368. *See also Methodology.*
Scientific societies 166
Scientific unity 166, 242
Scientists and Mathematicians
   as audience for AK's work 380-383, 386
   behavior of 9, 253
   AK's contacts with 190, 193, 384
   help from 276, 292, 297, 301
Scripps, Ellen 189, 190
Scripps, E. W. 189, 190-191, 636
Scripps Institute for Biological Research (Scripps Institution for Oceanography) 175, 177, 189, 191-192
Scripta Mathematica 521-522
Selections from Science and Sanity (1948) 590
Self-reflexiveness 223, 334-335. *See also Maps, self-reflexiveness of mapping (Royce).*
   Carrel quote 431, 649
   Eddington quote 188
   Keyser quote 121

'Semantic reaction' (s.r) *See also Evaluation; General Semantics; Neuro-semantic environments, factors, reactions, etc.*
   equivalent to evaluational reaction, evaluation 17, 343
   not limited to responses to 'language' 17, 343
   non-verbal in nature 343, 376, 411
   'semantic' or 'neuro-semantic' relaxation 344, 646
   AK's gradual abandonment of term 345-346
'Semantics' 273, 323
   confusion with 'general semantics' (GS) 17, 343, 344, 506
   study of linguistic 'meaning' 17
"Semantics Book Club" of the ISGS 17
Semiotics 244
"Senate of Humanity" 243
Serbia 50
Shaw, James Byrnie 205, 206
   Lectures on the Philosophy of Mathematics 205
Shaw, Ruth Faison 400
   Finger Painting: A Perfect Medium For Self-Expression (1934) 400
Shearer, Julie Gordon 516
Shub, David 593
   Lenin (1948) 593, 611
Significs 548-549. *See also Welby, Lady Victoria.*
   Dutch circle, and the International Society for the Study of Significs 548-549
Simons, Reverend George A. 116
Simultaneity 188
Sinkiewicz, Henryk 42
Skepticism 253
Skolimowski, Henryk 324
   Polish Analytical Philosophy 324
Slossen, Edwin E. 191, 326
Smith, Adelaide 179
Smyser, Selden 307, 395
Smyth, William Henry 175-176
Snafu(s) 545, 557
Sobanski, Captain 71, 82
"Social Credit" movement 113, 113-114, 116. *See also Antisemitism*
Socialism, Socialists 150, 589, 49, 128
Social Justice 116
Society for General Semantics 505, 506, 520 *See also ETC.: A Review of General Semantics.*
   plans for 488
   organization of 495-496
   AK's frustration with 552-557, 563-566, 587
      by-laws changes, Nov. 1946 563-564
      public representations of 'general semantics' in *ETC.* and elsewhere 564-565
   AK's 1947 protest letter "To the Editor of ETC." 565
   name change in 1948 to "International Society for General Semantics" (ISGS) 587
   fateful 1949 ISGS presidential election battle between Francis P. Chisholm and S. I. Hayakawa 608-609
   ISGS (1950) 17
Sommerfeld, Arnold 642
Sophia, Electress of Hanover 332
Soviet Union. *See Russia, Soviet.*
Sowell, Thomas 113

Space-Binding 124, 128
Space-Time 189
   disorientation 261
"Spanish Flu" (1918 Flu Epidemic) 92, 92–93
Spaulding, John Gordon 498
Speech Communication 455
Speech pathology 455
Spengler, Oswald 303
   The Decline of the West 303
Spiritualism 196
Sprengler, Otto 214
Stalin, Josef 461
   Hitler-Stalin pact 461
   hegemony in Eastern Europe 545
Stein, Gertrude 106
Steinmetz, Charles 152–153
Stevenson, George S. 452
Stimson, Henry 491
Straus, Robert K. 546, 559
Structural Differential 255. *See also Abstracting, Abstractions.*
   genesis 224–228
      summarizing AK's outlook 226, 227
         difference between animals and humans 226
         self-reflexive map of mapping/modeling/abstracting process 334
         stratifications, vertical and horizontal 331
         turning it upside down 270
   manufacturing of 228, 230–231, 268
   patent for 228–229, 232, 267
   early names as "Anthropometer", "Time-Binding Differential" 229
   teaching/learning applications 230-231, 232–233
      how to 'think' 227, 232–233, 278
   with rotary fan ('disk' where there is no disk) 231
   scrolling wall-charts 231, 617
   "the bug" 241
   special suitcase/trunk for 244
   copyright for 245
   misrepresentations as 'Thought Machine'. *See Houck affair.*
   copyright infringement lawsuit by Korzybski 293–294
   name changed from Anthropometer 331
Structure 183
   as a complex of relations consisting of multi-dimensional order 328–329
   as major unifying term of AK's work 328–329
   organic chemistry 36
Stupidity 9, 545
Sturtevant, G.H. 244
Stuttering and stammering 434, 455
Submarine Accident 8
Sullivan, Harry Stack 261, 539
   "one genus postulate" 261–262
Suri, Surindar Singh 575
Swift, Jonathan. *See Gulliver's Travels.*
Sword fighting 40–41, 60
Symposium on "Perception: A Focus for Personality Analysis" at University of Texas (1949–1950) 618
Synge, John L. 243, 639
   Science: Sense and Nonsense 639
Synthese (journal) 549
Syz, Hans 301, 303. *See also Trigant Burrow.*

T

Taft, William Howard 110
   AK's English bulldog named after 47
"Tar baby" 232–233
Tarski, Alfred 324
Tchaikovsky, Pyotr Ilyich 33
   Manfred Symphony 623
   Sixth (Pathetique) Symphony 622
Terechoff, Lieutenant Colonel 54, 56–57, 58, 59, 64, 65
Terminology, choice of 346. *See also Elementalism: terms; Multiordinality: of terms; Non-Elementalism: terms; Over/Under defined terms; Undefined Terms.*
Thalhimer, William 204
"The Great War." *See World War I.*
Theism 33
The Journal of Nervous and Mental Disease 237
The New York Masonic Outlook 269
'Thinking'
   how to 9, 139, 174, 227, 229, 232
   postulational 210, 214–215, 272
   probabilistic 36
   physico-chemical basis of 139
   time-dependent character 191–192
   biological aspects 191, 267
Thompson, D'arcy 248
Thomson, J. J. 36
'Thought' 224, 239
   economy of 207
   process of 'thought' 216–217
Tillotson, Kenneth 418
Time-Binding 17. *See also Manhood of Humanity.*
   incubating questions of AK 122–123
   influence of Charles Ferguson 123–124
   eureka moment 124
   definition 124
      theological and zoological definitions, opposition to 127
   chemistry-binding 124
   space-binding 124, 128
   exponential factors in 125–127
   basic formula, PR^T 126
   social collapse, explanation of 127
   political-economic implications of 127–128
   forerunners of notion 128–131
      Polish roots of 128
      Jewish tradition 129
      humanist tradition 129
      George Boole 129–130
      Abraham Lincoln 130
      August Comte 130
      Henry George 130
      Henry Adams 131
   childhood and manhood of humanity 130
   originality of Korzybski's formulation 131
   "spiral theory" of 139–140, 201–202
   problems with formulation 159–160
   mechanism of 161
   general theory of 165
   rate of 166
   attitude 191
   importance of language and symbolism 195

Time-Binding *continued*
  continuum of 255–256
  importance as foundation to AK's later work 604
  democracy and dictatorship 612
Time-Binding Club (1920-1923) 151–152, 213
Time Magazine 447, 482, 603, 614
Toklas, Alice B. 104
Tower of London 325
Trainor, Joseph C. 388
  research on effects of GS instruction on I.Q. scores 388–389
  "Experimental Results of Training in General Semantics Upon Intelligence-Test Scores" 645
Triple Self-Portrait (Norman Rockwell, 1960) 335
Truman, Harry 523, 545
Tsar Nicholas II. *See Russia, Tsarist.*
Turing, Alan 133
Tuyl, Marian Van 447
Twining, Luella 172–173, 175, 309
Tygodnik Polski: The Polish Weekly 502
Tyler, A. Ranger 373–374
Types, theory of 179–180, 204

U
Uncertainty 8
  Heisenberg's principle of 300, 338
  implications for living 341
  knowledge and 337–340, 341
  Korzybski's general principle of 338
Uncle Remus: The Complete Tales (Julius Lester) 233
Undefined terms 214–215, 639
  "structure", "relation", "order" as basic 328–329
Understanding 348
Uniforms 90
United Nations 529. *See also League of Nations.*
University of Amsterdam 549
University of Chicago 440, 441, 551
  GS at 551
  location of first self-sustaining, controlled nuclear fission 525
University of Denver 456
  GS-oriented curriculum 546–547, 592
University of Illinois-Urbana 205, 217
University of Iowa 455
University of Michigan 218
'Unknowable' 245
'Un-sanity'. *See 'Sanity'*
Un-speakable 342
"The Unsubdued" (Niepokorni) 44
Urwick, Lyndall 394.
  Graicunas "Span of Control" diagram 501
  Papers on the Science of Administration 501
U.S. Fuel Administration (U.S.F.A.) 89–93, 94, 630
U.S. Horseshoe Company (Erie, Pennsylvania) 83–84
U.S.N. San Francisco (submarine) 8

V
Values 541
  knowledge and 541
  military 55
Vandervoort, Henrietta 616
Van Vogt, A.E. 494
  The World of Null-A 584–585, 604–605
  'Null-A' confusion 584, 652–653
  The Voyage of the Space Beagle 652
Vasiliev, A. N. 242–243, 270, 326
Vatican 40, 41
Verbalism, detached 260
Verwiebe, Frank L. 586
Victor Emanuel III 40
  bodyguard 40
Virtues 541–542
Vitvan (Ralph M. deBit) 458–459
Vogt, William
  Road to Survival (1948) 585

W
Wade, Douglas E. 586–587
Wagner, Richard 33
  "Siegfreid's Funeral March" 622
Ward, Henry 380
Warsaw, Poland 24
  premature evacuation by Russians at start of WWI 53
  Russian loss to Germany in WW I 68, 70
  Warsaw Ghetto Uprising, 1943 503
  Warsaw Uprising, 1944 518
    destruction of "Royal Castle" 530
Warsaw Polytechnic 35–38
Washington Psychopathological Society 263
Washington State Normal School (now Central Washington University) 395
Waterston, G. C. 468
Watson, John B. 224
Weaver, Richard M.
  Ideas Have Consequences (1948) 580–581
Weil, Richard Jr.
  The Art of Practical Thinking (1940) 467
Weinberg, Alvin M. 456–457
Weinberg, Blanche 22, 384, 645
Weinberg, Harry L. 22, 384, 476, 493, 566
  Levels of Knowing and Existence (1959) 493
Weiss, Paul 357
  "The Theory of Types"- Supplement II of *Science and Sanity* (357
Welby, Lady Victoria 343, 548–549.
Wells, H.G. 538
Western Civilization 303
Weyl, Hermann 296
  "The Mathematical Way of Thinking" (1940) 611
Wheeler, William Morton 235, 330
  editing help to AK 358, 360
  "profound impression" of *Science and Sanity*, 381
  death 431–432
Whitehead, Alfred North 48, 179, 185–187, 216. *See also Principia Mathematica.*
  The Organization of Thought (1917) 185
  An Enquiry Concerning the Principles of Natural Knowledge (1919) 185
  The Concept of Nature (1920) 136, 185, 216
  The Principle of Relativity With Applications to Physical Science (1922) 185
  Process and Reality (1929) 185
  "Nature is a process." 186, 636

Whitehead, Alfred North *continued*
  AK's 1930 meeting with 330
  AK's 1933 meeting with 381–382
  influence on AK 216
"White race" 146, 639
White, William Alanson 197, 239, 256, 257, 258
  and "one-genus postulate" 262
  relationship with AK 262–263
  review of *Science and Sanity* 376
  Twentieth Century Psychiatry (1936) 263, 430
  death 430
Whorf, Benjamin Lee 481–482
Whyte, L. L. 179, 180, 182, 211
Why They Behave Like Russians (John Fisher, 1946/1947) 593
Wiener, Norbert 655
  Cybernetics (1948) 202. *See also Control theory.*
Wilcza Street, #66 (Warsaw) 45
Wilhelm II (Kaiser of Germany) 50
Wilkinson, John (official of United Mine Workers Union) 93
Williams, Cora Lenore 174
  Williams Institute of Creative Education 174
  death 438
Williams, Frankwood E. 197, 256
Williams, H. B. 303
Willis, John (head of the U.S.F.A. Speaker's Bureau) 90
Wilson, E. B. 382
Wilson, Edwin 499
Wilson, Woodrow 80, 89, 107, 114
  "Fourteen Points" Speech to Congress (Jan. 1918) 85, 97
  "war to end all wars" 99
Winchell, Walter 650
Winters, Eunice 363
Witherspoon, Mrs. and Mr. 311
Wittgenstein, Ludwig 219–222
  comparison and contrast with AK 219–221
  Tractatus Logico-Philosophicus (1922) 219–222, 638
Wolfenden, Dr. and Mrs. 309
Wolf, Hugo
  "Weyla's Song" 622
Wolf, Robert B. 152
Wolf, Simon 145
Wood, Charles W. 213
  "Witchcraft and Human Engineering", May 25, 1923 talk at New School 224
Woolworth Building (New York City) 123, 632
Worldview, new scientifically-based 186
World War I. *See also Korzybski, Alfred (World War I Service/Activities); Germany; Russia, Tsarist.*
  prediction of 49
  start of 50
  Allied Powers 50, 54
  Central Powers (Austria-Hungary and Germany) 50, 52
  geopolitical role of Poland 52–54
  appeal for Polish help and recruits by respective sides 52, 54
  August 1914 (Solezhenitsyn, Aleksandr, 1972) 629
  Tannenberg 1914 (Sweetman, 2002) 629
  The Eastern Front: 1914–1917 (Stone, 1975) 629
  entrenchment of forces 78
  United States entry on side of Allies 80
  uncertainty of outcome 88

World War I *continued*
  defeat of Germany and Central Powers 94–95
  Armistice declared (Nov. 11, 1918) 94–95
  origin of Korzybski's work 99
  Paris (Versaille) Peace Conference 97, 99, 107, 110
  Peace Treaty, struck down by U.S. Senate (1919) 114
  devastation of Poland 70, 78, 99
  analysis by AK of the causes of 128
World War II. *See also Korzybski, Alfred (at IGS, 1938–1950): World War II responses/activities; Germany, Nazi; Japan, Imperial; Russia, Soviet.*
  AK's prediction of 397, 443, 461
  appeasement of Nazis by British and French 442–443
  Hitler-Stalin pact 461, 588
  Gleiwitz deception 461
  1939 invasion of Poland 461–462
  Japanese attack on Pearl Harbor and U.S. entry in war 488
  'Battle of Los Angeles' (Feb. 1942) 490–491
  German propaganda and wartime morale in the U.S. 491–492
  "criminal destruction of Poland" 502
  Yalta Conference of Stalin, Roosevelt, and Churchill (early 1945) 545
  Unconditional surrender of
    Germany 523
    Japan 525
  legacy of post-war difficulties 527, 530, 545

X
X-Rays 36

Y
Yahoos. *See Gulliver's Travels.*
Yealland, Lewis R. 302–303
  Hysterical Disorders of Warfare 302
Yes and no 117, 181
"Yes, We Have No Bananas!" (popular American song of 1920s) 181, 279, 413
Young, W. H. 325
Yurkowski, Tadeusz 90

Z
Zel'dovich, Yakov (Russian physicist) 585
Zionism, Zionists 146. *See also Jews, Jewish culture/civilization.*
  First Zionist Congress in Basel (1897) 115
  Zionism (Richard J. H. Gottheil) 146
  AK favorably inclined towards 314, 504
  Revisionist Zionist movement 504
Zipf, George Kingsley 615–616, 655
  Human Behavior and the Principle of Least Effort: An Introduction to Human Ecology (1949) 616
Znaniecki, Florian 193
  The Social Role of the Man of Knowledge 193
Zurowski (friend of AK in Russian army) 55, 56, 61–62, 64

About the Author

Bruce I. Kodish had the privilege of studying and working as a colleague with some of Alfred Korzybski's closest co-workers, and their students and co-workers, at the Institute of General Semantics (IGS) during its post-Korzybski but still quite korzybskian heyday in the final decades of the 20th Century. Bruce served for many years on the staffs of the IGS seminar-workshops, the *General Semantics Bulletin*, and *Time-Bindings*, the IGS Newsletter. He helped edit the Fifth Edition of *Science and Sanity*, and as publications chairman oversaw the production of the Third Edition of Korzybski's *'Olivet Lectures'*, as well as the books *Developing Sanity in Human Affairs* and *General Semantics in Psychotherapy*. One of only a few individuals certified by the Institute as an "Approved Teacher of General Semantics", Bruce graduated from the IGS's former *Teacher Training Program* in 1992. He earned a PhD in GS/Applied Epistemology from the Union Institute and University in 1996. He has taught advanced, university-level seminars on *Science and Sanity* and on "The Scientific Roots of GS". With his wife Susan Presby Kodish, he wrote the renowned introduction to korzybskian GS, *Drive Yourself Sane: Using the Uncommon Sense of General Semantics*, recently published in its Third Edition. Susan and Bruce received the Institute's J. Talbot Winchell Award in 1998 for their "...many contributions severally and together to the wider understanding of general semantics as authors, editors, teachers, leaders."

Presently an independent scholar-teacher, Bruce is widely recognized around the world for his comprehensive research and authoritative knowledge of Alfred Korzybski's life and work, having spent seven years producing this first book-length biography, which contains many never-before-told details of Korzybski's extraordinary career. Bruce also wrote the books *Dare to Inquire* and *Back Pain Solutions*. A practicing physical therapist, Bruce lives in Pasadena, California. As a speaker, teacher, and consultant, for individuals and groups, on *radical* general-semantics—the *korzybskian* approach to *applied epistemology* (epistemics)—his presentations and seminar-workshops, offered world-wide, focus on the science-art of awareness, self-management, and innovation. If you're interested in inviting Bruce to speak, or in sponsoring a seminar-workshop, etc., contact him at *bruce.kodish@gmail.com*

www.ingramcontent.com/pod-product-compliance
Lightning Source LLC
Chambersburg PA
CBHW081212170426
43198CB00017B/2592